BALTIC SEA
RÜGEN
ODER R.
NETZE R.
VISTULA R.
WARTHE R.
NEISSE R.
ODER R.
GIANT MOUNTAINS
ELBE R.
MARCH R.
CARPATHIANS
DANUBE R.
DRAVA R.
SAVA R.
DANUBE R.
N
W
E
S
Miles
0
100
map by palacios

Germany: a history

Germany: a history

John E. Rodes
OCCIDENTAL COLLEGE

HOLT, RINEHART AND WINSTON
New York · Chicago · San Francisco · Toronto · London

j. t. a.

Library of Congress Catalog Card Number: 64–12757

27536–0114
Printed in the United States of America

Preface

MANY HISTORIANS, and in fact many Germans, look upon Germany as largely the product of historical development. They believe that nations are formed by the sum total of a people's experiences in a given region. Others however see in Germany an ethnic entity imbued with a "folksoul," the spiritual embodiment of a people's will and destiny. The former is essentially a rational approach; the latter, a romantic and more mystic interpretation. Both ideas have been vital forces in German history, particularly during the last two centuries; both remain influential today. If Germany is a historical entity, the present division into two Germanies can well be accepted as a new historical reality; the two states can each tread their separate paths and find their own development. But if, on the other hand, Germany is an organic realization of the German folksoul, then unification or reunification—as in past centuries—is a matter of inevitable destiny.

To understand these two views, one must study the background of Germany's past. Naturally the last century and a half present the greatest interest and have therefore been treated in more detail in this volume. But to omit entirely the centuries before 1815, as is done by most contemporary writers on the subject, would be to undermine the purpose of this study by depriving the reader of the essential bases for understanding recent and contemporary Germany. Too much of German development in the nineteenth and twentieth centuries is unintelligible to those who lack at least a background knowledge of its earlier history. Why, for instance, did the statesmen and poets of the nineteenth century and the nationalists of the twentieth strive with such assiduity to glorify Germany's medieval past? Why did so many Germans during the last 150 years dream of restoring the empire? Why did the Germans for centuries feel a cultural affinity while lacking political unity? What is the basis for the strange dichotomy in Germany where strong localism and particularism have persisted side by side with an equally strong proclivity for acceptance of authoritarian rule? These questions cannot be answered and Germany's troubled history in our century cannot be understood unless one examines, at least cursorily, the entire stream of Germany's development.

For this reason, the author has found it essential to devote a third of the present volume to an analysis of pre-Napoleonic Germany, particularly to those trends that foreshadow the more recent period. Because most college courses on German history tend to concentrate on the nineteenth and twentieth centuries, these early chapters should be particularly useful for filling in the students' background.

This book is not intended to be a cultural history, or an encyclopedic reference work. The inclusion of an infinite number of names of people with whose works or deeds the American college student is not familiar, and which moreover he need not know unless he wishes to become a specialist in the field, has been meticulously avoided. Primary emphasis has been placed on the development of Germany's political and social institutions, with the necessary inclusion of economic changes. Intellectual and artistic trends have been included only as part of German life, to give the reader a better appreciation of the German scene as a whole.

To cover 2000 years of a people's history within the limitations of a single volume requires selection and evaluation. Von Ranke's injunction to the historian to depict the past "as it actually happened" is clearly unobservable, since pruning and selecting itself distorts the past. What bias and preconceptions, besides those hinted at above, have guided the writer in this process of selection and evaluation? Unashamedly I confess that I have been brought up in the liberal and humanistic tradition. I have little sympathy with totalitarian ideals—under whatever form or color—that invariably stifle human freedom for the sake of dubious advantages. Admittedly then, when I look at German history, I tend to regard with apprehension whatever coercive features it embodies, whether found in Luther's doctrine, in the Prussian monarchical tradition, in Treitschke's historical philosophy, or in a host of similar developments. Aware of this bias on the part of the writer, which guided his selection and emphasis without, I hope, falsifying "historical truth," the reader is free to form his own opinions of the relative importance of the various threads that form the web of Germany's past.

J. E. R.

Altadena, California
January 1964

Contents

Maps and Charts

MAPS

CHARTS

1

Two Fundamental Questions

The historian discovers frequently that the development of a country is influenced by certain fundamental problems that reappear century after century. Such problems may come to the fore dramatically—in a revolution or in time of war. They may also lie dormant, seemingly settled or forgotten, yet actually molding policies, causing turmoil in domestic and foreign affairs —in fact, shaping the destiny of the people. Thus the need for a strong navy to keep Britain's sea lanes open for supplies has affected its political life ever since the sixteenth century. Similarly Russia's drive for warm-water ports has influenced the actions of its rulers for centuries and frequently involved them in wars. American history, according to Frederick Jackson Turner, also contained in the existence of the frontier a potent force that shaped American attitudes and developments. In a like manner, German history presents at least two such fundamental problems that deserve special attention in this study, since they affected the entire development of the German state.

THE FIRST PROBLEM: WHERE IS GERMANY?

The first problem has plagued Germany for over a thousand years. It is as acute and unsolved today as at any time during its history. It is the question: Where is Germany, or what peoples belong to Germany?

Some nations are endowed with readily defined political boundaries, determined by prominent geographical landmarks, linguistic homogeneity, or long historical tradition. But Germany is not so fortunate. The vast plain that stretches for some two thousand miles across northern Europe from the Ural Mountains in Russia to the English Channel is unbroken except for a number of rivers. The Erz Mountains and the Bohemian Forest in the east, the Vosges Mountains in the west, and the Alps in the south do not coincide with linguistic or ethnic boundaries. There is, in fact, no neat line of demarcation between Slavic and Germanic peoples, between religious affiliation, or between those speaking Romance and those speaking Germanic languages. Throughout her history, therefore, Germany's boundaries depended little on geographic or ethnic considerations, but were primarily the result of wars and power politics. As the German historian Johannes Haller noted, "the unity of the German people is not a natural one, but is the product of history." And, one might add, their concept of unity has been in a constant state of re-evaluation.

Where, then, is Germany? What territories and peoples should be included within her borders? When attempting to answer this question, one is at once aware of a dilemma: What criteria should be used as a basis for decision? Since geography appears to give no clue, could one use such criteria as historical precedents, race, or language? Upon closer analysis, none of these is satisfactory.

Historical Precedents of German Boundaries

A glance through any historical atlas will show that Germany's boundaries during the past thousand years have changed several times in almost every century. If history is to provide a basis for assigning boundaries to Germany, at what point can we assume that the political boundaries of the past coincided with the "true" limits of Germany?

Germany arrived late upon the scene as a full-fledged nation-state. But the fact that the unification of Germany took place less than a century ago and that a united Germany existed only from 1871 to 1945 is not the preponderant reason for the difficulty in establishing its borders. The equally young Italian state, despite its recent origin, has fairly fixed boundaries—except for minor fluctuations in the northeast. Rather, the quandary of Germany's borders dates from long before 1871. In every century of its history it is difficult to determine the exact geographical extent of Germany because of the existence of certain factors, such as German particularism, the superposition of an empire on the German Kingdom, the drive to the east, and the presence of a zone of fragmentation in the west—all factors that in themselves were also impediments to German unification. Since they persisted throughout the greater part of German history, they will appear again and again in this volume. For better focus, however, it seems advisable first to analyze them apart from the larger picture of German historical development.

German Particularism

One of the factors that complicate the determination of German boundaries is a deep-rooted particularism. In this respect, German history resembles that of Greece. Ancient Greek history is not really the history of Greece, but rather the history of numerous independent city-states. When a unified Greek state finally emerged in the nineteenth century, it was difficult to determine how many of these separate sections properly belonged to this larger political unit. Similarly, German history is largely the history of the separate tribes and areas. Even today there is no agreement as to which of these should be included in a German state.

THE STEM DUCHIES During the Middle Ages, such states as England and France developed strong monarchies as the centers of the future English and

French nations. Germany, however, failed to effect such political coherence. It was plagued by the existence of immensely strong tribal duchies, such as Bavaria, Swabia, Thuringia, and Saxony—often referred to as stem duchies, from the German word *Stamm,* meaning tribe (see Map 1). The exact origin of these duchies is not quite certain, but one may assume that they derived from former tribal organizations, each with its own customs, traditions, and dialects, and each imbued with a fierce love of independence. The known history of some of them goes back as far as late Roman times.

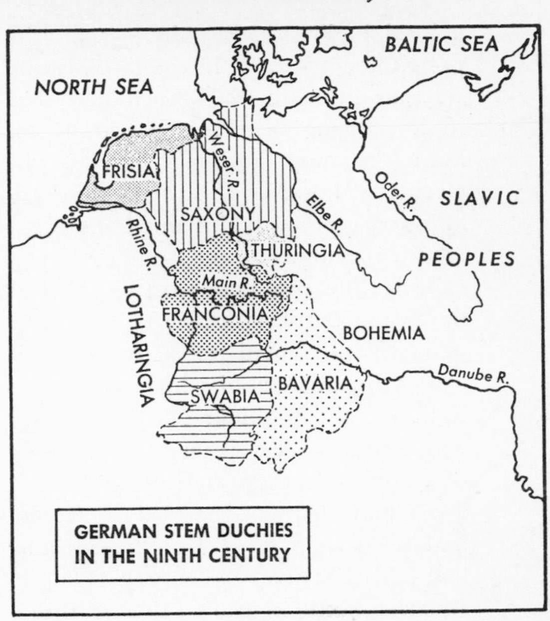

MAP 1

Bavaria, for example, was colonized by the Romans in the first century after Christ. Yet the Bavarians managed to retain some sort of semi-independence under their own dukes. Later, during the eighth century, when Charles the Great built up a powerful empire, he conquered Bavaria and turned it into a fief of the Frankish Kingdom. The Bavarian Duke Tassilo III refused at first to acquiesce in this loss of independence, and revolted against his Frankish overlord. In 788, Charles caught the rebel and banned him to a monastery. He abolished the Bavarian ducal title, divided the lands among his own Frankish lords, and turned Bavaria into a mere province of the Frankish Kingdom. Even then the Bavarians did not submit to their fate. Although defeated by the superior arms of the Franks and deprived of their duke, they tried to find consolation in the false claim that Charles the Great was actually a descendant of one of their own dukes (Tassilo I). Rather than admit that they had been conquered, they clung to the fiction that the Frankish Kingdom was in reality ruled by a Bavarian.

Other tribal duchies experienced a similar fate. In the late eighth century, the Franks tried to suppress the Swabians, Thuringians, and Saxons by imposing on them territorial rule by Frankish counts. Despite these measures, they failed to eradicate local tribal allegiances. When the Frankish Kingdom disintegrated in the early ninth century, the separate duchies reappeared as independent political units. Nor was their love of independence stifled after a so-called German Kingdom began to emerge in the tenth century.

The nature of these duchies changed in the course of the succeeding centuries. The old duchy had been based primarily on ethnic unity. Gradually the geographic boundaries and ethnic composition of these duchies were altered so that the new units came to be largely feudal, dynastic, and territorial in character. Yet, despite this transformation, particularism persisted.

To be sure, similar provincialism

existed in France. But there it lost its political significance in the late Middle Ages, and the kings of France succeeded in impressing their rule gradually on even the most outlying districts. In Germany, however, the rulers were unable to accomplish this until the nineteenth century.

This difference between the political development of France and Germany may be attributed to a number of causes, an analysis of which also sheds light on the problem of determining Germany's borders. It may be the result of different backgrounds. The French lands had all been occupied by Rome, had been thoroughly Romanized, and had been Christianized at an early date. By the sixth century, the Catholic Church had extended its organization throughout France. Thus all the French lands enjoyed more or less the same cultural and political background. This was not true of Germany. Only a small part of Germany had been occupied by the Romans, and Christianity came to Germany much later and much more slowly than to France. Furthermore, the lands forming the later German state were not all included from the beginning in the territories of the German Kingdom; many were added as a result of wars and colonization over a period of many centuries. There was therefore little uniformity in the background of the lands that belonged to the Kingdom of Germany by the end of the Middle Ages. Finally, there was an important difference between the dominant groups in the two countries. Although France was still inhabited by various peoples who had ruled the area in former times, such as Celts, Romans, and Goths, the conquering Franks had acquired domination in the early Middle Ages over the entire territory later included in the French state. France was thus ruled by members of a single tribal organization. Germany, however, was settled by numerous tribes, each retaining its identity; and no single one of them ever came to dominate the entire area for very long.

THE QUESTION OF ALLEGIANCE While it is easy to see that this strong particularism acted as an impediment to political unification, one may wonder in what way it complicates the determination of Germany's borders. The problem is one of allegiance. Throughout most of the Middle Ages, there was a German king and theoretically a Kingdom of Germany existed. Yet down to recent times the allegiance felt by the people to their king was always overshadowed by loyalty to their own duchy. Politically and culturally, Bavarians, Swabians, Frieslanders, and Bohemians, for instance, belonged to the same Kingdom of Germany, but in most cases they followed the dictates of their local leaders and paid little heed to the welfare of the kingdom as a whole. This absence of allegiance to a central unit —an allegiance that in most other nations developed rather naturally over hundreds of years—may account for the somewhat frantic and artificial attempt to instill nationalism in the Germans during the last century. It is surely also one of the reasons that there is today no general agreement as to which of these areas should be incorporated within the realm of Germany.

To use the examples of Swabia, Friesland, Bohemia, and Bavaria: almost everyone today takes it for granted that northern Swabia is German and that southern Swabia belongs to Switzerland and most of Friesland to the Dutch. No such common agreement, however, exists in relation to Bohemia and Austria. Ever since the creation of Czechoslovakia in 1918, quite a few Germans—not merely Hitler's National Socialists—expressed the conviction that parts of Bohemia properly belonged to Germany. Similarly, Bavaria for some five centuries included many of the lands that today are incorporated in Austria, giving rise to the question whether Austria in effect should be a separate state or whether it belongs to Germany—a question that may well be reopened in the future.

The Existence of the German Empire

A second factor which complicated the problem of German boundaries was the existence of the Roman Empire of the German Nation, usually referred to as the Holy Roman Empire. From 962 to 1806, most of the kings of Germany also bore the title "Emperor of the Holy Roman Empire." As kings of Germany, they claimed suzerainty over certain lands, most of them lying north of the Alps; as emperors, they claimed universal sovereignty over all Christendom as well as specific political control of territories situated both north and south of the Alps—in other words, much more territory than was manifestly German (see Map 7). The Empire therefore included lands where the German language was not spoken, and on the other hand, as Germans began to colonize toward the east, there came to be lands in which German was spoken, but which did not form a part of the Empire.

Thus the German Empire and the German Kingdom were not the same, despite the fact that most of the time the two were ruled by the same person. Moreover, the boundaries of neither give a clue as to the exact extent of what should now be German.

The German Drive to the East

A third major difficulty in regard to the determination of the exact location of Germany involves its eastern boundary. In fact, even today the question of where to draw this border provides one of the most critical unsolved international issues of our time. The problem involves much more than the fate of the inhabitants of the border districts and the political repercussions on Germany and Poland. It bears on the very existence and position of Poland between Russia and Germany and on the question of whether Poland is to be an eastern or a central European nation. It affects Russia's desired expansion toward the heart of Europe, and concerns as well the economic problem of Poland's direct access to the Baltic Sea. Moreover, it is linked closely with Germany's demand for "living-space" and the question of a balanced German economy. Finally, the fate of Germany's eastern boundary today forms an integral part of the entire conflict between the "iron curtain" countries and the West.

This eastern boundary has always been fluid. Since the early Middle Ages, the line between Slavs and Germans has varied almost from generation to generation, depending on the outcome of battles, the success of colonization or Christianization, or the result of diplomatic maneuvers.

From the fourth to the seventh century, at the time of the *Völkerwanderungen* (peoples' migrations), the predominant direction in which most of the tribes moved was toward the west.

After this westward movement had ceased and the various migrating tribes had settled down, Germanic[1] tribes generally occupied the lands west and south of the Weser River. The territory between the Weser and the Elbe contained a mixture of Germanic and Slavic peoples, while the districts east of the Elbe were almost exclusively Slavic. One might say that by the eighth century the Weser more or less delineated the furthest limits of the Slavs' expansion toward the west (see Map 2).

Thereafter the trend was reversed. With Emperor Charles the Great, in the late eighth century, began the Germanic drive to the east—the *Drang nach Osten.* Charles first subdued and Christianized the neighboring Germanic tribes across the Weser, and then pushed the various Slavic peoples he encountered farther to the east. Thus by the end of his reign, the limits between Germans and Slavs had been moved eastward and generally followed the Elbe between the North Sea and the mountains of Bohemia.

It is interesting to note that this line of demarcation along the Elbe—although it did not last for very long—became of considerable importance for the later political, social, and economic life of Germany. Down to recent times, the lands west of this line were known as "old Germany"; those later to be conquered to the east of the river were referred to as "new Germany." "Old Germany" is a region that has been settled by Germans for a longer period. In time, it became more industrialized than the "new" region, somewhat more democratic and liberal, and more densely populated, with much small-scale farming. "New Germany," on the other hand, long retained the characteristics of a conquered colony, with its small group of powerful, aristocratic, conservative landholders—the so-called Junkers—with large estates, dominating a numerous peasantry living in servitude. Seemingly by historical accident, this line of demarcation between "new" and "old" Germany more or less coincides with today's boundary between East and West Germany.

After the tenth century, the German drive toward the east continued along two different lines. On the one hand, it was colonization, frequently without concomitant political expansion. On the other, it was political expansion, an extension of the territorial limits of political control, regardless of the wishes of the populations thereby subjugated.

EXPANSION BY COLONIZATION German colonists pushed eastward primarily in three broad avenues: along the shores of the Baltic, up the valleys of the Oder and the Elbe, and down the broad plains of the Danube. This colonization was carried on by monks and bishops, peasants and noble lords, and religio-military organizations such as the Teutonic Knights, as well as by enterprising merchants and artisans. German-speaking cities were founded to exploit local commercial resources; strategically located German monasteries became spiritual, cultural, and eco-

[1] *Germanic* is the designation given a great number of tribes—such as the Angles, Saxons, Jutes, Franks, Burgundians, Goths, and Alemanni—who spoke related Germanic languages. Several—such as the Saxons, East Franks, and Alemanni—settled in the region between the Alps and the North Sea, the Rhine and the Bohemian Mountains; and the languages they spoke gradually evolved into modern German. Other Germanic tribes, settling in Scandinavia, England, and along the Channel, laid the foundations for such modern languages as Swedish, Norwegian, English, and Dutch.

nomic centers; German peasants built villages and introduced the three-crop system for better exploitation of the soil.

During the ninth and tenth centuries, the main effort at colonization was devoted to present-day Austria and adjacent territories; thereafter it shifted toward Bohemia, Silesia, and the Baltic coast. The high point of colonization in the northeast, carried on largely by the Teutonic Knights and facilitated by a temporary decline of the Polish Kingdom, was reached in the thirteenth and fourteenth centuries. A second wave of settlers moved into Poland primarily in the eighteenth and nineteenth centuries. In the south, the decline of the Ottoman Empire and the opening of Russia in early modern times reactivated the push into the upper Balkans and farther east. Especially after 1763, great numbers of settlers moved into southern Russia.

The results of these colonizing moves were astonishing. In the south, the drive to the east provided the basis for the expansion of the Hapsburg dominions and the creation of the Austrian Empire. All of Austria, Styria, Carinthia, Carniola, and parts of Bohemia, Moravia, Ruthenia, Hungary, Slavonia, Serbia, and Rumania became Germanized. Moreover, Germans established large-scale settlements in Bessarabia, the Ukraine, the Crimea, and along the Lower Volga. In the north, the eastward movement laid the foundation for the eventual establishment of the state of Prussia. Germans settled Silesia, Pomerania, East Prussia, much of the Baltic littoral to Estonia, and portions of western Poland and White Russia (see Map 3).

But what was the political significance of this expansion through colonization?

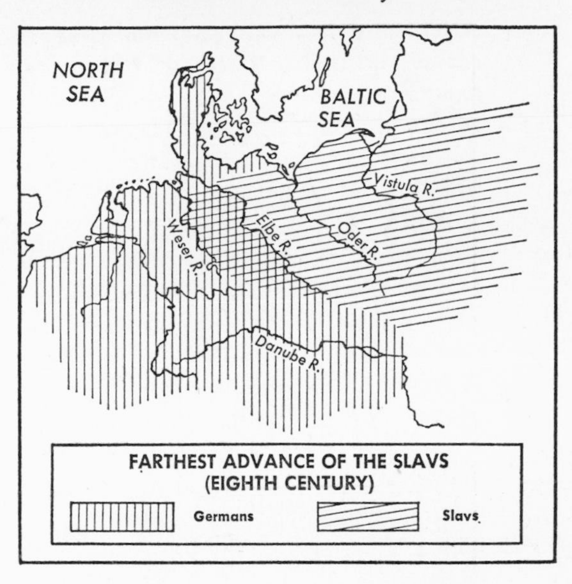

MAP 2

Was it an extension of the frontier, similar to America's westward movement? One must remember that much of this *Drang nach Osten* was not undertaken by emperors or kings in the name of Empire or kingdom, but by enterprising individuals or such organizations as the Teutonic Knights or the Hanseatic League of merchants. Moreover, in some areas it involved the creation of military, religious, or commercial outposts at certain strategic spots; in others, scattered peasant settlements were established. In both cases, thousands of Slavs were left inhabiting the intervening territories. The same pattern occurred, of course, in the westward movement in America. But the Indians displaced by the American frontiersmen rapidly lost their power, whereas the Slavic peoples, overrun by the Germans, periodically were to resurge to considerable strength. There is an added difference. The American Congress admitted into the Union the new states created in the West. The

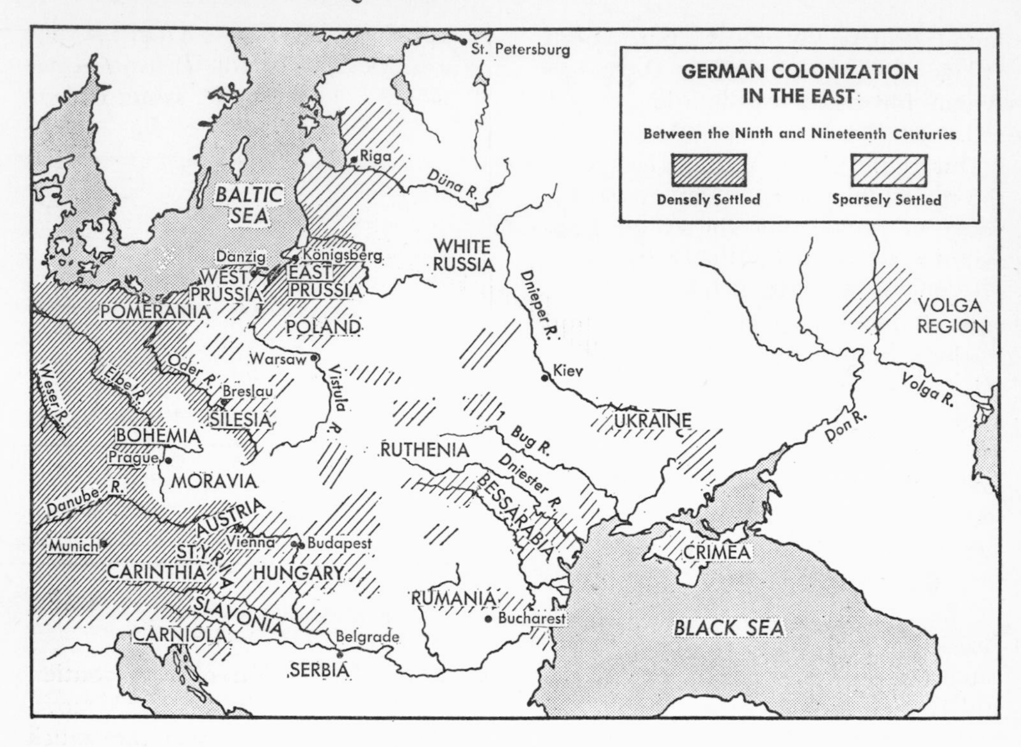

MAP 3

same did not occur in Germany's eastward drive. Only in some cases—Bohemia and Silesia, for example—was colonization followed by political annexation and incorporation into the Empire. In most areas, the political limits of the Empire were not extended eastward to include the colonized lands. In the case of East Prussia's colonization by the Teutonic Knights, for instance, the emperors—with the exception of a brief period in the thirteenth century—clearly recognized that these lands were not under their jurisdiction. Similarly, the emperors never extended the borders of the Empire into the area of present-day Hungary to incorporate into the Empire the German colonies that had sprung up in that region. Only in early modern times were East Prussia and Hungary taken over politically by the Hohenzollern and Hapsburg dynasties, respectively—but even then they were not incorporated into the Empire.

POLITICAL EXPANSION Besides expansion through colonization, there was growth through political aggrandizement. From the tenth to the fourteenth century, the boundary of the Empire continued to shift eastward. Ambitious princes conquered for themselves vast territories along the eastern fringes, and gradually these lands came under imperial jurisdiction. By 1100, the boundary of the Empire had been moved from the Elbe to the Oder, and in the southeast up to the river March, thus enlarging the Empire by a strip some two hundred miles in width and seven hundred miles in length, including Bohemia and Moravia. During the next two centuries the border was pushed beyond the Oder to embrace Pomerania and Silesia. Thereafter the eastern limits of the Empire became more or less stationary (see Map 7). If the imperial boundaries could be taken as a basis for determining the limits of the German state, this settling down of the border would have helped adduce a solution to our problem. But as pointed out, the borders of the Empire cannot serve as such a basis.

Moreover, political expansion toward the east did not cease with the fourteenth century. After 1400 the eastward political drive was carried on not by the Empire, but primarily by two quasi-independent states—Austria and Brandenburg-Prussia—or, more properly speaking, by two dynasties: the Hapsburgs in the southeast and the Hohenzollerns in the northeast.

Between the fifteenth and eighteenth centuries, the Hapsburgs added to their domains vast territories along the valley of the Danube, including the regions of modern Hungary, eastern Czechoslovakia, western Rumania, and northern Yugoslavia. The height of this expansion was reached in the eighteenth century (see Map 13).

In the northeast, the growth of Brandenburg-Prussia had been prepared for by the Teutonic Knights, who during the thirteenth and fourteenth centuries conquered most of the Baltic coast from Pomerania to the Gulf of Finland. Although the Teutonic Knights lost most of their Baltic possessions during the fifteenth century, they remained firmly entrenched in East Prussia, with their center at Königsberg. The Hohenzollern dynasty began its long eastward drive in the early seventeenth century, when the Margravate of Brandenburg and the former lands of the Teutonic Knights—then called the Duchy of Prussia—came under the rule of the same Hohenzollern prince. Thereafter the Hohenzollern rulers engaged in repeated wars during the seventeenth and eighteenth centuries to round out their eastern possessions and establish a land bridge between Berlin and Königsberg. At first they gained Pomerania and Silesia, which already belonged nominally to the Empire but not to Brandenburg-Prussia. Then in the late eighteenth century, in the course of the three partitions of Poland, the Hohenzollerns acquired West Prussia, Poznan, and the city of Warsaw. This marks the high point of their political expansion toward the east (see Map 15).

FORCED RETRENCHMENT IN THE EAST

After 1800, the seesaw movement of the eastern border started its pendulum swing in the opposite direction. During the nineteenth century, Austria gradually lost control over the lands it had acquired in the preceding four centuries, and by 1918 its boundaries had been pushed back to their present dimensions. A similar shift occurred in the northeast. Napoleon took the first step when he created the Duchy of Warsaw, carved primarily out of Prussian-controlled territory. The general European peace treaty of 1815 shifted the Prussian border even farther westward. This new line of 1815 remained unchanged until the end of World War I, and formed the eastern limits of the united German state that Otto von Bismarck created in 1871. The Treaty of Versailles of 1919 involved a further shift of the border by recreating an independent Poland and providing it with access to the Baltic Sea. West Prussia, Poznan, and Upper Silesia were taken from Germany and awarded to Poland. East Prussia was thus once again isolated from the rest of Prussia by the establishment of the Polish Corridor. Finally, after World War II, the tentative Polish-German border was shifted even farther west, to the Oder-Neisse line—giving Russia the northern portion of East Prussia and awarding the remainder of East Prussia as well as Silesia and Pomerania to Poland (see Map 15).

This survey of the migrations and the shifts in the eastern borders of Germany demonstrates the impossibility of determining its political frontiers solely on the basis of historical precedents. There were two major Slavic migrations toward the west, interrupted by a long German drive in the opposite direction. Which position should be accepted as basis for a permanent settlement? Each of the more recent solutions appears unsatisfactory. The border of 1815, which closed the gap between East Prussia and Brandenburg through annexation of the intervening lands, included within Germany much territory that was manifestly Polish in terms of language. The border of 1918 again separated East Prussia from the rest of Germany, while the present boundary of 1945 includes on the Polish side many districts where primarily German is spoken, although much of the German-speaking population of these regions either fled or was forcibly transferred to the west.

The Zone of Fragmentation in the West

Germany's western boundary presents a similar problem to its eastern limits, though one not so acute. The clouded state of its western boundary goes back to the very beginning of the histories of France and Germany. For several centuries before A.D. 843—in the days of the Merovingians and Carolingians—the future French and German states were frequently so intermingled that it would be difficult to draw an exact distinction between the two. To be sure, there were certain differences between the regions east and west of the Rhine; yet both sides were dominated by related Frankish tribes and much of the time were ruled by the same Frankish lord.

The more or less permanent division between the two occurred in 843, when the grandsons of Charles the Great settled the dispute over their inheritance by dividing their patrimony into three shares (see Map 6). This threefold division became the source of infinite difficulties. The western portion formed the basis for the French monarchy; the eastern part gradually developed into Germany. But the central strip, running from the Lowlands in the north, through Luxemburg, Alsace, Lorraine, and Switzerland down to Italy, never came to form a nation-state. Down to the present day, it remains a zone of fragmentation. Soon after the division of 843, the western and eastern Frankish kingdoms (or the future France and Germany) began to fight over this zone. This fight has continued some eleven hundred years, with the political boundary between Germany and France seesawing east and west.

At first, the East Frankish Kingdom absorbed the lion's share of the intermediary zone. In 870, in the Treaty of Mersen, Germany obtained all lands east of a line generally following the rivers Rhone and Meuse. During the subsequent two centuries, after the East

Frankish Kingdom had grown considerably in power, the border between France and Germany was shifted even farther westward. By the eleventh century, it ran west of the Rhone, near the Upper Loire, the Saône, and west of the Meuse. Thus the German "state" embraced much territory in which Early French was spoken (see Map 7).

Thereafter the trend was reversed. Just as Germany pushed its drive to the east against the Slavs, so France now had its eastward expansion. Starting in the late twelfth century, the rising French monarchy began the growth that later French statesmen hoped would eventually acquire for France its *natural boundaries.* This meant that its northern and eastern boundaries should be formed by the Rhine and the Alps. This expansion was at first most successful in the south. By 1500, the Alps had come to form its southeastern limits. Then came the slow but steady push toward the north and the east during the sixteenth, seventeenth, and eighteenth centuries. By 1766, France had obtained more or less the same boundaries that it holds today. The Rhine formed its boundary in the east but not in the north.

Thus the greater portion of the zone of fragmentation was taken from Germany in the course of six centuries—not merely by France, but also by the new states of Holland, Belgium, Luxemburg, and Switzerland that gradually came to be formed. Since a large part of this zone is inhabited by people speaking some type of German rather than French, here as in the east, there is little coincidence between linguistic and political boundaries. Furthermore, during the last hundred years the repeated transfer between France and Germany of the Saar, Alsace, and parts of Lorraine points up the fluidity of this border.

The Criterion of "Race"

Anthropologists have attempted to categorize mankind on the basis of a variety of measurements and tentative criteria—the shape of skull, eyes, or nose; stature; type of hair; or pigmentation—and have advanced many different categories. But all would agree that it is manifestly absurd to speak of a "German race," and that the criterion of race could never be of use in arriving at a definition of what is German. Yet emotional racialism was so pronounced among many Germans during the past century that it became a significant factor long before Hitler's National Socialists extolled it to the zenith of absurdity.

Starting with the myth of the *Volk* in the late eighteenth century, and adding a belief in the transcendent importance of heredity, many Germans used the word "race" as a synonym for "nationality." The shibboleth of the superiority and uniqueness of the "Germanic race"—the tall, blond, blue-eyed Aryans—propagated so enthusiastically by Houston Stewart Chamberlain in his *Foundations of the Nineteenth Century,* was shared by many nationalistic Germans of the late nineteenth and twentieth centuries. Enthusiasts—among them Richard Wagner and Pastor Adolf Stöcker—proclaimed that "German blood" flows in German veins and that Germans can be recognized by their superior courage and energy. With such a heritage, Hitler could readily claim that German boundaries should embrace all members of the German "race," because German soil was best suited for the development of the German *Volk.*

While these emotion-filled myths do not aid this investigation, they are worth recalling as factors complicating the determination of Germany's boundaries.

The Criterion of Language

If historical precedents and concepts of "race" are unworkable, what of the linguistic factor? Since the unity of some states is based on homogeneity of language, could one not decide that all who speak the German language are Germans? Closer examination reveals that language cannot serve as a suitable gauge for determining the limits of Germany. The reason lies primarily in the development of certain European languages.

It is assumed that most of the people now inhabiting Europe and the southern and western regions of Asia speak languages that developed originally from one common tongue, the so-called Indo-European. Philologists believe that these people at one time lived in a common territory and that their languages developed and changed as they migrated in different directions. Those settling in northern and central Europe spoke a derivation of Indo-European know as Germanic. As time passed and various tribes settled in different areas, further differentiation occurred and a distinction developed among three main branches of the Germanic language: East, North, and West. While the first category developed into Gothic and the second became the basis of Scandinavian and Icelandic languages, the last branch, West Germanic, provided the foundation for the development of such modern languages as English, Dutch, and German. Thus their common origin explains the great similarity among these languages, and accounts for the fact that neighboring tongues frequently shade gradually over from one to the other.

The various types of West Germanic languages changed over the centuries. One of them, for instance, gradually developed into Anglo-Saxon, then Middle English, and finally Modern English. Similarly, German went through a long development based on local needs and variations. Although many types of languages arose within the German branch of the West Germanic group—such as Franconian, Thuringian, and Bavarian—one can recognize three main groups based on geographical differences. Along the North Sea developed "Low German," immediately to the south "Middle German," and south of the Main River, in Bavaria and the Alpine regions, "High German." The designations "Low," "Middle," and "High" derive merely from the geographical nature of the land, since Low German originated in the flat plains of the north and High German in the mountainous areas of the south. In terms of linguistics, the differences among the three types are reflected in the extent to which they respectively developed away from the original Germanic parent language. Low German—as incidentally also Dutch and Old English—is closest to its Germanic origins; the farther south one travels, the more one finds that the language has shifted away from this origin.

How do these philological considerations affect the question of German boundaries? It means that among those who speak derivatives of West Germanic, few abrupt differences can be noted in adjoining territories. To be sure, there is considerable difference in language between an Austrian and an Englishman. On the other hand, there is more linguistic difference between a resident of Bavaria in the south of Germany and one of Schleswig in the north than between a German of Munich and his Austrian neighbor across the Alpine border. Similarly, Flemish, Dutch, Frisian, and *Platt-deutsch*—Low German—spoken along the German North Sea coast—all shade gradually one into the other, since all four are essentially a type of Low West Germanic.

This gradual linguistic transition from the Alps to the Channel would make the drawing of boundaries on the basis of language an impossibility. Unless we were to conclude that all derivatives of West Germanic—from the Austrians and Swiss with their High German to the Dutch and English with their Low German—should be included in the same state, we would have to fashion some absurd definition of how "high" or how "low" the language may be to warrant inclusion within Germany.

On the other hand, it is equally difficult to draw sensible boundaries between regions in which languages with different roots are spoken. The linguistic dividing line between French and German or between German and Polish seldom follows a line that could conveniently be taken as basis for a political frontier.

Finally, linguistic criteria for determining boundaries would have the drawback of disregarding the feelings of the people involved. A good example is Switzerland. On a basis of language affinity, the northern Swiss who speak *Schwyzertütsch* would have to be incorporated into Germany. Their political sentiments, however, clearly indicate that they do not wish to form a part of the German state.

THE SECOND PROBLEM: THE QUESTION OF LEADERSHIP

The second question that has affected German history, particularly since early modern times, is not so acute today as the question of German boundaries. It is the problem of what region, what state, or what peoples should lead Germany. In some respects, this question was temporarily answered during the last century. Some of its corollaries, however, still remain unsolved, and it is even possible that the question may be reopened some time in the future.

To someone not familiar with German history, it may seem strange that this question of leadership should present a problem. No equivalent existed in French or English history. From the time of Hugh Capet (A.D. 987) onward, Paris developed gradually and naturally into the metropolis of the new kingdom. Although on rare occasions the provinces tried to challenge the extreme centralization of government in Paris, there was never any doubt that Paris would continue to rule France. Similarly, from the time of William the Conqueror (A.D. 1066) onward, London was on its way to becoming the heart and center of the rising English monarchy.

The question, however, is not merely one of geography—whether the capital should be in this or in that region. A problem of leadership is involved. The American colonies, newly united under the Articles of Confederation, present a somewhat similar case. Regardless of the location of the capital itself, the question remained whether the southern or the northern states were to dominate the new Union. The answer not only affected the character of the new nation, but has remained a significant factor in American history.

Germany for many centuries before its unification in 1871 faced a similar problem. During the Middle Ages, the various powerful duchies and rising dynastic families vied for pre-eminence in the German Kingdom, and Germany as a whole was seriously weakened through these internal feuds and thereby deprived of a single center around which the future state could develop. Starting in the fifteenth century, it appeared as if a solution to the question of leadership might be found when the Hapsburg dynasty began to consolidate its holdings in Austria and tried to impose a more centralized rule on the entire German Empire. However, the religious split of the Reformation, which occurred more or less at the same time, put a rapid end to this hope. Rather, it added momentum and complications to the problem. The northern princes wanted complete independence and full sovereignty; they were therefore anti-Hapsburg. Since the Hapsburgs remained staunchly pro-Catholic, many a prince turned to Protestantism unquestionably not so much because of religious conviction, but because to be Protestant meant to be even more anti-Hapsburg. Thus the religious divisions resulting from the Reformation reinforced the political fragmentation of Germany and further complicated the question of leadership.

This north-south split, originating in a power struggle between rival dynasties and religious groups, became more crystallized during the succeeding centuries. With Prussia's rise during the seventeenth and eighteenth centuries and its growing dominance over northern Germany, this rivalry for leadership tended to focus on a struggle between this new northern kingdom and Austria, the center of the Hapsburg possessions. Since the victor of this prolonged contest was likely to put his stamp on the whole of Germany, the outcome was of vital importance, for, as will be seen in the ensuing chapters, there were considerable differences between the two states. The 1860s finally brought an outward end to this struggle when Bismarck's Prussia inflicted an overwhelming defeat on a declining Austrian Empire, and Prussia became the undisputed leader of the newly united Germany in 1871.

That the most acute and apparent aspect of this question was solved with Prussia's defeat of Austria is indisputable. But it is interesting to speculate whether even today all its underlying corollaries are solved. To be sure, the question of Austrian leadership over Germany has been answered definitely in the negative. But what, for example, happened to the concomitant religious struggle? Certainly Prussia's victory did not mean that Germany would become an entirely Protestant nation. Rivalry between the two branches of Christianity continued to affect the life of Germany, and religion still plays an important role in the policies of many German political parties. This portion of our problem is still smoldering today. The stronghold of Protestantism lies in northeastern Germany, whereas the Rhineland and Bavaria are predominantly Catholic. This means that the present division of Germany makes the eastern German Democratic Republic an essentially Protestant state—about 82 percent Protestant—while the western Federal Republic of Germany contains the bulk of the Catholic population and is in fact largely led by Catholics—although the Catholics, with 45 percent, do not represent an absolute majority. The question now is what will happen when and if Germany is reunified. Is the Catholic leadership in the West, as represented by Konrad Adenauer's Christian Democratic party, not likely to be challenged and the question thus reopened?

But the problem was not merely whether Prussia or Austria should lead a united Germany or whether the one or the other religion should predominate. It also was a question of whether all the other German states would be content with following the leadership of any one state. Such subordination went counter to their long tradition of independence. Therefore, after Prussia came to dominate Germany in the last century, it was not easy for such particularistic states as Bavaria to submit gracefully to Prussian hegemony. Bavaria still dreamed of partial or complete independence, and similar particularism was still strong in most regions. Hence the separate states within the unified empire of 1871 were allowed considerable local autonomy, and Germany became a strange mixture of a federated and a unitary state. This question of how much centralization or how much federalism should predominate is still a critical issue in German political life today.

The Early Middle Ages and the Rise of the Empire to 1125

THE GERMANIC TRIBES

The Roman Era

Our earliest and fragmentary knowledge of the German lands and their Germanic inhabitants comes from the Romans. Conquest of this territory started in the days of Julius Caesar, in 55 B.C., reaching its greatest extension during the reign of Emperor Trajan, about A.D. 110. Caesar's writings contain a number of brief references to the Germanic peoples whom he encountered in many skirmishes. He contrasts them sharply with the more civilized and sedentary Gauls whom he had just conquered. He expresses surprise to find among these Germanic tribes no organized priesthood, no hereditary nobility, and on the whole very little political organization. Their main subsistence at the time apparently was derived from hunting rather than agriculture, presumably because of their nomadic life.

The Romans occupied less than half the area that we today think of as Germany. The limes, or fortified boundary walls, which they built across Germany as defense against the unconquered Germanic and Slavic tribes to the north, ran from Holland along the Rhine to the Taunus Mountains, near Mainz. Thence the wall turned eastward to a few miles north of what is now the city of Frankfurt on the Main, and then southeast toward the Danube near Regensburg (see Map 4). Since the area south of this line was dominated by the Romans for almost four centuries and the regions to the north remained entirely unoccupied, it is interesting to speculate how much the centuries of Roman occupation influenced the later development of the southern territory. One difference between north and south resulting from this occupation is obvious. The Romans founded many cities in the south, built roads, and organized the land politically—activities that began in the north only many centuries later. Another difference is that Christianity came to the southern regions much earlier than to the north. But one wonders about others, less easily proved to be the result of Roman occupation. Conceivably, for example, it is no mere coincidence that those regions occupied by the Romans have generally remained Catholic after the Reformation, whereas the nonoccupied lands, with few exceptions, embraced Protestantism.

A more detailed account of the customs and mores of the early Germanic tribes was written by the Roman historian Tacitus (A.D. 55–117), whose description probably exaggerated their virtues and minimized their vices in order to teach a moral lesson to his own countrymen. Still, his account is useful because it contains information on certain social and religious institutions that apparently were common to most Germanic tribes and that influenced the Middle Ages, not only in Germany, but in all lands where Germanic peoples made their influence felt. Tacitus stressed the love of freedom and fighting of these "blue-eyed, tall" people with "red-blond" hair. According to him, their conception of family life was strictly moral, although women did all the hard work while men drank, gambled, and fought. There were relatively few class differences, and slavery hardly existed. Tacitus was impressed with the democratic nature of their political meetings, all the men assembling in the village square to approve or reject some important decision. Furthermore, he tells us that many of these people formed small groups (*comitatus* or *Gefolgschaftswesen*) around devoted leaders, whom they followed in times of war and peace alike. This arrangement was to play a considerable role in the later formation of feudalism. It also reveals an inherent clannishness that later reinforced political particularism. In social, military, and legal relationships, the Germans believed strongly in the inviolability of oaths, a concept they were to retain down to the present day. Finally, Tacitus describes their religion, which to some extent has influenced all of Western civilization, since Christianity, rather than attempting to eradicate all local customs, absorbed many into its own practices. The Germanic rites of fertility, for example, which celebrated the reawakening of nature in the spring, were fused with the Christian commemoration of Christ's resurrection, resulting in the festival of Easter; and the names of some Germanic gods were taken to denote days of the week—Thor, the god of thunder, for Thursday; Fria, wife of Wotan, for Friday.

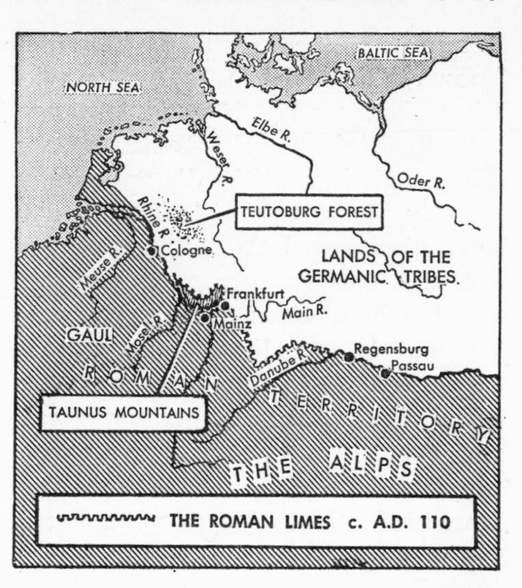

MAP 4

A single event that took place in Roman times has indirectly continued to have repercussions in German history down to recent times. In A.D. 9 the Roman general Varus crossed the Rhine, probably in an attempt to conquer the lands between the Rhine and the Elbe. But the German tribal chief

Arminius of the tribe of the Cherusci, known to the Germans as Hermann der Cherusker, managed to inflict a resounding defeat on the Roman legions. This event in itself hardly appears extremely important, although it may have discouraged the Emperor Augustus from further attempts at conquering northern Germany. But later in German legend, literature, and folklore, Arminius' victory took on tremendous significance. Again and again the event was celebrated in poems, plays, and novels. In 1875, after German unification, a huge monument to Hermann was erected in the Teutoburg Forest as a symbol of the achievement. To many Germans, Hermann represented the strength and virility of the early Teutonic tribes, a sign that the Germanic peoples could outfight and conquer the Romans, and a portent of Germany's future victories over the Romance peoples. To chauvinists, it even served as proof of the ultimate superiority of the Teutonic race. "Our Fatherland owes its freedom to this great victory," wrote a superpatriotic nineteenth-century German historian, "and we, the descendants of those races, are indebted to it for the unmixed German blood which flows in our veins, and for the pure Germanic sounds pronounced by our tongue."

The Era of Migration

In the middle of the third century began the *Völkerwanderungen.* During the next three centuries, tribe after tribe of Germanic, Celtic, Slavic, and other peoples migrated across the face of Europe, first infringing on and finally obliterating the boundaries of the Western Roman Empire, profoundly changing the political and ethnic map of Europe. Although few accurate historical details are available, it was in this period that the separate German tribes first appeared as recognizable political units. Some scholars even date the beginning of German historical awareness to the days of the *Völkerwanderungen,* which they call the heroic period of the Germanic peoples. For these centuries of unrest gave rise to a number of legends of heroes and memorable deeds which form the background of many Germanic epics, such as *Beowulf,* the *Volsunga Saga,* and the *Fall of the Niebelungen.* The latter, put into literary form in the late twelfth century, gave the Germans not merely a wealth of plots and symbols for much of their later literature, but also furnished them with a prototype for a national hero in Siegfried, who, like Arminius, played an important role in the nationalistic era of the nineteenth and twentieth centuries.

By A.D. 500, Europe had been completely transformed. All sorts of barbarian, that is, non-Roman, kingdoms had taken the place of the former Western Roman Empire. For our purposes, the most important of these was the Frankish Kingdom, established during the fifth century in what is now northeastern France and along the Lower Rhine.

THE FRANKISH KINGDOM

Under the Merovingians

The Frankish Kingdom, under its two successive dynasties—the Merovingians and the Carolingians—lasted roughly from 481, the year Clovis I became "King of the Franks," until 987, when the last Carolingian ruler in the west (Louis V) was replaced by the newly elected Hugh Capet, the founder of the medieval French monarchy. Initially Clovis ruled only the territory called Austrasia, which Frankish tribes had seized during the fourth and fifth centuries. Austrasia was situated along the lower Meuse and Rhine rivers, from the English Channel east to the Upper Main River region (which still today is called Franconia). Through conquests Clovis added Neustria and Aquitaine (the bulk of present-day France) and later the lands of the Alemanni (today's southwestern Germany). The Kingdom of the Franks therefore formed the basis for the future French monarchy as well as for the Kingdom of Germany. During most of the Merovingian period, Neustria, Austrasia, Aquitaine, and Burgundy (added in 533) were under control of the same Frankish king, and, superficially at least, similar customs were impressed on all regions. But the fundamental differences between the eastern and western portions of Francia remained profound (see Map 5).

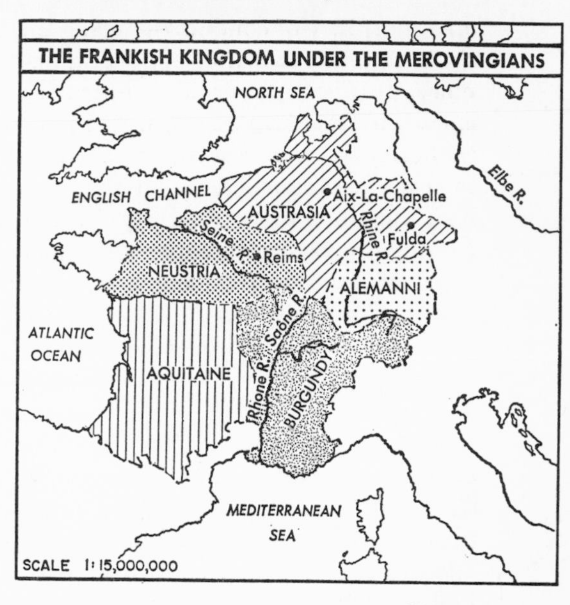

MAP 5

The western and southern regions had been thoroughly Romanized, whereas the north and east had experienced little if any Roman occupation. Consequently, the Frankish conquerors in Neustria, Aquitaine, and Burgundy generally adopted Roman customs and the Latin language, whereas the Franks in the north and east retained their Germanic tongue. Another divergence occurred in the process of Christianization. When King Clovis embraced Christianity around 500, his Frankish followers in the west readily joined his conversion, since the local population of the region had already been Christianized for centuries. East of the Rhine, however, there was no local Christian population. Hence the east Rhenish Franks did not become converted. These regions were Christianized considerably later: southwestern Germany during the sixth century; the areas north of the river Main only during the seventh and eighth centuries, partly by missionaries, such as the Anglo-Saxon Wynfrith (680?–754), and partly by forcible conversion by their Frankish overlords.

Concomitant differences between the two regions can be seen in the roles played by the bishops of the Church. Clovis and his successors found it opportune to base their rule on friendship with the Church of Rome and alliance with local bishops. But the power of the bishops varied. West of the Rhine, where the bishoprics had developed under the Roman administrative system, the bishops tended to display less independent power, and the Frankish rulers could exercise more control over them. In the north and east, however, the bishoprics had experienced no Roman domination. They developed in an atmosphere of conquest—during the sixth to tenth centuries—and retained more political power and independence. The Frankish rulers, whose royal authority in the east never assumed such great proportions as in the west, had therefore more difficulty in controlling the eastern bishops—a development of considerable importance in later German history.

Under the Carolingians

A little over a century after the death of Clovis I, the Merovingian rulers started to decline in power. Although they retained the official kingship for another century, their control over the kingdom decreased rapidly. Decentralization and feudalism made their appearance. The turning point came in the middle of the eighth century, when the impotent Merovingians were replaced by the new dynasty of the Carolingians. Pepin the Short (741–768),[1] the first king of the new dynasty, began his reign with an entirely new policy. That he would collaborate intimately with the Church was nothing new, since all Merovingian rulers had followed this policy. But far from contenting himself with working in harmony with the Church, he initiated the practice of interfering in Italy.

The pope of the time, Stephen II (752–757), was in need of a strong ally. He was trying to maintain political control over central and southern Italy and thereby came into conflict with the Byzantine emperors. Since he was actually usurping Byzantine rights over Italy, he needed the powerful backing that only the newly strengthened Frankish Kingdom could provide. Moreover, the pope's Italian holdings were threatened by invading Lombard tribes, who by 751 had already conquered the city of Ravenna and were beginning to threaten Rome itself.

Under these circumstances, Pepin and Stephen concluded a bargain. The pope came to Gaul, recognized Pepin as the legitimate ruler of the Franks, and anointed him as king. This act was in itself a significant precedent. In the minds of many, it sanctioned the prerogative of the pope to decide who was to be king and to confirm his coronation by the symbolic act of anointment. It raised the whole question of who was superior, pope or king, church or state, and—as we shall see later—it helped lay the foundation for the bitter controversy between later emperors and the papacy. In return, the pope requested Pepin to come to Italy and subdue the Lombards in order to free the papacy from the danger threatening it. As further inducement for this enterprise, Stephen II bestowed upon Pepin the old Roman title *patricius,* which delegated to the bearer the honor as well as the duty of protecting Rome and Italy. Thus by consent of the pope —though not by permission of the emperor at Constantinople, who might be considered the legal ruler of Italy at this time—Pepin and his descendants could lay claim to Italy, provided that Pepin could make his claim valid by conquering the Lombards.

After conclusion of the agreement, Pepin invaded Italy and defeated the Lombards. As *patricius,* he retained over-all protectorship of the peninsula; but in the Donation of Pepin, 756, he entrusted the papacy with specific au-

[1] For secular rulers and popes, dates in parentheses indicate reigns; for all others they refer to life span.

thority over central Italy, thereby providing it with the basis for the Papal States, which remained the property of the Church until 1860.

The Frankish Kingdom emerged from these events as the strongest state in Europe—with the possible exception of distant Constantinople. Its claim to dominance over Italy was later assumed by the German branch of the Carolingians, and thence to the German emperors, and led to centuries of German involvement in Italian affairs.

Charles the Great

Pepin's oldest son was Charles the Great, better known as Charlemagne. After a short period of joint rule with his brother, Charles became sole ruler in 771, and until his death in 814, he remained the undisputed master of the largest European realm ever brought under the rule of one man in the Middle Ages. After inheriting a domain considerably larger than present-day France, he spent almost his entire reign extending the borders of his lands by conquests. In the northeast, he pushed the boundaries to the Elbe River and advanced into Schleswig; in the east, he occupied the western half of what is today Czechoslovakia and Hungary; in the southeast, he conquered as far as northern Yugoslavia; and in the south, he pushed his dominion over the Pyrenees into northern Spain (see Map 6).

The motives for these conquests were many. He sincerely felt it his duty to extend and consolidate Christianity in Europe, and when people were unwilling to accept the blessings of the cross peacefully, he imposed the new religion by the sword. Moreover, his conquests fitted his desire to re-establish the defunct Roman Empire. To be sure, many of the lands he conquered never had been a part of the former Empire. Yet the ideal of empire stood for universal rule and obedience, and Charles may have found it expedient to apply this criterion of universality as an excuse for imposing his rule on other peoples. Finally, his conquests—especially those against the Wends, the Avars, and the Arabs—may also be termed defensive. To secure his lands against raids from across the borders, he extended his boundaries and formed so-called marches, defensive border states from where trusted officials, the margraves or counts of the march, had the duty of guarding the outlying districts of the kingdom. Some of these marches—such as the Dane Mark, the Mark Brandenburg, and the Ost Mark (Austria)—became kernels for later political units.

But Charles the Great's importance goes beyond the fact that he consolidated a huge kingdom and actively spread Christianity. His reign marks the culmination of the period of the Frankish Kingdom during which there was little, if any, separation between the future French and German states. After him, the Frankish Kingdom rapidly declined and then disintegrated completely. For the histories of France and Germany, Charles marks the end of one era and the beginning of another. In the century after his death, France and Germany were permanently separated. Charles the Great is the last significant common link between them. Both nations later looked back upon him as one of their founding fathers; both claim him as their own. To the French, he is *Charlemagne,* the French king and emperor under whom France

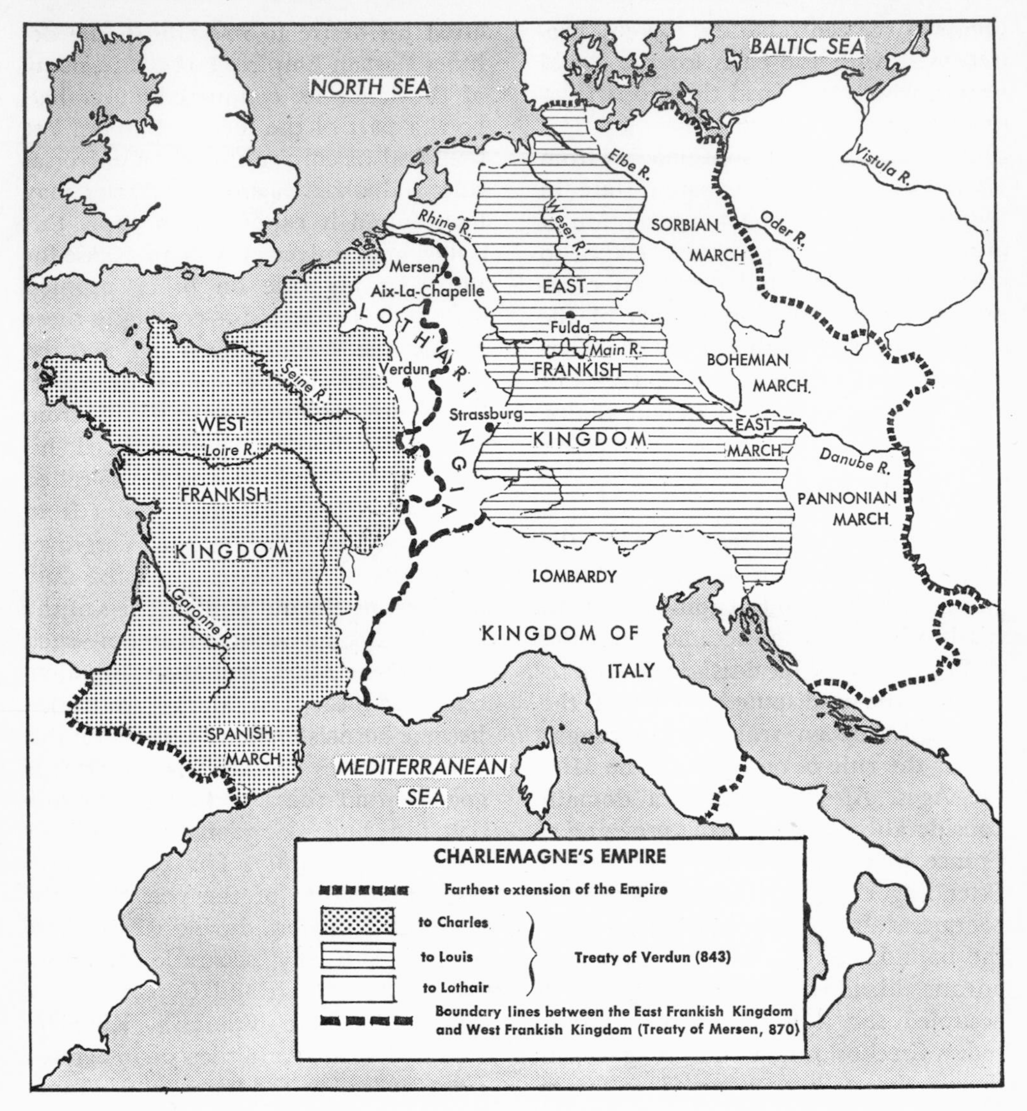

MAP 6

was larger than under any subsequent ruler except Napoleon I. To the Germans, he is *Karl der Grosse,* the first of the great kings and the founder of the German Empire.

Establishment of the Empire

The revival of the Empire, effected by Charles in A.D. 800, appears in the long run as the most significant of his acts. Like his father, Pepin, Charles intervened in Italy. After failing to subordinate the Lombard tribes by marrying the daughter of their king, Charles crossed the Alps, defeated the Lombards, and assumed the iron crown of Lombardy, thereby uniting under himself the Frankish and Lombard kingdoms. After gaining complete control of northern Italy, Charles was in a position to dictate his terms to the rest of the peninsula. Under normal circumstances, this might have brought him into conflict with the Church and with the emperor of Byzantium, who continued to hold claims of suzerainty over Italy. But neither event occurred. Byzantium (ruled at the time by Empress Irene) was not strong enough to challenge Charles, and in Rome, Pope Leo III (795–816) was barely able to control the city itself. In fact, in 799 the pope had been driven from Rome by a local revolution and had been restored only with the help of Frankish soldiers. He was therefore readily submissive to Charles's wishes.

After several conferences between pope and king, Charles went to Rome in the year 800 and was crowned emperor. We need not be concerned here with Charles's motives for accepting the imperial title nor with the reasons for the pope's eagerness to bestow it on Charles. Einhard, Charles's biographer, would have us believe that the king was not aware of the pope's plan to crown him, and felt filled with humble chagrin after the event. Most later historians insist that this was merely an outward show of humility and that Charles had actually worked out all the plans himself. Whatever the motives, the consequences of this act were enormous for all European history, and more particularly for the history of Germany.

By accepting the imperial crown, Charles in effect revived the dream of the old Roman Empire. Since the remainder of the original Empire still existed in the east, the revival of the Empire in the west actually re-created conditions as they had existed in late ancient times, after Rome had split into two empires, one with its capital in Rome, the other in Constantinople. But by 800, the Byzantine Empire was on the decline, and the rulers of Central and Western Europe had become accustomed to shaping their political destinies without imperial interference. The reconstitution of a strong Empire in the west, therefore, signified for most European rulers the reappearance of an imperial overlord who might claim their allegiance. By definition and tradition, this emperor would have universal rule. Such political universality, so well known in Roman days, had not existed in early medieval times. Separate kingdoms had arisen, particularistic and antiuniversal in nature. Thus the revival of the Empire by Charles the Great in a way went against the current stream of political development and was to create new complications for the rulers of Europe.

In the field of church-state relations, the revival of the Empire was to produce similar problems. The disappearance of universality in the political domain, after the fall of Rome, had no exact parallel in the field of religion. As the mantle of universality fell from Rome in the fifth century, Byzantium in the east and the papacy in the west both tried to assume it—one in the political, the other in the spiritual realm. But such an attempted separation between religion and politics proved impossible. The emperors at Constantinople continuously interfered in matters of religion, while the popes in Rome felt forced to assume political power. In fact, one of the main differences between the Greek Orthodox Church led by the patriarch of Constantinople and the Roman Catholic Church led by the pope was the question of subordination to an emperor. The patriarch in the east was completely subservient to the Byzantine emperors, whereas the pope in the west had succeeded in emancipating himself from such control. After

Pope Leo I, in the fifth century, the papacy had acquired almost complete sovereignty in spiritual matters and had grown more and more into a political power, unchallenged by other forces in western or central Europe. In the eighth century, the invasions of the Lombards and Pepin's interference in Italy were the first step toward limiting the political power of the papacy. Now the revival of an Empire in the west, with Charles the Great, threatened to bring the issue to a head. Since strict separation of politics and religion was impossible, conflict was bound to arise. The universal power claimed by the pope was contingent on absolute sovereignty, just as was that claimed by the emperor. But there could not be two universal and sovereign powers in Europe at the same time. Either the western Empire had to be subordinate to the papacy, or the pope had to obey the emperor.

This new question did not prove a dilemma in the days of Charles the Great. He was too powerful to be challenged effectively by the pope. Besides, the pope needed his protection. Under Charles, the Church was definitely subordinate. The emperor considered himself a Christian ruler, instituted in his position by God, responsible not merely for the political, social, and economic but also for the spiritual welfare of his people. He filled vacant bishoprics at his own discretion with candidates who would cooperate with him. In the realm of dogma he granted the pope considerable responsibilities, but in political matters he permitted him to exercise little more power than any ordinary bishop.

The so-called Roman Empire which Charles the Great set up was, of course, not a real revival of the old Roman Empire of the Caesars. The name it received later—from the twelfth century on—"The Holy Roman Empire of the Germanic Nation," is really quite apt, although it has often been ridiculed. Voltaire's statement that the Holy Roman Empire was "neither holy, nor Roman, nor Empire" is frequently quoted. Actually, the adjective *Holy* indicates the religious overtones of this political structure and its relations to the papacy. The words *Germanic Nation* properly label it as a German Empire. And the term *Roman* denotes that the new Empire was supposedly based on the model of the Empire of Augustus. *Roman* certainly does not signify that the center was to be at Rome. In fact, Italy represented hardly more than an annex, important for the past glory of the city of Rome itself and the connection with the Catholic Church, as well as for the economic wealth, particularly of northern Italy. The center of this Empire was at all times north of the Alps.

Besides setting up this new imperial structure and organizing a fairly efficient and centralized administration, Charles also contributed to the revival of learning. The years between the fifth and the eighth centuries had witnessed an alarming dissipation of the intellectual climate. Language itself had undergone rapid changes with much resulting confusion as the developing Germanic tongues mixed with or replaced the existing Latin. By far the greater part of the knowledge of classical times had been destroyed by the invading barbarians, or lay forgotten in musty scrolls, or was unintelligible to the scholars of the day because of their limited intellectual horizon or their inability to read Latin.

In his palace school at Aix-la-

Chapelle, Charles the Great gathered some of the best minds of his day for the purpose of consolidating existing knowledge and raising the level of education, particularly among the clergy. The teachers he employed came from many lands: Alcuin from York, Einhard from Fulda, Paul the Deacon from Lombardy. The language they used was still a vulgar form of Latin, closely approaching medieval Latin, but it is evident from documents that the vernacular languages had sufficiently crystallized to be used for purely local matters as well as for some works of literature. Much of the work consisted merely of copying classical documents in the beautiful Carolingian minuscule, but the period also produced auspicious beginnings of German literature in the *Wessobrunner Prayers,* the epic *Hildebrandslied,* and the story of Jesus, the *Heliand.* The latter, written in Old High German, is one of the earliest Christian epics known and shows an interesting attempt to fuse the various fountainheads of medieval culture: the Christian, the Germanic, and the classical traditions.

Finally, Charles also left his imprint on architecture. Here he leaned heavily on southern and eastern models, and even imported Byzantine architects. His beautiful, mosaic-studded palace chapel in Aix-la-Chapelle is a remarkable adaptation of Byzantine architectural and decorative styles.

Disintegration of the Frankish Empire

The ninth century was a period of renewed disintegration. Under the impact of Magyar and Norse raids, which afflicted most of central and western Europe, feudal decentralization set in. The outlying districts of the Empire looked to local rulers for protection, and gradually cut their ties of allegiance to the Emperor. The so-called Dark Ages began.

A strong ruler might perhaps have stemmed this tide of political dissolution, but Charles the Great had been the last strong Carolingian. His only surviving son, Louis the Pious (814–840), wasted his resources on civil wars with his own heirs over questions of inheritance. Like the preceding Merovingians, the Carolingians had failed to establish the right of primogeniture, and this failure helped accelerate the disintegration of the Empire and brought about the gradual separation of the future German and French states.

In the 840s, after the death of Louis the Pious, the three remaining grandsons of Charles the Great again took up the fight over the division of the patrimony. Charles the Bald had been assigned the western portion of the kingdom, and Louis the German was in charge of the eastern regions. The two allied themselves against Lothair, who, as the eldest son, had received the imperial title during the lifetime of his father but had not been awarded any particular share of the land as his own. At Strassburg, in 842, Charles and Louis took an oath of friendship in the presence of their troops. The text of this oath reveals the linguistic difference between the eastern and western parts of the Frankish Kingdom. So that the troops led by his brother could understand him, Louis the German pronounced his oath in what is easily recognizable as Old French, whereas Charles the Bald used a language much more Germanic in basis and close to Old High German.

In the ensuing struggle, the Church favored Lothair, presumably because he bore the imperial title and therefore stood for universality and order. It appears symptomatic for the future that Lothair, as emperor, had at his disposal less power and fewer resources than his brothers, who were supposed to be subordinate rulers. This was an obvious consequence of the initial legacy of Louis the Pious, when Lothair was given only the title and honors of emperor, whereas the land—the real basis of political power—was assigned to his brothers. Such relative weakness of the emperor vis-à-vis his subjects was to become a quasi-normal condition in the history of the Empire.

In 843, in the Treaty of Verdun, the three brothers came to an agreement. They now divided their patrimony into three instead of two portions. Charles the Bald received essentially what was to be the basis of modern France: Neustria and Aquitaine. In the east, Louis received almost all the lands east of the Rhine, including parts of present-day Austria. In the center, Lothair obtained the zone of fragmentation already referred to in Chapter 1. This purely political creation without ethnic or even dynastic justification, consisted of a narrow strip of land from Frisia in the north to below Rome in the south —a region partly Germanic and partly Romance in language, containing areas that were either thoroughly or very little Romanized. In addition, Lothair was allowed to retain the imperial title. This Treaty of Verdun tentatively marks the beginning of "French" and "German" history: except for a few brief years in the late ninth century, the two countries were never again united but developed as completely separate and frequently antagonistic units.

When Emperor Lothair's direct descendants died, a new division between the two remaining rulers was necessary. This was accomplished in the Treaty of Mersen in 870. The imperial title was taken over by Charles the Bald, but the bulk of Lothair's lands passed into the hands of the East Frankish ruler. The boundary set up in this treaty again was a political creation, ignoring all ethnic considerations. Following more or less the rivers Schelde, Meuse, Argonne, Saône, and Rhone, it incorporated the Romance-speaking regions of Lorraine and Burgundy into "Germany," while leaving the German-speaking Flemish peoples in "France." (see Map 6).

The Carolingian dynasty in the east —in what we shall from now on refer to as Germany—lasted another three generations after Louis the German before dying out in 911. These early years of German history pointed up certain developments that were to become familiar phenomena in succeeding centuries. The amount of land controlled by Louis the German and his successors varied constantly. Different regions here and there made themselves independent and, at times, were again brought under the rule of the German kings. Moreover, the early German rulers never quite managed to gain complete control of their kingdom. They were weak and conditions were against them. These were the days when Norse raiders plundered deep into the heart of central Europe and when local nobles grouped themselves around strong leaders for the sake of better defense, in an ever more ramified feudal arrangement. The natural leaders in this system were certain powerful bishops as well as counts and dukes whose families had been former tribal leaders or whose position of authority had been confirmed by Charles the Great when he incorporated them into his administrative system. Consequently, although the shadow of a kingdom was superimposed on the land, the real power remained with the rulers of the smaller units.

THE EARLY GERMAN DYNASTIES

When the last Carolingian of the German branch died in 911, the German duchies followed the example set by other regions and permanently broke with the Carolingians in the west. Rather than unite Germany again with France under the rule of the French Carolingian (Charles the Simple), the dukes elected Conrad of the House of Franconia as their new king. With this new dynasty on the German throne, a dynasty whose roots lay east of the Rhine in Franconia, it can be stated without hesitation that *German* history has started. From then on, the German crown was to be passed on by a mixture of hereditary and elective principles—that is to say, the new ruler was always elected, though most of the time the son of the former king was chosen as the next in line—but, with few unimportant exceptions, the crown always remained in the hands of families from German-speaking lands.

This separation of 911 should not be considered as a conscious rejection of a "French" ruler by "German" tribes. Both kingdoms continued for a long time to use the same term, *regnum francorum* (Kingdom of the Franks), to designate their realms. It was not until a century later that the eastern duchies adopted the new name *regnum theutonicum* (Kingdom of the Teutons or Germans). The simplest explanation for the separation of 911 lies probably in factors of local convenience and necessity. The Carolingian ruler west of the Rhine was weak and occupied with local problems. The German duchies to the east needed a nearby leader who could guide them against the invading Magyars and Norsemen. Hence they chose one of their own for this largely military task.

The new state that arose in 911 turned out to be a loose federation of duchies under a relatively powerless ruler. Its first king, Conrad I, ruled for only eight years. Upon his death in 918, the crown passed to the house of Saxony, in which it remained for over a century.

The Saxon Dynasty, 919–1024

The Saxon rulers, for the most part, were strong, able, and skillful. They vigorously repelled the invasions that continued to threaten Germany, especially by the Slavic Wends in the northeast and the Magyars in the southeast. Pushing the latter out of present-day Austria, the Saxons made Bohemia a tributary of the Empire and defeated the Poles, who had a strong and rising monarchy. They also extended their dominion in the west by reclaiming the Duchy of Lorraine, which had temporarily receded to the western branch of the Carolingians, and expanded to the southwest by gaining protectorship over Provence and Burgundy. Their main efforts, however, were directed to the south toward the conquest and retention of Italy. In this manner, Germany was converted into the most powerful European state of the tenth century.

In addition, the attempt was made

to reduce the power of the stem duchies. For this purpose, the Saxon rulers sought to ally themselves with the Church, which favored more centralized rule and opposed particularism. But lessening the powers of the dukes and turning Germany into a centralized state was hardly an easy task. The king's power depended, after all, on the resources he could muster from his family domain, and for all major undertakings he required the goodwill and cooperation of the dukes. It is symptomatic that when Henry I of Saxony became king in 919, he was initially recognized as such only by the Saxons and the Franks. The entire federation of duchies seemed on the verge of disintegrating. The Swabians and the Bavarians agreed to tender him recognition only after he assured them that he would not interfere with their sovereign powers and after he had won some important victories over the Hungarians, thereby acquiring the respect of the dukes.[2]

Even the second ruler of the Saxon line, Otto I (936–973) —one of the most powerful of the medieval kings—was unable to eradicate the strong stem duchies. Although he tried to lessen their independence by skillful marriage alliances and to overcome their opposition by force, particularism remained the stigma of German political life.

One may wonder why the German dukes, so staunchly intent on maintaining their independence, bothered to elect a king, thereby obligating themselves to give tacit recognition to an overlord. Would it not have served the interests of the dukes if the German Kingdom had been allowed to disintegrate into its component parts? The need felt by the nobles for a military leader to unite them in joint action against outside enemies was not the only reason for the continued existence of the kingdom. A more cogent reason lies in the relations between the kings and the Church. The clergy, the only learned men of the day, had retained some notion of the Roman idea of *respublica*—more or less equivalent to the modern idea of *state* or *commonweal*—whereas the dukes and lesser nobles were concerned only with personal relations. The Church was thus the prime supporter of the idea of a kingdom. Moreover, the bishops fared better politically and economically when they were not subject to local lay lords but merely paid homage to a distant king. The kings, for their part, could gain valuable economic benefits as well as added political and military power by being on friendly terms with the powerful bishops and by exercising some measure of control over episcopal lands and elections. This explains to a large extent the bonds of alliance formed at an early date between the German kings and the German bishops and abbots. It also reveals the perhaps startling fact that, to a large degree, the continued existence of the German Kingdom was due to the support of the Church.

OTTO THE GREAT Otto I is often called Otto the Great. It is he, rather than Charles the Great, who is frequently considered the founder of the Holy Roman Empire—although this name was not used in his day. Between Charles the Great and Otto I, the institution of empire had continued to

[2] By this time, the six stem duchies—Bavaria, Franconia, Frisia, Saxony, Swabia, and Thuringia—had been reduced to four, Frisia and Thuringia having been absorbed by their more powerful neighbors, the Saxons.

exist, but it had lost all effective power. Few of the emperors had been important. In fact, some, such as Guido of Spoleto and Hugh of Provence, were so insignificant that the title threatened to become meaningless. Other rulers, such as Henry I, although quite powerful, never had themselves crowned and were technically not emperors.

But Otto I looked with deep interest upon the institution of the Empire. His concern for the religious implications and overtones of universality was probably less great than his desire for political and economic control of Italy. He undertook several expeditions to the peninsula, established his dominance over its northern portion, and in the year 962 he formally re-established the Empire by being crowned in Rome, thereby underscoring German claims to permanent control over Italy.

The Empire thus reconstituted was essentially similar to that created by Charles the Great, and the dispute among historians whether it was a continuation of Charles's creation or a new beginning seems academic. Yet there were some fundamental differences. Charles's Empire was the work of one man, and although it continued to exist in theory, it actually hardly outlived its creator. The Empire set up by Otto I, however, was a lasting institution. It gained strength for several centuries before starting its gradual decline, and was ultimately abolished only in 1806, by Napoleon I. Moreover, the core of Charles the Great's Empire lay west of the Rhine, whereas the center of Otto's was to its east. Finally, another significant difference is that in Charles the Great's time there was no other political unit strong enough to challenge his rule; hence Charles could be considered a "universal" ruler. In the days of Otto that assumption no longer held true. Although the Germany of Otto was the strongest European power, there were other growing political units, such as England, France, and Poland, that clearly lay outside the realm of the new Empire, thus making universality a fiction (see Map 7).

In addition to establishing himself as emperor, Otto tried to make his hold on Italy as secure as possible. For this reason he sought to acquire Provence in order to have better access to the peninsula without having to rely exclusively on the one Alpine route over the Brenner Pass. The papacy of this period had fallen under the domination of local Roman noble families and was extremely weak and unstable. In the ninth century alone, twenty-eight different popes occupied the papal throne. Otto took full advantage of this situation. He brought about the deposition of two popes and the election of two others. He also forced the popes to concede that no papal elections were valid until approved by the emperor, thereby clearly underlining that the Church was to be subordinate to the Empire. Finally, he also arranged for the marriage of his son, the future Otto II, to the daughter of the emperor of Byzantium and claimed that his daughter-in-law's dowry was to be the remaining Byzantine claim to southern Italy, so that henceforth the emperors could pretend to legal rights to all of Italy.

Although the tenth century still belongs largely to the so-called cultural Dark Ages, a good deal of literary activity took place at the court of Otto I and in the monasteries of the Empire. Most of these works were written in Latin, such as the comedies of the nun Roswitha of Gandersheim, who at-

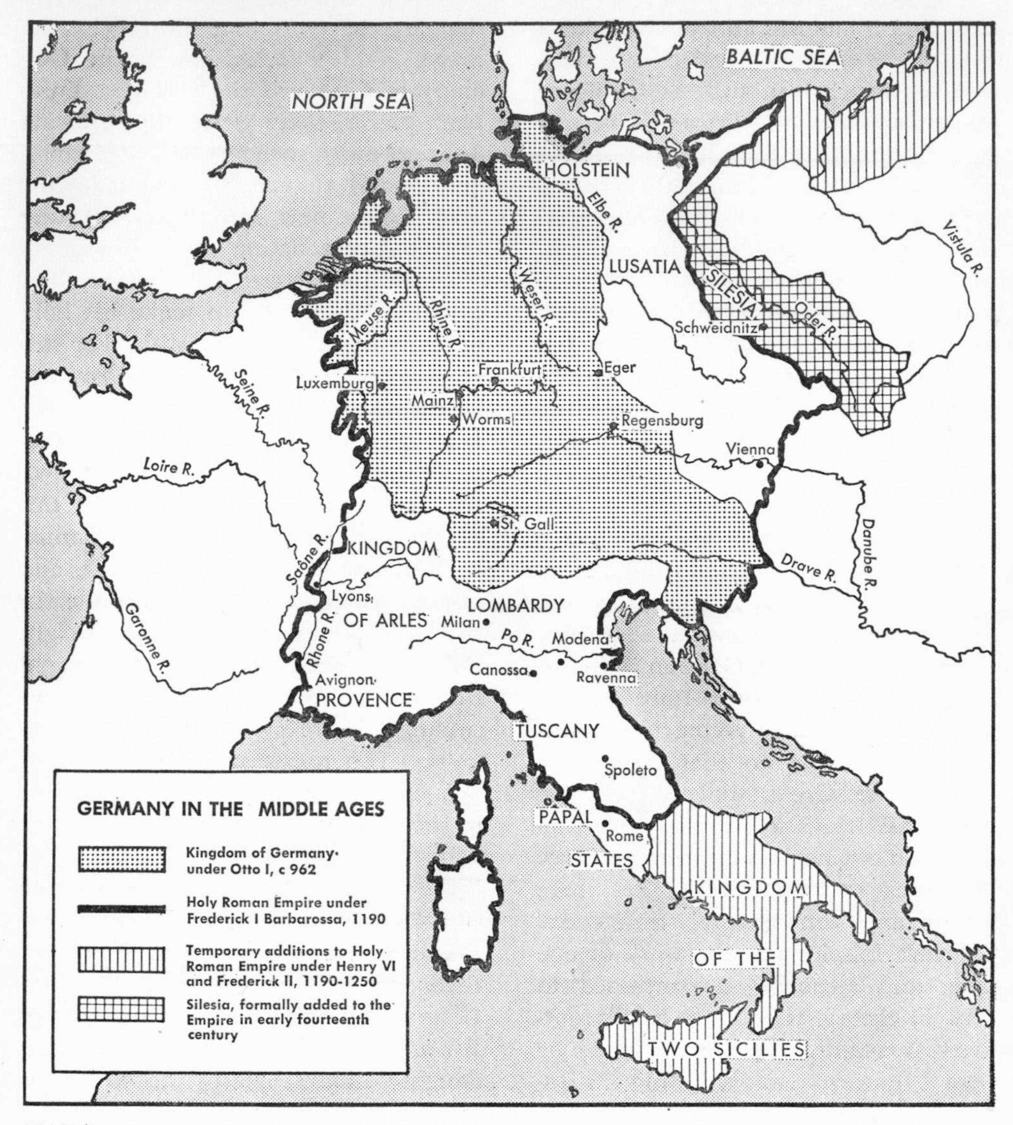

MAP 7

tempted to imitate the comedies of Terence but felt obliged to purge his works, since her aim was to praise the Christian life of virgins. There was also a Latin chronicle about the Saxon rulers, written to glorify the deeds of Otto the Great and others. It was composed by the Benedictine monk Widukind of Corvey, who is sometimes called "the first German historian." In addition, some works appeared that are more directly related to the beginnings of German culture. The *Waltharilied,* probably written by Ekkehard, a monk of St. Gall, is one of the earliest of the extant medieval legends that exerted a profound influence on German literature in later centuries. The Walther of this story is the son of the king of Aquitaine, a brother-in-arms of Hagen and Gunther, and a hostage of King Attila of the Huns. Many of the characters of this epic later reappear in the more famous and much larger saga of the *Niebelungen*.

THE LATER SAXONS The later emperors of the Saxon line in general continued the policies of Otto I. Besides expanding the kingdom in the northeast at the expense of the Slavs, they devoted much effort to keeping Italy subdued. Also, they constantly interfered in the affairs of the papacy. In fact, they tended to spend more time in Italy than in Germany. Emperor Otto III, for instance, adopted manners that were more southern than northern. He appeared so fascinated by Italy that a popular legend arose to the effect that the young emperor—he died at twenty-two—had fallen hopelessly in love with a beautiful girl called "Roma," who eventually killed him.

In Germany, the Saxon rulers faced many revolts by powerful dukes. Although these rebellions were usually put down successfully, the duchies were acquiring more and more power. The dukes and some of the lesser nobles even made their realms hereditary, establishing strong local dynasties. On the other hand, the power of the emperors over German bishops increased steadily, since the emperors were able to retain the privilege of electing new bishops. Consequently, the high ecclesiastics continued to be the emperors' best allies in the struggle against the rebellious dukes. In this connection, it is interesting to note that as the emperors pushed east, rather than entrusting more power to the dukes of the border districts, as Charles the Great had done, they created new bishoprics as outposts against the Slavs.

The Salian Dynasty, 1024–1125

In 1024 with the death of the Saxon Henry II, a new dynasty, the Salian or Franconian house, replaced the Saxon line. The new dynasty, which ruled the Empire until 1125, became involved in several developments that greatly affected later German history. In their attempt to weaken the powerful dukes of Germany, the Salian emperors encouraged feudalization of the smaller fiefs and condoned efforts by lesser nobles to make their fiefs hereditary. This, of course, produced a further splintering of political power. The Salians also increased their dominions in all directions: in the east, they gained parts of Poland and extended the boundary of the Empire to include Bohemia, Moravia, and the march of Austria (Ost Mark); in the west, they incorporated the kingdoms of Arles and Burgundy into the Empire. These acquisitions enabled them to dominate southern France and achieve an even tighter hold on Italy.

The most spectacular occurrence in the eleventh century was no doubt the prolonged fight between the papacy and the emperors known as the investiture controversy. To understand this struggle, one must examine the changes that took place in the Church during the late ninth and tenth centuries. At the beginning of this period, the papacy had reached one of the lowest points in its history. The popes had little or no power over the bishops, and the centralized structure of the Church had practically disintegrated. The See of St. Peter itself was in the hands of local Roman nobles who bought, sold, or conquered the privilege of being pope with no regard for its spiritual significance. The clergy at large were deeply involved in the rising feudal structure of society. When the emperor did not exercise this privilege himself, local nobles appointed bishops and clerics so as to control the church lands and benefit from their revenue. Simony and pluralism flourished, and since celibacy was practically unknown, many a clergyman raised a family and was more intent on arranging for the succession of his children to his own church benefice than on caring for the souls of his parish.

THE CLUNIAC REFORM These conditions within the Church evoked cries of protest and stimulated the powerful monastic order of Cluny to spearhead a movement for reform. To recentralize the Church and strengthen the papacy, to establish celibacy of the clergy and abolish simony, to eliminate lay influence over church lands, church elections, and church revenues—these were the main ideals promoted by the Cluniac reform. This movement gained momentum after 1000, and started to bear fruit in the second half of the eleventh century. It was to reach its climax in the powerful pontificate of Gregory VII, better known by his German name, Hildebrand (1073–1085).

The sudden attempt by the Church to free itself from outside interference and if possible to impose its will on lay rulers created antagonisms among all secular princes. Pope Gregory, in his famous *Dictatus Papae,* was to assert that "he may absolve all subjects from their fealty to wicked men"—that is, to lay rulers; that furthermore "it may be permitted to him to depose emperors"; and that "he alone may use the imperial insignia." Such statements were likely to provoke any ruler attempting to make himself sovereign. But in the eleventh century there existed no strong states, and the kings of feudal monarchies such as France and England were as yet too weak to challenge the papacy seriously. The emperors, however, were bound to take up the gauntlet. The Empire was the strongest political unit of the time. It dominated much of Italy, which the popes hoped to make their own domain. It had, in fact, for a long time dominated the papacy itself. Moreover, the emperors aspired to universality, and therefore both emperor and pope claimed ultimate sovereignty.

By the last quarter of the eleventh century, the papacy had gained considerably in strength. Its security had been increased through alliance with the Normans who had conquered southern Italy and Sicily. Above all, the popes had adopted the Cluniac reform program and had attempted to render the clergy independent of all lay rulers and more directly subordinate to the papacy.

THE INVESTITURE CONTROVERSY The clash between pope and emperor came into the open during the reign of Emperor Henry IV (1056–1106). Henry tried to concentrate all power in himself. To this end, he wished not only to subdue the lay princes, but at the same time to retain power over the German bishops. To strengthen his treasury, he freely made use of church revenues. In addition, he started the practice of granting charters to towns, thereby turning the burghers, then gaining in wealth and power, into friends of the monarchy and valuable allies against the powerful princes.

Since Henry was trying to use the

Church as a means of controlling his realm, he was bound to clash with those attempting to free the Church from lay influence. Hence he disputed with Pope Stephen IX (1057–1058) over control of the northern Italian bishoprics; with Pope Nicholas II (1059–1061) over the creation of an electoral college of cardinals, which was to remove lay interference in papal elections. He even contested the validity of the election of Pope Alexander II (1061–1073), since he had not been consulted. Under his auspices, the Synod of Basel elected a second or "antipope" (Honorius II). In all these struggles, the German bishops usually sided with Henry, since they opposed many of the projected reforms of the popes.

At this point, in 1073, Gregory VII ascended the papal throne. Gregory was not only the most ardent of the reformers, but he was also highly skilled at the diplomatic game of gaining allies and playing one enemy off against another. His desire to make the papacy supreme was almost a mania. His writings contain some of the strongest declarations ever made in the Middle Ages concerning the popes' superiority to kings and emperors.

In 1073, Henry IV was again involved in civil war. Saxony was in rebellion, and he was for a time unable to suppress the revolt. Most of the powerful princes of Germany sided against Henry, since they wished to maintain their independent power. Thus it was natural that they found a ready ally in Pope Gregory VII. Hard pressed, Henry decided to submit to papal demands. He promised obedience to the pope. This submission proved merely an expedient. As soon as he had overcome the rebellion in Germany, Henry quickly forgot his promises and continued to practice lay investiture, that is, electing new bishops and investing them with their insignia of office without consulting the pope.

But Gregory did not let matters rest. In December 1075, he accused Henry of breaking his promises. The pope wrote:

> Since thou doest confess thyself a son of the Church, it would have beseemed thy royal dignity to look more respectfully upon the master of the Church . . . to whom, if thou art of the Lord's sheep, thou wast given over by the Lord's voice and authority to be fed.

From Henry's point of view it was clear that he could not submit to Gregory's demands. Had Henry relinquished control over the bishops, the Church would have become an independent organization within his Empire, just at a time when he was trying to consolidate and centralize it. Henry therefore decided to defy the pope. "As if we had received our kingdom from thee!" he replied in the following year. "As if the Kingdom and the Empire were in thine and not in God's hands!" He then called his German bishops to a meeting at Worms, in 1076, and induced them to condemn Gregory on all sorts of charges and to demand his abdication.

Gregory replied by excommunicating Henry and absolving his subjects from their oath of fealty. In addition, he sought active allies. These he again found in the German princes. The latter, hoping to weaken Henry, demanded that he make his peace with the pope or be deposed. They invited the pope to come to Augsburg to preside over a session at which Henry would be tried for his crimes. The princes probably felt certain that no reconciliation between Henry and Gregory was possible; they therefore could feel justified in deposing an excommunicated king and electing in his stead a weaker and more pliable one. If, contrary to expectation, a reconciliation took place, Henry would be so humiliated that his power would be reduced to a minimum.

King Henry now lost all his support in Germany and was faced with a strong alliance against him. Even most of the German bishops abandoned him, fearing the emperor was no longer strong enough to protect them and not wishing to be on the losing side. With only a few towns, such as Worms, faithful to him, Henry was forced to submit. Rather than face the pope at a large gathering of German princes in Augsburg, he decided to journey to Italy for the purpose of coming to terms with the papacy. Meanwhile, Gregory had started north toward Germany. In the year 1077, the two met in northern Italy, at Canossa, near Modena. The scene of the supposedly penitent king standing barefoot in the snow below the walls of the fortress of Canossa has moved many playwrights and painters. The pope hesitated for three days before admitting Henry to the castle and bestowing upon him his forgiveness.

Canossa certainly seemed a tremendous triumph for Gregory. The king of the Germans, the ruler of the universal Empire, lay prostrate in the snow waiting for three days to be allowed to kiss the pope's feet! Was more proof needed that the papacy was superior to the Empire? And yet, in the long run, the penitence at Canossa did not hurt Henry, and the fight between the two in fact terminated in Henry's victory.

When Henry returned to Germany, the princes refused to retender their allegiance. They continued their rebellion and elected an "antiking," Rudolf of Swabia. Civil war again broke out, the towns siding on Henry's side while most princes opposed him. Gregory for his part hesitated for three years in choosing between the two German kings. He had forgiven Henry at Canossa and should therefore have again recognized him as legitimate ruler. But Henry hardly seemed penitent, for he continued to practice lay investiture. Rudolf of Swabia, on the other hand, promised Gregory not to interfere in episcopal elections. This move finally convinced Gregory, for he was determined to push his policy of reform. In 1080, he again excommunicated Henry and proclaimed Rudolf the rightful ruler of Germany, thereby asserting the prerogative of the papacy to decide on the legitimacy of German elections. This time, however, Henry was not abandoned in Germany. The bishops now feared Gregory's motives. They sided with Henry, met in synod, deposed Gregory, and elected an antipope (Clement III). Europe now witnessed the spectacle of two kings and two popes, both respectively claiming the same thrones.

Henry proved to be the stronger contestant. He was victorious in battle and defeated Rudolf in 1080 in an encounter in which the antiking was slain. Henry then began an invasion of Italy, and the pope found himself without allies except for the Norman Robert Guiscard. For several years, the Normans protected Rome from Henry's assault, but in 1084 the city became weary of its Norman protectors, who apparently acted more like conquerors than allies. Gregory was forced to flee to the south, where he died in the same year, and Henry entered Rome with his antipope.

The death of Gregory VII in no way ended the investiture controversy. It is true that Henry's antipope (Clement III) lived until 1100 and was succeeded by various antipopes, all subservient to the emperor. But the real power and prestige of the papacy reverted to Gregory's successors, Popes Victor III (1087), Urban II (1088–1099), and Paschal II (1099–1118), who were, of course, staunch enemies of Henry IV.

The emperor's triumph of 1084 was short-lived. His dream of establishing the supremacy of the Empire over the Church came to nought. Even more ominous for the future of Germany, he was unable to make himself master in his own kingdom. His enemies, in alliance with the papacy, were able to win to their side Henry's own sons, Conrad and Henry. Thus Henry IV finally lost control not only of Germany and Italy, but also of his own household. In 1104, the princes elected the young Henry as their new king, Henry V, without the consent and even against the will of his father. It is somewhat tragic and ironic that the father, after having withstood so many political storms in his fights with princes and popes, was to end his career betrayed by his own son. The latter tricked him into accepting a bogus invitation for a reconciliation. When Henry IV arrived, the son had his father thrown into prison, and by reducing him to helplessness, forced him to abdicate.

The era of Henry IV, with its civil wars and rebellions, points up the strong self-interest of the German princes, a heritage that became one of the banes of German political life. Also, struggles between father and son, such as that between Henry IV and Henry V, were to be a frequent occurrence in German history. It often happened that while the father was alive, the son advocated a policy diametrically opposed to that of his father. But, usually, when the son succeeded to the responsibilities of office, he realized the merits of his father's policies and adopted them himself.

HENRY V'S COMPROMISE Henry V (1106–1125), the last of the Salian emperors, was such a ruler. As soon as he began his reign, he found himself following in his father's footsteps. He started to oppose the papacy and practice lay investiture, and he attempted to reduce the power of the independent princes. In the east, too, he took up the expansionist drive, fighting wars in Hungary and Poland.

But the pope whom Henry V opposed, Paschal II, was more conciliatory in nature than Gregory VII. When Henry invaded Italy in 1111 to reclaim his Italian possessions and to obtain the imperial crown in Rome, Paschal offered to come to terms. The solution proposed by the pope, if it had been put into effect, would have ended forever the fight between church and state. But it would also have changed the fundamental character of the Church as a whole. Paschal proposed that the Church should devote itself exclusively to spiritual matters; that it should disentangle itself from all secular affairs and resume the original ideals of apostolic poverty by giving up all lands, fiefs, and secular power, retaining jurisdiction only over the city of Rome and over church tithes. In return for this renunciation by the Church, Paschal asked Henry to guarantee complete noninterference in the nomination, election, and investiture of churchmen. Henry appeared agreeable to such a solution. If the bishops would renounce their secular rights, they would cease being powerful princes. Under such conditions Henry could well forfeit the right of investiture.

It appeared, however, that the pope was the only churchman ready to take this momentous step. When the pact between Henry and Paschal was announced, the clergy rose in rebellion against their own pope, for they were in no way ready to relinquish their feudal rights and immense land benefices. The agreement therefore could not be consummated. Thus thwarted, Henry resorted to his father's policy of force. He imprisoned the pope and forced him to sign a renunciation of all the pretensions that had been set forth by Gregory VII, especially the Church's right of investiture. But this one-sided victory of the emperor did not last long. After Paschal had been freed from imprisonment and had strengthened his position, he retracted all concessions made to Henry and excommunicated him for having "dared lay hands on the Apostle of Saint Peter."

Thus the war between papacy and Empire was renewed. Henry elected a new antipope. Once again the allegiance of clergy and lay Christians was divided between two popes. Paschal's immediate successors at first continued the same policy and renewed the ban against Henry, but finally in 1122, Calixtus II (1119–1124) was ready to try another compromise. At Worms, a concordat was signed between the papacy and the Empire. The ceremony of investiture was to be divided into two parts, one spiritual and the other lay, thus assuring the concurrence of both pope and emperor in the choice of bishops. The spiritual consecration or investiture with the staff and ring was to be performed by the pope or his legate, while the temporal power was to be bestowed by the emperor or his representative in the form of the scepter. In Germany, lay investiture was to precede spiritual consecration; in Italy and Burgundy the opposite sequence was to be followed.

Technically, this Concordat of Worms of 1122 ended the fifty-year-long investiture controversy between Empire and papacy, although, in fact, quarrels over the control of bishops reoccurred in later times. But the theoretical settlement of this issue in no way solved the problem of supremacy. On the contrary, the fights between Henry IV and V and the papacy had merely sharpened it.

Outwardly the Concordat of Worms has the appearance of a compromise. In reality, it was a victory for the papacy. The popes now at least had gained the recognition of their own claims. Before 1122, the emperors had practiced the right to appoint as bishop whomever they pleased. Now in the concordat they conceded that the pope had as much right in this matter as they. Furthermore, the papal position was strengthened by the diminution of lay influence over bishoprics, particularly in Italy. And for the Empire, the investiture controversy proved highly detrimental. By granting to the popes the right to select new bishops in Italy and to bestow on them the spiritual consecration, the emperors lost almost all control over the north Italian bishoprics, which had previously been one of their main supports in their attempted hold on Italy. Even in Germany, the new arrangement tended to reduce imperial power over the bishops. Moreover, at a time when the French and English monarchs were working hard at consolidating their royal power and turning their feudal realms into centralized monarchies, the Salian emperors wasted much of their strength on these fights with the papacy. To be sure, conditions in Germany differed in many respects from those in France and England, and it is fruitless to speculate whether without this church-state struggle the Salians could have succeeded in the manner of the Normans in England. Yet it is obvious that their task was made immeasurably more difficult if not hopeless through the continuing opposition of the Church.

3

Zenith of the Empire, 1125–1250

RIVALRY BETWEEN GUELFS AND GHIBELLINES

It seemed that Germany never was to experience peace for very long. No sooner had the investiture controversy temporarily subsided after the signing of the Concordat of Worms in 1122, when strife broke out between two rival princely houses, both of which aspired to pre-eminence in Germany. This rivalry between the Guelfs and the Ghibellines—which foreshadowed similar struggles between other dynasties during the thirteenth and fourteenth centuries—lasted for almost a hundred years, plunged Germany into numerous civil wars, and contributed to keeping it from developing into a unified nation.

The house of Guelf had its stronghold primarily in Saxony; the house of Ghibelline, whose dynastic name was Hohenstaufen, was centered in Swabia and southern Germany. Besides being a struggle for power, the controversy had other overtones. The Guelfs are sometimes called by historians the more patriotic, the more devoted to German interests, since they concentrated on building up their own strong state, particularly in northern Germany. Other historians simply label them more parochial, more selfish than the more "imperial-minded" Ghibellines, who, although also enlarging their holdings in southern Germany, tried to carry on the imperial tradition of Charles the Great and Otto I. These superficial judgments overlook the fact that the Guelfs were the not-so-loyal opposition party and that their interests consequently had to be different from those of the Ghibellines, who usually ruled the Empire. The one time the Guelfs obtained the kingship, with Otto IV, their actions were clearly in the old imperial tradition. The controversy also had its counterpart in Italy, a fact that further complicates the process of labeling the two parties. The followers of the Guelfs in Italy represented the papal party, which, at least in the popular mind, favored papal rule over Italy; whereas the Ghibellines advocated imperial control of the peninsula.

The rivalry between Guelfs and Ghibellines arose after the death of the Salian emperor Henry V in 1125, for Henry left no heir. The logical successor would have been Duke Frederick of Swabia (1090–1147), the leader of the house of Hohenstaufen. He was the nearest relative of the Salian line, a renowned general, powerful and wealthy, who, in addition to his own Swabia and Alsace, had inherited the vast Salian possessions. Henry himself had designated Frederick as his successor. But the imperial election of 1125 was conducted under conditions quite different from those of the preceding century. During the eleventh century, in the course of the investiture struggle and the unfortunate battle between Henry IV and his son, royal power had declined while the authority of the dukes had increased. Also, the bishops no longer automatically supported the king. In fact, the opposite of what Henry IV had hoped to achieve had occurred. Instead of gaining more influence over the selection of bishops and popes, the kings were finding that the popes were acquiring a powerful voice in the choice of new rulers. It was to the interest of both high ecclesiastics and dukes to undermine the notion of hereditary kingship that the Saxon and Salian dynasties had encouraged and to substitute for it a purely elective system. The custom of the Saxon and Salian rulers of having the son elected during the lifetime of his father had warped the whole elective process. The extinction of the Salian dynasty opened new possibilities to redress the balance.

Lothair II

Thus the election of 1125 was dominated by the propapal forces, certain powerful bishops and princes. They opposed the election of Frederick of Swabia because he appeared too strong and because, as a former loyal supporter of Henry V, he was likely to continue the antipapal policy of his predecessor. In his stead, they elected a bitter foe of the Salians, Duke Lothair of Supplinburg, who had respectable, but not very wealthy, holdings in northern Germany. By electing Lothair, the dukes and bishops also circumvented the principle of hereditary succession that seemed implicit in an election of Frederick. Choosing Lothair had an added advantage: he was old and without male heirs. Hence a new election would soon be required and the elective principle would be strikingly underscored. Moreover, it could be expected that the new king would cooperate with those to whom he owed his election.

In all his acts, Lothair II (1125–1137) differed from both his predecessors and his successors. Believing in peace through compromise, if not through submission, he deferred almost completely to the bishops and the papacy. Not using his prerogatives under the Concordat of Worms, he permitted spiritual investiture to precede lay investiture not merely in Italy, but also in Germany, thereby losing effective control over the choice of bishops. Symbolically his most significant step was his acceptance of the role of vassal to the Church when he took central Italy as a fief from the papacy in return for imperial coronation by the Pope in 1133. He then dissipated his forces fighting two unsuccessful campaigns for the pope, one against an antipope, the other against the Norman rulers of Sicily.

In Germany, Lothair tried to strengthen the Guelf position by investing the leader of that family (Henry the Proud) with as many lands as possible. Not surprisingly, this action brought him into conflict with the Hohenstaufens. It also opened a complicated question that was to plague Germany for several centuries: how to distinguish among imperial, royal, and dynastic property. During the tenth and eleventh centuries, there had been little need to separate imperial from dynastic possessions. Both had been freely mixed in the same family, since the Salians had acquired the royal and imperial titles as well as the property of the Saxon rulers. But the election of 1125 produced a new problem. Although the royal and imperial titles were bestowed upon Lothair, the Hohenstaufens had been designated the heirs of Henry V. The question arose as to which part of the Salian legacy was their private property and could be deeded by them to their heirs, and which part was "public domain" and should devolve upon the new ruler. Germany, of course, was not the only country to experience this dilemma. The same problem had existed in England, France, and other monarchies. In these lands, however, the hereditary system was adopted at an early date. In Germany, the victory of the elective system and the constant alternation among the dynasties on the German throne between 1125 and 1438 turned the problem into one of long-range consequences. As the highest lords of the land, the kings possessed the feudal right of sequestering the property of noble families who died out and of vassals who defied the crown. Most rulers made ample use of this prerogative to acquire additional lands during their reign. Upon their death and the succession of a new ruler from a different dynastic house, the question arose each time whether the property thus accumulated would remain the private possessions of the family of the deceased or should be transferred to the new ruler, together with the titles and prerogatives of the crown.

Since Lothair claimed the Salian lands that had passed as family property into the hands of Frederick of Swabia, civil war broke out. The Hohenstaufens replied by proclaiming a brother of Frederick as antiking in 1127 and by waging a drawn-out struggle against Lothair, who was supported by the Guelfs and the papal forces. The civil war ultimately ended in Lothair's victory, but he ruled for only twelve years; with his death in 1137, civil strife erupted again.

Conrad III

The successor to Lothair should have been the Guelf duke (Henry the Proud) who had inherited the domains of the emperor and was the wealthy and powerful ruler of Saxony, Bavaria, and large sections of Italy. But again the Church and the princes preferred a weaker candidate and elected Conrad of Hohenstaufen, who had been antiking since 1127. Hence the election of 1138 brought to the throne the first of the Hohenstaufen rulers.

The Hohenstaufen era lasted from 1138 until 1250. During this time the Empire reached its greatest expanse, as well as the height of its splendor and glory. The period also coincided with a great cultural and economic upsurge in Germany.

It was the age of the minnesingers (literally "singers of love"), who, like the French troubadours, sang of courtly love and chivalric themes. The greatest among them and one of the best of the Middle High German period, Walther von der Vogelweide (1170–1230)—a favorite of the Hohenstaufen rulers—also wrote political poems, staunchly antipapal and in support of German grandeur and unity. Around the turn of the century, epic poetry reached its zenith. An unknown author composed the *Niebelungenlied,* freely mixing twelfth-century concepts with the earlier legends. Probably inspired by a French narrative, the German troubadour Gottfried von Strassburg (around 1200) described the famous legend of *Tristan and Isolde.* Another lyric poet, Wolfram von Eschenbach (1170–1220), depicted the romance of the Holy Grail in *Parsifal*; and Hartmann von Aue (around 1200) developed themes from the Arthurian legends in *Iwein* and *Erek,* as well as strongly mystical ideals in *Gregorius on the Stone* and *The Unfortunate Henry.* This literary flourishing gave a strong impact to the development of the German language and furnished a substantial heritage of themes to later German literature. At the same time the development of Romanesque and early Gothic church architecture and sculpture produced numerous masterpieces. Linked with political power, this flourishing of German culture greatly enhanced the aura surrounding the Empire under the Hohenstaufens.

Yet this was by no means a peaceful century. Except under Conrad, there were almost constant clashes between the Empire and the papacy, which attained its own zenith during the later Hohenstaufen era. Moreover, the struggle between Guelfs and Ghibellines continued to plague the land until the early thirteenth century. Conrad III, for example, spent the greater part of his reign fighting the young Guelf leader Henry the Lion (1129–1195), who succeeded his father in 1139 and whose wealth and power threatened the emperor's pre-eminence.

While Conrad III (1138–1152) was occupied in civil war, the princes either fought one another or resumed their expeditions toward the northeast. During the tenth century, raids against the Slavs had been conducted primarily by the kings themselves, most prominently by Henry I and Otto I. In the following century, the eastward drive had been more in the form of missionary work under the aegis of powerful bishops, such as those of Bremen and Bamberg. Now, in the twelfth century, the work was again taken up by the secular powers. Following the example of the crusades to the Holy Land—and receiving similar encouragement from the papacy—some lords organized expeditions against the heathens of the northeast. More effective were the efforts of powerful princes of the border districts to conquer adjacent lands to the east. Albert the Bear (1100–1170) pushed his domain almost to the river Oder and assumed the title "Margrave of Brandenburg." Shortly thereafter, Henry the Lion pushed across the Elbe into Holstein and helped found the Baltic city of Lübeck, soon to become the most important German commercial center in the north. Both Albert and Henry transplanted German settlers to the conquered regions and thereby laid the foundation for the "New Germany" beyond the Elbe.

Like his predecessor, Conrad was dominated by the papacy. His only independent and successful action was to obtain the pope's agreement to have his son elected king, in an effort to arrest the progress of the elective system and to return to the hereditary succession practiced by the Salians. But even here Conrad failed, for the son died while his father was still alive.

Finally, unable to create order at

home, Conrad III heeded the supplications of St. Bernard of Clairvaux for a new crusade against the Turks. The First Crusade, in the late eleventh century, had been primarily a western European undertaking. Few Germans had participated. It is even possible that the news of Pope Urban's famous speech at Clermont, calling on the nobles of Europe to gather for a fight to recapture the Holy Sepulcher, never reached Germany. Besides, the Germans were then busy fighting one another, and the emperor himself would scarcely have thought it wise to absent himself from Europe for such a long time. The Second Crusade (1147–1149), of which Emperor Conrad was a leader, was the first such undertaking with major German participation. Even so, many German lords remained at home to safeguard their local interests or to fight heathens in the northeast.

Conrad and his stepbrother (Bishop Otto von Freising) led the imperial armies across the Balkans, followed by a French contingent under King Louis VII of France. When the Germans appeared before the gates of Constantinople, a question of protocol delayed their movement for days. Almost a week was spent negotiating for a possible meeting between the two emperors, Conrad of the Holy Roman Empire and Manuel of Byzantium. In the end, none could be effected because of problems of rank, aggravated by suspicion on the part of the Byzantines. The two emperors, although related to each other by marriage, refused to meet because neither was willing to recognize the superiority of the other. Conrad moved on toward the Holy Land, but his expedition met with little success. The local population of Asia Minor harassed the movement of the crusading armies, and much energy was dissipated through internal squabbles, particularly between German and French crusaders. Moreover, Conrad became sick and was unable to give forceful direction to the enterprise. Like his rule at home, the emperor's crusade was a failure.

FREDERICK BARBAROSSA

When Conrad III died in 1152, the electors passed over his only surviving son, who was but seven years old. This time they chose a strong king, perhaps in the realization that order was desperately needed in the realm. Frederick I (1152–1190) was an active ruler, intent on restoring the power of the Empire. Through his mother he was related to the Guelfs, through his father to the Ghibellines, and it was hoped that he would heal the feud between the two families. Besides, his election was facilitated by the benevolent attitude of the Church, which needed the aid of a strong ruler to regain mastery of Rome, and by a bargain Frederick made with the Guelf Henry the Lion. By confirming the latter's rights in Saxony and restoring to him Bavaria, which his father had lost, Frederick received the Guelf's support and cooperation.

Frederick I, whose red-blond hair gave him the nickname Barbarossa (Red Beard), was ambitious, fairly intelligent, and a good soldier. One may assume that he was the typical embodiment of a medieval knight. Surrounded by a splendid court, he became a colorful ruler who fired the imagination of the writers of his time and captured the love of succeeding generations. He acquired great popularity in German literature, and countless legends gathered around his name. Curiously, many of these stories were originally connected with his grandson, Emperor Frederick II. In the minds of the people, however, the splendors of the two Fredericks became fused. Later Germans looked upon Frederick I as a model emperor, admirable for his strength and determination. He came to embody the German dream of Empire. Especially in the nineteenth century, when Germans longed for political unification, Barbarossa was often evoked as the ideal ruler. One legend, revived by a nineteenth-century romantic poet (Friedrich Rückert), described him asleep inside the Kyffhäuser Mountain, his long red beard grown through the marble table on which his head rested. Above the mountain soared ravens, and as long as the ravens flew, Barbarossa would continue his centuries-long sleep. But one day, the legend ran, the ravens would cease their flight: Barbarossa would then awake from his magic sleep, and with his awakening, the splendor of the Empire would be restored.

Barbarossa's reign appears dominated by the aim of making the Empire again a reality. His internal policy, his relations with neighboring countries and with the Church, even his participation in the crusades, all seemed designed to serve this purpose. Restoring the imperial tradition meant, above all, controlling the Italian peninsula and uprooting all notions of imperial subordination to the papacy.

To gather strength for this enterprise, Frederick expanded the Empire north of the Alps, granting considerable privileges to the great princes to obtain their cooperation for his Italian campaigns. His expansive moves, some of long-range consequences, extended in all directions. In the north, he compelled the Danish king to become an imperial vassal. In the east, he subdued the Poles in a brief war and forced them to pay tribute. He bestowed the royal dignity on Bohemia, increasing the power and prestige of that eastern outpost of the Empire. He also separated Austria from Bavaria and turned the former into an important independent duchy and a powerful bulwark in the southeast. In the west, he tried to reconfirm imperial power over Burgundy by marrying into the Burgundian family (see Map 7).

Barbarossa felt an emperor should not be *primus inter pares* (first among equals), but of infinitely higher rank than kings and dukes. To realize this concept of the role of emperor, he did not consider it necessary to render the dukes powerless; on the contrary, he wanted them to be strong and respected territorial lords. True to his policy, he supported even his potential rival Henry the Lion against rebellious nobles and cities as long as the truce between Guelfs and Ghibellines lasted. To render his own position more august, he solicited support from Italian lawyers then busily engaged in reviving Roman law. Except in cases where Roman jurisprudence had been incorporated into canon law, much of it had been lost during the early Middle Ages and had been supplanted by feudal relationships and justice. Now, in the twelfth century, as part of a revived interest in classic antiquity, professors at Italian universities were studying Roman legal procedures. An attempt was made to apply Justinian's Law Code to contemporary conditions. In the days of Justinian, the Byzantine emperor of the Eastern Empire, the emperor's position had been quasi-omnipotent, his person well-nigh divine. The Eastern emperor had been the supreme legislator: his will was law. The lawyers now proclaimed that the same should apply to the Western emperors of their own day, and official statements to this effect were read at imperial gatherings. Such concepts added immeasurably to Frederick's prestige, if not to his actual power.

The emperor also arranged for a series of imposing imperial diets, (*Reichstage*), at which he presided in all his majesty. Frederick saw to it that these meetings were attended by princes and delegates not merely from all parts of the Empire (*Reich*) but also from countries over which he had no jurisdiction, such as England, France, Spain, Hungary, and even the Byzantine Empire. Thus Barbarossa could assert that, like the Roman emperors of ancient times, he was the supreme lord of Europe, in fact, of more or less the known world. The flattering respect shown him by the rulers of Europe is exemplified in a letter written by the powerful and ambitious King Henry II Plantagenet of England:

> At Your Majesty's feet we place our kingdom and all we command, so that everything will be executed according to Your wishes and that Your will be done in all things. . . . You, whose rank is above ours, may command and in intended obedience we shall not be found wanting.

In his efforts to enlarge the Empire and strengthen his rule, Frederick Barbarossa encountered problems which had not particularly vexed his predecessors. Most significant of these for the political and economic life of Europe was the reappearance and growth of towns.

The Revival of Towns

With the decline of the old Roman Empire after the third century A.D. and the subsequent barbarian invasions, many towns had gradually decayed or actually disappeared. Not enough trade had survived to sustain a town economy. Most of Europe had been reduced to an agricultural society based on local self-sufficiency. Under these conditions, which dominated the early Middle Ages, a social structure had arisen in which towns had little significance. This feudal society was essentially divided into two main classes. On the one hand were the serfs and free peasants who tilled the soil and performed menial labor. On the other were the nobles who owned most of the land, acted as administrators, and fought one another over possessions and prerogatives. Both these classes were provided for in the social system, with feudalism regulating the relations among nobles and manorialism controlling the lives of the serfs and tenant farmers. In such a social system there was no room for the inhabitants of towns, who were neither noble nor tillers of the soil. Artisans and merchants whose wealth lay in money did not fit into an economy based on land.

Yet towns began to revive noticeably in the eleventh century. Old towns grew in population and wealth, and new ones were founded. Sometimes former Roman centers were infused with new life. Sometimes new combinations arose as nuclei of future towns; these usually consisted of a fortified place—a *Burg* (castle) or episcopal palace—surrounded by artisans' workshops and markets. A class of citizens came into being that was neither noble nor serf, and was therefore referred to as the "middle class." These "burghers" had new aspirations and ideals. Above all, they wished to be free from interference from the local noble lord or bishop who might own the land on which the town was situated. They desired freedom to trade with other towns, to govern themselves, and to fashion their own laws, for feudal customs did not suit their needs.

At first their aims and achievements were modest. In the tenth and eleventh centuries, a few towns acquired the right to mint their own coins, establish their own tolls, and hold free markets. As trade increased during the eleventh and twelfth centuries, towns grew stronger and more prosperous, first in northern Italy, then also north of the Alps. The townsmen based their fight for civic freedoms on new concepts of bourgeois law. To effect their aims, many formed communes or sworn associations, built walls around their cities, and finally organized citizen armies. Since most local lords tried to keep these growing towns in check, frequent fights occurred between townsmen and nobles or bishops. In their drive for independence and, if possible, full sovereignty, the townsmen often turned to the king or emperor for protection. They demanded that he grant them charters stipulating and guaranteeing their rights and liberties; in return, they might aid him financially and support him in his struggles with powerful princes. This alliance between bourgeois and king against feudal nobility became a common phenomenon in many European countries.

In the era of the Hohenstaufen emperors, some towns, particularly in Lombardy, were becoming so rich and powerful that they rejected even imperial interference and tried to attain complete independence. To protect themselves, they began to organize leagues, an arrangement that became common practice in the thirteenth and fourteenth centuries. Whereas earlier emperors had had to appease principally the powerful princes and the Church to gain mastery of the Empire, Frederick I now had to deal in addition with this rising class of merchants and artisans—whose obstructionism complicated his relations with the papacy and undermined his control of Italy.

Relations with the Papacy

In his relations with the popes, Barbarossa refused to recognize any actual or implied superiority of the papacy over the Empire. He was always ready to cooperate with the Church and to assist the popes in maintaining their ecclesiastical rights. In 1155, for instance, in order to enable the pope to regain admission to his capital he helped capture Rome from republican antipapal forces (led by Arnold of Brescia). But when it was a question of subordination, Frederick was adamant. He broke into a rage when told of a portrait in the Lateran Church in Rome showing Emperor Conrad, his uncle, receiving the crown from the pope as well as an inscription stating that the emperor was a vassal of the pope, and he ordered the immediate destruction of the painting. Other incidents occurred that underscore Barbarossa's intransigence. When on his way to the imperial coronation, he met the pope in the vicinity of Rome, symbolic protocol threatened to destroy all their previously arranged political agreements. The two met on horseback and the emperor refused to alight first to hold the stirrups for the pope.

Only after friendly dukes assured him that it was a meaningless tradition did he dismount and perform the ceremonial act.

Another incident had more far-reaching consequences, since it added to the growing estrangement between Frederick and the pacacy. In 1157, papal envoys presented to Barbarossa a complaint about the imprisonment of a bishop. In the letter, the pope reminded the emperor of the great "benefice" he had bestowed upon him. Frederick interpreted the phrase as meaning that the pope considered the emperor his vassal. A struggle then ensued between Church and Empire. The pope tried to rally to his side all northern bishops in order to undermine the emperor's position, but they remained loyal to Frederick. The pope was therefore forced to back down. In an apologetic letter of explanation to Frederick, he indicated that he had used the word "benefice" not in its new legal sense—denoting a "fief" and implying vassalage—but in the original Latin sense of a "good deed."

During the early years of Frederick's reign, relations with the papacy on the whole remained relatively cordial. The pope needed the emperor's assistance to regain control of Rome and to prevent the Normans of Sicily from becoming unwelcome strong neighbors. After the failure of Frederick's first Italian campaign, however, the pope ceased to rely on imperial assistance. Instead, he switched to the opposite camp and sided with Sicily and the Italian cities in their resistance to imperial domination. The ensuing struggle between Empire and papacy lasted for almost two decades. In 1159, Frederick took advantage of a split papal election. By siding with one pope against his opponent, who was supported by France and England, Frederick hoped to weaken the Church. Meanwhile, he used the temporary decline in the power of the Church to reassert imperial control over episcopal elections in Germany. Only in the last decade of his reign, after he realized that he could not triumph over the papacy by military force, did he switch to a policy of compromise. In 1177, pope and emperor came to terms and thereafter continued to cooperate for the remaining years of Frederick's reign.

Imperial Domination of Italy

Frederick's attempt to restore imperial control over Italy as it had existed in the days of Otto the Great occupied his attention for many years and involved him in numerous wars. His first Italian campaign (1153–1154) was a failure. He succeeded neither in subjugating the northern Italian towns nor in regaining lasting control of Rome. He abandoned the plan to conquer lower Italy and Sicily even before beginning the undertaking. His second campaign lasted four years (1158–1162). An imperial army roamed about northern and central Italy, seeking everywhere to impose political control by Frederick's agents. But the military defeat of a town and its resultant submission did not guarantee its loyalty. Often towns rebelled against their imperial administrators as soon as the emperor's army had departed. After one such rebellion in 1162, Frederick ordered the complete destruction of the city of Milan and the scattering of its population to the four winds. But even this frightful vengeance did not help for long; the emperor's power was not sufficient to break permanently the strength of the Lombard League, the alliance of northern Italian towns joined in a pact of mutual assistance. No sooner had Frederick left for Germany when neighboring townsmen helped rebuild Milan. The towns again refused to pay imperial taxes and proceeded to expel the imperial agents. Frederick tried again in 1167 and in the 1170s to force obedience on them; that he failed is perhaps a measure not of his weakness but rather of the strength of these towns. Trading had supplied them with the money necessary for building intricate fortifications. Frederick's failure was also a portent of the impending transformation in warfare, which enabled foot soldiers, fighting for the towns, to hold their own against well-armed knights on horseback and which gradually broke the fighting monopoly of the nobility.

A last effort to subjugate the Lombard League in 1176 ended in disaster. A portion of the imperial army was actually defeated in open battle by the Milanese and their Lombard allies in the vicinity of Legnano. This defeat and the simultaneous rebellion of the Guelf Duke Henry the Lion prompted Frederick to change tactics in Italy. Since military means had repeatedly failed, he resorted to diplomacy. A reconciliation with the papacy was now arranged, and a peace treaty was concluded with the Lombard League. Frederick agreed to recognize the autonomy of the cities; he withdrew his imperial agents, and permitted the townsmen to elect their own government officials. In return, the cities promised to pay taxes to the emperor and to acknowledge his overlordship. Even more important was his peaceful acquisition of Tuscany, which permitted him to exert pressure on both Lombardy to the north and the papacy to the south. Finally, he solved the problem of Sicily, against which he had been unable to undertake effective military measures. He entered into an alliance with its king and sealed it by arranging the marriage of Constanza, the daughter of the king of Sicily, to his son Henry, the future emperor. Thus in the last decade of his reign, Frederick succeeded by diplomatic maneuvers in gaining predominance over most of the peninsula and raising the Holy Roman Empire to greater heights of splendor.

The Administration of Germany

Meanwhile, Frederick had not completely neglected affairs in Germany, although they were to some extent of secondary importance to him. He realized that he needed the full and loyal support of the great nobles and ecclesiastical lords at home if he hoped to succeed in his Italian undertakings. Although some princes made occasional attempts to support the papal and Lombard forces, in the expectation of weakening the emperor's power, Frederick was master in his own house so long as the truce between Guelfs and Ghibellines lasted. But Henry the Lion had used the years of "peaceful coexistence" between the two princely powers to build up his own strength in northern Germany and Bavaria. The inevitable clash opened in 1176 when, despite Frederick's insistent pleas, Henry refused to give the emperor military aid against the Lombard League. Refusal to serve the emperor violated the old feudal as well as the new imperial concepts of public duty. To permit Henry to persevere in his disobedience would have undermined Frederick's whole concept of government. Consequently, as soon as Frederick had settled his Italian affairs, he proceeded with vigor against Henry. It is a measure of Frederick's power that he could deal so summarily with the rebellion of the most powerful duke in the Empire. He placed Henry under the imperial ban and confiscated all his possessions, except for a small bit of the original Guelf lands around Braunschweig-Lüneburg. Bavaria was transferred to the house of Wittelsbach, which, except for brief intervals, remained the dynastic house of Bavaria until 1918. In line with Frederick's policy of strengthening the bishops, Saxony was divided and the western portion assigned to the archbishop of Cologne. Henry the Lion himself was banned from the Empire and went into exile in England, to the court of his father-in-law, King Henry II. Thus the Guelf-Ghibelline struggle once again was temporarily settled in favor of the Hohenstaufens.

Having gained control of Italy through diplomacy, and having reasserted himself in Germany by defeating the rival Guelf, Frederick Barbarossa reached the apogee of his power and prestige. With confidence he could turn his back on the Empire and assume the role of the leader of Christendom by directing the Third Crusade against Sultan Saladin, who had seized Jerusalem in 1187. Supported by the kings of England and France, by most of the princes of Europe, and even by the Byzantine emperor, Frederick departed for the Holy Land in 1189. His life ended when he seemed about to reestablish the old Roman Empire in all its glory and expanse. His sudden death by drowning, in 1190, gave rise to the legend that he had not really died but would someday return to resume his glorious reign.

THE INTERIM PERIOD

Henry VI

Frederick bequeathed to his son an excellent basis on which to build an even more powerful reign. Young Henry VI (1190–1197)—who succeeded his father at twenty-four and died at thirty-one—was cold, deliberate, and almost fanatically bent on acquiring power. His actual and potential might in the last years of his short reign was greater than that of either his glorious father or his famous son, Frederick II. Yet because of his ruthless methods, his personality, or the brevity of his reign, he did not endear himself to the imagination of the people and has remained in relative historical obscurity.

The first four years of his rule were filled with strife. Through his wife he inherited the Kingdom of Sicily, but it was not until 1194 that he completed the conquest of the island with the help of Pisan and Genovese ships and subdued the anti-imperial faction of Sicilians. He was able to obtain the imperial coronation from the pope, but only in return for recognizing papal overlordship over Tuscany. Finally, he faced rebellion in Germany. As soon as Frederick I had departed on his crusade, Henry the Lion had returned from exile in England. The death of the emperor and the succession of a young son afforded an opportune moment for reopening the Guelf-Ghibelline struggle. Joined by some of the German princes, the Lion again raised the standard of rebellion, and Henry VI at first was unable to overcome the uprising.

In 1194, however, the emperor's fortune changed through a sheer coincidence of which he quickly took advantage. Returning from the Holy Land, King Richard the Lionhearted of England was captured in Vienna and turned over to Henry VI as prisoner. Such proceedings against a foreign ruler in transit through the Empire may seem outrageous, but Richard was the brother-in-law and ally of Duke Henry the Lion and hence could be considered a Guelf. The emperor refused to release Richard until the latter had mediated a truce between him and the Guelfs, paid a huge ransom, and even accepted England as an imperial fief.

Henry now reached the height of his power. He controlled Germany, northern Italy, and Sicily. The papacy was surrounded and impotent. With several fleets at his disposal, he aspired to control the Mediterranean and hoped to incorporate even the Byzantine Empire into his domains. Henry conceived a grandiose plan for turning his realm into a hereditary Empire. He offered the dukes unlimited rights of inheritance in their own lands if they would renounce their electoral powers and recognize the permanent privilege of the house of Hohenstaufen to wear the royal and imperial crowns. In addition, he wished to incorporate Sicily into the Empire. Sicily at the time was united with the Empire only in a personal union, since Henry was both Holy Roman emperor and king of Sicily. But he desired to make this union permanent so as to establish one grand realm all the way from Sicily and the Mediterranean to the Baltic and North seas. In order to round out his Italian holdings, he also proposed a plan to the papacy: in return for obtaining possession of the Papal States, including the city of Rome, Henry offered the papacy a fixed annual revenue from all the churches in the Empire (a plan that almost parallels the modern solution to Italy's church-state problem worked out by Mussolini). However, this ambitious scheme, which would have completely transformed the political structure of central and southern Europe, was fated to remain an imperial dream. Most of the dukes gave their approval, since they stood to benefit; but the powerful archbishops and bishops rejected the proposal: they would lose their electoral rights without being able to profit from the offered guarantee of hereditary succession. The pope also refused to accept the plan, even though Henry suggested he would take the Empire as a fief of the papacy—a symbolic offer he could well afford since in reality he would control the papacy if he possessed all the land and thus the purse strings of the Church.

Thus Henry's grand design was stillborn. Since his hereditary plan failed, he resorted to the methods of the Salians and had his baby son crowned king in 1196. One year later the emperor died, his task unachieved; the Empire was left to his three-year-old heir. Immediately upon Henry's death, German power collapsed everywhere in Italy; the Lombard League reformed; and anti-German forces got the upper hand even in Sicily. North of the Alps, the Guelf rebellion broke out anew.

Civil Wars between Guelfs and Ghibellines, 1198–1214

Since the Ghibellines needed a leader, not a boy ruler, they elected as king Henry VI's brother, Philip of Swabia (1198–1208), even though the young Frederick had already been officially made king. The Guelfs refused to recognize this election. Together with the archbishop of Cologne and other anti-Hohenstaufen lords, and with money provided by King Richard of England, they chose as king Otto IV, the youngest son of Henry the Lion. This split election of 1198 threw the Empire into chaos for some twenty years. Civil war again became the order of the day. This time it was more than a renewal of the old Guelf-Ghibelline struggle. It became part of an international conflict, the German civil war being but an appendage of the larger Anglo-French struggle between the Plantagenets of England and Philip II Augustus of France. The latter helped the Ghibellines while Richard the Lionhearted and his successor, John I, supported their Guelf relatives against the Hohenstaufens. It was symptomatic of the future that the outcome of the fight in the Empire was dependent largely upon the relative strength of two foreign powers. Of equal importance was the fact that the year 1198 brought to the papal throne Innocent III (1198–1216), probably the strongest of the medieval popes, who seized the opportunity created by civil strife in Germany and the Franco-English wars to extricate the papacy from the relative impotence it had experienced under Barbarossa and Henry VI.

Of the two rulers, Otto IV (1198–1218) was initially the stronger, since he was able to conclude an agreement with the new pope. Innocent III asserted his claim to all of central Italy in order to prevent future emperors from again dominating the entire peninsula. He also proclaimed the right of the pope to judge the validity of imperial elections. Since Otto IV secretly promised to recognize these claims, Innocent pronounced the Guelf's election valid and placed Philip of Swabia under the ban of excommunication. But Otto's position soon deteriorated. With the death of Richard the Lionhearted, the emperor lost his most valuable supporter. The new king of England, John I, was not of much aid to Otto, and after his defeat by France in 1204, he withdrew all support from the Guelfs. The French victory over the English turned the tide in favor of the Hohenstaufens. Pope Innocent, always ready to take advantage of a new situation, sought a compromise with Philip of Swabia, since Otto's government had become ineffectual. But just as he was about to win the struggle, Philip was murdered in 1208 as the result of a private quarrel.

Otto IV was now sole ruler of the Empire. The Guelfs seemingly had triumphed. The uncrowned emperor reconfirmed his previous promises to the pope and agreed not to interfere in episcopal elections. In return, Innocent performed for him the imperial coronation. No sooner had the Guelf Otto become powerful then he adopted the old Ghibelline policies. Despite his promises to the pope, he occupied central Italy and planned to conquer Sicily, thereby threatening the papacy with encirclement. Thus the understanding between the Guelfs and the papacy and with it, Otto's supremacy, was of short duration. In 1210 Innocent placed Otto under the ban for laying hands on church property and shifted his support back to the Hohenstaufens.

The young Frederick of Hohenstaufen, the son of Henry VI, had meanwhile reached the age of sixteen. He had grown up under the tutelage of Pope Innocent III, who had acted as his guardian and as regent for the Kingdom of Sicily. Innocent could use him well in his fight with the Guelfs. Although he had already been crowned king as a child of two, Frederick induced some electors to crown him again in 1211. For the second time in a generation, the Empire was confronted with the existence of two kings. With papal help, the young Frederick secretly traveled from his native Sicily to Germany in order to seize his hereditary domains and rally the German princes against Otto IV. Again foreign forces were to decide the fate of Germany. As friend of the pope, Frederick naturally had the same allies as the papacy. Therefore, the Hohenstaufens sided with France in the struggle against England and the Guelfs. Philip II's victory at Bouvines in 1214 over John of England and Otto IV assured the Hohenstaufen cause. The dukes abandoned Otto and rallied to Frederick. Without political support and deep in debts aggravated by his wife's costly gambling habits, Otto spent the remaining four years of his life in relative obscurity. Meanwhile, the new Hohenstaufen ruler began a reign that was to last almost four decades.

FREDERICK II

Frederick II (1212–1250) was the last of the great medieval emperors; his reign marks the apogee of the Empire (see Map 7). Frederick himself was a strange progeny of the thirteenth century. Diverse elements were mixed in him, and sundry epithets have been applied to his person. A contemporary chronicler, Matthew Paris, called him *stupor mundi,* the wonder of the world, in view of his manifold achievements and the miraculous splendor of his reign. Churchmen and popular opinion of the time labeled him the antichrist: born of a dragon, according to some; conceived by a nun, according to others. Many historians see him as the first modern ruler, because of his rationalism and his "unmedieval" ideas on government, while the philosopher Nietzsche called him "the first European," the first ruler with an appreciation of the culture of Europe as a whole.

Born in Sicily, the son of a Norman mother and a Hohenstaufen father, Frederick grew up in a Mediterranean environment permeated with Arab influences. He loved the south, made Sicily the center of his Empire, and spent as little time as possible in Germany. He started his life as a ward of the papacy and as a *Pfaffenkönig* (pope's king), yet he gradually became one of the bitterest foes of the institutionalized Church. Frederick was highly intelligent, a clever statesman, and a good linguist. He showed deep interest in the arts as well as in the sciences. An emperor who could play chess with the sultan while conversing with him in Arabic, who could write a book on the art of hunting with falcons which remains definitive today, who could devise a political constitution that was a model for its period, naturally astounded his contemporaries.

Church-State Relations under Frederick II

One of the important issues that occupied Frederick during most of his reign was an attempted settlement of church-state relations. Initially, during the powerful pontificate of Innocent III, who died in 1216, there was no conflict between the papacy and the Hohenstaufens. Innocent was mighty and the young Frederick was dependent on him for gaining mastery over the Guelfs. Frederick reconfirmed Otto's promises to respect papal rights over central Italy and to stop interfering in episcopal elections. During the reign of Innocent's successor (Honorius III, 1216–1227) papal-imperial relations remained friendly at first, and Frederick received the imperial crown in 1220 in return for granting to the Church exemption from taxation and awarding bishops the right to judge clerics without reference to lay courts. During this period he consolidated his claims in Sicily and Germany, and molded a base for gradual encirclement of the Papal States, while the pope did little to oppose these moves. Toward the mid-1220s, however, friction arose. The pope protested that Frederick misused his powers by dominating the churches in Sicily and accused the emperor of not undertaking the crusade he had promised to lead. Frederick in turn objected to the secret papal support offered to the rebellious Lombard cities.

In 1227, with the accession of the vigorous Pope Gregory IX (1227–1241), whose ideas on church government resembled those of Innocent III, the fight with the emperor broke out in earnest. Apart from a few truces, the struggle lasted until Frederick's death. In essence it was a rivalry for supremacy in Italy and control over the churches within the Empire, particularly in Sicily. The points of contention were often mere pretexts, obscuring the real issues. Gregory began his pontificate by excommunicating the emperor for abruptly calling off a crusade a few days after sailing from Italy. The pope chose to overlook Frederick's explanation that a plague had raged aboard the ships and that the emperor himself had contracted a fever. Pope Gregory was perhaps more interested in seeing the emperor absent himself from Europe than in having the Holy Land freed from the infidels. The following year, Frederick, although under papal ban, resumed the crusade. This time the pope opposed the emperor not only with spiritual and political sanctions but also by military means. He tried to prevent the emperor's success in Jerusalem while sending military forces to occupy Sicily during his absence. Frederick quickly returned from the Holy Land, defeated the papal forces, and arranged a compromise with the pope, rendering control over the churches in Sicily to the papacy in return for the lifting of the papal ban.

The truce was of short duration. In 1235 the battle reopened in conjunction with a new rebellion of the Lombard cities. The pope considered it suicidal to permit Frederick to control Lombardy, as he would then find himself in the encircling grasp of the emperor. Frederick, on the other hand, had to dominate the Lombard Plain or risk losing all control over passage to Germany. The papacy came to the aid of the Lombards, and the ensuing struggle rapidly engulfed most of the peninsula. The papacy was supported by the Lombard League, by the city-states of Genoa and Venice with their strong navies, and in general by all Guelf elements in Italy. The emperor, in addition to the aid of the Empire, Sicily, and the Pisan fleet, received assistance from the Italian Ghibellines, who believed Italian unity could be better accomplished under an emperor than a pope. The struggle was not solely a war of military campaigns. Calumnious pamphlets were freely disseminated by both sides. In the end, Frederick carried the field militarily but was unable to impose on the Church a lasting settlement.

Gregory's successor (Innocent IV, 1243–1254) was an equally bitter opponent of the emperor. Unable to achieve his designs in Italy, he fled to France and convoked a Church council in Lyons, which pronounced the deposition of Frederick. The fight was now no longer limited to Italy. The pope placed all Hohenstaufen lands under anathema and offered them to whoever could conquer them. This incited numerous defections in Germany, and the civil war spread to north of the Alps. Many bishops and princes deserted the emperor, and several antikings proclaimed themselves as new rulers in opposition to Frederick. The pope even urged the sultan to ally himself with Frederick's rivals. This final struggle lasted from 1245 to 1250. Despite frequent setbacks, Frederick's strength was astounding. On several occasions, he seemed about to overcome his many opponents, but in the end neither side attained a clear-cut victory.

Frederick's Religious Views

On the whole Frederick was sympathetic to the Church's ideals and problems. He passed laws prohibiting taxation of the clergy in the Empire, granted extensive privileges to the bishops, and staunchly supported the Church's efforts to stamp out heretics, a movement that assumed vehement proportions in the first half of the thirteenth century. Frederick made lay rulers legally responsible for apprehending heretics and even imposed the imperial ban automatically on all those who remained under excommunication for six weeks without seeking absolution. Yet his behavior was rather unorthodox for the thirteenth century. The strong Arab influence during his youth had made him somewhat more flexible in his Christian beliefs than were his contemporaries. And although his struggle with the papacy was largely based on political rivalry, the Church found ready ammunition for its campaign of calumny to the effect that he was the antichrist incarnate.

Certainly his attitude toward Jews and particularly toward Muslims differed considerably from the tenor of the times. His behavior during the crusade of 1228–1229 hardly epitomizes the most militantly "Christian" of all medieval centuries. Frederick undertook the crusade despite the fact that he was under papal excommunication and that the pope had prohibited the collection of special levies for the undertaking. Once in the Holy Land, the emperor, instead of making war on the infidel, negotiated with the sultan and established friendly relations with the Muhammadan foe. The sultan agreed to cede to the Christians certain fortified places for the protection of pilgrims, and he granted them free access to most of the holy sites in Jerusalem, Bethlehem, and Nazareth. In addition, the Muslim prince granted freedom to numerous Christian prisoners. This diplomatic settlement achieved better results than the preceding fighting crusades, but such peaceful agreements shocked most pious Christians.

Frederick felt so secure in his agreement with the sultan that he proceeded from the coast to Jerusalem without the bulk of his army, accompanied by only a small staff of attendants. According to one chronicler, the Knights of the Temple were so outraged by Frederick's behavior that they sent secret messengers to the sultan with the intelligence that the emperor was moving to Jesusalem almost unprotected and that the sultan's forces could easily capture and kill him. Supposedly, the sultan respected Frederick so much that he forwarded the treasonous message to the emperor to show him what sort of Christian allies he had. The Christian pilgrims in Jerusalem welcomed the emperor with wild acclaim, but the Church immediately placed an interdict on the city for having received the excommunicated Frederick. In 1229 he crowned himself "King of Jerusalem" in the Church of the Holy Sepulcher, uniting Jerusalem and the Empire in a personal union. Since he was under the ban, he could not receive the crown from an ecclesiastical representative. He therefore placed it on his own head, an act that further underscored his independence from the Church.

In the meantime, as was noted, the pope had declared war on him and had initiated military action against Sicily. Frederick therefore hastily returned to Europe. It was perhaps significant for the future that while the emperor was condemned by the Church for having negotiated with the infidel, in Germany he was hailed as a hero who had freed the holy places against the will of the Church. A popular song at the time north of the Alps began with the words: "Just look what an emperor can do, when heathens and priests struggle against him in great numbers. . . ."

The Position of Jews in the Empire

Equally at variance with the tenets of his time, although in line with the usual Hohenstaufen policy, was Frederick II's attitude toward the Jews. Under the Carolingian, Saxon, and Salian dynasties, the Jews had lived generally unmolested in the Empire. Naturally there had been some exceptions, such as their expulsion from Mainz by Emperor Henry II, but on the whole they had been well treated and frequently protected by imperial fiat. Jews were allowed to worship freely, but were not permitted to intermarry with Christians. Neither could they convert Christians to Judaism nor be appointed to high governmental office. Actually emperors frequently employed them as diplomatic envoys, since their travels as merchants made them acquainted with foreign lands and languages. A number of Jews also became physicians at the imperial court. While Jews were officially permitted to own land, they were prohibited from holding slaves or serfs and were thus unable to undertake large-scale farming, a condition that induced the Jews to seek their livelihood in trade and commerce rather than in agriculture. Of course, the relative security of the Jews at this time depended not solely on papal policy or imperial protection, but also on local pressures and attitudes. In the city of Worms, for example, Jews lived for years completely unmolested—supposedly because of a legend that Jews had lived in Worms before the time of Christ and hence could not be held responsible for His death.

But the era of the crusades had initiated a new period for the Jews. The enthusiasm of the First Crusade incited large-scale persecutions throughout Europe. The aim seemed to be to exterminate the enemies of Christ at home before killing the infidels abroad. French, English, and Lotharingian crusaders butchered countless Jews in France, and the Jews of the Empire feared a similar massacre when the crusaders passed through their lands. They appealed to Emperor Henry IV, who, true to Salian tradition, ordered all bishops and counts to protect the Jews in their territories. In some places this order was carried out with vigor, and citizens helped hide and protect the Jews against the crusaders. But in numerous cities, especially in the Rhineland, the imperial order remained unheeded. Local citizens zealously joined the crusaders in plundering and slaughtering the Jews of their community. Hatred of Judaism was certainly more important than racial anti-Semitism, since many converted Jews escaped the butchery. In many instances, however, desire for plunder outweighed ideological considerations.

After the storm had swept over Germany, Emperor Henry renewed his promises of protection to the Jews and even permitted those who had been forcibly baptized to revert to Judaism. But imperial promises henceforth were regarded by the Jews of Germany with less confidence. The climate of the twelfth century became increasingly intolerant. Official papal and imperial policy remained unchanged, but the lower clergy and fanatic citizens engaged in frequent rabble rousing. Despite the fairly effective preaching of St. Bernard against molesting Jews at home, bloody anti-Jewish outbreaks characterized the Second Crusade led by Emperor Conrad in 1147.

In spite of this increase in anti-Judaism, the Hohenstaufens insisted on a policy of toleration and protection. The three great emperors, Frederick I, Henry VI, and Frederick II, professed it their duty to protect Jews, not merely during times of crusades, but also in time of peace. In a special letter of protection sent to the Jews of Regensburg, Frederick Barbarossa declared:

> It is the duty of His Imperial Majesty —sanctioned by Law and demanded by Reason—to guarantee . . . peaceful possession of their goods, enjoyment of life, and retention of their customs to all his loyal people; not merely to those of the Christian religion, but also to those who deviate from our faith by exercising the traditions of their forefathers.

During the reign of Frederick II, such a policy was more difficult to enforce because it opposed the trend of the time. By the thirteenth century, Jews had generated additional hatred because of their dealings in usury. The canonical prohibition on usury for Christians, initially adopted as law by Charles the Great, had been reproclaimed by Frederick I and Frederick II. This opened the field more and more for the Jews to engage in trade and moneylending, and the increase of prosperity and available specie during the twelfth and thirteenth centuries further augmented their financial activities. In addition, persecution of Christian heretics, such as the Waldensians and the Little Brethren of St. Francis, fanned popular fanaticism in general. Even the popes no longer accorded the Jews their protection. On the contrary, Pope Innocent III ordered all Jews to wear special pointed yellow hats to distinguish them from Christian burghers and perhaps to make them look ridiculous.

In this altered climate, it is noteworthy that Frederick II—although supporting the Church in its attempt to eradicate heresy in Christian circles—continued to extend imperial protection to the Jews. In 1236, for example, many Jews were killed during a riot in the city of Fulda because Jews supposedly had murdered a small boy to obtain Christian blood for the performance of a religious ceremony. The news of the massacre spread through Germany, and Emperor Frederick convoked an assemblage of learned men to examine the specious charges. As a result, an imperial *diet* at Augsburg proclaimed that the story was spurious, that the Jews were not guilty of the purported crime, and that they remained under special imperial protection.

Frederick II and Germany

Frederick appeared in Germany for the first time in 1212. Eager that the crown remain in his family, he had his young son Henry elected king of Germany in 1220, the same year in which Frederick received the imperial crown. Since his son was still a minor and Frederick was not interested in governing Germany himself, he entrusted the reins of the administration to two regents and left for a fifteen-year stay in the south. By 1230, young Henry had come of age. He took personal charge of the government in Germany and initiated his own administrative policies. He attempted to solidify his power by forming an alliance with the new bourgeois elements in opposition to the powerful princes. Since this policy differed from that of the emperor, Henry soon found himself in open rebellion against his father. In 1235, Frederick subdued his son and imprisoned him until his death. Two years later, Frederick had another son, Conrad, elected king, but this time he retained greater control over German affairs and made more frequent trips north of the Alps until the last five critical years of his reign, 1245–1250, when domination of the northern lands gradually slipped from his hands.

Despite Frederick's relative disinterest in German affairs and his preoccupation with Italy, his reign produced developments highly significant for Germany's future. One such change concerned the power of the German princes; others, the accelerated expansion into the northeast, together with the rapid rise in strength and wealth of the cities.

In his relations with the princes, Frederick continued the policy of his father and grandfather. Both Barbarossa and Henry VI had bestowed favors on the great lords and had helped them increase their power at the expense of the smaller nobles and the cities. These emperors had accepted the progress of territoriality as an irrepressible development, and as good *Realpolitiker,* had decided to follow the trend and build their own territorial power, while, at the same time, trying to make the crown hereditary in their family. After the death of Henry VI, during the period of the civil wars, 1198–1214, the princes, both lay and ecclesiastical, had acquired further privileges and prestige and had acted more or less like sovereign rulers in their own lands. Frederick accepted these changes as a *fait accompli.* Rather than seeking to diminish their power, he awarded additional rights to these lords and legalized their new status. He required their support both for his struggle against the papacy and for his plan to make the Empire a hereditary possession in his family.

In 1220, he took the first, far-reaching step in this direction by according certain privileges to the abbots, bishops, and archbishops of the Empire. Instead of remaining mere royal fiefs, the bishoprics and abbacies now acquired the rights of territorial states. The ecclesiastical lords received exclusive rights to set up new tolls and control passage through their lands, and to permit the founding of cities in their territories. With some limitations, even secular justice was transferred to their jurisdiction.

Twelve years later, in 1232, the emperor issued an even more extensive decree in favor of both lay and ecclesiastical lords. The princes were given quasi-exclusive rights over striking coins, regulating commerce, establishing their own courts and police, and controlling the construction of fortifications within their territories. Above all, the edict granted them almost unlimited rights of justice, thereby undermining the basis for both royal justice and the extension of common law. During the eleventh and twelfth centuries, the main efforts of the kings of England and France in their drive to assert their royal power were directed toward an extension of royal justice. These rulers rightly ascertained that royal justice constituted the mainstay of their increasing governmental power, as well as an excellent source of revenue for the central government. However, with the decrees of 1232, Germany turned in exactly the opposite direction. In fact, these edicts of 1220 and 1232 represented a long step toward granting virtual sovereignty to the individual territorial lords. The opportunity to create a unified state—if ever it had existed in Germany as it had in England and France—was forfeited, and the splintering of Germany became a legal reality.

Even though many royal rights were thus transferred to the territorial princes, Frederick II was left with considerable power. His prestige was immense, as seen by the ease with which he subdued his rebellious son and the might he displayed in his fight with the papacy. He had built up his own domains to the largest extent possible, rounding out his inherited possessions into a powerful base in southern Germany. In addition, he possessed his native Sicily. In these private domains he could exercise the same privileges he had granted to other territorial lords. On this basis alone, he could be considered the most powerful lord in the Empire, since his lands were the largest and wealthiest.

Frederick's attitude toward the territorial lords does not necessarily mean that he had abandoned all hope of keeping Germany a political entity. In his native Sicily he showed considerable forbearance toward the noble lords, while at the same time attempting to effect a transition from feudal government to a centralized administration based on civil service. He elaborated on experiments conducted by his Norman predecessors in Sicily, appointing royal agents to administer the island in the name of the king. Possibly Frederick hoped to lay a similar foundation in Germany for the transition from a feudal to a bureaucratic administration. In 1235, he had the famous *Landfriedensgesetz* (Decree on the Maintenance of Internal Peace) promulgated at an imperial diet at Mainz. This lengthy document—the first imperial law written in German rather than Latin—sought essentially to maintain peace among the territorial lords. It proposed instituting an imperial judge, appointed by the emperor on a yearly basis and charged with the duty of supervising all legal matters in the Empire. The decree was larded with clauses reassuring the territorial lords of their rights, and yet it pointed hopefully toward the establishment of a strong central agency. It is difficult to ascertain whether Frederick was merely trying to preserve a last shred of royal justice, or whether he was hoping to establish an aristocratic federation subject to a single legal system. In spite of this attempt to impose a legal superstructure on the Empire, the long-term effects of the Hohenstaufen policy of letting the princes consolidate their territorial realms were to push the Germans irrevocably toward what they call *Kleinstäaterei,* territory divided into many small states.

The Growth of Towns in the Thirteenth Century

Although the emperors ranged themselves on the side of the princes, the Hohenstaufen period ushered in a new era in the history of the German *bourgeoisie.* Prior to 1200, the history of Germany, like that of many other lands, was really the history of the nobility and the clergy; now the bourgeois element made itself felt not merely in economic but also in political matters. The cities of Italy had already achieved importance in the twelfth century. After 1200, this new element in society made itself felt north of the Alps as well. In southern and western Germany, towns gradually withdrew from the domination of the territorial princes and exerted strong political power by banding together in defensive alliances. That the nobility sensed the danger of this development can be seen in repeated legislation passed by Frederick II prohibiting alliances of towns. Hence the first legitimate association of towns, the League of Rhenish Cities, could be founded only in 1254 in the period of disorders following Frederick's death.

In northern Germany and in the new lands to the northeast, the new cities acquired wealth and assumed political power even more rapidly. Here the possibilities of trade were unlimited, and the sparsity of settlement and the greater distance from the imperial armies made self-defense and self-administration more urgent. Trade relations led to political alliances, as in the development of the famous Hanseatic League, which reached its height in a later period. Some of these northern towns, such as Lübeck—though founded only in the second half of the twelfth century—quickly rose to the status of imperial cities, which means they were subject solely to the emperor's jurisdiction. They developed their own constitutions, took care of their own defense, were run by their own patrician lords, and extended wide economic and political influence along the shores of the Baltic. In some cases, Emperor Frederick granted these cities special rights and privileges and supported their aspirations, but in case of conflict between cities and princes, he almost always supported the latter. The development of city life was of vast importance for Germany's economic and political future, but it would seem erroneous to credit the Hohenstaufens for this. Rather, the development occurred in spite of their policies.

The cities of northern Germany were vitally interested in the expansion toward the northeast. In the days of Frederick Barbarossa, the drive across the Elbe had been pursued with vigor. Then, after the fall of Duke Henry the Lion and during the period of civil wars, there had been a lull. A few missionaries and merchants from Bremen established settlements in Estonia and in Latvia, where they founded Riga, and some Cistercian missionaries started to infiltrate Prussia. But on the whole the Germans did little, and the king of Denmark took advantage of the disorder in Germany to seize Holstein, Mecklenburg, Pomerania, and even the cities of Lübeck, Hamburg, and Bremen. Denmark thus controlled the important outlets to the sea and consequently threatened all German trade in the Baltic.

A new phase opened during the reign of Frederick II. The turning point came in the 1220s with the defeat of Denmark and the retaking of the lands previously seized by the Danish king. Thereafter the cities and the dukes of the border districts redoubled their efforts to occupy and colonize land along the Baltic. By far the most important work in this new wave of conquest was carried on by the Teutonic Knights.

The Beginnings of the Teutonic Knights

The Teutonic Knights had been founded in the Holy Land in 1190 as the "Order of the Knights of the Hospital of Saint Mary of the Teutons in Jerusalem." It had rapidly grown in membership and power, acquiring wealth and landed properties in the Near East, southern Italy, and Germany. At the beginning of the thirteenth century, the Knights had shifted their activity from Jerusalem to Europe by entering the services of the king of Hungary to help him fight Mongol tribes in Siebenbürgen (Transylvania). The Order of the Teutonic Knights was an anomalous brotherhood in which the ideals of monasticism and medieval knighthood were combined with modern ideas of trade and political administration. To become a member, a candidate had to swear that he was a celibate freeman, neither sick nor in debt. Once a member, he could be used by the order as a fighting knight, a provincial official, or for a variety of political, financial, or monastic positions. Apparently the Knights quickly became inconveniently powerful, as evinced by the request in 1225 by the king of Hungary that they leave his lands. At the same time, the duke of Masovia in Poland asked them to come to his aid against the unruly Prussian tribes constantly raiding his lands. In dire need of protection, the duke assured the leader of the Teutonic Knights, Grand Master Hermann von Salza (1170–1239), that the order could keep all lands it conquered from the Prussians. The Knights immediately applied for permission to Emperor Frederick II, who granted their request in 1226. The imperial decree read:

> We confirm . . . that Grand Master Hermann von Salza, his successors and his House may, for all times, take possession of the land which . . . they will obtain from Duke Conrad [of Masovia], in addition to all territories which he might later bequeath to them or which . . . they might conquer in Prussia . . . with all rights . . . and without obligation for service or taxes; and that they need to account for this land to no one.

The document granted the Knights the privilege of setting up tolls, establishing markets, minting coins, collecting taxes, regulating traffic, mining precious metals, and establishing a judicial and administrative system. "We add as special favor," the decree ended, "that this Grand Master and his successors are empowered to enjoy the same privileges of sovereignty as are exercised by the . . . princes of the *Reich*." This document has been hailed as "the hour of creation for the future Prussian state." In view of the subsequent success of the Teutonic Knights and the repercussions on German history, there can be no doubt that the decision to send this order to the northeast was of paramount importance. Yet it would be an exaggeration to call Frederick the founder of the new state of Prussia.

The Knights immediately started their new task. They built fortresses, founded cities, and conquered lands with astounding success. Before the middle of the century, they had gained dominant control of the entire Baltic coast from Estonia to the borders of Germany. They organized their conquests under an effective administrative system. New trade routes were opened whereby timber, furs, honey, and wax could be obtained from Russia. In most areas, the Knights used the labor of the local Latvians, Lithuanians, Prussians, and other native peoples, establishing the large estates that were to become characteristic of these lands. In some regions, the immigration of German peasants was encouraged so that colonization was more thoroughly effected. And in the wake of the conquests by the Knights, new cities—such as Reval, Thorn, Elbing, Greifswald—were founded, further expanding German trade and colonization.

4

Decline of the Empire, 1250–1410

WANING OF IMPERIAL POWER

With the death of Frederick II, the medieval Empire passed its zenith. Its power, the awe inspired by its rulers, and the magic of its name never regained the same splendor and intensity. After a generation of chaos, there were to be occasional efforts, sometimes partially successful, to restore vitality to the imperial framework and to fulfill the possibilities inherent in its structure. As a political entity, the Empire continued to exist for some 550 years, perhaps frequently inhibiting the normal development of the German state. As a social phenomenon it remained important, sometimes strangely at odds with the current of the times. And the memory of imperial glory, like an enchanting dream, left a strong impact on the mind of the German nation. But as a major political power, as molder of vital policy, as wielder of important military strength, the Empire experienced its demise with the disappearance of the Hohenstaufens.

The Interregnum

The period from Frederick's death in 1250 to the election of Rudolf of Hapsburg in 1273 is usually called the Interregnum because there was no effective ruler. Dukes, counts, and knights fought each other in incessant private feuds, plundered the countryside, or raided the caravans of defenseless merchants. It was an epoch of anarchy and disorder that left its mark on all territories belonging to the Empire. Various kings and antikings who probably had bought their elections sported the title of ruler without having effective control. The three Hohenstaufen princes who attempted to follow the path of Frederick experienced tragic but heroic failures. Frederick's son Conrad IV (1250–1254) sought to assume the entire Hohenstaufen inheritance, but as soon as he left Germany to conquer Italy, an antiking (William of Holland) seized control of parts of Germany while Conrad fought and died in the south. Manfred, Frederick's illegitimate son, followed Conrad in 1254. He gained Sicily and much of Italy, but was powerless north of the Alps. Ultimately, the pope invited the French Charles of Anjou to take Sicily, and Manfred was killed in battle against Anjou in 1266. The last of the Hohenstaufens, Conradin, the fifteen-year-old son of Conrad, then tried to reconquer Italy, but in 1268 he was captured by Anjou and executed in Naples.

Germany, meanwhile, was thrown into disorder. Not much political direction could be expected from such impotent absentee rulers as Alphonso of Castille, who, although calling himself king of Germany, did not even dare leave Spain; or from Richard of Cornwall, who spent most of his time in England. As a result, the splintering of political power in Germany continued. Dukes, abbots, knights, and cities seized the imperial Hohenstaufen properties and undermined the effective revival of the emperorship. As this process continued, the decaying stem duchies were gradually replaced by ever smaller territorial units based on dynastic holdings. Now even the lesser nobles—the margraves, counts, and knights—asserted their sovereign powers, and towns assumed the prerogatives of "free cities." Furthermore, the territory of the Empire began to shrink. The hold over Italy was lost, Burgundy and the Swiss cantons were leaning toward independence, and the Lowlands were growing restive. The changes in Italy went beyond mere loss of German control. The Hohenstaufen Empire had imposed on the peninsula at least an outward unity. This, too, was now lost, and Italy split into the multiple independent sovereign states — Venice, Genoa, Savoy, Florence, Milan, Naples, Sicily, and the Papal States—that were to dominate so much of its later history. The arrival of the French Charles of Anjou brought additional outside influence to Italy, further complicating its development.

Historians have debated for a long time whether the loss of Italy was a detriment to the Empire or a blessing in disguise. For two and a half centuries, Germany had exercised intermittent domination of the peninsula—although it could also be asserted that under the later Hohenstaufens Italy had dominated the north. Undoubtedly, Germany obtained much wealth from the south and reaped immeasurable cultural benefits. But probably even under strong leaders and more auspicious conditions, an Empire stretching from Sicily to the Baltic could not have been maintained as the Renaissance approached and with it the trend toward nation-states. Also, through coincidence or by design, the losses in. Italy were rapidly balanced by acquisitions in the northeast. As the hold over Italy declined, the drive to the northeast was intensified, and new wealth and trade in the Baltic to a large measure compensated for the loss of influence south of the Alps. In the course of the thirteenth century, Germany's centers of gravity shifted toward the east. Whereas before they had been in southwestern Germany, by the fourteenth century new political and economic nuclei arose east of the Elbe: Lübeck, the Mark Brandenburg, and such cities as Prague and Vienna.

The Empire had declined but imperial traditions were not forgotten, even though the need for reviving the Empire may have been felt more strongly by the papacy than by the dukes of Germany. In the 1270s, the pope (Gregory X) urged the Germans to elect a ruler and even threatened to appoint one himself if the princes would not re-establish order in their lands. The pope now saw an emperor as a possible counterbalance to Charles of Anjou, who had assumed more power in Italy than was consonant with the interests of the papacy.

RESTORATION OF THE EMPIRE BY RUDOLF OF HAPSBURG As a result, the dukes in 1273 elected Rudolf I (1273–1291), the first of the Hapsburg rulers. The new king, although relatively strong, was more a symbolic than an actual ruler. He was not even powerful enough to bring order to the Empire. Merchants, nobles, and ecclesiastics hoped he would enforce internal peace, and Rudolf acted as harshly as he could against the robber barons infesting the countryside and making life miserable for trade caravans and peasants. But his armies were insufficient for the task, and the cities refused to pay the additional taxes needed for strengthening his forces. Hence private warfare did not cease.

In external affairs, Rudolf was not very successful either. He was unable to ward off the gradual inroads made by Philip IV of France into Burgundy and Provence. Furthermore, he never went to Italy to obtain the imperial crown, which the pope had promised him in return for concessions Rudolf was willing to make. Although never officially crowned, however, Rudolf enjoyed most of the imperial honors and prerogatives.

Rudolf's main importance lies in the successful expansion of his *Hausmacht* (dynastic territorial possessions), whereby he created a new basis of imperial power to replace that of the Hohenstaufens. As a friend and faithful follower of the last dynasty, he had obtained a few minor possessions from their legacy and had skillfully built up a respectable foundation in southern Germany. His domains lay mainly in Swabia, Alsace, and northern Switzerland. Through an efficient governmental and tax system, he was able to derive adequate revenue for his own purposes. But his main success in aggrandizing his dynastic possessions lay in the east. Here he turned against King Ottokar II of Bohemia (1253–1278), who had refused to recognize the validity of the election of 1273. Rudolf invaded Austria, occupied Vienna, and forced Ottokar not only to acknowledge the election and cede Austria, but also to take Bohemia and Moravia as a fief. Two years later, in 1278, Ottokar rebelled against this settlement. Rudolf met the challenge successfully. He defeated the Bohemian in a famous encounter, the battle of the Marchfeld, in which Ottokar was killed. It is renowned because Rudolf's clear-cut victory assured the Hapsburgs possession of Austria, Styria, Carinthia, and Carniola and gave them the foundation of their future power, which was to last for many centuries (see Map 8). Ottokar's young son (Wenceslas II) was allowed to retain only Bohemia and Moravia, but even here Rudolf laid plans for future aggrandizement by embarking upon the policy of political marriages that was to characterize much of Hapsburg history. By arranging for the marriage of his son and daughter to Ottokar's heirs, Rudolf hoped to bring the Bohemian lands gradually under Hapsburg domination.

THE BEGINNINGS OF SWITZERLAND The death of Rudolf I in 1291 plunged Germany into renewed chaos. It also gave rise to further losses of territory with the rebellion of the Swiss cantons. Since the beginning of the thirteenth century, the three districts of Uri, Schwyz, and Unterwalden had belonged to the Hapsburgs. In 1231, however, Emperor Frederick II had "mediatized" Uri in order to secure passage over the Saint Gotthardt Pass, which had re-

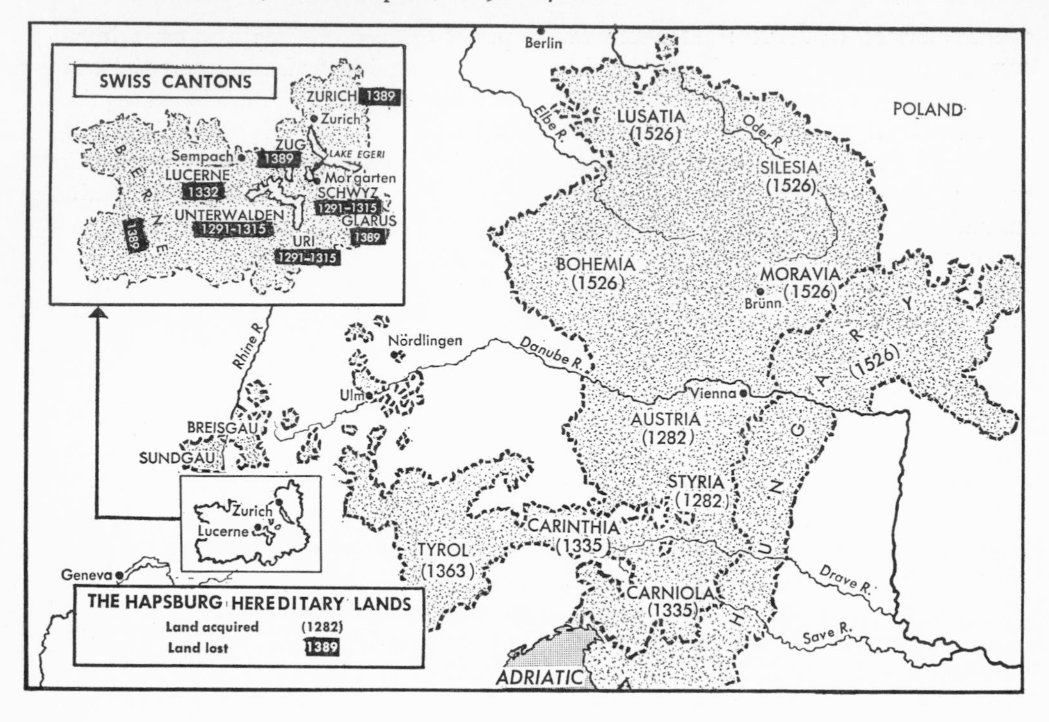

MAP 8

cently been opened to traffic. Mediatization meant that Uri was placed under imperial justice and freed from local Hapsburg jurisdiction. Such favored status was soon sought by the other two cantons, and successfully obtained by Schwyz. After the death of Frederick II, during the period of the Interregnum, the Hapsburgs had regained all rights in Schwyz, had consolidated their power in Unterwalden, but had left Uri temporarily mediatized. The cantons were unhappy, and friction multiplied between local citizens and Hapsburg governors.

During Rudolf's reign, the Swiss had no alternative to Hapsburg rule, since emperor and Hapsburg overlord were the same person. But Rudolf's death raised questions for the future, for it was uncertain whether the emperorship would remain in the Hapsburg family. On August 1, 1291—without the legendary aid of William Tell—the three cantons took an oath of mutual protection that became the basis for the future Swiss confederation. This entire period of Swiss-German history is shrouded in myth. It is clear, however, that this oath alone—if, indeed, it is a historical fact—did not ensure their independence. During the next decades, the three cantons were caught up in the strife between rival dynastic houses that plagued the German scene. Since the cantons always sided with the emperors, they were in constant conflict with the Hapsburgs, except during the reign of Albert I (1298–1308), who, after Rudolf, was the only other Hapsburg emperor during the thirteenth-century.

The Period of Dynastic Rivalries, 1292–1322

All this time, disorders in Germany continued—seemingly the natural legacy of the Interregnum. Originally the privilege of electing a king had been shared by the entire German nobility. Over the centuries, the group of electors had become restricted to only the higher and more important nobles and clergymen. During the thirteenth century, the number of electors was further reduced, until by 1257 it became fixed at seven: the archbishops of Mainz, Trier, and Cologne; and four lay rulers—the count Palatine, the duke of Saxony, the margrave of Brandenburg, and the king of Bohemia. There is no historical evidence as to why or how these seven rulers gradually assumed this privilege that raised them immensely above their fellow princes. The new tradition—which was not fixed into law until 1356—naturally lent itself to endless intrigue and bribery, and was better designed to further a power struggle among the great dynastic houses than to ensure orderly continuity of government in Germany.

The generations after Rudolf I suffered the consequences. Harmful rivalry among the great nobles shifted the crown back and forth from one family to another at the expense of political stability. Self-interest became the primary motive underlying the choices made by these electors.

In 1292, they by-passed Rudolf's son Albert in favor of a poor count, Adolf of Nassau (1292–1298). Seemingly, the electors had achieved their purpose of strengthening their own position by choosing a weak and destitute ruler. Adolf, however, used his office to enlarge his possessions and did not hesitate to do so by means of conquest and bribery. For these purposes he obtained financial aid from King Edward I of England, who desired Germany's assistance in his fight against Philip IV of France. The disgruntled electors felt deceived, and widespread discontent with Adolf grew; the emperor was finally killed in battle against a coalition of Bohemian and Hapsburg factions.

As a result, Albert I of Hapsburg became king by right of conquest as much as by right of election. He ruled from 1298 to 1308, devoting his major efforts to increasing the Hapsburg domain by confiscating the properties of landed families who had died out. For a short time it looked as though the Hapsburgs might succeed in reviving a strong monarchy. Since his domestic enemies sided with King Edward of England and with the strong Pope Boniface VIII (1294–1303), Albert allied himself with King Philip of France. His policies were generally successful; he was a good ruler in his own lands, a rather skillful soldier, and an adroit politician. But his unending greed for land gradually antagonized most of the lords of Germany, and he eventually found himself at war with the archbishops of Cologne, Trier, and Mainz. In 1308, however, he was murdered by his nephew, for personal rather than political reasons.

HENRY VII AND ITALY It is a strange coincidence that during this period France was ruled by particularly powerful kings—such as Philip II around 1200 or Philip IV around 1300—when Germany was in the throes of civil war. This imbalance gave France the opportunity of interfering in Germany, as in the electoral campaign of 1308. Philip IV, counting on the cooperation of the French pope Clement V (1305–1314), even hoped to have his own brother (Charles of Valois) elected to the emperorship. The scheme failed, however, since the pope hoped to gain more independence from France through the election of a German prince and since within the electoral college the three powerful archbishop electors had the dominant voice at the time. The election therefore resulted in a compromise. Henry VII (1308–1313) was a German prince; but he had received a French education, his language was French, and as duke of Luxemburg, he was technically a vassal of the king of France. The electors chose him presumably because he was not a wealthy prince and also because he was the brother of the powerful electoral archbishop of Trier. Despite the brevity of his reign, however, Henry, too, managed to lay the foundation for a future dynastic domain by having his son marry the heiress of Bohemia-Moravia. By his maneuver he snatched this rich prize from the expectant grasp of the Hapsburgs, at the same time making the new Bohemian-Luxemburg dynasty a temporary counterbalance to growing Hapsburg power.

But Henry's chief interest lay in Italy, which was then suffering from civil wars. This was the initial period of the so-called Babylonian Captivity of the papacy, when the French pope Clement V took up residence in Avignon, unable to return to Rome. The pope hoped to regain control over Italy with the emperor as intermediary, and Henry readily seized the opportunity. The Guelf-Ghibelline struggle still persisted in Italy, although its significance was now altered. The Guelfs, by now the majority, had become the revolutionary group, while the Ghibellines, remaining more conservative, still saw Italy's salvation within the framework of the Empire. When Henry invaded Italy, he was initially hailed by both factions, who momentarily united behind him in the hope that he could bring to Italy the peace it needed so much. With his attention focused on Henry, the poet Dante wrote his famous *De Monarchia,* advocating the imperial solution for Italy's problems. In 1312, Henry VII was crowned emperor in Rome by papal legates, and for a brief period the Empire seemed to regain a measure of its former glory. But the revived imperial aura was short-lived. The Italian cities quickly tired of their new overlord and rebelled against him in alliance with the king of Naples. In the following year, Henry suddenly died in Italy.

The death of Henry VII was followed by still another civil war in Germany. The imperial crown was sought by both the Hapsburg and the Luxemburg-Bohemian factions, and the year-long election campaign finally terminated in a split vote. Some of the electors chose the head of the Austrian[1] house (Hapsburg Duke Frederick the Handsome); others voted for his cousin, Louis of Bavaria, who obtained the support of the Luxemburgers and Bohemians, since the head of their own dynasty was too young to be an effective leader. Much remained to be clarified in the electoral procedure. By tradition the vote was to be unanimous, but no arrangements existed as to what to do in case of a mere plurality of votes. Therefore both elections of 1314 were essen-

[1] Starting in the fourteenth century, the house of Hapsburg is often referred to as the house of Austria, since Austria became the basis of the Hapsburgs' dynastic territory.

tially invalid. As the opposing parties were more or less equal in strength, it took a civil war of eight years before a decision could be reached between the two contestants. Finally, in 1322, Louis of Bavaria defeated his rival and imprisoned him. As a result of this victory, Louis IV (1314–1347) became the sole ruler of the kingdom, and Hapsburg pretensions were laid low for over a century.

INDEPENDENCE FOR THE SWISS CANTONS

The three Swiss cantons took advantage of the civil war to enhance their own cause. Emperor Henry VII had reconfirmed their rights, and during his short reign the three cantons had been ruled as a unit by an imperial provost. But after the double election of 1314, their fate was again uncertain. They decided to side with Louis, who offered them good terms and exhorted them to rebel against his Hapsburg opponents. In 1315 an Austrian duke (Leopold, brother of Frederick the Handsome), an excellent general and a shrewd politician, set out to subdue the cantons. What followed became a legend in the annals of Swiss history and a milestone in medieval warfare. At the battle of Morgarten, the stately ducal army was ignominiously defeated by the peasants of the three cantons, who used the startingly simple device of rolling heavy rocks down the hills onto the charging knights and then chasing the fleeing horsemen with their pitchforks into nearby Lake Egeri. With this victory, rather than with the quasi-legendary oath of 1291, originated the gradual independence of the cantons. They now formed a "Perpetual League" for mutual protection, which received immediate recognition from Louis the Bavarian. The privileges enjoyed by this league seemed so attractive to neighboring townships that it soon received additional adherents. Joined by Lucerne in 1332, it became the *Vierwaldstättenbund* (League of the Four Forest Cantons), from which was derived the name of the lake around which these districts are situated (also called the Lake of Lucerne). Despite Hapsburg attempts to prevent further secession from their domain, Zurich, Bern, Zug, and Glarus joined the Swiss league during the subsequent decades, augmenting the number of cantons from four to eight. The addition of these wealthy cities changed the character and interests of the confederation. Mercantile considerations began to outweigh the more restricted and local interests of the peasants inhabiting the original cantons.

In the late fourteenth century, the league not only continued its successful defensive actions, but started to make commercial and political alliances with other leagues of cities in southern Germany and assumed the offensive against the Hapsburgs. In 1385, Lucerne seized the Hapsburg-owned district of Sempach, and when in the following year an Austrian army came to retake the territory, the peasants from the four lake cantons again won a resounding victory, mercilessly slaughtering the attacking knights. Finally, after another Austrian army had been routed in 1388, the Hapsburgs conceded that the Swiss cantons had won their *de facto* recognition. Peace was concluded in 1389, but *de jure* recognition of their legal independence was not accorded until 1648.

The Fight between Louis IV and Pope John XXII

After the victory of 1322 over his rival, King Louis started successfully to enlarge his dynastic territory. His defeat of the Austrians afforded him enough power and prestige to enforce relative peace at home and to embark on an adventuresome foreign policy. His proceedings in Italy and his dealings with the Avignonese papacy showed a strange blending of medieval tradition and modern concepts. Like the Hohenstaufens, he coveted the traditional imperial prerogatives, but he was willing to gain them in a rather revolutionary manner. This was especially evident in his long fight with Pope John XXII (1316–1334). This struggle dealt with the age-old questions of leadership in Italy and respective jurisdiction in papal-imperial relations, but it was complicated by a variety of new factors: the growing strength of France, conflict within the Church itself, and the dawning of new ideas of government.

FRANCE AND THE PAPACY To understand Louis's foreign involvement, one must keep in mind contemporary conditions in France and Italy. During the twelfth and thirteenth centuries, the French monarchy had steadily gained in power, enabling it to engage in a policy of expansion. It is therefore hardly surprising that the French kings began to covet the imperial crown, as Philip IV had done at the time of the election of 1309. Philip's counselor (Pierre Dubois) bolstered this aspiration of the monarchy in his plan to transform the Empire into an instrument for assuring world peace by placing the French king at its head. Control of Italy and the papacy were two essential prerequisites for the implementation of such a scheme. The initial steps had been successfully taken in the thirteenth century, when Charles of Anjou had captured the Kingdom of Naples from the last of the Hohenstaufens (see page 61. By 1305, the second aim also seemed accomplished through the establishment of a French pope at Avignon.

The accession to the papal throne of the strong-willed Frenchman John XXII opened further possibilities to the French. Like his predecessors, Pope John wished to regain control over Italy, but realized that this could not be achieved through the help of a German emperor. He therefore decided to rely on French assistance and appointed the king of Naples—the French Robert of Anjou—imperial vicar to rule the peninsula in the name of the pope. The Neapolitan gladly tried to impose his rule on all of Italy. His attempt, however, provoked war between the propapal Guelf party—led by the king of Naples and aided by the French—and the Ghibellines, who based their support on northern Italy and soon received assistance from Germany.

The war, which raged throughout most of the 1320s, was complicated by a violent religious controversy. Pope John XXII, whose insistence on administrative centralization and heavy tax levies was alienating many churchmen, found particular opposition among a branch of the Franciscan Order called the "Little Brethren of St. Francis," after their Italian nickname *Fraticelli.* These Franciscans believed in apostolic poverty, and staunchly defended the thesis that in emulation of the life of Jesus and his followers, neither individual monks nor the Franciscan Order as a whole should own property. They believed that this ideal of apostolic poverty should extend to all clergymen and particularly to the papacy, which under John XXII maintained itself in great splendor in the magnificent palace of the popes in Avignon. The ensuing fight was acrimonious. The pope condemned the Little Brethren as heretics, sent Inquisitors to arrest them, and ordered a crusade to exterminate them. The Little Brethren, for their part, sided with the Ghibellines and other antipapal forces and did all they could to undermine papal power.

LOUIS'S INTERVENTION IN ITALY In 1323, the ingenuous King Louis IV became involved in a long struggle with the papacy when he dispatched an army to Italy at the request of the Ghibellines, who wanted his aid against the French, Guelf, and Neapolitan forces. John XXII, whose political ambitions were reminiscent of those of Innocent III, resented Louis's interference in Italy. Hence Pope John declared Louis's election invalid on the grounds that the pope had not been consulted, placed him under the ban of excommunication, and then imposed an interdict on his lands. Behind the scene, he worked during the next decade to transfer the German crown to the French monarch. In this maneuver, he found an ally in the Hapsburgs, who, thwarted in their own aim of obtaining the crown, were willing to help the pope transfer it to France. In return, they asked for French assistance for their project of acquiring more land in southern and eastern Germany.

Instead of forsaking their excommunicated king, as had happened when Henry IV was under the papal ban, the dukes and cities in Germany, with the exception of the Hapsburgs, rallied to Louis's side. In some towns, citizens forced clerics to read Mass in spite of the papal interdict; in others, the Little Brethren of St. Francis replaced the regular clergy when they refused to cooperate. A spark of national spirit seemed to kindle the fire of resistance against the "French" pope. Urged by the Franciscans, King Louis in 1324 charged the pope with crimes and heresy and demanded that a church council be convened to try him. To be sure, popes had been accused by emperors before, but the demand that the pope be tried by a church council was revolutionary, since by inference such a proposal assigned more power to the council than to the pope.

To bolster his position, Louis gathered at his court leaders of the antipapal factions and theologians with "new ideas," who unleashed a war of pamphlets against John XXII. The most influential of these pamphleteers was Marsiglio of Padua, who had fled from the Inquisition in Paris to settle at Louis's court in 1326, and soon became a trusted adviser to the king. Marsiglio had written a revolutionary book, *Defender of the Peace,* which assumed great importance during the next two centuries. In it he suggested that the Church should hold no property and exercise no secular power. Church and state should be strictly separated. He rejected the Petrine theory of apostolic succession and insisted that the pope had neither divine nor historical right to supremacy within the Church. The Church, moreover, was to embrace not merely the ordained clergy but—foreshadowing Protestant theories of the priesthood of all believers—was to include all lay adherents as well. Marsiglio asserted that the church council, and not the papacy, was the supreme organ of the Church and should decide on matters of dogma on the basis of Holy Scriptures. This emphasis on church councils—later called the "conciliar movement"—and stress on the Bible as authority had been voiced before by discontented groups and heretics. But now these ideas were supported by the German king and found echo in the imperial diet. Their boldness and latent consequences augured a new era.

The antipapal forces actively sought to implement Marsiglio's ideas. The Italian Ghibellines seized Rome; expelled the Neapolitans, the papal legates, and the pro-French nobles; and proceeded to set up a republican government (under Sciarra Colonna). They then invited Louis IV to come to Italy to resume imperial control of the peninsula. Since Louis's position in Germany was secure, he acquiesced and crossed the Alps. In Italy he was warmly acclaimed by the Ghibellines, the Little Brethren, and numerous antipapal and anti-French factions. In 1327 he accepted the Lombard crown from the hands of excommunicated bishops in Milan. A year later he went to Rome to assume the imperial title voted to him by the republican syndics of Rome. The crown itself he received from the hands of the revolutionary chieftain (Sciarra Colonna). Heretofore the imperial crown had always been bestowed by papal blessing, even if at times by an antipope with doubtful credentials. But to become emperor by the grace of the revolutionary republican syndic of Rome broke with all traditions. The carefree Louis probably scarcely understood the implications. His subsequent failure to exploit the possible advantages perhaps demonstrates that a penchant for adventure rather than preconceived plans prompted his actions. After the coronation, the Franciscans in Louis's entourage persuaded him to elect a Franciscan monk as antipope, and the populace of Rome was allowed to acclaim the candidate as pope—again underscoring a precept of Marsiglio's that the Church as a whole, both lay and ordained alike, should elect its ecclesiastical leaders.

But this revolution from above could not endure long without strong and efficient support from the emperor. Louis's inactivity allowed the Guelfs to resume the offensive. The propapal forces (under the Orsinis), aided by the Neapolitans, retook Rome and captured Louis's antipope, whom they dispatched to a prison in Avignon. In many Italian cities, the people tired of paying for the support of German troops. Pope John XXII, whose strength had not been impaired, again declared Louis a heretic, divested of all lands and rights. Seemingly matters stood where they had before Louis's invasion of Italy. By 1330, the emperor was back in Munich, and, although he vowed to return to Italy, never undertook another campaign south of the Alps.

SECULARIZATION OF THE IMPERIAL CROWN Louis now made several efforts to achieve a reconciliation with the papacy. But political complications, papal intransigence in demanding a Canossalike humiliation of the emperor, and the proud attitude of the German princes made this impossible. Matters were also complicated by the outbreak of the Hundred Years' War in 1337. Louis, whose wife's sister was married to King Edward III, was allied to England and even sent military forces against the French in the initial phase of the war. The resultant anti-French feeling in Germany made any dealing with the "French" papacy at Avignon difficult.

As in 1324, the papal pronouncements against Louis were ineffectual. The German electoral princes even proceeded to legalize the secularized concepts of imperial elections. Hitherto, the elected kings of Germany had all aspired to imperial prerogatives but had not really been looked upon as emperors until crowned by a pope in Rome. In 1338, however, the electoral princes proclaimed that the "tradition and constitution" of the German Empire awarded to the electors the right to bestow the royal title as well as the royal and imperial powers. Only bestowal of the imperial title was left to the pope. The words "royal" and "imperial" were used to distinguish between the Kingdom of Germany and the Empire. The electors then demanded that the pope remove the ban from the king without stipulating penance. The pope (Benedict XII) refused the demand, and at an imperial diet in Frankfurt on the Main the princes went even further in their effort to secularize the crown. After rejecting all papal accusations against their emperor and commanding that Masses be read everywhere in the Empire despite the papal interdict, they promulgated a revised electoral law that took from the pope even the last shred of prerogative. Bestowal of the imperial title was now also claimed as a right of the electors. Henceforth, they asserted, no papal assent was required for the candidate chosen by the electors to carry the royal and imperial titles and to exercise the powers of both king and emperor. In the accompanying explanation, the document pointed out that the powers and titles of a ruler come from God and not from the pope. Mysticism and Marsiglio's teachings seemingly had become influential in Germany, and St. Paul's ideas were being revived at the expense of church tradition. The concept of "an emperor by the Grace of God" and not by the grace of the pope went far toward undermining the power of the medieval papacy.

But the unity of the Empire and Louis's triumph in the face of papal opposition were short-lived. Internal jealousies reappeared in Germany. The Bavarian's ambition for expanding his dynastic holdings annoyed the princes and antagonized particularly the Luxemburg faction, which had a new and ambitious leader in the young Charles of Bohemia. The latter had been reared in Paris and had fought at the battle of Crécy on the side of the French. With the support of France and the pope (Clement VI), Charles rallied all elements jealous of Louis and finally managed to be elected as antiking in 1346 by five of the electors. Civil war again seemed imminent, but in the following year, 1347, Louis IV died on a hunting foray, leaving the stage to Charles of Bohemia.

Louis the Bavarian cannot be classed among the strong medieval rulers. He was kindhearted and friendly, but not always the master of the situation. The dynastic holdings he acquired soon diminished, although Bavaria remained one of the great states of southeastern Germany. His interference in Italy, too, was without lasting results, unless one considers that by delaying French domination of the peninsula he helped preserve the independent Italian city-states that were to be the seedbed of the Renaissance. Yet his reign of thirty-four years was of considerable importance for the transition from medieval to early modern times. It fanned national stirrings and enhanced the power of the imperial diet, thus giving impetus to the incipient conciliar movement, which during the subsequent century played an important role in undermining medieval ideas of authority (see pages 83–85). Moreover, by following Marsiglio's views, Louis had given vitality to the whole concept of political secularization, and had helped strengthen the resistance of the German Kingdom to papal interference. At the same time—though perhaps this was not evident to his contemporaries—his reign proved that the fates of Empire and papacy were intimately bound together and that the embryonic forces of national consciousness were inimical to both. A *French* pope could no more retain his universal power than could a *German* emperor. Pope and emperor had to remain above the particularistic ethnic or political entanglements and, despite centuries of antagonism, the two "universal" institutions had to cooperate if they wished to survive.

Charles IV of Bohemia

Charles IV (1347–1378) of the Bohemian-Luxemburg dynasty was the last strong medieval king. His first wife was a French princess, and he was a Gallophile in political and cultural ideals. In his youth, he had formed bonds of friendship with the pope, with whose aid he obtained the German throne, and he remained a friend of the Church during his entire reign.

His assumption of power gave evidence of his ruthless character. When, after the death of his predecessor, Charles was not at once acclaimed by all the princes as the legitimate ruler, he felt it expedient to hand out bribes and favors. To obtain the necessary funds, the young king adroitly seized the opportunity presented by one of the frequent waves of anti-Jewish outbreaks. He confiscated the property of Jews who had been killed and awarded it to his supporters; and he demanded payments of his Jewish subjects in return for protection. To some persecutors, he sold pardons for having massacred Jews; to others, he offered as prizes the property of Jews not yet slain.

Yet Charles was an intelligent ruler. He was interested in government and in the arts and sciences, but not in military ventures. His founding of the University of Prague, the first in German-speaking lands, was an important step in itself, and his autobiography reveals a youthful, romantic self-analysis quite uncharacteristic of the period. In politics, he was a realist, willing to break with past tradition, astute enough to perceive that forms without substance were meaningless. Hence he was ready to forgo the futile attempt to revive by-gone imperial glory, restricting his activities in Italy to obtaining additional revenue. Nor did he fight with the popes over the peninsula. Rather, he worked in harmony with the Church throughout his reign—not because he was weak, but because he seemed to have realized, as Louis had not, that Empire and papacy were interdependent institutions and that one was doomed without the support of the other. In 1377, shortly before his death, he reconfirmed the Church's right to freedom from taxation and exemption from the jurisdiction of lay courts, while also according it full power to choose and institute bishops in Germany. These steps were to be of considerable importance in the years before the Reformation.

THE GOLDEN BULL OF 1356 In foreign and internal affairs alike, Charles IV was interested in imposing order and a sense of legality on *de facto* conditions, provided that such arrangements would fortify or at least not diminish the power of his dynasty. This was especially noticeable in his governmental ideas and practices. In his own lands, he was a careful administrator, attending personally to the details of government. In the kingdom at large, he accepted as permanent the increasing power of the electors and, as it were, turned the electoral college into a royal cabinet with the king acting as prime minister. His most famous step in this direction was the promulgation of the Golden Bull in 1356, which has often been considered the first written constitution of the German Kingdom. This document recognized as "eternally valid" the power and duty of the seven electors to choose a king. It stipulated that elections were to take place as soon as possible after the death of the king—so as to avoid lengthy interregna and harmful bargaining for votes; that the candidates had to be "just, good and gifted as a ruler"; and that the decision was to be based on a majority vote. No mention was made of any required papal agreement. The Golden Bull remained in effect until 1806. Its primary importance was the grant of additional power to the seven electorates. To safeguard their territorial integrity and to avoid the splitting of votes, the Golden Bull specified that lay electorates were indivisible and were to be passed on by primogeniture—a stipulation not enforced for several centuries. It also granted additional rights to the electors, making them more or less completely sovereign, removing even those checks on their authority that had been included in the decrees of Frederick II. The electors were thus raised to a status high above that of other territorial lords. As regents, they were to meet with the king once a year in the spring to discuss problems of government, and in the event of his absence or death, they were to supervise the administration of the kingdom.

This Golden Bull did not result solely from Charles IV's solicitude for the government of Germany. By stipulating the indivisibility of electorates and increasing the power of the electors, he hoped to strengthen his own Bohemian dynasty, for he owned or indirectly controlled all four lay electorates and could thus hope to assure for his descendants a permanent voting majority in the electoral college. In the final analysis, despite his greater administrative skill and wider political interests, Charles IV resembled all German kings of the fourteenth century in being primarily devoted to strengthening his own family holdings.

EXPANSION OF THE BOHEMIAN DYNASTIC POSSESSIONS Germany experienced relative peace after 1347 and Charles, who did not dissipate his efforts on too many projects, was in a strong position and could devote his attention to the interests of his dynasty. He overcame most opposition at home through diplomatic rather than military pressures. His father had already added Silesia to the family possessions, and Charles now collected additional territories (Egerland, Oberpfalz, Lusatia, Schweidnitz, Brandenburg). Unlike the Hapsburgs and the Wittelsbachs of Bavaria, he added contiguous territory, thereby constructing a better base for any future operation. Potentially his greatest success was his action against the Hapsburgs. Their rebellion forced him to use military means to subdue them, and in the resulting treaty of reconciliation (Brünn, 1364), he laid the basis for the future union of the two houses through matrimonial arrangements. Furthermore, through the marriage of his son Sigismund to the daughter of the king of Poland and Hungary, he hoped to bring into his family even these lands, together with their vast dependencies — Galicia, Walachia, Serbia, and Bosnia. Acquisition of all these lands would have turned Bohemia into a gigantic kingdom covering most of central and eastern Europe. He could hardly have foreseen that ultimately the Hapsburgs and not the Bohemians were to profit from most of these grandiose projects. Finally, he saw to it that during his own lifetime his son Wenceslas was elected king of Germany. Charles was the first ruler in a long period to have sufficient power for such an undertaking.

His foreign policy was unspectacular. He abandoned Burgundy by bestowing upon the king of France "eternal vicarship" over the Burgundian lands. His actions in Italy evinced a similar retrenchment. In line with a promise given to the papacy before he became king, he did not cross the Alps until invited to do so. In 1354 he went south upon the invitation of the pope and received the imperial crown. But even though the Venetians requested his aid against the Milanese, he did not intervene militarily; instead, he contented himself with mediating between the opposing parties. He used this opportunity, as well as his second Italian expedition in 1368, primarily to obtain financial benefits, by charging for his mediation and by selling imperial vicarships, prerogatives, and titles of nobility. The revenue obtained went to fill the Bohemian coffers.

The Chaos of the Late Fourteenth Century

By the time Charles died in 1378, Prague had become a flourishing cultural and intellectual center, vibrant with university life and adorned by beautiful palaces. But Charles left behind a sad legacy for Germany. His reign had whetted the patriotic appetite of the Bohemians, thereby creating seemingly insolvable problems for the subsequent century. The grand designs for his dynastic holdings were only partially and temporarily realized. His younger son was able to inherit Hungary—although the enforcement of his claim required heavy fighting—but Poland and Brandenburg were lost to the house of Bohemia. Of sadder consequence for Bohemia and Germany was the fact that the new king, the nine-year-old Wenceslas IV (1378–1400), developed into a failure. Uninterested in government and showing a taste only for hunting and drinking, he ultimately became a useless alcoholic.

The period from 1378 to 1410 was a time of political chaos and disintegration for much of Europe. The papal schism split the Church first into two and ultimately into three papacies. The Hundred Years' War, despite several truces, locked France and England in an exhausting struggle. England, under Richard II and in the early reign of Henry IV, was plagued by religious, social, and political rebellions, and weakened by constant fighting with Scotland. France, ruled by an impotent and insane king (Charles VI), its strength sapped through the secession of Burgundy, was torn by factions. Germany in those years fared no better. Wenceslas had no power over the German Kingdom and could not even maintain peace in Bohemia. He retained the throne initially only because the Roman pope supported him in opposition to the pope at Avignon, who favored the Hapsburgs. But when Wenceslas attempted to interfere in

Italy, the Roman pope withdrew his support and arranged for his deposition in 1400 and for the election of a new king, Rupert (1400–1410), the unimportant elector Palatine. Since Wenceslas refused to abdicate, Germany now had two kings, just as the Church had two popes. Both kings interfered in Italian affairs, not as in former times under the aegis of imperial prerogatives, but because Italian cities, such as Florence and Milan, bought their services. That its kings now acted as mercenaries for the Italian city-states was a measure of the decadence of the German Kingdom.

The year 1410 brought even worse chaos. The death of Rupert was followed by another split election, in which Sigismund of Hungary (1410–1437), the younger son of Charles IV, and a duke of Moravia were both elected. Since Wenceslas was still alive and claiming his rights, three kings now purported to rule Germany, just as there were three popes after the fateful papal election of 1409. Finally, in the following year, the duke of Moravia died and Wenceslas compromised with his brother Sigismund, leaving the latter more or less in sole control of the kingdom.

THE RISE OF NEW FORCES

The fourteenth century, however, was not merely a period of disintegration. On the contrary, the period witnessed the development of new ideas and nuclei of power that were vital foundations for early modern times.

Growing Territorialism

The territorial lords had acquired their initial strength under the Hohenstaufens. The fourteenth century added impetus to this trend, aided by the weakness of the central government and the increasing wealth of Germany. Following the pattern set by the Italian city-states, the German territories were gradually transformed into *Ständestaaten,* states based on estates, in which relationships among people were no longer based on individual feudal arrangements. In such a state the various strata making up a society—clergy, bourgeois, nobility, and sometimes also peasants—were to be treated as groups or estates. Coupled with the gradual establishment of a nonnoble civil service based on Italian concepts of law, this system provided a skilled ruler with greater control of his land and pointed the way toward more centralized states. The introduction of firearms around 1400 and the beginning of mercenary armies also strengthened the territorial lords.

But the growth of the estates—usually representing the cities, the lesser nobility, and the clergy in opposition to the territorial lord—posed an inherent threat to the power of the rulers. By the end of the fourteenth century, the estates in many territories had acquired considerable power, and had the status of quasi-permanent institutions. They held regular meetings, assumed the rights of granting and withholding taxes and of acting as spokesmen for the people. Since the territorial lords rarely drew sufficient revenue from their own domains, their financial dependence on the growing estates led to frequent friction. Yet this dependence was not one-sided, for the merchants and bankers, whose financial contributions were vital, for their part needed the protection and peace that only a strong territorial lord could offer.

The designation "territorial lords," one must recall, does not refer solely to the king or the great princes. During the fourteenth century, territoriality was gradually assumed by counts, margraves, bishops, and all sorts of lesser nobles, as the atomization of the German Kingdom increased.

The Bourgeoisie

The cities for their part prospered and multiplied in this period. Around the year 1200, there had been an estimated 250 towns with their own municipal administrations in the Empire north of the Alps. By 1300 there were about 811, and by 1450 some 3000. Trade flourished during this century, particularly in the northeast, and the bourgeois accumulated wealth, and gained in political importance. Emperor Louis IV granted some of them participation in the imperial diet, and during the next few centuries, delegates from the important towns had a voice in its deliberations.

In the course of the rise of these towns, much friction developed with local nobles who threatened their commercial life. Class hatred between nobility and bourgeoisie made its appearance. To defend themselves, the cities resorted to the use of leagues. In the second half of the fourteenth century, leagues of towns—such as the Swabian and the Rhenish League—became so powerful that the nobles formed a *Herrenbund der Fürsten* or League of Noble Lords as a counterbalance. The resulting clash was an odd mixture of civil and class war. The leagues of towns, founded originally to protect trade and to safeguard themselves from interference by the nobles, ultimately became so powerful that the imperial diet of 1389 outlawed them, and the territorial lords did their best to enforce the prohibition.

But individual German towns did not develop into powerful political units during the fourteenth century as did their counterparts in the south—Milan, Venice, Florence, and others. Lack of wealth is not the explanation, nor is the gradual shift of trade to the Atlantic, which occurred only later. Moreover, there was no central authority, such as existed in England or Spain, to prevent such a development. The explanation, rather, lies in the fact that, with few exceptions, such as Nuremberg and Ulm, the German towns did not develop into city-states ruling the surrounding territories. The countryside of Germany remained the property of the landed nobility. These lords could exercise strong pressure on the life lines of trade and dominate the food supply of the cities. Unlike their Italian counterparts, governments of the towns were not much interested in political power and expansion. Trade was their primary concern and they seemed only too willing to leave the administration of the kingdom in the hands of the territorial lords. Perhaps this apolitical frame of mind might help account for later developments in German political life.

In short, although during this century the towns reached the height of their commercial power and political independence, they did not try to wrest political control from the territorial lords. On the contrary, they permitted the princes to retain the upper hand. During the following century, there were a few more attempts by towns to form protective leagues, but each one was motivated by commercial and not political issues, and each one provoked the formation of an effective counter-league of nobles. Ultimately the territorial lords retained their dominance.

The Hanseatic League

A similar attitude of the bourgeoisie was noticeable in the phenomenal development of the Hanseatic League, which also reached its high point during the fourteenth century. The exact origin of this association of towns is somewhat obscure. The term "hanse" apparently meant a merchant association and was used loosely to designate merchants from the same German town who cooperated in their activities at a foreign trading depot. During the thirteenth century, commercial depots were established in important trade centers, such as London and Bruges. Here the agents from particular German towns—for instance, Bremen or Hamburg—learned to cooperate in dealing with local merchants. Toward the late thirteenth century, distinction by towns was gradually eliminated, and all German merchants, no matter whether from Lübeck, Bremen, or Stralsund, formed a Hanse at the foreign depot. It was only a matter of time before the home cities, too, learned to work together in protection of their foreign trade. By the middle of the fourteenth century, one can speak of a *Deutsche Hanse* or German Hanseatic League, which at its height had a membership of some 70 towns.

The league stretched its commercial territory all the way from Novgorod, deep inside present-day Russia, to Bruges in Flanders. It included cities in Sweden and Holland and as far inland as Breslau, Warsaw, and Göttingen; it had trading concessions in England, Iceland, and even Venice, and exercised a virtual monopoly on all trade in the Baltic and North seas. No formal organization or constitution existed. Some cities, of course, were more important than others. Lübeck, Bremen, Cologne, Riga, Danzig, and a few others tended to impose their wishes on the weaker ones, but there were no official leaders. Occasionally representatives of all the towns gathered in consultative meetings.

The aims of the association, it should be stressed, were purely economic: the protection of trade interests and the assurance of trade monopolies. The Hanse took political steps only when its commercial interests were endangered. The most memorable such action was the fight with the Kingdom of Denmark, a struggle that demonstrated the power of these wealthy cities. In the middle of the fourteenth century, Denmark tried to break the Hanseatic monopoly on shipping in the Baltic. A Danish expeditionary force destroyed the Hanse's depot at Wisby on the island of Gotland, which had been an essential stopover for taking on fresh water. The league immediately made war on Denmark (1362–1365), but was unable to carry a military victory. Hence they built the water tanks of their ships large enough to obviate the stop at Wisby. Emboldened by his success, the king of Denmark now attempted to destroy the Hanse's fishing monopoly north of Jutland. This presented a direct threat to the league's commercial interests, and almost all Hanseatic cities cooperated to put such military and economic pressure on Denmark that she had to capitulate. The Peace of Stralsund (1370) between the Hanse and Denmark was an astonishing victory for the German cities. Denmark returned the fishing rights under dispute, and was forced to award to the Hanse important trading rights within the Danish Kingdom. This victory inaugurated the high point of Hanseatic power and prosperity, which lasted until the middle of the fifteenth century. The league now even interfered in the internal politics of the rest of Scandinavia and helped to set up the Union of Kalmar in 1397, uniting Sweden, Norway, and Denmark. The league's motives again were purely commercial, for this union offered vast trading concessions to the German merchants. Even during the height of its power, the Hanse developed no interest in forming a political alliance, which could have developed into a powerful force in northern Europe. In fact, the league's cooperation was effective only in times of danger, when selfish demands of the individual cities took second place below the common peril.

Bourgeois Culture

The prosperity of the cities in the fourteenth century was reflected in many aspects of German life. Cities spent vast sums building imposing town halls, and vied with one another in erecting beautiful churches and cathedrals. Merchants built splendid town houses that surpassed in comfort and even luxury the unattractive strong forts and drafty castles occupied by most of the nobility of the time. During the late thirteenth and the fourteenth centuries, bourgeois culture came of age, paving the way for the Renaissance and the Reformation in Germany. Town life produced a new class in the patrician merchant families who formed what would later be called the upper middle class. To gain prestige, they imitated the customs of the nobility. These patrician merchants organized their own clubs, the so-called *Adelsgemeinschaften,* associations of noblemen. They devised their own coats of arms and arranged jousts in the style of knightly tournaments. They listened to love songs performed by the meistersingers —members of the musical guilds—at their festivals, just as the knights a century before had enjoyed the epics and love songs of the minnesingers. To embellish their spacious homes, they commissioned portraits of members of their families or still-life paintings showing the comforts of their existence. This growing trend of secularization of the arts was shown even in literature. The courtly epic, with its deeds of legendary heroes and Christian passion, gave way to didactic morality plays, tales of bourgeois pranks, and earthy stories of adventure.

Similar changes took place on a lower social level. The growth of production and trade and the resulting increase in wealth brought power to the guilds of artisans, whose aim had originally been to assure a decent livelihood for their members by limiting production and establishing standards of manufacture. By restricting the number of artisans and workmen allowed to enter a particular trade, the guilds attempted to eliminate unemployment. But the system had grave flaws that became apparent during the fourteenth century. Social and economic differences grew between masters and artisans, causing friction within the guilds. The leaders of the guilds aspired to a greater voice in the government of the cities and looked jealously upon the patrician families. During the fourteenth century, there were a great number of uprisings of artisans against the patrician city governments. These revolts were usually caused by excessive taxation or simply by class jealousy. In many cases the patricians were temporarily expelled from the cities and regained admission only with the military aid of local nobles who, although disdaining the merchant patricians, still felt more affinity with them than with the lower classes of artisans. In a few towns, such rebellions helped the guilds acquire permanent representation in the city government, but in most cases the patricians retained their monopoly of political power. Some cooperation between patricians and artisans was, after all, needed, for the lower bourgeois were essential as foot soldiers for the defense of the city and as producers of the goods that brought wealth to the town.

The Teutonic Order at Its Height

During the same fourteenth century that saw the Hanseatic League extend German influence to its high point in the northeast, the Teutonic Knights reached the peak of their power. Both did this without the aid of the emperor or the great territorial lords. By the end of the thirteenth century, the Knights had lost their last possessions in the Near East, had transferred their headquarters to Königsberg, and were devoting their full energies to the exploitation and administration of their new state. The additional conquest of West Prussia, Danzig, and the mouth of the Vistula, all of which had belonged to Poland, gave them huge possessions along the Baltic shore. During the reign of Emperor Louis IV, a temporary threat to their domains developed in the alliance of Poland with the Grand Duchy of Lithuania, which at that time was a huge state reaching from the Baltic to the Black Sea. But the Teutonic Order emerged victorious from the war against Poland, and even increased its holdings by purchasing Estonia from the King of Denmark (see Map 9). During the second half of the fourteenth century, the lands under its jurisdiction flowered economically as well as politically. The missionary task of the order lay forgotten and the Knights gave their full attention to the development of an advanced and efficient administrative system. They elaborated an intricate civil service and set up academies to train government officials. Schools were established and the economy was managed in a paternalistic fashion. In some respects one can recognize in the activities of these Knights the antecedents of later Prussian governmental ideas. The importance of their work cannot be overestimated. Unaided by the German Kingdom, they gained important areas for German influence and eventual political infiltration, and laid the groundwork for Germany's *Ostpolitik,* or eastern policy, for centuries to come.

But the Teutonic Order had its weaknesses even in the period of its greatest power. Where possible, German peasants were imported to replace the decimated population, and cities were founded that were dominated by German merchants and artisans. However, no effort was made to befriend or assimilate the native groups, so that the order retained an essentially colonial character. As a result, the native peoples kept their identity, remained antagonistic to their conquerors, and readily resorted to uprisings, especially in times of danger from abroad. The same was true of the local nobility. The Knights needed reinforcements, and recruited nobles from all over Germany rather

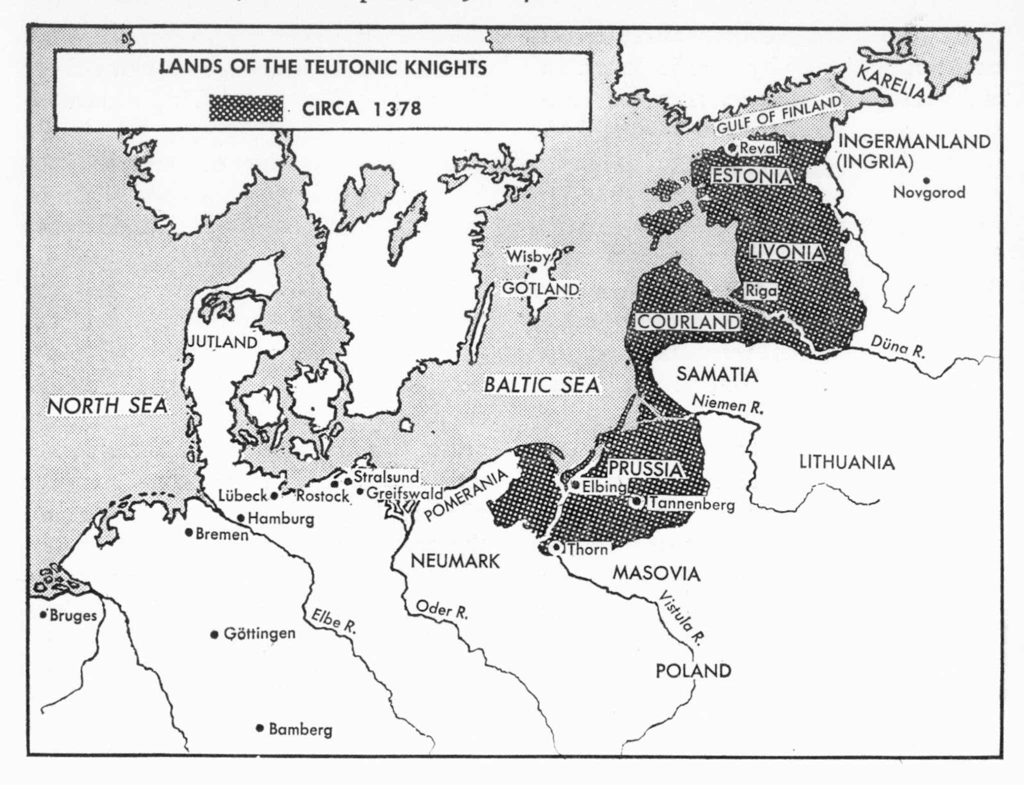

MAP 9

than admit members of the local aristocracy into their ranks. This separation between conquerors and conquered presented a grave problem to the social and political development of the region. Finally, there was also rivalry between the merchants of the Hanseatic cities on the one hand and the Knights on the other. Since the order itself engaged in trade and economic dealings, competition with the cities led to repeated conflicts during the following century.

Yet these internal frictions were less important than the danger from abroad. During the days of Emperor Charles IV, Poland was friendly to Germany and the Teutonic Order, and presented no threat to the latter's existence. But after the house of Bohemia had failed in its attempt to assume control over Poland, the Polish crown eventually fell (1386) into the hands of the grand duke of Lithuania (Jagello). The fate of the Teutonic Knights now seemed sealed. With Lithuania and Poland in the hands of the same aggressive ruler (who later became King Ladislas II of Poland), and with no succor from the Empire, the possessions of the Knights were in jeopardy. In a last effort to protect itself, the Teutonic Order conquered additional territories (Neumark and Samatia), but the inevitable war opened in the beginning of the fifteenth century. The smashing defeat the Knights suffered in 1410 at the battle of Tannenberg at the hands of an army of Polish, Lithuanian, and Russian attackers marked the beginning of the decline of the order. For a short period it survived, saved by its excellent fortifications and by dissension within the ranks of its enemies, but the decimation of its manpower from the battle, the financial ruin brought about by the huge indemnity with which the Peace of Thorn was concluded, and its loss of prestige pointed to its inevitable decline.

Thus Germany reached the demise of the Middle Ages. The Empire was dead, except in the memory of the nation and in the futile claims of some of its rulers. Even the kingdom had lost much of its reasons for existence, for it had failed to develop into an efficient nucleus of power and administration. The great nobles had cemented the cornerstones for their political domination of the land, which was to last until deep into the nineteenth century. The merchants and the Teutonic Knights, the Hapsburg and Bohemian dynasties had given Germany an eastern orientation, thereby shifting her further away from the West, where she was forsaking her former spheres of influence west of the Rhine and south of the Alps. Finally, the bourgeois of the cities, with their new secular interests, their accumulated wealth, and their thriving universities laid the groundwork for the social and religious upheaval of the approaching Reformation.

5

Germany in the Era before the Reformation, 1410–1517

THE FIFTEENTH CENTURY

During the fifteenth century much that was characteristic of the Empire in the Middle Ages was disappearing: the Teutonic Knights and the Hanseatic League lost strength, the Empire shrank in size, the power of the Church, of the emperor, and of knighthood diminished, and the remaining concepts of imperial universality all but vanished. The dominant themes of the century were those foreshadowing the future: the Hussite rebellion with its social, religious, and national overtones, the consolidation of *Kleinstäaterei,* or small states, the meteoric ascent of the Hapsburg dynasty, and the German Renaissance. Furthermore, the fifteenth century—or, more specifically, the period from 1410 to 1555, the generations from John Hus to Martin Luther—offered Germany its last chance for centuries to acquire the cohesion of a national state. The conciliar movement, growing national feeling, the successful examples of England, France, and Spain, and the fervor of the Reformation might have helped the Germans update their political framework. But Germany failed to unify and entered the early modern era not as a nation-state, but as a patchwork of independent powers, basted with a few shaky stitches of tradition.

The Reign of Sigismund

Many of these nascent forces were evinced during the reign of Emperor Sigismund. The younger son of Charles IV of Bohemia and the last non-Hapsburg to occupy the German kingship, Sigismund possessed considerable diplomatic skill, intelligence, education, and even some political power. But his reign proved far from beneficial. He devoted excessive attention to Hungary, of which he became king before being elected to the German throne. He became too deeply involved in questions of church reform, and neglected his governmental duties to the Empire.

THE CONCILIAR MOVEMENT Sigismund's reign coincided with the high point of the conciliar movement—rule by council—in the Church. Based in part on a revival of Aristotle's notion of popular sovereignty, the conciliar theory had flourished in the realm of secular politics during the fourteenth century, when the estates of many countries tried to establish restrictive controls over the ruler: the Cortes in Castile, the Estates-General in France, Parliament in England, and, in a pale fashion, the electoral princes and the imperial diet in Germany. If this political movement had succeeded, if delegates of the estates had gained permanent supervisory powers over the actions of their king, absolute monarchy would not have become the norm of early modern history. But although the estates gained considerable power in some of the German states, the movement as a whole rapidly spent its force and, except in England, the conciliar idea in the field of politics gradually faded out in the sixteenth century.

The movement was of similar if not greater importance in the Church. During the period of the Babylonian Captivity at Avignon (1305–1378), discontent with papal centralization and fiscal rapaciousness had spurred the desire among clergy and reformers for greater decentralization of the pope's authority. Based partly on the writings of Marsiglio of Padua and William of Occam, the conciliar theory was largely developed by reformers at the University of Paris (Henry of Langenstein, Jean Gerson, and others). With the papal schism, starting in 1378, the conciliar movement steadily gained adherents and soon assumed the proportions of a swelling tide. The theory aimed at making church councils superior to the papacy, and many ecclesiastics began to look upon such a council as the only possible agency for healing the schism, provided it be endowed with power to judge the validity of the claims of the two competing popes. The basic tenets of the conciliar theory were succinctly summarized in a decree (*Sacrosancta*) adopted by the Council of Constance in 1415:

> A General Council, lawfully assembled, and guided by the Holy Spirit, obtains its power directly from Christ; and every Christian, including the Pope himself, must obey its decisions in matters concerning the Faith, the abolition of the schism, and the reform of the Church of God in its head and its members.

The inherent consequences of implementing such a theory can be easily perceived. It could lead to abandonment of papal supremacy within the Church and of her entire pyramidical structure, and herald the first steps toward protestant atomization.

Reform-minded bishops finally called a church council to meet in Pisa in 1409 to seek a solution to the split in the Church. The Council of Pisa, however, only aggravated the problem. It elected a new pope (John XXIII, 1410–1415),[1] but the other two popes refused to recognize the council's jurisdiction and rejected all thoughts of abdicating; hence the election of 1409 resulted in a triple papacy. One pope was supported by most Italians, another by the house of Aragon, and a third by France. Hence it became evident that a solution to the triple schism needed the cooperation of political forces.

[1] Since the authority of the fifteenth-century papal pretender was later not recognized, the number XXIII could be assumed by Pope John XXIII (1958–1963).

THE COUNCIL OF CONSTANCE Under these circumstances Emperor Sigismund entered the conciliar fray. It is hard to assess the true motives that led him to help organize the Council of Constance (1414–1418) and to become its most active presiding officer. Presumably the emperor hoped for help from the council in his problem with the Bohemian Hussites. It is also known that he expected the reunited Church to organize a general crusade against the approaching Turks, who were threatening his Hungarian possessions. But one should not exclude the possibility that the emperor realized that the fates of the Empire and the papacy were interwoven and that weakness in the one undermined the strength of the other. Perhaps he also considered the emperor the only logical arbiter among the three popes and their political supporters.

Under pressure of the emperor, one of the popes (John XXIII) convoked the Council of Constance and recognized its jurisdiction in advance. The meeting was attended not merely by clerics, but also by theologians and representatives of secular powers. Besides 33 cardinals, 350 bishops, 564 abbots, it included thousands of university professors, politicians, and secular delegates. Unlike previous church councils in the Middle Ages, in this council the delegates did not vote as individuals but as "nations." At first there were four: the French, the English, the Italians, and the Germans—who included Scandinavians and Slavs. After Aragon recognized the council, the Spanish delegates constituted a fifth "nation."

The Council of Constance involved interminable discussions and bargaining as well as threats and pressures by the emperor. Sigismund even imprisoned one pope (John XXIII) and journeyed to the Pyrenees to meet with the king of Aragon and to persuade him to withdraw his support from another one (Benedict XIII). With such active imperial help, the council at last succeeded in healing the schism. All three popes abdicated, the council elected a new one (Martin V, 1417–1431), and the Church was finally reunited under a single head. But the council was by no means content with this achievement. The reformers pressed for enactment of other conciliar theories in order to make the pope permanently dependent on the council. After much discussion, the delegates passed various decrees that future popes were to accept as a condition for wearing the papal tiara. The most famous of these decrees (*Frequens*) aimed at making the council a permanent institution by specifying regular meetings at five-year intervals, without the necessity of papal convocation. It also stipulated that a church council was to convene automatically in the event of a dual papal election. Other decrees were aimed at reducing the administrative powers and financial independence of the papacy by limiting revenue and at assigning to the College of Cardinals supervision of papal appointments to high church offices.

The Council of Constance marks the high point of the conciliar movement. Although it left many problems unclear, especially in the realm of church-state relations, it undermined the entire traditional structure of the Church. No wonder that the popes spent the next decades fighting against all the implied innovations of Constance in order gradually to re-establish papal supremacy within the Church. The new pope elected by the council (Martin V) was forced to accept the conciliar decrees, but he had already planted the seeds for their future destruction by initiating unilateral negotiations with the various political rulers—a method that was to become the pattern for the papacy throughout the centuries.

THE CONDEMNATION OF HUS Besides attacking the problem of the papal schism, the Council of Constance faced the difficult Hussite question. During most of the fourteenth century, the Church had maintained an excellent reputation in Bohemia and was well served by educated priests and efficiently supported by the University of Prague, founded by Emperor Charles IV. But as in England, the Low Countries, and elsewhere, a reform movement appeared that stressed mysticism and apostolic poverty and also stimulated distrust of the clergy. Toward the turn of the century, under the incompetent rule of Wenceslas, various developments turned Bohemia into a hotbed of religious, social, and political discontent. The transformation had various roots, all of which became intertwined with national passions.

Friction had existed for some time between Czechs and Germans, particularly at the university, where the numerically superior Czechs objected to control by German teachers and students. The tension became aggravated during the papal schism, when the Czechs supported the French pope, while the Germans in Bohemia rallied to the side of the pope in Rome. This antagonism finally came to a head in 1410, when the German teachers and students resigned en masse and crossed over into Saxony, where they eventually founded the University of Leipzig.

In the late fourteenth century, the local reform movement was strengthened when some of the ideas of Wyclif were introduced into Bohemia from England. Wyclif's ideas found adherents at the University of Prague and fortified the demands voiced by John Hus (1369?–1415), a priest and fiery orator who rose with astounding rapidity to the post of rector of the School of Philosophy of Prague University. Hus stirred the crowds with his sermons in the Czech language, denouncing indulgences, simony, and the political power of the Church and rejecting oral confession, the celibacy of priests, and the miraculous presence of Christ in the Eucharist. He demanded that lay believers help clean up abuses in the Church; that all Christians, ordained and lay alike, be given the right to preach and teach; and that during Holy Communion the entire congregation be allowed to partake of the wine as well as the bread (a demand called "utraquism" since it called for communion in *both* kinds). Above all, Hus sought the establishment of a national Bohemian Church, and recognized as justification for his demands no authority other than Holy Scripture. Clearly Hus's ideas foreshadowed many of Luther's.

Hus's sermons added to the restlessness of the time, raised expectations among various segments of Bohemia, and then engulfed him in a religious and national revolution that he probably never intended to unleash. He became the spokesman not merely for the new religious ideas but also for the Czech national cause, drawing upon himself the anger of pope and emperor alike. Requested by the pope to appear in Rome, Hus refused, explaining that he would recognize only the jurisdiction of a general church council. The pope (John XXIII) consequently condemned him as a heretic in 1413 and placed him under the ban of the Church.

At this point, the Council of Constance convened, and the Bohemian requested a hearing before this body. His eagerness was unquestionably motivated by the double incentive of religious conviction and national fervor. Since a church ban, under laws passed by Emperor Frederick II and still valid in the fifteenth century, carried with it an automatic imperial ban, Hus demanded and obtained an imperial safe-conduct to attend the Council at Constance. There is reason to doubt that the imperial pass clearly stipulated protection on the return trip. Moreover, the Church had no reason to honor the imperial safe-conduct. On his part, Hus did not seem to worry. Hailed as a hero even by Germans and confident of obtaining vindication from the council, he traveled unmolested without worrying about a safe return trip.

At Constance, Hus was at first allowed to talk freely and to dispute with anyone. The emperor and many others urged him to confess his errors, or at least to keep silent about his heretical ideas. But Hus, like Luther a century after him, demanded public hearings, and persisted in his view that only Holy Scripture could be used as basis for his conviction. The council, it would seem, had problems enough without having to face this question of dogma, and since it was attempting to assume papal powers, it felt obliged also to discharge the papal responsibility of defending the faith. It condemned Hus and his views as heretical. To question whether Emperor Sigismund should have protected Hus after his condemnation by the council is not valid. Sigismund had issued his safe-conduct when there was no certain proof that Hus was a heretic, but after condemnation by the council, there could be no question of Hus's status. To expect the emperor to have protected Hus for the sake of an abstract ideal of civil liberty is to judge the fifteenth century by twentieth-century standards. Sigismund also had good political reasons for withdrawing his support from John Hus. The Bohemian's fiery patriotism could hardly have been welcome to the emperor. If Sigismund had countermanded the decision of Constance, he would have risked the collapse of the council, which he had helped to organize and from which he expected useful results. In consequence, Hus was burned as a heretic in 1415.

THE HUSSITE REBELLION The execution at Constance provoked an immediate reaction in Bohemia. The country flared up in rebellion, which rapidly spread over the land and assumed extensive complications of a political, social, and religious character. Bohemians fought Germans in the hope of preventing Emperor Sigismund, the reputed murderer of their hero Hus, from inheriting the crown of Bohemia. The lower classes rose against the wealthy and the nobility in the hope of achieving social equality. Finally, conservative Catholics fought the adherents of Hussite ideas. Adding to this confusion of conflicting currents, the Hussites themselves split into many factions. Most important were the moderate Utraquists, later often called Calixtines, and the more radical Taborites. The former, led by supporters in the University of Prague and some wealthy Bohemian nobles, demanded mild church reforms, insisted that the cup as well as the bread be given to the faithful during Mass, and held that the clergy should stay out of politics. Since they were members of the upper classes, they voiced no social demands. The Taborites, however, who derived their name from their chief stronghold, Tabor, became highly radical in their demands. The peasants, artisans, country clergy, and poor nobles who joined this group sought to bring about an immediate heaven on earth. They wanted to abolish the clergy, give each man the right to preach in open-air services, share all property in common, and establish equality of the sexes.

The fury of the rebellion was astounding. The conservative and moderate elements of the land were unable to put an end to the bloodshed. Under their fiery leader (John Ziska), the Taborites successfully repelled two imperial and papal crusades sent by Sigismund against the Bohemians. Strong forces of knights from all over Germany were unable to subdue the Hussite peasants and artisans. In the 1420s, under their new leader (the priest Procop the Great), the Taborites even assumed the offensive. They temporarily conquered neighboring Moravia and Silesia, and made forays into Hungary, Austria, Bavaria, Saxony, Brandenburg, Poland, and as far as Danzig. No power in Europe seemed capable of defeating the fanatic Hussites.

Since the revolt could not be quelled by the sword, certain German princes proposed offering the Hussites a compromise on the religious issues, in the hope of driving a wedge between the moderate and radical factions of Bohemians. The papacy, however, which was gradually regaining power after its weak position during the schism, objected to any compromise with heretics on questions of dogma. Sigismund was forced once again to try to achieve a military victory. The imperial army assembled for this purpose in 1431 supposedly numbered over 100,000 men. Yet as it entered Bohemia, all factions of Hussites again united and dealt the Empire another resounding defeat.

A policy of compromise was now inevitable. Another church council was meeting at the time at Basel to discuss further questions of church reform. Despite papal opposition, the council offered the Hussites a compromise solution, granting them permission to offer the cup to the laity during Communion, allowing anyone to preach in the Czech language, and permitting the establishment of a Czech National Church. The only Bohemian demand the council refused was the confiscation of all church property. This compromise, sometimes called the Prague Compact, was potentially of far-reaching consequences. By permitting the Czechs to deviate from the dogma of Communion in one kind, it augured the flood of dogmatic splintering that occurred in the sixteenth century. And by agreeing to the Czech demands, the council put into question its own decision of eighteen years earlier when it had condemned John Hus for the same views.

The papacy, now under Eugene IV (1431–1447), realized that the unity of the Catholic Church was at stake, and initially refused to condone the decisions of the Council of Basel and the Prague Compact. Emperor Sigismund, desirous of pacifying Bohemia, again intervened. He journeyed to Rome and persuaded the pope to accept the compromise of Prague. So close and effective was the new understanding between pope and emperor that Sigismund at the same time received the imperial coronation (1433).

In Bohemia itself the compromise had the desired effect. Stripped of the religious issue which had bound them together, Taborites and Utraquists now split over their social disagreements. The moderate Bohemians allied themselves with the Germans to end the social threat represented by the Taborites. By 1434, the back of Taborite resistance was broken, and moderate forces assumed control of the land. Emperor Sigismund finally could take possession of the country and be recognized as King of Bohemia in 1436, just one year before his death. But tension between Hussites and Catholics continued to smolder, and in the long run the rebellion helped alienate the Bohemians from the Empire.

SIGISMUND'S FAILURES The twenty-seven years of Sigismund's reign left many tasks unfinished and yielded few successes. The emperor never succeeded in marshaling the forces of Europe against the inroads of the Ottoman Turks, who gradually began to engulf the Balkan lands even before the fall of Constantinople itself (1453). In view of the wars and unrest this Turkish peril brought to European politics for the next four and a half centuries and the losses it was to inflict on the Hapsburgs, failure to stem the Ottoman tide turned out to be a major catastrophe. Moreover, Sigismund made no concerted effort to help stay the waning of German influence and prevent the contraction of German territory. He sat idly by while the dukes of Burgundy seized more and more imperial lands. He did nothing to support the exhausted Hanseatic League in its death struggle with Dutch shippers and traders, nor did he offer aid to the Teutonic Knights in their final fight against Poland. In Italy and in the Swiss cantons, he was unable to prevent the consolidation of the city-states and cantons when they threw off the last shreds of German jurisdiction. In Germany itself he could not put an end to the countless feuds among territorial lords, knights, and cities.

But even his church policy, to which he devoted so much attention, brought no benefits to Germany. In a way, the two church councils he had helped convoke were successful. The Council of Constance had healed the schism, and that of Basel had alleviated the Bohemian problem by arranging the compromise of Prague. But neither council had instituted church reforms, nor found a solution to the question of church-state friction. Actually, the Council of Basel—which in most respects marks the end of the conciliar movement—made one last, bold attempt at reducing the centralized power of the papacy by trying to impose restrictions on its financial independence. By this time, however, the papacy had regained sufficient strength to reject the attempts summarily. Pope Eugene IV simply adjourned the meetings of the council to Italy (Ferrara), where he could control its deliberations more effectively.

ATTEMPTS AT ECCLESIASTICAL AND POLITICAL REFORM A rump of radical reformers remained at Basel in defiance of the papal order, and even elected an antipope (Felix V), again splitting the Church. This last challenge of the "conciliarites," although seemingly futile, was nonetheless of considerable consequence for the future of church-state relations. The strong monarchies of the West—England, France, Aragon—took advantage of the decisions of the Council of Basel and of the renewed split in the Church to acquire more control over ecclesiastical affairs in their lands. France, for example, took the decrees of Basel as a basis for the elaboration of the Pragmatic Sanction of Bourges (1438). This step initiated the establishment of the Gallican (or French) Church, in which national interests were stressed and ultramontane ties loosened. Increased national independence in church affairs, as achieved by the western powers, was of vast importance during the era of the Reformation. It was also a seemingly indispensable step for the achievement of royal absolutism.

But Germany did not seize this same opportunity. During the last years of his reign, Sigismund insisted on maintaining the same amicable relations with Eugene IV that had procured for him the imperial coronation, and he was loathe to encourage division in the Church. Besides, he felt no more sympathy for German national aspirations than he had shown for similar Bohemian ambitions.

But certain forces in Germany saw the need for reforming the political as well as the ecclesiastical structure of Germany in order to bring her abreast of the western nations. The two types of reform went necessarily hand in hand. As long as there remained a political vacuum at the center, as long as Germany could not speak through the voice of a powerful monarch, a lasting political settlement with the papacy could hardly be achieved. And without greater control over the vast ecclesiastical lands and over the jurisdiction of the church hierarchy in Germany, the rulers could not establish a more unified, centralized state. Already in 1424, at the time of the Hussite crisis, the electoral princes had attempted to form the so-called *Kurverein,* or electoral union, as a substitute government for the ineffectual king. The chairmanship of this administrative commission was to rotate, although in reality the archbishop of Mainz came to assume the dominant role. This first reform attempt of the 1420s failed to gain ground, largely because of disunity and jealousy among the electors but also because the princes used this electoral union to augment their own power.

The Council of Basel and the resulting split in the Church offered a new opportunity for reform. The Germans looked with jealousy upon the French and their Pragmatic Sanction of Bourges. By maintaining neutrality between the two popes and withholding their recognition from both as a bargaining point, the archbishop of Mainz and certain electors hoped to achieve a similar independence for the German Church. They drew up the "Pragmatic Sanction of the Germans," which was accepted at an imperial diet in Mainz. In essence, the document stipulated that the Church in Germany should enjoy considerable political and financial autonomy. Of course, to be effective this measure had to be signed and actively supported by the king. Efforts to obtain this support and to implement the German Pragmatic Sanction motivated the political actions of most of the electors during the next decade. After Sigismund's death, they bargained with his son-in-law, the Hapsburg Albert II, exchanging their vote for his election in return for his consent to the decrees of Mainz. In this way, the Hapsburgs finally regained the German throne, which they were to retain without interruption until the demise of the Empire in 1806. But Albert II ruled for only a year and a half (1438–1439), and died before signing the Pragmatic Sanction.

Eager to enact their reforms while the time seemed auspicious, the electors rapidly chose Albert's cousin Frederick. The choice of the lethargic, proud, and incompetent Frederick III, whose reign of fifty-three years (1440–1493) was the longest of all German emperors and kings, proved disastrous for Germany. Moreover, the electors failed to obtain from him the expected approval for their reforms of the Church. Immediately after his election, Frederick began to obstruct the work of the electors and the imperial diet in all matters that might adversely affect Austria's development. Establishment of an independent German Church could offer few advantages to the Hapsburgs, whereas cooperation with the papacy was likely to benefit their interests. Hence, to gain time for negotiation with the papacy, Frederick delayed giving his consent to the Pragmatic Sanction. While keeping the electors in suspense, he came to an agreement with the Church and by throwing his support and recognition to the Roman pope (Nicholas V, the successor to Eugene IV), he undermined the bargaining position of the Germans, who had maintained neutrality between the two popes (Nicholas and Felix). Negotiations with Rome ultimately led to the conclusion of the Concordat of Vienna (1448), which was useful to the Roman pope as well as to the Hapsburgs, but which effectively annulled the German Pragmatic Sanction and put an end to the hopes of the reformers for a more independent German Church.

The failure of the German Pragmatic Sanction and the signing of the Concordat of Vienna, which remained valid until 1806, were of considerable importance to the entire religious development of Germany. The concordat, besides recognizing the legitimacy of the Roman pope as opposed to his rival (Felix V), awarded the papacy wide financial and political power in Germany at a time when the strong monarchies of the west were restricting papal powers in their domains. The right of the papacy to bestow church offices and collect first fruits and annates was reaffirmed. Frederick III, in turn, received the promise of the imperial coronation, which took place in 1452. Moreover, the Hapsburgs obtained special ecclesiastical rights in their hereditary lands: permission to elect six bishops and to collect church revenues, as well as outright suzerainty over all monasteries and convents in the Austrian lands. Finally, the agreement was sealed with a papal gift of 200,000 ducats to Frederick. By these negotiations the emperor proved that he was little interested in Germany as a whole, but intent mainly on consolidating Hapsburg power. By granting the Church added power in Germany, the concordat augmented the tension between church and state that plagued Germany in the decades preceding the Reformation.

The perturbed electors briefly thought of deposing the king. They also negotiated with the Roman pope to get him to accept the decrees of Constance and Basel. Neither move bore any results. The papacy—under the guidance of the skillful and strong Aeneas Piccolomini, first as papal chancellor and then as Pope Pius II—was rapidly regaining considerable strength, whereas the customary disunity set in among the German princes. Thwarted in their effort to achieve an all-German solution, the more powerful princes initiated bilateral negotiations with the pope. Since the papacy did not confront a united German Empire, but was able to deal with the princes one by one, it granted only minor concessions and succeeded in retaining Germany as a main source of income. Yet some of the princes acquired fragmentary control over the Church in their territories. This development not only increased their power, but also had profound repercussions on the development of Lutheranism.

Frederick III and the Hapsburg Dynasty

Frederick III's long reign proved disastrous to Germany in many other respects. Although crowned emperor in 1452—the last emperor to be crowned in Rome—he harbored neither imperial nor royal pretensions. He freely bartered German territory and showed no interest in supervising the administration of Germany. He rarely attended a meeting of the imperial diet, and for one period of twenty-seven years (1444–1473) never left his Austrian lands, except for a single journey to Italy. He was interested only in furthering Hapsburg aggrandizement. He was imbued with a fanatic belief in the future greatness of his dynasty, as expressed in the monogram he adopted for his family: "AEIOU" (*Austriae est imperare orbi universo,* or, in German, *Alles Erdreich ist Oesterreich unterthan*), which might be rendered in English as "Austria's Empire Is the Overlord of the Universe." His efforts to promote the fortunes of his dynasty were not successful during his lifetime. He was unable to retain Bohemia and Hungary, he could not even exercise complete control over his hereditary lands, and he failed in his attempt to regain the Swiss cantons. But his policies were built for the future. Here he was the real founder of the greatness of the house of Austria. By siding with the papacy and assuring the Church's support for Hapsburg policies, by skillful negotiations for the future reacquisition of Bohemia and Hungary, and above all by marriage arrangements, he laid the foundation that made the Hapsburgs within two generations the most powerful dynasty of western Europe. An enemy of Frederick's (Mathias Corvinus, king of Hungary) wrote about him contemptuously: "Let others fight wars! You, blissful Austria, marry! For the realms others get through Mars, you get from Venus."

POLITICAL ATOMIZATION AND TERRITORIAL LOSSES Ruled by an emperor without interest in its affairs, Germany moved rapidly toward disintegration. In fact, for the second half of the fifteenth century, it is a question whether the political superstructure of a German kingdom still retained any meaning. *Kleinstäaterei* now really came into its own. The king showed no intention of trying to end the constant civil wars among princes, nor did he attempt to prevent the territorial lords from making inroads on the independence of the free cities, which might have served as the foundation for a centralized monarchy. Meanwhile many princes wasted their strength on family disputes, while imperial knights preyed on one another or waylaid trading caravans. Some states, however, were led by skillful rulers, adept at building up their ducal powers to the level of regular monarchies. Brandenburg, the Palatinate, Württemberg, Saxony, and

Bavaria were particularly successful during this period in consolidating their power by elaborating their financial and administrative systems in imitation of those of the western monarchs.

Demands for reforming the structure of the Empire continued. Some princes still sought to make the imperial diet the supreme authority, and submitted various proposals to Emperor Frederick. They demanded an imperial court of justice capable of ensuring peace in the land; regular tax levies, to be paid largely by the cities; and an imperial ministry to govern Germany. Naturally they expected to form such a ministry from their own members. But by procrastinating, by playing on the mutual distrust of the princes, by dispensing lavish bribes, and by relying on the support of the Church, Frederick evaded these demands. Neither pope nor emperor had any sympathy for the conciliar ideas—whether of a political or religious nature—and ultimately the political reform movement suffered the same collapse as had the religious one a generation earlier. Hapsburg dynastic strivings and papal concentration of power went hand in hand, and both carried the field.

Meanwhile the shrinkage of German territory and influence so evident under Sigismund proceeded at ever-increasing speed. Schleswig-Holstein was joined to Denmark in personal union under the Danish king—with Holstein remaining in the Empire but Schleswig being separated from Germany. The Teutonic Knights suffered further defeats, and ultimately lost their independence. After their defeat at Tannenberg, the Knights had more and more difficulty controlling rebellious cities and local nobles, and several revolts occurred in which the order was barely able to keep the upper hand. The greatest threat to its existence came from the united Kingdom of Poland and Lithuania, which was constantly growing in strength. From 1454 to 1466, the order was involved in a final war with Poland, complicated by renewed rebellion of its own subjects. Once again the Knights were decisively defeated. In the second Peace of Thorn (1466), which concluded the war, the Knights were forced to cede to Poland the territories of Danzig and West Prussia—lands that were to form the famous Polish Corridor in the twentieth century. The order was allowed to retain merely East Prussia, which eventually became one of the bases for the future Prussian state, but it had to recognize Polish suzerainty over these lands, an act that carried complications for later centuries. After this disastrous war, the Teutonic Order continued to exist with its narrow base in East Prussia, but it had lost all effectiveness and importance.

Similarly, the Hanseatic League lost all significance during the reign of Frederick III. The Dutch employed bigger and faster vessels, and began to compete for the shipping trade in northern Europe. From 1438 to 1441, there was even open warfare between the Dutch and certain Hanseatic towns. The Dutch were victorious and acquired the right to sail the Baltic. Hereafter, the most lucrative trade routes rapidly slipped from the hands of the Hanse. In addition, the league was losing control over its terminal depots. In 1478, the duke of Moscow (Tsar Ivan III) seized Novgorod, and shortly thereafter destroyed the German colony in that city. In the West, Bruges gradually lost much of its importance as neighboring Antwerp undermined its commercial monopoly. As a shadow institution, the Hanseatic League continued to exist for a long time. Certain Hanse towns survived the decline and continued to be relatively prosperous for several centuries, but as an effective commercial league dominating northern Europe and spreading German influence in that region, the Hanse ceased to exist in the late fifteenth century.

RELATIONS WITH BURGUNDY To these losses in the north and east must be added the forfeiture of lands in the west. By 1400, the bulk of the southern portion of the "zone of fragmentation" —the old Lotharingian middle strip of the ninth century—had already been separated from Germany. Italy, the Swiss cantons, and the Kingdom of Arles were all but lost. Then, during the reigns of Sigismund and Frederick III, most of the northern portion also began to slip from German control. The remarkably successful dukes of Burgundy, originally a branch of the royal family of France, were taking possession of the prosperous strip of land between France and Germany. Between 1383 and 1442, they conquered or inherited Burgundy, Flanders, Artois, Picardy, Brabant, Holland, Hennegau, and Luxemburg. These regions were among the richest areas of Europe—particularly the trading and manufacturing centers of Flanders, Brabant, and Holland. As a result, the dukes of Burgundy rapidly became powerful and immensely wealthy. As rulers of Burgundy, they were technically vassals to the king of France, and as dukes of the Lowland counties they were supposedly vassals of the emperor. But by the fifteenth century, such notions of feudal obligations had lost much of their stringency, and the Burgundians were strong enough not to bow before either German or French overlordship.

Burgundian might and expansionism became even more marked under its last duke, the adroit and ambitious Charles the Bold (1465–1477). Charles's two main aims were to round out his possessions so as to control a continuous land mass from the North Sea to the Alps, and to acquire for his family the distinction of a royal title. The usual distrust between France and the Empire, which prevented their cooperation against the common Burgundian menace, made it relatively easy for Charles to succeed in his first aim. By purchase and conquest, he obtained Lorraine, Upper Alsace, and even the southern part of the Black Forest, thus acquiring the desired bridge between his northern and southern possessions. He was aided by Emperor Frederick III, who was not worried that these lands might be lost to the Empire: he contemplated the grander design of turning the entire northern "zone of fragmentation" into a Hapsburg possession. Although the German electors hardly agreed with him, Frederick felt these lands were not being separated from Germany, but would ultimately remain "German," provided the Hapsburgs continued to wear the German crown. Frederick pursued this design just as tenaciously as Charles the Bold worked on implementing his own dynastic dreams. The Hapsburg's opportunity lay in the fact that the Burgundian had no male heir. Charles had only a marriageable daughter, Mary of Burgundy, who was already betrothed to the dauphin of France. But Frederick held a trump card with which he hoped to force the Burgundian to consent to the marriage of Mary with the Hapsburg heir, Maximilian: as overlord of Lorraine, Frederick could thwart Charles's retention of this vital territory, and as emperor, he alone had the power to bestow upon Charles the royal title. Negotiations between the two lasted for years, always disrupted by mutual suspicion. Even when agreement had finally been reached and Charles appeared at an imperial diet in Trier in 1473, distrust between the two exploded the bargain. Charles insisted on first obtaining the crown, while Frederick demanded that the marriage contract be signed first.

The final solution came through Frederick's tenacity and luck, rather than through successful negotiation. For Charles the Bold overplayed his hand, and began to antagonize his neighbors and subjects alike. In 1475, he attacked Cologne in order to acquire additional territories along the Lower Rhine. The German princes united in their hatred and fear of the Burgundian, and rushed to the defense of the bishopric. At the same time France, eager to regain some lost lands, attacked Charles from the west, while the Swiss cantons threatened him from the south, and rebellions occurred inside Alsace and Lorraine. Charles was forced to back down on all sides. Actually, to prevent the destruction of the Burgundian lands, which he still hoped to acquire for his son, Emperor Frederick kept the imperial armies from pressing the attack. France also undertook only minor military campaigns, but the Swiss and the rebels within Burgundian territory attacked vigorously. Between 1474 and 1477, Charles's troops suffered three defeats at the hands of the renowned Swiss armies, which had become the most powerful infantry in Europe. To gain respite in the east and possible assistance from the Hapsburgs, Charles finally consented to sign the marriage contract for his daughter Mary and Maximilian, but soon thereafter he was killed in battle by rebellious Lorraine subjects.

The marriage of the eighteen-year-old Maximilian of Hapsburg and Mary of Burgundy took place in 1477, the year in which Charles the Bold was killed. The Hapsburg policy had succeeded. Although Frederick had seriously neglected affairs at home, the successful conclusion of the Hapsburg-Burgundian marriage alliance was sufficient to assure the meteoric rise of his dynasty. Actually it took over a decade before the fruits of this policy could be realized. The 1480s remained a period of reverses for the Hapsburgs. War broke out with the king of France (Louis XI), who sought to acquire a portion of the Burgundian inheritance. A compromise that was finally arranged assigned to France the Duchy of Burgundy and the counties of Artois and Picardy, but gave the remaining lands to Mary and Maximilian. But Mary died within a few years, and Maximilian experienced great difficulties in establishing himself as regent for his infant son, Philip. The Low Countries revolted against him, and in 1488 the rebels even captured and imprisoned him in Bruges. Maximilian was rescued by an army of German princes who helped him subdue his new subjects. They also supported him against the French, who still hoped to acquire Flanders.

PRE-LUTHERAN GERMANY

The Rise of Maximilian I

It may seem strange that the German princes were willing and even eager to help Maximilian assert his Hapsburg rights. The explanation lies in a variety of factors. For one, Maximilian was extremely active, quite in contrast to his lethargic father. An enthusiastic and magnetic persuader, he knew how to acquire popularity, and could readily impose his will on his compatriots. Moreover, this was a period of curiously inflamed "antiforeign" feelings, and the German princes admired Maximilian's tenacious stand against French encroachments. Finally, the electors had pinned their hopes for reform on the young prince, who professed a willingness to agree to certain structural changes within the Empire. Hence they sought to make him king of Germany as quickly as possible. It is ironic that the aging and distrustful Frederick III, who had dreamed so much of the future greatness of his dynasty, opposed the election of his son, and even refused to help him against his enemies. It took lengthy negotiations, pressure from the electors, and a disaster in his own Austria before Frederick finally agreed to have his son elected to the kingship of Germany in 1486. Even then, there was little cooperation between father and son during the remaining seven years in which both shared in the government of the Empire, the one as emperor and the other as king.

During the time that Maximilian was gaining dominion over the Lowlands, his father suffered one reverse after another in the east. The king of Hungary (Matthias Corvinus) conquered most of Austria, including the city of Vienna, while the Turks invaded Styria and Carinthia. The German princes, in their resentment against the emperor, refused to extend help, and Frederick found himself a wandering refugee in the Empire. Only after the death of the Hungarian conqueror (1490), and after Maximilian had settled his claims to the Burgundian inheritance, did events turn in favor of the Hapsburgs. The young king now came to the rescue of his father and freed Austria from foreign occupation. Although his forces were not strong enough to conquer Hungary, he was able to conclude the Peace of Pressburg (1491), which reconfirmed the cherished Hapsburg right to ultimate inheritance of Bohemia and Hungary originally established in the family compact of 1368. Thus in the last years of Frederick's rule, the future of the Hapsburgs seemed assured, even though the senile emperor had done nothing to protect the legacy toward the end of his reign. The death of the ninety-year-old Frederick was regretted by none. He died in 1493 of blood poisoning in the foot, incurred when he kicked open a door because he was too lazy to open it by hand.

Maximilian I (1493–1519) now began his flamboyant and turbulent reign of twenty-six years. He was the first and perhaps the only Renaissance king of Germany. Like his English and French counterparts—though they were not his exact contemporaries—Henry VIII and Francis I, he was intelligent, well educated, and rather cosmopolitan in outlook. He patronized the arts, encouraged scientific investigation, and aspired to be a writer. In some respects he was still a medieval knight: he delighted in tournaments, fighting, and hunting; he was devoted to the chivalric courtship of ladies; and he dreamed romantically of such heroic deeds as a grand crusade against the Turks. Some have called him an unrealistic dreamer who "tried much and accomplished nothing." On the other hand, he was the first modern ruler. He ran much of the government himself like an absolutist, based his policies on secular calculations, adopted the mercenary system for his armed forces, and appeared to sense the impending realignment of the European powers along antagonistic, national divisions. Maximilian was the first strong German ruler in a long period, and one of the last for many centuries. He appealed to the national feelings of the lower bourgeois, and delighted the educated classes with the intellectual atmosphere at his court. But the princes and the knights gradually came to distrust him, for he failed to bring about the desired political reform of the Empire, and did nothing to alleviate the economic plight of the knights. Besides, the princes finally realized that all of Maximilian's expenditures, wars, marriage arrangements, and foreign ventures neither aided the welfare of Germany nor increased their own power, but were designed primarily to further the dynastic interests of the Hapsburgs.

Yet, in the long run, the adulation of the middle class was of more consequence than the antipathy of the princes. Something had to take the place of political coherence if the concept of a "Germany" was to survive. Maximilian's reign, aided by new Renaissance ideas, furnished such a substitute. It generated aspirations for a "German entity" by stressing cultural affinity, and it stimulated feelings of national coherence by popularizing the image of a strong "all German" leader. Leaflets, poems, and songs proclaimed the miraculous powers of the handsome emperor and hailed him as the conqueror of the French and the future subjugator of the Turks. Like the legends of Charles the Great and Barbarossa, the hero worship of Maximilian inflamed the patriotic ideal.

Germany at the End of the Fifteenth Century

THE TERRITORIAL LORDS Germany at the time of Maximilian might still be called a nation, but it was no longer one state. The big territorial units had assumed almost complete sovereignty. In the more important ones, the right of primogeniture was being enforced, so that the constant splitting of family inheritances became a matter of the past. As a result, the various governments were more stable than they had been and their territorial borders began to have some permanence. To be sure, the frontiers of these lands continued to be altered through wars and other contingencies, but the former constant and chaotic changes in the map of Germany began to subside. At the same time, the rulers of these states assumed more power over internal affairs. The church-state struggle, which formerly had been waged between emperor and pope, was assumed by the principalities. The territorial lords tried to gain whatever influence they could over the Church within their region. Moreover, many of the petty lords were acquiring military forces with which they could dominate their subjects and defend themselves against inroads from neighboring states. Levies of feudal knights with their personal loyalties and outdated armor had become unreliable. The citizen armies, so effective in the defense of the local interests of towns during the fourteenth century, were also falling into disuse. On the other hand, the superiority of trained infantry had been shown by the feats of the Swiss soldiers, especially in the Burgundian wars. The emperor therefore began to hire professional mercenaries, and the territorial lords, as far as their finances permitted it, rapidly followed this example and hired their own armies. This gave rise in Germany to the same military plague that afflicted Italy during the Renaissance. Professional generals assembled trained armies, and either engaged in private warfare and plunder or hired themselves and their armies out to whichever territorial lord could afford to pay the price.

SOCIAL CHANGES During the late fifteenth century, the social structure of Germany also underwent changes. Many cities were losing their precarious political independence. Their inhabitants, on the other hand, were steadily becoming wealthier and more influential in the cultural, the economic, and even the political life of the land. Important discoveries of mineral wealth, especially in copper and silver, aided Germany's export trade as well as her financial resources. Manufacturing, particularly of cloth and also of iron products, was expanding. Above all, the accumulation of wealth permitted the rise of vastly important banking families in southern Germany, such as the Fuggers and the Welsers in Augsburg, who supplanted the Italians of Florence and Genoa as the dominant financiers of Europe.

But this wealth of the merchant class was not shared by members of the lower nobility, who were entering a final period of economic decay. These thousands of petty knights, each of whom owned but a few acres of land, were a pitiful vestige of medieval times. Seemingly excluded from the progressive vitality of the society, they could not rise to the status of territorial lords, for they lacked the power, resources, and landed possessions for such aspirations. In fact, the territorial lords did their best to suppress the knights. Nor could they improve their economic status by engaging in trade or manufacture, for the conventions of the time prevented a noble from doing any remunerative work. Since prices of manufactured goods were more inflated than those of agricultural products, these petty nobles were caught in a severe economic squeeze: their small holdings did not produce the revenue needed to buy essential consumer goods. Moreover, they were socially ostracized; despised as petty nobility by the territorial rulers, they in turn remained aloof from the bourgeois. The plight of this class was pathetic. They retired to their petty strongholds, ready to defy the territorial lord or anyone else who threatened their independence. They engaged in raids on neighboring knights or on defenseless cities. Recognizing neither territorial nor imperial laws that condemned *Fehde,* private feuds, and as though living in the early Middle Ages, they obeyed only the time-honored *Faustrecht,* the law of the stronger. The insecurity and emotional dilemma of this dying class is well pictured in Goethe's drama *Götz von Berlichingen.*

While the towns acquired more wealth and the knights declined, significant changes were taking place among the peasantry. Although the peasants did not benefit much from the commercial prosperity of the period, on the whole their economic position had improved considerably. They were not prosperous, but they suffered few famines; they were passably housed, and they enjoyed a relatively secure existence. Numerous new possibilities of livelihood, such as joining mercenary armies or finding employment in the growing cities, had widened their economic prospects. On the other hand, those peasants who remained on the land were still bound by the manorial system of the Middle Ages, subject in body and soul to the whims of the lord of the manor. It is probably this dichotomy between their improved economic status and their vestigial social and political dependence that lay at the heart of their restlessness during this period. During the second half of the fifteenth century, peasant uprisings, especially in southwestern Germany, became more frequent. Peasants organized into groups, called *Bundschuh,* and learned how to fight from those who had served in mercenary armies. At frequent intervals these peasant groups rose against the landlords in futile attempts to gain freedom from manorial restrictions.

THE GERMAN RENAISSANCE At the time of Maximilian, German humanism and the German Renaissance came of age. Despite its contact with Italy, Germany, like much of Europe north of the Alps, had been slow in adopting the new ideas. No signs of a Renaissance were visible in Germany before the fifteenth century. Even in the early 1400s, the Germans lacked eminent scholars and artists, and still clung tenaciously to Gothic ideals and medieval scholasticism. The only important break with the scholastic tradition came with the widespread movement of mysticism, which rapidly assumed importance in the religious and intellectual life of Germany. Despite, or perhaps because of, their growing antipathy to the organized Roman Church, the Germans were intensely fascinated by religious questions and devoted much effort to finding new ways of satisfying their spiritual needs. The ascetic and mystic approach of a Thomas à Kempis (in his *Imitation of Christ*) and the unrestrained emotionalism of other mystics (such as Tauler or Suso) on the whole appealed to them more than the intellectual approach of the southern humanists.

Eventually Germany, too, produced its share of humanistic scholarship. Before the middle of the fifteenth century, the learned Nicholas of Cusa (1401–1464), a forerunner of humanism, propounded a tightly reasoned defense of the conciliar movement, attacked the authenticity of important church documents such as the Donation of Constantine, and even announced that the earth turned around the sun. By the second half of the century, German humanism moved into full bloom, aided immensely by Gutenberg's invention of printing, which greatly facilitated and also made less expensive the dissemination of information. University life became more active. New universities were established with great speed, as the rulers vied with one another in turning their lands into centers of learning. The princes were also eager to have theologians who had not been trained in Italy. Freiburg, Basel, Ingolstadt, Mainz, Tübingen, Wittenberg, and Frankfurt on the Oder opened universities in the span of half a century (1457–1506), raising the number of German universities to over sixteen. Although medicine, law, and some liberal arts were taught at these institutions, theological studies still dominated the curriculum.

Throughout German lands, segments of the *bourgeoisie* avidly espoused the new ideas, especially at such humanistic centers as Nuremberg, Augsburg, Heidelberg, Tübingen, and Vienna. A new intellectual nobility arose, forming literary societies and exchanging correspondence on their latest discoveries. Many of them (such as John Reuchlin) studied Greek and Hebrew in order to investigate Biblical problems and examine the validity of the Vulgate Bible, a task ultimately culminated in the important work of Erasmus. Others (such as Ulrich von Hutten and Sebastian Brant), less interested in theoretical religion, wrote pamphlets and essays on political issues or on the general themes of human virtues and foibles. Probably the best known among them is Brant's *Ship of Fools,* a widely imitated didactic poem satirizing the weaknesses of mankind. But it should be stressed that the majority of the academicians were interested above all in matters of religion, and delved with fervor into disputes on exegesis, the documentary tradition of the Church, or the relative merits of Judaism and Christianity. Belles-lettres as such claimed their attention relatively little.

At another level, the Renaissance provided a powerful stimulant to the growth of a popular culture. Between 1450 and 1550, the meistersingers, especially those of Nuremburg, attained the height of their achievements. Most celebrated among them was Hans Sachs (1494–1576)—best known to non-Germans as the protagonist in Wagner's opera *Die Meistersinger von Nürnberg* —who wrote over two hundred plays and farces, well over a thousand comic tales, and hundreds of lyric poems. Although Sachs's humor was coarse and his language hardly refined, he left a vital impact on German popular culture, and together with Martin Luther helped stabilize the development of the German language.

At the same time, the age of Maximilian was fruitful for German art, which began to abandon Gothic styles and turn with interest to new media and new ideals of expression. Southwestern Germany—especially Nuremberg and Augsburg—was particularly active. The Vischer family of Nuremberg produced six sculptors and ironsmiths, of whom the best known is Peter Vischer (1460–1529), who fashioned the bronze tomb for Emperor Maximilian. Adam Kraft (1460–1508), who sculptured mostly in stone, and Veit Stoss (1440–1533), who preferred carving in wood, both combined expressive strength with intense realism, especially in their depiction of suffering; while Tilman Riemenschneider (1460?–1531) mingled sweetness of expression and Gothic love of detail with Renaissance *joie de vivre.* In painting, the mixture of medieval Gothic and Renaissance was even more apparent. Matthias Grünewald (d. 1530), who did much of his work in Mainz and northern Germany, remained thoroughly medieval in his sharp details and intense preoccupation with pain. Albrecht Dürer (1471–1528), probably the greatest of German Renaissance painters and engravers, was thoroughly Renaissance in his individualism. Yet the somber, necrotic aura permeating many of his paintings and woodcuts underlined the difference of northern art from the joyful and colorful affirmation of life exhibited by his Italian contemporary Botticelli. Lucas Cranach (1472–1533), who became court painter to the elector of Saxony and painted many of the best-known portraits of Luther, completely abandoned the medieval style in his sensuous nudes and his frank portraiture.

Although humanism, with its emphasis on the revival of antiquity, is often looked upon as a cosmopolitan movement, many a German humanist was an avid propagator of "nationalistic" ideas. Strictly interpreted, the term "nationalistic" should not be applied to the period before the French Revolution, since it denotes acceptance of the national state as the sole determinant of the fate of its subjects. But feelings of xenophobia and veneration of all that was considered *teutsch* were pitched at such an emotional level during this period that the word "patriotism" or "national feeling" seems inadequate.

Ulrich von Hutten (1488–1523), an intellectual knight-errant, preached intense hatred of all things foreign. German historians (Wimpfeling, Schedel, Celtis, Aventinus) stressed the historical unity of German culture. They searched for common characteristics among the regions of the Empire, looked in vain for determinants of what should comprise an ethnic or political Germany, and attempted to shape for their country a place in the stream of world history. In this connection, some of them freely invented legends; one such, for example, asserted that the Germans descended directly from Noah. The rediscovery of Latin sources, particularly of Tacitus, helped provide information on the background of German history. And while some intellectuals dug in the archives to discover a glorious past, the bourgeois admired the feats of German mercenaries on the many fields of battle. They also launched a violent campaign against the Roman Church, which in their eyes came to represent foreign domination and foreign exploitation. This surge of "nationalistic" feeling, probably more violent in Germany than in the surrounding countries, could have provided the German states with an opportunity for uniting into a single monarchy had Maximilian been willing to neglect his Hapsburg interests and devote his full power and resources to this task.

The Conflict of Hapsburg and German Interests

Maximilian was first and foremost a Hapsburg, and as such he faced enormous tasks that taxed his strength. As Burgundian heir, he had inherited the enmity of France, which could not reconcile itself to the loss of this rich legacy. In the east, the inheritance of Bohemia-Hungary had again not been accomplished. In the southeast, he was threatened by constant inroads by the Turks, and in the south, he had to deal with the French, who were acquiring the Milanese territory. Not only preoccupied with these tasks, Maximilian was also engrossed in projects for increasing the Hapsburg dominions by successful marriage alliances.

To German affairs as such, the emperor devoted neither much time nor interest. Always in need of funds for his many enterprises, he considered Germany as primarily a source of revenue. But the German estates supported his Hapsburg ventures only intermittently and tried to exact a heavy toll for their aid.

LAST EFFORTS AT POLITICAL REFORM

Maximilian's need for funds provided the electors with a final opportunity to attempt a reform of the government of the Empire. Before his election, he had promised his consent to such reforms, but after assuming power he showed little readiness to keep his word. Yet a bargain seemed possible, since the king was eager to obtain from the German lands a regular revenue as well as fixed contributions of manpower for the standing army he wished to establish. The estates, for their part, were primarily interested in the enforcement of internal peace and the setting up of an expeditious, independent judiciary to replace the distrusted royal court. A compromise was struck in 1495 at the Diet of Worms at a time when Maximilian needed funds for his campaign against France. The Worms decrees provided for the collection, over a period of four years, of an income and head tax, the so-called Common Penny. Since the electors hoped to legalize the widely accepted tradition that the estates had the power of granting or withholding the right to collect tax revenues, they insisted on a clause that placed the Common Penny under the administration of an imperial treasurer who would release funds only with the approval of the estates at their yearly meeting. Hence this measure pointed toward quasi-parliamentary control of the imperial finances. Although pleased with the prospect of additional revenue, Maximilian could hardly welcome such an arrangement, since the estates were not likely to approve expenditures of imperial funds for Hapsburg aggrandizement. A second decree agreed to at Worms in 1495 established the *Reichskammergericht,* the imperial court of justice, in which the king or his representative was to preside over a body of sixteen judges, chosen and furnished by the estates. This court was to have supreme authority for enforcing the third decree of Worms, the Edict on Perpetual Peace, which based itself on similar legislation by Emperor Frederick II in 1235. The edict outlawed private warfare. It was aimed primarily at the constant feuding of the lawless knights, and specified the type of breaches of the law to be judged by this court.

These decrees of Worms have often been hailed as an act of statesmanship on the part of Maximilian to give more coherence to Germany. To be sure, by awarding to the estates more financial and judicial power, they pointed the way for transforming Germany into an aristocratic republic. But the decrees were not the product of the emperor's political vision. Rather, they were imposed upon Maximilian and accepted by him because he was in desperate need of funds. Besides, the decrees of Worms remained largely a dead letter. Very little money was collected under the guise of the Common Penny. Only a few cities paid their share. Many of them, especially the Hanseatic towns, begged off because of the decline in trade. Clergy and nobility refused to pay altogether; and whole regions, such as those under the Teutonic Order, as well as Bohemia, Lorraine, and the League of Swiss Cantons, indicated that they no longer considered themselves as part of the imperial territory and hence not subject to imperial taxation. They also refused to recognize the jurisdiction of the new imperial court of justice. The latter, too, was a failure. There was no money to pay the judges and the court lacked the means with which to enforce its sentences and to ensure the peace of the land.

Nonetheless, the estates made another attempt at reform in 1500, led by the active archbishop of Mainz (Berthold von Henneberg. Again the emperor was in need of funds and troops. His armies had been defeated by the Swiss in 1499 when he had attempted to impose on them recognition of the decrees of Worms and the obligation to pay the Common Penny. Also he was about to undertake another campaign in Italy against the French. At the Diet of Augsburg in 1500, the estates issued an army law that stipulated that every four hundred citizens in Germany were to provide for the arming and support of one foot soldier. Maximilian was promised that this measure would result in a levy of 30,000 soldiers—although it seems somewhat astounding that the imperial diet should have at its disposal such statistics on population as to be able to estimate this figure. In return for this promise of funds and troops, Maximilian agreed to the establishment of a *Reichsrat,* an imperial council or cabinet. This provision would have transformed the emperor into a rather weak president of an aristocratic republic. The imperial council was to be composed of thirty-eight members: six spiritual lords—archbishops, bishops, or abbots; six princes or territorial lords; six counts; six prelates; six knights; six doctors—presumably lawyers; and two city deputies. The minute representation of the bourgeois element indicates the relative strength of the estates at the time. The chief officer of this cabinet was to be the archbishop of Mainz, and the body was to meet regularly in Nuremberg, under the presidency of the emperor or his delegate, to deal with the internal and external affairs of Germany.

This far-reaching measure, the last serious attempt at reforming the political structure of Germany, was also doomed to failure. The estates were not strong enough to impose their will on the emperor. For two years the imperial council led a turbulent existence. Its members questioned Maximilian's unsuccessful Italian campaigns and his constant need for additional funds. The emperor, in turn, refused to heed their advice and did not feel bound by the agreements of 1500, since the promised troops had never been furnished. In 1502 he dissolved this new body and abolished the farce of "parliamentary government." The demands for reform continued but were ineffectual. The decrees of Worms were retained on the statute books and the kingdom was even divided into ten imperial circles (in 1512) for the purpose of staffing and assigning jurisdiction to the imperial court of justice, but the time for serious reforms had passed.

EXTENSION OF HAPSBURG POWER

Maximilian was acquiring more and more power in Germany. He finally regained complete control of all the Austrian hereditary lands, expanded Hapsburg possessions in southern Germany by seizing additional areas from the defeated duke of the Palatinate, and made valuable alliances with certain of the German princes—all of which made him by far the most powerful lord in Germany. Moreover, a few important princes, such as the electoral duke of Brandenburg, forsook the party of the reformers and again concentrated on strengthening their own positions, leaving the emperor undisturbed in his activities.

But Maximilian became more independent of the estates and less subject to their pressure for reforms primarily because of the improvement in his financial resources. His need for funds continued, but his credit and revenue were vastly increased. The famous banking house of the Fuggers in Augsburg loaned him more and more money, so that the time came when one could say that the emperor was owned by Jacob Fugger the Rich (1459–1525).

Hapsburg marriage policy was beginning to pay dividends. In 1495, an alliance with Spain against the French had been sealed with a double marriage. The crown prince of Spain (John), the son of Ferdinand of Aragon and Isabella of Castile, married a daughter of Maximilian (Margaret); Ferdinand and Isabella's daughter (Joan the Mad) married his son, Philip of Burgundy (see Chart 1). Through a series of untimely deaths—John, Isabella, and Philip all died within a few years after the beginning of the century—Maximilian gained the regency for the Lowlands and Castile in the name of his grandson, Charles. And after the death of Ferdinand of Aragon, Charles would inherit the entire Spanish lands with their dependencies in Italy and the new world. Consequently Hapsburg power and credit became vastly enhanced.

THE WARS WITH FRANCE Maximilian's foreign policy, which required such huge expenditures, involved him primarily in wars with France over the Burgundian inheritance and over Italy. The campaigns in the north, in which the emperor was at times allied to England, produced a few imperial victories and netted Maximilian some territorial gains, but failed to weaken France in any decisive way. In Italy matters were more complicated. Here the prosperous Venetian republic and the strong Papal States under the powerful Renaissance popes, Alexander VI (1492–1503) and Julius II (1503–1513), were vying for pre-eminence over the remaining Italian states, while three foreign powers—Spain, France, and the Empire—intrigued for spheres of influence. Spain had its foothold in Naples, and the French entered the fray with Charles VIII's invasion of the peninsula in 1494. In 1499 the French threat assumed more serious proportions with Louis XII's conquest of Milan. In addition, the picture was clouded by the activities of the lesser Italian princes and by the constant interference of Swiss mercenary troops, the best fighting forces of the period. For over two decades, Maximilian found himself involved in this Italian maelstrom. His main aim was to prevent French encroachment south of the Alps. But despite some successful battles, his several military campaigns failed to achieve his purpose. Neither did his marriage to the heiress of Milan (Bianca di Sforza) aid him in dislodging the French. Even his constant shifts in alliances—in which he fought now with Venice, now against it, sometimes against the pope and sometimes as his ally, at times on the side of Swiss mercenaries and at times as their enemy—were of no avail. Nor was he successful in an attempted reconciliation with France, to be sealed by the proposed marriage of his grandson Charles to the daughter of the French king, Louis XII. In the long run France managed to retain Milan, and Spain kept Naples. The frequent campaigns proved costly and fruitless. They helped to fan the growing "nationalistic" spirit among the Germans and to sharpen Franco-German antagonism; to some extent, they also ushered in the era of international wars—if one can legitimately apply such a term to the sixteenth century. But they brought no benefits to Germany.

HAPSBURG EXPANSION TO THE EAST On the other hand, Maximilian was uncannily and perhaps unexpectedly successful in his marriage policy. In 1515, he was finally able to conclude marriage contracts with the king of Bohemia and Hungary, (Ladislas II). For over two centuries, the Hapsburgs had worked assiduously to acquire these valued lands. Various marriages and inheritance stipulations had been arranged, but each time the Hapsburg aim had been thwarted in the

Chart 1 THE RESULTS OF THE HAPSBURG MARRIAGE POLICY

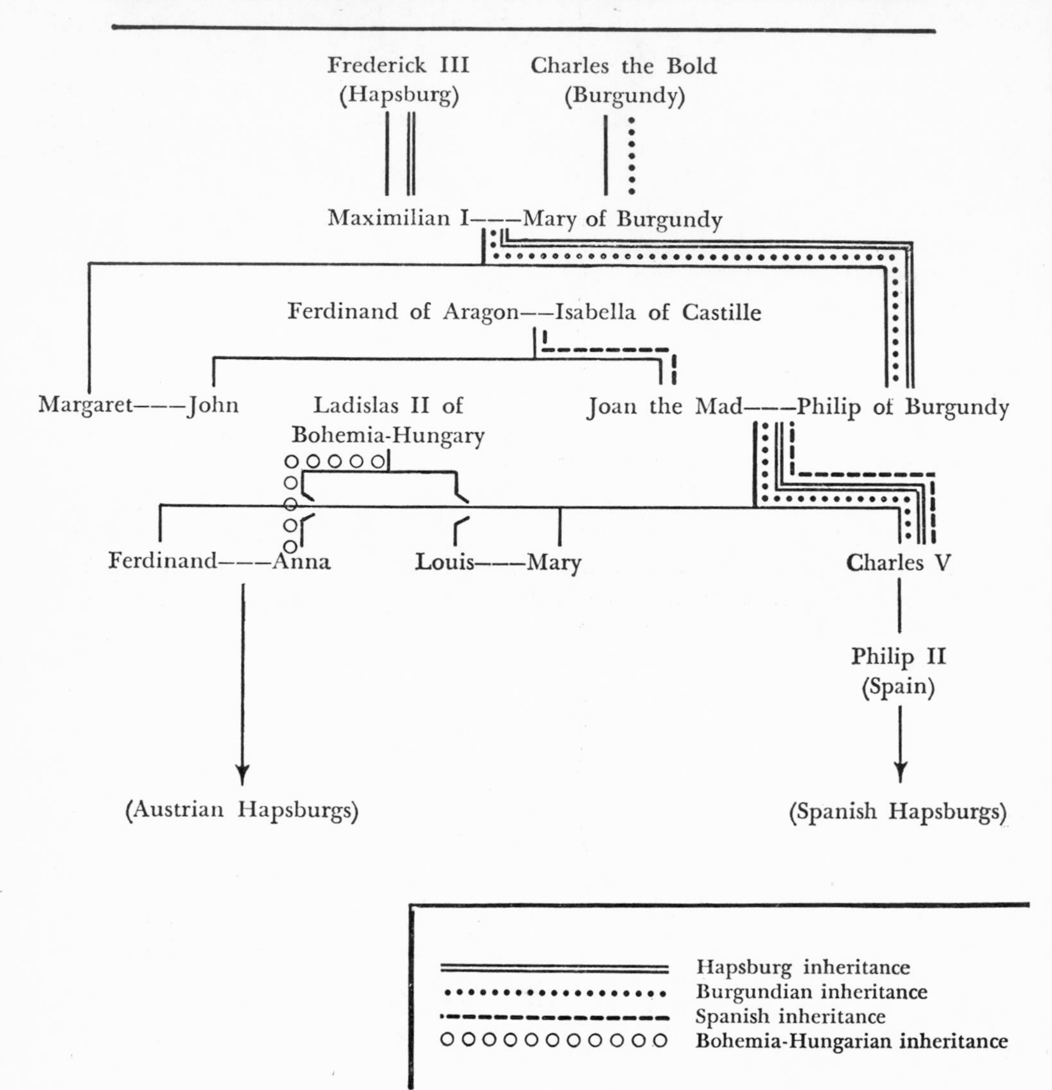

end. Maximilian's undertaking was finally successful. Marriages were concluded between his grandson Ferdinand and a daughter of the king of Bohemia and Hungary (Anna), and between his granddaughter (Mary) and the king's son, Louis (see Chart 1). The marriage contract stipulated that if Louis died childless, Crown Prince Ferdinand would inherit the two kingdoms. This actually occurred. The Hapsburgs at last came into possession of these huge eastern domains, which they were to retain until the twentieth century and which caused the center of gravity of their dynasty to shift away from the west. These acquisitions were therefore of lasting importance. The Hapsburgs' western inheritance, in contrast, though momentarily impressive, was doubtful and ephemeral. After the death of King Ferdinand of Aragon in 1516, Maximilian's grandson Charles came into outright possession of the entire Spanish inheritance. To his Burgundian lands, the seventeen-year-old Hapsburg prince thus added Castile, Aragon, and Naples, as well as the vast overseas territories recently discovered and claimed by Spain, including most of the American continent. Within two centuries—from Rudolf I to Charles V—Hapsburg domains had grown from their small Swabian holdings to an imposing part of the known world.

THE FINAL YEARS OF MAXIMILIAN'S REIGN During the last years of his reign, Maximilian increasingly demonstrated his lack of political realism. Some of his projects assumed rather fantastic proportions. In 1511, at the time of his fight against Pope Julius II, Maximilian—aided by his temporary ally, Louis XII of France—convoked a church council in Pisa for the purpose of having the pope deposed. The council actually convened to deliberate the matter, and Maximilian proposed that he be elected pope. His second wife had died, and he obviously thought himself eligible. Apparently in all seriousness, he actually signed himself "Maximilian, future Pope" in a letter to his daughter. But he lacked sufficient resources to garner the necessary votes for his elevation to the papal throne. Moreover, the ailing Julius II recovered his health as well as his political strength, and Maximilian's scheme came to nought.

His plans for a projected crusade seem equally fantastic. The idea of a general European crusade against the Ottoman Turks had always filled him with enthusiasm. From the point of view of protecting Hapsburg interests along the valley of the Danube, repulsion of the Turkish threat was, of course, a military necessity. But Maximilian's plans were hardly based on such realistic considerations. They seemed guided by his quixotic ideals of medieval knighthood, and were quite out of place in the sixteenth century. While Pope Leo X proclaimed a general war against the Turks at the Lateran Council of 1517, Maximilian met with the new king of France, Francis I, to project a grandiose plan for the undertaking. The emperor proposed a three-year campaign, to start with an invasion of Africa and, hopefully, to end with the recapture of Constantinople from the Turks. It was not difficult to fire the enthusiasm of the anachronistic German knighthood for such a venture. Their useless existence, whiled away by petty feuds and their disgruntled, medieval outlook made them embrace the idea with fervor. But the project was impractical. Maximilian had been unable to fulfill his more limited aims on the Continent and was incapable of enforcing peace at home. A three years' absence in Africa would have been disastrous. Moreover, the German estates, which had already shown their indifference to his European ventures, and had refused to support him with sufficient funds and troops, could hardly be expected to pay for the emperor's conquests in North Africa. Hence the projected crusade was abandoned.

Maximilian in no way perceived the significance of the anti-Roman outburst and of the indulgence controversy that raged through parts of Germany during the last years of his reign. The German estates were loud in their complaints against Rome and were vehemently demanding the establishment of a German Church. Numerous pamphlets denounced the drainage of gold to Rome. The forceful and celebrated Ulrich von Hutten was preaching German unity and fulminating against all foreigners. The Dominican Tetzel was provoking agitation through his indiscriminate sale of indulgences. On October 31, 1517, Martin Luther published his ninety-five theses on the indulgence problem, and in October of the following year was defending his views before a papal legate at the Diet of Augsburg. Maximilian seemed to take little notice of these developments, which occurred during the last years of his life. Of course, one should not make judgments based on hindsight; the emperor's failure to grasp the potential consequences of Luther's action is entirely understandable. But it is less easy to exonerate his obtuseness in not appreciating the new bourgeois fires of national consciousness that, ironically, he himself had helped to fan. All indications were at hand that Germany was ripe for a change, and that the Germans were eager to develop their own institutions without interference from foreign elements. Above all, the emperor should have realized that what was useful to the Hapsburg dynasty was not necessarily beneficial to Germany as a whole. Certainly, Maximilian did not comprehend that it was senseless to tie the German lands to the fate of the new Spanish-Burgundian dynasty and thereby turn them into an unnatural appendix to the Spanish Empire.

Moreover, he misjudged the strength of the political, social, and economic forces that precipitated the initial outbreak of Luther's movement. Had German interests and desires been considered during this crucial period, much of the steam would undoubtedly have been taken out of the reform movement—as occurred in England and France. But during his last years Maximilian was principally concerned with getting the electors to choose his grandson Charles as king of Germany, even though Charles by then had become king of Spain. That he failed to achieve this during his lifetime was not for want of effort on his part. Rather, certain electors, particularly Duke Frederick the Wise of Saxony (1463–1525), could not be readily persuaded to vote for the Spaniard, and Pope Leo X and King Francis of France were both intriguing actively against the choice of the young Emperor Charles. Hence when Maximilian died in 1519 at the age of sixty, no successor had been designated to succeed him as ruler of the Empire.

The Reformation, 1517–1555

THE RELIGIOUS PROTEST AND ITS CONSEQUENCES

The Election of 1519

The election campaign of 1519 to choose a new emperor was a shameless spectacle of backstage maneuvers. The German throne lay at the disposal of whoever bargained with the most effective promises—and had enough funds to buy the necessary votes. To be sure, throughout the centuries the electors had displayed evidence of self-interest in bestowing their vote on candidates useful to themselves. The general welfare of the land had rarely guided their choices, but in 1519 they completely disregarded the needs of the German lands. The electors flirted openly with the foreign candidates who presented themselves, and unhesitatingly welcomed foreign interference for the sake of personal benefits in the form of bribes and promises.

The candidates were numerous. Henry VIII of England and young King Louis of Hungary and Bohemia both made themselves available on the basis of vague promises they had received from Maximilian. But neither candidacy was pushed very much in the face of the indifference of the electors. From Germany itself there were two likely applicants. One was the ambitious duke (Joachim I) of Brandenburg, who until the end hoped to be a successful dark horse, and who intrigued for this purpose with the king of France; another, the benign electoral duke of Saxony, Frederick the Wise, stood a good chance of winning as a compromise candidate, but lacked the drive and zeal to assume the burdens of the emperorship. Besides, he preferred to use the opportunity to acquire additional power for his state of Saxony.

The two most serious contenders by far were the kings of France and of Spain. Francis I devoted large sums and efforts to swinging the election in his favor. Through lavish bribes and reckless promises, his envoys rapidly obtained the tentative assent of five of the electors. Charles I of Spain, on the other hand, was equally intent on gaining the German crown, which he regarded as a part of his Hapsburg legacy. Agents of the two monarchs competed with their enticing overtures to the electors, many of whom secretly offered their vote to both. The electors regarded both candidates as foreigners. Charles, born and brought up in Flanders, was then living in Spain and rapidly adopting Spanish customs. Despite his Hapsburg blood, he was as alien to Germany as was the king of France. Dukes and knights, cities and papal emissaries—all entered freely into the pre-election intrigues, which lasted for half a year. The pope, Leo X (1513–1521), whose voice in these matters was no longer final but still exerted some influence, hesitated between the candidates, who were both equally inconvenient neighbors on the Italian peninsula—the Spaniard through his possession of Naples, the Frenchman through his hold on Milan. In the end, Pope Leo preferred to see the German crown in Hapsburg hands.

Despite his initial advantage, Francis I lost. A tactical mistake of his emissaries may have contributed to his defeat. His agents, eager to discredit the opponent, spread the tale that the young Spaniard, whom few knew personally, was a sickly, inexperienced, phlegmatic prince, lacking the energy required of an effective ruler. Their own King Francis they painted as powerful and active. Such tactics were poorly suited to sway the electors, who had always preferred a weak ruler on whom they could impose their will. Moreover, Charles gained advantages by offering better promises. Charles's plenipotentiaries agreed to sign the so-called "election capitulations," thirty-four articles that obligated the future king and emperor to consult the electors in all matters concerning the government of the Empire, to collect no taxes without the consent of the imperial diet, to reinstitute the imperial cabinet outlined but not put into practice under Maximilian, and to take up the German complaints against the Roman Church.

On the basis of these promises, Charles was finally elected. Known as Charles I in Spain, he became Charles V in Germany (1519–1556). Thus at the time when the Lutheran movement was gaining ground, Germany came to be ruled by a twenty-year-old prince whose vast interests and tasks, ranging from the gold mines of Peru to the Turkish border in the Balkans and from Dutch trade problems to Moorish remnants in Granada, made it impossible for him to devote to German affairs the attention that they required (see Map 10).

Luther's Work

HIS EARLY CAREER Two years before the election of Charles V, the smoldering religious discontent had broken into the open with Luther's publication of his now famous ninety-five theses. Luther was born in Eisleben in 1483. His mother came from a bourgeois family, and his father, from peasant stock, had acquired a measure of prosperity through part ownership of several coal mines. Martin Luther received an excellent education, thorough and strict in accordance with the pedagogical theories of the time. At an early age, he demonstrated his musical talents, and as a young high school student devoted much time to caroling. He was probably well provided with financial support from his father. In 1501, he entered the University of Erfurt for the *studium generale* and some courses in law, and four years later obtained his master's degree at the age of twenty-two. In this same year, he suddenly changed his career. For a long period

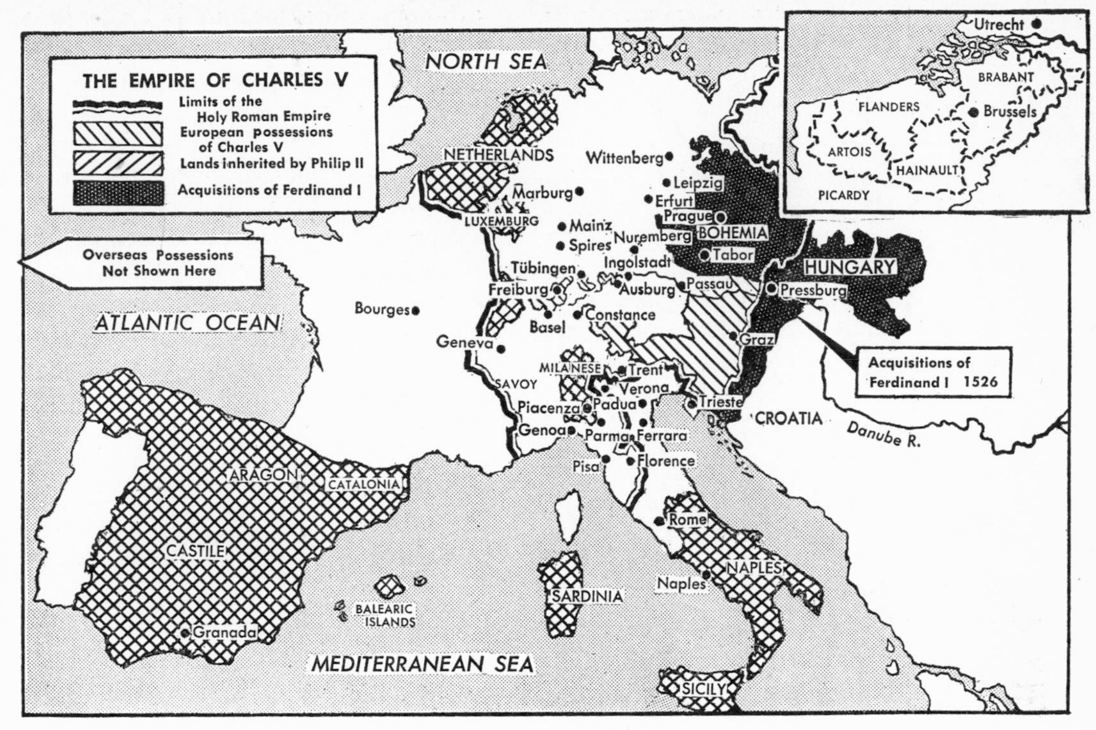

MAP 10

he had been preoccupied with religious questions. An emotional experience similar to those that have converted many religious leaders, occasioned perhaps through the death of a friend in a duel, finally led him to abandon the university.

In 1505, Luther entered the Augustinian monastery in Erfurt, where he sought the sense of calm and security that would convince him that his salvation in the eyes of the Lord was assured. He participated in the normal monastic practices, and through asceticism and self-castigation tried to free his soul in order to become reconciled to God. But he failed to achieve the inner conviction he was seeking. His mentor the vicar-general of the Augustinians, John of Staupitz (d. 1524), whose mystic tendencies approached those of Luther, tried to console the young monk by making him read the works of Augustine and the writings of the later medieval mystics. In 1507, Luther was admitted to the priesthood. Even then, he found no spiritual peace. He avidly studied Paul and medieval church writers, and gradually placed increasing emphasis on trust in Christ and faith in God's love as a way to religious knowledge and salvation. Yet it was a long time before he finally found the certainty for which he was groping.

Meanwhile Staupitz continued to support his scholarly career. In 1508, he obtained for Luther the position of Professor of Philosophy at the University of Wittenberg, an institution founded by the Saxon elector in 1502. Luther rapidly became a respected teacher and a popular preacher in the small university town. He also gained the esteem of Elector Frederick the Wise, which was to be of vast importance for his future career. In 1510 Luther was sent to Rome on a mission for the Augustinian Order. Upon his return to Wittenberg, Luther resumed his theological studies, his lectures at the university, and his preaching in the local Augustinian monastery. Gradually his former doubts subsided, and he acquired the conviction that man's salvation depended on the grace of God and could not be bestowed by any earthly representative of the Lord, not even the pope. Salvation, in his mind, was grounded on faith and based on the Gospel. Paul's statement in his Letter to the Romans that "the just shall live by faith alone" became his guiding motto. Mystically inclined as he was, he increasingly looked upon salvation as a matter between God and man through Christ's intermediation, but unaffected by outward activities, such as good works, or by the intercession of any organized church. This emphasis on inner conviction, expressed by many mystics before him, would have remained the guiding light for his own personal life had it not been for a variety of circumstances that drove the monk into the center of the German political stage and turned his personal beliefs into the faith of much of the nation.

THE INDULGENCE CONTROVERSY The immediate occasion for the change arose with the indulgence controversy. Indulgences were based on what is sometimes referred to as the treasure house of merits: the doctrine that Christ, through his passion and sacrifice, has stored up an infinite abundance of grace that lies at the disposal of the Church and can be bestowed on believers. For the remission of guilt after confession of sins, the act of penance in medieval Christianity required both inner repentance and outward signs of contrition in the form of good works. Such acts included giving alms, making pilgrimages, and going on crusades. The last, of course, were costly affairs, and not everyone could participate in such expeditions. Hence the custom arose that some would donate the money, while others would undertake the actual fighting. The crusader and the donor of money each considered his participation as a part of penance, for which he received an indulgence. But over the centuries, the nature of indulgences underwent misinterpretation and abuse. Originally regarded as a remission of time to be spent in purgatory and earned by prayer and good works, indulgences were erroneously taken to ensure salvation. Furthermore, the act of contrition came to be neglected, and indulgences, in the mind of the laity as well as in the eyes of unscrupulous sellers of indulgences, were thought to become effective through the mere act of purchase. In the thirteenth century the idea was also added that the treasury of merits was being constantly replenished through the merits of saints—a theory particularly objectionable to Luther.

By the early sixteenth century, misinterpretation of indulgences and abuse in their sale became flagrant. In 1516, for example, a new series of indulgences was being sold in Germany. Pope Leo X needed funds for the reconstruction of St. Peter's Basilica in Rome. To obtain the necessary revenue, he decided to issue a new indulgence to be sold primarily in Germany, a land that remained the papacy's best source of funds. An arrangement was made between the Augsburg Fuggers, financiers to emperors and popes alike, and the young, ambitious archbishop of Magdeburg, Albert of Hohenzollern (1490–1545), a brother of the elector of Brandenburg. In 1513 the twenty-three-year-old prince, then already archbishop of Magdeburg, had purchased the wealthy archbishopric of Mainz with money loaned to him by the Fuggers, who now requested repayment of the loan. Hence a three-way arrangement was concluded among Pope Leo, the Fuggers, and Archbishop Albert. In return for advancing funds to the papacy, which usually leased to a banking house collection contracts for indulgences, the Fuggers obtained the right to collect the indulgence revenue in Albert's territories. Half the income was to be counted against the money advanced to the papacy, the other half to reimburse the Fuggers for their loan to Albert. In this way all three stood to benefit: the pope could build his basilica, the Fuggers could retrieve their loan, and Albert would be absolved of his debts. Consequently, Fugger agents accompanied the indulgence sellers in the districts of Mainz and Magdeburg to supervise the collection of their share of the revenue.

The Dominican John Tetzel (1465–1519), who was entrusted with the task of selling indulgences in Albert's territories, was an unscrupulous salesman who was not reluctant to promise heaven and earth to his listeners, provided the effect on his audience would result in high revenues. The contemporary slogan, "When the coin in our coffer rings, the soul from purgatory to heaven springs," well illustrates Tetzel's practices. Many a German readily accepted this easy way of supposedly ensuring salvation, but many objected violently, not motivated so much by religious reasons as by economic considerations and antiforeign feelings. They hated to see their money flow abroad to the city of Rome. To prevent the drainage of gold from his electorate, the Saxon elector, for instance, forbade the sale of indulgences in his territory. Others, of course, objected to the indulgence campaign on purely religious grounds. Among them was Luther.

When Tetzel preached on the borders of Brandenburg in the vicinity of Saxon Wittenberg and some of Luther's parishioners crossed the Elbe to buy the indulgences, Luther could not restrain his wrath. He objected not merely to the abuses and to Tetzel's attitude, but also to some of the assumptions underlying the doctrine of indulgences. He rejected the concept of the treasure house of merits, since it awarded to the Church the key to salvation, whereas he had come to believe that salvation depended solely on the faith of the believer and the grace of God. Moreover, he insisted that for a moral life, inner repentance rather than outward good works was the decisive factor, and he was genuinely shocked by the expedient offered by the Dominican monk. An irascible man, he burned to expose the abuse. Since he believed the archbishop of Mainz ignorant of Tetzel's activities in his diocese, he set down his objections in the form of ninety-five theses, a copy of which he sent to the archbishop. At the same time Luther hoped he would get a chance to engage in a theological debate on the indulgence theory and the increasingly mechanical concept of salvation of his time. Whether he actually posted a copy of the theses on the doors of the court chapel of Wittenberg on October 31, 1517, has recently been questioned by some historians.

The theses acted as a catalyst of the Reformation. Translated from Latin into German, they quickly found wide distribution and raised a storm of controversy. The reason lay hardly in their nature. To be sure, Luther's language was concise and straight to the point, and his attacks were challenging. But similar ideas voiced before had caused relatively little commotion. Decisive, rather, was the climate of 1517, which was so filled with tension that the slightest spark sufficed to ignite the powder.

ISSUES UNDERLYING THE LUTHERAN REVOLT Germany at the time was frayed with religious, political, and social unrest. Peasants, knights, and many bourgeois were unhappy with the restrictions imbedded in the incongruous development of society. In defying the dictates, first, of his superiors, then of the pope, of the church councils, and of the emperor, and in grounding himself solely on his own concept of God's justice, Luther unconsciously furnished a common bond for all these discontents. This explains the enthusiasm with which the ninety-five theses and his subsequent writings were reproduced and scattered over the land, making Luther within a few months renowned throughout Germany.

The forces under tension that Luther's actions further incited were manifold. Within the Church, many critical voices throughout the fifteenth century had built up resentment and frustration. Apart from the more famous Wyclif and Hus, many precursors of Luther had inveighed against excessive papal authority, decried abuses among the clergy, satirized the immorality and ignorance of monks and priests, and criticized monastic life as useless. The mystics, with their objection to the impersonal approach to salvation offered by the medieval Church, added their voice to the swelling criticism. The humanists also had written scathing satires on the worldliness of ecclesiastic life, for which the ostentatious and immodest habits of certain Renaissance popes had provided ample material. Despite the scholastic attitude evident in their reverence for the classics, they tended to question authority by insisting on investigation and examination. Through their studies of original sources, they challenged the validity of church tradition and furnished arguments to those wishing to defy the Church.

At the same time, the humanists and the upper *bourgeoisie* were re-evaluating the intrinsic worth of man. In classical times, a this-worldly attitude toward life had prevailed, extolling the charms of life on earth and its fullest enjoyment. A similar outlook had been held by the early Germanic tribes. But in later Roman times, disenchantment with this world had gradually altered the climate of opinion. The need for certainty had been filled by Christianity, so that the City of God had slowly overshadowed the City of Man, and negation of the physical life had become the order of the day. Monastic asceticism, Neoplatonism with its disdain for the flesh, and stress on salvation with resulting neglect of the earthly life, had become the ideals. Of course, classical and Germanic tendencies had not been completely eradicated. Remnants of heathen superstition, an undercurrent of worldly desires, and an intrinsic interest in the earth and in nature for their own sake had lingered, and had caused a certain dichotomy between the City of God and the City of Man. Then, in the course of the fifteenth century, increasingly strong voices were heard in favor of the earthly City. The humanists, nurtured on Greek and Roman descriptions of the worth of rational man, rejected the thought that man was a ward under the guardian eye of the Church. The humanists were not pagan nor antireligious. On the contrary, they sought a compromise between their strong religious feelings and acceptance of the world about them. Similarly, for the bourgeois, surrounded in their comfortable townhouses by the fruits of their earthly labor, fear of purgatory was receding. They remained pious and deeply religious, yet chafed under the restrictions imposed upon them by the clergy.

A strong spirit of secularization also marked the political realm. The territorial rulers felt uncomfortable under a system in which all phases of life—from baptism to death, from education to the determination of truth, from social services to political theory—were supposed to be dominated by the Church. For a century, they had tried to gain within their lands the same controls over the Church as had been achieved by the kings of England and France. Of course, some princes and town councils had succeeded in increasing their power over the churches in their territory, but their ultimate success had been frustrated through their own disunity and through the effectual alliance of Hapsburgs and popes. They were now determined to achieve complete domination over their own territories, including absolute power over the churches in their land and termination of the fiscal exactions by the papacy. Here, too, the Lutheran movement, regardless of its religious content, could provide the remedy by giving the princes and towns a chance to unite against the pope.

The discontent unleashed by Luther also provoked political and social unrest among the knights, whose frustration and lawlessness were increasing at the beginning of the sixteenth century. Grievances also worked the patience of other classes: artisans chafed under the restrictions of the guilds, peasants decried their bondage, and small merchants vituperated against the monopolies of the large trading houses and the usury of the bankers. Luther, one should remember, was to write not merely of religious freedom. His pamphlets also contain denouncements of the big bankers, accusations against unscrupulous merchants, and discussions of a whole gamut of social and economic injustices. Finally, there was the swell of antiforeign sentiments. In their opposition to foreign cardinals, to the outflow of gold to Rome in the form of church revenue, to domination by a "foreign" emperor, the estates of Germany could bury their jealousies and unite for a moment of fraternal enthusiasm. And here, too, Luther seemed to point the way.

The ninety-five theses were not in themselves revolutionary. They did not directly reject papal supremacy, nor did they in any way suggest secession from the Church. Still, in their insistence on the supreme importance of inner repentance, they could be construed as an indirect attack on the fundamental function of the Church. In his early explanatory letters, sent to the archbishop of Mainz and Pope Leo X among others, Luther also showed moderation in his tone and his demands. Yet the wide gap between his ideas and church doctrine soon became apparent, as when he wrote to the pope in May 1518 that the question of church reform was a matter on which God alone could decide.

THE PEACEFUL PROGRESS OF THE REVOLT Despite these relatively temperate beginnings, Luther's attitude changed rapidly. More quickly than he himself expected, he progressed from merely questioning papal authority to completely rejecting it. By the spring of 1518, the Germans began to take sides for the impending dispute. Most of the humanists, the bulk of the knighthood, and the majority of the middle bourgeois applauded the monk of Wittenberg. Even the princes, including the elector of Saxony, looked with interest on this new development. Tetzel and his Dominican brothers, certain theologians and cardinals, as well as the Fuggers, looked with dismay upon the dwindling sale of indulgences. Pope Leo X himself and Emperor Maximilian, busy with the graver problem of manipulating the impending election of a new emperor, paid relatively little attention to the "monks' dispute" between Luther and Tetzel.

The more ardent Catholics, of course, were displeased with the papal and imperial inactivity. The theologian John Eck (1486–1543), of the University of Ingolstadt, was especially eager to debate the theses with Luther, in the hope of proving the heresy of the monk's opinions. Eck continually urged intervention by the Holy See against the "spreader of Bohemian poison," as he called Luther, in allusion to John Hus. When the papacy acceded to this pressure and commanded the Wittenberg monk to appear in Rome in defense of his views, Luther rejected the invitation, but agreed instead to meet with the papal legate (Cardinal Cajetan) at the Diet of Augsburg in the fall of 1518.

The discussion at Augsburg between the legate and the monk brought about no reconciliation. A compromise between the Church's definition of indulgences and Luther's stand on individual salvation seemed almost impossible. Luther refused to tender the demanded retraction of his statements and finally fled from Augsburg, not wanting to give anyone a chance to violate the imperial safe-conduct provided by Emperor Maximilian. The proceedings at Augsburg were complicated by political considerations. The emperor still hoped to get his grandson elected to the German throne, and cooperated with the pope to gain his support for the Hapsburg candidacy. Yet both pope and emperor had to proceed with caution in their dealings with Elector Frederick of Saxony, whose vote was crucial for their plans. The Saxon, for his part, was not averse to using the little monk of Wittenberg as a bargaining point, and extended to him his protection. Consequently, when the papal legate faced Luther at Augsburg, in essence Church and emperor were confronting the elector of Saxony. The cautious attitude of the Church in 1518 was therefore to an extent politically inspired. The pope contented himself with issuing a bull in November that merely restated the Church's view on indulgences without alluding to the Wittenberg monk. Finally, during the winter, a papal nuncio (Karl von Miltitz) was sent to confer with Luther in order to persuade him at least to refrain from further inflammatory proclamations.

But those forces on both sides not so much interested in the political overtones of the dispute as in its religious significance could not be silenced. Eck was pushing for public disputation with Luther, hoping to prepare for him the fate of John Hus. Luther wrote to the pope, whom he called a "lamb among the wolves," in order to "better inform" him of the errors in the indulgence question. By the summer of 1519, the dispute was heading irretrievably toward the final break. On the day on which Charles V was finally elected to succeed Maximilian, the debate opened in Leipzig between Eck and Luther's friend and colleague, Karlstadt (1480–1541). In the course of the disputation, Luther himself joined the discussion and was led to state publicly that a pope as well as a church council could err, and that the Council of Constance had been partially wrong in condemning all of Hus's doctrines, some of which Luther accepted as correctly based on Holy Scripture. This fundamental rejection of papal and conciliar authority marked Luther's definite break with the Church. When the Leipzig debates appeared in print, his more moderate supporters abandoned him, but the radicals enthusiastically flocked to his side. Luther's rejection of church authority became the cornerstone of Protestant doctrine on which all other points of dogma were based. By accepting only Scripture as authority, and insisting on the right of individual interpretation, he prepared for the atomization of Christian thought. Together with his new friend and colleague at the University of Wittenberg, the learned Philip Melanchthon (1497–1560), Luther now proceeded to analyze all church dogma on the basis of his own understanding of Holy Scripture, and began to reject everything for which he found no justification in the Bible. Only Baptism and the Lord's Supper were retained as true sacraments instituted by Christ. The intermediary role of the priesthood, the celibacy of the clergy, monasticism, and other points were rejected. Luther insisted that faith in the love of God alone was the duty of Christians, whose ultimate salvation depended on His grace.

Luther's ideas spread rapidly over Germany, aided by the general political confusion. Despite Charles's election, Germany was without a ruler, for the new emperor was detained by affairs in Spain and the Lowlands and did not appear in Germany for over a year. Much tension existed between Charles's emissaries and the German princes, who were awaiting fulfillment of the "election capitulations." Those who saw advantages in the spread of the new teachings did nothing to stop their dissemination, and those who opposed them anxiously awaited the arrival of the new ruler.

Meanwhile hundreds of inflammatory pamphlets and circular letters stirred up bourgeois and peasants against the Church of Rome. The printing presses, especially in south German cities, busily issued tracts against pilgrimages, monasticism, and other Catholic practices. Chain letters were sent to nuns and monks, urging them to forsake the cloisters. Pope, cardinals, bishops, and abbots were depicted as "wild beasts," "devils," "traitors," and "monsters." The impetuous Hutten called on "the proud nobility and the pious cities" to unite. "Have pity on your fatherland, you worthy Germans, act now! The time has come to achieve freedom." And he dispatched threats to the "Roman courtesans," as he called the ecclesiastical hierarchy, and planned to waylay papal envoys.

In the face of these challenges, the papacy took firmer action. The imperial election was over, and there no longer existed the same need for the Church to mollify the Saxon elector. In June 1520, a papal bull condemned Luther as a heretic and placed him under the ban of the Church, unless he recanted within sixty days. Luther reacted with characteristic defiance. Rather than recant, he publicly burned the papal bull and accused the pope of being the antichrist.

In this same year, he also produced some of his most important polemical writings. He addressed the emperor and the German princes in his *Letter to the Christian Nobility of the Germanic Nation,* in which he implored the lords to save Christendom, especially in Germany, from oppression by pope and cardinals. He exclaimed: "It is time the glorious Teutonic people should cease being the puppet of the Roman pontiff." He insisted that every man has "the power of discerning and judging what is right or wrong in matters of faith." Since "we are all consecrated as priests by baptism," he proclaimed the equality of all Christians in the eyes of God, denying the priesthood greater powers over salvation than the average believer. This hint at equality among Christians found echo among the lower classes, particularly the small artisans and the peasants, who mistakenly saw in it a call to social revolution. A similar theme ran through his *On the Freedom of a Christian,* which he sent to the pope in answer to the papal bull. Finally, his most vehement attack on the entire institution of the Church and one in which he propounded his major doctrinal views, particularly in respect to the sacraments, was contained in the pamphlet *On the Babylonian Captivity of the Church.* With these writings, Luther established the basis for his new faith—although many changes were to occur in the succeeding years, and it was to be a long time before the new ideas took the form of an organized religion.

Under normal circumstances, the ecclesiastical ban placed on Luther in the summer of 1520 should have been followed automatically by pronouncement of the imperial ban within the requisite period of time. There was no question that the young Charles, who in part owed his election to the pope, to the house of Fugger, and to other enemies of Luther, would in the end place the monk under the ban of the Empire. As friend of the Church, as king of Spain, and as ruler of vast domains outside Germany, Charles could neither protect religious schism nor condone German nationalism, both inimical to his interests. But the mood in Germany did not allow summary proceedings by the emperor. When the emperor opened his first imperial diet in Worms, in January 1521, the strained relations between him and the Germans were at once evident. Ironically, the electors who had hesitated to vote for Francis I because he was a foreigner now faced the Hapsburg-Burgundian Charles, who could not even speak German, much less understand the religious and political unrest in the land. The diet at once demanded measures against the Roman Church, and the princes requested fulfillment of Charles's pre-election promises. Whether agreeing with Luther's religious views or not, a majority in the diet was willing to use the Lutheran issue as a level to increase pressure on the emperor. Above all, the powerful Saxon elector, although showing no sympathy for the new religion, gave vent to his annoyance with pope and emperor by protecting the excommunicated Luther. Hence a compromise was arranged. A decision would not be reached on the imperial ban until Luther had been given the chance to clear himself before the diet. A safe-conduct was issued to protect him on his journey to and from Worms, regardless of the verdict reached. This compromise was in a way revolutionary in itself, since it implied that the German diet could pass on the validity of a papal judgment.

As a result, Luther appeared in April 1521 before the Diet of Worms, after a triumphant trip that recalled Hus's journey to Constance. Despite the pompous assembly of emperor, cardinals, princes, and bourgeois, Luther adhered to his views unless, as he proclaimed, he could be convinced of his errors on the basis of Scripture. In the end, he announced his faith in his own conscience and in God, and refused to recant. After further debates behind closed doors among the papal envoy (Aleander), the emperor, and the princes, the imperial ban was placed on Luther and his followers, and episcopal censorship of all printed materials was established throughout Germany to intercept the further spread of the new ideas. This Edict of Worms marks the end of the initial and peaceful phase of the Reformation, which had started so modestly three and a half years earlier and had developed with such astounding rapidity. Luther's self-assurance before the diet brought him even more adulation from peasants, bourgeois, and lower nobility. Hans Sachs, in a celebrated pamphlet, hailed him as the "Wittenberg nightingale" who sang the evangelical truth in the face of the pope, whom he described as a lion threatening innocent animals.

After the diet, imperial envoys informed Luther that his safe-conduct would expire within twenty-one days, after which time he would be beyond the protection of the law. On his return from Worms, he was apprehended by agents of the elector of Saxony disguised as highwaymen and taken to safety in the Wartburg, a castle near Eisenach. For a year Luther remained in seclusion, busy translating the Bible into New High German. Luther's translation became not only a vital adjunct to Lutheranism, but also exerted vast influence on the formation of the modern German language.

The Violent Stage of the Revolt

The authorities proceeded only sporadically against the followers of Luther. In few regions were serious attempts made to enforce the Edict of Worms. The emperor, occupied with his wars against Francis I, showed little interest in eradicating the new teachings. Moreover, Saxony remained an impregnable fortress for the Lutherans and an untouchable base of operation. Yet the years after 1521 were filled with confusion and chaos, resulting not so much from the dissemination of controversial religious thought as from the misappropriation of the new ideas by diverse groups. Uprisings and rebellions occurred everywhere, exerting profound influence on both the course of Lutheranism itself and on the sociopolitical development of Germany. Among the more important of these explosions were the excesses of the radical evangelists, the knights' rebellion, and the peasants' revolt.

It is difficult to find an all-inclusive label for the many radical groups that arose in various parts of the land, all justifying their actions on the basis of the Christian freedom and inherent equality propounded by Luther. The splintering of Protestantism was starting even before a Lutheran Church as such had been established. Social and political grievances, the forceful appeals of demagogic leaders, or simply rebelliousness against organized society pulled the misinformed followers of Luther in myriad directions.

Luther's overly ardent friend Karlstadt roamed the Saxon countryside with bands of lawless enthusiasts, compelling the people to take the Lord's Supper in both kinds, clearing convents and monasteries of their members, and forcing nuns to marry. Others engaged in iconoclastic orgies, smashing statues and pictures, and even burning churches in their zeal to purify the Church. Still another group, loosely labeled Anabaptists because most of them practiced adult baptism, spread a new social gospel of equality. This movement rapidly assumed widespread proportions, and gained a strong foothold, particularly among the peasants and artisans of the Lowlands and Westphalia. Proclaiming that the Kingdom of Heaven could be established on earth, frenzied Anabaptists plundered the rich and defied all authority in their attempt to bring about social equality and community of property, including the sharing of wives. Many of these extremists added emotional evangelism and mystic orgies to their social programs. The excesses and the radical demands of these groups, as well as their lawlessness, frightened the middle and upper classes, who united to suppress them in bloody massacres in which thousands of these rebels were hanged, burned, or drowned. Luther himself was horrified that his religious gospel had provoked such bloodthirsty outbursts. He always asserted that love and persuasion, and not force, should be used to impart true religious knowledge to Christians, and that traditional rites and practices could be retained, provided they were not incompatible with the Gospel. He left his retreat at the Wartburg in order to try to stem the excesses of his followers. In some parts of Saxony, he succeeded in reducing the ardor of the reformers and in lessening the violence of the outbreaks, but in Germany as a whole his voice was barely heard above the tumult.

THE KNIGHTS' REBELLION Worse outbreaks were ahead. The knights' rebellion of 1522 was also indirectly provoked by Luther's teachings. Many of the knights, among them the prominent Franz von Sickingen (1481–1523), had adopted Lutheran doctrines, and decided to use the national and Lutheran ferment to their own advantage. Under the guise of unifying the Empire on a new national basis, they hoped to improve their lot by overthrowing the territorial princes, who had undermined their social position and their political usefulness. Ulrich von Hutten approved their project, and Sickingen opened the campaign by attacking the archbishop of Trier. The resulting war turned out to be the death knell of the German knightly caste. The territorial lords, even though themselves flirting with Lutheran ideas, supported the Catholic archbishop with all available forces. Solidarity among princes seemed to overshadow religious disagreement. And Luther, who had disapproved of Sickingen's rebellion under the false guise of the new gospel, applauded the victories of the princes. Despite Luther's own hopes for a political transformation of Germany, he realized that only the territorial princes could help safeguard the religious reform, and he therefore disassociated himself from the violent crusade preached by Hutten and Sickingen. By 1523, the princes had won the field. Sickingen was killed during the siege of his fortified castle, and Hutten fled to exile in Switzerland.

THE PEASANT UPRISINGS What forced Luther to rely even more on the princes was the Peasant War of 1524–1525. Social upheavals in the lower classes, particularly peasant rebellions, had frequently accompanied heretical movements within the Church. This had occurred with the Lollards in England and the Taborite uprisings in Bohemia. It was hardly surprising that Lutheranism produced similar results, especially since the wrath of the peasants had been increasingly directed against the Church in general and the parish priests in particular, whom they held partially responsible for their subjugation.

The uprisings began in the southwest, and quickly spread through most parts of Germany and as far south as the Tyrol. In some places peasants joined in local Anabaptist rebellions, and almost everywhere disgruntled artisans and foot-loose knights flocked to join the rampaging peasants. The risings had been planned in advance through the organization of so-called Christian Associations with networks over parts of Germany. The rebels also produced a charter of grievances, the Twelve Articles, which they disseminated as widely as possible and on the basis of which they called on Luther to judge the righteousness of their cause. The Twelve Articles showed a curious influence of the new gospel. Most demands dealt with typical peasant grievances against landlords: improved contractual arrangements, guarantees against the lord's ruining the crop during hunting expeditions, permission for the peasants to use the common lands for grazing their cattle. But they also showed the spirit of Wittenberg. Serfdom was to be abolished as contrary to "Christian freedom," and the parish priest was to be elected by the parishioners. Finally, in the last article was the simon-pure Lutheran assertion that the peasants would abandon their demands only if they could be proved to be contrary to Holy Scripture.

The uprisings were frightening in their violence. Manor houses were burned, and landlords massacred unless they complied with the demands of the rebels. Within a few months Germany was in flames. The alarmed princes and the propertied classes recruited armies to crush the rebellion. Luther, who previously had urged the lords in vain to grant concessions to serfs, now admonished the peasants to lay down their arms and return peacefully to their cottages. When they did not heed his exhortation, he turned his full wrath against them. His pamphlet *Against the Pillaging and Murderous Hordes of Peasants* is of unbelievable violence in language and content. He urged the princes to "strangle" and "stab" the rebels, and to smite them as though they were "mad dogs." No penalty, no torture could be too severe a fate for such lawless beasts. At the same time he tried to justify his stand against the revolt. After all, he himself had rebelled against authority only a few years earlier. Basing himself on Paul, he defined Christian freedom as *spiritual* and not bodily freedom. The peasants had no right to rebel against their masters, he wrote, for "some must be free, and others slave." The Bible did not oppose bodily servitude. On the contrary, Paul had indicated that God placed everyone in his station in life, some high, some low, some free, and some in chains. Despite serfdom, the peasants could be "good Christians and enjoy Christian liberty."

Meanwhile the armies of the princes met the rebels in two military encounters in which the poorly equipped peasants were routed by the trained mercenary forces. The rebel leaders were executed, and a massacre of peasants followed which has few parallels in history. With their companions burned alive, crucified, or mutilated, the more fortunate ones returned to their hearths to sink into conditions of subjection and servitude worse than they had suffered for centuries.

Luther and the Princes

The stand taken in these critical years determined the future course of Lutheranism. In both rebellions, Luther had sided with the princes. Although in theory retaining his love for the common man, he had come to distrust the lower classes because of their resort to violence and because they used his teachings for social purposes for which they had not been intended. Yet he now had to condone the princes' use of his ideas for political designs. The former revolutionary thus was forced to accept a new authority. Henceforth, the fate of Lutheranism rested increasingly in the hands of the territorial lords, who turned it to their own advantage. In theory, Luther would have preferred some type of congregational church, and for the remainder of his life he clung to the hope that the princes would act merely as "emergency bishops." But conditions prevented establishment of a "popular" church structure. Since he remained in defiance of pope and emperor and had condemned the lawless rebellions of knights and peasants, reliance on the princes was for him a necessary expedient to save his movement from extermination. This turn of events was of profound influence on Germany's religious as well as political development. After 1525, the Lutheran movement became more and more involved in politics, and some of the princes and city councils tended to overshadow the theologians as leaders of the new movement.

Several great princes now adopted the new gospel, and turned their lands into Lutheran states. Saxony under its new elector, Hesse under Count Philip (1509–1567), then in quick succession most north German princes and many southern towns abandoned the Church of Rome. Many princes or city patricians embraced the new faith out of purely religious conviction. But there can be no doubt that some were motivated more, if not entirely, by economic and political reasons. The shift from Catholicism to Lutheranism furnished the rulers the opportunity to seize complete control over the Church in their own states. In addition it brought them economic benefits. The princes confiscated all ecclesiastic property—land, buildings, monastic institutions, precious jewels, and other valuables. Some monasteries were turned into schools, hospitals, or orphanages; some of the real estate and revenue was used for other social services, for financing the upkeep of the new state church, or for rewards to friendly subjects. But the bulk of this harvest went to enrich the princes and to fill the coffers of the states. Luther not merely approved of this trend, but encouraged the princes and cities to proceed more speedily with this secularization of church property. He forwarded this same admonition to bishops and other ecclesiastical leaders, urging them to turn their sees into hereditary secular states. To Albert of Hohenzollern, the general of the Teutonic Order, he gave the advice to "discard the stupid monastic regulations of the Order, to marry, and to turn Prussia into an archduchy." The general gladly complied with the suggestion, dissolved the Teutonic Knights, and transformed the lands of the order into a duchy, which became the personal property of the Hohenzollern family.

This secularization of ecclesiastic property—the drawing card, as it were, to attract some princes and city councils to the Lutheran cause—had repercussions on the politics of Germany as well as on the development of the new religion. It added considerable power and resources to the already powerful princes, and once and for all assured the future of particularism in Germany. It also changed Lutheranism. Papal authority was to be replaced not by the congregation, but by the authority of the territorial lord. The concept of having church ministers elected by the community of believers was gradually abandoned in favor of appointment of church officials by the government. The theory of individual or communal interpretation of Scripture gave way to adherence to Luther's catechism, which he elaborated in the later 1520s. The Lutheran church thus became a state church.

Uneasy Coexistence of the Two Faiths in the 1520s

The course of the Reformation in the period 1525–1555 may be described in less detail, for the essential direction had been set by the late 1520s. The ultimate outcome was to be determined by the endless struggle—interrupted by truces and attempted compromises—between the princes of Germany and Emperor Charles V, who most of the time was busy fighting the French, campaigning in Italy, battling the Turks, or solving other problems not connected with Germany. The Protestant cause lay in the hands of princes and city fathers, most of whom gradually banded together to form a Protestant league in opposition to pope, emperor, and such Catholic states as Bavaria.

This Protestant association, founded originally in 1526 by the princes of Saxony and Hesse as well as by certain south German towns to ensure reciprocal guarantees of confiscated ecclesiastical properties and to fight possible restoration of Catholicism, ultimately developed into the so-called Schmalkaldic League of Protestants. The emperor's reactions to these moves varied in accordance with the changing status of his foreign involvements. He was personally a devout Catholic and abhorred the Lutheran ideas. But in German affairs he seemed less concerned with protecting the integrity of the Catholic Church than with re-establishing peace and harmony. He interfered in the religious controversy only when he perceived a threat to his position as emperor or to his Hapsburg interests. The formula for temporary coexistence, first elaborated at the Diet of Spires in 1526 as a compromise between the Protestant princes and the rest of the estates, appeared to become the standard expedient: the Edict of Worms against Lutheran teachings was to be disregarded until a general church council could determine the validity of the conflicting claims. In the meantime, "everyone should live, rule, and act as he could justify in the eyes of God and

Emperor." In fact this meant that until an all-German solution could be found, every prince was more or less master in his own house and could act in matters of religion according to his own conscience or for his personal advantage. Naturally, it was tacitly understood that until a church council could settle the matter, the *status quo* would be maintained, and no further states would go over to Protestantism —a hope that was not borne out by the actions of the princes and city councils.

While the politicians saw advantage in such a formula for coexistence, the religious leaders abhorred it. Luther on the one side and the pope on the other both worked against it. Although Lutheranism continued to gain adherents, Luther was worried about the slackened progress of his movement. Some peasants and artisans were disillusioned by his attitude during the rebellion of 1525. Some bourgeois, traditionally lovers of an orderly and regulated life, also looked with suspicion on a movement that had produced so much disorder and so many revolts. Luther feared that too many conversions were shallow and superficial, and that any toleration of coexistence would endanger all that had been won so far.

Besides, some of the princes, who used the existence of the two faiths as bargaining weapons, gave him much trouble. A case in point was the powerful Count Philip of Hesse, one of the leaders of the Protestant league. Although personally a convinced Lutheran, Philip did not scruple to use pressure on Luther and Melanchthon in his effort to get their consent to a bigamous marriage. Since his wife refused to agree to a divorce and since the young lady he loved would not accept the role of a mere mistress, Philip saw no solution other than bigamy, considered according to pre-Mosaic law a lesser evil than adultery or divorce. Under threat of sabotaging the Protestant cause, he forced Luther and Melanchthon to pronounce that bigamy was not exactly contrary to Scripture, even though forbidden by imperial law. Such disagreeable bargains made Luther all the more aware of the dangers that could arise from coexistence of the two faiths, and he urged the Protestant princes to remain adamant in their stand against Catholicism.

In addition, Luther lost the support of some of the older humanists who disliked his intolerant attitude. The disagreement between Erasmus and Luther has become famous. Erasmus had at first hailed Luther for his courage and his critical analysis of what the Dutchman regarded as worthless tradition and superstition. The two engaged in an earnest correspondence, and it was thought that Erasmus would become a close associate, if not a leader, of the new movement. But Erasmus did not want to become deeply implicated in the Lutheran dispute. "It is not every one who has strength for martyrdom," he wrote, insisting that he had "no inclination" to risk his life "for the truth." Moreover, Erasmus believed fervently in the value of human reason as part of God's creation, and was repelled by Luther's dogmatism and violent emotions. "This man is mad enough anyway, without anyone to stir him up," he wrote about Luther. He considered "many of his teachings and exhortations excellent," but wished the German reformer "had not vitiated the good in his writings by his intolerable faults." Above all, the two parted on the issues of toleration and the attainment of salvation. Erasmus accused Luther of being more dogmatic than the pope himself and of destroying the value of the individual by making him a tool in the hands of God. He insisted that man had been given free will, the power to choose good and evil, whereas Luther—without being a predestinarian—placed primary emphasis on the love and grace of God for the attainment of ultimate religious certainty. The dispute was led by Luther with his customary vigor and violence of language. He called Erasmus a "stinking bedbug" to be squashed without remorse, and naturally alienated from his cause some of the humanists who, as Erasmus put it, disliked the "violent spirit" of his writings, "by which he brought immense discredit to all the friends of good literature."

Nor did Pope Clement VII (1523–1534) condone the idea of coexistence. Remembering the conciliar movement, he feared the threat to papal supremacy of a church council and he hesitated to call such an assembly. Instead, he put pressure on Charles V and the German diet to enforce the Edict of Worms and to put an effective end to the spread of Lutheranism. At a second diet at Spires in 1529, a majority of the estates acted accordingly. They revoked the three-year-old formula of coexistence, and demanded enforcement of the legislation against Lutherans. The Lutheran leaders within the diet—five princes and fourteen cities—*protested* against this decision, thereby giving rise to the term "Protestants."

Actually, the majority decision at Spires in 1529 proved ineffective, as did the attempt to arrive at a compromise solution at the Diet of Augsburg in the following year. In the winter of 1529, the Turkish danger had momentarily receded, and Charles had found a temporary settlement for his Italian problems. Freed from foreign preoccupations, Charles called a new imperial diet, which was to meet in Augsburg in the summer of 1530 in order to deal with the problem of German unity. The time seemed auspicious from the Catholic point of view, since disunity among the Protestant forces had brought about a split between the southern cities and the northern princes.

Zwingli and Luther

The disunity was caused by disagreements between Luther and the Swiss reformer Ulrich Zwingli (1484–1531). The latter had guided the reformation of Zurich and neighboring cantons along lines similar to those advocated by Luther. As a fundamental Protestant, he accepted Holy Scripture as the sole basis of his teachings. An enthusiastic patriot, he denounced foreign interference in Swiss affairs, particularly by the French, and urged the Swiss cantons to follow an isolationist policy in their relations with surrounding states.

But there were profound differences between the more politically oriented Zwingli and the mystical Luther. Zwingli interpreted the Eucharist as a memorial service. He placed emphasis on the words "Take this in memory of me," and interpreted the word "is" in "This *is* my body" as signifying "recalls." He could not accept Luther's more intricate dogma, usually called "consubstantiation," in which the body and blood of Christ coexist mystically with the elements of bread and wine during Communion. Moreover, there were differences of temperament and political background. Zwingli was not an intellectual but a man of action who enjoyed politics and even participated in battles. He was interested in the moral improvement of his parishioners rather than in the finer points of dogma. In some respects he was more of a fundamentalist than Luther, approving iconoclasm and even objecting to organ music in church as contrary to Scripture. Since the Swiss cantons were run on a pseudo-republican basis by city magistrates, Zwingli did not face Luther's problem of the role of the princes in his solution to the church-state question. He thought the city councils should control the religious as well as the political life of the state.

The disagreement between the two reformers threatened to split the Protestant camp. The south German cities, used to greater political freedom and not accustomed to political control by territorial lords as were their compatriots to the north, had more sympathy with Zwingli's Reformed Church than with Lutheranism and started to secede from the Protestant league. Luther, more interested in the purity of his faith than in political consequences, was hardly disposed to compromise with Zwingli. But the leaders of the Protestant league felt differently. In 1529 they arranged a religious colloquy in Marburg, at which Zwingli faced Luther and Melanchthon, in the presence of various Protestant theologians eager to mediate their differences. Some agreements were reached, but to the chagrin of the political leaders, no theological compromise resulted on the vital question of the Eucharist. Hence the colloquy in Marburg failed to achieve its purpose, and the south German cities remained devoted to Zwingli's teachings and doubtful allies of the Protestant camp. Only Zwingli's death in 1531 in battle against the Catholic cantons gradually weakened the Germans' interest in the Swiss type of Protestantism and returned them to the German Protestant league.

The Augsburg Confession

In the summer of 1530, the Diet of Augsburg finally convened. Charles V hoped the discussion would produce a compromise that would pacify Germany. Both sides were asked to submit their stand in a written declaration. Melanchthon, the chief nonpolitical representative for the Lutheran cause—the excommunicated and banned Luther could not appear at an imperial diet—composed the Augsburg Confession, which became a principal document of Lutheranism. The content of the Confession was as conciliatory as possible; in fact, it was so conservative that Luther decried it as a dangerous compromise. Yet it differed fundamentally from the Confutation issued by the Catholics, and no effective compromise between the two dogmas was possible. Between acceptance of papal pronouncements and reliance on individual interpretation of Scripture — even though in reality tempered by ecclesiastical pronouncements—there could be no middle way. Hence the Diet of Augsburg failed in its aim. It had helped clarify the issues between the two faiths, but had not achieved German unity. Once again an interim policy of coexistence was approved, until a church council should settle the entire question.

During the 1530s, the Protestant camp grew in strength and numbers. Turkish threats against Hungary and

Austria forced Charles to make concessions to the Lutherans in order to obtain military assistance from Germany. In 1532, the legal action instituted against Protestants under provisions of the Diet of Worms was suspended. Besides, the emperor was again occupied by other affairs. A successful campaign against the Turks in Tunis, repeated wars against Francis I, affairs in America and the Lowlands consumed his time. Even within Germany, friction with his brother Ferdinand, who had been elected king in 1531 to help in the task of governing the vast domains, selfish plots by individual princes, and a violent Anabaptist uprising in Westphalia in 1535 diverted Charles's attention from the task of healing the religious split.

Luther meanwhile settled down to establish the pattern for Protestant pastoral life. With his wife, Catherine von Bora, a former nun, and his many children, he tried to set an example for German conjugal life and morality. He lectured at the university, composed musical hymns—among them some of the most popular contained in Protestant hymnals—wrote homilies on family life, and continued to work on the Lutheran catechism and his translation of the Bible. Despite the success of his life's work, age did not mellow him. Some of his writings continued to be vehement in language as well as thought. He persisted in denouncing the "devilish papacy," advised that all witches be burned, and wrote harsh pamphlets against the Jews because of their refusal to be converted to Christianity. He died in 1546, admired by his followers, yet largely neglected by the political stream of the times he had influenced so much.

THE BEGINNING OF CATHOLIC MILITANCY

By 1540 the mood for compromise and coexistence was ebbing and mutual suspicion increased on both sides. Repeated talks between the Schmalkaldic League of Protestants and King Ferdinand or Emperor Charles had led to nothing but exasperation, since the imperial and papal conditions for a reconciliation stipulated not only the Protestants' return to the Catholic fold, but also restitution of confiscated ecclesiastical property. The expected church council that was to furnish the final solution had not yet been held. Charles became gradually convinced that Protestant opposition had to be broken if the imperial framework for Germany was to be preserved. The Protestant princes in turn realized that open warfare seemed imminent. Hence they did not hesitate to plan the overthrow of the emperor by intriguing with Charles's archenemy, the king of France. Francis I gladly entered negotiations that were to lead to a three-pronged attack on the Hapsburgs. He paid subsidies to the German Protestant princes to attack Charles from the north, made an alliance with the Turks to prompt their invasion of Hapsburg lands from the east, and prepared to relaunch his own campaign from the west. These negotiations, in fact, represented the opening moves of what became French policy for the succeeding centuries. To gain freedom of action along their own eastern frontier, the French monarchs initiated the practice of trying to keep the Hapsburg emperors busy at home and threatened from the east. This could best be accomplished by concluding anti-imperial alliances with German princes and by encouraging Turkish expansion in the Balkans. That this policy forced the Catholic king of France to conclude alliances with and pay subsidies to Protestant and Muslim forces was further proof of the degree to which politics had become secularized.

Pope Paul III

The decisive change of the decade may be attributed to the elevation to the papal throne of the intelligent and skillful Pope Paul III (1534–1549). With the exception of a brief interlude (Pope Adrian VI, 1522–1523), the popes of the first three and a half decades of the sixteenth century had been too occupied with political affairs in Italy and with their predilection for Renaissance culture to devote their full energies to the religious problems of the time. The pontificate of Paul III marked the turning point by initiating the Counter Reformation. This movement, partially in response to an inner need and partially in answer to the secessionists, reformed the Catholic Church, purified it of abuses, reaffirmed its dogma, and, above all, revitalized it for centuries to come. Its long-range results were felt only after the end of Charles V's reign, particularly in the second half of the sixteenth and in the seventeenth centuries, but Paul's energetic leadership attempted to force the emperor to change his policies immediately.

The all-important decision of Pope Paul III was the affirmation that the strength of the Catholic Church remained in its hierarchical structure, and was rooted in the tradition of fifteen centuries. Although it might be necessary to re-examine dogma and to eradicate abuses, it would be suicidal for the Church to compromise with the Lutherans. As the pope saw it, there could be no halfway point between church authority and an individual approach to the Scripture. Hence he tried to undermine the emperor's attempts of 1540–1541 to negotiate a compromise with the Protestants, and he pressed for abandonment of the vacillation of the 1530s in favor of a definitive stand. He thought a church council, which his predecessors had hesitated to convoke, could be used to reaffirm dogma and thereby clearly demonstrate the errors of the Protestants. After that, the emperor should proceed firmly and without delay with the suppression of the deviants. With this policy in mind, Pope Paul urged Charles to assume greater firmness in his dealings with the Lutheran princes, and issued the call for a general church council to meet at Trent in 1545. This Council of Trent, which met in three sessions over the next two decades, became the last and certainly the most important church council of the early modern period, and marked the turning point from Reformation to Counter Reformation.

As Paul III must have known, it was too late to draw the Lutherans back into the fold. In the 1520s, the Protestants had still hoped for the convocation of a council to debate the religious issues. But by the 1540s, their strength had grown to such an extent that they no longer saw any reason for submitting their views to a council in which they did not have a majority. Consequently they refused to recognize the jurisdiction of the Council of Trent, and instead urged the convocation of a German national assembly—in which they would have a clear majority—to decide on the religious differences.

Although he was urged by the pope,

Charles V hesitated, because of foreign commitments, to launch a military campaign against the Protestants. Mindful of the emperor's predicament, Pope Paul had mediated a ten-year truce between France and the empire in 1538, in order to free Charles's hands for action in Germany. But the truce did not last. After Charles's unsuccessful attempt to conquer Algiers in 1541—to reduce the Muslim threat in the western Mediterranean—Francis I reopened the war by attacking the Netherlands. Rather than fight the Protestants, Charles had to ask again for their military help. To obtain their cooperation against France, he agreed at a diet in 1544 to recognize the legality of the state churches established in the Lutheran lands. The pope was, of course, displeased, but to Charles these were but temporary expedients. As soon as he had overcome France, he hoped to take decisive action in Germany. Ironically, the Protestant forces hastened the final denouement by helping Charles defeat France. In the subsequent peace treaty (of Crespy) with Francis, Charles showed his hand. The defeated French monarch was forced to agree to help the emperor restore the unity of the Church. This clause lent itself to two different interpretations. The pope feared it was directed against him, in that the combined French and imperial forces might attempt to impose a solution of the religious problem on the papacy. He therefore hastened to convoke the Council of Trent (see pages 135–137). The Protestants, on the other hand, feared that it was directed against them, and some of them called for military action before it was too late. Charles, for his part, freed of the French threat, was also ready to take up the challenge. By the beginning of 1545, war seemed imminent between the Protestant league and the emperor and his allies—Bavaria and other Catholic princes. Charles merely lacked an excuse, legitimate or not, and an opportunity to split his opponents. A suitable occasion was furnished by John Frederick of Saxony (1532–1547) and Philip of Hesse, when they suddenly invaded and conquered the Catholic state of Brunswick in 1545 and introduced Protestantism by force.

The Schmalkaldic War

The emperor called a diet to condemn the two princes for breaching the peace of the land. This skillful maneuver divided the Protestant camp, for a majority of the estates and princes, including many Protestants, decided to side with the emperor, who in this case represented law and order. Only a few Protestant towns in southern and central Germany stuck by their commitments to the Schmalkaldic League and aided the reckless Saxon and Hessian princes. Hostilities opened in 1546. The resultant Schmalkaldic War, really a series of skirmishes and truces, lasted for a decade, until 1555. During its first phase, most of Germany stood on the side lines as Charles campaigned against the two leading princes of the Protestant camp. His justification for fighting was "the breach of the peace." But, as he wrote to his sister, "this pretext may deceive nobody of the fact that in reality the issue is religion." Charles received ample financial support from the pope, the Spanish Church, and the Fuggers. His resources grew constantly, while those of his opponents remained static. Within two years he forced the surrender of most of the Protestant cities, who were obliged to sue for peace and pay high fines. He also vanquished the two princes through military and diplomatic victories. His most effective coup was the bribing of the ambitious Maurice of Saxony (1547–1553), a cousin of the Elector John Frederick. Maurice was given money to hire an army and promised recognition as elector if he would agree in advance to accept the decisions of the Council of Trent and would help defeat his cousin. Maurice lived up to the bargain. While John Frederick was in the south fighting the emperor, Maurice seized Saxony and thereby deprived his cousin of his home base. The result was the defeat of John Frederick and soon thereafter the capitulation of Philip of Hesse. Both princes were seized by the emperor and condemned to life imprisonment.

Charles had succeeded beyond expectations. He had undermined Saxony, the stronghold of Lutheranism. The leaders of the Schmalkaldic League were in imperial prisons. Although Maurice, the new duke of Saxony, was himself a Protestant, Charles had faith in his promise to accept the verdict of the Council of Trent. He felt the Saxon could be trusted, since he owed his newly won electorate to the emperor. Meanwhile, Charles's archenemies Francis I and Luther had died.

While Charles was reasserting his power in Germany, disagreement flared up between him and the pope. The experience of decades had taught him to appreciate the tenacity with which the Protestants clung to their beliefs. Charles had therefore hoped that the Council of Trent would bring forth some conciliatory gestures that might make it possible for the Lutherans to return to the fold, and he had begged Pope Paul not to publish prematurely any decision of the council that would further alienate the Protestants. His aims, after all, were political and not religious. The pope, however, in line with his strict policy, had not complied with these wishes. The first session of the Council of Trent had been filled with vituperations against the Lutherans and had not produced even a minor compromise. Then in January 1547, Pope Paul had published the results of the Tridentine deliberations as if to fling them into the faces of the Protestants. Moreover, to safeguard the meetings against possible imperial pressure, he had adjourned them from Trent to Bologna. Finally, to strengthen his position and to protect himself against possible imperial demands for policies he considered contrary to the interests of Roman Catholicism, Paul had encouraged anti-Hapsburg uprisings in Italy and had negotiated with France for support against the emperor.

Under these conditions Charles V thought it best to seek his own solution. He called a diet in 1547 to meet at Augsburg to discuss peace for Germany, so that he could free his hands for action in Italy. Although his momentary strength would have allowed him to deal rather peremptorily with the German estates, he decided on a conciliatory religious policy, in defiance of the papal exhortations. He issued the "Augsburg Interim," which contained the usual formula indicating that a solution to the religious question had to await the final decisions of the Council of Trent, which, it was hoped, would be reconvened shortly. The complicated question of what to do with the secularized lands was not touched. But the Augsburg Interim drew the wrath of the Catholics because it gave in to Protestant demands on two issues: it permitted priests to marry and it allowed the faithful to receive Communion in both kinds. On the other hand, it raised a storm of protest from the Protestants because it referred to the Roman Church and papal authority as unalterable institutions; reaffirmed papal supremacy, the dogma of transubstantiation, and the veneration of saints; and ordered the reintroduction throughout Germany of all seven sacraments, and the traditional rites of the Church. Despite the two concessions to the Protestants, the tone and content of the Interim made it evident that the emperor intended to reintroduce Catholicism throughout the land.

The reaction in the Protestant regions of Germany varied. Some of the towns recently conquered by the emperor complied with the imperial edict and reintroduced Catholic rites into their religious services. A few of the weaker princes also submitted, and a few Protestants even planned to attend the second session of the Council of Trent. But the diehards rejected the Interim and retained their Protestant services. The emperor's attitude also revived the fears and suspicions of those Protestant princes who had stood by while Hesse and Saxony were crushed for "breaching the peace." As a result, the Schmalkaldic League was revived. The unscrupulous Maurice, who had gained the Electorate of Saxony through his secret deals with the emperor, now made plans to betray and, if possible, overthrow him and perhaps take his place as leader of Germany. He rallied the Protestant princes to his side, and negotiated with the new king of France, Henry II. The latter offered to attack the emperor from the west in return for cession of the important fortresses of Metz, Toul, and Verdun, which France had coveted for some time. In 1552 Maurice suddenly reopened the war by invading the Tyrol. Charles barely escaped capture in Innsbruck, and the Council of Trent, then in its second session, dispersed in fear of the approaching Protestant army.

But disunity among the Protestants, fear of the intentions of Henry II, and Charles's unexpectedly rapid assemblage of an army kept Maurice from pushing his momentary advantage. A truce was arranged in the same year, 1552, at Passau. During the negotiations, Charles doggedly insisted that the Council of Trent be reconvened, and refused to submit the religious question to a German national assembly. But he gave way on all other points: the controversial clauses of the Augsburg Interim about the sole authority of the Roman Catholic Church and the reintroduction of Catholic services were repealed, and the equal rights of both faiths affirmed. Both sides were enjoined to tolerate members of the opposing faith in their territories. Above all, Charles recognized as permanent the confiscation of ecclesiastical property that had taken place.

The Religious Peace of Augsburg, 1555

After the truce of Passau, the Schmalkaldic League once again disintegrated. A few radical princes continued to fight for a while, unwilling to accept coexistence and bent on exterminating the Catholics. But relative quiet gradually returned to the land. By 1555, arrangements for what was hoped would be permanent peace were completed. The resultant Religious Peace of Augsburg, negotiated by Ferdinand of Austria in the name of his brother Charles, marks the end of the Reformation period. Hope for a solution from the final verdict of the Council of Trent—which actually reconvened for its third and last session in 1562—was abandoned. It was realized that the decisions of a council which the Protestants refused to recognize as valid and binding could be implemented only by force. And force had failed spectacularly to achieve results during the preceding decade.

The new formula of 1555 recognized the legality of the *status quo* and of territorial sovereignty also in matters of religion: *cuius regio eius religio* gave to each lord the right to determine the religion of his subjects. The territorial princes could present their subjects with the choice of adhering to the official faith—Catholic or Lutheran—or of emigrating without taking along their possessions. In imperial cities, a majority of the ruling body was to decide on the official religion, but members of both faiths were to be tolerated within the limits of the town. While this decision made both Lutherans and Catholics coequal in the eyes of the law, other faiths, such as the Swiss Reformed Church of Zwingli or the more recently founded Calvinistic Church, were not included. The question of confiscated ecclesiastical properties was dealt with in clauses that left much room for future complications. The truce of Passau was taken as a model. All secularizations effected prior to 1552 were recognized as permanent and legal. Those undertaken after 1552 were declared null and void, and their restitution to the Church was ordered. Future secularization was prohibited—a blow to the Protestants, whose potential growth would be undermined if this provision were enforced.

A further problem was dealt with at Augsburg: the rights of Catholic Church officials — particularly abbots and bishops—to change their religion and turn their sees or abbacies into family possessions. In the past decade, a number of ecclesiastic officials had turned to Lutheranism, married, raised families, and turned monastic or episcopal properties into hereditary possessions for their children. A compromise was finally achieved at Augsburg. Princes of the Church had the right to convert to Protestantism, but under the Ecclesiastical Reservation clause they could not secularize the property of their see or monastery which, it was asserted, had merely been entrusted to them by the Church. Consequently, the new regulations enjoined them to leave their sees or abbacies so that a new bishop or abbot could be appointed. To make this compromise acceptable to the Protestants, King Ferdinand declared that Protestant subjects were to be tolerated within a Catholic see. But this declaration was not made a part of the written peace treaty.

The Religious Peace of Augsburg has been called a compromise because neither side had won the war and neither was strong enough to impose its will on the other. Yet it was clearly a victory for the Catholic forces. The only major success of the Lutherans was the legal recognition of their existence, a fact that had already received tacit approval at several previous diets. For the Catholics, however, the stipulations on the secularization of ecclesiastical property and the Ecclesiastical Reservation—if enforced—spelled a victory in that they would slow down, if not halt altogether, the spread of Protestantism. Of course, the formula of 1555 would not prevent individual conversions to the new faith for truly religious motives, but it would stop the widespread conversions for political and economic reasons so harmful to Catholic interests. The exclusion of the Calvinists from the provisions of the treaty was another major success for the Catholic forces. But the real victors emerging from the Religious Peace of Augsburg were neither Lutheranism nor Catholicism but the territorial lords. Whether Protestant or Catholic, they had gained immense additional powers through the formula of *cuius regio eius religio,* as was to become evident during the succeeding century.

In the ultimate analysis, of course, the Religious Peace of Augsburg was no peace, but merely the cornerstone for a long and uneasy truce. The next decades would show whether the emperors in the future would accept as permanent the reduction of their power. whether the two faiths could live peacefully side by side, whether the *status quo* could be maintained in the face of the introduction into Germany of militant Calvinism and the revived Catholicism of the Jesuits.

The Abdication of Charles V

Charles V, for one, could hardly have felt that the Religious Peace of Augsburg pointed to the successful conclusion of his task. He had failed to prevent the spread and consolidation of the new faith, and his fight with the territorial lords had ended in a draw, if not in his defeat. To be sure, considering the enormity of his burdens and the overextension of his domains, he had been relatively successful in maintaining himself in power. But he had failed in most, if not all, of his major designs. Despite his one successful campaign against the Turks in Tunis, he had neither swept their navies from the western Mediterranean nor prevented the growth of their power in the Balkans. His long, costly wars with France, which had diverted so much of his resources from other tasks, had brought him acquisition of the Duchy of Milan, but had not weakened the power of the French monarchy nor dissipated the French threat to the Burgundian inheritance. His hope of further expanding Hapsburg power and perhaps regaining England to Catholicism by marrying his son Philip to his niece Mary Tudor of England proved equally vain, since the marriage produced no children.

Disillusioned and weary of politics, the emperor abdicated in 1556 and retired to spend the last two years of his life in a monastery in Spain. Although he had contemplated for a while transferring the imperial crown to his son Philip, he had gradually recognized the impossibility of ruling over the vast legacy he would leave behind. Hence he decided to divide his inheritance (see Map 11). To his brother Ferdinard, who had become king of Hungary and Bohemia in 1526 and king of Germany in 1531, he bequeathed the Austrian hereditary lands of the Hapsburgs, and urged the electors to appoint him emperor, as they did in 1558. To his son Philip, who now became king of Spain, he gave his remaining possessions: Spain, the Spanish overseas territories, Naples, Milan, and the Burgundian inheritance, including the Lowlands and the Free County of Burgundy. This division established two separate Hapsburg dynasties; that of Spain, which was to last until 1700; and that of Austria, which continued until 1918. It ended the unnatural connection between Spain and Germany, although it by no means relieved Germany of foreign encumbrances, since the Austrian Hapsburgs maintained their Balkan interests. But by awarding the Burgundian inheritance to the Spanish branch, it sealed the future loss of these lands to Germany.

7

Germany Divided: The Counter Reformation, 1555–1618

THE AFTERMATH OF 1555

Germany after 1555 suffered primarily from two disturbing legacies: the religious split and the division of the Hapsburg inheritance between Philip of Spain and Ferdinand of Austria. Other factors also colored the succeeding century, among which four deserve special attention: the Counter Reformation; the disunity among the Protestants, particularly the distrust between Lutherans and Calvinists; the increasing influence of foreign powers on the political and cultural life of Germany; and the absence of strong and intelligent leaders on the German political stage.

The Counter Reformation

Of these factors, the Catholic Counter Reformation was unquestionably the most important, for its influence was widely felt. It began, as was seen, with the papacy of Paul III in the 1540s (see page 126). By the beginning of the second half of the sixteenth century, it was in full bloom in most parts of central, western, and southern Europe and spreading to other continents. The Counter Reformation was a rededication of Catholics to their faith and a reaffirmation of their way of life. It was also an active effort to regain ground lost during the Reformation period. Its overt activities and outward signs are easily identifiable—the Council of Trent, the work of the Jesuits and other new ecclesiastical orders, the establishment of the Index, the revitalization of the Inquisition, the flowering of baroque art, and the indefatigable efforts, especially of the papacy and of Spain, to undermine the Protestant cause. All these activities were important for Germany.

The Counter Reformation also further sharpened the differences between Protestants and Catholics. Here actual divergences of dogma or policy are perhaps less important than popular views and misconceptions held by each group of the other, since these opinions influenced historiography and affected German intellectual and political life. Although a brief summary of these views must inevitably be oversimplified and distorted, it throws light on the climate of opinion of the sixteenth century and the ideas that partially motivated many Germans during subsequent centuries.

Protestants tended to view the Reformation as a liberal movement. They saw the essence of Luther's work as freeing the individual from church-imposed shackles. Freed from needless tradition, they thought, Protestants—self-reliant and seeking direction only from their inner conscience and their respect for Holy Scripture—could carry on independent inquiry leading to new discoveries in thought, art, and music. According to this view, the Catholic Counter Reformation was almost exclusively a reaction to the Lutheran revolt, antipodal in all respects to Protestant liberalism. All that was conservative and medieval—Loyola's stress on coercion of mind and body, the Inquisition's merciless persecutions, the restrictive spirit of the Index, the revitalization of monasticism, and the emphasis on obedience to authority—was underscored in opposition to the Protestant spirit of freedom. The conservative tendencies of Catholic universities, the suppressive attitude of the Church in condemning Galileo, and the absolutist behavior of many Catholic rulers were contrasted with the less restrictive atmosphere at certain north German institutions, the free inquiry of Kepler, and more democratic states like Holland and England. Protestants regarded German history as torn between two forces, the conservative Catholic and the liberal Protestants, and interpreted events in this light.

Catholics, on the other hand, looked upon Luther's movement as a revolt or rebellion rather than a Reformation, since he did not reform the Church, but broke away from it. They saw in the movement of the 1540s (which they labeled the Catholic Reform or Reformation rather than the Counter Reformation) not solely a reaction against Lutheranism, but a series of successful steps to adapt the Church to modern times.

Moreover, Catholics did not necessarily interpret Luther's stand as liberal, for they disregarded his basic ideas and concentrated more upon the ultimate outcome of the Protestant movement. They stressed his call for obedience to state authority and his failure to separate state and church, which gave petty tyrants, whose position Luther regarded as God-entrusted and untouchable, considerable power over the bodies as well as the souls of their subjects. In consequence, they contrasted the development of Protestant authoritarianism, as eventually instituted in Prussia, with the more tolerant atmosphere of Catholic states.

These criteria were also applied to cultural and intellectual movements. Catholics asserted that the Church retained only those parts of tradition essential for their spiritual content, while fusing the new ideas and ideals of the Renaissance with medieval emphasis on salvation. Baroque art—in architecture, painting, sculpture, and music—was cited as the best proof of the success of this attempt. Whereas strict Protestants were adamant in their rejection of many Renaissance ideas, the Catholics embraced them, adopting those compatible with their way of life. Protestants destroyed art, preached an ascetic bourgeois morality, burnt witches, relished pseudo-Gothic architecture, and produced literature soaked with the mysterious, the demonic, and the occult; Catholics accepted the Renaissance lust for life, turned to the amusements of opera and the theater, incorporated realism in their literature, and gradually adopted an attitude of increasing tolerance. According to this view, therefore, the Catholic became the liberal, the Protestant had become the fundamentalist. The Catholic, provided he accepted the authority of the pope and the basic dogma of the Tridentine Confession, could afford to explore the realms of the mind and deviate from dogma on minor points. The Protestants, not held in one camp by submission to one authority, such as the pope, could not permit such latitude among their believers: deviation even on minor points meant splintering and the establishment of a new faith. In frantic efforts to reduce the multiplication of sects, many a Protestant became fundamentalist, bigoted, and opposed to free inquiry. The Catholics, according to this view, were more flexible because they incorporated tradition within the framework of their concept of authority, and tradition could change with the centuries. The Protestants, on the other hand, basing their religion exclusively on the Bible, were bound to rigidity, since Scripture remains unchanged with the passage of time.

These two views, both permeated with elements of truth as well as exaggeration and misconception, existed side by side, and down to the nineteenth century frequently exerted a strong influence on the coexistence of the two creeds in Germany.

THE SOCIETY OF JESUS The driving force behind the Counter Reformation was the Society of Jesus, conceived by Ignatius of Loyola in the 1530s, and established with papal approval as a full-fledged religious order in 1540. Members of the Society of Jesus had to take the three monastic vows of chastity, poverty, and obedience, and, in addition, to make a special promise to "dedicate their life to the constant service of Christ and the Pope, and to fight under the banner of the cross." Initially Loyola had thought that the fighting of this society should be done on crusades in the Holy Land, but he soon perceived the greater need of protecting the Church at home by fighting heresy and Protestantism. The Jesuits never initiated crusades as such. Instead, Loyola directed his religious order to take Catholicism to the newly discovered Americas as well as to Asia.

The Jesuits were organized in military fashion under the command of a general, the first of whom was Loyola. By papal authorization, they received important privileges that made them more powerful than ordinary monks or ecclesiastics. The society was placed directly under the papacy and local church officials had no control over it. It thus became an effective instrument for increased centralization of papal authority. Its members were awarded the same powers as were ordained priests, and could hear confession and act as spiritual advisers without requiring the permission of local bishops. Moreover, they were not required to wear special ecclesiastic garb, an exemption that made it easier for them to work within the circles they wished to influence.

Jesuit training, as outlined in Loyola's *Spiritual Exercises,* was rigorous in the extreme. It was designed to turn the members of the order into fervently obedient servants of a fighting church organization. The aims of the

Society of Jesus were the strengthening of the Church, the eradication of Protestantism, and the propagation of the faith. Its main efforts were devoted to education. By establishing institutions, by educating the coming generation of leaders among the upper classes, the Jesuits thought they could best ensure the ultimate triumph of their faith. Their schools, which spread rapidly through many parts of Germany, provided free education of such excellence that even Protestant parents eagerly enrolled their children. In addition to teaching, the Jesuits were active in politics. Hoping to influence governmental policies, they became advisers to princes. Because they believed that the masses are more easily moved by emotional impressions than by reasoned argument, they actively promoted the impressive baroque style in religious art to further their work of reconversion. Within the church hierarchy itself, they rapidly assumed positions of leadership. The third and last session of the Council of Trent was largely their work.

Seldom has a religious organization grown so fast in membership and importance and worked so assiduously as the Society of Jesus in the second half of the sixteenth century. Its success was phenomenal. Until about 1560, Protestantism had spread with unbelievable speed. By then all of Scandinavia, three quarters of Germany, much of Poland and Switzerland, parts of Austria and Hungary, the Lowlands, and the greater part of England had turned to the new faith. France wavered, and even Spain and Italy were affected. Thereafter Protestantism made little headway. The aggressive spirit of Calvinism turned Holland and Scotland to Protestantism and won some colonies in America to the new faith. But in most other lands, the crest of the Protestant wave had passed by 1560 and the countertide had set in. During the next few decades, Austria, Poland, parts of Hungary, South Germany, the Rhineland, France, the southern parts of the Low Countries, and much of Switzerland were firmly regained for the old faith. Although not the sole cause of this reversal, the work of the Jesuits was unquestionably of prime importance. In Germany, they were particularly active and influential.

THE RESULTS OF THE COUNCIL OF TRENT

As the Jesuits were the chief propagators of the Counter Reformation, so the Council of Trent was its primary instrument. The decision to call such a church council, as has been seen, had been a calculated risk on the part of Pope Paul III; there was always the danger that it might revive conciliar theories or make concessions to the Protestants that were inimical to the fundamental doctrines of the Roman Catholic Church. Hence the pope had to make sure that he could dominate its deliberations or at least control its final conclusions. As a concession to the emperor, Trent, a German town south of the Alps, was chosen for the meeting, but the pope tried to ensure that the membership was dominated by trustworthy Italian delegates.

Had the Church been let alone to deal with its affairs, a single session would have sufficed for settling all problems. But the Church could not operate in a political vacuum; it was buffeted about by Hapsburg-Valois (French) antagonisms and subjected to political pressures from the Empire. The main interests of the Church lay in defining doctrine, and in establishing a clear dividing line between those who accepted it and those who deviated from it. Indefiniteness on points of dogma could be only harmful to its position. Unlike the Church, the Hapsburgs, especially King Ferdinand, were more interested in finding a solution to German disorders than in defining dogma. As ruler of Spain and other Catholic territories, however, Emperor Charles V had to respect the sensibilities of many non-German peoples, and so he hoped the Council of Trent would produce agreements acceptable to all his domains. Under these circumstances, the first two sessions of the Tridentine meeting were unable to produce definite solutions.

But when the third session opened in 1562, conditions had changed. Ferdinand I of Austria (1556–1564) was now emperor. Although a devout Catholic, he was by nature accommodating and willing to compromise with the Protestants for the sake of peace and unity in the Empire and in his inherited domains. In the hope of finding reconciliation with the Lutherans, he urged the pope to make the widest possible concessions. But unlike Charles V, Ferdinand had little if any power over the pope. Pius IV (1559–1565), a convinced and ardent proponent of the Counter Reformation, was influenced rather by the Spanish Hapsburg Philip II, who could exert strong pressure on Italy through his possessions to the north and south of the Papal States, and who rejected compromise with the Protestants. Hence the third and last meeting of the Council of Trent, 1562–1564, was militantly guided by the Jesuits and Pope Pius IV, with no sympathy for the political problems of Emperor Ferdinand.

The council produced a reaffirmation of Catholic doctrine in its traditional form. It retained as authority for church dogma the Bible as well as tradition, which included the writings of the Church Fathers. It reiterated the value of good works in the attainment of salvation, certified the validity of the seven sacraments, demanded the celibacy of priests; in short, it reconfirmed all the points attacked and rejected by the Lutherans. To eradicate abuses, it issued strict regulations for the conduct of ecclesiastical officials and the supervision of monastic orders. To improve the educational level of priests, it provided for the establishment of cathedral schools in every see, and issued a catechism to regulate performance of religious services and to instruct believers. Except for the extirpation of abuses that had contributed to the Lutheran protests, none of the decisions of Trent were designed to entice the Lutherans back into the Church. Papal supremacy, so vehemently rejected by the Protestants, was reaffirmed in full force.

While the results of the final meeting of the Council of Trent were not helpful in reconciling the two faiths, they were of immeasurable aid to the Counter Reformation. The final decisions were approved by the pope and issued in a bull as the Tridentine Confession, which became the clearly defined dogma of the Church. Its definiteness and clarity immensely strengthened the Catholic Church, for the Protestants in their disunity had nothing similar as counterbalance. In addition, the Council of Trent established the Catholic Index of prohibited books, authors, and publishers, which attempted to slow down or stop the dissemination of anti-Catholic ideas. Whereas individual bishops had previously been enjoined to censor objectionable materials, now the council's intention was to make the regulations uniform for all Catholic lands. Protestant princes in Germany also resorted to censorship to preserve the purity of the religious beliefs of their subjects. But Protestant individualism and disunity allowed for countless different concepts of censorship, as opposed to the uniformity of the Catholic Index.

The Divergence between Calvinism and Lutheranism

Disunity among the Protestants became particularly evident in the distrust and even hatred between the established Lutheran faith and the new Reformed sect of Calvinism that began to spread across Germany in the 1550s. Enmity made cooperation between their adherents almost impossible—and facilitated the progress of the Counter Reformation.

The leader of the new faith, John Calvin, belonged to the second generation of reformers. He was eight years old when Luther published his ninety-five theses. Born in northern France, the son of a well-to-do middle-class family, he received a good education and, like Luther, studied law. After a sudden conversion, he left the university to devote his life to religion, and gradually abandoned Catholicism to evolve his own religious concepts, which he delineated in his *Institutes of the Christian Religion,* published in 1536. After some years of wandering, he settled in Geneva, which he slowly turned into the stronghold of his new faith.

Despite great differences in character, Luther and Calvin were in agreement on some points. As Protestants, both accepted only the Bible as authority, although Luther stressed the New Testament, and Calvin, the Old. But the fundamental disagreements between the two were wide. Basic differences in dogma, aim, and approach not only made it impossible for Luther and Calvin to cooperate but turned the two faiths into bitter adversaries. Luther emphasized the love of God and the possibility of finding salvation through His love and grace. Calvin, on the other hand, believed in a stern, righteous, and just God resembling the Biblical Jehovah. Moreover, he preached predestination of man either to eternal salvation or to perdition. Those predestined to be saved were the Elect to whom Calvin assigned special duties within his politico-religious system. Luther, moreover, retained much of the Catholic ritual in his services so as to facilitate transition to the new faith, and sought to expel from existing dogma and ritual only what he believed to be contrary to the Bible. Calvin was more revolutionary. He saw no reason to compromise or adjust, and rejected everything that in his view was not supported by the Bible. Calvinist churches were to be plain and unadorned, the ritual as simple as possible; even the elaborate music and sermons of the Lutherans were to be cut to the bone.

Above all, there was divergence between the development of their respective church organizations in relation to the state. On the basis of Paul's writings, Luther had advocated obedience to state authority, and Lutheran churches had gradually become state churches, with princes and city councils acting as the highest church officials. The Lutheran Church was thus in a way the spiritual department of a government whose over-all duties were to take care of and protect the citizens. Calvin, on the other hand, worked in the more republican atmosphere of Geneva. He attributed sovereignty to the religious community rather than to the state. In theory, the parish as a whole was led by God and, as in a republic, the individual was subject to the dictates of the community. Such a concept of government was well suited to Swiss conditions and could also be easily adopted in such countries as Holland, which had a strong middle class, or in Scotland, which had a weak government. In practice, however, Calvin believed that the community needed the guidance of law-abiding, morally upright, and God-fearing people—the Elect—who in the form of a Council of Elders or some other organized body were to supervise political activities of the state as well as the behavior of the citizens. In this sense, the Calvinist Church had vastly greater powers and tasks than the Lutheran. It had to purify the morals of the congregation; prevent indecent behavior, such as dancing, drinking, gambling, and blaspheming; guard the purity of the faith by ruthlessly exterminating all doctrinal deviationists; and supervise the political, social, and economic activities of the government.

On the whole, Lutheranism, especially under the leadership of the gentle Melanchthon, who guided the movement from the early 1540s to his death in 1560, was much more compromising, accommodating, and adaptable. Its initial burst of energy had been rapidly spent in the first two decades after 1517. Thereafter conversions slowed down markedly. In the face of the vigorous counterpressure exerted by the Catholics, Lutheranism assumed a primarily defensive attitude. Calvinism, on the contrary, was more militant and aggressive. It kept the expansive spirit of Protestantism alive in the second half of the sixteenth century, at least to the extent of completing the conversion of Holland and Scotland and helping to retain England in the Protestant camp. In Germany, too, it furnished the most active resistance to the Catholic resurgence, but received little cooperation from the Lutherans.

Foreign Influences on German Affairs

The third factor coloring German history in this period was the increasing pressure of foreign powers on German affairs, a pressure that gradually assumed such dimensions that almost every facet of German political, religious, and cultural life became dominated by foreign influence. To be sure, outside interference in German politics had been a frequent occurrence in preceding centuries. Germany's central geographic position, its internal disunity, and the combination of a local kingship with a universal emperorship had always made Germany particularly vulnerable to pressures from abroad. But the experiences of the medieval centuries were a pale prelude to what awaited Germany in the period from 1555 to the beginning of the nineteenth century. Among the many reasons for the growth of outside pressures, perhaps the most important was the division of the Hapsburg inheritance of 1555.

The territories allotted to Emperor Ferdinand—Austria, Bohemia, and Hungary—preserved for the members of the Austrian branch of the Hapsburgs their position as the most powerful lords in Germany; yet they were distinctly secondary in importance and wealth to the Spanish branch. His overseas possessions alone made King Philip II potentially the wealthiest and most powerful ruler of Europe. With the addition of the rich Italian lands, the Free County of Burgundy, and the Lowlands, he became the dominant lord of Europe. As a result, the Austrian branch was continually dependent on Spanish support. Its own resources were not sufficient to deal with the constant Turkish attacks, let alone to solve the problem of keeping Germany pacified. Many of the Austrian archdukes and future emperors were educated at the Spanish court and were under the influence of their wealthy Spanish relatives. Marriages between Austrian and Spanish Hapsburgs kept the bonds between the two branches as tight as possible. Consequently, Philip II and his successor, Philip III, could force the Austrians to act in accordance with Spanish interests, no matter how such action affected Germany. Spanish policy at the time was linked inextricably with the Counter Reformation, and was devoted to the weakening if not the annihilation of the French monarchy. Philip II was fanatically determined to restore the Catholic faith throughout Europe and to bring his father's prolonged wars against France to a successful conclusion. Germany was drawn into both designs. Unfortunately for Germany, Philip had inherited Burgundy and the Lowlands, territories that in theory still belonged to the Empire. Possession of these lands provided the Spanish king with the capabilities for a three-pronged attack on France. It also made it easy for his troops to interfere in Germany. On frequent occasions during the next century, Spanish soldiers appeared on German soil, under the banner of the Counter Reformation, to depose Protestant princes or to enforce Catholic edicts.

In addition to this constant intervention by the Spanish Hapsburgs, the actions of the German princes invited other outside interference. The Religious Peace of Augsburg had made them even more powerful in their own lands by awarding them jurisdiction over ecclesiastical affairs. Even in Catholic territories, the ruler had acquired at least permissive control over the Church, which could not maintain itself without his support, and which was always subject to his threat of turning Protestant. These princes now adopted the policy of making alliances with foreign powers. What had previously been an exception—such as Maurice of Saxony's agreement with Henry II of France—now became common practice. Unity and cooperation among them was impossible. Religious antagonism among Lutherans, Calvinists, and Catholics, as well as other jealousies, kept them apart. Each prince sought to bolster his position by gaining the backing and frequently the financial support of a foreign power. In most cases the foreign state was the stronger partner in any such arrangement, and used the hired German princeling for its own advantage. As a result, the German lords became the puppets of Spain, France, England, Sweden, and other states.

At the same time, the German aristocracy and upper middle class rushed to adopt foreign customs. Perhaps in antipathy to the Hispanicized Hapsburgs, or in appreciation of the advanced state of French society, they turned to France for inspiration for their cultural life. It became fashionable for the nobles to send their sons to study in France, to adopt the French language in polite society, to read French rather than German literature, to copy French manners and architecture, and to wear French clothing. Thus started a trend that by the end of the seventeenth century made German cultural life of the upper classes a pale and unnatural replica of its French counterpart.

Political Leadership after 1555

The fourth and final characteristic of the period was the appalling lack of strong and intelligent leaders on the German political stage. The emperors in the generations after 1556 lacked political aptitude and qualities of leadership. Some, such as Ferdinand I and Maximilian II (1564–1576), were too accommodating and hesitant; others, such as Rudolf II (1576–1612) and Ferdinand II (1619–1637), were too stubborn and too blind to political realities. For one reason or another all were mediocre rulers.

And among the princes of the chief territorial states, whose actions were now vitally important for Germany, there were few if any statesmen. Two of the Calvinistic electors of the Palatine—Frederick IV (1592–1610) and his son Frederick V (1610–1623)—showed some political sagacity: they appeared to recognize the larger issues involved in the Hapsburg policy, and attempted to rouse their fellow princes from their apathy. But the vast majority were stupid and inept, lethargic and narrow-minded, devoting more time to drinking and to women than to government. Above all, they acted from day to day, seeking momentary advantages, incapable of forming long-range plans that might have deflected the impending disaster of the Thirty Years' War.

Only one ruler stands out from this crowd of nonentities: Duke Maximilian I (1597–1651), who took over the government of his Duchy of Bavaria in 1597, became the leader of the Catholic League throughout Germany, and assumed a highly influential position in the Empire. By surrounding himself with skilled advisers instead of docile lackeys, he set up an efficient government that brought order to Bavaria. He was one of the first territorial lords to organize a permanent militia and a small standing army: the one to ensure order at home, the other to make him respected by his neighbors.

THE INTERIM YEARS

The Lenient Policy of Ferdinand I

Ferdinand had ruled as king of Germany since 1531, and therefore had had ample experience with the political and religious conflicts of the Germans when he became emperor in 1556. He had frequently tried to act as mediator between the German estates and his obstinate brother. As emperor, his policy was leniency, or perhaps indifference, toward the spread of Protestantism (see page 136). His apathy can be partially explained by the fact that the pope did not acknowledge him as emperor until 1560, asserting that the imperial election had been invalid because Protestant electors had participated in it. Moreover, there was as yet no Spanish pressure on the Austrian Hapsburgs. The young Philip II was still busy establishing his own power, and could hardly exert much influence on his older and more experienced uncle.

Consequently Ferdinand made no serious attempt to prevent the spread of Protestantism even in Austria and Hungary, where despite loss of momentum, Lutheran ideas continued to acquire new adherents. In some regions

Protestantism was not accepted, but Catholics adopted portions of Lutheran teachings without interference from the territorial lords or the emperor. For example, many priests married, although remaining within the Catholic Church. In Bavaria, fasting was abolished and the congregation was permitted to take Communion in both kinds. The religious clauses of the Peace of Augsburg were obeyed. Each lord could do as he pleased in ecclesiastical affairs, and the mood of the hour encouraged noninterference. This erosion—more harmful to the Church than outright secession—explains papal insistence that the final session of the Council of Trent take a clear and firm stand on all fundamentals of dogma.

In this relatively relaxed period of the short reign of Ferdinand I, before the full impact of the Counter Reformation was felt in Germany, there were further attempts, some sponsored by the emperor, to find a compromise that would reunite all Christians. But all theological discussions failed to produce the slightest accommodation. The Protestants themselves no longer agreed on all points. Strict Lutherans derided the moderate Melanchthon and his followers because of their repeated efforts to elaborate formulas for compromise. When the elector of the Palatinate (Frederick III) abandoned Lutheranism, and in 1563 issued the Heidelberg Catechism of the "Reformed Church" as a basis for spreading Calvinism in Germany, all hope for Protestant unity seemed lost. At this time, the Council of Trent was nearing completion of its statement of dogma, and Jesuit activity in Germany was increasing. The Counter Reformation was about to be launched in full force. In their defense, the Protestants had little to offer but theological bickering and political disunity.

Maximilian II and the Turkish Threat

Ferdinand did not live to witness the inevitable clash. He died in 1564, and was succeeded by his son Maximilian II, whose twelve-year reign marked the transition from imperial apathy toward religious problems to firm support of the Counter Reformation movement.

The incompetent Maximilian II had even less power than his father, who by dividing his patrimony and assigning Tyrol and Styria to two other sons, had further reduced the resources of the emperor. Maximilian had been raised by Protestant tutors, and there are reasons for believing that he had secret leanings toward Protestantism. Initially he refrained from enforcing any anti-Protestant measures; he even did not officially publish the papal bull summarizing the conclusions of the Council of Trent. But his neutral stand was tenuous. He needed resources for his fight against the Turks, and since he lacked power and firmness, he was unable to resist the pressure of his Spanish cousin Philip II. Had he lived longer, there is little doubt that he would have become a malleable instrument of the Counter Reformation party.

The Turkish threat that Maximilian had to face was the climax of a long period of constant inroads. The Ottoman Turks had started their invasion of the Balkans in the late fourteenth century, and had consolidated the conquest of its major portion by the middle of the fifteenth. Hungary, through its strategic position, had always been a defensive bastion against further Turkish expansion, and battles between

Hungarians and Turks had taken place as early as the beginning of the fifteenth century. When Ferdinand I inherited the Kingdoms of Bohemia and Hungary in 1526, the Hapsburgs also inherited the task of defending Europe against further Turkish expansion. Charles V and Ferdinand had been constantly occupied with this problem. The Ottomans at the time were led by the active and skilled Sultan Suleiman II (1520–1566). By 1529, his raids had led him as far as Austria, where he laid an unsuccessful siege to Vienna. In the course of his reign, he made a total of sixteen separate incursions into Hungary, during which he gradually seized large portions of the country. In 1566 war broke out again, and although Maximilian had a large imperial army, he was defeated by the Turks and was forced to pay annual tribute to the sultan. However, the warlike Suleiman II died during the war, and with his death passed the first long phase of Turkish pressure. A few years later, in 1572, the Spanish Hapsburgs were able to destroy the Turkish fleet at the famous battle of Lepanto, thus reducing Turkish power in the Mediterranean. The Turkish threat then ebbed for a while until it once again became one of the primary problems of the Austrian Hapsburgs in the late seventeenth century.

Progress of the Counter Reformation under Rudolf II

Under Maximilian's son, Rudolf II, the Counter Reformation gained ground in many parts of Germany. The young emperor had been brought up at the court of his uncle, Philip II, who, through marriage to Anne of Austria had also become his brother-in-law. Although Rudolf was more interested in astrology than in politics, his uncle's influence imbued him with uncompromising devotion to royal prerogatives and to the Catholic faith, and turned him into an influential propagator of the Counter Reformation.

While the Catholic forces prepared to regain the allegiance of Germany, the Protestant princes undermined one another in ecclesiastical maneuvers. Gone were the days of the Protestants' insistence on the right to individual or congregational interpretation of Scripture. In a vain effort to prevent deviation from strict Lutheranism, the elector of Saxony had Lutheran theologians prepare a "concordance formula" to which all Lutherans were to subscribe. The result was not harmony but additional splintering. By the 1570s, religious persecution among the Protestants was in full swing. Decapitations of "lenient" Lutherans by "strict" Lutherans became as frequent as the torturing or burning of Lutherans by Calvinists. In many instances, of course, political jealousies motivated the quarrels, which involved the various princes and their respective religious sects. But often theological questions alone animated the murderous hatred.

Protestant disunity made it easier for the united forces of the Counter Reformation to accomplish their tasks. There is no need to relate in detail how the Catholic princes and the ubiquitous Jesuits, backed when necessary by Spanish troops, rolled back the tide of Protestantism. Description of a few instances should suffice to show the modes of action available to the Catholics and the typical reaction, or inaction, of the Protestant defenders.

One method was for the Catholic territorial lord to use his rights under the provisions of the Religious Peace of Augsburg. Maximilian I of Bavaria, for example, stopped all concessions to the Protestants and tried to purify the faith of his land along the lines suggested by the Council of Trent. He declared Protestantism illegal—a right he enjoyed under the formula of *cuius regio eius religio;* he had Protestant preachers arrested; and he forced the important Bavarian nobles and bourgeois to return to the Church under penalty of imprisonment. Since Protestant roots had not gone very deep there, such methods sufficed to make Bavarian Protestantism wither away within a few years. The duke then rebuilt the Catholic Church in his territory. He did not interfere in matters of dogma or in episcopal jurisdiction, but used the state to supervise execution of all Tridentine enactments and to control the school system in an effective attempt at cooperation between church and state. Moreover, throughout his state he encouraged the educational, religious, and artistic work of the Jesuits.

A second typical case involved an ecclesiastical lord and the interpretation of another clause of the controversial Religious Peace of Augsburg. In 1570, the abbot of the monastery of Fulda, which had under its jurisdiction a sizable population, decided to prohibit the performance of Protestant services, which were being attended by the majority of bourgeois and nobles in his land. The Protestants asserted that Ferdinand's Declaration of 1555 at Augsburg was still binding, and that Protestants living within Catholic ecclesiastical territories had the right to exercise their own religion (see page 130). The Catholics responded that they were bound only by the written clauses of Augsburg and not by personal assurances of a former emperor, and the abbot proceeded to enforce his decision. Since he succeeded rather easily in the implementation of his policy, other ecclesiastical lords soon imitated his example and prohibited the performance of Protestant services in their territories.

In view of the number of ecclesiastical states in Germany and the fact that many inhabitants of these territories were Protestant, this development was of considerable importance to the Protestant cause. Yet the reaction of the Protestant princes showed their political ineptitude. When, in 1575, shortly after the Fulda affair, the succession to Emperor Maximilian II was discussed, the Calvinist elector of the Palatinate (Frederick III)—by nature and religion more inclined toward political action than his Lutheran colleagues—insisted that the candidate for election be forced to give his written agreement to Ferdinand's Declaration of 1555 before receiving the vote of the Protestant electors. But his proposal found no support in the electoral college. The Lutheran elector of Saxony, for one, was more bent on opposing his Calvinist coelector than on furthering the Protestant cause as a whole. Consequently Rudolf II was elected without giving any guarantees that Protestantism could legally exist in Catholic ecclesiastical territories. Ferdinand's Declaration of 1555 became a dead letter. Catholic bishops and abbots had received a tacit signal to proceed with their attempt to enforce religious uniformity among their subjects.

The question of the equality of the two faiths in imperial free cities also gave rise to a number of incidents. Here, as in most matters, the Catholics acted with unity and determination, whereas the Protestant princes did little to aid their coreligionists—perhaps they were also motivated by the long-standing disdain of territorial lords for the independent *bourgeoisie*. An example was the city of Aachen (Aix-la-Chapelle) in which, by 1580, the Protestants had gained so large a majority that they took over the city council and began to expel the Catholics. Since Aachen lay in a strategic position near the rebellious Netherlands, the Catholic forces decided to take action. The city's trade routes were cut off and its representatives refused admission to the imperial diet. The city council appealed to the Protestant princes, who contented themselves with verbal protests at the diet and ineffectual threats to withhold aid to the emperor for an impending campaign against the Turks. The Catholic forces, for their part, continued their firm pressure, and finally, when all else failed, dispatched a Spanish army (1589) from the Low Countries to occupy the city and return it to Catholicism by force.

Two final examples that illustrate the trend under Emperor Rudolf II deal with the ambivalent Ecclesiastical Reservation of the Religious Peace of Augsburg, and demonstrate the increasing shift in power from Protestants to Catholics. One such incident occurred at the imperial diet of 1582. During the lenient regimes of Ferdinand I and Maximilian II, the Protestants, particularly in northern Germany, had found an easy way of circumventing the Ecclesiastical Reservation, which prohibited a bishop or abbot from becoming Protestant and turning his abbacy or bishopric into a secular possession. If an ecclesiastical prince changed his faith, the reservation enjoined him to abandon his see and make way for a Catholic candidate to be appointed by the Church. In this way, the ecclesiastical property would remain in the hands of the Church. The method used to by-pass this stipulation was simple: usually under pressure of a neighboring Lutheran prince, the Protestant clergy in the see elected a Protestant noble—frequently a relative of a nearby ducal house—to replace their Catholic bishop. Naturally, such an election was not recognized as valid by the papacy, but it permitted the Protestants to assert that they had not violated he Ecclesiastical Reservation, since no Catholic bishop had turned Protestant. Under this ruse, a great number of north German abbacies and bishoprics had become secular states in the first two decades after 1555, and Ferdinand and Maximilian had recognized the new incumbents as official "administrators" of these territories.

Under Rudolf, however, matters were to be different. At the imperial diet of 1582, the "administrator" of the powerful former Archbishopric of Magdeburg (Joachim Frederick), a relative of the neighboring elector of Brandenburg, was refused a seat in the assembly on the grounds that he merited no legal place in any of the estates. He was neither an ecclesiastical nor a territorial lord, but simply the "administrator" of his lands. By this decision, the emperor disenfranchised all owners of former ecclesiastical territories and deprived them of influence in the imperial diet. Since the majority of governing officials—in the diet as well in the imperial court of justice—who had to pass on the validity of such a decision continued to be Catholic, the emperor won his point. The matter was debated at several succeeding diets, and a few Protestant princes threatened to withhold all taxes unless the emperor reversed his stand. But in the long run, the Protestants feared to act energetically, and eventually abandoned their resistance, thereby further weakening their position in the imperial diet.

The other example of the progress of the Counter Reformation is often called the War of Cologne. The Archbishopric of Cologne was one of the most important states of Germany. Its territories were vast and its geographic position gave it control over strategic portions of the Lower Rhine. Furthermore, the archbishop was one of the seven electors, and since three lay electors had already turned Protestant, a change of hands in Cologne would have given the anti-Catholic forces a majority in the electoral college. In 1582 the archbishop of this vital ecclesiastical state became a Calvinist, and indicated his intention of marrying and of transforming Cologne into a secular state. This action would be clearly in violation of the Ecclesiastical Reservation; yet its accomplishment would have been of immense value to the Protestants. Nonetheless, they took no advantage of this opportunity. The Lutheran princes would not come to the aid of the Calvinist ex-archbishop. On the contrary, they proclaimed that he had violated the Ecclesiastical Reservation—which they themselves had helped to by-pass so frequently in the preceding decades —and admonished that the Ecclesiastical Reservation be observed in the interest of peace. Since the incumbent of the formerly Calvinist electorate of the Palatine was as the time (1576–1583) a Lutheran, the Calvinists in Germany lacked a strong leader.

Under these conditions, it was easy for the Catholics to act. The pope excommunicated the ex-archbishop and appointed in his stead a Bavarian prince (Ernest). That this prince was already bishop of Freising, Hildesheim, and a number of other sees, and that plurality of offices was contrary to the edicts of the Council of Trent, was less important to the Catholic forces than that all high ecclesiastical posts be staffed with reliable candidates. The Wittelsbach princes of Bavaria were considered among the most trustworthy. The new archbishop of Cologne was not at once admitted to his see, but Bavarian and Spanish troops defeated the opposition in a few swift skirmishes and helped him take firm possession of his lands. The Cologne War of 1583 marks the beginning of the effective enforcement of the Ecclesiastical Reservation—a severe blow to the main Protestant hope for further expansion.

The Counter Reformation outside Germany

While the Counter Reformation was asserting itself in Germany, developments in many neighboring states brought less success to the policies of its chief advocate, King Philip II of Spain. His most obvious failure was in the Low Countries. The Dutch rebellion had begun in 1568. When Philip II died thirty years later, it had become obvious to all but the fanatical king that the northern provinces of the Netherlands were permanently lost to Spain. The truce of 1609 finally gave tacit, though not legal, recognition to the fact that the United Provinces had formed a new, independent Protestant power. During the same period, England under Queen Elizabeth overcame the religious difficulties of the mid-century, and after the execution of

Mary Stuart (1587) and the defeat of Philip's Armada (1588), was firmly placed in the Protestant camp.

The last decade of the sixteenth century also saw important developments in France that affected the future of Germany. Philip II's assiduous efforts to eradicate French Protestantism and to acquire dominant control over French affairs had failed. The disorders of the French wars of religion had given him every reason to believe that Spanish influence over the French monarchy might prevail. But neither military intervention by Spain, nor intrigues with French parties, nor even his marriage to the heiress of France (Elizabeth of Valois, the daughter of Henry II) had prevented the survival of the French monarchy as a strong, independent, anti-Hapsburg power. When the Protestant Henry IV, even though officially reconverted to Catholicism, took over the government in 1589 and nine years later issued the Edict of Nantes to award toleration to the Huguenots, it became evident how thoroughly Philip had failed.

Finally one must recall that the Counter Reformation made no inroads in Scandinavia. In fact, during this same half century Sweden rose to the position of a powerful Protestant force. After its independence from Denmark had been established in 1521, Sweden rapidly assumed a dominant place in northern Europe under its energetic new dynasty, the house of Vasa. It embarked on the conquest of the southern shores of the Baltic Sea with the acquisition of Estonia, and thereby became a continental power, locked in frequent struggles with Russia and Poland, and vitally concerned with the affairs of northern Germany.

Prelude to the Thirty Years' War

Without these developments in the neighboring countries, there would have been no Thirty Years' War and even no major armed conflict between the contending religious faiths in Germany. It is probable that the successes of the Catholic party would have continued. It is even conceivable that within a few more decades Protestantism would have all but disappeared as a political force in Germany, with Lutheranism and Calvinism remaining, at the most, unimportant, tolerated religious sects. That this did not occur, that the fairly peaceful progress of the Counter Reformation gave way to the more violent antagonism of the early seventeenth century, and finally to the Thirty Years' War, was due primarily to foreign interference and foreign pressures on German princes, particularly on the Protestants. The kings of France and Sweden, the leaders of the Dutch Republic, and to some extent even the rulers of England used the Protestant princes as pawns for their own designs and gradually altered the atmosphere of Germany.

The prelude to the Thirty Years' War opened in 1607. A minor quarrel in the imperial town of Donauwörth in Swabia between the Protestant citizenry and Catholic monks who wanted the right to hold religious processions led Emperor Rudolf to place the citizens under the ban of the Empire for disturbing the peace of the land. The energetic Duke Maximilian I of Bavaria, who was entrusted with the execution of the ban, occupied the city militarily, more or less annexed it to Bavaria, and forcibly reintroduced Catholicism. At the diet in the following year, the Protestants demanded the withdrawal of Bavarian troops from Donauwörth and a reconfirmation of the Religious Peace of Augsburg. The Catholic counterdemand calling for restitution to the Church of all ecclesiastical lands secularized since 1555 in contravention of this peace effectively prevented all agreement.

THE UNION AND THE LEAGUE The Protestant princes finally realized that in Maximilian of Bavaria they faced a dangerous opponent, intent on extending Bavarian power while furthering the cause of his faith. Spurred by the active and restless Duke Frederick IV of the Palatinate, the Protestants became sufficiently alarmed to conclude a ten-year pact, setting up the so-called Protestant Union of 1608. It was to provide mutual territorial guarantees for its members and protection against the Catholics, particularly the Bavarians. Common contributions were to pay for the recruitment of a Protestant army to be placed under the leadership of the elector Palatine. Many southern territorial lords and cities joined the union, and after a few years, even Brandenburg and Hesse adhered to it, despite the religious distrust between Lutherans and Calvinists. But it was symptomatic for the future that the elector of Saxony, the traditional protector of Lutheran interests, kept apart from the union. Hence from its very beginning, this Protestant association failed to garner the efforts of all German Protestants. Moreover, it retained throughout its existence the character of a loose association in which individual interests always outweighed common aims. Like its Schmalkaldic predecessor, the Protestant Union sought promises of assistance from outside powers. When Duke Frederick V succeeded his father as elector Palatine and leader of the Union in 1610, negotiations were started with his father-in-law, James I of England, with the cantons of Switzerland and the stadholder of Holland, and with Henry IV of France and Christian IV of Denmark.

Maximilian of Bavaria, for his part, was equally busy with diplomatic maneuvers. In answer to the Union, he formed in the following year the Catholic League, which soon embraced most of the German Catholic princes, including the three powerful electoral archbishops of the Rhineland: Mainz, Trier, and Cologne. The league was formed to defend Catholicism and to safeguard Catholic domination of the imperial diet. But initially the dominant position of Maximilian also made the Catholic League a useful instrument for promoting the interests of the Wittelsbachs. Just as the Protestant Union sought alliances with major foreign powers, so Maximilian negotiated for the support of the Spanish Hapsburgs.

At first the Catholic League did not include the Austrian Hapsburgs, who were then locked in a family struggle that made them incapable of firm action. Rudolf II's inefficient government had provoked discontent in his own lands and tempted his ambitious brother Mathias to replace him as ruler. To gain the required forces, Mathias promised the Hungarian, Moravian, and Austrian estates both increased freedom from royal interference and permission to practice Lutheranism in return for their support against Rudolf. The coup was successful. Rudolf was forced to relinquish the Austrian, Moravian, and Hungarian territories to his brother. To get backing against further reduction of his power, Rudolf granted even more far-reaching concessions to the Bohemian Protestants and estates. Despite this maneuver, he was soon supplanted by his brother also in Bohemia. Mathias now became sole ruler of the Hapsburg lands, and upon Rudolf's death in 1612 he also assumed the emperorship. The concessions and promises granted to the Hapsburgs' subjects in the course of this struggle, especially those to the Bohemians, were to bring grave consequences in the future.

THE INHERITANCE CRISIS The division of Germany into two armed camps, each allied with foreign powers, made the outbreak of full-scale war an imminent danger. In fact, twice during the period 1609–1614, a minor inheritance quarrel in northwestern Germany threatened to provoke a general war. The Catholic duke of Cleves, whose lands near the Lower Rhine (Jülich, Cleves, Berg, Mark, and Ravensberg) were inhabited mostly by Protestants, died in 1609 without leaving a male heir. Both the Catholic and Protestant forces hoped to acquire the inheritance. Among the seven pretenders to this legacy, who all based their claims on the female line of succession, the most serious were three: the elector of Brandenburg, John Sigismund (1608–1619); a Palatine count (Wolfgang William of Neuburg), and the duke of Saxony (John Frederick). All three were Protestants. The ultimate authority to decide on such disputed inheritances belonged to the emperor, who naturally preferred the lands in Catholic hands. But before any imperial pronouncement had been made, the Brandenburg elector and the Palatine count jointly occupied the lands. For once Emperor Rudolf reacted swiftly and with energy. He sent his nephew to sequester the lands in the name of the emperor. Supported by the Catholic League, the Hapsburgs gained control of a few cities and fortresses and ordered the surrender of the remaining territories. But the new occupants would not relinquish their prize so readily, and, to protect their acquisitions, they requested the aid of France. Henry IV, averse to seeing the Hapsburgs installed on the Lower Rhine, responded at once. In alliance with the Protestant Union, Savoy, Holland, and England, he initiated an attack against the Hapsburgs. Hostilities had barely begun in Alsace when Henry IV was murdered in 1610, and the anti-Hapsburg coalition collapsed. Emperor Rudolf, by then busy defending himself in Bohemia against his brother Mathias, decided not to push the matter further, and awarded the inheritance to the elector of Saxony who, although a Protestant, was not a member of the Protestant Union and was therefore a potential ally of the Hapsburgs. But after imperial troops were withdrawn from the disputed lands, Brandenburg-Palatinate forces reoccupied all the territories in disregard of the Saxon claim and the imperial decision. For the moment the Hapsburgs had to acquiesce in this violation of imperial rights.

Three years later, the issue was reopened when a quarrel arose between the two rulers who now shared possession of the inheritance. Both again sought foreign help. The Palatine count converted to Catholicism to gain help from Spain and if possible from the league; in answer, the elector of Brandenburg changed from Lutheranism to Calvinism to obtain the backing of Holland. Religion again became an extension of politics. General war seemed imminent. Spanish and Dutch troops invaded the disputed land and clashed in minor skirmishes. It seemed as though the Dutch-Spanish war was to be reopened on German soil. But neither the foreign powers nor the new Emperor Mathias was prepared for major hostilities. Consequently, the two contenders were forced to compromise. In 1614, a treaty between the two divided the inheritance. The Palatine count obtained Jülich and Berg, while John Sigismund of Brandenburg retained the other three territories—Cleves, Mark, and Ravensberg, acquisitions that marked an important step in Brandenburg's expansion in northern Germany. Once again, a general war was postponed.

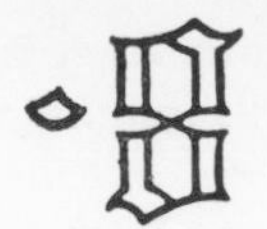

Germany Divided: The Thirty Years' War, 1618–1648

THE THIRTY YEARS' WAR

The Immediate Causes of the War

The postponement of fighting was to be of short duration, for the expected war broke out during the last years of the brief reign of Emperor Matthias (1612–1619), who proved incapable of mastering the problems he faced. On the one hand, his subjects put constant pressure on him to live up to the promises he and his brother Rudolf II had granted during their fight for the crown. On the other hand, his Austrian brothers and his Spanish brother-in-law, King Philip III, pressed him to disregard these concessions and to work instead for the complete restoration of Catholicism in the Hapsburg hereditary lands. Confronted by this dilemma, Matthias entrusted the task of government into the hands of his conciliatory minister (Melchior Khlesl) and gradually withdrew from public affairs to devote his attention to music and to his art collection.

Unhappy with the inactivity of the emperor and the lenient policies of his administration, the Catholic forces decided to replace him with someone who would promote their interests more vigorously. Since none of his brothers cared to assume the burdens of government and none of them had any male heirs, the succession to Matthias devolved either upon Ferdinand of Styria (the son of Maximilian's brother Charles) or upon Philip III of Spain (the grandson of Maximilian II through the female line; see Chart 2). The Spanish king claimed the crown for his younger son, Charles, and was eager to gain control of the Austrian branch of his family in order to further his designs against France and to institute a more adamant anti-Protestant policy in Germany. But the Austrians wanted to avoid Spanish domination, and in 1617 made a contractual settlement with Philip: Spain was to support the candidacy of Ferdinand of Styria in return for cession of the Austrian possessions in Alsace, which Philip coveted to improve his strategic capa-

Chart 2 HAPSBURG INTERMARRIAGES

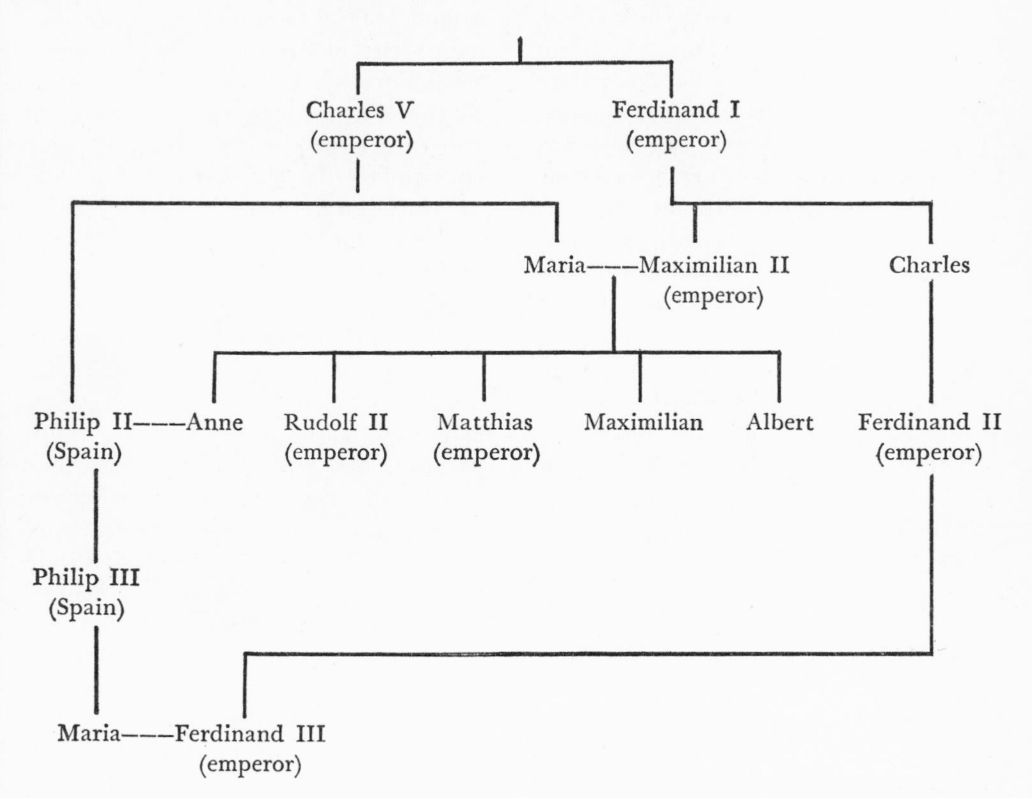

bilities for attacking France from the east.

Assured of this backing, Ferdinand used against his cousin Matthias the same methods the latter had previously employed against Rudolf. Through intrigues and pressures, he expelled Matthias from Austria and Hungary, and even succeeded in getting himself recognized as king of Bohemia. As a result, Ferdinand in effect became ruler in 1617, even though Matthias lived another two years. Ferdinand II (1619–1637) was a devout Catholic who had succeeded in ruthlessly exterminating Protestantism in his own Styria. Educated by the Jesuits, he resembled Philip II of Spain in his devotion to the interests of the Church as well as in his tactlessness and impulsion. The lack of restraint in his policies contributed not only to the eruption of the war, but also to its continuation at several critical stages of the fighting.

As soon as Ferdinand had assumed power in Bohemia, he introduced Hapsburg agents to initiate the suppression of Bohemian Protestantism and nationalism. Remnants of the Hussite movement were to be eradicated, and despite the promises of Rudolf, the Bohemian estates and nobility were to be deprived of their special rights. In protest against these measures, the Bohemians organized a resistance movement that culminated in the spring of 1618 in the famous "defenestration of Prague." To force an open break with

Vienna, certain Bohemian Protestant leaders decided to murder the imperial agents in Prague, invaded their castle, and threw two of them, as well as an innocent secretary, out of the palace window. Miraculously all three escaped serious injury, as their long fall was cushioned by a dunghill on which they landed. This event did not lack its humorous side, for the hapless secretary was afterward ennobled by the Austrian court under the appropriate title of *Ritter von Hohenfell* (Knight of Highfall). Ferdinand for his part immediately prepared to take up the challenge and suppress the Bohemian rebellion. Hence the "defenestration of Prague" marked the opening of the Thirty Years' War.

Underlying Causes and Aims

The underlying causes of the protracted struggle that devastated so much of Germany are suggested by the description of the period after 1555. Yet the character of the war defies precise labeling: each participant was guided by his own distinct motives. To some it was primarily a religious war, in defense of one of the three faiths involved. In this respect it was a resumption of the Schmalkaldic War, which had been interrupted by the Religious Peace of Augsburg. It was also a determined fight by the Calvinists for recognition as coequals with the other faiths, a status denied them in 1555.

For most rulers it was a political struggle, with religious issues furnishing at times a welcome excuse, at others an inconvenient obstacle. Within the Empire as a whole, it represented a last-ditch fight by the Hapsburgs to retain some measure of control over the innumerable political units in Germany and to determine whether the shadowy framework of an empire could be maintained. It was also a civil war among jealous territorial princes as well as a series of dynastic struggles among various ruling families. The ambitions of the Wittelsbach dynasty of Bavaria, the vain hopes of the elector Palatine to supplant the Hapsburgs as the head of the Empire, and a host of other political motives—important and trivial—complicated the picture. It was also a predatory war fought by mercenary generals for fame, power, and booty.

Finally, the Thirty Years' War was an international war for territorial and economic gains. The German states actually had little control over their own destinies and were wafted about by strong foreign currents. The Dutch Republic wanted to ensure its independence from Spain and to acquire international recognition of its new status. The Swedish monarchy hoped to gain control over northern Germany and to seal off the Baltic for its own purposes. England vacillated in its stand, wanting to aid its coreligionists on the Continent against its traditional enemy, Spain, while, on the other hand, growing apprehensive of French power and Dutch commercial competition. France desired to break the encircling noose of the Austrian and Spanish Hapsburgs and at the same time push its expansion toward the Rhine. These and other purposes guided the various nations in their conduct of the war. As on so many other occasions, Germany furnished the main battleground on which these diverse issues were to be decided.

The Stages of the War

The war, which began in 1618 and lasted until 1648, gradually became a general European conflict in which, at one time or another, almost all European states participated. It was interrupted by truces and even temporary peace treaties, such as those of 1629 and 1635. Among the states, the years of actual participation varied greatly. The Austrian and Spanish Hapsburgs, together with Bavaria, remained in the fighting throughout the thirty years, whereas other states entered the war and withdrew from it at intervals. Some, like England, changed sides in midstream. For most it started much later than 1618, and for a few it ended later than 1648, since France and Spain continued the fighting until 1659.

The thirty years are traditionally divided into four major periods: the Bohemian, Danish, Swedish, and French. Each period is named for the chief opponent of the Hapsburgs during the particular phase of the fighting. Although such a simplified subdivision is convenient, the actual conduct and issues of the war were infinitely more complicated than these divisions suggest.

The Bohemian Phase

Ferdinand's initial attempt to counter the Bohemian insurrection proved fruitless. He lacked the funds, troops, and allies needed to invade Bohemia. On the contrary, the insurgents invaded Austria twice in 1619 and, in league with rebellious Hungarians, attempted to rouse all Ferdinand's subjects to overthrow their oppressive ruler. Both sides looked for allies, but neither the German princes—both Protestant and Catholic—nor the foreign powers showed any eagerness to intervene. Each side received only insignificant outside support, and the fighting of the first year made it appear as though the war might remain localized.

All this changed when Emperor Matthias died, and the electors faced the decision of choosing a new emperor. Ferdinand, already nominal ruler of Austria, Hungary, and Bohemia, presented himself as the only serious candidate. The three Protestant electors well knew the firmness of his character and the steadfastness of his aims. Even though his power had been temporarily undermined by the Bohemian uprising, they knew he would soon receive the necessary outside assistance to overcome the rebellion and become a formidable foe of the Protestants. Nonetheless they voted for him, as if eager to sign their own death warrant. The pliable elector of Saxony (John George) bargained away his vote for territorial advantages in Silesia, even though admitting: "I know no good will come of it; I know Ferdinand." His motto was "One must leave the decision up to God." Elector John Sigismund of Brandenburg voted for Ferdinand even without concluding a bargain, although his envoys warned him that the choice would be a great misfortune for Germany. Only the more active and ambitious elector Palatine, Frederick V, vehemently opposed Ferdinand's election. Unable to make himself acceptable as an opposition candidate, he attempted to persuade Duke Maximilian I of Bavaria to stand for election—a doubtful political move in view of Maximilian's fervor for the Counter Reformation and his leadership of the Catholic League. But Maximilian refused, and in the end Frederick withdrew his opposition, and Ferdinand II was elected.

THE "WINTER KING" While Ferdinand was being elected and crowned, Austrian and Hungarian rebels joined the Bohemians in an association for the protection of their rights. They reaffirmed their ancient privilege of electing their own king, and declared Ferdinand deposed "as an arch-enemy of freedom of conscience, and a slave of Spain and the Jesuits." Thereupon they scanned the political horizon to find a new king who commanded the resources requisite to help their cause. The anti-Hapsburg duke of Savoy, the king of Denmark, and a prince of Hungary (Bethlen Gabor) all were considered as candidates. The crown was actually offered to the elector of neighboring Saxony, whose Lutheranism was compatible with the Bohemians' religious views. But the Saxon refused because he was afraid of antagonizing the Hapsburgs. In the end the crown was offered to Frederick V of the Palatinate. Despite his Calvinism, which might clash with their own faith and which made him suspect to the Protestant princes of Germany, Frederick appeared to be an appropriate candidate. His possessions in the Upper Palatinate made him a neighbor of Bohemia. His presidency of the Protestant Union, his family connections with England, and his close relations with France made it likely that he could obtain foreign support, and his aggressive nature would make him a strong leader of the anti-Hapsburg rising.

Frederick accepted the crown, despite warnings that he was taking up a challenge that surpassed his skill and resources. In the fall of 1619, he moved his residence to Prague, from where, as king of Bohemia, he directed the anti-Hapsburg forays of his small Bohemian and Palatine contingents. He soon realized that he had to face the Hapsburg onslaught almost singlehanded. Some Hungarians and Austrians stood at his side, but most of the hereditary lands were soon brought under firm Catholic control. His father-in-law, James I of England, vacillated between his own pro-Spanish policy and the pro-Protestant sentiments of Parliament. He finally contributed some funds, but could not be persuaded openly to aid the Bohemian rebel king. From Germany itself, little aid appeared. A few lesser Protestant princes dispatched some contingents. But the Protestant Union, of which Frederick was the official leader, refused to support him. Even in Bohemia, Frederick's support was far from unanimous. The Calvinist zeal of some of his Palatine followers, who subjected Hussite churches to iconoclastic destruction, alienated many Bohemians.

The Catholic forces, on the other hand, displayed remarkable unity. Ferdinand received generous papal and Spanish funds, and Spanish troops were dispatched to attack the Palatine possessions along the Rhine. Most important, the Catholic League came to the aid of the emperor. Maximilian of Bavaria demanded that Ferdinand promise him the electoral dignity that would be taken away from Frederick as punishment for his sedition, and that the Hapsburgs pay for the cost of the war. Actually Maximilian trusted Ferdinand so little that he occupied parts of upper Austria as a guarantee for the conclusion of the bargain. But the armies of the Catholic League, led by the skillful General Johan Tserclaes of Tilly (1559–1632), were essential to Ferdinand. To obtain their participation in the war, the emperor agreed to Maximilian's requests, though he had no legal right to alter the constitution of the Empire and to award the electoral dignity to another dynasty without the consent of the electoral college. Finally, even Saxony joined the anti-Bohemian forces. Jealous of the Palatine elector's rise to the kingship and always eager to come to terms with the Hapsburgs, the Saxon elector sent troops to aid the emperor in return for permission to expand toward Silesia.

Under these conditions, the new king of Bohemia could not maintain himself for long. During the winter of 1619–1620, he kept control of Bohemia, still hoping for outside help. But his luck was of such short duration that in early 1620 his opponents were already nicknaming him the "winter king," since his glory lasted for but one winter. The small Bohemian and Palatine forces could not prevent the invasion of the Hapsburg, Saxon, and Catholic League armies. The decisive battle was fought in November 1620. Near the White Mountain in the vicinity of Prague, Frederick's forces were completely annihilated by Tilly, Maximilian of Bavaria, and the imperial army (under Buquoy). The "winter king" was forced to flee with his wife and children, and eventually found asylum in Holland, where he lived until his death in 1632.

SUBJUGATION OF BOHEMIA The Battle of the White Mountain opened all Bohemia to Ferdinand's occupation. It ended the rebellion, and put an end to any traces of semiautonomy in Bohemia. Within the next few years, the severest political and religious measures were applied to turn Bohemia into the meekest of Hapsburg provinces. The Hussite dream was ended. Protestantism was outlawed and the Jesuits were returned to positions of influence. The rebel leaders were executed, their confiscated lands turned over to transplanted German nobles so as to impoverish the unruly Bohemian nobility. The Czech language was outlawed. The elective kingship was replaced by the hereditary rights of the Hapsburg dynasty, and most of the privileges of the local estates were abolished and transferred to Vienna. The king henceforth was given the right to legislate and to appoint all important officials. Government by the estates was replaced by royal absolutism.

After the subjugation of Bohemia, Ferdinand proceeded to stamp out Protestantism and tighten the reins of royal control in Austria and Hungary. At the same time, Spanish and Bavarian troops rushed in to occupy the Palatinate, each contingent eager to gain the major portion of the booty. The Spaniards established themselves along the Rhine, and Tilly occupied all of the Upper Palatinate and part of the Lower Palatinate. The capital city of Heidelberg was sacked, the countryside devastated, and Catholicism forcibly reintroduced. Maximilian of Bavaria made it clear that he intended to annex the Upper Palatinate to Bavaria, and Ferdinand kept his part of the bargain by placing the fugitive Frederick under the ban of the Empire and bestowing his electoral dignity upon the house of Bavaria.

By 1622 the Bohemian-Palatinate phase of the war had ended. Bohemia had been reconquered, and the Palatinate occupied by the Catholic forces. Wittelsbachs and Hapsburgs had been successful beyond all expectations. The major foreign powers had not interfered to prevent the astounding Hapsburg successes. France, most threatened by expansion of Spanish power along the Rhine, was suffering from internal disorders during the minority of King Louis XIII, and did not exercise a strong voice in international affairs until Richelieu's assumption of power in 1624.

Quite conceivably the war could have been ended at this point. To be sure, the Hapsburg and Catholic success frightened some foreign powers. Maximilian's greed and Ferdinand's high-handed behavior in banning Frederick and transferring the electorship without consulting the diet alarmed even the lethargic German princes. But moderation on the part of the victors and cessation of provocative acts by certain minor German princes might have permitted the conclusion of a compromise peace. Instead, during the period 1622–1625, the intransigence of both sides caused the continuation and enlargement of the war. Certain lesser German princes and mercenary generals (Ernest of Mansfeld, George Frederick of Baden-Durlach, Christian of Brunswick, and others) continued the war by roaming with their armies over parts of southwestern Germany. It is impossible to judge how much their military campaigns were motivated by love of adventure and quest for booty and how much by their desire to defend the cause of Protestantism. Their maneuvers led to several battles with the Catholic League in the years 1622 to 1625, and gave General Tilly the excuse to move his armies into northern Germany—the base of operation of his opponents. In these campaigns, Tilly and the Catholic League did not restrict themselves to military actions and pillaging, but also suppressed Protestantism and reinstituted Catholicism by force. Despite a few reverses, Tilly's armies were on the whole successful, and their success in northern Germany provoked the second phase of the war.

The Danish Phase

The Danish phase, which turned the Thirty Years' War into a general, international conflict, is frequently also called the Danish–Lower Saxon phase, since the region of Lower Saxony was the principal, though by no means the only, area of battle. By 1625 England, France—now under Richelieu—and Holland had become thoroughly alarmed at Hapsburg successes in northern Germany. Holland feared complete encirclement by Spanish forces along its land frontiers, and Richelieu could hardly look with equanimity on the prospect of seeing the chaotic and disunited state on France's eastern border replaced by a strong, centralized empire. But whereas Holland was already at war with Spain, and England was willing to provide some troops and funds, Richelieu was as yet too busy consolidating royal power and dealing with Huguenot uprisings at home to put France actively into the war. Hence French policy for the time being was to interfere only indirectly. Two effective means lay at Richelieu's disposal: to fan distrust between Hapsburgs and Wittelsbachs so as to undermine their unity, or to persuade other powers to take up arms against the Hapsburgs.

The kings of Denmark and Sweden were both likely candidates for such a role: they were devoted to the Protestant cause and opposed to the extension of Hapsburg power to the north. But King Gustavus Adolphus of Sweden was at the time engaged in war with Poland (1621–1629), and traditional distrust between the two Scandinavian powers made their cooperation in a common venture unlikely. Hence only Christian IV of Denmark responded positively to Franco-English pressure. As duke of Holstein, he was also a prince of the Empire, and as leader of the Lower Saxon circle, he felt a genuine responsibility for the protection of the region. Furthermore, his religious motives were bolstered by prospects of material gains, for he hoped to acquire the valuable ecclesiastical properties of Bremen and Verden. In the spring of 1625, his armies appeared in northern Germany, supported partially by French and English funds. His appeal to the North German princes and cities to join in a united effort against the league and the imperial forces received a most disappointing response. Despite the devastations of Tilly's troops, whose greed for plunder and zeal for the restoration of Catholicism recognized no neutrality, Brandenburg refused to commit itself, Saxony remained on friendly terms with the emperor, and most of the cities contributed nothing to the Protestant cause. Denmark's small army obtained the assistance of merely a handful of the lesser princes.

At the time of the Danish entry into the war, a change of policy was taking place in Vienna. Until then, Ferdinand had been occupied with the re-establishment of absolute control over Bohemia, Hungary, and his hereditary lands. In Germany itself he had played a somewhat secondary role behind Maximilian of Bavaria and the league. He now decided to assume greater control over the conduct of the war, hoping to acquire a larger share of the booty, most of which had previously fallen into the hands of the Wittelsbachs. To implement this decision, Ferdinand had to decrease his dependence on the armed forces of the league and create his own army.

THE APPOINTMENT OF WALLENSTEIN

Ferdinand's instrument for this purpose was Wallenstein, whom he appointed as commander in chief of all imperial armies. Albrecht Eusebius Wenceslas of Waldstein (1583–1634), whose name was somehow changed to Wallenstein, quickly became the decisive figure of the war, and remains to this day one of the most disputed personalities in German history. Born of petty German-Czech nobility, he abandoned the Protestant faith of his father to enter a Jesuit school. Two profitable marriages provided him with considerable resources, which he used to buy up estates confiscated from the rebels after the Bohemian revolt. Good fortune, successful financial speculation, and careful administration of his estates made him within a few years the richest and most powerful lord of Bohemia and one of the strongest princes in the Empire. In 1625, he assumed the title of Duke of Friedland, the name of one of his estates, which was loosely applied to the entire agglomeration of his possessions.

Wallenstein was an excellent organizer and administrator. From the beginning of the war he devoted himself to soldiering, and the minor victories of his armies gave him the reputation of a useful commander. Above all, he had perfected a new system for the support and recruitment of an army that was to change the character of the war. In the fifteenth and sixteenth centuries, the conscription of a mercenary army had depended almost exclusively on the availability of funds. Normally, a *condottiere,* a professional mercenary leader, was provided with money to hire colonels who in turn recruited their regiments. Noncommissioned officers and soldiers received a specified salary, for which they had to furnish their own equipment and subsistence. Even under this system, soldiers often plundered the countryside instead of paying for the necessary supplies, but such procedures were exceptions rather than the rule. During the early stages of the Thirty Years' War, this old system had gradually broken down. Scarcity of funds rarely permitted regular payment of troops, who became increasingly accustomed to satisfying their need through pillage and plunder. Tilly's armies had set the example afterward imitated by others. They lived off the land, whether it was friendly soil or enemy territory.

Wallenstein perfected this system. Rather than payment, he offered the prospect of booty as enticement to his recruits. He concluded that a larger army would be easier to maintain than a small one, since it could exert greater pressure on local populations to provide the necessary logistical support. He developed a system for protecting peasants and burghers from excessive violence so as not to annihilate the economy that was to support his troops, while at the same time he forced the population to contribute enough in money and kind to keep his soldiery content.

There is no question that Wallenstein was inordinately ambitious. His meteoric rise to wealth and power gave him every reason to believe in the accuracy of Kepler's horoscopic prophecy that "he was destined to rise to great heights." The only question about which historians dispute is whether his was solely a personal ambition or whether he was motivated by statesmanlike considerations for the reconstruction of Germany.

His opportunity came in 1625, when Denmark entered the fray and Ferdinand was in need of an army. Wallenstein offered to put 80,000 men into the field within the shortest possible time and without cost to the Hapsburg treasury. He would advance from his own funds the necessary capital to purchase military equipment and advertise his recruitment. In return, he merely asked for imperial consent to his plan for systematic plunder and for his appointment as commander in chief. The emperor hesitated, not because he was averse to legalizing the pillaging of Germany, but because it seemed dangerous to entrust the fate of the Hapsburg dynasty to the ambitious upstart Wallenstein. But in the end he agreed, and within a few months Wallenstein fulfilled his bargain. He collected a motley force of some 80,000 mercenaries, German as well as foreign, Protestant as well as Catholic, held together through the administrative genius of Wallenstein and their common love for plunder.

THE DEFEAT OF DENMARK In 1626 the war was resumed with full force in northern Germany. On a few occasions, Tilly's league forces and Wallenstein's own army cooperated in common campaigns, but differences in the characters of their generals and Maximilian's distrust of Wallenstein made their collaboration, for the most part, difficult. During the next three years, both armies were almost continually successful. Christian IV and his German Protestant allies were repulsed and defeated everywhere. Brandenburg and Saxony attempted to retain their neutrality, but Wallenstein showed no respect for neutral territories. His armies freely passed through neutral lands and even occupied parts of Brandenburg. Wherever possible he seized former ecclesiastical territories, expelled their Protestant "administrators," and returned them to Catholic hands. By 1628 he had conquered the Duchy of Mecklenburg, and with the reluctant permission of the emperor proclaimed himself its new duke. While Tilly occupied Holstein, Wallenstein's forces invaded Schleswig and Jutland and put an effective end to Danish resistance. In the spring of 1629, Christian IV was forced to conclude peace. In the Treaty of Lübeck, Denmark was treated with great circumspection, possibly so as not to antagonize unduly its friend and protector, England. Denmark was permitted to retain all of its territory, including Holstein, and merely had to withdraw from the war and desist henceforth from interfering in the affairs of the Empire.

The successful conclusion of this second phase of the war greatly increased the power and prestige of Wallenstein and Emperor Ferdinand II. Although unable to seize the fortified city of Stralsund, which was supplied by sea from Sweden and Denmark, Wallenstein controlled significant stretches along the Baltic shores. From the emperor he received the title of "General of the Oceanic and Baltic Seas," and he proposed to make his new position of "admiral" a reality. He urged the emperor to build a Baltic fleet and to wrest control of all trade from Holland and England by forming an association with the Hanseatic towns and with Spain. Realizing that Sweden would object to Hapsburg control of the Baltic, he sent an expeditionary force to aid the king of Poland against Sweden. He even suggested to Ferdinand far-reaching plans for using his victories to reshape the political frame of Germany by turning the Hapsburgs into the absolute, hereditary rulers of Germany.

Emperor Ferdinand made use of the victories in his own way. Even before the conclusion of the Peace of Lübeck, he promulgated the Edict of Restitution, which provoked new discord in the Empire. The edict reconfirmed the Religious Peace of Augsburg, in particular the clause of the Ecclesiastical Reservation. Accordingly, it declared as invalid all confiscations of ecclesiastical lands that had taken place since the truce of Passau in 1552. These lands were to be restored to the Church. Moreover, Ferdinand I's declaration that Protestants in Catholic ecclesiastical territory would enjoy special privileges was specifically declared null and void, and it was reiterated that only adherents of the Augsburg Confession (Lutherans) were to enjoy any legal rights in the land. Execution of the edict was entrusted to imperial commissioners supported by the imperial armies.

The Edict of Restitution and its high-handed promulgation by the emperor without consulting the estates shocked even the complacent elector of Saxony, although it did not stir him to more than verbal protest. The demanded restitutions involved two archbishoprics, twelve bishoprics, countless abbeys, and other religious territories, some of which had been in the hands of Protestant families for over three generations. Complete implementation of the edict would have amounted to annihilation of Protestantism as a political force in Germany. It would also have greatly augmented Hapsburg power, for the emperor seized the opportunity offered by the restitutions to enlarge his family's influence. Archduke Leopold William, his youngest son, for example, already bishop of Passau and Strassburg, was now awarded the two important archbishoprics of Bremen and Magdeburg.

Thus the second phase of the war, like the first, terminated with the unquestionable victory for the cause of the emperor and his Catholic supporters. In fact, by 1630 imperial and Catholic power had reached its high mark. The power of Wallenstein and the emperor had become so great that it provoked disunity among the Catholics. At the imperial diet of 1630, this discord came into the open. The electors refused to comply with Ferdinand's wish that they elect his son as king. Instead, they joined the princes, Catholic and Protestant alike, in bitter complaints about the increasing power of the imperial government. They felt their princely rights threatened, and accused Ferdinand of acting like a tyrant without consulting the estates. Maximilian of Bavaria showed particular irritation, and demanded the immediate dismissal of Wallenstein, whose military successes had relegated the league to secondary importance. Moreover, all the estates complained about the harrowing devastations caused by Wallenstein's marauding armies. Indirect pressure on Ferdinand was also exercised by foreign powers. Spain had become alarmed at the growth of Austrian power, while Richelieu's envoys encouraged Bavaria in its sudden opposition to the emperor, on the theory that any disunity within Germany would benefit French interests. Ferdinand finally gave way, and in the summer of 1630 Wallenstein was deprived of his command and dismissed from the imperial service. Most of his troops were incorporated into the armies of Tilly, who received supreme command of the imperial forces.

The Swedish Phase

Wallenstein's dismissal occurred at the moment when the third, or Swedish, phase of the war was being opened with the landing of Gustavus Adolphus in Pomerania. The Swedish monarch was unquestionably one of the strongest personalities of his time. Born in 1594, he became king in 1611, and soon acquired the reputation of skillful ruler and vigorous champion of Sweden's foreign interest. Aided by his diplomatic Chancellor Axel Oxenstierna, he put Sweden's internal administration in order so that he could devote more attention to expanding its foreign influence. Sweden already possessed Finland, Estonia, and Latvia, so it seemed reasonable for Gustavus Adolphus to try to acquire for Sweden political and economic monopoly over the Baltic Sea. While his rival Denmark was engaged in the Thirty Years' War, he continued to fight against Poland until 1629. From the Polish war, Sweden obtained the Lithuanian coast and important bases in Prussia. The Swedish ring around the Baltic was beginning to close. Aside from the Danish isles, it was primarily the German coast line, with its wealthy trading centers, that was not yet under Swedish control. This fact alone might explain why Gustavus Adolphus decided to enter the general European war.

But there were other considerations. As an ardent Lutheran, the Swedish king looked with misgiving at the progress of the Counter Reformation under the Hapsburgs and the Catholic League, and in particular at the promulgation of the Edict of Restitution. Many Protestant historians stress this religious devotion and explain Swedish intervention in the Thirty Years' War largely on the basis of the king's desire to defend his faith. On the other hand, many Catholic historians, as well as those less given to idealization of their heroes, see the primary motive as

Sweden's quest for land and economic advantages. Both interpretations essentially misread the temper of the times and misjudge the nature of Lutheranism, for both reasons are valid. They are not mutually exclusive. On the contrary, religion, politics, and economics at this period were so intertwined that one falsifies history by trying to separate them. The political and economic power of the Swedish monarchy—as well as that of Denmark—was based on Lutheranism. In defending his faith, Gustavus Adolphus defended his political position as well. The establishment of Hapsburg power along the southern shores of the Baltic would undermine Sweden's political position in the Baltic area and its economic future as much as the survival of Protestantism.

In addition, France urged Sweden to enter the fray. Richelieu by then had overcome the Huguenot resistance at home and was prepared to assume a more aggressive role against the Hapsburgs, although he was not yet ready to commit France to fullfledged hostilities. He mediated a truce between Poland and Sweden, so as to free the Swedish king's armies for an invasion of Germany. In 1631, after Swedish armies were already on German soil, France entered into its first alliance with Sweden. In return for the French subsidies, Gustavus Adolphus promised to fight until the German princes regained their former possessions—that is, until German particularism was re-established—and not to suppress the Catholic faith in the lands he conquered.

SWEDISH CAMPAIGNS IN GERMANY After the Swedes landed in northern Germany, they occupied the city of Stettin as a base of operation, and then in quick succession cleared Promerania and Mecklenburg of imperial troops. Mecklenburg, which had been awarded by the emperor to Wallenstein, was rereturned to its former lord, a relative of the Swedish king. Pomerania received different treatment. Although the elector of Brandenburg possessed the legal title to the inheritance after the death of the reigning duke (who died in 1637), Gustavus Adolphus announced that Sweden intended to retain Pomerania.

While the Swedish army was securing the shores of the Baltic, and the imperial forces under Tilly were marching north to meet it, the Protestant princes were in their usual quandary. They were frightened by the overbearing power of the emperor and the ruthlessness with which the Edict of Restitution was being executed; yet they hesitated to abandon their lethargic neutrality and to accept the overtures made to them by the king of Sweden. The pusillanimous elector of Brandenburg, George William (1619–1640), was under the influence of his minister (Schwarzenberg), who favored friendship with the emperor. Instead of reacting against the armies of Tilly, which were violating the Brandenburg border, George William complained above all about the Swedish occupation of Pomerania, which threatened his inheritance rights. Even though Gustavus Adolphus was his brother-in-law—the king had married the elector's sister in 1620—George William refused him the right of passage through Brandenburg territory. The drunken elector of Saxony (John George) also refused to commit himself. The major Protestant princes seemed bent on standing on the side lines during the impending fight between Sweden and the Catholic

League, even though the battles would take place on their soil, the armies would devastate their lands, and the outcome of the war would determine their future. Only the city of Magdeburg, a secularized ecclesiastical territory, rose against the Catholics, made an open alliance with Gustavus Adolphus, and was promptly besieged by Tilly's armies.

By 1631, the progress of both the Swedish and the imperial armies caused the Protestant princes to adopt a slight change of policy that considerably affected the war during the next few years. Saxony, Brandenburg, and others made an alliance at Leipzig and decided to collect an army—not for entering the war, but for safeguarding their neutrality. This attempt at armed neutrality had the opposite effect: the emperor called on the princes to demobilize their forces immediately, and rejected their meek explanation that they merely intended to guard their frontiers against Tilly's inroads. Ferdinand even instructed Tilly to prevent further arming on the part of Saxony and Brandenburg—if necessary by force.

In May 1631, Magdeburg had to surrender to Tilly. It had not received any Swedish reinforcements and was unable to resist the siege any longer. The city was burned to the ground. Only the cathedral, a convent, and a few huts remained standing. To this day there is no proof whether the fires were set by Tilly's forces or by the defending citizens, or whether they were accidental. But the raping, murdering, and plundering by Tilly's hordes, which decimated the population of the once prosperous city, can be laid at the feet of the general, who apparently took few measures to impose moderation on his soldiery. The gruesome example of the fate of Magdeburg spurred some of the Protestants into action.

Without further hesitation, Gustavus Adolphus now marched into Brandenburg and forced the elector to abandon his neutrality. At the same time, Tilly's forces invaded Saxony, thereby compelling the Saxon elector also to change his stand. Brandenburg decided to contribute to the cost of the war, and Saxony actually made an alliance with Sweden and put an army into the field against the Hapsburgs. Shortly thereafter, Gustavus Adolphus encountered Tilly near Leipzig and inflicted a resounding defeat on the imperial forces.

This victory turned the Swedish king into a German hero overnight. Since his mother had been from Holstein, Gustavus Adolphus spoke fluent German, and his new admirers overlooked the fact that he was first of all a Swedish nationalist and not a new Siegfried. The respected soldier-king now saw the Protestant forces flock to his side. Alliances and treaties were made, North Germany was at his disposal. He directed the Saxon forces to invade Bohemia—with the admonition to spare Wallenstein's estates, so as not to jeopardize secret negotiations then being conducted with him and not to throw him into the emperor's camp. By the winter of 1631, the Swedish armies had crossed into southern Germany, had seized Würzburg, and had taken up winter quarters in Mainz.

WALLENSTEIN'S REAPPOINTMENT In the following spring, Wallenstein was back in the field on the emperor's side. After the Swedish victory over Tilly, Ferdinand had turned in desperation to the general whom he had dismissed so peremptorily in 1630. For a while, Wallenstein, who lived in temporary retirement on his Bohemian estates, had negotiated with both sides. But mutual suspicion between the Bohemian general and the Swedish king had prevented any understanding between the two, and in the end Ferdinand had accepted the harsh conditions for which Wallenstein agreed to return to the field. The exact concessions the emperor had to make are still a matter of speculation for historians. Some describe them as granting Wallenstein powers coequal with, if not superior to, those of the emperor. Supposedly Wallenstein received lifelong supreme command over the imperial armies, supreme power to confiscate lands and issue amnesties, feudal suzerainty over all lands in the Empire, the expectancy of a portion of the Austrian hereditary lands, confirmation of his right to Mecklenburg, as well as a large financial payment. Whatever they were, the concessions were so exorbitant as to place the emperor in embarrassing dependency on his unpredictable general, and ultimately to bring about the latter's doom.

Wallenstein's first action, after recruiting a new army with amazing speed, was to expel the Saxons from Bohemia. Meanwhile Gustavus Adolphus invaded Bavaria, defeated Tilly in another battle in which the latter was mortally wounded, and even occupied Maximilian's capital, Munich. In the summer Wallenstein finally came to the relief of the fugitive Maximilian. For the first time, the two military geniuses of the war faced each other on the field. Both hesitated engaging in open battle and spent their time in long maneuvers for position. Finally Wallenstein abruptly rushed north to subdue Saxony. In November, when Wallenstein was about to retire to winter quarters, the two armies unexpectedly met. At Lützen, the Swedish forces carried the day, but Gustavus Adolphus, who always charged at the head of his troops, died in the fighting. The story of his bloodstained, riderless white charger roaming the foggy battlefield after the death of his master became renowned in the annals of Germany.

History is more than the story of great men, and events are caused by many forces other than strong personalities. Yet it cannot be denied that certain individuals exert enormous influence on the course of history. The death of Gustavus Adolphus and the subsequent fate of Wallenstein provide ample proof of this assertion.

Swedish power in Germany was at once dimmed by the disappearance of the king-general. His young daughter Christina, who succeeded him, could hardly take his place on the battlefield. Direction of the Swedish forces was taken over by Chancellor Oxenstierna, an excellent diplomat but not much of a military mind. Under him, the famed discipline of the Swedish army began to disappear. Foreign mercenaries, greedy adventurers, and lawless vagabonds began to replace the Swedish peasant recruits, so that the Swedish forces soon resembled the motley, rowdy bands of the continental armies. Nor could Oxenstierna exert the same magnetic authority over Sweden's allies that had been exercised by the admired king. Saxony, Brandenburg, and the others resumed their own policies. Oxenstierna's only major diplomatic victory was the Alliance of Heilbronn in 1633, concluded between

Sweden and the majority of the cities and princes of southwestern Germany. Encouraged by Richelieu, this alliance aimed at restoring the privileges of the German estates and at re-establishing Protestantism where it had been suppressed in the course of the war. The allies promised to work for peace, and agreed to grant compensations to Sweden for her efforts in behalf of "German liberty."

The year 1633 was relatively inactive. The main reason was Wallenstein's enigmatic behavior. After the battle of Lützen, he had resumed his usual winter quarters in Bohemia. In the spring he conducted some successful attacks against Saxony, but instead of taking advantage of his victories, he repeatedly interrupted his campaigns to negotiate with the enemy. Shortly thereafter, Swedish forces again invaded Bavaria (under Bernhard of Saxe-Weimar), and the harassed duke of Bavaria asked for Wallenstein's assistance. But Wallenstein delayed his movements, it was thought purposely, until it was too late, and the city of Regensburg had fallen to the Swedes. Whereupon Wallenstein again retired to early winter quarters.

THE MURDER OF WALLENSTEIN Since his reappointment to the generalship, Wallenstein had spent as much of the time in negotiations as in fighting. Although the ultimate purpose of these negotiations is still open to question, their content is fairly clear from available sources. With the Swedes he bargained for an alliance against the Hapsburgs. To Saxony he proposed a common fight against all foreigners—Swedes, French, and Spaniards, on the basis of an equal acceptance within Germany of all contending religions. With the Bohemians he bargained for the possible position of king of Bohemia, while he asked French assistance for a plan to acquire the Palatinate and its electoral privileges. Although the nature of these negotiations was initially kept secret, Wallenstein made no attempt to hide the fact that he was negotiating with the various powers. It is still not clear whether he assumed the right to conduct such diplomatic discussions on the basis of authority delegated to him by the emperor, or whether he tried to play these powers against each other in order to further his own ends. Wallenstein was always careful to use intermediaries, whose word he could repudiate if necessary. In the final analysis, he committed himself to nothing, since all discussions were undermined by the suspicions of the parties involved. Hence to this day no one can be sure of the true aims of this enigmatic, ambitious general. It seems unlikely that, as some have asserted, he was principally motivated by the desire to avenge himself for the humiliation of his dismissal in 1630. It is more probable that he was primarily interested in personal gains, but it is quite possible that these personal motives went hand in hand with larger aims of a more selfless nature, such as furthering Czech national ambitions or bringing peace to Germany as a whole.

In a strictly legal sense, Wallenstein's connections with other powers could perhaps not be termed treasonous, but Emperor Ferdinand soon became suspicious of his general's hesitant campaigns and multifarious negotiations, and decided to remove him. Wallenstein himself provided the needed excuse. Afraid of disloyalty in his army, the general forced his major officers to sign an oath of allegiance to him. This oath of Pilsen (January 1634) thoroughly alienated some of his officers, who had already become wary of their commanding general. Swearing allegiance to him rather than to the emperor was like reviving the personal armies of the last days of the Roman Republic, and might obligate the officers to undertakings contrary to their political views. After Ferdinand was notified, he issued a decree—at first kept secret—deposing Wallenstein on the charge of high treason, declaring the oath of Pilsen invalid, and freeing all officers and men of Wallenstein's army from obedience to the general. As yet the emperor did not dare an open break, although discussions were freely held at his court as to how best to get rid of Wallenstein. Finally, after a month's hesitation, the imperial decree was published. Three days later, Wallenstein was murdered during the night on orders of some of his rebellious generals. Ferdinand had not arranged for nor authorized the murder, but, like Henry II in the murder of Thomas à Becket, he carries a share of the responsibility. No attempt had been made to convict Wallenstein in open court. A simple imperial edict had been issued, and scheming lackeys, eager to please the emperor and to serve their own cause, had rushed to fulfill the verdict. The emperor rewarded the murderers by granting them some of Wallenstein's confiscated possessions.

After Wallenstein's death, the Catholic forces became more active. In the summer of 1634, the Swedes were beaten near Nördlingen, and forced to evacuate most of southern Germany, which fell into the hands of Spanish and imperial forces. Thereupon Saxony abandoned its Swedish ally and arranged for a separate peace that became the prelude to a general attempt at pacification.

THE PEACE OF PRAGUE In May 1635, the Peace of Prague was concluded between the elector of Saxony and Ferdinand II. Saxony received some concessions: it was allowed to retain a few territorial acquisitions made during the Bohemian war, and Saxon princes were awarded the former ecclesiastical properties of Magdeburg and Halberstadt. The main clauses of the treaty dealt with the religious issue and with an attempt to establish a general peace. Since the truce of Passau and the Religious Peace of Augsburg were reconfirmed, the Calvinists were still denied legal status. But the execution of the Edict of Restitution was to be suspended for a period of forty years, after which a new settlement was to be attempted. Sweden was to be offered an indemnity of three and a half million thalers, provided it would evacuate German territory immediately. If it refused, Saxony and the Empire would join in making war on Sweden. Furthermore, all other German princes, except those still allies of Sweden, such as Baden and Württemberg, were asked to adhere to the Peace of Prague immediately. Saxony agreed to help the emperor force the peace on the recalcitrant princes. Finally, the treaty outlawed all alliances and leagues of German princes, and prohibited the recruitment of private territorial armies. Even the Catholic League was asked to disband, and only Bavaria and Saxony were given the right to participate in the command of the imperial army.

Although many Protestant princes were disturbed by Saxony's unilateral action in concluding this peace, Brandenburg, Brunswick, other princes, and certain cities adhered to the pact. Most of them were weary of the war and deluded themselves into believing that they had won, since the emperor had in fact yielded on the issue of the Edict of Restitution. Yet this was mere self-deception: the character of the war was changing. What had started for Ferdinand II as a religious war with strong political undercurrents had become a political war with religious overtones. The emperor realized this, much to the discomfort of the papacy. His concessions in matters of religion were minor compared with his political gains, if the political clauses of the Peace of Prague were fulfilled. The dismantling of the Catholic League relieved him of an uncomfortable rival and weakened his dangerous neighbor, the house of Wittelsbach. The prohibition of private armies and alliances of princes would considerably increase his power within the Empire.

Thus the tenacious Ferdinand II had won again. In the following year, he succeeded in having his son elected to the German throne. At the beginning of 1637 he died, and Ferdinand III (1637–1657) assumed the burden of the final phase of the war. Although most of the German princes temporarily resigned themselves to the increase in imperial power, France could not acquiesce in this development. A strong Hapsburg Germany went counter to all of Richelieu's policies. Hence France now launched itself fully into the war, opening the last stage of this long struggle.

The French Phase

In 1635, France declared war on Spain and Austria, and began full-scale operations in the Pyrenees, in the north against the Spanish Netherlands, and in the east against Spanish and Austrian possessions in Germany. In the course of the next decade, it trained and equipped ever-larger forces and developed the resources that rapidly made it the foremost military power in Europe.

From the military point of view, the period 1635–1648 presents considerable confusion. Instead of two prominent generals, such as Wallenstein and Gustavus Adolphus, countless capable commanders (Bernhard of Saxe-Weimar, Piccolomini, Baner, Wrangel, Torstenson, Condé, Turenne, and others) and their armies crisscrossed Germany in never-ending forays, none of which was decisive, but each contributing to the final outcome.

It should suffice to indicate the main characteristics of this military seesaw. During his first few years in office, Ferdinand III, although less resolute and tenacious than his father, was able to maintain the strong position the imperial forces had achieved through the Peace of Prague. In the main, only those princes who had been excluded from the Peace of Prague remained loyal to their Swedish ally, and the strength of France was not yet felt on the field of battle. After a few years, this was to change. The power of Spain began to wane. Rebellions in Portugal and Catalonia, and French attacks on all its possessions made it less able to devote resources to the German theater of operations. Moreover, some of the German princes ended the unnatural honeymoon of the Peace of Prague and resumed their customary independence of the emperor. The new elector of Brandenburg, Frederick William, who began his reign in 1640, withdrew his state from the war and built up an army to protect his neutrality, in spite of the imperial prohibition of independent armies. Saxony followed this example after a few years, and in the end, even Bavaria abandoned the imperial ship and sought its own safety in a separate armistice with France and Sweden. The imperial forces continued to win minor battles, but in the long run, Swedish-French power prevailed almost everywhere. It became evident that the emperor could not win the war. Moreover, Germany was thoroughly exhausted. Its economic resources could not supply the large numbers of foreign troops trying to live off the land. As a result, armies had to get smaller or keep moving in order to find the required subsistence.

Peace talks had been initiated as early as 1641. Yet only in 1644 did representatives of the warring powers commence negotiations in the cities of Münster and Osnabrück in Westphalia. It took another four years before treaties were finally agreed upon and the fighting in Germany ceased. Intrinsic difficulties of the task, intrigues by the papacy, and wrangling over questions of ceremony and precedence are usually given as reasons for this interminable delay. Yet a more simple explanation lies in the failure of the belligerents to conclude an armistice before attempting to discuss the actual terms of peace. While the debates were dragging on in Westphalia for four years, the armies continued to fight, and the relative strength of the combatants continued to shift. Demands or concessions by each party varied with the most recent reports from the battlefront, and no one would agree to permanent concessions while the final test of arms was not yet completed. The peace was at last concluded in 1648, when the cause of the imperial forces seemed lost after the Swedes had seized Prague, and the French had inflicted a severe defeat on the Austro-Spanish forces near Lens.

The Terms of the Peace of Westphalia

The Treaties of Münster and Osnabrück, usually referred to as the Peace of Westphalia, count among the most important events in German political development and exerted profound repercussions on the rest of Europe. There were in reality two separate treaties: one between Ferdinand III on the one hand and Queen Christina of Sweden and her German allies on the other; the other between the emperor and King Louis XIV of France. Both contain identical clauses concerning a religious and territorial settlement in Germany, but the one deals with matters of Swedish interest, the other with matters of French interest. It should be noted that although delegates from all interested powers participated in the peace conference, not all agreed with the ultimate document. The Spanish envoys signed it, although France and Spain remained at war for another eleven years. The papal envoy protested it and refused to affix his signature. The all-embracing aspect of the issues involved in the war can best be seen from a list of the adherents to the peace, as enumerated in Article 17 of the Treaty of Osnabrück: the emperor; the kings of England, France, Poland, Portugal, Spain, Sweden, and Denmark-Norway with its dependencies; the house of Austria; the German electors, princes, knights, cities, and other estates; the grand duke of Moscow; the dukes of Lorraine, Savoy, and Schleswig; the prince of Siebenbürgen; the United Provinces of the Netherlands; the republics of Italy; and the Swiss cantons.

POLITICO-RELIGIOUS SETTLEMENTS The religious settlements were essentially a compromise, with broad concessions to the Protestants, whereas the political arrangements for Germany signified a clear-cut victory for the territorial lords. A general amnesty was declared for all who had been deprived of their rights because of religious affiliation or political activities. Restitution of property confiscated as a result of the war was to be made so that the status of 1618 would be restored or equitable adjustments made. The validity of the Religious Peace of Augsburg was reconfirmed, except where superseded by the Peace of Westphalia, and its provisions were extended to include the Calvinists. But no other faiths besides Lutheranism, Catholicism, and Calvinism received legal status, and it was specifically stated that the stipulation concerning religious equality would not apply to the Hapsburg hereditary lands. The all-important question of the Ecclesiastical Reservation was also solved on a basis that favored the Protestants. All ecclesiastical territories secularized prior to January 1, 1624, could be retained by the Protestants. These included the bulk of the secularized lands. Only those few that had changed hands after 1624 were to be returned to the Church.

The political clauses concerning the Empire's internal structure restored and legalized the rights that the territorial lords had lost to the emperor during the war. In fact, imperial power was not only reduced to its prewar status, but suffered further infringement. The German princes and estates were reassured their "rights, prerogatives, liberties, privileges, territorial jurisdiction in ecclesiastical and political matters." Except as far as his own hereditary lands were concerned, the emperor lost all power to act independently, for the treaty stipulated that the estates had to be consulted and were to be given the right to vote on all deliberations concerning matters that affected the Empire: legislation, taxation, mobilization, foreign policy, alliances, and the like. Although the medieval fiction of imperial suzerainty was maintained, the free cities and the territorial lords—from powerful dukes such as those of Brandenburg and Saxony to the petty lord who owned a square mile of independence—were given complete *de facto* sovereignty. They received absolute power to deal with their subjects according to their own designs. In foreign affairs, they obtained the right to make alliances among themselves or with foreign powers to ensure their own "preservation and security." The only proviso was that such alliances should not be directed "against emperor, Empire or the public peace," a condition easily forgotten in the succeeding years. Finally, in contrast to the restrictive clauses of the Peace of Prague, the treaties of 1648 gave each German state the right to establish and control its own army, its size being vaguely limited to the requirements of its need for security.

TERRITORIAL SETTLEMENTS The territorial and international settlements, of course, favored the victors, but even those on the imperial side gained some concessions (see Map 11). The Austrian Hapsburgs lost their possessions in the Rhineland—which they had already bargained away to Spain in the compromise of 1617—and forfeited much

MAP 11

power in Germany, but they at last received international acknowledgment of their hereditary rights to the Bohemian crown. The wartime destruction of Bohemia and the hereditary privilege solved, as far as Austria was concerned, the "Bohemian problem," which had plagued the emperors since the days of Hus and which was not to be reopened until the nineteenth century. The other major Catholic power, Bavaria, actually gained through the war. Its equivocal position vis-à-vis the Hapsburgs and its repeated intrigues with France produced results at the peace conference. Bavaria was allowed to retain the Upper Palatinate and the electorship it had won during the first phase of the war.

The German states that had fought on the Protestant side received mostly small territorial acquisitions of varying importance. Brandenburg had to renounce its inheritance rights to western Pomerania and the island of Rügen, but received a small stretch of Baltic coast in eastern Pomerania and a number of important former ecclesiastical properties, such as Minden, Halberstadt, and the succession rights to Magdeburg and Halle. The minor states, such as Mecklenburg and Hesse-Cassel, all received some compensations. Only the unfortunate Palatinate, which had suffered so much devastation during the war, was not restored to its former size. An eighth electorship was created, so that the son of Frederick, the "winter king," (Charles Louis) was made an elector, even though his father's electoral seat was retained by Bavaria. Only the Upper Palatinate, along the Rhine, was returned to him.

The most important benefits were reaped by Sweden and France. Sweden was allowed to tighten its grip on the Baltic by retaining western Pomerania, which included Stettin and many good harbors. In addition, it received parts of Mecklenburg, the former Archbishopric of Bremen—without the city of Bremen itself—the territory of Verden, and other minor areas. It could thus exercise strong commercial and political control over northern Germany. As "Duke of Bremen, Verden, Pomerania, [*et al.*]," the king of Sweden was given a seat among the estates of Germany, legally had to recognize the emperor as his suzerain, and could therefore legitimately influence the political course of Germany as a whole. Finally, Sweden received five million thaler as indemnity for its war effort, parts of which it was to use to pension off its soldiers in order to rid Germany of this military plague.

France received equally important concessions. Richelieu's dream of making the Rhine the eastern border of France was not realized, but the treaties represented an important step in this direction. Toul, Metz, and Verdun, which had been occupied by France since 1552, were permanently awarded to the French. From the Hapsburgs, Louis XIV received ten imperial cities and other valuable territories in Alsace, giving France the basis for the eventual acquisition of all of Alsace. At the same time, the connections of these lands to the Empire were maintained, so that, like the king of Sweden, Louis XIV was legally a "German prince" with a vote in the diet and could meddle in German affairs. France's intention of making its voice felt in Germany was clearly indicated in the treaty. France was given the right of occupying Breisach and Philippsburg on the right bank of the Rhine, opposite Alsace. Military occupation of these two places gave France a valuable bridgehead from which to move its forces into southern Germany whenever needed. Paragraph 75 of the Treaty of Münster stipulated specifically that "the King [of France] has the right to pass through the *Reich,* by water and by land, with troops, logistical support or other, in such quantities and as often as he deems it necessary." Such "movement through the *Reich*" was obviously aimed at future military expeditions against the Hapsburgs, each of which was to involve Germany in war or turn it again into a battlefield.

Finally, the treaties recognized the independence and sovereignty of Holland and of the Swiss cantons, thereby permanently and legally separating these lands from the Empire.

The Consequences of the War and the Treaties

Ratification of the treaties was completed in 1649, although delegates of the powers continued to meet periodically in Nuremberg for two years to iron out minor details of implementing the peace. By 1650 the war indemnity had been paid and foreign troops were officially withdrawn from Germany, although roving bands of discharged soldiers continued to infest the countryside for many years. Peace at last had returned to Germany and the famous composer of hymns, Paul Gerhardt, could write:

> Thank thee, oh Lord,
> the bells of peace resound!
> Now pike and sword
> can cease their murd'rous round.

The consequences of the war and the contents of the peace treaties are of incalculable importance for Germany. Of course, no exact statistics exist on the material damage and the loss in human life. Historians have long argued whether the population was reduced by a half, a third, a quarter, or less. The more recent the studies, the more the estimates of losses decrease. Germany's rapid recovery after the destruction in World War II and modern demographic studies have made it obvious that the former Armageddon-like descriptions of the Thirty Years' War need revision. Yet damage and losses were extensive and recovery was slow, so that Germany suffered for several generations from the material consequences of the war. War casualties, disease, and famine had underpopulated certain areas. Agriculture and livestock resources had declined, and the oppression of peasants was intensified as landlords tried to recover from the war by increasing the exploitation of their land. The commercial life of Germany was weakened immensely. In contrast to the blossoming trade of the Renaissance period, stagnation had set in. Money had again become scarce. The constant clipping of coins and minting of cheap substitutes, practiced during the war by both rulers and profiteers, had depreciated the value of money and affected its acceptance as a means of exchange. Above all, Germany was more or less cut off from all sea trade. The mouths of its important rivers were all owned or controlled by foreign powers. The Rhine was blocked by Holland, the Weser and the Oder by Sweden, and the Elbe by Denmark, which controlled Hamburg. The Hanseatic glory was gone. Germany could not profit from the commercial boom which now enriched such nations as England and Holland.

Besides the material and economic consequences, there were the moral, psychological, and social ones. A generation and a half of peasants had grown up knowing little else but the bestiality of the plundering armies, the futility of raising crops to see them pillaged or of rebuilding their huts to see them burnt down again. The contemporary *Simplicius Simplicissimus* by Hans von Grimmelshausen (1625?–1676) gives a good picture of the moral impact of the war on the lower classes. The middle class also underwent degeneration. Its love of freedom and proud sense for self-government of the Renaissance period were undermined. The economic changes, the war, and the rise of the territorial lords to the status of absolute rulers extinguished almost all of the former free cities. With fewer opportunities of making fortunes in commerce and finance, many bourgeois sought a new haven of respectability in the civil services that the rulers began to establish. The high nobility, on the other hand, had retained its privileged status. With the final triumph of territoriality, the upper aristocracy could act like kings and emperors in their own domains, and elevate their social status far above that of the other classes. Important positions in the army and the bureaucracy were reserved for the nobility, and many a burgher purchased his letter of nobility from emperors eager to sell them during the bankrupt postwar years. In this manner, he obtained the high position and cherished social acceptability he formerly could enjoy within his own class.

Finally, there were religious and political repercussions. The war and the peace treaties terminated the period of the Counter Reformation and initiated the era of secularized politics. Open religious struggles ceased after equal rights had been awarded to the three faiths. Although religion and politics could not always be separated, in public matters political considerations henceforth assumed dominance over religious motives. Religious toleration, however, had not been achieved, and rivalry among the religions continued. The pope issued a bull protesting against the peace treaties of Westphalia, and continued his efforts in behalf of the waning Counter Reformation; the Jesuits, meanwhile, persisted in their own successful campaign to increase the strength of the Church. But in the ultimate analysis, everything depended now on the whims of the territorial lord. Bigotry and persecutions were practiced by some; increasing tolerance became the policy of others.

The peace treaties of Westphalia were also regarded as a sort of written "constitution" for the Empire, and accepted as such by subsequent diets. From the standpoint of modern politics and international law, it may seem strange that an "international" treaty should contain provisions for an "internal constitution," and that foreign powers, such as Sweden and France, should be named as guarantors for political arrangements inside the Empire. Had Germany been a unified nation-state, there would have been two completely separate documents: one an international treaty settling the war between Germany and the other powers; the other a written instrument for settling the political structure of Germany. But Germany was not such a unified political entity. Relations between the princes and the emperor, and among the princes themselves, were assuming as much of an international character as relations between them and such foreign powers as Sweden or Holland. France in particular was interested in maintaining this disunity among the Germans, and therefore guaranteed the instrument that legalized it.

The "constitution" spelled out the failure of imperial absolutism and confirmed German particularism, often facetiously called "German freedom." Its provisions remained more or less unchanged until the dissolution of the Empire in 1806. A ninth electorate was created in 1692 with the admission of Hanover into the electoral college, but the change was hardly significant, for this body had lost most of its importance. The imperial diet under the new system sank more and more into a meaningless formality. Its three houses had to agree before any action could be undertaken, and agreement was seldom reached. Even a unanimous decision carried little meaning, for no one could guarantee its execution by the territorial lords. The Empire had no income of its own and was dependent on special levies in an emergency.

It had no army, except in times of crisis, when stipulated numbers of troops were to be furnished by the ten administrative circles into which Germany was divided. The imperial court of justice continued to function, but acceptance of its verdicts depended largely on the good will of the accused. Yet the fiction of the imperial diet was maintained. Starting in 1663, it even assumed the character of a continuous body, with regular sessions in Regensburg attended by permanent delegates. Although derided by foreigners and Germans alike, this assembly at least kept the three hundred or so political units informed of one another's activities and gave a semblance of cooperation.

Besides these "constitutional" provisions, the treaties produced other political repercussions. Brandenburg and Bavaria had gained relatively the most in strength and importance. Bavaria, of course, had been a strong state before, and had always exerted a considerable influence in southern Germany, but Brandenburg was a relative newcomer. The informal position as leader and protector of the Protestants that Saxony had enjoyed before the war was now taken over by Brandenburg, whose territorial acquisitions permitted it gradually to become the dominant power in northern Germany.

Above all, the war and the peace treaties introduced a new age in international affairs in Europe in which the predominance of a single state or dynasty was replaced by the new concept of a balance of power among groups of competing states. At the same time, Germany's dependence on foreign powers was legalized. As the history of the century and a half after 1648 would demonstrate, the German lands were to serve as pawns for other European nations in their seesaw attempts to establish a balance of power.

THE AGE OF THE BAROQUE

The second half of the sixteenth and all of the seventeenth centuries are the age of the Baroque in German culture. The religious controversies of the period affected art, thought, and literature. Universities particularly reflected the religious divisions. The Lutherans took over some existing universities, and founded new ones of their own (Jena, 1558; Helmstedt, 1567: and Giessen, 1607). Lutheran scholars, particularly in history, philosophy, and the humanities, faced the task of reinterpreting and re-evaluating knowledge on the basis of their new doctrines. For their part, the Catholics, mostly Jesuits and Benedictines, busily revitalized old and established new universities (Ingolstadt and Dillingen, 1563: Würzburg, 1582: Graz, 1585; and Salzburg, 1622). Catholic scholars dealt with the problem of reconciling Renaissance humanism with their traditional emphasis on salvation and otherworldliness. Both Protestant and Catholic savants produced research of some importance, especially in astronomy and mathematics, but, on the whole, much energy was dissipated on stultifying religious polemics between Lutherans and Catholics. These controversies ranged from debates on minutiae to discussions of differences in their respective world views and their historical interpretations of the Protestant movement.

The literature of the Baroque reflected this concern with religion. Perhaps to counter the arid effects of current theological debates, both Catholic and Protestant writers seemed concerned with stimulating the revival of deeper religious feelings. During and after the Thirty Years' War, mysticism flourished in literature, perhaps because it offered people an escape from harsh and uncertain times. Among the Catholics, Jakob Böhme's (1575–1624) *Aurora* set the trend for a plethora of mystic speculation and for moralizing about the vanity of earthly life. Angelus Silesius (1624–1677) and others produced a flood of spiritual poems filled with an almost sensuous passion for the Savior. The Jesuit Friedrich von Spee (1591–1635), in addition to writing playful pastorals and mystic love poems, also attacked the popular religious excesses of the time, particularly the burning of witches. The most active centers of this literary activity were Silesia, Königsberg, and Heidelberg. The Protestants also showed an inclination toward mysticism. Much of their energy was devoted to the composition of hymns. Paul Gerhardt (1607–1676) of Wittenberg, one of the most famous hymnists, produced more than a hundred religious songs, in which he combined a deep expression of faith in God with appreciation for popular joy in living.

The Protestants showed relatively little interest in religious art. But for the Catholics, the baroque period was extremely fruitful, particularly in architecture. Jesuits and Benedictines helped introduce the Italian baroque style, primarily in Austria and Bavaria. The Cathedral of Salzburg, constructed between 1614 and 1628 and designed by an Italian architect, became a model for other regions. From the south, the baroque style gradually spread to other areas of Germany. German baroque churches were lighter in structural form and their interiors more airy and bright than their Italian counterparts.

The social and political changes of the period and the increase of foreign influences are also reflected in the thought and letters of the times. The growth of the state produced new problems for scholars and writers. The emphasis on individualism popular during the Renaissance clashed with the seventeenth-century idea of political absolutism, which demanded that the individual be integrated into the state. Moreover, much Renaissance literature had been bourgeois in spirit. The temporary decline in the vitality of city life and the growing importance of courtly society changed the interests of writers. Aristocratic themes dominated much of the literature of the seventeenth century, and the style and language of the period reflected the artificiality of the atmosphere at the courts.

This trend was accompanied by a revival of humanism. Much of the force of the earlier Renaissance humanism had been sapped by involvement in the Lutheran controversy. The Germans now showed the interest in the classical motifs and forms that had captivated many European literatures a century earlier. One of the most important initiators in this field was the Silesian Martin Opitz (1597–1639), who in his *Treatise on German Poetry* attempted to set up new poetic rules for German poetry on the basis of Latin studies. The influential work of Opitz and his followers, however, led to much misuse and adulteration. Courtly writers, in imitation of Roman literature, produced a plethora of epigrams, pastorals, and allegories, most of which were shallow in content and overwrought in form. Dramatic literature in particular suffered at its very inception. Before the seventeenth century, Germany had produced almost no drama. Then troups of English players touring Germany in the time of Shakespeare awakened interest in this form of literature. But translations and adaptations of Seneca soon displaced Shakespeare. Preoccupation with form, bombastic expressions, and gory plots of adventure characterized most of the tragedies produced in seventeenth-century Germany. Despite their poor quality, they were received with enthusiasm at the many princely courts.

Opitz' emphasis on style was also important for the development of the German language. Luther's German translation of the Bible had furnished the beginnings of New High German, and had helped bridge the gap among the many spoken dialects. But a German literary language with its own forms was needed to permit the development of a unified modern German culture. In this area much was contributed by Opitz and his followers. Literary societies, modeled on those of the Italian Renaissance—the most famous in Weimar, Hamburg, and Nuremberg—were dedicated to the task of creating a German literary language and particularly to eradicating foreign words. The work of these societies spurred the development of German culture in other fields. In 1627, Heinrich Schütz (1585–1672) composed the first German opera, *Daphne,* based on a libretto written by Martin Opitz.

But the interest in purity of language and style soon degenerated. Poetasters who believed that writing was a craft and not an art preached and practiced mechanical versemaking. A Nuremberg school taught the writing of poetry in "six easy lessons." Similarly, the mania for purification of the German language became absurd. Enthusiasts, for example, even sought to ban the German word *Nase* (nose) as a "foreign" derivation from Latin, and to replace it with *Gesichtserker* (facial bay window). As a result, this movement to purify the German language became discredited, and foreign influences in all German culture increased even more in the second half of the seventeenth century.

Brandenburg-Prussia and Austria to 1740

POLITICAL CONDITIONS IN GERMANY

Foreign Entanglements of German Politics

The traditional division of a country's history into internal and foreign affairs is hardly applicable to the Empire after the peace treaties of 1648. Germany as a unit had almost no national political history. Rather, each of the many political territories within the Empire aspired to be a full-fledged state with a life of its own. The relations among them resembled the foreign relations of the big powers, while connections between some of these German states and other European powers were so close that one can hardly term such relations "foreign." One merely needs to recall the German princes who during this period acquired foreign thrones without abandoning their German possessions, or to contemplate the legal or family ties that bound other territories to foreign powers. In 1654, the Palatine duke of Zweibrücken became king of Sweden; three decades later, the duke of Saxony assumed the crown of Poland; and in 1714, the duke of Hanover ascended the throne of England. As a result, close ties were established between parts of the Palatinate and Sweden, between Saxony and Poland, and between Hanover and England. Moreover, Pomerania and Bremen belonged to Sweden; Oldenburg became Danish; and the duke of Brandenburg was a vassal of the king of Poland.

If, in addition, we recall that the king of France was the legal guarantor of the so-called German "constitution," that the kings of Sweden, Denmark, and France were members of the imperial diet, and that every German prince was by law entitled to conclude alliances with foreign powers, it becomes obvious that the development of the German states was intricately interwoven with the fate of their more powerful neighbors. This involvement with foreign powers was particularly noticeable in the relations between France and the Hapsburgs. During the entire age of Louis XIV (1643–1715), rivalry between France and the Austrian Hapsburgs kept the German states in an almost continuous turmoil.

Final Emergence of Particularistic States

There existed at the time over three hundred quasi-sovereign territories—electorates, duchies, counties, bishoprics, abbacies, principalities, free cities, and other political units. Most of these states were minuscule in size and importance, so small in fact that it has been facetiously said that, when going for a walk, the ruling princes had to be careful not to step outside the boundaries of their "empires." In addition to these quasi-sovereign units, there existed some fourteen hundred tiny "immediate" territories, which lay under the "immediate" jurisdiction of the emperor and had no right to engage in independent foreign policy. In terms of power over their subjects, however, the rulers of these "immediate" lands were as unrestricted as the princes of the larger states.

Whether large or small, almost all the states experienced during this period the same trend toward political absolutism that was realized in France under Louis XIV. Basing their positions on Roman law, which stressed the omnipotence of the territorial lord; applying the new theories on internal sovereignty elaborated by political scientists, such as Jean Bodin; or simply copying the system practiced by Louis XIV, the Sun King of France, the German rulers attempted to make themselves absolute lords of their land. They recognized responsibility for their actions to no one, unless it be to God. They objected to any limitations of their political activities by the estates of the land, by a parliament, or by a constitution. The much-vaunted *raison d'état,* the view that the requirements of the state should be supreme, elaborated by Machiavelli in the preceding century, became their sole guide in political actions.

In order to achieve such absolutism, which often resulted in petty tyranny, the rulers had to destroy or at least weaken the remaining powers of the estates, particularly the latter's traditional right of approving the collection of revenue. In some cases this was a difficult undertaking, but the princes won in almost all parts of Germany. Since in most principalities the peasants were not even represented in the estates, they presented few obstacles to the designs of the rulers. Servile tenure was ruthlessly enforced by most landlords, and except during a few peasant uprisings, the voices of these people carried little political weight. The bourgeois, for their part, once so vocal in their insistence on rights of self-administration, had lost much of their economic power, and in the long run proved incapable of resisting the centralizing drive of the little monarchs. The aristocracy, on the other hand, was absorbed into the system. It is interesting to note that the absolutism of Richelieu and Louis XIV was based on opposition to the upper nobility; that in fact French absolutism could be established only after these nobles had been crushed in the middle of the seventeenth century. In Germany, however, the upper nobility did not lose its political power and influence as had the French nobility. With so many states and rulers needing advisers at their court, generals for their armies, and administrators for innumerable subterritories, the nobility could work hand in hand with the rulers. The resultant continuing strength of the German aristocracy—in contrast to that of France, where it rapidly declined into a parasitical, impoverished class—was of great importance for the later development of Germany.

Despite variations among the states, the establishment of absolute rule followed similar patterns throughout Germany. Not merely Brandenburg and Bavaria, but also the smaller states learned from the experiences of the Thirty Years' War and, in imitation of France, organized their own standing armies. Although recruitment of the rank and file was still largely left to junior officers, the rulers insisted on the right to make appointments to the higher ranks themselves, to demand the personal allegiance of the general officers, and to supervise the conduct and employment of these armies. Since these troops were available also in time of peace, the army served not merely for fighting wars or for strengthening demands of foreign policy. On the contrary, its size, except in the case of Brandenburg and a few others, was so small that it could hardly be a weighty factor in foreign affairs. The purpose of the troops was, rather, to support the power of the ruler at home, to aid in the collection of revenue, and to act as a police force.

A second step undertaken by most of the princes was the establishment of a civil service. In some states, the new administrative system was elaborated to a high degree of efficiency and became a powerful bulwark of absolutism. In most, however, it was a patchwork riddled with favoritism and corruption. Its function everywhere was to aid in the collection of revenue, the supervision of territorial justice, the control of tolls and tariffs, and the enforcement of commercial policies.

In essence all these methods aimed at bringing financial independence to the rulers. The income from their own domains could not suffice to support the elaborate state machinery. New and regular sources of revenue, based on the productivity and wealth of the entire state, had to be found. As will be seen in the history of Brandenburg, this was a period of constant experimentation with methods of taxation, adapted from French and Dutch models. Yet hardly a single ruler was able to secure from his state the enormous revenues required. Consequently most of them were open to bribes and eager to receive foreign subsidies. A great number of German potentates, from the powerful dukes of Brandenburg and Bavaria to the obscurest count, balanced their yearly budgets with funds secured from Louis XIV or other neighboring rulers. These subsidies were naturally reflected in the foreign policies of such states, and their armies frequently acted as mercenary forces for France or other powers. Some princes eventually recognized the logical consequence of this system and made a lucrative business of selling the services of their soldiers to other nations.

The financial requirements of the rulers were aggravated by their pretentious way of life. Most of them indulged in ridiculous attempts at rivaling the splendor of Versailles. They built enormous castles, insisted on court ceremonies of ludicrous dimensions, and turned their lands into parks and hunting grounds. Everything French had to be imitated at any cost. Costumes, wigs, furniture, art academies, court jesters, princely favorites and ducal mistresses —all were copied on a scale bound to surpass the resources made available by even the most efficient collection system.

THE GROWTH OF BRANDENBURG-PRUSSIA

Among this multitude of states, particular attention must be devoted to the growth of Brandenburg-Prussia [1] and the development of its institutions. Seventeenth-century Germans probably considered Austria, Bavaria, Saxony, and perhaps others more powerful and more important than Brandenburg-Prussia, but here major attention must be devoted to Brandenburg-Prussia because it eventually became the most important German state and ultimately imposed on most of the others its own idea of national union. Such selectivity, though it may distort the significance of events in a given century, is adopted for the sake of providing a better understanding of later developments. It uses the advantages of historical hindsight without endorsing the once popular theory of most Prussian historians who spoke of the "destiny" of their dynasty, implying that the Hohenzollern rulers had been God's chosen instrument for the special mission of unifying Germany.

The Early Beginnings of Brandenburg

The history of Brandenburg had its vague origin when Charles the Great established fortifications against the Slavs along the Elbe River. During the next three centuries, the territory was expanded to the Oder and several bishoprics were founded; but the frequent splits in the inheritance and repeated uprisings by the conquered Slavs kept Brandenburg from growing into a powerful province. During the twelfth and thirteenth centuries, under the Ascanian dynasty, the Brandenburg rulers assumed the prerogatives of margraves; and conquests by such aggressive leaders as Albert the Bear increased the size and power of their state (see page 41). Settlers were imported from the west to populate the country, and many towns were founded. The city of Berlin, for example, dates back to 1240. Relatively important by the thirteenth and fourteenth centuries, Brandenburg's rulers became members of the electoral college when it gradually evolved in that era.

Upon extinction of the Ascanian line, the area passed from one imperial family to another—from the Bavarians to the Luxemburgers, and finally to the Bohemians—until Emperor Sigismund awarded it to the house of Hohenzollern in 1411. This dynasty had originated in Swabia. In 1227 the family had split, one line staying in Swabia, the other, the Franconian line, assuming control of the area around Nuremberg, Ansbach, and Bayreuth. The first Hohenzollern elector of Brandenburg (Frederick I) came from the Franconian line, and the connection between Brandenburg and the southern possessions of the family was maintained for many centuries.

During the fifteenth century, Brandenburg continued to grow through conquests, purchases, and profitable marriages. The Hohenzollerns (in the so-called dynastic disposition of Albert

[1] Before 1618, Brandenburg and East Prussia were separate states. Between 1618 and 1660, the term "Brandenburg-Prussia" is used to label the two territories, which were then under the same ruler. After 1660, the term "Prussia" designates both states.

Achilles, 1473) were one of the first princely houses to enforce primogeniture to make sure Brandenburg would cease to be weakened through divided inheritances. In the following century, Brandenburg rose to the status of a first-class power within the Empire. The Hohenzollern family spread its influence in many directions. Albert, a brother of the elector (Joachim I), became the archbishop of Magdeburg and Mainz who played such an important role in the Lutheran controversy. Another Albert, from the Franconian line, became grand master of the Teutonic Knights. Through marriages and inheritance contracts, Brandenburg gained possession of or expectancy to various territories that eventually gave it a dominant position in northern Germany—Pomerania, East Prussia, Jülich, parts of Silesia, and others. Moreover, the Hohenzollern electors learned that diplomatic bargaining and opportunism could enhance their power. Thus in opposition to its Saxon neighbor, Brandenburg remained staunchly Catholic and an ally of the emperor until 1539, when it turned Protestant to take advantage of the opportunity to secularize ecclesiastic properties.

The Union of Brandenburg and Prussia

The most important step in the growth of the Hohenzollern realm was the establishment of increasingly close connections between Brandenburg and East Prussia, which ultimately led to the merger of the two states. As mentioned before, the Teutonic Knights had lost the bulk of their Baltic possessions during the fifteenth century and retained only the eastern portion of Prussia, which the order continued to hold as a fief from the king of Poland. Shortly after Albert of Hohenzollern became grand master of the Teutonic Knights, he was converted to Lutheranism; he dissolved the order and secularized its lands, turning East Prussia into a family possession. The feudal rights of Poland were maintained, so that Albert, as duke of East Prussia, was theoretically a vassal to the Polish king. In 1539 the two branches of the Hohenzollern family took the first step toward working more closely together. The elector of Brandenburg, now also a Protestant, was awarded the rights of covassalage over East Prussia together with Albert of Hohenzollern. This right of covassalage was renewed for each successive elector. Then, late in the sixteenth century, the bonds between the two Hohenzollern branches were drawn even closer. The future elector of Brandenburg, John Sigismund (1608–1619), married the eldest daughter of the duke of East Prussia (Albert Frederick), who had no male heirs. This profitable marriage provided for the inheritance of East Prussia by the Brandenburg Hohenzollerns, and also served as the basis for their claims to the western territories (Cleves, Jülich, Mark, Berg, and Ravensberg) that were the object of the inheritance quarrel of 1609–1614 (see pages 148–149). Shortly before the outbreak of the Thirty Years' War, Brandenburg was successful on both counts. In the east, the elector inherited the Duchy of East Prussia; in the west, he obtained Cleves, Mark, and Ravensberg (see Chart 3).

The latent economic and political strength of Brandenburg-Prussia was greatly enhanced through these territorial additions of the early seventeenth century, but during the Thirty Years' War this potential could hardly be

Chart 3 GROWTH OF BRANDENBURG THROUGH INHERITANCES

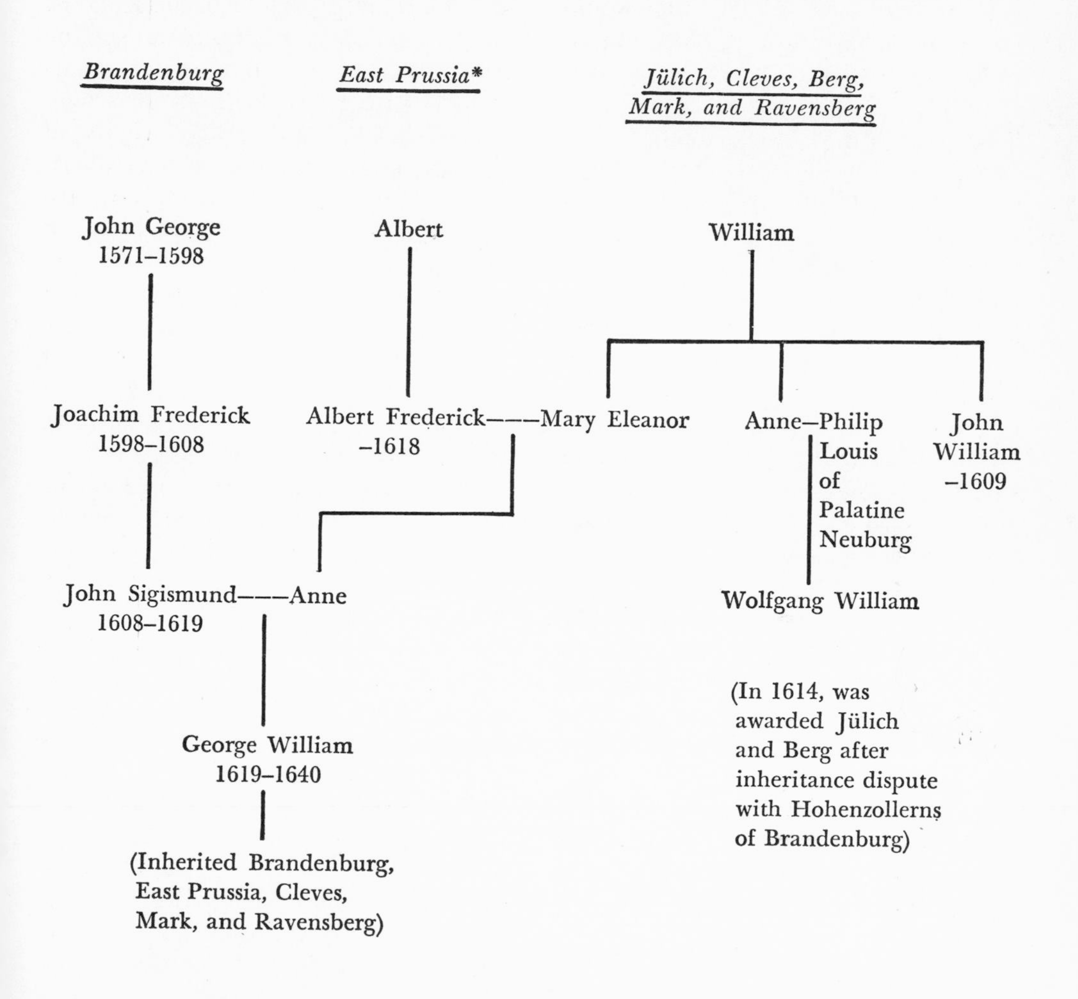

* Lands of the former Teutonic Order

realized. Brandenburg was drawn into the war against its will, and its lands were devastated by Swedish and imperial troops. Its incapable Elector George William was not respected by his own subjects nor by the other powers. In fact, by the 1630s, it seemed likely that his state would disintegrate under the impact of the war and of the internal friction between the estates and the upper nobles of the various territories. It was saved in 1640 largely by the accession of a new elector, the energetic and skillful Frederick William.

The Reign of Frederick William

THE ACCESSION OF THE GREAT ELECTOR Frederick William, who during his lifetime was given the sobriquet "The

Great Elector," was the first truly gifted ruler of the Hohenzollern dynasty. Without oversimplifying history by attributing too much importance to the actions of a single man, it must be conceded that Frederick William's work is the most important single factor in the creation of the basis for the powerful Brandenburg-Prussian state.

Frederick William was born in 1620. His education was completed in Holland, where he lived from 1634 to 1638 at the court of the stadholder, Frederick Henry of Orange. Here he studied military tactics, Dutch commercial policies, and diplomacy, and became acquainted with the daughter of his mentor, Louise Henrietta of Orange, whom he later married for personal as well as political reasons. Much of what he observed in Holland, with its staunch Protestantism mixed with occasional flashes of toleration, its wealth acquired through sea trade and the work of a diligent *bourgeoisie,* and its use of inland water transport, he put to use in his later years. Moreover the young prince despised his inept father, and hated his languid pro-imperial policy, as well as the venal advisers who carried so much influence at the electoral court.

When Frederick William began his reign in 1640, Swedish troops were occupying parts of Mark, Cleves was threatened by his opponents, the estates of his territories were in open rebellion or in clandestine alliance with foreign powers, and the Brandenburg mercenary armies obeyed the emperor or their own generals rather than the elector. The new elector faced a formidable task: he had to create order at home and rebuild the devastated economy of his country; he had to unify the territories under his own control if Brandenburg-Prussia were to rise above the level of the average German state; and he had to acquire the means for assuring peace for his land or, in case of war, for turning the military operations to his advantage.

On the whole he succeeded in these tasks with astonishing speed. Some of the means he employed have given him a reputation of unscrupulousness. Many historians are dismayed at his constant shift in alliances, whereby the ally of today often became the enemy of tomorrow—a policy so frequently imitated by his successors that it became almost a byword for Brandenburg-Prussian diplomacy. His behavior, however, was no more than the logical application of the theory of *raison d'état.* Brandenburg-Prussia's scattered position across northern Europe was its weakness as well as its strength. None of the other German states had so many powerful neighbors: France and Holland in the west, Denmark and Sweden in the north, Poland in the east, and the emperor to the southeast. Self-interest alone dictated that it was best to let the neighbors fight among themselves while Brandenburg-Prussia, shifted from one side to the other to obtain the best possible bargain. Frederick William became a master at this game.

He demonstrated this agility at the very beginning of his reign, when he managed to conclude a truce with Sweden in 1641 without, however, abandoning the emperor. In this way he could use the remaining war years to begin the internal reconstruction of his state and to acquire a small but well-disciplined army with which he could make his voice better heard at the peace conference. This policy was successful, for the Peace of Westphalia brought territorial accretions to the electorate: eastern Pomerania with the former bishopric of Kammin, Halberstadt near the Elbe, and Minden on the Weser, adjacent to Ravensberg. In addition, Brandenburg was awarded the expectancy of Magdeburg, which it finally obtained in 1680.

GEOPOLITICAL ASPECTS OF BRANDENBURG-PRUSSIA A glance at Map 12 reveals the obvious geopolitical factors that influenced the policies of Frederick William and his successors. The scattered location of his possessions demanded the acquisition of the intervening territories so as to unite the various pieces into a continuous state from the central Baltic to the Lower Rhine. Once this was accomplished, Brandenburg-Prussia would control all land routes from the north to central or southern Europe and could exert strong influence not merely on Germany but also on Scandinavia. Although unable to achieve this territorial unification, Frederick William sought to tie his lands together by other means. He instituted a reliable regular postal service and improved the roads needed for it. Passengers and mail could move in ten days from Cleves in the Rhineland to Königsberg in East Prussia. Besides helping to bring the people of his lands into closer communication and facilitating the control of the various local governments, the new postal service functioned as a steady source of revenue. The elector also ordered construction of the Frederick William Canal linking the Oder with the Spree, a tributary of the Elbe, an important connection that was to be the beginning of a wide system of canals eventually linking all the important rivers in Brandenburg-Prussia. The first canal was of great aid to Brandenburg trade and permitted the growth of Berlin, whose situation on the Spree now placed it in the center of the trade routes.

Its geographic position in Europe also determined Brandenburg-Prussia's foreign policy. Friendship with Holland was to protect the Rhenish possession of Cleves. Affinity between the two Protestant states should have made this easy, and Frederick William's marriage with Louise Henrietta of Orange was designed to cement good relations. In practice, however, the friendship was frequently disturbed by commercial rivalry and by the fact that Frederick William repeatedly sided with Holland's enemy, Louis XIV.

Relations with England were also determined by developments in northern Germany. The Great Elector coveted the former Welf lands between the Elbe and the Weser that separated Brandenburg from Ravensberg. These lands were a patchwork of disjointed political units, but Frederick William did not yet possess the required strength to acquire any of them. By the end of the century, the situation had changed. The major share of this territory was then united under the skillful control of the duke of Brunswick and turned into the Electorate of Hanover, for which a ninth electoral seat was created in 1692. At the same time, the duke of Hanover's marriage to the granddaughter of James I of England gave Hanover the expectation of succeeding to the English throne, a hope confirmed by the Act of Succession passed by the English Parliament in 1701. When George of Hanover became the king of England in 1714, the splintering of Brandenburg-Prussia seemed sealed by the existence of an

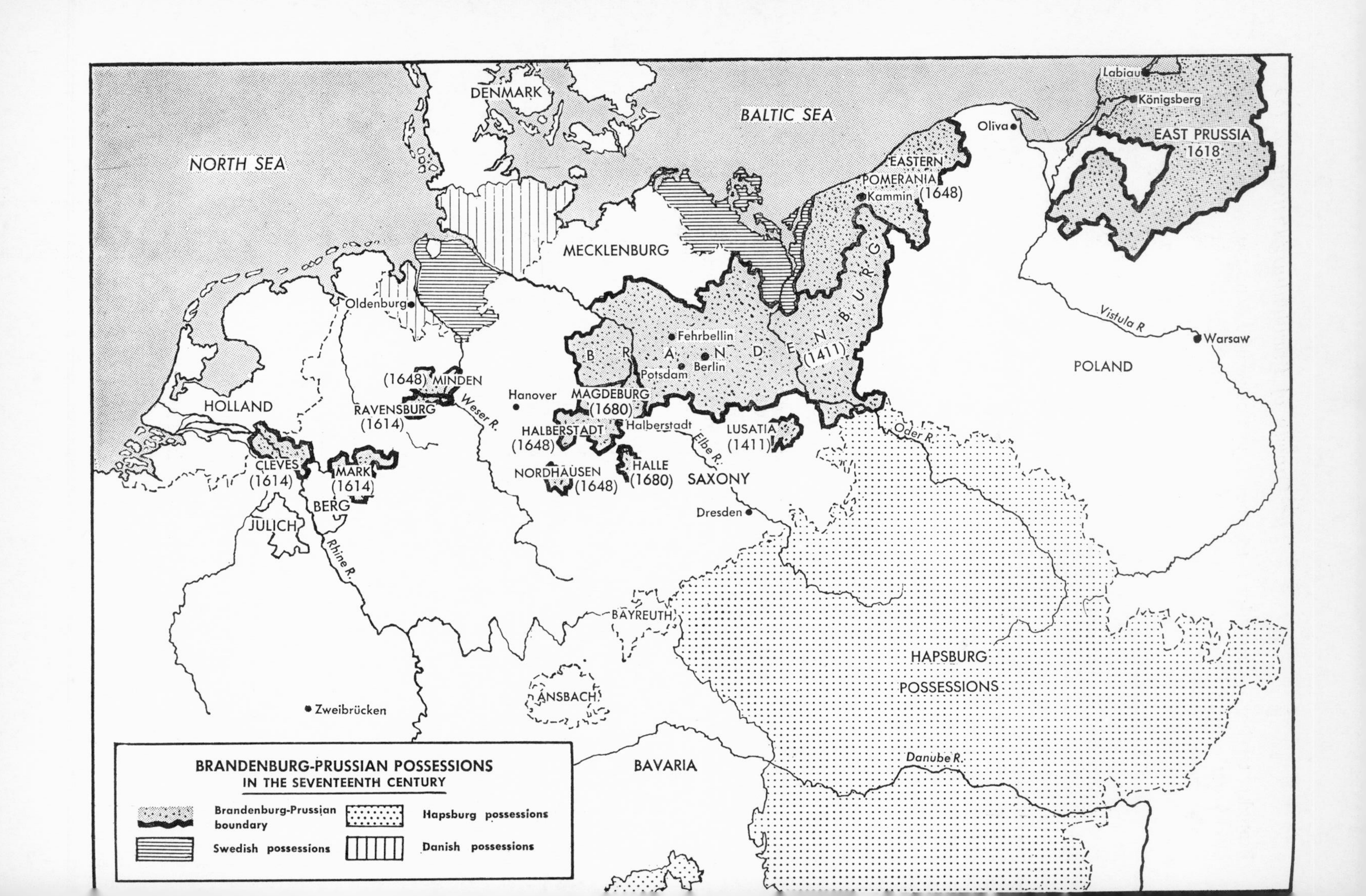

BRANDENBURG-PRUSSIAN POSSESSIONS
IN THE SEVENTEENTH CENTURY
Brandenburg-Prussian boundary
Hapsburg possessions
Swedish possessions
Danish possessions
NORTH SEA
DENMARK
BALTIC SEA
Labiau
Königsberg
Oliva
EAST PRUSSIA 1618
EASTERN POMERANIA
Kammin (1648)
MECKLENBURG
Oldenburg
BRANDENBURG
(1411)
Fehrbellin
Potsdam
Berlin
Vistula R.
Warsaw
POLAND
(1648) MINDEN
RAVENSBURG (1614)
Weser R.
Hanover
MAGDEBURG (1680)
HALBERSTADT (1648)
Halberstadt
LUSATIA (1411)
Oder R.
Elbe R.
HOLLAND
CLEVES (1614)
MARK (1614)
BERG
JULICH
NORDHAUSEN (1648)
HALLE (1680)
SAXONY
Dresden
Rhine R.
BAYREUTH
HAPSBURG POSSESSIONS
ANSBACH
Zweibrücken
BAVARIA
Danube R.

English Hanover in its midst. Brandenburg's only hope became friendship with England and the possibility of eventually inheriting the territory. This policy was reflected in the marriages of the three succeeding generations of Brandenburg-Prussian rulers after the Great Elector—Frederick I, Frederick William I, and Frederick II—to Hanoverian or Brunswick princesses.

Relations with Denmark, Sweden, and Poland were equally determined by territorial considerations. At the conclusion of the Thirty Years' War, Brandenburg had failed to obtain western Pomerania with its good harbors. Until this coastal strip would be annexed—a little over half of it was transferred to Brandenburg in 1720—friction between Sweden and Brandenburg was inevitable. As a result, Brandenburg fought four major wars against Sweden in the century following the treaties of Westphalia. Similarly, Brandenburg's determination to obtain a land bridge between Pomerania and East Prussia placed her in frequent conflict with Poland. Relations with Denmark were marred less by territorial claims than by economic considerations, since Denmark could block Brandenburg's outlets to the sea until the latter acquired the North Sea port of Emden in 1744.

INTERNAL REFORMS UNDER FREDERICK WILLIAM To create a strong and viable state, the Great Elector had to overcome the obstacles represented by the internal differences among his various territories. Prussia and Brandenburg were largely agricultural, grain-producing areas. As part of the "new Germany" east of the Elbe, which had been slowly conquered from the Slavs during the Middle Ages, these lands consisted mostly of large estates owned and administered by powerful nobles, called Junkers. The peasants in this region were generally poor and under complete domination of the aristocracy. Only in a few towns, particularly in Königsberg in East Prussia, did the middle class have any importance. The acquisitions in the west were different. To be sure, the local aristocracy also carried the dominant voice in the estates, but the more active economic life of the western towns gave greater power to the *bourgeoisie* and more social and economic opportunities to the peasant population. Cleves had an important cloth and silk industry, linen was produced in Ravensberg, and iron and steel were exported from Mark. In addition, both Cleves and Mark had important coal deposits that assumed vital importance in the succeeding period. To these social and economic differences must be added the divergence in religion. Brandenburg and East Prussia were more or less purely Protestant, whereas there was much Catholic strength in the western possessions.

Most of Frederick William's internal policies were devoted to the establishment of a governmental absolutism that would help fuse the different regions into a unified state. To accomplish this, he had to eliminate the governing powers of the local estates. The fight was long, and involved military force, arrests, and executions, as well as persuasion and concessions. On several occasions, the Prussian Junkers did not hesitate to request Polish help in their

MAP 12

fight against Hohenzollern centralization, while the bourgeois in the west tried to gain Dutch and French support in defense of their cherished privileges. The local estates also engaged in conspiracies and rebellions that the elector had to overcome through military intervention. In the end, Frederick William succeeded in depriving the estates in all his provinces of most of their essential powers, and thus laid the foundation for later Prussian absolutism.

It was significant for the future social and political configuration of the Brandenburg-Prussian state that the elector could not achieve his aim without granting concessions to the Junkers of Brandenburg and Prussia. They received reconfirmation of various political and economic rights that gave them added power and prestige, both as individuals and as a class. Their tax exemption was reaffirmed, and they were given other economic benefits—among them the right to export grains—and freedom from certain customs restrictions. Their police powers over their own estates were recognized anew. Most important of all, they were guaranteed increased manorial jurisdiction over the peasants. As a result, the servile status of the peasant became more firmly entrenched. Serfdom in Brandenburg-Prussia remained harsh and severe until its abolition in 1807—except on electoral lands, where it was gradually eliminated during the eighteenth century. These concessions also provided the Junkers the opportunity of increasing their landholdings, for they were given permission to confiscate any land that the peasants could not prove to be their own freehold, regardless of whether the nobles themselves could produce valid titles to it.

The chief purpose in reducing the power of the estates was to make the elector independent of their approval in financial questions. Frederick William's own court was maintained in relative austerity and his administrative habits were equally frugal. But the elector's own domain could not furnish sufficient revenue to establish a standing army and to finance an ever-expanding governmental machinery. Hence he decided to reform the tax structure of the state. The former direct head and land tax, the so-called war contribution paid only by peasants and *bourgeoisie,* was retained in places where he was not strong enough to alter it. But in most cities, particularly in the western provinces, he introduced a general indirect tax on consumption, the assize, in imitation of a similar tax in Holland. This tax affected the poorer classes more than the wealthy, but it could be collected more or less on a "pay-as-you-go" basis and soon brought substantial revenue. Of equal importance was that under the new system the task of assessing and collecting all taxes was removed from the estates and placed in the hands of special electoral tax agents working from a central office in Berlin.

To make the whole machinery of government more efficient, Frederick William organized new agencies and a civil service that, together with the army, ultimately became the backbone of Prussian government. The elector's privy council was enlarged and supervised the administration of the provinces. Specialization of tasks was introduced by the creation of two new departments; the general war commission, in charge of finances and the army; and the court chamber, in control of all the electoral domains. The staffs of these agencies, as well as their representatives in the field, were placed on a regular salary and imbued with the ideal of serving the state as a whole rather than local provincial interests. The important posts in this civil service were reserved for the nobility, usually the Junkers of Brandenburg or East Prussia.

Coordination of the provinces also involved less tangible policies than the creation of a centralized administration. Where possible, Frederick William tried to eliminate differences among the populations of the various areas. As noted earlier, his postal system and improved roads helped draw his subjects somewhat closer together. Equally important were his efforts to mix the populations by dispatching people from the east for military and administrative service in the west and vice versa. Also the religious differences between his eastern and western provinces forced the Calvinist elector to adopt religious toleration. Insistence on religious uniformity was his legal right, but it would have been political suicide, for Lutherans and Catholics would have looked to outside forces for protection of their religious interests. Consequently, toleration in religion was a political necessity, as the elector early realized. He urged Lutherans and Calvinists to halt their internecine quarrels and did not permit discrimination against Catholics. This policy was, of course, resented by various militantly pious groups. But although the second half of the seventeenth century was by no means an age of toleration, Frederick William's tolerant attitude was gradually accepted and became a general principle of later Hohenzollern rulers.

His power was based on the army. The small but reliable force he had organized immediately upon his accession to clear his lands of foreign troops and to carry more weight at the peace conferences in Westphalia was gradually increased from about two thousand to thirty thousand, a relatively large standing army in proportion to the population of his lands. To finance his army, he was forced initially to rely on contributions from the estates. His first major victory came in 1653, when the western estates decided to grant him the funds requested for military purposes on a six-year basis, eliminating the onerous yearly supervision. By the time the six-year period expired, the elector had found the way to circumvent his financial dependence on the estates, and the army increasingly became his own personal instrument of control, an indispensable tool for welding together the various territories of the state and imposing the military absolutism that would make the Hohenzollerns respected and all-powerful at home. The elector reserved for himself the right to form regiments and appoint officers, although the latter retained considerable power over the poorly paid and harshly disciplined peasants who served in the ranks. Moreover, the officers all belonged to the same Junker class that also dominated the civil service. This marriage of the Prussian aristocracy with army and civil service, both of which were increasingly imbued with loyalty to the Hohenzollern dynasty, proved to be of long-standing influence in Brandenburg-Prussian affairs.

To build his state and support his military machine, the Great Elector also developed economic resources. The examples of Colbert in France and of the Dutch *bourgeoisie* served as models, but it proved more difficult to introduce mercantilism in Brandenburg-Prussia than it had in France. The middle class was as yet rather weak, and manufacturing was unimportant except in the western provinces. There was a lack of capital as well as of labor, since the peasants were retained on the land through strict enforcement of serfdom. Still, Frederick William did his best to further the economy in a paternalistic fashion.

He imported Dutch peasants to introduce improved agricultural methods, particularly the use of better means of drainage and fertilization. He ordered the planting of potatoes, distributed seeds, gave money and material to rebuild villages destroyed by the war, and frequently used his army in time of peace to help with public works—land reclamation, road improvement, canal construction, or other projects of benefit to agriculture and commerce. The court chamber also tried to convert the electoral domains into model farms as examples for neighboring landlords and peasants.

Although Frederick William lacked the capital to sponsor state manufactories in the style of Colbert, he attempted to stimulate commercial activities and to stabilize trade. He concluded a monetary convention with some of the neighboring states, fixing the gold or silver content of coins in order to end the coin clipping prevalent during the Thirty Years' War and to rekindle confidence in coined specie. He also evinced a vital interest in overseas trade, despite the lack of good harbors in his provinces. The Great Elector had grand visions of Brandenburg-Prussia's capturing the trade of the Baltic and rivaling the English and Dutch on the high seas. He created an East Indies Trading Company in 1647, and in 1681 established a trading company for Africa. The company opened a trading station on the Gold Coast of West Africa—it was to be the initial step in a colonial empire that never got off the ground, and the station was finally sold to the Dutch in 1721. To support his merchant vessels, Frederick William had a number of warships built. His fleet never became very important, but served to elevate Brandenburg-Prussia in the eyes of the world as its flag suddenly appeared in various European waters. In 1680, his warships even defeated the Spanish navy off the Portuguese coast in an attempt to force Spain to pay a debt. Unable to collect the money, Frederick William then used his ships to capture Spanish galleons and bring them home as booty.

The various political and economic reforms of the Great Elector had far-reaching consequences. They charted the course for Brandenburg-Prussian policies for generations to come. The new army, the civil service, and the centralized administrative system helped the elector approach the position of an absolute monarch and raised the strength of the state in relation to its neighbors. It was to seem only logical to Frederick William's successors that they should follow a similar course to complete the unfinished tasks. As a result, Brandenburg-Prussia was launched on the path toward conservative rule and absolute monarchy at a time when Holland and England were moving in the direction of greater decentralization of government, more civil freedoms, and increasing emphasis on the political rights of the *bourgeoisie*.

THE ELECTOR'S FOREIGN POLICY Frederick William's reign was also a turning point in the foreign policy of Brandenburg-Prussia. It emerged from the Thirty Years' War as the leader of the German Protestant princes. Initially Frederick William tried to take advantage of this position by forming an ephemeral league of northern princes, ostensibly directed against a resumption of Hapsburg encroachment on the territorial rights of the princes. But his policy could hardly be exclusively anti-Hapsburg. He had to take into account the existing rivalry between Louis XIV and the Hapsburg emperors, and found he could best serve his own purposes by shifting judiciously from one side to the other. On the one hand, he cultivated friendly terms with the emperors and occasionally became their ally, professing a quasi-feudal respect that became a Hohenzollern tradition. This alignment also allowed him to pose as the defender of German soil against French encroachments—a mere pretext, wrongly interpreted by some historians as evidence of national feelings in the elector. On the other hand, he often sided with France. Brandenburg-Prussia's increase in power was rapidly turning it into a serious rival of the Hapsburgs within the Empire, and its position could best be enhanced through the political and financial backing of the Hapsburgs' strongest opponent, Louis XIV. Although he never fell into complete dependency on France, as did some of the Rhineland states, he maintained close relations with the court of Versailles during many years of his reign. In particular, he had come to realize that he needed France's acquiescence if he ever hoped to wring territorial concessions from its ally, Sweden.

It is typical of Frederick William's two-sided diplomacy that during the late 1650s he concluded a military alliance with Emperor Leopold I (1658–1705) and at the same time adhered to the Rhine League of Louis XIV, thus keeping his foot in both camps. This league, which lasted from 1658 to 1668, joined France, the electors of Mainz, Trier, and Cologne, the dukes of Bavaria and Brunswick, and many other German princes in a pact of mutual assistance and a "sincere union for the maintenance of the Peace of Westphalia." It was a skillful device of Louis XIV's to maintain the favorable *status quo* created in 1648 and to increase French influence, particularly in the Rhineland. It was, of course, directed especially against a revival of Hapsburg power.

THE FIRST NORTHERN WAR AND ACQUISITION OF SOVEREIGNTY In the First Northern War (1655–1660), Frederick William used skillful diplomatic shifts, punctuated with military intervention, to achieve advantages for his state. The war was caused by political and territorial disputes between Poland and Sweden. Upon the abdication of Queen Christina, her ambitious cousin (the Palatine count of Zweibrücken, Charles Gustavus) had become the king of Sweden as Charles X, and had resumed his uncle's plans for conquering parts of Poland and completing Swedish domination of the Baltic Sea. The king of Poland (John Casimir) for his part not only was prepared to defend Polish lands, but also claimed the crown of Sweden as a direct descendant of the Swedish royal house of Vasa.

The Great Elector was bound to be drawn into this war, since Prussia lay in the path of the Swedish armies. Moreover, as vassal to the king of Poland—a vassalship he had acquired together with the territory of East Prussia—he was obligated to aid his suzerain. At first he temporized, waiting to see who would be the stronger of the adversaries. His tentative offers to aid the Swedes in return for concessions were rebuffed by Charles X, who felt his own resources adequate to defeat Poland. Hence Frederick William made a protective alliance with Holland to assure himself of a fleet in case of necessity, increased his military strength, and awaited further developments.

Within a few months, the Swedes had defeated the Poles and began to invade East Prussia. After a few skirmishes, the elector realized that his troops were not yet strong enough to deal with the powerful Swedish forces, and he was forced to sign a humiliating treaty. Instead of Polish suzerainty, he had to accept vassalage to Sweden and to permit the Swedes to use Prussian ports and collect half of the revenue from these harbors.

Frederick William's first efforts had failed, but his luck soon turned. The Poles rose again and placed the Swedish armies in a dangerous position. Frederick William immediately offered to help Charles in return for better terms, and in a new treaty he received complete sovereignty over four Polish districts to be conquered in ensuing engagements. Vassalage to Sweden, however, was retained. Thereupon the combined Swedish-Brandenburg armies invaded Poland and defeated the Poles in the three-day battle of Warsaw. This time Frederick William's new army proved its mettle, and the battle started Prussia's reputation as a military power. It also enhanced the prestige of the Great Elector, who conducted his forces in person. The ideal of the soldier-statesman, so much admired by the subjects of the Hohenzollerns, henceforth colored the aura that surrounded the rulers of Brandenburg-Prussia.

But the battle of Warsaw did not end the war. The king of Poland rallied his forces and acquired allies. Russia was induced to attack the Swedes in Latvia as Polish armies advanced north. Frederick William seized the opportunity to raise his demands in exchange for continued cooperation with Sweden. In a new treaty (Labiau, November 1656), he was finally promised complete sovereignty in East Prussia on condition that he would stay in the fight against Poland and that he would not build warships for the Baltic.

In 1657, however, the conflict widened. The Austrian Hapsburgs were preparing to help Poland, and Denmark launched an attack on Sweden. The latter was forced to withdraw its troops from Poland in order to fight the Danes, and Frederick William found himself facing Poland alone. Deftly, he took the occasion not merely to desert his Swedish ally but to propose to Poland an alliance against Sweden. The king of Poland thereupon offered the Great Elector the same complete sovereignty in East Prussia he had been promised by Sweden, in return for evacuation of all occupied Polish lands. Not satisfied, Frederick William hoped to take advantage of Sweden's involvement against Denmark in order to conquer Swedish lands. In return for his vote for the election of Leopold as emperor, he received Hapsburg aid for his military campaign; soon a mixed army of Brandenburg, Hapsburg, Polish, and Danish soldiers, commanded by the Great Elector, was invading Swedish Pomerania and advancing in Denmark to attack the Swedish armies in the north. With the help of Dutch ships, he even hoped to conquer some Swedish islands.

It looked as if Frederick William would be successful in his maneuver.

But he suddenly realized that he had not considered the attitude of France. In 1659, Louis XIV at last ended the war with Spain started under Richelieu in 1635. France's victory allowed Louis XIV to devote more attention to German affairs. To permit a combination of Brandenburg and Hapsburg forces to defeat Sweden and possibly expel it from northern Germany was contrary to French interests. Such a result would upset the settlement of Westphalia and weaken the hold on the Empire exercised by the Franco-Swedish combination. Hence Louis XIV allied himself with England to save Sweden. He put pressure on Holland not to let its fleet be used against the Swedish islands, and mobilized an army along the Rhine to threaten Hapsburgs and Hohenzollerns alike. Under this pressure, and because Emperor Leopold was not ready to risk war with France on behalf of Brandenburg aggrandizement, Frederick William agreed to peace. The Treaty of Oliva, 1660, deprived Brandenburg of all conquests made during the war. Again the good harbors of western Pomerania were kept from Brandenburg, but the treaty did recognize the validity of the elector's agreement with Poland, in which he was granted full sovereignty over East Prussia.

It may seem strange that such feudal concepts of vassalage and sovereignty still remained important in an age of absolute monarchy and *raison d'état*. Meaningless as they seem today, they still possessed vast social and political significance, even though their legal obligations were rarely observed. The elector's acquisition of complete sovereignty in East Prussia, which lay outside the Empire, raised him above all other German princes except the emperor. In an age so conscious of rank and ceremony, Frederick William could now face the rulers of the world as an equal—just as in our own day the prince of Monaco receives the same official welcome as a head of state as does the president of France or the queen of England.

Since in Brandenburg and his western provinces, Frederick William remained technically a vassal to the emperor, whereas he was sovereign in East Prussia, the Great Elector began to emphasize the designation "Prussian" in all official matters. The Brandenburg postal service became the Prussian post; his army was called the Prussian army. *All* the lands under his control came gradually to be called Prussian. To distinguish the Hohenzollern lands as a whole from the original territory of the Teutonic Order, the latter was called East Prussia, the term "West Prussia" being reserved for the Polish lands between East Prussia and Pomerania.

PRUSSIA AND LOUIS XIV The era after the conclusion of the First Northern War was filled to a large extent with the wars of Louis XIV. These wars, which the Germans considered "predatory," were waged by France to gain land in the north and east and to make the Rhine the frontier. Although opponents and allies in these wars tended to shift, Louis XIV's natural enemies were Spain, Holland, and the Austrian Hapsburgs. To gain freedom of action, Louis again and again resorted effectively to diplomatic maneuvers. He tried to keep the Austrian Hapsburgs occupied in southeastern Europe by urging the Turks to push their attacks along the Danube Valley. Second, he attempted to keep the Empire immobilized by retaining certain princes in his pay, sowing disunity among others, and using his Swedish ally on occasion to divert their attention to the north.

During the first of these wars (the War of Devolution, 1667–1668)—in which Louis seized parts of the Spanish Netherlands he claimed as his wife's inheritance—the Empire stood idly by, and each German prince made his own deal with the French monarch. The Rhine League maintained its neutrality and then disintegrated in the wake of French successes in the Netherlands. Emperor Leopold, instead of supporting his Spanish relatives, made a secret agreement with France concerning an eventual division of the Spanish inheritance between Austria and France. The Great Elector was one of the few German princes to urge the establishment of an anti-French alliance—apparently not because he feared the consequence of French expansion toward the Rhine, but because Louis XIV was supporting a French candidate (the prince of Condé) for the Polish throne. A strong Poland tied to an even stronger France would have weakened Prussia's position immeasurably. Frederick William readily abandoned his anti-French designs and even signed an agreement with Louis XIV when the latter agreed to withdraw the French candidate for the throne of Poland. In the end, Louis concluded the war with Spain primarily because Holland and England threatened to intervene, since neither power wished to see France established along the estuaries of the Rhine.

Four years later, Louis XIV opened his second war (the Dutch War of 1672–1678)—aimed against Holland, which had prevented his acquisition of the entire Spanish Netherlands, and the Duchy of Lorraine, which partially blocked his advance to the Rhine. Careful diplomatic preparations preceded the attack on Holland. England, Sweden, Cologne, Münster, and Bavaria were made into allies; Hanover, Osnabrück, Mainz, Palatine-Neuburg, and even the emperor were bribed into benevolent neutrality; and the duke of Lorraine was expelled from his lands through military invasion. Frederick William alone spoke of defending the independence of German territories and offered to aid Holland with his armed assistance. He urged the emperor to declare war on France, but Leopold played a double role. Officially he organized against France a defensive league that included Denmark, Brunswick, and Hesse-Cassel; actually the emperor reaffirmed his secret pact of neutrality with Louis XIV.

As a result, the war opened with Holland and Prussia facing an overwhelming array of enemies. Holland was nearly defeated within the first year of operations, saved only by the decision to pierce the dikes so that large sections of inundated lands presented an impassable barrier to the French armies. Frederick William could not defend himself against the French, and withdrew from the war by concluding a separate peace with Louis XIV in 1673. France, however, did not halt its conquests. French troops continued their incursions along the Rhine and finally goaded the emperor into action. In alliance with Spain, Leopold declared war on France and soon persuaded most of the German princes to abandon France or their neutral position and come to the rescue of Lorraine and Holland. By 1674, the anti-French coalition had grown to large proportions; Frederick William decided to re-enter the war and join the alliance, after making a nonaggression pact with

Sweden and receiving the assurances of Holland, Spain, and the emperor that they would not make a separate peace. The war was waged furiously along the Rhine and in the Spanish Netherlands, with the French generally carrying most of the victories. In the following year, Sweden, as an ally of France, suddenly broke its pact with Prussia and began an invasion of Brandenburg. Frederick William immediately asked the German princes for aid. The response was characteristic of German disunity: Saxony declared its neutrality, and Bavaria and Hanover even offered Sweden armed support against Prussia.

Hence the Great Elector at first had to face Sweden without the support of allies. He withdrew his troops from the Rhine and rushed them to Brandenburg to meet the invading Swedes. At the battle of Fehrbellin, in 1675, he routed the Swedish armies. His success demonstrated the tremendous improvement in his military power since he had first faced the Swedish armies in 1655. During the next three years, Frederick William achieved almost uninterrupted success against the Swedes. He conquered most of Pomerania, and attacked Swedish possessions in Latvia. In these undertakings, he received the assistance of a few German princes who had finally declared war on Sweden, as well as support from the Dutch and Danish navies.

In 1678, when Frederick William had seemingly achieved his aim of obtaining the entire Pomeranian coast, his allies suddenly deserted him and concluded peace with France, despite their promise not to sign a separate peace. The emperor looked with suspicion upon the sudden increase in Prussian power and saw no reason for further support of the elector's ambitions. Thus Frederick again found himself alone. Louis XIV, freed from other commitments, immediately came to the aid of his Swedish ally. He dispatched an army across the Rhine and Weser to force the submission of Prussia. Realizing the futility of his position, Frederick William signed the Peace of St. Germain-en-Laye in 1679, by which he had to restore almost all of his conquests to Sweden.

For a second time, the Prussian ruler recognized the hopelessness of relying on imperial support, and the need for coming to terms with France as a prerequisite for changing the *status quo* in Germany. Consequently Frederick William effected a *rapprochement* with Louis XIV. He joined the many German rulers—Saxony, Bavaria, and others—who were already obtaining subsidies from France, in return for his promise to vote for a French candidate at the next imperial election, a promise he had no occasion to keep or break, since there were no more imperial elections during his lifetime.

Louis XIV now opened an era of peaceful expansion. With the aid of *chambres de réunion*, groups of lawyers who provided the legal grounds, he claimed all territories in the Rhineland, particularly in Alsace, that had ever been dependencies of lands France had acquired in the treaties of 1648 and 1679. Once the French courts decided which lands fell into this category, Louis's armies moved in to occupy them. In this manner, many small territories were seized, including the important areas of Strassburg, Trier, and Luxemburg, for which no "legal" claims were presented. The Empire was faced with a strange threat to its territorial integrity. Emperor Leopold became alarmed, and some of the more important German princes, among them those of Bavaria and Saxony, decided to cut their ties with France. Frederick William, however, still sulking over his diplomatic defeat, refused to join the Empire, which had abandoned him in 1678. Moreover, he was in dispute with the emperor over possessions in Silesia, which he had expected to inherit in 1675, but which the emperor had sequestered in favor of the Hapsburgs.

The intended war against France was delayed through Louis XIV's superior diplomatic maneuvers. He subsidized a gigantic Turkish offensive against the Hapsburgs, forcing Leopold to use his German allies not against France but against the Turks, who besieged Vienna in 1683 (see page 206). The danger of the Turkish threat forced Leopold and the imperial diet to agree in 1684 to conclude a twenty-year armistice with France, according to which Louis was allowed to retain all his "peaceful conquests" in the Rhineland, including the city of Strassburg, and had to restore only Luxemburg and Trier.

THE HUGUENOT ISSUE In the few remaining years of his reign, Frederick William changed sides once more. In 1685, Louis XIV revoked the Edict of Nantes, which his grandfather, Henry IV, had issued in 1598. With one stroke of the pen, Louis expected to eradicate Protestantism in France and enforce religious uniformity. Huguenot ministers were given fifteen days either to convert to Catholicism or to leave the country. The children of Protestant parents were to be raised in the Catholic faith. Emigration of lay Calvinists was prohibited. In spite of this prohibition, several hundred thousand Huguenots soon fled to Holland, England, Switzerland, and some of the German states.

The Great Elector particularly antagonized his French ally by issuing the Edict of Potsdam, in which he urged the Huguenots to leave France, invited them to settle in Prussia, and guaranteed them economic, social, and political advantages to help them get established. He even offered to help defray travel expenses, to lend them money for opening businesses, and to award them the rights of Prussian citizens. As a result, fifteen to twenty thousand Huguenots came to settle in cities of the Prussian electorate. The French colony in Berlin rapidly became influential in the cultural life of the city and remained important for centuries to come. Whether motivated by devotion to the Calvinist cause, by a desire to follow the example of Holland, or by purely economic self-interest, Frederick William's action proved highly beneficial to Prussia.

After this break with Louis XIV, Frederick William effected a *rapprochement* with the emperor which inaugurated a long period of better relations between Prussia and the Hapsburgs. A compromise was arranged in regard to the disputed territories in Silesia, and Frederick William at last agreed to help the emperor against the Turks and sent an army to fight in Hungary. Soon after, Louis XIV resumed his expansionist drive by claiming the Palatinate for a French prince. This time, however, there was more resistance to the French demands. Temporary successes in Hungary allowed the emperor to prepare for war against France; the major German states were ready to join him; Holland, England, Savoy, and Spain appeared willing to form a grand anti-French alliance. But Frederick William died in the spring of 1688, before Louis issued his declaration of war against the Empire. Hence the elector was spared the final decision of whether to fight with the Empire or with France, or to remain neutral. His main occupation during the last few weeks of his reign was to help the anti-French coalition in a completely different way. He assisted his nephew William of Orange of Holland in preparing the coup that a few months later resulted in the Glorious Revolution in England—the substitution of William and Mary for the Catholic James II. On the day of the elector's death, the password for the special guards at the palace was "London and Amsterdam."

The legacy of the Great Elector was of profound importance to the Hohenzollern dynasty, to Prussia, and to Germany as a whole. He had raised Prussia in power and prestige considerably above such other strong states as Bavaria and Saxony. He had implanted a certain sense of cohesion in the scattered parts of his electorate. After the gains of 1648, he had not succeeded in expanding Prussian territory, despite his skillful political and military maneuvers, but the acquisition of sovereignty alone was, in the long run, worth more than a few square miles of land. His zigzag diplomacy demonstrated to his successors how to further Prussian interests, regardless of the actions of the other princes or the fate of the Empire. His internal work of reconstruction and reorganization, perhaps his most important legacy, laid the foundation for the economic development that allowed Prussia in the eighteenth century to become one of the first powers of Europe. It also mapped the direction for the internal and external development of Prussia: military absolutism in conjunction with the Junker class, religious tolerance, and a vigorous foreign policy.

Elector Frederick III

The active, robust, and thrifty Great Elector was succeeded by his languid and pretentious son, Frederick III, who ruled Prussia from 1688 to 1713. The twentieth-century German emperor William II, in a biography of his ancestors, ranked Frederick as "one of the guiding spirits" of the house of Hohenzollern, "because he elevated Prussia to the status of a kingdom and created the basis for the Prussian officer corps." In reality, the new elector was a mediocre ruler. A baroque prince fascinated by ostentatious splendor and ceremonial magnificence, he was more interested in his glittering collection of jewels than in the daily tasks of administration. As was to happen frequently in subsequent Hohenzollern successions, he was in most respects the antithesis of his father.

His last years as crown prince had been complicated by troubled relations with his stepmother. After the death of his first wife, Frederick William had remarried, and his second wife (Dorothea of Holstein-Glücksburg), had tried to persuade him to bequeath the government of Prussia to their sons. In 1674 the elector's eldest son by his first marriage died, and the rumor spread at court that he had been poisoned. When, in 1687, the youngest son of the first marriage also died, the surviving Frederick fled from Berlin, ostensibly for fear of being murdered. Upon his father's death in the following year, it was revealed that, in spite of the law of primogeniture in effect among the Hohenzollerns since the fifteenth century, the Great Elector had divided his patrimony. Some territories had been awarded to the sons of the second marriage, although the major portion, including the electorship, had been bequeathed to Frederick. It is strange indeed that Frederick William, whose whole life had been dedicated to enhancing the position of his state, had agreed to satisfy his wife's demands. Frederick, however, did not feel bound to execute his father's testament and kept the entire inheritance himself.

In Frederick's reign of twenty-five years, Prussia saw only three years of peace, not because the king loved military adventure or expected significant advantages from the wars, but largely because he drifted along in the policies followed by his father at the end of his reign. Unlike the Great Elector, Frederick did not shift his course even when Prussian interests were at stake. In the Wars of the League of Augsburg (1688–1697) and the Spanish Succession (1701–1713), his troops were ranged at the side of the emperor against Louis XIV—and on several occasions, their victories enhanced the Prussian military reputation. At other times, the elector was temporarily at odds with the emperor and partially withdrew his armies. In essence, however, Frederick sacrificed much of his independence in foreign policy by becoming, as it were, the mercenary of the emperor, as well as of Holland and England, all of whom jointly paid for the upkeep of his army. During the first of the two gigantic wars, Frederick at least could claim that his troops were fighting in defense of Germany against the renewed incursions of Louis XIV. During the second war, however, no such reason existed. Who occupied the vacant throne of Spain was not of vital interest to Prussia. If it was of consequence at all, then a French prince would have been preferable to an Austrian Hapsburg, since a strengthened Hapsburg dynasty would reopen the whole question of predominance over Germany. Hence it might be argued that Frederick was fighting on the wrong side as far as Prussian interests were concerned.

During the first decade of his rule, Frederick enjoyed the services of an excellent adviser (Danckelmann), who kept the finances of the country in a semblance of order. After this minister was removed in 1697 as the result of court intrigues, the administration came into the hands of incompetent courtiers and embezzlers. Frederick's excessive spending was no longer held in check. Internal revenues and foreign subsidies did not suffice for both the war effort and the lavish court expenditures. An attempt was made to raise additional revenue by permanently leasing land from the electoral domain. Potentially such an operation might have procured additional revenue, provided employment for a greater number of peasants, and increased agricultural production. But Frederick's greedy administrators spoiled the project by demanding exorbitant initial payments—most of which they embezzled—thereby siphoning off the resources of lessees who would have developed the land. Consequently, the venture represented neither a successful effort at land reform nor a new source of revenue for the state. Lack of resources and the incompetency of his advisers may also explain why Frederick failed to seize the opportunity afforded by the Great Northern War (1700–1721) for acquiring the Swedish possessions along the Baltic. After Sweden had been defeated, and Russia, Poland, and Denmark were seizing Swedish lands, it would have been in Prussia's interest to have joined the coalition in order to acquire part of the booty. His father, Frederick William, would undoubtedly have quit the war in the west against Louis XIV and used his troops for this purpose. But Frederick was not an activist, nor was he quick in making decisions; hence he stood by while Poland and Sweden fought it out. It is conceivable, of course, that Frederick was simply motivated by jealousy of his neighbor, the elector of Saxony and king of Poland, and was loathe to fight on his side.

ORIGIN OF THE PRUSSIAN KINGDOM

One of Frederick's main achievements was his acquisition of a crown for Prussia. His love of pomp and display, his sensitivity to questions of rank and prestige imbued him with the burning desire to assume the title of "king." It is said that he was intensely annoyed at the prerogatives enjoyed at the peace conference of Ryswick in 1697 by his cousin, King William of England, who a few years before had been only stadholder of Holland. Moreover, his neighbor in Hanover was looking toward inheriting the crown of England; the crown prince of Bavaria—before his death in 1699—was heir presumptive to the throne of Spain; and the Saxon elector had become king of Poland in 1697. Frederick, who needed a crown if only to keep up with his neighbors, worked assiduously on the project. As a sovereign ruler, he could simply assume the royal title without consulting anyone; but if the other powers refused to recognize this action, Prussia would have lost face rather than gained prestige.

When the powers were on the brink of the War of the Spanish Succession, Frederick finally found a way of forcing the recalcitrant emperor into an agreement. Frederick offered to support the Hapsburg candidate to the Spanish throne with a contingent of 8000 troops, in return for a yearly payment of 100,000 thaler for upkeep of the troops and for the emperor's agreement to extend recognition to a Prussian kingship. After conclusion of this agreement, and to avoid any possible cancellation of it, Frederick made hurried preparations for holding the coronation before the outbreak of the war.

On January 18, 1701, he crowned himself in Königsberg and then placed a crown on his wife's head. Not wishing to appear subject to any ecclesiastical authority, he did not permit a clergyman to perform the act of coronation. Elector Frederick III thus became King Frederick I. Most states soon recognized his new dignity. Only the Vatican withheld recognition until 1787, since it had been not merely a Protestant, but also a lay coronation. As was true of the question of sovereignty, the royal dignity applied officially only in East Prussia, which lay outside imperial jurisdiction. In practice, however, the new king started to carry his title also in his other territories. His residence in Berlin became the "royal palace," his troops the "royal Prussian army."

Acquisition of the kingship produced no immediate, far-reaching political changes. It merely hastened the impending bankruptcy of the state, for Frederick I now squandered additional sums to add regal splendor to his court. In the long run, however, the newly won kingship no doubt was of advantage to the Hohenzollerns. There were no legal differences of any consequence between the sovereign powers of a duke and those of a king. But to his subjects, obeying the dictates of a king seemed to signify an infinitely greater honor than following those of a mere duke. Loyalty and devotion to the crown, particularly by the Junker class, were considerably enhanced through this increased prestige of the Prussian ruler.

Frederick's internal achievements were far less impressive than those of his father. He showed little interest in the army and did not lead it in the field. Still, some of his reforms further strengthened it as an instrument of power. In imitation of the practice initiated by Louis XIV in the 1670s, he provided uniforms for the various regiments, thereby improving the *esprit de corps* so vital to a modern army. He also reserved for himself the right to appoint and promote all officers, not merely those in the higher echelons, and thus tightened royal control over the Prussian armed forces.

FOSTERING OF CULTURE In the promotion of cultural activities he far overshadowed his father. The Great Elector had shown some interest in the advancement of education. He had established a Gymnasium (humanistic high school), a publishing house, and a state library in Berlin; he had founded a university at Duisburg in his Rhineland possession; and he had reinstituted the university of Frankfurt on the Oder; but he had allotted few funds for the cultural and educational life of his state. During his reign a few academicians, such as the political scientist Samuel Pufendorf (1632–1694), rose above the level of mediocrity, but on the whole, Brandenburg-Prussia had remained culturally unproductive.

Theological dogmatism, stultifying Latinity, bombastic drama, and slavish imitation of foreign models had characterized Prussian culture. Frederick I attempted to change this. It is impossible to ascertain whether he was truly interested in the arts and sciences, or whether his efforts were another aspect of his love of display and splendor. He spent enormous sums on beautifying his capital, importing architects, painters, sculptors, and landscape artists. He established an Academy of Arts in 1696, and four years later, upon the urging of the philosopher Gottfried Leibniz (1646–1716), who was then in the service of the duke of Hanover, he founded an Academy of Sciences in Berlin, of which Leibniz became the first president. The two academies proved of less importance than the University of Halle, which he founded in 1694. It rapidly assumed wide importance in the fields of theology, philosophy, and law, and gradually became a center for the emancipation of German culture from foreign influence. There the theologian August Hermann Francke (1663–1727) led a strong pietistic movement that was to free Protestantism from theological pedantry and invigorate it with a revived sense of personal dedication. The lawyer Christian Thomasius (1655–1728), who shocked his contemporaries by lecturing at the university in German instead of in the customary Latin, pointed the way toward the approaching Enlightenment by attempting to apply natural law to all facets of society and by fighting all remaining forms of superstitions, in particular the burning of witches.

Prussia under Frederick William I

In 1713 King Frederick I was followed on the Prussian throne by his son, Frederick William I (1713–1740). Pomp and splendor now gave way to austerity, and Prussia was turned into a bleak garrison. In contrast to his father, the new king was parsimonious in all matters except expenditures for his army. A hard worker and a difficult taskmaster, he tried to supervise personally every step of governmental operations. Personally pious in a rather prosaic way, he abhorred sentimentality on the one hand and the increasingly popular rationalism of the philosophers on the other.

The bleakness of his character has perhaps sometimes been exaggerated and its importance overstressed. Yet this "garrison king" came to symbolize Prussia in the eyes of many a subject as well as countless foreigners, and his character set the tone for certain strata of Prussian society for generations to come. Frederick William was a militarist in his public as well as his private life. He was rigid and strict as husband, father, and ruler, always ruthlessly conscious of his duties as well as his prerogatives. He believed in the value of Spartan discipline, and thought that even the love of his subjects for their ruler could be obtained on command. His sense of justice was severe, and he insisted on the same treatment for civilians and military alike. He had no intellectual or cultural interests, and made fun of esthetic pleasures. His chief delight and recreation consisted in observing and conducting parade drills, and in spending hours in his *Tabakskollegium* (tobacco den), smoking Dutch pipes, consuming pailfuls of beer, exchanging garrison jokes, and watching the antics of his court jester, whom he called the "president of his academy of sciences."

In its foreign policy King Frederick William's reign of twenty-seven years was rather colorless. His gruff manner and blunt ideas of order and discipline hardly fitted him to deal with delicate intrigues, and he was worsted in most diplomatic encounters. In internal affairs, however, to which he devoted most of his efforts and administrative talents, his achievements were of far-reaching consequence.

INTERNAL REORGANIZATION In the course of his reign, Frederick William undertook the gradual reorganization of the Prussian government at all levels in order to provide greater centralization and increased efficiency. He reshaped the central government, placing all separate agencies and offices under the control of one superministry, the General Directory, thereby eliminating overlapping jurisdictions and conflicting activities of the various departments. The General Directory supervised not only the central agencies for the administration of finances, army, and the royal domain, but also all provincial bodies. The local estates had by then lost almost all power, and Frederick William took the next step in centralization by depriving the cities of home rule by local patricians. District governors for the territories, *Landräte* (councilors) for the *Kreise* (administrative subdivisions, like counties), and *Steuerräte* (tax councilors) for the cities were directed from Berlin, and gradually exercised dominant supervision over all lands. The king also initiated judicial reforms to establish common legal practices and a single civil code for all Prussian territories, but this work was far from completed when he died in 1740.

Frederick William devoted much attention to the training of government officials and civil servants. Obedience and loyalty to the state were stressed, corruption was eliminated as far as possible, and each official was indoctrinated with the ideal of exclusive dedication to the duties of his post. The king inspected the activities of his staff in all echelons of government and severely punished even the most minute negligence. It is said that he became enraged when he found an improperly tied knot in the black and white ribbon used to bind office files together.

In the interest of the efficiency of his state machinery, the king also emphasized education. In 1717, Prussia became the first state to initiate compulsory elementary schooling. All children were to be taught the four R's, the fourth being religion, and many schools were opened throughout the land. In keeping with his military and administrative interests, the king endowed a faculty for military surgery and established chairs for the teaching of public finance, public administration, and police science.

Changes in financial administration brought a considerable increase in the resources of the central government. The lavishness of his father's court was replaced by strict austerity. All governmental expenditures, except for the army, were reduced. On the other hand, revenue was almost doubled, so that the royal treasury accumulated a sizable surplus. This was achieved partly through improvement of the system of taxation. Taxes were now made uniform throughout the country. The land, which furnished the "contribution," was divided into tax classifications on the basis of fertility of the soil. The assize, which had been started by the Great Elector, was paid by the middle class in all the cities. By means of strict supervision and severe punishments, graft and embezzlement were greatly reduced.

In the realm of economic administration, Frederick William espoused mercantilism to the extent permitted by the relatively poor resources of his state. He prohibited the import of manufactured items that could be produced inside Prussia, and stopped the export of raw materials, especially wool. In this way he hoped to promote local industries. Like his grandfather, he encouraged immigration, particularly of skilled craftsmen. Thousands of Germans from Swabia, Franconia, Saxony, Salzburg, and other districts flocked to Prussia at the king's invitation—Protestants escaping local discrimination or persecution, malcontents looking for new opportunities, or peasants searching for land. Underpopulated Prussia absorbed them easily and increased its labor resources. The king also built villages, gave subsidies to new manufactories, and tried to augment productivity by reducing the restrictive powers of the guilds.

Frederick William's most ardent and persistent efforts were spent on his army. From his father he inherited a well-trained and experienced standing army of somewhat fewer than 40,000 men. He used this army only once: during the first years of his reign, in the Great Northern War. Thereafter he spent some twenty years increasing his regiments and perfecting their training, afraid to enter another war, as it has been facetiously said, for fear of losing one of his beloved parade-ground grenadiers. By the time of his death, the troops had been more than doubled in strength, to a total of about 83,000 men, giving Prussia the fourth largest army in Europe. About two thirds of Prussia's budget was allocated for military purposes. To recruit such a large force, the king introduced in 1733 a new regulation that might be considered a first step toward general compulsory service. Prussia was divided into military cantons, each obligated to furnish a required number of soldiers from among its peasants and artisans. To obtain the needed officers from the aristocracy, the king insisted that it was the duty of at least one son of every noble family to serve as an officer in the Prussian army. In addition, royal Prussian agents roamed foreign lands, buying or enlisting new recruits. Foreign recruitment was particularly used to fill the ranks of the famous Potsdam Guard of grenadiers, composed of the tallest men the king could find in Europe. Frederick William attended personally to details of discipline, training, and armament. Exactness in military drill—soon to be called the Prussian drill—the handling of the new bayonet, improved techniques in muzzle-loading, and above all the enforcement of prompt and unquestioning obedience, all received his personal attention. Even though the army lacked experience in actual combat, it became remarkably efficient and enabled the king's son, Frederick the Great, to astonish Europe with his military exploits and turn Prussia into a first-rank European power.

The results of Frederick's reforms were memorable. At a time when France was being corroded by favoritism and inefficiency in government and was nearing financial chaos, Frederick William built an efficient, uncorrupted state with strong financial resources. The tensions in France that led to the great revolution at the end of the century were not permitted to exist in the Prussia of Frederick William I. Nobility and monarchy cooperated in close harmony, while loyal civil servants —unimaginative, incorruptible, hard working and efficient—built the state into an instrument of power too strong to be toppled by discontent among certain segments of the population. His son, Frederick the Great, was to bring Prussia more glory and infinitely more territorial aggrandizement, but the credit, for better or worse, for completing the foundations of the Prussian military state belongs to Frederick William I.

PRUSSIAN GAINS FROM THE GREAT NORTHERN WAR Frederick William I's one major success in foreign affairs was derived from the last years of the Great Northern War (1700–1721). By the time of his accession, Sweden's strength had been undermined through its defeat by the Russians (at Poltava in 1709). The Swedish king himself, Charles XII, was a refugee in Turkey. The Saxon elector had regained most of Poland and reassumed the Polish kingship after expelling the Swedish protégé (Stanislas Leszczynski) who had temporarily ruled Poland. Russian, Polish and Danish armies had seized most of the Swedish lands to the east and south of the Baltic. King Frederick I had for a moment contemplated joining the anti-Swedish coalition after Sweden's defeat in 1709. But under imperial pressure he had remained on the sidelines and had not interfered even when Russian and Polish forces crossed Brandenburg territory to reach Swedish Pomerania. The anti-French coalition of the War of the Spanish Succession, particularly Holland, England, and the emperor, were eager to avoid a possible intermingling of the two wars—the one in the north against

Sweden, and the other in the west and south against France—so as not to divert Prussian troops and resources to the north. The pliable Frederick had complied with their wishes.

Frederick William I, however, changed this policy. Less than two months after his accession, the War of the Spanish Succession ended with the peace treaties of Utrecht (1713). From the twelve years of fighting against France, Prussia received only minor acquisitions, most of them in the Rhineland. Some of these gains were actually exchanges for territories in Burgundy and elsewhere, to which Prussia renounced its claims. Conclusion of peace allowed Frederick William to bring back his armies from the French front for use against Sweden. He promptly effected a *rapprochement* with Tsar Peter the Great, and signed a treaty by which the Russians ceded to Prussia the occupation rights to Stettin and those portions of western Pomerania that they had seized from the Swedes, in return for a payment of 400,000 thaler—the estimated cost of the Russian war effort in this region. Frederick William was happy to see the Russian armies depart and proud to have acquired this valuable coast line without having fired a shot.

The following year, however, Charles XII reappeared on the scene, rallied a small army, and reopened the fighting by attacking the Prussians in Pomerania. Prussia, Denmark, and Hanover agreed on coordinated offensives and on a postwar division of Sweden's continental possessions. Charles XII was unable to withstand the attack. In 1715 Frederick William conquered the island of Rügen and the fortified city of Stralsund. Wismar, a Swedish enclave in Mecklenburg, fell the following year. In 1718, the Swedish king was killed in battle in Norway. The death of the adventure-loving conqueror considerably slackened the Swedish war effort. On the other hand, England-Hanover, Poland-Saxony, and the emperor were urging a termination of hostilities. The balance of power would be upset if Sweden were crippled beyond repair or if Prussia gained too much strength.

Consequently, military action ceased and peace negotiations were started. Hanover and Sweden signed a treaty in 1719, by which Hanover received the territories of Bremen and Verden—which Sweden had acquired in 1648—in return for a payment of one million thaler. The following year, the Peace of Stockholm awarded to Prussia the city of Stettin, some islands (Usedom and Wollin), and the part of Pomerania lying between the rivers Oder and Peene. In return, Prussia had to restore to the Swedes Stralsund and Wismar, and to pay them two million thaler. Finally in 1721, Peter the Great also concluded peace. He returned Finland to Sweden, but was allowed to retain a part of Karelia, and all of Ingermanland, Estonia, and Latvia, for which he paid Sweden two million thaler.

The results of these treaties were of considerable consequence to Germany. They amounted to a forced sale of the Swedish overseas empire. The century-long Swedish domination in the Baltic was broken, and Sweden descended to the rank of a second-rate power. Despite its retention of a seat in the imperial diet and a few square miles of territory in Germany—it lost Stralsund in 1815 and Wismar in 1903—its powerful influence in northern Germany was ended. Only

Poland-Saxony received no particular benefits from the war; rather, the war represented a substantial loss. A peace treaty between Poland and Sweden was not actually concluded until 1729, when the Saxon elector was again officially recognized as king of Poland.

The remaining four powers that had fought against Sweden were all strengthened as a result of the war. Denmark received territorial benefits in Holstein as well as commercial privileges in Germany. Its main gain was, of course, the decline of Sweden, which relatively enhanced Denmark's own power in the Baltic. Hanover's territorial gains gave it a considerable increase in strength, and the addition of new harbors provided better contacts with England. In fact, Hanover emerged as a potential rival to Prussia for the domination of northern Germany. Prussia itself had at last partially acquired what the Great Elector had worked for so assiduously: good ports in western Pomerania that would allow it to become a strong force in the Baltic and to participate to a greater degree in sea trade. This achievement, however, was somewhat offset by Russia's emergence from this war with the greatest gains. Before 1700, Russia had been an eastern nation. Its political influence had been felt in Poland, in Turkey, and sometimes in Sweden, but had made hardly a ripple in the diplomatic fabric of central and western Europe. Peter the Great and the Great Northern War changed all this. Russia emerged more or less as the dominant power in the Baltic. Russian armies had fought on German soil and hereafter were to be seen in central or western Europe during every major conflict of the eighteenth century (1733–1735, 1740–1748, 1756–1763, and 1795–1815). The cabinets of central and western Europe henceforth had to take into consideration the political and military capabilities of this gigantic power. Prussia and Austria were most affected by this new development, especially because the gradual decline of Poland during this period weakened the buffer that separated Russia from these two states.

FREDERICK WILLIAM'S BLAND FOREIGN POLICY After this success in the Great Northern War, Frederick William's conduct of foreign affairs was characterized largely by inactivity. Until the death of Peter the Great in 1725, he relied to some extent on friendship with Russia to achieve a stronger position in Germany. He also tried on several occasions to revert to the policy of the Great Elector by establishing a *rapprochement* with France. But primarily he maintained friendly relations with the emperor, placing himself at times into almost servile submission to the imperial interests. His main hope was to assure for Prussia the inheritance of the duchies of Jülich and Berg, two vital territories near the Lower Rhine that Prussia had failed to obtain in 1614. To further this end, he negotiated with Austria, with England, and with France; yet each one of these arrangements failed to bring the desired guarantees.

His lack of resolution in foreign affairs also made him reject any serious attempt to seek advantages for Prussia from the War of the Polish Succession (1733–1735). In this war, France, aided by Spain and Sardinia, tried to reestablish Louis XV's father-in-law (Stanislas Leszczynski) on the throne of Poland. In opposition, Saxony, Austria, and Russia supported the son of the deceased king, the new elector of Saxony. France tried to induce Frederick William to support its candidate in return for the acquisition of West Prussia, the Polish lands lying between East Prussia and Pomerania. Despite the danger of fighting Russia and Austria, Frederick William might well have considered the proposal, since the annexation of West Prussia would have been invaluable for his state, and since it was hardly to his advantage to see another Saxon on the Polish throne. Instead, he practiced his customary "loyalty" to the emperor and sent 10,000 troops—hardly used in the battles—to the Rhineland to help the emperor against France. Its role in this war was so unimportant that Prussia was not even represented at the peace conference nor mentioned in the Treaty of Vienna (1735), which terminated hostilities.

AUSTRIA AFTER 1648

Although in the long run Brandenburg-Prussia's influence on German development was to be paramount, Hapsburg Austria, with its dependent lands, was unquestionably the strongest German state in the period 1648–1740.

To be sure, the Thirty Years' War and the treaties of 1648 had weakened the emperor's position in the Empire, and the decline of Spain, which had provided the Austrians with strong backing for over a century, deprived the emperor of valuable support in the rivalry with France. On the other hand, Austria emerged from the war strengthened in many respects. Except for parts of Bohemia and much of Silesia, Austria's lands had not suffered much devastation, and its population was less reduced than that of most of central and northern Germany. Furthermore, economic recovery in the damaged areas was relatively rapid. The reduction of the emperor's power in the Empire, although a blow to his dignity and prerogatives, may be regarded as a blessing for Austria. Less entangled in imperial affairs, the emperors henceforth devoted more energy and resources to the interests of their own state. The Hapsburgs' loss of most of their possessions in the Upper Rhineland through the Peace of Westphalia and the subsequent wars of Louis XIV produced similar results. The more they relinquished their scattered holdings and were pushed out of Germany, the greater became the compactness of their state and the more intense their preoccupation with Danubian affairs. Whether this development in fact lessened Austria's "German" character poses an unanswerable question (see pages 5–10). Finally, in the century after the Thirty Years' War, Austria also derived strength from its considerable religious cohesion. The hereditary lands of Austria had been exempted from the religious provisions of 1648. This permitted the emperors, in conjunction with the Church and the Society of Jesus, to eliminate Protestant roots wherever possible. As a result the power of emperor and Church was measurably increased in most parts of the hereditary lands, with the notable exception of Hungary.

Attempts to Weld Austria into a "State"

The attempt to transform the dynastic holdings of the Hapsburgs into a unified modern state was initiated by Emperor Leopold I, the son of Ferdinand III. Only moderately capable in political matters, Leopold was confronted by internal and foreign problems that would have taxed even a better ruler's abilities. He did not have much power in Germany, and his attitude toward the princes of the Empire was particularly irresolute. In many respects, he would have been content to work in his own realm and to let the German princes drift wherever they wanted. But foreign affairs did not permit such a policy. Leopold was constantly forced to accommodate the more powerful German princes to obtain their help in his frequent wars against Turkey and France.

The Hapsburg lands included many ethnic groups, each with different local customs and political backgrounds. To weld these varied subjects into a state, Leopold thought he could adopt the absolutist structure of government practiced by most European monarchs of the time. But absolutism of the Prussian or French type could not readily be applied to Austria. The emperor and his successors succeeded in turning Vienna gradually into the real capital of the Hapsburg lands—the center of trade and communication and the source of major administrative power. But this centralization had to take into account the enormous differences among the territories that composed the Austrian "state." At best, it seemed, Austria could be transformed into a highly centralized "state of nationalities," in which the German element from Austria proper would dominate the local populations.[2] Moreover, the problem was complicated by the strong position of the nobility and by the status of the peasantry. It soon appeared that the nobles of the other territories, particularly in Hungary, insisted on retaining wide privileges in matters of local administration. At the same time the peasants in most of the territories remained in oppressive serfdom, except in parts of western Austria, where they enjoyed certain rights. Because of these conditions, a tacit agreement could be reached between the central government, supported by the Church, and the landed aristocrats of the different territories. The dominant interest of the nobility as well as of the Church, itself a holder of vast landed properties, was to guard their almost exclusive control of the land and to retain the use of serf labor. For this purpose the nobles required the aid of the government to put down periodic rebellions of the peasants.

Hence there arose among the landed aristocracy of the various regions—Austria, Bohemia, Hungary, and the others—a feeling of class solidarity that, cemented by the backing of the Church, became a unifying factor helping to hold the Austrian realm together. The powerful position of the nobility undermined the potential strength of the central government, for the absolutist desires of the Hapsburgs were thwarted by the need to placate the local nobility. This was particularly evident in the treatment of the various local diets or estates. Like most of the rulers of the time, Leopold tried to suppress their powers but could not eliminate them: the nobles in the estates presented too strong a resistance. Hence the estates had to be retained, although they were gradually turned into administrative bodies.

[2] The term "Austria" refers to both the German-speaking province around Vienna and the sum total of the Austrian Hapsburgs' possessions: the provinces of Austria, Tyrol, Styria, and Carinthia; the kingdoms of Hungary and Bohemia; and other properties.

In economic and financial matters, Leopold's efforts were much less successful than those of some contemporaries. The tax structure remained extremely haphazard, with infinite local variations. Revenue was not sufficient for Austria's costly wars, so that the state neared bankruptcy by the turn of the century. Mercantilism (the Austrian variation is called cameralism) was slow in coming to Austria. The *bourgeoisie,* on the whole, was weak. A few big merchant families derived their income from importing manufactured products and with well-placed bribes tried to keep the government from adopting the mercantilist principles of reducing imports. In consequence, the growth of local manufacture was relatively slow, whereas trade was kept at a high level. This was to the liking of the Austrian cameralists, who were more interested in increasing tax revenue from tolls, tariffs, and other trade assessments than in raising the productivity of the land.

Besides attempting to form a more unified state, Leopold was occupied by two major foreign questions: settling the Spanish succession and turning back the Turks. The latter was by far more important.

The Hungarian and Turkish Wars

Austria had inherited Hungary in 1526, but most of this inheritance had remained a mere claim. Only a small portion of Hungary along the eastern frontiers of Austria, Styria, and Carinthia had come under the control of the emperor, whereas the main central portion stayed under Turkish rule, and the eastern part (Siebenbürgen) was retained as a vassal state of the Ottoman Empire. Even control of the non-Turkish portions had not become very firm. The Hungarian nobles insisted that their kingship was elective, and forced each new emperor to reconfirm their local privileges before consenting to make him their king. If Austria wanted to compensate for its loss of territory and influence in the west by becoming a Balkan power, it had to overcome Hungarian resistance and break the power of the Ottoman Empire in the northern Balkans. Efforts to accomplish this occupied the late seventeenth and early eighteenth centuries.

The first Turkish war of this new series was in the 1660s (1663–1664). The Turks attempted to get complete control over eastern Hungary, but the Austrians interfered and defeated them, although this victory brought them no territorial gains. A more serious and longer war broke out in 1683. The Hungarian magnates in the mountains of northwestern Hungary, largely Protestant and nurtured by a fierce love of independence, rebelled against Jesuit attempts to enforce Catholicism and against political dictation from Vienna. They requested aid from the Turks, who responded readily. As allies of Louis XIV, they were expected at least to divert Hapsburg attention to the east whenever the French monarch was making a move from the west. The Turks promptly advanced with an overwhelming force of some 200,000 men, invaded Austria, and laid siege to Vienna. Emperor Leopold had to flee, since the small imperial army did not dare risk battle. With only a small defensive force, the city of Vienna resisted for three months. The king of Poland (John Sobieski), a traditional enemy of the Turks, and a few German states—primarily Bavaria and Saxony—finally responded to Leopold's plea for help, and dispatched an army which, together with the Austrians, inflicted a decisive defeat on the Turkish forces in the vicinity of Vienna (Battle of Kahlenberg).

The routing of the Turks opened Hungary for invasion by the western forces. For the next five years, all efforts were concentrated on its conquest. The Turkish war became popular in Germany; even Prussia sent troops, and many of the German princes assisted the emperor either by serving as generals or by dispatching contingents. This German solidarity against the Turks is surprising because the conquests could not benefit anyone but the Hapsburgs. Between 1683 and 1688, the combined forces of the Empire conquered Buda (the western portion of Budapest), subdued the Hungarian magnates who had rebelled against the emperor, and captured the city of Belgrade. An imperial diet held at Pressburg in 1687 even awarded the Hungarian crown to the Hapsburgs on a hereditary basis, thereby giving Vienna a stronger claim to the Hungarian lands. These military successes brought most of Hungary and the northern portion of what today is Yugoslavia under Hapsburg control.

At this point, however, the War of the League of Augsburg broke out in the west. The allied troops had to veer about and march to the Rhine. This allowed the Turks to recapture Belgrade in 1690 and begin a slow reconquest of the lost territories. They were successful until 1697, when Prince Eugene of Savoy (1663–1736) assumed command of the small Austrian forces which remained in the east. The young and energetic prince, who had initially offered his services to Louis XIV but had been rejected, had entered the Austrian army in 1683 and rapidly risen in rank. His decisive defeat of the Turks in 1697 established his reputation as one of the best and most popular generals of his time. This defeat and the end of the war in the west, which permitted troops again to be shifted to the Balkans, forced the Turks to agree to the Peace of Carlowitz (1699), a treaty which was extremely favorable to Austria. The Hapsburgs obtained parts of Slavonia with the city of Belgrade, Siebenbürgen, and Hungary except for the Banat of Temesvar (see Map 13). This peace treaty was the first step in allaying the Turkish danger. It strengthened Austria by laying the foundation for the development of the Austro-Hungarian monarchy.

The Spanish Succession of 1700

While these developments were going on in the southeast, the question of the Spanish succession occupied Austria in the west. In the mid-seventeenth century, it had seemed likely that King Philip IV would have no male heirs, when the unexpected birth of a son, Charles, delayed but did not close the issue. A sickly, fragile child not expected to survive long, Charles II surprised the world by living to be thirty-nine. He reigned from 1665 to 1700, but had no heirs. Consequently the European powers negotiated and debated for over three decades about the ultimate disposition of the vast Spanish Hapsburg possessions.

If inheritance through the female line was accepted as legal, there were three major heirs—France, Austria, and Bavaria—not counting Savoy, which

MAP 13

lacked the power to enforce any demands. England, Holland, and the German princes naturally looked warily upon all three possibilities. A merger of the Austrian and Spanish Hapsburg dynasties, which seemed the most likely solution in view of their constant intermarriages and traditional cooperation, would re-create the days of Charles V. It would threaten the independence of the German princes and once again encircle France. A union between France and Spain, on the other hand, might prove fatal to English and Dutch commercial and colonial interests, and would render Louis XIV so powerful as to place Germany in permanent dependence on its western neighbor. Possible inheritance of the Spanish lands by Bavaria appeared least ominous to the western powers. But the prospect of such an increase in Bavaria's strength was hardly to the taste of Austria and the German princes.

King Charles of Spain desired above all to maintain the integrity of his realm, and rejected the various projects designed by the powers to partition the Spanish inheritance. He appointed as sole heiress his younger sister (Margaret Theresa), the first wife of Emperor Leopold I (see Chart 4). When his sister died in 1673 without a male heir, Charles transferred the inheritance rights to her daughter by Leopold (Maria Antonia). This lodged the claim in the Bavarian house of Wittelsbach, for the new heiress was married to the elector of Bavaria. In 1692, when the new heiress died, the claim was once again shifted to the next generation. The crown prince of Bavaria (Joseph Ferdinand) became the official and sole heir, and was so designated in Charles II's testament of 1698. All appeared settled in a manner agreeable to England and Holland, but Austria and France refused to acquiesce. Emperor

Chart 4 THE SPANISH AND AUSTRIAN SUCCESSIONS AND THE WITTELSBACH CLAIMS

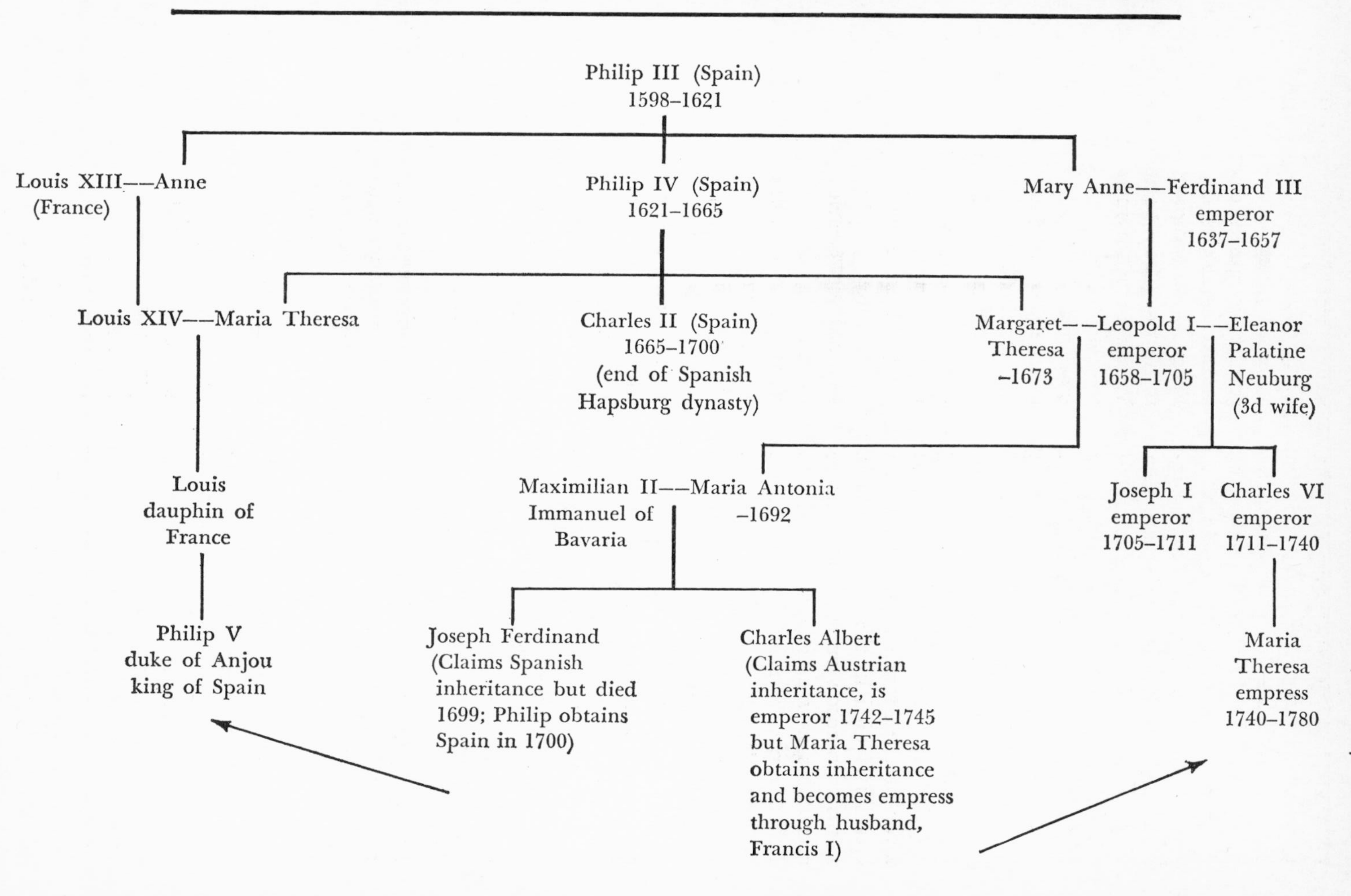

Leopold had never recognized the Bavarian claims. He insisted on the rights of Charles—his younger son by a third wife—as the great-grandson of King Philip III of Spain. Louis XIV, on the other hand, demanded the inheritance for his grandson Philip, who also could trace his lineage to the same King Philip of Spain. In 1699 the Bavarian crown prince suddenly died. Once again the question of the Spanish inheritance was opened. Louis XIV immediately interfered at the court of Madrid, and persuaded the dying Spanish king to issue a new will in favor of the French candidate. When Charles II died in the following year, Louis's grandson rushed to Spain to accept his new kingdom as Philip V. But the powers refused to acquiesce. Austria felt cheated of the inheritance. England and Holland feared a union of Spain and France, despite Louis XIV's promises to keep the two states separate. As a result, war broke out in 1701.

In this War of the Spanish Succession, Austria, the Empire, Holland, England, Portugal, and others formed a Grand Alliance to dispute Philip's rights in Spain. Philip, for his part, was supported by his grandfather, Louis XIV, by a few smaller states, and by the Wittelsbach electors of Bavaria and Cologne. Bavaria hoped to get some compensation for the loss of the inheritance—possibly the Spanish Netherlands as well as a royal title.

The war was fought in Spain, Italy, the Low Countries, and Germany. Prince Eugene proved not only a superior general, but also a highly successful statesman who did much to strengthen internal conditions in the Austrian lands. Despite a few French victories, Louis XIV was gradually defeated on all fronts. French predominance was waning, and starting in 1708, Louis tried repeatedly to obtain a termination of hostilities before his armies collapsed completely. In the end, several strokes of luck saved France from severe losses. A change of ministry (the Tories replaced the Whigs in 1710) made England eager to conclude peace. A change in the emperorship in 1711 made Austria's allies hesitant to continue the war.

Leopold I had died in 1705, and had been succeeded by his more active and energetic son Joseph I, who, however, ruled only a few years. When he died in 1711 without heirs, the electors of Germany chose as emperor his brother Charles VI (1711–1740), even though he was in Spain as claimant to the Spanish throne. Although now ruler of the Holy Roman Empire, Charles had no intention of relinquishing his claim to the Spanish throne. But his allies refused to condone such an inordinate increase in Hapsburg power. One by one they abandoned him, negotiated with Louis XIV, and finally concluded the Peace of Utrecht in 1713. Of the many clauses of the treaty, only a few need be mentioned. Philip V was recognized as king of Spain, but his possessions were limited to Spain and the colonies. The stipulation was included that Spain and France should never be united under the same ruler. Savoy was turned into a kingdom and received the island of Sicily—which it soon thereafter traded for Sardinia. Holland obtained the right to occupy certain barrier fortresses south of its borders to protect itself against possible future French aggression. Austria received the lion's share of Spain's continental possessions: the Spanish Netherlands, Milan, Mantua, Naples, and Sicily (in a trade with Savoy).

Neither Emperor Charles nor Philip V of Spain was happy with these treaties. Austria and a few German princes continued to fight against Louis XIV until forced to sign the Treaty of Rastatt in 1714. Even then, the emperor did not recognize Philip as the legitimate ruler of Spain, so that Austria and Spain remained officially at war for another six years. In 1720, Anglo-Dutch-French pressure finally forced Philip V to acknowledge Spain's territorial cessions to Austria, while at the same time Charles relinquished his claims to the Spanish crown.

Austria emerged from the war with considerable additional strength. Its acquisitions in Italy and northwestern Europe extended its power and influence. Its many military victories had helped break French domination of Europe. But the acquisition of Italian and Belgian lands again increased the non-German populations of the Austrian realm.

The war in the west had barely terminated when Austria saw a new opportunity to increase its strength and widen its non-German possessions. The occasion was presented by another Turkish war.

Austria under Charles VI

During the War of the Spanish Succession, the Ottoman Empire had been relatively inactive, although the Hungarian nobles, with some Turkish aid, had again risen in rebellion. Since Austria was busy in the west, it had been forced to grant large concessions of local privileges to the Hungarian magnates, so that the rebellion of 1703–1711 marked another step in the rise of the Hungarian aristocracy toward quasi equality with the Austrian nobles within the framework of an Austro-Hungarian Empire. Shortly after the end of the war in the west, the Turks opened an offensive against Venice, and seized the Peloponnesus, which they had lost in 1699. Venice appealed for aid to the emperor, and Prince Eugene again defeated the Turkish armies. The short war (1716–1718) was terminated with the Treaty of Passarowitz. For a second time, Austria made immense territorial gains, acquiring the Banat of Temesvar, northern Serbia, and eastern Wallachia (see Map 13).

After these two profitable wars, Austria enjoyed a decade and a half of relative peace under Charles VI. The emperor improved roads and communications, laid the foundation for an Austrian navy, and adopted some mercantilist policies. A Central Mercantile Directorate was established for economic planning. An oriental trading company was set up in Vienna, operating from Adriatic ports, and an East Indies Company opened in Ostend in the newly acquired Austrian Netherlands. Although various economic enterprises received government subsidies, Austrian mercantilism still centered more on expanding trade than on increasing internal production. Moreover, the emperor frequently sacrificed economic for political benefits as, for example, in 1732, when he gave way to English and Dutch pressure to close the ten-year-old East Indies Company, which had quickly become a flourishing enterprise. He was more concerned with the question of the Austrian succession than with the profits of this commercial undertaking, and acceded to the Anglo-Dutch demands in return for their guarantee to his Pragmatic Sanction.

The Pragmatic Sanction of 1713 stipulated the indivisibility of the Austrian monarchy and its dependent territories, and appointed Charles VI's eldest daughter Maria Theresa and her descendants as sole heirs should Charles die without producing a son (see Chart 4). The emperor well realized, in view of the experience of the War of the Spanish Succession, that the integrity of the Austrian realm would be in jeopardy if he could not obtain from the major powers firm guarantees that they would respect his testament. Consequently Charles's primary concern during most of his reign was to get such commitments. To obtain them, he sacrificed economic advantages and committed political blunders. The agreement of Spain was obtained in 1725; Prussia gave its consent in 1726 in return for promised inheritance rights to Berg, a promise on which Austria in the end defaulted; Holland and England accepted the Pragmatic Sanction in 1732, in return for dissolution of the East Indies Trading Company; when Saxony received Austrian support during the War of the Polish Succession (1733–1735), it gave its guarantee to Charles's arrangements; and finally French concurrence was included in the 1738 Treaty of Vienna, which ended the war over Poland. As events in 1740 were to show, the value of these guarantees given by the powers depended ultimately on the international situation at the time of Charles's death. At the critical moment, a majority of the signatories reneged on their promise to recognize Maria Theresa's rights to succeed to the Hapsburgs' hereditary lands.

Hence it appears that Charles VI wasted his political and military resources on the dubious Pragmatic Sanction. During the last decade of his reign, Austrian power began to wane. He entered the War of the Polish Succession to help the Saxon elector gain the throne of Poland. What advantage he expected from this war is not clear. With few exceptions, his armies were everywhere defeated by the French, and the resultant peace treaty showed the first trace of Austrian decline. In the Treaty of Vienna, Austria ceded Lorraine to France (indirectly through Louis XV's father-in-law) in exchange for Tuscany. Austria's position in western Germany was reduced to a few tiny possessions east of the Upper Rhine. In addition, Austria turned over Sicily and Naples to the Spanish Bourbons, in exchange for the Duchies of Parma and Piacenza. The only advantage of such an arrangement was that Austria's Italian possessions became more compact and closer to the homeland proper. At the time that Austria was concluding the fighting in the west, a new Turkish War (1736–1739) reduced its influence in the Balkans. The Austrian Army had lost its strength and leaders, and succumbed to the Turks on all fronts. By the Peace of Belgrade, Austria had to return to Turkey all gains made in 1719, except the Banat of Temesvar.

BAVARIA AND SAXONY

The Brief Ascendancy of Bavaria

Besides Prussia and Austria, a number of other lands occupied commanding positions among the German states. Bavaria, of course, had been important during most of the Middle Ages, and now assumed a dominant role in southern Germany. The Wittelsbach dynasty —which had acquired the duchy in 1180 and was to rule it until 1918—

furnished a number of skilled rulers during the seventeenth and early eighteenth centuries, who tried to use to their own advantage Bavaria's position between France and Austria. Moreover, the Wittelsbachs usually had large families and in addition received strong support from the Church, two circumstances that helped them branch out beyond the confines of Bavaria. In the early eighteenth century, for example, Wittelsbachs held four electorates—Bavaria, the Palatinate, Cologne, and Mainz—in addition to nine or more bishoprics and countless other lesser territories. Since the Wittelsbach relatives cooperated much of the time, the power of this dynasty was far greater than would be expected on the basis of the size of Bavaria.

Duke Maxmilian I had deftly guided his state through the Thirty Years' War, which brought Bavaria gains in territory and the electorship. He had begun earlier than other German princes to establish an absolutist government. The weakness of the *bourgeoisie* in his lands, the rigorous serfdom of the peasants, and the assiduous support of the Jesuits helped him in this endeavor. He ruled without consulting the estates, established a fairly reliable civil service, collected high taxes, and gradually turned his mercenary forces into the nucleus of a standing army. In almost every measure, he received the support of the Church, whose interests closely coincided with his since the Church owned over half the landed wealth of Bavaria. Maximilian's successor (Elector Ferdinand Maria, 1651–1679) continued the work of centralizing the state by simply abolishing the estates. In the incipient struggles between the Austrian Hapsburgs and Louis XIV, he initiated a policy that became the pattern for Bavarian foreign relations for over a century: he tried to maintain friendly relations with the Hapsburgs, whose possessions enclosed Bavaria on almost three sides and to whom he was bound by common religious interests; in times of crises, however, he relied on alliance with France.

During the reign of the next elector, Maximilian II Immanuel (1679–1726), Bavaria became one of the focal points of European intrigues because of its involvement in the Spanish succession. Louis XIV's continued pressure on Germany and the Turkish threats to Austria made Maximilian II side temporarily with the Hapsburgs, but in the end the Spanish inheritance question threw him back into the arms of France. This was also the result of economic considerations. Bavaria was poor and its tax revenues were small. It became increasingly difficult for the elector to pay for his standing army, which he was trying to perfect along French and Prussian models. In 1686 he even opened an artillery school, the first of its kind in Germany. For all these expenses he required foreign subsidies, which Louis XIV was always willing to provide. In fact, the Bavarian army came gradually to be paid for exclusively by French subsidies, thereby tying Bavarian policy to the coattails of France. Bavaria became one of the battlefields of the War of the Spanish Succession, Austrian troops devastated the land, and the elector himself had to flee. Even though he was restored to his lands and dignities in the treaties at the end of the war, Bavaria suffered severely. Economic progress remained slow. Maximilian initiated no mercantilistic reforms to help the country revive economically, unless one considers the establishment of a gobelin factory as vital pump priming.

The sad experience of the War of the Spanish Succession, from which Bavaria reaped no benefits, did not discourage the next elector, Charles Albert (1726–1745), from engaging in similar chimerical adventures. Although his state was usually on the verge of bankruptcy, he thought the backing of France was sufficient for him to dispute the Pragmatic Sanction and the inheritance claim of Maria Theresa to the Austrian possessions (see pages 220–223 and Chart 4). Neither the effectiveness of his administration and his army, both of which were shot through with venality and favoritism, nor his economic resources should have encouraged him in such an ambitious undertaking as challenging the Hapsburgs. Yet he attempted this in 1740, much to the detriment of Bavaria.

The Decline of Saxony

Saxony also quickly regained its importance after the Thirty Years' War, during which it suffered enormous devastation. Although none of Saxony's rulers was especially competent, economic recovery after the war was rapid. Always rather prosperous, Saxony's geographic position made it a natural trade center. The *bourgeoisie* was stronger here than in neighboring Brandenburg or in Austria and Bavaria, primarily because local production of metals and linen, as well as the mining of silver and other resources, furnished the middle class with means of securing independent wealth. This was evident in the lucrative trade fairs that had become a tradition in the country and were greatly expanded during the seventeenth and eighteenth centuries. As a result, the electors of Saxony never succeeded in establishing the absolutism that existed in Brandenburg and Bavaria. The estates retained a measure of power, and the standing army, established in 1682, was used more for foreign wars than for oppression at home. The lot of the peasantry, too, was better than that under the harsh Prussian system, serfdom was less rigid, and the landed aristocracy exercised fewer rights vis-à-vis the local population.

During the second half of the seventeenth century, the government was a fairly progressive one, especially in finance and economics. A stock exchange (1678) and a sort of Chamber of Commerce (1682) were opened, boosting the financial and commercial activities in the state. An excellent postal service was organized and communications were vastly improved. True mercantilism was not adopted, since the electors lacked the requisite centralized power as well as interest in the concept. Saxony's foreign policy during this period resembled Prussia's in that it wavered between accepting subsidies from the king of France and supporting the emperor against France or against the Turks.

A great change occurred with the accession of Frederick Augustus I (1694–1733), often called Augustus the Strong. His decision to accept the elective crown of Poland in 1697 was highly detrimental to the development of Saxony. Frederick Augustus I (who as king of Poland was called Augustus II) squandered money on his magnificent court in Dresden—which became one of the most splendid and costly courts of Europe—on his residences in Poland, and on the wars in behalf of his Polish interests. The Great Northern War, which involved Saxony merely because of its unnatural link with Poland, cost heavily in Saxon men, money, and matériel. Although the economy continued to grow under Frederick Augustus I, its improvement was slower than its potential indicated and it did not furnish enough revenue to keep pace with the expenses of the state.

Yet despite the elector's lavish excesses and his political mistakes, his rule was beneficial to Germany. In order to become king of Poland, he had converted to Catholicism. The presence of a Catholic ruler at the helm of a thoroughly Protestant state forced a further increase in the acceptance of tolerant coexistence between the two faiths. Furthermore, although Augustus I was pompous, he was easygoing and not inclined toward tyranny. He went no further in the direction of absolutism than his predecessors had gone. The combination of Poland and Saxony, at any rate, complicated all attempts at centralization. As a result, Saxony remained an island of relative liberalism amid the current of absolutism. This was particularly noticeable in the cultural realm, where Saxony had been a center for a long time, and its relatively freer atmosphere encouraged this trend. Leipzig became a center for the book trade and for the production of influential newspapers and learned journals. This in turn encouraged some of the smaller neighboring princes to devote their resources to the advancement of knowledge and culture. The little principality of Weimar gradually became the home of German enlightenment and literature, attracting to its court such figures as Goethe, Herder, and Schiller. Frederick Augustus I encouraged the arts at his own court, making Dresden a model of baroque architecture, its art gallery one of the best in the north. Saxony, the home of the Bach family, also became one of the important musical centers in Germany.

Politically, however, Saxony declined after Frederick Augustus I. His successor, Frederick Augustus II (1733–1763), fought the costly War of the Polish Succession and succeeded in becoming king of Poland as Augustus III. Again the fates of Saxony and Poland were joined, to the detriment of both. The new elector was even more lavish than his father, and his advisers were even more corrupt than his father's had been. He engaged Saxony in the two major wars of the mid-century in disregard of her meager resources, with the result that Saxony moved toward an inevitable decline.

Besides Prussia, Austria, Bavaria, and Saxony there were other important states: the Palatinate, Hanover, Württemberg, Baden, Hesse, and Mecklenburg, as well as others. Their rulers worked at increasing their territorial possessions, although some, such as Mecklenburg and Hesse, suffered diminutions because of dynastic divisions. The absorption of territories by the larger states resulted, of course, in an over-all reduction of the political units within the Empire. However this did not constitute a trend toward unifying Germany; on the contrary, the larger and stronger the more important states became, the more they desired to retain their sovereignty and the less they showed a willingness to sacrifice their sovereign rights for the sake of a German union.

10

Frederick The Great and the Enlightenment, 1740–1786

During the mid-eighteenth century Germany was dominated by Frederick II, who ascended the Prussian throne in 1740. Frederick, called "the Great" even during his lifetime, transformed Prussia into a first-rate European power. He not only fired the imagination of most Germans and rekindled their predilection for hero worship, but also fascinated his contemporaries abroad, where his fame achieved legendary proportions. His writings and correspondence, his interest in the arts and sciences, his innovations in military strategy, his enlightened philosophy, and his sheer perseverance in the face of adversity made him the cynosure of military, political, and intellectual circles; even his enemies admired his victories and clever diplomatic maneuvers.

FREDERICK'S YOUTH

The story of Frederick's youth and upbringing has become famous in German popular literature, and has offered attractive material for modern psychobiographers. He was born in Berlin in 1712, the third son of Frederick William I and Sophia Dorothea. The death of both older brothers made him heir presumptive at an early age, and turned his father's solicitous attention to his education. The "garrison king" hoped to rear his son in his own image: young Frederick was to become a God-fearing Christian, a duteous soldier, and a frugal ruler. According to his father's instructions, the boy was to be "kept away from operas, comedies, and other worldly amusements and, as far as possible, be made to dislike them." Parental discipline was harsh, and Frederick William did not hesitate to whip him before the assembled court, even when his son was in his young adulthood.

To the father's chagrin, his pedagogical efforts produced the opposite effects from those desired. Having to memorize psalms as a form of punishment or being forced to watch parade ground exercises for hours made Frederick neither a Christian nor a militarist. On the contrary, he showed no religious piety, contracted debts, and did not hide his boredom at tedious parades and military maneuvers. To the martial atmosphere of the barracks and the confinement of a uniform, which he called a "death shroud," he preferred his rococo salon and his soft French silk robe, in which he liked to lounge while reading philosophy or reciting French verses. His French-German tutor introduced him to French literature and thought, which became his favorite intellectual milieu. His mother arranged for secret flute lessons, and he composed works still performed today. During these early years, his older sister Wilhelmine became his devoted companion and frequently strengthened him in his opposition to his father's way of life.

Dissension between Father and Son

Tension between father and son permeated the court of Berlin during the entire 1720s. Although he felt sick at heart, a sense of obedience held Frederick's aversion toward his father within bounds until he resorted to open rebellion in 1730. The occasion was provided by his proposed marriage to an English princess. A few years earlier, King George of England had sought to protect his Hanoverian possessions through a marriage alliance with Prussia, and Frederick William had given his tentative assent. Although Frederick did not know his bride-to-be, he pinned great hopes on the proposed marriage as an opportunity to escape the vigilant supervision at his father's court. When political considerations suddenly made Frederick William withdraw his approval, the desperate young Frederick—possibly with encouragement and a promise of funds from London—made preparations to escape to England.

Frederick's plans were revealed to his father by a page boy entrusted with preparing the carriage for the flight. In addition, an intercepted letter revealed the complicity of a friend, a Lieutenant von Catte. Frederick William's reaction and the events of the next few months are shrouded in legends that still baffle historians, but have become part of German lore. Supposedly the enraged father would have killed his eighteen-year-old son on the spot had a general not stepped between the two. Frederick was imprisoned and sent before a military court-martial on a charge of treason, but the frightened court declared itself incompetent to pass a verdict on the prince. Foreign powers sent pleas to the Prussian king to act mercifully toward his son, perhaps in an effort to portray him in even harsher colors than his stern nature warranted. It is unlikely that Frederick William contemplated having his son executed, but evidence suggests that he intended to disinherit him and exclude him from the succession.

After three months, Frederick was finally granted a conditional pardon and imprisoned in the fortress of Küstrin. His friend Catte was condemned by a military court to life imprisonment on the charge of being the prince's accomplice, but the king changed the penalty to death. The young lieutenant was executed in the courtyard of the fortress of Küstrin within earshot of the prince, but, contrary to legend, Frederick was not forced to watch the execution.

During the next year, Frederick remained in light confinement. Forced to work in the local financial and governmental office, he learned much about the economic administration of the kingdom. Although he continued to brood about the death of his friend and about his relation to his father and the state, he gradually abandoned resistance to paternal authority. His rebelliousness had always been an inner one, but he was a Hohenzollern: obedience overshadowed personal considerations. Hence he was sad and dejected, but not broken in spirit. The experience made him more pliable and was probably good training for the rigors of later diplomatic and governmental activities. In 1731, he accepted his father's conditions for complete rehabilitation: he was to re-enter the army, devote himself seriously to training in government and military science, and marry a princess chosen by his father for political reasons. This arrangement brought about a reconciliation between father and son.

Two years later, the twenty-one-year-old prince married Elizabeth of Brunswick-Bevern, a niece of the emperor—a union through which Frederick William hoped to cement good relations with Charles VI. Frederick disliked his wife from their first meeting until his death. He treated her with polite deference, but remained a lonely man throughout his life. The marriage at least gave him a certain amount of freedom. He was allowed to set up his own household at Rheinsberg, where he spent the seven happiest years of his life—not because of conjugal bliss, but because he could do largely what he wanted.

The twofold character that eventually turned him into a true "philosopher king" now came to the foreground. He was a rare combination of an intellectual and a man of action. In preparation for his eventual duties, he studied military tactics and applied politics, and analyzed problems of government and the international scene with astounding perspicacity. He fulfilled his military duties by training with a regiment in the vicinity, and in 1734 joined Prince Eugene during several battles of the War of the Polish Succession in order to learn the art of generalship and to observe an army in action. On the other hand, much of his attention was devoted to discussions with chosen friends. He read Greek and Latin philosophy, studied history, composed music, and wrote poetry. He delighted in losing himself in literature and art, speculative philosophy, and sentimental reveries. His lifelong correspondence with Voltaire began during this period.

Assumption of the Kingship

During these years at Rheinsberg, the young prince was kept completely isolated from his father's policy decisions. Yet he used his time to outline his own plans for the future, both in domestic administration and in the field of foreign affairs. Consequently when he succeeded to the throne in 1740, he plunged into action with a speed and resolution that astonished his contemporaries. His father's legacy of a large, well-trained army, a full treasury, and an efficient bureaucracy enabled the ambitious young ruler to move in many directions. The fast pace of the first few days of his reign, the firmness of his decisions, and the variety of his initial measures showed immediately that the young king was inaugurating a new era for Prussia.

He also demonstrated at once that

he was determined to control everything by himself, not only supervising finance and government as had his father, but also acting as his own foreign minister and as commander of his armies in the field. He seemed to trust no one with secrets or vital assignments, and reduced his ministers to unimportant functionaries. Only his secretaries who wrote his letters and a few trusted counselors shared his plans and negotiations with foreign powers.

During his first four whirlwind days in office a plethora of royal decrees showed his interest in diverse reforms. Evidence of his paternalism was the arrangement for grants and loans to paupers, and the sale of food from government granaries at a reduced price to people suffering from the preceding harsh winter. In line with his concepts of enlightened government, he abolished torture in almost all judicial proceedings (although this decree was at first kept secret). Changed judicial procedure made the courts sole agents for judging and pronouncing sentence, the king retaining only the right to grant pardons. In the army, cruel punishments and manhandling of soldiers were outlawed and forced recruitment was abolished. Frederick also promised not to interfere with the press—a promise not always respected later; and he announced tolerance for all religions with the famous dictum that in his state, everyone was free to assure his salvation in his own fashion.

He immediately demonstrated his intellectual and artistic interests. Funds were restored to the Academy of Sciences, founded by his grandfather but neglected by his father. Frederick invited the French scientist Maupertuis to reorganize it and become its president. He also asked the German philosopher Wolff to return to the university of Halle as its vice-chancellor. Wolff had been expelled by Frederick William I, who had been told that the professor was an atheist and a believer in predestination. Finally, Frederick ordered the immediate construction of an opera house in Berlin.

These first four days also produced an important reorganization of the government. Worried about the annual trade deficit and the lack of industry, Frederick ordered the establishment of a fifth ministry, a central agency for commerce and production. Finally, immediately after his father's funeral he disbanded the famous but impractical regiment of tall Potsdam grenadiers, allocating the funds saved toward the addition of 10,000 men to the regular standing army.

At this time Frederick made a detailed analysis of the international scene as well as the strengths and weaknesses of the major powers that could affect Prussia's foreign policy (later included in his book *History of My Time*). Two major interrelated problems concerned him. England and Spain were then engaged in a colonial war (the War of Jenkins' Ear, 1739–1748), and Frederick foresaw that the conflict would spread to the Continent, with France siding against England, and that a general European war might ensue. The second problem concerned the eventual Austrian succession. Despite the various paper guarantees given to the Pragmatic Sanction, the death of Emperor Charles VI was likely to provoke international friction and perhaps war. Few statesmen expected that Maria Theresa would succeed her father without the interference of the other powers. On the contrary, everyone was calculating the possible advantages to be gained from the inevitable dispute. The Bavarian Elector Charles Albert, in particular, had never abandoned his claims to the Austrian inheritance (see Chart 4). Moreover, Austria had just been worsted by the Turks, and appeared weak and unprepared to resist foreign pressure and attempts at dismemberment.

PRUSSIAN FOREIGN RELATIONS UNDER FREDERICK II

Frederick the Great was determined to carry on an active foreign policy that would make Prussia strong and independent. He saw no reason for continuing his father's pusillanimity, particularly toward Austria. Over the past century, Austria had always acted in its own interests and had even frequently prevented the growth of Brandenburg-Prussia. Frederick was convinced that Prussia could become a first-rate power only in opposition to the Hapsburgs. He also felt that Prussia's population of three million was too small, that the income and resources of the state were too meager to permit it to become truly independent in foreign affairs and to achieve the status of a first-rate power. He was not interested merely in gaining the connecting links between his scattered territories, as the Great Elector had been, but in acquiring additional resources and inhabitants.

The Polish regions between East Prussia, Pomerania, and Brandenburg at first attracted his attention, although they were not densely populated. But in 1740 Frederick could hardly have attacked Poland without risking a war against the combined forces of Russia, Saxony, and France. The Hapsburg-owned province of Silesia, on the other hand, with its large population, its mineral resources, and its vigorous industry seemed a more attractive prospect. Frederick could advance inheritance claims, dating back to the sixteenth century, to certain areas of Silesia. Moreover, he knew that the Saxon elector, Augustus III, hoped to annex the province as a link between his Saxon and Polish possessions. Such a step would have resulted in the partial encirclement of Brandenburg by an enlarged Saxon-Polish state. The transfer of Silesia from Austria to Prussia, on the other hand, would weaken the Hapsburgs' position in northern Europe while presenting tremendous advantages for Prussia. These considerations determined the Prussian king to plan the acquisition of Silesia as soon as an opportunity arose.

The First Silesian War

The opportunity arrived sooner than expected. In the fall of 1740—five months after Frederick's accession—the emperor died. As anticipated, the powers showed little respect for the Pragmatic Sanction. Bavaria, Saxony, and Spain immediately voiced demands for Hapsburg territory. The international situation seemed hardly favorable to the Austrian heiress Maria Theresa. Russia was momentarily weakened by a disputed succession to the throne. Spain and England were at war, and Franco-British tension was increasing. It seemed likely that Prussia could count on the friendship of either France or England if it attacked Austria. Frederick therefore did not hesitate to make the first move. He did not feel bound by his father's signature to the Pragmatic since Austria had not kept its treaty obligations to help Prussia obtain the Duchy of Berg.

Actually such justification was merely a façade. The young king had long decided to use as his sole criterion in international relations whether or not an action brought benefits to Prussia. Although in 1738, with the aid of Voltaire, he had published a book entitled *The Anti-Machiavel,* in which he had rejected Machiavelli's concept of political morality, his refutation had been primarily an intellectual exercise. In foreign affairs, the king of Prussia proved one of the Florentine's best pupils.

Two days after receiving the news of the emperor's death, Frederick wrote: "It's merely a matter of executing projects which I have long ago elaborated in my mind." And a few weeks later, his armies moved into Silesia "to safeguard it." He had debated whether to negotiate with Maria Theresa first or march with his troops first. In the end, like Hitler two centuries later, he decided that it would be most effective to do both simultaneously. While his armies occupied most of the undefended province in a short "military parade," his envoy negotiated in Vienna. Maria Theresa was told that Frederick was occupying Silesia to protect it from Austria's enemies, and that he would make an alliance with her, help protect her possessions, and vote for the election of her husband to the emperorship in return for permanent cession of Silesia. Some Viennese statesmen were ready to accept the offer, afraid that Austria could not maintain itself against the many enemies likely to make demands on its territory. But Maria Theresa declined, and Frederick faced war.

Although Frederick was a firm practitioner of *Realpolitik,* he recognized the need for mollifying the powers that might become alarmed at his occupation of Silesia. Hence he set up what today might be called a public relations office with the task of influencing opinion in foreign capitals. Various pamphlets were circulated abroad to prove the legitimacy of his claims to Silesia. One such anonymous leaflet suggests a similar technique used by Hitler. It asserted that the Protestants of Silesia felt oppressed by the Catholic Hapsburg government and that the Prussians were seizing the province as protectors of the local inhabitants.

In Silesia itself Frederick tried to be a model occupier, and instructed his troops to treat the local population with utmost circumspection. Army provisions were shipped in from Brandenburg and not requisitioned locally. Freedom of conscience was proclaimed so as to assuage the fears of the Catholics, and Frederick gave a lavish festival for the inhabitants of Breslau, as if to celebrate their emancipation from Austrian domination. These measures, of course, did not prevent Austrian reprisals.

Within a few weeks of Prussia's occupation of the province, Austrian armies poured over the mountain passes from Bohemia to open the First Silesian War (1740–1742). The first major battle was fought in the spring of 1741 (Battle of Mollwitz). It was won by Prussia, but the Prussian cavalry was routed in the early stages of the engagement and Frederick's first essay as commander was a fiasco. Completely discouraged, he fled from the field and was almost captured by the enemy, while one of his generals (Count Kurt von Schwerin) turned the initial rout into victory.

THE SPREADING OF THE WAR Negotiations now started among the various states that hoped to acquire portions of the Hapsburg inheritance. Louis XV of France as yet cared little about politics, and his minister (Cardinal Fleury) preferred peace at almost any price. But the war party at Versailles (led by the adventure-loving Marshal Belle-Isle), hoping to seize the Austrian Netherlands from Maria Theresa, finally persuaded the king into action. An anti-Austrian alliance was made among Prussia, France, Spain, Naples, and Bavaria in preparation for the War of the Austrian Succession (1740–1748). At this time, France and England were becoming involved in hostilities in the colonies (King George's War). The Austro-Prussian war over Silesia thus became linked to an almost world-wide conflict. The four nearly simultaneous wars—First Silesian War, War of Jenkins' Ear, War of the Austrian Succession, and King George's War—were in some respects separate military ventures for distinct aims, while at the same time they represented one gigantic conflict, with interlocking alliances and constant repercussions of one struggle on the conduct of the others.

As Prussian and Austrian forces skirmished in Silesia during the summer of 1741, the anti-Austrian coalition laid plans for the dismemberment of the Hapsburg dominions even before they had launched an effective campaign. To weaken Maria Theresa and prevent the election of her husband, Francis, to the emperorship, they decided to support the candidacy of Charles Albert of Bavaria. The Wittelsbach family still commanded three electoral votes (Bavaria, the Palatinate, and Cologne); French agents and their bribes persuaded the archbishops of Mainz and Trier to join the group; the others were promised territorial or other advantages. Saxony agreed to vote for Charles Albert in return for gains in Moravia and Upper Silesia, while Hanover bargained its vote for guaranteed neutrality and integrity of its territory. Prussia, of course, was ready to cast its vote for the Bavarian in exchange for the retention of Silesia. In addition to the stipulated cessions of Moravia and Silesia, the allied plan for dismembering the Hapsburg dominions included other cessions of territory: Bavaria was to get Bohemia and Upper Austria, Naples demanded Austrian lands in Italy, and France hoped for gains in the Austrian Netherlands.

But within four months of the conclusion of this alliance, friction developed between France and Prussia. The French had been slow in moving their troops across the Rhine. Although Austria lay in front of them almost undefended, French and Bavarian forces reached Linz in Austria only in September 1741, so that Frederick began to doubt the sincerity of his French ally. Moreover, he had realized that his resources did not suffice for a prolonged war. Hence he adopted a principle he was to follow throughout his reign: it was to avoid a long war by making a few quick, decisive forays and then concluding a truce or a peace to recuperate.

Consequently the Prussian king resorted to his first "double cross" in October 1741. With the help of secret

English mediation, he concluded a clandestine agreement with Maria Theresa (Convention of Klein Schnellendorf), stipulating a truce of at least three months. Frederick was to cease all military action, in return for which the Austrians were to vacate the fortress of Neisse after a simulated resistance, and withdraw the scattered troops they still had in Silesia. The agreement was to be kept secret so as not to alarm Frederick's allies. It implied, of course, that Frederick would obtain permanent possession of Silesia; but Maria Theresa agreed to the sacrifice to be able to devote all attention to the seemingly greater danger posed by the Bavarian claims.

Frederick justified this secret truce on the usual basis of *raison d'état*. Not only did Prussia need time to recuperate, but France, he feared, might be interested more in seeing the German states fight one another than in weakening Austria.

While Prussia sat on the side lines, Maria Theresa rushed her troops south from Silesia and Bohemia to protect Austria proper against further inroads by the French and Bavarians. But instead of marching on Vienna, the Franco-Bavarian forces turned north and with the help of some Saxon troops conquered Prague, where Charles Albert of Bavaria was crowned king of Bohemia. Four months later, he was elected emperor in Frankfurt as Charles VII (1742).

Meanwhile the unpredictable Frederick had reopened hostilities. Since the Austrians had leaked the secret of the truce—to discredit him with his allies—he felt free to break the agreement. Even without this excuse, he would have resumed military activities for fear the French might not let him keep Silesia if he did not further participate in the war. The short truce had given him a few months to replenish his stores. Beyond that it had earned him nothing except the reputation of an untrustworthy ally. With the aid of some Saxon and French contingents, he now invaded Bohemia as far as Olmütz. But his campaign was desultory and produced no victories. Moreover, there was poor coordination among the allies. The French forces for the most part were again inactive, but Maria Theresa regained strength, expelled the Franco-Bavarian army from Linz, and even conquered Munich the same day that the Bavarian elector was crowned emperor in Frankfurt.

PRUSSIA'S WITHDRAWAL FROM THE WAR. Again Frederick contemplated withdrawing from the war. His supplies were running low and he suspected the French might make a separate peace. In the spring of 1742, he vacated Moravia and attempted to negotiate peace with Maria Theresa. The Austrian queen, however, felt more confident now, and refused Frederick's overtures until her armies had again been defeated by the Prussians. Thereupon she agreed to peace negotiations, which were mediated by England. Discussions dragged for some time, and Frederick, eager for a cessation of hostilities, ceded a number of points. Finally peace was concluded (Peace of Berlin, 1742). Frederick agreed to abandon his allies and received from Austria Silesia and the county of Glatz in Bohemia, but not certain other districts he had claimed (Teschen, Troppau, Jägerndorf). This treaty ended the First Silesian War.

Once again Frederick had deserted his partners. In correspondence, leaflets, and planted newspaper stories, he attempted to justify his conclusion of a separate peace. Again he claimed that France had been trying to negotiate peace itself but that he had outmaneuvered it, and insisted that Prussia's lack of resources did not permit continuation of the war.

During the following year, 1743, Maria Theresa regained even more strength. She expelled the foreign armies from Bohemia and occupied most of Bavaria, with the possible intention of seeking compensation in Bavaria for her loss of Silesia. She also succeeded in gaining firm allies. England, which had been fighting France in the colonies for over two years, now entered the conflict on the Continent. King George made a firm commitment to aid Maria Theresa, and organized the "Pragmatic Army" of English, Hanoverian, Dutch, and Hessian troops, which inflicted a severe defeat on the French in the summer of 1743 (Battle of Dettingen). At the same time, the elector of Saxony was persuaded to renounce his claims to part of the Austrian inheritance, for which Austria promised him a financial reward and a slice of Silesian territory. Sardinia also made an alliance with Austria and assumed part of the task of fighting the Spaniards in Italy. As a result, Maria Theresa's position suddenly improved immeasurably, and Frederick became worried about the safety of his Silesian acquisition. He spent the year 1743 replenishing his treasury by requisitioning additional revenue from his subjects, including the people of Silesia, whom he gradually incorporated into the Prussian state. He also raised the strength of his army to 140,000 men, improved the Prussian cavalry, and trained his armies in field maneuvers—a new practice in those days.

During the winter, Frederick negotiated with German princes for the creation of an "imperial army" to come to the aid of the hapless Emperor Charles VII, who was living in exile in Frankfurt after Maria Theresa's conquest of his homeland. Frederick's plan called for the establishment of an all-German army, of which the Prussian king would be the permanent commander in chief. The army's task would be to help Charles VII restore dignity and authority to the emperorship. Unquestionably Frederick was interested only in constructing a counterbalance to Maria Theresa's growing strength. The concept of acting in the national interest of a German state lay far from his intentions. But the plan failed. Most of the princes displayed an ingrained respect for the Hapsburgs. They were jealous of Bavaria's possible rise to power and were wary of subordinating their armies to the Prussian king. In short, the princes exhibited the same feelings that made the unification of Germany in the nineteenth century such a difficult task.

The Second Silesian War

In the end, only a few states (Cologne, the Palatinate, Württemberg, Hesse-Cassel) made an alliance with Frederick and encouraged him to re-enter the war against Austria. In the spring of 1744, the Prussian ruler renegotiated an alliance with France, which had become more active after control of the government had been assumed by Louis's mistress, Madame de Pompadour. According to the pact, France was to obtain a part of the Austrian Netherlands, Bavaria was to acquire Bohemia, and Prussia was to get certain mountain passes in northeastern Bohemia to protect its Silesian possessions. At a time when the bulk of the Austrian forces was committed on the Rhine, Frederick launched his campaign that opened the Second Silesian War (1744–1745).

In two months, he conquered the major part of Saxony and Bohemia and seized the city of Prague. But again luck turned rapidly against him. The Bohemian population evinced great hostility toward Frederick's "Imperial Auxiliary Troops" and made their supplying difficult. Two months later the Prussians were forced to evacuate Bohemia and retreat to Silesia. Maria Theresa had shifted her armies from the Rhine, and, contrary to Frederick's hopes, the French had made no attempt to pursue them. Again the Prussian king felt that France was letting him down.

In the spring of 1745, Frederick's position grew continually worse. His funds were running low, and Austrian troops were infiltrating into Silesia and maneuvering skillfully to avoid open battle. His allies were deserting him. Charles VII had died in January, and the new Bavarian elector (Maximilian III Joseph) followed the advice of his dying father and promptly concluded peace with Maria Theresa (Peace of Füssen), by which he renounced all claims to the Austrian lands and agreed to vote in the impending imperial election for Maria Theresa's husband, in return for restoration of the Bavarian lands that Austrian troops had occupied. Frederick was further disturbed by the sudden hostile attitude of Russia, by rumors of French plans for a separate peace, and by reports of new English, Dutch, Saxon, and Austrian plans, devised in Warsaw, to partition Prussia.

His letters of the period alternate between despondency and a doughty tenacity to hold on to Silesia regardless of the consequences. His admiration for Stoic ideals, which he studied during these campaigns, vied with his predilection for dramatic heroism. "If all my resources and all negotiations fail," he wrote to a minister, "if, in short, everything turns against me, I would rather perish with honor than live out my life without glory and fame." His extremism—again reminiscent of Hitler—was also plain: "I have crossed the Rubicon," he wrote, "and either I will assert my power, or else all shall perish and everything Prussian shall be buried with me."

By early summer his own hopes and the morale of his troops were lifted by news of a great French victory over the Austrians (Battle of Fontenoy, 1745). This was soon followed by Frederick's own victory of Hohenfriedberg, a fast and decisive battle fought at dawn, which showed the results of the Prussian cavalry's vigorous training and established Frederick's reputation as a consummate general. Feeling more secure, Frederick once again sought to conclude a separate peace. But Maria Theresa had not given up hope of reconquering Silesia. In the summer, she had succeeded in having her husband, Francis of Lorraine, elected to the emperorship as Francis I, despite the abstentions of Brandenburg and the Palatinate in the electoral college. An additional half year of fighting was an almost intolerable strain on Frederick's budget, but three more Prussian victories in Bohemia, Silesia, and Saxony, as well as Austrian defeats by the Spanish and French in Italy, were necessary to convince Maria Theresa to conclude a peace with Prussia. The Treaty of Dresden (1745) finally ended the Second Silesian War. Prussia's possession of Silesia was reconfirmed, Saxony was ordered to pay a million thaler indemnity, and Brandenburg and the Palatinate agreed to recognize Francis I as emperor.

Despite some strategic blunders and miscalculations of Austrian resilience, Frederick emerged as victor, thanks to Prussia's military strength, auspicious international conditions, and the king's unscrupulous attitude toward his allies. Violation of treaty obligations did not disturb him, since he clearly distinguished between personal or bourgeois morality for the conduct of individuals, and political or state morality for the guidance of rulers. In all cases of conflict, according to Frederick, state morality had to supersede personal scruples. And since his behavior had served the aggrandizement of Prussia, he deemed that it should not be labeled treacherous or immoral. However, to justify his conduct during the war and his triple desertion of his allies, his "public relations" office in Berlin, with its network of agents, was busier than ever propagating the Prussian point of view throughout Europe's governing circles. The main justification this time was that his allies had engaged in secret deals to the detriment of Prussia.

The war in the west continued for three years after Frederick's separate peace. England, kept busy with fighting in the colonies and with internal problems, became less active on the Continent. France made some gains in the Lowlands, but in the end she was threatened by Russian troops, which Empress Elizabeth suddenly dispatched to the Rhine to help her new ally Maria Theresa. By 1748, all belligerents were ready for peace. The Treaty of Aix-la-Chapelle (Aachen) restored the respective conquests of France and England and reconfirmed the possession of Silesia to Frederick. Only Austria lost some territories: in Italy, ceding Parma, Piacenza, and Guastalla to a younger son (Infante Don Philip) of the king of Spain. But aside from these Italian losses, Maria Theresa and Francis, despite all expectations, had succeeded in maintaining the integrity of the Hapsburg inheritance. Like Prussia, Austria emerged from the war considerably strengthened. Bavaria, on the other hand, had once again failed to attain the rank of a first-rate state. As a result, there were now two major powers within the empire. Austro-Prussian dualism had become a prime factor in German politics, and their jealous striving for pre-eminence was to color German history until the final denouement in 1866.

The Interwar Years

Frederick the Great proclaimed in 1745 that he desired peace to devote all resources to the welfare of his subjects, but in reality he prepared for the next war. He realized that Prussia's settlement with Austria and the Anglo-French arrangements were little more than truces. At the same time he felt isolated on the diplomatic stage. Russia, in firm alliance with Austria, showed on several occasions disquieting eagerness for war against Prussia. Relations with France had cooled considerably. In fact, it seemed that the three most powerful women of Europe—Tsarina Elizabeth, Empress Maria Theresa, and the Marquise de Pompadour—harbored a passionate hatred for Frederick. There were also quarrels with England over indemnity payments for damage inflicted on Prussian merchants during the war, and differences with Hanover over the Duchy of East Frisia, with its important port of Emden, which the Hohenzollerns had inherited in 1744. Frederick did not even succeed in concluding an alliance with the Turks so as to put pressure on Russia and Austria from the south. His actions during the War of the Austrian Succession had made him suspect to possible allies and distrusted by potential enemies.

His attitude during these years of peace hardly altered his reputation. He acted as though Prussia's safety lay exclusively in its armies and devoted much of the state's resources to strengthening the military. He studied the campaigns of the last war to improve his strategy, conducted yearly maneuvers, wrote a treatise on *General Principles of Warfare,* and devoted much of his *Political Testament* of 1752 to plans for the training and supplying of the army, which by 1756 had reached a peacetime strength of 156,000 men. Whenever the threat of war appeared, Frederick almost automatically rattled his saber. In his eyes, Prussia's armaments program ensured peace although it convinced other powers that Prussia was assuming an intolerably aggressive attitude. As a consequence, designs to weaken Prussia by dismemberment were frequently voiced in the 1750s, particularly at St. Petersburg, Vienna, and Dresden.

By 1755, a new European war seemed imminent. Hostilities between France and England had reopened with clashes in the Ohio Valley of North America; and England, unhappy with its former partner, Austria, was looking for a new continental ally for the protection of Hanover against France. Russia offered to protect Hanover with 50,000 troops in return for English subsidies. But in January 1756, Frederick persuaded England to switch its favor from Russia to Prussia. A Prussian guarantee of Hanover's integrity appeared more effective to London than the same offer by Russia, largely in view of Prussia's military strength and its proximity to Hanover. In the Convention of Westminster, England offered Frederick protection against Russia, while Frederick guaranteed Hanover against France. At the same time, the treaty stipulated that Prussia should remain neutral in case of an Anglo-French war.

But in the spring of 1756, Austria's highly skilled chief minister (Count Wenzel von Kaunitz) finally implemented a plan on which he had worked for half a decade: an alliance between the traditional archenemies, Austria and France. This pact, so contrary to customary European alignments that it is labeled a "diplomatic revolution," was potentially of great value to both partners. It was negotiated with the help of the politically sagacious Madame de Pompadour, who was not averse to avenging herself against Frederick for defamatory poems the Prussian king had written about her and circulated anonymously in Paris. The alliance—initially defensive, but changed into an offensive pact after one year—stipulated large French subsidies to Austria and its ally Russia. France was to receive the Austrian Netherlands, which it had coveted for two centuries, and Austria was to get back Silesia. In addition, the German states were to participate in a general partitioning of Prussia in order to reduce it to about the size of sixteenth-century Brandenburg.

During the summer of 1756, the schemes for carving up Prussia widened.

Sweden spoke of regaining Stettin, Saxony advanced demands, and Tsarina Elizabeth pressed for an immediate offensive against Frederick. Maria Theresa, however, insisted on a year's delay. Frederick's agents reported the various plans of his enemies, although not always accurately, and he decided to act quickly to prevent their execution. He sent two successive notes to Vienna to inquire whether Austro-Russian mobilization was directed against Prussia and whether the two powers had abandoned or merely postponed their planned attack. To both notes he received vague replies. Consequently he launched a sudden invasion of Saxony without issuing a declaration of war. In a move by then typical, he dispatched a third messenger to Vienna while his troops were invading Saxony, offering to withdraw his troops if he received written assurances from St. Petersburg and Vienna that neither would attack him within the next twelve months.

The Third Silesian War

Frederick's preventive campaign opened the continental phase of the Seven Years' War (1756–1763), which in Prussian history is called the Third Silesian War. While his troops were on their way, the king wrote to his brother Henry: "This war is not my fault. I did all I could to avert it. But honor and security must not be sacrificed to love of peace." Even though he took the first aggressive military action, Frederick could easily assert that it was a defensive war, since his opponents harbored aggressive designs. But there is no justification for glorifying Frederick II as a heroic defender whose sole aim was to safeguard Prussia's existence. There might have been no need to "defend" Prussia if he had not seized Silesia in 1740 and if his behavior had not antagonized the courts of Europe. One should also note that in his *Political Testament* of 1752 Frederick had pointed to Swedish Pomerania, West Prussia, and Saxony as desirable future acquisitions for Prussia; hence Swedish and Saxon fears were not unwarranted.

Frederick had decided to capture Saxony so that he could seize its resources, take advantage of additional manpower, and perhaps use the occupied lands as a bargaining point to achieve a quick peace. Within a few weeks he defeated the bulk of the Saxon troops and incorporated them into his own armies. In Saxon archives he found documents tending to prove the allied plans to partition Prussia, and these he published to justify his actions. He then invaded Bohemia, defeated a small Austrian force, and hoped that peace could be restored after these brief, lightning successes.

But Frederick had completely miscalculated the effect of his Blitzkrieg. It did not intimidate his opponents, but reaffirmed their aim to destroy Prussia. In the spring of 1757, his enemies increased in numbers and tightened their alliances. Russia dispatched an army; Sweden entered the field; the Empire, represented by most of the German states, collected troops against Frederick, who was accused of having breached the peace with his invasion of Saxony; and the Franco-Austrian alliance was turned into an offensive pact. Frederick for his part looked in vain for allies. Turkey could not be persuaded to attack Russia. England alone agreed to renew the Convention of Westminster, to pay a million pounds sterling in subsidies, and to assign some Hanoverian forces to fight France. A few minor states of northern Germany sided with Prussia. Otherwise Frederick, alone against an overwhelming coalition, had only one hope of survival: that his enemies would not mount a united campaign and that he could meet them one at a time. The situation was admirably suited to his penchant for self-pity and classical heroism. In his letters he underlined his stoic sense of duty while bewailing his unfortunate fate. He issued instructions to his minister (Count Finck von Finckenstein) not to pay ransom if he fell prisoner in the ensuing campaigns: "If such a misfortune befalls me, I shall sacrifice myself for the state."

THE CAMPAIGNS During the next six years, Frederick astounded the world with his tenacity. He raced with his armies from one front to another, attacking or defending as the occasion demanded, he outmaneuvered his opponents, and he refused to give up despite numerous defeats and a seemingly hopeless position. His reputation as an excellent strategist and his fame as a "fighting philosopher king" were fully confirmed during this war.

In the course of the first full year of war alone (1757), the Prussians were involved in nine major battles, of which five were victories. Prussia was attacked on all sides, and Frederick had to abandon his offensive in Bohemia to defend his own lands. In the east, the Russians seized East Prussia; in the north, Swedish forces took parts of Pomerania; in the west, the French forced Frederick's allies, the Hanoverians, into accepting a humiliating armistice; French and imperial forces approached from the southwest; and the Austrians captured parts of Silesia from the south. By the end of 1757, Frederick's position was slightly improved through two great victories (at Rossbach against the French and south Germans, and at Leuthen against the Austrians), but his resources were low. He forced the population of occupied Saxony and Mecklenburg to pay huge contributions and marshaled all possible reserve manpower, but he doubted that he could survive a long war. His only bright news at the beginning of 1758 was that George II of England repudiated the armistice of the previous year and recommitted the Hanoverian troops, this time under the command of a Prussian general, so that the French forces were kept occupied in the Rhineland during 1758. In the east, however, the Russians reached the River Oder. Frederick was able to defeat them in one of the bloodiest battles of the war (Zorndorf), but his losses in manpower were enormous and the Russians were not permanently repulsed. By the end of the year, Prussia lay exhausted. Frederick gained a breathing spell only because the Swedes, Russians, and Austrians failed to coordinate their military efforts and retired early to their respective winter quarters.

In 1759, Prussia suffered one defeat after another. The French again approached from the southwest, the Austrians invaded Brandenburg, and Frederick lost half of his force of 53,000 men to a combined Russo-Austrian army (in the Battle of Kunersdorf). After this battle, Frederick was so despondent that he seriously contemplated suicide, in the manner of his Plutarchian heroes whose lives he had studied so avidly. To his minister

(Finckenstein) he wrote: "I have no resources left, and to tell the truth, I believe all is lost. I shall not survive the collapse of my fatherland. Good-bye forever."

But the worst was yet to come. For two more years, his luck and resources went downhill, his total available forces dwindling to 60,000. In 1760, Berlin, which had been raided by Austrian detachments before, was captured a second time by Russo-Austrian troops, which collected an indemnity of two million thaler before vacating the city. Moreover, the death of George II and a subsequent change of ministry determined England to slacken its aid to Prussia. At the end of 1761, Frederick controlled only a small part of his state and a corner of Saxony. By all standards, he should have given up. But the following winter and spring brought an abrupt change to the war.

THE PEACE SETTLEMENTS In January 1762, Tsarina Elizabeth died and was succeeded by Frederick's admirer, Tsar Peter III, who at once made peace with Prussia, restored all conquests, and even offered Frederick an alliance against Austria. At Russia's behest, Sweden withdrew from the war, and Frederick was suddenly freed from danger in the north and east. Even though England ceased all payments of subsidies, Frederick felt encouraged to resume the offensive against Austria with the help of 20,000 Russians. Then in the summer, another change in Russian policy, occasioned by Peter's murder and the accession of his wife, Catherine II, caused Russia's withdrawal into neutrality. But Frederick continued his offensive, won two more battles against Austrian and French armies, and even sent small cavalry forces on raids into southern Germany to force the German states into neutrality.

Meanwhile France had become weary of the war with England, which had brought it nothing but colonial losses. An armistice between England and France was signed in November 1762, which was converted into the Peace of Paris in the following February. England, France, Spain, and Portugal settled their colonial differences to the advantage of England and the detriment of France. Five days later, Maria Theresa agreed to conclude peace with Prussia, with Saxony as intermediary. In the Peace of Hubertusburg (1763), it was agreed that Saxony was to be restored to its prewar size, that Silesia would be retained by Prussia, and that Frederick the Great would vote for Maria Theresa's son Joseph as emperor when the occasion should arise.

Thus Frederick the Great emerged from the war unscathed, even though his country had suffered badly. Having maintained itself in the face of a coalition of four major and many lesser powers, Prussia had proved its status as a first-rate power. Of course, luck had rescued Frederick the Great in the last years of the war; still, the outcome of the war could largely be credited to his armies. In fact, his diplomatic failures in the prewar period had been redeemed by military miracles. More than ever, Prussia's militarism was becoming its greatest asset.

THE LESSONS OF THE WAR The war taught Frederick diplomatic lessons that he tried to impart to his successors in various writings, particularly his second *Political Testament* (1768). Unlike many of his predecessors, whose policies had had a French orientation, Frederick had learned that relying on French support against the Hapsburgs had become obsolete. In the preceding two centuries, France had supported minor German princes against the house of Hapsburg, not merely to weaken the Hapsburgs but also to keep Germany disunited. But its growth had removed Prussia from the ranks of the minor German states and the French no longer found any advantage in unconditionally supporting the new "giant of the north." The dualism between Austria and Prussia that now existed within the empire demanded a change in French as well as in Prussian policy. The Austro-French alliance of 1756—followed fourteen years later by the marriage of Maria Theresa's daughter Marie Antoinette to the dauphin of France, the future King Louis XVI—showed the new trend. The two Catholic states could band together to clip the wings of Protestant Prussia, or France might conveniently switch her support back and forth between the two contenders for primacy in Germany, in an attempt to keep either from gaining preponderance. In either case, France ceased to be a reliable ally for Prussia.

In these circumstances Frederick cast about for other allies. The smaller German states had neither the resources nor the stamina to become trustworthy anti-Austrian bulwarks. Moreover, most of the German princes distrusted the new militaristic Prussia even more than they distrusted Hapsburg Austria. Frederick found the only logical ally in Russia, whose growing influence along the Baltic Coast and in Poland was of vital importance to Prussia. The Third Silesian War also had proved to Frederick the danger of facing an encircling coalition of Russia in the east and the Austro-French in the south and west. The prototype of Germany's twentieth-century nightmare of a two-front war was thus born in the 1750s. Like all European statesmen, Frederick the Great had initially vastly underrated the potential power of Russia and the effectiveness of its armies. He had spoken contemptuously of the ill-trained, undisciplined eastern hordes. However, as a result of his experiences during the war, in which the Russians defeated his forces more frequently than he was able to vanquish them, he reacted in two ways.

On the one hand, he launched a campaign of vilification against Russia. His "public relations" office in Berlin disseminated numerous dispatches detailing the cruelties and horrors committed by the "barbarian Tartars," labelling them inhuman, uncivilized monsters. He subsidized anti-Russian poems and sanctioned the falsification of statistics of Russian misdeeds. In the three-day occupation of Berlin in 1760, for example, Austrian troops had plundered the local population, whereas the Russian soldiers had been kept under exemplary discipline. Frederick's accounts, however imputed the worst possible behavior to the Russians. His motives for this psychological warfare are not quite clear. Perhaps he hoped to account for his defeats by the Russian armies by insinuating that his civilized Prussian grenadiers had been overwhelmed by the wild, barbarian Mongols. Whatever his motives, the campaign bore fruit. Its specific effects are hard to measure, but unquestionably public opinion in central and western Europe was influenced by this concept of Russia as a fearsome, greedy bear.

On the other hand, Frederick decided that Prussia's future foreign relations should be based on friendship with Russia. As long as Russia maintained benevolent neutrality, Prussia could stand up to Austria and play a dominant role within the Empire. With Russia as an ally, it could confront almost any combination of westtern opponents. But, he warned his successor in his *Political Testament,* with Russia as an enemy, Prussia always faced the dilemma of a two-front war. This political maxim guided most Prussian and later German statesmen in the succeeding two centuries; it was disregarded with calamitous consequences on only a few rare occasions —during the revolutionary period of 1848–1850, and during the two world wars of the twentieth century.

After the end of the war in 1763, Frederick turned to rehabilitating his country. He resumed his economic, political, and judicial reforms and labored to increase the revenue from his state, but much of his interest still centered on his army. The army corps were reorganized, the cavalry further improved, and the over-all strength continually increased. By 1772, his standing army amounted to 186,000 men. His first postwar allocation of reserve funds shows the disproportionate resources devoted to the military. Of a total of 29.5 million thaler in the treasury he assigned 14.5 million to a war fund (sufficient to conduct about two campaigns), 8 million for mobilization costs, new guns, war vehicles, and war matériel, and 5.5 million for the repayment of war loans. Although professing to devote primary attention to alleviating the war-caused misery of his subjects, he allotted only 1.5 million thaler for relief.

The First Partition of Poland

Frederick's next important foreign venture revolved around Poland. In 1763, he concluded with Catherine of Russia an eight-year mutual defense alliance (renewed in 1769). When the king of Poland died in the same year, Frederick aided Catherine in getting her former favorite, a Polish nobleman (Stanislas Poniatowski), elected to the Polish throne. This maneuver gave Russia paramount influence over Poland. Five years later, however, a segment of the Polish nobility revolted against their puppet king, who was supported by Russian troops, and called for Turkish aid. The Polish problem thus became linked with the centuries-old friction between Russia and Turkey, since the rebellion provoked a major Russo-Turkish War (1768–1774) in which the Russians were victorious on all fronts. This war and the Russian successes alarmed Prussia and Austria, as well as Turkey's traditional friend France, and led indirectly to the first partition of Poland.

Austria was then under the joint rule of Maria Theresa and her son Joseph II, who had succeeded his father, Francis I, in 1765. The new emperor, according to Frederick, was "charming, attractive, and of vivid intellect." Intent on enlarging and strengthening Austria, he built his policy on friendship with France, which encouraged him in his anti-Russian stand. Joseph feared that Russia might reap excessive gains from the Turkish War, and he hoped to obtain compensatory acquisitions for Austria by seizing certain strips of Polish land.

In view of the Prusso-Russian alliance, however, Joseph hesitated to antagonize Russia, for fear an Austro-Russian War would involve Frederick as an ally of Catherine. The Austrians therefore attempted to wean Prussia away from Russia.

Joseph visited Frederick in 1769 and feted him on a return visit in 1770. The emperor, himself an intellectual of sorts and an aspiring enlightened despot, greatly admired Frederick, and the two monarchs formed a friendship. But the description so often repeated of the young Joseph II sitting worshipfully at the feet of his older master to learn from him the secrets of enlightened government is a sentimental invention. Although Frederick liked Joseph, he distrusted his political designs. "He assured me that he had forgotten Silesia," Frederick reported to his minister after the first meeting with Joseph, "and then proposed a mutual reduction in our troop strength, which I refused as politely as possible." The Prussian king complained that Joseph was "devoured by ambition," and that it was "certain Europe will go up in flames as soon as he assumes [sole] rule." Joseph had no great confidence in Frederick, either. He regarded him as a genius but at heart a scoundrel.

But their visits were primarily motivated by political considerations. Vienna desired an alliance with Berlin, or at least assurance of Prussia's benevolent neutrality if Austria became involved in a war with Russia. No alliance resulted, but Frederick promised to use his good offices with Catherine in behalf of Austrian demands on Polish territory. For Frederick and Joseph were in accord on at least one point: a unilateral aggrandizement by Russia from gains made in the Turkish War was undesirable, and Austria and Prussia should make equal acquisitions at the expense of Poland.

To improve their bargaining position, Austria and Prussia each occupied a slice of Polish territory in 1770. In the same year, Frederick sent his brother Henry to St. Petersburg to sound out Catherine's views on a possible partition of Poland. The empress reacted rather coolly, since she regarded Poland as being in her own sphere of influence. But Austria made it clear that it would not permit Russia to dismember Turkey, and Catherine finally agreed to reduce her demands for Turkish territory in return for a portion of Poland.

In this way agreements were finally reached among the three powers concerning the partition of Poland, which was effected in 1772. Russia obtained the largest section (2200 square miles): Polish Lithuania east of the river Düna, and those portions of White Russia to the east of the Dnieper. Austria took Galicia (1300 square miles), whereas Prussia received some 600 square miles of Ermeland, West Prussia, and the district along the river Netze, except for the cities of Danzig and Thorn. Although Frederick obtained the smallest slice in this partition, his acquisitions were of great importance to Prussia. A land bridge was now established between Frederick's central possessions and the outlying region of East Prussia, and important agricultural districts were added to his state.

Aside from the question of morality, there has been much historical debate about the advisability of this partition of Poland. Unquestionably Prussia's expansion to the east into territory outside the boundaries of the Empire raised difficult questions for its future role in Germany. The same, of course, applied to Austria's acquisition of Galicia. Nationalistic German historians have always hailed Frederick's eastern annexations as the reconquest of "lost German lands." "Frederick regained," so runs a typical though moderate account, "for the German way of life [*Deutschtum*] original German [*urdeutsch*] land which had become utterly neglected under Polish rule." Other historians justify the acquisition on the basis that it "finally rounded off the eastern wing of the kingdom into a contiguous and tolerably defensible territory." On the opposite pole are the historians who stress the largely Polish character of the population of the annexed territories. "The theft of Polish territory was a misfortune not merely for the Polish but also for the German people," writes one of them. It "strengthened the feudal reaction in Germany and created additional difficulties for a progressive, peaceful, national development of Germany."

The Bavarian Succession

During the 1770s, Frederick's alliance with Catherine the Great remained the backbone of his foreign policy, while Joseph II relied on friendship with France—of which Marie Antoinette, his sister, became queen in 1774. The ambitious emperor took advantage of Russia's victory over Turkey to seize a portion of Bucovina and looked about for further aggrandizement. The question of the Bavarian succession seemed to present an excellent opportunity. The elector of Bavaria (Maximilian III Joseph) died childless in 1777. His nearest heir, the elector Palatine (Charles Theodore), of another branch of the Wittelsbach family, promptly concluded a pact with Emperor Joseph, ceding most of the Upper Palatinate and Northern Bavaria to Austria in return for good sincecures for his many illegitimate children. Joseph immediately occupied the territories, and the new elector of Bavaria assumed control over his rump state. The international situation favored Joseph's undertaking. The revolt of the American colonies, supported by France after 1778, kept English and French eyes averted from the Continent; and Catherine of Russia, threatened by possible renewal of the Turkish War, had no desire to become involved in Bavarian affairs. Frederick alone voiced objections against such Austrian aggrandizement. Together with Wittelsbach claimants, including Saxony, whose duke was a nephew of the late Bavarian elector, Prussia protested against Vienna's actions.

Emperor Joseph did not take Prussia's remonstrance seriously, but Frederick acted with resolution. He declared war on Austria and sent his troops into Bohemia (July 1778), opening the War of the Bavarian Succession. The ensuing struggle was derisively called the Potato War, since no battles were fought, but both armies ran low on food supplies. Unlike her ambitious son Joseph, Maria Theresa was interested in maintaining peace, and all other nations were eager to avoid another general conflagration. France and Russia, as allies of the two belligerents, immediately offered their mediation and peace was concluded in the following year (Peace of Teschen, 1779). The new Bavarian elector (Charles Theodore) retained the Palatinate and all of Bavaria, except for a small section between the Inn, the Salzach, and the Danube, the so-called Inn Quarter, which was ceded to Austria. Saxony received a financial indemnity for its claims, and Prussia was given permission to incorporate into its state the Hohenzollern possessions of Ansbach and Bayreuth, upon extinction of the local branches of the dynasty.

The Potato War satisfied Frederick's desire to prevent the aggrandizement of Austria. This was to remain the guiding thought of his foreign policy during the last years of his reign. In resisting Austrian expansion, he acted as protector of the smaller German states, accentuating ever more the dualism within the Empire, in which Prussia and Austria vied for predominance.

In 1784, Joseph II—who had assumed sole rule after the death of his mother in 1780—concluded a new bargain with the elector of Bavaria: the latter was to receive the Austrian Netherlands and the rank of king in return for cession to Austria of all of Bavaria. The scheme suited Joseph's plans to exchange all his outlying districts for territory contiguous to Austria's homelands. In a similar move, he hoped to exchange Limburg and Luxemburg for Salzburg and Berchtesgaden. Most European powers looked with equanimity on Joseph's plans, but Frederick again objected. Acquisition of Bavaria would have made Austria preponderant in southern Germany and possibly throughout the Empire.

In 1785, he created a League of German Princes, consisting of Saxony, Hanover, Mainz, and eleven other states, for the protection of the "constitution" of the Empire. Its stated aim was to prevent Joseph from executing the proposed exchange of territory with Bavaria, because it contravened the Treaties of Utrecht. This League of German Princes has often been hailed as an eighteenth-century attempt to unite Germany, to expel Austria from German affairs, and to create a state on the basis of *Kleindeutschland* under Prussian leadership. Neither the pact itself nor Frederick's intentions warrant such an explanation, for the aim of Frederick and the princes was to maintain the *status quo* and reinforce the powers of the princes, and not to reform the "constitution" of the Empire.

The League of German Princes was Frederick's last major foray into foreign policy. His health had never been very strong. Gout, dropsy, and a stroke were sapping his last physical resources. He died at seventy-four in the summer of 1786.

The fruits of his foreign activities can be summed up thus: through conquest, annexation, and inheritance—Silesia, the Polish lands, and the Duchy of East Frisia (see Map 14)—he had increased Prussian territory by over half; he had made Prussia into a first-rate European power; and he bequeathed to it the reputation of a militaristic and aggressive state. The role as one of "Europe's bad boys," played by Spain in the late sixteenth century and by Sweden and France in the seventeenth century, was temporarily assumed by Prussia under Frederick's rule.

FREDERICK'S INTERNAL ADMINISTRATION

Frederick's importance for Prussia and Germany of course transcends his activities in foreign affairs. Besides the years of war, there were

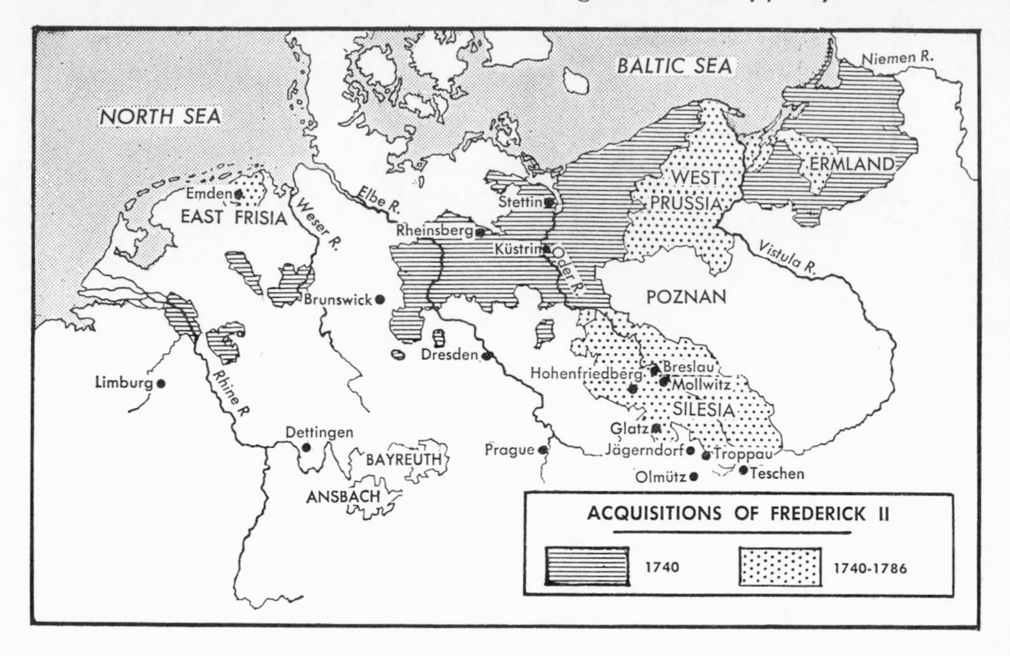

MAP 14

thirty-five years of peace during which he left a considerable impact on his age and implemented a large-scale reform program.

The Philosopher King

Frederick was a typical representative of the Age of Reason and a philosopher in the sense of the French eighteenth-century *philosophes.* At Rheinsberg in the 1730s and later in his rococo retreat of Sans-Souci near Potsdam, he surrounded himself with enlightened intellectuals, especially Frenchmen like Maupertuis, d'Argens, and Voltaire. With those whom he could not attract to his court, like Montesquieu, Diderot, and d'Alembert, he corresponded, discussing their works, the classics, questions of moral or political philosophy, or the writings of recent authors such as Hobbes, Locke, and Fénelon. His workday at Sans-Souci followed a strict schedule. Certain hours of the day were devoted to writing, composing, making music, and participating in intellectual discussions. Considering that he conducted the affairs of state like an autocrat, acting as his own minister of foreign affairs, of the interior, of finance, and of war, it is surprising that he found time for so many intellectual pursuits.

Our conceptions of the ideas, policies, and administration of the *Philosophe de Sans-Souci* are colored by a peculiar legacy. Few, if any, important rulers have left so many writings as Frederick has. The thirty-one volumes of his collected works—apart from more than forty-six volumes of political correspondence—include works on history, political science, government and administration, religion, military strategy, philosophy, and ethics, as well as poetry. Much of his writing is heavily didactic, but most is of good literary quality. As a result, historians are almost better informed about Frederick's thoughts and plans than about his actual accomplishments, and their views are invariably influenced by this legacy.

Frederick was rather eclectic in his philosophical tastes, and somewhat of a skeptic in the manner of Pierre Bayle, the French thinker whose works Frederick admired. Like Bayle, he liked to investigate and speculate, but he always doubted that definite knowledge could be attained, for he lacked the optimistic convictions of most of the French Encyclopedists. Perhaps as a result of his skepticism, he grew increasingly morose and lonely, and became in the last decades of his life a misanthropic cynic.

In his eclecticism, he freely adopted ideas and transformed them to suit his devices, regardless of possible contradictions. From the German philosopher Wolff, he accepted a measure of determinism suited to his predilection for Stoic fatalism. He fully agreed with John Locke's theories on the importance of environment in shaping human character, but rejected his conclusions about innate equality among men. To Locke's contractual theories of government—in which the people have the right to rebel against their ruler—he preferred Hobbes's theory of an original contract, made in prehistoric times between ruler and ruled, which is irrevocable and imposes no limits on the power of the ruler other than the responsibility of protecting his subjects. Frederick also studied Montesquieu and agreed with his stress on the importance of law in all social organizations. To a degree, he implemented Montesquieu's suggested divisions of power in government by partially separating the judicial and executive branches, but he retained executive and legislative powers in the hands of the king.

He particularly liked Fénelon's didactic writings, and subscribed to the Frenchman's advice that rulers were responsible for the happiness of their subjects. But as an autocrat, of course, he reserved to himself the right to determine what was best suited to make his subjects happy. In religious beliefs, Frederick can be generally classed as a Deist. He believed in the existence of a God as the original source of all power and in the impossibility, or at least unlikelihood, of divine interference in the everyday affairs of the world. But, unlike the Deists, he was not sure of the immortality of the soul, and professed complete disinterest in a possible life after death.

The Enlightened Despot

The theory of enlightened despotism, elaborated by the French *philosophes,* called for a ruler who governed according to principles of reason and on the basis of law. Arbitrary actions had no place in such a system. An enlightened despot, furthermore, was to be responsible for the welfare of the state and the people, but not accountable to his subjects.

Frederick the Great, who fits these criteria on the basis of his philosophical ideas and governmental theories, is usually labeled as a model enlightened despot. Yet there were considerable differences between the enunciated principles of the French *philosophes* and their implementation by the

Prussian ruler, not merely because theory often differs from practice but also because Frederick held certain concepts that deviated radically from those of the French theorists. This was particularly true in regard to the role of the state and the question of individual rights and equality. These differences throw light on Frederick as a ruler and on general conditions in Prussia.

Enlightened despotism in theory stressed that the ruler's actions should benefit the people and the state, but Frederick always stressed the latter. To him the state was of prime importance, and the people's value lay in their worth to the state. This state was so important and all-embracing that it was also above the ruler. Frederick's famous dictum that "the king is the first servant of the state," so frequently misinterpreted to show his humility, was meant rather to underline the ruler's duty to subordinate his personal wishes to the higher political ideal of the state.

The French *philosophes,* predominantly members of the middle class, generally supported Locke's view of the state's duty to guarantee "life, liberty, and property." Frederick agreed that the state should respect the safety of the individual and the security of his personal material property. In Prussia, unlike France under Louis XV, people were relatively safe from arbitrary arrest or unjustified confiscation of property. But as for "liberty," Frederick's concept was not free choice and action but rather obedience to willingly accepted authority in the sense developed by Rousseau: individual actions were at all times subordinate to the requirements of the state.

In his ideas on equality, Frederick was almost reactionary. He believed in a strict *Ständestaat* (state composed of estates), similar to what had existed in the Middle Ages. The classes to him were not equal: each had its own abilities, rights, and, above all, duties. The nobles were considered the pillars of the kingdom. Aristocrats invariably had a "greater sense of honor" than bourgeois or peasants. The sons of the nobility "must defend the country," he wrote; "their race is so useful that they deserve to be conserved in every way." Only nobles could serve as officers or high government officials. Frederick even dismissed the nonaristocratic officers who had served under his father and during the Silesian wars. He also stopped the conferring of noble patents by the king, for he believed that one could only be born into the aristocracy. Frederick thus completed the creation of a *Junkerstaat,* a state in which closest harmony existed between king and nobles. The bourgeois on the other hand, were to take care of trade, commerce, and manufacturing. No longer allowed to purchase noble estates, they could not slide laterally into the ranks of the nobility. Conversely, no aristocrat was allowed to engage in commerce or industrial production. The peasants had their own obligations—paying the onerous taxes on land, tilling the soil, and acting as soldiers in the royal armies. Although there was no class mobility in this medieval castelike system, neither in theory was there any oppression of one class by another. Frederick insisted that the government owed protection to all three classes, since all their activities were essential to the well-being of the state.

These differences between theory

and application of enlightened despotism may also explain why Frederick attracted, and yet repelled, the intellectuals of his time. In general, he was admired as a philosopher, but hated as a grouchy tyrant. Those at a distance, particularly the French *philosophes* who knew him primarily from his writings and correspondence, praised him as if he were Socrates and Caesar combined. Even the young Goethe, from outside Prussia, called him "the Northern Star about which revolve Germany, Europe, nay, even the world!" But those who saw his government in action quickly voiced their disenchantment, finding in Prussia, with its harsh financial, military, and police pressures, a regime more despotic than enlightened. Voltaire's disillusionment after three years in Potsdam resulted not merely from personal disagreement with the king, but also from the fact that Voltaire had not found in Prussia the political paradise he had expected. And Lessing, who had lived in Prussia, called it "the most enslaved land of Europe."

Governmental Policies and Reforms

RELIGION AND EDUCATION Keeping in mind his enlightened theories, one can more easily understand the nature of Frederick's governmental policies and reforms. In religious questions he was broad-minded and tolerant without believing in equality for all faiths. He did not care how people worshiped, perhaps because of his personal indifference to spiritual matters, and showed equal favors to Lutheranism and Calvinism, hoping the two would bridge their doctrinal differences and merge into a single Protestant movement. He built a church in Berlin for his Catholic subjects, and hired an Orthodox priest as chaplain for soldiers of that faith. When the Society of Jesus was dissolved by the pope in 1773, he seized the income of their establishments, but did not expel the Jesuits as did some other rulers. Rather, he used them as teachers, particularly in Silesia, which had a heavily Catholic population.

On the other hand, his tolerance was limited and he was hardly free from prejudice. No Catholic was admitted to the upper posts in government. In his *Political Testament* of 1752 he even advised his successor "not to trust the Catholic clergy, unless certain proof of their loyalty is at hand." And although he showed respect to a number of Jewish intellectuals and bankers, his general attitude toward them was one of prejudice. "The state cannot use Jews. . . . We must see to it that their number does not increase. . . . They should be kept out of the wholesale business and allowed only to deal in retail."

Like all rationalists of the eighteenth century, Frederick was interested in education. He expanded the educational system fostered by his father, and issued special school laws for Protestant and Catholic elementary schools (*Volksschule*). Significantly, the curriculum in the upper classes was modified to include logic, German grammar, Latin, geometry, religion, and history. History, a relatively new field of study in the eighteenth century in which Frederick was particularly interested, was made a requirement for all future officers. Frederick also devoted much attention to specialized advanced education, particularly for the army and the bureaucracy. The practical and theoretical training of civil servants was improved, a military academy for the training of officers was established in 1755, and twenty years later, a school for engineers was opened.

LEGAL AND ADMINISTRATIVE REFORMS. Frederick the Great appreciated the importance of law in government and society. In fact, one of the prime differences between the typical monarch by divine right of preceding periods and the enlightened despot of the eighteenth century was the latter's rejection of arbitrariness and his acceptance of the rule of law. "Let the laws speak and the ruler be silent" was his motto and, to a considerable degree, he aimed at realizing this concept. Far-reaching reforms of the legal systems and court procedures were undertaken during his reign (by Cocceji and later by Carmer). To regulate legal procedure, speed up trials, and make them uniform throughout his lands, a *Codex Fridericianus* was issued (1747–1748). New legal procedures were first tried in Pomerania and gradually extended to the other provinces. The multiplicity of courts with overlapping jurisdictions was reduced to distinct organs at three levels. The highest courts were the *Tribunale* in Berlin and Königsberg. Below them came various superior courts, called *Hofgericht* in Prussia, *Kammergericht* in Berlin, and *Regierungsgericht* in the provinces; at the bottom of the scale were the ordinary courts on the royal domains, on the estates of the nobility, or in the cities.

The selection and remuneration of judges were radically altered. To eliminate the customary bribery by litigants, judges received regular, adequate pay. Litigants paid the state for use of the courts, and the state in turn paid the judges. After 1755, only trained lawyers who had passed a special examination were allowed to practice as judges, and members of the legal faculty of the universities were prohibited from acting as judges, their function being restricted to the training of lawyers. In this way the judges became state employees rather than remaining an independent class as in France. To make the laws uniform for all his lands, Frederick's legal advisers continued the collection of laws started by Frederick William I, which as *Corpus juris Fridericiani* was finally published in 1794 and became the basic law code (*Allgemeines Preussisches Landrecht*) for all of Prussia.

At the same time Frederick insisted that the laws of the state be obeyed by all, regardless of rank and station, and he used every available occasion to demonstrate that in Prussia even the upper nobility had to submit to equality before the law. As a result, his Prussian subjects acquired an ingrained respect for law, no matter how harsh, which was to differentiate them considerably from most of their contemporaries in other lands. But Frederick's reforms did not create a true *Rechtsstaat,* a state in which the law is supreme not only over the individual but also over the government. Despite the wishes of some reformers, the administration of justice and the administration of government remained separate. Governmental bureaus were not made subject to the law courts. Every ministry and administrative service retained its own judicial powers to investigate, judge, and assess fines and punishments. Civil and criminal cases were judged by the regular courts, but a question of tax evasion, for instance, was judged by the

Ministry of Finance. Thus the individual had no recourse against the government. The new legal system provided speedy and fair justice to the people in their relations with each other; but in the relations between subjects and government, Prussia lacked protective safeguards for the individual citizen.

During his reign of forty-six years, Frederick also reformed the governmental machinery. Primarily these changes were aimed at increasing efficiency and at assimilating the newly acquired territories. As the task of government grew more complex, Frederick established new ministries under the direction of the General Directory. After creating the Ministry of Trade and Commerce in 1740, he added six years later a special Department for the Army, primarily to handle logistical support; in 1768, he established a Ministry for Mining and Mineral Resources, and finally, in 1770, a Ministry of Forestry. The civil service grew constantly in size, and foreigners were amused by the large number of Prussian officials. Despite its size, the system remained fairly efficient under the strict supervision of the king. Inspectors in the field checked the work in the provinces, and regular promotion lists were prepared for approval by the monarch. Centralization continued to be the basic criterion for the organizational framework. The granting of local privileges was usually mere window dressing. Frederick, for instance, wanted to please the bourgeois by returning to the cities certain rights of local administration that had been canceled by his predecessors. In reality, such concessions were meaningless, for the fiscal agents (*Steuerräte*) sent to the cities by the central government remained the primary authority within the municipalities.

ECONOMIC PATERNALISM In financial and economic policies, Frederick the Great mixed mercantilistic theories with his own brand of paternalism. On the basis of regular reports from the provinces on imports, exports, production and consumption, working conditions, quality of goods and prices, he gathered detailed statistics used to determine policies that would strengthen the state by aiding all vital sectors of the economy. He retained the three main taxes inherited from his predecessors: the indirect consumption tax in the cities (assize), the land tax paid by the peasants (contribution), and the feudal dues of the nobles, which amounted to very little, except in Silesia where the nobility had not traditionally been tax-exempt. The main revenue of the state, however, was still derived from the royal domains, which consisted of almost a quarter of all land in the state. Later he changed the assize into the *Regie* and entrusted its administration, assessment, and collection to French agents, who increased the revenue but also turned the tax into a harsh and hated institution. Assessments on some essential items were reduced, but taxes on luxury goods were raised considerably. Frederick also introduced state monopolies on tobacco and coffee, and set up a state lottery. Through these various measures, the state's annual income rose from 7.4 million thaler in 1740 to over 20 million at Frederick's death.

His policies for agricultural and industrial production were basically mercantilistic, and achieved for Prussia a highly favorable balance of trade.

In some cases total import restrictions were enforced, resulting in trade wars with neighboring states (Saxony and Austria). To reduce smuggling, customs patrols guarded the borders. The lumber industry and the mining of iron, coal, copper, and salt were encouraged by state subsidies. The government set up "royal factories," and particularly furthered the production of cotton, silk, china, and metal articles, such as knives, scissors, and armaments. Frederick imported and helped settle skilled craftsmen to develop these industries, constructed or supervised public housing and even set up production quotas.

Similar attention was paid to agriculture. New arable land was opened, partly by draining swamps along the Oder, Warta, and Netze Rivers. New villages were constructed with state funds, and the immigration of peasants was encouraged. The newly created Ministry of Forestry controlled the lumber reserves of the country and made reforestation compulsory in certain regions.

In some respects, Frederick's trade and financial policies followed the ideas of the French physiocrats. He encouraged a freer flow of goods within Prussia by reducing internal tolls, improving transportation facilities, constructing additional roads and canals, and making rivers more easily navigable. Emden in East Frisia was turned into a free port, and Prussia's participation in external trade was encouraged by the establishment of an Overseas Trade Office (*Seehandlung*) in 1772. To facilitate commercial credit, he also founded a state bank in 1763.

His reputation for paternalism was also based on his solicitude for the various classes of the state. The nobility received his special attention. He protected the landed rights of the nobles by prohibiting the bourgeois from purchasing noble estates. To ease their financial difficulties, he opened a mortgage institution in 1770, which would extend credit to the noble landowners up to an amount of 50 percent of the value of their land. Moreover, he did not want to undermine the nobles' political and economic hold on the peasants by abolishing serfdom—although the abolition of serfdom was one of the tenets of the Enlightenment. On the other hand, he helped the bourgeois with his economic policies, and improved living conditions for the workers by subsidizing housing and attempting to stabilize the cost of living. To achieve the latter, he tried to equalize the cost of grain. When in the period 1770–1774, for example, poor harvests threatened to raise the price of grain and cause a famine, Frederick ordered grain to be sold cheaply from the state granaries. When three years later good harvests made the price of grain fall to the point where landlords suffered losses, the state purchased large quantities for storage in its warehouses and the price of the commodity again rose to a normal level. Finally, there was the peasant class, the "nourishing fathers of the state" (*Nährväter*) as Frederick called them. The king abolished serfdom on the royal domains and suggested that on the noble estates the labor services (*corvée*) of the peasants be reduced to three or four days a week, so that they would have more time to work on their own plots. He also prohibited confiscation by nobles of peasant plots for which the peasant could not prove his rights of ownership. Needless to say, despite these royal measures, the plight of the peasant continued to be exceedingly harsh.

Frederick's Views on German Culture

It is strange that Frederick, who became one of the most beloved heroes of the Germans, was completely at odds with the cultural development of Germany. His love of French culture made him almost blind to the gradual cultural revival in Germany during his lifetime. In fact, his judgments were frequently unenlightened in that he considered almost anything good if French, and poor if German. He was so thoroughly rococo in his tastes that he adored Rameau, but had no understanding of Bach or Handel.

His literary tastes were equally one-sided. He hated the German language, "a jargon devoid of grace," which he spoke very poorly and used only rarely in his correspondence, and he did not think German writers worthwhile unless they copied or imitated French models. The few German authors he graced with his favor were second- or third-rate writers—Christian Gellert (1715–1769) with his sentimental plays and his fables, both in slavish imitation of French models; or Johann Gleim (1719–1803), who produced heroic poems such as the *Kriegslieder eines preussischen Grenadiers* (*Warsongs of a Prussian Grenadier*). But for the real awakening of German literature inspired by England rather than France he showed no appreciation. Friedrich Klopstock (1724–1803), Gotthold Lessing (1729–1781), and the beginning of the *Sturm und Drang* movement (see page 249) that initiated the high period in German literature, he rejected. Goethe's *Götz von Berlichingen* he called a "horrible imitation of those bad English plays," presumably in reference to Shakespeare, who was then becoming popular in Germany, and whose plays Frederick deemed "fit only for the savages of Canada." As late as 1780, in his book *On German Literature,* Frederick could discover no outstanding writers among his German contemporaries, although for some reason he predicted an era of greatness after his death, when "we shall have our classic authors," and when "our language, polished and perfected by our writers will be spoken . . . throughout Europe."

THE RESILIENCE OF AUSTRIA

While Prussia grew in power and cohesion under Frederick the Great, Austria not merely survived but emerged strengthened from the onslaught of the War of the Austrian Succession. Its territorial losses were largely balanced by gains in other areas: it lost Silesia (1742), Parma, Piacenza, and Guastalla (1748); but acquired Galicia (1772), Bucovina (1774), and the Inn Quarter (1779).

Austria under Maria Theresa

From 1740 to 1780, Austria was ruled by Maria Theresa, archduchess of Austria and queen of Hungary and Bohemia. After her husband's coronation as emperor in 1745, she assumed the title of empress, although she did not officially become the head of the Empire. In theory, the Empire and the Hapsburg lands were during this period under separate rulers: the former ruled by her husband, Francis

I (1745–1765) and later by her son, Joseph II; in the latter, Francis and Joseph acted only as coregents with Maria Theresa. In fact, however, the empress exercised primary power over the Hapsburg lands as well as over the Empire, particularly during the lifetime of her ineffectual husband.

Maria Theresa was essentially peace-loving, a devout Catholic, and conservative. But her conservatism did not prevent her from being interested in reforms, particularly in softening the penal code, improving education, and ameliorating the conditions of the peasantry. And in foreign affairs, her much-publicized scruples did not keep her from practicing ruthless *Realpolitik,* while praying, "God grant that I be not held accountable for it in the next world!" In fact, she did not hesitate to emulate the tactics of her antagonist Frederick II. While protesting about the ignominy of annexing territory without legal claims, she participated in the "unfortunate" partition of Poland, which threw her into "blackest melancholy" and, as she explained, poisoned and embittered her life. Similarly, she tried to soften her son's tempestuous attempts to aggrandize Austria. But she certainly did not prevent him from acting like Frederick when he simply seized Bavaria so as to negotiate from strength rather than first negotiating and hoping to gain Bavarian territory later.

Within the hereditary lands, certain administrative reforms were undertaken. In the absence of a workable system of confederation, not considered possible at the time, Austria needed to centralize its government if the state was to remain viable. Considering the ethnic and geographic differences among the various Hapsburg lands, such a task was considerably more complicated in Austria than in Prussia. Maria Theresa reduced the vast number of regional administrative organs, and consolidated their tasks into six central governmental departments set up on the basis of function rather than geography, and subject, as in Prussia, to a single directory. This initial step made the local estates obsolete by removing their residual administrative powers. At the same time, it increased Vienna's need for a large civil service, and heightened the domination by the German element from Austria proper over the other peoples in the state—Slavs, Magyars, Italians, Belgians, and others. To reinforce this trend, Maria Theresa made German the official governmental language throughout the Hapsburg possessions.

Meanwhile, Maria Theresa's husband busied himself with financial reforms, the only field in which he showed some aptitude. In 1747 Austria received her first state budget, in which contemplated revenues and expenditures were enumerated. But whereas Prussia usually accrued a surplus during years of peace, Austria's revenue remained inadequate, and its budget was balanced for the first time only in 1775. Like her contemporary in Prussia, Maria Theresa applied some mercantilistic practices to improve the economy of the land. A central commercial agency established in 1746 promoted the commercial and industrial life of Austria and Bohemia. But trade and manufacture did not develop as fast as expected, since Austria lacked capital. There was also a resistance to modernizing the tariff structure and to granting equal trade opportunity to all regions of the Austrian state. Tolls between the various parts of the Hapsburg possessions were not removed and markets remained restricted. Certain regions were kept in a quasi-colonial status. In Hungary, for instance, and later in Galicia and Bucovina, the government settled German peasants and aided agricultural undertakings, but the expansion of industry was discouraged, and ultimately the establishment of new manufactories in these lands was prohibited.

The Reign of Joseph II

When Joseph II took over sole control of the state in 1780, he rushed to implement reforms with a speed that betrayed the impatience he had felt under his mother's tutelage. Joseph, a doctrinaire reformer, attempted to put into practice at one stroke all the innovations and improvements suggested by the rationalist *philosophes.* Unquestionably his motives were good. He wanted to make his subjects happy, if necessary by force, by applying rationalism to government, but he was hasty in his measures and, unlike Catherine or Frederick, he showed little judgment in distinguishing between ideal and feasible theories. As Frederick said of him, "Too bad he always takes the second step before the first."

In 1781, he emancipated the peasants from serfdom throughout his lands—a step his mother, as well as Frederick in Prussia, had applied only to the royal domains. The obligation of forced labor of the former serfs was commuted into contributions in kind payable to the lord of the land. But few preparations were made for the economic welfare of the freed peasantry and for the functioning of the landed estates; hence the measure failed to produce the blissful conditions envisioned by the reforming emperor. In actual fact, the serflike obligations on the peasantry remained in effect until the Revolution of 1848. A second reform dealt with the legal system. Joseph hoped to eliminate the differences among the legal practices in the various parts of his state by promoting common procedures and a common code. He even suggested abolishing the death penalty. Although improvements were achieved, it proved impossible to coordinate all systems on an equal basis throughout his lands.

His attitude toward the Church was close to that of the French rationalists, and quite in contrast to the traditional Hapsburg policy of close support for the Catholic Church. Essentially, he sought to withdraw all power from the Church, and make it strictly subordinate to the state. He confiscated about one third of all monastic institutions in his state, some 783 monasteries and convents not engaged in social work: operating hospitals, schools, or similar institutions. The funds gained were used to pay the salaries of bishops, who now became state employees, to open seminaries for the "enlightened" training of clerics, and to enlarge the school system, for which he proclaimed an obligatory attendance of seven years. He also placed the activities of the clergy under the strict supervision of the state. Papal bulls and pastoral letters could not be published without approval by the government, and priests were no longer to be educated in Rome. In addition, Protestants and Jews were awarded freedom of worship; censorship laws were eased so that liberal ideas could more easily be published.

Above all, Joseph showed a passionate interest in charitable and social institutions. Hospitals, orphanages, homes for the indigent, insane asylums, reformatories, institutions for the deaf and dumb were established by the state or with state funds, according to the ideal rationalist theories of the duties of a secular ruler. At the same time, he continued his mother's attempts to centralize and strengthen the state, albeit at a rapidly accelerated pace.

Army reforms along Prussian lines and intensified support for commerce, industry, and navigation generally produced lasting results. But the forced "nationalization" of the subject countries provoked resistance and ultimately rebellion. The Hungarians, deprived of their remaining rights to appoint their own officials, were henceforth governed by envoys from Vienna. Joseph announced his concept of a unitary state rather peremptorily by refusing to be crowned in Prague and Budapest as king of Bohemia and of Hungary, respectively, as had his predecessors for centuries. He proclaimed the head of Austria to be automatically ruler over all Hapsburg lands. To show that Hungary had ceased to exist as a separate entity, he even ordered the revered crown of St. Stephen—Hungary's symbol of national independence—brought to Vienna to be placed in a museum, an order that had to be rescinded because of violent Hungarian opposition.

But Joseph's reforms were too drastic and hasty, and the differences among his various subject peoples more ingrained than he had realized. Toward the end of his short reign, Hungarians and Belgians rose in rebellion, and most of his reforms had to be dropped. Many historians have concluded that Joseph's impatience threw Austria into turmoil instead of strengthening it. It is, of course, true that Prussia at the death of Frederick II in 1786 was stronger than Austria at the end of Joseph's reign in 1790. But the Prussian state contained an inherent weakness: its power depended largely on the strength of one man. Under Frederick's rather incompetent successors, Prussia fell rapidly from its pinnacle, and finally experienced complete disintegration during the Napoleonic period. Austria, on the other hand, despite inherent weaknesses, retained its resilience. She not merely withstood the onslaughts of the revolutionary and Napoleonic eras with surprising vitality, but was to emerge stronger than ever in 1815.

THE LESSER STATES

Under the shadow of the rivalry between Prussia and Austria, the other states of Germany lost more and more power. Neither resources nor population permitted them to compete with the first-ranked nations of the Continent. Even the larger ones, such as Saxony, Bavaria, and Hanover, gradually diminished in political and economic importance. But most of the rulers of these states hardly seemed to appreciate the insignificance of their power. In fact, it would seem that the less their significance, the more their pretentions to status. With a few notable exceptions, the princelings were almost ludicrous in their demands for recognition. Unfortunately many of them were determined to compensate for their lack of external power by enforcing internal despotism on their subjects. Even the obscurest ones insisted on the need for a sizable army, an expensive court, and quasi-royal prerogatives. In most cases, they engaged in bitter fights with the estates, which hoped to retain some measure of control over the prince's expenditures.

Opposition to princely absolutism came from the lower nobility and the bourgeois, who felt the impact of the Enlightenment. But in only a few states, Württemberg and Mecklenburg, for example, did the long struggle between the estates and the rulers result in a compromise, whereby some limits were imposed on the power of the princes. In most states, the nobles moved gradually to the side of the princes, while the bourgeois were too weak to resist ducal absolutism. In these states, the underlying tension between ruler and ruled continued and made itself powerfully felt during the revolutionary and Napoleonic periods. The princes, for their part, tried to bolster their independence by satisfying their financial needs in ways not requiring approval by the estates. The favorite device continued to be acceptance of foreign subsidies. Other schemes included the sale of soldiers to foreign powers, practiced assiduously by the dukes of Hesse-Cassel.

The plethora of courts produced certain cultural advantages, especially in the fields of architecture, music, and drama. A sort of social and artistic rivalry among the princes led them to allot disproportionately large sums to the construction of beautiful castles, art galleries, parks, theaters, opera houses, or other public buildings. Soon dozens of German towns boasted one or more theaters, academies for the sciences or the arts, and conservatories of music, all of which gave a boost to the cultural awakening of Germany during the second half of the eighteenth century.

11

The French Revolution and Germany, 1786–1813

THE FERMENT OF NEW IDEAS

The pervading atmosphere in Germany in the days of Frederick the Great had been essentially conservative. Rationalism and enlightenment had provided a comforting prop for the genteel courtly society. Didactic neoclassicism in literature, still leaning heavily on French models, and classical forms in music as found in Haydn's work, had appealed to the love of order characteristic of the aristocracy. But during the last quarter of the eighteenth century, Germany experienced a cultural flourishing that not only produced literary and musical works of permanent value and affected European culture in general, but ultimately exerted great influence on the sociopolitical development of the country. Revolutionary trends were astir long before Frederick's death in 1786, stimulating new styles in art and music, renewed vigor in literature and thought, and liberal currents in politics.

The new trend was heralded in a little booklet published anonymously in 1773, *Von Deutscher Art und Kunst, einige Fliegende Blätter* (*Pamphlets on the Nature and Art of the Germans*). This small, poorly printed volume contained three essays directing German literature and intellectual thought toward new goals. In it the barrister Justus Möser (1720–1794) drew an original sketch of German history, extolling the freedom of the old Germanic peoples in contrast to the Germans' eighteenth-century servitude. The young counselor Johann Gottfried von Herder (1744–1803) praised German folklore, urged the collection of German folksongs and tales, and pointed to Shakespeare as a worthy model for German dramatists. Finally, the twenty-four-year-old Johann Wolfgang von Goethe (1749–1832) attacked the current uncritical reverence for classical architecture and lauded the medieval Gothic style as embodied in the cathedral at Strassburg.

The three essays initiated a revolution in German thought, and roused the young intelligentsia of the period. Although not chauvinistic, the movement enhanced the patriotic tendencies of the decade following the Seven Years' War. It demanded a return to the popular art of former generations, in spirit as well as subject matter. It rejected the notion that Germans were incapable of producing their own art and pointed to Germany's past, its folk spirit, and its native genius as inspiration for a renaissance in German thought and letters. The three authors espoused Rousseau's emotionalism rather than the cold reason of Voltaire, "nature" rather than artificial "culture," passion rather than reason, faith rather than skepticism. Above all, in the arts they hoped to enthrone the ideal of the creative genius as opposed to esthetic rules and regulations. And in his later works, Herder developed his theory of the *Volksseele,* the essence or soul of a people which determines its character and destiny—a notion which undermined the cosmopolitan rationalism of his age.

In the same year that the first *Fliegende Blätter* appeared, Goethe revolutionized drama with his *Götz von Berlichingen,* a play that in many respects epitomized the new movement. Inspired by Shakespeare, Goethe broke with the rules of classical drama in form, style, and subject matter. The hero Götz, a powerful representative of the dying class of knights of the sixteenth century, is portrayed as fighting a gallant but hopeless battle on the side of the peasants against the territorial lords. Violence and rebellion intermingle with sentimental longing for bygone days of justice and freedom. In the following year, Goethe published *The Sorrows of Young Werther.* The emotional outpourings of the novel's young hero, whose hopeless love finally drives him to kill himself, brought Germans and Europeans to tears and despair, and inspired many "romantic" suicides.

In its full bloom, this new movement, which rapidly embraced large segments of German intellectual life, was called *Sturm und Drang* (Storm and Stress). In essence, it was a poetic and religious movement with political overtones. In poetry and drama *Sturm und Drang* signified a bursting of all fetters, with sole reliance on the genius and emotional inspiration of the poet. In religion the stream ran counter to the worship of mathematical order popular in the Enlightenment, and favored an intense, inner faith and a belief in the occult and mysterious.

In politics the call was for more freedom from arbitrary rule and petty tyranny, and occasionally for more national coherence. The examples of England's parliamentary system and of the concepts of popular sovereignty implemented in the American War of Independence were not merely stirring prerevolutionary France but also raising expectations among the German middle class. The newly awakened interest in politics, absent in previous generations, can be seen in the works of many poets, dramatists, and ballad writers of the period. They attacked the oriental tyranny of petty princes and their practice of selling soldiers, the immorality of the aristocracy and their court intrigues, the nobles' exploitation of the land and their disdain for the *bourgeoisie.* Students organized literary societies and spent evenings singing new drinking songs that praised their German fatherland and vented their hatred of tyranny and foreigners, especially the French. Their new literary heroes were William Tell, Arminius (Hermann der Cherusker), and Brutus, who had stood by his convictions and murdered the tyrant Caesar. Gradually these poets became bolder and no longer masked their attacks by allegorical or fictional devices. Instead of laying their scenes in distant lands or past times, they dealt with contemporary affairs in Germany.

Among the poets who became politically minded was Goethe's friend Friedrich von Schiller (1759–1805), one of Germany's great playwrights. Schiller, an angry young man of his generation, was a fugitive from the tyranny of the duke of his native Württemberg. His drama *Die Räuber* (*The Robbers*) is even more emotional and more politically barbed than Goethe's *Götz*. The hero is not an individualistic knight of the sixteenth century, but a robber of the eighteenth who glories in excesses of cruelty and ruthlessness. Unlike the sentimental Werther, Schiller's hero turns a weapon not against himself but against an unjust society.

Sturm und Drang was essentially a transitional movement and, like all rebellions, short-lived. The excessive revolt against rules in drama and poetry soon gave way to the new poetic conventions of romanticism. The religious rebellion was gradually replaced by a reinvigorated Enlightenment or a return to more traditional forms of religion, particularly Roman Catholicism. And the political demands in the days before the French Revolution never went beyond the boards of the stage or the recitations of students and poets. The exclamation of the hero in *Die Räuber,* "Put me in front of an army of fellows like me and Germany will be turned into a republic," had hardly more effect on German politics than the equally provocative demand by Marquis Posa in Schiller's *Don Carlos*: "Sir, give us freedom of thought!"

It is significant that throughout this period the German intellectuals remained cosmopolitan—despite the literary and cultural revival that made them increasingly conscious of Germany's cultural unity and despite occasional flashes of extreme patriotism evoked by the *Sturm und Drang* writers, in particular Herder. They looked upon German nationalism as a "political monstrosity," an obstacle to human usefulness, and considered *Weltbürgertum* (world citizenship) the only proper calling for the leading men of the nation. As the dramatist Gotthold Lessing wrote: "To be praised as a zealous patriot is the last thing I desire—a patriot that is, who would teach me to forget that I must be a citizen of the world." The German writers actually rejoiced that Germany did not exist as a nation that might confine their realms of thought by claiming a narrow allegiance. The young and freedom-loving Schiller boasted that he wrote "as a citizen of the world who serves no prince." He was proud to "belong to no nation," and exclaimed: "I lost my fatherland to exchange it for the great world. What is the greatest of nations but a fragment?" Even Johann Gottlieb Fichte (1762–1814), later one of the strongest advocates of German patriotism, proclaimed before his "conversion" that the fatherland of the truly educated Christian European should not be a particular region but "that European state which leads in culture."

Although it produced no immediate, tangible political results, *Sturm und Drang* turned Germany from the cultural desert it had become in the seventeenth century to the proverbial land of poets, thinkers, and musicians. And this cultural flourishing was vital in providing Germany with the coherence not furnished by its loose political structure.

GERMANY DURING THE FRENCH REVOLUTIONARY PERIOD

Frederick William II

The new king of Prussia was Frederick William II (1786–1797), the eldest son of Frederick the Great's younger brother. The succession showed the weakness inherent in Prussia's highly centralized governmental system. Although efficient and well organized by Frederick William's predecessors, the Prussian administrative machinery was not yet capable of functioning under a poor ruler. And the good-natured Frederick William II was indeed incompetent. During his ten-year rule, Prussia began the rapid decline that finally ended in the disaster of 1806. Although personally immoral and preoccupied with sensual pleasures—after divorcing one wife, he committed bigamy while retaining a string of mistresses—he pretended to be deeply religious and fell under the influence of a number of spiritualistic charlatans who guided his decisions of state. Eagerness to gain easy popularity led him to discard many successful policies of his predecessor. He cut taxes and reintroduced favoritism in military promotions, thereby dissipating the fiscal reserves of the state and reducing the efficiency of the army. Within a few years of his accession, Prussia was heavily in debt and its prestige had waned.

Frederick William's foreign policy was marked by vacillation. Except in relation to Poland, he missed opportunities to maintain or improve Prussia's position, and he failed to comprehend the real dangers that threatened Germany from revolutionary France. Austria, suffering from internal unrest and economic failures in the last years of Emperor Joseph II's reign, became involved in a joint Russo-Austrian War against Turkey. For a moment the court of Berlin thought of strengthening Prussia's position by seizing Polish territory while Austrian and Russian eyes were turned toward the Balkans. But Frederick William II rarely acted with determination. He permitted Prussia to be sidetracked into the triple Anglo-Dutch-Prussian alliance of 1788. England was interested in protecting Holland from possible French interference and in maintaining Europe's peace and equilibrium. Hence the new alliance, which put pressure on Russia and Austria to restore their conquests to Turkey, was of little benefit to Prussia.

INITIAL REACTION TO THE REVOLUTION The storming of the Bastille in Paris and the spread of the revolution in France at first affected Germany relatively little. Prepared by the ideas of Rousseau, the French Encyclopedists, the American Revolution, and the German *Sturm und Drang,* most German intellectuals immediately proclaimed their enthusiastic adherence to the French principles of 1789. Poets, historians, pamphleteers, and journalists hailed the era seemingly inaugurated by events in Paris. But the princely governments of the German states were naturally opposed to the revolutionary ideas of liberty and equality. They feared that this "strange, nameless, wild, enthusiastic thing," as Edmund Burke called the

French Revolution, might stir unrest among their subjects and endanger their traditional prerogatives. Yet during the initial years of the revolution, France as a state appeared hardly to pose a threat to Germany. On the contrary, some German statesmen welcomed the events in France on the theory that they would sap France's strength and undermine its ability to meddle in German affairs.

Even in 1790, Frederick William thought Prussia had more to gain from unrest in Poland than to fear from revolution in France, and he might never have interfered in French affairs if it had not been for Austrian persuasion. The new emperor, Leopold II (1790–1792), was vitally interested in French affairs, since Queen Marie Antoinette was his sister, and since France had been a useful ally of Austria for three decades. He talked Frederick William into signing a treaty of friendship whereby Prussia temporarily abandoned its independence in foreign affairs to play second fiddle to Austria. Within two years this friendship involved Prussia in war with France for which the former was militarily and financially unprepared.

There were, of course, many reasons for the outbreak in 1792 of the first of a long series of French revolutionary wars, all of which engulfed Germany in one way or another. On the one hand, many French revolutionaries, particularly the Girondists, actively and enthusiastically sought war "for the maintenance of liberty and independence." On the other hand, many people within the Empire were equally eager for war. Dozens of German princes—among them the archbishops of Mainz, Trier, and Cologne, the duke of Württemberg, the elector Palatine, the margrave of Baden—had possessed feudal lands in Alsace that, according to the Treaties of Westphalia, had been placed under French sovereignty. These lands had all been confiscated in 1789 when the French revolutionists abolished feudalism. The German princes protested against this unilateral decision. After a debate in the imperial diet, they appealed to the French National Assembly, which rejected their claims on the basis of the new ideal of popular sovereignty but offered to pay an indemnity. The Germans refused to be satisfied by indemnity payments, and were considering military action to recover their lands. By 1791 most of the princes also became alarmed at the increasingly Gallophile tendencies among large segments of their middle-class subjects. Exhortations to follow the French example, demands for a written constitution, even proposals for establishing republics or incorporating the Rhineland with France were heard with greater frequency and were pushing the governments toward opening a war against revolutionary France.

The French aristocrats who had emigrated with the brother of Louis XVI also helped drive Germany into war. Their headquarters was at Trier, where the archbishop supplied them with weapons. From here they issued appeals to the German princes to launch an anti-French crusade for the rescue of the honor and traditions of royalty. Although the German rulers officially rejected the appeals of this army in exile, its very presence on German soil, close to the border of France, did much to stimulate the war fever.

THE FIRST COALITION AGAINST FRANCE

In the summer of 1791, Emperor Leopold pushed Austria closer to the brink of war with France, even though he officially and perhaps sincerely desired to maintain peace. He invited the sovereigns of Europe to espouse the cause of his brother-in-law Louis XVI, massed troops along the French frontier, and drew Prussia into a military alliance. At a conference in August of that year, the emperor and the Prussian king discussed the affairs of France and finally issued the undiplomatic Declaration of Pillnitz. While informing the French *émigrés* that they could no longer use imperial territory for their military preparations, the two rulers promised to "employ the most efficient means, in proportion to their resources, to place the king of France in a position to establish" a government that would be "in harmony with the rights of sovereigns." It is fairly evident that this declaration was intended as a bluff. It was hedged with loopholes, for it called for action on the condition that all major powers would participate, and Leopold was fairly certain that Britain would not join the proposed coalition. Rather, Leopold hoped to frighten the revolutionaries in Paris into treating his brother-in-law and sister with more circumspection, and neither he nor Frederick William made the required war preparations implied in their declaration. The French revolutionaries, on the other hand, found in this unfortunate manifesto powerful ammunition for whipping up enthusiasm for an eventual armed conflict.

In April of 1792, France finally declared war on Austria. Although the declaration of war was directed only against "the King of Hungary and of Bohemia," Prussia and most German states immediately ranged themselves on the side of the new emperor, Francis II (1792–1835, after 1804 also known as Francis I of Austria), who succeeded his father in the spring of 1792. The allied armies were placed under the poor leadership of the duke of Brunswick, who issued the so-called Brunswick Manifesto in the names of the emperor and the king of Prussia, announcing the Austro-Prussian war aims of helping the German princes regain their rights in Alsace and of freeing the French king from the restraints imposed by the revolutionaries. The manifesto threatened to punish all Frenchmen who took up arms against the invading Germans and to "inflict an ever memorable vengeance by delivering over the city of Paris to military execution and complete destruction" if the Parisians did not at once submit to Louis XVI.

The subsequent invasion of eastern France turned into an almost immediate fiasco for the German forces, and showed particularly how far the Prussian armies had deteriorated since the death of Frederick the Great. Undaunted by his lack of military knowledge, Frederick William II accompanied the armies and constantly interfered in military decisions. Poor logistical support and insufficient training undermined the spirit of the small Austro-Prussian forces, who faced a motley army of French regulars and volunteers, inferior in equipment and experience, but superior in numbers and enthusiasm. The Prussian officers had been misled by the exaggerations of the *émigrés,* and had disdainfully assumed that the hordes of undisciplined French revolutionaries would quail before the "invincible Prussian army."

When the two armies met at Valmy,

some hundred miles east of Paris, the German forces fled in disarray before the wildly screaming, spirited French. Militarily this battle of Valmy was unimportant. Except for exchange of cannon fire, there was little contact between the opposing forces and few casualties on either side. But its psychological and political consequences were immensely significant for the course of the revolution in France, as well as for the ensuing policy of Prussia. The frequently quoted words of Goethe who, as court historian to the prince of Weimar, witnessed the battle and observed the patriotic zeal of the French, are still apt: "From today begins a new era of world history." The French victory gave renewed confidence to the revolutionaries in Paris, who on the day of the Battle of Valmy deposed Louis XVI and proclaimed the First French Republic. At the same time it made the Prussians less eager to remain in the war. Complaints about lack of Austrian support were voiced at the court of Berlin, and distrust of Austria threatened to overshadow fear of the revolutionaries.

After the retreat of their opponents, the French took the offensive on all fronts. They defeated the Austrians in the north and seized Brussels and the Austrian Netherlands; in the south they occupied Nice and Savoy; and without officially declaring war on the imperial princes, they invaded the Upper Rhineland, captured Spires, Worms, and Mainz, and Frankfurt on the Main. These successes intoxicated the French and convinced them of the invincibility of their armies and the righteousness of their cause. They executed Louis XVI, declared war on England, Holland, Spain, and a host of other countries, and officially offered assistance to all peoples who wished to overthrow their own "tyrannical" governments. In consequence, the war changed in character. The principle adopted in the initial French constitution "not to undertake any war with a view to conquest" was transmuted into an offer of assistance to bring the "inestimable blessing" of French liberty to all peoples. This offer was immediately accepted by republican forces in Belgium, the Rhenish provinces, Savoy, and Nice when they requested to be united with France on the basis of popular sovereignty.

Stirred by the French victories and excesses, the coalition forces resumed their offensive on all fronts and achieved temporary successes during most of 1793, until the threatened French revolutionaries declared a general mobilization of all manpower, reorganized their forces, and reversed the allied advances. Frederick William II meanwhile attempted to play a double role. His armies helped in the temporary reconquest of the Rhineland and he accepted British funds for continued participation in the war against France. His main attention, however, had shifted to the east.

THE FINAL PARTITIONING OF POLAND

In 1791, Poland had changed its constitution to strengthen the central government and decrease the power of the unruly nobility. In the following year, Empress Catherine II of Russia took advantage of Austro-Prussian involvement in the French War by invading Poland, officially to prevent the spread of French revolutionary ideas into eastern Europe. In reality, she feared that the new constitution might strengthen the Polish state. Without consulting his Austrian ally, who was bearing the brunt of the anti-French war effort, the Prussian king sent troops into western Poland and forced Catherine to share the spoils of her conquest. The two states then agreed upon a second partition, awarding eastern Poland to Russia and transferring some 25,000 square miles with a population of about a million people to Prussia—the cities of Danzig and Thorn, with the districts of Poznan, Gnesen, and Kalisch which came to be called South Prussia. At the same time the revised Polish constitution was set aside in favor of a return to Poland's traditional anarchy.

Emperor Francis II was naturally bitter about this Russo-Prussian action that left Austria without any spoils. Cooperation between Vienna and Berlin suffered accordingly, and the emperor revived the scheme of seeking compensations in Bavarian territory and abandoning the Austrian Netherlands, which had proved difficult to defend. But England, Holland, and Prussia opposed this Austrian plan.

Meanwhile the Polish patriots, led by Thaddeus Kosciusko, made one final attempt to resuscitate their truncated nation, giving Prussia an excuse for interfering again in Polish affairs. Prussian army units moved into Poland, soon followed by Russian troops from the east. After prolonged fighting and a siege of Warsaw, the insurrectionists were defeated and Poland was obliterated from the map of Europe. This time Austria, having rushed back troops from the French frontier, was permitted to take its share. The third and last partition of Poland, completed in 1795, awarded Cracow to Austria, Central Poland to Russia, and Warsaw with the surrounding districts and another million inhabitants to Prussia. These territorial accretions, marking the high point of Prussia's expansion in the east, created new problems because the population was primarily of Slavic stock, and even harsh administrative methods could not achieve its assimilation (see Map 15).

THE PEACE OF BASEL In the same year Frederick William II withdrew from the war in the west: Prussia's resources were exhausted, despite British subsidies, its finances were depleted, and little had been done to improve or enlarge its army. Prussia's relations with its so-called Austrian ally were strained, not merely because of the events in Poland but also because of rivalry between Francis and Frederick William for the role of preeminent protector of the Empire against French encroachment. Moreover, conditions in France had changed. The Terror had gradually subsided after Robespierre's execution, and the more moderate leaders in Paris spoke of abandoning the missionary zeal for revolutionizing all of Europe. On these grounds, Frederick William felt justified in abandoning Austria and concluding a separate peace with France.

In the resulting Peace of Basel of 1795, Prussia recognized the legal status of the republican government of France, which in turn promised to respect the neutrality of the German states north of the river Main. In a secret clause, Prussia agreed to permanent French annexation of the entire left bank of the Rhine, including the small territories Prussia owned west of the Rhine. In exchange, Prussia would be allowed to annex as yet unspecified lands in northern Germany. Soon Spain also arranged for peace with France, and most of the German

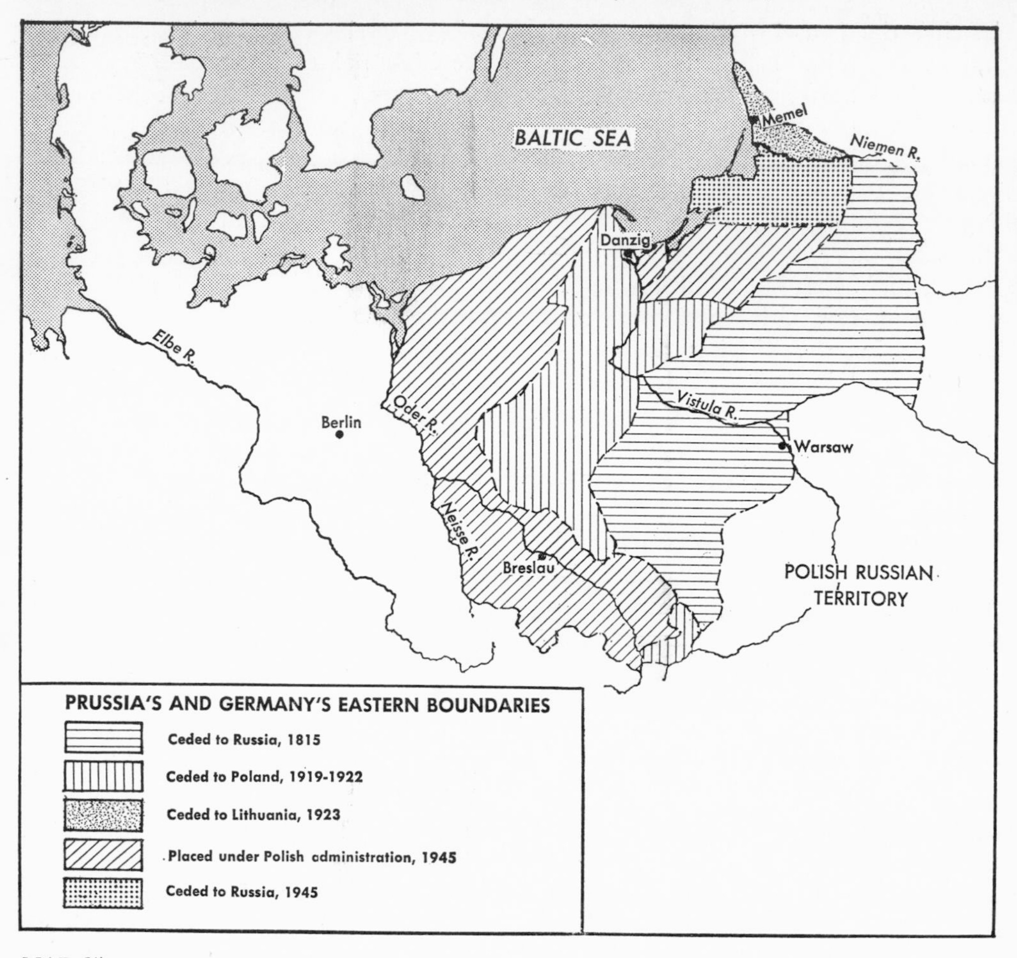

MAP 15

princes—Saxony, Hesse-Cassel, Württemberg, Baden, Swabia, and Bavaria—followed suit. Meanwhile Holland was transformed into the Batavian Republic under the protection of France. Austria and England thus remained alone in the field against France, each refusing to cease hostilities and to recognize the permanence of the French Republic.

For France the Peace of Basel marked a major victory and an important step toward the long-desired recognition of its "natural frontiers." Within the Empire, the treaty provoked varying reactions. In his *Perpetual Peace* the philosopher Immanuel Kant (1724–1804) acclaimed it as the beginning of a new era. Some praised Frederick William for drawing to his side most of the German princes and giving Prussia a respite to absorb its Polish acquisitions while France and Austria continued to weaken each other in a prolonged war. Such judgments proved shortsighted, for in reality Prussia did not gain prestige in the Empire through the Treaty of Basel, but instead lost its strong position in Germany. By permitting France to seize German land that Prussia did not own and by claiming territory in northern Germany that belonged to others, Prussia endangered its pretended role as protector of German interests. Unlike England and Austria, Frederick William did not realize that the moderate spirit of the French was merely an interlude during which France could regain its strength. Finally, contrary to the precepts of Frederick the Great, Frederick William did not use the years of peace to build up his resources and to reorganize his armies in preparation for the inevitable ultimate battle. While Austria and England continued the struggle, he kept Prussia on the side lines, where it remained, growing more and more impotent, until 1806, when it was too late.

Austria and the Lesser States

A few months after the conclusion of the Peace of Basel, France established the Directory, a short-lived experiment with republican forms of administration. In the war against England and Austria France was increasingly successful; its armies were superbly organized and led by excellent generals, including the young Napoleon Bonaparte. During the campaigns of 1796 and 1797, French strategy against Austria was based on a pincer movement: the armies under Napoleon operated in Italy to attack Austria from the south, while the northern forces pushed through the Rhineland, Baden, and Württemberg into Bavaria to invade Austria by way of Germany. As a result, southern Germany became a battlefield. Neutrality was of little help to the states in the path of the opposing armies. Some envied Prussia and the northern states that appeared to be safe behind the line of demarcation set up in the Treaty of Basel. They appealed to Frederick William to intercede in their behalf with the French. The Prussian king enjoyed the role of protector of German interests and negotiated with Paris about an extension of the line of demarcation, an effort that proved fruitless as long as Austrian and French armies faced each other in the field. Not obtaining protection from Prussia or Austria, some of the small southern and western princes concluded that an understanding with France offered the only chance to safeguard their territories from military devastation. This pro-French attitude in the south and west became an important trend during the ensuing decade, with repercussions on Germany as a whole.

For two years, Austria showed astonishing resilience in its war against France. Skillfully led by Archduke Charles (1771–1847), the brother of Emperor Francis, its armies held their own in southern Germany; in Italy, however, the Austrians could not counter Napoleon's successful campaigns. By 1797 Austria was ready to come to terms with France. The resulting Peace of Campo Formio was the counterpart of the Treaty of Basel. Austria officially ceded Belgium to France and recognized the French gains in northern Italy, while claiming for itself compensation in eastern Venetia. In a secret clause Austria agreed to French annexation of the left bank of the Rhine as far north as the city of Andernach. The Prussian possessions north of that point were excluded, presumably to allow France to make its own deal with Prussia—an arrangement already secretly made in

1795. On the other hand, another secret clause stipulated that Prussia was not to receive compensations for lands it might lose to France west of the Rhine. Finally it was agreed that France would help Austria get Salzburg and a strip of southeastern Bavaria. The Treaty of Campo Formio was concluded by Francis only in the name of Austria. The Empire was to be dealt with separately. Vienna and Paris merely agreed that a congress should be called at which France would negotiate with the imperial princes about conclusion of peace and possible indemnification—for those German princes who would stand to lose possessions west of the Rhine in consequence of the secret clauses of Campo Formio.

As a result of this treaty of 1797, the spheres of influence in central Europe were radically altered. Through the loss of Belgium, Austria was withdrawing from western Europe. By not acting as the spokesman for the Empire, it was abandoning its pre-eminent role in Germany. On the other hand, it was consolidating its position in southeastern Europe. At the same time France was offered what amounted to a *carte blanche* for reorganizing Germany. With Austria and Prussia abdicating their former roles, France could henceforth assume protectorship over the small German states. Before long the ambitious Napoleon drew the logical consequences from this treaty and made full use of the opportunity.

The conference to establish peace between the Empire and France convened at Rastatt in Baden at the end of 1797. Its deliberations lasted seventeen months without accomplishing more than showing the self-interest and disunity of the German princes. Although Prussia and Austria had just bartered away portions of imperial territory in their treaties with France, their envoys at Rastatt pretended to be guardians of imperial interests. Francis II did not even blush at the hypocrisy of admonishing the assembled princes "to uphold the common interests of the fatherland" and "to promote a just and enduring peace, founded upon the integrity of the Empire." The lesser princes and their ambassadors, however, fully realized that the tables had been turned on Prussia and Austria. While intriguing against one another, they took care to ingratiate themselves with the French envoys in order to obtain favorable concessions. In the end, France alone benefited from the meeting. Officially granted possession of the entire left bank of the Rhine, it proceeded to annex these territories. Moreover, France skillfully fostered distrust among the German princes, promoted jealousy between Prussia and Austria by appearing to favor the former, and pretended to act as protector of the smaller states against both Hohenzollerns and Hapsburgs. But before compensations for dispossessed rulers or peace terms for the Empire were set the conference was dissolved in the face of renewed hostilities.

THE ERA OF NAPOLEON

Even during 1798, while these negotiations were taking place, the insatiable French armies had been on the move in Italy, Switzerland, and Egypt. Finally in the winter of 1798–1799, the big second anti-French coalition was formed. Russia this time assumed the initial leadership, and Austria was easily persuaded to re-enter the fray at the side of Britain, Naples, Turkey, and Portugal. Once again Italy, Switzerland, Holland, and Germany became battlefields during three years of almost uninterrupted campaigns. Only Prussia, now ruled by the young Frederick William III (1797–1840), refused to participate in the struggle that was to determine the fate of Germany. In spite of occasional reverses, the French won most of the battles. In 1799, Napoleon consolidated his grasp on France through his *coup d'état,* and acquired the power that permitted him to initiate his interminable revisions of the map of Europe—annexing conquered territories, setting up satellite republics, and ultimately creating kingdoms at will.

Reorganization of the Empire

In 1801, Austria, forced for a second time to withdraw from the war, signed a peace treaty with Napoleon and agreed to recognize the territorial changes he had imposed on other states. Once again Emperor Francis had left the Empire to shift for itself.

The German princes now began to dance the last minuet of an era. Unable to agree among themselves on reapportioning the truncated territory of the Empire, they called on France and Russia to act as arbitrators. Actually, Russia was given little opportunity to make its voice felt; France alone called the tune, which in effect became the imperial funeral march.

Between 1801 and 1803, Napoleon, by then First Consul of France, and his Minister Talleyrand supervised the reorganization of the Empire. It is symptomatic of the state of German affairs that the dissection of the German body politic was not undertaken at a conference deliberating on German soil, but that all important issues were settled in Paris, where Talleyrand had great sport receiving envoys of the German princes, each trying to undermine his competitor through larger bribes and more obsequious flatteries.

The initial reorganization of the Empire eliminated over half of the more than 300 political entities that had claimed sovereign status since the Treaties of Westphalia. Forty-five imperial cities were deprived of their independence, and only six—Hamburg, Bremen, Lübeck, Frankfurt on the Main, Nuremberg, and Augsburg—survived as free cities. Of seventy ecclesiastical states—archbishoprics, bishoprics, abbacies, and the like—only one, the former electorate of Mainz, now transferred to Regensburg, retained sovereignty. The 112 cities and territories deprived of their independence were incorporated into other states, and the arrangements were set down in the so-called *Reichsdeputationshauptschluss* (Principal Decree of the Imperial Deputation), confirmed at a diet in Regensburg in 1803.

After this first reorganization, under French guidance, the German princes themselves continued the process of secularization and consolidation. Imitating the example set by the French Revolution, the states confiscated all religious establishments, including monasteries, universities, and hospitals. Furthermore, all remaining "immediate" knights, over one thousand of whom still claimed quasi sovereignty, were deprived of their lands and political power.

It seems noteworthy that in the course of this reorganization, the outdated framework of the Empire was retained—at least for the time being. The former archbishop of Mainz, now bishop of Regensburg, kept his electoral voice and his post as archchancellor of the Empire. To replace the abolished electorates of Trier and Cologne, now annexed to France, Hesse-Cassel, Württemberg, Baden, and Salzburg were given electoral privileges. Hence the electoral college was not only retained but enlarged, as if it were still endowed with meaningful power and authority.

As a result of these changes, the number of German states was considerably reduced and the surviving ones were enlarged and consolidated. The secondary states in central and southern Germany, particularly Bavaria, Baden, Württemberg, and Hesse-Cassel, received territorial compensations for lands lost west of the Rhine, as well as additional increases in territory and population. Prussia was awarded none of the lands it coveted south of the river Main, but was allotted some 5000 square miles of former ecclesiastical territories in northern Germany in compensation for the 1000 square miles lost to France west of the Rhine.

The territorial rearrangements of Germany were, of course, extremely favorable to France: they gave Napoleon a dominant voice east of the Rhine. By heaping favors upon the secondary states, he bound them closer to France, and could reasonably expect they would support his future ventures lest a French defeat deprive them of their territorial gains. In case of need, the southern "client" states might also act as a buffer against Austria or coalesce into a third force within the Empire as a counterweight to Prussia and Austria. On the other hand, it was to Napoleon's advantage to reward Frederick William for his benevolent neutrality and, as Napoleon wrote to Talleyrand, encourage "increased opposition between Vienna and Berlin," as well as to assure that the affairs of the Empire "will be directed from two different centers."

It would be erroneous to assume that the decrease in the number of states ended German *Kleinstäaterei,* the small-state system, or marked a first step of unifying Germany. By building up the secondary states and cultivating friendly relations with them, France in effect made unification of Germany more difficult, since these states were placed in a better position to defend their sovereignty against possible encroachment by either Prussia or Austria. The nineteenth century was to prove the soundness of this hypothesis. On one score, however, France unwittingly improved Prussia's chances of later assuming a dominant role in Germany: the elimination of the ecclesiastical states and the secularization of church institutions weakened Catholic Austria while enhancing the political prestige of Prussia, Germany's most powerful Protestant state.

The Confederation of the Rhine

In the same year, 1803, Napoleon's troops actively interfered in northern Germany, to the dismay of King Frederick William III. After a brief truce that followed the Peace of Amiens (1802), England and France had resumed hostilities. In answer, Napoleon had rushed his troops to the north and seized the Duchy of Hanover, which still belonged to the English crown. This move placed Napoleon's troops between Brandenburg and Prussia's Rhineland provinces, and the French promptly closed the mouths of the Elbe and Weser rivers, thereby blocking Prussian commerce. Although Prussia's dream of dominating northern Germany was thus endangered, the only response of the peace-loving, pious, and irresolute Frederick William was to issue a mild protest. Even when two years later the allies organized the third anti-French coalition, Frederick William stuck by his neutral course. Neither Russia nor England could entice Prussia to join their alliance. On the contrary, the Prussian king listened willingly to French overtures for a treaty, signed in 1805, whereby Prussia promised to remain neutral and ceded additional territories to France (including Ansbach and Neuchâtel), in return for the promised cession of Hanover after the conclusion of the war with England.

The ensuing War of the Third Coalition, in which England, Sweden, Russia, and Austria were allied against Napoleon, again turned southern Germany into a battlefield. This time, however, German conditions were different. Napoleon's reorganization of the Empire was bearing fruit. The states he had favored with territorial aggrandizement, Bavaria, Württemberg, and Baden, joined the French against Austria, making Napoleon's passage through southern Germany much easier. Hence Napoleon could invade Austria with unexpected speed, capture Vienna itself, and disrupt the coalition through his brilliant victory at Austerlitz. The Russians were forced to retreat, and Austria agreed to still another peace treaty. For a third time in less than a decade, Austria was defeated by the French and obliged to accept territorial losses. In the Treaty of Pressburg of 1805, Austria ceded a further strip of Italian territory to France. Napoleon's "client" states Bavaria, Württemberg, and Baden received valuable gains, mostly at the expense of Hapsburg territory. Württemberg and Bavaria were also turned into kingdoms.

In the following year (1806), Napoleon and his retinue of German princes further reorganized Germany by eliminating several minor states, depriving Nuremberg and Frankfurt of their free status, and finally establishing the Confederation of the Rhine with Napoleon as its official protector. Within a short time all states of the Empire joined this league, with the exception of Austria, Prussia, Brunswick, and electoral Hesse. Even Saxony eventually became a member of this Napoleonic creation with which Napoleon presumably hoped to frighten Prussia and Austria into further submissiveness.

The creation of the Confederation of the Rhine entailed the final demise of the Holy Roman Empire. The first step in this denouement had already been taken in 1804, when Napoleon had proclaimed himself Emperor of the French. The days of Charles the Great seemed revived, but was there room in central Europe for two emperors? While the southern German princes hailed their French protector as emperor and extended congratulations to him, England, Russia, and Prussia notified Francis II that they still recognized him as emperor and ruler of the Holy Roman Empire. Francis, however, preferred to be realistic, and placed more reliance on his hereditary Austrian possessions than on the elective imperial title over regions rapidly slipping from his control. The structural reorganization of the Empire effected by Napoleon made it doubtful that a Hapsburg would be elected upon the death of the incumbent, since the occupants of some of the newly created electorates were rivals of the Hapsburgs and could not be expected to follow the traditional pattern of seeking their emperors in Vienna. Consequently Francis decided to negotiate with Napoleon. Although not yet relinquishing his title of Holy Roman Emperor, he agreed to recognize the Frenchman's imperial dignity in return for his own recognition as Emperor of Austria. Francis II thus assumed his new title: Francis I, His Imperial and Royal Apostolic Majesty of Austria. (*Seine Oesterreichisch-Kaiserliche und Königlich-Apostolische Majestät*).

This interim solution was finally cast aside in 1806. When the German princes met to establish the Confederation of the Rhine, they were encouraged by Napoleon to renounce all residual allegiance to the Hapsburg emperor. Napoleon then proclaimed that the German states had ceased to be states of the Empire and that "the Diet no longer has a will of its own." He acknowledged the complete and absolute sovereignty of these states and so notified the court of Vienna. In reply Francis admitted that conditions in Germany no longer permitted him "to fulfill the duties which we have assumed by the conditions of our election." And he concluded:

> We proclaim, therefore, that we consider the ties which have thus far united us to the German Empire as dissolved; that we look upon the office and dignity of the Imperial headship as dissolved by the formation of a separate federation of the Rhenish States, and regard ourselves as freed from all obligations to the German Empire. Herewith we lay down the Imperial crown which is associated with such obligations and we relinquish the Imperial Government which we have thus far conducted. . . .

The Defeat of Prussia

The year 1806 and the establishment of the Confederation of the Rhine finally shook Frederick William III out of his lethargy. Events in Germany and the arguments of the war party in Berlin led him to the hesitant conclusion that Prussia's ultimate survival no longer rested on neutrality and reliance on Napoleonic promises but on its own army. France's annexations in Germany north of the Main, its alliance with the German princes, and the stationing of French troops on German soil in time of peace made Frederick William realize at last that Prussia could never dominate northern Germany so long as Napoleon retained his present position. Moreover, he was jealous of the added power and prestige of the southern princes. His resentment came to a head over the issue of Hanover. As a reward for his neutrality, Frederick William had been permitted to occupy Hanover, an action that ruined Prussian overseas trade by provoking British retaliatory seizures of Prussian merchant vessels. In the summer of 1806 Frederick William learned to his surprise that Napoleon, eager to negotiate peace with the English, had offered to return Hanover to them. The Prussian king then realized that he was being duped by Napoleon and ordered mobilization of the Prussian army. But it is characteristic of his sentimental behavior that shortly before the outbreak of war, he wrote to Napoleon and, like a cheated lover, reminded the emperor of their past harmonious relationship and of the services he had rendered to him: "I have been insensible to threats as well as to promises when it was a question of making me false to our good relations."

Prussia's call to arms unleashed enthusiastic demonstrations in Berlin, encouraged by exaggerated royal proclamations. Frederick William promised to liberate all Germany from the French yoke, and privately hoped at least to unite northern Germany under Prussian auspices. Napoleon was hardly dismayed by Prussia's mobilization nor by Frederick William's proclamations. "The suggestion that Prussia could campaign against me by itself," he wrote to Talleyrand, "seems to me so ridiculous as not to warrant discussion." The Prussian king actually was counting on Russian assistance, having made a secret military agreement with Emperor Alexander I, in whom he had great confidence. (His wife, Queen Louise, wrote to the tsar): "I believe in you as I believe in God.") In accordance with the secret Prusso-Russian arrangements, Alexander I canceled his truce with France, and in late September Prussian troops marched into Saxony, with which a prior understanding had been reached.

Thus Prussia supposedly had two allies against Napoleon. But the decisive military clash with France occurred so quickly that neither Russia nor Saxony could be of much help. Moreover, the Prussian armies were unprepared for the ordeal. Little or nothing had been learned from the defeats of 1792 or the Napoleonic campaigns against Austria. Superannuated officers from the days of Frederick the Great led regiments that were not even brought up to full strength because of embezzlement and inefficiency in the system of recruitment. A demoralizing mixture of disdainful self-confidence and hero worship of Napoleon affected the fighting spirit of the Prussian army; the irresolute Frederick William hardly helped matters by accompanying the army and interfering in its military command.

Early in October 1806, French and Prussian armies met on Saxon soil. Despite adequate warning, the Prussians failed to concentrate their forces, giving Napoleon the opportunity of attacking two separate contingents in the same day. In two battles on October 14, one at Jena, the other at Auerstädt a few miles away, the Prussians were routed. The remnants of the army fled in disarray. The king sought refuge in East Prussia, hoping to find safety in the proximity of Russian troops. After Jena, the French forces rapidly occupied almost all of Brandenburg. One Prussian fortress after another surrendered to the French, frequently without attempting defense, despite adequate supplies and manpower. Berlin itself opened its gates to Napoleon on October 27.

THE AFTERMATH OF JENA

Had Prussia been alone, the war would have ended in a few weeks. Immediately after Jena, the king requested a truce, hoping for lenient terms from the conqueror he secretly still admired. But Napoleon, who still faced the Russian forces, rejected the appeal. While treating the occupied portions of Prussia as conquered provinces, collecting indemnity payments, and even incorporating Prussian lands west of the Elbe into his ever-growing empire, he marched east and urged the Poles to revolt against their Prussian and Russian masters. By December, he was encamped in Warsaw, ready to risk a winter campaign. The ensuing battle of Eylau (February 1807) against Russians and Prussians was indecisive. Heavy losses forced both sides to withdraw while awaiting reinforcements, and induced Napoleon to tempt Frederick William to abandon the tsar and conclude peace.

But Frederick William had been too rudely shocked by French behavior; one incident was particularly galling—Napoleon had ordered the victory statue toppled from the Brandenburg Gate in Berlin and dragged off to Paris. Lacking confidence in Napoleon, he decided to remain at the side of Alexander I and rejected the French enticements. He even negotiated secretly with England and Austria in the hope that they might help Prussia out of its predicament. But by June Napoleon had gathered sufficient reinforcements to resume his campaign. At the ensuing Battle of Friedland, in June 1807, Russia was defeated so decisively that Alexander abandoned his Prussian ally and requested an immediate armistice and peace negotiations.

The Peace of Tilsit

Russia's defeat at Friedland sealed Prussia's fate and produced a diplomatic reversal in Europe. Alexander decided to throw in his lot with the conqueror of Europe. Just as Stalin and Hitler came to terms in 1939 in order to destroy Poland, so Alexander thought it opportune to divide Europe with Napoleon over the prostrate body of Prussia. The two rulers met on a raft in the river Niemen near Tilsit to discuss an economic and military offensive against England, the disposition of Prussia and Poland, the future of Turkey, and their respective spheres of influence on the Continent. While the two ambitious emperors secretly conferred for two days in the seclusion of their raft, Frederick William and his beautiful wife, Louise, had to wait on the shores of the Niemen before they were finally allowed to hear the sentence of Tilsit. Seldom had royalty been treated with so little respect. Not even Queen Louise, who is said to have supplicated Napoleon on her knees, was able to avert the complete destruction of Prussia.

The Treaties of Tilsit, which resulted from this conference, marked one of the low points in Prussian history. Napoleon had even contemplated dismembering Prussia completely, but partly at the behest of the tsar he agreed merely to reduce Prussia by over half in size and population and eventually limit its army to only 42,000 men. The treaty even included the humiliating statement that Prussia owed its survival to the intercession of the tsar, as if to say that the Prussian state had no right to existence on its own basis. Prussia was deprived of all its lands west and south of the Elbe, most of which were incorporated into the Kingdom of Westphalia, which Napoleon had just created for one of his brothers. The Polish lands that Prussia had acquired in the partitions of 1792 and 1795 were taken to create the Grand Duchy of Warsaw. In addition Prussia was forced to pay a large indemnity to France and to permit French garrisons on Prussian soil until full payment was made. Finally, Prussia had to join the economic blockade against England that Napoleon had proclaimed from Berlin.

A further humiliation for Frederick William resulted from Napoleon's treatment of Prussia's rival, Saxony. During the campaigns of 1806 and 1807, the Confederation of the Rhine had proved highly useful to the French emperor. Not only could he establish troop and supply bases, unmolested, close to the borders of Prussia; his German allies also furnished contingents for the invasion. Consequently, Napoleon expanded the confederation by giving Saxony the same generous treatment he gave Bavaria and other southern states. He made the duke of Saxony a king, awarded him the newly created Grand Duchy of Warsaw with rights of passage across Silesia, and gave Saxony full membership in the Confederation of the Rhine.

The catastrophic collapse of Prussia can, of course, be largely explained by the overwhelming power concentrated in the hands of Napoleon, who at this point in his career would have been capable of dealing similar blows to most European states. But the Prussian government also carried a large share of this responsibility. The administrative framework of Prussia required an efficient ruler at its helm, and Frederick William III was anything but that. His internal government was disorderly, his foreign policy shortsighted. Moreover, the army, hitherto the backbone of the Prussian state, had been allowed to deteriorate. Perhaps all can be summarized by Queen Louise's explanation in a letter to her father: "We have gone to sleep on the laurels of Frederick the Great."

With the downfall of Prussia, the question of leadership in Germany became more vexing than ever. During the eighteenth century struggle between Prussia and Austria, the balance had begun to tip in favor of the former. But now all was radically altered. To be sure, Austria retained some strength despite its repeated defeats by Napoleon, but it had been expelled from Germany and forced to turn to the southeast. On the other hand, Prussia had lost its strong position in the north. Now only the kingdoms of Bavaria, Württemberg, and Saxony could boast of some importance. Yet their mutual jealousies, their subservience to Napoleon, and their lack of resources made it unlikely that any one of them might rise to leadership in Germany. Hence the French emperor could justly feel that France alone had become the leader of the German states.

Napoleon's Impact on Germany

Abruptly, Prussian overweening pride had turned to humble servility. French patrols walked the streets of Berlin, and the population stepped back in awe and respect. In the Rhineland and in parts of the south, the French armies had at first been welcomed as liberators bringing popular sovereignty, equality, and the benefits of the Napoleonic Code. This cordiality was naturally diluted with the passing of years as the French troops, although officially regarded as allies, became a burden on the local populations. In Prussia, however, the French were from the beginning looked upon as conquerors.

While the bulk of the population lay in stunned apathy, strong voices were heard demanding action to regenerate Prussia. Despite the watchful presence of Napoleon's army of occupation, these demands were transformed into action with astonishing speed and led to a thorough reform of the entire Prussian state. Their aim was well expressed by Prince Karl August von Hardenberg's (1750–1822) famous suggestion to the king: "Your Majesty, we must do from above what the French have done from below."

The resulting reform movement was made practicable through a significant transformation of the thinking of the people of Prussia and of Germany in general: cosmopolitanism was giving way to nationalism. Initially, the nationalistic outbursts of the French Revolution had not evoked a similar reaction in Germany. The enthusiasm produced by events in Paris had quickly died down east of the Rhine. Frightened by the excesses of the Terror and the growing imperialism of the French, most Germans had turned away in disappointment. Hence in the final analysis it was not the French Revolution but the constant inroads by the French armies and their occupation of Germany that gradually incited German feelings of nationalism. Slowly and in growing numbers, the German intellectuals began to shed their cosmopolitanism and deplore the lack of national feeling that seemingly had enabled the French to achieve so many prodigious feats. Confronted with constant French successes, they called for changes in Germany's political, social, economic, and educational structure that would help the Germans to resist French aggression, and might in the end lead to a unified Germany. As the poet Christoph Martin Wieland (1733–1813) explained in 1798, when war was about to resume between Austria and France: "Now or never! The moment has come to create a truly German policy. But I forgot that we are not a nation, but merely an aggregate of over 200 peoples."

The crushing defeat of Jena, the humiliation of Prussia, and Napoleon's conquest of what remained of Germany marked the turning point. The romantic poets had helped lay the groundwork with their glorification of the German past. Collections of German folklore and epics, descriptions of Germany's heroic past, and the deification of the German *Volksseele* underlay the ardent nationalistic outburst that rocked Germany in the years after 1806. Feverishly, many of the German writers joined this call for a national awakening. "As a writer," said the poet August Wilhelm von Schlegel (1767–1845),

> there is at this moment but one aim for me: to point out to the Germans the picture of their old glory, their old dignity and freedom in the light of former times; I must kindle every spark of national sentiment wherever it may slumber. Sentiments must reunite what external circumstances have kept apart.

The playwright Heinrich von Kleist (1777–1811) not only wrote ardently nationalistic dramas, such as *Die Hermannsschlacht* (*The Battle of Arminius*) and *Der Prinz von Homburg,* but also composed vitriolic anti-Napoleonic pamphlets and the highly chauvinistic *Catechism of Patriotic Love.* The journalist Joseph von Görres (1776–1848) published a periodical in which he admonished his countrymen to battle the invader, to create one strong and unified country, and to be ready to sacrifice their lives for the fatherland.

That this nationalistic outburst rapidly touched the borders of fanaticism is illustrated by the writings of Ernst

Moritz Arndt (1769–1860), a poet who for many years of French occupation of Germany lived in voluntary exile in Sweden. There he admired the national spirit of the Swedes, and looked sadly across the Baltic upon "our miserable German disunity, our so-called humane all and nothing." In 1806 his patriotism blossomed fully, and he proclaimed in his book, *Der Geist der Zeit* (*The Spirit of the Time*); "Oh fatherland, you do not lack brave, bold hearts; you lack brave and bold voices which will proclaim with fervor and love your needs and your salvation."

Arndt now sought to become the prophet of a new age. Battle songs and patriotic hymns poured from his enthusiastic pen. He hoped to march in the vanguard of an army of writers who battled for the fatherland. "I shall never desert my German fatherland and its holy cause so long as there is a drop of blood left in me." From a mere admirer of German culture, he rapidly turned into one of the most ardent proclaimers of German supremacy of his time.

> We live in a beautiful, large, rich land, a land of glorious memories, undying deeds, unforgettable service to the world in remote and recent times. We are the navel of Europe . . . we are as good as the best . . . German! What a name and what a people!

Finally, in his battle songs, he became extreme in his damnation of all foreigners, especially "the French apes."

It was, of course, not clear at first whether this patriotic swell would retain the traditional particularism, or whether it would become an all-German movement. Many a rising patriot, particularly in Prussia, was thinking only of his own state and not of a larger German entity. But others thought that the Napoleonic upheavals could serve as a prelude to the formation of a unified German state. When the theologian Friedrich Schleiermacher (1768–1834) issued his *Proclamation to the Saxons,* his literary friends acclaimed it but criticized its narrow viewpoint. "Why Saxony?" asked Friedrich von Schlegel (1772–1829):

> It's just this division which has always been our misfortune. Unfortunately I see traces of it creeping up again everywhere; of all times now, when it matters so much that it should not be a question of Saxony, Prussia, Hanover, or the like, but of Germany. . . .

Similarly, Baron Heinrich vom Stein (1757–1831), the most influential of the reformers of Prussia, insisted that he recognized but one fatherland: Germany.

The philosopher Fichte, whose public lectures entitled "Addresses to the German Nation" (delivered in Berlin from 1807 to 1808) were a clarion call for the national awakening, also looked beyond the horizon of Prussia. "I speak for Germans," he stated in his opening lecture, "brushing aside all the divisive differences which unhappy events have created during the centuries in the single nation." These lectures also raised another question about the regeneration of Germany. Some reformers, such as General Neithardt von Gneisenau (1760–1831), hoped that the transformation of Germany would follow democratic lines, believing that the inherent powers of the nation could best be awakened by giving every individual a suitable field for his ability. Others, such as Minister Karl von Hardenberg, aimed at a more authoritarian centralization of power, and stressed duty and service more than liberty, which he felt might easily degenerate into license.

Fichte's views were even more conservative. He was largely instrumental in promoting a concept of the relationship between the individual and the state that became highly influential in German history. Starting with Herder's theory of a German folk soul (*Volksseele*), Fichte raised the "nation" onto a pedestal where it became the highest embodiment of a people's striving. The nation, to him, was more than a political state with its laws and physical boundaries. It became a spiritual and living entity endowed with the "unquestionable right of requiring of all, whether they consent or not, and if necessary of compelling them, to give up everything, including life." The nation thus became the primordial force in the lives of the people, the "embodiment of the Eternal." True patriots would serve this nation joyfully; others would be compelled to serve it. Fichte also looked upon the Germans as the primordial race, the fairest and only true representatives of Western civilization. From these theoretical premises, Fichte then pointed to the practical tasks that faced the reformers. Primarily the "Addresses" dealt with the development of a system of national education whereby the state would educate its subjects to be useful and loyal citizens and instill in them the highest sense of duty and devotion.

The Prussian Reforms

While poets and philosophers rekindled the patriotic flame, politicians and generals embarked on the task of reforming the Prussian state. King Frederick William III, although hardly wiser after the debacle of 1806, at least showed the good sense to entrust more power to his advisers, and permitted a group of aggressive innovators to assume the direction of government. It is curious and perhaps significant that three of the five most influential reformers were not Prussian by origin. Baron Stein came from Nassau, General Gneisenau from Saxony, and General Gerhard von Scharnhorst (1755–1813) from Hanover. Yet these men all placed themselves devotedly in the service of the Prussian state, which they regarded as the best hope for Germany's future.

THE WORK OF STEIN The initial social, economic, and administrative reforms of Prussia were directed by Baron Stein, who had entered the Prussian civil service in 1780, and had held many administrative positions. After 1804, he had been entrusted with the supervision of customs and trade, a position that gave him firsthand knowledge of the financial disorders and inefficiency permeating the central government. He had offered various suggestions for reforms and had done what lay within his power to improve Prussia's monetary resources. He proved a skilled and devoted administrator. He certainly was no revolutionary, but his civil liberalism was as outspoken as his contempt for the prevailing aristocratic paternalism and for the pretensions of the petty German princes.

After the debacle of Jena, Frederick William III offered Stein the post of minister of foreign affairs, but aware of the entrenched opposition to innovation at the court of Berlin, Stein declined and retired from public affairs. It is ironic that the king recalled him in the following summer, largely at the behest of Napoleon, who distrusted the incumbent Chief Minister Hardenberg and believed that Stein's financial abilities would make it easier for Prussia to pay off its obligations to France. As a result, Stein now accepted the post of chief minister, and with it responsibility for salvaging what was left of the Prussian state.

Supported by the king and a few colleagues in the government, Stein proceeded with astonishing speed to lay the foundation for Prussia's regeneration. To help pay the indemnity demanded by France and the upkeep of the 150,000 French troops of occupation, he mortgaged large portions of the royal domain, reorganized the tax system, and contracted loans with bankers and merchants.

His next step was the issuance of the Reform Edict of October 1807, aimed at removing "every obstacle which in the past has prevented the individual from attaining that prosperity which he was capable of reaching." By complying with the "demands of justice" and the "principles of a wise economic policy," the edict was supposed to unshackle the productive capacity of the people of Prussia. The rigid caste system, with its distinctions among nobles, burghers, and peasants, was abolished. Freedom of exchange of property was legislated, so that nobles henceforth could buy and sell "nonnoble" land, just as burghers and peasants could purchase land hitherto labeled "noble." Similarly there was to be free choice of occupation, with its concomitant class mobility: nobles could engage in trade, burghers could farm, and peasants could enter bourgeois occupations. Talents would thus be encouraged, "whatever the rank," and the equalization of classes would, according to Gneisenau, convert "the living strength of men and the dead strength of resources into productive capital." Serfdom was to be abolished by 1810, but the ex-serfs were to remain financially obligated to their former landlords and masters for all feudal land they occupied and all debts they had contracted. Finally, in line with its fundamental tenet of emancipating trade and production, the Reform Edict restricted the privileges of the guilds and limited their monopolistic powers.

The edict went a long way toward modernizing Prussia. By equalizing the classes and giving incentives to peasants and bourgeois, it awakened civic pride and proved a sound foundation for the economic boom of the succeeding decades. But it would be erroneous to assume that this law eradicated class distinctions in Prussia or freed the peasantry on the large estates from the traditional manorial jurisdiction of the noble lords.

As a next step, Stein initiated administrative reforms. By the Municipal Act of 1808, city dwellers were allowed to elect their own councils to replace the local nobles or agents of the central government. Stein thus gave the burghers a feeling of responsibility and self-respect that, he hoped, would make them better citizens. He hoped to extend this principle of home rule to rural districts and cap the entire system with a constitutional framework somewhat like England's. The central government he conceived in the form of a real cabinet, its members working as a group and responsible to the king.

But Stein's administrative reforms

did not go beyond the establishment of municipal home rule. For such an undertaking, his ministry was too short-lived and opposition too strong. The aristocratic Junkers were undermining his position lest he weaken their autonomy in the provinces, and the entrenched bureaucrats were agitating against him. Napoleon was also applying pressure on Frederick William III to dismiss his reforming minister who was unduly strengthening the Prussian state and, according to intercepted messages, conspiring to alter conditions in Germany as a whole. In December 1808, less than a year and a half after he had taken office, Stein resigned and departed for a three-year exile in Austria.

After Stein's departure, Hardenberg returned as chief minister. Although more conservative than Stein, Hardenberg continued the reform program initiated by his predecessor. He awarded equal political and economic rights to the Jews, lifted certain trade restrictions, and secularized what was left of Catholic and Protestant church property. To raise more revenue for payment of the increased indemnity called for by Napoleon, he sold some of the royal domain that had been mortgaged by Stein. He also attempted to free the peasants from their financial obligations to their former masters. Instead of paying rent for their land or incurring indebtedness for land they had appropriated, they were to surrender one third of their property to the lord as full payment in return for outright ownership of the remaining two thirds of the land. Even this measure of 1811, however, did not prevent the gradual purchase of much of the land by bourgeois and nobles, with the resultant creation of an agricultural proletariat that hardly comprised the self-respecting citizens Stein had hoped to create. Finally, Hardenberg took up his predecessor's plan to create an assembly representative of all the people. Die-hard opposition by the conservative aristocrats of Brandenburg and East Prussia forced him to transmute the original designs into a mere parody of Stein's intentions. The assembly that finally met in 1812 was elected not by the people as a whole, but by the three classes, acting separately, and it was so arranged that the nobility retained the major voice.

THE REGENERATION OF THE ARMY

While Stein and Hardenberg were revising the political, economic, and social framework of Prussia, two generals were at work reshaping the army. Stein had appointed General Scharnhorst as head of a commission for reorganizing the military establishment. Scharnhorst had served in the Hanoverian army in the early revolutionary wars, and later had taught at the military academy in Berlin and had written widely on military subjects. He was assisted by the resolute General Gneisenau, who had started his military career in the service of the emperor, had then served as a British mercenary in the American War of Independence, and had finally entered Prussian service in 1785.

Scharnhorst and Gneisenau set out to revamp the Prussian army. On the principle that "all the inhabitants of the state are its defenders by birth," they instituted universal military service. Since the treaties with France restricted the Prussian army to 42,000 men, they devised the system in which recruits served only short tours of active duty, sufficient for learning the rudiments of military service, and then were placed in active reserve components to make room for a new contingent of inductees. In this manner, the state could count on a large number of trained army personnel without exceeding the limits imposed by Napoleon. Furthermore, the existing army was reorganized and brought up to date. Superannuated officers were dismissed, caste restrictions were replaced by advancement by merit wherever possible, and the logistical service was improved. The entire army was reorganized into regiments and brigades, partly in imitation of Napoleon's successful innovations. Finally, at the time of the wars of liberation, the regular army was augmented by two new branches, the *Landwehr* (home or territorial guard) and the *Landsturm* (militia), which represented an adaptation of the French idea of "the nation in arms."

The aim of these reforms was not merely to improve the fighting ability of the Prussian forces, but also to convert the old-style aristocratic army into a more popular organization rooted in the people and not feared as an oppressive instrument of the ruler. On the whole the reforms proved successful, and Prussia's armed forces emerged strengthened. They were to have a good record in the fighting that finally ended the Napoleonic supremacy in Europe. But the plan to "democratize" the army made little progress.

The military reforms in Prussia were accompanied by a curious new movement, the establishment of gymnastic societies. Their originator, Friedrich Ludwig Jahn (1778–1852), devoted himself to the physical and moral regeneration of Prussia's youth. The gymnastics he prescribed were not merely to develop the muscles of the future soldiers but also to stir the patriotism of the future citizens. The rhythmic beat of the exercises performed in unison by groups of young men was to stimulate obedience and comradeship. *Turnvater* Jahn's societies spread throughout Prussia and Germany with astonishing speed. The youth from the cities were delighted to exercise their bodies away from the dust of the factory or the stale air of the office. On the *Turnplatz* they could develop a proud bearing and self-respect. And everywhere the gymnastic societies became centers for intolerant patriotism.

Education of the mind was equally stressed. Even King Frederick William III remarked after the war with France that "the state should replace by intellectual strength the material forces it had lost." Fichte, Schleiermacher, Stein, and others pointed to the vital role of education in the rejuvenation of Prussia. "The written word has more influence on Germans than on any other people," wrote Stein in 1810. Although the French had won through force of arms, he thought the Germans might ultimately triumph "through ideas and public opinion." And all recognized the influence teachers could exert on the minds of their students.

The king appointed Baron Karl Wilhelm von Humboldt (1767–1835), the brother of the scientist Alexander von Humboldt, as chief of the Department of Worship and Public Instruction. Humboldt revised the system of elementary education along the theories advocated by Pestalozzi. He also promoted secondary education, in particular the so-called humanistic *Gymnasium,* and instituted the *Abitur,* a comprehensive examination given at the end of high school and required for entrance to a university. In 1810 the king provided funds for the establishment of the University of Berlin, which, Schleiermacher hoped, would make Berlin "the center of all intellectual activity in northern, Protestant Germany." The new university immediately attracted some of the best professors, and became a powerful tool in the political reorientation of Prussia.

Rising Opposition to Napoleon

After the Peace of Tilsit, Napoleon's power reached its zenith. To be sure, he could not relax and enjoy the fruits of his conquests. The commercial warfare with England constantly increased in bitterness; rebellion and civil war sapped French strength in the Iberian Peninsula; and the reports of military reforms in Prussia and Austria, of restlessness in Holland and other satellite regimes were casting shadows on the future of his empire. But on the whole Napoleon's power was such that he could dictate at will to the nations of Europe—with the noteworthy exceptions of Russia and England.

In September 1808 he forced new humiliations on Prussia, making it cede additional territories to the kingdom of Westphalia, raising its indemnity obligations, and obtaining permission to establish French military roads to strategic points in Prussia. In the following month, he invited Emperor Alexander I to a congress in Erfurt so that the two emperors could discuss their respective spheres of influence in Europe. During three weeks of gaudy celebrations, which included a rabbit hunt on the battlefield of Jena, Russo-French flirtations reached the high-water mark. Austria and Prussia were pointedly omitted from the list of invited guests, but the kings and princes of the Confederation of the Rhine were present, encircling the two luminaries like satellites. It was at this occasion that Napoleon met Goethe and presented him with a cross of the Legion of Honor. Goethe, almost alone among the German poets, had not turned against the French and had not been caught up in the fever of political patriotism. In his Olympian aloofness to the banality of the international struggle, Goethe retained his unqualified admiration for the genius of Napoleon, just as the emperor openly revered the poet.

In 1809 the peace in Germany was again broken. Austria was ready to risk another trial of strength rather than sink permanently into the rank of a secondary power. Not only was the Austrian ruler irritated at not being invited to the Congress of Erfurt; he was fearful lest the Russo-French plans were to undermine Austria's position in the Balkans. Unable to woo the tsar to their side, the Austrians decided to act alone, and mobilized their forces. In March, Archduke Charles concentrated his forces in Bohemia for an invasion of Germany, where he expected the local populations to rise against the French and to join the Austrians in a war of liberation. If such a maneuver had succeeded, Austria might have won over Prussia as the future leader of Germany.

But Archduke Charles's appeal to the Germans to rise against Napoleon was premature. To be sure, here and there ardent patriots were itching for action, and minor sporadic uprisings occurred in various parts of the Empire. The Tyroleans under Andreas Hofer rebelled against the Franco-Bavarian occupiers and even captured Innsbruck. Small bands of armed men, led by impetuous officers, enacted dramatic rebellions in central and northern Germany, but there was no general anti-French uprising. Prussia maintained strict neutrality, and Napoleon's "client states" in Germany, the members of the Confederation of the Rhine, placed their troops at his disposal for use against rebels in Spain or the Austrians.

Failure to evoke a general rising against the French left the Austrians alone to face Napoleon and his satellites. Although they inflicted several defeats on the Franco-German forces, they could not withstand the onslaught for very long. Vienna and western Austria fell to Napoleon, and after his decisive victory of Wagram in July 1809, an armistice was arranged. In the ensuing Peace of Vienna (Treaty of Schönbrunn), Austria was further mutilated. Bavaria, Saxony, France, and even Russia—not a participant in the war—received territorial cessions. Austria's new boundaries deprived it of access to the Adriatic. In addition, it was forced to pay a large indemnity and to join the economic blockade against England.

As a result of this war, Austria's position became almost as precarious as Prussia's and led to a complete reappraisal of its foreign policy. Renewed friendship with France seemed to offer the only salvation. By uniting the ancient house of Hapsburg with the new family of the Bonapartes, Emperor Francis could hope to prevent further dismemberment of his empire. Hence Austrian envoys worked behind the scenes to prepare for Napoleon's divorce from his wife Josephine, and his marriage in 1810 to the Austrian Archduchess Marie Louise.

Although Napoleon was reasonably secure, unrest in Europe continued to mount. The Tyrolean rebels held out for almost a year until their leader, Andreas Hofer, was captured and executed, to become a quasi-legendary martyr to German liberals. The civil war in Spain continued unabated. The Prussian reform movement, student agitation, and sporadic risings continued to foment anti-French hatred. And driven by his *idée fixe* of bringing England to its knees through an economic blockade of the Continent, Napoleon increasingly overextended himself by annexing Holland, central Italy, northwestern Germany, and the German port cities as far east as Lübeck on the Baltic.

The Franco-Russian War

In the winter of 1810, the harmonious relations between Russia and France began to disintegrate. There were many causes for friction besides Napoleon's obvious unwillingness to share the limelight of Europe. Russia's successful war against Turkey worried the French, just as Alexander looked with misgivings on French scheming for a strengthened Poland. Moreover, the Hapsburg-Bonaparte marriage and alliance was resented by the tsar as a snub to the Romanov dynasty and as a potential threat to Russian expansion in the Balkans. Finally, Russia suffered so severely from the economic blockade that the tsar finally renounced his adherence to the Continental system and reopened Russian ports to English trade.

By the summer of 1811, Napoleon started open preparations for the inevitable conflict with Russia. Intense diplomatic maneuvers occupied the succeeding months. Russia concluded treaties of friendship with England and Sweden, and Turkey agreed to terminate the war against the tsar despite French efforts to keep this front open. Napoleon's German satellite states continued to side with their French benefactor, and consented to furnish sizable contingents of troops for the projected invasion of Russia. Prussia's position was more equivocal. The reformers made secret contacts with the tsar regarding a possible anti-French alliance. But Alexander was not eager to extend his front by sending troops for the defense of Prussia: he had decided on a defensive campaign against Napoleon rather than risk open battle far away from his bases of supply.

Actually Prussia did not have much choice. Napoleon concentrated his troops on the Prussian borders and without much difficulty forced Frederick William III into an alliance whereby Prussia was to furnish 20,000 men to be incorporated into the French army of invasion. Austria, for its part, was in a better bargaining position, and negotiated a treaty with France whereby it was to obtain the retrocession of Illyria in return for furnishing contingents to Napoleon. But the 30,000 Austrian troops were to remain under the control of their own Austrian commanders.

On June 22, 1812—129 years to the day before Hitler attempted a similar undertaking—Napoleon launched his war against Russia. Less than half of his Grand Army of about 600,000 men consisted of French contingents. A majority of his troops came from France's assorted allies and satellite states: Germans from the Confederation of the Rhine, Austrians, Prussians, Poles, Swiss, Italians, Dutch, and mercenaries. After crossing the river Niemen at the end of June, the huge army advanced rapidly, although with constant losses, toward Moscow, which fell in the middle of September. But the burning of Moscow, Russia's scorched-earth policy, successful guerrilla warfare and hit-and-run tactics by Russian Cossacks, and an early, severe winter turned Napoleon's momentary triumph into utter defeat. Within five months, the Grand Army was reduced by over five sixths of its strength. By early December, the remaining 100,000 invaders were painfully struggling back across the Niemen. Russia had successfully withstood the invasion, despite tremendous losses. Napoleon hastened back to Paris to quell a palace revolt. Emperor Alexander hesitated for a moment whether to pursue the enemy and possibly free all of Europe from French domination.

His closest adviser since the spring of that year had been the same Baron Stein who had initiated the reform movement in Prussia, and who now saw the best hope for Germany's liberation in the youthful and ambitious tsar of Russia. Largely at his urging, Alexander agreed to persevere in the war until its logical conclusion: the overthrow of Napoleon. Thus Napoleon's disastrous rout in Russia and the tsar's decision to continue the war opened the way for the German wars of liberation—whose signal was Prussia's desertion of the French and its alliance with Russia.

·12

Napoleon Expelled and Conservatism Restored, 1813–1840

THE WARS OF LIBERATION

The news of the Napoleonic disaster in Russia stirred the hopes of patriots throughout Germany, while it perplexed the rulers of Prussia and Austria. Fortunately for the vacillating Frederick William III, he was forced into a decision by the rebellion of one of his trusted generals.

Yorck's Defection

On December 30, 1812, General Hans von Yorck (1759–1830)—later known as Yorck von Wartenburg—the commander of the Prussian contingent in the French Grand Army, withdrew from the French alliance. "With aching heart," he is supposed to have written the king of Prussia, "I break the bond of obedience and wage war on my own account." He announced that the Prussian people desired war against Napoleon, but that their king was not free to heed the needs of his nation. Without royal orders, he signed an agreement with the Russian general in the field—the Convention of Tauroggen—stipulating the neutrality of his Prussian troops and promising to occupy East Prussia to safeguard the right flank of the advancing Russian army. Yorck was no reformer or rebellious hothead, but he saw the only hope for the rebirth of Prussia's grandeur in the defeat of Napoleon. And he acted out of conviction, without regard for his personal future. His flagrant breach of oath to the king made Yorck a disputed symbol of justified insubordination to generations of Prussian and German officers, including those who contemplated rebellion against Hitler.

Yorck's defection meant the liberation of East Prussia. Stein immediately proceeded to Königsberg to supervise the administration of the province. He convoked the local diet, opened the ports to English trade, and called up the reserves for the expected fight against France—all without the approval of the Prussian king.

Frederick William III was in a quandary. He ordered Yorck's arrest, disavowed the Convention of Tauroggen, and even sent his apologies to Napoleon. The king's behavior has been traditionally termed shortsighted and cowardly. But it should be recalled that Frederick William had learned in 1806–1807 that Prussia could not stand up to Napoleon alone, and that the tsar could not always be trusted. Frederick William's hesitation seems justified, for Alexander's troops waited a month before proving his intention of staying in the war by crossing the Niemen to pursue the retreating French. Moreover, Austria as yet opposed any action against Napoleon.

Rising popular pressure and the advancing Russian armies finally swept Frederick William into the anti-French camp. Tactitly he sanctioned anti-Napoleonic uprisings in many parts of Prussia. Despite the presence of French occupation troops, an unofficial levy en masse was authorized, resembling a secret military mobilization. Volunteers, especially students, swarmed to the colors, although no war had been declared. Meanwhile negotiations were opened with Russia, with Stein acting as intermediary. The question of Poland's future complicated the discussion. Alexander demanded a major part of Poland, whereas Frederick William would not forfeit what his father had obtained in the last two Polish partitions. A vague compromise finally permitted conclusion of a Russo-Prussian alliance (Treaty of Kalisch, February 1813). Russia was awarded most of Poland, and in turn promised to help restore Prussia to its former size and importance through adequate territorial compensations in northern Germany.

Prussia's Entry into the War

Prussian armies were now officially mobilized, and Russo-Prussian forces gathered in Silesia to launch the liberation of Germany. On March 17, proclaiming that "the moment has come when we can no longer harbor the slightest illusion as to our situation," Frederick William declared war on France. It was to be characteristic of his behavior during the next decade that his "Appeal to My People" was so worded that it was not clear whether he was addressing only his own subjects or all Germans, for his preoccupation with Prussia now vied with his temptation to seize the role of an all-German leader. His "Appeal" also contained the first hints of a more liberal attitude that raised false hopes in many of his subjects. "Remember the blessings for which your forefathers fought," he reminded his people; "freedom of conscience, national honor, independence, commerce, industry, learning"—an eclectic array of ideals, likely to attract all varieties of liberals.

From March to June 1813, the Wars of Liberation were waged in full force in eastern Germany. Although the French won some minor battles, they were gradually driven across the Elbe. Only isolated French garrisons in the east—Magdeburg, Stettin, Danzig, and others—held out for another year. Prussia and Russia received financial aid from England and some ineffective assistance from Sweden, who sent a corps. But essentially they alone bore the brunt of the fighting. Russia assembled additional contingents in Germany as fast as they could be transported from the east, and Prussia proved the effectiveness of its military reforms, within a few weeks quadrupling its armies, financed largely by citizens' contributions. Austria stayed neutral, while the German states of the Confederation of the Rhine—with the exception of Mecklenburg, which deserted France after being overrun by Prussian and Russian armies—remained actively in the Napoleonic camp. The secondary princes who owed their royal dignities and territorial aggrandizement to Napoleon had no intention of deserting their benefactor unless guaranteed retention of their gains by the advancing "liberating" powers. And the liberals in the southern and western states, in no hurry to jeopardize the constitutional and legal benefits brought by the French revolutionary army, hardly welcomed the advancing forces of conservative Prussia and Russia.

By early summer, both France and her foes were exhausted. Wooed by both sides, Austria mediated a truce that lasted two months. The adversaries used the temporary lull to assemble reinforcements, while Austria under Metternich reassumed a more dominant role in the diplomacy of Europe. Prince Klemens von Metternich-Winneburg (1773–1859) had served in the diplomatic service of various German states, had acted as Austrian ambassador to Berlin and Paris, and had become Austrian minister of foreign affairs in 1809, a post he was to retain until 1848. Marie Louise's marriage to Napoleon had been largely arranged by Metternich, whose plans seemed to succeed when Empress Marie Louise gave birth to a son in 1811. The heir of France was the seed of a new Hapsburg-Bonaparte dynasty that would cement Austro-French relations and serve as a welcome support to a restored and powerful Austria. Consequently, Metternich had every reason for trying to act as mediator, and he attempted to effect permanent peace on the basis of French withdrawal from east of the Rhine in return for a reaffirmation of the Rhine boundary. Moreover, Metternich could hardly disregard developments in Germany if he hoped to regain Austria's first-rank status. If Prussia—rather than Austria—liberated most of Germany, it would assume preponderance over the German states. Nor was Metternich unaware that Stein was preparing to weld the liberated German territories into a unified state rather than return them to the jurisdiction of their former princes.

Austria's Assumption of Leadership

But Napoleon refused Austria's offer, although it would have left France considerably larger than before 1789. Consequently, Metternich persuaded Francis I to enter the struggle against his son-in-law. In August 1813, Austria declared war on France, opening the second and final phase of the Wars of Liberation. Prussian, Russian, Austrian, and Swedish armies soon engaged Napoleon in minor skirmishes in Saxony, seeking an opportunity for a joint attack on the newly reinforced French armies.

Meanwhile Metternich tried to gain diplomatic advantages. In early October, he forced the first major breach in the Confederation of the Rhine through the Treaty of Ried, in which Bavaria agreed to desert Napoleon and join the anti-French coalition. By promising Bavaria retention of its territorial increases, Metternich outfoxed Napoleon. Bavaria was to restore the Tyrol and Salzburg to Austria in return for compensations in Germany, leaving Bavaria the third largest German state next to Austria and Prussia. The Bavarian king was permitted to keep the royal dignity. In some respects this treaty sacrificed the long standing Austrian goal of absorbing parts or all of Bavaria to strengthen its foothold in southern Germany. By accepting the continuance of a relatively strong Bavaria, Metternich abandoned this policy. On the other hand, by taking the initiative in dislodging Bavaria from the French camp, Metternich hoped to wrest from Paris the role of protector of the secondary states of Germany. Certainly the Austro-Bavarian agreement opened the way for other German princes to desert the French alliance on the assumption that their newly enhanced status would also be recognized by Vienna. Finally, Metternich's success with Bavaria dealt a mortal blow to Stein's hopes of using the Wars of Liberation to effect a fundamental transformation of Germany.

Shortly after Bavaria changed sides, the opposing armies concentrated near Leipzig in Saxony. For the first time, the allies cooperated in their strategic moves. The resulting "Battle of the Nations," one of the biggest battles of the entire Napoleonic era, lasted four days. Amidst the fighting, Napoleon, caught in semiencirclement, requested an armistice that the allies rejected. Toward the end of the battle, most of his Saxon and Württemberg troops deserted to his opponents. In the end, the French were totally defeated and began their retreat toward the Rhine. By early November the bulk of the French forces had crossed the river, leaving only isolated garrisons in Germany.

Without French support, the Napoleonic puppets collapsed everywhere. The Kingdom of Westphalia was dissolved, and Württemberg, Baden, Hesse-Darmstadt, and others now joined the coalition and declared war on France, but their future status seemed unclear.

Stein meanwhile pursued his aim of liberalizing and, if possible, unifying the conquered states. As head of the Central Administration for Conquered German Lands, he assumed control of some "liberated" territories—Saxony, Frankfurt, Berg—and attempted to implant constitutions and prepare them for some sort of German union. Not expecting firm support from King Frederick William, he hoped that Emperor Alexander, with his "persistence and noble spirit" and his ideals of liberalism, would help set up a new Germany. Stein insisted that he was working not for Prussia nor any other particular German state, and that he considered dynasties to be "of no importance whatsoever in these critical moments; they are mere instruments." He might have added that dynasties were actually an impediment to his plans. For if in the critical moment of the collapse of Napoleonic power, the former princelings could have been prevented from resuming control of their states, or could at least have been forced partially to abandon their sovereignty, some kind of unification might have been possible. And this is what Stein hoped to achieve, with the backing of Russian and Prussian power. His motto was "unity" and he desired that "Germany become strong and great; that she find her independence, her liberty, and her nationality." Like Bismarck half a century later, he advised a pragmatic approach. "Let us do whatever is practical; only stop thinking about these quarrels between Montagues and Capulets."

But Stein's efforts were doomed. In many of the liberated areas—Electoral Hesse, Brunswick, Hanover, and Oldenburg, for example—the former princes reappeared, determined to restore the *ancien régime* with the backing of Metternich. In the other states—again with the encouragement of Metternich—the rulers retained their authority by following the example of Bavaria and deftly shifting from Napoleon to the allied side without relinquishing any power. And as the armies of liberation moved west, Stein encountered added complications. Germany had in fact fought two decades of civil war. The armies of the Confederation of the Rhine had helped devastate Prussia in 1806. Prussian and Russian armies now ravaged the western lands. The Prusso-Russian armies might approach under the banner of liberation, but most of the inhabitants looked upon them with fear and suspicion.

In the winter of 1813, Napoleon again rejected an offer by Metternich to conclude an armistice and negotiate peace. Hence the allies decided to invade France. The French emperor and his generals displayed astounding military skill in delaying the Prussian, Russian, Austrian, and English armies, but in the long run were unable to impede their advance. Paris was captured by the allies on the last day of March, and soon thereafter Napoleon abdicated and departed for his exile on the island of Elba. One month later, on May 30, 1814, the first Peace of Paris was signed between the allies and the newly restored king of France, Louis XVIII.

THE SETTLEMENTS

While the heads of the allied governments prepared for the conference that was to reshape Europe, the old regimes were restored wherever they had been extinguished by revolutionary or Napoleonic armies. The pope returned to Rome, Ferdinand VII assumed control of Spain, the German princelings settled back in their autocratic saddles. Repression of revolutionary ideas and institutions was the order of the day.

The Congress of Vienna

The European congress finally opened at Vienna in September of 1814. Its sessions lasted for almost ten months. All the states of Europe, except Turkey, were represented, many by their rulers and chief ministers. The congress was easily dominated by the four principal allied nations, Russia, Prussia, Austria, and England, but disagreements among them permitted the skillful French envoy Talleyrand to introduce France as a fifth power in the inner circle. Mutual suspicions did not permit much cooperation between Prussia and Austria, and each sought the backing of the more powerful victors—Russia and England. The four powers disagreed particularly over the division of territorial spoils. Prussia and Russia supported each other's claims: Russia expected to absorb all of Poland, and Prussia hoped to acquire Saxony. On the other hand, Austria—and to some extent France—joined England in the hope of preventing undue aggrandizement by the others.

While the congress debated, Napoleon attempted his famous return to power. After landing in southern

France with a handful of soldiers, he made a triumphant re-entry into Paris, gathered a new army, and forced the allies to re-form their coalition forces. One hundred days later, he was defeated at Waterloo and forced into his second and final abdication. Once again the allied forces entered Paris and replaced the aged Louis XVIII on his throne. Emperor Alexander then persuaded his hesitant colleagues to subscribe to the Holy Alliance, a vague declaration on the behavior of princes toward one another and toward their subjects—later confused in the popular mind with the reactionary measures of the Quadruple Alliance. Motivated "by an overflow of pietistic feelings," as Metternich privately characterized him, the tsar wanted to apply Christian principles to politics and to get "the three allied princes, namely Austria, Russia, and Prussia, to regard themselves as delegated by Providence to govern as three branches of the same family."

After this flight into romantic mysticism, the allies turned to the harsher business of imposing on France a new peace treaty. By the Second Peace of Paris, November 20, 1815, France agreed to additional minor territorial cessions: Saarlouis and Saarbrücken in the coal-rich Saar district were given to Prussia, and the fortress of Landau assigned to Bavaria. This time a heavy indemnity was imposed on France, and seventeen border fortresses on French soil were to be occupied by allied troops for a period of up to five years at the expense of France. Prussia's Hardenberg had pressed for further territorial dismemberment of France, particularly the ceding of Strassburg and other portions of Alsace-Lorraine, but although the powers wanted to contain France and prevent another Napoleonic revival, they hesitated to undermine the prestige of the restored Bourbon king by imposing on France an unduly harsh treaty. After completion of the Peace of Paris, Austria, England, Prussia, and Russia reaffirmed their wartime Quadruple Alliance "for the maintenance of royal authority" and preservation of the "tranquility" of Europe, and agreed to periodic consultations on international problems, a decision that became the basis for the series of international congresses of the succeeding decade.

Meanwhile the Congress of Vienna had finished its labors. The main states of Germany, except Saxony, emerged more powerful than before the revolutionary wars. Austria, now excluded from the Rhineland, was restored and even enlarged by Salzburg and Venetian territory. Its influence in Italy through Hapsburg family connections further increased its dominant position in southeastern Europe. Bavaria retained the Rhenish Palatinate and the acquisitions received from Napoleon, and acquired the former Prussian territories of Ansbach and Bayreuth, thus depriving Prussia of a useful bridgehead south of the river Main. Hanover, which still belonged to the British crown, was considerably enlarged, but Saxony was reduced by about one half. The lion's share of Poland was awarded to Russia, and Prussia retained from the Polish partitions of the eighteenth century only West Prussia, Danzig, and the province of Poznan (see Map 15). On the other hand, it received substantial increases throughout northern Germany: Swedish Pomerania, half of Saxony, and the greater portion of Westphalia and the Upper Rhineland. As a result, Prussia considerably increased its hold over northern Germany.

While consolidating the German states along seemingly modern lines, the Vienna settlements contained curious remnants of feudal and dynastic concepts. The king of Bavaria again obtained the Palatinate along the Rhine, a territory in no way contiguous to Bavaria. Prussia reacquired Neuchâtel in Switzerland, which King Frederick I had inherited (from his mother, Louise-Henrietta of Orange-Nassau). This retrocession was merely a dynastic arrangement, for at the same time Neuchâtel was admitted as a new canton into the revised Swiss Confederation. Similar anachronistic dynastic considerations affected many new boundaries drawn for the German states, particularly in Hanover, Brunswick, Holstein, and Luxemburg—all readily apparent from a glance at Map 16.

The Creation of the German Confederation

The best evidence of the influence of dynasticism is the Act of Confederation, which established the new German *Bund* (Confederation). A special commission consisting of Austria, Prussia, Bavaria, Hanover, and Württemberg deliberated for months on a constitutional reorganization of Germany to implement Article VI of the First Peace of Paris, which stipulated the independence of the German states and their association in a federal league.

The debates on the reconstruction of Germany were acrimonious. Stein, though not a member of the commission, worked behind the scene for a more centralized state strong enough to limit the absolutism of the German princes and ensure a modicum of basic liberty to the citizens. When this plan encountered fierce opposition, he proposed as a compromise the formation of two federal states, one under Prussia and the other under Austria. But his views could not prevail. Austro-Prussian rivalry, the claims of the lesser princes, and the soft pressure of the European powers against the formation of a strong Germany created an atmosphere that favored the revival of Hapsburg influence in Germany. Metternich feared that a centralized Germany might breed liberalism and in the end become strong enough to escape Austrian influence. Limiting the sovereignty of the German princes might undermine Vienna's own autocratic regime, and at the same time Metternich wished to keep Prussia from gaining undue influence over the German states. On the other hand, he realized that a completely atomized Germany would constitute a political vacuum dangerously susceptible to French infiltration.

The final solution accepted by the powers at Vienna and by the other German princes and free cities bore the mark of Metternich. His ideals of dynastic legitimacy and stability characterized the so-called constitution that was to regulate intra-German affairs from 1815 to 1866. By insisting on a loose federation of sovereign and absolute states under the permanent presidency of Austria, most of Metternich's aims seemed to be satisfied.

The new German Confederation consisted of thirty-five sovereign principalities and four free cities. It was to be a "perpetual confederation" aimed at maintaining "the external and internal security of Germany and the independence and inviolability of the

MAP 16

individual German states" in the interest of Europe's "repose and equilibrium." Like its predecessor, the Holy Roman Empire, the Confederation accorded equality and sovereign rights to its members, with power to enter foreign alliances, provided such engagements were not "directed against the safety of the Confederation or that of any individual state in the union." Similarly the members agreed to defend "Germany as a whole" or a single partner of the confederation and to guarantee one another's possessions, "so far as they are included within the Confederation." Only those Prussian and Austrian territories that had belonged to the Holy Roman Empire prior to 1806 were included in the confederation, which for example, was under no legal obligation to help Prussia or Austria if East Prussia or Hungary were attacked. Finally, the constitution required members to pledge not to make war among themselves, and to submit their differences to arbitration by the central diet.

The diet, meeting at Frankfurt on the Main under the permanent presidency of Austria, was to be the central organ of the confederation. Its theoretical powers were considerable: matters of war and peace, support of the federal army—consisting of contingents from member states—mediation of disputes, conclusion of treaties, and adoption of confederate legislation were to be within its jurisdiction. In fact, however, the diet was impotent and usually no more than a rubber stamp for Austrian policy. The delegates were merely ambassadors or spokesmen for their sovereigns, and were not interested in an all-German policy. The diet had no executive powers with which to enforce its resolutions. Its complicated voting procedures reserved undue power for the smaller states, since unanimity was required in the resolution of basic issues. In fact, each sovereign could act as he pleased, although most of them were strongly influenced by Austria.

On paper, certain of the Articles of Confederation followed the principles that had emerged from the French Revolution. Article XIII stipulated that "each of the confederate states will grant a constitution to the people based on the system of estates." Furthermore, equality for all Christian faiths was guaranteed, as were uniform regulations on freedom of the press.

The Congress of Vienna had been largely concerned with the prevention of any further outbreak of Napoleonic imperialism; hence the confederation was assigned its part in the containment of France. The constitution provided for federal fortresses along the French border to be manned by federal troops—a clause embodying potential friction, since distrust among the states prevented the creation of any real federal army.

Vienna and Berlin had resisted all suggestions of reviving the Holy Roman Empire, but the new confederation was in essence not greatly different from the old framework. Particularism once again had triumphed. The Hapsburgs had regained sufficient prestige to sway the princelings of Germany but not enough real power to dominate them. And again foreign elements in German affairs clouded issues of allegiance and unity. Austria possessed more non-German than German territory; about a third of Prussia lay outside the confederation. The kings of England, Denmark, and Holland were members of the confederation, respectively for Hanover, Holstein, and Luxemburg, all of which lay inside confederate territory. Although the number of political units of the former Empire had decreased to about one tenth, the new framework of 1815 brought Germany hardly closer to the unification so ardently desired by many patriots.

THE SPIRIT OF THE TIMES

The decades after 1815 in Germany are usually labeled the Age of Reaction or the Age of Metternich. To be sure, Metternich exerted wide influence on German affairs, and many princelings adopted reactionary methods to obliterate the ideals of 1789 and fortify their shaky prerogatives. But such labels are oversimplifications, as are those that unduly stress the liberal and revolutionary ferment of the period.

The Popular Mood

In 1815, relatively few Germans were politically conscious. Three quarters of all Germans still worked in agriculture. In the southwest, the serfs had been freed during the French occupation; many now owned small plots of land and some displayed an occasional interest in political and economic matters. But in Prussia, despite the reforms of 1807 and 1811, matters were different. Only in the Rhenish provinces had a few peasants been able to acquire land of their own. In central and eastern Prussia, the nobility generally had retained all land, whereas the agricultural population was little more than a peasant proletariat, living apart from the political stream.

The urban population was, of course, more intimately involved in political life, but the importance of cities at this time should not be exaggerated. In 1815, most German towns were little more than overgrown villages. The twelve largest cities of Germany together had only about 750,000 inhabitants, at a time when London alone had about a million. In fact, most German towns still fitted within their medieval walls. The process of tearing down these ramparts and turning them into broad avenues to connect the new suburbs with the old inner city was not even started until the early nineteenth century.

The availability of newspapers and magazines enabled city dwellers to keep abreast of political trends, and it was here that new ideas clashed with the forces of tradition bolstered by the aristocratic governments. Yet all was not ferment or reaction within the cities. The upper bourgeoisie and the merchant patricians were more interested in security and comfort than in political innovations. Similarly, the middle bourgeois settled back to enjoy the stodgy "Biedermeier" period. German culture was flourishing; economic progress appeared adequate; above all, there was stability and peace after a generation of war and insecurity. The Biedermeier generation, with its hoop skirts and stiff collars, was hardly in a mood to mount the barricades of revolution. Ferment and unrest, on the other hand, existed in a few small groups: the intelligentsia, the new class of commercial and industrial entrepreneurs, and the growing proletariat. It was between these potential innovators and the ruling aristocracy that the ideological battles of the period were fought.

The Conservatism of the Romantic Movement

During the last decade of the eighteenth century, *Sturm und Drang* had given way to the romantic movement, which continued to dominate the intellectual climate after 1815. Most of the early romantic writers had been liberal, although their liberalism, unlike that of the Jacobins, was based on emotion rather than on eighteenth-century rationalism. Although some writers retained this liberalism, many turned conservative or even reactionary, largely in response to French revolutionary excesses and Napoleonic abuses. Reverence for tradition, admiration for things medieval, pietistic ideals, and a strong current of conversions to Catholicism marked this group of influential conservative romantics. Thus Romanticism in Germany lent support to liberalism, conservatism, and reaction alike. But of the three, conservatism became the strongest, producing ideas of lasting importance to German political thought.

The famous poet Novalis (pseudonym of Baron Friedrich von Hardenberg, 1772–1801), for example, was a romantic who underwent rapid conversion from almost revolutionary liberalism to conservatism. In his *Christianity or Europe* (1799), he rejected the eighteenth-century insistence on equality and natural rights. Divine Providence, he insisted, had placed rulers over the people, and society could best be regenerated if the pope and the Jesuits would help reintroduce medieval authoritarianism.

A similar transformation occurred in Friedrich von Schlegel, who strongly influenced other romantics, especially Fichte and Schleiermacher. At first a cosmopolitan rationalist, then a nationalistic liberal, and eventually a romantic conservative, he embraced Catholicism and moved to Metternich's Vienna. His later writings underscored the change in his ideas. In his *Philosophy of History* (1829), he asserted that truth lay in the irrational alone. If the Holy Roman Empire could not be revived, he thought a confederation under the pope might revitalize the medieval spirit of faith he admired so much.

The journalist Joseph von Görres—another example of this transformation—had been a leader of the anticlerical movement, a liberal whose newspaper, the *Rhenish Mercury,* was for a time the chief advocate of the Rhenish Secessionist movement favoring the union of the Rhineland with revolutionary France. In 1816, his newspaper was suppressed by the Prussian authorities as seditious and inflammatory. Görres himself soon changed his views. He converted to Catholicism and became a professor at the University of Munich, the center of ultramontanism. Here he turned intensely antiliberal and nationalistic. He advocated a Catholic German nationalism, demonstrating what later became obvious: that nationalism was not necessarily intertwined with liberalism but could also become a formidable bulwark of conservatism.

Conservative Theories of the State

Constantly attacked by liberals who demanded changes under the aegis of abstract ideals, such as liberty, fraternity, and equality, the conservatives sought backing from philosophers and political theorists. Burke's stress on *tradition* as a guiding principle in political considerations influenced the Germans. Metternich himself, in theory at least, was a "traditionalist," not a reactionary. He declared that "one must not dream of reformation while agitated by passion; wisdom directs that at such moments we should limit ourselves to maintaining." Stability, he proclaimed, need not be "immobility." In practice, of course, Metternich "moved" very little, concentrated on "maintaining," and at times even turned the clock back.

But more than "tradition" was needed to bolster conservatism. By following in the footsteps of Herder's cultural nationalism and Fichte's concepts of the state, the theorists made conservatism nationalistic, and attached it to the ideal of an all-powerful organic state (pages 249 and 267). New conservative and nationalistic political philosophies thus guided many German statesmen during the nineteenth century.

One such influential theorist, despite his exaggerations, was the political economist Adam Müller (1779–1829), also a Prussian who converted to Catholicism and moved to Vienna. He extolled the Christian state and asserted that man derived his value not from his individualism, as claimed by the liberals, but from the state. The Swiss political theorist Karl L. Haller (1768–1854), whose writings were much admired by Frederick William III and German conservatives, further elaborated on the theory of an all-powerful state. Also a convert to Catholicism, he hated all notions of popular sovereignty and insisted that the state was the property of the prince. The ruler could do with state and subjects as he liked, for the moral order rested in power and not in abstract concepts of natural rights. The prince was supreme, since might made right, although Haller suggested that rulers might well use the Catholic Church to help preserve social order.

Historians, too, were helping the conservative cause. A study of Roman and medieval history and of Herder's philological and ethnological theories led the historian Friedrich Karl von Savigny (1779–1861), who lectured at the University of Berlin, to stress not merely tradition but also organic growth in the history of states. In his *History of Roman Law in the Middle Ages* he showed his dislike for Roman legislation because it was based on rational theories. To Roman jurisprudence he preferred Germanic common law, which grew organically with the people and their customs, and was shaped by the *Volksgeist* (people's spirit).

Finally, the philosopher Georg W. F. Hegel (1770–1831) welded many of these ideas into a conservative theory of the state that was much abused and misinterpreted in later years. In his *Natural Rights and Polical Science* (1821), he rejected all contractual notions of government in favor of the organic development of the state. He made the state all-powerful and amoral, and tried to show that freedom lay only in the state and could not exist apart from it. In practical matters, Hegel actually stood on the liberal side, but his ideas of an all-powerful, organic state could be conveniently misused by German rulers to bolster their petty tyrannies.

The frequent conversions to Roman Catholicism were not merely a religious phenomenon denoting a revival of the Catholic faith. The liberals of the revolutionary period had been fiercely anticlerical, forcing the Church to become antiliberal. This dichotomy between liberals and the Roman Church became a characteristic of the nineteenth century. The Church stood for tradition, stability, and legitimacy. The restored papacy upheld the monarchic principle; hence the conservatives found in the Church a welcome ally against the revolutionary ideals, so much so that even Protestant Prussia and Orthodox Russia actively helped restore the papacy to its former power.

The Aims of the Liberals

Many of the intelligentsia and the middle class, of course, rejected the traditionalism of the conservatives, insisting that their task was to construct a better future rather than remain tied to the past. For them, eighteenth-century rationalism and the revolutionary era had undermined tradition, and to by-pass these changes would not be simply conservative but reactionary.

There were two main groups of liberals. Romantic writers like the poet Heinrich Heine (1797–1856) and the dramatist Georg Büchner (1813–1837) had rejected the conservative trend of most followers of romanticism. Their liberalism was enthusiastic; they extolled freedom and individualism; and their emotional appeal should not be underrated, but their ideas lacked concreteness. Other liberals derived their theories from eighteenth-century rationalism and pursued more pragmatic aims. These rational liberals, in turn, were sharply divided among themselves, according to their respective class interests.

Most writers, teachers, and members of the middle class primarily sought political changes. Particularly in the west and the southwest, they demanded constitutions to limit the political power of the rulers and to guarantee fundamental rights of the citizens. The merchants, the financiers, and the rising industrial entrepreneurs interested in improving trade and manufacture showed less concern for constitutionalism than for economic liberalism. Finally, the liberalism of the lower classes was primarily social. No factory legislation of any kind had as yet been passed in Germany. The traditional systems of production and distribution —putting-out, home manufacture, and guilds—were disintegrating before the slowly rising factories. Women's and children's labor, inhuman working hours and employment conditions, slums and alcoholism—all demanded remedies not furnished by the "tradition" of the conservatives.

The Question of Unification

Looming in the background of these conservative and liberal currents was the problem of unification, which plagued the Germans in the decades after 1815 until Bismarck found a solution in 1870. The main question was whether a liberal or a conservative program might more readily achieve unification.

"Traditionalist" conservatives, including Frederick William III and many Prussian aristocrats, opposed unification: it would put an end to Metternich's concept of "legitimacy" by depriving all but one of the German rulers of their sovereign rights. Those conservatives, however, who espoused the concept of an all-powerful, organic state were divided in their attitude. Many saw the organic state that represented the wave of the future embodied in Prussia and the Hohenzollern dynasty, rather than in an artificially created all-German body politic. Hence they also opposed programs for unification unless the other states would become subordinate to Prussia so that the integrity of the Prussian monarchy would be guaranteed. Only those conservatives, in Prussia and other states, who harked back to Herder's ethnic nationalism saw the future in an all-German union of quasi-equal states.

Among the liberals there was generally greater interest in unification, although here, too, there were different viewpoints. Most students, many intellectuals, and some business groups agreed with Stein that Germany had to be unified into a single state in order to ensure the triumph of liberal ideas by destroying the power of the petty autocratic princes. Conversely, liberalism had to succeed before unification could be achieved. "Freedom and Unity," was the cry of these enthusiasts, which sent shivers of apprehension through Metternich and the princes.

Doctrinaire liberals were more concerned with liberalism than with national unification. To them the status of the individual seemed the most important issue, and they thought individual freedom could more easily be secured within the framework of a smaller state. Particularly in the southwest, many liberals feared that German unification, by including conservative Austria and Prussia might endanger the fate of liberalism in the smaller states.

A third and very influential group of liberals—the budding industrial entrepreneurs—saw the unification of Germany as the dominant issue. Their expanding trade and industry required a unified Germany more than it needed political liberalism. Free speech, free assembly, and a free press might be pleasant luxuries, but they were hardly essential for the development of their manufactories. A unified state—and incidentally a strong state—would best serve their economic interests. This group in the end forsook many of their liberal ideals for the sake of unifying Germany.

But the bulk of the people as yet showed no burning interest in the question of unification. They were happy to enjoy increasing prosperity and material advancement, a tremendous outburst of cultural flourishing, and, above all, decades of peace and tranquility after twenty-three years of war and unrest. As Heine wrote sarcastically, Germany was content to "sleep peacefully under the protection of her thirty-six [*sic*] monarchs," who enjoyed wearing their crowns and their "nightcaps."

Cultural Flourishing

The period 1815–1840 witnessed a continued flourishing of literature, music, education, scholarship, philosophy, and scientific inventions. Romantic music reached its zenith with Weber (1786–1826), Beethoven (1770–1827), Schubert (1797–1828), Mendelssohn (1809–1847), and Schumann (1810–1856). Romanticism in poetry blossomed with Goethe, Heine, and other lyric poets. Popular ballads, medieval romances, and idyllic country tales became the favorite literary fare of the nation, while in the 1830s, political overtones in literature reappeared with the revival of liberalism. In philosophy, this was the age of Arthur Schopenhauer (1788–1860), whose *The World as Will and Idea,* with its study of man's "ungoverned will" in conflict with unattainable desires and ideals, appeared in 1819 and gave rise to a strong stream of pessimism. Hegel's "Idealism" of the same period provided a more optimistic and positive view, and became a guidepost for German metaphysics. His dialectic and affirmation of the "Absolute" were soon misinterpreted by both the nascent materialists and the pseudo philosophers of might and violence.

Meanwhile astonishing strides were taken in education and scholarship. King Louis I of Bavaria (1825–1848) worked assiduously at turning Munich and its university into an artistic and scholarly center. He endowed museums, supported the arts, and sponsored a romanticized Greek revival. In 1817, Frederick William III of Prussia established a special Ministry for Public Education. In many states, universities and scientific laboratories, expanded with government support, encouraged fruitful research and the painstaking thoroughness that during this period became a synonym for German scholarship. The Germans showed particular interest in mathematics, chemistry, engineering, archeology, philosophy, philology, and history.

Much was accomplished in the field of history. Libraries and archives were established, and documents collected and studied. Greek, Roman, and early German history were of particular fascination to the scholars of that period. The original version of the *Niebelungenlied* was discovered and edited, and the famous collection of source materials, the *Monumenta Germaniae Historica* started by Stein, became a model for similar collections in other countries. At the same time, the historian Leopold von Ranke (1795–1886) began his careful investigation into medieval history, employing scientific methods that earned him the reputation of a founder of modern historical research.

THE GERMAN CONFEDERATION AFTER 1815

Prussia

Prussia emerged from the settlement of Vienna considerably strengthened. The Polish and East Frisian territories ceded to Russia and Hanover, respectively, were largely agricultural, whereas the lands gained in Saxony and the Rhineland, particularly the Ruhr district, were commercially highly productive and potentially extremely valuable for Prussia's industrial development.

FREDERICK WILLIAM'S PSEUDO LIBERALISM In the early years after the Congress of Vienna, Frederick William III paid lip service to liberalism. Possibly he realized that the liberal reforms of 1807–1808 had contributed to Prussia's rebound in 1813 and to her restoration as a first-rate power. In 1815, he publicly promised a constitution, and encouraged the hope that he would permit the creation of some sort of central diet by allowing the provincial estates to send representatives to an all-Prussian body in Berlin. A council of state was created in 1817, consisting of the royal princes, the generals of the army, the heads of the various governmental departments, and certain important noble landlords. The king's conservative bent was seen in the membership of this council, which was drawn from the four elements on which Prussian strength had traditionally been built: the crown, the army, the bureaucracy, and the landed nobility. This organ, consequently, was a poor substitute for the legislature and cabinet demanded by the liberals, but it provided Prussia with a semblance of an executive-advisory council, which at least might impose some limitations on royal absolutism.

At the same time, the financial and tax structures of the new and old provinces were overhauled, the judiciary was reformed, and the army was improved—all with a view toward greater efficiency. The educational reforms started by Humboldt were carried forward. To the humanistic Gymnasium, a counterpart was added, the *Realschule,* a secondary school emphasizing the sciences rather than the liberal arts. Teacher-training colleges were established, and the universities were further enlarged

Finally, partly to still the demands for a constitution and a central legislature—a promise the king had no intention of keeping—the old provincial estates were reorganized in 1823. They still retained their essentially medieval character, with their tripartite class distinctions between nobility, bourgeois, and peasantry, but were given additional powers over taxes and awarded a semblance of authority over minor local legislation.

Frederick William's pseudoliberal period was short-lived, however. Even when permitting these minor reforms, he had instinctively distrusted such moderates as Stein and Hardenberg. Stein was never recalled to serve the Prussian government. The king apparently could not forgive his rebellious action in mobilizing East Prussia in January 1813, and feared that Stein's proposals for reorganizing Germany might diminish the Hohenzollern prerogatives. Even Hardenberg was not retained in office beyond 1817, despite his growing conservatism and his services to Prussia at the Congress of Vienna. Soon ultraconservative ministers gained ascendancy at the Prussian court and political stagnation set in.

PRUSSIA AND THE GERMAN CONFEDERATION On the international scene, Prussia under Frederick William III played a secondary role to both Metternich and Alexander. It participated in the various European congresses—Aix-la-Chapelle, Troppau, Laibach, Verona—at which the five big powers (Austria, Russia, England, France, and Prussia) discussed the peace of Europe, but Prussia's voice at these summit meetings was not a loud one. Nor could Prussia exert a commanding role in the German Confederation. Metternich frequently made a show of consulting with Berlin about all-German affairs, but in reality had little trouble persuading the Prussian king to adopt Austria's views.

A major difference between Austrian and Prussian policy derived from the fact that Frederick William despised the German Confederation and disregarded it, whereas Metternich, although equally contemptuous, used it to his own advantage. The Hohenzollern showed a gleam of interest only at the possibility that the German Confederation would actually create the federal army stipulated in the articles of confederation. In such an army Prussia hoped to play a dominant part, so that it could be a welcome instrument for the extension of Prussian influence or the suppression of liberal movements within Germany. Precisely for these same reasons, however, the smaller states rejected the idea, and attempts to create a federal army were abandoned. Prussia thereupon lost its last interest in the activities of the diet at Frankfurt and became frankly obstructionist. In fact, Prussia's indifference and hostility toward the confederation and its diet rapidly became an ingrained part of Prussian policy that Bismarck later found difficult to eradicate, even when he attempted to unify Germany under Prussia.

On the other hand, Frederick William indulged in such chimerical ventures as trying to unite all German Lutherans and Calvinists. In 1817 he created the Evangelical Union, for which the theologian Schleiermacher and his colleagues drew up a sort of German Book of Common Prayer. By uniting the Protestants and stressing pietistic tendencies, the king hoped to create a counterpart to Catholicism as a bulwark against liberalism. Various other German states actually accepted the idea; but, in the long run, theological differences between the two faiths doomed their unification.

Austria under Metternich

While Prussia was reorganizing internally but losing power abroad, Austria was taking the opposite path. Under Metternich's skilled diplomacy, its foreign influence grew, whereas few changes were effected internally. Vienna's influence, one might almost say dominance, reached throughout central Europe from northern Germany to Sicily. Austria's presidency of the Frankfurt diet was more than honorary, since it was used to sway the other German states. Similarly, Metternich employed the international congresses, at least until 1822, to exercise a paramount position in the "Concert of Europe."

Within the vast Hapsburg dominions, however, Austrian policy remained static. The anachronistic provincial diets were useless as administrative units and, although lacking in substantial power, were even harmful for the long-range viability of the Austrian Empire, since they served as symbolic rallying points for the centrifugal elements of the various subject populations—Italians, Hungarians, Czechs, and others. The only ties that bound the empire together were a precarious loyalty to the emperor at Vienna, police surveillance, and the power of the army. But even the ubiquitous police, the army, and the civil service lacked the efficiency and effectiveness of similar institutions in Prussia.

Possibly more important was the slowness of Austria's economic advance in the decades after 1815. Old-fashioned paternalism allowed the new entrepreneurs little chance for initiative. Consequently the middle class, except in a few cities, such as Vienna, Prague, and Milan, remained small. It is interesting to speculate whether this slow economic development and the tardy growth of a middle class did not in itself preclude Austria from ever leading a unified Germany. Since Germany was eventually unified not so much by Bismarck's "blood and iron" as by economic forces, it is conceivable that the Metternich system, by stressing political factors rather than economic development, ruined Austria's chances for leadership of a united Germany.

Clashes of Liberalism and Conservatism

SUBSERVIENCE OF THE DIET The diet of the confederation had its first session in 1816. Its debates over the next decades seldom led to action. In the rare cases that did not involve the interests of any of the major states—such as a minor territorial exchange among various Saxon duchies effected in 1826—the diet could act as a useful mediator. But on all points touching the spheres of the bigger states, the diet's course depended on the desires of these states, or ultimately on those of Austria. When, for instance, the incompetent

Duke Charles Frederick William acceded in Brunswick and initiated a regime of tyranny, the more liberal delegates to the diet voiced strong objections. Their complaints went unheeded, since Austria and Prussia refused to undermine the principle of legitimacy. When, on the other hand, Prussia demanded a piece of Hessian territory in Westphalia to round out its borders, the diet agreed, and the cession of land was implemented.

The diet's subservience was particularly noticeable in regard to the liberal movements. When Metternich showed no alarm about the constitutional movements in southern and central Germany, the diet, too, remained silent. But when the Austrian minister pushed for action against liberal and revolutionary ideas among students and intellectuals, the diet became an instrument for repressing liberalism. Article XIII of the confederate charter had stipulated that all states were to be endowed with a constitution "based on the system of estates." Although the proviso concerning "estates" stripped such constitutions of much of their progressive nature, Austria, Prussia, and other conservative states showed no intention of implementing this clause. A few of the more progressive states, however, whose populations had lived under the constitutional system of the French occupation, implemented Article XIII. Between 1817 and 1819, Saxony-Weimar, Hesse-Darmstadt, Bavaria, Baden, and Württemberg granted constitutions and set up central assemblies, most of them on the bicameral system. These constitutions were, of course, very conservative. Suffrage was strictly limited, all notions of popular sovereignty were omitted, and the powers of the assemblies were tightly restricted. Hence Metternich, although displeased, decided not to intervene so long as the fundamental sovereignty of the rulers of these states did not appear endangered. Moreover, interference would have been complicated, since the states stayed within the legal limits of the confederate charter.

THE STUDENT MOVEMENTS The liberal and nationalistic movement among students and intellectuals, however, presented a different challenge. As an all-German phenomenon, it threatened to undermine the whole settlement devised at Vienna, so that Metternich felt compelled to force the diet to adopt suppressive measures.

After the Napoleonic Wars, students at various universities had rapidly reformed older organizations and inspired them with new political flavor. These fraternities, or *Burschenschaften,* quickly grew in membership, opened new chapters at many universities, and united into a national federation. Many members were veterans of the 1813 campaigns, from which they had retained the nationalistic ambition for a united Germany, and they adopted the black-red-gold banners carried by the volunteers of the Wars of Liberation. Encouraged by liberal professors, the students dreamed of freedom, justice, and a united fatherland. On specific plans they were vague and on the whole their demands were moderate, but an occasional spark of republicanism lit up their emotion-charged sessions.

The movement attracted the alarmed attention of the governments for the first time in 1816, when the *Burschenschaft* of the University of Erfurt was suspended because of alleged radicalism. In the following year, students from the University of Jena in the relatively liberal state of Weimar invited delegations from other Protestant universities to attend a festival in the Wartburg (castle) in commemoration of the three-hundredth anniversary of Luther's ninety-five theses. The festivities had the tacit approval of King Frederick William III, who at the time was trying to strengthen Protestantism through his Evangelical Union. But in addition, the students decided to celebrate as well the fourth anniversary of the battle of Leipzig as the decisive event in the liberation of Germany from Napoleonic occupation.

The very place chosen for this festival, the Wartburg, was charged with symbols appealing to the emotional romanticism of the students. The Wartburg had been a center of German medieval culture with its minnesongs, epics, and legends, such as those of *Tannhäuser*. As the former home of Ste Elizabeth of Hungary and the hiding place of Luther, it evoked religious piety and fervor. Above all, the memory of Luther, who had translated the Bible into German while residing in the Wartburg, and the recollection of the battle of Leipzig, inspired nationalistic enthusiasm. Hence it is no wonder that the Wartburg Festival was transformed into a sort of patriotic revival session. Some five hundred students from various universities drank, sang, and reveled. Speeches by students and professors from nearby Jena, extolling freedom and fatherland, prompted the intoxicated revelers to light a bonfire in imitation of Luther and to burn symbols of what they despised. Amidst harangues deriding militarism and the torpid conservatism of the princes, they consigned to the flames a corporal's cane, a Prussian military manual, and stacks of conservative pamphlets.

Metternich and Frederick William quickly sensed that the Wartburg Festival of 1817 was more than an overgrown student prank, particularly since the local police and militia, instead of suppressing the riot, joined the celebration. The worried Prussian king immediately sent his Chief Minister Hardenberg to investigate the incident and consult with the duke of Weimar, while Metternich initiated plans for squashing this challenge to his system.

INITIAL REPRESSION The first step was taken in 1818. Metternich's work was facilitated by the changed attitude of Emperor Alexander. Discovery of a supposed plot against his life had undermined his earlier idealistic liberalism. He now dropped all intention of granting his subjects a constitution and fell more and more under the influence of the Austrian minister. Metternich easily convinced the tsar that revolutionary seeds anywhere in Europe were a potential danger even to far-off St. Petersburg, and Alexander promptly denounced the German universities and press as a hotbed of revolution. With such support, Metternich could assume the offensive. At the five-power Congress of Aix-la-Chapelle in 1818, he convinced Frederick William III that "the revolutionists . . . have planned to educate the next generation for revolution," and that German high schools and universities had become subversive. Prussia and Austria then agreed that all German states should restrict the freedom of the press, initiate police surveillance of universities, close high schools where necessary—especially those Prussian Gymnasiums afflicted with the subversive spirit—and prohibit the establishment of parliaments and the granting of new constitutions.

Not all German states felt obliged to follow this mandate from Vienna and Berlin, but initial measures against the press and against certain universities increased the ferment among students and intelligentsia. Nationalistic emotions were further enflamed by the "foreign" interference of Metternich and Alexander. This resentment led to another incident that, like the Wartburg Festival, was largely symbolic, but Metternich used it as justification for further action. Students and liberals had concentrated their antagonism on the playwright August von Kotzebue (1761–1819), then editor of a weekly newspaper in Mannheim. Kotzebue apparently received financial support from the tsar. His paper inveighed against German nationalism and liberalism, and the students came to look upon Kotzebue as a spokesman for the court of St. Petersburg. Caught in this fever of hatred, a young student (Karl Sand) vowed in a religious and patriotic trance to annihilate this symbol of conservatism. For months he lived in the intoxication of his self-imposed mission, keeping a diary of his emotions. In March 1819 he entered the house of Kotzebue and stabbed the playwright in the circle of his family. His attempted suicide having failed, the assassin was later executed.

Provoked by Kotzebue's murder, Metternich and Frederick William III met at Töplitz to devise concerted repressive measures, and called a conference of the more important German states at Carlsbad. Even before the conference met, Austrian and Prussian police took action. Liberals and nationalists were arrested or were dismissed from government posts. Homes of professors were searched and newspaper plants seized. Many writers and teachers, sometimes with their students, fled to asylum in Switzerland, France, or America. Even the prominent were not spared. *Turnvater* Jahn was arrested in Berlin, Stein was placed under police surveillance; the journalist Görres, at the time not yet converted to conservatism, had to flee from the Rhineland; the poet Arndt was dismissed from Bonn University because of his extreme nationalism; and Humboldt resigned his post as minister of education. In Prussia students were arrested en masse for wearing the subversive black-red-gold ribbons and some were even condemned to death.

THE CARLSBAD DECREES Meanwhile at Carlsbad eight German states devised a series of resolutions for submission to the Diet of the German Confederation. The resulting Carlsbad Decrees embodied far-reaching measures for ferreting out subversives and crushing the spreading liberal and nationalistic movement. Special government agents were to be appointed for every university, to "observe carefully the spirit shown by the instructors in their lectures, . . . to give salutary direction to the teaching," and to ascertain that "morality, good order, and propriety" were promoted among the students. The governments pledged dismissal of all professors caught propagating doctrines "harmful to public order or subversive of existing governmental institutions." The *Burschenschaften* and other subversive student unions were outlawed, and students found to be members of a secret organization were to be expelled and denied public employment anywhere. Teachers or students prosecuted under these articles were not to be rehired or readmitted at any other university on confederate territory. At the same time, Jahn's gymnastic societies and all political clubs were prohibited, and strict censorship of newspapers and books was established.

The Carlsbad Decrees tended to undermine the absolute sovereignty of the states. Metternich evidently had no confidence in the ability or willingness of some of the smaller princes to repress liberalism in their own states. Consequently, in matters of censorship, each state was made responsible "to the whole Confederation for every publication appearing under its supervision in which the honor or security of other states is infringed . . . or their administration attacked." Presumably such a clause made the king of Bavaria accountable to the diet if one of his subjects insulted the king of Prussia. An investigating committee was established at Mainz to conduct investigations throughout confederate territory into the "ramifications of the revolutionary plots and demagogical associations" that might endanger the peace of the union or of individual states. This commission had to report its findings to the diet, which thereby assumed the right to interfere in the internal affairs of the member states.

Although some of the lesser states disliked the new decrees, the diet ratified them barely a month after their formulation at Carlsbad. The king of Württemberg, particularly, protested the implied undermining of his sovereign rights. As if to spite Metternich, he relaxed some of the laws limiting the political rights of his subjects and talked loudly of resisting Austro-Prussian attempts at dominating the smaller states. Metternich tried to placate him by reaffirming the principle of the sovereign independence of the states, while at the same time proceeding to enforce the Carlsbad Decrees.

Enforcement of the repressive decrees, undertaken only perfunctorily in some of the lesser states, quelled many outward signs of unrest. It is, however, difficult to estimate how it affected the liberal movement as a whole. Because the 1820s were relatively free from revolutionary signs and because the revolutionary year 1830 did not produce any major upheaval in Germany, it is often asserted that Metternich's measures were highly effective. One should recall, however, that the liberal and nationalistic unrest had not been spectacular before the Carlsbad Decrees. It is fairly obvious that Metternich exaggerated the danger and strength of the liberal movement for his own purposes. Quite conceivably, the indignities of Metternich's attempt at muzzling public opinion fanned the discontent of the middle class instead of eliminating it.

The Revolution of 1830 and Its Aftermath

While Germany remained tranquil in the 1820s, revolutions abroad rattled at the foundations of Metternich's system. Spain and its colonies, Naples, Greece, Portugal, and even Russia experienced the tremors of nationalistic or liberal revolts. Finally, 1830 turned into a year of wholesale revolution.

The overthrow of the Bourbon dynasty in Paris coupled with major revolutions in Belgium, Italy, and Poland aroused hopeful excitement in Germany. For a while it seemed as though the entire confederation might go up in revolutionary flames, but in the end only a few minor uprisings occurred. Conservative Prussia and Austria remained quiet; the more liberal states of the south and west experienced mild disturbances, usually in the form of demonstrations and petitions for greater political participation and better guarantees of civil liberties. Actual revolts threatening to overthrow the ruling princes broke out in only a few intermediate states. In Saxony, Hesse-Cassel, and Hanover these outbreaks were quelled by promises of political concessions. Only in Brunswick did the revolution force the abdication of the hated duke and the substitution of his more liberal brother.

Austria and Prussia in 1830 faced problems of a different nature. The rebellions in Italy fanned the nationalistic unrest among the subject peoples of the Austrian Empire. The resulting demands for equal status, autonomy, or even complete independence strained the energies of the Viennese government. At first Metternich seemed confident that Austria was strong enough to ensure survival of its empire while retaining domination of the German Confederation. But it soon became obvious that both tasks could not be accomplished simultaneously; and Metternich—unlike his successors—never questioned that the survival of the empire was more important than domination of the confederation. This decision profoundly affected the unification movement of Germany: it demonstrated that in times of general crisis Austria would be occupied primarily with non-German affairs; hence the secondary states in the confederation had no choice but to look to Prussia for possible assistance. Each Austrian crisis therefore allowed Prussia to tighten its influence over the other states, and only an energetic and self-confident leader at the helm of Prussia was needed to take full advantage of Austria's recurring dilemma.

Frederick William III, of course, was not that leader. When in 1830 the southern states, afraid of a possible French invasion unleashed by the revolutionary forces in Paris in the style of 1792, asked Prussia to establish a military league of German states for the protection of German territory, the hesitant king asked for Metternich's advice and approval. Vienna naturally suggested a delay until it had suppressed the revolts among its subject peoples and could resume its preponderant role in the German Confederation.

Although the revolutionary unrest in Germany had been insignificant in 1830, Metternich, fearful that the new bourgeois spirit of Paris might undermine legitimacy in Germany, insisted on increased vigilance against all possible subversive elements. New press laws were proposed that merely antagonized the growing middle class. In answer, liberal journalists organized a festival at Hambach in the Bavarian Palatinate in the spring of 1832. Some twenty to thirty thousand people gathered to drink and dance together, listening to inflammatory speeches on German unity and liberalism, and calling for an end to all absolutism, particularly in Prussia and Austria. Finally, the celebrants dispersed peacefully long before a Bavarian army, dispatched against them, reached the scene of the supposed revolution. Notwithstanding its moderation, the Hambach Festival served Metternich to convince Frederick William and others of the persistent dangers of the liberal movement. Consequently, the diet at Frankfurt passed new restrictive resolutions, shoring up the powers of the princes and undermining the existing constitutional assemblies. The new measures of 1832 authorized the diet to interfere in the states in case liberal forces appeared to threaten the authority of a prince.

Whether or not as a result of these measures, Germany enjoyed relative political calm during the remaining 1830s. There was a minor revolt in Frankfurt, where a small band of diehards attempted to overthrow the diet, and a constitutional struggle in Hanover in 1837 upon the accession of the reactionary King Ernest Augustus.[1] Meanwhile the middle class concentrated on developing the prosperity of Germany. It is, of course, impossible to ascertain how much latent discontent was building up under this outward tranquility. The historian is probably on surest ground if he does not overrate the revolutionary temper of the Germans.

Economic Unification

While Metternich and Frederick William III were dissipating their efforts in suppressing the liberal movements, economic changes began to transform Germany—preparing the path for its eventual unification, although not necessarily assuring the triumph of liberalism.

PRUSSIA'S ECONOMIC GROWTH In 1815, Prussia, like most of Germany, was economically still rather backward. The newly acquired regions in the Rhineland were only beginning to be developed. There was little mining, machines were scarce, and industrial entrepreneurs were few. Prussia's trade was largely in agricultural products. Its banking and credit system lagged far behind those of France, England, and Holland. On the other hand, Prussia was favored with potentially valuable resources of industrial raw materials, the beginnings of a good network of roads and canals, and a labor force noted for fine workmanship.

With this foundation Prussia could commence its economic growth. The speed of this development in the first half of the nineteenth century should not be exaggerated. It was a slow process until 1830, became noticeably faster after 1835, and turned into a phenomenal boom only in the 1840s with the widespread introduction of steam power and an extensive net of railways. Although private enterprise and initiative were largely responsible for this industrialization, the state from the beginning helped by supervising, planning, and occasionally financing many of the new activities. An important step was the establishment in 1821 of the Prussian Institute of Trades to spread knowledge of new industrial processes and machinery. Moreover, Prussia, more than most German states, continued to stress im-

[1] Since the Salic Law did not permit inheritance through the female line, Hanover became independent in 1837 when Queen Victoria ascended the throne of England.

provement of its internal means of communication and exchange: roads and canals were continually expanded; from 1825 on, steamships were employed on the Rhine; and after the introduction of railways in 1835, Prussians became expert builders of commercially profitable railroads.

At the same time, enlarged trade and production in many of the German states, as well as improved communications and transport, increased contact among the populations and pointed the way toward unification. Prussia's creation of the Zollverein (customs union) was in part the logical extension of this development.

THE PRUSSIAN TARIFF SYSTEM The background to the establishment of the Zollverein was the initiation of a new Prussian tariff in 1818. Its originator (Karl G. Maassen), an economist of the school of Adam Smith, probably had no political aims in mind, and certainly could not foresee that his fiscal ideas could ultimately be used to help unify Germany. The primary purposes of the tariff of 1818 were to increase trade, improve transport and communications, and raise the revenue of the government. This could best be achieved by creating a large free market through the internal economic unification of Prussia, as well as by modernizing and simplifying its tariff structure.

The tariff law established complete freedom of trade within all Prussian lands. The sixty-seven different tariff rates on imported goods that existed in the various provinces were equalized and generally lowered to about 10 percent. It was thought that such low rates would eliminate smuggling, a perennial problem for Prussia, with its jagged frontiers bordering on twenty-eight different states. The simplified reduced rates would also lower the cost of collection and still produce an adequate revenue for the government. Certain raw materials needed for industries were admitted free of duty, while mildly protective tariffs of about 20 percent were applied to goods, such as sugar and coffee, imported from colonial lands. Only the importation of items produced by government monopolies, such as salt and playing cards, was prohibited.

A further feature of the 1818 law lent itself admirably to economic warfare, although it probably was not so intended by its framer. Goods in transit that merely passed through Prussia, for consumption in a different state, were to be assessed with a very high tariff. Since Prussia lay astride most trade routes between northern and southern Europe, from the Niemen to the Rhine, and since there were enclaved states whose external trade had to pass through Prussian territory, this high transit tariff produced a good revenue without burdening the Prussian consumer. This measure rapidly forced some of the enclaved and neighboring states to join Prussia in a customs union in order to escape the prohibitively high tariff. In the late 1820s, Prussia also realized that it could use this measure in economic rivalry with its more independent neighbors, especially Hanover. The only north-south trade route in Germany that did not pass through Prussian soil went from Bremen via Hanover, Göttingen, and Kassel into southern Germany. In order to attract trade away from this route and to induce other states to join Prussia's growing customs union, the Prussian government used some of the revenue from transit tariffs to build up the best possible north-south roads, and even offered to construct connecting roads in states that joined the union. The majority of Prussia's neighbors soon thought it advantageous to join the Prussian system in order to avoid the high transit tariffs. For Prussia the scheme proved to be self-financing: the improved roads brought more transit revenue to finance more roads, which in turn attracted more trade.

THE ZOLLVEREIN In this manner, the original tariff law intended solely for Prussia became the basis for the Zollverein. By 1928, some seven small states had joined Prussia in this budding customs union. In every case, the smaller state turned the administration of its customs over to the Prussian government, in return for which it received a share in Prussia's revenue from import and transit tariffs. While economically advantageous to both states, the stationing of Prussian customs officials at the borders of the smaller states seemed to diminish their sovereignty and was easily interpreted as Prussian imperialism.

Hence there were economic as well as political reasons for the dismay shown by the southern and central states. They appealed to the diet to set up an economic union for all states which would be devoid of the political implications of Prussia's Zollverein, but Austria showed no interest and the diet took no action. Bavaria and Württemberg then formed their own southern economic league, while Hanover and some of the northern states tried a similar experiment. Prussia's system, however, was more viable, and it was able to expand its customs union after eliminating the politically objectionable features of the earlier customs treaties. In 1828 Prussia induced the Duchy of Hesse-Darmstadt to join the Zollverein on the basis of complete equality. Hesse was to retain its own customs service. A joint council was to determine the policy on which the two customs services would operate. The total revenue from import and transit tariffs was to be shared on a basis of population. As in earlier treaties, there was to be free trade between the two states.

This new arrangement did not infringe on the touchy sense of sovereignty of other states, but in essence it left dominant power in the hands of Prussia, whose economic preponderance was increasing. It proved to be the "open sesame" for the Zollverein. In rapid succession, the ephemeral central and southern leagues dissolved and its members climbed on board the Prussian system.

Finally, an all-encompassing economic treaty was signed in 1833 among most of the German states, thereby inaugurating the German, as opposed to the Prussian, Zollverein. A customs parliament with annual meetings was set up to decide tariff policy on the basis of unanimity. The essential features of the old Prussian tariff were retained, establishing free trade among its members and low protective tariffs against foreign goods—although tariffs tended to increase in the 1840s.

By 1842, all German states had joined the Zollverein with certain significant exceptions. In the south, Austria remained completely aloof; in the north, Hanover, with nearby Oldenburg, Mecklenburg, Holstein, and the free cities of Bremen, Hamburg, and Lübeck, preferred to keep unrestricted trade with England. Austria and Hanover were to remain for decades undaunted opponents of any kind of German unification.

Even in its own day, the Zollverein was hailed as the great unifier of Germany. A current song hailed the power of such commodities as matches, lard, cheese, and wax, which were tying the nation together better than the confederation established at Vienna. Unquestionably it marked a major step toward unifying the German states. It also underscored what was becoming increasingly evident—that Austria was excluding itself more and more from the German Confederation, whereas Prussia was constantly increasing its influence over the states. Furthermore, the creation of a wide area of free trade acted as a strong stimulus to the economy. Greater trade provided the capital needed to finance the industrial growth that was to blossom forth in mid-century.

To be sure, the consequences of the Zollverein should not be exaggerated. A measure of the relative importance of the customs parliament can be gathered from the fact that it could not even persuade its members to create a uniform system of coinage. And the industrial boom was based as much on improved transport and communications, new inventions, a better-educated and more scientific-minded middle class as on the creation of a free-trade area. Finally, the success of the Zollverein should not obscure the fact that the economic unification, although a precondition for German unification, could not by itself overcome all political obstacles. The history of the three decades from 1840 to complete unification in 1871 shows only too well that German particularism was indeed tenacious.

13

Years of Decision, 1840–1858

THE DECADE BEFORE THE REVOLUTION

During the 1840s, the Biedermeier period of relative quietude gave way to an era of expectation and restlessness. Economic and social changes, intensified nationalism, and a new critical attitude increased the ferment that finally erupted in the revolutionary year 1848.

The Temper of the Times

SOCIAL AND ECONOMIC UNREST The economic and industrial transformation of the 1830s gained momentum after 1840. Railroads and the electric telegraph—the use of which was at first reserved to governments—helped bind the German states closer together and exerted a far-reaching impact on the socioeconomic structure of the land. A fairly comprehensive net of railroads, constructed with considerable speed, provided Germany with some three thousand miles of track by 1848. Improved communications hastened economic expansion and began to alter the hitherto sleepy character of rural life. Growing industrial enterprises, although insignificant by later standards, increased output and attracted labor to the city, while railroads carried a new dynamic impetus to the rural communities.

As a result, the exclusively agricultural aspect of Germany began to give way. Cities grew quickly. Berlin increased by about 30 percent in the decade of the 1840s. A city proletariat arose to man the new factories, and city slums bred the new generation that was to build the barricades of 1848. Simultaneously, industrial and commercial expansion increased the power and numbers of the upper middle class—the manufacturers, merchants, and financiers who demanded German unity and a share in the affairs of state.

Social injustices and occasional economic crises added to the ferment. The plight of the agricultural laborers, who constituted a large segment of the rural population, grew worse. Natural disasters, such as failure of the potato crop in 1846–1847, brought them near starvation and made them tinder for revolutionary fires. The semirural population, such as the Silesian weavers who depended on the textile cottage industry, suffered from the introduction of machinery. In Silesia the open rebellion in 1844 was bloodily repressed by the Prussian army. Saxony, Hanover, Württemberg, and most of the other states experienced periodic disorders and minor uprisings frequently caused by economic failures and unemployment. The years 1846 and 1847, particularly, were filled with swelling agitation: a Polish revolt in Cracow in 1846, ruthlessly suppressed by Austria, scattered across Germany Polish refugees eager to propagate their revolutionary invectives against authoritarian Austria, Russia, and Prussia. At the same time, a plague swept across Germany, leaving death and misery in its wake. A world-wide trade and financial crisis shook the security of the middle class. Coupled with crop failures, it brought food shortages to the cities. Rye, normally an export item, had to be imported into the Zollverein area. Price increases and shortages of bread and potatoes caused riots in Berlin, where women pillaged foodstores and beat up merchants who tried to profiteer from the food crisis.

THE PULSE OF NEW IDEAS The general restlessness was intensified by new nationalistic, liberal, and materialistic ideas. The threat of war with France in 1840 produced in the German middle class an outburst of nationalistic elation that was fanned by the patriotic poets of the day. "The Song of the Rhine," with its stern warning to the French not to touch "the free German Rhine," "The Watch on the Rhine," and the poem "Deutschland, Deutschland über Alles" stem from this period and rapidly acquired a symbolic role in German nationalism. This movement was not merely negative in its antiforeign aspects, but also highly dynamic in its quest for German unity.

In literature and thought, some conservative followers of Hegel continued to champion existing institutions, especially church and state, but, generally speaking, romanticism had spent its force. Many intellectuals were searching for new philosophical and literary ideas, and considered the political framework no longer compatible with changing socioeconomic conditions. Hence they regarded tradition and authority as stultifying rather than as guides for conduct. Poets and critics of this new wave, after 1830 loosely grouped together and labeled the "Young Germany" movement, turned their pungent satire on all that seemed staid and venerable in the social and cultural life of Germany. Most of these iconoclasts lived in exile in Paris, London, or Zurich, where they were not hampered by censorship or political police. But although they lived abroad, they wrote about Germany and for Germans. Among them were the revolutionary poet August von Platen (1796–1835), famous for his ballads, and the satirist and journalist Ludwig Börne (1786–1837). Inferior in literary skill but more ardently active in political matters were Georg Herwegh (1817–1875) and Ferdinand Freiligrath (1810–1876). The most famous of these Young Germans was the lyric poet Heinrich Heine, who resided in Paris after the revolution of 1830. A curious dichotomy polarized his emotions. He was strongly attracted by French rationalism and the intellectual atmosphere of his adopted French home. But France could never become his "fatherland." His lyric poems are among the greatest in the German language, his criticisms of German political conditions are among the most penetrating ever written. Like his fellow exiles, Heine was passionately devoted to the ideals of freedom and cultural emancipation, but unlike many of the boisterous nationalists of his day, he was violently opposed to chauvinistic nationalism.

New and liberal currents also entered Germany from other sources. From Switzerland, France, Poland, Italy, and even the United States, democratic and revolutionary ideas spread across Germany, fanned by pamphlets and newspapers that circumvented censorship and surveillance. As always, these new currents found the strongest foothold in southwest Germany, politically and geographically closer to republican Switzerland and liberal France. But even in Austria, intellectuals gathered in "reading circles" to discuss democratic concepts and search for some alleviation of their political frustrations.

This search for the new was noticeable in many fields. Advances in the sciences and a reinterpretation of Hegel's dialectic by the so-called Young Hegelians furthered a growing materialism inimical to spiritual and pietistic values, and tended to undermine the hallowed authority of rulers and church. Even in Catholic Bavaria, pressure was exercised against the ultramontanism that had characterized the Metternich era. An even more devastating movement against the Church was launched by David Friederich Strauss (1808–1874) with his *Life of Jesus,* a materialistic reinterpretation of Christ's life. Strauss depicted Jesus as a socially conscious man rather than as divine, and rejected His miracles as spurious. At the same time, Ludwig Feuerbach (1804–1872) shocked his contemporaries with his uncompromising materialism in his *Nature of Christianity.* He denied all spiritual and supernatural essence, insisting that "man is what he eats." Since God was merely the product of human imagination, Feuerbach believed man could better his fate only by mutual aid and an improvement of social institutions. Some groups used these irreligious and humanistic ideas to launch renewed attacks against pietism and orthodoxy in the Lutheran Church, or against ultramontanism, both of which were anathema to the liberals of the day. Others adapted the new materialism of the Young Hegelians and Feuerbach to bolster the growing socialist movement.

Prussia in the 1840s

THE NEW KING: FREDERICK WILLIAM IV The hopes of the liberals in Prussia and other German states were raised in 1840 by the death of the seventy-year-old Frederick William III, who had patently failed to fulfill his reform promises of the liberation period and had meekly submitted to the influence of Metternich. The initial acts of the new king, the forty-five-year-old Frederick William IV (1840–1858), confirmed the expectations of the intelligentsia. He granted an amnesty to political prisoners, relaxed censorship, and restored political suspects, such as the poet Ernst Moritz Arndt and the historian Friedrich Dahlmann, to their positions. The new Prussian ruler seemed kind and warmhearted, imbued with a genuine though paternalistic love for his people. Intelligent and cultured, he showed deep interest in the arts, especially painting and music. Above all, his corpulence and personal distaste for soldiering presaged an end to the militarism of Prussia's rulers.

His early speeches, characterized by

the historian Heinrich von Sybel (1817–1895) as "grandiloquent, oratorically sublime, but politically meaningless," kept popular enthusiasm at a high pitch. Frederick William hinted at reforms in Prussia as well as in Germany. He granted more importance to the eight provincial estates and, one year after his accession, permitted them to send committees to Berlin to discuss common financial and legislative problems. Even though he resisted pressure to establish a central diet for all of Prussia, he complied with the request for regular meetings of the provincial diets with free and public debate, and allowed the new central committees to hold frequent consultations in Berlin. A remark attributed to him—that he loved a convinced opposition—appeared at first correct.

But the honeymoon between the liberals and their new ruler lasted barely two years. Frederick William was at heart a romantic and a traditionalist. Although as vacillating as his father and as politically inept, he held strong, almost unflinching beliefs in the divine rights of kings. Morbidly afraid of revolution, he abhorred popular sovereignty and similar rationalist notions. He was rather attracted by the mysticism of the Middle Ages, by the orderliness of the medieval state composed of estates (*Ständestaat*), and by the splendor of the Holy Roman Empire. He would probably have felt more at ease on the throne of a medieval castle, surrounded by armored knights and vested bishops, than in industrial Berlin with its challenge of onrushing changes.

Despite his sympathy for the people, Frederick William IV hardly understood their needs or demands, and proved unequal to the opportunities presented to him. With few exceptions, he surrounded himself with ultraconservative ministers and friends who isolated him from his changing environment. His foreign policy was colored by traditionalist views. Despite the altered positions of Austria and Prussia, he could not shed the time-honored Hohenzollern reverence for the Hapsburgs, and looked upon Vienna as the natural head of any possible German union. Even when the inevitability of Austria's gradual withdrawal from Germany became obvious, Frederick William remained in favor of *Grossdeutschland* (unification of the German states including Austria). He wrote to his friend and advisor Joseph Maria von Radowitz (1797–1853) in 1847: "May God in Heaven save me from any attempt to drive Austria out of the Confederation."

By 1843, the increased demands of the diet committees for constitutional safeguards, and the vigorous criticism of his regime appearing in newspapers and pamphlets had instilled new fears in the king. Strict censorship and police surveillance were reactivated; the "Metternich system" reappeared. To some, the cause of liberalism began to look as hopeless as ever.

But Prussia's economic and social transformation could not be thwarted by Frederick William's conservative faintheartedness. The restlessness of the growing middle class and the agitation of the lower classes could not be obliterated by censorship or mild repression. Minor disorders, disturbances in Prussian Poland, and the weavers' rebellion were portents that reached even the insulated king.

PRESSURE FOR A REPRESENTATIVE ASSEMBLY In the end it was largely a financial problem that forced the Prussian king to listen to the middle class and open a Pandora's box of revolutionary demands. At the beginning of his reign in 1840, Prussia's income had sufficed to balance the state budget. But in the ensuing years the revenues no longer met the increased demands. The expenses of the central government, particularly of the court, owed its alarming growth to Frederick William's delight in opulent festivals and his lavish grants to the nobility. Economic expansion increased the governmental bureaucracy and raised the cost of the civil service. Above all, the boom in railroad construction placed new burdens on the state budget. Initially, Prussian railroads had been built by private joint-stock companies in accordance with over-all plans laid down by the state. But in the 1840s, largely to keep up with progress in neighboring states, the government encouraged construction of railroads by granting yearly subsidies and guaranteeing shareholders' interests. Plans were also being drawn for ultimate government purchase of all railroads.

The funds needed for these new commitments were unattainable from current revenues. Tariffs could not be raised without permission from all members of the Zollverein, and taxes could not be increased without consent of the estates. A law of 1820 even stipulated that the government could not contract new loans without agreement of the estates.

Frederick William naturally felt disinclined to show dependence on the diets. His device of calling committees of the various estates to Berlin in 1842 —rather than permit establishment of an all-Prussian assembly—was an attempt to achieve financial solvency without admitting constitutional limitations. But the committees refused to grant funds except in return for constitutional concessions. In the long run, failure to compromise would threaten the success of the railroad program. For a few years the industrial boom and speculation furnished enough private funds to continue construction, but by the mid-1840s, further progress was endangered. Fearful of a bursting of the bubble, the government had issued a law in 1844 to limit speculation. As a consequence, joint-stock companies suddenly found it harder to obtain investment capital. To keep up railroad construction, the government was forced to commit ever-larger sums, thereby increasing the need for either raising taxes or borrowing more money.

At the same time, a pressure group developed in unexpected quarters. Because they seemed unprofitable to private investors, two vital railroad lines had not yet been constructed. One was a spur to Saarbrücken, in which only the government was particularly interested because it could transport coal from state-owned mines in the Saar—and be of value in the event of war with France. The second was a main line to the east, from Pomerania to Königsberg. This Eastern Line (*Ostbahn*), also of strategic importance in connection with the restless Polish situation, primarily interested the Junker landlords, who hoped to ship their grain more cheaply into central Prussia and Germany in order to compete with American and Russian imports. Hence the government and its close supporters, the Prussian aristocrats, now urged the construction of these two lines, which no private company cared to finance.

Frederick William IV gradually realized that the increasing financial pressure might ultimately compel him to convoke an all-Prussian assembly in order to achieve financial relief. Despite Metternich's warning, he began consultations in 1845 to determine what form of meeting would placate the estates without undermining the royal prerogatives. Various plans were produced by the king's advisers during 1846, but he waited until February of 1847 to convoke the new assembly. The poor harvests and business failures of 1846–1847 and the state's increased financial distress made all delay unwise, and prompted the king to call the meeting of a United Diet (*Vereinigter Landtag*) in Berlin in April, 1847.

THE UNITED DIET The calling of this United Diet, representing the estates of all eight provincial diets, was hailed by liberals as a momentous event. Even foreigners speculated that it might mark the beginning of the transformation of Prussia and Germany, and eventually of all eastern conservative monarchies. For the first time, representatives from all the provinces were to sit jointly to debate all-Prussian problems. The liberals firmly expected that Prussia would at last obtain a constitution.

Frederick William, of course, had not called the meeting for such a purpose. Above all, he needed money. At the most he was willing to counteract the increasing unrest among his subjects by acceding superficially to certain popular demands, provided the substance of royal power remained untarnished. The very composition of the United Diet showed the king's distaste for democratic forms and his predilection for medieval corporate representation. The diet was divided into two houses on the basis of classes: the upper house contained 70 princes and lords; membership in the lower house was made up of 237 minor nobles, 182 burghers, and 124 peasants. A two-thirds majority in both houses was to be required before any petition or report could be submitted to the king. In view of the social composition of this body, it is surprising—and indicative of the strong mood of discontent—that the United Diet tried to act so determinedly against royal absolutism.

The hopes of the liberals were quickly dashed by the king's opening speech to the assembled delegates. In typical Hohenzollern fashion, he reminded them that it had "pleased God to let Prussia become great through the sword—abroad through the sword of war, at home through the sword of the spirit"—the spirit of order and discipline. The only task he laid before the diet was to grant taxes and authorize new loans. On other matters, the members could act in an advisory role, provided the king requested their opinion. The diet was to be given no legislative function. "As in military campaigns a single commander is needed," the king reasoned in his speech, so the fate of Prussia "can be directed only by a single will." At the discretion of the king, special committees of the diet could be reconvened, presumably every four years, to discuss current matters, but Frederick William made it clear that he had no intention of creating a permanent parliament. And he concluded with the famous solemn pronouncement that "no power on earth" would ever force him "to transform the natural . . . relationship between prince and people into a contractual and constitutional one," and that he would neither then nor ever "permit a blotted parchment to thrust itself, like a second Providence, between our Lord in Heaven and this land, to rule us with its paragraphs and to replace the ancient and sacred bond of loyalty."

Despite this inauspicious opening, the diet immediately debated political problems. A surprising number of members from the upper middle class and the lower nobility delivered impassioned speeches proposing a constitution for Prussia, which they regarded as requisite also for a closer German union. As an initial demand, they stipulated regular meetings of the entire diet and parliamentary control over the state budget. Frederick William, of course, was not ready for such concessions. Bitter fights ensued between moderate parliamentarians and the supporters of unlimited royal absolutism. The opposition was led by the moderate liberal Rhineland industrialist Ludolf Camphausen (1803–1890). The king found strong support in his minister of the interior, Otto von Manteuffel (1805–1882) and in a newcomer to the political stage, Otto von Bismarck (1815–1898), who established a reputation as a defender of the system. In the end, the diet refused to grant the requested loans for railroad construction unless given concessions by the king. Hence Frederick William dismissed the delegates in June with a faint promise to reconvene them within four years.

Although short-lived, the meeting of the United Diet had far-reaching consequences at home and abroad. The experience revealed the wide gulf separating the king from even the most moderate opposition. The lines seemed drawn between the monarchy and the nation at large. Frederick William had demonstrated his inflexibility when, according to Camphausen, an outstretched hand, "a word would have sufficed to terminate the constitutional struggle in Prussia." His brother, the future William I, had flaunted before the delegates his conservatism and his infatuation with the army. Most of the delegates had shown surprising docility and patience. Their loyal submission to the crown seemed to outweigh their discontent and revealed their ingrained respect for authority.

In Germany as a whole, the king's attitude toward the United Diet discredited Prussia in the eyes of the liberals; on the other hand, the moderation of the delegates renewed the confidence of the conservatives. Finally, an unexpected reaction of long-range consequence came from St. Petersburg. Frederick William's brother-in-law, the ultraconservative Emperor Nicholas I, regarded the very convocation of the United Diet as an unwarranted concession to popular demands and henceforth looked upon the Prussian king with undisguised misgiving. The resulting cooling of relations between the two autocracies proved of considerable importance in the failure of German unification in 1849–1850.

The Unitary Movement before 1848

While the Metternich system gradually became effete as well as ossified and socioliberal unrest increased, the question of unification continued to occupy many Germans. The hope for a closer union that was bright during the Wars of Liberation and had sparked the enthusiasm of student and other liberal and nationalistic groups was now stronger. The demand was also taken up by the growing industrial and commercial classes, which saw in unification a guarantee of future prosperity.

The upsurge in nationalistic feelings

became so intense that even the ruling classes found it expedient to pay lip service to the ideal of unity. At a festival in Cologne in 1842 inaugurating the projected completion of the famous cathedral that had stood unfinished for centuries, Archduke John of Austria (1782–1859) and German kings and dukes vied with one another in their toasts to German unity. Frederick William IV lauded the "spirit of German strength and unity" that had built the cathedral and had freed the adjacent Rhine from foreign domination. Archduke John, uncle of the reigning emperor of Austria, Ferdinand I (1835–1848), endeared himself to the nationalists by his widely reported toast: "No Austria, no Prussia; but a great united Germany!"

Throughout the decade there was speculation as to how Germany could be unified. Writers, poets, historians, and university professors discussed various proposals. Deputies from the more liberal southern states held occasional meetings to deliberate on the problem. Frederick William himself discussed the question with his advisers and hinted at reviving the old Holy Roman Empire, with the Prussian ruler as "Captain-General."

The task of unifying Germany raised countless questions. Three possible solutions concerning the size of the union were advanced: *Grossdeutschland,* including all the lesser German states, together with Austria and Prussia and their dependent alien populations; *Kleindeutschland,* embracing the lesser states and Prussia with its Polish possessions, but excluding the entire Austrian Empire; or an ethnically homogeneous state, including only German-speaking peoples—a solution that would require the dismemberment of Austria and Prussia by forcing them to loosen or even relinquish their ties to non-German territories. There were also problems of leadership: Hapsburgs or Hohenzollerns might assume control; a lesser state, such as Bavaria, might act as mediator between the two giants; or a directorate of the five kings and the emperor, with rotating chairmanship, might be established. Moreover, there was the problem of finding a balance between Protestant and Catholic states. Finally, questions of political and social reforms inextricably affected all other considerations: liberals and conservatives, constitutional monarchists and republicans, social reformers and moderates—all produced their own programs.

Most answers to these questions remained where they originated—in the drawing room—or they were no more than exercises in journalistic imagination, or emotional vagaries of street-corner harangues. Only a few were elaborated into complete programs. Frederick William's friend Radowitz evolved a plan to turn Germany from a loose confederation into a federal state. The five kings were to exercise more power than the dukes and the cities, and were to control an invigorated central diet. But this scheme had little influence outside the royal court of Prussia.

Two programs developed in central Germany carried considerable weight during the revolutionary years. One was framed in 1847 at a meeting at Heppenheim, near the Rhine, attended by influential leaders from several central and southern states. It was essentially a moderate proposal, reflecting the opinions of its chief author, Baron Heinrich von Gagern (1799–1880) of Hesse. It called for the convocation of an all-German parliament and the establishment of a German constitutional monarchy. The program avoided all reference to social problems. Its moderation attracted the middle class and made it a forerunner of the unification attempts by the Frankfurt National Assembly of 1848.

The other program, elaborated in greater detail, was evolved in the same year at Offenburg under guidance of the more radical liberals Gustav Struve (1805–1870) and Friedrich Hecker (1811–1881). Besides an all-German parliament and state assemblies, all elected by universal male suffrage, the program called for a whole gamut of civil liberties which became a common ingredient of the revolutionary demands of 1848: trial by jury; freedom of speech, press, and assembly; and guarantees of religious rights. To weaken the power of the petty states over their subjects, it called for a common German citizenship. In its demands for a national militia in lieu of royal or ducal armies and for oaths to be given to the constitution instead of to the ruler, it displayed outright republican tendencies. Finally, the Offenburg platform contained proposals that inevitably frightened the middle and upper classes: abolition of all class privileges, a graduated income tax, and state powers to guarantee the laborer's right to work and to regulate relations between capital and labor.

The socialistic demands in the Offenburg program reveal the changing attitude of the lower classes during the 1840s. The romantic ideals of harmonious communal living espoused by the utopian socialists no longer satisfied the new proletariat. Instead, workers began to organize in defense of their own interests and to champion more practical demands. Self-proclaimed socialist leaders were active in Switzerland, France, England, and other countries developing "scientific socialism." In 1846, Karl Marx (1818–1883) and Friedrich Engels (1820–1895) wrote *German Ideology* (published *in toto* only in 1927), in which they advocated the "overthrow of the existing social order" through the "Communist revolution," and called for "the abolition of private property." In the following year they prepared the *Communist Manifesto,* published in January 1848. Soon the radical demands of these socialists found an echo in newspapers, in pamphlets, and in the proposals of certain political reformers.

THE REVOLUTIONARY YEARS, 1848–1849

During the first four months of 1848, revolutions spread like an epidemic over large areas of Europe. The Italian states, France, Austria, the German states, Hungary, Poland, and Rumania were scenes of major revolts; pressure and demonstrations in Belgium, Denmark, Holland, and Switzerland forced the governments to grant concessions or new constitutions. Only Russia, England, Spain, and a handful of smaller nations escaped the revolutionary disorders.

The various revolutions were essentially interrelated. The initial sparks of revolt jumped from capital to capital like signals of a semaphore, and some revolutionaries collaborated on an international scale. Most of the revolutions produced radical shifts in foreign policy that in turn affected the revolutionary movements in neighboring states.

An Over-all View of the German Revolutions

Within Germany, revolutions occurred in almost all the states—some involving armed clashes and bloodshed, others consisting of peaceful demonstrations and petitions, followed by more or less gracious concessions on the part of the rulers. Taken as a whole, these revolutionary outbreaks were complex and confusing, for they lacked unity of purpose. On the one hand, there were over thirty separate revolts in the various states; on the other, there was one all-German revolution aimed at uniting the states into a single political entity. Different classes—serfs and peasants, workers and small artisans, middle and upper bourgeois—participated in the revolts, each fighting for its own aims, which usually were different from, if not antagonistic to, those of the other classes. Class war appeared in 1848 as it rarely had before in Germany and complicated the revolutionary struggle.

At least three major aims can be crystallized: one was the nationalistic goal of unifying Germany, which served to some degree as a coalescing factor for the revolts. A second goal was political. The revolutionaries everywhere demanded basic civil rights and a measure of popular sovereignty, although they differed on the degree of desirable changes. Finally, a third set of aims was social and economic. Those still in serfdom wanted freedom; the agricultural proletariat desired emancipation from the dominance of the landlord; city workers demanded shorter hours, higher wages, and a guarantee of employment; merchants called for freedom from economic restrictions; and the ultraradicals preached socioeconomic egalitarianism.

The three aims—one might call them three types of revolution—national, political, and social, interacted and were frequently at cross-purposes. Germany actually was not ready for a social revolution, and it is doubtful that the aims of the socialist extremists could ever have been implemented in 1848. But the same judgment does not apply to the national and political revolutions. Conceivably either one of them alone might have succeeded, but the intertwining of the three confused the issues. The middle class was ultimately forced to choose between unification and liberalism. They chose unification and doomed both. Similarly, fear of the egalitarian aims of the lower classes drove the middle class into reliance on the conservative forces of order and stability—thereby aborting the social revolution and undermining their own liberal aspirations.

Despite the complexity of the years of insurrections, they can be divided into distinct periods. The months from late February to May 1848 constituted the phase of initial revolutionary outbreaks, marked by liberal and national revolts with an occasional social rebellion. A new period began in June 1848, initiating the first phase of reaction. The fall of the insurgent city of Prague to the forces of the Austrian general, Prince Alfred Windisch-Graetz (1787–1862), proved that the Austrian army was still an effective bulwark of conservatism. Reaction began to reassert itself in Germany and the Austrian Empire, causing the failure of most of the liberal movements. The period ended in April 1849, when Frederick William's refusal of an all-German crown seemingly dashed hopes for the national unitary movement (see pages 330–331). Finally, there was a brief third phase: a new wave of revolutions swept over most of the states between April and August of 1849. Liberals and nationalists rose, hoping to salvage at least a portion of their initial gains. The lower classes in the south and the west rebelled when they realized that their initial sacrifices on the barricades had brought them no social or economic benefits. This second wave of revolutions was in the end mercilessly crushed by the armies of Prussia, Austria, and Württemberg, and prepared the way for a decade of conservative reaction in the 1850s.

German Reaction to the French Revolution of 1848

It is commonly stated that when news of the overthrow of King Louis Philippe in Paris crossed the Rhine in February 1848, it immediately unleashed revolts in its wake. Although this assertion is generally correct, German reaction was considerably more complicated.

REVERBERATIONS AMONG THE MIDDLE CLASS Among the middle class there was joy at the Paris revolution. Establishment of the Second French Republic bolstered the liberal aspirations of the Germans and seemed to augur well for their future. Groups of citizens in the western German states sent professions of friendship and admiration to the provisional government of France. Initially the main worry of the German liberals was that Austria, Prussia, and others might launch a monarchical crusade to deny the French those liberties that the Germans sought for themselves. Such a war would benefit only the conservative forces, particularly reactionary Russia. This feeling was reflected in a petition presented on March 4 to King Louis I of Bavaria by a large group of Munich students: "If a Franco-Russian war is inevitable and Germany is involved, German liberals will fight with France against Russia."

On the other hand, the French Revolution of 1848 reminded Germans of 1792 and Napoleon. Rumors of imminent French invasion stalked the countryside of southwest Germany and made the people wary of the blessings of imported liberty. This fear of invasion strengthened their desire for unity. "Unite to be strong" became a common slogan in the press, accompanied by demands for common defense measures by the federal diet or for the creation of a stronger federation capable of defending German soil against expected French aggression. Thus from the very beginning, nationalism was being appreciably strengthened while the banner of liberalism was being raised.

The paniclike fear of French aggression lessened somewhat after the revolutions had gained ground in the various German states, and after Alphonse de Lamartine, France's provisional head of government, had proclaimed his peaceful intentions. In fact, popular fear shifted from west to east. Friendship between French and German liberals seemed assured, but Russia's attitude remained an enigma. Gradually the fear of a Russian war to re-establish autocracy outweighed all misgivings about France. In late May, the revolutionary National Assembly (see pages 324 ff.) at Frankfurt even agreed enthusiastically to conclude a "fraternal pact" with the

French National Assembly, although the French were warned not to entertain designs on the Rhineland.

THE ATTITUDE OF THE GOVERNMENTS

The attitude of the German governments and the ruling circles was, of course, vastly different. As early as 1847, Frederick William IV of Prussia had predicted a French upheaval, and had unsuccessfully tried to persuade Victoria and Albert of England to join a coalition to prevent a revolution in France. When the news of the revolt in Paris reached Berlin, the Prussian king felt bewildered. Secretly he was delighted at the overthrow of King Louis Philippe, the usurper who owed his throne not to legitimacy and divine right but to the popular revolution of 1830. On the other hand, he was filled with fear. He felt certain the French would invade Belgium, the Rhineland, and Italy, and propagate their revolutionary doctrine by the sword. To Victoria, Metternich, and Nicholas I, he proposed re-establishing the anti-French coalition of 1814 to safeguard the settlement of 1815. The four powers were to restrict the subversive disease to France, and to prepare for a counteroffensive in case the new French Republic should launch a revolutionary war. England assured Berlin that it would fight if France violated Belgium or the Rhineland, but refused to join an a priori coalition that might needlessly antagonize Paris. The tsar offered troops if needed for the defense of Germany, and Metternich entered into vague discussions with the Prussian envoy Radowitz concerning common defensive measures. On the whole, however, neither the other courts nor Frederick William's own cabinet welcomed the proposal for a coalition.

Among the governments of the lesser German states the news from Paris evoked varying degrees of panic. Initially, the princes feared the spread of the radical ideas more than an invasion by French armies, but they did not dare call for a crusade against Paris lest such a war unleash revolts among their own subjects. Many requested the federal diet to take defensive measures for safeguarding the Rhine frontier. But even in these critical days, they displayed their usual particularism and distrust of one another. Bavaria made an offer of friendship to Paris, and at the same time called for a German conference on defense against the French. Baden objected to letting Prussian troops cross its territory to man the federal fortress of Rastatt.

But after the revolts had struck the German states and liberal cabinets had been installed, the princes became more fearful of invasion. Lamartine's famous Manifesto of March 4, in which he proclaimed that the policy of the French Republic would be based on peace and friendship, assuaged but did not still this fear across the Rhine. Most German rulers hardly considered the moderate Lamartine strong enough to maintain his course against the radicals in Paris. Moreover, there were ambiguous phrases in the manifesto likely to create conflicts. France, Lamartine proclaimed, no longer recognized the treaties of 1815 and desired to regain the influence and position it deserved. And his promise of aid to all oppressed nations, especially Poland, sounded ominously like a similar offer in 1792 that had preceded the revolutionary wars. If the Poles rose against Russia and Prussia, French armies might stream across Germany to come to their assistance, or revolutionary groups within Germany might demand French aid to overthrow their local rulers.

Although Lamartine vaunted his love of peace to all ambassadors, events in Paris, the activities of German and Polish exiles in France, and the bellicose speeches and articles of the French radicals hardly reassured the German princes. "France would be happy," cried the revolutionary *La Réforme,* "to fight once more for the salvation of the world and to implant her sword in the breast of the last king." And in a public speech, the republican leader Alexandre Ledru-Rollin urged all Germans to shake off their "odious yoke" and prophesied that "soon the breath of the people will blow away the dust of the throne where idle kings used to slumber."

ACTIVITIES OF THE EXILES These foreign complications loomed in the background of the revolutionary events in the German states. The possibility of a revolutionary war launched by France clouded the western horizon until June 1848: meanwhile the chance of a Russian war in favor of monarchical reaction lurked in the east.

A particular problem was presented by the German refugees in Paris who had organized the German Democratic Club and were exerting increasing pressures on the weak French provisional government. Together with *émigré* Poles and exiles of other suppressed nationalities, they sought aid in order to establish liberal regimes in their homelands. The intimidated provisional government allowed them to deliver before the French Assembly rousing speeches in which they demanded money, arms, munitions, and clothes for launching their own campaigns of liberation. Lamartine, hard pressed by sympathetic French radicals, and eager to rid Paris of these revolutionary mobs, finally had the government vote the Germans a grant of 60,000 francs. With Lamartine's tacit approval, the poet Herwegh (with the journalist Bornstedt and others) then organized the refugees into a German legion, numbering between fifteen and eighteen thousand men. To preserve amicable international relations, Lamartine notified the German governments that he was "repatriating foreigners." Baden, by then led by a liberal ministry, replied that it would gladly welcome the returnees, provided they came "in small groups and unarmed." But Lamartine had to confess his impotence, and admitted that the German legion had already left Paris. Thereupon the German federal diet issued a call for mobilization and sent Baden, Hessian, and Württemberg troops to protect the Rhine frontier. Even liberal Germans denounced this foreign meddling in German affairs and expressed fear that the so-called "German" legion might be a disguised prelude to a full-fledged French invasion.

Although emotions ran high, the episode did not lead to war with France. Encouraged by the news of new revolutionary outbreaks in Baden, the German legion crossed the Rhine on April 24. But insufficiently armed and poorly led by the idealistic Herwegh, the motley legion was rapidly defeated by the armies of Württemberg and the whole "liberation" movement collapsed.

The Revolutions outside Prussia and Austria

After news of the Paris revolution reached the German states, demonstrations occurred almost everywhere. In

Munich, where tension had run high for some time—partly because the infatuated King Louis I insisted on awarding a title of nobility to his lowborn Irish mistress, the dancer Lola Montez—popular pressure forced the abdication of the king and the flight of the courtesan. Lola departed to seek gold in California, and Maximilian II (1848–1864) ascended the Bavarian throne, supported by a moderately liberal ministry.

Few other rulers were forced to abdicate. In most states, as in Württemberg and Hesse, the uprisings merely brought about installation of a more liberal cabinet and satisfaction of some of the people's demands. The most common petitions called for the basic freedoms, for trial by jury, and for an extension of the people's rights under the constitution. In some regions, especially those close to revolutionary France, the uprisings were more violent and the demands more radical.

The Grand Duchy of Baden, for instance, deeply influenced by neighboring Switzerland and France, experienced early sporadic uprisings of a more radical nature. Peasants rose against their noble landlords, and members of the middle class protested against paying taxes without a voice in the government. On February 27, Gustav Struve raised the standard of revolt in Mannheim and proclaimed his intention of establishing a republic. Two days later, demonstrations in Heidelberg and Karlsruhe forced the grand duke to accede to certain popular demands. He permitted freedom of the press and trial by jury, and allowed the middle class to form an armed militia, which they demanded both as a counterweight to the ducal army and as a protection against social revolution from below. The duke agreed to set up a liberal and constitutional ministry and to press for the convocation of an all-German parliament.

Up to this point, the revolution in Baden paralleled those of many other states. The moderate revolutionaries had seemingly gained their aims by early March. But fear of the radical left made the new ministry overly legalistic and slow in its reforms—a phenomenon common to upper-middle-class revolutions. Hence the lower classes and the radicals took matters into their own hands. New bloody peasant risings occurred, manor houses were burned and proprietors massacred. On April 12, Hecker and Struve proclaimed the establishment of a Baden republic near Constance, hoping to obtain assistance from Herwegh and his German legion on their way from Paris. This republican experiment was short-lived. Its supporters were routed in clashes with the army even before Herwegh's legion crossed the Rhine to meet a similar fate. The grand duchy as a whole then settled down to a quiet, benevolent liberalism. But the indomitable Struve attempted a third republican revolt on September 21; once again his cause was suppressed by the army.

The strength of radicalism and republicanism in Baden was perhaps not typical, but two important phenomena of this revolution were paralleled in most German states. Almost everywhere the incumbent governments softened the revolutionary *élan* of the upper-middle class by granting immediate moderate concessions. Although these concessions deprived the governments of few, if any, essential elements of power, they pleased the middle classes and turned them into defenders of the regime against the more far-reaching demands of the lower class. Second, in all states the army generally remained loyal to the governments. Despite the creation of national militias, the armed forces retained a monopoly on military power and remained an instrument with which the rulers could crush those rebellions that threatened to undermine their real power or the privileges of their class. Failure to subvert the armies ultimately doomed the chances of the revolutionaries.

Revolution in Austria

The revolutions in the Austrian Empire differed from those in Germany. The social and political aspects were, of course, similar, but whereas the national revolution in Germany was centripetal, aimed at uniting the German states, in Austria it was centrifugal, aimed at securing autonomy for the component nationalities (see Map 17).

REBELLIONS AND DISINTEGRATION The February revolts in Sicily, rapidly reverberating up the Italian peninsula, soon created unrest in Austria's possessions south of the Alps. Tension in Lombardy and Venetia, in turn, unleashed currents of revolt among other subject populations and in Vienna itself. Prepared by revolutionary propaganda and encouraged by the news of other revolts, Viennese students and bourgeois staged a demonstration on March 12 that led to clashes with imperial troops. Despite the mildness of the uprising, Emperor Ferdinand felt obliged to compromise, since not only his own Viennese but also most of his other subject populations were in rebellion. Metternich was forced to resign, and control of Vienna was turned over to a national guard. The repressive Metternich laws were revoked and the convocation of a constituent assembly was promised.

Meanwhile, the Hungarians adopted their own constitution, the March Laws, and obtained from the vacillating emperor recognition of autonomous status. The Croatians rose to demand self-rule, the Milanese forced the withdrawal of Austrian troops, the Venetians set up an independent republic, and the Czechs clamored for autonomy. By early April, Moravia and even the outlying districts of Galicia, Transylvania, and Dalmatia rebelled against the central authority of Vienna. In addition, the Kingdom of Piedmont-Sardinia declared war on Austria in defense of its Italian compatriots in Lombardy.

The Hapsburg emperor gave way on all sides. He promised autonomous rights to Croatia, Bohemia, and Hungary, and issued a fairly liberal constitution for Austria itself—acting hastily before the Austrian Constituent Assembly might propose a more radical political frame. Although it permitted creation of a responsible ministry, Ferdinand's constitution did not mollify the Viennese liberals. The emperor's attempt to disband the national guard and dissolve the radical student committees in the middle of May, together with disappointment with the imperial constitution, provoked a second wave of uprisings in the Austrian capital. Even the emperor's permission for the re-forming of the student committees and his promise to revise the constitution failed to soften the revolutionary mood. To escape the pressure of the agitators, Ferdinand finally fled

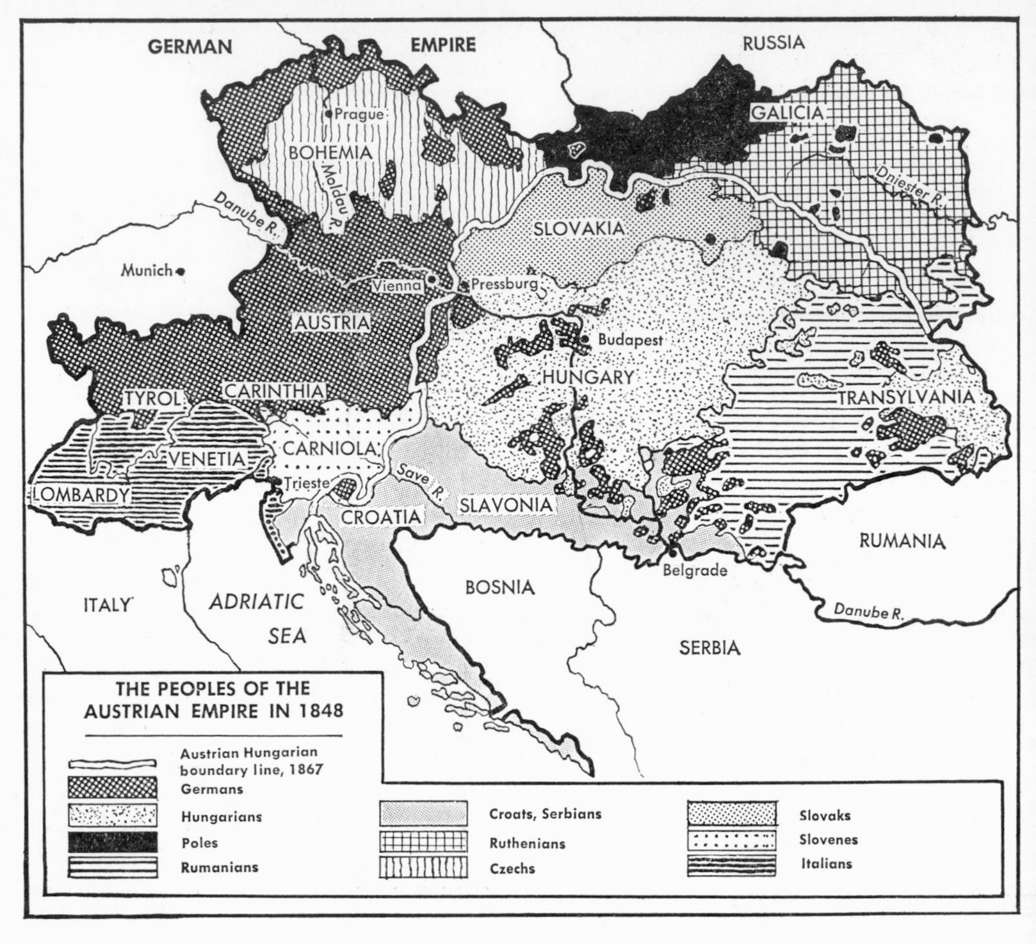

MAP 17

from Vienna to Innsbruck, and the Austrian capital fell under the complete control of a revolutionary committee of public safety.

Thus, by the end of May, the Austrian Empire seemed on the verge of disintegration. The revolution had been temporarily successful in Vienna, while Czechs, Magyars, and other subject peoples were apparently gaining independence or at least autonomy. The war against Piedmont was going badly, and the emperor, urged by England and discouraged by the initial success of Piedmontese troops, was ready to grant independence to Lombardy. Obviously, during the spring of 1848 Austria was in no position to exert much influence on German affairs.

THE FIRST PERIOD OF REACTION But in the end the commanders in the field proved more resilient than the imperial court. In the middle of June, Prince Windisch-Graetz, commander of the Austrian troops in Bohemia, put an end to the autonomous movement among the Czechs by bombarding Prague into submission and placing all of Bohemia under tight military dictatorship. Six weeks later, General Joseph Radetzky (1766–1858) defeated the Piedmontese in the decisive battle of Custozza, signed a temporary armistice with Piedmont, and re-established Austrian control over all of Lombardy. Thus the energetic action of two Austrian generals and their armies reinstituted imperial control over portions of the empire during the early summer months of 1848, initiating the first period of reaction. Only Vienna itself and Hungary remained in the hands of disaffected forces.

In late July, the Constituent Assembly that Emperor Ferdinand had promised in March finally opened its meetings in Vienna. Its liberal members rejected Ferdinand's constitution as inadequate and started to frame their own more democratic instrument. The new assembly also attempted to assume control over the revolutionary forces in Vienna, trying to act as a provisional executive and legislative body. It passed some liberal measures of which only a few—such as the final and complete eradication of serfdom—survived the revolution.

In early September, the imperial government tried to reassert its authority over Hungary and Vienna itself. To use one subject people against another seemed the most convenient expedient. The Croatians, under Baron Joseph Jellachich (1801–1859), were urged to invade Hungary to help repress the rebellion in Budapest, but this first attempt failed. The Hungarians not only repelled the Croatian invasion but advanced to the gates of Vienna to give encouragement to the revolutionaries in the Austrian capital. Ferdinand, who had meanwhile returned to his capital, fled once again, and a new revolt occurred in Vienna. The constituent assembly itself split into two factions. Its moderate members withdrew to the provincial town of Kremsier, where they hoped to work undisturbed, while the more radical delegates remained in Vienna to support the revolution. By the middle of October, Vienna was again in the hands of the insurgents, while the armies of Windisch-Graetz and Jellachich were advancing to invade the city. After a thunderous bombardment on the last day of October, Vienna was forced to open its gates to the imperial and Croatian armies. The fall of the Austrian capital signaled the triumph of reaction. Those revolutionary leaders who were unable to flee were promptly executed. Except in Hungary, the revolution collapsed. In Austria, Bohemia, and Lombardy, imperial power reasserted itself.

In late November, the highly skilled Prince Felix von Schwarzenberg (1800–1852) assumed the post of chief minister, determined to maintain the integrity of the Austrian dominions. One of his first acts was to persuade the weak emperor, who had become compromised through political pledges, to resign in favor of his eighteen-year-old grandson, Francis Joseph I (1848–1916). The inexperienced new emperor left the tasks of government almost completely in the hands of his capable, conservative minister. Thus Austria and the Hapsburg Empire came to be ruled—and restored—during the next four years by the diplomatic skill of this "new Metternich."

SCHWARZENBERG'S REGIME Schwarzenberg's tasks were clear: he had to eradicate the remaining pockets of rebellion among the subject peoples and quickly strengthen Austria's international position, so that Vienna could resume its dominant role in Germany before the German states fell completely under the yoke of Prussia.

The most important preliminary step was to subdue Hungary. In January 1849, Prince Windisch-Graetz seized Budapest but even this military success did not settle the Hungarian problem. The Magyars desired not merely autonomous rights but also a share with the German-speaking Austrians in controlling the other subject populations of the empire. Schwarzenberg's constitutional ideas of centralizing all power in Vienna clearly went counter to such Hungarian hopes. As a result, the Magyars rose again in April, expelled Windisch-Graetz' army of occupation, and proclaimed an independent Hungarian Republic under the leadership of the radical Louis Kossuth (1802–1894). Since many Austrian troops were then again in Italy campaigning against Sardinia, Schwarzenberg gladly accepted Russia's offer of help against the Hungarians. Emperor Nicholas I, ever the guardian of conservatism, had become frightened at the progress of republicanism in neighboring Hungary. Proclaiming that the rebellion "endangers the tranquillity of the two Empires" and that "it was but natural that the two Cabinets should understand one another on this point of common interest," Nicholas dispatched troops into Hungary. Crushed between Russian and Austrian forces, the Hungarian rebels were finally forced to lay down their arms in August. Kossuth's republic was dissolved, Austrian power firmly re-established, and a new bond of friendship created between the two conservative emperors, Nicholas and young Francis Joseph.

Meanwhile Schwarzenberg had also met the threat in Italy successfully. When Sardinia-Piedmont reopened the war in March 1849, Radetzky quickly defeated the invading armies at Novara. The armistice this time was followed by a peace treaty that reconfirmed all of Austria's rights over Lombardy. In the summer, Austrian troops then laid siege to Venice and finally bombed and starved the Venetians into surrender. With the fall of the Venetian Republic in August, Vienna reestablished its authority over all its subject peoples. The Hapsburg Empire had been saved; the movements for autonomy and liberalism had been crushed everywhere.

Schwarzenberg had also broached the problem of a new political framework. On March 1, 1849, the moderate rump of the constitutional convention, sitting at Kremsier, produced its constitution. As expected, it was a mildly liberal document that took account of the aspirations of the subject peoples by prescribing decentralization for the empire. However, Schwarzenberg, true to his principles, dissolved the constitutional convention and disregarded its work. He could neither condone the notions of popular sovereignty implied in the document nor accept its federal character. Instead, he issued his own constitution with a highly centralized administrative system. The local diets of the subject peoples were to have little authority, all essential power emanating from Vienna. His one concession to liberalism, at least on paper, was the provision for a central diet representative of all subjects, and for a ministry responsible to this diet. The centralized character of Schwarzenberg's system had a profound effect on developments in Germany. By binding the various ethnic groups of the Austrian Empire into a tighter union, it complicated the prospect of creating a state embracing only German-speaking peoples. For Austria itself, however, Schwarzenberg's constitution had a merely symbolic value, for the minister and his young emperor continued to base their government on military autocracy, with the explanation that unsettled conditions did not yet permit implementation of the new constitution.

Revolution in Prussia

Even more important to the future of Germany than the uprisings in Austria was the fate of the revolution in Prussia. Ever since the dismissal of the United Diet in 1847, tension and speculation had run high among Frederick William's subjects. When the news of the fall of King Louis-Philippe was received in Berlin on February 26, tension gave way to bewilderment and consternation. Every successive dispatch telling of revolts in southern Germany and bringing more details from Italy and France reminded the liberals that it was time to act in behalf of their ideals. The streets of Berlin rapidly abounded with rumors of impending plots. Yet the "loyal Berliners"—as the king later called his people—seemingly made docile by centuries of indoctrination in obedience, were slow to react to the challenge. It is noteworthy that Berlin was the last major city to enter the revolutionary fray.

Disorders within Prussia first broke out in the Rhineland, in Silesia, and in East Prussia. On March 3, crowds entered the city hall of Cologne to place six demands before the startled city fathers. Besides the usual call for suffrage, civil rights, and a popular militia, the petitioners requested protection for labor, a guaranteed minimum standard of living, as well as state education for all.

THE MARCH DAYS IN BERLIN A week later, unrest in Berlin produced the first overt action. Middle-class groups organized political meetings to request a reconvening of the United Diet and a free press. At the same time, the lower class made itself heard. Among Berlin's factory workers, numbering about 40,000 (not counting families and apprentices), poverty was again on the increase. The price of potatoes was still high, a typhus epidemic was spreading through the city, and a recession had produced layoffs at the big Borsig factory and other enterprises. Radical leaflets appeared and socialist leaders urged the workers to organize for action. On March 11, a group of workers sent a petition to the king, begging him to "speedily do away with the present distress among laborers and make their future secure," and suggesting establishment of a labor office composed of wage earners and employers, elected by their respective groups, to help improve labor conditions.

Despite the moderation of these petitions, Frederick William IV displayed the hesitancy and vacillation characteristic of his actions during the next crucial month. On March 13, the first incidents occurred between crowds, police, and army. A single barricade was put up and promptly destroyed by the army without bloodshed.

During the next four days, Berlin was in a continual emotional seesaw. Ever-larger crowds gathered daily to demand royal concessions, haphazard barricades were erected and quickly destroyed by roving cavalry, occasional stones were thrown at the palace of Prince William—the symbol of conservatism—but except in two cases, bloodshed was avoided. The king, for his part, continued his ambivalent stand. He made vague promises of reforms while calling for additional troops and police to keep the petitioners in check.

The news of Metternich's fall convinced even the timid Berliners that the "impossible" was possible. Late on March 17, crowds signed a petition to the king calling for withdrawal of the hated troops from the capital. The following morning the same crowds gathered before the royal palace to present their petition. To their surprise, several deputations were admitted to the palace and the king agreed to discuss their grievances.

During the preceding night, Frederick William had once again changed his course. Perhaps frightened by the fall of the once-mighty Austrian minister, the king had determined to make concessions. He decided to form a more liberal cabinet under Camphausen, and prepared two proclamations to his people. In these, he reconvened the United Diet for April, presumably to write a constitution for Prussia, lifted most censorship restrictions, and promised to work for changes in the German Confederation. On the other hand, he dismissed the moderate commander of the 15,000-man Berlin garrison and replaced him by the more conservative and reliable General Max von Prittwitz—a step of long-range significance, since assured assistance of the army proved infinitely more important for the course of the revolution than all the royal proclamations and promises.

When the two proclamations appeared on the billboards of Berlin in the early afternoon of the eighteenth, the crowds in front of the palace swelled to threatening proportions. The people had presumably gathered to thank their monarch for his liberal concessions, but the sight of the masses frightened the king. General von Prittwitz was ordered to clear the square in front of the palace. As the grenadiers advanced, two musket shots were discharged. Although no one had been injured, the people felt betrayed; the crowd turned into an angry mob. Fighting ensued, barricades were erected in many quarters of Berlin, and all through the night there was street fighting between the army and the population.

The court immediately admitted that the shots had been fired by two soldiers (later brought before a court-martial that acquitted them), but it was asserted that the shots were accidental and that the troops had not received orders to fire on the crowd. Although this explanation may be correct, it is equally conceivable that the two grenadiers acted on secret orders of General von Prittwitz in order to frighten the king into determined opposition to the mob. If so, the scheme failed, for Frederick William was horrified and frightened by the bloodshed. No military man, he craved love and obedience from his people. During the night of fighting, he oscillated between pity for his subjects and indignation at their defiance of his authority.

In the early morning hours he ordered his troops to cease fighting, and had a white flag raised over the royal palace. Royal couriers then roamed through the city, posting the king's tender letter "To my dear Berliners" (*"An meine lieben Berliner"*). "By reasons of my proclamation of this day, convening the Diet," he wrote, "you received proof of the loyal sentiments of your King toward you and our common German Fatherland." He indicated that the happy occasion had been marred by "a band of rowdies," and that royal troops had been asked to clear the square merely to avoid "insults to my brave and faithful soldiers." The two shots had been accidental and had hurt no one, but "a band of rascals, mostly foreigners . . . a week in hiding here," had misused the incidents to put "thoughts of vengeance into the heated heads of many of my loyal and beloved Berliners." He swore that the troops had acted merely in self-defense, and concluded with pathos: "Your loving Queen, prostrate with suffering, joins her heartfelt and tearful prayers to mine."

On the same Sunday morning, March 19, Frederick William took the next step in concessions. After the truce became effective, he attended church and then negotiated with envoys from the barricades. He agreed to withdraw his troops from Berlin if the people in turn would tear down the barricades. As a result, the royal garrison immediately began to evacuate the city, even before the insurgents started to dismantle their strongposts. By oversight—or again by design of General von Prittwitz—not even a small protective detachment was left to guard the royal palace.

Frederick William had placed himself completely at the mercy of his people. The prisoners taken by the army during the night were released, the mob controlled the streets, and a motley band of students and merchants made themselves voluntary guards of the royal palace and its frightened occupants. On the same afternoon, the king and queen had to submit to their first open humiliation. The insurgents carried their dead into the courtyard of the palace, and the royal family had to participate from the balcony in a ceremony honoring the fallen rebels. It seemed that revolution in Prussia had triumphed.

The power of the crowds also frightened the middle classes, which feared the workers might make social demands and endanger property and business. Bourgeois groups volunteered as a militia to maintain law and order and safeguard their interests. But the period of humiliation for Frederick William had not yet ended. On March 20, crowds gathered again, demanding the release of all political prisoners and demonstrating against the conservative Prince William. The king not only had the prison doors opened, but also sent his brother William, the future emperor of Germany, to England. On the following day, he even seemed to enjoy himself in a fraternal honeymoon with his subjects. He rode through the streets of Berlin wearing the revolutionary colors, black-red-gold, the symbols of German unity and of the Wars of Liberation, but not the colors of the Hohenzollerns or of Prussia. He made flattering speeches to the insurgents and praised their worthy sentiments. "To my people and to the German nation" he made his famous ambiguous remarks: *"Preussen geht fortan in Deutschland auf,"* which could mean either that "Prussia will henceforth be dissolved in Germany," presumably through the creation of a union of coequal states, or that "Prussia will henceforth prosper in Germany," that is, that Prussia would gain even more power by uniting with the other states. This and similar pronouncements by Frederick William, at a time when he had seemingly accepted liberalism, brought him into the limelight of the movement for German unification, which was gaining ground during this same month.

GRADUAL REASSERTION OF ROYAL POWER But the honeymoon between the king and his Berliners did not last much longer. The king's attendance at the burial of the revolutionary dead, on March 22, was the last major act in the drama of revolutionary cooperation. During the month of April, the citizen guards experienced increasing difficulty in maintaining order in Berlin. Radical elements grew in strength, and many a bourgeois longed for a return of royal troops as a safeguard against a possible social revolution.

When the United Diet met, it acted in the legalistic fashion that characterized other German revolutions of 1848. Instead of assuming additional powers, it arranged for the election of a constituent assembly for Prussia and then disbanded. The elections for this constituent assembly, based on universal but indirect male suffrage, were held in early May and produced a surprisingly liberal, almost radical assembly that opened its meetings in Berlin on May 22. With Berlin in the hands of liberals, and a constituent assembly gathered to write a constitution for all of Prussia, the cause of liberalism seemed assured.

Yet the apparent victory was a deception. The constituent assembly engaged in interminable debates throughout the summer, whereas prompt action on a constitution was required. Frederick William left Berlin in May for Potsdam, where he felt more secure under the protection of his army. There he forgot the days of the liberal honeymoon and came again under the influence of reactionary advisers. Although the insurgents in Berlin did not realize it, the revolution was, in fact, lost. The liberal Camphausen ministry meanwhile drifted along, awaiting the outcome of the constitutional convention. Although well intentioned, this government provided little succor to the liberal cause in Prussia, and devoted its main attention to foreign affairs and the national unification movement.

Camphausen's minister of foreign affairs (Heinrich Freiherr von Arnim-Heinrichsdorff) championed a mixed course of liberalism and German nationalism. He hoped to unify Germany under Prussia while guaranteeing a modicum of liberal safeguards. Unlike most Prussians—and for that matter, most Germans—he advocated at least a partial restoration of Polish autonomy. Because he realized that championing autonomy for Poland would arouse the displeasure of Russia, he sought an anti-Russian alliance with France. The reactions to this proposal throw an interesting light on conditions in 1848. Paris showed interest in the plan, since French liberals had always had an affection for Poland. They favored friendship with a liberal Prussia, but feared an anti-Russian alliance, which they thought might lead to war. German liberals, on the other hand, favored the anti-Russian aspect of the scheme but looked with suspicion on its pro-Polish features. But the future of the plan depended on the attitude of Frederick William. The Prussian king had always been pro-Russian. While he might be persuaded to extend a diplomatic smile to the Second French Republic, he would never consent to an open break with the tsar. The bulk of the Prussian officers shared the king's feelings. German liberals might flirt with Paris and flaunt St. Petersburg, but the Prussian officers held the French republicans in contempt, whereas they had an affinity for conservative Russia.

Under these circumstances, no anti-Russian alliance was made. It became clear that the king and his military advisers still determined policy, although Prussia was officially governed by a liberal cabinet. This was particularly evident in the Danish, Polish, and all-German questions, in which Prussia sided with the conservative forces (see pages 326–329).

On November 2, three days after Vienna was retaken by the reactionary forces, Prussia, too, embarked on an official change of policy. The liberal Camphausen ministry was dismissed and replaced by a new government under the conservative Count of Brandenburg, a natural son of King Frederick William II and an outspoken advocate of monarchical supremacy. Baron Otto von Manteuffel was brought back to the Ministry of Interior. The king disregarded the assembly's protest against the change in ministry. In fact, a week later he exiled the constituent assembly to the city of Brandenburg, even though it had not yet completed a constitution for Prussia. A month later, Frederick William reasserted his authority even further. He re-entered Berlin with troops, dissolved the civic guard and the assembly, and issued his own constitution. The royal document, prepared by Manteuffel, embodied some features elaborated by the delegates, but was clearly a monarchist constitution reserving full powers for the king. Elections on the basis of the new constitution took place in January 1849, and the newly elected delegates convened in February. But even then new quarrels erupted between the king and his subjects.

As occurred in many parts of Germany, a second wave of uprisings shook Prussia in the spring of 1849. The Rhineland, in particular, was the scene of democratic and socialistic risings. Following the mood of the people, the diet attempted to revise Frederick William's constitution to make it more democratic. Annoyed, the king thereupon dissolved the new assembly and changed the electoral procedure in the hope of excluding the liberal and democratic elements. Thus by the summer of 1849, Prussia had returned firmly to the conservative camp. Despite astonishing early successes, the revolution had failed in its over-all aims and had produced few permanent gains.

The Unitary Movement

While rebellions were sapping the strength of the state governments, determined groups were working for German unification. On March 5, 1848, fifty-three liberals met at Heidelberg to discuss a closer union of all German states. The conferees, mostly from southwestern and central Germany, generally agreed with Heinrich von Gagern's suggestion that a union could best be achieved under a constitutional monarchy. Some, however, convinced that Germany could never be unified so long as the particularistic princes retained power, saw Germany's salvation only in the establishment of a united republic. In the end all agreed to work for unity by legal means, and called on present and past members of German state legislatures to convene at Frankfurt at the end of March to discuss plans of action. A committee of seven was to arrange the convening of this Frankfurt preparliament, or preliminary parliament.

On March 31, some 600 voluntary delegates appeared at Frankfurt. Attendance reflected the varying degrees of liberalism of the states: 124 came from all of Prussia, while tiny Hesse-Darmstadt furnished 84, and Baden 72. The five-day meeting evoked violent debates between the small republican minority, led by Struve and Hecker, and the large majority of moderate monarchists. In the end the moderates carried the day, although they did agreed to have the all-German constituent assembly elected by universal male suffrage. They asked the federal diet in Frankfurt to order the election of 1 delegate for every 50,000 Germans for the purpose of attending a national assembly and framing a constitution for all of Germany. Before disbanding on April 4, the preparliament elected an organizational and preparatory committee of fifty to remain at Frankfurt.

THE NATIONAL ASSEMBLY AT FRANKFURT Elections of delegates were soon held all over Germany. Although suspicious of a popular body created by universal suffrage, no prince dared prevent the elections in his state. In the absence of strong support from Austria—itself in the grip of revolution—and under pressure from his liberal cabinet and excited subjects, even Frederick William consented to the elections. At best the princes could hope that moderate delegates would be elected and that the Frankfurt assembly would be an advisory rather than a constituent or legislative body. They hoped that the federal diet and the individual governments would retain power to discuss, reject, or ratify whatever constitution the delegates might produce at Frankfurt.

The National Assembly—often called the Frankfurt Parliament—opened its first session in St. Paul's Church in Frankfurt on the Main on May 18, 1848. Although 830 delegates had been elected, usually only about 500 attended the sessions. The delegates represented almost the entire political spectrum, but the majority stood for middle-class forces of order and moderation. The extreme right-wing conservatives generally boycotted the sessions, and few really left-wing radicals had been elected. The membership was largely composed of the professional classes—lawyers, university professors, businessmen, doctors—and members of the clergy, the officer corps, and local diets. The lower classes were omitted, and even regional representation was very uneven. Austria with its 18 million subjects should have sent 360 delegates, but sent only a handful, since the non-German groups boycotted the elections. Prussia, too, was notably underrepresented; the smaller liberal states shared the bulk of the membership. Yet despite irregularities in the haphazard electoral proceedings, and even though it lacked political skill, the Frankfurt Parliament represented an astounding array of talent and intellect.

When the sessions began, there were, of course, no political parties to facilitate parliamentary maneuvers. But soon like-minded people began to congregate in local restaurants to discuss possible programs of action and thus fashioned a modicum of party life. The many factions can be divided into four groups. On the Right were the Prussian conservatives, representing the aspirations of Frederick William IV and certain groups of Prussian nobles and intellectuals (led by Radowitz and Baron Georg von Vincke). They sought a German constitutional, military monarchy or empire in which Prussia would dominate. Such a government should be founded on monarchical and not popular sovereignty, and rest on the consent of the princes of Germany, who would continue to play an important role in the new state. To the left of this group were the non-Prussian conservatives, representing the interests of the kings and princes who were wary of Prussian leadership. These monarchists, while wishing to reserve considerable power to the ruling princes, were willing to accept certain liberal, constitutional measures. One such plan called for the addition of a popular assembly representing all Germans to be added as a lower house to the existing federal diet in Frankfurt.

The third and largest group may be labeled constitutionalists or democratic monarchists. It contained some of the most brilliant minds of the assembly, including Heinrich von Gagern, the poet Arndt, the historian Dahlmann, the journalist Georg Gervinus, and the writer Jacob Grimm. Essentially, they represented the majority view of the Heidelberg meeting that had launched the whole program for unification. They were divided on such details as whether or not to include Austria, whether to have a hereditary or an elective ruler, and whether to make him an emperor or not. But they essentially sought to establish as liberal a regime as compatible with their concept of monarchy. Finally, on the left stood a fourth small but vociferous group of republicans, led by the enthusiastic orator Robert Blum (1807–1848). The republicans came mostly from southwest Germany, and some espoused socialistic ideals. The group gained little power at Frankfurt, and ultimately hoped to impose its ideas through popular uprisings outside the framework of the Frankfurt Assembly.

The opening of the meetings at St. Paul's Church was greeted with mixed feelings by the old federal diet. It was not clear whether the new assembly had any legal right to supersede the diet or whether its function was merely that of a constituent body. In the absence of clear instructions from their home governments, most delegates wavered in their attitude. The congratulatory message of the diet to the new assembly reflected this confusion. It spoke of "the force of extraordinary events" and the "ardent desire of our whole fatherland" that had produced an "assembly such as had never before been seen in all our history"; and ended with the noncommittal phrase: "The German governments and their common organ, the Diet, . . . gladly yielding to the spirit of the time, extend a hand of welcome to the representatives of the nation."

On May 19, the assembly elected as its president Heinrich von Gagern, whose skilled parliamentarianism was to guide the stormy debates during the coming months. In his opening speech, Gagern proclaimed: "We must frame a constitution for Germany, and we derive our authority for this purpose from the sovereignty of the nation." It appeared as though Gagern was to launch the assembly onto a truly revolutionary path. During the succeeding weeks, he made it clear that the assembly's task was not merely to write a constitution, but also to act as a central legislative and executive government for all of Germany. For this purpose, he had the federal diet suspended, a move the princes at the time did not dare oppose. The assembly was thus free to create its own executive. On June 28, after prolonged debate, the delegates in St. Paul's chose Archduke John of Austria as imperial regent, and authorized him to appoint his own cabinet and form a provisional central government. The choice of the Hapsburg duke, who was known for his mild liberalism, showed Gagern's acumen. The installation of a legitimate prince as provisional ruler was bound to give comfort to the moderates, and might secure for the central government the respect of the princes of Germany. Archduke John immediately set up a provisional ministry, including the Austrian Anton von Schmerling (1805–1893) as minister for foreign and internal affairs, a Prussian (Peucker) as minister of war, and a Hamburg lawyer (Heckscher) as minister of justice.

From its inception, the new provisional government enjoyed a strangely ambiguous status. It was officially recognized by the German states, but not obeyed on vital issues. Foreign democratic nations, such as France and the United States, sent accredited ambassadors, but other states ignored its existence. Above all, Archduke John's government carried an empty mandate, for it lacked diplomatic and military resources with which to enforce its decisions in Germany.

While the executive in Frankfurt acted as an all-German shadow government, study committees of the assembly worked on the proposed constitution. In sublime oratory and with remarkable intellectual acuity, the delegates lost themselves in the intricacy of seemingly insolvable details. The questions of a *Gross* versus a *Kleindeutschland*; of republic, empire, or monarchy; of imperial versus states rights; of fundamental civil rights; of the rights of ethnically non-German groups; and a thousand others occupied the delegates for the remainder of the year 1848. Failing to comprehend that revolutions must be accomplished rapidly, the delegates debated interminably while the forces of reaction in Austria and Germany were regaining ground.

THE FRANKFURT ASSEMBLY AND GERMAN NATIONALISM Almost all the questions studied at Frankfurt involved the nationalistic feelings of the delegates. As the French envoy to Frankfurt remarked: "A dizzy feeling seemed to seize the Parliament of Frankfurt every time a question of conquest presented itself to them or when they could foresee the possibility of enlarging their territory under pretext of protecting the German nationality." Even most liberals displayed surprisingly intense Pan-German feelings in regard to Schleswig-Holstein or to the subject populations of Austria and Prussia. Hegel's mythical entity, the "state," seemed to outweigh considerations of humanity and liberty. Pointing with pride to Generals Radetzky, Windisch-Graetz, and Jellachich, who were crushing the rebellions of the subject peoples, a deputy declared: "Let us first found real power, and then establish freedom, which is impotent without power." The moderate

Gagern sounded equally chauvinistic. We must "embrace as satellites in our planetary system," he declared, "those peoples in the Danubian basin who have no talent for and no claim to independence." Nor did the delegates show any qualms about their inconsistency. With equal relish they invoked the principle of nationality to secure Schleswig-Holstein from Denmark, and appealed to authoritarianism to deny this same ideal to the Poles.

Three events in the summer of 1848 exemplify this nationalistic attitude of the Frankfurt parliamentarians. By playing into the hands of the reactionaries, they ultimately undermined both liberalism and the chances for unification. One such event concerned the Czechs of Bohemia. They had been invited to send delegates to the Frankfurt Assembly on the assumption that they would form a part of the future united Germany. The Czechs, however, preferred a political future apart from Germany, and called their own Pan-Slav Congress in Prague—an action that provoked the delegates at Frankfurt into lengthy tirades against the Czech secessionists. In a manifesto of June 12, the Czechs complained: "The Germans threaten many Slavic peoples with violence if they will not agree to assist in the building up of the political greatness of Germany." The manifesto continued: "We Slavs utterly decry such pretensions, and reject them the more emphatically the more they are wrongfully disguised in the garb of freedom," and ended with a plea to the Saxons and Prussians to "abandon at long last the systematic denationalization of the Slavs . . . in East and West Prussia." But the shortsighted representatives at Frankfurt understood only German nationalism. When five days later, General Windisch-Graetz bombarded Prague into submission and destroyed the hopes of Czech secessionists, the Frankfurt Assembly applauded this "victory of German weapons." Few stopped to think that it spelled a triumph for reaction.

A second test of the nationalistic feelings of the Frankfurt parliamentarians concerned Poland. During the honeymoon period with his "dear Berliners," Frederick William of Prussia had granted an amnesty to the Poles and hinted that his Polish subjects would be given the right to stay outside the proposed new German state. As a result, the Poles immediately established a National Polish Committee in Poznan, and sent a deputation to Berlin to request re-establishment of a Polish kingdom, and to offer the crown to a Prussian prince. Although Prussia's foreign minister (Arnim) showed sympathy toward such a project, Frederick William could not allow the establishment of an independent Polish kingdom through which he would lose Prussia's eastern lands and probably provoke war with Russia. But he granted temporary concessions. On March 24, he issued a decree allowing the establishment of a Polish national guard, the development of local autonomy for the Poles, and the creation of regiments in Poznan.

This decree provoked consternation in St. Petersburg, but it was wildly acclaimed by the Poles as well as by German and French liberals. In early April, however, radicals gained the upper hand in Poland, and refused to accept Frederick William's concessions as sufficient, insisting instead on complete independence. Anti- Prussian uprisings followed, and soon turned into outright revolt. The Prussian government consequently reversed its stand and decided on repression. By mid-April, there was open warfare between the Polish rebels and the Prussian army. When in May, the French provisional government decided against assistance to the Poles, Prussian troops could complete their crushing of the rebels without fear of international involvement.

By the time the Frankfurt Assembly opened, the Prussian armies were getting the upper hand over the insurrection. The parliamentarians immediately showed much interest in the Polish question, and a few voiced sympathy for Polish aspirations. But a three-day debate on the issue, begun on July 24, revealed that the mood of most delegates had changed. The Polish insurrection offended their idea of German grandeur, and its radicalism frightened even the moderates. Finally, in the style of a debating society, the assembly put to a vote the question whether the "partition of Poland had been a shameful wrong." Only a hundred delegates cast an affirmative vote. The accompanying debate showed that the majority of conservative and moderate delegates, and even some liberals, felt that Prussia had the right, if not the duty, to subdue the Poles for the sake of expanding German culture.

The third event involving nationalism concerned the two duchies of Schleswig and Holstein (see Map 18). Schleswig, containing a slight majority of Danes, did not belong to the German Confederation. Holstein to the south, overwhelmingly German in population, had become a member in 1815. Both duchies were tied together politically and loosely joined to Denmark in personal bond to the Danish crown. In 1846, the Danish king, (Christian VIII) had asserted his intention of eventually integrating both duchies into Denmark, and his pronouncement had provoked indignation in the duchies as well as in Germany. The question became acute in January 1848 upon the accession of a new king, Frederick VII, who issued a constitutional draft that clearly threatened the political independence of the two duchies. The affected populations agitated in favor of their autonomous rights, and refused to grant allegiance to the new king. They chose, instead, to recognize as ruler Duke Christian of Augustenburg, from a side line of the royal house of Denmark. When the Danish king sent troops to enforce his decision, the duchies rose in revolt under the leadership of Augustenburg. On March 24, 1848, they seceded from Denmark, established a provisional government in Kiel, and appealed to the federal diet in Frankfurt for support.

Thus Germany was forced to take a stand on the matter. Without hesitation, the diet championed the rights of the duchies, and requested Prussia to send military aid in the name of the German Confederation. Even the moderates then preparing for the Frankfurt assembly applauded this decision. Since Frederick William of Prussia was not averse to championing German expansion, he dispatched Prussian troops to the duchies. By May, they were fighting against Danish troops and invading southern Jutland.

But matters changed in June. Prussian troops made little headway, and, without a navy, Prussia could expect a long campaign. Moreover, Britain and Russia, both interested in maintaining an independent Denmark as guardian of the entrance to the Baltic, exerted pressure on the belligerents to accept mediation. Most important, however, was the change at Frankfurt. When the federal diet abdicated its powers to the new National Assembly, Frederick William suddenly saw himself no longer fighting for the confederation of princes, but in the name of a revolutionary body with doubtful credentials. Consequently, on August 26, he signed the armistice of Malmö, providing for the evacuation of Danish and Prussian troops from both duchies, and their administration by a joint Danish-German commission.

Since Frederick William had never acknowledged that he had been fighting in the name of the National Assembly, he concluded this armistice without consulting the delegates at Frankfurt. News of the armistice provoked tumult and indignation there. The delegates had faithfully applauded every minor victory of Prussian arms, and had even collected money to purchase a navy for the war against Denmark. They considered their nationalistic aims betrayed by Prussia's abandonment of the inhabitants of Schleswig-Holstein. Heated debates followed. A majority wished to reject the armistice and continue the war, until the realization that the assembly lacked all military power made them recognize the futility of this course. Therefore, on September 16, Parliament voted by a small majority to accept the armistice. The vote provoked a symptomatic rebellion in the city of Frankfurt. The nationalists proclaimed that the assembly itself had betrayed the German cause, and called for its overthrow. Radicals roamed the streets, murdered some delegates, and disrupted proceedings in St. Paul's Church. The assembly finally had to call on nearby Prussian and Austrian troops stationed in the fortress of Mainz to protect the delegates and crush the rebellion.

Thus the Danish problem not merely underlined the nationalistic fervor of the parliamentarians, but also ended ominously, with the assembly pitifully dependent on the soldiers of reactionary Prussia and Austria.

THE FRANKFURT CONSTITUTION After September 1848, the majority of the Frankfurt delegates grew increasingly conservative. The radical uprisings in Frankfurt, Struve's renewed attempt to establish a republic in Baden, and occasional flickers of social revolt made the delegates wary of liberalism. The Frankfurt riots also made them recognize their reliance on the armies of the princes, and realize that Germany could probably never be unified "by the people" against the will of the princes.

Between spurts of pretending to act as the government of all Germany, the delegates worked diligently in committee to hammer out the proposed constitution. It is typical of their lack of practical vision that they devoted their first major effort to the formulation of abstract ideals. In January 1849, the assembly accepted a declaration of fundamental rights, an eloquent tribute to the idealism of the majority of the delegates.

The more urgent question of a new political framework was infinitely more difficult to solve. Possibilities changed every month, as various princes regained power lost in the spring of 1848. In October a first and tentative compromise was reached regarding the size of the union. The assembly voted to include only German lands that had no organic ties with non-German territory. But the delegates did not agree on what was to be considered German land. Strictly interpreted, this stipulation would have required Prussia and Austria to divest themselves of territories with non-German-speaking populations, or to transform the organic links to these lands into a personal union under the crown. The first solution was unlikely to be acceptable to Berlin and Vienna, whereas the second seemed impractical in an age of rising nationalities. Austria, at any rate, could hardly follow such a policy and hope to survive as a major European power. In fact, Prince Schwarzenberg was to pursue a diametrically opposite course by forcing increased centralization on the Austrian patchwork of nationalities. And it soon appeared that the Prussian delegates looked upon Prussia's Polish lands as inherently German territory, but considered Lombardy, Venetia, Hungary, and some of the other subject states of the Austrian Empire clearly non-German territories. Hence they voted for this resolution, because they favored a *Kleindeutsch* framework, and hoped to use this maneuver to exclude Austria from the proposed new union.

On March 27, 1849, the completed constitution was finally accepted by the National Assembly. It created a federal state in which the central government was to be endowed with considerably more authority than the old federal diet, including control over a federal army, foreign policy, and economic affairs. The government was to be headed by a hereditary emperor empowered with merely a suspensive veto over legislation. The national legislature was to consist of two houses: a *Staatenhaus,* half chosen by the state governments and half elected by the lower houses of the state legislatures; and a lower house, the *Volkshaus,* elected by universal, direct, male suffrage on the basis of secret and equal ballots. The federal ministry was to be responsible to the national parliament.

The strongly democratic character of the constitution was largely the result of a last-minute political stratagem of Austrian and other delegates who did not want the king of Prussia to obtain the headship of a unified Germany. They voted with the democrats and liberals for universal manhood suffrage and only a suspensive veto in hope of prejudicing Frederick William against the constitution. This seemed the only way to prevent Prussian absorption of Germany, since Austria had obviously forfeited its chances of leading the new state. Schwarzenberg's centralizing policies and his constitution of March 4, with its insistence on the unity of all Hapsburg lands, had torpedoed the last hopes for a *Grossdeutschland* solution. The reconquest of Budapest in January and the victory of Novara over the Piedmontese on March 23 showed that Schwarzenberg's intentions were not a hollow boast. At the same time, Austria's resurgence made it probable that it would not let events in Germany go unchallenged.

FREDERICK WILLIAM'S REFUSAL OF THE CROWN On March 28, the National Assembly elected Frederick William IV as "Emperor of the Germans," and sent a delegation to Berlin to offer the crown to the Prussian ruler. Actually, the stratagems of the Austrians to make the crown distasteful to the Hohenzollern prince had not been necessary. Frederick William's "March liberalism" had never been more than a brief infatuation, and his proclamations on

German unification had always been mere window dressing for his desire to extend Prussian power. In August 1848, in a public speech in Cologne, Frederick William had already addressed a friendly warning to the Frankfurt assembly: "Gentlemen, do not forget that there are still princes in Germany, and that I am one of them." But the assembly had largely ignored the warning. The king's actions in Schleswig-Holstein should, of course, have shown how little he respected the Frankfurt assembly, but the delegates could not know how thoroughly he actually despised it. By December 1848, he had decided never to accept a crown "created by an Assembly born of revolutionary seed, even if offered with princely approval." Just as the Prussian diet had infuriated him in November by attempting to strike from the royal title the phrase "by the Grace of God," so he felt that only the Almighty and the princes could resuscitate the "thousand year old crown of the German nation." Whatever Frankfurt could produce would "stink of the revolution."

When the delegation of parliamentarians offered him the crown, Frederick William made a conditional refusal. He would accept provided all princes and states of Germany gave their approval, and provided the Frankfurt Constitution served merely as a proposal that all the German governments could then discuss and modify. The latter proviso amounted to a complete repudiation of the work of the parliamentarians. The news of these conditions dismayed the monarchists in Frankfurt. Having battled republicans and radicals for a year in an effort to preserve the throne of Germany, they now felt betrayed by the Prussian ruler, who did not seem to understand that their constitutional frame work was the best possible compromise. For their part, the princes and state governments immediately acted on Frederick William's challenge. The bulk of the small states, and even the kings of Saxony and Hanover, expressed approval. But under Austrian pressure Bavaria, Baden, and Württemberg hesitated. Austria, whose delegates had been officially withdrawn from Frankfurt on April 5, of course, had no intention of concurring. Hence on April 21, Frederick William felt justified in announcing his outright refusal of the German crown.

When the hapless delegation returned to Frankfurt, the hope of unification had evaporated. Some governments had recalled their delegations; other members had left of their own accord. Only a small group of liberals remained, still hoping to find some way to unify Germany. In May, this rump of the old assembly was forced to leave Frankfurt, and adjourned to Stuttgart to continue for a short time its ephemeral existence. These liberal delegates felt temporarily encouraged by new waves of revolts in many parts of Germany.

THE LAST REVOLTS Once again, the radicals in Baden led the way. This time even the bulk of the army defected to the liberal forces, the grand duke fled, and a republic was proclaimed in Baden. Soon democratic uprisings—evoked by the failure of the Frankfurt experiment and by apprehension that the revolution had been lost—occurred in Saxony, Bavaria, and the Rhineland. Spurred on by socialistic organizers—including Karl Marx, whose newspaper *Neue Rheinische Zeitung* appeared regularly in Cologne until it was closed by the government on May 19—workers and peasants also rose to turn these rebellions into social revolutions. The workers could justly feel that their barricades had brought them no gains.

This time Prussia showed no hesitation in applying military suppression. After putting down the revolts in the Rhineland, Prussian armies turned south. On June 18, they helped the troops of Württemberg disperse the rump assembly in Stuttgart. By July, the rebellion in Baden was crushed and the grand duchy placed under Prussian military occupation. The last rebels either fled or fell before firing squads. In Saxony, Bavaria, and the other states, the rulers firmly re-established their power.

On May 15, while this final rebellion was at its height, Frederick William once again issued a famous proclamation "to my people," in which he explained his views and justified his conduct. "Taking as a pretense the interests of Germany, the enemies of the fatherland have raised the standard of revolt to overturn the order of things established by both divine and human sanction." He explained that he had refused the emperorship because "the assembly has no right to bestow the crown without the consent of the German governments." He asserted that he had tried to reach an understanding with the assembly, but that most members had departed, and the rump was dominated by terrorists who used German unity as a pretense for "fighting the battle of godlessness, perjury, and robbery—a war against monarchy." Showing his true concept of government, he continued: "But if monarchy were overthrown, the blessings of law, liberty, and property would be doomed." Finally, he concluded that he had by no means given up hope of unifying Germany—on his own terms—and that his government had "taken up with the more important German states the work on the German constitution begun by the Frankfurt Assembly."

The Failure of the Revolutions

All these events indicate why the revolutions failed. An excess of nationalism, of intellectual idealism, and of reliance on moderate, legal means among the Frankfurt parliamentarians; middle-class fear of social revolution, which forced the bourgeois to look to autocracy for the protection of property and social privileges; political inexperience; diffusion of aims; innate strength of the autocratic regimes—these and other explanations help interpret the failure of the unification movement and of the separate revolts in the states. Carl Schurz's observation may be correct: "The Parliament would have been sure of success in creating a constitutional German Empire, if it had performed that task quickly and elected and put into office its *Kaiser* while the revolutionary prestige of the people was still unbroken." That would have been within the first few months after the March revolutions. But, as Schurz continued, by searching for a perfect solution, these "noble, learned, conscientious, and patriotic men" of the Frankfurt assembly became bogged down in minutiae of little consequence. They lacked the "genius that promptly discerns opportunity," and were not "mindful of the fact that in times of great commotion, the history of the world does not wait for the theoretical thinker."

Moreover, the unification movement was hampered by distrust among the various states and jealousy among the princes. During the republican revolts in the Black Forest, for instance, the army and the bourgeois of Baden, although unable to quell the revolt by themselves, did not want the aid of Württemberg troops. Above all, there was the dislike of most southerners for Prussia. When Frederick William's proclamation of March 21, regarding the possible merging of Prussia and the rest of Germany became known in the south, anti-Prussian demonstrations flared up in many states. In Stuttgart, the Prussian ruler was publicly burnt in effigy. In Munich, rioters in front of the Prussian embassy warned that "the people of Germany and the princes will rise united to repulse the dictatorship of one man." In addition, there was the continued Austro-Prussian rivalry, lessened only by Frederick William's attachment to the Hapsburgs that made him refuse to take advantage of Austria's preoccupation with its subject peoples during the greater part of 1848.

Although they describe conditions in Germany in the mid-nineteenth century, such explanations should not be interpreted as throwing light on the "German mind" or on the "nature of the German people"—an attempt lately undertaken by many historians. Instead of stressing the uniqueness of the German revolutions and attributing their failure to "German characteristics," one should recall that the revolutions in Italy, Austria, and other states failed as spectacularly, and that even the Second French Republic was abortive and led to the dictatorship of Louis Napoleon.

Despite failure, the revolutions left important legacies. All German states emerged at last with constitutions, giving the German middle class, if not actual power, at least a sense of participation. At the same time, the acrimony of socialist agitation and the violence of some uprisings had brought class hatreds into a new focus. The workers felt bitter and frustrated, while among the propertied classes, fear of the "red specter" became permanent.

It is often asserted that the legacy of the revolution included a loss of faith among the liberals that permanently colored German history. In isolated cases, this no doubt occurred. The re-establishment of conservatism after 1849 may account for the wave of pessimism and lack of self-reliance that afflicted certain groups in the succeeding two decades. But it must be remembered that the princes failed as much as the liberals. Only much later, after unification was achieved by their opponents, did many liberals feel frustration and hopelessness.

Among the legacies of 1848 were the lessons of what not to do—although one may wonder how often statesmen learn from the past. Prince William later observed that "whoever wants to rule Germany must conquer her. À la Gagern [that is, by words] it does not work." Bismarck was to reiterate this idea in his famous speech of 1862: "The great questions of the day will not be settled by speeches or by majority votes—that was the mistake of 1848 and 1849—but by blood and iron!" Thereafter it became popular to assume that the primary lesson of 1848 was that Germany could be unified only by force. In reality, such a statement foreshadows a justification for the use of force rather than a deduction from the lessons of 1848. The failures of 1848 could legitimately provide future statesmen with many guiding caveats: not to underestimate the power of the princes; to create a favorable climate among foreign powers, particularly Russia; to construct the new state with the support of the mass of the people. But it is a perversion of historical interpretation to read into these lessons a mandate for the use of force.

Prussia's Last-Minute Attempt at Unification

As Frederick William IV had proclaimed on May 15, 1849, he still hoped to unify Germany on his own terms. Radowitz elaborated a plan to unite the states into a close federation, with the king of Prussia as president of a college of princes. This proposed state, sometimes called the "Prussian Union," was to enter into a close economic and political alliance with the Austrian Empire.

At the end of May, delegates from the states met at Berlin to discuss the new scheme. Austria and Bavaria withdrew after a few days, but Saxony, Hanover, and Prussia worked out a draft constitution for the new union. Twenty-eight minor states eventually agreed to join, and arrangements were made for the convocation of a federal parliament to discuss a final constitution. Briefly it appeared as if Prussia might succeed where Frankfurt had failed.

But when elections for the federal parliament were held in January 1850, the likelihood of failure became apparent. From the beginning, Saxony and Hanover had asserted that they would enter the union only if all other German states would join. Bavaria's and Württemberg's failure even to hold elections now prompted Saxony and Hanover to boycott the scheme. Hence the federal parliament at Erfurt, opening on March 20, 1850, was attended only by delegates from Prussia and the small states. The four kingdoms—Saxony, Bavaria, Württemberg, and Hanover—and Austria remained on the side lines. The hopelessness of the scheme was further stressed by the alienation of the moderates. Prussia had meanwhile returned to thorough conservatism. The revised Prussian Constitution of January 1850 amply demonstrated the king's reawakened authoritarianism. Consequently, the Prussian delegates at Erfurt had been instructed to insist on conservative modifications of Radowitz' draft constitution. Although formally accepting the revised draft, the moderates now lost their remaining faith in the Prussian ruler. Boycotted by the four kings and distrusted by the moderates, the Prussian Union was doomed.

Prince Schwarzenberg sensed Austria's opportunity to seize the initiative from Prussia. On May 16, he recalled to Frankfurt the old Diet of the German Confederation, insisting that it had never legally ceased to exist, but had merely suspended its functions during the turbulent days of 1848. Some of the small states promptly seceded from the Prussian Union, and rejoined the old diet under Austrian leadership. But Frederick William was not ready to concede defeat. He claimed that the diet of 1815 no longer existed, and called some of the small states of his union to a meeting in Berlin. Prussia and Austria stood in clear opposition, and some believed that only war could settle the issue. In such a contest, Austria clearly held the trumps. It enjoyed the backing of Russia and the unmatched diplomatic skill of Schwarzenberg. Its armies were well prepared and strengthened by recent victories in Italy and Hungary, whereas the Prussian forces were in a poor state of training. Tension between the two states approached the breaking point over an insignificant incident in Hesse-Cassel that was skillfully exploited by Schwarzenberg. With Austrian encouragement, the autocratic duke had dismissed his liberal ministry and had begun collecting taxes without consent of the estates. When his subjects protested and even his army officers joined the opposition, the discomfited duke appealed for help to the federal diet at Frankfurt. In September, the diet, now consisting of Austria, the four kingdoms, and a few minor states, voted to uphold monarchical sovereignty, and promised the duke help against his unruly subjects. The Hessian people, however, appealed to Frederick William, and since Hesse-Cassel was in the Prussian union, the king considered its affairs within his sphere of influence.

Frederick William was baffled by the problem. Intervention in Hesse-Cassel might lead to war with Austria, and would also align Prussia on the side of rebellious subjects. Nonintervention, on the other hand, would place Prussia on the side of monarchical solidarity, but at the price of abandoning to Austria attempted leadership in Germany. Crown Prince William urged action, and Radowitz advocated boldness. Prussian troops were dispatched to Hesse. Schwarzenberg immediately prepared for war, and the frightened Frederick William sought the mediation of the tsar. A meeting in Warsaw at the end of October was attended by Nicholas, Francis Joseph, and Prince Charles of Prussia. Despite the close family ties that united Berlin and St. Petersburg, Nicholas backed Austria. Russia, dismayed by Frederick William's vacillation during the revolutionary days, by his flirtations with the liberals, and by his attempt to weaken Denmark, awarded Austria carte blanche in Germany.

With this guarantee from Russia, Schwarzenberg acted at once. Bavarian troops were sent to Hesse in the name of the federal diet to aid the duke. If Prussian troops engaged them on the field, an Austro-Prussian war would result. On November 2, Frederick William decided to capitulate. He dismissed the aggressive Radowitz, who had been minister of foreign affairs for only a few months, and called for the resignation of Count von Brandenburg. In his stead, Otto von Manteuffel, a reactionary thoroughly opposed to war with Austria, was appointed chief minister. Schwarzenberg understood the new mood in Berlin and pressed his advantage. He demanded the dissolution of the Prussian Union as well as the evacuation of Prussian troops from Hesse. To stress his determination, he sent Austrian troops toward Hesse.

Prussia offered to negotiate, and Manteuffel and Schwarzenberg finally met at Olmütz in Bohemia on November 29. Prussia made so many concessions that this meeting is frequently called the "Humiliation of Olmütz." Prussia agreed to withdraw its troops from Hesse (with the exception of a single face-saving battalion), to recognize the re-establishment of the old federal diet under Austria's leadership, and to disband the Prussian Union. To soften Prussia's humiliation, Austria agreed to hold a conference in Dresden to discuss a possible revision of the federal statutes. But this conference, which lasted four months, proved fruitless. The diet was reconstituted in its old form, as if no revolution had occurred. In May 1851, Austria and Prussia even concluded a three year antirevolutionary alliance, whereby Prussia promised to help Austria in case of rebellions in Italy, although Austria extended no similar guarantee regarding Prussia's subject Poles. Germany returned to a modicum of the stability that preceded the events of 1848. Clearly Prussia had lost the first round in the struggle for pre-eminence in the unification movement.

THE 1850s

The enthusiasm and idealism of the revolutionary interlude were followed by years of sober realism. Stodgy conservatism based on princely power and a duteous bureaucracy again became dominant in politics. Realism in literature turned from political interests to the life of the commercial middle classes or to bourgeois tragedies. Fear of socialism, of the revolutionary proletariat, and of radical liberalism was so pronounced that the diet annulled the Declaration of Rights of 1848 passed by the National Assembly.

But this new conservative period was not an age of reaction like that inaugurated in 1815. Industrial, commercial, and social changes and the revolutionary years had ushered in the "age of the masses." Even petty autocrats felt compelled to pay lip service to popular demands. In France, Napoleon III veiled his dictatorship with plebiscites and social paternalism. In Germany, constitutions, no matter how imperfect and restricted, endowed the governments with a semblance of popular support.

In international affairs, too, the Metternich system had disappeared. The 1815 settlement had become shaky, and the Concert of Europe had disintegrated. During the following decades, wars became the order of the day for settling international questions.

The Prussian Constitution

The year 1850 opened with Frederick William's promulgation of the final version of the Prussian Constitution, which he had revised several times during the previous year, each time making it more conservative. According to its terms, the king appointed all ministers, who would be responsible only to him. The ministers, composing the Ministry of State (*Staatsministerium*), did not form a cabinet in the British sense, but simply represented the responsible heads of the nine administrative departments of the government. The king, furthermore, had power to propose or veto legislation, and his proclamations had the force of law. At his side was a Council of State (*Staatsrat*), appointed by him and endowed with largely ornamental functions. The task of debating bills submitted by the crown and of approving all financial appropriations was entrusted to the bicameral diet (*Landtag*). The upper chamber (*Herrenhaus*) of 365 delegates was to consist of 115 hereditary lords—including former sovereigns of territories absorbed by Prussia—200 civil servants and clergymen, and 50 members appointed by the king for life, mostly city patricians, university professors, and members of professions.

The 433 delegates to the lower chamber (*Abgeordnetenhaus*) were to be elected in open ballots by indirect suffrage based on a three-class voting system. The first step occurred in the primary electoral districts, in which one elector was to be chosen for every 250 inhabitants. Here all qualified male voters over the age of twenty-four were divided into three groups on the basis of direct tax payments. Those paying one third of the taxes were assigned to the first voting category, those paying the second third to the second category, and all others—including those paying no taxes—to the third category. Each of the three categories voted for the same number of electors. Under this system, the category with the highest tax assessment in a given district often was composed of only one or two individuals, while the group with the lowest tax assessment normally included the bulk of the population. The upper two categories together controlled two thirds of the votes in the primary districts, but represented only an estimated 17 percent of the electorate. The remaining 83 percent of the population possessed only one third of the votes. In the second step of the voting procedure, the elected representatives of the three groups in turn voted by absolute majority for one delegate to be sent to the lower house of the parliament—a device that further tended to underfranchise the lower-income groups.

This intricate system, which remained in effect until World War I, was, of course, designed to exclude the liberals from the parliament. During most of the 1850s, when many liberals sulked under the dull repression of Frederick William's regime and boycotted the elections, the three-class scheme produced the desired effect: conservative majorities dominated the parliament. But when the liberals again took hope in 1858 after the retirement of the king, the sociological miscalculations inherent in the system became apparent. Liberalism, it turned out, was concentrated in the well-to-do middle class, which was comfortably represented under the three-class vote. The conservative peasantry, numerous but not wealthy, had been largely disenfranchised, on the other hand. Hence even this system produced liberal majorities in the years after 1858, even though it always underfranchised the proletariat.

The Last Years of Frederick William's Reign

The conservative tenor of the 1850 constitution reinforced the Manteuffel regime. While the king became more estranged from his people, Manteuffel developed a system based on tyrannical pettiness and degradation. Eavesdropping and police surveillance, arbitrary arrest of liberals, censorship of the press, and political favoritism for the nobility marked his administration. The Junkers again enjoyed unlimited esteem, and were even given back some feudal powers over the peasants on their estates. In 1854, the constitution was again altered toward greater conservatism. Public meetings were prohibited and political clubs dissolved. A new school regulation instructed teachers that the main aim of education was to impart to students Christianity, patriotism, and love of their king.

The stultifying atmosphere of the Manteuffel regime evoked disgust rather than rebellion. Because of the numerous restrictions, political parties as such could not be formed, but likeminded groups built a basis for future party life by forming around certain influential newspapers. The ultraconservatives gathered around the *Kreuzzeitung,* of which Bismarck had been a founder in 1848. The more moderate monarchists, including Prince William, the heir to the throne, assembled under the banner of the *Preussische Wochenblatt.* The harassed liberals for the moment had no such standard-bearer.

Despite political oppression, Prussia made phenomenal strides in its economic expansion. Growing industrialization, banking, and communications made it more prosperous and economically sound. This was also reflected in Prussia's foreign trade. The *Zollverein* not only survived the troublesome revolutionary years but emerged more successful than ever. By 1853, even the last recalcitrant states had joined, so that all but Austria were included. Because of Prussia's low tariffs, Vienna could neither afford to join the customs union nor succeed in breaking it up by luring the southern states out of their profitable arrangement. Hence the Zollverein assumed importance as a unifying factor on the basis of *Kleindeutschland.*

Conservatism also marked Prussia's foreign policy during the 1850s. The decade opened with a temporary settlement of the Danish problem. In March 1849, Denmark had broken the armistice of Malmö. Three months of inconclusive fighting by the Prussian army and Schleswig-Holstein volunteers against Danish forces had finally led to a second armistice in July 1849, followed by a peace treaty with Denmark, which Prussia concluded in the name of all Germany. But the rebels continued to defy Copenhagen, and Austria, once again a champion of monarchical authority, insisted on quelling the disorders. At Olmütz Prussia was forced to concur with Schwarzenberg's scheme. The federal diet in Frankfurt was authorized to restore order in Schleswig-Holstein, and Austro-Prussian troops and commissioners were sent to the duchies to help Denmark subdue the rebels. Against such formidable opposition, the rebellion collapsed, and in 1852 the great powers gathered in London to settle the international aspect of the problem (see page 350). The conclusion of the Danish episode demonstrated the change in Prussian policy. In 1848–1849, Prussia had fought on the side of the duchies for the sake of German nationalism. After Olmütz, it threw its weight into the opposite camp to uphold monarchical sovereignty and suppress the rebellious subjects.

Frederick William's next problem in foreign affairs stemmed from the Crimean War (1854–1856). His mind was already clouded by approaching insanity and his policy was unsure. Despite Russia's unfriendly attitude in 1850, Frederick William could not conceal his admiration for Nicholas I, whom he called "one of the noblest of men, . . . one of the truest hearts, and . . . one of the greatest rulers." Consequently he was disturbed when England and France sided with Turkey to make war on Russia. He was also horrified on religious grounds at the "help which England in unchristian folly gives to Islam against Christians."

But, afraid that Napoleon III might violate the Rhineland borders, Frederick William did not dare aid Russia. Although both England and Russia wooed him, he remained on the side lines. At one point he was ready to help England if it guaranteed the Rhineland against French attack. At another, he became anti-British when he heard rumors that England and France might stir up revolutions in Austria if the latter did not join the war against Russia. When free shipping on the Danube was threatened by Russia's occupation of the Danubian Principalities, he agreed to a defensive alliance with Austria, but at the same time made sure that this action would not antagonize Russia.

In the end, Prussia's neutrality had advantages as well as disadvantages. The inactivity entailed a serious loss of prestige, so that Berlin hardly figured at the peace conference in Paris in 1856. On the other hand, benevolent neutrality gained Prussia the gratitude of Alexander II, who ascended the throne of Russia in 1855. It marked the beginning of a switch in Russian policy from a pro-Austrian stand to renewed friendship with Prussia, a shift that was to be of vital importance in the decade of the 1860s.

Incipient Decline of Austria

Austria made an astonishing recovery from the revolutions that had almost destroyed it. Outwardly the nation appeared as powerful in 1850 as it had in the days of Metternich; internally its system was rotting. After Prince Schwarzenberg's death in 1852, Alexander von Bach (1813–1893) assumed the work of governmental centralization, as minister of the interior. The Constitution of 1849 was revoked, and the Viennese bureaucracy ruled the sprawling empire, with the support of army and police. The subject peoples, especially the unruly Hungarians, were everywhere suppressed and the German minority was entrusted with ruling power. The emperor and his ministers openly catered to the nobility, the army, and the clergy, who had all helped overcome the revolution. A new concordat concluded with the papacy in 1855 awarded wide powers over education and financial support to the Church.

But this Bach system, as it was called, produced neither administrative efficiency nor financial solvency. The subject populations were momentarily quiescent but unreconciled to their fate. And unlike Prussia, Austria failed to make decisive economic strides.

In foreign relations, Austria was also unsuccessful. In 1849 and 1850, after the collapse of the rebellions, it joined Russia in demanding from Turkey extradition of Kossuth and other Hungarian rebels given asylum in the Ottoman Empire. When Britain and France threatened war unless the Austro-Russians withdrew their demand, the latter complied. Their vindictive request thus brought them nothing but the scorn of the western powers.

The disputes over Russian influence in Turkey, which led to the Crimean War, placed Austria in a difficult position. Nicholas at first expected that Austria would side with him in gratitude for his help in subduing the Hungarian rebellion. But Schwarzenberg supposedly remarked in 1849, "We will astonish the world by our ingratitude," and Emperor Francis Joseph fulfilled this prediction. Austria tried to protect its Danube interests by leaning toward England and France and making a defensive alliance with Prussia, but to the western allies these maneuvers smacked of duplicity. Repeatedly Austria mobilized its forces to threaten Russia's flank, but in the end remained neutral.

The Crimean War brought Austria no benefits; instead, it hastened Austrian decline. Austrian finances had been strained through mobilization and the country had become isolated among the European powers. Its diplomatic equivocation made it suspect to England and France, and its anti-Russian attitude made it permanently lose the friendship of the tsar. Estrangement from Russia and political isolation from the West became of paramount importance during the subsequent decade, when Austria was toppled from its pinnacle by France and Prussia.

14

The Unification Period, 1858–1871

BEGINNING OF A NEW ERA

The years 1858–1859 opened a new era in German history, which initiated the gradual disintegration of the Austrian Empire, and pointed toward the ultimate triumph of Prussia. These years were marked by the end of ultaconservatism in Prussia, the first of a series of military defeats for Austria, and the revitalization of German nationalism. The period began with a change of leadership in Prussia.

The Accession of William I

The health of King Frederick William IV had been failing for some time. Attacks of insanity finally forced him to appoint his brother William as regent. Although the mentally deranged Frederick William lived another three years, William in fact assumed complete control of the government in 1858 and ultimately became king in 1861, as William I.

Born in 1797, William had participated in the final battles of the Wars of Liberation as a lad of seventeen, and thereafter spent a lifetime in service to his beloved army. After becoming a general in 1825, he trained troops, served on army commissions, and became better versed in military affairs than any other Hohenzollern ruler since Frederick the Great. During the Revolution of 1848, the conservative prince had been temporarily exiled to England, but he had returned in time to participate in the counterrevolution of 1849 by commanding the Prussian troops sent to quell revolts in Baden. After 1850, he obtained some administrative experience by acting as governor of the Rhineland and Westphalian provinces.

William believed in monarchical untouchability, but he lacked the romantic and reactionary tendencies of his brother. His conservatism had become more moderate, and more appropriate to the times. He accepted the existence of a parliament and constitutionalism as unalterable, albeit unpleasant, facts of his reign, and was willing to work with them, provided they did not impinge on the honor of the Hohenzollern dynasty and the Prussian army. In political matters, foreign as well as internal, he trusted bold action more than had his vacillating predecessor, and he usually followed a course with perseverance and determination. Vital decisions in German history during the succeeding several decades are usually credited to Bismarck. Although this view is largely true, even a Bismarck could have achieved little without the support of a determined ruler. In view of Bismarck's aim of unifying Germany, William's main failing was that throughout his life he remained more Prussian than German.

A sigh of relief throughout Prussia greeted William's assumption of power in 1858. The sixty-one-year-old prince, a shrewd judge of character, immediately dismissed the reactionary Otto von Manteuffel. He refused to appoint the vehement Otto von Bismarck, who was ambitiously hoping to become chief minister, and instead chose the moderate Prince Anthony of Hohenzollern-Sigmaringen (1811–1885), the head of the Catholic branch of the dynasty. All political groups, except the ultraconservatives, were pleased by this appointment. The parliamentary elections of 1859 showed the result. With the reestablishment of civil liberties, the liberals ceased their boycott of elections, and voting resulted in a majority for the moderately liberal representatives. Only one action by the new ruler warned the liberals of impending conflicts. William knew from experience the relatively poor state of training and organization of the Prussian army. He promptly appointed as minister of war the conservative Count Albert von Roon (1803–1879), a close friend and adviser of Bismarck's. Roon in turn made General Helmuth von Moltke (1800–1891) chief of the Prussian General Staff. Together with Roon and Moltke, William soon embarked on army reforms that enabled Prussia to win the wars of the 1860s, but engendered the most vehement conflict in its constitutional history.

The Italian War of 1859

A second event that ushered in the new era was the Italian War of 1859. Largely for reasons of prestige, Napoleon III had agreed to help Sardinia dislodge Austria from northern Italy, provided the Viennese government could be made to look like the aggressor. Despite British and Russian efforts at mediation, Austria actually blundered into declaring war on Sardinia, and the French emperor fulfilled his promise of aid. The campaigns against the Franco-Sardinian forces, fought in Lombardy, went badly for Austria. It evacuated the province, although its armies were not destroyed in the field. Clearly Austria lacked the leadership and determination shown in 1848 and 1849, and after a campaign of barely three months, Austria and France agreed on an armistice.

It is interesting that both Napoleon and Francis Joseph desired a rapid termination of hostilities because of the attitude of Prussia. The war had evoked much sympathy for Austria among southern Germans, and had rekindled the fear that Napoleon III might violate the Rhineland border in a repetition of the campaigns of his uncle, Napoleon I. Prussia had taken advantage of this anti-French mood and begun to mobilize its troops. William had offered military aid to Austria on the condition that Prussia be allowed to command all the troops of the German Confederation in the war against France. Vienna, however, feared that consent to such a stipulation would represent abandonment of its own preeminent position in Germany. Hence it refused and hastened to make peace with France. As Moltke later remarked, "Austria would rather give up Lombardy than see Prussia at the head of Germany." Austria and France concluded a peace whereby Lombardy was ceded to Sardinia and the way opened for Italian unification. The dismemberment of Austria had begun, and in accordance with previous agreements between Napoleon and Cavour of Sardinia, France was enlarged by the addition of Nice and Savoy.

The effects of this war on Germany were manifold. The dismemberment of the Austrian Empire in Italy raised hopes among Austria's other subject populations and weakened its international prestige. At the same time, Austro-Prussian rivalry, dormant since the days of Olmütz, was revived. French successes also gave a boost to German nationalism, which had been fairly quiescent during the 1850s.

Above all, the victory of little Sardinia and the initial steps toward uniting Italy acted like an electric shock on the German unification movement. State governments resumed discussion of possible schemes for union. Groups of former members of the Frankfurt Assembly met to devise new plans. In 1859, the Hanoverian Rudolf von Benningsen (1824–1902) founded the *Nationalverein* (National Association), which was to play a vital role in the creation of a united Germany. Everywhere, it seemed, liberals revived their hopes. Extreme conservatism was weakened by the loss of Frederick William IV and by the failure of the Austrian experiment with centralization. Even southern liberals, although still pro-Austrian and suspicious of Prussia, began to conclude that unification under Prussia's new ruler might be the only feasible, if not the best, solution. And applying the lessons of Italy to the problem of German unity, the radicals proclaimed that "Austria must be crushed, dismembered, destroyed, . . . its ashes . . . strewn to the four winds!" They reasoned that "the executioners of Italy are also our oppressors, and our freedom requires separation from Austria."

The Prussian Army Reform and the Constitutional Struggle

The feverish revival of the unification movement and of liberal aspirations formed the background for Prussia's constitutional struggle that led to the appointment of Bismarck as head of the Prussian ministry. This struggle arose over William's and Roon's determination to reorganize the Prussian army.

For many reasons the army was in need of reform. It was still organized on principles developed during the Napoleonic campaigns, even though Prussia's population had nearly doubled and its military requirements had vastly altered since 1815. The mobilization of 1859 had shown the army's inefficiency and there were many besides William, in both Prussia and other states, who agreed that the renewed French menace and the impending task of unifying Germany demanded an effective military force.

Roon proposed to increase the

peacetime strength of the army from 150,000 to 213,000 men, and to enforce the legal three-year period of compulsory service for recruits, which had not been applied because of lack of funds. He wanted to reduce total liability for service from nineteen to sixteen years, placing men three years on active duty with the line forces, then four years in the stand-by reserve, followed by nine years in the *Landwehr*—an emergency reserve force. Above all, the *Landwehr,* more democratic in composition and rules of conduct, was to be placed under stricter supervision by the regular army. Finally, the minister of war wished to supply the forces with up-to-date equipment, in particular the breech-loading needle gun, which could be loaded and fired in the prone position and thus revolutionize infantry fighting.

When these proposals were submitted to the lower chamber in the spring of 1860, they were voted down by the liberals and moderates, who commanded a majority. The Progressives—as the new moderate liberal party was called—admitted the need for an efficient and enlarged military establishment but opposed the Prussian style of militarism. At heart, they wanted a "parliamentary army," which could become a pillar of a more liberal and popular regime. Moreover, they were not averse to using the reform issue as a lever for extracting constitutional concessions from the king, in particular a decrease in the power of the upper chamber. Consequently, they refused to approve the proposed enforcement of three years of service for recruits and the contemplated tighter control over the *Landwehr*.

Although the diet had legislative power of sorts, the king could have legally circumvented the legislature's rejection of the army bill by issuing a royal proclamation. But the projected reforms required additional funds, and the lower chamber had the power of granting or withholding taxes. William was in a quandary. He regarded the army as being solely under the jurisdiction of the crown, and thought the parliament's duty was to vote the required funds without attaching strings. The revolutionary days had shown that without control of a reliable army, the entire monarchical structure would be in jeopardy. And William was convinced that a semi-independent bourgeois-oriented *Landwehr* might be easily subverted, and that a three-year period of service was needed to indoctrinate recruits in proper allegiance to the crown.

Rebuffed by the diet, the government withdrew the reform bill and simply requested additional appropriations in the general budget. When these were granted, Roon commenced his reforms. The same maneuver was repeated in 1861, although this time the parliamentarians were aware that the government was circumventing their powers, and approved the larger budget only by a scant majority. New elections in the winter produced an even greater majority for the liberal forces, and when the crown tried in early 1862 to outwit the diet by the same scheme, it met defeat. The lower chamber refused to approve the budget without a detailed breakdown. William rejected this demand, which would have implied parliamentary control not merely over the army but over the entire executive. He dissolved the lower chamber and called for new elections.

When the elections of 1862 increased

liberal representation, the constitutional struggle reached an impasse. William, now king in his own right, contemplated abdication rather than submission to the will of the parliament. "I will not reign," he is supposed to have stated, "if I cannot do it in such a fashion as I can be answerable for to God, my conscience, and my subjects." But Roon advised him instead to request Bismarck to lead the struggle against the parliament. Bismarck was quickly recalled from his post as ambassador to France, and when he promised to advocate reorganization of the army "in opposition to the majority in parliament," William agreed "to continue the battle and . . . not to abdicate." Bismarck was thereupon appointed chief minister. The so-called era of incipient liberalism was ended and Prussia fell under the shadow of a new spirit.

BISMARCK'S INITIAL WORK

Early Career

Otto Eduard Leopold von Bismarck-Schönhausen (1815–1898) was a tall, robust Junker from Brandenburg, the son of a middle-class mother and an estate owner of petty though ancient nobility. He had received a good education at the universities of Göttingen and Berlin, and had acquired an astonishing fluency in French and English that facilitated his later diplomatic career. At the age of twenty-one he entered the Prussian civil service, but his arrogant love of independence and hatred of city life with its "stink of civilization," as he called it, soon filled him with disgust and contempt for the career of a bureaucrat. He withdrew to his estate to indulge in boisterous drinking and to try his hand in rural management. He loved the country life of a gentleman farmer, and was proud of being "no democrat," but of being "born and raised as an aristocrat."

In 1845 he represented his district and his class in the provincial diet and two years later became involved in general Prussian politics, as a member of the United Diet. On this brief occasion, he emerged on the national political scene as a staunch defender of monarchical conservatism and a loyal supporter of the king, whom he later called "'the central point of all my thinking and all my actions." His speeches on behalf of royal absolutism were precise in thought and distinguished in language, but suffered from poor delivery and an excessive amount of sarcasm.

From that time he remained in public service and in politics, although he frequently spoke of his desire to retire to his estate. In 1848 he served in the Prussian assembly, and the following year became a member of the lower chamber in the Prussian diet. Frederick William, though grateful for such loyal support, was somewhat fearful of the vehemence of the "terrible Junker," and hesitated to offer him a major post. However, in 1850 Bismarck was sent to the Erfurt Parliament, and from 1851 to 1859 served as Prussian envoy to the federal diet at Frankfurt. While at Frankfurt, Bismarck kept up his political connections in Prussia, continuing as a member of the lower chamber in the Prussian diet until 1852, when the king appointed him to the upper chamber. Finally, in 1859, the new regent of Prussia made Bismarck ambassador to Russia, and in 1862 transferred him to the court of Napoleon III.

Hence when in September 1862 Bismarck was made minister-president and minister of foreign affairs, he was well prepared for his new post. Through his various positions, his frequent travels, and his correspondence, he had become well acquainted with conditions in Prussia, in the German Confederation, and at key capitals of the world. Through his years at Frankfurt, he knew most of the influential officials in the other German states. The Prussian king had sent him on special missions to Vienna and other capitals. And although only an ambassador, Bismarck had frequently tried to influence Prussia's foreign policy through memoranda and advice, which he freely dispatched to his home government. His training and experiences had thus made him ready to become what Carl Schurz called "a veritable Atlas carrying upon his shoulders the destinies of a great nation."

As borne out in his later actions when in control in Prussia and Germany, his experiences provided him with a keener interest in foreign than in domestic affairs. His work in the various Prussian parliaments had instilled in him not only a deep hatred of parliamentarianism, but also the conviction that foreign affairs were generally more important than domestic matters. His letters, dispatches, and conversations of the 1850s show the keen grasp of foreign relations that helped him become one of the most skilled manipulators of diplomatic crises in his time.

Ideas on Government and Unification

The ideas he expressed before 1862 on Prussia's foreign relations are of interest since they foreshadow his later actions. His work at Frankfurt made him fully aware of the unsatisfactory functioning of the federal diet. In the end, he looked upon the German Confederation as then organized as "an oppressive and sometimes perilous tie" for Prussia. He repeatedly advocated that either the federal framework be altered, or Prussia's relations to the diet changed before it had to be transformed *"ferro et igni"*—a favorite expression of Bismarck's, meaning "by iron and fire."

His experiences at the diet also changed his earlier admiration for the Hapsburgs into hatred of Austria. He gradually came to suspect the sincerity of every Austrian proposal and finally became convinced of the inevitability of "a death struggle" between Prussia and Austria. For an eventual war with Austria, Prussia needed allies, and Bismarck scanned the international horizon. Repeatedly he seized on Russia as a logical candidate. He considered a pact with Russia "the cheapest among all continental alliances," since Prussia could obtain it without sacrificing vital interests. During the Crimean War, he warned against siding with Britain and France, and thereafter he continued to insist on friendly relations with the tsar.

On relations with France, his views were more ambivalent. Always a pragmatist in politics, he derided his colleagues who objected to cooperation with France because of Napoleon's revolutionary background. He pointed out that many European thrones were not truly "legitimate," and that many other nations were imperialistic. In international politics he felt that "standards of morality and justice" could hardly serve as criteria for action. Bismarck did not fear France, nor did he trust Napoleon. But he perceived advantages in smiling at France without committing Prussia to a full-fledged alliance. During the Austro-French War over Italy, he was pleased to see France weaken Austria. When the regent mobilized Prussian troops against France, Bismarck dispatched memoranda to Berlin objecting to support for Austria and even suggesting military aid to France in order to crush Vienna once and for all.

Bismarck's lukewarm preference for France was also conditioned by his knowledge of the prevailing mood in southern Germany. This area had always looked for outside support to either Vienna or Paris. In a Prussian struggle against Austria, the southern states might be more at ease if Prussia and France were at least tacit friends.

Most significant among Bismarck's early suggestions to the foreign office was his insistence on flexibility in international commitments. Diplomatic planning should always open onto two possible courses. The opponent could be permitted to guess both plans as long as he could not ascertain which would ultimately be followed. He objected to the dull rigidity with which foreign affairs had been conducted under Frederick William IV, and suggested a pragmatic and flexible approach, which under his own direction later sometimes bordered on sheer opportunism.

Although a Prussian Junker to his marrow, Bismarck had extended his horizon through his political apprenticeship in Frankfurt and at foreign courts. He did not lose his "Prussian national consciousness," as he called it, yet unlike many of his fellow Junkers, he recognized the contributions that other German states and German national feeling as a whole could furnish to a united Germany. But apart from his conviction that Austria should be expelled from Germany and that this would probably require force, prior to 1862 he produced few specific ideas on the subject of unification. That Prussia would have to assume leadership in Germany Bismarck did not doubt, but how this could be accomplished was not yet clear.

Many historians, relying excessively on Bismarck's own memoirs written in the 1890s, ascribe to the Prussian minister an almost Mephistophelean adroitness in manipulating the diplomatic chessboard to obtain his ends. They infer that, from the outset, Bismarck planned the myriad steps required for the unification of Germany, including each of the three wars that Prussia was to fight in the 1860s. Everything, according to these writers, fits into a neat pattern the chancellor had worked out in advance. Actually this is part of the legend that Bismarck delighted in bequeathing to posterity. Bismarck was a masterful diplomat, a sagacious judge of men and situations, but his success derived not from adherence to a rigid pattern—a political behavior he rejected as unsound—but from brilliant improvisations. With more speed and perspicacity than most of his opponents possessed, Bismarck could assess a new situation and decide on a successful course of action. Herein lay Bismarck's success.

Bismarck's Solution to the Constitutional Struggle in Prussia

In his first speech to the budget committee of the Prussian diet after his appointment as minister-president, Bismarck said prophetically: "The eyes of Germany are not fixed upon Prussia's liberalism, but upon her armed might." In another speech, he remarked: "Our strength cannot spring from cabinet or newspaper politics, but only from the actions of a great armed power." He thus announced his determination to support the king and Roon in the proposed army reforms at the price of destroying liberalism and constitutional government. He authorized collection of taxes without a budget and without parliamentary approval, thereby enabling the army to continue its reorganization.

To the Prussian diet he showed no willingness to compromise. He scornfully asked the parliamentarians: "Are we to be ruled monarchically like a great power, or, as conceivable for a mere small state, by professors, judges, and small town politicians?" When informed by the delegates that they represented the will of the people, he advised them that true statesmen mold public opinion rather than being influenced by it. When the diet persisted in its refusal to grant funds, he dismissed the lower chamber, to the applause of the conservative minority. There was much agitation throughout Prussia, and most of the press vituperated against Bismarck's highhanded actions. Even King William feared a revolution. But Bismarck felt secure and pursued his chosen course.

When the diet reconvened in January 1863, it reiterated its refusal to approve the budget. Once again Bismarck lectured the delegates in a famous speech. He contended that the constitution of 1850 provided no solution in case of conflict between the crown and parliament. "Necessity alone is the determing factor," and Bismarck reasoned that since the state must continue to exist and requires funds for its existence, the state also has the right to collect taxes, regardless of the attitude of parliament. When the parliamentarians protested and criticism grew louder, Bismarck resorted to sterner measures. In June he again dismissed the diet and called for new elections. Strict censorship was reimposed, liberals were imprisoned, and the civil service was purged of those who showed open sympathy with the representatives. The repressive atmosphere of the 1850s returned. A few advocated refusal to pay taxes. Accused of sedition, they were thrown into jail. The moderate forces, including Crown Prince Frederick, publicly complained about the return of unlimited authoritarianism, but the civil service and the army supported the king, and William in turn stood behind his chancellor. The old Prussian combination of power had been revived, taxes continued to be paid, and there was no open rebellion.

The divergence between public opinion and the government can be seen in the results of the new elections of October 1863. The country sent to Berlin an even more liberal representation, which proved as frustrated and powerless as its predecessor in the face of the crown's determination. The deadlock was to continue for another three years, but starting in 1864, Bismarck and Prussia became increasingly involved in foreign affairs; and because of his success in the foreign arena, his arrogant treatment of the Prussian diet was less and less criticized.

First Successes in Foreign Affairs

RELATIONS WITH RUSSIA A few months after assuming power, Bismarck had an opportunity for implementing his pro-Russian policy. In

1862, Emperor Alexander II had whetted the appetite of the freedom-minded Poles by granting them increased political rights. Not satisfied by the tsar's offers, Polish radicals demanded complete independence and began an insurrection in January 1863. Rather than grant more concessions, Alexander sent his army to beat down the rebellion. Polish uprisings in the nineteenth century, especially after the revolutions of 1830 and 1848, always attracted the sentimental interest of Europe. It was not surprising, therefore, that England, France, and Austria sent protests to the tsar concerning the repressions in Poland. These protests, of course, were not serious, since France was then occupied in Mexico, England showed no interest in active intervention, and Austria was unlikely to desire a free Poland that could become a rallying point for its own Polish subject populations. Yet the tsar resented the interference in what he considered his own affairs.

Bismarck, however, refused to join the European powers. Instead he dispatched Count Constantin von Alvensleben to St. Petersburg to offer Prussian aid against the rebels. In February 1863, by the Convention of Alvensleben, Prussia agreed to mobilize troops along its Polish border to prevent the spread of the revolution and, if called upon, to assist Alexander in his territory. By May Russia had crushed the revolt without Prussian military aid, but the tsar was grateful to Bismarck, and Russia's friendship was to be of value to Prussia during the ensuing decade.

Bismarck's action had not been designed merely to gain Russia's friendship. As early as 1848 he had remarked that an "independent Poland would be the irreconcilable enemy of Prussia." And a successful rebellion in Russian Poland might all too easily provoke a smilar rising of Poles in Prussia's eastern territories. The Prussian conservatives and Junkers, for their part, were delighted with Bismarck's action, whereas the liberals deplored Prussia's realignment on the side of autocratic Russia.

AUSTRO-PRUSSIAN RIVALRY IN THE EARLY 1860s After the war with France in 1859 and the loss of Lombardy, the Austrian Empire once again seemed at the brink of collapse. Its financial resources were depleted and its subject populations quivered with unrest. It was symptomatic that the Hungarians had sent volunteers to help the Italians against Austria. Moreover, Austria's prestige in Germany had suffered through the Italian debacle.

To strengthen Austria's internal structure, Emperor Francis Joseph experimented with a slight relaxation of centralized authoritarianism. He took as his minister Anton Schmerling, the comparatively liberal lawyer who had served as minister of foreign affairs in the Frankfurt provisional government of 1848. In October of 1860, Schmerling issued the "Diploma," which instituted a measure of decentralization by granting local rule to the former diets. Since these diets were not based on national divisions but on feudal arrangements, the Diploma satisfied none of the aspirations of the subject peoples and proved unworkable. In 1861, the emperor produced a different plan, the "February Patent," providing for a central parliament of the empire based on an electoral system in which classes rather than regions were to be represented. It was a renewal of the old

Hapsburg hope of governing the multifarious empire with the support of the upper classes of the various peoples.

The central parliament worked fairly smoothly, although the Hungarian deputies were ominously absent. Hungary had been promised re-establishment of its own parliament with supreme powers over the Magyar lands. Since the emperor was unwilling to implement this concession, the Hungarians continued their passive opposition, which vitiated the whole new system. Hence in the long run, the February Patent too, proved a failure, and Vienna resorted to its tried methods of absolutist repression of the local nationalities.

Despite internal instability, Austria attempted to enter the German scene more actively. In 1861, Prussia had proposed revisions of the federal constitution to entrust more power to the federal diet. The attempt was thwarted, but continued submission of similar proposals finally goaded Vienna into action. In August 1863, Francis Joseph summoned to Frankfurt a congress of all German princes to discuss a reform of the diet. Since King William and Bismarck were at the time occupied with the Prussian constitutional struggle, the emperor thought his proposals would encounter little opposition. The king of Saxony in person delivered the invitation to William, who considered it unwise and impolite to refuse. Bismarck, however, thought otherwise: attendance by the king of Prussia at such a conference would enhance the prestige of Austria and possibly spoil the chances of German unification under Prussian auspices. Bismarck's reasoning finally prevailed over the king.

When the conference opened, it was attended by all German states except Prussia. Vienna proposed the establishment of a tighter union, governed by a directory of five princes under the presidency of Austria. A parliament of deputies was to be established, with members drawn from the diets of the various states. Always more suspicious of Prussian than of Austrian intentions, the princes accepted the proposal in principle. But the absence of Prussia killed all chances of success, and the plan remained a dead letter.

Immediately thereafter Bismarck made a countermove that evoked astonishment and even cynical derision. He proposed that the German parliament of deputies should not be drawn from the state diets, but should represent all of Germany on the basis of universal suffrage. Since Bismarck was at the time locked in battle with Prussia's diet—which was not elected by universal suffrage, but based on the three-class vote—his proposal was considered insincere by many Germans and ridiculed by the Prussian liberals. But as he proved in 1867, when establishing the Reichstag of the North German Confederation on the basis of universal male suffrage, Bismarck was not in principle opposed to such a representative body for Germany. In fact, he considered such a body the only sound basis for uniting German public opinion, provided it had no real power over the executive. Moreover, his proposal was an example of masterful diplomacy. It was bound to let Prussia take the initiative from Austria, which on principle and in practice could not allow universal suffrage. And it was likely to mitigate some of the distrust felt by German liberals for Prussian authoritarianism. His proposal was, of course, rejected, but it helped put Austria once again on the sidelines.

THE DANISH PROBLEM After the Prusso-Danish War of 1848–1849, the Danish problem had in theory been settled by the London Protocol of 1852, subscribed to by England, France, Russia, Prussia, Austria, Denmark, and Sweden, but not by the German federal diet (see pages 328, 338, and Map 18). Since King Frederick VII had no heirs, the protocol vested succession to the Danish crown as well as to the duchies of Schleswig and Holstein in Christian of Glücksburg, a relative of the king through the female line. It also guaranteed the integrity of the existing Danish boundaries, and stipulated that Holstein would remain in the German Confederation and at the same time enjoy autonomy within the Danish Kingdom. The Augustenburg claimant was indemnified for his lost expectancy of the duchies by a monetary payment. For the moment all participants seemed content, except for the heirs of the Augustenburg line and the nationalists at the Frankfurt diet, both of whom withheld their consent to the protocol.

But the problem was far from settled. During the 1850s, King Frederick VII and the Danish nationalists repeatedly tried to integrate the duchies into the Danish monarchy. A revised, more centralizing constitution for Denmark was to be applied also to Schleswig and Holstein. These attempts invariably resulted in unrest in the duchies and in appeals to the German Confederation, which forced the Danish king to postpone his plans under threat of war. The Frankfurt diet also warned Frederick against separating the two duchies, although legally only Holstein could claim some form of German protection. But despite English and French admonitions to exercise caution, the Danish king submitted to his parliament in March 1863 a bill stipulating that the new Danish constitution would apply to Schleswig, and that Holstein, although remaining semiautonomous, would have to pay national taxes to the Danish state. When he rejected German demands to withdraw these proposals, the diet at Frankfurt voted for federal execution against Denmark and called on Hanover and Saxony for military action.

Six weeks later, King Frederick VII suddenly died. In accordance with the London Protocol, he was succeeded by Christian IX of Glücksburg. The new ruler was as nationalistic as his predecessor, and with the support of parliament, he proceeded to incorporate Schleswig into his kingdom. An outburst of indignation shook the duchies and large segments of German nationalists. At the same time, Duke Frederick of Augustenburg disclaimed his father's renunciation and styled himself the rightful ruler of Schleswig-Holstein. Prussia and Austria hesitated, but the German diet, not being a signatory to the London Protocol, dispatched Hanoverian and Saxon troops into Holstein and Lauenburg, which were both federal territories. With the support of the German diet, the Holsteiners then proclaimed Frederick of Augustenburg their ruler on the theory that the Salic Law did not recognize succession through the female line and thereby voided King Christian's legal title to the duchy. They also talked of complete secession from Denmark. To avoid conflict with the German forces, Danish troops were temporarily withdrawn from Holstein.

The course of the crisis depended largely on the attitude of Austria and Prussia. Austria actually had no direct interest in the northern duchies, but its desire not to let Prussia derive any advantage from the situation drew it irretrievably into the crisis. As an initial step, Bismarck decided to uphold the London Protocol and persuaded the court of Vienna that the duke of Augustenburg, whom the federal diet had recognized, represented a revolutionary element. Jointly Vienna and Berlin then recognized King Christian IX, an action that complied with the stipulations of the London Protocol. Throughout Germany, Bismarck's recognition of King Christian was decried as a betrayal of German national interests. The federal diet had hoped to bring about the secession of both Schleswig and Holstein from Denmark and their consolidation into a new federal German state under the duke of Augustenburg. But Bismarck had different ideas. The creation of a new small state that might side with the other petty principalities in opposing Prussian leadership could hardly appeal to him. Moreover, he wanted Prussia to be free to act independently and not become a mere executor for the will of the Frankfurt diet, as had happened in 1848. Ultimately he hoped to find some way whereby both duchies, or at least Holstein with Lauenburg, could be annexed to Prussia. Their acquisition would furnish Prussia an outlet to the North Sea, the important Baltic port of Kiel, control of the mouth of the vital Elbe River, and welcome additional pressure on Hanover. In exaggerated respect for Bismarck's political machinations, many historians falsely look upon his intervention in the Danish affair as merely a means to destroy the

MAP 18

German Confederation, expel Austria from Germany, and bring about German unification under Prussian leadership. To be sure, the Danish crisis weakened the federal diet and eventually embarrassed Austria; but Bismarck's main aim in 1864 was the aggrandizement of Prussia.

Acting as a champion of international treaties, Bismarck made an alliance with Austria providing for joint action and the exclusion of the Frankfurt diet from further negotiations with Denmark. In January 1864, Austria and Prussia demanded that King Christian abide by the London Protocol and safeguard the semiautonomous status of the two duchies. The Frankfurt diet opposed this action because it implied a reversion to the *status quo ante*; naturally the Danish king rejected the request because it contravened the aspirations of his nationalistic supporters.

THE WAR AGAINST DENMARK Upon Denmark's rejection of their demand, Austria and Prussia agreed on military action. On February 1, 1864, 37,000 Prussian and 23,000 Austrian troops began their invasion of the duchies. Bypassing the Hanoverian and Saxon troops, which still occupied Holstein, they invaded Schleswig and then Jutland. By April, the superior power of the Austro-Prussians had forced the Danes to evacuate their troops to the islands, and the mainland of Denmark had fallen to the invaders. The federal diet in Frankfurt, of course, was deeply disturbed, since this military action was conducted by Prussia and Austria on their own account and not in the name of the German Confederation. The powers, on the other hand, stood by while Denmark was being defeated. Napoleon was busy in Mexico; Russia was friendly to Prussia; and Britain, although worried about Denmark's independence, could hardly interfere against military action by Austria and Prussia ostensibly designed to uphold the London Protocol: it could only urge another conference.

With. defeat of Denmark in sight, an armistice was made on May 12 and a conference was held in London to debate the fate of the duchies. Various suggestions were made: one was to partition Schleswig, but the intransigence of the Danes and of the German federal diet prevented agreement, much to the delight of Bismarck, who preferred a total defeat of Denmark so that he could dictate his own terms.

Fighting resumed in late June. Prussia ferried troops to the islands and was successful in several minor engagements. Realizing the hopelessness of his position, King Christian agreed to a final armistice on July 20. Bismarck now asserted that the London Protocol had lost validity and that peace was to be made solely by the three belligerents—Denmark, Austria, and Prussia. After lengthy negotiations, Denmark signed the Peace of Vienna in October 1864, whereby Schleswig, Holstein, and Lauenburg were completely detached from Denmark and ceded not to the German diet but to Austria and Prussia for their joint disposal.

Prussia had succeeded in its first maneuver: the duchies had been separated from Denmark but not combined into a new state under the duke of Augustenburg. Many unsolved problems remained, involving agreement with the federal diet and with Austria. The diet still insisted on turning the duchies into a new, independent German state. Since it could hardly expect to annex the duchies itself and it was opposed to Prussian aggrandizement, Austria, too, now favored this solution. The best it could hope for was territorial compensation, letting Prussia absorb the duchies in return for the cession of Prussian territory—perhaps in Silesia—to Austria. But Bismarck would not sanction the loss of a square foot of Prussian land. He was willing to accept the diet's proposal only on condition that the military forces of the new state would be incorporated into those of Prussia, and that its railroads and communications would be run under Prussian direction—in short, the duke of Augustenburg would be a puppet of Berlin.

Prussian determination and Austrian vacillation decided the issue on a temporary basis. Hanover withdrew its troops from Holstein, as did Saxony under threat of war from Berlin. The Austrians were then persuaded to accept the compromise Agreement of

Gastein (August 1865). Prussia was allowed to annex the tiny Duchy of Lauenburg, in return for paying 2.5 million Danish thalers to Austria. Joint sovereignty over the two large duchies was retained by Austria and Prussia, with Schleswig under temporary administration by Prussia, and Holstein under Austria. For the purpose of communications with Schleswig, Prussia was awarded two military roads through Holstein. The important harbor of Kiel, in Holstein territory, became a joint port but was put under Prussian administration. The Agreement of Gastein represented no permanent solution. Joint sovereignty over the duchies by the two rival powers was a legal fiction not likely to endure for long. Essentially the agreement favored Prussia, for Austria had abandoned its support of the duke of Augustenburg, and Prussia had attained military and economic power over the duchies. But again the Machiavellian character of the agreement is frequently exaggerated. It is said that Bismarck devised the arrangement because he knew it would embarrass Austria and make an Austro-Prussian war inevitable. Although aware that German unification under Prussia was unlikely without a military defeat of Austria, in 1865 he was primarily concerned with obtaining the duchies for Prussia, and the Gastein Agreement embodied a step in this direction.

The Beginning of Unification

The temporary settlement of the Danish problem brought Bismarck little popularity at home. Most Prussian liberals had favored the Danish War, but the victories had not been spectacular enough to convert their distrust of Bismarck into admiration. Hence they continued to oppose Bismarck on the issue of the army budget, even though the reorganization of the army had proved of some value in the Danish War.

Bismarck, however, paid little heed to the internal discontent. His attention was devoted to convincing King William of the inevitability of war with Austria and to making the necessary preparations for such a conflict. In the end, it proved more difficult to persuade the king than to arrange for a favorable international alignment.

FOREIGN PREPARATIONS In October 1865, Bismarck vacationed at Biarritz, and seized the opportunity to discuss German problems with Napoleon III. He hinted at the possibility of an Austro-Prussian war and tried to find out whether France would maintain benevolent neutrality. Napoleon, never the shrewdest of diplomats, was no longer at the height of his political power. The failure of the Mexican adventure, the miscarriage of his Italian plans, loss of popularity at home, together with his own failing health, seemed to make him desperate for cheap success that might restore him to glory. As a champion of the ideals of nationalism, he was not averse to the establishment of a unified German state. On the other hand, he believed in a European equilibrium that required French aggrandizement if a large German state were created beyond the Rhine. During the preceding years, Napoleon had repeatedly sent secret negotiators to Bismarck to suggest that France would not oppose Prussia's attempt to reorganize Germany, provided France obtained commensurate compensations in the Rhineland. At Biarritz Bismarck referred to these offers, and without committing himself, made Napoleon feel that such an arrangement could be worked out. The French emperor presumably expected any Austro-Prussian war to be long and exhausting for both sides, so that France could seize the desired Rhineland possessions while Austria and Prussia were busy fighting in the east.

Convinced of his diplomatic skill, Napoleon then offered Bismarck his mediation to bring about a Prusso-Italian alliance. From such a combination, Italy might gain Venetia, which Napoleon had failed to obtain for the Italians in the 1859 war. On the other hand, Napoleon hardly expected Prussia to derive much military support from such an alliance.

With Prussia's right flank reasonably secure, Bismarck concentrated on the Italian alliance. Negotiations between Turin and Berlin were protracted, for the Italians distrusted Bismarck, and King William was loathe to make an alliance with a foreign power against Austria, which he still considered a German state. In the end, William contented himself with striking from the draft treaty a clause that would have required Italy to declare war also on the south German states should they side with Austria in the impending conflict. The offensive and defensive alliance between Prussia and Italy was signed in April 1866. Italy promised to declare war on Austria and not sign a separate peace, provided war between Prussia and Austria broke out within three months of the signing of the treaty. In return, Italy was to obtain Venetia.

Thus by the spring of 1866, Bismarck had completed his preparations. Roon's army stood ready, Russia's friendship had been assured, and French neutrality more or less certain. He had even found in Italy a welcome ally for keeping a number of Austrian divisions engaged south of the Alps.

APPROACH OF THE AUSTRO-PRUSSIAN DUEL It would be incorrect to conclude that Bismarck alone was preparing for the war he considered inevitable. Nor was he the only statesman who during the spring of 1866 was searching for pretexts that would unleash such a war. The Austrians, too, had concluded that the economic, political, and military progress of Prussia was such that Austria would permanently lose its position in Germany unless Prussia could be brought down. A mere political humiliation, such as that of Olmütz, seemed no longer sufficient. A military defeat was required, and Austria expected the bulk of the German states to help it crush Prussia. Hence, Austria also prepared for the war and was busy stirring up pretexts.

During 1865, Austria had gained some internal stability through the emperor's decision to conciliate the Hungarians. Four years of unsuccessful attempts to implement the "February Patent" had convinced Francis Joseph that Hungarian cooperation was essential for the survival of his monarchy. The moderate Hungarian liberal Ferencz Deák (1803–1876), who in the Revolution of 1848 had been pushed aside by the radical republicans, offered to work out a compromise to satisfy the autonomous aspirations of the Magyars while safeguarding the unity of the empire. A committee under Deák began to elaborate a draft proposal that eventually led to the establishment of the Dual Monarchy. When in the same year Italy had offered to settle its differences with Austria by purchasing Venetia for a sizable sum, Austria had declined unconditionally. It felt strong enough to hold its own against Italian demands, and at the same time to stand up to Prussia in the Danish duchies and at the federal diet.

In May 1866, the Viennese government found out about the Prusso-Italian alliance. To avoid a two-front war, the emperor offered Italy outright possession of Venetia, provided it would break its alliance with Prussia. But Italy felt bound by its commitment to Berlin, and rejected the offer. Vienna then made overtures to Paris, which on June 12 ended in the conclusion of a secret Austro-French treaty. In return for French neutrality, Austria agreed to cede Venetia to Napoleon, who in turn would present it to Italy. This clause, which was to obviate Italy's entry into the expected war on the side of Prussia, showed again that Austria considered its position in Germany more important than its possessions in Italy. In another clause, Napoleon awarded Austria a free hand to change the German federation, provided France received adequate territorial adjustments. In two separate agreements, Napoleon thus promised neutrality in return for territorial compensations, bestowing French blessing for a reorganization of Germany in one case to Prussia, and in the other to Austria.

Meanwhile, friction between Austria and Prussia increased from week to week in the Danish duchies as well as in the federal diet. Realizing the tenuousness of his hold on Holstein, the emperor gave encouragement to the supporters of Augustenburg. The establishment of an independent state of Schleswig-Holstein within the German confederation seemed the only way to keep the duchies from falling into the hands of Prussia. Bismarck promptly accused Vienna of contravening the Convention of Gastein. He then reintroduced his proposal to reform the federal diet by the addition of a lower house based on universal suffrage. To bring matters to a head, he suggested that Austria be excluded from the confederation, since it opposed establishment of a democratic federal parliament. Austria countered not merely by rejecting Bismarck's plan, but by proposing that the federal diet be empowered to decide the fate of Schleswig and Holstein, a suggestion that clearly violated the Gastein Agreement.

By mid-April 1866, Prussia and Austria both began to mobilize. King William became gradually convinced that Austria would not abide by the Gastein Agreement and could not be trusted. Incidents in the duchies, where Prussian troops had to pass through Austrian-held territory, began to multiply. Sensing the imminence of war, Russia, Britain, and France on May 28 proposed a European congress to settle the fate of the duchies and mediate among Italy, Austria, and Prussia. Turin and Berlin promptly accepted the invitation, but Austria's reply stipulated that none of the three powers should be permitted territorial gains as a result of the conference. Since both Italy and Prussia sought territorial aggrandizement, whereas Austria was on the defensive, such a stipulation was understandable, but the powers interpreted it as unwillingness to negotiate. As a result, no congress was held and Austria remained diplomatically isolated during the ensuing critical months.

A week later, on June 6, Austria provided Bismarck with the desired excuse for action. The Austrian governor of Holstein called a session of the members of the Holstein diet to discuss their own wishes for the future of their duchy. Bismarck notified Vienna that this action nullified the Convention of Gastein, and that henceforth the Treaty of Vienna would again be in force, according to which both duchies were entrusted to the joint administration of Prussia and Austria. Accordingly he dispatched Prussian troops to occupy Holstein. Austria promptly withdrew its own outnumbered troops from Holstein to adjacent Hanover, and asked the diet at Frankfurt to order federal execution against Prussia for having violated the federal territory of Holstein.

A paroxysm of emotion and anti-Prussian feelings ran through the German states at the news of Prussia's occupation of Holstein. Bavaria, Saxony, Hanover, and most other states sided with Austria and voted in favor of war against Prussia to keep it from swallowing the Danish duchies. War was declared on June 14. Only Weimar, Mecklenburg, and a few other small states in northern Germany sided with Prussia. The Prussian envoy promptly left Frankfurt, declaring that Prussia henceforth considered the federal diet dissolved, and hostilities commenced.

THE SEVEN WEEKS' WAR William I felt uncomfortable as a protagonist in a civil war among Germans. He saw the war more as a defensive action than as a possible step toward the unification of Germany. On June 18, he issued an address to the Prussian people, stressing that only recently he had cooperated with Austria "to free a German land from foreign domination." But, he complained, Austria was jealous of the "more youthful Prussia," and had incited the German states against Berlin. "Throughout Germany we are surrounded by enemies," he proclaimed, who falsely thought Prussia "paralyzed by internal discord." Stressing his love of peace and readiness to negotiate, he concluded by warning his enemies of the preparedness of his army, and reminding his subjects that they were fighting for the very existence of Prussia.

The ensuing military operations proved the value of the army reforms undertaken by William, Roon, and Moltke. They also revolutionized concepts of warfare. In less than a week, Prussian armies were fully assembled and on the move. By June 29, two weeks after the outbreak of war, Hanover had capitulated, and the Prussian central armies turned to threaten the states south of the Main. Meanwhile on June 22, three Prussian armies had poured into Bohemia from three different points. One of them had passed through Saxony unhindered. By the judicious use of railroads and the telegraph, Moltke coordinated and directed the movements of his armies from headquarters in Berlin in such a way that they converged with frightening speed and precision on the bulk of the Austrian forces gathered northeast of Prague.

As early as July 1, the Austrian High Command sensed the inevitable catastrophe. After a few minor skirmishes, they urged the emperor to request an armistice. Two days later, the debacle occurred. At the Battle of Sadowa (or Königgrätz) the Austrians were routed, and Bohemia lay open to the Prussian forces. The breech-loading needle gun, which the Prussians lying prone fired at the standing Austrians, had proved its value. And King William, who during the battle had exposed himself to cannon fire, had shown that despite his age he was a "soldier king" of the old type, worthy of the respect of his subjects.

Meanwhile the Italians had honored their commitment and had entered the war on June 20. Four days later they were soundly defeated by the Austrians at the second battle of Custozza, and in the following month, the Italian fleet was beaten by the Austrian navy. Despite their victory, the Austrians were eager to conclude hostilities in the south to have a freer hand against Prussia. On the day of Sadowa, July 3, they kept their secret bargain with France and ceded Venetia to France, to be transferred to Italy. This gesture came, of course, too late, for after Sadowa, Austria was in no position to continue the fight against Prussia, even if it could have rapidly transferred all its troops north of the Alps.

After Sadowa, Prussian armies started to move south through Bohemia toward Austria and Hungary. Napoleon III now offered his mediation. Not anticipating Prussia's lightning warfare, he had not readied his own forces. Yet he wished to prevent the complete collapse of Austria, which would have fundamentally disturbed the balance of power in central Europe. Bismarck and Francis Joseph accepted the offer of French mediation, although Bismarck insisted that his terms be accepted by Austria before conclusion of an armistice. King William and the army, however, favored continuation of the war to achieve the final prostration of Austria.

The king, the royal council, and Bismarck argued fiercely about termination of the war and conditions for peace. William assumed a pseudomoral posture, insisting on the need for punishing Austria for its breach of agreements and demanding sizable territorial cessions. Similarly, he claimed annexations from every German state that had opposed Prussia in the war. The excellence of his military machine and the taste of victory at Sadowa had apparently changed his views about the defensive character of the war.

Bismarck stanchly resisted William, and apparently under threat of resignation, finally carried his view. He opposed continuation of the fighting on military and diplomatic grounds. He pointed out that the defeat of Italy gave Austria renewed resilience north of the Alps, that Hungary was intact and in its present mood would firmly oppose a German invasion. Moreover, cholera and dysentery were sapping the Prussian army, and fighting in the hot Danubian plains might easily lead to a military fiasco. Above all, he suggested that a prolonged war would give France the time needed to prepare its forces and throw its weight into the balance. He was against "wounding Austria too severely," and according to his memoirs, derided William's ideas of "punishing the opponent." In international rivalries, he claimed, both parties are guilty, and it was not Prussia's task to mete out punishment, but to "found German unity." He reasoned that destruction of Austria would result in the rise of numerous Magyar and Slavic states and that such fracturing of southeastern Europe would create permanent instability. The annexation of Bohemia or other Austrian lands would drive Austria into the arms of France or Russia. Primarily he warned against creating "needless bitterness or desire for revenge" among the Austrians or the other German states, so as not to jeopardize future alliances.

Having overcome his sovereign's resistance, Bismarck concluded an armistice with Vienna. The Preliminary Peace of Nikolsburg, signed on July 26, seven weeks after the beginning of the war, contained all decisions ultimately incorporated into the Treaty of Prague signed a month later. Prussia demanded no territory from Austria and only a small monetary indemnity. On the other hand, the old German Confederation was legally declared dissolved and Austria in effect deprived of its position among the German states. Prussia was awarded Schleswig and Holstein and agreed to hold a plebiscite in Schleswig to determine which of the Danish-speaking areas wished to be retroceded to Denmark—a plebiscite held only after Germany's defeat in World War I. Moreover, Prussia was allowed to annex the states of Hanover, Nassau, Electoral Hesse, and Frankfurt, and was given freedom to organize a new federation among the states north of the Main. The southern states, Bavaria, Württemberg and the others, were allowed to retain their independence, and to be free to organize their own southern confederation or to join an alliance with Prussia.

An armistice with the southern states was signed only on August 2. Not certain that Bismarck would persist in his policy of lenient treatment of the vanquished, Bavaria and the others appealed to Napoleon to assist them in obtaining the best possible peace terms from Prussia. But Bismarck held a political trump. On August 5, Napoleon's ambassador to Berlin, Count Vincente Benedetti (1817–1900) presented to Bismarck an official demand for compensations in the Rhineland. This was no longer a secret request presented by private agents of the emperor, but a public demand for the cession of all or parts of the Bavarian Palatinate and the west Rhenish possessions of Hesse-Darmstadt, including the city of Mainz. Bismarck rejected the request on the pretext that it was distasteful to German nationalism, and sent copies of the French demand to the southern states, at the same time offering them peace terms of extreme leniency. Except for minor border rectifications, he stipulated no territorial cessions and only an insignificant war indemnity. Perturbed by the revival of Napoleonic designs on the Rhineland and impressed by Bismarck's apparent selflessness, the southern states not only signed the offered peace treaties but also entered into secret defensive and offensive alliances with Prussia, whereby they agreed to place their armies under Prussian command in case of war with France.

REPERCUSSIONS OF THE WAR IN AUSTRIA AND PRUSSIA Austria's lightning defeat sealed its exclusion from Italy and Germany, and the battle of Sadowa sounded the death knell for hopes for a *Grossdeutschland,* until they were revived by Hitler under vastly different auspices. Despite its defeat, Austria remained a foremost European power, but its eyes were thenceforth cast down the Danube Valley, and its center of gravity was shifting from Vienna toward Budapest.

The war gave greater urgency to the task of achieving a compromise with the Hungarians. The plans of Deák's committee were more or less completed, but a major decision was still to be made: whether to adopt a federal or a dual system. The former Saxon prime minister, Count Friedrich von Beust (1809–1886), who was now the chief minister in Vienna, was a stanch champion of German superiority. A federation in which all nationalities shared equal power would have submerged the German-speaking minority. Hence Beust favored a dual system, in which the Magyars and Germans together would hold the reins over the remaining nationalities. Together with the Hungarian statesman Count Gyula Andrássy (1823–1890), Beust and Deák finally agreed on terms for the "Compromise" enacted in 1867, creating the Dual Monarchy of Austria-Hungary under the personal rule of Emperor Francis Joseph. Only foreign and military affairs and over-all finances were to be regulated by joint Austro-Hungarian ministries. In other matters, each state was governed by its own parliament, and controlled its own subject populations. Yearly meetings of sixty delegates from each parliament were to be organized for the discussion of joint problems. The new constitutional framework afforded relative stability to the Austro-Hungarian monarchy, but the increased power of the Hungarians made it impossible for the emperor to resume any significant role in German affairs.

The defeat of Austria and the resulting aggrandizement of Prussia also had profound repercussions within Prussia. As a liberal from the Rhineland noted, countless thousands "acclaimed the god of the moment, success!" The king and his army, the conservative Junkers, and, above all, Bismarck, with his authoritarian methods, stood vindicated. The unconstitutional acts of the government had led to a glorious victory. The question arose whether liberals thenceforth could conscientiously claim that the people's representatives deserved a voice in the affairs of government.

A realignment of political thought and allegiances became immediately evident. Elections to the Prussian lower house produced a conservative majority for the first time in seven years. The country was in a mood of compromise and forgiveness. Only certain Catholics, Socialists, and die-hard Progressives stood steadfast in their opposition to Bismarck and refused, as Wilhelm Liebknecht (1826–1900) put it, to let his halo of fame wash away the stain of his violation of the constitution. King William was ready for conciliation, and admitted that the tax collections of the preceding years had been illegal. Even Bismarck agreed to make the gesture of a concession. He submitted to the diet a Bill of Indemnity that retroactively sanctioned the budgets of 1862 and subsequent years and legalized the illegal collection of taxes. The bill also stipulated the total allowable expenditures for the current year, for which the government promised to submit a budget in 1867. This bill was accepted by a 3 to 1 majority in September of 1866. Subsequently the diet gave Bismarck a resounding vote of confidence, and requested the king to reward the successful minister. William made him Count von Bismarck.

True liberals looked upon the Bill of Indemnity as a dark omen for the future. To be sure, by even requesting such a bill, the government seemed to confirm the right of the diet to vote on the budget. But by retroactively legalizing the government's unconstitutional acts, the diet had undermined its position. In the future, the crown could always point to the precedent of the 1860s when the diet *ex post facto* conceded its shortsightedness and accorded apparent infallibility to the executive. Many liberals considered it a worse defeat than the one in 1848, since in 1866 the people had not succumbed to military suppression but had been dazzled by military glory.

The Bill of Indemnity caused a significant split in the Progressive party. The old-style Progressives stuck to their constitutional principles and voted against it. The majority, however, veered to the right and joined the members of the *Nationalverein* to found the National Liberal party. This group voted for the bill. Their liberalism was directed more toward economic aims and the maintenance of free trade than toward doctrinaire constitutionalism. The National Liberals found adherents in other North German states that Prussia was about to annex or incorporate into the North German Confederation. Their commercial interests made them particularly faithful supporters of Bismarck's attempt to unify Germany. The National Liberals thus became one of the first parties to extend its program and membership beyond the confines of Prussia.

At the same time, the Conservatives split over Bismarck's reorganization of northern Germany. The old-style Conservatives mistrusted Bismarck's National Liberal supporters and his proposals for unifying northern Germany on the basis of universal suffrage. They began to suspect that Bismarck had abandoned his Junker principles and saw no reason for the Bill of Indemnity. They thought that after the victory on the battlefield, the army should have destroyed the diet. Instead, the crown had lowered itself by asking forgiveness from the representatives of the people. Moreover, the Conservatives objected to the deposition of the princely dynasties in the annexed territories as a violation of the monarchical principle. Certain Conservatives, however, abandoned their party and sided with Bismarck. Coming more from industrial and financial than agricultural circles, these upper-middle-class representatives, who ultimately formed the Free Conservative party, applauded Bismarck's success in the effort to unify Germany. This group, like the National Liberals, quickly found adherents outside the confines of Prussia.

It is perhaps ironic that the year that witnessed the surrender of liberalism also became the year in which Prussian and Germany party life sprang into full bloom. Within a few years, these parties, with their numerous splinters, became a formidable echo of German public opinion, although under Bismarck's system they were never to enjoy political power. It is also interesting that the pragmatic Bismarck thenceforth found support among those groups, whether liberal or conservative, that adopted an equally pragmatic attitude. The doctrinaires—liberal, socialist, conservative, or Catholic—remained in the powerless opposition.

THE NORTH GERMAN CONFEDERATION

By the Treaty of Prague, Prussia was allowed to annex Hanover, Nassau, Electoral Hesse, and the city of Frankfurt, and had the option of reorganizing the states north of the Main into a new federation. When the Prussian lower chamber protested against the annexations, Bismarck replied: "Our right is the right of the German nation to exist, to breathe, to unite." But actually these annexations were undertaken not to unite Germany, but to unite Prussia. The work begun by Frederick William, the Great Elector, in the seventeenth century was finally consummated by Bismarck. Until then, no continuous link had existed between Prussia's possessions in the Rhineland and those in north-central Germany. Absorption of Hanover and Electoral Hesse made Prussian lands contiguous from Königsberg to the French border. Annexation of Frankfurt can perhaps be explained on ideological grounds, since it was the former symbolic capital of Germany. The fate of Nassau appears less subject to justification. According to Bismarck, its dukes were dangerously devoted to the Hapsburgs; moreover, King William harbored a traditional Hohenzollern dislike for its dynasty.

Yet Bismarck was firmly opposed to Prussian absorption of all the northern states. The resulting accretion in Prussia's power would have antagonized too many Germans and alarmed the foreign powers. A federal system, however, was more likely to assuage the powers, and would also make it easy for the southern states eventually to join the north without abandoning their independence. Federalism would also respect the rights and privileges of the various ruling houses, and the upper chamber representing the state governments would act as a welcome conservative influence.

The North German Confederation was essentially Bismarck's own creation, tailored to suit his purposes. In August 1866, Prussia concluded treaties with the twenty-one remaining states north of the Main, guaranteeing the territorial integrity of all parties and stipulating their agreement to enter into a common federation. Meanwhile the armies of all states were placed under the control of the Prussian crown. Plenipotentiaries from all states were called to Berlin to discuss Bismarck's constitutional draft, which was later submitted to a popularly elected constituent assembly. The Prussian minister was evidently in a conciliatory mood. His democratic respect for the rights of the small states and the demands of public opinion astonished his contemporaries. On certain points, he even permitted the assembly to modify his draft—substituting the secret ballot for his proposed open vote. In essentials, of course, the North German Constitution as finally promulgated in July 1867 contained all Bismarck's requirements (see Map 19).

The king of Prussia was made the hereditary president of the confederation and its permanent chief executive. He was given full control over foreign and military affairs, supervision over the federal civil service, and power to declare war and peace. As commander in chief, he controlled all federal forces. Prussian military law, uniforms, organization, and recruitment were extended to the confederate armies so that the confederate forces were in fact an extension of the Prussian army. No similar arrangement was made for the navy, since Prussia as yet had no navy to speak of. A new federal naval ministry was therefore created.

The rulers were permitted to retain a semblance of sovereignty. With their own diets, they could dispose of local affairs and collect provincial taxes. Recognizing the vanity of the petty princes, Bismarck even allowed them to maintain their own representation abroad, a meaningless gesture since all

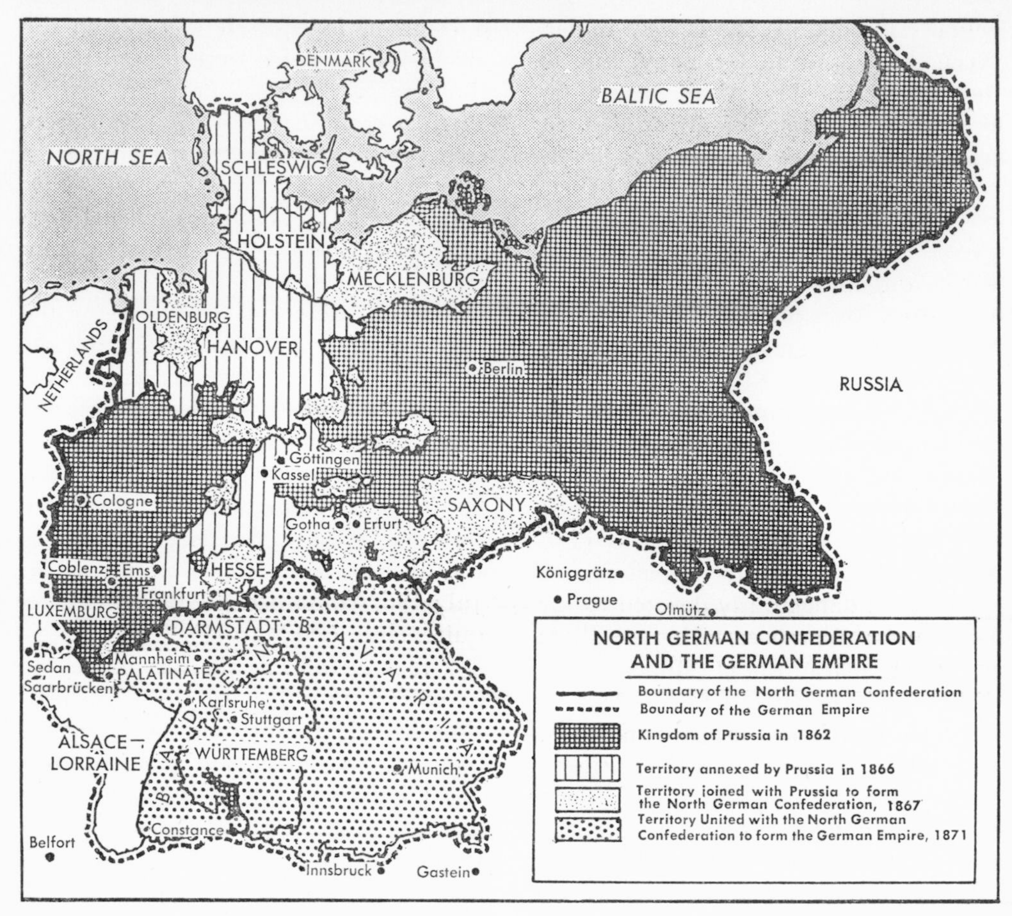

MAP 19

foreign affairs were handled from Berlin. Yet some of the princes—the king of Saxony was one—actually continued to send ambassadors to the major courts of Europe.

The legislature of the confederation comprised two houses. The upper house or *Bundesrat* consisted of delegates who represented the state governments and hence resembled the former federal diet, except for its increased powers over federal legislation. The delegates voted en bloc, as instructed by their governments, casting a total of 43 votes, of which 17 were assigned to Prussia. Since 14 votes sufficed to veto any constitutional amendments, Prussia could prevent any change in the constitution. The lower house or *Reichstag* was elected on the basis of universal male suffrage from the entire territory of the confederation. It shared in the legislative process with the upper house, but the Bundesrat possessed more legislative power than the Reichstag.

All essential power rested in the executive—the king of Prussia and his federal chancellor. Bismarck was immediately appointed to this all-important post, while at the same time, as minister-president of Prussia and first minister of the King of Prussia, he became the presiding officer of the Bundesrat. Since Bismarck also acted as foreign minister and ran various governmental departments in Prussia, he now held so many posts that to keep his files straight he sometimes corresponded with himself in his various capacities. In true Bismarckian spirit, he refused to establish parliamentary responsibility. To make the federal government responsible to the Reichstag would undermine the authority of the states and give power to political parties and popular representatives, whom Bismarck at heart despised. He thought it essential that the states—primarily, of course, the Prussian state—retain their supremacy. Consequently, his constitution made the federal government responsible only to the chief executive, the king of Prussia. Since Bismarck always preferred to work alone and bully others, he did not permit the organization of a ministerial cabinet. Cooperation with colleagues of more or less equal rank was to him an impossibility. He insisted that governmental "responsibility existed only when there is a single man who can be held accountable for any mistakes."

The North German Constitution, which with some modifications later became the constitution of the German Empire, was a skillful mixture of constitutionalism and authoritarianism. It functioned with amazing smoothness under Bismarck's direction, but after his dismissal, it became quickly evident how very personal a creation it was. The historian Heinrich von Sybel, a member of the constituent assembly in 1867, lauded the constitution as a product of pragmatic analysis of political conditions rather than the issue of academic imagination, as had been true of the Frankfurt constitution of 1849. He thought that the three main "political facts" of 1867 were well represented in the framework. The presidency embodied the power, prestige, and military might of Prussia. The Bundesrat represented the "vitality" of the smaller states and their princes, supported by "historic tradition and local sentiment," and the Reichstag embodied public opinion. Since Sybel was a supporter of Bismarck's he failed to add to this astute analysis that public opinion was given only a sounding board in the Reichstag, and was left without true political power.

THE FINAL ROAD TO UNIFICATION

The annexations of 1866 and the creation of the North German Confederation made Prussia the undisputed master of northern Germany. The process of unification had begun. It remained to be seen whether it could be completed without another war.

The Question of War

According to most evidence, Bismarck apparently convinced himself that a war against France would rekindle the patriotic all-German fervor of 1813 needed to draw the south German states into a unified Germany. "A common national war against our aggressive neighbor," he wrote in his memoirs "would serve better than anything else to bridge the historical gulf which dynastic and ethnic feelings and modes of life had created between the south and the north of our fatherland." Once unification had been achieved, he remarked, "our feeling of nationality . . . was conserved and strengthened mainly through war. . . . It is regrettable that it could not have been done peacefully—but it is grounded the more firmly for all that." But Bismarck did not concede that such a war was the *sine qua non* of unification.

Unquestionably there were many obstacles to bringing the southern states into a union with Prussia. Most southern Germans distrusted the militarism and authoritarianism of the Prussian government and harbored a residual, rather sentimental love for the Austrian Hapsburgs. Many Prussians, for their part, remained suspicious of southern ultramontanism. Moreover, the traditional particularistic jealousies among the southern states themselves were still alive. It is characteristic that the Baden envoy, when negotiating the peace treaty with Prussia in 1866, suggested that since Bavaria's size might be a hindrance to a closer bond among the German states, it should be reduced in size—the Rhenish Palatinate transferred to Baden and northern border strips ceded to Prussia. Bismarck reports a similar enlightening incident. When hearing rumors of Hesse being compensated for territorial losses north of the Main by the addition of sections of northwestern Bavaria, the populations of the affected areas voiced complaints. As Catholics, they objected to being transferred to Protestant Hesse, and as subjects of a king, they resented becoming citizens of a mere duchy.

But these problems were not insurmountable. Hanoverians felt an equally deep-seated antagonism toward Prussians, and after its annexation by Prussia in 1866, Hanover was a center of friction. Yet this animosity was gradually overcome and, as Bismarck had to admit, even Hanoverians became loyal Germans. The federal ties of the North German Confederation were loose enough so that the southern states could have been persuaded to enter in 1866. But Bismarck's excessive caution at the time made him forfeit the opportunity, and later, when France was better prepared for war, it was too late.

Perhaps because Bismarck was a Junker, he tended to overlook the fact that industry, science, engineering, banking, and trade were unifying the German states at an ever-increasing pace, just as the Common Market in our day is drawing the western European countries together, irrespective of the lag in common political institutions. In the 1860s, banks and joint-stock companies, chemical and electrical industries, and, above all, coal and steel consortia were spreading over the German lands, regardless of state boundaries. Almost all regional tolls were abolished on river transport to allow faster and cheaper shipping. Roads, railroads, telegraph, and improved postal services, conventions on monetary units and credit arrangements—all helped to draw the states together. As Lord Keynes later remarked, "The German Empire was built more truly on coal and iron than on blood and iron."

Prussia's Zollverein was also expanding in the 1860s. Until 1863, Austria had made repeated, though unsuccessful attempts to break up the customs union. But the tariff arrangements were so favorable for the various states that during the Austro-Prussian War tariffs throughout Germany were collected as usual, the funds transmitted to Berlin, and from there distributed to the member states of the Zollverein —even though the outbreak of hostilities had legally invalidated the treaties, and the German states were at war with Prussia.

The creation of the North German Confederation also brought about changes in the Zollverein. The old tariff congress, in which each member state had a veto, was transformed into a bicameral customs parliament. In the upper house, the states were represented, and questions were decided by majority vote. The lower house, inaugurated in 1868, was based on popular elections throughout Germany. This parliament, with its representation from the southern states, debated common economic and political problems. Although it accomplished little in its first two years, it was another medium for closer cooperation.

But the German states did not exist in a vacuum. Unification in 1866 would have been feasible, since France had anticipated a long Austro-Prussian war and an Austrian victory, and was ill prepared for intervention. Once this opportunity for unification had been missed, the attitude of France became of vital importance. Repeatedly in the period 1866 to 1870, Bismarck expressed his conviction that France would seek to gain by force those compensations out of which it had been cheated by the lightning victory of Sadowa. Moreover, he fully realized that Napoleon needed to restore his prestige, and might choose to find the opportunity in a Franco-Prussian war. Time and again Bismarck predicted a war with France, while stressing his own love of peace. "I shall never consent to a war that is avoidable, much less seek it. But this war with France will surely come. It will be clearly forced upon us by the French Emperor."

One may, of course, contend that if Bismarck wanted such a war in order to unify Germany, he merely used clever tactics by repeatedly predicting it and pushing the blame in advance, onto Napoleon. But there is sufficient evidence that large segments of the French ruling classes desired such a war as much as Bismarck did. Internal political problems of the imperial regime, the traditional fear of a strong Germany, and perplexity over the lightning victory of Sadowa, among other reasons, made the French government yearn for a spectacular diplomatic, if not a military, victory. Napoleon's championing of the rights of nationalities had made him sympathetic in principle to German aspirations for unity. But the French fiasco in Mexico, caused largely by Mexican nationalism, and his ambivalent involvement in the Italian unification movement—in which he favored Italian nationalism but felt compelled to give the pope in Rome military protection against the Italian nationalists—had cooled the emperor's idealistic ardor. "If Bismarck draws the southern German states into the North German Confederation," he remarked in 1868, "our guns will go off by themselves."

The Approaching Conflict with France

During the years 1866–1870, Napoleon fostered many diplomatic intrigues for territorial compensations. Each French step was parried by Bismarck, eager to seize every opportunity to coalesce German public opinion against France. From these critical years, Napoleon emerges as bungling and impatient,

Bismarck as a resourceful superb improviser. But again the exaggeration of the popular picture of Bismarck pulling all the strings to set up the Franco-Prussian War in Prussia's favor should be noted. In fact, the initiative for the most part lay with the French, but Bismarck's countermeasures usually were effective in stimulating German nationalism and in improving the chances for unification.

After the rejection of his demand for territorial cessions in the Rhineland in early August 1866, Napoleon looked elsewhere for compensations. In late August, the French Ambassador Benedetti discussed with Bismarck the possibility that France might seize Belgium and Luxemburg, in return for allowing the unification of all of Germany. The French later insisted that the proposal originated with Bismarck. Actually the suggestion evolved from Napoleon's desire to shift French eyes away from Mexico, where he was about to abandon Maximilian, and Bismarck seized the occasion for his own purpose. He urged Benedetti to submit the scheme in writing—thereby acquiring a useful document that, at the needed moment, could be shown to prove French expansionism.

During the winter of 1866–1867, while French troops were being withdrawn from Mexico, France negotiated with the king of Holland, the sovereign of Luxemburg, for the cession of this strategic district. Luxemburg had been an official part of the old German Confederation and was still occupied by Prussian troops. After the demise of the old German Confederation in 1866, Luxemburg's legal status lacked clarity, and the French asserted that Prussia had lost the right to man its fortresses. In private conversations with the French ambassador, Bismarck pretended to concede that France should be allowed to acquire the duchy, but he cautioned that German public opinion might oppose the loss of territory that had belonged to the German Empire for a thousand years.

By the spring of 1867, the king of Holland had given his agreement to the intended transfer. Napoleon seemed on the verge of obtaining at least a part of his desired compensation. But in April, Bismarck was interpellated on the matter in the Reichstag of the North German Confederation. There is good reason to believe that Bismarck had arranged the questioning himself to bring the matter to public attention, while he assumed the role of mediator between German national feelings and French demands. The German press immediately echoed with anti-French proclamations, while demands were voiced in Paris for the forceful ouster of Prussian troops from Luxemburg. The frightened king of Holland withdrew his assent to the transfer of his duchy.

A Franco-Prussian war appeared imminent. It was avoided because neither side felt prepared for it. Strikes and political unrest were debilitating the French state; the army was not effectively prepared; and the emperor was loathe to spoil the impending grand opening of the International Exposition at Paris, through which he hoped to bolster his prestige and repair his reputation as a man of peace. Nor was Prussia ready for a general war. Even the General Staff was not certain that the army was prepared to engage the French forces, which still enjoyed a formidable reputation. King William feared risking the recent gains, and, contrary to legend, even Bismarck was not yet convinced that a war with France was the only path to unification. Consequently the chancellor pursued an ambivalent course. To frighten Napoleon, he published the secret defensive and offensive alliances Prussia had concluded with the southern states in the previous year, while at the same time he cautioned the Reichstag "to take into account the understandable apprehensions of France." He believed the crisis would enhance German national feeling, and hoped a display of German unity might make Napoleon acquiesce in German unification.

In the end, both Paris and Berlin felt relieved when the matter was taken out of their hands by the European powers, which, at the urging of Russia, called an international conference to deal with the problem of Luxemburg. The London Conference (May 1867), attended by France, Prussia, Austria, Russia, England, and Holland, produced a compromise embodying a setback for Prussia and a rebuff for France. Luxemburg was officially separated from the defunct German Confederation and declared a sovereign grand duchy, united in family bonds to the dynasty of Holland. All Prussian troops were to be evacuated, Luxemburg's fortresses were to be dismantled, and her perpetual neutrality was to be guaranteed by the signatory powers.

Conclusion of the Luxemburg crisis dispelled the overt clouds of war. In the following month, the Prussian royal couple, accompanied by Bismarck and Moltke, attended the Paris International Exhibition and were warmly entertained by Napoleon. These signs of Franco-Prussian friendship, however, could not conceal the fact that the outcome of the Luxemburg crisis had fundamentally altered Napoleon's views on Germany. He blamed Prussia for foiling his designs on Luxemburg, and concluded that war with Prussia might, after all, be inevitable. Hence he decided to strengthen his military resources, and cast about for allies.

A law of January 1868 provided for a sizable increase in the French army. At the same time new weapons were introduced to bring the forces up to Prussian standards of modernization. Above all, the French General Staff pinned much hope on the development of its secret weapon, a machine gun based on a Belgian invention and considerably more powerful than the American Gatling gun invented in the early 1860s.

Finding allies proved difficult for Napoleon. In August 1867, he visited Francis Joseph in Salzburg, and a few months later, the Austrian emperor went to Paris. Discussions of a possible alliance continued for two years, and produced a tentative draft treaty in 1869. But no firm anti-Prussian alliance was ever concluded, although Napoleon continued to delude himself that Austria would aid him in a war against Prussia. The Austrian minister Beust, a bitter enemy of Bismarck's, actually favored such a pact, but the Hungarian Andrássy saw no reason to help Vienna regain influence in Germany. Since Budapest carried much weight in the newly created Dual Monarchy, Austria in the end maintained neutrality.

Napoleon was equally unsuccessful in gaining an alliance with Italy, whose aid in a war with Prussia would actually have been of little benefit to the French. In 1867, when Napoleon had felt obliged to dispatch another expeditionary force to Rome to protect the pope from attacks by Italian nationalists, he had revived Italian animosity against France. As long as French troops occupied Rome, no firm alliance between Italy and France was conceivable. Thus France found itself alone in the crucial year 1870.

Bismarck had also learned from the Luxemburg crisis. The rallying of an all-German national enthusiasm after the civil war of 1866 seemed the only positive result. Besides entailing the loss of Luxemburg, the maneuver had merely antagonized France to the point that war with France seemed to be likely as soon as the French felt ready. Although King William was stanchly opposed to such a war, Roon and Moltke speeded plans for the training of the enlarged army of the North German Confederation and for a joint offensive with the armies of the southern German states. By 1870, the Prussian General Staff felt ready, and hoped for a speedy outbreak of the war before the French would catch up with their own training and equipment.

The Hohenzollern Candidacy and the Outbreak of War

In September 1868, a liberal revolution in Spain had overthrown the corrupt regime of Queen Isabella II and resulted in her flight and deposition. Throughout 1869, the Spanish provisional government had searched for a new ruler among the dynasties of Europe. The Spanish crown had been offered to Italian, Portuguese, and German princes, all of whom had declined. By the spring of 1870, only Prince Leopold of Hohenzollern-Sigmaringen (1835–1905) was still under serious consideration, having neither accepted nor rejected the proffered crown. Prince Leopold was the son of Charles Anthony of Hohenzollern-Sigmaringen, who had been prime minister of Prussia under Frederick William IV. As a Catholic and a brother-in-law of the king of Portugal, he seemed well suited to lead the Spanish nation. He was a distant relative of both King William of Prussia and Emperor Napoleon of France. Moreover, in 1866, both France and Prussia had secretly helped his brother Charles assume the newly created throne of Rumania as Carol I. It appeared, therefore, that Leopold might be equally acceptable to Spain, France, and Prussia.

Leopold's candidacy, however, became the immediate cause of the outbreak of the Franco-Prussian War. The French government objected vehemently to the elevation of a Hohenzollern prince to the throne of Spain. It feared such action would revive the empire of Charles V and imperil the honor of France as well as the equilibrium of Europe. Napoleon felt that Prussia had gained enough power in 1866 and should not extend its influence over the Iberian peninsula. The French did not look upon Leopold of Hohenzollern-Sigmaringen as just any German prince. His father, Charles Anthony, was a friend of Bismarck's, and had shown his subservience to Prussian interests by voluntarily ceding the Sigmaringen lands to Prussia. Moreover, the war party in Paris, encouraged by certain cabinet officers and Empress Eugenia, sensed in the issue an opportunity for restoring Napoleon's prestige by humbling Prussia diplomatically or militarily.

Contrary to the impression left by Bismarck in his memoirs, which discretely omit all references to his own activities during the spring of 1870, the Prussian chancellor was involved in the question of the candidacy from the very beginning. Officially Bismarck considered the matter as a family affair of the Hohenzollerns. Whether Leopold accepted the throne or not, he claimed, was no concern of the Prussian government. Behind the scenes, however, he worked assiduously to promote Leopold's cause. By 1870 the prospect of war was no longer unwelcome to him, since the Prussian General Staff had assured him of the readiness of the army. But to assert that his sole aim was to goad France into declaring war on Germany so that the Germans could unite in defense of their fatherland is another oversimplification of the Bismarck legend. The chancellor saw other advantages in the Spanish candidacy besides a possible war. A Hohenzollern in Madrid, even though he might not remain completely subservient to Prussian interests, could always exert pressure on France when Prussian diplomacy required it. A friendly Spain would also open new markets to Prussia. Finally, the issue seemed such that even without war Napoleon was bound to lose further prestige, provided Bismarck could arrange it that the Prussian government did not seem directly involved. It was important that the members of the Spanish Cortes should elect their own ruler. If Napoleon then forced the Spaniards to rescind the election, European opinion would accuse him of gross interference in Spanish internal affairs and France would add to its isolation resulting from the Mexican fiasco. Or if the Spaniards refused his demands, Napoleon's prestige would be further dimmed and he might even be toppled from power.

Hence Bismarck negotiated secretly with envoys from Spain and with representatives of the Hohenzollern family. Leopold showed little eagerness to accept the crown, but declared himself ready to obey his father's command. Charles Anthony, in turn, placed his son at the disposal of King William. But it was difficult for Bismarck to persuade William to approve the candidacy. The Prussian king feared a war with France and saw little value in the venturesome scheme. Negotiations within the Hohenzollern family council, which Bismarck secretly attended, dragged on throughout the spring. The chancellor sent agents to Madrid to ascertain the mood of the Cortes. For his plans it was important that the Spaniards elect Prince Leopold with a resounding vote, so that there could be no accusation that Prussia had imposed its candidate on the Spanish people. When assured of the cooperation of the Cortes, William finally acquiesced, and on June 19, Leopold privately communicated his acceptance to the Spanish envoys. It had been agreed that Leopold's acceptance was to be kept secret until the Cortes had officially elected him, so that Napoleon would be confronted with a *fait accompli.* To give further credence to the fiction that the affair had been wholly a family matter, the members of the Prussian government dispersed to their respective summer resorts. The king went to Ems, Bismarck retired to his estate, and even Roon and Moltke left the capital.

But the Spaniards bungled the arrangements. The Cortes disbanded before electing Prince Leopold. Instead, on July 2, Madrid simply announced that he had accepted the crown. The French now had proof of what they had suspected for some time. The Parisian press immediately clamored for war against Prussia. Violently anti-Prussian speeches were launched in the French assembly, and the duke of Gramont, Napoleon's foreign minister, warned that unless Leopold's candidacy were forthwith withdrawn, "Frenchmen would know how to do their duty without hesitation and without weakness." Gramont then instructed Ambassador Benedetti to demand immediate satisfaction from the Prussian king.

On July 9 and again two days later, Benedetti spoke to King William at Bad Ems. In essence, he demanded that the Prussian ruler order Prince Leopold to renounce the Spanish crown. The interviews were friendly. William was concerned about the prospect of war and disturbed by the bellicose mood of Paris, but he felt his royal honor would suffer if he accepted the French order. Hence, he officially rejected it, while secretly urging Prince Leopold to withdraw his name for the sake of peace.

On July 12, Charles Anthony of Hohenzollern-Sigmaringen officially announced his son's withdrawal from the Spanish candidacy. Those who had feared war were delighted by the announcement. The friction between France and the Hohenzollerns appeared dissolved without loss of prestige to either party. But those who wanted war felt frustrated. When hearing of Leopold's renunciation, Bismarck felt dumfounded. He even considered resigning, fearing that Germany had been humiliated and his own plans undermined. In his memoirs he noted:

> I felt very dejected, for short of picking an artificial excuse for a quarrel, I saw no means of repairing the corrosive damage which a timorous attitude was about to inflict on our national position. In those days I already looked upon the war as a necessity, realizing it could no longer be avoided without loss of honor.

The war party in Paris felt equally disturbed. The Hohenzollern candidacy had been thwarted, but in such a way that France could not honestly claim a diplomatic victory. Furthermore, there was the possibility that Prince Leopold might again change his mind, since as a private citizen he was not bound by any official government promises. The duke of Gramont decided to push for a diplomatic triumph over Prussia, even at the risk of war. He telegraphed Ambassador Benedetti to demand a third audience with King William and extract from him a written promise that no Hohenzollern would ever again be a candidate for the Spanish throne. On July 13, the French ambassador complied with this crucial demand of his government. Rather than wait for an official audience in the afternoon, Benedetti approached the king during his morning promenade at Ems. This informal violation of traditional protocol in itself led to misinterpretations. William naturally refused the requested guarantees and promises. Quite possibly Benedetti's somewhat emotional importuning embarrassed and irritated William, who had never felt comfortable with Bismarck's intrigues and longed for an end to the disagreeable cabal of the candidacy. Despite the tension, however, the interview was cordial. When during the same afternoon, Leopold's official renunciation of the candidacy reached Ems, William sent Benedetti a copy of the statement, with a note that the matter now seemed closed and that he saw no need for Benedetti to come to the afternoon audience. When the king left Ems that evening by train, Benedetti was at the station to pay his respects, and William extended to him the customary compliments. It is clear, therefore, that the events at Ems, although personally disagreeable to William, represented no affront to either France or Prussia.

Yet they were turned into a *casus belli* by Bismarck's now famous version of the Ems Telegram. Before leaving Ems, the king had authorized a dispatch to Bismarck, who had returned to Berlin, informing him of the events of the day, with permission at his discretion to relay this information to the press and to Prussian embassies abroad. With the tacit approval of Moltke and Roon, who assured him that the army was ready for immediate action and that a "speedy outbreak of war was more favorable than delay," Bismarck edited the dispatch from Ems before sending it to the press and the foreign office. By deletions and change of tone, Bismarck's version of the Ems dispatch implied that the Prussian king had been insulted by the French ambassador, who in turn had been rebuffed by the king. Bismarck was confident that his telegram would "act like a red cloth in front of the Gallic bull" and that he had found a way to safeguard German honor. Moltke is said to have called it "a clarion-call to arms."

The telegram appeared in the press and on embassy bulletins on the following day, and produced the desired effect on both sides of the Rhine. Parisians clamored for revenge against Prussia for the insult to their ambassador. Mobs shouting "To Berlin!" roamed the streets of Paris, and, despite warnings by the opposition, the French cabinet demanded war credits and mobilization. In Berlin and even outside Prussia, crowds gave vent to their hatred of France by singing "The Watch on the Rhine" and demanding satisfaction for the insult to King William. Only William himself, who knew what really happened at Ems, still opposed war when he arrived at Berlin on July 15. On the same day, however, news arrived that France had declared general mobilization. The war fever in Paris had triumphed. William promptly authorized Bismarck to proceed with Prussia's own mobilization. Four days later, on July 19, France issued a declaration of war. The magic telegram had worked its miracle: Bismarck had his war with France at a time of his own choosing and in a manner that made France look like the aggressor.

The Franco-Prussian War

Napoleon III had hoped that Austria, and possibly Italy, would side with France, and that the South German states would retain a benevolent neutrality despite their treaties with Berlin. The strategic plans of the French High Command had envisioned assembling forces in southern Germany for a push into Central Prussia by way of Saxony, where they could receive the assistance of Austrian armies from Bohemia. Such hopes proved to be vain. Austria, Italy, England, and Russia maintained strict neutrality, and the south German states honored their treaty obligations and mobilized alongside Prussia.

Württemberg, Baden, and Hesse immediately placed their troops at Prussia's disposal. Among Bavarians there was a brief hesitation between their dislike for Prussia and their hatred of the "French aggressor" before they, too, decided "to show their German heart" and join the war against Napoleon. For the first time since 1814, the German states were united in a common effort. As had occurred during the Wars of Liberation, enthusiasm for the war was fanned by poets, journalists, and pamphleteers. Gruesome tales of French behavior in the first military skirmishes made the Germans self-righteous in their anti-French pronouncements. "May God punish the sinful French and destroy the new Babylon," became a war slogan.

The military campaigns once again proved the efficiency of Prussia's preparations. Within ten days the North German army was raised from 300,000 to 900,000 men; even the forces of the southern states assembled speedily. Skillful use of railroads allowed massing the bulk of the German forces in the Palatinate and completion of total mobilization within eighteen days. Thus France was invaded in early August, before the French army had completed its own preparations. During August, three German armies maneuvered in Alsace and Lorraine, encountering the French in numerous minor engagements. To gain time, they bypassed or invested fortresses instead of stopping to capture them. Moltke's primary goal was to envelop the main part of the French army before attempting to push inland toward Paris. Losses on both sides were heavy, but the French had to give ground almost continually. Emperor Napoleon, in the field and pretending to command the armies, proved no match for the skillful Moltke.

By the end of August, most of the land east of the Meuse River had fallen to the Germans, except for several important fortified towns, such as Metz and Strassburg, in which strong French garrisons had been encircled by the invader. The discouraging news from the front toppled the cabinet that had helped push France into the war. Empress Eugenia, acting as regent, was barely able to retain control of the government.

Disaster struck the French on September 1. A sizable French army, with Napoleon himself in its midst, was encircled by superior German forces at Sedan, near the Belgian frontier. Massive German artillery fire foiled all French attempts to break out of the encirclement. With 13,000 men killed and 30,000 captured, the pathetic emperor, who had always dreaded the carnage of battle, decided to surrender. "Not having been able to die in the midst of my troops," he wrote to King William, "it only remains for me to surrender my sword to the hands of your Majesty." The capitulation of Sedan was negotiated, and on September 2, Napoleon, together with some 40 generals and 83,000 men, accepted imprisonment by the Germans. The confrontation between the shattered emperor of the French and the robust and gleeful Bismarck, who had donned a Prussian uniform for the occasion, has frequently been depicted in print and on canvas. Emotionally, it was a memorable event, but politically it lacked significance, for Napoleon no longer spoke for France. The following day, the emperor departed for his residential prison, the castle of Wilhelmshöhe near Kassel.

The victory of Sedan opened northern France to the invaders, although the fortresses of Metz and Strassburg continued to resist capture and held down sizable units of the German army. Nonetheless, a German army reached the outskirts of Paris on September 19 and began investing the city.

Meanwhile the news of Napoleon's surrender had caused a revolution in Paris. On September 4, Parisian mobs had forced the empress to flee, had proclaimed a republic, and had installed a provisional government pledged to repel the invader and "not abandon a foot of French soil." Mindful of the prodigious success of the French republican armies in 1792, the French liberals vowed that the unleashed forces of the Third Republic would sweep the aggressor from the land. They expected that the German forces would be pinned down in the sieges of Strassburg, Metz, and Paris while new French armies were being raised in the provinces.

The overthrow of Napoleon and establishment of a republic intensified the question whether the Germans were fighting against Napoleon or against the French people, and whether their aim was to unify Germany or to conquer territory. The historian Heinrich von Treitschke proclaimed in an article entitled "What we demand from France": "The nation [France] is our enemy, not this Bonaparte, who rather obeyed than led it." A desire for belated revenge against injustices suffered by earlier generations fanned the emotions of many Germans. When asked, "Against whom is Germany fighting now that Napoleon III, who declared the war, is vanquished and imprisoned?" the historian Ranke tersely replied: "Against Louis XIV!" Not all sounded as vindictive as the composer Richard Wagner, who urged Bismarck to obliterate Paris from the earth. But to justify their nationalistic and expansionist desires, many Germans assumed a moralistic tone that sounded arrogant and insincere in an age of *Realpolitik.* Treitschke wrote of the "idealistic and moral forces [of the Germans] which can only be released through a just war." He intoned against "the sins of France," and insisted that "the sense of justice to Germany demands the lessening of France." He pointed to Alsace and Lorraine, which he called "the beautiful homelands of the German stock where the old *Reich* once suffered its deepest humiliation," and insisted that "these territories are ours by the right of the sword, and [that] we shall dispose of them in virtue of a higher right—the right of the German nation." Questions of self-determination did not perturb the Prussian historian. "We Germans," he wrote, "know better than these unfortunate ones what is good for the people of Alsace."

For strategic reasons, the Prussian generals demanded cession of all of Alsace and Lorraine, including the fortresses and fortified towns west of the Vosges mountains, so that German outposts would henceforth stand at the edge of the plains of northern France. Bismarck himself showed similar arrogance toward the French, though his demands were more moderate. During the Sedan negotiations, he complained of the pride and jealousy of the French, whom he accused of having attacked Germany some thirty times in two centuries. When the question of immediate peace negotiations was raised, he replied to the French: "If we make peace now, as soon as you could, in five or ten years, you would reopen the war." He insisted on the need of a buffer between France and Germany. "We need land, fortresses, and borders which in future will protect us from all French attacks." His territorial demands, however, were not so far-reaching as those of the Prussian generals.

Since the French refused to negotiate peace on the basis of territorial cessions, the war was continued. The long siege of Paris (132 days) was started, engendering the radical revolution of the Paris Commune against the forces of moderation. The city of Strassburg fell on September 28, and a month later, Metz surrendered with a garrison of 173,000. Despite the civil war inside Paris and the increasing futility of their cause, the French hoped for a reversal of fate, based on the slender success of their provincial armies, fighting primarily in the Loire Valley. By the end of 1870, most of France north of the Loire, except Paris and Brittany, was under German control, and food and supplies in the capital were running low. Finally, on January 28, Paris capitulated. Even then, savage fighting continued in the area of Belfort and Dijon near the Swiss border, where Garibaldi with a volunteer army attempted to help the French republicans in a last-minute effort. But in early February, the fortress of Belfort also surrendered, and the French armies in Burgundy were dispersed or escaped into neutral Switzerland to avoid capture. The Germans had won the war, and France was ready to submit to its fate.

Meanwhile French elections had been held, and a new government established provisionally at Bordeaux under the leadership of Louis Thiers. Peace negotiations with Bismarck were undertaken. The harshness of the German terms and Bismarck's inflexibility mortified the French negotiators, but France was in no position to reject the terms and resume fighting. Protracted pleading saved only Belfort for the French. On March 1, 1871, the French National Assembly accepted the preliminaries that were then incorporated into the Treaty of Frankfurt of May 10. According to its provisions, France ceded eastern Lorraine and all of Alsace, except for Belfort, and was to pay an indemnity of five billion francs. German troops were to occupy northern France until full payment had been made.

Creation of the Second German Empire

In early August 1870, after the initial German victories near the frontier in which troops of the southern states participated effectively, Crown Prince Frederick of Prussia (1831–1888), the heir to the throne, developed his own plans for creating a united Germany. But his liberal tendencies and his predilection for the British style of parliamentarianism made him suspect in the eyes of Bismarck, who in any case disliked interference in what he considered his own domain.

Disregarding the crown prince's views, Bismarck opened official negotiations with the southern states in September. They were asked to join the North German Confederation on the basis of mutual treaty arrangements. Bavaria at first refused to commit itself, and presented counterdemands that Bismarck found unacceptable. For the moment, Bismarck decided to proceed without Bavaria. Delegates from the four southern states were invited to sign the treaties of accession at Versailles, which had become William's field headquarters. Baden and Hesse acceded at once and without reservations. At the urging of Bavaria, however, Württemberg delayed its commitment. Bismarck then tried to entice the two recalcitrant southern rulers by a mixture of threats and promises. He threatened to exclude them from the customs union, but at the same time offered them special concessions to sweeten their loss of sovereignty. Württemberg was easily persuaded, but Bavaria resisted until November before finally signing the treaty. The *Sonderrechte* (special rights) granted to the two kingdoms included the right to control their own armies in time of peace, administer their own postal and telegraph services, and run their own railways. Bavaria obtained additional concessions: a permanent seat on all important committees of the Bundesrat, the federal upper house; freedom to determine its own laws on marriage and citizenship; and—a vital point to Bavarians—the right to establish their own taxes on beer.

The signing of the treaties between the North German Confederation and the four southern states did not touch on the question of the official framework for a unified Germany. The southern states could simply have adhered to an expanded North German Confederation without changing its leadership from a president to an emperor and without adding all the other imperial paraphernalia. In fact, William I himself, most Prussian Junkers, and many others in and outside Prussia objected to the creation of an "imperial" superstructure. To William, no honor could be higher than the revered title of King of Prussia, borne by his illustrious Hohenzollern ancestors. But Bismarck looked upon the imperial title as "a political necessity." He believed that the ideal of *Kaiser* and *Reich* retained a romantic aura, particularly for non-Prussians. German nationalists saw in the establishment of a Reich not the re-creation of the pitiful Holy Roman Empire of more recent centuries, but a revival of the glorious days of the Hohenstaufens. For decades, historians, journalists, novelists, and poets had been rekindling admiration for Germany's medieval past. The patriots now saw the day when their wishes could be fulfilled. Conceivably, also, Bismarck found a symbolic meaning in the imperial title. For centuries it had been held by the Germans until wrested from them by the first Napoleon. The Germans had now vanquished Napoleon III and recaptured the title, together with Lorraine, the ancient homeland of imperial dignity.

It is impossible to generalize on the symbolic and emotional values attached to the concepts of *Kaiser* and *Reich*. In medieval times, they had signified in a vague way power and universal dominion, but after 1300 they had gradually become hollow dignities. With Napoleon I, they had acquired new significance, denoting imperialism and expansionism. Louis Napoleon, before becoming emperor in 1852, had tried to convince France and the world to disregard the slogan "Empire means war," insisting that his "conquests" would be solely for "religion, morality, and comfortable living." Yet his regime had been a long series of colonial and European wars. Bismarck also asserted that the Reich would be peaceful and not bent on expansion. But the wars of the 1860s and, to no small extent, the assumption of the now hexed imperial title gave Germany the reputation of an aggressor nation.

After persuading William to accept the dignity, Bismarck still had to determine the precise title. The southern kings would not brook the name "Emperor of Germany," which would make the Hohenzollern ruler of all the states and hence superior to ordinary kings. "Emperor of the Germans—in the style of Napoleon's "Emperor of the French" —was rejected by William as sounding too democratic. "Emperor in Germany" was considered but pleased no one. The final proclamation made William "German Emperor." It was a designation all could accept; in popular language it soon became simply *Der Kaiser*.

Finally, the question remained of how the new crown should be offered to the Prussian king. Recalling the fiasco of 1849, Bismarck threatened that if the princes did not offer the crown to William, he would have the ceremony performed by the North German Parliament. After long pressure and possibly some financial bribing, he finally persuaded the mad king of Bavaria, Louis II, to face the inevitable and to enhance his own personal dignity by taking the initial step. Louis then invited his princely colleagues to join him in offering the crown to William. After obtaining their consent, he sent a letter—dictated by Bismarck himself—to the Prussian king, requesting him to accept the crown.

At last the empire was ready to be proclaimed (see Map 19). The North German Parliament had voted its approval, but the coronation had to be postponed until the Bavarian Parliament consented. On January 18, 1871, the imperial coronation took place in the Hall of Mirrors in Versailles. The ceremony, as well as William's Proclamation of the Empire, bore a characteristic Hohenzollern imprint and foreshadowed a German Empire that was to be no more democratic than the Kingdom of Prussia had been. The official accounts in the gazettes described the splendor of the coronation, with King William "surrounded by sovereigns, generals, and soldiers." "Owing to the necessities of the times," the reports indicated, "the German people were represented at the ceremony only by the German army." Actually a delegation from the North German Parliament had reached Versailles but was not admitted until after the imperial coronation. It is not known who first devised the plan to hold the coronation at Versailles, a decision most insulting to France. But it is interesting that the humiliation of France seemed to outweigh any need to have the new emperor crowned on German soil. There was no reason why William and Bismarck had to be near the battle front, for by January 18 the war was almost over, and their presence was not necessary for completing the campaign.

William's proclamation stressed that he owed his imperial crown not to the German people, but, if to anyone, to the army and the princes. "The German princes and the free cities," he said, "have unanimously called upon us to renew and to assume the German imperial office." Throughout his speech, William referred solely to the princes and to the governments of the free cities—which, no doubt to his regret, were not run by noble lords. No mention was made of the German people; no role was assigned to them in the creation of the Empire and, as the constitution was to show, no rights were to be reserved for them under the new framework.

The Imperial Constitution

The constitution of the Second Reich, adopted by the new Reichstag in April 1871, was essentially an extension of the constitution of the North German Confederation, now enlarged to include twenty five states and Alsace-Lorraine. The latter was organized as a *Reichsland* under an imperial governor, and not given the status of a federal state. Unlike the draft of 1849, the instrument of 1871 contained no bill of rights, and all attempts to append a list of fundamental rights were defeated. On the other hand, the document contained numerous articles dealing with fiscal matters, customs, railroads, commerce, the postal service—particulars not normally included in constitutions. Article 54 even stipulated that "every German . . . should serve in the standing army for seven years," a specification usually left to statutes or other legislation.

The Prussian king was made hereditary German emperor and commander in chief of the army and navy, and awarded power over foreign affairs and all imperial appointments, including the selection of the chancellor and his cabinet ministers. He could even "enter into alliances and treaties with foreign states" without consulting anyone. With the consent of the Bundesrat, he could declare war, dissolve the Reichstag, and enact federal execution against a recalcitrant member state—except Bavaria, which had been granted special immunity from this clause.

The bicameral legislature paralleled that of the North German Confederation. The Reichstag, whose members were elected for five years on secret district ballot by direct suffrage of all males over twenty five years of age, was largely a forum for discussion. Together with the upper house, it could legislate on all matters under the jurisdiction of the federal government—army, navy, customs and taxes, industry, trade and communications, currency and banking, patents, weights and measures, censorship, criminal and civil law, and others—but actually the Bundesrat dominated legislation, since no laws could be promulgated without its consent. Except for its powers over the budget—a doubtful privilege in view of the constant threat of dissolution and the outcome of the constitutional struggle in Prussia in the early 1860s—the Reichstag acted more as a steam valve for popular opinion than as a real parliament. It could exercise no control over the executive. There was no parliamentary responsibility for the cabinet, and no vote of confidence. Moreover, until 1906, its members received no pay and its system of representation became quickly grossly outdated. Elections were based on geographic districts rather than on population, and no reapportionment of districts was undertaken during the empire's forty-seven years of existence. Hence the agricultural districts continued to exert strong influence in the Reichstag despite the progress of urbanization.

The Bundesrat retained the preeminent position it had enjoyed under the North German Confederation. Its members were appointed like ambassadors by the rulers of the twenty-five states and were forced to vote en bloc. The number of seats was raised to 58, and Prussia retained its 17—later increased to 20 by treaties with small states that relinquished their vote to Prussia. But since the veto of 14 votes for all constitutional amendments was kept, Prussia retained its power to prevent constitutional changes.

The constitution turned Germany into an odd mixture of federalism and centralism under the aegis of Prussia. "Imperial legislation" was to "take precedence over state legislation," but its enforcement was often left to the states. Moreover, the states retained control over their own judiciary, police, taxation, and educational and other policies. And through the Bundesrat, each state could potentially exercise important powers. On the other hand, the federal superstructure was a powerful extension of the authority of the Prussian king, and had the effect of merging the German states in Prussia. The king of Prussia was automatically "the presiding officer of the Federation." It is interesting to note, for example, that no arrangements were made for an imperial salary or an imperial castle. Even as emperor of Germany the king of Prussia derived his income solely from Prussia and resided in Berlin's "royal Prussian castle." As a state, Prussia dominated the federation through its size, population, wealth, and army. It represented three fifths of the territory of the empire and sent to the Reichstag 235 out of a total of 397 delegates. In terms of political power, the Prussian king and the chancellor, who was appointed by and was responsible to the Prussian ruler, dominated the Bundesrat and the Reichstag and were in fact the fountainhead of all power within the Reich. Prussia's predominance was symbolically evident in the new flag adopted by the empire: it was not the black, red, and gold of 1813 and 1848, but black, white and red—the colors of the Hohenzollerns mixed with those of the commercial Hanseatic cities.

15

The New Reich, 1871–1890

BISMARCKIAN GERMANY

The Germany that arose from the battlefields of the Franco-Prussian War of 1870 might well be called Bismarck's Germany—not merely because Bismarck laid its foundations, but also because he virtually controlled its destiny during the next twenty years.

Bismarck had guided Prussia successfully through three wars, and had procured the imperial crown for his king. Yet in 1871, he evidently had no intention of withdrawing from the political scene. No doubt he was motivated partly by personal ambition and love of power, but more important was his realization that the process of unifying Germany had not been completed. He was habitually distrustful of others, and hesitated to leave this task to less experienced men. Moreover, William I apparently considered governing without him an impossibility, and Bismarck remained in office partly because of the wishes of his sovereign.

The Temper of the Gründerzeit

The decades after the formation of the empire, called *Gründerzeit* (period of the founders) by the Germans, were characterized by nationalism and materialism. The Germans were proud of their achievements on the battlefield, and a tremendous industrial and commercial expansion made them self-confident and prosperous. Nationhood also seemed to unleash latent energies in the fields of letters, arts, and sciences. Press and theater, concert halls and opera houses, universities, libraries, and laboratories—all were vibrant with activity.

Sentimental patriotism was encouraged more than ever in the so-called *Heimatkunst,* short stories, dramas, and novels depicting the life of country folk living in close communion with the beautiful though mysterious German countryside. Local patriotism was fostered by numerous historical societies, which collected source materials in the various regions of Germany. In Prussia particularly education was designed "to sow the seeds of patriotic, religious, and moral sentiment in the children." The Prussian school of historians asserted that the historian's task was to educate the public in nationalism and to guide the statesmen by revealing the glories of the nation's past. Treitschke, Sybel, and Johann Gustav Droysen (1808–1884), the foremost members of this school, interpreted

German history in the light of the "destiny" of the Hohenzollern dynasty; they praised German nationalism and waged relentless attacks on France, Austria, and the Catholic Church.

Perhaps because the Germans had waited so long to achieve nationhood, they now reveled in it. Hence in some circles, nationalism, formerly directed toward the clearly defined goal of achieving unity, now became a noisy creed mixed with elements of Pan-Germanism and anti-Semitism. An excellent example is furnished by the composer Richard Wagner (1813–1883). A romantic rebel in his youth, he had been occasionally embroiled in politics, although he had devoted his main attention to composing and conducting. Because of his involvement in the revolution of 1848–1849, he had fled to Switzerland, where his writings and compositions had become increasingly nationalistic. He returned to Germany only after proclamation of a political amnesty in 1861. Three years later, King Louis II of Bavaria became Wagner's patron. The opera house at Bayreuth that the king had constructed for Wagner soon became a mecca for lovers of grandiose opera and for German superpatriots. During Wagner's Bayreuth period (1872–1881), he composed the gigantic *Ring des Niebelungen,* a perfect embodiment of mystic nationalism. But besides writing operas, Wagner wrote eight volumes of prose works, among them articles on "Judaism in Music," "What Is German?" and "German Art and German Policy." In these and other writings, he stressed the superiority of the German *Volk* and his belief that a "Barbarossa-Siegfried will some day return to save the German people in time of deepest need." The Jews, whom he thought incapable of speaking the German language or producing German music, he regarded "with repugnance" as the "demons of the decline of mankind." To Wagner, democracy was alien and disgusting, an invention of Jews and Frenchmen. Above all, he revered the mystic primeval force of the German folk soul (*Volksseele*), which he tried to capture in his music dramas. Richard Wagner societies sprang up all over Germany to venerate their master's German music as "the ideal bond" for cementing the unity of the German fatherland.

The materialism of the *Gründerzeit* found newly invigorated expression in both philosophy and literature. Realism, which had first appeared in the novel and the drama in the mid-nineteenth century, continued to dominate literature. The novelist and essayist Theodor Fontane (1819–1898), who for a while had edited the *Kreuzzeitung,* remained the idol of the conservatives with his realistic novels of contemporary life. Fondness for prosperity and for solid middle-class standards was echoed in the novels of Gustav Freytag (1816–1895), a champion of commercial life. Soon the literature of the period began to reflect the increased misery that industrialization and urbanization had brought to the lower classes. In the late 1880s, German naturalism burst into bloom with the dramas of Gerhart Hauptmann (1862–1946). His early plays *Before Sunrise* and *The Weavers* pointed up the poverty of the lower classes, and gave great impetus to the literature of social consciousness.

Whereas most Germans basked in the comforts brought by unification and nationhood, not all could joyfully accept Bismarck's creation. Some regretted that unification had not been achieved on the basis of *Grossdeutschland.* Others opposed the chancellor's autocratic tendencies. Certain ethnic, religious, and political groups—Poles, Alsatians, ultramontanes, and socialists in particular—were leery of the new Reich. In addition a few perspicacious observers, such as Friedrich Nietzsche (1844–1900), objected to the superficiality and chauvinism of the new German spirit. In his *Unzeitgemässe Betrachtungen* (*Untimely Observations*), he warned that the victory over the French did not necessarily herald a victory for German civilization. And he complained that "today everything is determined by the coarsest and most evil forces, by the egotism of an acquisitive society and by military potentates."

Industrial and Commercial Expansion

Political unification by itself, of course, was not likely to eradicate entrenched particularism. Of more importance for uniting the Germans was the rapid industrialization transforming the Reich. It drew the Germans together economically, and produced an unprecedented prosperity that made many of them forget the past.

Between 1871 and 1890, Germany's population rose from 41 million to over 49 million (56 million by 1900, and 64 million by 1910), despite the emigration of well over 2 million Germans to the New World. Parenthetically, it might be pointed out that the population of France during this period increased only from 36 million to 38 million. The demographic balance was shifting in Germany's favor.

Prior to 1850, Germany had been essentially an agricultural area. Between then and 1870, industrial and financial progress had been considerable, especially in the construction of railroads and the promotion of banking. But the really spectacular expansion started with the founding of the empire, as seen by the shift of the population from country to city. Whereas there were only eight towns with more than 100,000 inhabitants in 1871, there were twenty-six by the time the chancellor retired in 1890. The number of those gaining their livelihood in agriculture fell from 60 percent of the population in 1871 to about 40 percent in 1890. The greatest economic stimulus occurred during the first five years of the empire. The new central government encouraged industrialization, and the 5 billion francs of war indemnity provided easy credit, which, incidentally, led to considerable speculation in financial circles.

The Germans emphasized heavy industry. In iron and steel production, they soon surpassed England, as can be seen from the table.

STEEL OUTPUT IN METRIC TONS

Year	*Germany*	*England*
1870	169,000	286,000
1890	2,161,000	3,637,000
1900	6,645,000	5,130,000
1910	13,698,000	6,374,000

German industry also specialized in chemicals and electrical equipment. Transportation, too, was stressed. The merchant marine soon became the second largest in the world, lagging behind only that of England. The expansion of the railroads and the development of inland water transport aided both industry and agriculture.

This rapid development that transformed the German economy within a few decades into one of the most industrialized in the world is frequently called the "German miracle." Similar superficial assertions are often made today concerning Germany's astounding recovery after World War II. To be sure, the Germans worked with efficiency and assiduity, devoting much time and energy to the development of science and its application to industry. But hard work and perseverance alone did not bring about this expansion. Starting almost from scratch, Germany was not handicapped by outmoded models and methods. Consequently its industrial plant was up-to-date and the Germans could rationalize and streamline industrial processes. Moreover, the German government played an important role in this economic development. Despite the ideals of certain liberals, classical economists had relatively little influence in Germany. German industry never experienced a long period of *laissez faire*. The government assumed ownership of the railroads, regulated industry, encouraged large-scale amalgamations for the sake of greater efficiency, and provided subsidies, tax privileges, and tariff protection. Big industry and government therefore cooperated closely in the aim of making Germany powerful, both politically and economically. In the tradition of German paternalism, the government exercised supervision over the economy. In turn, economic interest groups exerted pressure on the government so that it would operate in their favor. Thus industry grew more and more powerful. The trend favored the establishment of huge cartels that covered entire industries, such as steel, coal, and chemicals, and dominated whole segments of German life. This concentration of industry and the close relationship between government and industry were of considerable importance in later years, and were probably not auspicious for the development of democracy in Germany.

Expansion of industry was accompanied by the growth of German financial institutions. A number of important credit banks had been founded in the 1850s and 1860s, but as occurred in industry, the real period of growth started after the founding of the empire. German banks, especially the Reichsbank and the famous "D" banks (so called because their names all started with a "D"—the *Diskonto, Dresdner, Darmstädter,* and *Deutsche* banks), specialized in industrial production credit and frequently acted as holding companies for large industrial concerns. This amalgamation of financial and industrial interests produced a greater concentration of economic power in the hands of small groups of individuals than occurred in most other Western countries.

BISMARCK'S INTERNAL WORK

Perhaps the best explanation for Bismarck's remaining in office after 1871 was that he felt his task was not yet completed. With the promulgation of the constitution of 1871, Germany was outwardly united, but a thousand years of localism and particularism were not eliminated by a mere political proclamation. Hence, besides administering internal and foreign affairs, Bismarck had to weld the various states into a unified empire.

As soon as possible after the victory

over France, the new central government proceeded with the task of unifying the new Reich economically. A common currency was created, the postal and telegraph systems of the various states were united—except those of Bavaria and Württemberg—and the metric system of weights and measures was adopted everywhere. Construction of an extended railroad network was pushed with speed in order to link all parts of the country. Coordination of the different legal systems took more time, but the main step in this direction was taken in 1876 with the establishment of the Common Court of Appeals in Leipzig. This was followed by the issuance of a common code of criminal law and finally—though only in 1896—by a common civil code.

Political Life

Bismarck's Germany may be characterized as "absolutism in democratic forms." Although Germans enjoyed universal male suffrage and representative government of a sort, in the imperial constitution there were few of the checks and balances that Americans take for granted. Control emanated almost exclusively from above (see pages 377–378). As minister-president of Prussia and chancellor of the Reich, Bismarck was vested with tremendous power. Legally, he was not responsible to the Reichstag, although he did try to gain its support to further his legislative program and to receive a measure of popular backing. Bismarck's cabinet had no power of its own, but rather resembled a managerial staff. The chancellor hired and fired ministers—with the automatic consent of the emperor—much as an industrialist replaces divisional or departmental heads. The ministers were responsible to Bismarck for the conduct of their particular department but were not consulted on over-all policy.

Ultimately, Bismarck was dependent solely on the goodwill and confidence of his emperor. While William I was alive Bismarck's position was impregnable. After his old friend and protector died (1888), Bismarck was unable to maintain himself and fell from power.

However, Bismarck's power should not be overestimated. One is easily misled by the epithet the "Iron Chancellor," and by the usual photographs showing him as a stern Prussian Junker. To be sure, Bismarck was powerful, but he was no dictator, and his power was limited. Particularism persisted, and Bismarck knew that the princes of the larger German states—particularly Bavaria and Württemberg—would not easily be reconciled to a secondary role in the new Germany. Opposing these princes might push them straight into the arms of Austria or France and thus open the possibility of renewed international conflict, something Bismarck chose to avoid at all cost. He was therefore cautious in his dealings with the Bundesrat and proceeded warily in all matters affecting the rights of the states.

It is also significant that Bismarck, who had done so much for the aggrandizement of the Prussian army, was unable to control it. William I looked upon himself as a soldier, and while he was content to let Bismarck run the government, he jealously regarded the army as his private domain. Nor did the commanding generals, such as Moltke, brook any interference in military affairs.

The relationship between the civilian

authorities and the army in Germany deserves further consideration, for it presented problems that have remained acute in Germany. The inability to achieve civilian control over the armed forces was to plague the Weimar Republic; relations with the army were a problem even in the Hitler era, and the question is still being debated today in connection with Germany's present-day rearmament policies. In America, the armed forces are supervised by a civilian secretary of defense who, although appointed by the President, is ultimately responsible to the people through their electoral power. In Germany, however, the Prussian army had been created by the kings as their own instrument of power—one might almost say as their own property. There had been no revolution in Germany comparable to those in France and America; no "nation in arms," no minutemen, no national guard—except for brief periods during the Wars of Liberation and the Revolution of 1848—that might have evolved into a people's army truly independent of the ruler and subject to the people's direction. The army had stayed strictly apart during the nineteenth century, when a certain amount of democratization had been allowed to take place in government. It was not democratized internally, nor placed under civilian control. And the creation of a *German* army concomitant with the establishment of the Reich was in fact a mere expansion of the *Prussian* army. Prussian army laws and regulations were extended to all component units, and all soldiers and officers swore allegiance to the king of Prussia. Only Bavaria, Württemberg, and Saxony were permitted to retain their own semiautonomous regiments, within the framework of an all-German army under Prussian direction and leadership.

Since Germany had the forms of a democracy, Bismarck also had to contend with the various political parties that grew more numerous and active after 1871. Elections to the Reichstag were held every five years, unless required sooner because of dissolution by the Bundesrat and the imperial chancellor. Since parliamentarianism in the British sense did not exist, Bismarck himself could afford to belong to no particular party. Yet because he required a base of operation within the Reichstag to assure passage of legislation and approval of the budget, he aligned himself with this or that group as the occasion demanded, and felt free to switch his allegiance when such support no longer suited his purposes. In this kind of political maneuvering he proved a master.

In 1871 there were six major and over a dozen minor parties with national status, as well as countless parties operating only on the local level (see Chart 5). From the beginning, German parties tended to splinter with frightening rapidity. Germany was to be plagued as much as any other European country by the atomization of its political life. The usual political individualism and tenacious adherence to abstract principles, which may account for splintering in other European countries, only partly explains the problem in Germany. Regional differences, local interests, as well as past traditions of the various states, frequently made it impossible for people from different parts of the Reich to collaborate in a common party, even though they might be in agreement on most major issues. Ethnic

Chart 5 ELECTION RESULTS, 1871–1912

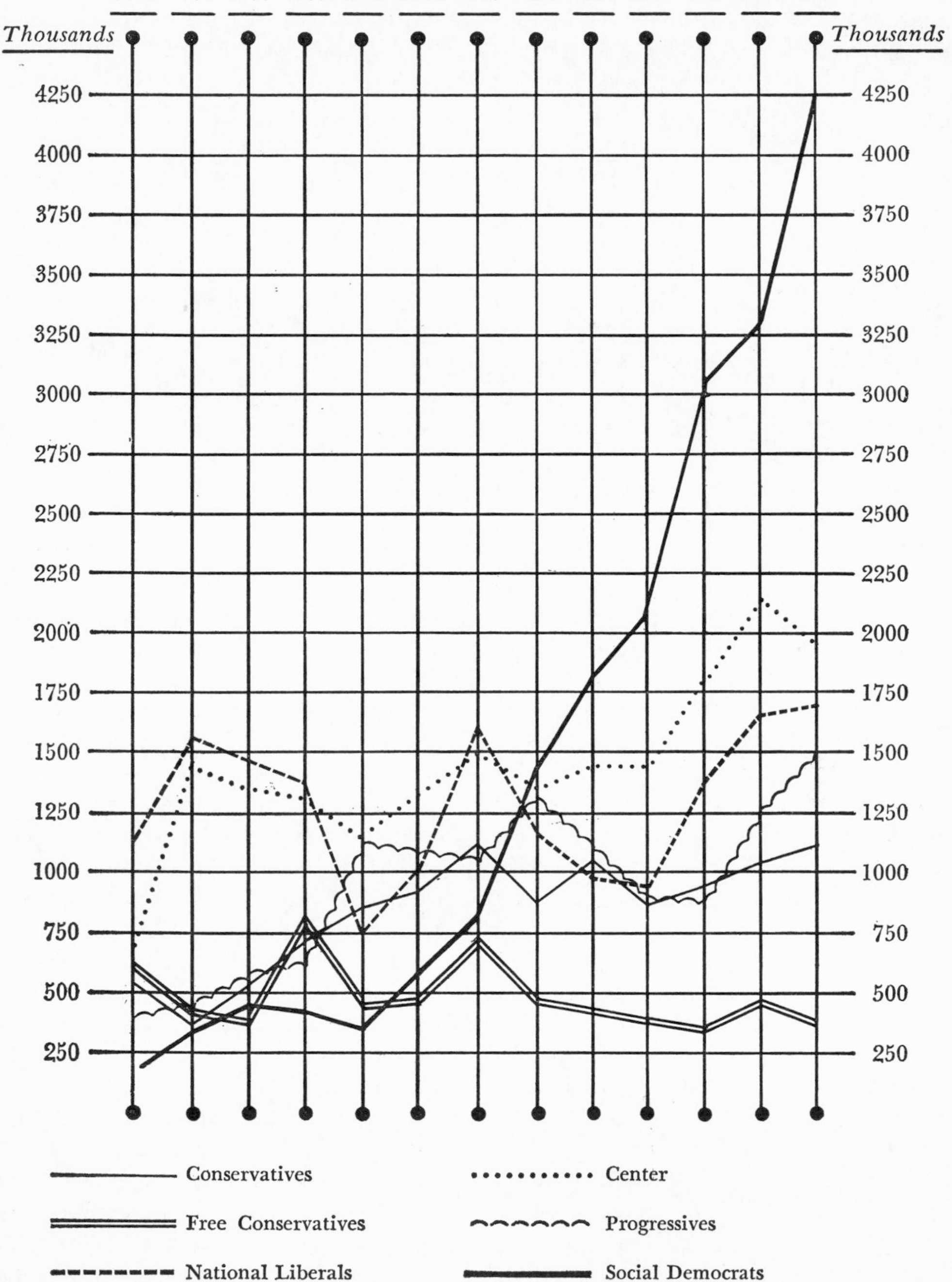

minorities—such as Danes, Poles, and Alsace-Lorrainers—and regional groups—such as Bavarians and Hanoverians—formed their own parties or splinters. At first, this subdividing was particularly characteristic of the liberals (who formed many different parties with similar names and usually similar ideals). Later the conservatives suffered from the same dilemma, so that the total number of parties constantly increased.

THE CONSERVATIVES On the right side of the political spectrum were the Prussian Junkers. They belonged to the loosely organized Conservative party, which in 1871 received slightly over an eighth of the votes and was the fourth largest political group. In addition to the landlords from the "new" Germany east of the Elbe River, this party generally included high-ranking army officers, Prussian government officials, and conservative Lutheran ministers. Since the strength of this group lay in Prussia, one might expect its members to be strong supporters of Bismarck, who had done so much to aggrandize Prussia and who was a member of their own Junker class. But, except for brief intervals, they remained distrustful of Bismarck's aims and opposed his policies. They were nationalistic in a Prussian rather than in a German sense, and revered the title and traditions of the Prussian Kingdom more than those of the German Empire. They considered Bismarck too "German" and too "un-Prussian," and feared he was submerging Prussia in the new Germany. That their apprehensions were partly justified can be seen from Bismarck's own memoirs. Prussian nationalism, he wrote, "has no more justification than the specific patriotism of the individual German states. . . . As soon as I became convinced that the Prussian national feeling was the anvil to hammer out the others, I ceased to follow lopsided Prussian aims." Moreover, the Conservatives regarded him as a traitor to his class because of his flirtations with democracy and because his sequestration of power from the landlords in local governmental affairs was undermining their remaining hold on the Prussian peasant population.

Since their stronghold lay in agrarian regions, the Conservatives tended to oppose rapid industrialization and the growth of modern capitalism. Initially, they were stanch supporters of free trade. But in the late 1870s, pressed by rising prices of both labor and industrial goods, and suffering from the heavy competition of Russian and American wheat, they became champions of protective tariffs. Finally, under William II, they participated in backstage bargaining with industrial interests to put a strong tariff wall around Germany.

The philosophy of this group, voiced in one of its newspapers, the influential *Kreuzzeitung,* was in some respects medieval. Its members believed in corporatism, in quasi-divine right monarchy, and in the social prestige and the political all-importance of the "modern knights," the Prussian officers. In addition, they favored strong and independent religious institutions, whether Lutheran or Catholic, and were against state interference in church matters. They therefore opposed Bismarck's attempt to subordinate the Catholic Church in the *Kulturkampf* (see below, page 390), not because they liked Roman Catholicism, but because they disliked Bismarck's insistence on civil marriages and state-controlled education. In other respects, this group echoed ideals of the romantic period. In a pseudo-Hegelian spirit, they revered the state—primarily the Prussian state—as a living organism to which the individual is subordinate.

In Bismarckian Germany, the Conservative party was not very powerful. But at that period Bismarck's manipulations kept all parties from acquiring true power. Nevertheless, its influence was frequently felt, and until World War II the party represented one of the fundamental aspects of German sociopolitical opinion.

THE FREE CONSERVATIVES Whereas the Conservatives usually opposed Bismarck, the Free Conservatives, Germany's third largest party in 1871, more frequently supported him. The philosophy of this party to a great extent resembled that of the Conservatives, from which it had split in 1866, but its stronghold lay primarily in the "old" Germany and therefore largely outside Prussia. Strongly pro-German in their nationalistic feelings, its members felt grateful to Bismarck for having achieved unification. In fact, in 1871 they adopted as alternate party label the name *Reichspartei,* presumably to show their enthusiasm for the new Reich. Besides landholders, this group also included some of the powerful industrialists and capitalists from the Ruhr, who quickly recognized the economic possibilities provided by an enlarged Germany. Many of the more influential members of this party became government officials in the 1870s.

THE NATIONAL LIBERALS More toward the center of political opinion were the many groups that at one time or another had split off from the Progressive party. During the first decade of empire under Bismarck, the most influential of these were the National Liberals, who had split off from the Progressives over the issue of the Bill of Indemnity (see page 360). The National Liberals, the strongest party in Germany, had polled over a quarter of the votes cast in the elections of 1871. To be sure, they had retained part of their liberal ideals, but as in 1866, whenever there was a conflict of interests between liberalism and national unity or furtherance of the Reich, they threw their support to the latter.

Most of the National Liberals came from the upper levels of the middle class. They were an urban group, not at all Prussian in outlook. Like the Free Conservatives, many had economic interests in industry or commerce. They consequently looked with favor upon Bismarck's efforts to unify Germany economically and financially and credited him with the increased prosperity resulting from Germany's expanded markets. One can easily see why Bismarck, in turn, relied on them heavily in the early years after 1871. They had helped him in the three difficult years preceding the Franco-Prussian War, and they now supported his fight against the Catholic Church, against the agrarian Conservatives, and against remaining particularism. Toward the end of Bismarck's first decade as chancellor, however, they became increasingly disenchanted with his administration. They disliked his compromise with the Catholic Church and his veering toward the Conservatives. On the other hand, they were pleased with some of his new policies and particularly welcomed Germany's entry into the colonial arena in 1883.

In due course, these National Liberals lost most of their liberal ideas. Like the Conservatives, many of them abandoned advocacy of free trade in favor of protectionism. As their liberalism declined, they became increasingly nationalistic. In party politics, they gradually lost importance. But just as the Conservatives were less significant as a party than they were as representatives of German thought, so the National Liberals represented views that are worth recalling. One of their premises remained important in German life: the idea that strengthening Germany is more vital than principles of freedom, democratization, or individual liberty.

THE PROGRESSIVES To the left of the National Liberal party were the old-style Progressives. They, too, were subject to constant splits, realignments, and changes of name. In 1866, this party had remained true to its principles of constitutional government, and had refused to vote for Bismarck's Bill of Indemnity. In 1871, it polled less than 10 percent of the vote and was the fifth party in size. Although pleased with the democratic measures embodied in the constitution of 1871, the Progressives were opposed to Bismarck's autocratic administration. They adhered to their belief in free trade, and disapproved of the tariffs of 1879 and later. They wanted to develop Germany rather than diffuse their energies through imperialistic adventures. They distrusted the Junker class and the army, and strove without success to subject the military to civilian control. And they would have preferred a constitutional monarch to their anachronistic "divine right" ruler.

In the course of the 1880s and 1890s, the Progressives modified their principles considerably. They changed from typical late eighteenth- and nineteenth-century liberalism, which called the "least" government the "best" government, to the modern approach that assigns to government certain protective functions. Although disagreeing with the socialists on methods as well as aims, the Progressives gradually called for state help in social work and labor relations. They came to approve of limited tariffs and government-run education, and called for a balanced consideration of the rights of the state as a whole versus those of individual citizens.

Their influence under the Bismarckian system was not very great, but they represented an important bridge between the spirit of '48 and the liberal democratic tendencies that were to assert themselves once again after World War I.

THE CENTER PARTY Although the parties discussed so far were largely Protestant in membership, religion did not form their primary base of cohesion. Rather, they were based on political, economic, or class ideals. The Center party, however, was of a different nature. Its basis was largely religious. It was founded in 1870 primarily as a political organ of German Catholicism, and immediately became very powerful. At the polls in 1871, it gained more votes than any other party except the National Liberals, and it continued to exert much influence in German political life for decades. Though largely a middle-class party, its support came from all walks of life, and class interests played a relatively minor role in its policies.

The religious division of Germany continued to have repercussions in German politics. Since the days of Frederick the Great, the rivalry between

Protestant Prussia and Catholic Austria had maintained a precarious balance between the two major religions of the Germans, but with the establishment of Bismarck's Reich and the exclusion of Austria, there could no longer be a balance. Prussia was in the saddle, and Germany seemingly was to become a Protestant nation. Hence it is understandable that the Center party in its early years was distinctly wary of the Reich and usually anti-Bismarckian in its policies. Its leader, Ludwig Windthorst (1812–1891), not merely supported the interests of the Catholic Church, but also encouraged the aspirations of various groups at odds with the new Germany—the Poles in West Prussia and Poznan, the newly conquered Alsatians and Lorrainers, the Bavarians who bewailed their lost independence, and certain Hanoverians who regretted their destroyed kingdom. The anti-Bismarckian stance of the Center party lasted for nearly the first decade of the new Reich, and provided the background for the famous *Kulturkampf*.

THE SOCIALISTS Finally, on the left side of the political scale were various socialist and workers' groups. In 1870, organized socialism was fairly new and relatively weak. Only 2 (out of 397) socialist representatives were elected to the Reichstag of 1871. The first German socialist organization of any importance, the General Association of German Workers, had been founded by Ferdinand Lassalle (1825–1864) in Leipzig in 1863. Lassalle had rejected most of the utopian solutions of earlier decades, but had refused to embrace the new theories of Karl Marx in their entirety. Thoroughly democratic in outlook, he had advocated universal suffrage to enable workers to influence legislation. His workers' organization was to use political weapons rather than violence to gain social and economic aims. In addition, Lassalle had hoped to eliminate the "exploitation by capitalists" decried by Marx—not through state ownership of the means of production but through establishment of industrial cooperatives owned by the workers.

Lassalle's premature death in a duel in 1864 left the German workers divided for almost a decade. Some continued to advocate his policies, but were willing to compromise with Bismarck. These followers of Lassalle were somewhat nationalistic and did not object to the existence of a strong state. Many of them supported Bismarck's Bill of Indemnity. Other groups of workers rapidly fell under the influence of Wilhelm Liebknecht, who had spent thirteen years of exile in London in the company of Karl Marx. When Marx founded the First International in 1864, Liebknecht tried to bring German workers into the new international movement. With August Bebel (1840–1913), he developed an anti-Lassallean and anti-Bismarckian program. His group vehemently opposed the Bill of Indemnity, Prussia's militarism and expansionism, and the impending war with France. In 1869, Liebknecht and Bebel formally organized their followers into the Social Democratic Workingman's party.

German socialism gained some strength during the early years of the Reich. The Lassalleans quickly grew wary of Bismarck's policies, and at a large congress held in Gotha in 1875, they agreed to merge with Liebknecht's followers. The result of the merger produced the Socialist Workingman's party, more frequently called the Social Democratic party (SPD). Although Liebknecht, the international Marxist, became the leader of the new party, the program adopted at Gotha was largely based on the ideas of Lassalle, so much so that Marx himself bitterly denounced it. The new combined party greatly increased its representation in the Reichstag, so that Bismarck soon considered it a danger to his system and devoted his energy to eradicating German socialism.

The Kulturkampf

Soon after the founding of the empire, the spectacular attempt to subordinate the Roman Catholic Church to the new imperial government split Germany into opposing camps. Although this attempt was essentially a fight for power between the government and the Catholic Church, some contemporary journalists called it a struggle between two ways of life or two civilizations, and hence gave it the inappropriate name *Kulturkampf* (battle of cultures).

There can be no doubt that the entire struggle was more political in nature than religious. Still religion had its share in the temporary reawakening of the rivalry between Catholics and Protestants. Protestants at the time looked with apprehension on the efforts of Pope Pius IX to reassert the power of the Catholic Church, while German Catholics regarded with suspicion the political victories of Protestant Prussia.

Historical forces were also involved. The last great fight between popes and emperors had ended in the fourteenth century. After that, with a few exceptions, such as Napoleon I, the emperors had been too weak to challenge the popes. As a result, there had been few quarrels between Empire and papacy for some six centuries. Significantly, the fight was reopened when the German Empire was re-established on a strengthened basis in 1871. The fact that the new emperor was also a Protestant, the first Protestant emperor in history, only heightened the mutual suspicion. Although Bismarck insisted that the Germany of 1871 was a satisfied nation and harbored no imperialistic ambitions, the very fact that the old Reich had been resurrected seemed to recall to life the ghosts of the Guelfs and the Ghibellines and set the stage for a new struggle. Bismarck himself must have been conscious of this, since he referred so frequently during this struggle to the days of Emperors Henry IV and Frederick II. But although much has been written about the *Kulturkampf,* it is even now impossible to ascertain the true motives behind the chancellor's actions. To justify his attempted curtailment of its power, Bismarck simply characterized the Catholic Church as *reichsfeindlich*—an enemy of the Reich.

Bismarck desired a thoroughly unified Reich. A strong independent Catholic Church that he could not control would have been as distasteful to him as it had been to all autocratic rulers of previous centuries. He therefore set out to weaken the Catholic Church in Germany and place it under the supervision of the state. Between 1871 and 1875, numerous laws and ordinances were passed for this purpose. In 1872, the Society of Jesus and its affiliates were banished from German territory. The so-called May Laws of 1873 transferred to the government the right to sanction church appointments, gave the state control over all clerical education, and restricted the jurisdiction of ecclesiastical courts. Two years later civil marriage was made compulsory, and pressure was brought on disobedient clergy by withholding government-collected church taxes. The Catholic press was censored and the publication of papal letters of remonstrance prohibited. Finally, all Catholic religious orders—except those devoted to tending the sick—were abolished and some recalcitrant priests fined and imprisoned.

For several years this new "investiture controversy" raged in bitter acrimony. Bismarck was aided by a split in the ranks of the Catholics themselves. Not all Catholics had readily accepted the strong stand taken by Pope Pius IX in his Syllabus of Errors of 1864 and in the subsequent dogma of Papal Infallibility. The so-called Liberal or Old Catholics had refused to follow the pope, and had split off from the Church. They sided with Bismarck, not because they wanted the Church's independence destroyed, but because they hoped to see the papal drive for centralization weakened. Their stand recalled the attitude of certain German bishops who sided with Henry IV in his struggle against Gregory VII. Besides this help from the Old Catholics, Bismarck also received support from the National Liberals, from many Protestant groups, and from nationalistic conservatives, who were instinctively opposed to "foreign" influence in Germany.

On the other hand, the Catholic Center party was not alone in opposing Bismarck in the *Kulturkampf*. All elements in the Reich that disliked Bismarck's policy of centralization sided with the Center party, particularly the Poles, Bavarians, and Alsace-Lorrainers. Many Protestants also favored the forces opposing Bismarck because they disapproved in principle of the subjection of church to state.

The *Kulturkampf* finally ebbed in the late 1870s. It can hardly be said that Bismarck called off the struggle because he felt he had accomplished his aim. On the contrary, as a result of the attack, the Center party had more than doubled in strength, and by 1878 almost equaled the National Liberals in the Reichstag. Rather, Bismarck came to realize that little could be achieved by continuing the struggle. Instead of helping to unify the Reich, the *Kulturkampf* crystallized the opposition of particularistic elements. Moreover, political alignments in Germany were changing, and Bismarck was losing some of his traditional supporters.

The chancellor therefore prepared to come to terms with the Center party. Good fortune helped his plans. After the death of Pope Pius IX in 1878, the papacy was led by the more conciliatory Leo XIII. Negotiations with the papacy were started at once, although neither side was officially willing to cede many points. Bismarck refused to abrogate the anti-Catholic laws immediately, and the pope would not negotiate on any other basis. But since Bismarck was eager to make peace with the papacy and gain the support of the Center party for his new policies, especially for the tariff legislation, he simply ceased to enforce the laws. Some of the anti-Catholic laws were later amended and some were abrogated entirely; only a few, such as the law on compulsory civil marriage, remained. The papacy was placated by these measures, and the *Kulturkampf* ended gradually after 1878. It was followed by a large-scale realignment of the forces that supported Bismarck.

The Tariff of 1879 and Political Realignments

In the elections of 1878, the Conservatives and the Free Conservatives each increased their Reichstag representation by 19 seats, while the National Liberals lost 29. These electoral results, coupled with the debate on impending tariff legislation, demonstrated to Bismarck the need for reshuffling his political support. The gains made by the two conservative parties and by the Center made it advisable for the chancellor to come to terms with them. At the same time, he realized that he could no longer rely so heavily on the National Liberals in his parliamentary maneuvers, since they were declining in strength and since some of them opposed him on the tariff question.

The chancellor had come to favor protective tariffs for German industry and agriculture to strengthen them against foreign competition and to increase the revenue of the Reich, which depended to a great extent on customs receipts. He also hoped to encourage German production in order to make the Reich as self-sufficient as possible. To procure adoption in the Reichstag of his tariff of 1879, he therefore relied on a combination of Conservatives, Free Conservatives, Centrists, and a few National Liberals, who voted for the bill in opposition to the remaining National Liberals, the Progressives, and the Social Democrats. The Conservatives, representing the agricultural interests, had been severely threatened by American and Russian imports, and offered general political support to the chancellor in return for tariff protection on their produce. Moreover, some of the National Liberals, especially those in industry who had suffered from the two minor depressions of 1873 and 1877, were also ready to abandon their doctrinaire stand on free trade and accept the tariff. A large part of the Center party was equally willing to vote for the tariff, provided their other contentions with Bismarck could be resolved.

The Anti-Socialist Struggle

Besides the tariff question there was another issue conducive to this political realignment: the rising strength of the Social Democrats. In the early 1860s, Bismarck had momentarily contemplated allying himself with Ferdinand Lassalle to gain the workers' support for his efforts to unite Germany. The two men admired each other's political sagacity and found common ground in their preference for a strong, centralized government. But during the 1870s, Bismarck had come to distrust the motives of the Socialists. Although their Gotha program of 1875 was fairly Lassallean and evolutionary, the Socialists were internationalists, pacifists, antimilitarists, and thus suspect to Bismarck. In the 1877 elections, they polled half a million votes—more than the Free Conservatives and almost as many as the Conservatives. Moreover, their leaders in the Reichstag, Bebel and Liebknecht, had led an incessant campaign against Bismarck's programs. And the conservative landowners and large industrialists who now sided with Bismarck gladly supported the chancellor in his efforts to nip in the bud the "red" danger to their way of life.

The purported justification for the suppression of German socialism were two attempts on the life of Emperor William. Although neither of the would-be assassins was connected with the Socialists, Bismarck at once called for strong measures against all socialist organizations. His bills failed to pass in the Reichstag, and he dissolved it. As was seen, the new elections of July 1878 gave him the support of the Conservatives that he needed to obtain a majority for his proposals. In October of that year, the chancellor's anti-Socialist legislation passed in the Reichstag. These laws were a curious attempt to reconcile discriminatory measures against a particular group with the democratic principles of free elections. On the one hand, Socialists were forbidden to organize into groups. They could hold occasional meetings, but only under strict police supervision. Their aims were decried as "subversive" to the public order and hostile to the interests of the state, and most of their publications were outlawed. Financial contributions to "subversive" groups were declared illegal. On the other hand, the new legislation permitted Socialists to be elected to public offices, for during the parliamentary debates, a majority in the Reichstag had refused to undermine the principle of free representation by disenfranchising the Socialists. Thus the anomaly existed that while officially the Socialists (and their publications) were forced to go underground and some of them were jailed on charges of subversion, they still could become members of the Reichstag and hold free debate therein.

Besides enforcing the anti-Socialist laws, which were periodically renewed until 1890, Bismarck tried to prevent the growth of German socialism also by adopting some of its goals for improving the lot of the German workers. In 1881 he launched a program of social legislation that was so comprehensive and farsighted that it immediately placed Germany far ahead of other nations in this field of national policy. Bismarck's aim was, of course, not solely to take steam away from the Socialists. In internal policies, the chancellor had never favored the extreme *laissez-faire* ideas of the nineteenth-century liberals. On the contrary, in the style of the old Prussian paternalism, he proclaimed that it was the obligation of the state to protect the weak. As a sincere Christian, he felt it the duty of everyone, especially of the government, to help alleviate the suffering of the sick, the old, and the weak. Finally, as a statesman he realized that the state as a whole would be strengthened if none of its members was so weak as to endanger the rest of the body politic. One must remember that he always saw social reform from the viewpoint of the state and not from that of the worker who demanded help as an inherent right. Bismarck "passed social laws because they were necessary; social reform was never to him a passion, but always a policy."

After some parliamentary delays, the first legislation was adopted in 1883. A Health Insurance Law provided for financial and medical aid to workers laid off because of sickness. One third of the cost of this insurance was to be borne by the employer and two thirds by the worker. The following year saw the passage of the Accident Insurance Law, under which disabled workers were to be compensated and widows of workers killed on their jobs were to receive pensions. Premiums for this system were to be paid entirely by the employers. Finally, in 1889, an Old Age and Invalidism Insurance Law made provisions for all retired workers over the age of seventy and for those permanently disabled at an earlier age. The cost of this program was to be borne by employers, workers, and the state itself. After Bismarck's dismissal from office in 1890, additional social legislation was passed to improve the lot of the lower classes. But Bismarck's system of social security alone considerably improved the material well-being of the German workers.

It is commonly asserted that Bismarck failed in his anti-Socialist struggle, since neither the anti-Socialist laws nor the social security legislation curbed the growth of German Socialism. In fact, between 1878 and 1890, the Social Democrats increased their representation in the Reichstag from 9 to 35 seats, and by 1912 became the largest party in Germany, obtaining 20 percent of all votes cast. But the increase in the party's numerical strength does not mean that Bismarck failed to steal some of the Socialists' thunder; in fact he may have contributed measurably to the incipient emasculation of Socialism in Germany. By helping the workers in some of their social problems and by heightening their sense of security, he softened their revolutionary ideals and strengthened the evolutionary, more middle-class-oriented wing of the party. He acted in the Prussian tradition (exemplified by Karl von Hardenberg) that revolution or change must come from above. By bestowing benefits from above instead of giving in to pressure from below, Bismarck weakened the political strength as well as the virulence of the Socialist movement.

In the long run, this development proved detrimental to German socialism and perhaps equally so to German democratization. The workers could claim no credit for their improved status, since they had not really fought for the benefits they received. On the contrary, many of them came to believe that their own political action was of little importance, since the state seemed ready to take care of them. There appeared to be less need for workers' associations, workers' parties and democratic or revolutionary political action, since the state was cognizant of their needs. Consequently German trade-unionism and socialism, although growing numerically, did not develop the same sense of fruitful achievement and political responsibility as did similar movements in England and France, where they were forced to a much greater extent to fight for their cause.

The Problem of Ethnic Minorities

Cementing German internal unity required more than fighting Catholic particularism and Socialist internationalism. Within Germany there were millions of Poles, Danes, Alsatians, and Lorrainers who spoke no German and had few reasons to be loyal to the new Reich. Revived Polish patriotism, Catholic solidarity—for with the exception of the Danes, these ethnic minorities were mostly Catholic—as well as French sympathy and tacit support for their cause, turned the treatment of these peoples into a constant problem for the German government. Since the central administration hoped gradually to eradicate exaggerated provincial patriotism, particularly in southern Germany, it considered it all the more essential to assimilate these alien elements into Germany's social and political body. Consequently, the federal and Prussian governments inaugurated a policy of forced Germanization. Prussia dealt with the Danes and the Poles, since they lived on territory under Prussian jurisdiction. Alsace and Lorraine, on the other hand, which were not given statehood until 1911, were governed as an imperial territory by the federal government directly from Berlin. In all these regions with ethnic minorities, the speaking of German was made compulsory in school and at public functions. Land was transferred, sometimes forcibly, from local owners to German colonists. Manifestations of non-German sentiments were suppressed, and Germans were induced to migrate to the critical regions in order to alter the ethnic composition of the population.

Yet this drive to Germanize the minorities, which reflected the nascent Pan-German movement, was on the whole unsuccessful, no matter how methodically conducted. The Poles tenaciously held onto their land and customs, and the resistance of the Alsace-Lorrainers was so persistent that the imperial government ultimately had to concede them a certain amount of local autonomy.

THE FOREIGN POLICY OF BISMARCK

The German Reich of 1871 was the product of three wars. In the process of its creation, Bismarck had repeatedly proclaimed that only force could unify Germany. This bellicose attitude alone aroused the apprehensions of the European powers. These fears were further nourished by certain extreme nationalists in Germany, who announced that its military might made Germany a world power destined to dominate the Continent. In addition, the emergence of a strong and united Germany with a burgeoning economy had radically altered the international balance in Europe. Russia was bound to be upset over the presence of a powerful neighbor on its western frontier. For over a century Russia had tried to prevent such an occurrence, since it would discourage Russia's possible future expansion toward the heart of Europe. Austria's status was fundamentally changed. Expelled from Germany, Austria turned its full attention toward expanding into the Balkans, an area in which it was fated to clash with Russian designs. Finally, France, defeated and deprived of Alsace-Lorraine through the Peace of Frankfurt, appeared unwilling to reconcile itself to being inferior to Germany. The chimera of a war of revenge hovered over Paris.

Thus Bismarck's role in foreign affairs after 1871 was not easy. He called Germany a satiated nation harboring no further territorial aims. This was not simply a deceitful diplomatic maneuver. His reiteration of Germany's peaceful intentions—in fact, all his assiduous attempts to maintain the peace of Europe—were based on shrewd political considerations. In connection with the war scare of 1875, he noted in his diary:

> Such a war [with France] would . . . probably have provoked an alliance among Russia, Austria, and England and possibly have brought about active intervention on

their part against the new and not yet consolidated *Reich*. This would have put Germany onto the same path which led the first and second French Empires to their downfall through a policy of continued war. Europe would have looked upon our action as a misuse of our acquired strength, and everyone, including the centrifugal forces in the *Reich* themselves, would have constantly been on guard, or at war with Germany. After the surprising proof we gave of our military strength, it was the peaceful attitude of German policy which contributed to conciliating the foreign powers and internal opponents sooner than we had expected. . . .

There were, of course, more than a few Germans who insisted that Germany was not "satiated," that the "gathering-in" of Germans on the Continent had not been completed, or that overseas expansion was the next essential step. But as early as the Revolution of 1848, Bismarck had opted in favor of a *Kleindeutschland* solution because he considered it the most feasible. He saw no reason to change his mind in 1871. To go beyond—to risk war—would be to run the chance of destroying his entire work. Any major European war that might upset the *status quo* of 1871 presented inherent dangers to Germany. Consequently, the Iron Chancellor proclaimed himself a guardian of peace during his entire remaining tenure of office and his foreign policy rested on these considerations.

Relations with France

In 1871, France was a weak nation. Its armies had been defeated and the empire of Napoleon III had collapsed. The civil war in Paris, the loss of territory, the payment of the war indemnity to Germany, as well as internal political dissension, were all sapping France's strength. The Treaty of Frankfurt of 1871 had specified that German troops were to occupy certain northern departments of France until the full indemnity of five billion francs had been paid. As long as France lay prostrate and partially occupied by German army units, Bismarck could feel relatively safe from a French war of revenge.

But French recovery was surprisingly rapid. Barely two years after its defeat, and one year ahead of schedule, France paid off its indemnity to Germany, forcing an early withdrawal of the German occupation contingents. Moreover, in 1873, the conservative royalists came to political power in Paris. Their program was fervently nationalistic and bellicose. They favored strengthening the army, spoke of supporting the pope against the new Italian monarchy, and hinted at a war of reprisal against Germany.

France's resurgence rekindled the distrust between the two countries and lay at the heart of several war scares (in 1875 and 1887–1888). Berlin and Paris made an occasional effort at establishing friendly relations, but the wound of Alsace-Lorraine would not heal, and no sincere reconciliation was effected. Persisting mutual suspicion produced an armament race that grew in intensity over the next decades. To keep French eyes averted from the Rhine, and to dim French hopes of recovering the lost provinces, Bismarck openly encouraged the French government to acquire more African colonies.

Bismarck was determined to keep France isolated at all cost. Germany, he felt, could always repeat the victory of 1870 over France alone, but if

France were to acquire a major ally, such as England, Austria, or Russia, any ensuing general conflagration would entail dire consequences for Germany. This decision to isolate France became one of the pivots of his foreign policy. To make a *rapprochement* between France and Italy more difficult, he encouraged both to covet Tunisia. Similarly, he tried to fan the distrust between France and England by pretending to support each in their competing claims in Egypt and Morocco. As long as these nations sought similar spheres of influence in Africa, Germany was relatively safe from the possible threat of an anti-German coalition. But it was even more important for Bismarck to keep Austria and Russia from befriending France: such an alliance would threaten Germany with a two-front war. In this case, Bismarck could not reach his aim by fanning conflicts between the nations. He had to rely on a complicated system of alliances. Critics have often asserted that the web of alliances he fashioned for this purpose was too complicated to be durable and that it ultimately led Europe closer to war—but it did accomplish Bismarck's primary aim. As long as he was in charge of Germany's foreign relations, France remained isolated.

Relations with Austria

Fundamental to the security system with which Bismarck tried to undergird the Reich was his alliance with Austria. A friendly Austria would at least guarantee a peaceful southern border. Above all, internal considerations made it important for Berlin to be on friendly terms with Vienna. If antagonized, Austria might easily reassume its old role—that of a rallying point for all discontented anti-Prussian, and especially Catholic, elements in Germany—and thereby endanger the internal unity of the Reich.

The new era of Austro-German *rapprochement* was opened when Emperors William I and Francis Joseph met in 1871 and again in 1872 to discuss relations between their countries. But in befriending Austria, Bismarck did not wish to alienate Russia. This was to prove difficult, for Russia and Austria clashed continually over spheres of influence in the Balkans, and it demanded more diplomatic dexterity than even Bismarck could muster to support at the same time two countries at loggerheads with each other. Russia was acting as protector of the Serbs against Turkey and Austria. Moreover, it hoped to extend its border into Rumania, and to acquire a protectorate over the central Balkans. Austria, on the other hand, hoped to inherit from Turkey at least the land along the Adriatic coast and to subjugate the Serbs, who were acting as a rallying force for a strong anti-Austrian Pan-Slav movement.

During the Near Eastern crisis of 1875–1878, Bismarck was repeatedly called upon to declare himself either for Russia or for Austria. The 1875 insurrection against Turkey in Bosnia-Herzegovina, followed in 1876 by the Bulgarian revolt and the Serbo-Turkish War, and in 1877 by the Russo-Turkish War, threatened to produce a general European war. Britain dispatched its fleet to the Straits at Constantinople, and tension between Austria and Russia nearly reached a breaking point. After much secret bargaining among the powers, an International Congress finally met in Berlin in 1878 to settle the Near Eastern question. England's Disraeli generally supported Austria's Andrássy because both wished to keep Russia from gaining paramount influence over the Balkans. Italy and France played distinctly minor roles, while Bismarck tried to act, as he put it, "the honest broker" among Austria, Russia, and Turkey. In the final settlement, Serbia, Rumania, and Montenegro were recognized as independent states. Turkey was reduced in territory but not completely destroyed, Austria was allowed to occupy Bosnia-Herzegovina, and Britain to take Cyprus. France, Italy, and Germany received no territorial awards. Russia, on the other hand, was permitted to keep some of its conquests from the Russo-Turkish War, but less than it had hoped. At the same time, Russia's role as protector of the Balkan Slavs lost some of its halo because of its inability to assert its demands.

During the Congress of Berlin, Bismarck managed to walk a tightrope between Russia and Austria for a surprisingly long period. Yet in the end his "brokership" was interpreted by Russia as unfriendly to its interests, and unleashed strong Russian recriminations against Germany. This crisis and the resulting clamor induced the chancellor to tie Germany more closely to Austria. He had not abandoned hope of retaining Russia's friendship if possible, and Emperor William I steadfastly favored close relations with his cousin Alexander II. But for the moment Bismarck decided to lean more on Austria than on Russia, because the former seemed the more reliable nation. Austria had gained much internal stability after its reorganization of 1867, and had proved its foreign prestige in the Near Eastern crisis. Russia, on the other hand, was in the throes of internal disorders that led to the assassination of Emperor Alexander II a few years later.

The result of Bismarck's decision was the Dual Alliance of 1879 between Germany and Austria-Hungary, a defensive alliance stipulating that both nations would fight together if either were attacked by Russia, and that either would observe benevolent neutrality if the other were attacked by a power other than Russia. In order not to antagonize Russia, Bismarck kept the treaty secret until he defiantly published it during the war scare of 1888, at a time when Russo-German relations had cooled off considerably. The Dual Alliance was renewed periodically until the outbreak of World War I. The nucleus of Bismarck's security system, it was the most stable of all the alliances in the European diplomatic network. Bismarck considered it advantageous because it kept Germany from being completely isolated. However, it undermined Russo-German relations and involved Germany in the tangled affairs of the Balkans by strengthening Austria's hand vis-à-vis Russia and by tacitly promising Germany's support in Austria's Balkan ventures.

Relations with Italy

During the 1870s and 1880s, conditions were auspicious for drawing Italy and Germany into friendship and possible alliance. Both were new nations, essentially isolated and in need of finding a place in the European state system. Their histories provided so many common bonds and so much similarity that the two countries might feel instinctively drawn together. Prussia and Italy had been allied in 1866, and Prussia's victory over Austria had sealed Italy's acquisition of Venetia. Four years later, the Franco-Prussian war had provided Italy the opportunity to seize Rome when Napoleon had to recall his troops. Finally, both nations could profit from such an alliance. To keep France isolated, Bismarck found it advantageous to support Italy in its struggle with France over trade relations, colonial expansion, and spheres of influence in the Mediterranean. Italy, for its part, gladly accepted German backing for its designs on Tunisia and for insurance against renewed French intervention in Italy on behalf of the pope.

Friendly relations between the two countries were cemented in 1873 when the king of Italy visited Berlin. However, no alliance was made until Italy had been completely rebuffed by France and alienated by French seizure of Tunisia in 1881. In 1882, Italy joined Germany and Austria in the Triple Alliance. This secret treaty, renewed periodically until World War I, was a defensive alliance guaranteeing mutual aid if one of the partners was "attacked [by] and engaged in a war with *two* or more great powers." If one of the three allies found itself at war with only *one* other power, the treaty stipulated that the other two were to observe benevolent neutrality. The Triple Alliance was thus useful to Bismarck for obtaining Austro-Italian assistance in a possible two-front war against Russia and France. So that this alliance would not contradict the secret Dual Alliance between Berlin and Vienna, a special clause provided that each of the three allies had the right to aid one of the partners "if it should see fit," even when the treaty obligations called only for benevolent neutrality. Thus, if Russia attacked Austria or Germany, Berlin and Vienna could still present a common front against St. Petersburg.

Each partner in this alliance hoped to gain security for recent territorial acquisitions—Germany for Alsace-Lorraine, Austria for Bosnia-Herzegovina, and Italy for Rome. Article 2 specified that both partners would aid Italy in case that country "should be attacked by France, without direct provocation on her part." The Italians, in turn, were treaty-bound to help the Germans if Germany were attacked by France. No similar special clauses were inserted for Austria, which felt sufficiently protected by the guarantee of Italian neutrality and the assurance of German aid (stipulated in the Dual Alliance) in any war with Russia.

Although this alliance strengthened Germany and became another cornerstone in Bismarck's system, it was punctuated by many question marks. Italian irredentist demands on Austrian territory—particularly the Trentino and Trieste—and Italian hopes of acquiring lands and influence in the western Balkans caused constant tension between the two southern partners in the Triple Alliance. Moreover, Italy stipulated in a specially appended declaration that it would not fight against Great Britain; hence the alliance did not strengthen Germany in the Anglo-German colonial duel about to open. Finally, Italy expected the alliance to act primarily as a support against France. After its differences with France over trade and colonies were settled—as happened by 1902—Italy cooled measurably toward its Austro-German friends and proved the weakest link in the alliance.

Relations with Russia

During his entire tenure of office, Bismarck tried to maintain friendly relations with Russia. This attitude was the continuation of long-standing Prussian policy. Frederick the Great, during the Silesian Wars, had been the last to experience a two-front war against Russia and France, and later statesmen continued to recall Frederick's advice that friendship with Russia was a prerequisite if Prussia hoped to undertake anything in central Europe that might antagonize the French. This lesson had been underscored in the two decades preceding unification. Russia's anti-Prussian and pro-Austrian attitude during the revolutionary period 1848–1850 had been important in preventing Prussia from unifying Germany and had contributed measurably to its humiliation at Olmütz (see page 335). Consequently, Bismarck had decided to cultivate good relations with Russia in the preparatory years of German unification. During the Crimean War, when he was Prussian envoy to the diet at Frankfurt, he had argued successfully against German intervention on the side of England. At the time of the Polish rebellion of 1863, he had earned the gratitude of Alexander II by aligning Prussia solidly on the side of Russian repression of the insurgents. Finally, Bismarck and William I were exceedingly grateful to Russia for maintaining benevolent neutrality during the critical years when Prussia crushed Austria and France in the process of unifying Germany.

As early as 1872, William I, Francis Joseph, and Alexander II met in Berlin. Their meeting recalled the days of the "Holy Alliance," when it was thought that solidarity among the three eastern powers would bring stability to Europe. They discussed outstanding issues and tried to devise solutions for the troubled Balkan area. The Austrians and Germans asked the tsar to curb the nascent Pan-Slav movement inside Russia, since they feared it might endanger their possession of Slavic lands. No formal treaties were signed, but the talks foreshadowed the Three Emperors' League concluded in the following decade. Bismarck hoped to create such a league in order to maintain peace in eastern Europe and "undergird," as he wrote in his memoirs, "the solidarity of the monarchical system of order as represented by the three Emperors . . . in the face of the disorderly tendencies of a social republic such as France." It is interesting to recall here that Bismarck had secretly tried to enhance the power of the republican elements in France during the founding of the Third Republic, when it was as yet undecided whether France would adopt republican or monarchical institutions. He did this largely to ensure that France and Russia would find it harder to come to terms, for he thought it unlikely that autocratic Russia would put much trust in a republican France, despite Alexander II's mild liberalism.

Then came the rapid French resurgence in 1873 and the ensuing war crisis with France. Bismarck was forced to lean even more heavily on Russia. The two emperors, William and his nephew Alexander, exchanged several more visits, and a Russo-German military convention was concluded that would help Germany in any trouble with France.

However, during the Near Eastern crisis of 1875–1878, as was seen, Bismarck thought it impossible to support all of Russia's demands. He found himself more and more in disagreement with the Russian foreign minister, Prince Gorchakov. Bismarck's decisions at the Congress of Berlin in 1878 earned him the friendship of England and the gratitude of Austria, but at the same time antagonized Russia. Despite William I's determination to side with Russia, Bismarck's view of Germany's over-all position between Russia and Austria had led him to tie Germany more closely to Austria by signing the Dual Alliance. Russo-German relations had reached a momentary low.

But Alexander II did not want to see Russia isolated in the face of an Austro-German alliance. Negotiators were sent to Berlin and Vienna to discuss new agreements among the three powers. The tsar was particularly disquieted by renewed war dangers in the Balkans, caused this time by disputes among Turkey, Montenegro, and Greece. Bismarck was equally interested in improving relations with St. Petersburg. Only Austria showed momentary hesitation. Hence the actual Three Emperors' League was not concluded until the summer of 1881, after the assassination of Alexander II and the accession of his son, Alexander III. This treaty obligated the other two partners to observe benevolent neutrality if one of them became involved in war with a fourth power. In any conflict with Turkey, the three agreed to hold mutual consultation in regard to territorial adjustments. The treaty gave Russia and Germany some reassurance in any conflict with England or France, respectively, but its primary aim was to prevent conflict between Austria and Russia. For this reason the treaty and appended protocol made specific disposition for the future of areas of outstanding Austro-Russian friction in the Balkans. The pact was to have a duration of three years and was kept secret.

For the moment Bismarck felt that Germany's position had once again been secured, yet he feared that this new alliance would disintegrate in the face of the frequent crises in the Balkans. Consequently, in the following year he concluded the Triple Alliance with Austria and Italy to gain added security against a possible two-front war. In 1883 he adhered to an alliance previously concluded between Austria and Rumania. Since Rumania lay in the path of Russia's advance into the Balkans, this Austro-Rumanian-German alliance was patently directed against Russian expansion toward the south, and once again showed that Bismarck preferred Austria over Russia.

Imperfect and fragile as the alliance of the three emperors was, it served Bismarck's purpose of keeping Russia friendly and discouraging it from forming an alliance with France. Consequently, despite recurring Austro-Russian friction, he managed to get the alliance renewed in 1884 for a second three-year term. Shortly thereafter, however, a new Near Eastern crisis flared up. War broke out between Serbia and Bulgaria, and Bulgaria itself was shaken by revolution.

The crisis lasted from 1885 to 1888, and involved Austria, Russia, Turkey, and England. In addition, there was renewed tension between Germany and France. Europe once again seemed dangerously close to war. The result of these crises was the breakdown of the Three Emperors' League, which Russia refused to renew in 1887. To protect Germany, Bismarck increased German armaments, and renewed the Triple Alliance with Austria and Italy. However, he still felt obliged to take special steps to keep Russia from aligning itself with France in order to avoid the encirclement of Germany. He therefore concluded with Russia the so-called Reinsurance Treaty of 1887, which was to replace the link lost through the demise of the Three Emperors' League.

Like that league, this Russo-German alliance was no military agreement. It did not call for either partner to aid the other militarily. It merely stipulated benevolent neutrality in case either power was involved in war, unless Russia should attack Austria or unless Germany should declare war on France. With this treaty in effect, Bismarck could face the war scare with greater assurance. Yet for added protection, he published the hitherto secret Dual Alliance to dampen Russian imperialistic ardor in the Balkans by convincing Russia of Austro-German solidarity. At the same time, he saw to it that France was informed of the terms of the secret Triple Alliance in order to dam the French clamor for a war of revenge.

The terms of the Reinsurance Treaty, which was kept secret until 1890, reveal Bismarck as rather unscrupulous. In order to please Russia, he encouraged its aspirations to dominate Bulgaria and the Turkish Straits, both areas in which he knew it would be steadfastly opposed by Great Britain and by his ally, Austria. Thus, the Treaty of Reinsurance was in effect contrary to the Dual Alliance, in spirit if not in actual terms. Yet despite these conflicting commitments, the treaty served its purpose for Bismarck. The failure to renew it in 1890—which was one of the issues leading to Bismarck's resignation—signaled the first step in the destruction of his security system and the beginning of the encirclement of Germany that was to be so disastrous for the nation in World War I.

Relations with England

During the two decades of Bismarck's chancellorship, Great Britain was concerned primarily with colonial expansion, while at home much of its energy was consumed by the Gladstone-Disraeli struggle, by questions of internal reform, and by the Irish problem. Hence, Britain remained aloof from Continental developments unless they directly affected its interests. Whenever Danish independence was threatened, England intervened on the diplomatic scene, for Denmark controlled the entrance to the Baltic Sea, an important waterway for British trade. Likewise it was British policy to safeguard the Low Countries, since Britain desired no major power to dominate the southern coast of the Channel. Finally, it entered the international fray whenever the fluid Balkan situation suggested that Russia might subjugate Turkey and gain possession of the Straits, since this would affect vital British interests in the eastern Mediterranean. However, Britain was reluctant to become involved in the numerous international squabbles of the Continent over areas where its own interests were not involved. Despite frequent wooing by the larger powers, Britain refused to enter alliances that would limit its freedom of action.

Britain generally favored a balance among the major Continental powers. It had not been frightened by the unification of Germany, but had rather welcomed the new country as a counterweight to French power. During the war scare of 1875, however, Britain tried to restrain possible German bellicose intentions, for it feared the new equilibrium between the two countries would be upset if Germany were to crush France a second time.

On the whole, it was therefore easy for Bismarck to chart his course in regard to Great Britain. He strove to cultivate friendly relations—although he never succeeded in drawing it into an alliance. During the 1870s, when Germany was not yet a protagonist in the colonial field, bonds between the two countries were strong. Bismarck did his best to encourage Britain in its colonial designs in areas where it might clash with French or Russian interests. Such a policy he thought would help prevent any possible Anglo-French or Anglo-Russian entente and might ensure the continuation of Britain's aloofness from the European scene.

But when Germany entered the colonial field in 1883, friction arose between the two countries. Bismarck found himself forced to effect a brief *rapprochement* with France in order to convince England of the dangers of opposing all German attempts to establish colonies. He urged France to show a united front with Germany, since both countries found their central African ventures threatened through British opposition. In 1884, Bismarck arranged for a joint Franco-German invitation to all powers interested in Africa to attend a colonial conference in Berlin. During the meeting, Britain and Portugal found themselves opposed by France, Belgium, and Germany and agreed to accept compromise solutions. Hereafter, disagreements between Germany and England again subsided. As Britain clashed more and more with France and Russia in the colonial world, it agreed to work out agreements with Germany and, as it were, to admit Germany gracefully into the colonial club. Thus relations between the two countries resumed their friendly tone after 1885, and remained so until Bismarck's dismissal in 1890, when William II embarked on his new imperialistic policy, which had little regard for assuaging the growing apprehension of Great Britain.

Creation of a Colonial Empire

Bismarck's policy was centered in Europe. He was not interested in *Weltpolitik*—world politics—as William II was to be later on. As late as 1881, he stated:

> While I am imperial Chancellor, we shall not engage in any colonial policy. We have a navy which is not seaworthy and do not need any vulnerable spots in other parts of the world which would fall as booty to the French as soon as war breaks out.

He appeared convinced that Germany should concentrate its energy on the Continent and not become entangled in international complications through a race for colonies.

On the other hand, manifold pressures were exerted on the government to push Germany into the colonial field. German traders and missionaries had begun to penetrate Africa as early as the 1840s; by the 1870s their increased importance made it more difficult for the government to refuse to recognize and support them. Merchants, industrialists, and shipbuilders favored the acquisition of colonies, insisting that Germany's rapid industrialization and growth of population made it essential to obtain new sources of food, markets for manufactured goods, and outlets for surplus population. Some proclaimed that Germany ought to collect colonies in order to gain the prestige of a first-rate power, while others reasoned that colonies could be used for deportees. Finally, there were those who believed that Germany's excessive vitality, which could no longer be expressed on the Continent without danger of provoking a major war, should best be diverted to overseas adventures. In the early 1880s Bismarck decided to give in. Some historians advance the theory that Bismarck was not really pressured into abandoning his anticolonial stand, but rather welcomed the opportunity to antagonize England and create inside Germany a national feeling that served his political purposes. Thus, A. J. P. Taylor writes in *The Course of German History*:

> Colonial disputes with England gave Bismarck an easy popularity with national feeling in the *Reichstag* and in Germany. ... In colonial affairs what mattered to him was the dispute, not the reward; and he was both astonished and annoyed at British acquiescence in his demands, which at once deprived him of his quarrel and saddled him with unwanted colonies.

But one should seek the cause of Bismarck's change of position not in Anglophobia, but rather in his desire to obtain added support from certain political groups in the Reich—the industrial and commercial interests and the ultranationalists.

In 1878, the German Africa Society had started to set up posts in East Africa. The *Kolonialverein* (German Colonial Society) had been founded in Frankfurt in 1882, and in 1883 German merchants claimed the territory around Angra Pequena, which was to become the southern portion of German Southwest Africa. Bismarck agreed to extend the protection of the German flag over these new ventures and defended the new colonial ambitions in the face of British opposition. The period from 1883 to 1885 became years of feverish colonial expansion. By 1885, Germany had asserted its sovereignty over all Southwest Africa, German East Africa, and the Cameroons, Togoland, and parts of Zanzibar in Africa, as well as northeast New Guinea, the Bismarck Archipelago, and the Marshall and Solomon islands in the Pacific. In fact, except for a few later acquisitions in the Pacific—such as Samoa, the Marianas, and Tsingtao on the Chinese mainland—Germany acquired all its colonial empire in the brief span of two and a half years. By 1913, this empire was organized into ten colonies, covering 1,231,000 square miles, with thirteen million people (see Map 20). In area it was the third largest agglomeration of colonies, after those of England and France. Although Bismarck henceforth defended and supported German colonial affairs, it was not the government but rather private merchants and trading companies who acquired these lands. Only after private interests had secured the land did the German gov-

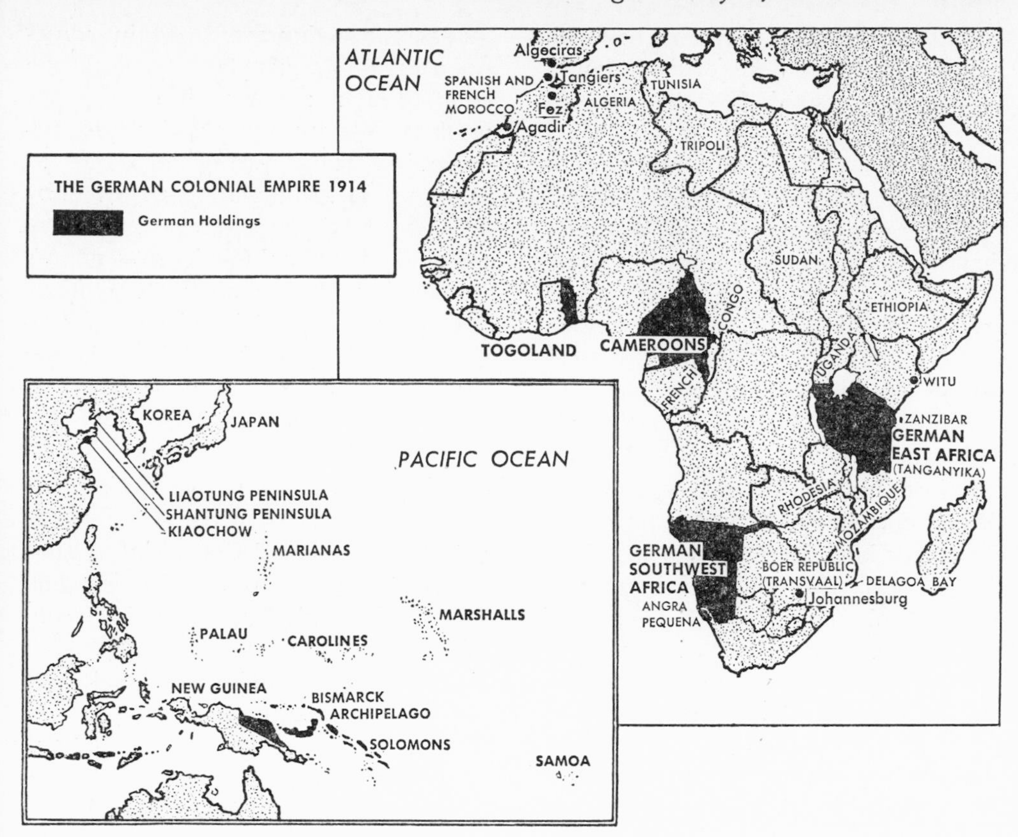

MAP 20

ernment step in to protect German interests, and it was not until after Bismarck's dismissal from office that a full-fledged Colonial Office was established in Berlin.

The main reasons traditionally advanced for Germany's entry into the colonial arena were these: (1) to obtain raw materials for its industry, acquire new outlets for manufactured goods, improve trade, and stimulate shipbuilding—in short, for economic profit; (2) to acquire land for its surplus population; (3) to achieve the prestige of a first-class power; (4) to find an escape valve for excess energy; and finally (5) to bring the benefits of European civilization to native peoples.

There is no consensus whether any of these aims were accomplished. To be sure, Germany soon imported considerable quantities of basic materials from its colonies—such as copper, cocoa, diamonds, rubber, and hemp. But no agreement exists among economists whether these imports warranted the large investments and corollary expenses. Perhaps greater profits could have been reaped from ordinary trade with other countries. When Germany lost its colonial empire in 1919, many observers suggested that it should be happy to be freed from this financial and economic liability. The second possible purpose—the acquisition of colonies for settling excess population—is unanimously regarded as a failure. By the outbreak of World War I, fewer than 30,000 Germans had migrated to the colonies, a truly insignificant number, especially when one considers that during the same period several million Germans migrated to the Americas.

This leaves three intangible purposes that are hardly susceptible to a clear definition. Unquestionably the German Empire after 1871 ranked among the first-class powers. But it is mere conjecture whether Germany could have held that position equally well had it eschewed colonization. One must remain as hesitant in judging how well the colonies served as outlets for excess energy, or how deeply and beneficially European civilization was implanted on the colonies. Many Germans, of course, stress that the brief span of years during which they owned colonies did not permit developing them for their intended purpose.

There are, however, certain consequences of Germany's entry into the colonial field about which there can be little disagreement and which became important during the reign of William II. Colonial expansion by whatever nation sooner or later provoked international friction. Germany's sudden imperialism was no exception. Advocates of colonialism and the various colonial associations joined the big industrial interests and nationalistic elements to become powerful lobbyists on the German political front. The acquisition of a colonial empire provided these groups with a motive for building a powerful German navy, and offered William II a world-wide arena for exercising his flamboyant *Weltpolitik*—two factors that contributed much toward clouding the international scene in the two decades preceding World War I.

16

The Empire of William II: The First Decade, 1890–1900

THE PERIOD OF TRANSITION

Bismarck's tenure of office lasted until 1890, but the last two years of his long "reign" were essentially years of transition to the "Wilhelmian Reich." The death in 1888 of the ninety-one-year-old William I, with whom Bismarck had built the empire, foreshadowed the end of an era. It jeopardized both Bismarck's power and the whole governmental and constitutional system that the chancellor had fashioned to suit his own requirements.

The Ninety-nine Days of Emperor Frederick

The new ruler, the fifty-seven-year-old Frederick III,[1] was mortally ill with cancer of the throat. An operation performed a month before his accession had temporarily prolonged his life, but he was not expected to survive more than a few months. Despite the gloomy atmosphere at the court, the change of rulers was greeted with enthusiasm by German liberals. The new emperor and his English wife, Victoria, were known to be more liberal and democratic than the usual Hohenzollerns. They shared a warm admiration for British parliamentary institutions and had many friends among members of the Progressive party and the liberal intelligentsia. But the frequent assertion that Frederick III could have turned Germany into a truly democratic empire is mere conjecture. It is quite possible that historians have overrated the strength of his liberal convictions.

Before their accession, Frederick and Victoria had often quarreled with Bismarck. The crown prince had openly objected to the authoritarianism of the regime, and the chancellor had not tried to conceal his contempt for the idealistic tendencies of the royal heir. But because Frederick knew how brief his

[1] As German emperor, he should have borne the title Frederick I, but he is known by his Prussian designation, Frederick III.

reign would be, his first act as emperor was to request "his father's faithful and courageous counsellor" to remain at the helm of the state. The new ruler—who had by this time lost the use of his vocal chords—and the wily old chancellor tacitly agreed to hide all signs of friction and disagreement. Even so, Frederick's three months' reign revealed so many points of difference between emperor and chancellor that it is fairly obvious that Bismarck would not have continued in office had the new emperor's health permitted a longer reign.

Bismarck did his best to isolate the royal pair. He feared the influence of the progressives on the sick emperor, as well as foreign interference through the empress, who, he complained, "never ceased to look upon England as her fatherland." Most of Frederick's proposed measures were opposed by Bismarck. The chancellor refused to let Frederick include the imprisoned Social Democrats in the traditional amnesty proclaimed by the new ruler. Nor would he permit the emperor to bestow special honors on his liberal friends. Frederick was not even allowed to dismiss the demagogic, anti-Semitic court pastor, Adolf Stöcker (1835–1909), the leader of the Christian Social party—not because Bismarck particularly liked Stöcker, but because he feared such a dismissal might be interpreted as a concession to the Progressives. Finally, Bismarck successfully interfered in a project dear to the empress's heart: to have her daughter marry Prince Alexander of Battenberg (1857–1893), who in 1886 had relinquished the throne of Bulgaria. The young prince had incurred the wrath of Emperor Alexander III, and Bismarck believed his marriage to a Hohenzollern princess might endanger Russo-German relations. Bismarck stirred up a violent press campaign against the proposed marriage, and finally won his point—together with the irreconcilable hatred of the empress.

Bismarck permitted only one imperial measure to pass unchallenged. In early June 1888, Frederick dismissed the Prussian minister of the interior, Robert von Puttkamer (1828–1900), a hated authoritarian who had delighted in persecuting the Social Democrats in Prussia and had used his police powers to influence elections. Puttkamer's dismissal gave the liberals added reason for loving the dying emperor.

But Frederick's reign was short. Ninety-nine days after his accession, he died, leaving the crown to the twenty-nine-year-old William II.

The Character of William II

William II, whom many Americans call simply "the Kaiser," was not prepared for the task he inherited in 1888. Two years before, his father had urged Bismarck to give the young prince some training in internal policy, so that he would acquire at least a minimum of administrative knowledge; and he had warned the chancellor not to let William dabble in foreign affairs because of his "immaturity," his "inexperience," and his "predilection for exaggeration." In accordance with his parents' wishes, the prince's education had been simple. The first Prussian prince to attend an ordinary public gymnasium—at Kassel—he had then studied at the University of Bonn, and finally served as an officer at Potsdam and Berlin. But, although a quick learner who dabbled in many fields, he showed no interest in learning the art of politics, and once even boasted that he had never read the constitution he was supposed to uphold.

His lifelong immaturity was marked by an almost childish love of drama and bombast. His temperament lacked a sense of moderation. His decisions were often impulsive, and his craving to be admired and to occupy a place in the forefront of the political stage knew few bounds. Addicted to assuming military poses, he owned about a thousand different uniforms, and on one typical occasion, decked himself out in an admiral's uniform to attend a public performance of Wagner's *The Flying Dutchman.* King Edward VII of England, his uncle, once remarked: "My nephew William must always strut about like a peacock; if he cannot do that, he feels inferior and unhappy."

Some psychologists attribute his conceit to unconscious compensation for a congenital defect that resulted in his left arm being shortened and crippled. Through Spartan self-discipline, he learned to ride a horse and to eat properly with a special fork. Yet it is felt that the incongruity of a "cripple" on the military throne of the Hohenzollerns led him to seek glory and admiration in other ways. Sadly susceptible to flattery, he liked being surrounded by obsequious courtiers who shielded him from criticism, so that he often was ignorant of the disastrous effect of some of his actions. Confident of his own capabilities and believing in the divine mission of the Hohenzollerns—as evinced in the biography he wrote about his dynasty, *My Ancestors*—he bragged that he ran the Reich almost singlehandedly and hence was often, and at times unjustly, blamed for all mishaps. "I chart the course correctly and it shall be followed!" he announced in the naval terms so dear to him. Ignorant of the constitution, he thought he had the power to command the princes of the Reich and even to levy taxes without consent of the Reichstag. "That is the trouble," he once said, "my subjects should simply do what I tell them; but they always want to think for themselves and all the difficulties arise from that." In reality, though, he was not interested in running the government, nor was he able to do so; he could not even dominate his own ministers nor surmount the fog of court intrigues. He loved to make speeches, but he hated work that required concentration. He displayed much interest in the army and the navy, where his activities were less circumscribed by the Reichstag, but primarily he liked to enjoy himself and was fond of hunting, fishing, and traveling. It has been estimated that he spent about one fifth of his entire reign on the pleasure yacht "Hohenzollern." Since he usually traveled for over half the year, when he was largely out of touch with political affairs, his claim of personal government was indeed a fiction.

Many of William's ideas were strangely contradictory. He believed in "divine right" monarchy and was undisguisedly partial to the nobility. His anachronistic views hardly fitted the new industrial society. On the other hand, he loved all things modern, and was vitally interested in industry and engineering. Industrialists and entrepreneurs, such as Friedrich Alfred Krupp (1854–1902) and the shipping magnate Albert Ballin (1857–1918), were among his frequent companions. He also professed deep interest in the social problems of his subjects; yet his first proclamations after his accession were directed to the army, and only after three days did he address the people, significantly without reference to the constitution. He was essentially kind and friendly, a man of peace; yet he loved taking a bellicose stance and rattling the sabers of his soldiers.

Much has been written about William and the source material on him is prodigious. Many unwarranted accusations have been flung at him, such as a French indictment of his entire reign as "a permanent conspiracy against world peace." He cannot be blamed for all the problems of the era that bears his name; greater onus must fall on the system of government that allowed the continuation of the Bismarckian framework without a Bismarck.

Bismarck's Dismissal

Soon after William II's accession, it became apparent that differences between the impulsive and vainglorious emperor and the experienced Bismarck would not permit long-term cooperation between them. The fault lay not merely in their respective infatuation with power, but also in the system. Under the constitution, all power was vested in the emperor. But William I had delegated most authority to his chancellor, and Frederick III had not lived long enough to alter the arrangement. The ambitious young William II, however, was bent on exercising the power he considered his prerogative. As the grand duke of Baden remarked so aptly: "The real question was whether the Bismarckian or the Hohenzollern dynasty should reign."

Besides this underlying struggle for power, there were many specific points on which emperor and chancellor disagreed. In foreign and domestic affairs, Bismarck was conservative and Continental in his outlook, content to remain in the tried and chosen path. He saw no reason for changing legislation or alliances or tampering with the system and showed little appreciation of the new demands of expanding industry, world markets, and an increased proletariat. William, however, was consciously fostering the image of a new era. Without definite aims or adequate preparation, he was impatient to embark on new paths and expected immediate results. As Bismarck complained, William wanted to have a birthday every day.

An early clash occurred in the spring of 1889, on the occasion of a miners' strike in the Ruhr. The emperor was eager to gain the love of his subjects by ostentatious concessions and, without consulting Bismarck, invited the strikers to send envoys to Berlin to discuss their grievances. Convinced of the justice of the strikers' demands, he publicly threatened withdrawal of all troops from the Ruhr so as to leave the industrialists at the mercy of the strikers, unless the mine owners immediately raised wages. Bismarck was shocked that the emperor would make such rash threats before hearing both sides in the conflict. But he could not dissuade William from making his impetuous pronouncement.

Bismarck spent the winter of 1889–1890 on his estate. During his absence from Berlin, various intrigues were engendered in the entourage of William II by those who hoped to profit from the chancellor's dismissal. When Bismarck returned to attend the Crown Council of January 24, the first public clash occurred between the emperor and his chancellor. William had decided that Bismarck's system of social security was insufficient. Partly under the influence of Pastor Stöcker and his Christian Socialism, the emperor had devised a new set of labor laws. He wished not merely to extend the insurance coverage, but also to regulate working conditions—abolish Sunday work, limit child and female labor, ensure fair treatment of workers, and safeguard their health and morals. An official body was to be set up to represent workers before employers and government. And finally he called for an international conference on labor problems, so that similar legislation might be adopted by all countries in order to avoid unfair competition. William had discussed these proposals with friends, but had not submitted them to Bismarck or any ministers. When the Crown Council convened, the draft was introduced as a surprise. Bismarck was annoyed that the bill was presented without his prior approval. He also objected to the implied excessive governmental interference in industry and the lack of forethought in not providing for compensation to the workers for the loss of Sunday wages. Despite Bismarck's objections, the emperor published the proposed social reforms in the official imperial gazette, without the customary countersignature of his chancellor. The rift between the two was thus communicated to the public at large.

Soon new disagreements arose. The anti-Socialist laws of 1878 came up for renewal. Bismarck insisted on new and harsher measures, which were opposed by the emperor and a majority of the Reichstag. In the end, Bismarck's refusal to accept less stringent legislation caused the lapse of all anti-Socialist legislation. At the same time, Bismarck's support in the Reichstag was undermined by new elections (see Chart 5). In 1890, the Free Conservatives, or *Reichspartei,* and the National Liberals each lost over half their seats —decreasing from a combined total of 140 to a mere 62—while Bismarck's opponents, the Progressives and the Social Democrats, increased from a total of 43 to 111. This electoral upset, so rarely mentioned by historians when discussing the fall of Bismarck, must have influenced his position and his outlook for the future. Constitutionally he was, of course, not dependent on a vote of confidence from the Reichstag. But the loss of support in that body at a time when he was also losing the confidence of his emperor unquestionably undermined his position. At a minimum, he was faced with seeking a realignment of supporting parties, without which a proper legislative program was impossible. According to some, Bismarck even contemplated forcing a constitutional reform that would do away with the anomalous pseudo parliamentarianism he himself had instituted.

At the same time, Bismarck and William disagreed on matters of foreign policy. William's watchword—"The course remains the same, full steam ahead!"—shows how little he understood Bismarck's more subtle policy, which never operated at full throttle. When in the early months of 1890, Russia inquired about renewing the Treaty of Reinsurance, the Kaiser hesitated. He wished to remain faithful to the alliance with Vienna, and felt that the treaty with Russia presented inherent dangers to Germany in any Austro-Russian war, even though it did not require German neutrality if Russia attacked Austria. Moreover, the Foreign Office, inspired by Baron Fritz von Holstein (1835–1909), opposed the alliance. Bismarck, however, always considered the Russian treaty a fundamental part of his international system and had lost some of his faith in the reliability of an Austria in which the Slavs and Magyars had increased their power at the expense of the Germans. Hence the question of renewing the treaty, while in no way a cause of Bismarck's dismissal, contributed to the tension between the emperor and his minister. William was openly jealous and suspected that the tsar had sent his ambassador (Shuvalov) to negotiate a renewal of the treaty solely with Bismarck and that Alexander III was maintaining a private correspondence with the chancellor. William had heard that in one of these letters to Bismarck, Alexander referred to him as an "ill-bred youngster." The emperor finally decided against renewal of the important Treaty of Reinsurance.

A question of administrative protocol brought about the final break. A royal decree of 1852 stipulated that all executive affairs had to pass through the hands of the chief minister before submission to the king of Prussia, and that only the chief minister and the minister of war could confer directly with the king. All other royal audiences needed the presence or the consent of the first minister. This rule had admirably fitted Bismarck's administrative requirements, and he insisted that its retention was requisite for administrative coordination. In fact, by allowing him to supervise all governmental activities, this regulation gave Bismarck his day-to-day basis of power. William, however, felt imprisoned by it. He complained that Bismarck could talk and negotiate with whomever he liked, whereas the emperor did not enjoy this privilege without the chancellor's permission. Moreover, he insisted that Bismarck's frequent absences from Berlin made the decree untenable. In March 1890, he finally ordered Bismarck to rescind the decree and made Bismarck's refusal a cause for dismissal.

Bismarck's "resignation" engendered bitter recriminations between the two protagonists, as seen in their private letters and posthumous memoirs. The emperor bestowed on the retiring chancellor the meaningless dignity of duke of Lauenburg—meaningless since William I had already made Bismarck a prince—and sent him his life-sized portrait as a "sign of never ending gratitude." In shortsighted vindictiveness he ordered the new chancellor, Caprivi (see below), not to consult his predecessor about current conditions. The Prussian government even requested the refunding of eleven days of salary by the chancellor, who retired on March 20, a few days before the end of the first quarter of 1890. The embittered ex-chancellor withdrew to his estate for the eight remaining years of his life, and launched an interminable barrage of criticism against his successors and their "new course" in foreign and domestic affairs.

The news of Bismarck's "deposition" provoked considerable consternation abroad. Bonds declined on the Paris market. Foreigners had generally come to look upon the German chancellor as a guarantor of the peace. Substitution of the impetuous young emperor seemed to forebode instability. But inside Germany there was surprisingly little excitement. Only two ministers considered handing in their own resignations, and on the whole, politicians and the people at large accepted the event passively. Some newspapers and Reichstag delegates even sighed with relief. Bismarck's most spectacular successes during the period of unification were almost a generation in the past. His rigidity and aloof, domineering manner had not endeared him to the new generation and had even begun to mark him as a man of the past. Buoyant with optimism and confident in their own ability to handle the future, those in government showed little regret at his disappearance.

THE FIRST DECADE

The four chancellors who succeeded Bismarck in the "Wilhelmian Reich" did not possess the abilities of their illustrious predecessor. The Prussian officer and bureaucrat General Count Georg Leo von Caprivi de Caprera de Montecuccoli (1831–1899) held the office from 1890 to 1894, and was followed by the Bavarian Prince Chlodwig Karl Viktor zu Hohenlohe-Schillingsfürst (1819–1901) from 1894 to 1900. The suave and talented Prince Bernhard von Bülow (1849–1929) was chancellor from 1900 to 1909, and finally the hapless Theobald von Bethmann-Hollweg (1856–1921) served from 1909 until the total collapse of the Bismarckian system in 1917. The relatively mediocre performance of these chancellors and their cabinets is frequently blamed on Bismarck, who had failed to train political successors, and whose authoritarian system had not allowed others to gain political experience. While it is true that the prevailing system was not auspicious for the development of political experience, it would be wrong to assert that no talented candidates existed for the important posts. Rather, they were not given a chance by William II, who had no desire to efface himself behind a new Bismarck.

Conciliation under Caprivi

Caprivi, the first of the four, was made chancellor of the Reich, federal foreign minister, and minister-president of Prussia—and thus in theory was vested with Bismarck's powers. He had had some forty years of military experience, as officer in the field, as administrator in the War Ministry, and as chief of the Admiralty, but in politics and diplomacy he was a novice. He felt duty-bound to the emperor, and worked faithfully on everyday problems and daily dispatches, but he failed to develop over-all views and a broad policy. He lacked the self-assertion as well as the vision necessary to dissuade the emperor from his grandiose ventures. Nor could he block the backdoor maneuvers of such intriguers as Baron von Holstein, the determined privy councilor in the Foreign Office, or Count Alfred von Waldersee (1832–1904), chief of the General Staff, confidant of the emperor, and husband of William's ex-mistress.

In his "new course," William was eager to placate all parties and inaugurate an era of harmony. Caprivi's gentle, conciliatory attitude fitted this mood. Compared with Bismarck, he was liberal in economic, social, and foreign matters. As a military man, he was free from all party affiliations, but contrary to political wisdom, he never tried to align reliable support in the Reichstag.

Many issues faced by Caprivi involved bringing government policies abreast of rapidly changing economic and social conditions. During the 1890s the population of Germany increased almost 15 percent—from 49.4 million in 1890 to 56.4 million in 1900—not because of an increase in the birth rate but because of a sharp reduction in the death rate and in emigration. Employment in industry, trade, and commerce rose quickly, while the percentage of those remaining in agriculture declined steadily. By 1895 only 36 percent earned their living from agriculture, almost 40 percent were engaged in industry, and 12 percent were in trade and communication; the remainder were in government, domestic, and other services. The larger cities doubled and tripled their populations without adequate provision for a corresponding increase in housing. By 1910, over 21 percent of the population were to live in cities with more than 100,000 inhabitants. Rents soared exorbitantly, and people were forced to sublet portions of rooms. In Berlin around 1900, for example, an average of 3.69 people shared each heatable room, and 10 percent of the one-room apartments were occupied by six or more people, many of whom were boarders. Production and trade indices were skyrocketing, and there was opportunity for many in the lower middle class to move from poverty toward prosperity. But wages remained low, and most of the proletariat rose no more than from want to bare subsistence wages. The cleavage between rich and poor remained exceptionally severe.

LABOR LEGISLATION AND TARIFFS One of Caprivi's early measures stemmed from William's continued desire to conciliate the workers by enacting the labor protection program that Bismarck had opposed. Although Bismarck had placed Germany in the vanguard of the social insurance system, it was backward in the field of labor legislation. In the summer of 1890, a law established labor courts. These industrial courts, consisting of an impartial presiding officer and elected associates representing both labor and management, were to mediate disputes between employers and employees. A year later, a law on labor protection made Sunday a legal holiday, limited child and female labor, prohibited payment of wages in kind, set up a protective code against harmful occupations, limited the power of employers to levy fines, and even suggested the establishment of workers' councils or factory committees to help determine employment policies. The powers of previously authorized government factory inspectors were increased to enforce these new regulations. Unquestionably much of this legislation was wholesome, despite the spottiness of its enforcement. But it neither conciliated the workers nor softened the opposition of the militant Socialists, who in this same year in their Erfurt Program, took a more doctrinaire, Marxist stand on the class struggle.

To secure outlets for Germany's growing industry, Chancellor Caprivi sought to create a sort of "common market" in central and eastern Europe. Bismarck's protective tariff of 1879 had helped German industry grow, but had not opened up new markets abroad. He had negotiated most-favored-nation clauses with a number of countries, but no reciprocal trade treaties, which might have forced him to lower tariffs on imports into Germany. Between

1891 and 1894, Caprivi concluded with eight European nations a series of trade treaties in which duties were reduced and fixed for a period of twelve years, thereby permitting German industry to plan a long-term price and production program. Actually, the government had not wished to lower agricultural tariffs for fear of undermining Germany's own food production and rendering it vulnerable to blockade in time of war. On the other hand, reduction of agricultural tariffs would result in lower food prices, which in turn would permit industry to pay lower wages and hence produce cheaper and more competitive goods. Furthermore, most of the countries desiring to import German industrial goods could pay for them only in agricultural produce. Hence, as a price for concluding the trade treaties, Germany had to agree to reduce import tariffs on grain.

The treaties were accepted in the Reichstag, since the industrialists stood to profit by them and the liberals favored the principle of free trade. Although the agricultural interests did not favor this tariff policy, they were not adequately organized to oppose the measures. Also, because droughts had pushed up the world grain price they did not feel immediately threatened by imports of grain. Nonetheless, Caprivi's tariff policies suddenly provoked a realignment of political forces. Argentinian exports and an unexpected abundance in the Russian harvest in 1892–1893 lowered grain prices and hurt the landlords east of the Elbe. Since the new treaties prevented raising the tariffs, the agriculturalists blamed their plight on Caprivi's administration. To fight for their economic interests, the Prussian estate owners organized the League of Landlords (*Bund der Landwirte*) in 1893. This league quickly became one of the most powerful pressure groups in Germany, more important than most political parties with their official representation in the Reichstag. The league, largely composed of Prussian conservatives from the "new Germany," also attracted estate owners from other regions, who had formerly belonged to the Center and National Liberal parties. To secure wider support, especially among the smaller peasant proprietors of the south and southwest, it made a tacit alliance with the League of German Peasants (*Deutsche Bauernbund*) and backed their demands for high tariffs on all agricultural products, not merely on grain. The League of Landlords gave a powerful boost to the conservative forces. In fact, agricultural interests quickly assumed dominance within the Conservative party—despite the fact that industry surpassed agriculture in importance on the national economic scene—and were partially responsible for Caprivi's fall from power in 1894.

William II's initial policy of conciliation extended in many other directions. To please the liberal majority in the Prussian legislature—and increase revenue—he authorized a bill for the levying of a progressive income tax in Prussia. To eradicate remaining resentment from the *Kulturkampf,* he ordered repayment to the Catholic Church of all funds withheld in the 1870s, and he even supported, although unsuccessfully, an education bill in 1892 that would have transferred more supervisory power over primary education to the Catholic Church. The emperor also insisted on fairer treatment for the people of Alsace-Lorraine, and attempted to reconcile the Polish minority to Prussian rule by suspending Bismarck's policy of forcible Prussianization of the eastern lands, which had been inaugurated in 1886.

THE ARMY BILL AND THE ELECTIONS OF 1893 Despite these attempts to placate so many groups, William encountered difficulties with the Reichstag in regard to his military program. In 1890, the Reichstag agreed to add 18,000 men to the standing army, and to allocate additional funds for an expansion of the artillery services. But neither William nor Caprivi was satisfied with these increases. French rearmament programs and growing cooperation between France and Russia —facilitated and encouraged by William's failure to renew the Treaty of Reinsurance with Russia—gave Caprivi nightmares of a possible two-front war. Hence in 1893, the government presented a new army law calling for an increase of 84,000 men and high expenditures for new weapons. To gain the support of the liberals, Caprivi offered a reduction of the period of obligatory military service from three to two years and quinquennial in lieu of septennial approval of the army budget—a step that would increase the Reichstag's supervision over the army. This proposed reduction of military service is often regarded as evidence of Caprivi's democratic idealism, yet one should recall that he also asked for increased draft quotas. The same number of soldiers formerly drafted in three years would now be recruited in two. The proposal would thus quickly strengthen the available number of trained reservists and make Germany better prepared for a possible war.

Despite the enticements held out to the liberals and despite Caprivi's warnings about the Franco-Russian threat, the requested army law was defeated in the Reichstag. Determined to increase the military establishment, the emperor authorized Caprivi to dissolve parliament and call for new elections. The ensuing electoral campaign of 1893 was fought largely on the issues of the recently defeated education and army bills as well as the trade treaties. The election results favored the extremist parties, with a corresponding loss in the center of the political spectrum (see Chart 5). On the Right, the fairly new Anti-Semitic party increased its votes fivefold over the 1890 election, and gained 16 instead of their previous 5 seats. The right wing as a whole —which, besides Conservatives, Free Conservatives, and Anti-Semites, now included the National Liberals—increased its representation from a combined 140 to a total of 169 representatives. The Social Democrats, for their part, gained 9 seats. But most important for the fate of the army program was a new split among the Progressives. After the various liberal elements had united in 1884 and joined a left-wing splinter of the National Liberals to reform the *Freisinnige Partei* (literally, Freethinking party, though usually translated as Progressive party), they now again divided more or less into their original components. The left wing, the Progressive People's party (*Freisinnige Volkspartei*), under the guidance of Eugen Richter (1838–1906), remained doctrinaire in its opposition to militarism and continued to oppose the army bill. The more compromising Progressive Union (*Freisinnige Vereinigung*) voted for the army bill to gain a reduction in the period of military service. Caprivi's military proposals were finally adopted by the new Reichstag, although by a scant majority.

But four years of the "new course" left Emperor William thoroughly disappointed: his longing for adulation was not satisfied; no one seemed conciliated; the Conservatives complained about the new tariffs; the Socialists opposed his regime, despite his social legislation and his refusal to renew Bismarck's anti-Socialist laws; even the minority groups whom he had tried to placate did not appreciate him. In 1894, he complained loudly about ingratitude, expressing his disappointment particularly about the opposition of the nobility. He finally decided to abandon the "new course," relinquished thoughts of conciliation, and determined to return to Bismarck's sterner policies, particularly the fight against all "subversive elements." Count Caprivi, hardly the proper instrument for such a policy, was dismissed.

The Chancellorship of Hohenlohe

As new chancellor, William appointed the seventy-five-year-old Prince Chlodwig zu Hohenlohe-Schillingsfürst, who had considerable experience for the position. Among many other political activities, he had been minister-president of Bavaria, had worked effectively for the unification of Germany, and served as an influential, somewhat liberal, and stanchly antiultramontane member of the Reichstag. From 1874 to 1878 he had been ambassador to Paris, then worked as German foreign secretary under Bismarck, and finally occupied the post of governor of Alsace-Lorraine. But by 1894, Hohenlohe had become a tired old man, polite and ineffectual. The emperor could easily dominate him, and William's personal rule henceforth assumed greater importance, subject to fitful interference by intriguing subordinates.

In some respects it was not difficult to arouse national emotions for a fight against what Bismarck had called the *Umsturzparteien* (revolutionary parties). The nation at large entertained an almost neurotic fear of the ever-increasing Social Democrats. Not only the conservatives and the solid middle classes inveighed against the red specter, but also many liberals and even status-conscious domestic servants hated the workers and were terrified by Socialist talk of class warfare and revolution. Any imputation of crimes to the Socialists was readily accepted by the general public, and Socialists were frequently beaten up in the streets, while the police—as occurred later in the Weimar Republic—closed an eye or even arrested the victims as violators of the peace. Even in normally liberal Saxony, fear of socialism resulted in a change of the electoral system. Universal suffrage was replaced by an indirect three-class electoral system similar to Prussia's, with the result that the Socialists lost 15 of their 16 seats in the lower legislature.

At the same time, the conservatives were becoming more vociferous and dogmatic. Conciliation and harmonious cooperation figured no more in their views than in those of the militant Socialists. Stöcker and his Christian Socialists vigorously pushed their demagogic agitation against Jews, Progressives, and Social Democrats, under the banner of vague "Christian and Germanic" principles. In their party program of 1892, the Conservatives demanded an unconditional fight against the Social Democrats as enemies of the state, as well as "local self-administration based not on universal suffrage but on the natural and organic subdivisions of the people," which in essence meant a return to medieval corporatism.

Yet William and Hohenlohe were unable to get the Reichstag to pass new anti-Socialist legislation. The proposed bill "for the suppression of agitation" did not specifically mention the Social Democratic party, and most parties therefore feared that the measure might be used to restrict their own freedom. Even inside Prussia, the government's efforts to suppress the SPD failed when the bill was declared unconstitutional by the Prussian Supreme Court. A final attempt in 1897 to introduce in the Reichstag a law making it illegal to incite a strike or to join an association that might hinder work or put pressure on employers was also defeated. The Progressives and the Center party saw no reason to weaken the SPD, which was frequently a useful ally in parliamentary maneuvers against the government.

Thus William's "aggressive course" (*Kampfpolitik*) fizzled out as had his "new course." The campaign for anti-Socialist legislation had shown that, despite the rising strength of the conservatives, the parties favoring constitutionalism were determined to defend the principle of equal political rights for all. Beyond this, it had accomplished nothing except to embitter the two million Socialist voters and their sympathizers. The government had talked a lot but had never applied much pressure to ensure passage of its program. Hohenlohe had hardly exerted himself, and William, more interested in foreign affairs, had done little to help his chancellor.

In domestic legislation, the era of Hohenlohe was unspectacular. In 1896, the Common Civil Code for the Empire, compilation of which had been started under Bismarck, was finally enacted. In 1899, the provisions of the laws on old age and invalidism were extended and a new Association Law was promulgated to allow greater freedom for the formation of clubs and associations. Of greater consequence than these purely internal matters was the enactment of the first German Naval Law of 1898, which will be examined below in conjunction with foreign affairs. The old chancellor himself was not much involved in its passage nor in the intrigues surrounding it. He retired from office in 1900, and died shortly thereafter.

The Beginning of Weltpolitik

As in internal affairs, the young emperor was eager to launch Germany's foreign policy on a "new course." In a speech in 1896, he proclaimed that "the German Reich has become a *Weltreich*," and he justified his view on the grounds that "everywhere in distant lands live thousands of our compatriots." Bismarck's outlook had been Continental. Once Germany had been unified in 1871, he had not wished to become involved in colonial ventures or imperialistic expansion. He thought additional frontiers would merely bring added dangers. But, in the long run, as was seen, his reluctance had been overcome by economic expansion. From the very first, however, William II showed no hesitation about removing the Continental limits from Germany's political horizon. His was to be a *Weltpolitik* and Germany not just a European but a world power.

William's deliberate and much-publicized shift from the Continent to the world arena is often regarded as a prime cause of World War I. Yet it should be examined within the context of the late nineteenth century, a period of rampant imperialism, through which ran a strong strain of social Darwinism [2] on the international scene. Economic expansion of the great powers—in shipping and banking, in the search for raw materials and markets, in the creation of large trusts and interlocking cartels—furnished the dynamics of much of their foreign policies. Similarly, Germany's own economic life continually expanded beyond its borders, and drew it, willy-nilly, into the maelstrom of world politics. The politically minded Bismarck conceivably never grasped the full significance of this development, which began during his chancellorship; William, however, was delighted to take full advantage of all its implications.

Most of the great powers—except Italy, which was defeated in 1896 in its attempt to seize Ethiopia—were gathering in imperialistic conquests during the 1890s: Britain and France primarily in Africa, Russia in Manchuria, Japan in Formosa and on the Chinese mainland, and the United States in Puerto Rico, Hawaii, Guam, and the Philippines. Naturally Germany was intent on garnering its share. Bülow, who became foreign minister in 1897, insisted that its *Weltpolitik* did not imply that Germany desired to dominate the world. But, he asserted, since others conquered, it deserved "equal rights," an open door to the world, "a place in the sun," as he put it.

Germany, Japan, the United States, and to some extent Italy, became world powers in the 1890s. As late-comers among the great powers, they were regarded by the other nations as upstarts and intruders on the world scene who threatened the established equilibrium. Yet there was an essential difference between rising powers such as Japan and the United States, and Germany. The imperialistic aims of the former appeared clear, well defined, and limited, with the possible exception of American acquisition of the Philippines. The emperor's *Weltpolitik,* on the other hand, was nebulous and noisy. Bolstered by unscrupulous advisers and supported by boisterous pressure groups at home, William played the role of a tactless and pretentious *parvenu.* Germany's yearning for influence seemed to know no limits; its actions betrayed no recognizable direction. In Bismarck's time, the powers could sense the extent of German aspirations. Under William, no one knew the bounds of German aims, perhaps least of all the emperor himself. From the shores of China and the Pacific Isles to the coasts of Africa and the rivers of the Near East, Germany interfered everywhere. As William announced in 1900: "On the seas and in distant lands, no great decisions should be made without Germany and without the German Emperor." Railroads in Turkey, the British fight with the Boer Republic, the Boxer rebellion in China, the actions of the United States in the Philippines—everything

[2] Social Darwinism, the attempt to apply Darwin's theories of natural selection and survival of the fittest to the realm of politics. The stress was put on the sword as the symbol of authority rather than on the rule of law, and it was asserted that the strongest individuals and nations, not necessarily those abiding by law and morality, were destined to survive the struggle among men and states. See also pp. 429 and 460.

presented William with an excuse for intervention.

William's craving for adulation and power was evident also in the manner in which he conducted foreign affairs. He constantly interfered personally in diplomatic matters normally handled by ministers and ambassadors, made impromptu speeches on foreign policy, and in 1905 even negotiated a treaty with Russia on the spur of the moment. His staff felt obliged to remind him that "solidarity between Your Majesty and the Foreign Office is an urgent necessity," and that it might well happen that "Your Majesty's personal intervention destroyed the functioning of the machine." But worried about Germany's insecure position and eager to find acclaim, the emperor smiled in all directions to gain friends, rather than pursuing the less spectacular but more steady course of a firm alliance system such as Bismarck's. His zigzag course earned him distrust rather than friendship, for when he failed to get instantaneous professions of friendship, he usually turned his back and smiled at others. This fitful behavior particularly characterized his relations with England and Russia. His methods were aptly described by an undersecretary in the Foreign Office, speaking of the famous Baghdad Railroad: "By now bowing before the British Lion and then curtsying to the Russian Bear, we will wiggle our railroad through to Kuwait."

Thus the expanding Germany, guided by the moody young emperor with his bombastic speeches, abandoned the cautious framework of Bismarck's Continental system and jumped into the wide arena of world politics. From his retreat, the aging Bismarck noted in his memoirs: "In the future, as in the past, we need not merely armaments but also a sane political course to guide the German ship of state through the coalitions to which we are exposed because of our history and our geographic situation." But William II and his advisers insisted on moving ahead unchecked, and even Bülow and Bethmann-Hollweg, the chancellors after 1900, in the last analysis relied more on armaments and bluff than on tact and politics.

PRESSURES BEHIND THE THRONE Officially, the government of the Reich was a one-man affair, with all power concentrated in William II. But in reality, various individuals in his public and private entourage exercised a strong influence on German policy. Since much of this power was exerted indirectly and secretly, it is difficult even now to evaluate its real importance in certain cases.

In William's confidence were his friend Count Philipp Zu Eulenburg (1847–1921) and Pastor Stöcker, both of whom encouraged the young emperor's supernationalistic fervor. There were the skillful Albert Ballin and Alfred von Tirpitz (1849–1930), one of the strongest personalities in the Wilhelmian Reich. Both sought to direct William's eyes ever more to the high seas and to naval expansion of all types. Besides these, Count Alfred von Waldersee, who succeeded Moltke as chief of staff in 1888, acquired considerable power through intrigues and well-timed flattery. Waldersee harbored a fierce hatred of Bismarck as well as of Russia, and helped turn William against both. In fact, from his intrigues in 1889–1890, it is difficult to judge whether he wished to topple Bismarck in order to destroy the Russo-German alliance, or to undermine relations with St. Petersburg in order to dislodge the chancellor. He looked forward to plunging Germany, on the side of Austria, into a war with Russia, and even entertained hopes of some day assuming the chancellorship himself, even though he noted in his private diary: "I have the conscious realization that I am not up to such tasks."

Most powerful, though least known at the time, was Fritz von Holstein, privy councilor in the Foreign Office, "the evil spirit in German politics," as one historian has called him. A misanthropic, lonely man, filled with bitter suspicions (he always carried a pistol), he had served in the diplomatic service in St. Petersburg, Washington, and Paris. In 1876, Bismarck had appointed him to the Foreign Office in Berlin. The chancellor had known how to dominate him and use his particular skills at diplomatic intriguing. He employed Holstein frequently for secret missions and backstage maneuvers, and noted of him: "To be used in the basement only!" After 1886, Holstein began to intrigue with Bismarck's opponents to gain in power through removal of the mighty chancellor. Blithely insisting that a Franco-Russian alliance was inconceivable, he worked against renewal of the Treaty of Reinsurance, and helped persuade William to remove the "Bismarck dynasty." During the 1890s, his influence on the new chancellors and on Germany's foreign policy increased steadily (see pages 441 ff.). Recently discovered sources reveal that in many instances, until his removal from office in 1906, he had the decisive voice in foreign affairs. Yet he always remained in the background, and few at the time recognized his pervasive influence.

Apart from these individual intriguers, various pressure groups affected the course of German foreign policy, sometimes more by embarrassing the government than by exerting direct influence on its actions. The League of Landlords and the Naval League were two such groups that, for reasons of economic gains, lobbied for measures with far-reaching repercussions in foreign affairs (the tariffs of 1902 and the construction of a powerful high-seas fleet). Perhaps the noisiest among these groups was the All-German League, founded in 1890 as a protest against the Heligoland Treaty, through which William attempted a *rapprochement* with England by compromising on competing colonial claims. The All-German League, which published its own *All-Deutsche Blätter* (*All-German Pamphlets*), preached a policy of might and expansionism. Although it always remained small in membership—never more than about 22,000—it became representative of vociferous Pan-Germanism. Its pamphlets appealed to "German honor" and engendered distrust of other nations by denouncing the activities of their "clandestine and evil" agents. Considering themselves "Germans first of all," these Pan-Germans always looked upon coexistence and compromise in foreign affairs as treasonous, stressed their readiness to fight at William's call, and stanchly demanded their "share of the world as a conquering nation." Their policies and aims foreshadowed the later annexationist demands of certain groups in World War I.

THE "NEW COURSE" IN FOREIGN AFFAIRS William's "new course" in 1890 consisted of loosening the existing bonds between Germany and Russia, placing more confidence in the Triple Alliance, and attempting to establish closer relations with England. The changed attitude toward Russia was of fundamental importance for all other foreign relations. William harbored no liking for Emperor Alexander III, and considered the Treaty of Reinsurance too binding in view of the Dual Alliance with Vienna. But unlike some of his advisers, he had no intention of bringing about a real split between Berlin and St. Petersburg, much less of provoking a war. In fact, there were frequent periods in the 1890s and 1900s when William entertained very cordial relations with the Russian court, especially after his young cousin Nicholas II became tsar in 1894. At times Germany and Russia even cooperated actively, as, for example, in 1895 and subsequent years when they fashioned a common front against Japan. But the lapse of the Treaty of Reinsurance marked the end of any formal alliance between the two nations in the period before World War I. It opened the door to the gradual splitting of Europe into two camps and to the eventual "encirclement" of Germany—two developments Bismarck had tried so assiduously to avoid.

Russia was in no mood to remain isolated. Faced with German refusal to renew the treaty, Alexander III showed more interest in the overtures of France, despite the traditional tsarist hatred of French republicanism. Reciprocal visits by high officials and by their respective fleets resulted in negotiations for a Franco-Russian military convention. Alexander's initial hesitations to commit himself to a firm alliance were gradually overcome as William II's stanch pro-Austrian attitude, German *rapprochement* with England, and Caprivi's new army law drove him more and more into the arms of France. In 1894, the two countries ratified the first of a series of military conventions. Russia was to aid France if the latter were attacked by Germany, or by Italy supported by Germany. Similarly, France would assist Russia if she were attacked by Germany or by Austria with German help. This pact, periodically reaffirmed and widened in its stipulations, was thus patently directed against the Triple Alliance. Its formation marked the beginning of the entente system that was to divide Europe into two hostile camps.

Rather than depend on Russia, William chose to rely on the Triple Alliance, which was renewed and tightened in 1891. Few in the Foreign Office seemed to question the value of this alliance. Yet it should have been clear that Austria's reliability and usefulness as an ally were becoming more doubtful. The Slavs and Magyars of the Austrian Empire were constantly gaining in power at the expense of the Germans and embroiling Vienna in Balkan affairs that were not necessarily of vital interest to Germany. At the same time, Italy did not develop into a strong ally. It showed an ever-growing interest in acquiring African colonies, and demanded German backing for these ventures as a price for the alliance. Above all, one should recall that Bismarck had created the Triple Alliance in the days when Germany's aspirations were limited to the Continent. Since all three nations were then land powers, with insignificant navies, such an alliance had been well designed to assure the peace in Europe. But William's *Weltpolitik* needed a different framework, and Austria and Italy could not serve as adequate supports for the new German foreign policy.

Perhaps a subconscious recognition

of the insufficiency of the Triple Alliance led William to seek a *rapprochement* with England. The story of the repeated attempts to bring about closer Anglo-German relations is a tortuous one. Time and again during the prewar period, the two nations seemed about to bury their disagreements and establish mutual trust and friendship, if not an alliance, but each time such steps were frustrated—usually, though by no means exclusively, through some thoughtless act of William's, who at heart despised the English. The Heligoland Treaty of 1890 was the first step. Bismarck had favored settling all colonial disputes with England, and Chancellor Caprivi, who thought that Germany had already acquired more colonies than it could use, was glad to complete the negotiations. Certain business circles and the Pan-Germans, of course, favored colonial expansion rather than retrenchment. But Caprivi and others in the government wondered whether the money and sacrifices expended were justified in view of the meager benefits attained. Also, the German government was becoming increasingly involved in suppressing native rebellions, especially in Tanganyika, where the East African Trading Company was unable to handle the insurrections. Consequently, Caprivi gladly subscribed to a withdrawal of certain German claims. According to the Treaty of Heligoland, Germany relinquished its protectorate over Witu and its claims to Uganda and Zanzibar. The German rights to the coast of East Africa were confirmed, and the frontier between German and British East Africa was defined. In return, England ceded to Germany the tiny island of Heligoland, some hundred miles off the mouth of the Elbe. This treaty, considered treasonous by the Pan-Germans, was followed by a state visit of William to London. The Anglo-German *rapprochement* was seemingly successfully started, yet this appearance was deceptive. England was basically cool to the German advances, and William's unsteady course could not furnish a basis for a real Anglo-German alliance.

THE ZIGZAG OF THE MID-1890s Within a few years after Bismarck's dismissal, Germany's foreign policy began to waver between contradictory courses. On the one hand, William made occasional attempts to pursue the Anglo-German *rapprochement*. On the other, he frequently turned his back on the Channel, smiled at England's rival, France, and tried to regain the friendship of Russia.

Anglo-German relations were complicated by many areas of friction, one of which was economic. The rising German industrial output of the 1880s had engendered a sharp trade rivalry. Rather than impose protective tariffs England hoped to dam the flood of German goods by appealing to British patriotism. It forced the Germans to stamp their wares "Made in Germany," but the label soon became a mark of quality workmanship rather than a deterrent to British buyers. At the same time, the rapid growth of the German merchant marine enabled Germany to carry most of its exports in its own ships and thus deprive Britain of this lucrative trade. English newspapers in the 1890s frequently spoke of a "commercial war" between the two nations; Germans even called the rivalry a "matter of life and death."

Another irritant was the beginning of German penetration into the Near East. In 1888, a railroad from Hungary to Constantinople had been opened, completing the line from Berlin to the Turkish capital. The sultan then invited German companies to build the next link, from the south shore of the Bosporus to Ankara in central Turkey. A German consortium headed by the *Deutsche Bank* created the Anatolian Railroad Company and launched the first leg of what was to become the Berlin-to-Baghdad railroad. German industrialists and financiers viewed the project as a welcome expansion in a new direction, but Bismarck had perceived its political implications and warned that the Reich would not lend its official support to the venture. William II's attitude was naturally different. A German-built and German-controlled railway into the heart of the Near East fitted his dreams of *Weltpolitik*. He had visions of possible German settlements in Turkey, of extending German political influence over the entire Near East, and of becoming, as he later announced in an official speech in Palestine, the "friendly protector of the 300 million Muslims in the world." Consequently, the railroad scheme received his full backing after 1890. When the link to Ankara was completed in 1892, negotiations with the Turks were at once undertaken concerning further concessions for extensions to the south. England promptly submitted bids of its own, out of commercial as well as political considerations. But the Germans successfully thwarted the British efforts, and received the contract for the link to Konia, which was completed by 1896. The German victory of 1893 thus added to Anglo-German friction.

Africa also remained a source of Anglo-German disagreements, despite the compromises of the Treaty of Heligoland. In 1893, the two nations clashed again over a disputed border in northern Tanganyika. Moreover, Holstein, together with Baron Adolf Marschall von Bieberstein (1842–1912), who directed the Foreign Office, elaborated the curious theory that England's friendship and alliance could best be gained by antagonizing it wherever possible: London would learn from experience that it was preferable to have Germany as a friend than as an enemy. This theory gradually found credence among many influential German policy makers and partly accounts for Germany's stand against England in the Sino-Japanese War of 1895 and in the Transvaal conflict.

The quasi independence of the Boer Republic had been recognized by Gladstone in 1884, but discovery of new gold and diamond deposits had caused British imperialists to have second thoughts about abandoning this territory. Unofficial plans were made, largely with the connivance of Cecil Rhodes, for British recovery of the Transvaal. The Boers, under the leadership of Paul Kruger, in turn pinned some hopes on German support against England. William II encouraged the illusion and in 1894 dispatched two warships to Delagoa Bay, in an ostentatious gesture to bolster the Boer Republic against possible British attack. The insufficiency of the German fleet in the face of the British Navy and the fact that Portuguese territory blocked all passage from Delagoa Bay to the Transvaal made such a demonstration militarily meaningless. Yet it was a typical Wilhelmian irritant.

Late in the following year, Dr. Leander Jameson, from the South Africa Company in Rhodesia, invaded the Transvaal with a few hundred men in the hope of unleashing a pro-

British revolution in Johannesburg. The German government deliberated immediately on possible steps to help the Boer president against Jameson's raiders. Portugal was asked to grant German troops free passage through Mozambique, but refused. Even Kruger rejected the proferred aid. In fact, within barely a week, the Boers captured Jameson and his troops and suppressed all seeds of rebellion in Johannesburg. Hence Germany was given no occasion for active intervention.

World opinion strongly condemned Jameson's raid, but the powers maintained a discreet silence, since England not only disavowed all complicity but even tried and condemned Dr. Jameson. William and some of his advisers, however, refused to adopt such a tactful path. They were intoxicated by bold ideas, such as offering the Transvaal protection against future English aggression. When news of the Boer victory reached Berlin, William dispatched a telegram to Kruger, congratulating him for having successfully repelled the "disturbers of the peace" without foreign help, and for having "safeguarded the independence of the country from outside attacks." The telegram raised a storm of protest in England, which resented German interference in its colonial problems. The incident also shocked most of the other powers, who were not accustomed to this style of diplomacy.

While attempting to antagonize Britain into friendship, William also sought to improve relations with Russia. The "new course" toward the Polish minorities in Germany had frightened Alexander III, who feared it might raise similar hopes among the Poles under Russian control. Moreover, a tariff war between the two nations had caused considerable tension. These irritants were now assuaged. In 1893, Caprivi negotiated a new tariff treaty with St. Petersburg, and in the following year, Prussia's conciliatory policy toward its Polish subjects was terminated. The accession of Nicholas II in late 1894 further improved the chance for better Russo-German relations. William at once set out to woo his young cousin, the tsar, in order to regain Russian friendship, but showed no willingness to enter a new alliance. William and Nicholas remained firm friends over the next decades, corresponding constantly and advising each other on vital issues; frequently they exchanged visits or joined in common vacations. Down to the very day Germany declared war on Russia in 1914, the two rulers consulted on how to safeguard the friendship between their two nations. Yet they never seriously attempted to re-form Bismarck's alliance and, of course, proved incapable of delaying the outbreak of war.

In 1895, Russia's eyes were turned to Asia. Japan had emerged victorious from the Sino-Japanese War, and by its annexations on the mainland was threatening tsarist designs on Manchuria and Korea. During the war, England had tacitly favored Japan, but Germany, France, and Russia intervened jointly in behalf of China and actually forced Japan to retrocede a part of its conquest (the Liaotung Peninsula). Since Russia and France at the time were joined in an anti-German military pact, the cooperation of Germany with these two neighbors seems indeed strange. Actually, Germany found it useful to cooperate now and then with France in colonial matters, particularly when the action was designed to frustrate British plans. And cooperation with Russia fitted William's mood of the mid–1890s.

But German intervention on behalf of China was not motivated solely by a desire to gain the favor of Nicholas. It marked the beginning of German penetration in the Far East—another phase of William's *Weltpolitik.* Germany's commercial interests in the area and William's longing for added prestige turned Germany suddenly into a strong contender for a sphere of influence in China. From this intervention, the Germans in 1897 secured Tsingtao and a dominant economic hold on the Shantung Peninsula.

THE GERMAN NAVY Before the accession of William II, Germany had almost no navy. The futile attempt of the National Assembly at Frankfurt in 1848 to acquire naval forces had discouraged the Germans from repeating a similar experiment. During the 1850s and 1860s, Prussia had acquired a few coastal vessels; but even after unification, the navy assumed no important role. Bismarck had finally allotted negligible funds for the construction of a small naval force, enough to lend perfunctory support in colonial problems, but not sufficient to constitute a fighting navy. When Caprivi took over the Admiralty, he stressed construction of coastal defenses and torpedo carriers, but showed no interest in developing a high-seas fleet.

The accession of William II brought about a fundamental change in the German navy. The young emperor, himself an avid yachtsman, took great interest in all naval matters. An expanded naval program clearly seemed to go hand in hand with the new world-wide arena of German activities. He proclaimed succinctly: "Imperial might means sea power." Starting in 1890, he placed technical experts at the head of the navy, and separated the Admiralty from army control. New ships were launched, although not according to any over-all planning and with relatively limited funds. In 1895, the important Kiel or Kaiser Wilhelm Canal was completed, linking the North Sea to the Baltic. German ships could now pass from one sea to the other without fear of a Danish blockade, and the fleet gained greater flexibility. But despite this progress, the German navy remained a negligible weapon. When the lack of naval strength became apparent in the Boer and China crises, William determined to construct a high-seas fleet commensurate with his ambitions.

In 1897, he placed Admiral Tirpitz in charge of the Imperial Naval Office (*Reichsmarineamt*). Tirpitz, the ennobled son of a civil servant, was a ruthlessly determined and skillful advocate of German naval expansion. Quite possibly he tried at first to avoid politics and develop his naval plans along purely technical and strategic lines, but before long, he was deeply involved in the internal political squabbles surrounding the naval program, as well as in the shaping of German foreign affairs. Tirpitz was a forceful advocate of a so-called German risk fleet, a navy so big that England would not risk a war with Germany for fear of sustaining such damage that its naval supremacy would be endangered. He was motivated by an intense hatred of England, and by the naïve belief, shared by William, that England could be frightened into friendship. In a famous memorandum of 1907, he was to write: "This constant danger of war with England . . .

will cease and even change into England's desire to befriend us only when our fleet is further strengthened." This theory, which required a constant increase in naval construction, was one of the causes of the naval armaments race between Germany and England in the prewar decade.

In 1898, Tirpitz proposed the first of a series of naval laws. He sought to build up the fleet and naval personnel through a program based on long-term budgets resembling those of the army. His first proposal stipulated a total of 17 ships of the line, 8 coastal vessels, 35 cruisers, and reserve ships. Seven ships of the line and 9 cruisers were to be built within seven years. The proposal was accepted by the Reichstag, although doctrinaire liberals disliked relinquishing financial control over naval expenditures by fixing the budget for seven years. But almost immediately Tirpitz and his supporters found the size of the contemplated navy inadequate. The Spanish-American War, in which Germany intervened perfunctorily, and the acquisition in 1899 of new possessions in the Pacific—the Mariana, Caroline, Palau, and Marshall islands—prompted Tirpitz to request a doubling of the naval strength in a new seventeen-year construction program proposed in 1899.

This second naval bill encountered more opposition. Many Centrists, most Progressives, and all Socialists fought the proposal. But Tirpitz was a master propagandist. The Navy League, which he had helped organize in 1898, became a formidable pressure group rallying public opinion behind the idea that a world power should also be a naval power. And William II echoed this thought with his call: "Our future lies on the seas!" The Pan-Germans, at any rate, desired a navy to protect the colonial empire and to endow Germany with the prestige and power of a first-rate nation. The industrial interests also favored construction of a large fleet, since it would increase production. Moreover, more than a few liberals favored the navy for purely domestic, political reasons. Not only would a large fleet be good for trade and industry; it would also act as a liberal influence on internal politics. The army had traditionally been the province of the nobility. An enlarged navy, without the aristocratic taint of the army officer corps, would increase prospects for bourgeois power. The navy would be run largely by middle-class technicians and could hardly be used for the repression of internal rebellions. In the eyes of the liberals, therefore, increasing the navy represented a step toward democratization. The revolution of 1918 was to prove that these considerations were not so farfetched as they seem.

A crucial question was whether the Conservatives could be induced to vote for the bill. In Prussia especially, they continued to be dominated by the League of Landlords, which opposed the idea of a large fleet but still sought the reintroduction of high agricultural tariffs. The industrialists, on the other hand, wanted their fleet but opposed higher tariffs on food. A compromise was finally effected between the two groups, with the aid of government intervention and pressure from Tirpitz's Naval League. The industrialists promised to vote for higher agricultural tariffs when the current treaties expired in 1902; in return, the agrarians supported the naval program. This anomalous alliance between industry and agriculture remained important in the domestic politics of the next decade.

After this political realignment, the second Naval Law was passed in the Reichstag in 1900. Germany was launched on the naval race with England. The government had wanted to finance this naval program largely on the basis of loans, but the Reichstag insisted on raising taxes. A new stamp tax on shares, lotteries, and commercial sea transports, and higher taxes on champagne, liquors, and beer were to help pay for the scheme that would turn Germany into the second greatest naval power in the world.

The Cultural Milieu

The lightning transformation of Germany through industrial and material progress continued unabated under William II. Cities burgeoned; production indices skyrocketed; self-assurance and optimism were comfortably bolstered by prosperity. New inventions enhanced the growing faith in science, and encouraged the application of scientific methods in nonscientific fields. In the popular mind, capitalists, industrialists, entrepreneurs, and scientists were ranked with army officers and civil servants as the heroes who had created the nation and were responsible for its amazing progress.

But while Germany experienced constant change, its social structure remained conservative, its class divisions entrenched. The numerous members of the upper aristocracy, although largely deprived of their governmental powers, still lived in a world apart. Even the lower nobility, many of whose members still dominated the officer corps and the higher echelons of the civil service, claimed and maintained a social status strangely discordant with an age of universal suffrage. As in earlier times, ambitious bourgeois aspired to be admitted to the sacrosanct milieu of the noble class.

Below the nobility and the officer corps, but still at a vastly elevated level, were those with titles or academic degrees. Everyone in the civil service of the federal and state governments, down to almost the lowest clerk, assumed a title, of which the German vocabulary contains a plethora. Each had its untranslatable distinctions. In the postal service, for instance, were *Postrat, Postdirektor, Postmeister, Posthalter, Postschreiber, Postsekretär, Postverwalter, Postwärter,* and a host of others. A title, even if it designated him only as a third clerk in a city post office, gained the bearer the humble respect of the nontitled burghers. University titles and degrees became a similar mark of distinction. The middle and lower bourgeois emulated the practice in order to maintain a respectful level above the proletariat and peasantry. Even technicians, merchants, artisans, and craftsmen who achieved some status adopted for themselves and their wives titles that they bore proudly and that they had inscribed on their tombstones. Thus the wife of a chimney sweeper who had passed his trade examination and had paid his admission dues to a master craft guild styled herself *Frau Schornsteinfegermeister* (wife of a master chimney sweeper). This mania for titles and craving for social distinction had a divisive and unhealthful influence on the development of the nation.

The comforts of prosperity and the pride in new nationhood persisted in buoying up materialism and militant nationalism. Among some groups this led to a boisterous social Darwinism in which racialism, nihilism, and "action for action's sake" combined into a powerful ethos. Nietzsche's *Thus Spake Zarathustra* and *Beyond Good and Evil,* both published in the 1880s, were misappropriated by these circles. The philosopher's devastating blows at militarism, socialism, chauvinism, factionalism, egalitarianism, and Christianity were turned into aimless nihilism. His self-reliant, rational superman was twisted into a muscular superbeast. These ideas also found currency among the youth. As in the days of the *Burschenschaften,* youth groups (such as the *Wandervögel*) organized hiking excursions or military games, sang war songs, and dreamed of heroic actions in which they could display valor and strength. But unlike the *Burschenschaften,* which advocated definable aims, such as German unification, their twentieth-century counterparts were nihilistic in their disdain for society and sought action largely for the sake of action.

A strong dichotomy marked the life at universities and the course of education as a whole. Humanistic and practical learning vied for predominance. Scholarship still brought surprising results and opened new fields. Historiography, for example, was infused with new vitality through crossbreeding with other sciences. Wilhelm Dilthey (1833–1911) applied philosophy to historical analysis, while Max Weber (1864–1920) and others fruitfully combined history and sociology. But much of this was accomplished almost in spite of the prevailing atmosphere at universities, at which learning degenerated into pedantry in research and veneration of "omniscient professors." At the same time, unlike in the revolutionary year 1848, most intellectuals disdainfully disassociated themselves from the stream of political life. Even students showed more interest in dueling and drinking bouts and in emphasizing their social superiority to the nonacademic world than in preparing to participate in the political life of their nation—a development that augured the unfortunate fate of the Weimar Republic after World War I.

Among writers and journalists there were many who could not wholeheartedly embrace the empire of William II. Despite occasional censorship and libel suits by the government, a steady stream of criticism was launched by numerous periodicals against the antiquated governmental framework, the pretensions of the aristocracy, the bombast of the military clique, and the extravagance of capitalists and industrialists.

Naturalistic drama thrived with new plays by Hauptmann and the works of the prolific Hermann Sudermann (1857–1928). A nostalgic regret at the decay of the peaceful though dull atmosphere of early nineteenth-century merchant life characterized *Buddenbrooks* (1901), the first major novel of the young Thomas Mann (1875–1955). But many of the writers shielded themselves from the crass reality of Wilhelmian materialism, and took refuge in belated romanticism or in the new movement of symbolism. Munich and Vienna became centers of neoromanticism in literature and music, as well as painting. Most famous among the symbolists were Stefan George (1868–1933) and his numerous disciples, who cultivated an extreme form of art for art's sake, remained aloof from the world about them, and sought spiritual satisfaction in the esthetic forms of their poetry.

17

The Empire of William II: The Bülow Era, 1900–1909

In October, 1900, Prince Bernhard von Bülow became chancellor after having served as minister of foreign affairs for three years. Bülow showed some skill in devising an over-all policy in domestic affairs, and at first seemed able to make Emperor William more tractable. Compared to his two predecessors, he was an able chancellor. But he never acquired the strength or determination to steer Germany's internal policy on a constant course in the face of the demands of the various pressure groups. In foreign affairs his diplomacy was superficial, and oblivious of the danger of Germany's growing isolation. Historians have traditionally blamed Bülow for the baneful turn of Germany's foreign relations during the first decade of this century. In his posthumous memoirs, Bülow placed the blame on William, Holstein, and others. The truth, no doubt, lies between these two indictments. A stronger chancellor could perhaps have saved Germany from the stigma of international distrust; but it is doubtful whether any minister could have overcome a system that permitted the nation's ruler, miscellaneous intriguers, and assorted pressure groups constantly to intervene in the administrative course.

CONSERVATISM UNDER BÜLOW

Guide lines for the Bülow era at home were based on a realignment of forces and a new policy. After the failure of conciliation (1890–1894) and *Kampfpolitik* (1894–1898), the administration chose to maintain the *status quo* wherever possible by uniting all conservative forces—especially agrarians and industrialists—into a common front against the growing proletariat. This program accentuated the internal divisions in the nation and enhanced the bitterness of the class antagonism preached by the left-wing Socialists. Moreover, it proved an inadequate policy for a society changing as fast as prewar Germany.

Yet Bülow and Emperor William II chose to treat all matters—tariff questions, colonial administration, the naval laws, the treatment of minorities, constitutional reform in Prussia, and the Reich—under the aegis of conservatism.

The tariff laws of 1902 provide a typical example of the government's new policy. Agricultural producers, particularly on the large estates of the northeast, had suffered an economic squeeze during the 1890s. The industrial boom had pushed up wages, the cost of production, and interest rates; while the relatively low tariffs of 1893 had depressed the price of grain because of foreign competition. Consequently, many estates were mortgaged and encumbered with debts. Despite increasing pressure from the League of Landlords and the government's recognition of the problem, only minor palliative measures were taken in the 1890s to aid the agrarians, for the tariffs were set by treaties that could not be altered before their expiration. The government reduced the land tax, lowered the import quota for live cattle, and made easier credit available to landowners. These minor remedies did not satisfy the agrarians, who were adamant about reintroducing high protective tariffs. All other government suggestions were rejected. The landlords refused to accept such proposals as government price fixing for all grain, domestic as well as foreign, the adoption of diversified instead of one-crop farming, or government aid for settling small peasant owners on the large estates, a sort of disguised land reform.

After 1897, the government showed more and more inclination to mollify the agrarians. The political maneuvers preceding the passage of the second Naval Law showed the value of using the agrarians as a counterweight to the industrialists and of combining both into a conservative coalition. There were other political reasons for favoring the agrarians. The rural areas furnished the bulk of the soldiers and noble officers for the army. Also, the steady increase in the number of Socialist deputies in the Reichstag and the obstructionism displayed by most Progressives and Centrists against William's foreign policy forced the government into greater reliance on the conservative parties.

In 1901, Bülow announced his willingness to raise minimum grain tariffs more or less to their pre-1891 level when the current treaties expired. The announcement produced a storm of opposition and months of debate in committees and on the floor of the Reichstag, ending with a six-week filibuster by the Social Democratic deputies. The extremist agrarians considered the proposed tariffs too low; all advocates of free trade continued to oppose tariffs on principle; and the Socialists campaigned against the "bread-usury" that would raise the cost of the laborer's food without other compensations. Bülow tried to mediate among the conflicting interests, but in the end sided largely with the Conservatives. In December 1902, the Reichstag, with the votes of the Conservatives, the National Liberals, and some Centrists, passed a bill authorizing negotiations with other governments on new tariffs. The treaties, finally completed by 1905, were effective for twelve years. Caught between agrarians and the industrialists, the government not only raised agricultural tariffs but also included additional protective barriers for German industry.

The tariff episode of 1902 cemented the alliance between the government and the Conservatives, and produced a deepened split between producers and consumers. In the electoral campaign of 1903, the Socialists campaigned largely on this issue, and as a result, increased their representation in the Reichstag to 81 seats, and obtained some 3 million votes, or about 30 percent of the total cast—thereby becoming the second largest party in the parliament and by far the largest in popular vote.

ECONOMIC AND SOCIAL CHANGES

Agriculture and Industry

Conditions in agriculture improved measurably in the years after 1902, aided by the new tariffs, by a general rise in world grain prices, and by greater productivity resulting from the use of better fertilizer. To compete with the large estates, the smaller farmers resorted to cooperatives. From 1900 to 1912, the number of such agricultural cooperatives doubled from 13,600 to 26,000. At the same time, speculation in land continued to boost the value of the highly mortgaged estates. But while the improved status of the landlords created better markets for industrial consumer goods, higher agricultural prices also raised the cost of living, adding to the tension between rich and poor, producers and consumers. Furthermore, the economic status of the simple agricultural laborers was hardly altered. Little social legislation protected them, and the 1891 colonization law, by which the government was to have financed the opening of small farms, had produced few results. In two decades, only about 22,000 new peasant farms were created under this program. To keep wages at a minimum, many landlords east of the Elbe imported cheap Polish agricultural workers. Hence the farm laborers failed to profit from the improved conditions in agriculture, and tended to share the bitterness of the city proletariat.

Increased home production was not enough to make the country self-sufficient in food. Meat and grains continued to be imported in large quantities to feed the bulging population—which increased from 56.4 million in 1900 to 64.9 million in 1910. Thus Germany, like England, remained vulnerable to blockade in time of war.

The continued large-scale industrial expansion, which pushed Germany past England in the production of many basic items, such as iron and steel, also accentuated politico-economic problems. Big industry grew bigger and politically more powerful, while small industry declined. In the two decades of industrial boom before World War I, the number of independent entrepreneurs and small enterprises decreased, whereas the total labor force increased sharply. Capital and industrial ownership became concentrated in fewer and fewer hands. The formation of cartels and syndicates, frequently owned or controlled by the large banks, was encouraged by the government to assure better utilization of scarce resources. The government was also engaged in commerce and industry, for it owned most of the railroads and many coal mines as well as other enterprises. Yet certain cartels became so powerful that the government occasionally found it impossible to resist their pressure; for example, in 1904, when the Prussian state tried to purchase more coal mines, it was prevented by the coal trust.

Besides increasing the political and economic power of big industry, industrial concentration also forged a widening gap between the growing mass of workers and the dwindling number of entrepreneurs. On the whole, the workers benefited from the rising standard of living; but higher food prices, importation of cheap foreign labor, lack of job security, and social envy fanned their dissatisfaction with the economic and political regime. Some additional social legislation raising the minimum age for child labor and regulating working hours was passed under Bülow, and the social insurance system was enlarged. But these measures did not touch the deeper social problems, for no attempt was made to incorporate the laborers into the fabric of society. The workers continued in their social limbo, feared and resented by the middle and upper classes.

The Labor Movement

During this period, the labor movement was determined to gain recognition for its unions. The Association Law of 1899 made it legal for unions to organize, and they rapidly grew in membership. The largest, the Social Democratic unions, increased from 680,000 members in 1900 to 2,500,000 in 1912. But the entrepreneurs formed associations in order to present a united front against the unions' demands, and steadfastly refused to recognize the workers' bargaining rights. On this point, the industrialists were supported particularly by the Prussian government. Hence the workers became distrustful of the government because they resented its apparent partiality toward big business. The strike of some 220,000 Ruhr miners in 1905 illustrates these conditions. When the miners' union presented its grievances—concerning layoffs, unhealthful work conditions, money fines, and increased travel time into deeper pits without added wages—the mine administrators refused to recognize the rights of the union to bargain for the workers. The government contemplated arbitration, but the workers had no faith in governmental mediation and began a strike. After a few days, the strike had to be called off because the workers lacked the requisite reserve funds. To show its good intentions, the Prussian government then attempted to pass a law making layoffs without provisions for the dismissed miners more difficult, but the law was rejected by the conservative upper house. Bülow, in the end, barely managed to get a law passed that permitted miners' unions to present grievances even though it did not accord them a legal title to collective bargaining. It was a pale measure, which hardly earned the chancellor the gratitude of the labor population.

The Workers and Socialism

In confronting business and government, the workers found few mediators. Stöcker's Christian Social party was unsuccessful in its efforts to absorb the labor movement on the basis of a demagogic reconciliation of the classes. Nor did Friedrich Naumann's (1860–1919) virulent and visionary National Socialist party succeed in bringing about social mediation. Naumann, a former disciple of Stöcker's, had conceived a mass movement to unite workers and bourgeois in a nationalistic fervor overriding all domestic issues. Since world commerce required the support of the workers, he favored mock democratization at home as a buttress for an aggressive foreign policy. Like Hitler's later movement of similar designation, Naumann's was at heart not interested in socialism but rather in nationalism. Sensing this incompatibility, the workers shunned his movement, and the National Socialist party was dissolved after its electoral defeat of 1903.

Hence the various workers' associations—the large socialist unions as well as the small Catholic and the even smaller liberal unions—and above all the Social Democratic party remained the only spokesmen for the workers. But the SPD itself was not united in its aims and aspirations. Officially the party continued to adhere to its Erfurt Program of 1891, which had demanded nationalization of all land, mines, natural resources, factories, tools, and means of transportation; the extension of suffrage to all men and women aged twenty-one or over; popular control over decisions on war and peace; popular election of government officials rather than appointment from above; free legal and medical aid; and abolition of all indirect taxes and customs. In fact, however, few Socialists deluded themselves into believing that such large-scale aims were about to be realized. The bulk of the workers pressed for more tangible, immediate gains—improved working conditions or fewer hours of work—while the intelligentsia of the SPD fought over the question of how the ultimate aims were to be achieved.

The radicals, led in the prewar period by Rosa Luxemburg (1870–1919), Franz Mehring (1846–1919), Karl Kautsky (1854–1938), and Karl Liebknecht (1871–1919), continued to preach Marxian principles. They insisted that reliance on electoral campaigns for the Reichstag and the prevailing wait-and-see attitude of the Socialists would never topple the conservative Prussian government nor overthrow the capitalistic regime. Instead, they advocated intensification of the class war and a revolutionary struggle employing strikes and violence where necessary, in order to plunge the entire monarchical and capitalistic system into chaos and ultimately annihilate it.

Opposed to the radicals were the revisionists, strongly influenced by Eduard Bernstein (1850–1932), whose *Evolutionary Socialism* had appeared in 1899. Bernstein decried the theory of the class struggle, since it prevented possible alliance of the proletariat with the liberal segments of the middle class. He saw no evidence of an impending collapse of bourgeois society, and disputed Marx's prediction of an inevitable acceleration in the concentration of wealth. He noted, on the contrary, that the propertied classes were becoming numerically larger rather than smaller, and that the progress of democracy and industry was slowly changing their character. Influenced by the Fabians in England, where he lived in exile, he urged the workers to struggle for democracy rather than for social upheaval, and to achieve their aims gradually, in alliance with the lower middle class.

The revisionist program was heatedly debated at the Dresden Congress of the Social Democratic party in 1903 and finally rejected by majority vote, on the grounds that it tended to obscure class differences and muddle the distinction between the socialist proletariat and the "bourgeois reactionaries." But this reaffirmation of orthodox Marxism—echoed two months later in London when the Russian Social Democratic party held its meeting of exiles and accorded Lenin and the extremists (Bolsheviks) a majority vote over the moderates (Mensheviks) led by Georgi Plekhanov—failed to unite the Socialists on a common basis. In Prussia, where Socialist representation was small because of the three-class vote and urban underenfranchisement, and where hatred of the aristocratic government was particularly pronounced, Socialists continued to be revolutionary. In the Reich at large, where Socialists had better representation and state governments were somewhat more liberal, the more evolutionary or revisionist tendencies prevailed—despite the Dresden pronouncement. But everywhere, the Socialists persisted in a rather negative attitude toward the state, which made it difficult for bourgeois friends of labor to effect any mediation.

TREATMENT OF MINORITIES

Besides the workers and the agricultural proletariat, there were many other groups who remained essentially unreconciled to the Wilhelmian Reich. Segments of the Catholic Center party, and such particularistic groups as the so-called Guelphs of the former state of Hanover retained their negative attitude toward the imperial government, despite William's occasional conciliatory gestures. Antagonism was even more pronounced among certain ethnic minorities, such as the Poles and the Alsace-Lorrainers.

German Poland

After William's unsuccessful attempt at conciliating the Poles, he had returned to Bismarck's policy of colonizing Prussia's eastern provinces so as to increase the German element at the expense of the Poles. The Prussian government protected and favored German merchants, and attempted to speed up German cultural infiltration at all levels. A German academy was established at Poznan, a technical institute was set up in Danzig, and German schools were multiplied throughout all Polish-speaking districts. But the government encountered problems when it tried to transfer Polish land to German ownership. The Prussian Land Commission, charged with this task, could not settle many Germans, since the Poles, peasants as well as nobles, steadfastly refused to sell their landholdings. Between 1891 and 1900, the Germans in the province of Poznan managed to increase by 3.75 percent; but this change hardly "Germanized" the region, since the Polish population increased by 10.5 percent during the same period. In 1898, the Prussian government appropriated millions for a "colonization fund" to help German settlers buy up Polish properties. Actually, over the succeeding ten years, few Polish estates were purchased by Germans, for most of the funds were required to help the Germans retain their own land. Many Poles worked in the Ruhr mines or elsewhere in the booming German factories and saved money with which, after their return to Poznan, they bid for land owned by Germans. Their financial offers were so attractive that the German landowners found them hard to resist. Consequently, the Prussian government found itself forced to loan money to German peasants to enable them to outbid or reject the Polish offers.

Realizing that it was fighting a losing battle, the Prussian government proposed sterner measures in 1907. Legislation was introduced to empower the Prussian Land Commission to expropriate Polish lands. But the diet rejected the bill. The Center party sympathized with the Catholic Poles, the Progressives objected on principle, and even the Conservatives feared possible later violation of their own property rights. Moreover, the government produced no adequate plans concerning resettlement of the Poles whose lands would be expropriated. A watered-down compromise law was finally adopted in 1908, giving the Land Commission power to expropriate a limited amount of land (about 173,000 acres), but under the new chancellor after 1909, Bethmann-Hollweg, the commission seldom availed itself of its expropriatory powers. Consequently, the new law merely further antagonized the Poles without achieving its purpose of Germanizing the eastern lands. In all their years under German domination, the Poles never became reconciled to their German overlords and continued to be a separate and distinct entity.

Alsace-Lorraine

A similar treatment was accorded Alsace-Lorraine. Organized as a *Reichsland* in 1871, the two provinces were placed under control of an imperial governor and a local committee, operating under the Bundesrat. During the first two decades after the Franco-Prussian War, while French demands for revenge were frequently heard, the Alsace-Lorrainers looked with suspicion upon their German masters. Their status seemed temporary and uncertain. The imperial governors favored the clergy and the upper middle class, but failed to reconcile the lower classes to the German regime.

In the 1890s, French talk of revenge receded, and German economic prosperity made itself felt in the two annexed provinces. The dictatorial regime of the governors was relaxed, and in 1902 their special police powers were rescinded. But the population now voiced new demands, in view of the likelihood that the provinces were to remain German indefinitely. They objected to the inferior status they held within the empire. Various political parties began to agitate for full autonomy for their provinces, and for the same semisovereign rights enjoyed by the German federal states. The Berlin government, however, refused to honor these demands, since it feared the Alsace-Lorrainers might use their greater freedom to cement better relations with France.

German suspicions concerning the reliability of their Alsace-Lorraine subjects were fanned anew by the increased Franco-German friction in the years after 1904. The population of these provinces continued to be an oppositional minority pressuring the government to concede autonomy. In 1910, under Bethmann-Holweg, the government finally tried to conciliate the provinces. A bill was introduced in the Reichstag to eliminate the Bundesrat's control over Alsace-Lorraine and to grant to the provinces a constitution establishing a two-chamber system—a lower elected house, and an upper chamber composed of members of the professions and imperial appointees. The Reichstag added a further provision granting the provinces three seats in the Bundesrat. But government and Reichstag refused to attach the rights of sovereignty and equal status with other states (*Länder*) to this constitution, which was finally promulgated in 1911. Emperor William continued to remain direct overlord of the provinces, and the governor, still appointed by him and supported by German army contingents, retained his supreme powers. The Alsace-Lorrainers were also deprived of any power to amend this constitution, a power expressly reserved to the Reichstag.

The new constitution pleased the moderates in the provinces and lessened friction with the Reich at large. But the more nationalistic Alsatians and Lorrainers were not mollified by the hollow favors bestowed upon them by the German Reichstag. Encouraged by the growing international tension between France and Germany, they used every blunder of the German military and civilian officials to stir up unrest. The famous Zabern affair in November 1913, in which German officers in the Alsatian town of Zabern acted rashly, injuring a civilian and illegally arresting others in reprisal for anti-German demonstrations, was such a case. The excitement it produced in the two provinces showed the deep-seated antagonism felt by most of the population. It appeared evident that after forty-three years of German rule, Germany had failed to absorb Alsace-Lorraine. At the same time in the empire at large, the Zabern affair afforded the opposition groups—Social Democrats, Center, minorities, and even certain liberals—a welcome opportunity for publicly venting their pent-up displeasure with the government's militaristic regime.

FINANCES AND PARTY POLITICS

Imperial Finances

Despite the increasing prosperity, the imperial government was constantly in debt, and neither Bülow nor the autocratic Emperor William was strong enough to redress this situation. The existing system of financial decentralization allowed the individual states to pocket most of the tax receipts. The Reich, dependent largely on income from customs duties and monopolies and on annual levies (called "matriculation fees") from the states, had no way of forcing the latter to increase their contributions. And when new taxes were proposed to augment the imperial revenue, the Reichstag usually voted them down.

Thus the debts of the Reich rose to 1400 million marks in the decade before 1892, whereas the various German states accumulated financial surpluses. Caprivi's proposed tax reforms were rejected, and the increased army expenditures were paid for from current revenues and loans. Increased prosperity rather than fiscal skill account for the fact that the national debt rose only another 200 million marks between 1895 and 1900. Furthermore, the Reichstag, in a rare mood of fiscal responsibility, insisted on financing the new navy through new and higher indirect taxes. Yet these measures hardly sufficed to balance the budget. After 1901, even ordinary expenses had to be covered partially by loans, and the imperial debt continued to spiral upward.

In his four last years as chancellor, Bülow repeatedly attempted to bring solvency to the empire. In 1905 and 1906, he tried to raise revenue by introducing a variety of new direct and indirect taxes—on beer, tobacco, receipts, bills of freight, railroad tickets, and automobiles—as well as a direct inheritance tax. But he was forced to compromise with the Reichstag opposition and settle for less than half the requested revenue, raised exclusively from indirect levies.

The naval construction law of 1906 and other increased expenses produced a new deficit in 1907 and a forecast for an even greater imbalance for 1908. The government therefore submitted new tax proposals, requesting a wider distribution of levies among the population in order to mollify all groups. It proposed abolishment of certain "nuisance" taxes—on sugar and railroad tickets, for example; it requested 400 million marks in new indirect taxes—on brandy, beer, tobacco, and other consumer items—a tax preferred by the Conservatives since it largely burdened the poorer classes; and it again demanded a progressive inheritance tax on land, favored by the Socialists because it placed the burden on the wealthier landowners.

These government proposals produced stormy debates in the Reichstag throughout the winter of 1908. The Progressives and Socialists opposed indirect taxes, but were willing to vote with the government, since the inheritance tax would strongly affect the rich and distribute the burden of taxation somewhat more fairly. The Conservatives, however, vehemently objected to an inheritance tax, adopted parliamentary obstructionism, and resorted to such dubious slogans as "spare the widows, tax the living." They had always disliked paying federal taxes, since these would indirectly increase the power of the Reichstag, which was suspect to them because of its popular base. They preferred paying taxes, if at all, to the Prussian government, which they controlled.

Bülow warned prophetically: "The Conservative Party is digging its own grave by misreading the signs of the time and refusing to recognize legitimate demands." He finally demanded a vote on his entire tax program, as if to make the matter a vote of confidence in parliamentary fashion. He emphasized the "all-or-nothing" aspect of his demands. The Conservatives, however, refused to approve the proposals unless the inheritance tax were omitted, and the Center joined them in an effort to split Bülow's party support and topple him from power. The inheritance tax clause was defeated in the end by 194 (Conservatives, Center, and Anti-Semites) to 186 (Free Conservatives, National Liberals, Progressives, and Socialists), and the emasculated tax bill was adopted by 226 to 127. Bülow, already at odds with Emperor William over questions of foreign policy, saw in the defeat of his tax legislation a rebuff to his administration, and handed in his resignation.

Party Politics Under Bülow

According to the constitution, there was no reciprocal connection between the executive and the legislative branches of the German government. William and his ministers were not accountable to the Reichstag, and the representatives shared no responsibility for the government's actions. Yet Bülow's resignation in 1909 seemed to demonstrate that Germany was drifting into a kind of parliamentarianism made necessary by political requirements that were rendering the government increasingly dependent on the support of the Reichstag. Unquestionably, over the decades, the search for a cooperative majority among the representatives had become a major task for all chancellors, for without the backing of enough votes, the government could not enact a legislative program. Bismarck himself had faced this problem, but to a large extent he had led the parties and dominated the Reichstag. In the 1890s, however, and even more in the 1900s, during Bülow's regime, the task had become more complicated. Legislative and financial requirements of the government were constantly increasing while its power over the Reichstag was decreasing. Party leaders and economic pressure groups were pulling first one way and then another, so that the government was frequently dragged helplessly along.

But despite the growing importance of the Reichstag, the imperial entourage retained its deprecatory view of this parliamentary body. Emperor William and his advisers seemed to share Treitschke's view, expressed in 1886: "An irresponsible parliament, produced by changing elections, split into small parties—an assembly that lacks all the traditions of a ruling estate—possesses neither the power nor the unity nor the moral stature to dominate the Reich." And, of course, they thoroughly agreed with Treitschke's prediction that "the great decisions of our history will be taken by the crown of the Hohenzollerns." Even among the population at large, the Reichstag enjoyed relatively little confidence. Fraudulent voting and failure to reapportion electoral districts undermined its representative nature, despite the heralded universal male suffrage. The constant splintering of the parties over minor doctrinal or economic issues prevented many voters from establishing deep ties with political groups and their representatives in the Reichstag.

The delegates themselves rarely showed any consideration of all-German problems. Since the system made it impossible for a party to "come to power," political leaders could indulge in unlimited bargaining or obstructionism without the sobering influence of exercising statesmanship. For the most, each delegate represented a class or a region, an economic interest or political doctrine, and bargained accordingly. The Prussian Conservatives, for example, refused to vote the money for a canal connecting the Weser and the Elbe—a vital link in Germany's inland water system—and insisted that the funds be spent instead on extending railroads in eastern Prussia, a measure that would benefit almost solely their own grain production. Similarly, the Center party in the Reichstag agreed to approve an increase in the number of noncommissioned officers only if in return the other parties would agree to alter the anti-Jesuit laws so as to permit individual Jesuits to reside in Germany. For their part, Socialists, Progressives, National Liberals, Poles, and Alsatians fought their own battles, pulling the Reichstag in myriad directions. And neither the absentee emperor nor his chancellor had the strength to set Germany on a definitive course.

A government crisis in 1906 gave Chancellor Bülow the opportunity to establish a new working relationship with the Reichstag and to set up a pseudo-parliamentary government based on cooperation between the executive and the legislative branches. Emperor William had become disillusioned with Bülow. Court intrigues fanned by the ubiquitous Eulenburg, the ill-fated Algeciras Conference of 1906 (see page 449), and Bülow's failure to obtain from the Reichstag sufficient funds for colonial administration had turned the emperor against his chancellor. Bülow, for his part, was unhappy with William's international *faux pas* and tired of the behavior of the Reichstag, which had refused his requested taxes and obstructed his colonial policy. Moreover, Bülow found that the Center party voted more and more frequently with the Socialists to block government action, so that he felt the need for a new alignment. To find a new *modus vivendi* with the parties and perhaps to prove his prowess to William, Bülow dissolved the Reichstag in the fall of 1906 and called for new elections.

The election campaign of January 1907 was fought in an aura of militancy and chauvinism. The government desired to allocate more funds to the construction of railroads, ports, and military installations in the colonies, particularly in Southwest Africa, where a rebellion had been seething for some time. But the Socialists and most bourgeois delegates had vetoed such funds, partly on principle and partly because they envisaged more profitable investments elsewhere. The colonial issue was therefore made a major campaign item. Government speakers and conservative candidates appealed to the emotions of the populace, and proclaimed that Germany's honor was at stake in the colonies.

Bülow added a second issue to the election campaign. He desired a new working majority in the Reichstag and thought it expedient to try to unite all bourgeois parties against the Socialists, ostensibly to strengthen the Reich against internal enemies, but actually to form a progovernment bloc and revive Bismarck's anti-Socialist *Kampfpolitik*.

Bülow's campaign was successful. The elections (see Chart 5) in which almost two million more voters cast ballots than in 1903, brought electoral gains to all parties except the Socialists, Guelphs, and Alsatians. In fact, the Socialists, although gaining a quarter of a million votes over 1903, lost half their seats—a measure of the inequity of the Reich's electoral districting. Bülow's new "bloc," consisting of Conservatives, *Reichspartei* (Free Conservatives), National Liberals, Progressives, and Anti-Semites gave him a working majority of 203—of a total of 397 votes—and made him independent of the Center and the minority parties. The chancellor could thus hope for a better chance to push his programs through the Reichstag.

As a result, Germany assumed an air of parliamentarianism in 1907 and 1908. Supported by his bloc, Bülow was able to enact parts of his program, which he termed "conservative with some liberal reforms." New social legislation was passed, the Association Laws were amended, the criminal code was revised, the stock exchange was regulated, and the stringent proceedings against lese majesty curtailed. On most national questions and foreign matters, the bloc parties could cooperate and defeat the Socialist and Center parties, which now clearly formed the opposition.

But at heart, the bloc was a fragile construction. The Progressives cooperated only reluctantly with the right-wing parties and frequently demanded concessions. The Conservatives for their part feared the spread of liberalism. In the end, the tax debates of

1908 split the bloc and ended Bülow's hope for cooperation between government and a majority of the Reichstag. Because he had been weakened in prestige by the famous *Daily Telegraph* affair (see pages 450 ff.) of 1908 and thwarted in his tax program, Bülow's resignation in 1909 appeared like the result of a vote of no confidence. With Bülow's departure his bloc disintegrated. Economic pressure groups, political splinters, and doctrinaire interests once again assumed dominance in the Reichstag and made it impossible for the new chancellor, Bethmann-Hollweg, to rule with the parties. The landed interests controlled the Right, and the Socialists—who had regained their electoral strength to become the largest single party by 1912—dominated the Left. In the middle, the bourgeois banded together in the *Hansa-Bund,* an economic association founded in 1909 in imitation of the League of Landlords. It advocated "equal opportunity for all trades, commerce, and industry," and aimed at "breaking the pernicious influence of the one-sided agrarian demagogues." The various progressive parties joined in 1910 to form the Progressive People's party, in a vain attempt to shore up the middle-of-the-road parties. In reality, Germany had lost its opportunity to establish a parliamentary system—short of altering the entire electoral and political structure of the Reich.

FOREIGN AFFAIRS UNDER BÜLOW

When Bülow assumed responsibility for the Foreign Office in 1897—three years before assuming the chancellorship—the international scene seemed auspicious for Germany, and the optimistic Bülow, anticipating easy success, glanced lightly at possible dangers. England was occupied with Egypt and the Boers; Russia and England were clashing in the East; France and England were in conflict over the Sudan; even Spain and far-off America were about to be embroiled in war. Germany, alone among the major powers, was free from entanglements and in a position to gain from the discomforts of the others.

In some respects, Germany skillfully used the occasion to enhance its power and prestige. It obtained the Carolinas and a major part of the Samoan Islands. Backed by French financiers, it received the concession for the Turkish railway to Baghdad, and in 1899 began construction of this vital link of the Berlin-to-Baghdad railroad—much to the dismay of Russia and Britain. In conjunction with Anglo-Franco-Russian contingents, Germany interfered in the Boxer Rebellion in China, and managed to reaffirm its newly acquired position in the Far East.

On the other hand, the optimistic Bülow and the obstinate Holstein did nothing to keep William from turning these years of opportunity into a field day for his bombastic *Weltpolitik,* which antagonized the powers without bringing concrete benefits to the Reich. In 1898, William visited Turkish Palestine and publicly promised to protect Turkish integrity—at a time when Britain and Russia were secretly suggesting to Germany that Turkey be partitioned into spheres of influence. In the same year, he ordered his nascent fleet to steam to the Philippines to run unwarrantable interference between the Spanish and United States navies. And in 1900, when German troops invaded China together with those of other powers, William again antagonized the world with his pretentious claims of vengeance for the murder of the German envoy to Peking.

Failure to Conclude an Alliance with England

Most damaging for Germany's future was its failure to achieve an alliance with England during this period. Great Britain, at odds with France and Russia, was seeking support on the Continent. Its overtures to Russia in January 1898 having been rebuffed, England turned to Germany. Joseph Chamberlain, Britain's powerful colonial secretary, and Prime Minister Salisbury made repeated offers to William to work out a fundamental Anglo-German understanding, if not an alliance. They assumed that Germany would welcome such overtures to help extricate it from the squeeze of the Franco-Russian alliance. Bülow and Holstein, it is clear, enjoyed this sudden wooing by England, but saw no reason for making these advances any easier. William himself was hesitant, for he liked his freedom from commitments, which permitted him almost unlimited international philandering. Yet he had qualms of conscience. At the end of May 1898, he wrote to the tsar, his "dearest Nicky," to tell him that "quite unexpectedly" he found himself "faced with a decision of vital importance" for his country. He informed Nicholas of the thrice-repeated offer of an English alliance, and begged his advice as a "friend and confidant." In typical Wilhelmian terms, he admitted that he had refused the previous overtures offhand, but that the last proposal seemed so good that "I deem it my duty toward Germany, to ponder thoroughly before answering." He finally begged the tsar to tell him what Russia could offer if Germany rejected the British alliance, and terminated his letter: "May God help you find the right solution and decision," as if asking Nicholas to decide what was best for Germany and for his "devoted friend Willy."

Nicholas II replied that three months earlier England had offered to iron out all differences with Russia by dividing Asia into respective spheres of influence, and that the proposal had filled him with suspicion: "Never before had England made such an offer to Russia." Hence, Nicholas confessed, he had refused it "without thinking twice," and implicitly urged William to do likewise.

William rejected the British overtures of 1898, and continued his aloofness in the succeeding years. Chamberlain tried to reopen the matter a few more times, but Bülow instructed his ambassador in London "to listen politely" but to agree to nothing. And Holstein, convinced that the threat of an English *rapprochement* with France and Russia was a hoax, gloated over Chamberlain's "feverish attacks of friendship," and insisted that "time is on our side."

Actually, the failure to bring about an Anglo-German alliance in the period 1898–1901 opened the doors to Germany's prewar encirclement. The fault, of course, lay not solely with Germany. Nor had the nascent German navy as yet become an insurmountable hindrance to an Anglo-German *rapprochement*. England, it must be remembered, was still a colonial power. Although it sought a Continental support for its clashes overseas with France and Russia, England was reluctant to tie itself to the Continent by a tight alliance that might interfere with its colonial objectives.

The Germans, for their part, did not reach for England's tentatively proffered hand. The Pan-Germans, the Navy League, and other fervent nationalists feared that friendship with England might curtail Germany's colonial opportunities and obviate the need for a large navy. Holstein and the Foreign Office, confident that an Anglo-French or an Anglo-Russian entente was impossible, expected high profits from Germany's waiting game. The emperor himself may have recognized the danger of Germany's continued isolation, but he hardly worked hard enough to provide a determined direction to German foreign policy.

By 1902, the chances for an Anglo-German *rapprochement* had passed. The accession of the Francophile King Edward VII, who flouted his German imperial nephew, dampened relations between London and Berlin. In 1902, England found in Japan the desired anti-Russian ally and hence no longer sought Germany's friendship so eagerly. Germany had missed the opportunity to emerge from its Continental isolation, and now entered the era of encirclement.

The Beginning of Encirclement

The problem of Germany's gradual encirclement and increasing isolation resulted from two different trends: on the one hand, the Triple Alliance with Austria and Italy was weakening, even disintegrating; on the other, England, Japan, France, and Russia were slowly drawing closer together. In the first decade of the twentieth century, this problem was barely recognized by the German Foreign Office. Holstein remained blissful and confident until dismissed in 1906, and Bülow showed little apprehension. Perhaps the government's fitful reactions to international developments showed its inner insecurity. But Bülow failed to identify the danger of encirclement in a positive sense by adopting a new course that would bring an end to Germany's growing isolation.

"Encirclement" actually involved more than international relations; it constituted the unconscious beginning of a German national psychosis of anxiety. Notably after World War I, this fear of encirclement (*Einkreisungsangst*) was to become quasi-paranoiac. But well before the war, many Germans, particularly conservatives, reacted with intense emotions to the chimera of a ubiquitous enemy, and attributed all national calamities to the hostile ring girdling the nation or to "the enemy within," whom they suspected of collaborating with foreigners. They tended to project their own xenophobia onto the world at large, and ascribed hostile feelings to all other nations. This anxiety made them appear quarrelsome and antagonistic to the foreign powers. A vicious circle developed. German swagger provoked among the powers anti-German alliances, which in turn heightened Germany's paranoiac reactions.

Germany thus became an outcast among the nations. The British and French press gleefully denounced every awkward step of German diplomacy, and labeled Germany the troublemaker of the world. Even before the advent of World War I, Germany acquired the reputation imputed to France, Spain, and other "aggressor" nations in previous centuries. This ill repute—stemming partly from the powers' jealousy of Germany's meteoric rise and largely from irritation with William's clumsy *Weltpolitik*—colored international relations in the prewar decade and, one might say, produced the theory of German "war guilt" well in advance of the war. In turn, it nourished Germany's brooding feeling of injustice and heightened its irritability and distrustfulness.

Much of the powers' suspicions of German intentions can be attributed to the incredibly undiplomatic behavior of the German Foreign Office and its spokesmen. At the first Peace Conference at The Hague in 1899, for instance, the German delegates acted like boorish novices. The majority of the twenty-six nations attending the conference distrusted the Russian proposals for disarmament, but tactfully circumvented the problem by directing the discussion to international arbitration and the need for limiting the horrors of war. The German envoys, however, supported by a press that decried pacifism as befitting only weak or rich nations but not growing states like Germany, talked squarely against disarmament. They proclaimed that Germany was not overarmed and that they saw no reason that it should stop arming. All the other major powers at the conference undoubtedly felt as Germany did but had the tact not to make the admission publicly. German frankness produced nothing but increased international suspicions.

A similar spectacle was presented at the second Peace Conference in 1907. Great Britain desired to safeguard its naval supremacy by an international agreement limiting future naval construction. Again none of the major powers cherished such a proposal, but Germany again aroused the suspicion of the nations by acting as a blunt spokesman for naval expansion.

WEAKENING OF THE TRIPLE ALLIANCE

The alliance among Germany, Austria, and Italy was renewed for a six-year period in 1902—as it was to be in 1908 and again in 1912. But its value to Germany had become doubtful. Even if the alliance had remained firm, the Continental character of Germany's two allies and the smallness of their navies made them poor support for Germany's global commitments. But the alliance did not even remain firm. Italy was becoming a dubious partner, and the Italians made it clear that inadequacy of their navy would discourage them from fighting France or England.

Above all, Italy had been drawing closer to France. The trade war between the two ended in 1898 with the signing of a Franco-Italian commercial treaty. In the following years, the two countries agreed on mutually respecting each other's spheres of interests in Africa, with France tacitly relinquishing Tripoli to Italy, and Italy abandoning all claims to Tunisia. The Italians felt that Germany would be of little aid in helping them conquer the African empire of their dreams, but that the acquiescence of Britain and France was essential, since their navies could frustrate Italian designs overseas. In 1902, Italy and France even concluded an agreement—the exact terms of which were not revealed to the German government—in which Italy more or less agreed to remain neutral in a Franco-German war. The Italian king emphasized the new amity by visiting Paris in the following year.

Perspicacious observers recognized that Italy's defection rendered the

Triple Alliance worthless to Germany. But Bülow shrugged it off as merely an "extra dance" with another partner that would not endanger the "Italo-German honeymoon." Actually, Italy's *rapprochement* with France also threatened to undermine its peaceful relations with Austria. Austro-Italian friction over the Trentino and Trieste regions had lain dormant after 1882. But French backing now permitted the Italians to resume anti-Austrian irredentist agitation.

Austria, too, was a weak link in the alliance. Apart from its entanglement in the Balkans, which sapped its usefulness to Berlin in the event of a Franco-German war, it was disintegrating internally. After 1897, antagonism among its minorities threw the tottering empire into continual parliamentary crises. There was also discord between Austrians and Hungarians over control of the military, with the result that no substantial increase of the army was undertaken between 1889 and 1912.

FORMATION OF THE ENTENTES While Germany's alliance system was losing strength, the other powers were drawing closer together. In 1902, Great Britain abandoned its long-standing "splendid isolation," and concluded a firm alliance with Japan. Two years later, France and England settled their many colonial differences, particularly in Africa, and signed the Entente Cordiale, despite the complication that their respective allies, Russia and Japan, were at the time engaged in the Russo-Japanese War. The German government at first saw few serious implications in this Anglo-French agreement, which was merely a *rapprochement* and not a full-fledged alliance. The Entente was to retain this appearance of informality until the outbreak of World War I. In fact, however, tighter bonds soon developed between Paris and London, especially after Sir Edward Grey became British foreign secretary and arranged for unofficial talks between military advisers of the two states to draw up plans for possible wartime cooperation. The German government had only vague suspicions of these arrangements.

Finally, England and Russia also examined areas of colonial friction and reached compromises that permitted the formation of an Anglo-Russian Entente in 1907. Informal and tenuous as these two Ententes were, they represented the beginning of the Anglo-Russo-French front that eventually surrounded Germany in 1914.

To counter this development, the German government had two choices: the positive step of befriending one of the great powers and thereby breaking Germany's own isolation, or the negative approach of attempting to split their nascent alliances. William, Bülow, and Holstein attempted both on various occasions, but failed in all their efforts.

THE ATTEMPT TO BEFRIEND RUSSIA The year 1904 offered the opportunity for a German *rapprochement* with St. Petersburg. Russia was engaged in a losing war with Japan. Its French ally stood on the side lines, and even concluded the Entente with England, which at the time was an ally of Japan. Great Britain was frankly anti-Russian and refused to let the Russian fleet pass through the Suez Canal on its way to the Far East. When Russian men-of-war mistakenly sank a British fishing vessel in the North Sea, open hostilities almost erupted between the two nations. Hence Russia stood seemingly alone, and William seized the occasion to attempt a *rapprochement.*

Despite British protests, Germany supplied coal to the Russian fleet on its long journey to the Pacific. William visited St. Petersburg to encourage his tsarist cousin, who was losing battle after battle against the Japanese and was facing an increasingly restless populace inside Russia. But William's reception was cool. Nicholas lacked confidence in the German ruler and was unwilling to jeopardize his alliance with France. For although France was not obliged to help Russia in the war against Japan, it reassured St. Petersburg to have a partner in Europe while Russia was engaged in the Far East.

In October, William tried to overcome the tsar's scruples in regard to France by proposing to unite the Triple Alliance of Germany, Austria, and Italy, with the Franco-Russian Dual Alliance. He wrote to Nicholas that he realized that France was obligated "to share Nicholas' bed," but suggested that France should also feel obliged occasionally to "caress Germany or give her a kiss," rather than go "crawling into the bedroom of that ever-intriguing grab-all on the island [England]." But France preferred to abide by its agreement with England, and Nicholas would do nothing without French participation.

In the summer of 1905, on the occasion of a yachting vacation with Nicholas, William tried more of his personal diplomacy. There was no longer any possibility of drawing France into a pact with Germany and Russia: Berlin and Paris stood on the verge of war in the first Moroccan Crisis. But by then Russia had lost the war against Japan, and numerous insurrections, strikes, and mutinies had shaken the tsarist regime in a prelude to the October Revolution of 1905. William simply wrote up a draft treaty, presented it to the tsar on the Russian yacht, and in a scene engendered more by emotion than by rational negotiations, persuaded Nicholas to sign it.

This so-called Treaty of Björkö, drafted, as William informed Bülow, "with the aid of God," was specifically limited to mutual Russo-German protection on the Continent. It could therefore be of no value to Germany in a conflict with Great Britain. Moreover, it lacked the safeguards of Bismarck's Reinsurance Treaty in regard to the Austro-German alliance. William's draft did not specify German neutrality if Austria attacked Russia. On the contrary, its terms would have forced Germany to fight on Russia's side. And since Russia was still firmly allied with France, the Treaty of Björkö could not have helped Germany in a Franco-German War. One wonders, therefore, what William possibly hoped to accomplish.

When notified ex post facto of the proposed treaty in a letter from the exuberant emperor, Bülow promptly asked to be relieved of his post. He was horrified at William's personal diplomacy and his thoughtless action in risking the alliance with Vienna without achieving at least equivalent gains. Softened by an ignominious defeat in the Far East and weakened by internal insurrections, Russia hardly appeared a worthwhile ally to Bülow.

It was typical of William that, when thus reprimanded by Bülow, he did not attempt to justify his impetuous behavior aboard the tsar's yacht, but appealed to his minister, "his best and most intimate friend," not to abandon him simply "because the situation seems critical." In a tearful, almost hysterical letter, he reminded Bülow of the heroic suffering he had endured at his minister's behest—chiefly in connection with his visit to Tangier in the course of the first Moroccan Crisis—and begged him to stay in office. "Jointly, we shall work together for the greater glory of Germany," he wrote. Although insisting that Bülow's resignation would embarrass him "eternally," he added paradoxically: "The day after your request for dismissal would not find the Emperor alive! Think of my poor wife and children!"

Bülow stayed and the Björkö draft was shelved. The Russian Foreign Office, anyhow, had refused to ratify the treaty proposal. Germany abandoned its attempt to befriend Russia, and turned with greater energy to Holstein's scheme for splitting the Anglo-French Entente by proper exploitation of the Moroccan Crisis.

The First Moroccan Crisis

Morocco, rich in natural resources, remained one of the few African regions still available for colonization. An international convention in 1880 had stipulated respect for Morocco's independence and guaranteed equal commercial rights for all nations. But by the turn of the century, Moroccan local government had become anarchical and European penetration had begun. Britain and France both had designs on the sultanate. Each offered Germany a share in the spoils in the hope of getting support against its rival, but Germany rejected all advances. Although Holstein could not conceive of the possibility of a Franco-British *rapprochement,* he preferred to leave Morocco as a point of friction between the two. Meanwhile all the powers continued their commercial penetration, and the French even began territorial encroachment across the borders from neighboring Algeria.

By early 1905, France had completed its preparations for openly proclaming a protectorship over the sultanate. Italian acquiescence had been obtained in return for a free hand in Tripoli. Agreement with Spain was reached when northern Morocco was reserved for Spanish penetration. And the Entente Cordiale, although officially guaranteeing the *status quo* of both Egypt and Morocco, had in fact placed the latter at the disposal of France. Thus only Germany had not indicated advance approval when France openly negotiated with the sultan for political control over his state.

At this point Holstein decided to use Morocco as a wedge for breaking the Anglo-French "ring" and convinced Bülow of the merits of his plan. William was to give official endorsement to Morocco's independence and demand continuation of the open-door policy established by the Convention of 1880. Bülow and Holstein were sure that England and the United States would endorse such a step, which was not pro-German but favored all nations, and that consequently England would have to renege on its promise of support to France. To make it more dramatic, they insisted that William make such a pronouncement on Moroccan soil. William disliked the plan, its diplomatic implications as well as his assigned role, but he reluctantly agreed to play his part.

On the last day of March 1905, he landed at Tangier and rode through the streets of the city, "mounted on a strange horse despite his limited riding ability," as he later described it, "acclaimed by crowds which included bribed anarchists." He was received by the sultan's uncle, to whom he expressed public assurance that Germany stood behind Morocco's independence. A week later, Germany and the sultan called for an international conference to discuss the Moroccan problem.

One of the first in a series of international crises that blackened Germany's reputation developed immediately. Europe was astonished by Germany's audacity and baffled by its intentions. Maurice Rouvier, the French premier, feared a possible war with Germany at a time when France was not prepared and when its Russian ally could not be expected to furnish much assistance. He therefore offered to meet the Germans in a bilateral conference to discuss compensations for Germany—possibly an Atlantic port in Morocco or parts of the French Congo—in return for German agreement to French occupation of Morocco.

But Bülow and Holstein were not interested in compensations or in a bilateral conference that would recognize France's special rights over the sultanate. They wanted to humiliate France at an international conference that would uphold the Convention of 1880, and hoped to split the newly formed Entente Cordiale. England had promised France diplomatic support for the conquest of Morocco, but because by tradition England favored a policy of free trade, the Germans expected that Great Britain would refuse to back French desires for exclusive control over Morocco, and thereby antagonize the French. As to France, Bülow felt confident that it would not risk war, although Holstein was not averse to an armed conflict. The German government actually was not in agreement about the results to be expected from the crisis it had created. Count Alfred von Schlieffen (1833–1913), the German chief of staff, favored a preventive war against France at a moment when its Russian ally still had the remnants of its defeated forces on the Pacific front. But William was adamant about guarding the peace. He still hoped to bring France—and Russia—into alignment with the Triple Alliance, and thought, as he had about England in the 1890s, that Paris could be frightened into a *rapprochement* with Germany.

The French foreign minister, Théophile Delcassé, the architect of the Anglo-French Entente, meanwhile consulted with London and drew the erroneous conclusion that Britain was ready to join France in a war against Germany if necessary. Although England agreed to support French aspirations to Morocco, it was hardly prepared to conclude a firm military alliance with France. Certain of British help, Delcassé urged a firm anti-German stance. But the French government as a whole was not convinced of British support. Anxious to avoid war, it forced Delcassé to resign.

The fall of Delcassé was a victory for Germany, and William promptly rewarded Bülow by making him a prince. France had been humiliated. But Holstein had not yet achieved his purpose of splitting the Anglo-French Entente, and he persisted in his demand for an international conference.

The powers were horrified at Germany's intransigence but finally agreed to a meeting.

When the nations convened at Algeciras from January to April 1906, Germany found itself isolated. England, Spain, Russia, and even Italy supported France. Austria alone sided with Germany, but made it clear that Austria would not fight for Morocco. Germany maintained its legalistic stand that it merely wished to uphold equal treaty rights for all, and continued to reject all French offers for a bilateral settlement. Legally, the German position was irreproachable, but the powers regarded it as further evidence of German pugnacity.

At several points, the deadlocked conference looked like a prelude to war. But William did not want war and ordered the withdrawal of one German demand after another. The obstructionist Holstein was finally dismissed from his post. The final acts of the conference upheld the fiction of the sultan's sovereignty and of free and equal trading rights for all nations, while awarding France and Spain special police powers and economic privileges that paved the way for eventual annexation.

As a result of this first Moroccan Crisis, Germany again gained nothing but ill repute. After grandiose promises, it had let down the sultan of Morocco and had rejected the chance for special economic rights or compensations in a bilateral deal with France. Its position had been legally sound but diplomatically foolish. It had not succeeded in splitting the Entente Cordiale; on the contrary, it had publicly revealed its own isolation. At the same time, Germany fanned the fires of French nationalism, which brought to power Georges Clemenceau, an inveterate foe of Germany.

Relations with England

Until 1906, Germany's growing navy had been primarily the kind of "risk fleet" advocated by Tirpitz. But when England launched the Dreadnought, a new type of battleship with heavy armor plate and 12-inch guns, Germany promptly passed a new naval law to increase its own fleet and to provide for the construction of similar ships. Since the armament and fire power of these new superbattleships rendered the older types obsolete, Germany could acquire parity with England if it could build dreadnoughts at the same speed as Great Britain. Thus began the second phase of the Anglo-German naval rivalry, which gradually drove England more firmly into the anti-German camp.

In the summer of 1906, King Edward visited William, and requested that Germany scale down its naval program in the interest of Anglo-German friendship. Bülow and his cabinet, made cautious by the Moroccan Crisis, urged William to make concessions. But he looked upon the German navy with personal pride. Acting on Tirpitz' advice, he rejected Edward's request, and Germany pursued its naval program.

In the following year, England attempted unsuccessfully to dam German naval expansion through the second Peace Conference at The Hague, and then concluded its *rapprochement* with Russia. Thus the naval race not only prevented improvement in Anglo-German relations, but also produced international friction and increased Germany's isolation. Even Tirpitz noted in a memorandum that England might attack Germany, as it had previous naval challengers, such as Spain, Holland, and France, in an effort to safeguard its supremacy on the seas. He concluded that Germany should speed up its naval program. However, the German ambassador in London, who questioned the wisdom of Germany's naval policy, reported that England would never attack Germany despite the provocative nature of its naval program.

Early during the Bosnian Crisis, in the summer of 1908, Edward once again visited Germany to discuss the naval question with his imperial nephew. William insisted that a large fleet was required to protect Germany's growing trade. When asked by Edward's undersecretary for foreign affairs (Sir Charles Hardinge), how the fleet could protect world-wide trade when it usually remained close to the home ports, William admitted: "Because our London embassy advised that the less the British see our fleet, the better." Edward and his secretary again urged a slowing down of naval construction, but William remained adamant and threatened: "Then we would have to fight, for it is a question of national honor and dignity." According to a report William sent to Bülow after this interview, he stressed his determination by looking the undersecretary "sharp in the eye" and "baring his teeth—which made a deep effect. One must always deal with the English in this manner."

Once again Bülow was embarrassed by his ruler's personal diplomacy. He wrote to William: "I know that the creation of a German fleet is the task which history has placed before Your Majesty." But he urged caution and warned that the English might be goaded into war if they "take it for certain that our naval armaments will be continued like this *ad infinitum*." He intimated that England's greater resources would at any rate always permit it to construct ships faster than Germany. To soften his tone, he pledged his eagerness to help William "achieve his life work," but insisted that England's offers to come to terms should not always be rejected categorically.

It soon became evident how little William understood the seriousness of the situation. On October 28, 1908, two months after the meeting of Edward and William, the *Daily Telegraph* in London published an interview with William, together with a tongue-in-cheek commentary by the anonymous English interviewer. In the interview, William repeatedly boasted of his love of peace and called the English as "mad, mad, mad as March hares" for always distorting German actions and insinuating that Germany "holds a dagger" behind its back. In bragging terms, he claimed that he had really favored England in the Boer War, that the German General Staff had worked out the military plans for England to defeat the Boers, and that he alone had resisted Franco-Russian pressure to embarrass England by joint intervention on the side of the Boers. Further, he insisted that he had wished only to safeguard private German interests in Morocco and that the German newspapers that had taken a bellicose stand on Morocco were run by "mischief makers." According to William, the German navy presented no threat to England, since its duty was to protect trade, "especially in the Far East." But he warned that only he and "a minority of the best elements in Germany" felt friendship for England. "Large sections of the middle and lower classes of my own people are not friendly to England." Yet, he assured his interviewer, he commanded the Germans, and he promised continued friendship toward Britain, provided his services were appreciated by the English.

William had made many previous *faux pas* in interviews and speeches, and in his fitful attempts at personal diplomacy. But never before had he managed to antagonize almost everyone at home and abroad in a single communication: He had revealed Russian and French diplomatic secrets in regard to anti-British intervention in the Boer War; the Japanese resented the statement that the German fleet was to protect trade "especially in the Far East"; and the whole content and tone of the interview naturally aroused the ire of the English—not least the insinuation that the bulk of the Germans hated England and that German military plans had helped England win the Boer War.

Inside Germany, the *Daily Telegraph* affair created an even greater storm. The liberal press vituperated against the insinuation that "the best elements" in Germany were those not belonging "to the middle or lower classes," and objected to the implication that William could command German feelings. Even the conservatives were aghast at his indiscretion. During a tempestuous three-day debate, the Reichstag demanded a curb on the emperor's personal diplomacy; but no united action resulted and the delegates failed to take advantage of the occasion by pressing for parliamentary responsibility. William simply laughed at the furor and went on a vacation. Bülow, officially responsible for the publication of the interview, tried to enhance his own prestige by acting as spokesman for the Reichstag and the nation at large vis-à-vis William. He claimed he had not approved the text of the press release before its publication, but had passed it on to a subaltern. In view of the unclear lines of responsibility that permeated the government, it is impossible to know whether Bülow had read the text and passed it on to embarrass his monarch and thus use the resulting scandal to put an end to William's personal diplomacy; or whether, indeed, some subaltern approved it, since both Bülow and the foreign minister were away from Berlin at the time.

In the end, Bülow had an official audience with Emperor William and announced the latter's promise to be more cautious in his private utterances. But nothing was done to change the governmental system that permitted such impulsive diplomacy. For a while, William was more careful in his speeches, but he probably never grasped the import of his indiscretion, which had further undermined Germany's international reputation.

The Bosnian Crisis

In most aspects, the complex Bosnian Crisis of 1908–1909 appears like a rehearsal for 1914, and brought Europe perilously close to war. Partly to put a halt to Austro-German penetration through the Balkans, Russia and England pressed for political reforms in Turkish Macedonia. At the same time, the Young Turk Revolution restored a constitutional regime to Turkey in an effort to strengthen Turkish national unity. This revolution not only frustrated Russia's hopes of gaining greater influence over Turkey and free passage through the Straits for its warships, but also undermined the position of Germany, which had acted as a friend of the reactionary sultan. Finally, Austria-Hungary used the Turkish upheaval as an excuse for annexing the provinces of Bosnia and Herzegovina, which it had administered since 1878, while Bulgaria on the same day broke away from Turkey and declared its complete independence. Serbia and Montenegro, which had nourished hopes of acquiring portions of Bosnia-Herzegovina, protested against Austria's actions and started military preparations against Austria. Russia threw its support to Serbia, and the Anglo-French Entente stood behind Russia.

The varied and complex aspects of this crisis, which involved every Balkan state and implicated all the major European powers, are not germane to this analysis. But Germany's reaction is significant. Instead of resuming Bismarck's arbitrative role of 1878 and 1886–1887, in which he had placed himself between Austria and Russia, in order not to lose its last dependable ally, Germany sided unequivocally with Austria. While sending reassuring messages to London and Paris, Germany flexed its muscles toward the east and rather peremptorily pressured Russia into abandoning Serbia. Thus the crisis passed. Austria retained its gains, but neither Russia, Serbia, nor Turkey received compensations.

The relatively easy victory of Austria-Hungary and Germany gave Berlin an illusory self-confidence. Bülow concluded that the Triple Entente was, after all, not to be feared in times of crisis. Unquestioning support of Austria had proved to be correct policy. In reality, however, the course of the crisis inspired Berlin with unwarranted optimism. Russia had backed down not because it feared the strength of the German army, but because it had not yet recovered from its defeat by Japan. Thereafter Russia was to recover the self-confidence it had lost in the Russo-Japanese War and thereby change the balance, whereas Germany was to adopt the same stand in 1914.

18

The First Storm, 1909–1918

THE LAST YEARS OF PEACE

Theobald von Bethmann-Hollweg, who came from a family of bankers and politicians, assumed the chancellorship in the summer of 1909. He was to be the last chancellor under the Bismarckian framework of politics. Within less than a decade after his appointment, the external might of Bismarck's Reich crumbled under the impact of World War I, and his internal system disintegrated under the stress of tensions and revolutions. The five remaining years of peace were characterized by frequent international crises and by internal frictions that inexorably led to the flare-up of war and revolt. To be sure, the Bethmann-Hollweg government made some accommodations to alleviate international tension. And, perhaps encouraged by the greater flexibility shown by the Socialists and the Liberals, the chancellor displayed occasional willingness to conciliate the internal opposition by progressive policies. But the right wing showed little inclination to make concessions. The system remained inflexible, and despite his good intentions, Bethmann-Hollweg lacked the force and foresight to impose radical changes.

Failure to Reform Prussia

One of Bethmann-Hollweg's first steps was an attempt at reforming Prussia's antiquated electoral system, a measure that had been vaguely promised by Bülow in January 1908. The representative character of the Prussian diet continued to be warped by the three-class system (see pages 336 ff.), which divided the electorate into classes on the basis of districts and tax assessments and which operated by use of indirect elections and open ballots. Only one minor change in the electoral law had been made since its promulgation in 1850, and all but the few who profited from its inequity had been demanding reform for decades. The public ballot permitted fraud and intimidation of voters. Assignment to electoral groups on the basis of tax payments grossly underfranchised the proletariat. And failure to redraw electoral districts despite the cityward movement of seventy years gave a vast advantage to the landlords of the east over the industrial entrepreneurs and the city proletariat of the west. This inequity is best seen in a comparison of electoral results in Prussia with those in Germany at large. In 1908, the Socialists succeeded for the first time in obtaining representation in the Prussian diet with the election of 7 deputies in a total of 443, at a time when they polled about 30 percent of all the votes cast in a Reichstag election. Conversely, the right-wing parties—Conservatives and Free Conservatives—dominated the Prussian diet of 1913 with 45.6 percent of the seats, even though they made up only 14.3 percent of the delegates in the Reichstag of 1912. Considering in addition the power of the upper house (consisting largely of the landlords from the area east of the Elbe) over the Prussian legislature, and the dominant position that Prussia itself held within the Reich, one can understand the clamor of the Liberals and the Socialists for electoral reforms in Prussia.

As chancellor of the Reich and minister-president of Prussia, Bethmann-Hollweg wanted to please the opposition parties in the Reichstag without unduly antagonizing the conservatives of Prussia. Hence in February 1910, he hesitantly submitted modest reform proposals to the Prussian legislature, together with the obviously contradictory implication that the existing electoral law actually allowed a fairly equitable representation of public opinion. He suggested abolition of the public ballot and of the indirect voting arrangement. Secret voting would be welcomed by peasants and workers; direct elections would eliminate the rotten borough system and please the urban population. But his proposals retained the three-class division under a highly complicated formula weighing each vote according to the financial status of the voter. One vote from the first class, those paying the most taxes, was to equal 4 votes from the second class and 5.3 votes from the lowest class. Since under the existing system a few very rich had dominated the first class, it was proposed that tax assessments over 5000 marks be disregarded when voters were assigned to electoral classes. And to mollify the middle class, intellectuals and professionals were to be raised into the next higher voting class than indicated by their tax payments.

But even these moderate proposals were defeated. The left wing demanded universal, equal, and direct suffrage. The Conservatives, and even the Center, looked upon the measure as a dangerous opening to the left wing. Bethmann-Hollweg, never a fighter, withdrew his proposals, and the anachronistic electoral system remained a cancer in the body politic of Prussia.

Bethmann-Hollweg and the Reichstag

In other less crucial legislative areas, Bethmann-Hollweg was more successful, although he was unable to establish a working arrangement with parties for support in the Reichstag. After the failure of Bülow's bloc, parties and pressure groups again split into mutually antagonistic sections, and parliamentary alignments resumed their chaotic course. The only major change occurred on the Left. The political leadership of the Social Democratic party, as well as that of the growing socialist trade unions, adopted an increasingly moderate and evolutionary path. After their electoral defeat of 1907, the Socialists rebounded in 1912 to gain 4.25 million votes—about 35 percent of all votes cast—and 110 seats, making them by far the strongest party in the Reichstag. Once again renouncing the doctrine of the class struggle, they agreed to collaborate with the recently united Progressives, who remained the fourth largest party in electoral votes. Jointly these two commanded 152 delegates out of the total of 397 in the Reichstag, and presented a vital power in the legislature.

Maneuvering among the parties, Bethmann-Hollweg succeeded in passing a capital gains tax that pleased the Socialists. He also managed to balance the budget for three consecutive years. A constitution was passed for Alsace-Lorraine, and the Imperial Insurance Code was enacted in 1911. The latter brought uniformity to all existing schemes for old-age pensions, accident insurance, sickness benefits, and provisions for invalidism. It also extended coverage to orphans, widows, domestic employees, and agricultural laborers, and increased some benefits, although many of the Socialists' demands for increases were refused because of financial considerations.

The chancellor also faced the question of the army budget when the regular five-year appropriations ended in 1911. The last major increase in the German army had been effected in 1893. After 1898, most of the funds had been allocated to the navy, the darling of the emperor, of the Reichstag, and of public opinion. The War Department itself had not particularly pushed for an increase in troop strength. In fact, General Karl von Einem (1853–1934) the minister of war, had favored improvement of the army's training and equipment rather than an increase in its size. "The German army," he wrote, "has now reached a size which clearly is beyond the limits of a healthful development and which constitutes serious dangers." Not the least of these "dangers" to the conservative minister was the threat of excessive democratization of the officer corps. On the other hand, the famous Schlieffen plan, evolved in 1905 as strategy in a possible two-front war, called for a considerable increase in troop strength. But its author, Count Alfred von Schlieffen, chief of staff from 1891 to 1905, had done nothing to convince the ministry of this need. Even in 1906, after the first Moroccan Crisis, the War Ministry had kept its demands moderate, although Bülow favored an increase in the strength of the army. In view of the financial problem of increasing the military budget, Bülow in the end had not pushed the matter in the quinquennial appropriations of 1906.

But a new trend opened in 1911, intensifying the armaments race with France. General Josias von Heeringen (1850–1926), the minister of war, complained that Germany devoted only 15.5 percent of its budget to the army as against 34 percent by France, and pressed for a considerable increase in troops and expenditures. Bethmann-Hollweg at the time was not yet worried about the international situation, and requested an increase of only 10,000 men, mostly technicians, to bring the peacetime army to a strength of 515,000. Shortly after passage of the army bill of 1911, international tension rose sharply with the second Moroccan Crisis. The chancellor and the War Ministry prepared to ask for an additional 30,000 men in 1912. Public opinion seemed to favor the proposed increases, for in the general elections of January 1912, the main issues were not foreign policy, defense budgets, nor armaments, but rather economic and tax questions. Despite the electoral triumph of the Social Democratic party, which opposed an increase in the army, the new Reichstag approved the requested military increase in 1912. This second increase, kept relatively moderate to avoid the need for new taxes, required an additional 56 million marks, most of it obtained through deficit financing.

By the summer of 1913, the need for a more vigorous armaments program seemed evident to Bethmann-Hollweg. The wars in Tripolitania and the Balkans, increases in Russian armaments, and the breakdown of Anglo-German naval discussions moved the new chief of staff, Helmuth von Moltke (1848–1916) to demand three new army corps. The government at once proposed a bill calling for the immediate addition of some 120,000 men and 20,000 regular and noncommissioned officers, at a cost of about 200 million marks, as well as an added 900 million marks for the strengthening of fortresses and armaments. In addition, the bill projected a further increase of the army by an additional 190,000 men. Only the Socialists, Poles, and Alsatians opposed these demands in the Reichstag, and the big army increases were quickly approved. However, financing the measures presented problems. All proposals for new indirect or direct taxes were rejected. In the end, by getting approval for a special one-time capital levy, the so-called defense contribution, Bethmann-Hollweg succeeded in raising a portion of the funds required. Although they continued their opposition to the increase in the army's strength, the Socialists voted for the tax levy because it would fall on the well-to-do classes.

The Prewar Crises

The conduct of Germany's foreign affairs did not change radically with Bethmann-Hollweg's appointment. The new chancellor was less optimistic than Bülow, and made several perfunctory attempts to break the "ring" around Germany. But he was unwilling to loosen the bonds with Vienna in order to improve relations with Russia, or to reduce the size of the fleet in order to achieve an understanding with Great Britain. He was not a forceful leader, and he received little support from Emperor William, who now remained more in the background of the political scene. Much power, on the other hand, was exercised by Alfred von Kiderlen-Wächter (1852–1912), a favorite of the emperor. He was secretary of foreign affairs from 1910 to 1912, and enjoyed a heyday of bluff and intrigue during the second Moroccan Crisis.

In 1910, there was a brief improvement in relations between Russia and Germany. The Balkans were momentarily quiescent, and Nicholas II visited William II at Potsdam. No fundamental agreement on the future of the Balkans appeared possible, but Russia finally withdrew its opposition to Germany's further extension of the Baghdad Railway system. Berlin, in turn, agreed not to interfere in Russia's penetration of northern Persia.

At the same time, Germany maneuvered skillfully among the various revolutionary and counterrevolutionary factions in Turkey and succeeded in cementing Turkish-German relations.

This *rapprochement* ultimately led to a full-fledged wartime alliance. Although militarily weak and politically unstable, Turkey could act as a minor wedge against Germany's total encirclement, provided the intervening Balkan area could be made safe for Austro-German contact with Turkey.

But the war between Turkey and Italy over Tripoli, which erupted in September 1911, presented Germany with a dilemma, since it was allied with Italy and friendly with Turkey. The war threatened Germany's economic interests in the Turkish Empire, and frightened Austria by endangering the *status quo* in the Balkans. The war lasted a year, and the Turks were finally forced to recognize Italy's seizure of Tripolitania. During the hostilities, Germany succeeded in maintaining a benevolently neutral attitude toward both antagonists. Abandoned by all the major powers, which had secretly promised Italy a free hand in Tripolitania, and nearly stabbed in the back by its Balkan neighbors, Turkey was glad to have the moral support of Germany—and to some extent of Austria—even though it received no military help. Italy, on the other hand, was appreciative of the tacit backing of the Triple Alliance, since military operations in the eastern Mediterranean proved difficult, and it could expect no Anglo-French support. The course and outcome of the war over Tripoli both strengthened and weakened the Triple Alliance. In recognition of its usefulness, the three partners renewed the alliance for another six-year term in December 1912 and added new agreements concerning naval cooperation, although the validity of the current treaty extended to 1914. On the other hand, Italy's acquisition of Tripolitania made it even more dependent on the good will of Britain and France, whose navies dominated the Mediterranean, and rendered it less willing to assume a firm anti-French or anti-British stand.

THE SECOND MOROCCAN CRISIS While fairly successful in guiding Germany's relations with Turkey and its conduct during the war over Tripoli, Kiderlen-Wächter meanwhile rekindled the suspicions of the powers during the second Moroccan Crisis. After 1905, France had pursued its penetration of Morocco. In 1909, it had finally made a bilateral arrangement with Germany, promising an open door to German economic interests in return for German recognition of France's political interests in Morocco. Hereafter the French moved ahead boldly, and in 1911 dispatched troops to the capital of Fez on the pretext of quelling disorders. After having rejected all proposals for compensation in 1905 and in the intervening years, Germany suddenly demanded indemnification. Believing France to be unwilling to offer compensations unless threatened, Kiderlen-Wächter sent the German gunboat *Panther* to Agadir in Morocco, ostensibly to protect German merchants and their property against raids by local tribes. Kiderlen-Wächter notified the powers that Germany's intentions were peaceful, while at the same time he accused France of unilaterally violating the Algeciras Convention. The German foreign minister evidently was resurrecting the old game of trying to frighten France, but at the same time he wished to press for maximum concessions.

The appearance of the "Panther" in Moroccan waters caused consternation in France and England, but was hailed with exuberance by the nationalists in Germany. France hesitated between picking up the gauntlet and offering timely concessions. England, pressed by David Lloyd George, then chancellor of the exchequer, warned Germany not to go too far, and made preliminary preparations to ready its fleet and to arrange for military cooperation with France. Emperor William and his foreign minister worked at cross-purposes. William wanted no war and so notified the French, but Kiderlen-Wächter assumed a harsher stand in order to obtain maximum concessions. Franco-German negotiations continued through July and August, but the crisis reached critical proportions when France, backed by England, decided to use intimidation itself and threatened to send warships to Agadir. This action in turn piqued the German ruler.

With war in sight, Kiderlen-Wächter finally agreed to negotiate seriously, and requested cession of the entire French Congo in exchange for Germany's abandoning all claims to Morocco. But his hand was weakened, since his mistress, the wife of a Russian diplomat, was in the pay of the French government and had revealed that Kiderlen-Wächter's secret correspondence showed that Germany was not ready for war. France therefore retained the upper hand in the negotiations, and succeeded in scaling down German demands. In a final convention between the two countries, France received a free hand in Morocco and in compensation turned over to Germany 106,000 square miles of Congo backland, infested with sleeping sickness and economically as yet worthless. Thus war was averted. Germany had obtained compensations of doubtful value, after having rejected a possibly better settlement in 1905. The crisis had once again given Germany an unsavory reputation and had cemented the Anglo-French Entente.

In early 1912, England made a last effort to come to terms with Berlin on the naval question. It offered to help Germany in Africa in return for German agreement to limit its naval expansion. But Tirpitz and Emperor William refused to agree to naval limitations and, on the contrary, called for increased construction of warships. This British offer, if indeed it was advanced seriously, probably represented Germany's last chance to loosen the Entente. Thereafter Berlin and London continued to cooperate on occasions, and even succeeded in ironing out colonial problems, as occurred in the summer of 1914 when they finally settled their rivalry in the Near East, and Germany agreed not to continue the Berlin-to-Baghdad Railroad to the Persian Gulf. But their relations always lay under the shadow of the naval race and could hardly lead to a permanent understanding.

THE BALKAN WARS The Balkan Crises of 1912 and 1913 were true overtures to the outbreak of World War I. In the First Balkan War of 1912–1913, Bulgaria, Serbia, Greece, and Montenegro fought against Turkey for territorial expansion, particularly in Thrace, Macedonia, and Albania. The Second Balkan War, in 1913, pitted Serbia, Greece, Turkey, and Rumania against Bulgaria in a fight over the spoils of the preceding war. All the European powers became deeply involved in both wars. Austria and Italy were intent on making Albania an independent state in order to keep it out of the hands of the Greeks, Serbs, and Montenegrins, who all coveted portions of this mountainous land. Austria, in particular, was adamantly against Serbian aggrandizement, especially Serbian acquisition of any part of the land along the Adriatic coast. Russia and France championed the cause of Serbia. Russia at first also supported Bulgaria, but gradually abandoned it when Bulgarian troops advanced into Turkey and threatened the Straits. Russia's abandonment of Bulgaria and its resulting defeat in the Second Balkan War eventually made Bulgaria turn toward Austria and Germany, on whose side it finally entered World War I in 1915. Germany, for its part, was sympathetic to Turkey and Austria during most of the crisis.

By the winter of 1912, the outbreak of a general war seemed likely. Russia and Austria prepared for mobilization, and it seemed unavoidable that their respective allies would be drawn into the conflict. England exerted pressure on the Balkan countries as well as on the major powers, and succeeded in getting up a conference of ambassadors in London to discuss the crisis. England hoped to enlist German help in mediation between Serbia and Austria. William and Bethmann-Hollweg felt somewhat perplexed. They showed little sympathy for Austria's harsh Balkan policy; yet they understood its interest in containing Serbia, since Serbian nationalism and expansionism created unrest in Austria's own Slavic territory. Hence they advocated conciliation, and at the same time assured Vienna of their support, since they did not wish to jeopardize the alliance.

In the end, the crisis once again passed when Russia, unprepared for war as it was, backed down and abandoned Serbia. Thus Austria was given a free hand to force Serbia and Montenegro to evacuate Albania. For the moment, it had achieved its aim. Again, the Triple Alliance and the Triple Entente had withstood a crisis. It was to be the last of the rehearsals.

The Outbreak of World War I

After a relatively calm spring, Europe was only slightly aroused by news of the assassination of Austria's heir to the throne at Sarajevo, on June 28, 1914. Murdering rulers or political opponents was not rare in the Balkans. The ruling princes of Montenegro and Serbia had been assassinated in 1860 and 1868, respectively. A similar fate had befallen the king of Serbia in 1903 and the grand vizier of Turkey in 1913. Yet three weeks after Sarajevo, friction between Austria-Hungary and Serbia approached the breaking point when the former issued its stern ultimatum demanding satisfaction for the murder, as well as concessions that the latter found degrading.

Fairly confident of Russian support, the Serbs rejected some of Austria's demands and readied their armies. Austria, in turn, ordered partial mobilization, and on July 28 declared war on Serbia. The next few days were filled with frantic diplomatic maneuvers by the powers to save the peace or achieve stronger positions in the event of war. Russia decided to aid the Serbs, and hesitated merely between a general mobilization and a partial mobilization directed against Austria only. At the same time, it negotiated with Vienna for a settlement that would satisfy Austria without destroying Serbia. Nicholas also appealed to William to restrain his Austrian ally. France for its part assured Russia of support, and England called for an international conference, but did nothing to restrain Russia. When on July 30 Russia opted in favor of a general mobilization, Germany on the following day sent an ultimatum to St. Petersburg asking for an immediate rescinding of the order. Berlin also inquired in Paris whether France would side with Russia in case of a German-Russian conflict. Meanwhile the German government tried to restrain as well as reassure the Austrians, who declared a general mobilization on the same afternoon.

On August 1, the die was cast. Russia refused to heed Germany's ultimatum—despite the tsar's tearful promises of friendship to William—and France mobilized. In accordance with strategy outlined in the Schlieffen plan, Germany then seized the initiative. It immediately declared war on Russia, two days later on France, and on August 4 also on Belgium. On August 4, after German armies had invaded Belgium, England declared war on Germany. The stage was set for World War I.

UNDERLYING CAUSES It would be impossible in a study of this type to analyze in detail the causes of the war or the problem of war guilt. The many analyses that have been published are familiar to most readers. The accusation that Germany and its allies alone caused the war—as stipulated in Article 231 of the Versailles Treaty—is today rejected by scholars. Popular among the Allied nations in the early years after World War I, it was revived during the height of Hitler's aggressions. But stripped of its emotional content, it cannot stand the test of historical scrutiny. Innumerable factors mingled to unleash the war.

Many underlying causes are often cited by historians: militant nationalism, the armaments race, competitive imperialism, the alliance system, commercial rivalry, and chauvinism. It is often customary to blame the war on German militarism. To be sure, a martial spirit had colored Prussian history for several centuries, the army and the officer corps had occupied a preferred position on the German scene, and social Darwinism had found widespread acceptance in the Reich of Bismarck and William II. Germany had produced more than its share of jingoists, and made more of a fetish of war and sheer power than had most other nations. Friedrich von Bernhardi (1849–1930), one of the prophets of this cult, had written in 1911: "War is a biological necessity . . . . without it an unhealthful development follows which excludes all advancement of the race, and hence all true civilization." And a great number of young people had embraced this creed with almost religious fervor. But again it must be recalled that jingoism was popular in many lands, and that force and violence had become acceptable to the generation nurtured on the glorious tales of colonial victories. In England the political thinker Walter Bagehot proclaimed as a "fundamental law" that "those nations which are strongest tend to prevail over the others; and in certain marked peculiarities the strongest are the best." In France, syndicalists, among others Georges Sorel, preached violence as the means to social salvation; even in the United States, Theodore Roosevelt had advocated a policy of force.

IMMEDIATE CAUSES Moreover, no single nation and no single statesman can be held responsible for the crucial act that lit the fuse.

Austria's demands on Serbia were unreasonably harsh, but the cocky nationalism and intrigues of tiny Serbia were unquestionably provocative and likely to goad any major power into action. Russia's clumsy eagerness to mobilize, the intrigues of its powerful ambassador to Paris, Alexander Izvolski, who had somehow concluded that Russia could gain the Straits only in the course of a general war, and Russia's determination not to abandon the Serbs again as it had done in 1912–1913 were hardly counterbalanced by Nicholas II's pathetic attempts to maintain the peace through personal appeals to William II. England's failure to take a clear and public stand during the crucial week before Germany's invasion of Belgium, as well as Sir Edward Grey's almost blind faith in the magic power of international conferences, gave London a nebulous role at the height of the crisis. France and Germany stood all too uncritically behind their respective allies, Russia and Austria, in an issue that, seen objectively, was not of vital national interest to either. Yet Emperor William's famous "blank check" to Emperor Francis Joseph, so often misrepresented in discussions of the war, was in fact nothing more than a report by Bethmann-Hollweg to the German ambassador in Vienna of a conference between the emperor and the Austrian ambassador to Germany. After discussing the Serbian crisis and its relation to Rumania and Bulgaria, William sent his assurances to Vienna that he would "faithfully stand by Austria-Hungary, as required by the obligations of his alliance and of his ancient friendship." This "blank check" can hardly be labeled as proof of guilt by making Germany an accomplice in Austria's declaration of war on Serbia. Poincaré, the French president, extended similar encouragement to his ally in St. Petersburg. Moreover, Berlin sent subsequent dispatches to Vienna urging caution in Austria's dealings with the Serbs.

THE QUESTION OF GERMAN WAR GUILT But its clumsy diplomatic behavior in the prewar decades had made Germany suspect in the eyes of world opinion long before 1914. And its invasion of neutral Belgium at the beginning of the war clinched the German reputation of being an aggressor.

Most Germans, long burdened by the chimera of encirclement, genuinely believed that the war was purely defensive. William II, probably in all sincerity, stated publicly that the war had been forced on Germany, and in his proclamation to the army and navy urged the armed forces to "protect the fatherland against the infamous surprise attack." Bethmann-Hollweg, in his Reichstag speech of August 4, insisted that Germany was fighting a defensive war, but admitted that the possibility of a French attack on the German flank had made it essential for Germany to violate Belgian neutrality. "We were forced to overlook the *justified* protest of the governments of Luxemburg and Belgium. We shall try to make up for this injustice—I speak openly—this injustice we are committing, once our military aims have been accomplished." Officially, the Germans also claimed that French officers had first violated Belgian neutrality by moving into Belgian fortresses before the outbreak of war, and that French flyers had dropped bombs on German territory a day before Germany declared war on France. But all these feelings and proclamations did not prevent the Allies from pointing to the invasion of Belgium as proof that Germany was the sole aggressor and responsible for the war.

The invasion of Belgium was undertaken on purely military considerations. The politicians were not consulted, and it was hoped that Belgium would not offer resistance and would agree to let the German army pass unmolested. German strategy was based on the Schlieffen plan, which assumed that Russia would take longer for its mobilization and movement of troops to the frontier than would France, and that it would be advisable to crush France first before turning to the east. Believing that the French would probably concentrate their troops in the west for a drive into Alsace-Lorraine and southern Germany, Schlieffen had proposed guarding the southern flank with only minor contingents, while throwing the bulk of the German armies through Belgium in a giant wheeling motion to envelop Paris from the west and then to sweep eastward to attack the main body of the French forces from the rear. The Schlieffen plan provided that after this lightning defeat of France, the German troops would be transferred to the eastern front to face the Russian armies. The success of this strategy depended in part on the speed of its execution. German troops had to pass through Belgium and invade northern France before the French had time to mobilize fully. This military requirement of speed, laid down by the General Staff, outweighed all political considerations. Once Russia had mobilized and a Russo-German war seemed inevitable, the Schlieffen plan assumed that France would automatically enter the war on Russia's side. The politicians were given no time for hesitation or accommodation. Strategy required that the German armies be hurled against the west within specified hours after the outbreak of war in the east. Hence Germany invaded Luxemburg less than twenty-four hours after declaring war on Russia, declared war on France on the following day, and then commenced the invasion of Belgium, thereby adding to its reputation of being the aggressor.

THE COURSE OF THE WAR

Upon the outbreak of hostilities the Triple Alliance disintegrated at once when Italy refused to support Austria's offensive against Serbia and announced its neutrality, which it exchanged a year later for active intervention on the side of the Allies. In November 1914, the Central powers were joined by Turkey, and in late 1915 by Bulgaria. The Serbo-Russo-Franco-Belgo-British Alliance, for its part, gradually grew to include eighteen other nations, adding Montenegro, Japan, Italy, Portugal, Rumania, the United States, Greece, China, and a host of Latin-American states. Ultimately, the four Central powers found themselves at war with twenty-three nations.

The Theaters of Operation

The war was fought in eight distinct theaters of operation: the western front in northern France and southern Belgium; the eastern front against Russia, from the Baltic to the Black Sea; the Balkan front against Serbia, Montenegro, and later Rumania and Greece; the Italian front in northeastern Italy; the various Turkish fronts on all the confines of Turkey's large territory, from the Dardanelles to Armenia and from Persia to Palestine. In addition, there were colonial campaigns in Africa, Asia, and the Pacific islands; an air war over England, Germany, and France; and naval fighting on and below the seas.

THE WAR IN THE WEST The German forces were mobilized swiftly in accordance with the timetable set up by the General Staff, and rolled across Belgium with surprising speed, despite more stubborn local resistance than anticipated. But the chief of staff, Moltke, did not execute the Schlieffen plan in all its bold aspects. It is therefore impossible to ascertain whether the failure of the German armies to achieve their goal resulted from defects in the plan itself or from Moltke's deviations from it. Fearing a French invasion of southern Germany, Moltke detached more units from the northern army to protect Alsace-Lorraine than called for by Schlieffen. Moreover, he prematurely transferred several divisions from the French front to the east because he felt overconfident of victory over France, and was frightened by Russia's rapid concentration of forces. Thus weakened, the northern German armies were not quite capable of achieving their mission. After wheeling across Belgium, they came within about twenty miles of Paris; but in early September, during the gigantic Battle of the Marne, they were hurled back and lost their initiative. Schlieffen's plan had failed, and according to many military analysts, Germany forfeited its chances for ultimate victory during these early months of the conflict. After consolidating their lines along the river Aisne, the Germans abandoned Schlieffen's strategy and attempted to push their northern flank toward the English Channel. They succeeded in gaining the ports of northern Belgium, but stubborn resistance by English, Belgian, and French forces prevented them from breaking through to the Channel and thereby shortening the front by about 100 miles.

Thereafter the western front hardened along hundreds of miles of muddy trenches and twisted barbed wire. Although there was fighting on many other fronts, both sides clung to the belief that the ultimate decision of the war would be achieved by a breakthrough or by attrition of the enemy on the front in France. Commanders were frequently changed, and every year masses of new recruits were assembled on each side and slaughtered in month-long battles that never altered the front by more than a few miles. In the late spring of 1915, for example, the French gained a strip of three miles in a battle that lasted six weeks and cost them some 400,000 casualties. In 1916, the Germans tried for five months to pound their way into Verdun and failed at the cost of about 300,000 men. During the same summer, the British lost 60,000 men in a single day in an unsuccessful offensive. Even the sudden employment of new weapons could not alter the stalemate. In the long run, the German resort to poison gas in 1915 helped no more than the British introduction of tanks in 1916.

Even in 1917, the fighting in the

west remained indecisive, despite its horrendous cost in lives and matériel. Germany was beginning to feel shortages caused by the blockade and by attrition of its resources. But success on the Balkan fronts against Serbia and Rumania, as well as the internal collapse of Russia, gave the German High Command confidence that the war on the western front could be won in 1918, before the arrival of large American reinforcements.

THE EASTERN FRONT In the east, along the extended front from the Baltic to Rumania, Russian forces concentrated more quickly and assumed the initiative more rapidly than expected by the Central Powers. They advanced successfully against the Austrians in southeastern Poland and Bucovina, and at the same time invaded East Prussia, which the startled Germans prepared to evacuate. A timely change of command among the Germans repaired the situation. The local commander was dismissed. In his place, old General Paul von Beneckendorff und von Hindenburg (1847–1934) was called from retirement and given the task of saving East Prussia.

Within three weeks after this change of command, the Russians were expelled from East Prussia in the course of two big battles that cost them enormous casualties and over 200,000 prisoners. Actually, Hindenburg was an undistinguished careerist more famed for his knowledge of East Prussian geography than for his military skill; a subordinate commander in the field had made all tactical dispositions to prepare for this victory before Hindenburg arrived on the scene. But the Battle of Tannenberg—which German patriots celebrated as symbolic revenge for the defeat of the Teutonic Knights on the same spot in 1410—made Hindenburg the hero of the nation. He was raised to the rank of field marshal, given command over the entire eastern front, and later, in 1916, over all German field armies. In fact, however, Hindenburg worked throughout the war in close collaboration with his highly skilled and ambitious chief staff officer, General Erich von Ludendorff (1865–1937), who made most of the strategic and political decisions officially credited to Hindenburg. Yet popular adulation was accorded to Hindenburg, who during these years built his undeserved reputation that served him as an eventual stepping stone to the presidency of the Weimar Republic.

During the winter of 1914–1915, combined Austro-German drives into Russian Poland failed to make much headway, but several offensives in the spring and summer of 1915 yielded far-reaching results. Memel, Lithuania, and the bulk of Poland fell into German hands, and the Russians lost their initial gains in the Carpathian region. The loss of about a million men and severe shortages in war matériel, aggravated by governmental inefficiency and breakdowns, were beginning to weaken the Russian war effort. Despite this impairment, Russia launched two counteroffensives in 1916, partly in response to Allied requests to draw German-Austrian pressure away from the western and Italian fronts. Russia's offensive persuaded Rumania to enter the war against Austria and Germany. In answer, Austrian, Bulgarian, and German forces rapidly seized most of Rumania and extended the eastern front to the Black Sea. But after some initial success, in the course of which

Austria suffered enormous losses, the Russians were again repelled by the Central Powers. Within Russia, these failures led to despair and demoralization and ultimately to revolution.

At first the revolution of March 1917 in Russia did not greatly alter the status of the eastern front. Despite disorder at home, the Provisional Government in Russia pressed for continuation of the war against the Central powers, and launched another great offensive in Galicia in the summer. Once again, initial success gave way to defeat. By September, the Russian armies, punctured by revolutionary and counterrevolutionary confusion, were beginning to dissolve in the field. While the Germans occupied Latvia in the north and straightened their lines on the rest of the front, Russian contingents and individual soldiers were tramping homeward to participate in the revolutionary upheaval. After the Bolsheviks assumed power in the November Revolution, one of Lenin's first acts was to negotiate for an armistice, which came into effect on December 15, 1917. No longer faced by an organized enemy in the east, the Germans now began to shift the bulk of their contingents to the western front.

But some troops were still needed in the east. The remaining Rumanian armies were finally defeated in the spring of 1918, and Rumania signed the peace treaty of Bucharest in May. The Russians at first rejected the harsh terms demanded by the Germans, whereupon the Germans resumed their advance until March 3, when the Bolsheviks agreed to the terms of the Treaty of Brest Litovsk. By it, Russia renounced sovereignty over Finland, Lithuania, Latvia, Estonia, Poland, the Ukraine, and the regions beyond the Caucasus, with Germany and Austria given the right to determine the future status of these areas. In addition, Germany was promised regular delivery of crude oil and other vital materials. The German armies now helped organize the newly independent states, sent troops to occupy Finland and the Ukraine, and soon found themselves involved in the Russian civil war.

THE SOUTHERN FRONTS The western and eastern fronts occupied the main attention of the German war machine, since France and Russia were direct neighbors of Germany. But German armed forces also had to assist the other Central powers in their battles against the Allies. In 1914, Austria twice failed in attempts to invade tiny Serbia. During the following year, when the Allies showed their intention of launching a campaign through the Balkans—which was finally initiated when the French and British landed some troops at Saloniki—Germany decided to assume a greater role in the Balkans. Bulgaria was persuaded to join the Central powers, and German troops were dispatched to support a new Austrian offensive against Serbia. In the fall of 1915, Serbia rapidly collapsed under the joint impact of an Austro-German offensive from the north and a Bulgarian push from the east. Although the Italians halted the Austrian advance in the mountains of Albania and the Allies helped evacuate Serbian troops, the Allied armies at Saloniki were unable to impede the drive of the Central powers. Much of the Balkan area was thus opened to Austrian and German occupation, and the Central powers gained direct contact with their ally Turkey.

During 1916, the Balkan front remained relatively stable from the Adriatic to the Aegean Sea. German, Austrian, and Bulgarian troops fought French, British, Serbian, and Italian units in Albania and Macedonia. In the following year, the Allies finally succeeded in forcing Greece into the war on their side, and they began to pour more men and matériel into the Saloniki front. But the lines of the Central powers held throughout the summer of 1918. Only by September 1918 had the Allies concentrated sufficient forces to launch a giant offensive. In rapid order, the Bulgarian, German, and Austrian lines were broken and Bulgaria was forced to seek an armistice, which it signed on September 30. During October the Italians seized Albania, the Serbs reconquered their own lands, while the Allies crossed Bulgaria to attack Turkey from the north and to liberate Rumania. The Balkan front, in fact, ceased to exist before the war ended in the west.

Germany also found itself ultimately embroiled in the Italian campaigns. During the first eight months of the war, Italy's status had been unclear. It had refused to join the Central powers on the pretext that Austria's attack on Serbia had not been defensive and that Germany had declared war on Russia and France without the justification of "sufficient provocation" stipulated in the Triple Alliance. Nevertheless, Italy had continued to negotiate with Vienna and Berlin in the hope of satisfying its irredentist demands in the Tyrol, Venezia Giulia, and along the Adriatic coast. By 1915, Germany had actually persuaded Vienna to make these territorial sacrifices, but the Allies had meanwhile offered Italy even greater concessions, at the expense of Austrian territory, and Italy decided to join them.

Italy declared war on Austria-Hungary in May 1915, but no official state of war existed between Italy and Germany until the following summer. For two years, the Italians attempted to breach the Austrian defenses north of Trieste. But in eleven separate battles they gained no more than a few miles. Their advances in fierce mountain fighting in the southern Alps were equally negligible. The Austrians, for their part, tried to break through from Trent toward the Adriatic in the spring of 1916, but were equally unsuccessful. Finally, in late 1917, the German High Command decided to intervene on the Italian front. Six divisions were dispatched to aid the Austrians in a fall offensive. Within a few weeks, the Italians were routed and thrown back to the river Piave, abandoning all of northeastern Italy. The Italians appeared demoralized and on the verge of collapse.

In 1918, the Allies furnished greater support to Italy. Austria-Hungary, on the other hand, began to disintegrate. Incited by Polish, Czech, and Yugoslav national councils in exile, local nationalities within the empire provoked disorders and weakened its fighting strength. Throughout the summer, the Austrian lines in Italy held firm, despite growing desertion of its soldiers. But when the Italians finally rallied for an offensive in late October 1918, the Austrian army simply collapsed. The Italians were able to advance rapidly and to force the Austrians to sign an armistice on November 3.

German forces became involved also in the Near East. Turkey concluded a military alliance with Germany on August 1, 1914, directed primarily against Russia. But before Bulgaria's entrance into the war and the defeat of Serbia, it was almost impossible for Germany to send effective aid to the Turks. The Germans merely dispatched two large cruisers to Constantinople in order to bind Turkey more firmly to the Central Powers. On October 29, 1914, a combined Turko-German naval force bombarded Russian Black Sea ports, whereupon the Allies declared war on Turkey. For the next two years, Turkey had to fight its campaigns alone, aided only by German military advisers and by clandestine attacks by German submarines in the Aegean Sea. Turkey fought the Russians in the Caucasus and along the borders of Persia, the British in the Sinai Peninsula and lower Mesopotamia, and the combined Allies on the Gallipoli Peninsula at the entrance to the Straits. In 1917, the Germans finally dispatched a small army to aid the Turks in Palestine, but logistical considerations kept this support fairly small. In the end, Turkey was overwhelmed by foreign invasions and local Arab uprisings, and signed an armistice on October 30, 1918.

THE LOSS OF THE GERMAN COLONIES At the outbreak of the war, Germany did not have sufficient local troops to defend its far-flung colonial empire. Within a few months, most of its colonies were seized by the British, Australians, New Zealanders, South Africans, Indians, French, and Japanese. The German Cameroons and German Southwest Africa held out a bit longer against foreign incursions, but only German East Africa was able to offer effective resistance, so that parts of it remained in German hands until the end of the war.

AIR WARFARE In the course of the war, England, France, and Germany, and later the United States, made considerable use of airplanes. Air mastery over the front lines in the west shifted back and forth between England and Germany, depending on experimentation with new types of planes and their relative rates of production. Airplanes were used most spectacularly for aerial duels between aces, but their true military value lay in general reconnaissance, artillery observation, and occasional support of ground troop movements. As the war progressed, planes of both sides were used in larger formations to carry out bombing raids on London, Paris, and the Rhineland cities of Germany. Property damage ran relatively high, but such raids always had more psychological than strategic value. Starting in 1915, the Germans plagued England with bombing raids by dirigibles, sometimes employing as many as seven at a time, until the English improved their defenses against such attacks.

THE WAR AT SEA During the first year of the war, roving German cruisers preyed on Allied shipping in the various oceans of the world, and made surprise raids on Allied outposts. By early 1915, these raiders had all been caught by the British fleet and had been sunk or had scuttled themselves. The British, meanwhile, had started their blockade of the North Sea, in order to strangle Germany's economy and at the same time bottle up the German fleet in home waters. Nonetheless, individual light cruisers repeatedly slipped through the blockade to lay mines around the entrances to British ports, bombard English coastal towns, or raid Atlantic shipping.

However, Germany's powerful high-seas fleet as such was never really used in the war. Despite repeated urging by Tirpitz that the massed fleet should steam forth and boldly challenge the British Grand Fleet, in order to break the British blockade and then blockade England not merely with submarines but also with surface ships, William II refused to sanction such plans. Like King Frederick William I, who feared to lose a single beloved grenadier, William II acted as though his fleet had been built to be admired but not to be risked in battles. After Tirpitz resigned in 1916, a portion of the fleet was finally permitted to challenge the British in the only major naval engagement of the war (May 31, 1916). Both sides claimed victory, and this naval battle, fought off northern Jutland, remains to this day a controversial subject among naval historians. After Jutland, most of the German fleet again remained in home waters until the end of the war.

Germany's primary efforts at sea were devoted to submarine campaigns. At first, submarines were employed almost exclusively against enemy warships. But in February 1915, the Germans decided to counter the British blockade of Germany by launching a submarine blockade of England. In this first phase of unrestricted underseas warfare, which lasted from February to September 1915, German subs attacked merchant shipping regardless of nationality, and sank, among countless others, the British liner *Lusitania,* which had many American passengers, thereby bringing Germany and the United States to the brink of war. During the next year and a half, German policy changed repeatedly. In order not to antagonize the United States, the Germans for a time concentrated their underseas attacks largely on British shipping; a brief second period of unrestricted warfare followed from March to May 1916.

Finally in January 1917, the German High Command decided on an all-out effort to starve Britain into submission. A total submarine blockade was proclaimed, even at the risk of driving the United States into the war, for it was expected that Britain would have to surrender before the United States could render effective military aid to the Allies. The resultant submarine campaign reached its height between March and October 1917. It not only brought the United States into the war, but also inflicted almost paralyzing damage on Allied shipping and the British economy. But in the end the Germans lost their gamble. The British perfected the convoy system and new methods for detecting and destroying submarines. The Allied shipbuilding program was also stepped up, so that soon more tonnage was built every month than the Germans could sink. By the winter of 1917, it was evident that Germany could not win the war by torpedoing Britain into submission. The German High Command then placed its last hopes on the spring offensive in France.

At the war's end, the remaining German fleet was surrendered to the Allies according to the terms of the armistice, and then interned at Scapa Flow in northern Scotland, where the German crews scuttled it in June 1919.

The German Home Front

MORALE On the whole, the Germans welcomed the outbreak of war with enthusiastic ardor. Volunteers from all walks of life rushed to enlist in such numbers that the army at first could not absorb them all. "To be honest," a recruit noted in his diary, "we were fed up with this lazy peace." A typical reserve officer described the spiritual fervor that filled the hearts of his comrades as they moved into the initial battles. "It was one of the most beautiful hours of my life," he wrote, "and I am proud to have experienced it." An observer in the capital depicted the departure of the jubilant troops who were leaving "to face a life of vigorous action, the highest type of existence." Everywhere the soldiers dedicated their lives to their emperor, "to the last drop of blood." A Socialist Reichstag deputy who had volunteered for service wrote from the front: "to shed one's blood for the fatherland is not difficult; it is enveloped in romantic heroism."

This initial enthusiasm soon dwindled. Mounting casualties, misery in the trenches, and shortages of food and supplies at home were stripping the "holy campaign" of its aura. By 1916, the Allied blockade, shortages of manpower and of fertilizer on the farms, as well as political and economic mismanagement, brought hunger to the cities and disillusionment to the civilian population. Thereafter, as food rations dwindled, disenchantment with war continued to grow. By the summer of 1918, famine, epidemics, and strikes had reduced civilian morale to the point where few, if any, were still ready to praise the glory of war.

However, it was a long time before this disenchantment altered the optimism of the nation. The German press monotonously reiterated that the Allies were patently failing to win the war, and that each onslaught against the German lines was being repelled. The German armies were deep inside Russian and French territories, and the population readily believed the frequent prophecies that the next major German offensive would crumble the Allied lines and overwhelm the enemy. By 1917, this extreme optimism began to wane, especially in those few political leaders who were better informed on the true status of the German war effort. Loss of faith in final victory led to greater internal tensions, which gradually forced the government to grant political concessions. But it is noteworthy that Ludendorff and Hindenburg, who assumed an almost complete dictatorship over political as well as military affairs in 1917, succeeded through censorship and propaganda in keeping the nation at large uninformed about the true military situation. Almost down to the day the front collapsed in the west, the average German clung to the belief that his armies were invincible. The sudden reversal from hope and confidence to the realization of total collapse and unmitigated defeat came to most Germans as a disillusioning shock, which in part explains the stunned pessimism of the early days of the Weimar Republic.

MOBILIZATION OF THE TOTAL ECONOMY No previous war had required so complete a use of the total resources of the participants as the Great War of 1914–1918. Like other nations, Germany had to devise new means to achieve total mobilization of the economy. Such measures tended inevitably to strengthen the powers of the central government. They also revealed the continued bitter cleavage between producers and consumers, industrialists and unions, conservatives and liberals, despite the much-heralded closing of ranks for the sake of prosecuting the war.

Fearing a British blockade and a consequent lack of raw materials, the Germans immediately set up a War Raw Materials Board in the Ministry of War. Its organizer and initial director was Walther Rathenau (1867–1922), the Jewish president of AEG, Germany's huge general electric corporation. Rathenau promptly appropriated vital raw materials, whether in industry, commerce, or private possession, and then created separate divisions for every type of material—chemicals, wool, jute, rubber, leather, and so forth. These divisions, approximately sixty in number, soon resembled distinct companies—many of them based on a mixture of private and state ownership—and were placed under the direction of the War Department. By supervising all industrial planning, including the production of chemical substitutes, the War Raw Materials Board acquired great power over the entire economy, not merely over raw materials. It assumed the authority to close small, inefficient plants and set maximum prices, and it tried to equalize profits. Rathenau's work proved successful, but he became the target of bitter attacks and denunciations. A number of big industrialists complained of Rathenau's "state socialism" and launched an anti-Semitic campaign against him. The press accused him of causing food shortages, although his office had nothing to do with food. In March 1915, Rathenau bowed before the storm and resigned, but the board he had organized continued to grow in power and importance.

Meanwhile the government also attacked the problem of food. About a thousand price-control and rationing offices, similar to the American OPA in World War II, were set up to establish maximum prices and attempt rationing. Various governmental agencies were created to centralize buying and the distribution of all food and animal fodder, but none of them proved very effective. Harvests and livestock constantly decreased, prices rose, and a black market flourished. Fertilizer, draft animals, seeds, and agricultural manpower were all in short supply. In addition, the situation was aggravated by a running feud between the agricultural producers and the state. General Wilhelm Groener (1867–1939) and others who directed the policy of the War Food Office frankly advocated protection of the consumer as opposed to the producers. The conservative landlords and many of the smaller peasants, however, objected to price fixing and governmental control of production. Like the industrialists, they decried the new state socialism, and refused to grow food to be sold at low prices. They insisted that the government should content itself with providing fertilizer, but leave the market free so that peasants had an incentive to produce. In retaliation against the government, and despite the famine in the cities, some let their lands lie fallow and others grew merely enough to feed themselves.

By late 1916, shortages in all resources, human and material, became so acute that the government adopted a new concept of total mobilization. While dictatorial powers over all political matters were gradually taken over by the army, every aspect of the economy was placed under control of a newly created War Office supervised by General Groener. All existing agencies, such as the War Raw Materials Board, the War Food Office, and the Munitions Board, were put under the over-all supervision of the War Office, which thus assumed control over the procurement and feeding of labor, weapons, munitions, raw materials, synthetics, transport, imports, and exports—in short, over every aspect of the nation's finances, economics, and labor.

One of Groener's first tasks was to help draft a compulsory labor law that gave the state power to assign work to all males between the ages of seventeen and sixty. Here again a struggle ensued. The industrialists in the Reichstag produced a draft law without consulting the unions or including protective clauses against the abuse of workers. Groener, supported by the Socialists and the trade unions, insisted on inserting into the law guarantees of workers' rights in regard to wages, working conditions, and related matters. Once again, despite the urgency of the situation, the bitter antagonism between labor and producers came to the fore. Most of the safeguards were included in the final law, and the industrialists again denounced what they regarded as growing state socialism.

THE POLITICAL TRUCE As late as December 1913, Emperor William had written privately to the retired Bülow: "First let us shoot down the Socialists, or behead them, or somehow make them harmless, then we can face an external war." Yet on August 1, 1914, he told the populace: "In time of war, all parties cease and we are all brothers." His conciliatory attitude produced an unofficial truce among political parties (*Burgfrieden*) and a temporary cessation of criticism of the government. Most Germans welcomed this closing of ranks behind the common war effort. But a few left-wing Socialists suggested that the government be first compelled to institute important internal reforms before support be granted to the war effort, and some extreme conservatives feared that the political truce gave the internal enemies of the Reich the opportunity to destroy Germany from within. As one conservative deputy put it: "For heaven's sake, this means we shall lose the war politically on the home front."

According to the constitution, the emperor needed only the approval of the Bundesrat to decide on war or peace. Hence the Reichstag was not consulted on the question of declaring war, but its consent was needed to finance the war effort. On August 4, 1914, the Reichstag unanimously approved an initial war credit of 5 billion marks. By voting this financial support, the parties in effect placed their stamp of approval on the war. The deputies of the Social Democratic party voted in caucus 96 to 14 in favor of war credits, and in accordance with customary party discipline, all 110 delegates accepted the decision of the majority. In view of the Socialists' heralded pacifism and the subsequent split in their ranks over the conduct of the war, it is worthwhile to examine the speech of their leader before the vote on the war budget.

Hugo Haase (1863–1919) declared

that the war was caused by imperialistic policies for which his party took no responsibility, since it had always opposed them. He indicated that the Socialists, together with their French brethren, had labored until the final moment to try to prevent the war. But, he said, now that war had come, there was danger of invasion. "It is not up to us today to decide for or against peace, but to grant the required means for the defense of our country." Above all, it was urgent, he proclaimed, to prevent a victory of Russian despotism. "In agreement with the Socialist International, we recognize the right of every people to national independence and self-defense, just as much as we condemn every war of conquest." And he ended by expressing hope for a quick peace and friendship among neighboring peoples.

The political truce not only put an end to disputes among the parties, it also brought about an abdication of power by the members of the Reichstag. Never having exercised much political power, they now disbanded after voting the war credits, and left the conduct of the war effort in the unsupervised hands of the executive and the military. Not even an attempt was made to deputize a standing committee of delegates to work with the government on the task of prosecuting the war. During the next two years, the Reichstag was only rarely convened. Not until 1917 did it again become an active forum for discussion in conjunction with the question of war aims.

THE QUESTION OF WAR AIMS William II had proclaimed that Germany was not motivated by lust of conquest, and Bethmann-Hollweg had clearly indicated that proper amends would be made for the violation of Belgium. On August 14, the SPD had issued a set of war aims designed to safeguard Germany's independence and integrity—including the retention of Alsace-Lorraine. The proclamation proposed that all colonial empires be opened to traders and immigrants from all nations. It demanded freedom of the seas, and opposed dismemberment of Austria-Hungary and Turkey. At the same time, it opposed German conquest of foreign soil, which would only "weaken the inner unity and strength of the German national state" and violate the principle of self-determination.

But as hope for a short war began to fade, divergent opinions on war aims came to the foreground and threatened to shatter the harmonious political truce. Certain ultraconservatives, in particular, distrusted Bethmann-Hollweg, and looked for ways to overthrow his regime in order to ensure their own war aims. In late August 1914, the All-German League, irritated by the news that the chancellor desired an early, quick, and lenient peace with France and England, started deliberations on this matter. They voiced the fear that the SPD, the Jews, certain weak officers, financiers, and other "traitors" might gain power over the government and introduce universal suffrage in Prussia. The chairman of the All-German League organized numerous meetings with leading industrialists and conservatives, such as Alfred Hugenberg (1865–1951), Gustav von Bohlen und Halbach (1870–1950), Hugo Stinnes (1870–1924), Emil Kirdorf (1847–1938), and others—many of whom later supported the rise of Hitler—and with representatives of the

League of Landlords, the League of German Peasants, the Union of German Industrialists, and other conservative pressure groups. From these meetings originated the first comprehensive set of war aims of the conservatives, which were circulated in a memo addressed to some two thousand influential citizens in the Reich.

The government attempted to stop this agitation by the All-German League. In January 1915, it ordered a search of the homes of several conservatives, confiscated the memoranda on war aims, and placed certain members of the All-German League under surveillance. Bethmann-Hollweg feared that publication of the annexationist demands of the conservatives would spoil the political truce by antagonizing the SPD and would make Germany look more than ever like an aggressor in the eyes of the world.

Despite this prohibition, the program of the All-German League received the adherence of numerous groups, including some Centrists, National Liberals, and university professors. The complete outline of war aims was finally sent to the chancellor in May 1915, under the guise of a petition, and was subsequently published in the press.

The petition stated that it would be folly to conclude a premature peace while Germany's position was militarily favorable, unless the peace brought better security for its western and eastern frontiers, an extension of its sea power, the "possibility of unchecked economic development," and a "stronger position in the world." Specifically, it demanded enormous territorial acquisitions: a large section of northern France, including the coastal districts to the Somme, to secure Germany access to the Channel; areas containing iron ore to make Germany more self-sufficient; and as much other territory as required by "military and strategic considerations." The petition also called for a protectorate over Belgium and vast expansion in the east to award Germany space for colonization, military security against Russia, and more agricultural lands. The populations of the ceded territories should be removed if possible so that Germans could be settled in these lands and that no new foreign elements would be introduced into the Reich. For similar reasons, the eastern borders should be sealed to prevent further influx of Jews. The petition also demanded a colonial empire "to satisfy Germany's manifold economic interests," and a weakening of England's domination of the seas. Finally, in view of the later treaties of Brest Litovsk and Versailles, it is noteworthy that these conservative war aims demanded a war indemnity "suitable to our requirements," and expressed the belief that Germany's future safety lay in a "serious economic and military weakening of our enemies."

Bethmann-Hollweg was not in sympathy with such extreme demands, but he was not a forceful leader and usually found it easier to straddle the fence. He reiterated his prohibition of public discussion of war aims, but in a speech in December of 1915, he expressed vague demands for "guarantees of security" against future threats to Germany and for German economic gains. By April 1916, he declared publicly that the prewar status could not be re-established, thus giving encouragement to the annexationists, who continued to push their demands clandestinely.

By the end of 1916, the debate on war aims could no longer be repressed. The government lifted its restrictions and permitted more or less free discussion. It at once appeared how deeply the nation was divided between those who insisted on peace without annexations and those who urged that the sacrifices borne by the nation required adequate compensation in the form of conquests. Slogans were devised to label opposing viewpoints. The conservatives derided the notion of a "peace of hunger"; the liberals opposed a "Hindenburg peace." In July 1917 the *Kreuzzeitung* editorialized: "Victory or peace of renunciation, this seems to be the big question of the moment," completely omitting the possibility of defeat.

Questions of war aims, of internal reform, and of peace proposals now became intertwined to shatter the political truce and to split the nation—seemingly as a prelude to the revolution of 1918. Between December 1916 and the summer of 1917, various attempts were made to bring about an armistice, through direct negotiations among the belligerents and through mediation by President Wilson and Pope Benedict XV (1914–1922). In principle, the German government agreed to proposals for future disarmament and international arbitration; but under pressure from Hindenburg, Ludendorff, and the conservatives, it avoided commitments about the evacuation of conquered territories and the rehabilitation of the devastated foreign lands. Actually, it appears that a peace of understanding could have been achieved in the summer of 1917. The German population was weary of the war; Russia was in the grips of revolution; French morale was low; the Italians were woefully unsuccessful; England was exhausted; and the United States was as yet ill prepared for the war it had just joined. But the conservatives and the military in Germany rejected the thought of a peace without victory and without gains, and successfully thwarted all attempts at mediation.

The more liberal groups and the lower classes, for their part, also demanded compensation for their sacrifices. But they sought such requital largely on the home front. They wanted political concessions from the government, as well as social and economic improvements. Bethmann-Hollweg and William II, who had been pushed increasingly into the background by the military, thus found themselves pressed from both sides. The conservatives insisted on a firm stand against political reform as well as on a vigorous war effort. The liberals pressed for internal reforms and a peace of understanding.

In his Easter Message of April 1917, Emperor William gave the first public indication that he recognized the demands of the liberals. He promised a revision of the Prussian electoral system after the war, although he did not pledge support for the introduction of universal suffrage. This was to be the beginning of a hapless attempt at revolution from above. In July 1917, William took a further step. In an imperial decree, he promised equal universal suffrage for Prussia in the next reform program.

Ironically, the first victim of these proposals was the imperial chancellor. The liberals had never been attached to him and did not consider him the proper man for negotiating a peace of understanding. The conservatives and the military now withdrew the little support they had given him. They feared that Bethmann-Hollweg lacked determination to resist the pressure for political reform and to push their war aims with sufficient vigor. Hindenburg and Ludendorff hurried to Berlin, and on the following day Bethmann-Hollweg was dismissed. The new chancellor, Georg Michaelis (1857–1936), was a colorless bureaucrat, an appointee of Ludendorff's. He carried neither prestige nor power, and his subservience to the High Command made it easier for Ludendorff to cement his military dictatorship.

Bethmann-Hollweg's dismissal and the ascendancy of Ludendorff acted as a coalescent on the opposition. The Social Democrats, the Progressives, and the Centrists now united, at least on the floor of the Reichstag—a union that foreshadowed the typical coalitions of the later Weimar period. The leader of the Center party, Matthias Erzberger (1875–1921), initially a proponent of a strong peace, had come to the conclusion that total victory was impossible. Even during the war he had frequently traveled abroad, and had realized that "Austria was at the end of her strength" and that the munitions ratio was constantly increasing in favor of the Allies. Moreover, he was convinced that the submarine campaign would not succeed in forcing England to its knees before the United States entered the war in full strength. Certain that "a peace *à la* Ludendorff" was unobtainable, he also believed democratization at home to be a *sine qua non* for a peace of understanding, since the entrenched military and conservative elements would never consent to such a peace so long as they retained a monopoly of political power. Erzberger communicated his convictions to his fellow delegates in various Reichstag speeches, and finally presented to them a Peace Resolution. This measure was adopted by the Reichstag on July 19, 1917. It was carried by a favorable vote of 212 Centrists, SPD, and Progressives against 126 negative votes, with 17 abstentions. It urged the government to seek a peace of reconciliation, and voiced its opposition to territorial conquests as well as to "political, economic, and financial oppression" of other peoples. At the same time, it demanded constitutional reforms that would democratize Prussia and impose parliamentary checks on the federal government.

As an attempt at opening the road to peace, the resolution of 1917 was a failure. Chancellor Michaelis pretended to heed the mandate of the majority parties, while at the same time remaining an obedient tool of the military dictators. He boasted privately that "one can, in fact, make any peace one likes, and still be in accord with the Resolution." Erzberger also failed to exploit the opportunity for using the resolution as a wedge for gaining greater political power for the Reichstag. As military dictator, Ludendorff had little difficulty in outmaneuvering the opposition and keeping the Reichstag powerless.

Despite these failures, the Peace Resolution had important repercussions. Besides paving the way for a coalition of the liberal and leftist parties, it also produced a frenzied reaction among the rightists and deepened the political cleavage of the nation. In September 1917, Admiral Tirpitz and the Prussian government official Wolfgang Kapp (1858–1922), together with other conservatives from various political parties, formed the German Fatherland party for the purpose of opposing Erzberger's "peace of hunger" and promoting a victorious or "Hindenburg peace." This group also launched a campaign of defamation against the advocates of a soft peace, labeling as defeatists and traitors those who signed the resolution. Thus was created the theory of the "stab in the back," the legend that was to grow into a gangrenous sore in the body politic of the Weimar Republic.

DISUNITY AMONG THE SOCIALISTS

While the High Command dominated the political scene—although, as Ludendorff complained, not always adequately supported by the emperor—and the liberals stood in passive dismay at the impending disaster, groups of workers, trade-unionists, and Socialists grew increasingly adamant in their opposition to the government. Socialist unity had long ceased to exist. The left-wing radicals in the Reichstag had submitted to the party's majority decisions at the outbreak of the war, but many of the rank and file had resented the apparent capitulation of their leaders to the capitalists and their war. As early as December 1914, when new war credits were requested, Karl Liebknecht—the son of Wilhelm Liebknecht, the founder of the Marxist wing of the SPD—opposed his more accommodating Socialist colleagues and voted against the budget. He then began to agitate openly against the war. To silence him, the government drafted Liebknecht into the army, and finally jailed him when he continued his demonstrations. Leadership of the left-wing dissidents then passed into the hands of Rosa Luxemburg until Liebknecht's release from prison. Encouraged by the success of the Bolshevik Revolution in Russia, this group rapidly gained additional adherents among war-weary workers, but it remained outside the Reichstag and in a status of semilegality. During the winter of 1917–1918, it helped foment a few strikes in war plants and circulated propaganda on the futility of the war effort among soldiers and, more particularly, sailors. Under the name of Spartacus League, organized in 1917, it became the forerunner of the German Communist party.

A larger and more influential splinter of the Socialists, with representation in the Reichstag and a broad following among the rank and file, was the USPD or Independent German Social Democratic party, formally organized in 1917. Its leaders, such as Hugo Haase, Karl Kautsky, and Eduard Bernstein, represented various Socialist views, revolutionary as well as revisionist. Starting in December 1915, the Reichstag members of this amorphous group had voted against further war credits, and because of their refusal to acquiesce in the more compromising stand of the central committee of the SPD—at this time usually called the Majority Socialists to distinguish them from the two splinter groups—they had finally been expelled from the party and formed their own organization. They insisted that the political truce was a capitalistic hoax to undermine the class struggle. They hated the middle and upper classes and the annexationist war aims. Particularly after the overthrow of the tsarist rule in Russia, they saw no reason for continuing the war, and became adamant in their demands for peace. Once formed, the USPD grew rapidly in membership, although differences among its leaders did not permit it to coalesce into a homogeneous party. It engaged in denunciations of the annexationists and at times cooperated with the Spartacists, but generally remained within the bounds of legality until the outbreak of revolution in the fall of 1918.

THE END OF THE WAR

The Last Months of Confidence

For almost a year after the Peace Resolution, the annexationists felt triumphantly sure that they had been wise in rejecting a peace of reconciliation. As Ludendorff noted in his memoirs, the High Command stood by its convictions in regard to war aims until "July/August 1918, as long, that is, as it hoped to safeguard the requisites of life for the German people." The Treaties of Brest Litovsk and of Bucharest (see page 465), providing for German territorial, political, and economic aggrandizement, were drawn up in harmony with the views of the annexationists. They were negotiated by the military, in conjunction with their new puppet chancellor, Count Georg von Hertling (1843–1919), who had replaced Michaelis in the fall of 1917. The Reichstag had not been consulted. Some of the liberals had already lost self-assurance in the face of Ludendorff's military victories. The pleas of others for an end to the mad dream of self-delusion were now rejected even more decisively. In such a mood, the German High Command merely smiled at the British war aims publicly announced by Lloyd George on January 5, 1918, and shrugged off as transatlantic reveries the Fourteen Points Wilson presented to the United States Congress three days later.

The rout of the Italian armies, Russia's withdrawal from the war after the Soviet Revolution, the defeat of Rumania, the anticipated success of the spring offensive in the west, all made Ludendorff confident that he could win a military decision over the Allies. The termination of hostilities on the eastern front allowed Ludendorff to transfer to the west large reserves with which he hoped to break through the Anglo-French lines. From March until June 1918, the Germans launched their last series of gigantic offensives. Although creating minor breaches and once again crossing the Marne toward Paris, the Germans failed. With the help of newly arrived troops from the United States, the Allies stemmed the German offensive. By July, a counterattack was launched, initiating the gradual rollback of the German armies that ultimately forced the Germans to request an armistice.

Request for an Armistice and Belated Democratization

As soon as the terms of the Armistice of November 1918 became known, the conservatives—the so-called National Opposition—intensified their complaints about a stab in the back. Briefly stated, this accusation amounted to an exculpation of the High Command and the annexationist forces by alleging that the German army had not been defeated in the field of battle but had been stabbed in the back by revolutionary elements at home, namely by Communists, Socialists, and other "un-German" factions. Since this theory became an essential steppingstone in the revitalization of conservatism after the revolution and in the ultimate rise of Hitler, the circumstances of the armistice and the events preceding the November Revolution warrant particular analysis.

In July 1918, the German offensive in the west gradually gave way to the Allies' counteroffensive. By early August, the Allied advance gained speed and the German position became increasingly hopeless. August 8, according to Ludendorff, was the "Black Day" on which the German lines began to crumble and on which the High Command was forced to weigh the need for peace. A week later, the government began to investigate possible avenues for arranging peace with the Allies. But nothing was done for a few weeks, although the armies in the field were gradually rolled back by the attacking French, British, and American forces. During September, the situation became desperate. The Balkan front collapsed, Bulgaria withdrew from the war, the Dual Monarchy was on the verge of disintegration, and the retreat in the west continued.

On September 28, Ludendorff noted that the collapse of the Balkan front might render Germany's position untenable "even if the western front could possibly hold out." On the following day, Hindenburg suddenly warned the government to seek an immediate armistice, which he and Ludendorff hoped could be concluded while German armies still occupied a strip of northern France. "As yet the German forces are holding out," Hindenburg notified Berlin, "but the situation deteriorates daily!" In view of the stab in the back theory, it is interesting to note that Hindenburg made no reference to the demoralization of his troops by Communist agitators, an accusation that later became popular.

The unexpected admission by the High Command of imminent disaster on the western front had far-reaching repercussions on the home front. Those who had remained blissfully optimistic were rudely plunged into realization of the catastrophe at hand. Count Hertling resigned at once, and Emperor William issued an edict promising a new government that would represent the will of the people. On October 4, Prince Maximilian of Baden (1867–1929), the liberal heir to the throne of the Duchy of Baden, was installed as chancellor. Belatedly, Germany was given quasi-parliamentary government, for Maximilian promised to govern with the consent of the majority in the Reichstag—those parties, in fact, that had supported the Peace Resolution of 1917. Erzberger joined the new government as minister without portfolio, and even the conservatives agreed to cooperate with Maximilian in order to gain an "honorable end to the war." The High Command's sudden relinquishing of power to the civilian government and acquiescence in the establishment of parliamentary government was a part of Ludendorff's calculated withdrawal from the political scene, so that the army could be exonerated from the blame of defeat.

Prince Maximilian, in conjunction with the Austrians, at once notified President Wilson that the Central Powers were ready to discuss peace terms on the basis of the Fourteen Points. While waiting for a reply, Ludendorff expressed hope that peace could be obtained soon, while his armies were still more or less intact, and could if necessary exert pressure during the negotiations. But the Allies unexpectedly injected a new problem. Woodrow Wilson made it plain that so long as Germany was ruled by military and monarchical authority, it could not expect a negotiated peace, but would have to surrender unconditionally.

Until this time, there had been relatively little "republicanism" in Germany. Discontent with William II and with his political system had seldom touched the imperial framework as such, perhaps because the notion of a Reich appealed to the romantic emotions of even the most discontented opposition. But now the question of the continuation of the monarchy seemed linked with the survival of Germany as a state. The SPD, joined by many liberals, promptly called for Emperor William's abdication.

Unrest, strikes, and minor outbreaks of rebellion marked the last days of October, while the field armies continued their slow retreat before Allied pressure. On October 26, General Ludendorff resigned his command, presumably to keep his hands untarnished by defeat, although Hindenburg remained as commander in chief. General Groener assumed Ludendorff's place and inherited the thankless task of supervising the army during the final two weeks of the war. General Groener and Maximilian now vainly attempted to persuade William to abdicate. According to an unverified story, Groener even urged William to go to the front, presumably in the hope that he would be hit by a bullet and thus gloriously leave the German political scene.

With Germany poised on the brink of disaster, militarily unable to prosecute the war and equally unable to conclude a peace so long as William II remained at the helm of the collapsing Reich, outright revolutions broke out in various sections of the country. The sailors at the Kiel naval base mutinied on October 29 and refused to set out to sea on a last-minute raid against England. By November 3, red flags were waving from the German fleet at Kiel, and the mutinous sailors, supported by USPD shock troops, were battling police and special army units in the streets of the city. The rebellion rapidly spread along the coast to Hamburg, Bremen, and Lübeck. On November 7, revolution erupted in Munich, resulting in the overthrow of the Bavarian monarchy. In all corners of Germany, Spartacists and Independent Socialists agitated against the regime, while the moderate Socialists warned against "Russianizing Germany." Still William II rejected all pleas for his abdication.

If the army had been able to maintain its position in the field, these revolutionary outbreaks at home could perhaps have been considered a stab in the back. But the front lines had given way long before the outbreaks occurred, and the revolts produced only two indirect results. Certain conservatives wished to speed up the return of the army so that it could effectively crush the rebellion at home. And Wilson hastened to inform the Germans that the Allies agreed to an armistice and to discussion of peace terms on the basis of the Fourteen Points, with the exception of certain British reservations regarding freedom of the seas, and of Allied demands for German payment for the rehabilitation of occupied lands.

The day after receiving Wilson's communication, Prince Maximilian sent Erzberger with an armistice commission to France to negotiate with the Allies. Hindenburg sent a personal message to Erzberger before the latter's departure for Compiègne: "Above all, the army needs a rest. Godspeed and try to salvage the best for our fatherland." Erzberger was accompanied by a general to advise him on military matters, but it is symptomatic that the High Command attempted to disassociate itself from the humiliating task of seeking an armistice. General Groener noted in his memoirs: "I was glad to see the army and the High Command remain as unsullied as possible in these unfortunate negotiations." The military thus tried to avoid responsibility for Germany's collapse; in fact, Matthias Erzberger later had to carry the brunt of the hatred of those who asserted that Germany had needlessly surrendered.

The Armistice demands presented to Erzberger at Compiègne on November 8 were harsh and amounted to almost unconditional surrender. The Allies wished to make sure that Germany would be in no position to resume the war. Erzberger tried in vain to obtain alterations of the terms, and finally wired to ask Hindenburg's advice. The latter advised Erzberger to seek certain changes, but urged him "to conclude negotiations in any case, even if the modifications cannot be achieved." The military situation was desperate and conclusion of peace essential. The army thus sanctioned the Armistice and it can hardly be asserted that surrender was the work of revolutionaries. After Erzberger received Hindenburg's advice on November 10, he signed the Armistice terms, which became effective on November 11.

Meanwhile Maximilian of Baden and General Groener had continued to press William to abdicate. No amount of persuasion seemingly could convince him to abandon the throne of the Hohenzollerns. When revolutionary unrest erupted in Berlin, the chancellor finally decided to force the issue. On November 9, he announced William's abdication without having received any authorization. The Socialists thereupon proclaimed the establishment of a republic, while William II, at his wartime headquarters, was still hesitant as to his course of action. Only after Hindenburg and Groener finally convinced him that even the army might no longer be loyal to him, did he take the course of prudence and flee to Holland during the night of November 9–10.

The Armistice Terms

The Armistice was originally to last thirty days, but its eighteen clauses reduced Germany's military strength to such a point that there could be no serious thought of a resumption of the war. The German armies were to withdraw immediately from all lands west of the Rhine and even evacuate a special neutral zone east of the Rhine. In the east, "all troops were to withdraw behind the boundaries of August 1, 1914," although no fixed time limit was given for this withdrawal, presumably because of the uncertainties of the Russian civil war. Rumania, Austria-Hungary, and Turkey were to be evacuated. The Treaties of Brest

Litovsk and Bucharest were declared voided. Large quantities of military and industrial matériel were to be turned over to the Allies: cannons, machine guns, mortars, airplanes, locomotives, railway cars, trucks, as well as the bulk of the battle fleet and parts of the merchant marine. The blockade of Germany was to remain in effect—a decision bitterly resented by the Germans—and Allied armies were to occupy the left bank of the Rhine, with the cost of occupation to be borne by the Germans.

Under the terms of the Armistice the German forces at once began their retreat and released all Allied prisoners. Where possible, the field armies were transported home in orderly fashion. But morale at the front was at its lowest point, transport was lacking, and discipline not always enforcible. Strikes and revolutionary outbreaks hampered orderly operations, and many field units simply dissolved, with individual soldiers making their way home as best they could.

The Allies followed on the heel of the retreating and disintegrating German forces. By early December, they had invaded the Rhineland and had begun to occupy the cities of Cologne, Coblenz, and Mainz, as well as surrounding districts.

·19

Germany's First Republic, 1918–1929

THE BASIS OF THE WEIMAR REPUBLIC

The German Republic of 1919 to 1933, popularly called the Weimar Republic, was Germany's first experiment with a republican form of government and with the parliamentary system. From its inception, the new regime was burdened by many serious handicaps. The aftermath of war and defeat, the harsh Treaty of Versailles, inflation, and disorder poisoned the soil on which the young republic was to grow. Moreover, the upheaval of November 1918 that brought forth the Weimar Republic was not a true revolution marking a clear break with the past. On the contrary, few fundamental changes were effected in Germany's social, economic, and even political structure when the empire of William II suddenly gave way to the fragile, democratic Weimar Republic. This semiabortive character of the revolution of 1918 was to be vitally important for the fate of the republic.

The Character of the November Revolution

The revolution in Berlin, as was seen in the last chapter, was preceded by upheavals in other parts of Germany. The mutiny of the sailors in Kiel and its spread had led to the formation of soviets (councils) of workers and soldiers in many regions. It seemed at first as if Germany were following the example of the Bolshevik Revolution. But in most cases, these soviets did not fall under the control of radicals; their members showed more interest in mild social reform than in outright revolution.

Not the establishment of the soviets but the overthrow of the monarchy in Bavaria gave the impetus to further changes. In the hope of ending the war and the "imperial fraud," and of goading his fellow Socialists into action, the Independent Socialist Kurt Eisner (1867–1919) proclaimed a Bavarian Republic on November 7, 1918. If necessary, he was willing to press for Bavarian independence. The abdication of the Wittelsbach monarchy acted as a green light all over Germany. Princes everywhere felt forced to lay down their scepters, and local government either remained in the hands of civil servants or was seized by soviets or other emergency bodies.

Only Emperor William II hesitated to abdicate, until Maximilian of Baden made a revolutionary decision and forced the issue. On November 8, without William's consent, the chancellor simply announced that "the Emperor and King has decided to relinquish the throne." Although constitutionally he had no right to appoint a successor, Maximilian then turned the chancellorship over to Friedrich Ebert (1871–1925), the leader of the Majority Social Democrats. Its illegality notwithstanding, this act was hardly very revolutionary, since the Majority Socialists, as the largest party, had earned the right to rule on the basis of the democratic procedures that had been tacitly accepted by William during the last year of his reign. Transference of the chancellorship to the leader of the Socialists did not even imply an automatic end to monarchy in Germany. Maximilian as well as Ebert initially thought of a regency. The unrevolutionary character of this transfer of power was highlighted by the cordial meeting between Prince Maximilian and his successor. The two met in a friendly conference to discuss the change of government, and Maximilian "entrusted the fatherland" to the care of Ebert, in whom he had considerable confidence. It was as if the retiring chancellor wanted to relinquish a bankrupt enterprise, hoping that new management might pull it out of the doldrums. And rather than grab power by force, the Socialists accepted it almost reluctantly, as if by default.

The second revolutionary step occurred on the same day when Philipp Scheidemann (1865–1939), an impetuous member of the executive committee of the SPD proclaimed the German Republic from the steps of the Reichstag—possibly to head off action by the more revolutionary left-wing radicals. Scheidemann had not consulted his colleagues. It was characteristic of the new regime that Ebert, who was convinced that only a legally elected Constituent Assembly had the right to decide for or against a republic, screamed at Scheidemann after the proclamation: "You have no right to proclaim the Republic!"

These two measures—the forced abdication of Emperor William and the proclamation of the German Republic—were the only truly revolutionary aspects of the change of regime. Beyond this, the disorders of November 1918 hardly constituted a *bona fide* revolution. No significant change occurred in the alignment of political power. The bureaucracy and the army, which had been so important since the days of the Great Elector, retained their prominent social position and political influence. The judiciary remained unchanged. Even social and economic changes were minimal. Although the kings, dukes, and princelings were deposed, the aristocracy preserved its social prerogatives. Despite a democratic constitution and universal suffrage, the ancient spirit of respect for titles—whether noble, academic, or bureaucratic—continued to foster wide class distinctions and warp the ideals of equality and fraternity that the Socialists and Progressives had preached. Moreover, no attempt was made to diminish the overwhelming power of the Prussian government by decentralizing Prussia or splitting it into a number of smaller states. The Prussian agrarians, the Rhineland industrialists, the aristocratic officer corps retained their conservative influence. It is interesting that the traditional term "Reich" was retained to designate the German state, even though Germany was no longer an empire. As the poet Rainer Maria Rilke (1875–1926) noted disappointedly, there had been "no change of heart."

The failure to effect a clear break with the past and to attempt a fundamental transformation that might have given Germany a vital and viable democratic structure was partly due to the circumstances of the period, as will be seen in subsequent sections. But in part, it can also be attributed to the idealistic and unrevolutionary character of the bulk of the Socialists. Like most of his colleagues, Ebert, in his own words, "hated social revolution like sin." Imbued with a deep respect for legality, most of the Socialists actually aspired to acquire traditional middle-class status rather than to transform German society. Many of them, including Ebert, who ultimately became the first president of the young republic, were not even antimonarchist at heart.

A comparison with the two Russian revolutions of 1917 is instructive. The Socialists and the Constitutional Democrats who overthrew the tsarist regime in March 1917 refused to sanction any critical reforms while the revolutionary temper was still hot. Consequently, they failed to extend their basis of power, and their revolutionary *élan* lost its appeal. In the November Revolution of 1917 however, Lenin's Bolsheviks acted quite differently. Intent on seizing complete power and gaining immediate popular support for their movement, the Bolsheviks directed their first revolutionary decrees to the nationalization of all land and industry. In Germany, Ebert and his friends acted like the Socialists and Constitutional Democrats in Russia, insisting that only the legally elected representatives of the people could decree reforms. Afraid that truly revolutionary social changes would play into the hands of the radical Left, they seemed more intent on safeguarding the purity of their evolutionary ideals than on consolidating their power. Unlike Lenin's first decrees, their initial proclamation of November 10 dealt with questions of moderate social and political reform, specifically the institution of the eight-hour day and of universal equal suffrage, and the guaranteeing of civil as well as property rights. Even more typical in its bourgeois and liberal preoccupation was the proclamation of November 12. It set as the task of the new government the "realization of the Socialist program." But the nine points of the proclamation did not touch on such fundamental Socialist principles as land reform, social security, nationalization of basic industry, or an extension of free public education. Instead, they were devoted to liberal demands such as guarantees of free assembly, free speech, free exercise of religion, an amnesty for political prisoners, and "the lifting of censorship of the theater."

The Provisional Government

On November 10, Ebert set up a provisional government to direct German affairs until nation-wide elections would establish a constituent assembly. The provisional government included three members of the Majority Socialists and three Independent Socialists. Since it lacked any other basis of authority, Ebert's cabinet called itself a committee of people's commissars, ruling in the name of the Central Committee of the moderate soviets of workers and soldiers. In reality, the soviets quickly lost the little importance they had enjoyed, and the provisional government acted more or less as an autonomous body. Among its most prominent members were Ebert, Scheidemann, and Hugo Haase, the leader of the Independent Socialists.

THE TASKS CONFRONTING EBERT The provisional government was at once beset by numerous problems whose solutions were to affect the outcome of Germany's republican experiment. For one, there was profound disagreement and distrust among the various factions of Socialists. The Spartacists, who were not represented on the governing body, favored a complete social revolution in the style of the Bolsheviks in Russia. The USPD, with its mixture of revolutionary and revisionist adherents, wanted government by the soviets of workers and soldiers, although not necessarily a radical overturn of the social spectrum. The Majority Socialists preferred the calling of a legally elected national constituent assembly that would decide on the future framework for Germany. These differences, particularly those between the Majority Socialists and the radical Spartacists, led Ebert at once to the fateful decision that he had to align himself with the forces of order and semiconservatism in order to crush the ultraradicals. In addition, the provisional government had to arrange for and supervise the execution of the Armistice, undertake the demobilization of the armed forces, deal with famine and economic chaos, keep law and order in the face of attacks from the radical Left as well as the conservative Right, and govern Germany until a constitution had been framed and a permanent government formed.

Most important of the problems faced by Ebert was the question of keeping order and maintaining the integrity of Germany. Mindful of the experiences of the Mensheviks during the Bolshevik Revolution, the provisional government did not want to become a tool of the soviets of workers and soldiers. Nor could they count on local police forces as sufficient protection against the more radical elements of the Spartacists. The Independent Socialists were urging the immediate creation of a citizens' militia, composed of Socialist and republican elements, which would defend the new regime, but Ebert feared that such shock troops might become vanguards of Bolshevism. Instead, he immediately made an arrangement with General Groener (Ludendorff's replacement) that was to have dire consequences for the Weimar Republic. Ebert and Groener agreed to cooperate against the extreme radicals. Groener indicated that he would persuade Hindenburg to remain for the time being as commander in chief —Hindenburg actually stayed at his post until Germany accepted the Treaty of Versailles in June 1919— and to have the army recognize and cooperate with the new revolutionary government. The army was to help keep order and to crush the extreme left wing. Support by the military would enhance the prestige of the provisional government. In return, Ebert agreed to let the old officers remain in charge of the military units. He promised not to destroy the army and not to create a people's militia or a "red army" in the manner of Lenin. No doubt, a German civil war was thus avoided. But this arrangement between the army and the government, reaffirmed a year later between Ebert and General Hans von Seeckt (1866–1936), the new chief of the *Truppenamt*—the Weimar euphemism for the former General Staff, which was outlawed by the Treaty of Versailles—threatened the future of German democracy. It entrusted the survival of Weimar into the hands of the conservative military, who at heart remained monarchists and imperialists. General Groener aptly remarked in his memoirs: "I and my colleagues saw to it to keep our daggers unsheathed and to safeguard the High Command unsullied for the future."

Order was threatened not only by the Spartacists but also by returning veterans. Countless demobilized soldiers, returning with their weapons to their starving families, found nothing but bitterness and disillusionment. There was no program for rehabilitation to civilian life. Many youngsters had left school to volunteer for the front, and now returned with no trade or training other than fighting. Few jobs were available. Consequently a dangerous number of them joined the Free Corps, bands of semiorganized fighting units grouped around a leader at whose direction they engaged in street fighting or open warfare, wherever chance might take them. The formation of Free Corps units was at first actively encouraged by Hindenburg and other officers. Some of these marauding Free Corps fought in the Baltic area in the Russian civil war and the Russo-Polish War; others made themselves available for suppressing uprisings or executing political murders within the Reich. A few of these units joined the radical Left, but the bulk turned to the extreme Right. Nurtured on the stab-in-the-back theory, they blamed the Socialists for the defeat and for their resulting plight, and were always available for attempts at overthrowing the "traitors of the fatherland." The Free Corps thus posed a serious threat to the provisional government. Yet the Majority Socialists lacked the power to disband them; in fact they were forced to accept them as a temporary ally against further subversion from the radical Left. Hence Ebert and his Socialist minister of war after December 1918, Gustav Noske (1868–1946), found themselves relying on the Free Corps and the army for repressing left-wing uprisings.

The provisional government was mainly intent on keeping the revolution from turning further to the Left. Ebert begged the old civil servants to stay at their posts to help maintain order. He resisted all suggestions for land reform lest they disrupt the production of food and worsen the famine caused by the war and the continued Allied blockade. And he refused to nationalize the basic means of production, not only because he awaited the verdict of a properly elected assembly but also because he was afraid of disrupting the already teetering economy. Above all, he feared that overly violent social and economic changes might open the door to a Communist revolution.

Ebert's moderate and antirevolutionary stand was, of course, not due solely to his bourgeois and evolutionary beliefs. One must recall that the German army had not disintegrated as had the Russian army and that it represented a power factor in German politics. Ebert was thus forced to pursue a middle course that might satisfy a majority of his SPD followers without provoking interference by the military. Moreover, Ebert had to take account of the international situation. The Allies were at the time supporting the anti-Communist forces in Russia and were gradually getting actively involved in the Russian civil war. It seemed obvious that the western powers, particularly the French, would not have tolerated the establishment of a radical regime in Germany and that the Allied armies would very likely have marched into unoccupied Germany to prevent its Bolshevization.

THE SPARTACIST UPRISINGS The Spartacists, who disapproved of Ebert's seeming conservatism, opposed the proposal for calling a national assembly, and favored immediate sovietization of Germany. They began to receive financial aid and advice from Lenin's newly created Third International, assumed the name of German Communist party (KPD), and made a bid for power in an uprising in December 1918. Ebert and his provisional government did not hesitate to call on the army to crush the Communists. The insurrection was successfully quelled by army and Free Corps units, but not without profound repercussions. Although the unions and most workers had not lent their support to the Spartacists, it was nevertheless difficult for them to understand why a Socialist government, supposedly representing the proletariat, should use the conservative army and the reactionary Free Corps to fire on the workers.

Some of the Independent Socialists had sided with the Spartacists. In protest over the government's action, the USPD quit the provisional government. Haase and his Independent colleagues insisted that the "blood bath of December 24" proved that Ebert had given his minister of war unlimited power to use the army against the workers. The USPD wanted no "responsibility for the fact that a representative of the old system of tyranny [General von Lequis, in charge of the troops that repressed the Spartacists] has been given discretionary power over the lives of the people." Haase insisted that one should negotiate with the Communists, not shoot them down.

A few weeks later, the Communists made a second attempt at insurrection in Berlin. They called for a strike, which was poorly supported by the workers, and tried to wrest control of the government from the Majority Socialists. A number of USPD members again sided with them. But once again, Ebert called for military help, and the army and the Free Corps crushed the rebellion. The Spartacist leaders, Rosa Luxemburg and Karl Liebknecht, were taken prisoner and shot on their way to jail, much to the consternation of the liberal elements in Germany. For the second time, the provisional government had suppressed the advocates of social revolution and given encouragement to the conservative forces. Further revolts during February and March were similarly subdued by Noske's armed forces.

THE REVIVAL OF THE BOURGEOIS PARTIES While the SPD turned more conservative and the extreme Left was being robbed of its *élan,* the bourgeois parties regained their composure, and the antirevolutionaries took heart. The

January 1919 election for the National Constituent Assembly, which was boycotted by the Communists, gave the SPD and the USPD 165 and 22 delegates respectively, while giving a total of 260 seats to the various middle-of-the-road and conservative parties. In Bavaria, a brief counterrevolution took place in February. Kurt Eisner was assassinated—the first of many prominent liberals to meet this fate—and an attempt was made to re-establish the monarchy. In reprisal, the Communists succeeded in gaining control of the government in April and in establishing a Bavarian soviet republic. But this radical experiment was crushed in the beginning of May by the combined efforts of the federal army and various Free Corps units. Hereafter radicalism was eradicated from Bavaria, and Munich became a stronghold of conservatism.

After the National Constituent Assembly convened at Weimar in early February, it chose a new interim government to serve until a republican constitution would come into effect. Friedrich Ebert was elected as first President of the German Republic, and Scheidemann was made Prime Minister. The cabinet consisted of seven Majority Social Democrats, five Democrats (see page 495), and three Centrists. The all-Socialist character of the government had expired with the revival of the bourgeois parties.

While the delegates to the National Constituent Assembly labored in the provincial town of Weimar, far removed from the revolutionary turbulence of the industrialized cities, the new provisional government faced not only continued internal disorder but also the problem of concluding peace with the Allies.

The Treaty of Versailles

In January 1919, representatives of the victorious nations convened in Paris and debated throughout the spring on the terms to be imposed on Germany. After much bickering and dissension (which is not directly of concern in a discussion of German history), the Allies submitted a draft to the German provisional government with the obvious implication that the stipulated terms had to be accepted. The German delegation protested vigorously against the terms of the treaty, asserting that it violated Wilson's Fourteen Points and represented not a negotiated agreement but a "dictated peace." Scheidemann refused to sign it and resigned from the government, proclaiming that the hand that "imposes such chains upon us [by signing the document] must wither." Groener advised that resumption of hostilities would be hopeless, but Hindenburg declared that although "the outcome of further military operations was highly doubtful," as a soldier he preferred "an honorable fall to an ignominious peace." Finally, the National Assembly appointed a new cabinet willing to accept the treaty, albeit under protest. The Assembly then voted 237 to 138 in favor of submitting to the Allied demands, and Hindenburg resigned from his post of commander in chief.

In many respects, the Treaty of Versailles, with its over 400 clauses and numerous appendices, was in agreement with Wilson's Fourteen Points. But in a few specific items and, above all, in its spirit, the treaty violated Wilson's idealism. It was no peace of reconciliation designed to undo injustice, but a document based on hate and vengeance.

TERRITORIAL AND DISARMAMENT CLAUSES Germany was to return Alsace-Lorraine to France and cede three small border districts to Belgium, after the holding of a plebiscite to determine the wishes of the population. A plebiscite was also to be held in Schleswig, as a result of which a large northern strip was transferred to Denmark in 1920, while a smaller southern area remained with Germany. In addition, the coal-rich Saar district was to be internationalized and governed by the League of Nations. At the end of fifteen years, a plebiscite was to decide whether the Saar should be returned to Germany or joined with France. Meanwhile, "as compensation for the destruction of the coal mines in the north of France and as part payment towards the total reparations due from Germany," all the coal mines of the Saar were to be handed to France "in full and absolute possession."

In the east, the territorial losses were even more extensive. To re-create an independent Poland with free access to the Baltic, the provinces of Poznan and West Prussia, which Prussia had acquired in the eighteenth century, were to be turned over to Poland. Danzig was to become a free city, under the protection of the League of Nations, with special port privileges reserved for Poland. East Prussia was thus physically separated from the rest of Germany, even though Poland guaranteed free passage to persons and goods over its territory. This Polish Corridor, as it came to be called, was to become an international irritant in the interwar period, much like the East German strip between West Berlin and the Federal Republic of Germany after World War II. Furthermore, Germany had to cede the Memel district, which the League of Nations eventually awarded to Lithuania, and had to submit to plebiscites in large sections of East Prussia, which, however, resulted in no territorial losses. Finally, plebiscites were to decide the disposition of Upper Silesia, which was meanwhile occupied by French troops. When the voting in 1921 favored Germany, the Polish minority, tacitly encouraged by the French occupation forces, rose in rebellion. The League of Nations eventually made a decision that was greatly resented in Germany. The bulk of the land and population of Upper Silesia was awarded to Germany, but Poland was given most of the mines and industrial complexes (see Map 21).

Despite Wilson's Fifth Point, urging "a free, open-minded, and absolutely impartial adjustment of all colonial claims . . . ," the Treaty of Versailles deprived Germany of all its overseas possessions, which were turned into mandates of the League of Nations, occupied and governed by various Allied powers. The total loss of their colonial empire created severe resentment among many Germans, even though the colonies had been more of a drain on the imperial budget than a boon to the economy. Deprivation of the empire was largely a blow to the German ego, a toppling from among the ranks of world powers.

As a preliminary step toward implementing Wilson's Fourth Point, reducing national armaments "to the lowest point consistent with domestic safety," the Treaty of Versailles sought to destroy the German war machine. The German armed forces were to be reduced to 100,000 men, including a maximum of 4000 officers, by March 31, 1920 at the latest. There was to be no

MAP 21

conscription. Enlisted men were to serve a minimum of twelve years, officers at least twenty-five; thus the Germans could not secretly train a large reserve by arranging for a rapid turnover of personnel. The German General Staff was to be abolished. Germany was to have no military planes, tanks, or poisonous gases; the number and size of guns was to be limited; the size of the navy was to be restricted; and no submarines were to be allowed. To safeguard France and Belgium, a strip of thirty miles east of the Rhine was to remain forever demilitarized, without fortifications and without military installations of any type. Finally, to ensure that Germany abided by these limitations, an Inter-Allied Commission of Control was to be established in Berlin, entitled to inspect German military matters at its discretion.

ECONOMIC AND PUNITIVE CLAUSES Besides the territorial and military clauses, the treaty contained many sections dealing with economics, most of them connected with the matter of reparations. "To enable the Allied and Associated Powers to proceed at once to the restoration of their industrial and economic life," Germany was to pay five billion dollars in the first two years. Meanwhile the Reparations Commission would assess by May 1921 the total payments required from Germany to compensate "for all damage done to the civilian population of the Allied and Associated Powers and to their property." The Germans were thus forced to sign, as it were, a blank check for an unspecified amount. They were also to deliver specific raw materials, such as coal and lumber, and surrender to the Allies their foreign assets as well as the bulk of their merchant marine. In addition, they were to build ships for the Allies, and permit Allied vessels to navigate freely on all German rivers.

The variety of punitive and special provisions inflamed the German temper as much as, if not more than, the material losses. "As a guarantee for the execution of the present Treaty by Germany," Belgian, British, American, and French troops were to occupy the western portion of the Rhineland, together with bridgeheads on the right bank of the river, for a period of fifteen years. Also, Germany was required to recognize the independence of Austria, Czechoslovakia, and Poland. While such recognition appears self-evident in line with international law, it was aimed at preventing Germany and Austria from merging, even if the two German-speaking states should desire it, unless special consent were given by the Council of the League of Nations.

To justify the demand for reparations and to mark Germany in the eyes of world opinion, the Allies inserted Article 231 into the treaty—the so-called guilt clause. It placed on Germany and its allies the responsibility for causing "all the loss and damage," and stated that the war had been imposed on the Allied powers "by the aggression of Germany and her allies." The Allies indicted Emperor William "for a supreme offense against international morality and the sanctity of treaties," in view of the violation of Belgian neutrality, and demanded the trial of persons "accused of having committed acts in violation of the laws and customs of war." On the basis of these clauses, England's prime minister, Lloyd George, tried to negotiate William's extradition from Holland so that he could be tried before a special tribunal of five judges, one each from Great Britain, France, Italy, United States, and Japan. Probably to the secret relief of the Allies, who were thus spared possible embarrassment, Queen Wilhelmina declined to extradite the former emperor. Since the German government also refused to surrender to the Allies any of the Germans whom the victors sought to arraign before military tribunals, a compromise was eventually arranged whereby the German Supreme Court at Leipzig was to try the accused. Of the 900 who appeared on the Allied list, the Germans eventually prosecuted 12 and pronounced 6 guilty.

Finally the treaty contained various petty stipulations regarding restoration of war booty from previous wars. "The trophies, archives, historical souvenirs or works of art" carried off during the Franco-Prussian War of 1870 were to be restored to France within six months. Also the "skull of the Sultan Mkwawa," which the Germans had taken from their former East African colony, was to be handed over to the British government.

Apart from the obvious economic consequences, the Treaty of Versailles produced far-reaching repercussions in Germany. Only the realization of their military impotence and the fear of civil war drove the more coolheaded legislators to advise acceptance of the treaty rather than risk reopening the war, as Hindenburg was willing to do. But those Socialists and Centrists who in the end accepted the treaty, albeit as an inescapable disaster, became saddled with the onus of having "betrayed Germany." Throughout the period of the Weimar Republic, denunciation of the so-called *Diktat* (dictated peace) of Versailles became the emotional shibboleth of the conservative parties. The "November criminals" who had perpetrated the stab in the back were now linked with the "red and black traitors" (Socialists and Catholics) who had signed the shameful peace. There is no question among historians that the Treaty of Versailles was not a wise peace. But its wisdom or folly is less important than what the Germans chose to make of it. From its inception the Weimar Republic suffered under the burden of the treaty, and Hitler rode to power on the promise of undoing it.

The Weimar Constitution

A month after the signing of the Treaty of Versailles, the Constituent Assembly enacted its republican constitution. It was an impeccably democratic document, with long sections devoted to guarantees of civil rights. It created a lower house, still called the *Reichs-*

tag, the delegates to which "were to represent the entire people." They were to be elected by universal, equal, direct, and secret ballot, at least once every four years, on a basis of proportional representation. The voters were to select their representatives by party lists, a system that made the party organizations more important than the political merits of the individual candidates. The system of proportional representation, practiced in many other European democracies, entailed the advantage of providing a voice for all political views, but it also encouraged the formation of countless splinter parties that were to become a scourge for the Weimar Republic and one of the causes of its political instability.

The upper house, or *Reichsrat,* was composed of delegates from the German states (*Länder*), which had been reduced from 25 to 18 by the amalgamation of 8 small central states into the single state of Thuringia. The separate states were allowed considerably fewer powers than they had enjoyed under the Bismarckian system. As a result the new Reichsrat could exercise little substantive authority. The Weimar constitution, although retaining the federal system, entrusted far more power—executive, legislative, judicial, as well as financial—to the central government than had the Constitution of 1871.

The president of the Reich was chosen for a term of seven years in direct elections "by the entire German people." Only in Friedrich Ebert's case was an exception made; the Constituent Assembly simply confirmed his provisional title of President without resorting to a formal national election. The president's powers were considerably less than those previously held by the emperor. For every action, he needed the countersignature of the Reich chancellor or of the cabinet officer concerned. He could be removed by a two-thirds vote of the Reichstag in conjunction with a popular referendum. Yet the president's influence over the affairs of the Reich remained considerable. It was his duty to appoint the chancellor, who, together with the cabinet, acted as the real executive. As is true of any parliamentary system, the chancellor and his ministers had to "enjoy the confidence of the Reichstag during their tenure of office." But in spite of this requirement of a vote of confidence, his power to choose the chancellor made the president quite important, particularly when it is recalled that Germany suffered twenty changes of cabinets in the period from 1919 to 1933.

Probably the most famous article of the constitution was Article 48, which dealt with the president's emergency powers. It empowered the president to compel a state government, if necessary with the help of the armed forces, "to fulfill the duties incumbent upon it." Similarly, if "public safety and order are seriously disturbed or imperiled," the president could employ the armed forces to restore order and could "temporarily suspend" the fundamental civil rights guaranteed by the constitution. Countless commentaries have been written about this Article 48, which has been denounced as containing the fatal seed that would later destroy the republic. Since it was employed over 200 times and ultimately abused to such a degree that it helped pave the way for Hitler's dictatorship, the article itself has been blamed as the lethal flaw in the constitution. Significantly, the present Bonn constitution contains no similar clause. Yet Article 48 was hedged with numerous safeguards giving the Reichstag power to repeal the emergency measures of the president. It is not the fault of the constitution that during most of the Weimar period, the Reichstag lacked the required working majorities essential to make the safeguards effective. Moreover, one must recall that the constitution was framed at a time of extreme instability. Attacks from the Right and the Left were threatening the existence of the republic. Just as French President Charles de Gaulle included a similar emergency clause in his 1958 constitution for the Fifth French Republic to deal with the threats to the republic, so the framers of the Weimar Constitution felt the need for such provisions.

The Weimar Parties

In many respects, the political parties of the Weimar period resembled those that had developed during the empire, with two exceptions: more parties existed, and their number kept on increasing as new groups splintered off from existing organizations; and the more extremist parties tended to gain in strength at the expense of those with more moderate programs (see Chart 6).

On the extreme Left was the Communist party (KPD), the former Spartacist League. It openly followed instructions from the Third International and advocated Communist policies as laid down in Moscow. The Communists boycotted the elections to the Constituent Assembly, but thereafter presented themselves at the polls, although they never participated in a coalition cabinet. Between 1924 and 1930, their voting strength hovered at around 10 percent, until it rose somewhat after 1930, in the dying years of the republic.

The Independent Socialist party (USPD), which as we saw had been formally organized in 1917, enjoyed a brief but important existence. After helping to run the provisional government immediately after the November Revolution, the USPD members refused to serve in further cabinets, in view of their opposition to the Majority Socialists' flirtation with the conservative forces. But they polled 2 million votes in 1919 and 5 million in 1920, briefly emerging as the second strongest party in the Reich. They supported the government in the crucial days of 1919 and 1920 when it was attacked from the Right and the Left, and helped push through the Reichstag acceptance of the colossal reparations bill presented by the Reparations Commission in 1921. Yet the meteoric rise of the USPD was reversed as suddenly as it had started. After 1922, most of the Independents rejoined the Majority Socialists, while a few of the more doctrinaire went over to the Communists. The USPD ceased to exist after 1924, when it polled a mere 98,000 votes.

The Majority Socialists (SPD), despite the loss of members to the KPD and the USPD, remained the largest party in the Reich until 1932, when it was suddenly surpassed by Hitler's National Socialists. But it is significant that the SPD was the largest party only in the sense that it polled a few more votes than any other single group. It obtained by no means a majority of the votes. From a high of 38 percent of the votes cast in 1919, it quickly dropped to 21 percent in 1920 and remained around this percentage ex-

Chart 6. THE POLITICAL BAROMETER OF THE WEIMAR REPUBLIC

Percent of votes cast

January 1919 · June 1920 · May 1924 · December 1924 · May 1928 · September 1930 · July 1932 · November 1932 · March 1933

100 · 95 · 90 · 85 · 80 · 75 · 70 · 65 · 60 · 55 · 50 · 45 · 40 · 35 · 30 · 25 · 20 · 15 · 10 · 5 · 0

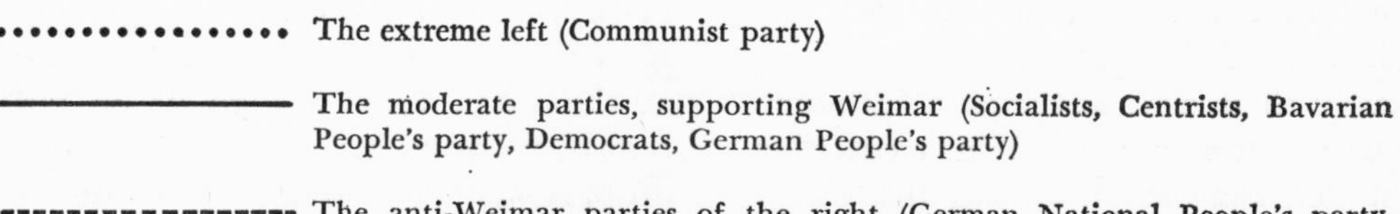

cept for a mild rise in the later 1920s. The failure of the Socialists to obtain a majority can be attributed not only to the existence of too many parties and the system of proportional representation, but also to the idealistic policies of the Socialist leaders. In a way, Ebert and Scheidemann were the founders of the republic, but although they were Socialists, they created no Socialist republic. By refusing to institute a program of nationalization, even though it was demanded by many of the rank and file in their party, by aligning themselves with the conservative forces of law and order, and by permitting the army to fire on the workers, the SPD lost much of its appeal among the proletariat, as evinced in the election results of 1920. Another explanation for this loss of popularity lies in the social structure of Germany and in the temper of the times. Unlike its counterpart in Soviet Russia, the German middle class represented the dominant element and was in no mood for further revolutionary experiments. The shock of the Treaty of Versailles, for which the Socialists were unjustly blamed, disillusioned the electorate. As the electoral results of the 1920s clearly show, either the middle class longed for a return to normalcy and voted for middle-of-the-road parties, or it was filled with nationalistic indignation and voted for the rapidly rising conservative parties. At any rate, the SPD lost control of the chancellorship in March 1920 and, with the exception of the period 1928–1930, was never again to recapture it. Until 1923, the SPD served in most cabinets, but thereafter, again except for 1928–1930, it was not even represented in the government.

Rather than the Socialists, the real "Weimar party" was the Center, which showed remarkable electoral stability, was represented in every coalition government until 1932 and headed 9 of the 21 cabinets that ran the Weimar Republic. In 1920, the Bavarian People's party split off from the Center, to pursue a slightly more conservative course and ride its hobbyhorse of Bavarian particularism. But on most national issues it continued to cooperate with its parent body. Taken together, the Center and the Bavarian People's party consistently polled between 15 and 20 percent of the votes cast. As was true during the empire, the Center remained a polygenetic party, held together loosely by the Catholicism of its members. Its political orientation is difficult to define. It supported the Weimar Republic and the latter's democratic ideals, but its basic philosophy, initially somewhat left of Center, veered to the right in the mid-twenties and gradually turned increasingly conservative.

Another "Weimar party" was the German Democratic party (DDP), formed in November 1918 by remnants of the former Progressives and the more liberal segments of the National Liberal party. It included doctrinaire liberals as well as idealists and humanitarians. During the political crisis provoked by the necessity of signing the Treaty of Versailles, the DDP withdrew from the government, but thereafter was represented in every cabinet between 1919 and 1931. Since this party helped constitute the backbone of the democratic institutions of the Weimar Republic, the history of its attraction to the voters is of interest. The DDP polled 5.5 million votes, 18.6 percent of those cast, in the 1919 elections to the National Assembly. As early as

1920, it dropped to 2.3 million votes or only 8.3 percent. Thereafter it gradually dwindled to less than 4 percent by 1930. To stress its increasingly nationalistic attitude, it changed its name to German State party, but even this did not help its survival. By 1932, it reached a low of only 1 percent of the votes cast, permitting it merely two delegates in the Reichstag.

Considerably to the right in the political spectrum was the new German People's party (DVP), with its leader Gustav Stresemann (1878–1929). This party represented business and industry, and embraced the bulk of the conservative wing of the former National Liberal party. Its orientation was at heart monarchist, but once the republic seemed more or less firmly established, Stresemann and his party supported it to the best of their ability. The DVP became the fourth largest party in 1920, gaining almost 14 percent of the votes cast, and it had representatives in every cabinet from 1920 to 1931. But it is symptomatic of the fate of the Weimar Republic that this party, too, lost its popularity with the voters. By 1930, it was down to 4.5 percent and continued to decline thereafter.

Among the truly conservative parties was the important German National People's party (DNVP), monarchist and ultraconservative in aspirations, representing big industry and the Prussian landlords. It opposed the very existence of the Weimar Republic and freely supported all oppositional ventures from the extreme Right, particularly the Free Corps and other nationalist and racialist groups. The DNVP grew rapidly during the early years of the republic. In 1924, it obtained over 6 million votes, and became the second largest party, the backbone of all opposition to democratic government, to compliance with the terms of Versailles, and to cooperation with the Allies. In the ensuing years of relative political and economic stability, it lost considerable strength. Although it rebounded somewhat in the dying years of the republic, it lost many adherents to Hitler's National Socialists, a group that was far more fanatic, far more conservative, and far more tightly organized than the DNVP.

The National Socialist party (NSDAP), which ultimately toppled the republic, will be dealt with in detail in the subsequent chapter. It is enough to note here that when the NSDAP first presented itself at the polls in 1924, it drew just under 2 million votes. In 1930, it suddenly emerged as the second largest party, and by July 1932, it received almost twice as many votes as the Socialists and became by far the largest party in Germany, with its 37.4 percent of the vote.

In addition to these nine major parties, the Weimar Republic was plagued by countless splinter groups, many of which attracted enough voters to qualify for representation in the Reichstag: the Economic party, the Christian-Social People's Service, the League of Landlords, the Christian National Peasants' and Agriculturalists' Popular party, the German Hanoverian party, the German Social party, the German Peasant party, the Christian People's party, and numerous others, some of which operated only at the state (*Land*) level. These parties represented social and economic interests, and most of them were at the far Right of the political arena. Their mere existence helped to proliferate political allegiances and imperil governmental stability.

The existence of these multifarious

parties necessitated the formation of coalitions to obtain parliamentary majorities in the Reichstag. The result was a merry-go-round of cabinets, similar to that experienced by the French Republic in the years after World War II. Of the twenty-one cabinets between 1919 and 1932, the most stable stayed in office twenty-one months, in the period of relative quietude of 1928 and 1929. Most cabinets survived barely a few months.

The Burdens of the Young Republic

The preceding analysis of the basis of the Weimar Republic highlights the burdens imposed upon it, and in part explains its ultimate failure. The Weimar Republic was born without much planning or preparation, almost as if by accident, and was largely the consequence of the military collapse at the end of the war. It was greeted with indifference by large segments of the German population and soon lost the support of many of the workers and most of the lower middle classes. After the disillusionment of the Treaty of Versailles, it faced the onslaught of oppositional forces that, fortified by the legend of the stab in the back, saw in the republic little more than a symbol of shame and national disgrace. The relative lack of experience with truly democratic forms, the failure to break significantly with the past, the disappearance—largely through assassination—of many of its more forceful and imaginative leaders, and the economic and financial disasters of the early 1920s turned the republican framework into a thin veneer hiding the cancer of discontent and disillusionment. In addition, the victorious powers of World War I, particularly France, showed little understanding of or sympathy for the sensibilities of Germany's new democracy, and thereby contributed considerably to the ultimate victory of the antidemocratic forces within the Reich.

THE YEARS OF UNREST, 1919–1924

Political Instability

The first five years of the republic revealed an alarming instability in the new regime. Governmental coalitions were patched together at frequent intervals, but none proved viable. Of the twelve cabinets between 1919 and 1924, only two lasted about a year; seven others survived less than six months. Only one of these cabinet changes resulted from normal political causes: the realignment of parties after the election of 1920, requiring the formation of a new cabinet. All other changes arose from resignations caused by internal attacks from right- or left-wing extremists or from repercussions of the Treaty of Versailles—the loss of Upper Silesia, the announcement of reparations schedules, French occupation of the Ruhr, and other national calamities provoked largely by French interpretation of that treaty.

"The shameful dictate of Versailles"—coupled with the legend of the stab in the back, with fear of communism, and with the disillusionment of demobilized veterans—produced, as we have noted, a strong resurgence of extreme conservatism and nationalism. This was evident in the electoral results of the period 1920–1924 as well as in the formation of numerous small groups of extreme nationalists, dedicated to anti-Semitism, anti-Bolshevism, the annihilation of democracy, and the abrogation of the Treaty of Versailles.

One such group, founded in 1919, was the German Worker's party, which later became the National Socialist German Workers' party (NSDAP) and which Hitler turned into his instrument for power. This antidemocratic mood provided the background for a series of attempts to overthrow the young republic from the Right and replace it by some type of dictatorial regime.

THE KAPP PUTSCH Among the more spectacular of these attempts was the Kapp *Putsch* of March 1920. A small group of army and naval officers, led by General Walther von Lüttwitz (1859–1942) and encouraged by Ludendorff, and groups of old-line conservatives brought together by the same Wolfgang Kapp who had sponsored the German Fatherland party in 1917 (see page 475) decided to overthrow the national government. As their shock troops, they enlisted the aid of a disaffected army brigade, which (under the command of its captain, Hermann Erhardt) acted more like a Free Corps than a unit of the regular army. Its members had fought as a Free Corps against the Communists in Poland during 1919, and were now threatened with unemployment, since the brigade was marked for disbandment in accordance with the disarmament clauses of the peace treaty. Hence they were readily persuaded to try to topple the government. The prospect of such an insurrection was welcomed by many conservatives, who, however, cautiously withheld overt support until its outcome could be foreseen.

When the insurrectionists marched on Berlin, the government requested the commanders of the regular army to organize the defense of the capital. Their reply was ominous for the future of the republic. Although willing to fight against Communist mutinies, they rejected the suggestion of dispatching the *Reichswehr* (regular army units) against fellow soldiers, albeit rebellious ones. The flaw in the Ebert-Groener bargain of 1918 (see page 485) at once became apparent. The army had agreed to support the government against the extreme Left, but had expressed no similar willingness in the case of attacks from the Right.

Left without armed support, President Ebert and the Socialist chancellor Gustav Bauer (1870–1944) appealed to the workers and to members of the SPD to "paralyze the economic life" of the nation by a general and complete strike and to "strangle the reactionary clique and fight with all available means against the return of William II." The members of the government then fled from the capital in order to escape possible imprisonment. Unhindered by police and regular army, the insurrectionists seized Berlin and announced the formation of a new government under the dictatorship of Kapp. But the workers rose to the defense of the Weimar Republic. Socialist, Catholic, and Independent unions called a general strike, which was also supported by the liberal and left-wing parties. Only the Communists withheld cooperation: chaos and revolution were favored by Lenin as means of achieving Communist ends. The general strike was extremely successful. Life in the capital came to a halt, and communications stood still. Kapp proved incapable of imposing his dictatorship on a passive population. After a few days he fled and was eventually jailed. Ebert and the cabinet returned to Berlin and persuaded the workers to return to their jobs. The Kapp *Putsch* had failed.

But the rapid collapse of the insurrection hardly concealed the sickness of the regime. It is symptomatic that the government did not profit from the experience. To be sure, a new chancellor, Hermann Müller (1876–1931), was installed, and Noske, who had shown his incapability of controlling the armed forces, was dismissed as minister of war. But the SPD leadership, still in command of a majority of the electorate, failed to placate the workers, who had stood fast against the "Baltic lansquenets" and the "military dictatorship." Labor demanded action on a program of nationalizing heavy industry, democratizing the civil service, and substituting a popular militia for the Free Corps and the *Reichswehr*. The government made promises, but in the end met none of the demands. It appeared that even the Kapp *Putsch* did not modify Ebert's overriding fear of sovietization. Of course, it should again be pointed out that Ebert's choice of action was limited. He could hardly have launched a determined fight against the Right so long as he required the army's support to remain in power. The Kapp *Putsch* had shown that the military could not be trusted to act forcefully against conservatism. On the other hand, army and Free Corps could always be relied on to crush risings of the radical Left. When violent Communist uprisings in the Ruhr followed on the heels of the Kapp *Putsch* in the spring of 1920, Ebert found no hesitation among the military when he dispatched them to subdue the rebellion.

Yet Ebert might conceivably have shown more foresight by at least attemping to bring the army into stricter obedience to the government. Instead, in March 1920, he transferred the command of the *Reichswehr* to the highly controversial General von Seeckt, who had been chief of the *Truppenamt* since November 1919. An excellent organizer and administrator, Seeckt was a stanch conservative and an admirer of power politics (see page 506) who believed that "the flourishing of the nation is inseparably tied to the *Reichswehr*," and decried as stupid the slogan "Never again war!" Above all, he hoped to build up the army. Since his plans contravened the Treaty of Versailles, he had to proceed secretly. Hence he hoped the military would, for the time being, stay apart from the political convulsions of the country and he ordered his officers to keep out of politics under threat of expulsion from the army.

The Communist uprisings in the Ruhr were widely supported by non-Communist workers. They were crushed mercilessly by the army and the Free Corps, an event that further disillusioned the proletariat about their government. The hapless republic, fighting against both extremes, was thus faced with a constantly shrinking base of power. And the French gleefully added to its troubles. Although the French government would hardly have welcomed the establishment of communism in the Rhineland, it insisted that the Germans had violated the Treaty of Versailles by sending troops into the demilitarized zone. In reprisal, French troops occupied Frankfurt on the Main and some towns in the Ruhr for a period of six weeks. The effect on Germany was a further weakening of the government's prestige and an increase of power for the vociferous nationalists.

Armed attacks on the republic from Left and Right continued during the next years at a subdued pace, until they flared up with greater violence in the troubled year 1923. The friction with France over reparations and the Franco-Belgian occupation of the Ruhr, coupled with runaway inflation, brought the Weimar Republic to the brink of dissolution by the autumn of that year. Supported by French and Belgian troops, a new wave of separatism, similar to the movement that had failed in 1919, swept over the Rhineland. Pro-French elements established a Rhineland Republic, claiming independence from Prussia. The movement ultimately collapsed in January 1924. Meanwhile Saxony went temporarily Communist, and a monarchical restoration was plotted in Bavaria. The famous Beer Hall *Putsch* of November 1923, in which Hitler and his National Socialists, supported by Ludendorff (who seemed to be present any time there was a chance to overthrow the republic from the Right), attempted unsuccessfully to gain control of the Bavarian government, was but one more in a series of attacks on the Weimar Republic. And the government's actions in each case were similar. The attacks from the left were crushed ruthlessly, while Hitler, for example, was jailed for less than a year.

POLITICAL MURDER Political instability also manifested itself in the inability of the government to ferret out subversive elements and maintain law and order. In the summer of 1920, the government was finally able to comply with Allied demands that the Free Corps be outlawed. This was possible because General Seeckt, as a strict disciplinarian, disapproved of the Free Corps with their relish for personal allegiance rather than for military obedience. The army therefore withdrew its tacit support from the Free Corps. But even after they were officially disbanded, many of them continued to flourish under various disguises, such as gymnastic clubs, trucking firms, or other cover organizations. They could thus retain their weapons and their *esprit de corps,* and be ready to engage in street fighting when it seemed opportune. Frustrated in gaining their immediate objective of overthrowing the republic, some of these organizations specialized in political murders. In secret meetings, they condemned to death leaders who, because of leftist leanings or willingness to fulfill the obligations imposed upon Germany by the Treaty of Versailles, had become "traitors to the fatherland." As Rosa Luxemburg and Karl Liebknecht had been shot in 1919, and Hugo Haase, the leader of the USPD, murdered shortly thereafter, so the roll call of death continued in the early 1920s. Matthias Erzberger, the former leader of the Center, who had accepted the armistice terms, was shot in 1921, and even his widow continued to be persecuted by the nationalist fanatics with written threats to desecrate the tomb of her husband. These same elements tried to intimidate government ministers with letters threatening to execute all "traitors" who accepted the imposed reparations and complied with Versailles. Walter Rathenau, who had helped organize the German war effort in 1914 and served as foreign minister in 1922, was assassinated in the heart of Berlin. Similarly, the leader of the separatist Rhineland Republic was murdered in January 1924. Besides these party leaders, innumerable lesser known liberals fell victims to political assassination.

The government seemed incapable

of stemming the activities of these fanatic exterminators, the forerunners, as it were, of Hitler's Gestapo. The Centrist chancellor Joseph Wirth (1879–1956) might complain in 1922 to the Reichstag that the ultraconservatives were "plunging Germany into an atmosphere of murder," and the "political morality of the jungle"; he might exclaim: "There is the enemy, . . . dropping his poison into the wounds of the nation . . . and there can be no doubt, the enemy is on the right." But in the final analysis, nothing was done to stop the erosion. The conservative judiciary, with its allegiance still halfway in the empire of William II, constantly meted out lenient sentences to those trying to assassinate the republic from the Right, while proceeding severely against similar offenses by left-wing elements.

Financial Instability and the Question of Reparations

Economically and financially, Germany emerged exhausted from World War I. The labor force was undernourished and reduced, the soil lay depleted, and raw materials were in short supply. Deficit financing during the war and the sharp decline in production of consumer goods had inflated prices and depreciated the German mark. The losses in territory, population, productive capacity, and raw materials resulting from the Treaty of Versailles, as well as from social unrest of the immediate postwar period, further aggravated the dislocation of the national economy.

THE DILEMMA OF REPARATIONS Besides suffering from the consequences of war and defeat and from shortsighted imperial financial policies, the economy wobbled under the indeterminate reparations claims of the Allies. Versailles had, in fact, presented Germany with a blank bill. Neither methods of payment nor a total and final amount had been stipulated. Hence neither the German government nor the business community could—if they had wished to—devise meaningful plans for settling their obligations. Initially, the Germans simply surrendered to the Allies the small gold reserves they had left, together with foreign assets, manufactured goods, and quantities of remaining raw materials. Meanwhile the Reparations Commission held interminable conferences to bring order to the Allied demands. At various meetings during 1920 and 1921 —at Spa, Paris, and London—the Allies agreed on a division of the spoils. France was to receive 52 percent of the total, the British Empire 22 percent, with the remaining 26 percent to be divided among Italy, Belgium, and other nations. The United States demanded no share. The Allies tacitly accepted the French proposal of sanctions against Germany if it should default on the imposed payments, and finally arrived at a total bill of 33 billion dollars, in gold marks as well as reparations in kind, to be paid over a period of thirty years.

This staggering demand produced an immediate government crisis in Berlin. The semiconservative German People's party resigned, forcing the formation of a new cabinet in which, significantly, a major role was again played by the Social Democrats, one of the few parties willing to accept the onerous obligations of defeat. The Allies threatened to invade the Ruhr unless Germany accepted the reparations bill. Hence the new cabinet signed the schedule of payments and promptly borrowed 250 million gold dollars in London in order to pay the first installment under the new arrangement.

Borrowing from the Allies in order to pay reparations or floating bonds in Allied capitals for similar purposes became one of the customary ways in which Germany paid some of the reparation demands. Similarly, foreign speculators, especially Americans, invested heavily in Germany, buying up German industrial shares, real estate, and paper marks. Between 1919 and 1922, about 1 billion dollars flowed into German hands, which the government turned over to the Allies as reparations. Considering in addition the complicated picture of inter-Allied loans contracted during the war, in which the United States and Great Britain alone had each loaned out some 7 billion dollars, one can get some idea of the intricacies of international finance during this period.

But Germany did not pay reparations merely out of Allied investments and loans. It transferred to the Allies railroads, real estate, buildings, equipment, ships, and raw materials in the ceded territories, and it also made annual deliveries of coal, chemicals, timber, ships, rolling stock, machinery, and vast quantities of other supplies demanded by the Allies for the reconstruction of their industries. These payments in kind produced further economic problems inside Germany, and led to sharp discord with the Allies, since no agreement could be reached on their exact value. Germany's inflation was continuing and the mark was further depreciating. Whereas before the war, the ratio of the mark to the dollar had been 4 to 1, and 8 to 1 by early 1919, it stood near 250 to 1 by late 1921. Under these conditions, the assessed value of deliveries in kind varied considerably between Allies and Germans. For the first three postwar years, the Germans calculated the value of total payments in kind at 10 billion, whereas the Reparations Commission set their book value at only 2 billion dollars.

Accepting the lower assessment of the Reparations Commission, France constantly accused the Germans of being in arrears with deliveries. In March 1921, the French seized Düsseldorf and surrounding towns in reprisal against Germany's defaulting on its deliveries, a charge heatedly denied by the Germans. During 1922, Franco-German friction over reparations became more acute. The German mark began to collapse. By August it stood at almost 2000 to the dollar, and the Reparations Commission agreed to grant a temporary moratorium on payments and deliveries. Great Britain, growing gradually more sympathetic to Germany, offered to cancel all war debts and withdraw all reparations demands, provided the Allies, in particular the United States, would do the same. The response of the United States to this proposal is well summarized through President Coolidge's succinct remark "They hired the money, didn't they?" Since the United States refused to cancel any debts—agreeing only to lower interest rates and lengthened periods of repayment—the Allies continued to press for reparations from Germany. England and France had already lost heavily when Lenin had repudiated all Russian debts, and France, in particular, was in no mood to accommodate the Germans. Prime

Minister Poincaré's whole policy of reconstruction was based on expectation of German payments. Despite British pleas for reasonableness and Italian proposals for a compromise, Poincaré was willing to grant a moratorium on reparations payments only in return for French acquisition of German factories and mines. On this basis he thought France could satisfy some of its demands for deliveries in kind and prevent Germany from completely defaulting on reparations.

OCCUPATION OF THE RUHR AND RUNAWAY INFLATION England and France began to differ sharply on the issue of reparations. The Entente Cordiale was crumbling, giving some Germans the hope of ending the years of "encirclement" and regaining a place among the western powers. But Poincaré remained adamant. In December 1922, he declared Germany in default in deliveries of coal and timber, and in January 1923, he sent French and Belgian troops to occupy the Ruhr and operate the German mines and factories for the benefit of France. England refused to participate in these measures and, in fact, criticized the French action.

The Franco-Belgian occupation of the Ruhr became the high point in the reparations drama, and led to the final collapse of the German economy and the German mark. Moreover, it dangerously undermined the weak underpinning of the Weimar Republic by rousing German nationalism to a feverish pitch and indirectly leading to the ruination of the middle class.

Unable to resist the invasion militarily, the German government ordered passive resistance. Once again the workers showed their loyalty to the Berlin government by heeding this call for a general strike. They refused to work for their new French masters, sabotaged the factories, and occasionally even attacked French occupation units. Only a few Rhinelanders cooperated with the occupiers and aided the abortive attempt to establish a separate Rhineland Republic. On the whole, the French reaped little but trouble. Unable to count on the local labor force, they had to use troops to operate the mines and factories, and in the end acquired few worthwhile economic benefits. Perhaps the only boon was the lesson that such peremptory treatment of Germany paid no dividends, a lesson that paved the way for the more cooperative spirit marking the subsequent years.

Passive resistance entailed for the Germans not only unemployment and famine but also runaway inflation. To meet its obligations and support the unemployed in the Ruhr, the government printed money without regard to its backing. Once this started on a grand scale, prices soared and the inflation ran amuck. By summer, prices were rising ten- or a hundredfold in a single day. Incapable of printing new money with sufficient speed, government presses overprinted old denominations by adding zeros in red. A 100-mark bill of one day became a million-mark bill of the next. Finally, city governments issued their own emergency money (*Notgeld*), printed on silk, leather, linen, or whatever was at hand, and permission to overprint was granted to reputable private concerns throughout the country, as money lost value so rapidly that it might be worthless by the time it was shipped from Berlin to other areas of the nation. It was the time when housewives had to shop many times a day, since a pound of butter costing 100,000 marks in the morning might cost 500,000 in the afternoon. These were also the days of the warm beer, when customers ordered two steins at a time, since the price might go up while they drank their first one. By November, a week's subscription to a Berlin newspaper cost 500 billion marks. In the end, paper money lost all value, except as a souvenir of frightening times. When the inflation ended and money again was stabilized, the rate of exchange was to be 1 trillion of the old marks for a single new one.

Much has been written about this inflation, and many false accusations have been made. To say that the German government inflated its currency to pay off reparations at a cheaper rate is an economic fallacy. The inflation had started long before the occupation of the Ruhr. The latter merely sent it on a gallop toward collapse. The transfer of payments as reparations could not be made in German marks, anyway, whether inflated or normal, unless these marks were backed by gold or productive capacity. The Allies could hardly have been expected to welcome the receipt of billions of paper marks unless these could be used for purchasing German goods. Hence it was German productive capacity and not German paper money that alone could pay off the reparations debt. Inflation helped the government solely by reducing its internal debt and by allowing it to pay less for the labor and other production costs of the goods delivered to the Allies as reparations in kind.

Part of the cause of the inflation was the government's inherited reluctance to raise taxes. Reconstruction, social services, welfare schemes, municipal improvements—including the ubiquitous public swimming pools for the lower classes—were financed largely through deficit spending. New demands were met through an increase in paper money rather than by an increase in taxes. At the same time, the growing supply of money was not balanced by an enlarged reservoir of production. On the contrary, deliveries in kind decreased the availability of these goods on the home market, thereby further cheapening money and again driving up the cost of living. The unstable cabinets between 1919 and 1922 lacked the strength to put a drastic end to this vicious circle by increasing taxes and decreasing the amount of paper money in circulation. The Franco-Belgian occupation of the Ruhr added to the financial deterioration. Sequestration of the Ruhr industries further lowered Germany's productive capacity and the amount of goods available, while, on the other hand, the printing presses produced more and more paper money to finance the added relief burdens assumed by the government. One cannot know with certainty whether in the end the galloping inflation completely escaped the control of the wobbly Berlin cabinet, or whether, as some have asserted, the final printing spree was a deliberate attempt on the part of Berlin to destroy the German financial structure in order to torpedo France's exploitation of the Ruhr and demonstrate to the Allies the impossibility of abiding by the reparations schedule.

Germany's International Position

The defeated nation, quite naturally, faced a hostile and unsympathetic world. The attitude of the powers at Versailles had clearly shown that the past was not to be forgotten. The pariah was not admitted to the newly created League of Nations nor allowed to participate in the early disarmament conferences. Germany remained isolated and despised, and Berlin could justly complain of constant interference by France, which did its best to antagonize Germany and, as it were, rub salt into the wounds of the defeated "Boche." By 1921, the specter of a new encirclement haunted the Foreign Office in Berlin. France signed a treaty of mutual assistance with Poland, and gave its blessing and assistance to the formation of the Little Entente by Yugoslavia, Rumania, and Czechoslovakia. The tottering Weimar Republic thus found itself in a potential east–west vise similar to that which had preceded World War I.

DESIRE FOR AN AUSTRO-GERMAN UNION

Immediately after the collapse of Austria-Hungary and Germany, there was a strong movement for the union of the two defeated states. Through the establishment of the independent states of Czechoslovakia, Hungary, and Yugoslavia, and through territorial cessions to Italy, Austria had been reduced to a tiny, economically weak state with some seven million inhabitants. Surrounded by hostile neighbors, a majority of Austrians thought the only chance for survival lay in union with Germany. After adopting a republican constitution in March 1919, the Austrian National Assembly promptly voted to integrate Austria into the new German Republic. However, the Allied powers, particularly France, opposed the extension of German influence into the upper Balkans. Hence they inserted clauses expressly prohibiting an Austro-German union in the Treaties of Versailles and of St. Germain (the peace treaty with Austria). When, despite this prohibition, the Weimar constitution included a clause that "other territories may be taken into the *Reich,* if their people desire it through the right of self-determination," the Allies forced Germany to modify the clause and again recognize Austrian independence. The Austrians' desire for union did not wane immediately. In 1921, Tyrol and Salzburg voted to apply for membership in the German federal system. Once again the Allies interfered to prevent this move. It was only after the Austrian economy recovered gradually with the help of loans by the League of Nations that the pressure for union with Germany subsided.

During the early years of the Weimar Republic, however, the question of an Austro-German union was less important than two problems that dominated the foreign policy of Germany: one dealt with the attitude toward the Treaty of Versailles and the related question of reparations; the other concerned the direction of Germany's foreign orientation.

THE ATTITUDE TOWARD VERSAILLES

The conservative and nationalistic elements in the nation sought to pressure the government into avoiding compliance with the treaty, particularly with those stipulations dealing with reparations and disarmament. Where open defiance was not possible, they advocated clandestine circumvention. The more moderate and liberal groups, on the other hand, favored at least nominal compliance. Where this was not possible, as was true of the question of reparations, they hoped to convince the Allies through a demonstration of goodwill of the impossibility of Germany's fulfilling the demands. Through this attitude, they expected to achieve Germany's readmission into the family of nations and the resumption of a strong voice in international affairs.

Germany's actual policy wavered between these extremes in the period 1919 to 1923. The moderates were not strong enough to pursue their preferred course without constant interference by the nationalists. Only the catastrophe of 1923—the Ruhr occupation and inflation—convinced enough political leaders of the folly of continued obstructionism and allowed the government at least temporarily to adopt an avowed policy of fulfilling the obligations incurred under the Treaty of Versailles.

THE ORIENTATION OF GERMANY'S FOREIGN POLICY The same divergence of political views affected the problem of Germany's foreign orientation. The conservatives and the army, like their predecessors in the nineteenth century, favored an eastern orientation, despite the fact that Russia was now Communist. Confident that friendship with Russia would not lead to a Bolshevization of Germany, they saw in an alliance with Russia the best means of regaining the lost territories in the east and of acquiring the strength needed to stand up against French demands in the west. It is symptomatic that during the Russo-Polish War of 1920, some conservative Free Corps units fought side by side with German Communists and the Red Army against the Polish defenders of Warsaw. Lenin and his successors also favored a *rapprochement* with Germany, which they thought would help sow disunity among the capitalist nations, and add ferment to the political turmoil within the Weimar Republic.

General Seeckt, the commander of the German *Reichswehr,* was a typical and highly influential proponent of the conservative point of view. He insisted that Germany "must carry on an active foreign policy," for without it, it would cease being a state. An active and purposeful foreign policy, in his view, required a *rapprochement,* if not a treaty, with Russia. Economic relations he considered useful, but more important were political and military links that would provide Germany with an immense "accretion in power." Seeckt considered himself to be a confirmed *Realpolitiker.* He scorned those who spoke of reviving Bismarck's formula of attempting friendship with both east and west. He insisted that politics be adapted to the needs of the moment and be based on the assumption "that every state is fundamentally egoistic in its policies." And France's policy he assessed as "a policy of annihilation, pure and simple." He thought that sooner or later England would woo Germany as a counterweight to France, and that England would be even more eager for such an alliance if Germany were strengthened through alignment with Russia.

The conservatives looked upon Poland as the core of the eastern question. "Poland's existence is intolerable and incompatible with Germany's vital interests," wrote Seeckt. "She must disappear." Russia and Germany, he concluded, had a strong common interest: the annihilation of Poland, which acted as France's buttress of the Versailles Treaty in the east. Hence he proclaimed the re-establishment of the 1914 borders with Russia as Germany's primary aim in foreign policy. To obtain it, he suggested that Germany help arm Russia, thereby strengthening a potential ally and indirectly fortifying the German army itself. Seeckt's views exerted a strong influence on Germany's policies, not only in foreign affairs, but also inside Germany, where they became the basis for German secret rearmament.

The moderate politicians, on the other hand, were wary of an eastern orientation, particularly of a military consorting with Soviet Russia. Count Ulrich von Brockdorff-Rantzau (1869–1928), chief of the German delegation to Versailles and, after 1922, German ambassador in Moscow, warned that a policy "exclusively oriented to the east" would be not only premature but dangerous. He thought that Russia could not be trusted, that Germany should not get involved in a possible war over Poland, and that an alliance with Moscow would bring no economic gains, but would merely cement the Anglo-French Entente. Granting the die-hard enmity of France, Brockdorff-Rantzau saw the best course as one of friendship with England, which before long would need German assistance against French threats. To be sure, the moderates were no more ready than the conservatives to acquiesce in a permanent loss of the eastern territories, but they advocated a wait-and-see attitude, hoping for an eventual collapse of the new Polish regime that might permit a rectification of the borders.

By 1922, the conservative outlook had won temporary ascendancy. When the powers, including Russia and Germany, met at Genoa to discuss the problem of international financial obligations, and in particular the tsarist debts that the Communist regime refused to acknowledge, the two outcast nations effected a *rapprochement.* By the Treaty of Rapallo, a resort not far from Genoa where German and Russian delegates met secretly, Berlin and Moscow agreed to resume diplomatic relations. Furthermore, the two nations canceled all mutual claims for reparations and extended to each other the most-favored-nation clause in their commercial relations. Rapallo thus marked the beginning of Germany's *rapprochement* with Russia and an end to its postwar isolation. The treaty was hailed by the conservatives as a first step toward resuming an "active foreign policy" and bewailed by the liberals as an invitation to disaster. It was soon followed by secret arrangements for military cooperation to build up the Red Army and initiate the clandestine rearmament of Germany.

The Psychology and Culture of a Defeated Nation

Since the campaigns had been fought beyond the German borders and air raids on German cities had been rare, Germany emerged from the war with little physical destruction. Moreover, by 1923 no Allied troops occupied German soil, with the exception of the left bank of the Rhine and the Ruhr. Finally, those who had run the government during the crucial years of fighting—William II and the military—had been allowed to depart with unsullied hands, without signing the onerous armistice and the treaty of 1919. It was the civilian forces of liberal republicanism that had assumed the burden of guilt and odium that, in the German mind, was associated with the defeat and the "dictate of Versailles." As the course of the Weimar Republic showed, this was a serious blunder by Allied diplomats and strategists, who should have insisted on surrender by William II and his staff, and on a brief military occupation of Germany, to convince the Germans that they had been defeated militarily, and that the war had been partially caused by the disastrous policies of their emperor.

Failure to convince the Germans of the incontrovertible fact of military defeat not only led to the insidious theory of the stab in the back but also helped produce a fatal cleavage in the psychological make-up of the young republic. The disillusionment of defeat, normally issuing in bitter resentment of the victorious enemy, was turned by the Germans into recriminations against their compatriots and particularly against the new system of government.

PESSIMISM AND ESCAPISM As might be expected, the horrors of war and the ensuing political and financial chaos launched the Weimar Republic on a note of pessimism and disillusionment. Much of the literature of the 1920s captures this feeling of futility and general revulsion toward war. *All Quiet on the Western Front* and *The Road Back* by Erich Maria Remarque (1897–) were representative of this powerful trend of disenchantment and are perhaps the best known works of this trend.

Of course, disillusionment evoked varying reactions among the writers of the period. Some tried to isolate themselves from the stream of politics and turmoil and escape the uncertain temper of the times. This reinforced what some have called the ingrained indifference of German intellectuals toward politics, an attitude that may have contributed to the failure of the republic. Thus Germany's greatest poet, Rainer Maria Rilke, living mostly in voluntary exile, looked sadly upon the crass materialism of his homeland, and withdrew increasingly into the seclusion expressed by his esthetic and spiritual poetry. The young novelist Franz Werfel (1890–1945) turned to mysticism in some of his novels and dramas. Gerhart Hauptmann, who in his youth had thrown himself so passionately into the social questions of his time with his naturalistic dramas, now remained aloof from the sociopolitical dilemma of the day. Psychology and religious visions play a part in his superb short story, *The Heretic of Soana* (1918) and in the drama *The White Savior* (1919), while his novel *The Isle of the Great Mother* (1924) is a tongue-in-cheek analysis of the birth of religions. Even Thomas Mann was caught up in the pessimistic escapism of the Weimar era. He had established his fame before the war with his long novel *Buddenbrooks* and numerous short stories. During the war, he had sided with the conservatives. In his *The Magic Mountain* (1924), however, the hero Hans Castorp loses himself for seven timeless years at a tuberculosis sanatorium in Davos, where he had gone to visit a relative. In an atmosphere of decay and disorder, far removed from the turmoil of the "flat land," Castorp attempts to discover himself and the meaning of life. But the mood of pessimism in the end gives way to reaffirmation, indicative of Mann's own gradual acceptance of the Weimar Republic and democracy. A wiser Hans Castorp returns home to assume what he considers to be his responsibilities in life.

The pseudohistorian Oswald Spengler (1880–1936) began on a similar tone of pessimism in *The Decline of the West* (completed in 1922), which brought him world-wide fame almost overnight. But to Thomas Mann's rationalism he opposed the antirational tradition of the neoromantics. His philosophy of history, describing the rise and fall of civilizations and predicting the decay and disintegration of the West, was based on the organic theory of the state so popular in the early nineteenth century. Once again the state, with its own destiny, its own instinct and feeling, was placed at the apex of all life. Spengler, like Mann, was disillusioned, but the remedy he suggested differed diametrically. Spengler complained that the Weimar Republic was not motivated by "power, honor, and glory," and followed no aims except those of selfish parties. "For five years," he wrote in 1924, "we have had no deeds, no decision, no thought." And in *The Decline of the West* he predicted that only a German Caesar could delay the decay of Europe by enthroning "life over reason," by channeling the animallike war of races into its final stage in which one race dominates all others. Thus pessimism led Spengler to grasping the straw of authoritarian salvation.

Albert Schweitzer (1875–), the musicologist, organist, physician, theologian, and philosopher, attempted to analyze the dilemma of his time. He perceived the "great inward lack of confidence," poorly concealed behind a "self-confident exterior." Although Schweitzer was looking at Europe as a whole from his African mission, his admonition was particularly apt for Germany. "The acceptance of authoritarian truth," he warned in his autobiography *Out of My Life and Thought* (1933), ". . . does not bring skepticism to an end; it merely covers it up."

LIBERALISM VERSUS CONSERVATISM

Two politically antagonistic streams of thought affected the literary trends of the period. On the one hand were those who fervently accepted the republic. As if infused with new vigor by the freer atmosphere of the period, literature flourished in the 1920s. Writers already important before World War I labored with new energy, and new faces appeared, making Weimar a rich period, particularly for the German novel. Liberal and rationalist in essence, these writers were generally violently antinationalistic and antimilitaristic. They exuded an almost revolutionary cosmopolitanism, and in politics varied from mild liberalism to confirmed socialism. Fritz von Unruh (1885–) with his antimilitary plays; Heinrich Mann (1871–1950) with his satirical novels against the old empire; Arnold Zweig (1887–) with his novels decrying the suppression of the individual by war and the impersonal state; Bertolt Brecht (1898–1956) with his experimental dramas against social inequities; Alfred Döblin (1878–1957), Hermann Hesse (1877–1962), and many others underlined their faith in the inherent dignity of the individual and saw in the overthrow of the empire the augury of a new era.

But opposed to this group were the more conservative, conventional writers. They detested the innovators, the coterie of those who experimented with psychological techniques and who championed liberal thought, rationalism, and social ideals. They hated them as passionately as they hated the political democracy of the Weimar Republic that seemingly had spawned them.

They considered these innovators subversive of Germany's true character, and labeled their writings "cultural bolshevism." Since many of the liberal and experimental writers were Jewish, the conservatives' hatred was marked by virulent anti-Semitism, which was also rampant in economic and professional circles.

Among the conservative writers was Stefan George (1868–1933) and his circle, who had gained fame before the war as the foremost exponents of German symbolism. Imbued with a conscious adoration of the elite, George despised the Weimar period, with its "decadent mass culture," and its debasing, democratic socialism. Like so many of his compatriots, George longed for the noble rebirth of the Reich under a new Siegfried whom the nation could follow into the dawn of a new glory.

Oswald Spengler, with his neoromanticism loosely clothed with scientific vocabulary, must be classed with this same group. Similarly, there were journalists and theoreticians, believing in the myth of an organic state and the ethnic legends of the past, who also despised democratic individualism. Railing at the rationalists, they became conscious forerunners of Hitler's ultimate "revolution to the Right." Most influential among them were Hans Grimm (1875–1959), whose *People without Living Space* (1926) bolstered the idea of a mystical relationship between ethnic cultures and the soil—an important doctrine of National Socialism—and Alfred Rosenberg (1893–1946), later Hitler's party philosopher whose books on racialism, written during the 1920s, all reveal the same contempt for the masses and advocate the myth of the racial elite.

THE DESIRE FOR EXPERIMENTATION

The Weimar period also experienced a great flourishing in many nonliterary fields. In science, philosophy, and some of the arts, Germany again achieved world fame. Since many of these scientists and philosophers ultimately emigrated from Hitler's Germany and settled in the United States, they are particularly well known to American readers: Albert Einstein (1879–1955) in physics; Wolfgang Köhler (1887–), one of the proponents of Gestalt psychology; the neo-Kantian Ernst Cassirer (1874–1945) in philosophy, and Martin Heidegger (1889–), who together with Karl Jaspers (1883–) helped found existentialism; Werner Sombart (1863–1941) the liberal economist, and numerous influential liberal historians, such as Friedrich Meinecke (1862–1954). In the arts, the Austrian-born Oskar Kokoschka (1886–) advanced the expressionist school, while Arnold Schönberg (1874–1951), also Austrian by birth, and Paul Hindemith (1895–) continued the musical revolution with experiments in atonal and twelve-tone compositions. Of greatest world-wide impact was the Bauhaus school of modern functionalism in architecture, launched in the 1920s by Walter Gropius (1883–), a development which revolutionized modern concepts of construction.

The Weimar period, in fact, scintillated with activity and experimentation. True to their democratic idealism, the national government, the states, and the municipalities demonstrated their solicitude for the masses by catering to their tastes for culture and amusement—regardless of the cost, which was usually borne by loans and deficit financing. Concert halls, theaters, public swimming pools, sports arenas were built in many small as well as large communities. The motion-picture industry flourished and made its impact on Hollywood. Experiments in progressive education at the elementary level abounded. Innovations in stage productions were introduced. Publishers propagated culture for the masses in millions of inexpensive paper-backed books, printing works of the masters and new trash literature with equal gusto. As they did everywhere, the roaring twenties made their mark on the Weimar era. With fervor, the Germans fled from insecurity by abandoning themselves to the stupefaction of jazz music, dancing, cults, and fads.

THE YEARS OF STABILIZATION AND COOPERATION, 1924–1929

By the fall of 1923, Germany was approaching complete disintegration. Famine, unemployment, and runaway inflation had made a shambles of the nation's economy and the morale of its population. Passive resistance had failed, and Franco-Belgian troops remained in the Ruhr. Rightist putsches in Bavaria and Küstrin, leftist uprisings in Saxony and Hamburg, and separatist revolts in the Rhineland threatened to destroy the fragile structure of the Weimar Republic. And relations between Germany and the Allies, particularly with the French, were so bitter that open conflict seemed imminent.

At this point, a change of attitude by both the German and the Allied governments inaugurated a new era. The near-fatal experiences of the preceding years of shortsighted vengeance and obstructionism led the Allies to adopt a more moderate policy of cooperation, and forced the Germans to seek internal stability and to resign themselves to accepting their international obligations. Conceived in late 1923, these new policies achieved the status of a credo in 1924 and in the succeeding years.

This era is often called "the period of fulfillment [of Versailles]" or "the period of the Locarno spirit." One might as well label it "the age of Chamberlain, Briand, and Stresemann," the three foreign ministers largely responsible for the tenor of the times. In England and France, initiation of the new policy coincided with a leftward shift in the government. In January 1924, the British Conservative party was succeeded by the first Labor government in English history, headed by Ramsay MacDonald, a stanch advocate of international cooperation. Although MacDonald's tenure of office was less than a year, the conciliatory Austen Chamberlain, foreign minister from 1924 to 1929, continued to guide England's foreign affairs in the new spirit. Similarly in France, the vindictive Poincaré was replaced by the more liberal Édouard Herriot, and then by the Socialist Aristide Briand, who remained in charge of French foreign affairs from 1925 to 1932.

Most responsible for the shift in German policy was Gustav Stresemann, the astute politician who as chancellor in the fall of 1923 initiated the measures that were to help German stabilization, and as foreign minister from 1923 to his death in 1929 worked for the reintegration of Germany into the family of nations. Stresemann, head of the mildly conservative German People's party, came to power with the aid of the Socialists and Democrats, those parties that, as was true in 1919, were willing to cooperate with the Allies in order to save the German Republic. During Stresemann's long tenure as foreign minister, however, his political moves depended mostly on the sufferance of cabinets that, with few exceptions, moved more and more to the right of center. Many hailed Stresemann as the savior of the Weimar Republic, but more recently, as more archives have been made available, historians have seen in him one of the gravediggers of the republic. His political coloring was indeed mixed. Nationalism and internationalism, idealism and *Realpolitik,* conservatism and mild liberalism breathed within him side by side. With consummate skill, he showed the proper color to impress those with whom he had to deal.

In a Reichstag speech in April 1923, at the height of tension with France, he advertised his cosmopolitan idealism by calling for an economic union with France that foreshadowed the Schumann plan of 1951 (see page 645). He suggested that a joining of the French and German coal and iron-ore industries would in the long run be more important than squabbles over reparations, and would heal the wounds of war and cement a political *rapprochement* between the two states. On the other hand, he was an ardent nationalist, unwilling to cede an inch of German soil. He called for a "strong and justified national feeling." His policy of "fulfilling Versailles" was not meant to be a surrender to the West. By displaying willingness to cooperate and by stabilizing Germany internally, he sought to strengthen his nation sufficiently to resume the defense of its national interests. While flirting with the West, he secretly permitted the conservatives to strengthen Germany's economic, military, and political ties with Russia. Although he publicly reprimanded the ultraconservatives at home for advocating continued obstructionism, he freely supported internal conservatism. His conviction that political action must confine itself to the "realm of the achievable" made him shrink from embracing extremes. Therein lay his strength and his success.

Stabilization of the Economy

In September 1923, Chancellor Stresemann called off the futile passive resistance in the Ruhr in order to "preserve the state and its people." He proclaimed in the Reichstag that reconciliation with France was possible and that Germany should honor its reparations obligations, provided France did not demand territorial cessions along the Rhine. In October, the Reichstag voted him extraordinary emergency powers, for a maximum of six months, to deal with the financial, economic, and social chaos. His powers included the right to "deviate from the constitutional civil rights." Stresemann promptly declared a state of siege and used the *Reichswehr* to suppress the disorders in the various states and to reimpose the authority of the central government.[1]

The next step was aimed at halting the inflation. The financier Hjalmar Schacht (1877–   ) devised a new cur-

[1] His firm action against the Communists in Saxony, contrasted with the mild treatment of the monarchist and Hitlerite rising in Bavaria, led to protests by the Socialists and their resignation from the cabinet, causing the fall of Stresemann's government at the end of November 1923, after which he served only as foreign minister.

rency, the *Rentenmark,* backed theoretically by the real estate and industrial equipment of the entire nation, but in reality by foreign loans and renewed confidence in the future of the economy. The value of the new *Rentenmark* was pegged at 1,000,000,000,000 to 1 in exchange for the old mark. The repercussions of inflation, deflation, and stabilization were drastic. The middle and lower classes lost their hard-earned savings, and the retired, the aged, widows, and disabled war veterans were deprived of their security. The reserves of labor unions were wiped out. These groups, normally the mainstay of a democracy, experienced profound disillusionment and loss of status that drove many to seek more radical solutions on the Left or the Right. Thus the foundation of the Weimar Republic was seriously undermined.

On the other hand, immense profits were made in the course of this financial maneuver. Government and industry were strengthened, since their debts were practically wiped out. Huge fortunes were made by speculators who bought up land, factories, and industrial equipment with inflated funds and had sufficient resources to retain them until after the stabilization of the new currency. Concentration of capital and industrial combines was thus favored and cartels grew more powerful, whereas the smaller entrepreneurs fell by the wayside. The small fortunate group thus strengthened and enriched boosted the power and resources of the conservative element. Many workers and many members of the lower-middle class, on the other hand, became impoverished and disillusioned. The results of the elections in the spring of 1924 showed the repercussions of this "stabilization." The conservative parties—the German National People's party and the National Socialists—almost doubled their representation over that of 1922, rising from a combined 65 to 127 seats. The Communists increased from 16 to 62, while the moderate parties—Socialists, Centrists, Democrats, and the People's party—dropped from 344 to 238 (see Chart 6).

Stabilization of the economy also involved a readjustment of the reparations claims. Various international committees labored for half a year on new agreements that were finally accepted by Germany and the Allies in April 1924. Known as the Dawes Plan, the new reparations schedule remained vague about Germany's total obligation, but scaled down the annual payments to a more reasonable level. To place Germany back on its feet and enable it to meet its initial quotas, new loans to the amount of 200 million dollars were extended to Germany. The Reparations Commission was empowered to supervise German finances, in particular the operation of the Reichsbank and the state-owned railroads. Revenues from the railroads and from certain indirect taxes were pledged as security for the loans, the bulk of which came from America. It is curious in this respect that the United States was unwilling to reduce or cancel Allied debts, but was ready to lend money to Germany so that it could pay reparations to the other Allied nations, who in turn paid some of their debts to the United States. In view of the heavy American investment in Germany and the repercussions of the United States depression five years later, it has been said facetiously, though with some truth, that

German democracy was stabilized and later unstabilized by United States loans.

Thanks to Schacht's financial wizardry, the Dawes Plan, and foreign investments and loans, the German economy and finances became relatively stable during the half decade following the disaster of 1923. It has been estimated that between 1924 and 1929, Germany received foreign loans totaling 8 billion dollars, mostly in short-term commitments, whereas it paid out in reparations less than 2 billion. The difference of 6 billion, a huge sum in the 1920s, was used to rejuvenate industry, support public works and social services, extend unemployment insurance, and pay for subsidies to agriculture, particularly in the northeastern regions of Prussia.

Consequently, there was a considerable, if hollow, recovery of the economy. Cartels grew bigger and more powerful, wages rose, unions regained some strength, and heavy industry was able to divert funds and resources for secret rearmament. Cities built lavish opera houses and recreation parks, factories replaced old machinery and spent money unsparingly to develop new processes. Prosperity had seemingly reappeared, inviting many Germans to look upon these years as a period of affluence and stability.

But it was a hollow recovery, laced with political as well as economic dangers. Foreign supervision of large sectors of German finances, called for under the Dawes Plan, was resented by German nationalists as incompatible with the dignity of a sovereign state. Although acceptance of the plan was followed by complete French evacuation of the Ruhr, the conservatives decried the new reparations scheme as another step in the enslavement of their nation. Moreover, from an economic point of view, the Dawes Plan was woefully shortsighted. Unless Germany started to earn foreign credits by exporting more than it imported or through other means—tourism, shipping, and the like—it could never repay the enormous loans it was contracting. But Germany's balance of trade was unfavorable during most of the succeeding years. It was not only living on borrowed funds, but sinking ever more deeply into debt. "If ever a crisis hits us," Stresemann remarked prophetically in 1928, "and the Americans recall their short-term loans, we face bankruptcy."

The Era of International Goodwill

After Stresemann became foreign minister in late 1923, he devoted all his energies to finding a *modus vivendi* with the Allies, despite the obstructionism of the conservative elements inside Germany. The first tangible result of this policy, after a year of difficult negotiations, were the five Locarno Treaties of October 1925. In the Treaty of Mutual Guaranty between Germany, Belgium, France, Great Britain, and Italy, the signatories guaranteed "the maintenance of the territorial *status quo*" and the "inviolability" of the borders between Germany, France, and Belgium. This agreement thus involved Germany's renewed recognition of the permanence of its western frontiers, as set by the Treaty of Versailles. The contracting parties furthermore undertook "in no case to resort to war against each other," unless such action were required by a mandate from the League of Nations. In four separate arbitration conventions with France,

Belgium, Poland, and Czechoslovakia, respectively, Germany subscribed to the peaceful settlement of all disputes, and declared that it would not attempt to change its eastern borders by unilateral force. The world hailed these treaties as an end to the years of distrust and the beginning of a period of international goodwill, the renowned "spirit of Locarno." Europe began to relax, and the three chief architects of the pacts, Stresemann, Briand, and Chamberlain, were awarded the Nobel Peace Prize.

Much has been written about the Locarno Treaties, in praise and in damnation. Many asserted that they were a logical first step in overcoming the age-old enmity between France and Germany, and that the ultimate failure was due to the economic collapse at the end of the decade rather than to any political flaws in them. The aura of idealistic optimism engendered by the pacts was such that Briand and Stresemann actually discussed such thorny issues as evacuation of the Rhineland, return of the Saar, termination of Germany's unilateral disarmament, and the retrocession of territories transferred to Belgium. But despite Locarno, France retained a strong residual fear of a German revival. As an added measure of insurance, it soon began construction of the Maginot Line in defense of its Rhineland border, and cemented closer relations with Poland and the Little Entente, particularly with Czechoslovakia.

Others were mainly critical of Locarno. Some Allied observers saw in it a German ploy for lulling France into lessened vigilance along the Rhine and for driving a subtle wedge into the Anglo-French alliance. Some called it "an ostrich policy" on the part of France, since the dangerous "powder keg" in the east—the question of Germany's frontier with Czechslovakia and Poland—remained. In recent decades, with the hindsight of experience in the Allied reaction to the rise of Hitler, some historians have seen in Locarno the inception of "appeasement."

More important here is the reaction inside Germany and the question of Stresemann's real intentions. German nationalists were horrified by the "sell-out" of Locarno. They accused Stresemann of signing the "enslaving" Treaty of Versailles a second time and treasonably abandoning Alsace-Lorraine by accepting the permanance of the Upper Rhine frontier. They also feared that his prowestern policy endangered their own eastern orientation.

Stresemann defended himself vigorously against these accusations. His speeches to the Reichstag and before conservative groups became so nationalistic that it is difficult to discern his true intentions. He may have been duping the West with his show of collaboration or else deceiving the conservatives at home with his patriotic boasting. A study of his private papers reveals that he was primarily an astute defender of Germany's national interests. He had "surrendered" to the Allies only what was at any rate lost—Alsace-Lorraine. All other German demands he held in abeyance. He boasted that he had rejected all notions of a nonaggression pact with Poland or Czechoslovakia, and that sooner or later the "impossible frontier lines in the east" would be corrected. "No German government," he claimed in a speech, "from the German nationalists to the Communists, would ever recognize this frontier." He did not even reject the possibility of war under certain conditions. The recovery of German soil, including the Saar, union with Austria, rectification of all grievances imposed by Versailles—all these he felt could be achieved, but only at the rate of one step at a time. Insisting that the final advantage alone counted, he publicly implored the conservatives not to meddle in foreign affairs, no matter how much they disliked his initial steps. And as tangible proof of his good intentions toward the conservatives, he promptly negotiated a new treaty of friendship and neutrality with Russia that expanded Russo-German cooperation in trade and armaments.

As a result of Locarno, Germany's relations with the Allies improved immensely. In December 1925, Allied occupation troops evacuated Cologne and vicinity. In the following year, Germany was admitted to the League of Nations and given a seat on the Permanent Council. Stresemann hoped to use the League as a means for effecting gradual adjustments in the Treaty of Versailles. As a first step, in early 1927, Allied control over German armaments was discontinued. Thereafter the question of Germany's military status became enmeshed with the larger problems of world-wide disarmament discussed at numerous conferences under the auspices of the League of Nations. In 1928, Germany also became a signatory to the abortive Kellogg-Briand Pact for the renunciation of aggressive war, a further step in its re-entry as an equal partner into the family of nations.

Finally, in 1929, the reparations question was reopened and a new schedule of payments devised. Germany had been drifting deeper into debt, and many Germans were chafing under the Allied supervision of their finances. Even the United States, as chief creditor, was worried about the disturbing conditions in Germany's balance of payments. Hence when the Germans requested a re-examination of the reparations issue, the Allies proposed the Young Plan, which finally fixed the total sum to be paid by Germany over a period of fifty-nine years. Annual payments were considerably reduced below those stipulated by the Dawes Plan, and emergency clauses were included as safeguards against sudden financial fluctuations. In recognition of Germany's sovereign rights, foreign controls over its economy were abolished. Instead, a Bank for International Settlements was created in Basel to help arrange the yearly transfer of payments. Despite the better conditions offered by the Young Plan, the German nationalists campaigned vigorously against its acceptance, since the very payment of reparations involved tacit acceptance of the guilt clauses of Versailles. Still, the Young Plan was eventually accepted. Concomitantly, the Allies began the withdrawal of their last occupation troops from the Rhineland. With the Young Plan and the evacuation of the Rhineland, Stresemann had gained yet another step in his rehabilitation of Germany. He had accomplished much through peaceful means and perseverance. In October 1929, he died, some three weeks before the stock market crash in the United States, that radically undermined the recovery of Germany and eventually brought to the fore those forces determined to complete Stresemann's work through violence.

Resurgence of Political Conservatism

The years 1930–1933, between the Wall Street crash and Hitler's seizure of power, are commonly called the declining years of the Weimar Republic. True though this may be, one must not overlook that the so-called period of stability and cooperation, 1924–1929, saw a resurgence of political conservatism that foreshadowed the revolution of the National Socialists.

THE ELECTION OF HINDENBURG The death of President Ebert in early 1925 and the subsequent presidential election gave the conservatives an opportunity to test their strength. On the first ballot the votes were divided among seven major and several minor candidates, so that none received the required majority. Of the votes cast, 10.4 million were for the conservatives, 7.8 for the Socialists, 3.9 for the Center, 1.9 for the Communists, and a total of 2.9 for a number of other candidates, including Ludendorff.

To prepare for the second ballot, a month later, at which only a plurality was required for election, the parties formed voting blocs and launched joint electoral campaigns. The conservative *Reichsblock*—consisting of the DNVP, DVP, Bavarian People's party, Economic party, Bavarian Peasant League—chose as their new standard-bearer the seventy-eight-year-old, twice-retired General Hindenburg, largely because of his expected sentimental appeal to the nation at large. The tone of the electoral proclamation of the *Reichsblock* ominously foreshadowed the propaganda slogans of Hitler's Third Reich:

> We deem it to be the irrefutable duty of all Germans . . . to labor with all force and devotion for our Hindenburg. Hindenburg was your *Führer* in glorious and difficult times; you obeyed him; you loved him! He never deserted you. Hence, fight for him now when, with the traditional loyalty of a leader, he wants to step again at the head of your columns, to serve his fatherland in peaceful reconstruction! Hence our motto: . . . Hindenburg, our savior from discord!

The Center, the SPD, and the DDP formed the *Volksblock* and jointly backed the former Catholic chancellor, Wilhelm Marx (1863–1946), a leader of the Center party. Their campaign slogan was "For the fatherland, for a popular government, for the Republic." The KPD, however, refused to join any voting bloc. Opposed on principle to the bourgeois Weimar Republic, they shortsightedly hoped to gain by undermining its structure.

On the second ballot, Hindenburg received 14.6 million votes, against 13.7 million for Marx and 1.9 million for the Communist Ernst Thälmann (1886–1944), and thus became the Weimar Republic's second president. In his inaugural address, the aged general promised to safeguard the laws and the constitution, to represent all Germans and not merely a particular party, region, or confession, and to act as the embodiment of the national will. Yet there was little doubt that Hindenburg's sympathies did not lie with the republic. He attempted to maintain official neutrality as demanded by his office, but did little to strengthen the republican forces. He cherished the memory of his army and of prewar Germany and hated all that was connected with the Treaty of Versailles.

Despite economic progress, there continued to be frequent cabinet crises during Hindenburg's regime, usually over sharp disagreements between conservatives and liberals. In 1925 the Prussian government, to the dismay of the Socialists, awarded a large financial indemnity to the Hohenzollerns, and returned to them many of their confiscated estates. When in the following year the central government proposed to compensate all former dynasties, the liberals forced the issue into a popular referendum. Since not enough votes were cast in favor of expropriation, the conservatives succeeded in passing a Reichstag bill granting compensation to all dispossessed princelings. Even the question of the German flag produced a cabinet crisis, at a time when the DVP, the party of Stresemann and Luther, was constantly growing more conservative. In 1926, DVP Chancellor Hans Luther (1879–1962) issued an order permitting the occasional use of the old black-white-red colors that had been the symbol of the empire. The Socialists and the Democrats, favoring the republican colors, black, red, and gold—the flag of 1848—protested vehemently and forced Luther's resignation.

GERMAN REARMAMENT Another stronghold of antirepublicanism resided in the *Reichswehr* and the various paramilitary organizations, particularly the nationalistic *Stahlhelm* (literally, steel helmet). The German professional officers had never resigned themselves to the disarmament and arms limitations stipulated at Versailles. The weakness of the Weimar regime and its experience with putsches had forced the government to continue to rely on the army, and had made strange bedfellows of the liberal government and the conservative officer corps. The ministers were therefore forced to close their eyes to the activities of the military. Thus even a semistabilized republic could not solve the age-old problem of German politics: putting the military under effective civilian control. Although reduced in strength and power, the *Reichswehr* retained a surprising independence of action and planning.

As chief of the *Reichswehr* from 1920 to 1926, General Seeckt devised a vastly efficient, modern army in which relatively small size was compensated for by excellence of training and equipment. It was, in effect, a cadre army of actual or potential officers, capable of rapid expansion in times of emergency. The problem of manpower was partially solved through training in numerous paramilitary organizations. Above all, in order to produce modern equipment the military and industry cooperated to the benefit of both. Civil aviation was built up largely with a view toward its military potential. Synthetics, chemicals, transport, and shipbuilding were perfected, where possible with an eye to military applications, and certain industries actually experimented with modern weapons.

In part this rearmament—actual and potential—was secret and in part quite open. It was begun long before the famous *rapprochement* with Soviet Russia at Rapallo. The idea of German-Russian military collaboration against the West was shared by some Soviet leaders and nationalistic Germans as early as 1918. By 1921, Lenin had requested German assistance in reorganizing the Red Army, and Seeckt had eagerly complied. Thereafter the military of the two states worked in close contact. German industrialists helped set up Russian war factories to produce experimental planes and tanks for both armies, and Russia's vast territory offered useful ground for the training of small German units in the use of special weapons. But the importance of this Russo-German cooperation should not be exaggerated. The Germans found it equally easy to set up branch factories in Holland, Denmark, Switzerland, and other neutral countries for the production of modern military equipment, particularly in the field of aviation.

The Allied Disarmament Commission in Berlin was, of course, not totally ignorant of these proceedings. But, short of complete military occupation of Germany, there was little the Allies could do to prevent them. Some British statesmen, in fact, were not averse to seeing a stronger Germany as a counterweight to France, whereas the French were thoroughly suspicious of German intentions. Inside Germany, the activities of the *Reichswehr* produced a political uneasiness. A few liberals and Socialists protested, but most remained silent for fear of being labeled traitors. The nationalists, of course, favored the development, and Stresemann, for diplomatic reasons, pretended ignorance.

In later years, much unwarranted defamation was directed against Germans because of this secret rearmament—primarily because of the subsequent militarism of Hitler. Yet it should be kept in mind that Versailles and the League of Nations had echoed Wilson's proposal for world-wide disarmament, but that in practical application only Germany had been disarmed. Only a highly idealistic German could be expected to remain content with such unilateral disarmament. To assert that all Germans who secretly or openly favored the rebuilding of an effective army were aggressive militarists is to let emotion override historical common sense. The damage to the republican structure was not perpetrated by the mere fact of secret rearmament, but by the failure to subordinate the military to the civilian government. The danger lay less in the desire of the military to strengthen Germany than in the fact that many of the officers and most of the members of the paramilitary organizations were opposed to the very republic itself. In a typical *Stahlhelm* proclamation of 1928, its members declared: "We detest the present form of government with all our heart . . . because it blocks all prospects for liberating the enslaved fatherland, for removing from the Germans the false stain of war guilt, for gaining the needed living space in the east, for rearming the German nation."

AGITATION AGAINST THE WEIMAR REPUBLIC In the elections of 1928, the conservative parties lost momentum, the Socialists gained, and for the first time since 1920, a Socialist, Hermann Müller, again became chancellor. Actually, the electoral losses merely led the antirepublican forces to increase their agitation. The presence in the cabinet of the "traitorous" Socialists who had signed Versailles made it all the easier for Hitler's growing National Socialist party to excoriate those in power. In 1928, Joseph Goebbels (1897–1945) called on his compatriots to "shed the red chains," and urged the overthrow of Stresemann. "As yet, the world bristles with arms, while Germany is disarmed down to the last leggings; as yet the Negroes are occupying the Rhine . . . but Stresemann remains."

The negotiations for the Young Plan in 1929 gave the nationalists a chance to flex their muscles. To prevent German acceptance of the new reparations schedule, Hugenberg's German National People's party, Hitler's National Socialists, and the *Stahlhelm* formed a "Reich committee for the Demands of the German People." This committee drafted a "Bill against the Enslavement of the German People," and obtained almost four million signatures to force its discussion by the Reichstag. The bill instructed the government to notify the Allies promptly that Germany rejected the guilt clause, that the occupied territories were to be vacated immediately and unconditionally, that the Germans refused all further financial obligations based in any way on the theory of war guilt, and that the German chancellor or any minister who signed an international agreement contrary to these instructions—that is, the Young Plan—would be guilty of high treason and punishable with imprisonment. Despite pressure from the extreme Right, the Reichstag defeated the proposed bill, 323 to 82, and adopted the Young Plan. In a subsequent popular referendum, the bill received 5.8 million votes, far short of the 51 percent required to pass it over the head of the Reichstag. Stresemann's successor rightly told the Reichstag that it was "sheer nonsense" to ask in a referendum whether the German people liked paying reparations. But he warned prophetically that the radical Right was proposing such cheap demagoguery less to free Germany from its foreign dilemma than to undermine the bourgeois republican government. Defeat in the referendum temporarily eclipsed the rising star of Hugenberg and Hitler, but, as became apparent in the following year, in no way destroyed it.

National Socialist Germany in Time of Peace, 1930–1937

THE COLLAPSE OF THE WEIMAR REPUBLIC

The period 1930–1933 saw the complete erosion of the republic's parliamentary structure and the gradual substitution of Hitler's dictatorship. Many volumes have been written attempting to diagnose the causes for the failure of Germany's republican experiment and for the rise of National Socialism. There is no need here to reiterate the well-known arguments. The preceding chapters on the Weimar Republic and on earlier periods described many weaknesses in the body politic of Germany as well as flaws in the international situation that eroded the young republic and paved the way for its totalitarian successor.

Yet a few words of caution against overly facile interpretations seem in order. Too many non-German analysts unconsciously adopt an inversion of Hitler's racialism. They attribute Germany's plunge into totalitarianism to the consequences of a supposed flaw in the German people. As Hitler saw in the *Volk* the driving power of spiritual and cultural superiority, so some writers have seen in the Germans an inherently cruel, militaristic attitude of which Hitler became the physical embodiment. Needless to say, such racialism is absurd. A second misinterpretation—equally misleading—rejects the theory of "racial guilt," but sees in Hitler and his disciples the incarnation of evil, which by deceit and revolution imposed itself on a naïve people.

Such black-and-white interpretations overlook the entire political, socioeconomic, and psychological frame that made National Socialism possible. They also disregard the aspirations of millions of people and distort the changeover to Hitler's dictatorship, which was pseudo legal rather than revolutionary. Interpretations of this type lead neither to a comprehension of the phenomenon of National Socialism with its appeal to the masses, nor to an understanding of the twentieth century itself, in which extremist panaceas for crucial problems vie for allegiance. Rather, the rise of National Socialism must be viewed against the background of the general social erosion that gripped Europe in the decades after World War I. In almost all European states, economic dislocation, social tension, and class friction led certain groups to advocate the use of force for the solution of social, economic, and political problems. Fascist parties became important even in democratic France, Holland, and Belgium. Dictatorships were established in Austria, Italy, Spain, Portugal, and in ten eastern European countries from the Baltic states to Greece—with the exception of Czechoslovakia. Germany's resorting to dictatorship was therefore part of a general European phenomenon. That the German version involved such excesses of cruelty and barbarism raises a question that has provoked much speculation among analysts and journalists, but which in essence is unanswerable on the basis of our present methods of social and psychological research.

The Economic Crisis

Primary among the causes for the fall of the Weimar Republic was the economic crisis of the early 1930s. Even before the crash of the New York stock market in 1929, the world economy had been in imbalance. Higher and higher tariff walls—adopted as a source of additional government revenue, as a defense against depreciated foreign currencies, or simply as an expression of blatant nationalism—had hindered international trade. Agricultural overproduction and inflation, unbalanced budgets and uncollected debts had produced economic and financial dislocations in many nations. The boom and bust of 1929 finally ended the era of speculation. Repercussions of the collapse of Wall Street were soon felt all over Europe. By 1931, most nations were in full depression, with Germany and Austria suffering the most.

The sudden recall of short-term United States loans, coupled with a decline in stock values and a reduction of trade, rapidly swelled the German recession to disastrous proportions. Between 1929 and 1932, the German national income dropped by 20 percent. Unemployment, not severe during the pseudoprosperous years of 1925–1929, rose to 5 million in 1930 and exceeded 6 million by January 1932, or almost as many as the number of unemployed in all other European states combined. By the end of 1932, 43 percent of Germany's labor force was unemployed —as compared with 25 percent in the United States. While unemployment rose and bread lines lengthened, countless businesses went bankrupt. In the summer of 1931, even the Darmstädter Bank, one of Germany's largest, became insolvent, and the government was forced to close all banks and savings institutions for two days in a desperate effort to halt the financial catastrophe.

The depression was accompanied by grave psychological, social, and political repercussions. Business failures shook the self-reliance of the middle class. Unemployment and hunger increased class antagonism between rich and poor. And even among nations hatred between the "have" and the "have-not" states rose to a new pitch and became a dominant theme of international relations in the 1930s. Almost everywhere, people hoped to escape from economic chaos by awarding more power to the central governments and by insisting that the state assume greater responsibility for the economic well-being of the nation. The remnants of nineteenth-century *laissez faire* gave way to increased state intervention, on the Continent as well as in the United States. And in many nations, the middle class and the proletariat were happy to escape from chaos by seeking their salvation in a dictatorship. The search for order was not limited to Germany.

Throughout 1931, Chancellor Heinrich Brüning (1885–) tried desperately to stem the economic and financial disaster. He hoped to balance the budget by reducing expenditures in all areas—lower salaries for government employees, lower pensions and welfare payments, less government housing, and other measures. Contrary to John Maynard Keynes's then current advocacy of pump priming, Brüning sought retrenchment everywhere. To put his unpopular—and unsuccessful—policy into effect, he was forced to resort constantly to Article 48 and rule by emergency decree (see page 492).

In the spring of 1931, Austria also neared economic collapse with the bankruptcy of the powerful Credit Anstalt, a bank that had dominated much of the Danubian trade. To help both nations and to improve trade, Berlin and Vienna negotiated the establishment of a Customs Union. The Little Entente—always fearful of Austrian resurgence—Italy, and France promptly protested against these negotiations. France even referred the matter to the World Court, which adjudged the proposed economic union contrary to the Treaty of Versailles. The German-Austrian Customs Union had to be abandoned, furnishing further ammunition for the propaganda of the German nationalists, and Great Britain, although itself in financial straits, came to the rescue of the Credit Anstalt in order to avoid a complete collapse in Austria.

The depression also required reappraisal of the question of reparations and international debts. In the spring of 1931, President Hindenburg appealed to President Hoover for his intervention in favor of a temporary cessation of reparations demands. The United States finally felt forced to acknowledge a relationship between reparations and inter-Allied debts. Hoover proposed a one-year moratorium on all intergovernmental debts and interest payments, a suggestion greatly resented by France, which had not been so hard hit by the depression and feared the moratorium might lead to a permanent cancellation of reparations. As the crisis deepened and most countries abandoned the gold standard, frequent international conferences were held to debate the question of debts and reparations. The Young Committee, recalled for the purpose, announced that it seemed doubtful whether Germany would be in a position to resume payment of reparations upon expiration of the moratorium, and Chancellor Brüning finally proclaimed publicly that "continued political payments" were impossible. In the summer of 1932, a general conference met in Lausanne to work out a permanent solution. Significantly, England and France were represented by the same MacDonald and Herriot who had helped to create the spirit of Locarno. Some escape clauses notwithstanding, the Lausanne Conference amounted to an abandonment of all reparations demands. The United States agreed to adjust but not to cancel the debts owed it—a useless gesture, for after 1934 all countries, except Finland, defaulted on their payments. For Germany, however, the decisions made at Lausanne represented another step in the unraveling of Versailles.

The Background of Hitler and His Movement

HIS EARLY CAREER Born in Austrian Braunau near the Bavarian border, Adolf Hitler was the third child of his father's third marriage. Intelligent but not well educated, Hitler aspired to become an artist in order to escape the narrower prospects offered by the career of a customs official, which his father had followed. In 1908, he moved to Vienna, where only frustration seemed to await him. He was not admitted to the School of Architecture because he had not graduated from an academic high school. Nor could he attend the Academy of Fine Arts, since he failed the requisite entrance tests. The examiners rejected the sample sketches he submitted—ironically on the required themes "Expulsion from Paradise" and "An Incident from the Deluge." During five years of poverty and occasional vagrancy, he earned his living by painting postcards, and devoted much time to haphazard reading. It was during these frustrating years in Vienna that he formed many of his ideas and prejudices. He came to hate the non-German peoples who crowded the polyglot capital of the Hapsburg empire. His German national feeling became intense. Liberalism, humanism, Christianity became hateful to him. He particularly despised Jews, Slavs, and intellectuals, and disdained the masses with a scornful contempt he retained all his life.

In 1913 he moved to Munich, and in the following year his aimless life was given a new meaning through the outbreak of World War I. He volunteered for service with a Bavarian regiment and served as a messenger at the front. His sudden sense of belonging and achievement was shaken only by Germany's collapse in 1918. The end of the war found him in a military hospital, gassed and half-blind. Unable to conceive that Germany had lost the war fairly, he ardently embraced the idea of the stab in the back. After convalescence, he returned to Munich and decided to devote himself to politics.

Postwar Munich was filled with the tumultuous seesaw struggle between opposing ideologies. Hitler thrived in this hotbed of intrigues and street fighting. He was given a job by the *Reichswehr* to spy on various sprouting political fringe groups, among them the German Workers' party (founded in 1918 by Anton Drexler) with its mixed program of nationalism and socialism. Instead of spying on it, Hitler harangued the group on several occasions, then joined it and rapidly rose to a position of leadership. Henceforth, he became a full-time politician.

THE BEGINNINGS OF THE NSDAP In 1920, the German Workers' party adopted an official program of twenty-five points, largely elaborated by the militantly anticapitalistic economist Gottfried Feder (1883–1942). In it, nationalism, socialism, and racialism were mixed in forceful, albeit contradictory, terms. The twenty-five points—in some respects similar to Mussolini's program of 1919—called for the union of all Germans, the return of Germany's colonies, the abrogation of the Versailles and St. Germain Treaties, and the equality of Germany with other nations. At home, the program purported to place the good of the community before that of the individual by threatening death to those who worked to the detriment of the public weal, by confiscating war profits, and by abolishing unearned incomes. The state, moreover, was to provide an adequate living for all citizens, nationalize the industrial trusts and share in the profits of big business, improve old-age pensions, aid small businesses, and institute agrarian reform. The state was to be purified by denying citizenship rights to Jews and expelling non-German immigrants. In public education, the program called for the teaching of "state ideals" and the improvement of the health of the youth. Nationalism was to be furthered by extirpating non-German—that is, Jewish and foreign—influences from the press, art, and literature, and by granting freedom of religion only when it did not "endanger the state or give offense to the moral and ethical feelings of the Germanic race." The program also called for abolition of the professional army in favor of a people's force.

Soon thereafter, the German Workers' party changed its name to the National Socialist German Workers' party (NSDAP), and began to extend its influence from Munich into other parts of Germany and into Austria. It acquired a party newspaper, the *Völkischer Beobachter* which, under the editorship of Alfred Rosenberg, propagated National Socialist ideas. In 1921, the growing NSDAP organized the SA (*Sturmabteilung,* or storm troopers) under the command of the socialistic former army officer, Ernst Roehm (1887–1934). These brown-shirted storm troopers, fully armed like members of the Free Corps and the *Stahlhelm,* were used to guard party meetings, disrupt the work of other parties, and engage in the street fighting common to the period. Besides Hitler, Feder, Rosenberg, and Roehm, the party numbered among its early important members Gregor Strasser (1892–1934), Rudolf Hess (1894–) —soon Hitler's favorite adjutant—the colorful and venal ex-air force officer, Hermann Göring (1893–1946), the publicist Joseph Goebbels, and eventually the inscrutable Heinrich Himmler (1900–1945).

Methodically organized and fanatically devoted to its cause, the NSDAP grew substantially during its first three years. The economic and political dislocations of the early Weimar Republic, Mussolini's success in 1922, and tacit encouragement by *Reichswehr* officers and by the nationalistic Ludendorff persuaded Hitler to attempt the premature Beer Hall Putsch of 1923 (see page 500). Its disastrous outcome not merely landed Hitler in jail but convinced him that seizure of power by his party had to be carefully prepared and could probably be achieved only through pseudolegal means.

Outlawed after the putsch of 1923, the NSDAP was re-created in February 1925. In the same year, it added a second fighting arm, the black-uniformed SS (*Schutzstaffel*), composed of elite members with special duties. But during the ensuing years of apparent stabilization following the Pacts of Locarno, the party's growth was slow. At the end of 1928, it numbered only some 60,000 members. Meanwhile its ideology was gradually being modified, and parts of the original program of twenty-five points were unofficially abandoned. Three books in particular helped change National Socialist dogma. In 1923 appeared *The Third Reich* by the journalist and literary historian Arthur Moeller van den Bruck (1876–1925). The author was not a member of the NSDAP, but exerted much influence in conservative circles. Moeller advocated "corporatism in state organization and economics," a system that would at first be revolutionary but would ultimately have a stabilizing and conservative effect. As an undaunted nationalist, he detested the international creed of the SPD and the KPD and insisted that Germany needed a "new Socialism" as the "foundation of Germany's Third *Reich*." Such a regime, he proclaimed, needed a leader who knew how to supplant international socialism by a new, nonliberal German type of socialism, which he labeled "National Socialism."

A few years later appeared Hitler's *Mein Kampf*, written during his imprisonment. With uncanny precision, Hitler depicted the future course of his movement, both in foreign affairs as well as in internal policies. Finally in 1930, Rosenberg's *The Myth of the Twentieth Century*, with its theories on the supremacy of the German race, was added to the party ideology. Meanwhile Hitler continued to deliver his inflammatory speeches in which he hammered again and again on the same few themes: denunciation of Versailles and the "November criminals" who had signed the armistice and created the Weimar Republic; condemnation of communism, socialism, freemasonry, and international Jewry; and a promise to redeem German honor and inaugurate for all Germans a glorious future. Although Hitler's speeches never deviated from these same themes, the basic party aims during the 1920s tended to lose the socialistic fervor of Gottfried Feder's original program and become more opportunistic.

After the stagnant period of the late 1920s, the NSDAP was infused with new vigor as a result of the economic crisis. By promising panaceas to everyone, Hitler suddenly attracted millions of discontents to his side. To the peasants, he offered higher agricultural prices; to labor, employment and higher wages; to the industrialists, safety from communism and unions; to the army and veterans, an expanded military machine; and to all German nationalists, the abrogation of Versailles and the establishment of a powerful *Grossdeutschland*. As membership and voter attraction increased, so did financial support of the party. Certain powerful industrial magnates of the Ruhr, such as Fritz Thyssen (1873–1951) and Emil Kirdorf, began to throw their financial support to the NSDAP. Banks and insurance companies contributed to party funds. Tired of the instability of the republican regime and fearful of a Communist coup, nationalistic conservatives saw in Hitler's movement a possible remedy. Hitler, for his part, abandoned even more the socialistic ideals of the party. He dismissed the anticapitalistic Gottfried Feder and took as his new economic adviser Walther Funk (1890–1960), whose conservative theories were more attuned to those of the Rhineland magnates, whom Hitler wished to attract to his movement.

The Political Disintegration of the Republic

When Hitler seized power in 1933, he did not have to overthrow the Weimar Republic. It had more or less ceased to exist. Never very stable during its brief life span, it had begun to disintegrate in the critical years of economic depression.

In March 1930, the Socialist Chancellor Müller resigned when the German People's party refused to remain in the government coalition. To raise additional funds for unemployment compensation, Müller had urged an increase in the contributions of both employers and employees. His plan was defeated by pressure from business and labor unions alike. When he requested permission from President Hindenburg to use the emergency powers of Article 48 to deal with the economic crisis and the growing disorders in the streets, he was also rebuffed. It seemed that Hindenburg would not entrust the powers of Article 48 to a Socialist. Hindenburg's court camarilla, primarily the influential intriguer General Kurt von Schleicher (1882–1934), was happy to use the occasion to topple the Socialists from power.

BRÜNING AND THE GROWING CRISIS To replace Müller, Hindenburg selected the conservative Centrist leader Heinrich Brüning, a fiscal expert and at heart a monarchist who was only half-reconciled to the republican regime. Brüning formed a conservative cabinet that excluded the SPD, but he made it clear from the start that the new cabinet would not be bound to any coalition. Insisting that he ran the country for the benefit of the nation as a whole rather than for that of specific parties and interest groups, he resorted constantly to Article 48, with the wholehearted approval of President Hindenburg. Whatever he could not achieve through ordinary legislative process, he ordered by emergency decrees. Although isolated voices warned that excessive use of Article 48 would lead to dictatorship, those opposed to its use could not muster a majority in the Reichstag to overrule the chancellor. And there were many who no longer cared about democracy. An apt headline of 1930 noted: "The people long for guidance." The ensuing article stated: "It is no longer vital whether the government has a popular base or not. What matters is that it governs well."

During the summer of 1930, while the economic situation worsened, street battles between opposing paramilitary factions became the order of the day. Brown-shirts, red-shirts, green-shirts, and black-shirts terrorized the cities and fought each other in pitched battles. Hampered by continued obstructionism in the Reichstag by members of the DNVP, the NSDAP, the SPD, and the KPD who opposed his budget and his rule by Article 48, Brüning dissolved it and called for new elections. The republic's fifth national election, in September 1930, produced ominous results (see Chart 6). The moderate parties dropped in strength, with the SPD, the DVP and the DDP —now called the German State party —losing the most votes. The extremists on both sides showed huge gains. The Communists obtained 4.5 million votes, rising from 54 to 77 representatives in the Reichstag. The manifold right-wing splinter parties doubled their representation. The NSDAP—increasing its vote at the expense of the

DNVP, which declined by almost 50 percent—rose from the 800,000 votes of the last election to 6.4 million, thereby increasing its delegation in the Reichstag from 12 to 107.

The landslide victory of Hitler's movement boded ill for the future of the Republic. In a Reichstag speech, Gregor Strasser warned: "We favor democratic Weimar and its Constitution, so long as it suits us." The legislative process of the central government reached an impasse. Communists and National Socialists, both equally determined to topple the republic, shouted and fought during legislative sessions, proposed silly amendments, or staged walkouts—whatever might best disrupt the regular functioning of government. Yet there were many who failed to recognize the dangers. Even the Socialist prime minister of Prussia, Otto Braun (1872–1956), pretended that the electoral results of 1930 threatened "neither the Constitution, nor public safety, nor the course of foreign policy," and expressed confidence that a "coalition of all reasonable people" could be formed to guide Germany out of its quagmire. Two years later, this same Otto Braun was to be the victim of a nationalist *coup d'état* in Prussia.

Despite these difficulties, Brüning's government lasted for over two years. Relying on Article 48, and ruling with the confidence of Hindenburg rather than that of the nation, Brüning attempted to solve the economic chaos and at the same time placate enough factions to remain in power. Essentially a nationalist, he continually promised to "rebuild Germany in peaceful cooperation with all people." He frequently denounced Versailles, favored *Anschluss* (union) with Austria, and at the Geneva Disarmament Conference in 1932 insisted on "equal rights and equal security for all *peoples*"—meaning equality of armaments for Germany. He showed favors to the army, and proudly called his cabinet a "government of war veterans." He attempted to alleviate the economic distress by retrenching social services, aiding agriculture, and trying to balance the budget.

But none of Brüning's measures helped stem the tide of National Socialism. The NSDAP gradually gained control of several states. Although intent on assuming power by legal means, the party also made careful preparations for a coup if one seemed appropriate. Ordinances arranging for the institution of military government, for the ruthless suppression of all opposition, and for the summary application of the death penalty for political offenses were meticulously prepared by the NSDAP should a sudden collapse of the central government make revolution advisable.

In October 1931, the NSDAP gained added power by the formation of the so-called Harzburg Front. Through the intermediary of the financier Hjalmar Schacht, a working agreement was formed among Hitler's movement, Hugenberg's DNVP, certain Rhineland industrialists, and the *Stahlhelm.* In a public proclamation issued at Harzburg, the coalition derided the government's long-standing failure to suppress the "bloody terror of Marxism" and the "growing cultural bolshevism," and promised to heal the disunity in the nation and end the subservience to foreign powers. The group declared its readiness to "seize power," and warned that "in the coming disorder" it would "protect life and property of [only] those who openly side with us, but [would] not safeguard the present regime." Not only was the Harzburg Front an open challenge to the Weimar Republic; it created discomfort within the ranks of the NSDAP. Although Wilhelm Frick (1877–1946) assured the members of his party that the "only aim of the coalition was to obtain power within the state," and that the NSDAP would see to it that it would lead the coalition, the more leftist members of the party objected to this "deal" with the ultrarightists and conservative industrialists. Hence the Harzburg Front increased the power of the party, but also contributed to its later split between the opportunists and those who took their "socialist" label more seriously.

In the midst of these political problems and the continuing economic crisis, new presidential elections were required upon the expiration of Hindenburg's term in 1932. It is symptomatic of the shift to the Right that Hindenburg, who in 1925 had been a candidate of the conservatives, became a candidate of the moderates and Socialists in 1932. Despite the senility of the eighty-four-year-old general, the Socialists rallied behind him as "a protective shield against the rise of Hitlerism." The aged Hindenburg himself felt uncomfortable in his new position. "Look at the situation into which Brüning has got me," he is supposed to have told his friend Franz von Papen (1879–). "Now I have been chosen by the Left, whereas the Right, my own people, have put up this lance-corporal."

On the first ballot, Hindenburg received 18.6 million votes against 11.3 for Hitler, 4.9 for the Communist Thälmann, and 2.5 for the *Stahlhelm* candidate. As in 1925, a second ballot was required. In the second election a month later, over a million fewer voters appeared at the polls—indicative perhaps of the feeling of futility among segments of the electorate. With the *Stahlhelm* deciding to throw its support to Hitler, the second ballot gave 19.3 million to Hindenburg, 13.4 to Hitler, and only 3.7 to Thälmann. The senile Hindenburg was thus elected for a second term.

THE MISCALCULATIONS OF PAPEN

Soon after the elections of 1932, Brüning, who had incurred the wrath of too many influential groups, was forced to resign. His proposal for a partial expropriation of the estates of East Prussian landlords for the purpose of settling peasants on unused Junker land had particularly infuriated Hindenburg and his circle of Junker supporters. Moreover, Brüning had incurred the deadly enmity of the NSDAP by outlawing the SA and SS in an attempt to quell the continued street fighting. Wilhelm Groener, the ever-optimistic minister of defense and of the interior, had hoped to absorb the paramilitary organizations of the NSDAP into a "gigantic sports club, supervised by the central government." But after Hindenburg's re-election and the continuation of street fighting, Brüning had decided on the sterner solution of a complete ban.

Since Brüning's cabinet had always existed at the sufferance of Hindenburg rather than through the support of a parliamentary majority, Hindenburg's displeasure was tantamount to Brüning's dismissal. On the advice of Schleicher and with the consent of the Harzburg Front, Hindenburg on June 1, 1932, appointed Franz von Papen as the new chancellor.

Papen, a friend of Schleicher's and Hindenburg's, and of many other aristocrats and nobles, was a self-confident master of intrigue who believed he could forge a coalition of conservative Junkers, Rhineland industrialists, and army men that would keep Adolf Hitler out of power. Conservative and aristocratic, he disdained the rabble-rousing nature of National Socialism while admiring the nationalistic fervor of Hitler. But to get into office, Papen made a bargain with the NSDAP: he would lift the ban against the SA and SS in return for support from the National Socialists. Joseph Goebbels anticipated the consequences of such an agreement when he noted in his diary: "The *Reichstag* will be dissolved; all compulsory laws will be abrogated; we will get freedom to agitate and will deliver a masterpiece of propaganda."

Papen's cabinet was nicknamed a cabinet of "army officers and barons." It included Schleicher as minister of defense, four barons, and one count, among them Baron Konstantin von Neurath (1873–1956) for foreign affairs and Count Johann Schwerin von Krosigk (1887–   ) for finance, both of whom also served in Hitler's first cabinet. In foreign affairs, Papen's first half year in office was marked by a single success: the ending of the reparations obligations at the Lausanne Conference. Within Germany, his regime marked the further corrosion of the republican forms of government, since he continued the practice of governing by decree. Papen dissolved the Reichstag June 4. A week later, the ban against SA and SS was lifted, and street fighting resumed its usual violence. In Prussia, the National Socialists provoked increasing disorder on the floor of the diet. Pitched battles were fought between SA and Communists in the streets of Berlin. These disorders in Prussia led Papen to take frankly dictatorial measures—much in the manner of Mussolini. He deposed the Socialist prime minister of Prussia, Otto Braun, on the charge that he was unable to maintain peace in his state, and placed Prussia under martial law. This unconstitutional move was designed to please the ultraconservatives. The Communists ordered a strike to protest against this outrage, but the Socialists and labor unions refused to cooperate with them, since they hated the KPD even more than they hated the Nazis.[1]

The new Reichstag elections took place on July 31, 1932. Once again Hitler's movement produced a landslide. His party polled 13.7 million votes and obtained 230 seats in the Reichstag, swallowing up most of the small right-wing splinter parties. Only the Center party and the Communists made slight gains, while all other groups declined (see Chart 6). As leader of the largest party, Hitler was clearly the man of the hour. The question no longer seemed to be whether he could come to power, but only how: whether legally or by *coup d'état*. Goebbels favored a pseudo-legal entry into the government, if necessary in coalition with the nationalistic DNVP, confident as he was that "seizure of power is fundamentally different from the ultimate aim" of the NSDAP. According to his later statement, Hitler opposed a *coup d'état*—perhaps in recollection of the Beer Hall Putsch—since he was afraid of the *Reichswehr*. Yet when Papen attempted to make a bargain with Hitler,

[1] The abbreviation "Nazi" was actually a term of contempt, used by Hitler's enemies, although foreigners gradually turned it into a general label for the movement.

the latter refused to join the government unless he were given full powers.

During the summer and fall of 1932, the Nazis straddled the issue. On the one hand, they acted as defenders of constitutionalism, deriding Papen for his dictatorial use of Article 48. On the other hand, they openly increased their terror. A famous incident revealed their real concept of the law. When five storm troopers broke into the house of a Communist worker and beat him to death in front of his mother, they were imprisoned by the government and condemned to death on the basis of a new law against political terrorism. Hitler at once sent a telegram to his imprisoned comrades: "Your freedom is a question of our honor!" And Rosenberg asked in the *Völkischer Beobachter* how one life, especially that of a Polish Communist, could possibly be worth the lives of five German veterans. "One soul does not equal another soul," he exclaimed, "one man not another. . . ."

At the same time, rifts seemed to appear within the NSDAP. Those Nazis who leaned toward Socialism became increasingly wary of Hitler's flirtation with big business. Gregor Strasser broke with Hitler, quit the party, and tried to induce others to follow him. Papen and Schleicher hoped to take advantage of Strasser's desertion to split the NSDAP. For this purpose, Schleicher negotiated with Strasser, and Papen once again dissolved the Reichstag and called for new elections, expecting the results would weaken Hitler's party. Another reason for dissolving the Reichstag was the chancellor's desire to anticipate a motion of censure by the conservatives, who disliked his economic measures. They had wanted to avail themselves of a safety clause in Article 48 in order to countermand the president's emergency powers. The Nazis and the DNVP complained that Papen's dissolution of the Reichstag was illegal on the grounds that it prevented them from maintaining the supremacy of the Reichstag over the chancellor. Since the use of Article 48 had been made necessary to a great extent by the legislative obstructionism of the Nazis and the Communists, such an accusation seemed ironic.

In the November elections of 1932, Hitler lost 2 million votes and 34 seats in the Reichstag. The excessive Nazi terror had frightened some voters, and the split with the left wing of his party had disillusioned others. The SPD sustained further losses, while the DNVP and the KPD both showed some gains. But there was no sign that Germany was regaining political stability. None of the moderate parties showed any gains, and 1.4 million fewer Germans went to the polls.

THE SCHLEICHER INTERIM The elections were followed by a new government crisis. For the second time, Hindenburg offered the chancellorship to Hitler, but withdrew his offer when the latter demanded unlimited power. Hindenburg insisted that "his constitutional oath and his conscience" would not allow him to grant exclusive powers to Hitler, a step that would necessarily lead to "dictatorship by one party." Papen urged a change in the constitution that would permit the chancellor to govern without the Reichstag, but Hindenburg also rejected this proposal as unconstitutional. Finally Papen resigned and a new Cabinet was formed by Schleicher.

The new cabinet, which was to be

the Weimar Republic's twenty-first and last, existed for only two months. Schleicher, who until then had intrigued in the background, was now the standard-bearer of the camarilla. He had persuaded Hindenburg that he was capable of solving the crisis without forcing the president to break his constitutional oath. He felt confident that he could woo Strasser and the Nazi left wing into a coalition with the bourgeois and Socialist parties and thereby undermine Hitler's movement. Fearful that his beloved *Reichswehr* might be overshadowed by Hitler's personal army, he was now belatedly determined to stop the Nazi steamroller. But all his schemes failed. Hitler successfully wooed the masses, in and out of his party, so that Strasser was given no opportunity to split the NSDAP. Schleicher's government proved as unable to deal with the continuing economic crisis as its predecessors had been. December 1932 and January 1933 saw endless secret intriguing by Hitler, Papen, Schleicher, Hugenberg, Strasser, and Thyssen, each of whom was trying to dupe the others; above them stood the senile, uncomprehending Hindenburg, who was still important because his consent was needed for the appointment of a new chancellor.

In the end, Papen succeeded in toppling Schleicher by concluding a second bargain with Hitler. The latter agreed to abandon his demands for exclusive power and to form a coalition cabinet with Papen, Hugenberg, and other conservatives. Papen in turn undertook to persuade Hindenburg that such a combination would be acceptable. As a result, the President appointed Hitler as chancellor on January 30, 1933. When Hitler moved into the chancellery in Berlin, he is supposed to have remarked to Goebbels: "No one will ever get me out of here alive!"

THE ESTABLISHMENT OF HITLER'S DICTATORSHIP

In view of the later Nazi excesses—so clearly foreshadowed even before 1933 in their speeches, in their party newspaper, and in the actions of their storm troopers—many foreigners have wondered why the Germans allowed Hitler's rise to power. To explain these events, one must recall that Hitler was made chancellor not by the vote of a majority of the German people but by presidential fiat, and that he established his totalitarian dictatorship in installments. One must also keep in mind the conditions of the period: the economic chaos, the political vacillations of the government, the street fighting and the national frustration, as well as Hitler's reiterated pledges to find immediate remedies for all ills. Although a few cautious observers in 1933 warned that Hitler not only would annihilate the republic and all democratic elements, but would also pervert justice and freedom and degrade human values, there were millions who naïvely flocked to his ranks or tolerated his movement for lack of a better solution. Indeed, provided they closed an eye to this or that in the Nazi creed or behavior, most discontents could find much attraction in Hitler's promises. What scruples existed were easily effaced by the rationalization that the Nazi movement "after all, contained much good." Above all, the unemployed were promised reintegration into the nation's economic life, and the bourgeois were guaranteed economic stability and safety from communism. Through remarkably skillfull propaganda, the insecure masses were given a sense of belonging, a feeling of achievement in helping "to reconstruct the Reich." Moreover, many citizens abided by their ingrained respect for governmental authority which, by tradition, deserved obedience regardless of the citizen's personal feelings. Finally, the new regime provided enough scapegoats to allow the masses to sublimate their prejudices and tension. The Nazis' much-publicized intention of fighting the "black, red, and yellow internationals"—the Catholic Church, communism and socialism, and the Jews—attracted the anti-Catholics, the anti-Communists, and the anti-Semites.

The Creation of a One-Party State

Hitler's first cabinet was essentially based on the Harzburg Front. Three Nazis—Hitler, Göring, and Frick (Interior)—were flanked by nine independent conservatives and members of the DNVP and the *Stahlhelm*. Among them were Papen (vice-chancellor), Neurath (Foreign Affairs), Schwerin von Krosigk (Finance), Hugenberg (Economics and Agriculture), General Werner von Blomberg (1878–1946, Defense), and the head of the *Stahlhelm*, Franz Seldte (1882–1947, Labor). Hindenburg naïvely expected that the presence of so many non-Nazis in the cabinet would dam Hitler's drive toward dictatorship. But the gigantic torchlight victory parade, in which thousands of brown-shirted storm troopers marched past the chancellery on the evening of Hitler's appointment—the day Hitler called "the day of the national rising"—should have been an omen. And two days later, Hitler appealed to the German people: "Give us four years and then judge us!" Promising to end its "suffering from fourteen years of Marxism," he vowed to restore Germany's greatness.

As an initial step, Hitler dissolved the Reichstag and called for new elections in March, hoping to obtain the two-thirds majority required to alter the constitution. Intimidation of the electorate was expected to produce the desired result. Göring, who had become minister-president of Prussia, used the Prussian police and the SA to begin his "clean-up action." He boasted that he knew but two types of people: "those who work for the *Volk* and those who only destroy and annihilate." Urging the police not to hesitate to shoot down all enemies of the state, "regardless of the consequences," he loosed the Nazi terror into the streets and the homes of the nation.

On February 27, the Reichstag building went up in flames. Within hours, Göring and Goebbels denounced the fire as "a monstrous deed of Bolshevik terror." Recently some historians have tried to substantiate the accusation that members of the KPD actually started the fire, but most continue to believe that it was set by the Nazis themselves to provide a spectacular excuse for sharper repression of the opposition. Certainly the Nazis had stronger motives and had more to gain from the fire than the Communists.

In face of the "red threat," Hitler persuaded Hindenburg on the following day to issue "Ordinances for the Protection of the German State and Nation." "As defense against communistic acts of terror endangering the state," the ordinances set aside, without time limit, most of the civil liberties guaranteed by the Weimar constitution, and converted the penalties for many crimes from imprisonment to death. Freedom of speech, press, and assembly; the secrecy of the postal service; habeas corpus; and the inviolability of home and property were all suspended. The powers of the central government were made clearly superior to those of the federal states. The Nazis promptly used the ordinances to close opposition newspapers, imprison opponents, and intimidate the population. "Enemies of the state," "traitors," "November criminals"—those who had helped establish the Weimar Republic in the November Revolution of 1918—were ruthlessly apprehended. As Goebbels noted gleefully in his diary: "Now Göring is cleaning up. What a delight! Now the red pestilence will be extirpated!"

Despite terror and intimidation, the elections of March 5, 1933, failed to give the National Socialists a majority (see Chart 6). In this last supposedly free election, with 88 percent of the eligible electorate participating, they received 44 percent of the votes or 17.3 million out of a total of 39.3 million. In coalition with the DNVP, which obtained 8 percent of the votes, the NSDAP could count on only a majority in the new Reichstag, far short of the 67 percent needed to change the constitution. The strength of the Center and the SPD parties had changed surprisingly little, and the KPD had dropped only slightly.

Actually, the electoral results were of little importance, since Hitler was busy undermining the remaining democratic institutions. During March, concentration camps were established; at first they were improvised in private homes, then they became specially prepared barbed-wire enclaves. The enemies of the regime began to disappear in the dead of the night. Interrogations, torture, or death awaited them. The concept of legality was giving way to that of the "national will" embodied in the Führer and his NSDAP. Three weeks after the elections, the Reichstag was deprived of all essential power. Through the Enabling Act of March 23 —officially labeled "Law for the Relief of the Distress of Nation and State"—Hitler's government was awarded the right to make laws and treaties without the approval of the Reichstag, even if they violated the Weimar constitution. The new law was to be valid for four years, unless Hitler's government should fall before expiration of this period.

The Enabling Act gave legal sanction to the establishment of Hitler's dictatorship. Of the delegates, 441, including all Centrists, voted for it, and only 94 Socialists (out of a total SPD delegation of 120) voted against it, warning that the act would destroy "legality, equality, and human values." The 81 Communists who had been elected to the Reichstag had been disqualified by a special law and hence could not vote on the issue. Since the 74 favorable votes of the Catholic Center—largely motivated by fear of Communism rather than by love of National Socialism—gave Hitler the required votes to pass the law, the Center was later accused of guilt by association with Nazism. After World War II, when Nazism was on trial, the German courts had to deal with this question and came to the conclusion that the Centrists had been unwise, perhaps even stupid, but not guilty.

During the next four months, Hitler

used the legislative powers awarded to him under the Enabling Act to transform Germany into a totalitarian state. The Socialist and Center parties were dissolved, the DNVP disbanded itself voluntarily, and the *Stahlhelm* was incorporated into the NSDAP. By a law of July 14, the NSDAP was made the sole legal party in Germany, and the attempt to organize new political groups was made a criminal offense. As Goebbels explained to the foreign press: "National Socialism requires all power and all responsibility." And he pointed out that "he who is convinced that his *Weltanschauung* [view of the world or philosophy of life] is correct . . . can suffer no competitor for power." To transform Germany from a federal into a unitary state, *Statthalter* (governors) were appointed by Hitler to supervise the administration of the various states. In addition, the Nazis divided all Germany into *Gaue*—an old Germanic word for "districts"—each of which was under the supervision of a specially appointed *Gauleiter* (district leader). Hitler was thus provided with two channels of authority over all German territory: the official government line through the *Statthalter* and the unofficial one through the party and the *Gauleiter*.

At the same time, the cabinet was rendered impotent when voting by ministers was abolished and the Führer was given all power of decision. A law for the "Rehabilitation of the Civil Service" also gave Hitler power to dismiss from government service all "non-Aryans"—that is, all Jews—all those who "show no aptitude," and "those who do not labor relentlessly for the national state." Strikes were forbidden in May, after which all labor unions were abolished, eventually to be replaced by an All-German Labor Front, including employers and employees, and closely supervised by the central government. Meanwhile, Goebbels began to infiltrate the fields of education, art, theater, newspapers, and literature, in order to eliminate from German culture all politically unreliable elements and impregnate it with National Socialist ideals.

Yet, despite Hitler's determination to eradicate voting, majority decisions, and any ideas of individual responsibility wherever pockets of democracy had left them, his political astuteness—like that of Mussolini and Stalin—required the retention of mock elections to demonstrate to the world the popular backing of his regime. Although the Reichstag had been disenfranchised through the abolition of all parties except the NSDAP, new elections were held in November 1933. The official party list of the NSDAP received 92.2 percent of the votes. Only 3.4 million Germans dared to brave reprisals by expressing their doubts about the regime and casting negative or invalid ballots. The new Nazi Reichstag was seldom called, since it had no legislative functions and served largely as a rostrum for Hitler's speeches.

The Elimination of Internal Opposition

The regular police forces, the SA, the SS, and the newly created Gestapo (secret state police) succeeded fairly rapidly in eliminating most overt signs of resistance. But before Hitler could claim to be a real Führer, he had to face the problem of disunion within his party and the related question of the obedience of the *Reichswehr*.

Once the Nazis had seized power, the rivalry between Roehm's SA, the "old fighters," and Himmler's SS, the black-shirted elite guard, had become more and more pronounced. Roehm and his brown-shirts represented the left wing of the party; they desired more of a social revolution, more of the spoils of victory, and incorporation of their units into the regular *Reichswehr,* a step that would give them more prestige and better weapons. Hitler, however, was losing his fondness for the plebeian SA that had helped him to power. To run the Reich he relied largely on the smaller, more tightly organized, and more fanatically devoted SS, and saw to it that its members were awarded choice posts in the government. Moreover, he hoped that by abasing the SA, he might gain the respect of the upper classes and the support of the *Reichswehr* officers, both of whom looked with fearful suspicion upon the inchoate mass of some three million brown-shirts.

In the early summer of 1934, Hitler decided to crush the independent power of the SA. To put its members off guard, they were sent on furlough, and Himmler spread among his most trusted SS officers the rumor that Roehm was plotting a conspiracy against the Führer. On June 30, the Nazis were ready for their St. Bartholomew Massacre. In a brief, savage week end, as the announcement later read, "Hitler acted as the Supreme Tribunal of the German people," and together with Göring, Himmler, and the SS "destroyed without mercy the undisciplined, the unsocial and sickly elements" within the NSDAP. Hitler personally went to Bad Wiessee near Munich to supervise the arrest of Roehm and other SA leaders. The arrested were taken to prison and promptly shot without legal procedures. Meanwhile, Göring and the SS similarly apprehended prominent SA leaders in Berlin and saw to their immediate execution. Accused of conspiring with Roehm, of being traitors or homosexuals, others were shot in homes and prisons throughout Germany upon advance orders of Hitler, Göring, Himmler, and Reinhard Heydrich (1904–1942), the head of the SS Security Division. General von Schleicher and his wife, Gregor Strasser, friends of Papen, prominent Catholics, suspected monarchists, personal enemies, and even victims of mistaken identity—all fell in this national blood bath. A few more fortunate suspects, such as Papen himself, were merely arrested, but not shot. The dead, by official count, numbered 74; the unofficial toll ran closer to 1000.

On the heels of this three-day purge, Hitler promulgated a law retroactively legalizing the killings of the preceding days as "emergency measures required for the suppression of treasonous attacks." And Göring elaborated the theory that no law could have been violated by the purge, since "law and the will of the Führer are one and the same," and Hitler had to save the nation. Meanwhile, Goebbels propagated the theme that Hitler had liberated the German people from the terror of Roehm's SA. In gratitude for the services of SS members in the purge, Hitler turned them into an independent organization within the party, subject only to himself and Himmler. In the end, Göring reassured the confused and terrified nation that

> the *Führer* accomplished great deeds out of the greatness of his heart, the passion of his will, and the goodness of his soul. Faith in him is alone the basis of our life. He who dares touch that faith has

ceased to be a German and must be destroyed.

Two months later, the death of President Hindenburg provided Hitler with an opportunity to attack another problem: the relationship of the army to his movement. He still hoped eventually to subvert the traditional spirit of the army officers through universal military service that would swamp the professional soldiers with politically indoctrinated recruits. But considerations of foreign policy forced him to delay this step until March 1935. Since there could be no thought of an open confrontation with the well-armed military, Hitler meanwhile devised other means to bring them into tighter control.

A day before Hindenburg's death, Hitler promulgated a law combining the offices of president and chancellor, designed to come into effect with the death of Hindenburg. Through this measure, Hitler sought to obtain the post of commander in chief of the armed forces, traditionally lodged in the presidency. On the following day, barely hours after Hindenburg's death, the *Reichswehr* was required to take an oath of allegiance to Hitler as its new commander. Significantly, the wording of the oath was changed from the days of the Weimar Republic. For "faithful service to my people and my fatherland" were substituted the words "unquestioning obedience to the Commander in Chief of the *Wehrmacht,* the *Führer* of the German *Reich* and people, Adolf Hitler." Moreover, to stress the break with the past, Hitler changed the name of the German army from *Reichswehr* to *Wehrmacht.* Trained by tradition to live and die by their military oath, the officers and men of the *Wehrmacht* henceforth became obedient, albeit reluctant, servants of the new regime. To get popular backing for this latest coup, Hitler ordered a plebiscite on the question of uniting the offices of president and chancellor. Only 5.1 million voted against it; 88.2 percent of the electorate approved the action.

THE NAZI STATE

From the beginning of their accession to power, Adolf Hitler and his associates, feeling responsible only "to the future of the German nation," started to construct the Third Reich, which, like the first German Empire, was to last a thousand years. Hitler felt convinced that destiny had chosen him to fulfill his task, which, according to Goebbels, was "the achievement of total revolution." The "National Socialist *Volksbewegung*" (popular movement) was to transform Germany in all aspects. Hitler asserted that he wanted to destroy all that was diseased (by which he meant the Weimar Republic), and then build up a new Germany. "Either Germany will become a world power," he had written in *Mein Kampf,* "or she will cease to exist." And so that Germany would win a possible future war and not again fall victim to a stab in the back as in 1918, he sought to construct the strongest possible home front by unifying the nation through total coordination and discipline.

Yet Nazi ideology and actions were more negative than positive. There was much the Nazis stood against, but little they stood for. National Socialism was anti-Communist, anti-Socialist, anti-Semitic, antiforeign, anti-internationalism, anti-Catholic, anti-Versailles, anti-Freemasonry, anti-League of Nations, and opposed to a plethora of other groups, ideologies, and institutions. Its "positive" aims were few: the purification of the race and the building of a new Germany in which the totalitarian state would be supreme.

The State and the Judiciary

In political and other matters, the Nazis' aim was expressed by their favorite term *Gleichschaltung,* meaning literally "coordination" but in fact connoting "subordination." All thought and action were to be subordinated to the state, which, according to Frick, resided in the Führer (leader) and his followers (*Gefolgschaft*). Private life apart from the state was not to be tolerated, since it was deemed meaningless. "What benefits the state is right" became a favored motto. The individual German was left only with *duties* to the state. The state, on the other hand, had no duties to its citizens or to humanity at large, but only *rights* vis-à-vis other states. Hegel's ideas on the organic state were now distorted beyond recognition, and Rousseau's General Will became the will of the Führer. As Frick explained to a meeting of *Gauleiter,* "The *Volk* is a being, leading its own life and following its own laws . . . with its own historically formed blood community. Individualistic, liberal thinking must be overcome."

This all-powerful state, according to Hitler, knew no moral scruples and lived by a primordial instinct of survival. "The strongest has the right to enforce his will," he had announced in 1923; forever intoxicated with the thought of battle and might, five years later he added: "Man does not survive on humanitarian principles, but only through brutal struggle."

To control the German state, Hitler used his party and its numerous affiliates. Besides the SA and SS, there were the National Socialist Motorized Corps (NSKK), the Gestapo, the German Labor Front (DAF), the German Labor Service Battalions, the League of German Women (DFS), the Hitler Youth (HJ), the Union of German Girls (BDM), and dozens of other organizations—some uniformed, some provided only with distinctive insignias, but all hierarchically organized, thoroughly disciplined, and subject ultimately to the Führer. Keeping the masses organized made them easier to control, while at the same time it gave them a sense of purposeful participation.

The Nazis also hoped to turn Germany into a unified and unitary state, more susceptible to totalitarian control. In 1934 they abolished the remaining sovereign rights of the states as well as of the Reichsrat in which the states had been represented at the national level. *Gauleiter* and *Statthalter*—often one and the same person—retained sole rights of local control, theoretically, "in the name of the German people"; in fact, under the direction of the party and the central government. To symbolize the final achievement of German unification in 1934, young people were sent into the fields to collect all border posts marking the traditional limits between the German states, to bring them to the market places of towns and villages, and to burn them in a nation-wide bonfire of unity. To unite the people still more, the Nazis tried to mix the population by sending Germans from one region to work and settle in other parts of the Reich. Yet despite all these efforts, the traditional particularism did not die out. Even after thirteen years of Hitlerism, the age-old antagonism between Bavarians and Prussians persisted.

Totalitarian control also required new concepts of law and legality. Law in all its aspects was deprived of its abstract or moral basis and became frankly political and opportunistic. Hans Frank (1900–1946), the Nazi Reich Commissioner for Justice, did his best to abolish "the old liberal idea of 'no penalty without a formal law.' " Nazi law, according to him, knew no equity or justice in the traditional sense, and people's actions were to be judged not on the basis of laws but rather on the basis of "the National Socialist *Weltanschauung*." In essence, the whole legal machinery was no longer to serve the individual, but solely the aims of the *Volksbewegung*. The protection of the law, according to Göring, was to be extended only to those who were true *Volksgenossen* (National Socialist-minded citizens). Since Hitler and his followers embodied the German people, those who disobeyed them were committing crimes against the German people and therefore deserved no protection of the law.

To implement these ideas, the judiciary was purged of all unreliable judges, and a special People's Court was set up in 1934 to judge cases of treason, which by definition could mean almost any political offense. The death penalty became common in the sentences passed by this court. Much of the law, however, was not administered through the courts; rather, it remained in the hands of the Gestapo, supervised first by Göring and later by Himmler. Proceedings here depended on the whims of the examiners and the importance of the case. Most frequently, those arrested were "interrogated" and sent to a concentration camp for a few months or a few years as a salutary warning to like-minded discontents and as an intimidation to the people at large. But even during the early years, some were given a mock trial and promptly executed. Occasionally others died as a result of the "interrogation." As the regime grew to maturity, concentration camps multiplied, ultimately reaching perhaps as many as three hundred. Communists, Socialists, Jews, recalcitrant priests and ministers, defeatists, financial speculators, intellectuals—in fact, almost anybody who displeased someone in the hierarchy—were gradually herded into the ghastly compounds that were to become a black stigma on Western civilization.

Blood and Soil

With the aid of the party philosopher Rosenberg and the application of pseudo-scientific ideas, the Nazis developed racial theories that came to assume the place of a creed in their movement. Nationalistic to the point of absurdity, Rosenberg asserted that race was the primordial force in society, the basis of language and cultural traditions, of art, beauty, progress, and achievement. Among the races, the Nordic Aryans were not only the best, but were destined to rule the lower races—the Latins, the Slavs, the Semites, and the Negroes. In *Mein Kampf,* Hitler had stated: "All human culture and civilization depend on the Aryans." Without them "the earth would sink back under the dark veil of primitive times." But superior racial stock alone did not suffice to make a people great. Race, according to Rosenberg, stemmed from the soil. Blood and soil together produced the true folk soul (*Volksseele*) that alone could aspire to greatness. Hence it was not merely politically wrong, but "religiously" blasphemous to allow "German soil" to be contaminated by an alien race.

The fetish of race and racial purity, in which the extermination of the Jews was only incidental, became an end in itself in the Nazi ideology. The Nazis were imbued with an obsession against "racial impurity." "Racial mixing," Hitler wrote in *Mein Kampf,* "is the sole cause of the demise of all cultures." And he became fanatically convinced that the German *Volk* could be saved only by ensuring its "racial purity." As early as July 1933, the Nazis passed their first in a series of Eugenics Laws, designed to supervise the breeding of future generations. Strict medical examinations were required before marriage, especially for all members of the SS elite. A Hereditary Health Court was established, with powers to issue sterilization decrees for the mentally or physically diseased. Those of good Aryan stock were encouraged to keep up their health through physical exercise and to propagate, in and out of wedlock, so as to increase "the best of the race." State subsidies were provided for large families, and Hitler personally acted as godfather to the twelfth child of every married woman.

To unite the German race, to justify demands for more living space *(Lebensraum),* and to ensure that "250 million Germans will live on this continent in less than 100 years," the Nazis actively encouraged the return of Germans—or descendants of German families—living abroad. Various organizations were established to keep contact with these Germans living abroad (*Auslandsdeutsche*), especially in the United States and South America. Reduced fares were offered to entice them to come "home to the Reich."

Racial fanaticism, ingrained anti-Semitism, and the need for an effective scapegoat stimulated the Nazis' persecution of the Jews, whom Hitler called "the eternal parasites." In *Mein Kampf,* in a discussion of leadership and propaganda, Hitler asserted that "all truly great leaders" know that they must keep "the attention of the masses concentrated on a single enemy." If there are too many opponents, Hitler felt, the people become confused, and "may question whether indeed all others are in the wrong." He applied this dictum in his policy toward the Jews. In countless speeches, he and his party bigwigs drummed into their audience the idea that the Jews lurked behind all enemies: Jews had instigated the 1918 stab in the back; Jews had made the 1918 Revolution; Soviet Communism was run by Jews; democracy, majority rule, and liberalism were nefarious Jewish devices; Freemasons were Jews; the stock exchange was manipulated by Jews. The ubiquitous Jew was the cause of all Germany's ills.

The consequent persecution of the Jews, so well known to most readers, initially lacked any formal policy. An unofficial boycott of all Jewish businesses and professional services was inaugurated in April 1933; Jews were occasionally beaten up and imprisoned; and the emigration of Jews started. Meanwhile, the Nazis indoctrinated the nation with their racial theories. The doctrine of race was to supersede all religious considerations. Catholics and

Protestants were instructed to investigate their origins, for their religion and personal beliefs were no safeguard if their lineage revealed a single Jewish grandparent. Countless Germans suddenly discovered they were labeled Jews and hence inferior to their friends and colleagues.

Those Jews who were prominent in the professions, in the wholesale or the retail trades, in banking and certain industries, and therefore readily identifiable to the public, were the first to suffer. Businesses were wrecked, Jewish merchants were terrorized by storm troopers, and some Jews disappeared into concentration camps. The Jewish exodus from Germany increased, just as did the flight of Communists, Socialists, intellectuals, and sincere liberals. But emigration was soon made difficult. An emigration tax (*Reichsfluchtsteuer*) was imposed on all those who wanted to leave the country; at first it was only a small percentage of the emigrant's assets, but soon it was raised to a confiscatory 100 percent. Their inability to take along at least some savings discouraged many Jews from fleeing the country. Moreover, many Germans, ignorant of their Jewish ancestry until the advent of Hitler, had no wish to leave their homes, and remained in the hope that the Nazis' threats were mere propaganda.

But by 1935, discrimination and persecution were becoming systematized. Through the Nuremberg Laws and the Nationality Acts of September 1935, Jews—now legally defined as anyone with a single Jewish grandparent—were deprived of their citizenship and designated as "members but not citizens of the state." This automatically barred them from the civil service, the legal profession, the Labor Front, and all official organizations. Mixed marriages between Jews and non-Jews, or sexual relations between them, were prohibited by law. In the fall of 1938, anti-Jewish legislation and harassment went into high gear. Using as a pretext the murder of a secretary of the German Embassy in Paris by a young Jew, the Nazis unleashed ruthless attacks on the German Jews. Synagogues were burned; Jewish homes, apartments, and shops were destroyed; and a collective fine of 1 billion marks was imposed upon them. Thereafter more anti-Jewish legislation was issued almost weekly. Jews were barred from attending theaters, concerts, movies, or other public performances; they were forced to sell their real-estate and business holdings at ridiculous prices; they were not allowed to buy jewelry or gold; they could not walk on certain streets; they had to assume special Biblical names, such as "Israel" and "Sarah," entered in special identity papers that clearly marked them as Jews. Finally, they were forced to wear a large yellow star. Before the outbreak of World War II, some Jews were being restricted to ghettos and there were rumors in the Nazi hierarchy that the decision might ultimately be made to exterminate the Jews.

The New Religion

Hitler often used religious terminology in his pronouncements. However, what he called spirit and soul—words often found in his speeches—were not Christian concepts, but mystical embodiments of nationalism. When he invoked God—which he liked to do in his public addresses—he envisioned some kind of Germanic god who could best be served by devotion to the German people. Despite his Catholic background, Hitler had no understanding of Christian ideals. Privately he insisted that "one is either a German or a Christian. One cannot be both." The Old and New Testaments and everything connected with Christian dogma were to him "all the same Jewish swindle." And he vowed: "In the end, I will eradicate Christianity in Germany, root and branch."

But in his early pronouncements of 1933, he promised, for obvious tactical reasons, not to meddle in religious affairs. He recognized the usefulness of seeking a temporary accommodation with the Catholic Church. And despite his personal conviction that "a German Church or German Christianity" was "sheer nonsense," he gave his consent to the attempt to create a Protestant Reich Church, which was to be coordinated with the state and act as a useful tool for the political orientation of the youth.

In July 1933, the German government concluded a Concordat with the Vatican. The Catholic Church hoped to obtain recognition of her traditional rights in the new Reich. In return for their assurance not to mix in politics, Hitler granted the Catholics freedom of religious activities. His main aim, of course, was to undermine the remaining strength of the Center party and of the Catholic unions, and to get valuable public recognition for his young regime. He had no intention of abiding by the agreements, for in the end the Catholics, too, were subjected to total integration.

Friction between the Nazis and the Catholic Church began in 1934. Catholic orders and schools were attacked, Catholic literature was censored, and church welfare agencies closed. Nazi interference and harassment finally led to an open break in 1937, when the pope publicly denounced Hitler's constant violation of the concordat and the heathenish deification of race and *Volk* practiced by the Nazi regime.

From then on, Catholicism was arraigned among the enemies of the people. Although some priests did not oppose Hitler, others were arrested and condemned on trumped-up charges, usually involving morals or devious financial dealings. A campaign of hatred and defamation against the church was launched in the National Socialist press. Churchmen in great numbers were herded into concentration camps. All possible means were used to deter the youth from attending religious services. In 1938, numerous Catholic churches suddenly burst into flames. On such occasions, the services of the local fire departments were usually unavailable or conveniently delayed, and the arsonists were never apprehended.

With the Protestant churches, Hitler faced a slightly different problem. Despite the outward union of the various Protestant sects in the so-called Evangelical Church in July 1933, the Protestants remained in fact disunited in dogma as well as in their attitude toward the new regime. On the one extreme, there were the "German Christians," wholly devoted to Hitlerism. They believed that God's law was being fulfilled in the Führer and the Nationalist Socialist state. Their motto was: "One *Volk!* One God! One *Reich!* One Church!" At the opposite pole were those led by Pastor Martin Niemöller (1892–) who opposed the Nazis's aims of converting their church into a political arm of the state. Between these two extremes, the bulk of the Protestants simply followed the Lutheran tradition of obedience to the constituted government, and tried to avoid becoming involved in the political struggle. Hitler hoped to use this division among the clergy to gain control of the entire church. In November 1933, he appointed a Protestant Reich bishop for the task of subordinating the church to the new regime. Clergy and dogma were to be gradually "Aryanized," that is, purified of all Hebrew-Christian influence. By 1935, religious *Gleichschaltung* had progressed to the point that Hitler created a Reich Ministry for Church Affairs with complete control over the Protestant churches. The minister, Hanns Kerrl (1887–1941), was given legal power to grant or withhold funds, confiscate church property, imprison ministers, and issue binding ordinances, all for the supposed purpose of "establishing order in the German Evangelical Church."

But a number of pastors refused to submit to the imposed ideology of the new Reich Church. Niemöller—although he had originally been a Nazi sympathizer—and like-minded ministers formed the Emergency League of Pastors in 1933, and in the following year established an independent church administration under the name of the German Confessional Church. The Confessionals refused to give the oath of allegiance to Hitler, required of all members of the Reich Church. They rejected the application of authoritarian principles within the church as well as the heathenish philosophy of the Nazis. By 1936, the fight between the regime and the Confessional Church was in high gear. Pastors were arrested in great numbers, and their religious activities were curtailed wherever possible. In 1937, Niemöller disappeared into a concentration camp from which, with the exception of a short interval, he emerged only at the conclusion of World War II.

Persecution of ministers and the closing of churches reduced the activities of the Confessional Church, but it did not help Hanns Kerrl in building an effective, all-embracing Reich Church. This led Hitler gradually to abandon all expectation for using the church as a positive instrument of government and education. The regime turned to indoctrinating the youth and the masses with a new German creed, in which Hitler was the second Messiah. Children learned that "Jesus freed men from sin just as Hitler saved Germany from ruin"; that "Jesus worked for heaven, while Hitler works for the German earth." Faith in Hitler was given truly religious significance, and party rallies and pageants were turned into gigantic acts of devotion. Extremists even claimed that Christ had been a Nordic martyr, crucified by the Jews, an act now avenged by the Führer, whom these fanatics actually believed to be Christ in a second coming.

The *Führerprinzip*

Totalitarianism on the scale practiced by the Nazis required effective organization and unquestioned obedience within the hierarchical scale. Through their myriad organizations, the leaders of the party achieved hitherto inconceivable control over the life of the nation. National Socialism in fact represented the militarization of all life. The state demanded full obedience.

and directed the individual in his work and leisure, his social, cultural, economic, and political activities. To establish lines of command, a pyramid of *Führer* was fashioned, from Adolf Hitler down to the lowest block warden, and at all levels of the ladder, obedience was stressed as a sacred duty.

While there was some semblance of collective leadership among the party bigwigs, Hitler stood far above the rest in the minds and affection of most Germans. He alone held in his hands all the vital powers. He was president—a title he never used—and chancellor; he was chief legislator, chief executive, and supreme judge—the division among the three branches having been abolished; he was head of the only legal political party and commander in chief of the armed forces. But more than all this, he was *der Führer,* the well-nigh infallible symbol of the race and the nation, the embodiment of the collective will. Some worshipers journeyed to Berchtesgaden to fill urns with earth on which the Führer might have stepped.

Hitler displayed tremendous self-assurance and an uncanny intuition—although some say that he actually suffered from a persecution complex and owed his success principally to good luck. Whatever his psychological aberrations, he was remarkably gifted for his chosen profession. He had stupendous oratorical gifts with which he swayed the multitudes and imbued in his audience the same fanatical devotion to his cause that he himself practiced. A vegetarian who loved Wagner's music but hated ordinary leisure and recreation, Hitler lived on a strange mixture of emotion and logic. He was no intellectual, in whatever sense the word is used. Success made him feel and act almost like a prophet, and one wonders whether his rage against those who disobeyed his will was not inspired by the conviction of his own infallibility.

Hitler believed that the end justified the means. He displayed no scruples, no political or moral principles. Only the ultimate goal counted, and could be attained through any opportune action. "I will do anything to facilitate the success of my policy," he announced, adding characteristically; "Why should I not make an agreement in good faith today and unhesitatingly break it tomorrow, if the future of the German people demands it?"

Among the echelon of secondary *Führer,* many occupied multiple posts, so that the ruling clique was surprisingly small. Göring, for example, headed the Reichstag, supervised the Four-Year Plan, commanded the air force, acted as minister of forestry and hunting, and later became a member of the cabinet council, besides discharging other tasks. Himmler ran the SS and the Gestapo, later commanded all military units inside Germany, and became Reich commissioner for "safeguarding German nationality." The party hierarchy consisted largely of lower-middle-class discontents who had used the party and the National Socialist revolution to emerge as *Bonzen* (which might be translated as "rowdy *nouveaux riches* with abusive political power). But a surprising number were university graduates and former high school teachers. Although most of those in the party hierarchy were convinced and devoted Nazis, there were the inevitable opportunists who climbed on the band wagon.

Below the hierarchy lay the masses

who made the movement possible. Despite their lower-class origin, most of the minor leaders felt contempt for the people at large, in whose name they supposedly ruled. Obedience was all that mattered; mutual respect was of secondary importance. As Goebbels noted: "The strength of a political party does not depend on the mental prowess of its members, but rather on their disciplined obedience."

Propaganda and Education

To weld the nation into flag-waving frenzy, the Nazis employed terror, propaganda, and educational devices with consummate efficiency. Hitler had predicted in 1923: "We will unleash a storm! People shall not sleep; they shall know that a thunderstorm is brewing!" In *Mein Kampf,* he had outlined most of the methods later adopted by Goebbels in his position as minister for propaganda and for the enlightenment of the people. Hitler advised that "all propaganda . . . must be at the level of understanding of the least intelligent." The greater the lie, he thought, the more readily the masses will swallow it, especially if it is accompanied by judiciously applied terror and intimidation. The Führer himself gave the example by pronouncing everything with utter conviction, and labeling all whose views differed as either stupid or criminal.

Through the Reich Chamber of Culture *(Reichskulturkammer)*, Goebbels supervised press, radio, and cinema, as well as literature, the theater, music, painting, and sculpture. Even architectural styles had to conform to the new ideal of regularity and massiveness. Writers and artists who did not wish to produce National Socialistic art either emigrated or grew silent. The Nazis even sought to purify the German language by eradicating foreign words where possible, and gradually developed their own vocabulary befitting the national struggle.

Above all, the educational system was revamped to fit the "new order." Special SS schools were created to foster a new elite. The staffs and students of existing universities and schools were purged of uncooperative elements. Textbooks were rewritten and new courses were added, such as geopolitics. Physical education was transformed into defense science. Instead of pitching balls, the young were taught to lob hand grenades; hide and seek games were turned into training in camouflage. And when not attending classes, young people were indoctrinated through various youth organizations.

In the educational process, Hitler was not interested in "improvement of the mind," but in developing "instinct, determination, and energy." Youth was to rediscover its "primitive nature." Frick insisted that the main purpose of schools was to produce students "whose thoughts and actions are dedicated to serving the nation and to self-sacrifice, if needed." With all means of communication controlled by the state, with the young indoctrinated to distrust, and if necessary to inform on their parents, young Germans were brought up to know little else but National Socialist morality and aims.

National Socialist Economics

Gleichschaltung was also the watchword for the national economy. But whereas most other Nazi accomplishments were of dubious worth, their achievements in the area of economics were outstanding, even phenomenal. By using a mixture of state socialism and free enterprise, under strict government control, by ruthless economic planning, and by trampling on the rights of "all enemies of the state," the Nazis pulled Germany out of its economic slump. It was largely Hitler's success in providing a good measure of prosperity and stability that accounted for his popularity and persuaded so many to overlook the sinister aspects of his regime.

Industry and agriculture, labor and management, transport, trade, and communications—all were reorganized and supervised so as to strengthen the state. Using the German Labor Front as a gigantic superstructure, its administrator, Robert Ley (1890–1945), tried to weld labor and management into a community of interests. Within each industrial enterprise, the owner or manager (as *Betriebsführer* or leader of the establishment) was made responsible to the German people for his firm's contribution to the reconstruction of the Reich.

Under the direction of Schacht—made president of the Reichsbank in March 1933 and minister of economics in August 1934—and later of Göring, a Four-Year Plan was devised with the announced aim of helping the peasants and workers. The eradication of unemployment initially received priority in government planning, and was effected with astonishing success. Large-scale public works projects, such as the building of superhighways, huge sports arenas, monumental government edifices, and public housing, were inaugurated. Economic growth was stimulated, especially in heavy industry and the production of armaments. Labor camps were set up and then converted into labor service battalions, to which all young men and women had to contribute a year of compulsory service. Jews, Communists, "undesirables," and many women were dismissed from their jobs, while more and more people were enrolled in full-time paramilitary or other party organizations. From 6 million unemployed in January 1933, the number dropped to 4 million by December of that year, to 2.6 million by December 1934, and to less than 1 million by the end of 1937. In 1938, when the huge fortifications were being constructed in the west, and rearmament was in full swing, there was a labor shortage.

Within the limits set by government requirements and the Four-Year Plan, the big industrialists enjoyed considerable power, prestige, and profits. During the early years of the regime those who had helped Hitler's rise had reason to feel satisfied with their decision. Although the government controlled prices and wages, and reduced profits to some extent by levying special taxes, the industrialists felt safe from the threat of general nationalization, were freed from labor troubles, and were guaranteed a booming market. The production of basic materials rose sharply. Between 1933 and 1938, hard-coal output increased from 110 to 186 million tons; soft coal, from 126 to 195 million tons; and raw steel from 7.6 to 22.7 million tons.

To bind the workers firmly to the regime and indoctrinate them with National Socialist ideology, the government asserted complete control over their economic existence. The state administered all welfare and social insurance plans as well as compulsory savings programs, set wages, supervised working conditions, and had arbitrary power to assign workers to jobs. Even vacations were made compulsory. The government established a special agency, Strength through Joy (*Kraft durch Freude*), to organize and supervise the workers' leisure time. Film showings or theatrical productions, family camps in the mountains or vacations at the seashore, ocean cruises on government-owned Strength-through-Joy liners, all accompanied by free indoctrination, were made "compulsorily" available.

Hitler also sought to make Germany as self-sufficient as possible. Food imports were reduced so that more foreign credits could be diverted to the importation of basic raw materials—used at first for industrial expansion and later for strategic stockpiling. The invention and production of synthetics were pushed with deliberate speed, particularly in the fields of motor fuels, buna (a substitute for rubber), and artificial fibers. When the Second Four-Year Plan was inaugurated in 1936, Hitler stipulated as its primary purpose the achievement of economic autarky. In a secret memorandum, he expressed his conviction that Germany would soon be at war, and that economic mobilization, regardless of the cost, had to proceed hand in hand with the strengthening of the *Wehrmacht* and the building of German armaments, so as "to make Germany the first military power on earth." Production of food as well as of synthetics and basic machinery, rationing and allocation of quotas, regulation of imports and exports were now oriented to rendering Germany as independent as possible of shipments from abroad, in case war should entail another blockade. The Second Four-Year Plan thus inaugurated the period of "guns rather than butter." In a speech much ridiculed because of Göring's own obesity, he asked the nation: "Shall we import lard or metal ores? Let me tell you: preparedness makes us powerful. Butter merely makes us fat!" Although he was a nationalist, Schacht resented the increased political interference in economics involved in this plan. In November 1937, he resigned as minister of economics and was replaced by Funk.

But Schacht remained as president of the Reichsbank to continue his task of financing Hitler's ventures. As he had in 1923, he devised ingenious schemes that at first produced astonishing results. Germany became a closed economy. All exports and imports were handled by the government, all private fortunes abroad had to be placed at its disposal under penalty of death. Under this system, the government alone held foreign currencies and foreign credits, which it could allocate to strategic imports. Where possible, barter was used between Germany and foreign countries, since Germany was perennially short of gold and hard currencies. Heavy machinery, precision instruments, chemicals, transport equipment, and other manufactured goods were exchanged for food and needed raw materials. By being sealed off from the money markets of the world, the German mark could be kept at a fictitious level and thus ensure relative financial stability at home. The barter system and governmental control of all foreign trade also permitted Hitler to initiate economic warfare. By judiciously buying up major crops, often at prices above the world market—particularly in Greece, Yugoslavia, Rumania, and Bulgaria—Germany was able to apply increasing politico-economic pressure on the states of southeastern Europe, a pressure that helped expand German influence.

To obtain the required funds for internal spending, Schacht and the government resorted to various devices. Special contributions and even forced loans were frequently demanded. The property of Communists and Jews was gradually confiscated. Patriotic citizens were enjoined to surrender their gold rings and jewelry. Special extra postage stamps were sold to raise funds for social services. Yet in the long run, the expedient resorted to was to print more paper currency to cover the yearly deficit. Because prices and wages were fixed, the mark retained its apparent stability. But as government expenditures continued to increase, especially with the heavy armaments program after 1936, and as revenue remained more or less stationary, Schacht warned that it would be impossible to keep up the artificial value of the currency forever. In January 1939, he was dismissed from his post as president of the Reichsbank—although he continued to serve in the government as minister without portfolio until 1943. The printing of money continued, and with it the devaluation of the mark. By 1945, it had depreciated to about 1 percent of its 1933 value.

HITLER'S SUCCESS IN FOREIGN AFFAIRS

In *Mein Kampf,* Hitler defined the task of foreign policy as the "creation of a healthy, viable, and natural balance between the size and growth of a country's population on the one hand and the size and quality of its land on the other." As the particular goal of National Socialism, he stipulated the acquisition of territory as required by the German people. He predicted that such action would demand sacrifices in blood, since "only the might of a victorious sword" could solve the territorial question. He advised that Germany should seek land not in colonies, but "almost exclusively in Europe." "We shall take up where they [our forefathers] stopped six centuries ago," he wrote, "and look for land in the east. Land can be gained primarily in Russia and in the border states dominated by her."

His more immediate aims, proclaimed in almost every speech in the 1920s and reiterated after his assumption of power, were the abrogation of the Treaty of Versailles, the breaking of Germany's isolation, and its establishment as one of the dominant powers in the world.

To achieve his aims, Hitler conducted a highly successful, intensely active foreign policy. By keeping Germany constantly on the diplomatic offensive while lulling his opponents into a false sense of security, he succeeded beyond all expectations. Like a master tactician, he knew when it was opportune to shift from stern demands to holding out the olive branch. He frequently proclaimed his love of peace. He announced in 1933 that all outstanding questions could be settled "peacefully and by treaties." "No war," he intoned, "even if successful, is worth the sacrifices." His demands were clothed in reasonable principles. Germany deserved equality of rights with other nations, and the theory of self-determination for all peoples should be applied to solve disputed boundaries.

In the conduct of foreign affairs, most of which he directed personally, he was helped by his fanaticism and his disregard for international morality. He was convinced that France would forever remain the deadly enemy of Germany, and constructed his policy accordingly. He felt equally certain that Russia, according to him dominated by Jews, would disintegrate, because the Jewish race was incapable of building a state. He could not conceive of alliances for the preservation of peace. "An alliance not aimed at war is senseless and without value," he wrote in *Mein Kampf*. "Alliances are only made for battle." In a sense, his pseudo Darwinism dominated his concept of international relations. Since all life was built on struggle, there was "really little difference between peace and war." Opportunism, guided by his intuition, dictated much of his action. "I am prepared to guarantee all frontiers and make nonaggression pacts and alliances with anybody," he once stated. "It would be stupid not to employ such measures merely because one might possibly one day have to break such solemn promises."

His success was, of course, also aided by the complicated international situation of the 1930s and the incredibly shortsighted selfishness of the nations. After the brief era of international cooperation from 1925 to 1930, during which statesmen had hoped to solve all problems at the conference table, the nations retreated to isolation and distrust. Each sought its own salvation, much to the benefit of the revisionist powers: Germany, Italy, and Japan.

Abrogation of Versailles

The first major breach of the Treaty of Versailles was made in October 1933, when Germany walked out of the sixty-nation disarmament conference in Geneva and renounced its membership in the League of Nations. To be sure, the disarmament talks were not likely to produce tangible results, and the League had been discredited by its failure to prevent the Japanese conquest of Manchuria in 1931. But Germany's action signified that Hitler intended to rearm the nation. As an official excuse, Hitler complained that although in 1932 the Allies had agreed in principle to grant Germany equal rights, they were apparently no longer willing to abide by this agreement—because of his assumption of power. He called this a "discrimination dishonoring the German people," who no longer wished to remain a second-class nation. At the same time, the Führer stressed his "unshakable love of peace and his readiness to negotiate," and boasted that a plebiscite would prove the German people's "concept of honor." In November, the Germans were asked to vote on the question of withdrawal from the League. The referendum resulted in an affirmative vote of 95 percent.

In January 1935, according to the schedule contained in the Treaty of Versailles, a plebiscite was held in the Saar to determine whether its inhabitants wished to remain under the government of the League of Nations, join France, or return to German sovereignty. Voting was preceded by a violent campaign, in which the Nazis displayed to the world their virulence and fanaticism. Since most Saarlanders spoke German, and Germany appeared economically more prosperous than France, the outcome was a foregone conclusion. Yet the lopsided result of the plebiscite, supervised by the League, with 90 percent favoring Germany, surprised the world.

Jubilant over this success, Hitler assured France that the German-French border was now settled, and that he renounced forever Germany's rights to Alsace-Lorraine, since he wished to spare Germany and Europe the bloody sacrifices of a war. He then launched his next step in the dismantling of Versailles. In March 1935, he publicly denounced the disarmament clauses of the treaty. A special law was promulgated, introducing universal military training and calling for an army of thirty-six divisions. At the same time, Hitler announced the official creation of a German air force. In reality, Hitler's announcements were merely a public avowal of an established fact. Secret rearmament had already brought the army to the proposed future strength; according to most estimates, the German air force at the time was as strong as England's.

The reaction of the powers to Hitler's unilateral destruction of Versailles revealed their disunity. They protested, but took no action. Italy, France, and England conferred at Stresa in Italy to discuss whether to seek safety in pacts with Germany or to take joint action against it. But this so-called Stresa Front produced no tangible results, and, in the end, each nation went its own way. France concluded an alliance with Russia, a step it had contemplated for some time in order to re-establish its traditional two-front pressure on Germany. France's answer to Hitler was to seek reinsurance rather than to deal with him. Italy, about to start its conquest of Abyssinia, preferred to remain completely neutral. England, however, decided to come to terms with Germany, at least in the area that concerned it most. In June, England concluded the Anglo-German naval agreement, allowing Germany to build up to 35 percent of Britain's tonnage. No limitations on submarines were included in the pact. England's accommodation with Germany boded ill for the peace of Europe. By sanctioning the construction of a German navy, no matter of what tonnage, it admitted that the Treaty of Versailles had in effect become invalid. Moreover, England took this step without consulting the other signatories to the Versailles Treaty, even though the pact was bound to worry Russia and France. The naval agreement abandoned the Baltic Sea to the German fleet, much to the dismay of the Soviet Union, and forced France to enter the naval race in order to keep up with Germany. Britain's action was also shortsighted in other respects. By allowing the recreation of a strong German navy, the pact forced the Anglo-French fleets to concentrate more in the North Sea, thereby abandoning the Far East to Japan.

The disunity of the Allies and their preoccupation with the Ethiopian crisis emboldened Hitler to undertake the final scrapping of the Versailles Treaty in March 1936. Using as a pretext the need for securing Germany's border against the new Franco-Russian alliance, he repudiated the Locarno Pacts and sent his army to reoccupy the Rhineland, which, according to the Versailles Treaty, was to remain demilitarized. Again he held the sword in one hand, the olive branch in the other. While German troops marched toward the Rhine, Hitler harangued the world by radio, boasting of the strength of the German "defensive forces." At the same time, he offered to come to terms with the powers. If the world would not accept his action, which he said was designed merely to gain equal rights for Germany, he proposed a demilitarized zone on *both* sides of the Franco-German border—a suggestion the French were bound to reject since it would require dismantling their Maginot Line. He also suggested a twenty-five-year nonaggression pact with France and Belgium, nonaggression pacts with the eastern states, and Germany's re-entry into the League of Nations.

Once again Hitler was successful. Britain, busy in the Mediterranean and increasingly pacifist in attitude, refused to consider countermeasures. Some Frenchmen desired action, but feared their army might be inadequate for the job of expelling the Germans from the Rhineland without full-scale mobilization, which might unleash a general war. According to testimony presented at the Nuremberg War Crimes Trials (see pages 608 ff), some German generals apparently felt that even a minor military demonstration by the French would have sent the German army in headlong retreat, since Hitler's army was as yet more bluff than reality. The question was finally turned over to the League of Nations, which found Germany guilty of violating the Treaties of Versailles and Locarno, but took no further action.

The End of German Isolation

While gradually dismantling the Versailles Treaty, Hitler was also busy strengthening Germany by expanding its influence abroad through various official and secret means. Besides economic penetration, the Nazis used what came to be known as fifth columns, local Nazi parties or organizations friendly to Germany. They received organizational help, financial support, and propaganda from Germany. Overseas, as, for example, in the United States, these pro-German associations never acquired much importance. In Europe, however, especially in the states bordering on Germany or in others with German-speaking minorities, local Nazi units became important instruments for spreading German influence. Austria, Czechoslovakia, Hungary, and Rumania were particularly affected by this internal subversion. Danzig, although officially remaining a free city under auspices of the League, was actually slowly taken over by local Nazis, and for all intents and purposes incorporated into the Nazi system long before the official annexation of 1939.

RELATIONS WITH POLAND AND RUSSIA

In order to concentrate on the opportune direction of the moment, Hitler found it advantageous to make temporary settlements in other areas. While working against the West on the abrogation of the Versailles Treaty, he found it expedient to avoid all tension in the east. In January 1934, he negotiated a ten-year nonaggression pact with Poland. The two nations, despite their previous distrust, agreed to maintain the existing borders and not to use force against each other under any circumstances. Since even the Weimar Republic had refused to accept the permanent loss of the eastern lands, it should have been obvious that Hitler's guarantee represented at the most a temporary expedient. Yet the Poles, wedged between Communist and Nazi states, accepted the pact at face value and relaxed their reliance on France. Hitler thus succeeded in undermining France's eastern security system. When in September of the same year, the French tried to bolster their power by proposing to guarantee a mutual security pact among Germany, Russia, Poland, Czechoslovakia, Finland, and the three Baltic states, Hitler brushed them aside. Without equality in armaments, he argued, Germany could not afford to become involved in eastern conflicts.

German relations with Russia were similarly opportunistic. Despite Hitler's savage suppression of Communism and his stated intention of conquering Russian territories, commercial relations between the two nations continued to flourish as they had in the 1920s. For a while, even their military collaboration was retained. Hitler's stand was ambivalent. He pretended to be not anti-Russian but only anti-Communist. In 1936, he told the Reichstag: "I have never refused to collaborate with Russia for peace; I am only opposed to Bolshevik expansion." But a boastful anti-Communist stand was not meant solely for internal propaganda. He also hoped to attract to his campaign other nations, particularly England. He publicly requested others to help him "preserve European culture and civilization" and safeguard Europe from the "incursion of this destructive Asiatic ideology which topples all traditional values."

Worried by Japan's expansion in Manchuria and Germany's renascence, Russia joined the League of Nations in 1934 and became the most ardent advocate of collective security against the revisionist powers. In 1935, Communists everywhere were instructed by Moscow to abandon their traditional boycott of bourgeois politics and to cooperate with all anti-Fascist parties. As a result, so-called popular front governments—comprising moderate parties, Socialists, and Communists—came to the fore in various countries with the aim of stemming the rising tide of Fascism and National Socialism.

ATTEMPTS AT UNION WITH AUSTRIA

In *Mein Kampf,* Hitler had stated that "related blood belongs in a common *Reich.*" One of his proposed tasks, therefore, was to unite Germany and Austria. During the early 1920s, the Austrian Socialists and liberals, mostly concentrated in Vienna, had also desired *Anschluss* with the Weimar Republic. The Austrian Catholics and the conservatives of the provinces had opposed it. But the question had remained academic, in view of the Allies' refusal to sanction such a union. During the late 1920s, Austria had become less and less stable. Economically it was always on the verge of bankruptcy. Street fighting was common. Three main groups, each with its own private army, vied for power: the Christian Socialists—growing daily more conservative; the Socialists; and the Nazis.

In 1932, the office of prime minister had been assumed by Engelbert Dollfuss (1892–1934), nominally a Christian Socialist. By this time, the Socialists of Vienna no longer desired union with Germany, whereas the Austrian Nazis and conservatives worked for it assiduously. An authoritarian at heart and an admirer of Mussolini, Dollfuss abrogated most constitutional freedoms in 1933 and ended parliamentarianism. To safeguard Austrian independence, he outlawed the Austrian Nazi party. Hitler retaliated by closing the flow of German tourists to Austria. By 1934, Dollfuss decided to establish a dictatorship, since he equally hated the Socialists on the one hand and the Austrian Nazis on the other. He outlawed all political parties except his own Fatherland Front, promulgated a semi-Fascistic constitution, and made an agreement with Mussolini designed to protect Austria's independence. A protest rising by the Socialists was quelled with much bloodshed.

Austria's turmoil and the fear that Dollfuss' independent dictatorship might be successful goaded Hitler into premature action. Encouraged by Berlin and more or less directed from Munich, the Austrian Nazis attempted a *coup d'état* in July 1934. They seized some government buildings and the radio station in Vienna and murdered Dollfuss, but failed to gain control of the government. Since Mussolini immediately sent troops to the Austrian border in order to help the Austrians against Germany, Hitler disavowed the entire affair and gave no further support to his fellow Nazis in Austria.

After the failure of this putsch, Dollfuss' successor, Kurt von Schuschnigg (1897–) pursued the same dictatorial policies. Like Germany, Austria began to rearm, and as a safeguard against German annexation, there was even talk of restoring the Hapsburgs. But Hitler had learned that he could not absorb Austria without first coming to terms with Italy; hence he decided on a temporary policy of conciliation. In 1935, he told the Reichstag: "Germany has no intention of interfering in Austrian affairs or of annexing Austria." What he wanted were merely "self-determination"—a principle Hitler could easily manipulate to Germany's advantage. In 1936, when he was eager to effect a *rapprochement* with Italy, he even concluded a treaty with Austria recognizing its sovereignty and promising not to interfere in its internal affairs nor to help the Austrian Nazis, provided Austria would always act "in a manner behoving a German state." The latter clause affords an interesting insight into Hitler's definition of sovereignty. The treaty of 1936, at any rate, was designed by Hitler merely as a stopgap. Once Germany's friendship with Italy was cemented, Schuschnigg's position rapidly became hopeless. The Austrian Nazis grew in strength and prepared for the eventual *Anschluss,* which took place in 1938.

ITALO-GERMAN FRIENDSHIP The Austrian question and Mussolini's growing influence over the Balkans, an area on which Hitler had his own designs, made Italo-German cooperation more and more important for Germany. Ideologically, the two dictators shared many beliefs. Above all, both Italy and Germany were revisionist powers, dissatisfied with the results of World War I. But by 1933, Mussolini was an established dictator, whereas Hitler was still a parvenu. Mussolini represented an Allied country of the wartime coalition; his ambitions lay largely overseas and not in Europe. Hitler's demands for the union of all German-speaking peoples might be aimed at the South Tyrol, which Italy had absorbed as a result of World War I. Consequently, Mussolini sided with England and France during the early years of Hitler's regime. When Hitler visited Mussolini in June 1934, presumably to ascertain Italy's attitude toward Austria, no agreement between the two powers seemed possible. During the Vienna Putsch, Mussolini remained anti-German, and in the following spring, when Germany announced its rearmament, he joined England and France in the anti-German Stresa Front.

The turning point came with the Abyssinian crisis in the fall of 1935. When Mussolini, after much hesitation and many negotiations, launched his invasion of Ethiopia in October, the League condemned Italy as an aggressor and imposed sanctions. But Germany, as a nonmember, continued its commercial support of Italy. Hitler made it clear to Mussolini that he could count on German benevolence during this crisis, and the Duce vowed that he would never forget that Germany did not join in the sanctions against Italy.

In 1936, Italo-German friendship ripened. The German-Austrian Treaty reassured Mussolini's fears, and Hitler's official recognition of Italy's new empire in Ethiopia pleased his vanity. Above all, the outbreak of the Spanish Civil War helped to cement the friendship between the two countries. Italian ground troops and German technicians and pilots cooperated in Spain in support of Franco. Italian relations with England and France, already embittered by the sanctions provoked by the Abyssinian War, further deteriorated, since the Anglo-French favored nonintervention in Spain. Italy was thus thrown into the waiting arms of Germany. In October 1936, Italy's foreign minister visited Berlin to sign various cooperative agreements. Thus the beginnings of the Rome–Berlin axis were laid.

Further collaboration in Spain thenceforth drew the two dictators closer together. In September 1937, Mussolini visited Berlin, where he praised the renascence of Italy and Germany, and professed that they shared the same aims of national independence and greatness. Although Mussolini, temporarily satiated by the absorption of Abyssinia, still felt tempted, as he said, to jump to the "other side of the barricades" and side with England and France, continued friction in Spain brought him more and more firmly into the German camp.

While wooing Italy, Hitler succeeded in getting other friends. A likely partner was Japan, which had renounced the disarmament pacts and the naval limitations, had flouted the League of Nations, and was conducting an expansionist war in China. In November 1936, Tokyo and Berlin signed the Anti-Comintern Pact. Officially the two states agreed merely to "keep informed about the activities of the Communist International and to consult about necessary defensive measures." The pact also stated that the signatories would welcome other states whose "internal peace was threatened through the subversive activities of Communism." In reality, the pact was directed against Russia, located between the two revisionist powers.

A year later, in 1937, Italy agreed to become a signatory to the Anti-Comintern Pact. The revisionist powers were drawing closer together. Hitler could now declare: "Germany today stands no longer alone! First a European axis, now a great world-wide triangle!"

21

War and Axis Supremacy, 1938–1942

THE TURNING POINT

The 1930s witnessed many international crises: the rape of Manchuria and Abyssinia, the Civil War in Spain, and Hitler's scrapping of the Versailles Treaty. Confronted with these emergencies, the League of Nations proved ineffectual and collective security collapsed. Yet until 1937, a major conflict seemed evitable. The year 1938, however, marked a turning point: war was no longer avoidable. Japan's renewed invasion of China in 1937, followed in 1938 and 1939 by Germany's absorption of Austria and Czechoslovakia, Hungary's annexation of Ruthenia and parts of Slovakia, and Italy's seizure of Albania, marked the opening of the more active expansionist drive by the revisionist powers. Despite these nations' reiterations of their love of peace, the question was in reality no longer *whether* war would come, but *how soon.*

The war crimes trials at Nuremberg after World War II, with their public revelation of Hitler's aggressive plans, reinforced the conclusion that the Nazis were guilty of starting the war. The unbelievable horrors committed by the Germans in butchering millions in extermination camps buttressed this conviction. Although this judgment is unquestionably correct, it bolstered an unwarranted attitude of self-righteous innocence on the part of other nations and governments. One must not forget that the French occupation of the Ruhr, Japanese actions in Manchuria and China, and the Italian conquest of Ethiopia had demonstrated that the use of force remained an acceptable solution to international problems. Unquestionably, primary blame for the outbreak of war in the summer of 1939 must rest with Hitler. But British and French vacillation between fear of fascism and dread of communism, the indifference of the nations toward Japanese and Italian aggression, the readiness of the powers, particularly Russia, to make pacts with aggressors, made them also culpable to a certain degree.

That the years 1937–1938 were the

turning point is evident from the continuing internal political crisis in France, which made it incapable of resolute independent action, as well as from the fact that the idealistic and pacifistic Neville Chamberlain became prime minister of England. Inside Germany, the turning point there resulted from Hitler's personal conviction in late 1937 that the period of preparation had ended and the time of action was approaching. The Anti-Comintern triangle of Germany, Japan, and Italy gave him confidence of foreign support; above all, the progress of economic reconstruction and of rearmament made him feel better prepared to face a possible trial of arms.

The Progress of German Rearmament

Rearmament had started with Hitler's seizure of power, but had been given full priority only in the Second Four-Year Plan of 1936. In 1937 alone, Germany spent about 4.5 billion dollars on armaments, three times as much as the combined total for Britain and France. In February 1938, Hitler announced to the Reichstag that the German army—he liked to call it the *Friedensheer* (peace force)—was built. "A gigantic air force protects our homeland, a new sea power our shores," and he boasted of his accomplishments in increasing the industrial production requisite for executing such unparalleled rearmament. This speech was designed to impress his own people as well as to intimidate other powers, particularly Austria. Many observers thought he was bluffing, and most informed German officers believed Germany insufficiently prepared for any conflict. Hitler, of course, did not mean that the task of rearming was completed and no further increase in armaments needed. The feverish build-up continued all through 1938. But his speech and actions revealed his conviction that the time for greater risks had come.

Despite frequent public protestations of his peaceful intentions, Hitler and his military planning staff had made preparations for war from the very beginning of his regime. By 1936, he was trying to convince his generals of the inevitability of war. In 1937, war plans became more specific. In June, Hitler ordered continuation of secret mobilization in case force were needed to crush Austria. The armed forces were ordered to be in position "suddenly to start a war and surprise the enemy."

In November 1937, Hitler held a secret conference with the leaders of the armed forces to inform them of his decisions regarding war. He argued that "the future of the German race of 85 million" rested exclusively on a solution of Germany's space requirements. Attainment of autarky in food, he asserted, was impossible on the basis of the arable land available in Germany, and reliance on world trade would place the Germans at the mercy of the British fleet. Hence, for the time being, Germany had to seek space on the Continent. "For Germany, the question is where can the greatest gains be made with the least risk." Since "history has proved that expansion always involves risks and requires the smashing of resistance," Hitler was convinced that "only force could solve the German question." He then laid out a timetable for this application of force. Under normal conditions, the action was to be launched at the latest in the period 1943–1945, before the armaments race might give an advantage to the opponents. But if social unrest in France should suddenly paralyze the French army, or other unforeseen conditions arose, the German forces were to be prepared at any time to crush Czechoslovakia and Austria in a simultaneous, lightning blow. It is interesting that when Generals Werner von Blomberg and Werner von Fritsch (1880–1939) cautioned Hitler at this meeting that France and England might fight and that the Czech fortifications were formidable, Hitler brushed them aside with the assertion that France and England would not enter hostilities, that they had at any rate "written off" the Czechs and "become reconciled to the fact that this question would one day be cleaned up by Germany."

Hitler's Control over the Military

To be able to act ruthlessly and promptly in the crises he planned to unleash, Hitler decided to eliminate the hesitators in his entourage and to subordinate the *Wehrmacht* more completely to the party. "The tasks of the future," he explained to the Reichstag, "demand a closer bond between the political and military power of the Reich." Relations between the NSDAP and the army had remained cool, even after Hitler had become supreme commander in 1934. Jealousy and distrust among the SS, the SA, and *Wehrmacht* had continued. Universal military service and the expansion of the armed forces had helped swamp the lower ranks with properly indoctrinated recruits. But among the officers, various attitudes prevailed. A few were so grateful to Hitler for freeing the army from the restrictions of the Versailles Treaty and helping to rebuild it to its former status that they became enthusiastic National Socialists. Many were simply opportunistic fence sitters who hoped to keep the army out of politics and, although not convinced of the blessings of the new regime, went along with it. Minister of Defense General Blomberg, a member of the original cabinet of 1933, belonged to this category. He was no convinced National Socialist; yet he played along with Hitler and supported him in his speeches, as when he pronounced in 1937 that "the *Wehrmacht* is the bearer and herald of the National Socialist *Weltanschauung*. Jointly with the NSDAP, with which it is indissolubly intertwined, the army forms the fundamental backbone of the *Reich*." Most of the tradition-bound higher-ranking officer corps, however, maintained a distinct aloofness toward the rabble-rousing Führer and his mob rule.

At the beginning of February 1938, Hitler suddenly purged the government and the High Command. Baron von Neurath, the nationalistic but moderate foreign minister who had learned his diplomatic formulas under the Weimar Republic, was replaced by the former champagne salesman Joachim von Ribbentrop (1893–1946). An obsequious admirer of Hitler, Ribbentrop had worked for eight years as the Führer's trusted diplomatic errand boy, and had performed rather tactless service as German ambassador to the Court of St. James's. The change from Neurath to Ribbentrop, in fact, signified Hitler's personal assumption of complete control over foreign affairs.

At the same time, sixteen generals and many other high-ranking officers were relieved of their positions of command. The Ministry of Defense was abolished and its head, General Blomberg, was dismissed. In its place a new High Command of the Army (OKW) was created, nominally in charge of the compliant General Wilhelm Keitel (1882–1946), but in fact under the personal supervision of Hitler. Moreover, General Fritsch was relieved as head of the army and replaced by General Walther von Brauchitsch (1881–1948), who was known to be more subservient and reckless than his predecessor. In this drastic reorganization of the upper echelon of the armed forces, Hitler not only gained added control but also tried to humiliate the officer caste in order to make its members more pliable. As commander in chief of the armed forces, he had the power simply to dismiss Blomberg and Fritsch. Instead, with the aid of Himmler's Gestapo, he disgraced the former by revealing that his wife was once a prostitute, and falsely accused the latter of being a homosexual.

EXPANSION IN TIME OF PEACE

Having completed economic preparations and gained more direct control of the army, Hitler felt ready to strike his first expansionist blow. Despite the Austro-German Treaty of 1936, the Austrian Nazis had continued their agitation under orders from Berlin. Schuschnigg's dictatorial regime had grown increasingly feeble, since it lacked support both at home and abroad. Within Austria it faced the hostility of the Socialists and the Nazis. Moreover, it had been abandoned by Mussolini after his *rapprochement* with Hitler. Schuschnigg was finding it more and more difficult to cope with Nazi provocations. Since the contemplated remedy of a Hapsburg restoration seemed impossible, the hapless Austrian chancellor looked abroad for French and Czechoslovakian support. Fearing that Austria's isolation might be broken, Hitler decided on immediate action.

Anschluss with Austria

On February 12, 1938, Schuschnigg visited Hitler at Berchtesgaden, the Führer's mountain retreat. Instead of discussing mutual problems, Hitler treated the Austrian with insolence and presented an ultimatum. Austria was to grant amnesty to all imprisoned National Socialists and permit them to join the only legal party, the Fatherland Front. The attorney Arthur Seyss-Inquart (1892–1946), one of the leaders of the Austrian Nazis since 1931, was to be made minister of the interior. Schuschnigg felt compelled to agree to these demands, hopefully telling Hitler that he expected the Nazis to respect the Austrian constitution.

A month of deceit followed. On February 16, Seyss-Inquart was appointed Austrian minister of the interior, and thereby given control over the police forces. On February 19, the Austrian Nazis were again given freedom of action. Supported by Berlin, they at once fomented disorders and riots throughout the tiny republic. Publicly, Hitler proclaimed once more he contemplated "no intervention in Austria." Secretly, he ordered his army to get ready to invade "in order to re-establish in Austria constitutional conditions and prevent further violence against her pro-German population." Mussolini agreed in advance not to interfere and to accept the Brenner pass as the future common frontier between Italy and Germany. So confident was Hitler that France and England would abstain from action that he told the army to take no special security precautions on the German frontiers.

Unable to control the increasing violence, Schuschnigg made a belated attempt to rally the country behind him. He appealed to the workers, whom his dictatorship had estranged, and offered to take Socialists into his cabinet—a proposal that Hitler labeled a violation of the Berchtesgaden agreement. As a last resort, Schuschnigg called for a plebiscite on March 13, in which the people were to decide for or against "a free and German, independent and social, Christian and united Austria." Hitler feared that the outcome of this plebiscite might be unfavorable to his own plans. Göring at once notified Schuschnigg through Seyss-Inquart that the plebiscite violated the Berchtesgaden agreement, that Germany had lost confidence in the Austrian chancellor, and that he should resign immediately and turn his office over to Seyss-Inquart. Noncompliance within an hour would result in a military invasion of Austria.

To avoid bloodshed, Schuschnigg resigned on the evening of March 11. Seyss-Inquart became the new chancellor, and Göring dictated to him the text of a telegram he was to send at once to Berlin "requesting the German government to dispatch German troops as soon as possible" in order to help the new Austrian provisional government "restore law and order." At dawn on the following day, German troops crossed the frontier and rapidly occupied the whole country without encountering opposition. On March 13, Seyss-Inquart passed a law abolishing Austrian sovereignty and making Austria an integral part of Germany. A day later, Hitler made his triumphal entry into Vienna. Thereafter the *Gleichschaltung* of Austria was accomplished with all speed. Members of the opposition were arrested; Schuschnigg himself disappeared into a concentration camp—from which he emerged only in 1945; and Jews were beaten. Nazi law, Nazi economics, Nazi education were introduced. Hitler proclaimed in Salzburg that he felt "convinced that he could rule Austria better than Schuschnigg or any one else." On April 10, the Austrians were asked in a plebiscite whether they approved of the merger with Germany. That 99.75 percent of the electorate gave their *ex post facto* approval of the *Anschluss* showed that Nazi intimidation was highly effective or that the Austrians expected miraculous economic benefits from union with Germany.

The seizure of Austria gave Germany an addition of seven million people and valuable raw materials, as well as greater influence over the Balkans and a common border with Fascist Italy. Moreover, it proved the effectiveness of Nazi methods—fomenting disorders in a neighboring country in order to have an excuse for sending in troops to re-establish order. The formula was to be used repeatedly until the outbreak of World War II.

The reaction of the powers to Hitler's coup was symptomatic. No more than whispered protests were heard from Paris and London. When interpellated in the House of Commons concerning Britain's inaction, Chamberlain replied that the government's only obligation toward Austria had been a commitment to consult with the

French and the Italians in the event of a threat to Austrian independence. He boasted that "we have fully discharged this pledge of consultation."

Annexation of the Sudetenland

Intent on retaining the initiative, Hitler eagerly rushed from crisis to crisis. Barely two weeks after the fall of Austria, he promised Konrad Henlein (1898–1945), the leader of the Nazis in Czechoslovakia, "to solve the Czech problem in the near future." The solution Hitler had in mind was the destruction of this relatively wealthy and rather heavily armed democracy that had shown surprising viability since its founding in 1918, despite the fact that it embraced countless mutually antagonistic minority groups. Under the guidance of President Eduard Beneš, Czechoslovakia had become an important link in the security systems of France and the Soviet Union and therefore presented an impediment to Hitler's projected eastward expansion.

Along the mountainous borders of western Bohemia lived some 3.5 million German-speaking Sudetens, who constituted a useful lever for Hitler's plan to annihilate the entire Czech state. By professing to protect kindred blood from alien oppression, he could advance his project under the banner of self-determination. As Seyss-Inquart had done in Austria, the Czech Konrad Henlein took his orders from Berlin. The success of the *Anschluss* made Henlein eager to try similar methods in the Sudetenland. At the end of March 1938, Henlein conferred in Berlin with Hitler and Ribbentrop. Jointly they elaborated the demands the Sudetens were to make on the Prague government. These included complete autonomy for the Sudetenland and a revision of Czechoslovakia's anti-German foreign policy. But Henlein was advised not to conclude agreements with the Czech government "which might leave the impression abroad that a solution is possible": no solution short of annexation was agreeable to Hitler.

THE FIRST CZECH CRISIS Confident of Germany's support and secretly aided by the German ambassador in Prague, Henlein publicly presented his program to the Czech government. Its repection by Beneš marked the opening of the first Czech crisis, April–May 1938. The Sudeten Germans provoked disorders, and England offered to mediate between Henlein and Beneš. Noting that Germany was concentrating troops on the Czech border, Beneš ordered partial mobilization. War or peace seemed to hang in the balance. By May, the crisis was at its height. England promised aid to France in case of "an unprovoked attack by Germany," but made it clear that it had no intention of undertaking "concerted military action in order to safeguard Czechoslovakia against a German attack." France and Russia, however, assured Beneš that they would fulfill their treaty obligations in case of aggression by Germany. Italy, although sympathetic to German aspirations, was still occupied in the Spanish Civil War.

These circumstances gave Hitler pause. Rather than take any military action that might provoke a war with the major powers, he preferred to wait for better political conditions. By June the crisis had abated. But the Führer had not abandoned his "unalterable decision to smash Czechslovakia through a military action in the foreseeable future." He ordered the armed forces to prepare not only for an invasion of Czechoslovakia, but also for a possible two-front war, involving France in the west. To protect the western frontier, and conceivably to lull France into a false sense of security through the misconception that Hitler's plans for expansion were solely aimed toward the east, he ordered the immediate construction of gigantic defense fortifications in front of France's Maginot Line. This so-called Siegfried Line was to protect Germany in the west while it was militarily involved in the east. At the same time, the army and air force were further increased in size.

Hitler's determined military build-up worried not only Paris, London, and Prague but also many high-ranking German officers. They insisted that Hitler was overplaying his hand and that Germany could not possibly win a general European war. They called it their duty to the German people to warn Hitler that a general war would not only undo his work but also spell ruin for Germany. As a last measure to save the army and Germany from certain destruction, some officers plotted to arrest Hitler if he unleashed a war over the Sudeten crisis. Since ultimately Hitler gained Czechoslovakia without hostilities, the conspiracy was abandoned.

During the summer, the crisis simmered. France continued to assure Beneš of its readiness to support him, but Chamberlain persisted in his ambivalent attitude; he refused "to indicate how and when Britain would act in circumstances which had not yet arrived." He urged Beneš to give in to Henlein to the maximum extent possible, and sent a mediator to Prague. But Henlein, on orders from Hitler, scuttled all attempts at compromise, while Goebbels launched his campaign to denounce Czech atrocities against the Sudetens.

THE SECOND CZECH CRISIS In May, Hitler had calculated that it would take until October 1 to complete all military preparations, including construction of the Siegfried Line. His timetable progressed on schedule, and he opened the second Czech crisis in mid-September. At the Nazi Party Congress at Nuremberg on September 12, Göring bragged of the Siegfried Line, of Germany's stockpile of raw materials, and of its invincible army, navy, and air force. Hitler then spoke of the riots in Sudetenland and upbraided Beneš. Sarcastically he exclaimed that "God did not create them [the Sudetens] to be surrendered by Versailles to a foreign power," and promised that "if these tortured souls cannot obtain rights and help themselves, they can obtain them from us!"

The crisis now flared up to new dimensions. The Sudeten riots became intensified to the point that Beneš declared martial law—thereby giving Hitler further excuse to rant about the oppression of German-speaking peoples. Konrad Henlein fled to Berlin, and called by radio on his fellow Sudetens to "march home to the Reich." He no longer demanded autonomy, but incorporation with Germany. German troops began to concentrate; France called up reservists.

At this point Chamberlain decided on personal intervention and visited Hitler at Berchtesgaden on September 15. After a lengthy discussion, in which Hitler alternated between threats and sweet reasonableness, Chamberlain agreed to discuss the question of self-determination for the Sudetens with

Prague and Paris. Presumably plebiscites were to be used to determine which areas contained 50 percent or more Germans, so that these regions could be ceded to Germany. With French approval, Chamberlain then pressured the reluctant Czech government to accept Hitler's demands, threatening to abandon Czechoslovakia to its fate if it did not comply. Meanwhile the German propaganda machine kept the crisis at a high pitch by constant, mostly inaccurate, reports about disorders and atrocities in Czechoslovakia.

On September 22, Chamberlain once again visited Hitler, this time at Bad Godesberg near Bonn. Although Chamberlain reported that he had been able to obtain Beneš's acceptance of Hitler's demands of September 12, the Führer now rejected the use of plebiscites. He insisted that time was of the essence to prevent further bloodshed in Sudetenland, and that "one way or another," the question had to be solved by October 1. He demanded immediate cession of all obviously German regions, with a possible later rectification of the new border after a subsequent plebiscite. He insisted that Czech property in the ceded areas be turned over to Germany without compensations, and that the territorial demands voiced by Poland and Hungary on Czechoslovakia be also satisfied as soon as possible. He curtly informed Chamberlain that German troops would act on October 1, unless a peaceful solution had been found before then.

Chamberlain's peace mission had failed, since the Czechs rejected these new demands of Hitler's. Instead, Beneš ordered mobilization, France called up some divisions, and even England readied its fleet. Russia again offered to aid Czechoslovakia in conjunction with France, but the West showed little eagerness to bring the Soviet Union into Central Europe. Moreover, Rumania and Poland refused to permit Russia, which lacked a common border with Czechoslovakia, either to fly over or march through their territory. Dread of Communism, it appeared, was as yet stronger than fear of expansionist Germany.

THE MUNICH AGREEMENT War was averted at the last moment when Mussolini, upon the urging of Chamberlain and Franklin Roosevelt, arranged an immediate conference to settle the Sudeten question. On September 29, Mussolini, Chamberlain, and French Premier Edouard Daladier met with Hitler in Munich, symbolically at the Brown House, the headquarters of the NSDAP. Hitler had refused to invite Beneš, and Chamberlain had not insisted, being more interested in safeguarding the peace than in saving Czechoslovakia. Beneš's presence at the vivisection of his country would be only a delaying hindrance. But failure to insist on Russian participation was most shortsighted of Britain and France. The Soviet Union was, after all, an ally of both France and Czechoslovakia, and the nation ultimately most threatened by Hitler's eastward expansion. As a result, Stalin inferred that the western powers were encouraging the Nazis' eastern designs so that they might accomplish their announced plans of exterminating Communism.

The Munich Agreement resulting from the conference awarded Hitler more or less what he had demanded at Bad Godesberg. Between October 1 and 10, the Czech forces were to evacuate the Sudetenland in advance of occupation by the German army. An international commission was to fix the exact boundaries. Further arrangements were to be made to satisfy the territorial demands of Poland and Hungary. Britain and France guaranteed the new Czech frontiers, whereas Italy and Germany reserved such an undertaking until the Polish and Hungarian claims were settled. Finally, Chamberlain and Hitler signed an additional protocol of dubious value, in which they agreed jointly to work for peace and "never to go to war with one another again."

Munich delayed war momentarily, and throughout Europe there was untold relief. But Czechoslovakia had been dealt a mortal blow. Germany received about 10,000 square miles of strategic territory rich in minerals, with a population of approximately 3.5 million. Within a few weeks, Czechoslovakia had to cede the small territory of Teschen to Poland, and almost 5000 square miles and a million people to Hungary. Beneš resigned, and the truncated Czech state braced itself for the next onslaught. Hitler's prestige at home and abroad had been immensely elevated. The army officers who had wanted to overthrow Hitler began to place more trust in his judgment; the smaller nations, especially in eastern Europe, started to wonder whether it might not be safer to come to terms with Hitler than to rely on their traditional, but evidently valueless, pacts with France.

Continued Prewar Expansion

Before Munich, Hitler had proclaimed that after the solution of the Czech question, "there were no further territorial problems for Germany in Europe." Optimistic observers therefore concluded that German demands had been satisfied by the Munich Agreement. But Hitler immediately prepared for the next step. As he admitted later, he had always considered the acquisition of the Sudetenland as only a "partial solution," since he required all of Czechoslovakia "as basis for the conquest of Poland."

Three weeks after Munich, he ordered the army to make plans for the seizure of Bohemia and Moravia. He cautioned the German press that endless invocations of peace might lead to softness among the Germans, and urged the journalists to help condition the people to demand force in the solution of future problems. To lull the suspicions of France, he concluded a pact with Paris that again stipulated the inviolability of the Franco-German border. But significantly, despite French requests, he refused to guarantee the new Czech borders, in accordance with the Munich Agreement.

During the winter of 1938–1939, the Nazis worked on undermining the truncated Czech state. To weaken the Prague government, they encouraged the independence movement of the Slovaks and the Ruthenians. They also exerted pressure on the new Czech president, Emil Hácha, to reshape his army and administration along lines suitable to Germany. Prague finally granted autonomy to the Slovaks and Ruthenians, but refused to award them complete independence. Hence Hitler again applied his trusted formula. Nazi agents encouraged disorders between Czechs and Slovaks, until, finally, on March 13, 1939, the leader of the Slovak independence movement rushed to Berlin to plead for Hitler's protection against Czech oppression. Hitler promptly ordered President Hácha to Berlin and re-enacted the scene he had staged with Schuschnigg a year earlier. He bluntly told Hácha that he had decided to dispatch troops into Czechoslovakia on the following day in order to restore order to the state and incorporate it into Germany. If Hácha would order the Czech army not to resist, his people would be spared the horrors of a crushing defeat and would be rewarded with a "certain amount of national freedom" within the German Reich. If not, Czechoslovakia would be mercilessly crushed within two days, and "the world would not blink an eyelash." The frightened Hácha promptly telephoned Prague orders not to resist the German advance, and Hitler's troops occupied Bohemia and Moravia.

Two days later, on March 15, Hitler made his triumphal entrance into Prague. Bohemia-Moravia was made into a German dependency, Slovakia a German protectorate, and Ruthenia turned over to Hungary. The latter had just joined the Anti-Comintern Pact, and was rapidly becoming a convenient outpost for Hitler's growing influence in the Balkans.

England, France, Russia, and the United States all protested against Germany's destruction of Czechoslovakia, but the German government simply refused to receive such protests, since they "lacked all political, juridical, and moral grounds." Even the optimists now lost confidence in Hitler's assurances that he wanted merely to undo the injustice of Versailles and extend self-determination to all ethnic Germans. Despite Hitler's assertion in Prague that "Bohemia-Moravia have belonged to the *Lebensraum* of the German people for a thousand years," the Czechs were clearly not German-speaking peoples. If these disillusioned optimists had read *Mein Kampf,* they might have recognized Hitler's unlimited thirst for *Lebensraum.* "To demand restoration of the 1914 boundaries is political nonsense of criminal proportions," he had written, for he considered those frontiers neither logical nor appropriate from a military and geographical point of view.

Since success had been so easy, Germany now ordered the Lithuanians to cede the territory of Memel which they had received as a result of Versailles. Lithuania submitted to these demands at once, and Memel was incorporated into the Reich on March 21. At the same time, Hitler reiterated his demands on Poland that had been previously rejected by the Polish Foreign Office. He called for the incorporation of Danzig into the Reich and for the construction of an extraterritorial railroad and superhighway across the Polish Corridor to connect East Prussia with the rest of Germany. And while Hitler was thus preparing for the next and final crisis, Mussolini slipped across the Adriatic on April 7 to conquer and annex Albania.

The Prelude to War

Destruction of Czechoslovakia brought about a drastic change in British foreign policy. Two days after the fall of Prague, Chamberlain voiced his disappointment at Hitler's flagrant violation of promises given at Bad Godesberg and at Munich, and warned that Britain "favored peace, but valued freedom even more." On March 30, London proposed to Paris, Warsaw, and Moscow the formation of a coalition to resist all future German threats against the independence of any state. France agreed at once. On the following day, England and France guaranteed Poland armed support "in the event of any action which clearly threatens Polish independence." A week later, this guarantee was converted into a mutual assistance pact. During the ensuing weeks, as the threat of war increased, the Anglo-French powers extended protective guarantees also to Rumania, Greece, and Turkey.

NEGOTIATIONS BETWEEN MOSCOW AND THE WEST But negotiations between the western powers and Russia—vastly more vital for the maintenance of peace—dragged on listlessly throughout the spring and early summer, until they were finally broken off on August 22. After Munich, Stalin had abandoned hope that collective security could ever be used effectively to contain Fascist aggression. The French ambassador in Moscow even warned that the Munich Agreement was bound to drive Russia into a *rapprochement* with Hitler, and that Stalin might attempt to divert Hitler's land hunger from the Ukraine by arranging for a partitioning of Poland between Russia and Germany. Stalin had become convinced that the western capitalists were afraid of a general war because they thought it might lead to revolutions and a strengthening of Communism. He believed they were happy to see the revisionist powers absorb the smaller states because they anticipated that the aggressors would ultimately hurl themselves against the Soviet Union. The appointment in May of the antiwestern Vyacheslav Molotov as new commissar of foreign affairs clearly indicated this change in Russian policy.

Despite mutual suspicions, proposals and counterproposals shuttled back and forth between Moscow, London, and Paris. Russia showed hesitant readiness to negotiate a general mutual assistance pact with England, France, Poland, Rumania, and the three Baltic states. But hatred of communism and fear of Russian imperialism, particularly on the part of the smaller eastern states, rendered conclusion of such a pact impossible. Questions of "indirect aggression" and of the stationing of the Red Army in case of a German attack presented the main stumbling blocks. In view of Hitler's proved method of preparing annexation through the fomenting of internal disorder in his victim and the use of fifth columns, Stalin demanded the right to dispatch troops to prevent Nazi subversion of the small countries. But Poland and Rumania, which had both gained land at the expense of Russia in 1918, refused to grant such permission. They even rejected the suggestion that in case of overt aggression by Germany, the Red Army should be allowed to traverse Polish or Rumanian territory, for they feared that once in the country, Soviet forces would remain in permanent occupation.

HITLER'S DEMANDS ON POLAND During these same months of fruitless negotiations between Russia and the West, Hitler made preparations "to solve the Polish problem." As usual, his official diplomatic offensive was accompanied by secret orders to the army to effect military preparedness. Since Germany now surrounded Poland on three sides, army and air force units were secretly deployed along a large perimeter, ready to accomplish the sudden and prompt destruction of the Polish army. Hitler's public demands on Poland—annexation of Danzig with safeguards for Polish economic interests, and permission to build a German railroad and highway across the Corridor—sounded reasonable and negotiable. But his true intentions reached much further. "Danzig is not the real objective," he informed his generals and confidants in May. "Our aim is to round out our living space in the east and to solve our food problem."

In their negotiations with Warsaw, Hitler and Ribbentrop alternated between intimidation and promises of friendly collaboration. At one point Hitler tried to convince the Poles that Berlin and Warsaw should work together against the Soviet Union, since communism was their mutual enemy. On the other hand, Hitler denounced Germany's nonaggression pact with Poland on the pretext that Warsaw harbored aggressive intentions against Germany after the conclusion of the Anglo-French-Polish pact. For good measure, he also canceled the Anglo-German Naval Agreement of 1935, in order to intimidate his opponents. There followed the usual incidents in Danzig and the Corridor, which Goebbels' propaganda machine enlarged to frightening proportions so that Hitler could promise aid and protection to the ethnic Germans, "oppressed" by their Polish masters. Since Hitler wished to destroy Poland and not solve the disagreements, the several months of negotiations brought no results, and lasted only until his military and political preparations were completed.

In view of Britain's change of policy, it seemed likely that Germany's planned action against Poland would lead to a general European conflagration. Hence Hitler thought it expedient to secure the benevolent neutrality of as many countries as possible, so that the number of enemies he had to fight at the same time would be reduced. After conclusion of the Spanish Civil War, Spain at once joined the Anti-Comintern Pact and thereby signaled its continued friendship with Germany and Italy. During May, Hitler concluded nonaggression pacts with Estonia, Latvia, and Denmark. Sweden, Norway, and Finland rejected similar offers. On the other hand, friendly relations were established with Hungary, Yugoslavia, and Bulgaria. On May 22, Mussolini, although by no means militarily or economically prepared for war, agreed to convert the vague Rome-Berlin Axis into a tight alliance. The "Pact of Steel," as it was called, was not simply a defensive alliance, but actually obligated the signatories "to support the partner with all military forces," in case he became "embroiled in a war."

THE NAZI-SOVIET PACT But Hitler realized that a two-front war, against Poland and Russia in the east, and England and France in the west, involved strategic risks that he preferred to avoid. If Russia could be kept out of the conflict—at least temporarily—Poland would remain isolated and could be crushed in a short time, after which German forces could turn west and either conquer France or conclude peace with the western powers. Consequently, Hitler decided on a *rapprochement* with Stalin. Preliminary negotiations began in May, and proceeded at first quite slowly. Understandably, Stalin and Hitler found it difficult to trust each other. But the Soviet dictator perceived the advantages of the situation: it offered easy territorial aggrandizement and at least a temporary breathing spell for the Soviet Union. As time passed, Hitler grew more and more eager. A trade agreement was finally concluded as a prelude to further political negotiations. At last, after much German pressure, Ribbentrop was invited to Moscow and left Berlin immediately, endowed by Hitler with full powers of negotiation. On the same day—August 23—Ribbentrop, Molotov, and Stalin agreed on a pact of friendship and nonaggression. The pact itself, drawing together the two bitter ideological enemies, was remarkable enough. The secret protocol that accompanied it was even more ominous for the future.

In this protocol, Germany and Russia agreed on a "delimitation of their respective spheres of interest in eastern Europe." Finland, Estonia, Latvia, and Bessarabia were granted to the Soviet Union. Lithuania was reserved for Germany—although in a subsequent secret agreement of September 28, after the fall of Poland, Germany transferred this claim to Russia in return for a larger share of Poland. The protocol furthermore drew tentative borders for a division of Poland, "in case of territorial changes" in that country, and stipulated that all further Polish problems would be discussed by the two nations in a friendly and cooperative manner.

This cynical Nazi-Soviet Pact not only removed Hitler's last hesitation about attacking Poland, but had other far-reaching repercussions. It was obviously a temporary arrangement, for it contravened Hitler's long-planned eastward expansion by allowing Russia to move westward. For a short while, by giving it access to Russian food and raw materials, particularly petroleum, it freed Germany from the fear of total wartime blockade. But these transitory advantages could not conceal the fact that Hitler had violated the spirit and letter of the Anti-Comintern Pact and had undermined the foundations of his anti-Communist ideology. Expediency had reached its high point. Rosenberg, the party philosopher, feared the consequences of Hitler's actions. "I have the feeling," he wrote in his diary two days after the signing of the pact, "that this Moscow Pact someday will backfire on National Socialism," for he felt that it negated the very essence of Hitler's movement. Less ardent Nazis saw even worse consequences for Germany and Europe. It is indeed ironic that Hitler, who always posed as the leading anti-Communist, granted Russia predominance over eastern Europe and awarded it the boundaries that Russia has since occupied and maintained.

Once Hitler was assured of Russian neutrality, only a few days of peace remained. Feverish diplomatic activity marked these last hectic days. Chamberlain, Daladier, Roosevelt, and even Mussolini tried to persuade Hitler to modify his stand. Mussolini made it plain that he would not join in a war in the foreseeable future unless Germany provided Italy with huge amounts of war matériel. Hitler hesitated for only a moment, hoping to get England to remain on the side lines. But Chamberlain re-emphasized Britain's guarantees to Poland in a new and stronger agreement, while at the same time offering to mediate between Warsaw and Berlin.

Despite the counsel of more cautious advisers, Hitler finally sent an ultimatum to Poland, and without waiting for a reply, issued his order of attack.

At dawn on September 1, 1939, German troops and air force went into action against Poland. Strict orders were given to provoke no hostilities on the French border, so that "the responsibility for opening of hostilities would be left up to England and France." After the German troops had begun their invasion of Poland, Italy once more tried to forestall war by calling for a conference. England and France mobilized, but informed Germany that negotiations could still save the peace if Hitler at once withdrew his invading forces from Polish soil. Since the troops continued to push on, and Hitler did not even bother to reply to the British demands for cessation of hostilities, England and France declared war on Germany on September 3.

THE PERIOD OF AXIS SUPREMACY, 1939–1942

In the gigantic war that followed, the Axis powers—consisting of Germany (with its annexed Austrian and Czech territories), later joined by Italy, Hungary, Rumania, Bulgaria, Finland, and Japan—enjoyed initial advantages that made them appear almost invincible. The Germans were better armed and far bolder in their employment of new tactics of surprise and mobility than the Allies, who at first relied on the old strategies that had won them World War I. Imbued with the revisionist myth of fighting for a new order, and streamlined in their command chain by dictatorial administration, the Axis powers at first also displayed far more unity of purpose and initiative than was possible in the loose coalition of the Allies. Long-term strategic planning, ruthless diplomatic pressure, skillful use of fifth columns, thorough exploitation of conquered territories, and readiness to employ total war tactics made it easier for Hitler and his allies to win astounding success. As a result, the Nazi steamroller gained stupendous victories during the first three years of the war, until the tide gradually turned in the the winter of 1942–1943.

Initial Triumphs of German Arms

BLITZKRIEG IN POLAND The German campaign against Poland, prepared meticulously down to the last required pontoon bridge, was a startling sample of *Blitzkrieg* (lightning warfare). The air force strafed and bombed military positions and civilian centers with ruthless precision; mechanized units of tanks and armored cars slashed through enemy lines to complete encircling movements. Within a few weeks, the Polish army of about 600,000 men was annihilated. After twenty-seven days, which included a prolonged and highly destructive siege of Warsaw, Poland lay prostrate and defeated.

During the last week of fighting, Russian armies crossed Poland's unguarded eastern border to seize their share of the spoils. Ribbentrop and Stalin then conferred again in Moscow to set a new Russo-German frontier across the heart of Poland. Each took approximately half the territory of Poland in this fourth partition, but Germany's western portion was more heavily populated. At the same time, Moscow and Berlin arranged for closer economic cooperation. Having pocketed without cost almost 80,000 square miles and 13 million new subjects, Russia then proceeded to seize the other awards made to Stalin in his pact with

Hitler. Within the next ten months, the Soviets acquired Lithuania, Latvia, Estonia, Bessarabia, and Bucovina, totaling another 92,000 square miles with about 9.5 million inhabitants. Only Finland resisted Russian demands but, after a short but hard-fought winter campaign, was finally obliged to cede to Russia some 16,000 square miles.

After the fall of Poland, Hitler addressed the Reichstag to boast of his accomplishment. Insolently mixing threats and enticements, he suggested to London and Paris that further bloodshed and destruction be avoided through prompt conclusion of peace and arrangements for general disarmament. Since Hitler showed no intention of restoring Poland, his peace offer was, of course, rejected.

Preparations were then made for the next campaigns. A special movie, "Blitzkrieg in Poland," showing the power of the German war machine and the horrors of modern warfare, was shown as widely as possible to bolster German morale and intimidate the nations of Europe. However, many German viewers, it appeared, were sickened by the cruelty in the film, and many a foreigner became more firm in his determination to resist Nazi aggression.

In the west, Anglo-French divisions behind the Maginot Line uneasily faced German troops in the Siegfried Line in the so-called *Sitzkrieg* (sitting war, as contrasted with the lighting war in Poland). Sporadic shelling was accompanied by propaganda leaflets and radio broadcasts sent across the trenches. Goebbels attempted to demoralize the French soldiers by reiterated insinuations that they were shedding their blood solely "for the benefit of the British capitalists."

Hitler's eagerness for action was not shared by many of his generals, who were not so convinced of the invincibility of their armies or the weakness of their opponents. They hesitated to launch a direct attack on France. In a memorable address to his staff, the Führer tried to demonstrate the advisability of speedy action in the west and the need for trust in his own infallible decisions: "I will attack and not capitulate. The fate of the *Reich* depends solely on me." And he assured them: "In all modesty I must speak of my own person as irreplaceable. Neither a military nor a civilian personality could replace me." And with similar modesty he continued: "I am convinced of the power of my brain and of my powers of decision."

But the Sitzkrieg continued throughout the winter, largely because of unfavorable weather. The only action of note occurred at sea, where German submarines sank Allied commercial and naval vessels, and where the German pocket battleship "Graf Spee" enjoyed her brief but memorable foray into the Atlantic, until she was overpowered by British pursuers and scuttled herself in the Bay of Montevideo.

SEIZURE OF DENMARK AND NORWAY

When the British decided to mine Norwegian coastal waters in order to halt the shipments of badly needed Swedish ores to Germany via the port of Narvik, Hitler suddenly shifted his attention to Scandinavia. Plans for German action had been previously elaborated, since the German air force and navy wanted to use Norway as a base of attack on England and on Allied shipping. On April 9, 1940, German troops suddenly occupied Denmark in a sweeping strike, and placed the frightened little kingdom under military occupation for the duration of the war. On the same day, German naval and air-borne units seized strategic areas of Norway, aided in places by local fifth columnists. The Norwegian forces, supported by the British navy and a small Anglo-French expeditionary corps hastily dispatched to Norway, resisted fiercely for a few weeks. But by early May, the Germans had crushed most opposition, and Norway gradually disappeared into the German orbit, controlled by the German army, and governed by the pro-German Vidkun Quisling, as the head of a Nazi-dominated dictatorship.

Flushed by the brilliant success in Denmark and Norway, Hitler promptly ordered the attack on the west. Not squeamish about violating treaties and neutrality arrangements, he based his strategy on a modified Schlieffen plan. By speedily overrunning the three neutrals, Holland, Belgium, and Luxemburg, the German armies were to plunge into France from the north, and thus by-pass the Maginot defenses.

DEFEAT OF FRANCE The attack was launched along the entire front on May 10. Once again surprise was achieved and maneuvers were executed with incredible speed. Highly mobile tank units, air-borne drops, bombing of cities, strafing of fleeing refugees, and occasional use of traitorous fifth columnists were all employed in efficient coordination. Within five days, air bombardment had reduced Rotterdam to a shambles, all strategic points had been occupied by German motorized units and paratroops, and Holland surrendered. Supported by British and French units, the Belgian army resisted for two weeks. But by driving straight to the Channel, the Germans succeeded in cutting off the Allied armies in Belgium from their main forces in France. The story of their evacuation from Dunkirk across the Channel to England has been depicted frequently enough. By early June, four German armies were streaming into France, preceded by dive bombers and fighter planes that had complete command of the air. French equipment was largely outdated and inferior. Here and there, horse-drawn artillery tried valiantly to delay approaching *Panzer* columns. Refugees clogged the roads, disrupting communications and making French military movements difficult. Despite an occasional display of heroic bravery, most French units were pitifully demoralized and defeatism was rampant.

A month after the initial attack, the Germans had completely by-passed the Maginot Line and were within reach of both Paris and the Atlantic Ocean. On June 14, they seized Paris, after the French government had moved south. On June 16, the aged Marshal Henri Pétain became head of the French state, and with almost half of France under German control, he decided on the following day to request an armistice. The German armies continued their advance for another five days, until Hitler met the French envoys at Compiègne on June 22 to sign the terms of surrender. To satisfy his feelings of revenge, he insisted that the humiliating surrender of France be concluded in the same railroad carriage in which the Germans had accepted the 1918 armistice.

The successful campaign against the four western countries, which had lasted a mere forty-three days, was filled with drama, heroism, and treachery. Mussolini, in particular, showed the baseness of his bravado. He stood on the side lines until certain that Hitler would be victorious in the west. Then on June 10, he declared war on France and Britain, and sent his troops over the poorly defended southern borders of France. An entirely different attitude was shown by the United States and England. Roosevelt urged the French to pursue the fight, even if the mainland of France had to be abandoned, and to continue the battle in North Africa. To aid in the struggle, he promised to dispatch war matériel. Churchill, who had become prime minister on May 10, begged France not to capitulate, and in a dramatic gesture offered to merge France and England in a Franco-British Union that would ultimately conquer the common enemy.

As a result of the armistice terms, France was temporarily divided into two sections. Northern France and the Atlantic seaboard were occupied by German armies and placed under military government. The remainder of France was allowed nominal sovereignty under Marshal Pétain who, with the aid of Pierre Laval, established a Fascist dictatorship that acted largely as a German puppet regime. Beyond the seas, however, in London and in most of the French dependencies, General Charles de Gaulle established a French National Committee to head the so-called Free French forces, which remained at war with Germany until the end.

Hitler's belief in his own infallibility now knew no bounds. In ten months of war he had conquered seven states. German domination extended from the Vistula to the Pyrenees, from the fjords of Norway to the Austrian Alps. But England remained undefeated, and in the east, Russia loomed as a question mark. Since his renewed peace offer was bluntly rejected by Churchill, Hitler issued orders for the invasion of England. Unable to gather enough suitable ships to cross the Channel for an immediate landing, the Germans launched their air fleet against Britain and intensified their submarine blockade of the island. For three months, in the Battle of Britain, German bombers battered English coastal installations, inland military depots and factories, as well as the major cities—particularly London and Coventry—in order to reduce England's potential resistance to invasion and demoralize the population. Damage was tremendous, and the losses at sea caused by prowling submarines were frightening. Yet Britain remained defiant. Despite the German blockade, American supplies of war matériel and foodstuffs arrived in ever-greater quantities. The Royal Air Force retained command of the air space over the island, although Göring's *Luftwaffe* enjoyed numerical superiority. In fact, the RAF even launched retaliatory air raids on Berlin and some cities in the Ruhr, giving German civilians their first taste of war on the home front. In October 1940, the impossibility of defeating England by air became apparent even to Hitler, who officially postponed the invasion plans until spring, when for a brief period the heavy air raids on London and the countryside were resumed. Actually, Hitler's attention had been turned eastward to the Balkans and to Russia.

The Invasion of Russia

Some of Hitler's military advisers proposed that Germany could best undermine Britain's strength by expelling it from the Mediterranean and conquering its Near Eastern empire. Italy, in fact, pursued this idea, since Mussolini had always dreamed of converting the Mediterranean into an Italian sea. In September 1940, the Italians launched their invasion of Egypt, and in the following month attacked Greece. But, poorly equipped and ineffectively led, they were defeated in both areas, so that Hitler ultimately was forced to bail out his ally by sending troops to North Africa and Greece and by stationing air squadrons in Italy to reduce attacks by the British navy on the fast-dwindling Italian fleet. In Hitler's view, these were useless diversions. He rejected the thought of concentrating German efforts on the Mediterranean, being determined to conquer the Continent. This meant, in fact, conquering Russia.

There were many reasons why Hitler was adamant about his decision to destroy the Soviet Union. For one, he was convinced of the inevitability of ultimate conflict with Russia, and therefore wished to attack it as soon as possible, while Germany's military machine was at its most effective. Moreover, he did not trust Stalin and was fearful that Russia would attack Germany unexpectedly at a time of its own choosing. Hitler was also worried about Soviet expansion (which he himself had approved and facilitated), possibly because he came to realize that Stalin was almost as adept as he in absorbing neighboring states. There was friction over influence in the Balkans and in Finland, which German troops had gradually infiltrated under the guise of transit to northern Norway. Hitler also disliked being dependent on Russia for shipments of raw materials, and constantly accused the Russians of being in arrears in their deliveries. Most curious among his reasons was his conviction that the best way to defeat England was to conquer Russia. "England's hope is Russia and America," he told his generals. Once Russia was defeated, he thought Japan would be the strongest power in East Asia and keep the United States so busy that it could no longer help England. Annihilation of Russia would thus deprive England of its main supply depot, the United States, and of its "continental dagger" against Germany. Except for his theories about Japan and the United States, Hitler's idea paralleled that of Napoleon, who, when his invasion plans of the island had to be abandoned, had also hoped to defeat England by attacking Russia.

POLITICAL AND MILITARY PREPARATIONS Preparations for the invasion of Russia were begun in the summer of 1940, to be implemented in the following spring. Actually, several delays occurred. Meanwhile Russo-German relations cooled steadily. Russia resented Hitler's expanding influence in the Balkans, and refused to be pacified by Hitler's insinuation that it look for compensations in central or southern Asia—for example Iran and India.

In September 1940, Germany, Italy, and Japan signed the Tripartite Pact, in which the two European powers recognized Japan's right to establish "a new order in greater East Asia," while Japan agreed to respect Axis leadership in creating "a new order in Europe." The three powers, moreover, agreed "on mutual political, economic, and military assistance in case of an attack on one of the contracting parties by a power not presently engaged in the European war or the Sino-Japanese conflict." This alliance was obviously directed against the United States, but could apply equally well to Russia.

Germany spent the winter and spring occupying the entire Balkan Peninsula, partly to help Mussolini and to expel the British who had landed in Greece, and partly to safeguard the right flank of the armies that were to be launched against Russia. Rumania, with its valuable oil fields, was taken in October 1940, after it had lost much territory to Russia, Hungary, and Bulgaria. Hungary joined the Axis alliance more or less voluntarily in the following month. In February 1941, Bulgaria was seized, followed two months later by Yugoslavia and Greece. Meanwhile an expeditionary force was dispatched to Africa, under Field Marshal Erwin Rommel (1891–1944), who helped the Italians launch another invasion of Egypt.

By June 1941, all the delaying tasks had been accomplished. With the Balkans secure, Hitler was ready to launch his gigantic attack against the Soviet Union. Like the *Grande Armée* of Napoleon, his forces included troops from client states—Italians, Rumanians, Hungarians, and Finns, later augmented by French, Spanish, and others. But significantly, he could not count on the assistance of Japan. Unwilling to become involved in a war in Siberia that would divert its forces from striking against Southeast Asia and the Pacific Islands, Japan had signed a nonaggression treaty with Moscow (April 1941).

INITIAL SUCCESSES On June 22, 1941, Hitler suddenly hurled over three million men against Russia on the entire front from the Baltic to the Black Sea. His pretext was that Russian troops had concentrated along the border with seemingly hostile intentions. The campaigns that ensued were of gigantic proportions, considering the vastness of the areas covered and the quantities of men and matériel involved. The Germans advanced in their usual lightning fashion, under an umbrella of thousands of planes, enveloping enemy units and strong points in huge pincer movements that netted them great numbers of prisoners. The tidal wave of German Panzers headed eastward so rapidly that most observers believed Russia would fall within a few weeks. During the first seven days, most of the buffer zone recently acquired by the Russians fell into German hands. By the middle of July, the Germans had seized Lithuania and Latvia, invaded the Ukraine, and on the central front, captured Smolensk, barely 250 miles west of Moscow. In September, German and Finnish forces laid siege to Leningrad, which, despite constant bombardment and near starvation, successfully withstood a siege of a year and a half. By October, almost the entire Ukraine, with its major cities Kiev and Kharkov, had been seized by the Germans, the Crimean peninsula was under invasion, and the battle for Moscow had begun. Vast tank battles rolled over the central Russian lands frozen by the early approach of winter, and at the end of November, the Germans reached the suburbs of Russia's capital and were almost within sight of the Kremlin towers. In five months, they had won innumerable battles, advanced some 600 miles, taken great numbers of prisoners, but, as they now were forced to realize, they had not defeated Russia.

The Russians had displayed unexpected tenacity and skill in defending their vast areas. They scorched the earth so as to leave no food for the advancing enemy; guerrilla fighters constantly interrupted German communications; hit-and-run attacks undermined German morale and took a great toll among German soldiers behind the front lines. Moreover, Russia possessed more war matériel than suspected by Hitler, who had perhaps been misled by the poor showing of Russian arms in the Finnish War of 1939. And Stalin expected aid and supplies from abroad. On July 13, Moscow and London signed a mutual aid agreement. In the following month, British and Russian troops occupied Iran in order to establish a supply line for aid to Russia, and Roosevelt's adviser, Harry Hopkins, visited Moscow to discuss the shipment of American supplies.

THE FIRST REVERSES In the winter of 1941, the Germans suddenly suffered their first defeats. On December 6, the Russians launched a heavy counteroffensive that gained immediate success and pushed back the German lines before Moscow and in the northern Ukraine. Throughout the winter the Red Army retained the initiative until warm weather returned in the following May. Unaccustomed to being subjected to serious attack, and poorly protected against the Russian winter, the German troops quickly lost their morale. Hitler, who had spent most of the months of the campaign at army headquarters meddling in the tasks of his generals with the delight of a boy playing with tin soldiers, now ranted at his officers. His infallibility seemed at stake. He reshuffled important commands, personally assumed the title of Commander in Chief of the Army, and directed the defenses against the Russian attacks, disregarding his subordinates' advice to establish shorter lines of communication by a general withdrawal. Under Hitler's fanatic direction, the troops gave way only under severe pressure, and no rout developed. Yet the tremendous suffering of the troops boded ill for Germany's future unless Russia could be defeated before a second winter.

Within a few days of the beginning of the Soviet counteroffensive, two other events forecast a turning point in Germany's chances for victory. After Japan's assault on Pearl Harbor, Hitler gleefully seized the opportunity to declare war on the United States, despite the counsel of more sober-minded advisers. He completely underestimated the industrial and military potential of the United States. His reason for challenging it was certainly not based on any sense of obligation to stand by his ally Japan. Rather, he expected that open hostilities against the United States would allow German submarines to patrol its coasts and successfully intercept the American supply line to Britain and Russia—particularly since the United States Navy would be fully occupied in the Pacific war against Japan. Actually, Hitler's calculations were exaggerated but not completely erroneous. Allied shipping losses through German submarine attacks during 1942 became almost catastrophic. But in the final analysis, Hitler did not have quite enough submarines, and the United States succeeded in building ships much faster than German submarines could sink them, so that by the middle of 1943, the Battle of the Atlantic was to turn in favor of the Allies.

The second event foreshadowing a change occurred on December 11, 1941, when British and Commonwealth troops invaded Libya and successfully drove back Rommel's *Afrika Korps*. Militarily this British drive bore few long-term consequences, but it afforded a great boost in morale to the British, for whom it represented the first outright victory over German troops.

Despite these temporary defeats, Germany resumed the offensive in the spring of 1942. Rommel in North Africa repulsed the British and burst into Egypt, as part of a vague plan to penetrate into the Middle East, where a link might be made with Japan in its drive through Southeast Asia and India.

In Russia, Hitler directed the summer offensive southward. Overly confident of his tactical knowledge and contemptuous of generals who warned against the risk, he divided his forces, sending one along the Black Sea toward the Caucasus, the other due east to Stalingrad on the Volga. For several months, the German steamroller again made fantastic gains. The southernmost spearheads came within 100 miles of the Caspian Sea, but in the end, the Germans succeeded neither in capturing the Caucasian oil fields nor in cutting Russia's major supply lines on the Volga. In the fall came the great turning point. The Germans had slowly fought their way into the center of Stalingrad, fiercely defended block by block by Soviet troops and partisans. Suddenly they found themselves threatened by strong Russian counteroffensives to the north and south of the city. Despite the threat of imminent encirclement, Hitler would not countenance a retreat. The Russians were allowed to close a tight ring around the 22 German divisions trapped in the city. After about 240,000 men were killed in the battle, in faithful obedience to Hitler's fanatic command to "stand and die," the remaining 90,000 troops, including 24 generals, capitulated at the beginning of February 1943.

Surprisingly, in addition to those used in the Battle of Stalingrad the Russians had enough men and supplies to mount a general winter offensive along the entire front. They forced the Germans to lift the siege of Leningrad, to withdraw along the central front, and to evacuate almost half of the Ukraine in the south. Only in March 1943 did the lines become temporarily stabilized. By then, it had become evident that the Russian winter offensive had once and for all broken the back of German power. Henceforth the initiative was to remain almost exclusively in Russian hands, and the Germans were to begin their two-year rear guard action that ended in the Battle of Berlin.

The fall of 1942 brought similar changes on the other fronts. In October, the British resumed their drive into Libya. A month later, a task force of American, British, and Free French troops landed in Morocco and Algeria. The Germans rushed reinforcements to Tunisia, but by May all North Africa had been conquered by the Allies. In their retreat, Germany and Italy sustained great losses in men, matériel, and shipping, and the Italian peninsula became exposed to possible Allied invasion. Germany's only success in these black months was the seizure of the rest of defenseless France in retaliation for the Allied conquest of Algeria and Morocco; but its aim of securing the remaining French fleet was frustrated when most of the ships were scuttled by their crews in the harbor of Toulon.

Even in the far-off Pacific, the fall of 1942 marked a turning point, in that the battles on and around the Solomon Islands signaled the end of Japanese victories and the beginning of the American offensive.

Retreat and Total Collapse, 1943–1945

RETREAT AND DEFEAT

The shift of power from Axis to Allies that occurred in 1943 was symbolized by the meeting of Roosevelt and Churchill in Casablanca in January of that year. Here the two western nations announced their determination to insist on the eventual unconditional surrender of the enemy powers. The two heads of state also discussed the strategy required to achieve this aim, and the Allied air staff adopted a policy of total air war against Germany, designed not only to destroy its military, industrial, and economic life, but also to undermine "the morale of the German people to the point where their capacity for armed resistance is fatally weakened."

To be sure, serious disagreements among the Allies in some cases delayed military action. Stalin continued to press for the immediate opening of a second front in western Europe so as to draw off German divisions from Russia. Repeated postponement of a second front made him increasingly suspicious of Allied intentions. Moreover, America, Britain, and China did not see eye to eye over the campaigns in southeast Asia and the treatment of India. Above all, Churchill wanted to invade fortress Europe through the Balkans, whereas the American military staff favored a direct cross-Channel invasion of the flat regions of northern France, where Allied armored divisions could operate more effectively under an air umbrella provided from nearby British airports. But these disagreements did not save Germany from an almost unbroken string of defeats.

The Reverses of 1943

In 1943, the Soviet Army launched its first summer offensive. Despite skillful defensive moves, the Germans were slowly driven back. By the end of the year, Hitler's armies had been pushed to the prewar border of Poland in the north, and retained only a precarious foothold in the western Ukraine and parts of the Crimea.

In the Mediterranean, the Allies crossed from Tunisia to conquer Sicily in a hard-fought, month-long battle. Faced with the prospect of invasion of their homeland, most Italians became disenchanted with their Duce. The Fascist Grand Council and the Italian king suddenly deposed Mussolini and had him arrested. The ambitious chief of staff, Marshal Pietro Badoglio, then dissolved the Fascist regime and secretly got in touch with the Allies to negotiate an armistice, even offering to let Italian troops aid the western powers against Germany. But negotiations between the emissaries of Badoglio and General Dwight Eisenhower were so protracted that the German army found time to consolidate its position throughout central and northern Italy. Consequently, when the armistice was finally agreed upon and Allied troops tried to take over Italy, they succeeded in seizing only the lower third of the peninsula before getting bogged down in front of the strong defenses that the Germans had rapidly thrown across Italy, halfway between Naples and Rome.

The fall of Mussolini thus represented a German loss but no clear-cut Allied victory. The liberated southern portion of Italy under Badoglio declared war on Hitler, and furnished the Anglo-Americans a firm foothold on the Continent from which to increase their bombing raids on the heart of Europe. But another year of costly fighting was to be required before central Italy could be conquered. The Germans meanwhile rescued Mussolini from prison and set him up as a puppet in charge of the so-called North Italian Republic, which furnished them some help against the Allies. Still, the loss of half of Italy as a cobelligerent and the need to concentrate more troops south of the Alps were serious blows to German morale and resources.

During 1943, the Germans faced other setbacks. Partisans in Yugoslavia and Greece, with the aid of air-dropped British and American supplies, were increasing their disruptive activities and pinning down dozens of German divisions that would otherwise have been used on the Russian front. The submarine campaign was rapidly failing as the Allies improved their convoy system, installed better radar devices, and increased their air patrols of the Atlantic shipping lanes. The air war was also changing in character. The Allies were building planes and training pilots at such a rate that they could afford to bomb German cities, industrial complexes, and transportation networks by day as well as by night, in raids frequently comprising 500 or 1000 bombers. Although the German air force and air defenses were still formidable and inflicted a heavy toll on the attackers, they could not save the German cities from ghastly destruction.

Russian Gains in 1944

In 1944, German defeats multiplied so rapidly that the final collapse became inevitable. Unquestionably, if Nazi propaganda had not misinformed the Germans and if Hitler's fanaticism had not inspired so many of them to fight to the bitter end, if fear of Russia and misgivings about Allied intentions in view of the much-publicized demand for unconditional surrender had not frightened many into blind resistance, the war would have ended in late summer of that year.

In the course of 1944, the Russians cleared their homeland of foreign troops. Then in rapid succession, they seized over half of Poland, forced Finland out of the war, occupied Estonia, Latvia, Rumania, and Bulgaria, helped Tito's partisans liberate most of Yugoslavia, and invaded eastern Czechoslovakia and Hungary. In December, the Red armies stood along a line from Memel on the Baltic, past Warsaw and Budapest, to the Adriatic near Fiume, poised to invade Germany.

The Soviet advance and the German retreat entailed further frightful massacres in eastern Europe. When the Red Army approached the Vistula in August, the Poles of Warsaw rose in rebellion to hasten their liberation from the Germans. But since the Polish rebels were mostly bourgeois and anti-Communist, the nearby Russian armies refused to aid them. Anglo-American supplies were flown in all the way from Britain, but without ground support, the premature rebellion could not succeed. After a costly siege of two months, the Germans once again seized Warsaw and massacred the rebels, while the Russians, entrenched across the Vistula, were apparently content to see the Nazis wipe out the non-Communist Polish resistance movement. A similar event occurred at the same time in Slovakia, where non-Communist resistance fighters were wiped out by the Germans in a bloody two-month campaign, while the Red Army, only a few miles away, refused to aid their fellow Slavs.

Hungary, like Italy, was thrown into civil war as a result of the German retreat. When the Russians invaded the country, the Hungarian government attempted to conclude an armistice and withdraw from the fighting. But the Germans arrested the regent (Admiral Miklós Horthy) and set up their own puppet government, while the invading Russians established their own pro-Communist regime. During the subsequent three-month siege of Budapest, Hungarians were thus forced to fight on both sides in support of their respective foreign masters.

The front in Italy changed relatively little during 1944. Heavy fighting south of Rome finally led to an Allied breakthrough in June and to the seizure of central Italy. But north of Florence the Germans had constructed a second defensive line that kept the Allies at bay for another eight months, until the total collapse of Germany in the spring of 1945.

The Second Front in the West

In the west, the Allied landing in Normandy on June 6, 1944, opened up the second front that the German military had always dreaded and that Stalin had requested for so long. In anticipation of such an assault, the Germans had fortified the entire coast line from Denmark to the Bay of Biscay and had stationed reserve divisions in strategic locations. But the Allies had made meticulous, long-term preparations. By this time they had gained unquestioned air superiority that permitted massive strategic bombing to disrupt the transportation system by which German supplies and reserves could reach the Normandy front. Actually, production of German airplanes, in factories placed underground or hidden in caves in the Bavarian Alps, was still increasing in 1944, despite constant Allied air assaults, but a growing shortage of both fuel and trained pilots was sapping the effectiveness of the once-formidable Luftwaffe.

The invasion was preceded by heavy

bombing and shelling of the coastal areas, and the landing of parachutists, who, together with French underground forces, cut communications between Normandy and the rest of the German-held territories. The landing operation itself was gigantic, involving thousands of ships, hundreds of thousands of vehicles, and millions of men, as well as almost unlimited supplies. Fuel was piped across the Channel in numerous pipe lines hastily laid under water from England to France. After establishing their beachhead, the Allies spent almost a month consolidating it and resisting tenacious counterattacks by the Germans. Field Marshal Rommel, who commanded the army group in northern France, warned Hitler in July that a disaster seemed imminent. In view of the Allies' domination of the sky and their logistical superiority, especially in artillery and armor, he saw no way of containing their armies and preventing them from overrunning all France. He complained that he was receiving practically no supplies and replacements: for 225 tanks lost, he had been sent 17 replacements, and 6000 men had replaced 97,000 casualties. He begged Hitler "to draw the proper conclusions without delay."

But as before, Hitler refused to countenance strategic withdrawals. He ordered the army to hold every inch of ground, no matter how hopeless. In mid-July, the Americans broke out of the beachhead, and Rommel's predictions came true. Within two months, the Allied armies, joined by new forces that landed in the south of France on August 15, occupied almost all France and Belgium. Paris fell on August 25, Brussels on September 4, and on September 11, American units crossed the German border at two points. Hitler refused to see the inevitable and threw all blame on his generals, some of whom became implicated in the plot on his life, on July 20 (see pages 592 ff.). After Rommel was forced to commit suicide because of indirect involvement in the assassination attempt, the trusted Field Marshal Hans-Günther von Kluge (1882–1944) was given the hopeless task of stemming the Allied tide. In August, when his failure became apparent, he, too, was relieved of his command. In a final letter, Kluge implored Hitler not to rely on last-minute miracles, but to spare the German people continued suffering. "You have fought an honest and truly great battle," he flattered Hitler. "Now prove your greatness by putting an end to a hopeless struggle." After writing this letter, Kluge committed suicide. His successor, Field Marshal Walther Model (1891–1945), who could hardly do any better, committed suicide in 1945.

The Final Months

With invasion imminent from two sides, some Nazis now looked at the political rather than the military aspects of their desperate situation. They properly assessed the inherent incompatibility of the Russians and the western Allies, and hoped to find a way not merely of driving a wedge between them but of possibly enticing the Anglo-Americans to join a German crusade against Communist Russia. Some advocated that, for this purpose, the eastern front should be held at all costs, while only token resistance should be offered in the west. Some even reasoned that if occupation of German soil was inevitable, it would be preferable to let in the western forces rather than the Red Army, which was clearly bent on avenging the horrors inflicted on Russia by the Nazis.

Hitler himself toyed with such ideas, but ultimately remained determined to fight on both fronts with equal vigor. In December 1944, he even ordered the famous counteroffensive in Belgium, designed to split the Allies by a quick thrust to the Channel between the American and British forces. But by January, this Battle of the Bulge, too, was lost, and the American armies were clawing their way through the Siegfried Line.

Thereafter, the final assault on Germany was started. In February, the Russians crossed the Oder River and raced to within thirty miles of Berlin, while the Americans conquered the left bank of the Rhine. In March, United States, British, and French forces crossed the Rhine and within five weeks occupied most of Germany west of the Elbe, while the Russians began their siege of Berlin. By late April, all resistance in Italy had ceased. Mussolini had been captured and hanged by Italian partisans. And German armies in most areas were preparing to capitulate. Only Hitler, in his Berlin bunker surrounded by a few faithful, was still speaking of ultimate victory until his suicide on May 1.

THE GERMAN HOME FRONT

The first two years of the war, until June 1941, were for most Germans a period of undiluted victories and delights. Hitler's easy triumphs, the perceptible growth of Greater Germany, and the unquestioned superiority of German arms swelled the breasts of all those who did not bother to analyze the likely consequences of ruthless application of might and violence. German casualties in the Polish and French campaigns were light; the occasional token air raids by the RAF barely interrupted the normal life of the cities; an acquaintance here or there might disappear, presumably into a concentration camp; a Jewish family next door might be deported; but relatively few Germans suffered. The exploitation of conquered lands permitted an increase in food rations and brought luxury items back on the market. The average German felt convinced that all was well with his world.

This mood changed with the invasion of Russia. Bewildered at first by the new twist in Goebbels' propaganda, which reconverted the Soviet Union into an archenemy, many Germans were soon shaken by the endless casualty reports from the Russian front. By 1942, morale in the fatherland began to sink. Shortages of food and consumer goods appeared; soldiers on leave from the eastern front reported the horrors of winter warfare on the frozen steppes; the destructive rain of explosives and fire bombs began to gut German cities and impress on their populations the reality of war.

Concomitant changes were felt in almost all areas of life, in and outside the Nazi spectrum. After 1941, the Nazi treatment of the Jews, of the conquered populations, and of their own German subjects became more and more ruthless and brutal, as if the leaders unconsciously sensed the impending doom. The more radical elements in the party came to the fore, and at the same time anti-Nazi resistance movements grew more active.

German Control of Occupied Territories

The Nazis soon learned that it was easier to conquer Europe than to establish their so-called New Order. By the fall of 1941, they found themselves in direct or indirect control of the entire Continent, with the exception of Portugal, Spain, Switzerland, Sweden, the British Isles, and the unconquered portions of Russia. Their basic aims were simple: to exploit Europe economically for the benefit of Germany, and to maintain control over the subject and dependent populations. But no clear-cut and consistent policy was ever evolved on how to organize the Continent for such a purpose. Partly because of the military requirements of the war and the haphazard way in which territories were acquired, administrative measures remained opportunistic, confused, and sometimes contradictory. Plans for the New Order had to be adapted to geographic and economic conditions and take into consideration the presence or absence of strong political cohesion in the conquered lands.

The conquest of the more sparsely settled, vast regions of the east afforded the racists the opportunity to experiment with schemes for the New Order. Rosenberg, as minister for occupied eastern territories, favored colonization of the Baltic region. He collected families of Germans, Dutch, and kindred "superior racial stock" and settled them on farms in the northeast. He held visions of "purified" colonial enclaves, gradually spreading throughout much of European Russia, surrounded by the local slave populations who toiled for their German masters. Himmler on the other hand, who in 1943 became minister for the interior and commissioner for "safeguarding German nationality," thought of establishing in the heart of Europe a racially pure paradise. For this purpose he hoped to eliminate within Germany all "impure" elements, and repatriate all ethnic Germans—from the Baltic region, the lower Volga, Yugoslavia, and other areas—for settlement in and around Germany. A kernel of "ethnic purity" would thus arise in central Europe that could easily dominate the outlying areas of "racial inferiors." Caught between these contradictory schemes of Himmler's and Rosenberg's, some families were actually uprooted twice, being first sent out to colonize the Baltic, and then repatriated by Himmler's orders.

Arrangements for the political control of occupied Europe remained multifarious. Areas that had belonged to Bismarck's Reich, or that contained many ethnic Germans, were directly annexed to Greater Germany, and either converted into *Gaue* (districts) or appended to a neighboring German *Gau*. Among others, these included Austria, the Sudetenland, Memel, Danzig, West Prussia, Poznan, Alsace-Lorraine, and even Slovenia in northern Yugoslavia. Some territories became directly or indirectly subordinate, such as Bohemia-Moravia and Poland, which were administered almost exclusively by Germans. Norway and Holland were controlled by a German Reich commissioner with the aid of German army, SS, and police units, since the legal Norwegian and Dutch governments had fled to London and established official governments-in-exile. Denmark, on the other hand, whose king and his government had remained on Danish soil, was placed under military occupation, although not, strictly speaking, under military government. The Balkan states, all occupied by German armies and controlled by puppet regimes, acted as nominal allies of Germany but actual administrative power resided in Berlin. The occupied portions of Russia, of course, remained a theater of war, where army and SS units clashed over policies and spheres of jurisdiction.

Where possible, the economic, political, and legal life of subject territories was "coordinated" along the lines adopted in Germany. Economic planning was applied to satisfy the requirements of total war, laws were redesigned to meet National Socialist ends, and anti-Jewish policies were enforced. Although countless German agencies and departments were involved in this gigantic task of exploitation and domination, overwhelming power resided in Heinrich Himmler, who not only commanded the SS and the Gestapo, but, as minister of the interior, also controlled the police.

The actual treatment of conquered populations varied from place to place—or one might say, from "race to race." The official hierarchy of "races" awarded preference to Nordic peoples. Latins were considered superior to Slavs, and the "sub-human" Jews were rated below all others. In Holland, Denmark, and Norway, the occupying soldiers generally treated the people with relative respect, even though the overbearing SS troops frequently acted as conquerors rather than "liberators." In France and Belgium, the Nazis' contempt for a "weaker race" mixed uneasily with the admiration felt by most officers for the cultural traditions of the Franco-Belgians. In the east, especially in Poland and Russia, the behavior of the SS army units (*Waffen* SS) and even of most regular troops ranged from mere contempt and exploitation to primitive barbarism. Polish and Russian prisoners and civilians, regardless of sex or age, were kicked, whipped, tortured, and exterminated at random. In one of Himmler's typical exhortations to his SS leaders in 1943, he warned that a show of sympathy for non-German peoples, particularly the Russians, was a crime against "our *Volk* and our blood. Whether the others live in prosperity or perish from hunger concerns me only in so far as we need them as slaves." And as a practical example, he added: "Whether during the construction of a tank trap 10,000 Russian women perish from exhaustion or not concerns me only if the tank trap should not get completed."

Besides violating all humanitarian considerations, the behavior of the German occupiers, particularly in the Ukraine, was also political folly. Many Ukrainians, at heart anti-Communist and proud of their former independence, might have welcomed the Germans as liberators from Soviet Russian domination. Instead, German atrocities quickly turned them into fierce anti-German guerrilla fighters. Instead of recognizing this tactical and political blunder, Hitler welcomed the guerrilla warfare: "It gives us the possibility of exterminating whoever opposes us," he bluntly told Rosenberg and other advisers.

German looting and arrogance naturally provoked the local populations, not only in the east but also in the west and north. Resistance groups were gradually forming everywhere, gathering arms, establishing contact with the Allies, helping the escape of downed Allied flyers, and engaging in sabotage. Some of these groups were dominated by Communists, others by moderate or right-wing elements. In Yugoslavia, where partisan activity was the fiercest, internecine civil war between Communist and non-Communist guerrillas sapped much of the energy that might have been used against the Germans. But everywhere the resistance movements grew more powerful and active as German military power declined in 1943 and 1944. In many countries, such as, for example, France, Yugoslavia, and Greece, these nuclei of resistance formed the embryonic bases of the provisional governments that helped govern their countries after the withdrawal of the German occupation troops.

But Germany could never have dominated most of Europe if it had been faced by nothing but hostility and active resistance everywhere. In most countries, from Norway, Holland, and France to the Balkans, the Nazis found surprising numbers of sympathizers who were eager and proud to help establish the "new order," either because of ideological conviction or because of sheer opportunism. Nationals from all occupied nations volunteered to work in Germany, where economic conditions were presumably better than in their own defeated or occupied countries. Thousands of them voluntarily enlisted to fight against Russia side by side with the Nazi troops, apparently persuaded that Communism was a greater danger than Nazism. Such local support by the so-called collaborators enabled the Germans to control and exploit surprisingly large areas with a relatively limited number of occupation troops.

Total War

The demands of total war, according to the Nazis, required total dictatorship. In April 1942, Hitler informed the Reichstag that everything—traditional rights, justice, and administration—had to be subordinated to the sole task of achieving victory. He requested the Reichstag to grant him legal power "to force everyone to fulfill his duty," using whatever penalties he saw fit, and leaving the definition of duty up to his conscience. Upon a motion by Göring praising "the wisdom, justice, goodness, greatness, and above all the genius of the Führer," the Reichstag approved Hitler's request by acclamation and granted him the right to act "without being bound by existing legislation."

Even more than before, every aspect of public and private life was now subject to arbitrary interference by the various agencies of the party. While Goebbels droned endlessly by radio and press that victory was in sight, terror and coercion increased in proportion to the real hopelessness of the situation. Special courts awarded death sentences on the slightest pretext and meticulously forwarded the bill for the cost of execution, including postage, to the nearest relative of the condemned. A typical example is that of a minor government clerk in Rostock, who in 1943, after the fall of Mussolini, said in a streetcar that what happened in Italy would happen in Germany, and that the Führer should resign, since victory was no longer possible. For this he was condemned to death on the charge of undermining the National Socialist defense effort.

As the war continued beyond its expected duration, stockpiles of strategic raw materials became depleted and the problem of shortages arose. The Allied blockade permitted no imports, except from Sweden and Spain, and the conquered lands provided less than had been anticipated. Moreover, strategic bombing by the Allies took its toll of industrial complexes. In 1942, Albert Speer (1905–) was appointed minister for armaments and munitions and awarded far-reaching dictatorial powers over industry and transport. At the same time, Fritz Sauckel (1894–1946) was made commissioner general for manpower in all occupied territories. The shortage of labor in Germany had become so severe that even careful and often forced assignment to jobs could not fill the required needs. Hence the German government began to recruit workers in occupied countries. Initially, sufficient volunteers could be found, but gradually Sauckel resorted to conscript labor. As in everything else, racial bias affected the treatment of these foreign workers employed in German industry and agriculture. Those from the east, working mostly on farms, were usually treated as slaves. By 1945, five million foreigners had been forcibly assigned to labor in Germany.

Even these measures could not furnish sufficient manpower to meet the demands of industry and replace the mounting civilian and military casualties. In September 1944, Hitler and his deputy Martin Bormann (1900–1945?) created the *Volkssturm,* a people's militia based on the compulsory enrollment of all able German males aged sixteen to sixty, with the task of "defending the homeland with all weapons and means, in as much as they appear suitable." With young boys and old men called into the fighting, with women and the handicapped manning the factories, with imported slaves working the fields, and daily air raids destroying the cities and burying their inhabitants under mountains of rubble, everyone was made to perform his duty in Hitler's total war.

Extermination of the Jews

The Nazi program for "racial purity" was instituted with the same gradualness as the abrogation of the Treaty of Versailles or the establishment of Hitler's dictatorship. If Hitler and his followers had attempted in 1933 to gas the 600,000 Jews of Germany, there is little question that a revolution would have toppled them from power. But by proceeding step by step, while securing their regime and indoctrinating the people in the morals of brutality, they could progress from discrimination to persecution, then to mass deportation, and finally to complete extermination without endangering their control of the government. The Nuremberg Racial Laws of 1935 and the pogrom of November 1938 were major turning points in the anti-Jewish program, but the decisive change came with the outbreak of World War II. Before 1939, the Jews of Germany—and eventually of Austria and Czechoslovakia—were subjected to discrimination, degradation, and persecution, and some died in concentration camps. After 1939, they were at first deported, and then massacred. It is a measure of the incredible brutalization of life and of the adaptability of man that, compared with the final bestial solution, the excesses of the earlier period appear almost humane.

There were many reasons why the outbreak of war added such impetus to the campaigns against the Jews. In *Mein Kampf,* Hitler had predicted that war would result "in the extermination of the Jewish race in Europe." He repeated this prophecy in a Reichstag speech of January 1939. Military exigencies always permit greater latitude of ruthlessness. The fanatic Nazis, convinced that Bolshevism, capitalism, and democracy were all a cloak for international Jewry, believed they had to eradicate the Jewish enemy within before being able to defeat the same enemy abroad. They were also practical considerations. In wartime, relatively more secrecy could be used to shield the extermination proceedings from the scrutiny of public and foreign opinion. An even more important link between the war and the intensified anti-Jewish program were the German conquests in the east. So many more Jews lived in eastern Europe—Poland alone having over three million—that the seizure of Poland, White Russia, and the Ukraine greatly multiplied the number of Jews under Nazi control.

From the outbreak of war to the invasion of Russia, the policies more or less followed the directive given by Göring to Reinhard Heydrich: "to prepare a solution to the Jewish question, in the form of emigration or evacuation, which favorably fits existing conditions." As head of the Security Division of the SS, Heydrich was charged with implementing this directive. To "purify" central Europe, Jews from Austria, Bohemia, and parts of Germany were deported to Poland, where ghettos were established at Lodz, Warsaw, and other communities. During 1941, Jews from western countries and the Balkans were rounded up where possible, and shipped in sealed trains to the new Polish ghettos. To make use of this concentration of cheap manpower, forced labor was ordered for all Jews in Poland.

The invasion of Russia in 1941 and Rosenberg's dream of colonizing the east with ethnic Germans led to the final step in the program. The increasing desperate pace of the war and the growing power of the fanatics in the party led to more radical "solutions." If eastern Europe was to provide *Lebensraum* and not merely be a food basket for Germany, then the concentration of millions of Jews seemed contrary to Nazi aims. In the fall of 1941, the final mass deportation of German Jews to the east was begun. On the pretext that they were being resettled or "going on vacation," the Gestapo permitted the deportees to take along 50 kilos of luggage and 100 marks. The rest of their property was confiscated by the state. But most of them were no longer destined for eastern ghettos, but for the new extermination camps that were being constructed at Auschwitz, Belzec, Chelmno, Sobibor, Treblinka, and other places.

The "final solution to the Jewish problem" was discussed and elaborated at a meeting of party and state officials and SS leaders in January 1942. Careful organization and planning was needed "to comb through Europe from west to east" so as to apprehend all Jews, to make available the transportation required to ship them to the extermination camps, and to cover the cost of such a gigantic operation by using the labor of the condemned and by extracting whatever profit there remained in their bodies—shoes and clothing, gold teeth and jewelry, and human hair for industrial purposes. On the basis of the "practical experiences" gathered in 1941, the conferees decided that the physically weak Jews should be exterminated forthwith, while those capable of heavy work should for the time being be used to build roads in the east. In the course of such work, it was assumed, "a great number would undoubtedly be lost through natural decrease." But, lest the survivors of these work teams form the germinal nucleus of a new Jewish renascence, these "would have to be treated accordingly," as soon as their work tasks were completed.

The nightmare now took on the most ghastly proportions. Unless hidden by friends or protected by local governments—as, for example, in the case of Denmark—Jews from all over occupied Europe were herded together, thrown into cattle trains, and gassed, shot, or beaten to death in the special extermination camps that rapidly increased in number in order to accommodate the constantly growing volume of the operation. Special task forces (*Einsatzkommandos*), consisting of between 500 and 1000 police and SS, roamed through Russian territory behind the invading troops to clean out Jews, gypsies, and Communist leaders, whom they either slaughtered on the spot or dispatched to death camps.

There is no need to shock the reader by a description of the horrors committed in these camps. The atrocities have received wide notoriety since the end of the war. Nor is it necessary to quibble over statistics concerning the number of victims—as if the inhumanity of the Nazis would have been less reprehensible if they had exterminated three million instead of five or six million persons.

The question of responsibility and of the abetting guilt of the Germans as a whole has been debated ever since 1945. Most Germans abide by the convenient claim that they knew nothing of the brutal excesses perpetrated by the Nazis. They insist that when they were occasionally informed about them during the last year of the war through Allied leaflets or radio broadcasts, they disregarded the reports as propaganda; and that only after the collapse in 1945 they became gradually, although hesitatingly, convinced of the truth of Allied accusations.

It is, of course, true that relatively few Germans were involved in the actual operation of the gas chambers. Wherever possible, the Nazis used prisoners and candidates for later extermination to perform the varied tasks required—sorting the clothes of the victims, cutting off their hair, dragging the bodies out of the gas chambers, pulling out gold teeth, digging the mass graves, and dumping in the bodies. Perhaps only a few thousand SS actually whipped the endless colums of naked Jews into the extermination chambers or pulled the triggers of the machine pistols on victims lined up before open graves. Yet hundreds of thousands of Germans were involved in, or were witnesses to, some part of this gigantic operation: doctors who performed medical experiments on prisoners, chauffeurs who drove the gassing trucks in which the victims were asphyxiated, engineers who ran the deportation trains, police and SS who guarded the camps, officials who visited the compounds, and soldiers near the front who saw the task forces in action. And these hundreds of thousands must have spoken about what they knew to millions of friends and relatives.

It is also certain that most Germans during these years of terror saw Jews being dragged out of their houses and kicked by a booted SS into a waiting truck. Perhaps they looked away or hurried to their local beer cellar. When the same Jew was never again seen, he was presumably deemed to be living comfortably in a new Polish ghetto. And when news came of his death, as it often did, one felt sorry for a minute, and then ordered another beer. The general attitude was less one of ignorance than of numb and convenient indifference. As the student resistance leaders Hans and Sophie Scholl proclaimed in one of the leaflets distributed in the winter of 1942–1943, in which they pointed out that since the conquest of Poland the Nazis had murdered 300,000 Jews, "Everyone wants to absolve himself of share in the guilt, everyone does it, and then falls asleep with the clearest of consciences."

Anti-Nazi Resistance

After the collapse of Hitler's regime, a great many Germans claimed that they had been members of the anti-Nazi resistance, and protested that they should not have to suffer because of crimes committed by the terrorists whom they themselves had fought for years. These claims raised not only the problem of collective guilt but also the question of the numerical strength of the opposition to Hitler. Actually, no precise answers can be given to these questions. The nature of the Nazi regime required utmost secrecy in all underground oppositional ventures. To escape detection by the Gestapo, the more effective resistance fighters were organized into small independent cells, working in ignorance of one another, so that the arrest of one member, who might reveal secrets under torture, would not result in the discovery of the entire organizational net. Moreover, the term "resistance" is subject to many different interpretations: silent, mitigating, and active—to mention three major types.

No doubt the vast majority of Germans belonged at one time or another to what might be called the "silent" resistance. These people felt—and sometimes showed—a lack of enthusiasm for the regime, or were disconcerted by some aspect of the Nazi program. This sort of mild disenchantment naturally grew stronger as victory turned into disaster, as food and supplies became scarce, and as German cities crumbled under incessant air bombardment. Needless to say, such behavior, which the Nazis on occasion punished with imprisonment or death, never presented a serious threat to Hitler's monopoly of power. Yet it infuriated Goebbels' vanity, for it seemed to prove a flaw in his program of total indoctrination.

The "mitigators" were those moderate sympathizers with National Socialism who disliked certain excesses of the regime, but remained at their posts and actively served Hitler with the expectation of being able to mitigate the more nefarious aspects of the system. Hjalmar Schacht, certain officials in the Foreign Office, and other civil servants and professionals might be placed in this category. By softening the execution of harsh decrees or resisting the total introduction of Nazi practices into their bureaus, they claimed to have obstructed the regime. It is, of course, impossible to establish how far they were successful in their professed aims, or how much they deluded themselves. Nor can one really ascertain whether they were sheer opportunists who later convinced themselves and the world of their basically honorable intentions, or whether they deserve a measure of moral praise for doing their best under difficult circumstances to diminish the horrors of the regime. The fact that Schacht was acquitted by the tribunal at Nuremberg hardly proves that he was a "mitigator," since the indictments were for specific crimes against peace or against humanity.

THE ACTIVE RESISTANCE The majority of those who participated in the active resistance labored to undermine the regime but did not actively attempt to overthrow it. There were various distinct groups, each engaging in minor acts of resistance. Some distributed anti-Nazi leaflets or listened to foreign broadcasts—acts punishable by death. Some helped Jews or political suspects to hide from the Gestapo or to escape abroad. Some engaged in economic sabotage. Others kept in contact with like-minded organizations abroad. Most of them were largely intent on preserving the ideals of their own fields of activity—religion, politics, the legal profession, academic life, and so on—from contamination by National Socialist ideology.

Their overriding interest in their own spheres of life, their different social backgrounds, and, above all their divergent hopes for the reconstruction of a Germany without Hitler prevented these groups from uniting during the entire peacetime period. Collaboration among them was effected only in the face of the disasters of the war. Although there were many such groups, a few deserve special attention.

Most of the Communist leaders fled from Germany in 1933 to escape imprisonment. They went to Russia, where they helped found the National Committee for a Free Germany. Except during the period of Nazi-Soviet collaboration, 1939–1941, they maintained contact with small Communist underground cells inside Germany, called the Red Chapel (*Die Rote Kapelle*). The Communist underground was particularly active in trying to sabotage factories, in slowing down production, or in attempting to weaken the war effort on the eastern front. A few of the Communists were convinced anti-Stalinists. Whether remaining in Germany or fleeing to France, England, or Mexico, they maintained their belief that a popular front, in which all antifascist groups would cooperate, might ultimately become the basis for the reconstruction of Germany.

The headquarters of the outlawed SPD moved to Prague in 1933, then to Paris in 1938, and finally to London in 1940. Until the outbreak of war, contact between Socialists in and out of Germany remained fairly close, and much illegal literature was smuggled into the Reich for clandestine distribution. The Socialists, however, were not united in their ultimate aims. The more radical wing resembled the USPD of 1919. They regarded the failure to adopt a thoroughly Marxist program after World War I as the cause for Hitler's rise to power and for the weakness of the Weimar Republic. Hence they believed that only an orthodox Marxist program could wean the workers away from National Socialism and offer hope for the future success of a socialistic democracy.

The official program of the underground SPD, however, remained revisionist and thoroughly anti-Communist. It rejected the thought of a Popular Front for fear that the SPD might fall under the domination of the better financed, though smaller, Communist underground. The most active leader of the underground SPD, Wilhelm Leuschner (1888–1944), a former trade-unionist and minister in the Hessian government, worked closely with secret representatives of the non-Socialist Christian trade-unions. Convinced that the workers alone could never overthrow Hitler and establish a Socialist government, Leuschner hoped to attract the middle class with a program resembling that of the Labor party in England. As a supplier to the German navy, Leuschner had relative freedom to travel, which allowed him during the war years to become an important link among various anti-Nazi circles and one of the organizers of the attempt to overthrow Hitler in 1944.

The churches were also centers of resistance. A number of courageous clergymen publicly denounced the Nazis' pagan ideology and virulent racialism. The Catholic Church, as well as the Confessional Church of the Protestants and other Protestant sects, such as Jehovah's Witnesses, tried to use moral pressure and sometimes even chose martyrdom in order to resist the inroads of National Socialist *Gleichschaltung*. A considerable number of priests and ministers suffered for their convictions in concentration camps. But most of this resistance by ecclesiastics was defensive in that they wanted to preserve Christianity and Christian morality. Only a few members of the clergy actually joined plots to overthrow the regime.

Besides political and religious bodies, there were other, less well-defined groups who participated in occasional acts of resistance. A few university professors, especially during the earlier years of National Socialism, tried to uphold the traditional values of western civilization and publicly denounced the chauvinism of Hitler's movement. Student organizations printed and distributed clandestine leaflets calling on the Germans to rid themselves of the Nazi nightmare. Some lawyers, economists, philosophers, and writers—the so-called inner emigrants—did what they could to resist the destruction of their professions, and a few joined the active anti-Hitler fighters. But most of the intellectuals who had not fled abroad maintained a tenuous and compromising appearance of apolitical indifference.

Finally, a considerable number of army officers formed a part of the resistance. Their motives varied. Fear and jealousy of the Nazi paramilitary units, class hatred of aristocrats for the upstart Nazis, and above all, the danger that Hitler would ruin the *Wehrmacht* through his flamboyant diplomatic and military ventures drove many an officer into quiet opposition to Hitler. But very few of them dared to violate the sanctity of their oath to the Führer and to participate in the active resistance.

It is impossible to estimate the magnitude of this active resistance. The fact that so many non-Jews were executed by the Nazis or lingered in concentration camps, or that about a quarter of a million joined the Society of Victims of Fascism after the war sheds little reliable light on the question. National Socialist justice and terror sent to the gallows countless people who were in no way members of the resistance. Telling a joke about Goebbels' clubfoot or Göring's obesity, hoarding an extra pound of lard, possessing foreign currency, or failing to salute the swastika during a parade of storm troopers—under the Nazi regime any of these insignificant acts might lead to a jail sentence or to death.

But even without the benefit of statistics, it appears that the size and effectiveness of this active resistance was not considerable. The ubiquity of police spies and informers, the octopuslike organization of party and state, and, above all, the cold-blooded brutality of Nazi coercion frightened all but the most resolute from expressing the slightest overt displeasure.

PLANNED COUPS AGAINST HITLER

There is no evidence of any serious, organized plot to overthrow the regime before 1938. In this connection, it must be recalled that Hitler's assumption of power was pseudo legal, and that his dictatorship was instituted by installments. Consequently, the opposition at first believed that Hitler's government might be terminated by similar pseudo-legal means. It is difficult to ascertain at what point the more active plotters concluded that only an armed coup could topple the entrenched Nazis.

Planning for a successful anti-Nazi coup involved three major problems, apart from the difficulty of avoiding detection by the Gestapo. For one, the conspirators required the collaboration of some armed organization in order to overthrow the regime and impose their rule on the country. A few thought that disloyal Nazi units, perhaps under the ambitious Göring, might be used to topple Hitler. But realizing that such boring from within the party was not likely to eradicate the objectionable aspects of National Socialism, most of the plotters concluded that their only hope lay in enlisting the aid of the regular armed forces.

A second problem involved the type of government to be installed after the overthrow of Hitler. Assassination of the Führer and his immediate subordinates would produce a political vacuum that the plotters would have to fill promptly with an adequate substitute government. In view of the Weimar experience, many of the conspirators were apprehensive about the viability of a democracy. Their divergent backgrounds also made it difficult for them to reach a conclusion about the degree of nationalization to be instituted after the overthrow of Hitler.

The third problem was perhaps the most complicated: in order to please the masses, the plotters would have to guarantee the preservation of the gains made by Hitler without resorting to Nazi tactics. The longer the underground waited, the more Hitler's almost unbroken string of successes complicated this aspect of their task. On the home front, for example, the conspirators could hardly risk sending millions of workers back into unemployment after Hitler had found jobs for them. Similarly on the foreign scene, lest they be accused of being less patriotic than the Nazis, they felt they had to match Hitler's success in scrapping the Versailles Treaty and aggrandizing Germany.

Even by 1938, the various active resistance groups had not found a common solution to these major problems. In that year, however, the unwelcome prospect of a war against Czechoslovakia stirred certain high-ranking army officers and civilian officials to adopt a plan for the removal of Hitler (see page 561). Among the officers, the most active was General Ludwig Beck (1880–1944), chief of the General Staff of the army until his resignation in August 1938. In addition, Field Marshal Erich von Witzleben (1881–1944), commander of the Military District of Berlin, General Franz Halder (1884–), Beck's successor as chief of the General Staff, and others formed part of the conspiracy. Among the civilians, who included diplomats, police officials, and members of the clergy, the driving force was Carl Goerdeler (1884–1945), the former mayor of Leipzig, who was to remain one of the most active members of the resistance until his imprisonment in 1944. During the Sudeten crisis of September 1938, the conspirators secretly urged the British government to take a firm, public stand against Hitler's demands on Czechoslovakia. If in the face of a determined Anglo-French stand, Hitler backed down, his regime would be seriously weakened by the resulting diplomatic defeat. If he attempted war, Goerdeler informed London, "the leaders of the army declared their readiness to countermand Hitler's policy by force of arms." The Munich Agreement vitiated all these plans. The conspirators were interested only in preventing a war for which they felt unprepared. They saw no reason to object to the peaceful absorption of the Sudetenland.

After the abandonment of the 1938 plot, the conspirators became less active for a number of years. Most army officers seemed bewitched by Hitler's stupendous success. Some of them feared the overextension of the theater of war and opposed the attacks on Scandinavia, France, and Russia. But Hitler's triumphal march through the west, the Balkans, and into the east made their caution seem hopelessly untenable. In the final analysis, they considered it treasonous to undermine the war effort while Hitler continued to be successful.

Hitler's victories also complicated the question of possible peace terms. Even during the early years of the war, Beck and Goerdeler made several contacts with the British government to discuss a possible settlement in case Hitler were overthrown. But no agreement was ever reached, for the British remained suspicious and the German demands were high—either because the members of the resistance were themselves supernationalists, or because they feared to lose face with the German people if they settled for less than Hitler had achieved. Even the peace note of May 1941, sent to England by Goerdeler, who was considered a moderate, contained far-reaching demands. While promising to restore the sovereignty of all neutral lands occupied during the war, the note demanded that Germany retain Austria, the Sudetenland, and Memel, regain its 1914 borders with Belgium, France, and Poland, and receive back its overseas colonies.

But a few convinced officers, such as General Beck, and a number of civilians, particularly Goerdeler, Leuschner, and Ulrich von Hassel (1881–1944), a member of the diplomatic corps, became increasingly disturbed by the immoral excesses of the regime in its foreign as well as domestic policies.

They came to fear military victory as much as defeat, since either would ruin Germany—the one by perpetuating National Socialism, the other by destroying the country. And they saw no solution. Goerdeler unceasingly tried to convince key generals of the need for prompt action against Hitler, but as long as they hesitated, nothing serious could be undertaken.

While waiting to find an opportunity for removing Hitler, various resistance groups began to coalesce into a more all-inclusive movement. Most influential of these groupings was the "Kreisau Circle," so named after the Silesian estate of Count Helmuth von Moltke (1907–1945). Starting in 1940, the young Moltke and his friend Count Peter Yorck von Wartenburg (1904–1944), both scions of famous Prussian noble families, gathered representatives from various opposition groups in order to debate solutions to the problem of Germany's postwar reconstruction. The Kreisau Circle represented many shades of sociopolitical opinion—Catholics and Protestants, trade-unionists and entrepreneurs, Socialists, liberals, and conservatives. Many members became key figures in the revolutionary plots of the later war years, and the deliberations of this group strongly influenced the program ultimately adopted by the plotters.

THE PLOT OF JULY 1944 Active resistance was infused with new vigor when Hitler's chain of victories suddenly broke before the gates of Moscow. In 1942, serious disaffection reappeared among certain army officers who recognized the hopelessness of the Russian campaign and the potential military strength of the United States. A new opposition cell was formed inside the Counter Intelligence Service by its chief, Admiral Wilhelm Canaris (1887–1945), while in Munich students organized a concerted campaign to distribute in many parts of Germany leaflets calling for the overthrow of Hitler.

In 1943, after the debacle of Stalingrad, a few officers were willing to risk their life and honor in an effort to oust Hitler. But apparently only one serious attempt was made, when the chief of staff of the Central Army Group in Russia (General Henning von Treschow, 1901–1944) smuggled a time bomb in the guise of two cognac bottles into Hitler's airplane. The timer failed to go off. Although a few more assassination plans were hatched, no more serious attempts were made in that year. The officer corps as a whole feared that a *coup d'état* might lead to a breakdown of the Russian front and a subsequent Soviet invasion of Germany. Moreover, the announced Allied insistence on unconditional surrender made them feel justified in continuing the war. Contacts of the underground with the American OSS in Switzerland failed to bring firm assurance that the overthrow of Hitler would permit Germany to expect more favorable armistice terms.

Spurred by the continuous military defeats and the example of the overthrow of Mussolini, the conspirators around Beck and Goerdeler finally completed their plans by the fall of 1943. They reached agreement on detailed plans for the reconstruction of Germany after the overthrow of Hitler. During the first days of disorder, a military government was to control Germany under a state of siege. Once order was established, a provisional government was to take over, with Beck as president, Goerdeler as chancellor, and Leuschner as vice-chancellor. The state of Prussia—which had retained its huge size despite the *Gleichschaltung* of the Nazis—was to be cut up, and Germany was to be divided into new states (*Länder*), each with about three to five million inhabitants. The administration was to be liberal but not completely democratic. Elections for the lower house were to be indirect, and the upper house was to be based on estates rather than on geographic distribution. The program called for nationalization of certain industrial monopolies and for special privileges to trade-unions.

After reaching this agreement, the conspirators were ready. In the thirty-six-year-old Count Klaus Schenk von Stauffenberg (1907–1944), whose position in the General Staff allowed him access to Hitler, they found a devoted activist who quickly became the soul of the conspiracy. But the contemplated action required the cooperation of more than merely a few ardent anti-Nazis, and months passed before the conspirators could persuade enough officers to join in the plot. The bulk of the officers continued to hesitate. Fear of committing treason, hesitation about violating their oath to the Führer, the absence of a promise of better terms from the Allies—these and a variety of other reasons served to justify their reluctance.

In the end, only the hopeless situation resulting from the Allied landings in Normandy and the Russian advances in the east persuaded enough officers to support the plot. They hoped the overthrow of Hitler would at least permit them to make peace in the west and throw their total strength against the Red Army. In July 1944, Stauffenberg was given the signal that all was ready. Twice he delayed setting the bomb because Himmler and Göring were not present, and he hoped to kill them together with Hitler. On July 20, during a meeting at Hitler's headquarters in East Prussia, Stauffenberg placed his briefcase, containing a time bomb, against Hitler's conference table, and flew to Berlin, where Generals Beck and Witzleben were seizing key buildings and notifying certain army commanders that Hitler had been killed and that they had assumed command. Actually Hitler was only slightly wounded by the blast, which blew him out of the flimsy wooden structure where the temporary headquarters were located. Many army officers refused to act until convinced of Hitler's death. Their hesitation, together with Goebbels' prompt action in telephoning Hitler from Berlin and convincing loyal army and SS units that the Führer was alive, doomed the plot from its very beginning. The conspirators were rounded up, and Hitler assured the Germans by radio that he had escaped the plot of a few "criminal and stupid officers, who are now being mercilessly exterminated." Stauffenberg and those most immediately involved were shot on the same day. Beck, Rommel, and others committed suicide. The People's Court held mock trials for Witzleben, Wartenburg, Moltke, Leuschner, Hassel, Goerdeler, and many others before executing them. Some conspirators or suspects simply disappeared behind the bars of Gestapo prisons or concentration camps. The total number of executions has never been established.

The attempt of July 20, 1944, was the last—and one should add the only thoroughly planned—attempt of the underground to remove Hitler. The repressions following its failure wiped out most of the leaders of the active resistance. With few exceptions, the army officers again cowered in awe before the Führer and stood by him to the bitter end of Germany's total destruction.

COLLAPSE

Germany could have been spared much of the devastation of its cities and hundreds of thousands of lives could have been spared by all belligerents if the war had been terminated in late 1944 or at least at the beginning of 1945. Had rational leaders governed Germany, they would have requested an armistice at the latest in January 1945, after the failure of the Battle of the Bulge and the collapse of the German central lines in the east. But Hitler's maniacal fanaticism prolonged the war for an agonizing four months.

The Suicidal Temper of Final Resistance

In order to keep the Germans fighting, the Nazis used whatever means they could devise. Goebbels constantly assured them that victory was in sight and that secret weapons would soon be used to hurl the invaders back on all fronts. Himmler appealed to all German women to spur their men into giving their last to assure final victory. "We stand by the holy conviction," he stated in a proclamation, "that God has given to Germany in our Führer Adolf Hitler the one man who can ward off this danger [the Bolshevik seizure of Europe], and that in the end He will award victory to our brave and heroic people and thus to the true Europe."

In a final effort, the propaganda machine tried to scare into fighting those who could not be enticed voluntarily to give their lives in a hopeless struggle. News of the atrocities committed by the advancing Russians on the eastern front and of the American Morgenthau Plan (see page 601) helped the Nazis in this task. Hitler warned the Germans that "the enemy's ultimate aim is the eradication of the German people." And many became convinced that they might as well resist to the end in the hope that the final catastrophe could somehow be averted.

Where enticement or fear did not help, ruthless terror was applied. In February 1945, soldiers were informed that if they surrendered at the front, their kinsmen at home would be imprisoned or shot. Special court-martial tribunals were set up throughout Germany to see to it that "all Germans"—civilians as well as military—prove their "readiness to fight and their devotion unto death." Acting under martial law, these tribunals—composed of a judge, a member of the NSDAP, and an officer of the army, police, or SS—were empowered to pronounce only one of two sentences: death or exoneration. Moreover, some fanatics devised the plan of concentrating all Germans in a central territory of the Reich, which would be turned into an impregnable fortress. A mass exodus from the east had begun, as German civilians fled before the advancing Soviet armies. The Nazis now forced further evacuations from the east, a gigantic operation that complicated military operations and added to the dangerous dislocation of food supplies. Martin Bormann contemplated applying this same idea to the west of Germany, so that the advancing Allies would find nothing but depopulated areas.

Even in early April, when American, British, and French troops were racing across Germany from the west, and the Russians stood within sight of Berlin, SS fanatics saw to it that every inch of ground was defended. Young boys and women were impressed into paramilitary formations to help defend towns by building tank barriers or sniping from rooftops. The SS issued an order prohibiting the surrender of a single house. If a white flag was hoisted in a house, SS detachments had permission promptly to shoot all male occupants.

During these months of carnage on the ground, made infinitely worse by incessant air bombardments, Hitler lived in the chancellery in Berlin, where he had returned in January, after the loss of the Battle of the Bulge, which he had personally directed from army headquarters. Daily injections of various concoctions were given him to calm his nerves, but his mood alternated between fits of rage and despondency. Air raids and later the bombardment by Russian artillery forced him to spend most of his time in an underground bunker, where he lost himself in a world of fantasies.

As late as April, he clung to his belief in ultimate victory, and distrusted the judgment of even his closest collaborators when they expressed fears about the imminence of defeat. Even after the Russians had entered the outskirts of Berlin, he predicted that the anti-German coalition would split, since the western powers would never permit the Communists to overrun Germany. Above all, he frequently spoke of his secret weapons that would still turn the tide. It is true that Germany had produced surprising new weapons during the last year of the war. In June 1944, England was suddenly subjected to devastating attacks by V-1 robot bombs, fired with surprising accuracy from installations on the Continent. By the fall, a new model, the V-2, which traveled faster than the speed of sound, made its appearance and was directed against Antwerp and other coastal towns used by the Allied armies for shipment of supplies and reinforcements. But despite the heavy damage caused by these new devices, they could not slow down the Allied advance. Nor could the new turbojet fighter plane that the dwindling German air force suddenly launched against the slower, propeller-driven Allied machines prevent the destruction of German cities and transport networks. And the atomic bomb, on which the Germans were feverishly working at the same time as the Americans, was not completed before the total collapse.

Despite his hopes for a miraculous turn of fortune, Hitler issued a vicious decree in March, ordering the total destruction of everything within the territory of the Reich, "which somehow sooner or later could be used by the enemy in the continuation of his struggle." Included in his list were all military installations, transport and communications facilities, industrial complexes, supply depots "as well as objects of value." The *Gauleiter* were made responsible for the execution of this scorched-earth policy, which aimed at turning Germany into a barren desert. Actually, Minister Speer interceded and to a large extent countermanded Hitler's order, insisting that only bridges be destroyed to delay the advance of the enemy, but not the agricultural and industrial basis of the nation's future existence.

But Hitler's destructive order had not been motivated by military considerations. Rather, it resulted from his manic determination to destroy everything that did not live up to his conception of Germany's destiny. Increasing megalomania had seemingly convinced him of the truth of Nazi propaganda that the Führer was the embodiment of the German people. Since Hitler had no intention of surviving defeat, he saw no reason for the people to outlive the war. To him their defeat merely meant that, contrary to his expectations, the Germans were the weaker people: there was no sense in safeguarding the bases of existence of a people who did not merit survival.

The Last Days

During the last ten days of April, contact among Hitler, the Nazi leaders, and the commanders in the field became increasingly difficult. Berlin was surrounded by a tightening ring of Soviet armies, and the rest of Germany was split by the rapid American advance across the center toward Czechoslovakia. Grand Admiral Karl Doenitz (1891–), the commander in chief of the German navy, was given command over all armed forces in the north, while Field Marshal Albert Kesselring (1885–1960) was placed in charge of all armies in the south.

On April 20, Hitler's fifty-sixth birthday, the last conference of the major leaders took place in the Führer's bunker in Berlin. Thereafter they scattered, some of them to engage in last-minute maneuverings for personal power. Hitler himself decided to remain in Berlin, rather than flee to relative safety in the Bavarian Alps. With him stayed Goebbels, devoted to the Führer until the end, and Bormann, eager to inherit Hitler's power. Once away from Berlin, Göring acted as if he were the chief of state, claiming Hitler was a prisoner in Berlin. He established contacts with the Allies in the hope of extracting better terms for himself. Infuriated by such "treason," Hitler expelled him from all his posts and appointed a new commander of the air force. Meanwhile Himmler had also left Berlin, had started his own futile negotiations with the Allies, and had attempted to persuade Admiral Doenitz to make a joint bid for power. Oblivious of the agony of Germany, the leading Nazis were busy fighting over the cadaver of the regime.

On April 28, it became evident that all efforts to break the Russian siege of Berlin were hopeless. On the following day, in a final fit of respectability, Hitler married his mistress Eva Braun. After that he wrote two testaments. One dealt largely with personal matters, the other concerned the fate of Germany. In the latter, he reiterated the claim that neither he "nor anyone else in Germany wanted war in 1939," and that he had done everything possible to avoid a war that, in the final analysis, had been "instigated exclusively by those international statesmen who were either Jewish or worked for Jewish interests." After stressing his own devotion to peace and to the German people, Hitler expelled Göring and Himmler from the Nazi party and transferred all power to a new government in which Doenitz was to serve as chancellor, Bormann as head of the party, and Seyss-Inquart as foreign minister. At the end of the testament, all Germans were enjoined to obey the new government unto death, and the leaders of the nation were commanded to observe the racial laws and put up "merciless resistance against international Jewry, the world poisoner of all people."

On April 30, Eva Braun took poison and Hitler shot himself. Despite his promise to Hitler to carry on the struggle, Goebbels on the following day poisoned his six children and then with his wife committed suicide. Bormann, the only other important witness to Hitler's death, tried to gain advantage from the confusion. Although he notified the surprised Doenitz of his appointment as successor to Hitler, he at first delayed the news of Hitler's death. On May 1, he finally informed Doenitz that the testament was in force and that Hitler had died on the preceding day, but urged the admiral to delay any action until he could join him. Bormann then left the bunker to make his way out of embattled Berlin, and disappeared. No certain proof of his death has ever been discovered.

In the afternoon of May 1, Doenitz announced over the German radio that Hitler had died and that he himself had assumed the arduous tasks of government. In view of the hopeless military situation—Berlin was lost, Hamburg had capitulated, the Italian front had collapsed, and over half of Germany was in enemy hands—Doenitz's only hope lay in concluding an immediate armistice with the Anglo-Americans, allowing him, if possible, to continue the war against the Russians. Disregarding Hitler's testamentary appointments, he chose his own, politically more moderate, provisional advisers and made arrangements to establish contact with Allied headquarters in the west. He was embarrassed in these actions by the increasing breakdown of communications, by the presence of Himmler, who persisted in hovering around the admiral despite his reiterated dismissal, and by the approaching columns of the Red Army.

On May 2, Doenitz moved his headquarters to Flensburg, near the Danish border in order to escape capture by the Russians. On the same day, all German forces in Italy surrendered unconditionally. Two days later, while negotiations proceeded with General Bernard Montgomery, a partial capitulation of the German armies in northern Germany, Holland, and Denmark was signed, all submarine warfare ceased, and German crews began to scuttle their U-boats in their home ports.

In accordance with inter-Allied agreements, the western powers refused to sign a unilateral surrender, and insisted on Germany's unconditional capitulation on all fronts. Finally, on May 7, Doenitz's plenipotentiaries signed the unconditional surrender terms with the western Allies at Reims, followed by similar agreements in Berlin with the Russians on May 8. The armistice came into force at one minute past midnight on May 9.

During the subsequent two weeks, American, British, French, and Russian forces quickly disarmed the German units and took over control of the entire country, while Doenitz, from his headquarters in Flensburg, attempted to supervise the dismantlement of the remaining German war machine and the dissolution of the Nazi regime.

Germany's Troubled Resurgence: Occupation, 1945–1949

ALLIED OCCUPATION

With the German unconditional surrender that became effective on May 9, 1945, the task of governing Germany was assumed by the occupying powers: England, Russia, and the United States, soon joined by France. Retention of a German central government under Admiral Doenitz was merely a transitional measure to facilitate the transfer of authority into Allied hands and to implement the Allied decision that the Germans be forced to dissolve the Nazi regime themselves and to demobilize their own war machine. On May 23, the pretense of the Doenitz government was terminated. The admiral was imprisoned to await trial as a war criminal, and the last shreds of a central German administration vanished.

Allied Military Government now assumed powers far surpassing those of previous military occupiers. According to the Hague Convention of 1907 on general rules of warfare, the rights of an occupying army are strictly limited and its duties largely confined to the maintenance of law and order. The Allied war aims, however, included the total reorganization of Germany as well as the reorientation of German political thinking. The occupying forces therefore set out to destroy German militarism and war potential, to obliterate the Hitler regime in all its aspects, to house and feed the German population, and to rebuild the German political, economic, and social structure. Even if the Allies had been in complete harmony on all facets of this formidable program, its accomplishment would have represented an enormous challenge.

Fruits of Total War

In the summer of 1945, Germany lay in ruins. Dire misery prevailed. Bombs and artillery shells had reduced the major cities to grotesque heaps of rubble. Apartments and shops, office buildings and factories lay in shambles;

water and gas mains were ruptured, electric and telephone wires were cut in thousands of places. Hamburg, for example, was 52 percent destroyed, with some 1.5 billion cubic feet of debris covering large sections of the town. In Cologne, 75 percent of the dwellings were uninhabitable. Over 25 percent of all German housing lay in ruins, at a time when the vast influx of refugees and expellees greatly augmented the need for shelter.

Communication and transport were at a standstill, major roads were impassable, all railroad bridges across the Rhine, the Weser, and the Danube had been blown up or damaged, and over half the locomotives and freight cars had been destroyed. In western Germany alone, inland shipping was blocked by almost 4000 obstructions—dynamited bridges, sunken barges, or damaged locks. Wartime losses and Allied seizures had reduced the merchant marine from 4 million gross tons (1939) to a mere 100,000.

Agricultural production was dangerously lowered through loss of food-producing areas (seized by Poland), lack of fertilizer and farm equipment, and disruption of transport. Shortages of food, clothing, and fuel brought threats of epidemics and starvation. The confusion was aggravated by the ceaseless flow of refugees from the east and by the chaotic streams of displaced persons crossing Germany in all directions. The population of Germany, although reduced by war casualties and by the millions that were still prisoners of war, was in fact vastly increased: 6 to 7 million aliens had been brought to Germany as slave laborers or had fled to Germany for other reasons. In addition, there were the millions of Germans who had fled before the advancing Red Army and were seeking shelter and support, and the millions of others expelled from eastern countries who arrived in the following months.

At the same time, the economic life of the nation lay in ruins. The German mark was worthless; the nation's total assets had been reduced by over 40 percent through the loss of territories, Allied seizures, confiscation of foreign holdings, and war destruction. Local government administration and normal police activities, educational institutions, news media, and municipal services—all had practically ground to a halt.

Added to the material devastation was the psychological trauma. Until the very end, Goebbels' propaganda machine had assured the Germans of imminent victory. The sudden realization of national humiliation came as a shock, and readjustment to the new reality caused anxiety and bewilderment. The generation that had come of age after 1933, had fought in Hitler's *Wehrmacht,* or had worked on the home front as a matter of duty, was suddenly confronted with the assertion that the ideals of their youth were not the pronouncements of an infallible Führer but the ravings of a war criminal. What had been sacred truth for twelve years was now declared a demoniacal lie. Their accepted system of values was swept away by the bombs and the occupation armies. Sitting beside the rubble of their former dwellings, nibbling on a crust of bread, smoking a cigarette butt saved from the crushing heel of an Allied soldier, many Germans faced the agonizing need for re-evaluating their lives. With their illusions dashed, some fell into self-effacing humility before the conquering occupants, some bolstered their ego with haughty self-exculpation. The bulk of the population, overwhelmed by the sheer exigencies of keeping alive, sank into a temporary stupor.

The Aims of Allied Occupation

For the purpose of reshaping Germany, the occupying powers attempted to work out common aims and policies.

WARTIME PLANNING The three principal Allied powers had discussed the projected treatment of Germany at numerous conferences between 1941 and 1945. In the Atlantic Charter (August 1941), Roosevelt and Churchill had denounced "territorial changes that do not accord with the freely expressed wishes of the peoples concerned." Yet it soon appeared that "the struggle for victory over Hitlerism" pledged by the Allies in the Declaration of the United Nations (January 1, 1942) required agreement not only on the political frame for postwar Germany but also on the question of Germany's frontiers. At two Moscow conferences in 1941, Stalin had suggested that after the war Austria and Czechoslovakia be restored, that East Prussia be turned over to Poland, the Ruhr detached from Germany, and that the Germans be forced to pay reparations. The western powers at the time considered such suggestions premature.

During 1942 and 1943, however, Churchill and Roosevelt became more interested in discussing postwar territorial settlements. The United States and Great Britain gradually accepted the suggestion of dividing Germany, either by encouraging separatist movements or by carving it up. They also lessened their opposition to ceding East Prussia to Poland, provided the local population be permitted to emigrate. But growing distrust between Stalin and the western powers prevented any agreement. Their delay in opening a second front in western Europe made Stalin increasingly suspicious of the Anglo-Americans, while rumors of separate Russo-German peace negotiations worried London and Washington. There was no consensus even on the terms of surrender. Stalin, who favored harsh but specifically stated conditions, objected to the stipulation of unconditional surrender announced at Casablanca (January 1943).

At the Quebec, Moscow, and Teheran Conferences of 1943, some decisions were reached. The surrender was to be signed by the Nazis themselves, so as to force the Germans to admit total defeat. The three Allies were to occupy Germany, assume political and economic power, and remove all Nazis from positions of influence. Thereafter the occupiers were to exercise minimum interference in local German government. Germany's political structure was to be decentralized, its arms factories were to be dismantled, its industry was to remain under permanent Allied inspection, and the Germans were to pay reparations. But no agreement on Germany's frontiers resulted.

On the one hand, the West shared Stalin's fear that Germany might recover rapidly after the war if it were not dismembered. Roosevelt was willing to see Germany divided into five states, whereas Churchill suggested that Prussia in the north remain more or less as it was and that the southern states be combined with Austria into a Danubian confederation. However,

Churchill and Roosevelt feared that the dismemberment of Germany would create a political vacuum in central Europe open to Soviet penetration. Hence they questioned the advisability of carving up Germany. For similar reasons, they sought ways to strengthen Poland as a possible buffer against Russian expansion. Since Poland was likely to lose territory in the east that Russia claimed and soon occupied, London and Washington came to favor Polish claims to East Prussia and to lands along Poland's western borders. As a possible boundary between Poland and Germany, the Big Three discussed the Oder-Neisse Line but reached no agreement.

At Quebec, in August 1944, Roosevelt and Churchill debated the assignment of occupation zones. They rejected plans for a combined western zone, which would have been politically and economically advantageous, although militarily and administratively more complicated. Instead, northern Germany was allotted to England, and the southern areas to the United States. At Quebec, the two heads of state also adopted the Morgenthau Plan, which had encountered much opposition in Roosevelt's cabinet and was to raise great controversy in the ensuing years. The Morgenthau Plan aimed at preventing "renewed rearmament by Germany" by closing down and dismantling the industries of the Ruhr and the Saar, and by having "some body under the world organization" ensure that these industries "were not started up again by some subterfuge." The dismantled machinery was to be used as reparations to restore the industries of countries devastated by the Germans. The proposed limitations on Germany's "metallurgical, chemical, and electrical industries" that could easily "be converted from peace to war," as well as suggestions for re-education, for political decentralization, and for the punishment of war criminals were later incorporated into the Potsdam Agreements. One statement, however—not contained in Morgenthau's original version, but somehow inserted in the communique signed by Churchill and Roosevelt—created discomfort in Allied ranks and provided useful ammunition for the Nazis' exhortation to their countrymen to fight to the bitter end. This was the phrase that the Allies were "looking forward to converting Germany into a country primarily agricultural and pastoral in its character."

At the Yalta Conference a few months later (February 1945), Stalin, Churchill, and Roosevelt reaffirmed their aims of destroying German militarism and Nazism and of bringing all war criminals to justice. Moreover it was decided that German reparations were to be extracted in three ways: (1) by removal of "equipment, machine-tools, ships, rolling stock, German investments abroad, shares of industrial, transport, and other enterprises in Germany," largely with the aim of destroying "the war potential of Germany"; (2) by "annual deliveries of goods from current production"; and (3) by Allied "use of German labor" for reconstruction of devastated areas in their own territories. An Allied Reparations Commission was to elaborate the details on the basis of a tentative total of 20 billion dollars, half of which was to go to the Soviet Union. At Yalta, the Big Three also decided that Germany was to be divided into four zones of occupation, with France receiving a portion of the regions previously assigned to the English and the Americans. Detailed zonal boundaries were to be fixed by a special commission. Germany as a whole was to be governed by a quadripartite Allied Control Council with headquarters in Berlin. Finally, Churchill and Roosevelt agreed that Poland should cede land to Russia in the east—along a border more or less following the Curzon Line proposed after World War I—and that in compensation, Poland should "receive substantial accessions of territory in the North and West" from Germany.

THE POTSDAM CONFERENCE Thus the general aims of the Allies had been outlined during the war and reaffirmed in the Berlin Declaration of June 5, 1945. In order to elaborate details and to discuss the continuation of the war against Japan, the Big Three held another summit conference at Potsdam near Berlin in July 1945. Of the wartime leaders who had participated in the previous meetings, only Stalin attended the session of two and a half weeks. After the Labor party victory in England, Clement Attlee replaced Churchill during the conference; President Harry S. Truman represented the United States.

The Potsdam Agreements, signed on August 2, 1945, were of decisive importance for the treatment of the German population and for the fate of Germany. Even though violated in many instances by one or another of the occupying powers, the Potsdam Decrees were regarded as the "Bible" of Allied Military Government for several years.

Like the Berlin Declaration, the Potsdam Agreements defined Germany's boundaries as those of December 31, 1937, before Hitler began his series of annexations. Within the frontiers of 1937, certain special, temporary arrangements were made (see Map 22). The coal-rich Saar was attached economically to France, and was to be treated differently from the remaining German territory, although its future political status was not stipulated. Furthermore, the Big Three "agreed in principle" to "ultimate transfer to the Soviet Union of the City of Königsberg and the area adjacent to it," and Truman and Churchill declared that their countries would support this cession "at the forthcoming peace settlement." It was also agreed that the territories to the east of the Oder and Neisse Rivers (with the exception of the Königsberg area) were to be separated from Germany and placed under temporary Polish administration, although it was stipulated that "the final delimitation of the western frontier of Poland should await the peace settlement." The area in question contained some 40,000 square miles (the former Prussian regions of East Prussia, eastern Pomerania, Silesia, and eastern Brandenburg), with a prewar population of about 9.5 million. Although this arrangement was provisional, the Potsdam Agreements exempted these lands from the jurisdiction of the Allied Control Authority (see page 605), and thus awarded Poland a free hand to treat them as it wished.

The remaining 138,000 square miles of Germany were divided into four zones of occupation, to be controlled by the four zone commanders, under the joint supervision of the Allied Control Authority. Soviet Russia was given some 43,000 square miles (all or part of the former regions of Pomerania, Mecklenburg, Brandenburg, Saxony,

MAP 22

and Thuringia), with a population of about 20 million. The second largest zone, some 42,000 square miles with roughly 23 million inhabitants, was occupied by England. It included Schleswig-Holstein, Lower Saxony, the city-state of Hamburg, and a new German state called North Rhine–Westphalia, comprising Westphalia, the Ruhr, and the Lower Rhineland. The American Zone, some 36,000 square miles with 17 million people, consisted of Bavaria, Hesse, and parts of Württemberg-Baden. In addition, Britain ceded to the United States the occupation rights to the port of Bremen to provide the American forces with port facilities for supplying their troops. Finally, a small zone of 17,000 square miles with 6 million inhabitants (including the Palatinate and the Upper Rhine Valley) was turned over to France. A special status was reserved for Berlin, which was to be divided into four sectors, each occupied by troops of one of the four powers, and administered jointly by an Inter-Allied Kommandatura. Separate bilateral arrangements, not contained in the Potsdam Agreements, were drawn up between the western occupants and Russia to permit free access by rail, canal, highway, and air between the western zones and Berlin.

The Potsdam Decrees contained directives designed "permanently to prevent the revival or reorganization of German militarism and Nazism." To this end, army, navy, air force, SS, SA, the Gestapo, the General Staff, military reserves, veterans' units, paramilitary outfits, and all Nazi organizations were to be abolished, all Nazi institutions dissolved, and all Nazi laws abrogated in so far as they contained "discrimination on grounds of race, creed, or political opinion." Nazis "who had been more than nominal participants" in the movement were to be removed from public office. The German educational and judicial systems were to be reorganized, war criminals put on trial, and the German people as a whole made to recognize that "their own ruthless warfare . . . [had] made chaos and suffering inevitable."

The political reconstruction of Germany was to be based on maximum administrative decentralization, with strong emphasis on local self-government, on the elective principle at all levels of government, and on the strengthening of democratic political parties. Freedom of speech, press, and religion was to be guaranteed, as well as the free development of trade-unions, "subject to maintenance of military security"—a phrase easily susceptible of misuse. In order to maintain a semblance of German unity, German central administrative departments for finance, transport, communications, foreign trade, and industry were to be set up under the supervision of the Allied Control Council, but "for the time being, no central German Government [was to] be established."

To disarm Germany permanently and to furnish the basis for reparations, the Allies projected various economic measures, many of which resembled those submitted by Morgenthau in his secret "Program to Prevent Germany from Starting a World War III." Industries producing aircraft, arms, or ammunition, as well as others easily converted to war production, were to be entirely prohibited, with the factories destroyed or turned over to the Allies as reparations. The level of industrial production, particularly in metals, chemicals, and heavy machinery, was to be fixed by the Allied Control Authority in order to prevent German rearmament, meet the needs of the occupying forces, and assure that the German standard of living would not exceed "the average of the standards of living of European countries." Agriculture and "peaceful domestic industry" were to be favored, and German industrial complexes broken up in order to eliminate "the present excessive concentration of economic power." To ensure the pooling of resources from the four zones, Potsdam stipulated that "during the period of occupation, Germany shall be treated as a single economic unit," a stipulation largely ignored by the occupiers, particularly the Russians and French.

Arrangements for reparations followed more or less the basis established at Yalta. The bulk of the claims of the Soviet Union and Poland were to be satisfied by removals from the Soviet Zone and by seizure of German foreign assets in Bulgaria, Finland, Hungary, Rumania, and eastern Austria. In addition, Russia was to receive from the Western zones 25 percent of the German industrial equipment declared "unnecessary for the German peace economy," in return for a portion of which it was to deliver to the western zones "an equivalent value of food, coal, potash, zinc, timber, clay products, petroleum products, and such other commodities as may be agreed upon." This arrangement led to considerable disagreement between Russia and the western powers. The claims of the eighteen other Allies were to be met from the western zones or from other

German foreign assets. The practice whereby each occupying power dismantled its own zone evoked much suspicion and recrimination, even though in theory quadripartite inspection teams were to decide which factories to remove. Moreover, it was specified that all dismantling of industrial equipment was to be completed within two and a half years—a stipulation that the western Allies accused the Russians of violating in 1948.

At Potsdam, the Big Three also acknowledged the need for transferring to Germany "German populations, or elements thereof, remaining in Poland, Czechoslovakia, and Hungary." These transfers were to "be effected in an orderly and humane manner," and the expulsions then in progress were to be temporarily suspended until the Control Council could undertake a census of those who had already fled to Germany from the east, could settle "the question of the equitable distribution of these Germans among the several zones of occupation," and establish "the time and rate at which further transfers could be carried out." The Allies acquiesced in this mass deportation, since the Germans (in prewar times an estimated five million) living in Poland, Czechoslovakia, and to a lesser extent in Hungary, had given Hitler an excuse for his drive to the east. No mention was made, however, of transfers from other countries from which Germans were then being expelled or from which they were fleeing —the Baltic states, Yugoslavia, Rumania, Russia and the Polish-occupied lands beyond the Oder-Neisse line.

Finally, the Big Three set up a Council of Foreign Ministers, including representatives of Russia, Britain, France, America, and China. This council was authorized to draw up peace treaties with Germany's five European allies (Finland, Italy, Hungary, Bulgaria, and Rumania), and was charged with the "preparation of a peace settlement for Germany to be accepted by the Government of Germany when a government adequate for the purpose is established."

The Allied Control Authority in Action

Soon after the Potsdam Conference, the Allies set up the Allied Control Authority (ACA) in Berlin. The four zone commanders, constituting the Control Council, met periodically to decide on policy for Germany as a whole. Below the Control Council sat a permanent quadripartite Coordinating Committee to supervise the functioning of the quadripartite directorates. The twelve directorates (respectively in charge of transport, finance, reparations and restitutions, prisoners of war and displaced persons, manpower, internal affairs and communications, as well as military, naval, air, political, economic, and legal matters) acted like all-German ministries, but lacked executive powers, which were vested in the individual zone commanders. Each directorate, with its committees, subcommittees, and working teams composed of delegates from the four occupying powers, attempted to elaborate common solutions for the treatment of Germany.

The occupying powers sought to deal immediately with the task of demilitarization and denazification. It was easy to disarm the population and dismantle military installations. Eradicating "militarism" was infinitely more complicated, and largely a matter of education and sociopolitical readjustments. The Control Council took the initiative by dissolving all military and paramilitary organizations and abolishing the state of Prussia on the grounds that "from early days . . . [it] has been a bearer of militarism and reaction in Germany." Equally difficult was the question of denazification.

DENAZIFICATION From the beginning, the Allies tried to distinguish between ferreting out and punishing those accused of specific crimes—a difficult though definable task—and eradicating Nazism—an immensely complicated and amorphous undertaking. During the early months of occupation, while the Control Council debated various drafts of anti-Nazi legislation, each zone commander initiated denazification proceedings in his zone according to the dictates of his own government.

The Russians and French generally favored summary removal of all Nazis from public positions, while the English and the Americans proceeded more slowly, attempting to observe legal formalities. In all zones, there were, of course, cases in which Nazis with technical skills were retained because of lack of non-Nazi replacements. Still, the early months of occupation were marked by a widespread removal of Nazis. Some were simply deprived of their jobs, while perhaps as many as one million (no detailed statistics are available for all zones) were herded into internment camps to await either trial or further disposition of their cases.

By early 1946, denazification proceedings had become more systematic. All Germans over eighteen years had to complete detailed questionnaires, so that intelligence personnel could distinguish among those Nazis criminally liable, those merely to be kept from positions of influence, and those to be completely exonerated. The United States favored turning over the denazification proceedings to the Germans themselves, on the theory that they should be forced to clean their own house. In each state (*Land*) in the American Zone, the Americans created German Ministries for Political Liberation, and forced the Germans to pass a "Law for Liberation from National Socialism and Militarism" (March 1946). By the end of 1946, 425 German denazification courts in the American Zone alone were combing through 11.5 million questionnaires and instituting proceedings as quickly as the dockets could be cleared for new cases. American authorities also turned over most internment camps to German control, retaining direct supervision only of those housing prisoners suspected of war crimes.

Detailed common policy for all of Germany was fixed by the Control Council in October 1946 in its directive on "The Arrest and Punishment of War Criminals, Nazis, and Militarists, and the Internment, Control, and Surveillance of Potentially Dangerous Germans." This directive delineated a clear distinction—already made in practice—between punishment of persons who had committed war crimes or crimes against humanity, and "internment of potentially dangerous persons who may be confined because their freedom would contribute a danger to the Allied Cause."

The Control Council directive defined five categories of Nazis: (1) *Major Offenders* were subject to penalties including death or life imprisonment, confiscation of property, loss of pensions, ineligibility for public office, or other punishments that would permanently remove them from public life. (2) *Offenders*—activists, militarists, or profiteers—those who actively helped advance Nazi tyranny but did not commit specific crimes, could be sentenced to a maximum of ten years in prison. (3) *Lesser Offenders* were those activists who, because of youth or other extenuating circumstances, deserved leniency; they were to be placed on probation for two or three years, during which time they could not operate or control a business, could not teach, write, or preach, or otherwise engage in public activities. (4) *Followers,* nominal supporters of the regime, were to be placed under police surveillance, could not stand for election to public office, and were obliged to pay a special contribution for reparations. (5) *Exonerated Persons* were former members of Nazi organizations who had been either passively or actively resisting Nazi tyranny and had themselves suffered from Nazi harassment. No sanctions were to be applied against the members of this category.

This Control Council directive gave a semblance of uniformity to the denazification proceedings throughout Germany, although differences of implementation continued among the zones. But the directive could not solve some of the problems inherent in the denazification process. In certain occupations, for instance, the number of Nazis or Nazi followers was so great that the occupiers had to retain at least "temporarily" the services of known Nazis. Moreover, the policy of forcing the Germans to do most of the denazifying themselves raised problems. The occupiers frequently had to interfere in German proceedings when they suspected the decisions of the German courts had not been just. Such interference created resentment; and those Germans who collaborated with the occupation authorities by informing on former Nazis, testifying against them, or participating in denazification courts were sometimes subjected to social ostracism. The treatment of hundreds of thousands of interned Nazis also presented difficulties. Inevitably some of those interned were mistreated, their food rations were kept at the lowest possible minimum, and some died in the camps. Germans who resented the Allied occupation were thus furnished ample ammunition for later denouncing the "atrocities of the Allies" and for comparing the internment centers for Nazis with Himmler's concentration camps. Finally, the exceedingly slow pace of the denazification process was denounced by many Germans who preferred to make a break with the past and to concentrate on building a new and different Germany.

Unquestionably, injustice was done in some cases, and many who deserved censure escaped it. Yet in view of the immensity of the undertaking, which no conqueror had ever before attempted in such scope, the denazification proceedings were relatively successful in accomplishing the desired aims.

WAR CRIMES TRIALS Considerably easier to accomplish was the punishment of Nazis for specific crimes. As early as 1942, nine Allied governments had declared their intention of trying Germans for crimes committed in occupied countries, such as "mass expulsions, execution of hostages, and massacres." In the Moscow Declaration of October 1943, Russia, Great Britain, and the United States had agreed to let individual countries try Germans for crimes committed on their territories or against their nationals. But a joint Allied tribunal was to try major offenders whose crimes involved more than one country. Thereafter, representatives from France, Russia, the United States, and Great Britain worked on detailed agreements for an International Military Tribunal. The study group faced countless questions: whether to advocate summary justice or formal legal proceedings; whether to try only individuals or also entire organizations; and whether people could be declared guilty on the basis of their association with a group. Furthermore, many Nazi crimes were not covered by existing international law. Hence the committee had to decide whether it was legal—and indeed advisable—to create new law.

The International Military Tribunal was finally established in August 1945 and endowed with a charter of jurisdiction. The tribunal was to prosecute "war criminals whose offenses have no particular geographic location whether they be accused individually or in their capacity as members of organizations or groups or in both capacities."

Eventually twenty-two individuals and seven organizations were tried by this tribunal in Nuremberg, in proceedings lasting from November 1945 to October 1946. There were four kinds of indictments: conspiracy to prepare aggressive war; crimes against the peace, namely "waging of a war of aggression, or a war in violation of international treaties"; war crimes, that is, violations of the customs of war (murder, use of slave labor, killing of hostages, plunder of cities); and crimes against humanity (extermination, enslavement, deportation, persecution). Of the seven organizations indicted, three were found innocent: the Reich cabinet, the General Staff and High Command of the army, and the SA. The remaining four—the Leadership Corps of the NSDAP, the SS, the SD, and the Gestapo were found guilty, but the verdict stipulated that membership in these organizations did not automatically make an individual a criminal. When passing judgments, the lower courts were to consider extenuating circumstances or the accused's possible ignorance of the aims of the organization.

Of the twenty-two persons tried before the tribunal, three were acquitted: Schacht, Papen, and the propagandist Hans Fritsche (1900–). Of the remaining defendants, twelve were sentenced to death by hanging—including Göring (who committed suicide before his scheduled execution), Ribbentrop, Rosenberg, Seyss-Inquart, and Bormann (*in absentia*). Hess, Funk, and Grand Admiral Erich Raeder (1876–1960), the head of the navy before he was replaced by Doenitz in 1943, were sentenced to life imprisonment. The remaining four, including Doenitz, received sentences of ten to twenty years' imprisonment.

In addition to the International Military Tribunal, special military government courts within each zone prosecuted Nazis for atrocities, murder, mass deportation, and other crimes against humanity or infringements on international rules of warfare. Allied nations not participating in the occupation of Germany—such as Czechoslovakia and Yugoslavia—also held trials of extradited Germans for crimes committed against their own nationals in the course of the German occupation of their country. After 1949, the Germans themselves gradually assumed responsibility for trying wartime offenders and criminals of the Nazi regime. These investigations and trials dragged on for years, at times in a somewhat desultory fashion, until new vigor was infused into the proceedings in 1958 (see page 661).

PROBLEMS OF GOVERNING GERMANY

The occupying powers faced many other tasks and problems. In the matter of permanent disarmament, for instance, it was relatively easy to prohibit the production of war matériel, but difficult to determine what factories could easily be reconverted to wartime production. For example, a plant that had manufactured periscopes for submarines could be used to produce mirrors or camera lenses; yet it might be easily reconverted to wartime use. A similar difficulty in delineating a clear dividing line between peaceful and military research faced the Allies in regard to surveillance of scientific activities.

Another problem of the ACA concerned agreement on a level at which to hold German industrial production. Since its industrial capacity had successfully supported Germany's war effort, and since many powerful industrialists in Germany had overtly or passively supported the Nazi movement, it seemed advisable to lower the German level of production and to break up the huge industrial cartels so that a few individuals could not wield disproportionate economic power. On the other hand, there were sound reasons for maintaining, if not raising, the level of German industry. Over 10 million more people were now crowded into an area reduced by almost 25 percent. Since the lands provisionally ceded to Poland were largely agricultural, industrial output might have to be raised so that more exports could pay for increased imports of food. A high level of industrial production might also provide surpluses to be used for reparations in kind. Finally, some Allied advisers pointed to the interdependence of the European economy as a whole, and argued that the creation of an economic desert in Germany might ruin all chances for a rapid economic recovery in the surrounding European states.

In March 1946, the Control Council finally adopted the Level of Industry Plan for all of Germany. It contained blanket prohibitions for certain industries, such as those manufacturing aircraft, seagoing vessels, radio transmitting equipment, ball bearings, and many synthetics and machine tools. Production rates in most industries were strictly limited: steel was fixed at 7.5 million tons a year, basic chemicals were limited to 40 percent of the 1936 level, and a ceiling was placed on the manufacture of trucks, busses, and tractors. Actually most of these limitations were never enforced, for inter-Allied disagreements during the following years completely altered the attitude of most nations, particularly the United States, toward European and German economic reconstruction.

One of the busiest of the ACA directorates dealt with prisoners of war, displaced persons, and expellees. Displaced persons were non-Germans found in Germany at the end of the war; expellees were ethnic Germans expelled from Eastern Europe. Initially, the repatriation of German prisoners of war, particularly from British and American camps, had proceeded rapidly. Yet by December 1946, almost 4 million German prisoners had not yet returned to their homes. Over half a million remained in France, working on reconstruction projects, and over 3 million were presumably working in the Soviet Union or being detained in Russian compounds. It proved impossible for the directorate or the International Red Cross to obtain precise reports on the number remaining in Russia.

The problem of displaced persons proved equally complicated. During the first half year of occupation, more than 5 million were repatriated to their homelands. But more than a million remained in Germany, about 70 percent of these being unacceptable to their native country or unwilling to return for political or other reasons. These lived in special camps—most of them in the American and British zones—under supervision of Allied Military Government. In 1946, the United Nations Relief and Rehabilitation Agency assumed the care of these persons, many of whom remained in German compounds for years before finding homes in Australia, New Zealand, Argentina, the United States, or elsewhere.

The greatest task of the Prisoner of War and Displaced Persons Directorate was to supervise the assignment of expellees from the east to one of the four zones. According to quadripartite agreements, some 5 million Germans were to be admitted. These were assigned to numerous reception camps, and statistics were prepared to show how many trainloads could be received in each zone in a given month. But the preparations fell far short of the needs. Czechoslovakia, Hungary, and Poland expelled more people than had been stipulated. In addition, Poland drove out over a million Germans from the territories under its provisional administration, Rumania, Bulgaria, and Yugoslavia also contributed to the stream of expellees, and countless Germans fled on their own into occupied Germany. As a result, instead of the 5 million expected, almost 10 million expellees and refugees surged into Germany in the first two years of occupation. A large proportion of the expellees were women and old people, many unable to work. Until German authorities could take over the care of these millions, the occupation forces housed them in emergency compounds or even in abandoned Nazi concentration camps.

Differences in Zonal Administration

The Potsdam Agreements had stipulated that "so far as is practicable, there shall be uniformity of treatment of the German population throughout Germany." Yet the basic directives of the ACA received widely differing interpretation and implementation by the four zone commanders, each of whom was in fact supreme in his own domain. As a result, Germany was subjected to four different policies of administration. As United States Secretary of State James Byrnes complained (September 1946): "So far as many vital questions are concerned, the Control Council is neither governing Germany nor allowing Germany to govern itself." The divergent policies of the four Allies were particularly evident in their respective plans for the political reconstruction of Germany.

CENTRALISM VERSUS FEDERALISM As might be expected, France preferred to see Germany emerge as a loose confederation of states. Throughout the centuries, France had benefited from the disunity among the German states; the unification of Germany in 1870 had paved the way for the three invasions that France suffered at the hands of a united and centralized German state. Consequently the French proposed that the sixteen individual German states (*Länder*) be turned into quasi-sovereign units, exercising all powers not specifically reserved to the confederation. The federal legislature was to consist solely of an upper house representing the several states. The proposal envisioned a long delay before such a confederation would be created. Meanwhile Allied Military Government would exercise the necessary coordinating authority, except in purely technical fields, which could be entrusted sooner to German agencies. The administrative policy followed in the French Zone reflected these views. Establishment of political organs was largely limited to the states. All-zonal organizations were created only in technical areas where over-all coordination was essential, such as price control, post and telegraph, social insurance, and finance. The French thus hoped to make the states politically as self-sufficient as possible in order to obviate the need for a strong central government.

The Soviet proposal for reconstructing Germany was diametrically opposed to that of the French. Russia favored a highly centralized state, more unitary than the Weimar Republic. Although the Russians did not wish to revive a strong Germany, their social theories required the creation of a strong central government. Through the aid of the Communist party, they hoped to direct the activities of this government in accordance with Russian interests. As early as September 1945, Soviet Military Government created German administrative agencies with jurisdiction over the entire Soviet Zone in such fields as industry, labor, education, agriculture, health, and justice. Initially only advisory in capacity, these central agencies were soon accorded substantial executive power. The state governments on the other hand, were never awarded much political power in the Soviet Zone.

The British Labour government, itself fairly centralized, also favored a unitary state, although one not so completely centralized as that supported by the Russians. The British allowed the states powers similar to those stipulated in the Weimar Constitution. Control over most fields, including economy, finance, and justice, was retained by Military Government, which acted as a sort of zonal government. As a result, the states in the British Zone exercised relatively unimportant functions until the beginning of 1947, when the economic merger of the British and American zones necessitated an adaptation of the political systems of the two zones to each other.

The United States hoped to turn Germany into a federal state. The three states of the American Zone were to receive legislative and executive powers similar to those exercised by the American states. To coordinate their activities, a zonal conference of the minister-presidents of the states was organized in the fall of 1945, with regular meetings supervised by Military Government. The American Zone was thus decentralized in administrative functions, although it enjoyed a certain amount of coordination among the state governments.

THE BEGINNING OF POLITICAL PARTIES
Similar divergences characterized the attitudes of the occupying authorities toward the formation of political parties. The Potsdam Agreements stipulated that "local self-government be restored throughout Germany . . . as rapidly as is consistent with military security," and that for this purpose "all democratic political parties with rights of assembly and of public discussion be allowed and encouraged throughout Germany."

But even before the Potsdam Conference, the Allies diverged in practice. When the western armies were streaming into Germany in April 1945, SHAEF (Supreme Headquarters Allied Expeditionary Forces) ordered its forces not to allow the Germans to publish political papers or engage in political activities. Although an occasional local military commander permitted former members of Weimar parties to hold meetings, as a result of the SHAEF order anti-Nazi underground forces could not form political groups and the formation of parties in the western zones had a late start.

The Russians, however, speedily pushed the formation of parties. On June 10, 1945, the Russian zone commander licensed four groups—the Communists (KPD), the Socialists (SPD), the Christian Democrats (CDU), and the Liberal Democrats (LDP). By late July, when the Allies were gathering at Potsdam, the four parties were fully operative on an all-zonal level, publishing their own papers (under Soviet censorship) and holding party meetings (under Soviet direction). From the beginning, therefore, the Russian occupation forces used centralized German political organs for influencing public opinion, under the guise of promoting cooperation among all "anti-Fascist parties."

The western powers proceeded more slowly with the reconstruction of German political life, and tried to introduce decentralized control at the grassroots level. The Americans were the first to authorize the formation of parties, at the county (*Kreis*) level in August 1945. All-zonal mergers of parties were allowed only in early 1946. Similarly, elections in the American Zone began with rural districts and small communities in January 1946, and ended with elections to the three state legislatures in December of that year. This slow pace, according to the American directive, was designed to promote the development of "genuine democratic institutions in Germany." American authorities carefully supervised the elections—regulating electoral codes, suffrage rules, and campaign procedures—and retained control over the licensing of parties until November 1948.

British authorities allowed the formation of parties immediately on an all-zonal level (September 1945). However, the first elections in the British Zone were held only in September 1946, and the British retained close control over all parties until 1950. The French, for their part, were extremely reluctant to permit the revival of political life in Germany. Initial permission for the reconstitution of parties was given in December 1945, but so many obstructions were placed in the way of politicians that parties began to form only in the spring of 1946, after local elections had already been held in the American Zone.

SOCIAL, ECONOMIC, AND EDUCATIONAL POLICIES In almost all other facets of occupation policy, there was little uniformity among the four zones. Economic unity was not achieved. Surpluses from the Russian Zone were not made available to fill deficits in other zones. Industrial complexes with branch factories located in different zones could not function as units. Even the normal interzonal exchange of railroad freight cars was hampered by obstructionism, usually by Russian or French authorities; and the Allies could not agree on uniform rations throughout Germany.

The attitude toward labor unions furnished a typical example of the divergent policies of the western and the Russian authorities. The reconstruction of labor organizations in the western zones received the active support of American, British, and French unions. The occupation authorities favored free trade-unions, organized democratically and based on free election of union officials. At the same time they insisted that unions be politically neutral. By the end of 1946, unions in the American Zone were allowed to operate on the level of the states, but not at that time on a zonal basis. In the other western zones, they were kept even more decentralized.

The Russians, however, asserted that grass-roots control of unions might permit their infiltration by neo-Fascist elements. Hence they immediately set up hierarchically organized unions on an all-zonal basis, with control tightly lodged in a Russian-picked executive committee. Membership in unions was made more or less compulsory, and unions were turned into political pressure groups. The Russian authorities could thus use the unions as another instrument for governing their zone.

In the field of education, the Potsdam Agreements had stipulated that "Nazi and militarist doctrines" be eliminated from German education, and the "development of democratic ideas" encouraged. But the ACA could reach no agreement on the implementation of these principles. At the beginning of the occupation, all schools were closed. By the fall of 1945, elementary schools in all the zones began to reopen, despite shortages of buildings, acceptable textbooks, and non-Nazi teachers. All four occupation authorities helped train new teachers and produce textbooks free from Nazi indoctrination, and they sought to eliminate the social distinctions imbedded in the former German school system. But wide differences among the zones arose in the organization of school administration, the curriculums at the higher levels, the admission policies of universities, as well as the establishment of youth movements.

Most of these differences in occupation policies also characterized the quadripartite administration of Berlin. Although in theory common procedures were determined by the Allied Kommandatura for Berlin, in practice each occupation sector of the city was administered differently—a situation full of complications, since it affected people living within the same city, sometimes only a few blocks apart.

BEGINNING OF RECOVERY AND THE COLD WAR

Starting in 1946, and especially in 1947, differences among the Allies coagulated into the cold war between Russia and the West. This tension gradually affected most facets of Allied occupation policy, and ultimately brought about the division of Germany into two separate states.

Rebuilding the Economic Life

During the first two years, primary efforts were devoted to satisfying the desperate need for food, shelter, and fuel. At the same time, considerable progress was made in clearing away the rubble—especially in the American and the British zones—and in restoring public utilities and transportation. By February 1946, for instance, almost 96 percent of the primary railroad lines in the American Zone were again usable. The British, meanwhile, concentrated on reactivating coal production. Special food rations were issued to miners, and by the spring of 1946, production of hard coal, almost at a standstill at war's end, stood at over 50 percent of capacity. But because a portion of this coal was allocated as part of reparations, shortages in Germany remained acute.

Some sectors of the German economy were in better condition than expected, and furnished a potential basis for German economic recovery. During the war, industrial capacity had been expanded, and Allied strategic bombing had hurt German production more by disrupting transport and keeping workers off their jobs than by obliterating plant facilities. Hence a relatively large number of plants, blast furnaces, and machine tools were either ready for operation in 1945, or reparable within a short time, provided sufficient transport, energy, manpower, and raw materials could be made available.

Still, this industrial recuperation was more potential than actual. Besides shortages of materials and manpower, there was financial instability and uncertainty about the future. In the western zones—especially in Berlin—the German middle class feared that the western powers might withdraw and abandon the Germans to Communist expropriation. Moreover, the German mark was being printed in reckless quantities, the price structure was erratic, and inflation was rampant. Three different price levels existed. Wages and rationed food were kept at a controlled level. A pound of bread at the official price cost the equivalent of 2 U.S. cents, and wages varied between 8 and 18 cents an hour. Prices on articles of current production were flexible. For instance, a cheap ashtray, made from scrap aluminum salvaged from a downed airplane, might sell for $1.50. On the black market, however, bread cost $4 a pound, a pack of cigarettes in Berlin up to $20, and two drinks and some poor food in an ordinary nightclub about $100. Without a stable price structure, it seemed impossible to initiate a sound revival of the economy.

Uncertainty in industry and commerce was also caused by the unclear policy concerning nationalization and decartelization. Starting in 1946, the Russians sponsored popular referendums in some states for the approval of laws to expropriate "reactionary" concerns. In this manner, mines and other basic industries were gradually nationalized. During 1947 alone, some two thousand enterprises passed from private ownership into the possession of county or municipal governments, or of specially organized cooperatives. The authorities in the western zones, on the other hand, left all decisions about nationalization up to a future all-German government. Even this policy did not reassure the industrialists, since the major political parties, including at first the various Christian Democratic groups, advocated some form of nationalization in their party programs. Moreover, the French adamantly demanded international ownership and control of the coal and steel industries in the Ruhr as a vital requisite for ensuring European peace.

The policy on decartelization was equally nebulous. In accordance with the mandate of Potsdam, this problem was frequently discussed at the ACA, and in November 1945 the Control Council enacted a law for the decartelization of the huge I. G. Farben concern. But it proved impossible to formulate a general law on the permissible size of industrial or financial complexes and on interlocking management. In 1947 and 1948, British and American authorities issued laws in their zones for the control and decartelization of coal, steel, iron, chemical, and electric industries, as well as of financial institutions. Few concerns were actually affected, and most cartels were never split up. In fact, after 1950, large enterprises were recartelized and vast new concentrations were created.

The unsettled issues of reparations and restitution also delayed economic recovery. So long as it was not determined which factories were to be earmarked for reparations, industrialists were reluctant to repair war damage or improve production facilities. Moreover, even after the Allies officially announced the Level of Industry Plan, it was obvious that their decision was subject to revision, so that it remained difficult for Germans to make long-range economic forecasts.

The question of restitution was also clouded. Although it was fairly easy to identify and restore foreign goods seized by the Germans during the war, restitution within Germany was more complicated. Thousands of industrial and commercial concerns had been confiscated by the Nazis from Jews or from other "enemies of the state," or acquired in forced sales. After the collapse of the Nazi regime, their ownership remained in doubt. The Allies merely stressed the need for making equitable restitution, and it was a long time before the Germans, lacking a central government, evolved a consistent policy of restitution and compensation.

AMERICAN ASSISTANCE In order to prevent starvation and economic collapse as well as to rekindle the economy, the United States and England furnished large-scale aid to Germany. In the first three postwar years, before the initiation of the Marshall Plan, American grants and credits amounted to almost 1.2 billion dollars. At the same time, American military establishments contributed heavily to Germany's reconstruction, and private American citizens mounted a relief campaign of magnitude. To coördinate the multifarious efforts of private organizations, the United States government in February 1946 recognized the Council of Relief Agencies Licensed for Operation in Germany (CRALOG), composed of eleven private agencies engaged in shipping food, clothing, and medical supplies to the American Zone. In 1946, also, the Cooperative for American Remittances to Europe (CARE) set up facilities for shipping relief parcels to individual German families in the American Zone, an arrangement soon extended to the other zones of occupation.

This public and private aid unquestionably helped tide the Germans over the first two harsh winters and alleviated some of the suffering. But the anomaly of the situation was soon recognized. The United States was extending grants and credits not only to Germany but to nineteen other European nations (a total of about 12.5 billion dollars between July 1945 and June 1948). As long as each European country was attempting to recuperate in economic isolation, waste and needless duplication in the aid program were inevitable. Moreover, it appeared shortsighted to keep the German level of production to a minimum when German productive capacity could be used to help rehabilitate the economy of Europe as a whole. Finally, the American government began to realize that it was shipping into Germany on an emergency basis some of the same materials that Russia was withdrawing from Germany under the guise of reparations. These considerations soon led to a fundamental reappraisal of American policy that resulted in the Marshall Plan for economic aid to Europe as well as in the establishment of Bizonia in Germany.

THE CREATION OF BIZONIA At the Paris meeting of the Council of Foreign Ministers in July 1946, United States Secretary of State Byrnes declared: "We cannot continue to administer Germany in four airtight compartments, preventing . . . exchange between the four zones of goods, communications, and even ideas." Complaining that the existing arrangement produced "inflation and economic paralysis" and resulted in "increased costs to the occupying powers and unnecessary suffering to the German people," he proposed the immediate "establishment of central German administrative agencies necessary to secure economic unity in Germany." In order to assuage French apprehensions, he suggested that the coal-rich Saar might be retained for a time under separate French control in order to aid the economic reconstruction of France. If all the other powers were unwilling to accept the American proposal, Byrnes offered to merge the American Zone economically with the zone of any other nation, on the theory that economic unity of two zones would be better than none.

Byrnes's proposal was rejected by both Russia and France. Intent on first satisfying its reparations claims, Russia was unwilling to pool all Germany's resources. And France persisted in opposing the creation of any central German agencies, except in return for wide concessions—the separation from Germany of the Ruhr, the Rhineland, and the Saar. The French, who had not participated in the Potsdam Conference, did not feel bound by the agreements made there concerning German economic unity.

A few weeks later, the United States representative on the Control Council (General Joseph T. McNarney), repeated Byrnes's offer. The British promptly accepted, and they and the

Americans established five German agencies for the administration of economics, finance, transport, communications, and agriculture for both zones, under the supervision of joint English and American control boards. Exports and imports for the two zones were merged, and the cost of necessary imports was shared by the two Allied governments. In order to make all vital resources available to Bizonia, British authorities withdrew control of the iron and steel industries in their zone from ACA jurisdiction, a move that infuriated the Russian and French governments. The establishment of Bizonia, officially inaugurated on January 1, 1947, thus marked an important step in granting more self-administration to the Germans, and signaled a beginning of the division of Germany.

The creation of Bizonia was also accompanied by a change in the American attitude toward Germany. As Secretary Byrnes noted in a speech in Stuttgart in September 1946, the policy of distrust and nonfraternization had given way to friendship. He also urged that, if reparations continued to be taken from current German output, the levels of industrial production should immediately be raised. Finally, he suggested that an all-Germany currency reform was essential to place the German economy on a sound footing.

The establishment of Bizonia in effect foreshadowed the creation of a West German state closely tied to the economic life of the western nations. While in their zone the Russians continued dismantling factories during 1947 and even tore up railroad tracks for shipment to the Soviet Union, the English and Americans temporarily suspended dismantling operations and attempted to raise industrial production so as to lessen the unfavorable balance in Germany's foreign trade. In August 1947, they officially revised the proposed level of industry, and permitted Germany to increase its steel production to 11.7 million tons a year. At the same time, free travel by Germans between the two zones was permitted, and, where possible, political, legal, and other matters were put on a common level.

Political Parties, Old and New

First on the scene was the German Communist party (KPD), formed with the active support of the Russian occupation authorities by *émigrés* returned from Russia. Initially there was a tendency also in the western zones to favor the KPD, since its members were known to be stanch anti-Nazis. Among the leaders of the party, officially founded in Berlin in June 1945, were Wilhelm Pieck (1876–1960) and Walter Ulbricht (1893–   ), both cofounders of the KPD in 1918 and members of the National Committee for a Free Germany formed in Moscow during World War II. The first program of the KPD was moderate. Hoping to attract liberals and democrats, the Communists announced that the Soviet system was not applicable to Germany, and that all anti-Nazi parties should cooperate in a joint program of denazification, economic and political reconstruction, freedom of religion, and cooperation with other nations. However, when left-wing leaders of the Social Democratic party (SPD)—Max Fechner (1892–   ) and Otto Grotewohl (1894–   )—suggested cooperation between the SPD and KPD so as to eliminate the traditional cleavage among the workers, Ulbricht at first rejected the offer, feeling confident that the

KPD alone, with financial, political, and propaganda support from the Russians, could seize the leadership of political life in Germany.

Soon, however, the Communists realized that their only hope of extending their influence, particularly in the western zones, lay in a merger with the numerically stronger SPD. They exerted pressure on left-wing SPD leaders in Berlin and in the Russian Zone, and appealed to SPD and KPD members in the western zones to present joint candidates at the elections. Western Socialists generally rejected this appeal, unless the union of the parties would be effected on an all-German basis, to assure the SPD a majority and thus safeguard the united party from Russian control. But the Russian authorities opposed the suggested grassroots approach of the Socialists. They jailed some recalcitrant SPD leaders, and harassed the activities of the Socialist party in their zone until preparations were completed to effect a forced merger of the two parties. Without consulting the rank-and-file members, Pieck, Grotewohl, and other hand-picked KPD and SPD leaders voted a formal union of the two parties in April 1946. The resulting Socialist Unity party (SED) was not a real merger; rather, it submerged the Socialists under Communist domination in the Russian Zone.

Despite the sham existence of other political parties, the SED became a real state party. In the 1946 Russian Zone elections, it obtained a clear majority at the communal level, and received an average of 48.7 percent in district and state-wide balloting. By the use of voting lists, by putting up sham parties in order to draw away votes from opposition groups, by rationing newsprint and employing other devices, the SED gained control of all state governments and legislatures in the Russian Zone. In the western sectors of Berlin, however, where the Communists had initially filled all important posts in the city administration, the SED failed in its avowed purpose. In city elections in October 1946 only 20 percent of the votes went to the SED, as contrasted with 48.7 percent to the SPD.

In the three western zones the KPD initially posed as a democratic, anti-Nazi organization favoring cooperation with all liberal parties. Its platform called for wide-scale nationalization of industry and expropriation of large landholdings. In all three zones, the KPD emerged as the third largest party, although it polled only between 5 and 8 percent in the various elections between 1946 and 1948. In some states (Hesse and North Rhine–Westphalia). Communists obtained posts in state governments. The strength of the KPD in the western zones, however, was short-lived. After the creation of a West German state in 1948, the party abandoned its policy of cooperating with other groups, and adopted a more clearly Moscow-oriented direction. Its attraction for the voters fell rapidly. In 1953, it captured only 2.2 percent of the votes, and in 1956, the West German Constitutional Court declared the KPD to be "unconstitutional," and outlawed it.

Simultaneously with the Communists, Socialist leaders in the various zones re-established the German Social Democratic party. The veteran Socialist Kurt Schumacher (1895–1952), who had languished for ten years in a Nazi concentration camp, early assumed control over the party's reconstruction, and became the official SPD chairman for all three western zones in May 1946. The party's platform, formed at Wenningen in October 1945, stipulated that all German Socialists should follow identical policies in order to preserve the unity of Germany, that cooperation with democratic parties should be encouraged, and that the Communists' offer to fuse the two workers' parties should be rejected. The Wenningen program was imbued with a strongly nationalistic fervor. Perhaps in bitter recollection of the 1920s, when the SPD had been accused of being traitorously un-German, Schumacher was determined to make his party the voice of German nationalism. It rejected the notion of collective war guilt for all Germans, and attacked the aims of the Morgenthau plan. Dismantling of industry was decried as economically unsound. The SPD demanded the rapid creation of a strongly centralized national government, in opposition to the federalism advocated by some of the other political parties. The state was to direct German reconstruction, control financial institutions, and nationalize basic industries. But the SPD platform rejected state ownership in favor of a system of cooperatives in which governments, local groups, and consumers participated.

The SPD grew rapidly during 1946 and emerged as the strongest or second strongest party in all the western states. It exerted much influence on the writing of many of their constitutions. In 1948–1949, it sent the largest number of delegates (although not a majority) to the Parliamentary Council charged with drafting a constitution for West Germany (the Basic Law of 1949). Although the SPD failed in its aim of maximizing the powers awarded the proposed central government, it was able to force a compromise with the bourgeois parties on other points of disagreement; the role of the churches in education, the social duties of the state, and other contended points were left undefined in the final draft.

Although the SPD of 1945 was essentially a revival of the Socialist party of the Weimar Republic, Schumacher gave it a wider base of appeal than its predecessor had. Instead of concentrating on workers and intellectuals, the new party also attracted lower bourgeois and small peasants. By toning down its anticlericalism, the party could court religious-minded Socialists. And its nationalistic, antiforeign stand appealed to German patriots.

Another party, the strongest in the West, was the Christian Democratic Union (CDU). Officially founded as an all-German party at Bad Godesberg in December 1946, the CDU at first remained a loosely knit organization, held together by the conviction that only a religiously oriented middle-class party with a moderate platform might counteract the strength of the SPD and KPD. The diverse Christian Democratic groups were gradually molded into a real party only through the need for nation-wide electioneering for the 1949 elections, and the party held its first formal all-German convention only in October 1950.

The CDU is both a new party and a revival of the old Center party. Like the former Center, it adheres to the middle of the road, without appealing to a specific class or region, reconciling within its ranks various conflicting economic interests. Like the Weimar Center, the CDU can shift to the Left or the Right, and enter coalitions with conservative parties or with the Socialists. Among its first executive committee of thirty, eighteen had been members of the Center party before 1933. But the CDU is also essentially a new and different party. The influential Cologne group within the party, among whose leaders was Konrad Adenauer (1876–), considered the Catholic framework of the former Center too restrictive, and insisted that Protestants be included to give the party a broader base. The Berlin group, founded by members of the Kreisau Circle (see page 592) and other anti-Nazis who had been involved in the plot of July 20, 1944, and had learned the need for cooperation between diverse points of view in the underground, advocated a program of liberal social legislation. The CDU thus embraced Protestants and Catholics, conservatives and liberals, members of the former DNVP as well as former Socialists. Its original executive committee contained industrialists, civil servants, scientists, agriculturalists, workers, lawyers, educators, artisans, as well as a journalist and a housewife.

Despite this broad base, the Bavarians who had formed their own Christian-Social Union (CSU) on the basis of similar ideals refused to amalgamate their party with the CDU. Although from its inception, the CSU usually cooperated with the CDU in all national questions, it remains to this day a separate party.

The initial platform of the CDU was quite liberal. In 1945, it demanded the strictest anti-Nazi measures, the abolition of monopolistic capitalism, the nationalization of coal mines and energy resources, and confiscatory taxes on war profits. By 1946, its anti-Nazi fervor had slackened, and with the ascendancy of Konrad Adenauer, its liberalism paled. Still, the "CDU Economic and Social Program" formulated at Ahlen in February 1947 was surprisingly liberal. It attacked "the unlimited domination of private capital," advocated decartelization of big industry and establishment of a planned cooperative economy, assuring "social justice." The program also called for "the right of codetermination" for workers by permitting labor representatives to participate in management councils. The Ahlen program was thus a frank attempt to bridge the cleavage between workers and capitalists and to attract labor votes, an attempt that proved successful even in the solid SPD territory of the Ruhr.

For a while the CDU seemed determined to implement its Ahlen platform. When Bizonia was created, CDU members called for agrarian and currency reform; for laws to equalize the burdens caused by war, reparations, and the need to care for refugees; and for a total reorganization of industry in accordance with the Ahlen proposal. Yet the cleavage between SPD and CDU remained severe. When the Bizonal Economic Council—consisting of 20 SPD, 20 CDU, 3 KPD, and 10 members of smaller bourgeois parties—elected its five directors in July 1947, the bourgeois majority showed its usual distrust of the Socialists by choosing a directorate composed exclusively of CDU members. The CDU thus assumed primary responsibility for planning the economic reconstruction of the western zones, just as in the following years, it was the dominant voice in the establishment of the West German state. Involvement in the leadership of the nation turned the CDU into the strongest political party in West Germany and rapidly gave its ideals an increasingly conservative coloring.

Besides the three major parties—CDU, SPD, and KPD (SED)—there were various smaller political organizations with moderate programs. In the British Zone, some former Centrists refused to join the CDU, and revived the old Center party, with a progressive program of socialization and federalism, combined with a strong stand against close collaboration with the west for fear of endangering German unity. The Center party distrusted the conservative wing of the CDU, and although working in coalition with the Christian Democrats in North Rhine–Westphalia, opposed Adenauer's party in the first *Bundestag*. It never acquired much national importance, gaining only 3.1 percent of the 1949 vote. Even its collaboration with the small Bavarian party (BP) did not prevent its decline. By 1953, it polled less than 1 percent in the national elections and sank to obscurity.

Of greater long-range consequence were the numerous semiconservative middle-class parties that in 1948 banded together in the three western zones to form the Free Democratic party (FDP). The FDP rapidly rose to national importance, and became the third largest party in 1949, with 11.9 percent of the votes. Composed mostly of businessmen, civil servants, and intellectuals, most of whom were members of the former Democratic and German People's parties, the FDP stood to the right of the CDU, advocating a nonsectarian program of free enterprise and individual freedom. It opposed all schemes for socialization or codetermination in industry. Like the SPD, it favored noninterference in religious matters, a strongly nationalistic program, and a more centralized government than that preferred by the CDU. Unlike the CDU, it opposed closer ties with the West until German reunification was achieved. But on most other matters it could readily cooperate with the CDU, so that in 1949, it formed a coalition government with Adenauer, assuring the election of its chairman, Theodor Heuss (1884–   ) to the presidency of West Germany.

In addition there arose many small conservative parties, only a few of which reached national stature. Many championed particularistic rights, such as the South Schleswig Association and the Bavarian party. The program of the German party (DP), a conservative group, some of whose members favored restoration of the monarchy, was federalistic, antiunion, and in favor of a completely private economy. It opposed the denazification program, demanded better treatment of former army officers, and enjoyed a long-lasting although relatively unimportant political existence. Finally, there were various authoritarian or neo-Nazi organizations, which gathered in former members of the DNVP and NSDAP. Among these were the German Conservative party (DKP) and the short-lived German Rightist party (DRP). The most successful, the German Social Reich party (SRP) was, like the NSDAP, socialistic only in name. Founded in 1949, it enjoyed a moment of national importance, but was quickly swept aside by the growing democratic current, and dissolved by order of the Federal Constitutional Court in October 1952.

The East-West Split of Germany

BREAKDOWN OF QUADRIPARTITE GOVERNMENT None of the foreign ministers' conferences held during 1946 and 1947 produced a quadripartite solution to the German problem. The four wartime Allies remained deadlocked over Russian reparations demands, German economic unity, and establishment of a German central government. For the United States the issue involved primarily financial considerations. Since its external assets of about 2 billion dollars had been confiscated, Germany could not pay for vital imports unless it increased its exports to earn the necessary funds. But so long as Russia was claiming Germany's excess production as reparations while America was paying for Germany's imports, American taxpayers were in fact financing German reparations to other countries. At the London Conference in December 1947, Secretary of State George C. Marshall sharply criticized Soviet intransigence and accused the Russians of wanting to impose "conditions which would not only enslave the German people but would seriously retard the recovery of all Europe."

Consequently the West decided to act unilaterally. France, Britain, and the United States joined delegates from the Benelux countries (Holland, Belgium, and Luxemburg) in a series of conferences in London between February and June 1948 at which they reviewed the German problem. The Russians promptly protested against these meetings, accusing the West of violating occupation agreements. When the meetings continued and the West publicly placed all blame on the Soviet Union for preventing German economic and political unity, the Russian delegates walked out of the Control Council meetings in Berlin on March 20, 1948, dramatizing the end of the quadripartite administration of Germany.

Meanwhile the western powers proceeded with the amalgamation of their zones. A German Bizonal Economic Administration, a German High Court, and the *Bank Deutscher Länder* (Bank of the German States) were established in February 1948. The six powers then decided at London to create Trizonia (effective June 1, 1948) by merging the French Zone with Bizonia, to allow the Germans to draft a provisional constitution for the three zones, and to establish a German federal government subject to only limited Allied supervision as defined in a special Occupation Statute. The conferees also agreed to make minor border adjustments in Germany's frontier with Belgium and Holland (involving some 52 square miles of territory), to set up an International Authority for the Ruhr, and to integrate Germany's economy into the European Recovery Plan.

The Russians, for their part, refused further invitations to merge their zone with those of the West and, in reprisal, initiated their harassment of Allied access to Berlin. On April 1, they imposed restrictive inspections on Allied military and freight trains, and then began to hamper all rail and barge traffic. On June 12, they closed the Autobahn bridge over the Elbe, ostensibly for repairs, and arranged for a time-consuming detour by ferry. These and other Russian measures brought to light the precariousness of western access to Berlin and gave rise to the "Berlin question" that was to plague Germany and the world in the ensuing years.

By the middle of June, the crisis became acute. It was unleashed by Russian reaction to western plans for a German currency reform. From the beginning of the occupation, the four Allies had issued special occupation money, but excessive printing of currency by the Russians and low German productivity had devalued the occupation mark as well as Germany's own currency. To stabilize the financial structure, kindle economic growth, and undercut the flourishing black market, the western powers decided to issue a new currency. They offered to supply the new mark for distribution in the Russian Zone, but rejected Russia's demand for locating the printing presses in Leipzig (in the Soviet Zone), lest the Russians print money without western control and re-create the inflationary conditions of 1945. Although the real points of contention were more far reaching, the Russians chose this incident as a pretext for their blockade of Berlin.

On June 16, the Russians withdrew their representatives also from the quadripartite Kommandatura for Berlin. Two days later, the West officially announced its currency reform for Trizonia, with the stipulation that the new *Deutsche Mark*—to be exchanged at the official ratio of one *Deutsche Mark* for ten *Reichsmark* or occupation marks for all legally acquired funds—was not to be introduced into Berlin. On June 19, the Russians replied by stopping all passenger trains and automobiles between Trizonia and Berlin, and restricting the movement of freight on trains and barges. At a four-power conference in Berlin three days later, Russia announced that it would issue its own currency not only for its zone but also for *all* sectors of Berlin, and that this currency would not be subject to four-power control. The dispute thus involved the control of Berlin as much as it did the financial reconstruction of Germany: a Russian currency in West Berlin would integrate this area economically into the Russian Zone. Although the West rejected their plan, the Russians proceeded to issue their own currency (later known as the *Ost Mark*) for their zone and presumably for *all* of Berlin. Thereupon, as a countermeasure, the west introduced the *Deutsche Mark* into the western sectors of Berlin on June 23, and the Russians retaliated with a full-fledged blockade of the city.

Allied and West German access to Berlin by road, rail, and canal was gradually sealed off; even delivery of electricity and food from East to West Berlin was stopped. The Russians at first gave "technical difficulties" as reasons for the severance of communications and access to Berlin, but soon admitted a relationship between the Berlin blockade and the currency reform. Actually, discussions between the western powers and the Soviet Union, which continued during the blockade at various ministerial levels, soon revealed that the issue was not merely the currency reform and Russia's hope of dislodging the other powers from Berlin, but also Russian intention of preventing the integration of West Germany into the economic net of western Europe.

In answer to the blockade, the West organized an airlift to Berlin, dubbed "Operation Vittles" by American airmen. From June 26, 1948 until the final lifting of the blockade on May 12, 1949, Allied planes from airports in Trizonia supplied the 2 million inhabitants of West Berlin with food, coal, and raw materials. In the fall, daily shipments rose to about 4000 tons a day; by April of the following year, the daily rate was 8000 tons. Meanwhile the dispute had been taken up by the U. N. Security Council, which voted in October 1948 for immediate removal of all Berlin travel restrictions. But the Russians rejected the U.N. resolution. Only the West's proved ability to supply Berlin by air for indefinite periods ultimately led the Russians to lift the unsuccessful blockade, which had aroused German enmity toward the Russians and evoked gratitude and admiration toward the western powers.

THE CREATION OF TWO SEPARATE STATES On July 1, 1948, the military governors of the three western zones met with the minister-presidents of the eleven western German states to discuss implementation of the London Agreements (see page 622). The Germans raised some objections regarding the proposed Constituent Assembly, the powers reserved to the Allies, as well as the intended limitations on the Ruhr industries. But on July 26, the German state governments accepted the London provisions in principle and called for a Parliamentary Council to convene in Bonn on September 1 in order to draft a provisional constitution. The drafting committee of 65 delegates, chosen by their respective state legislatures, consisted of 27 SPD, 19 CDU, 8 CSU, 5 FDP, 2 Center, 2 DP, and 2 KPD. Although the Socialists constituted the largest single party, the bourgeois parties, especially the CDU, CSU, and FDP, banded together and elected the CDU's Konrad Adenauer as president of the Parliamentary Council.

The labors of the drafting committee dragged on for eight months. The western military governors frequently interfered in its deliberations, either to break deadlocks or to guide the drafting along lines acceptable to the West. Interminable delays were caused by the general reluctance to accept the Ruhr Statute, as well as by disagreements, particularly between SPD and CDU/CSU council members, on the question of federal versus states rights. Moreover, despite the provisional character of the proposed constitution and the fact that membership in the new state was to be open to the Russian Zone, the representatives feared that setting up a West German government might split Germany permanently. This apprehension was particularly evident after February 1949, when the Russians offered to lift the siege of Berlin and rejoin the ACA in return for a four-power conference to discuss the entire German problem. The western powers had little faith that such a conference might succeed and rejected the proposal, but the Germans favored any step that might narrow the gulf between east and west.

Delays were also caused by disagreements among the three Allies over German economic rehabilitation, over the security measures to be imposed upon Germany, and over the constitutional framework for the proposed West German government. The three military governors debated for months on the formulation of the Occupation Statute to set limits to the sovereignty of the proposed German state and define the powers reserved for the occupation authorities. Eventually, the Allies adopted the Ruhr Statute setting up a Ruhr Authority, composed of Allied, Benelux, and German representatives, charged with supervising the decartelization of certain industries and with controlling the new, increased level of coal and steel production, set considerably higher than the French had hoped. During these negotiations, the Americans secretly promised Adenauer not to dismantle certain chemical and steel plants, in return for German agreement to join the international Ruhr Authority. When revealed, these promises infuriated the SPD because of the favoritism shown to big business, and disturbed the French because of the added power given Germany. Finally, in April 1949, Britain and France reluctantly accepted the United States proposal to permit German production of certain items prohibited by the Potsdam Agreements—such as ocean-going ships, ball bearings, and aluminum.

Cold-war strategy, which during the same period resulted in the formulation of the North Atlantic Defense Treaty (signed April 4, 1949), finally led the Allies to compose their disagreements on the Occupation Statute and to oblige the Germans to terminate their work of drafting the constitution. On May 8, 1949, the Parliamentary Council adopted its draft by a vote of 53 to 12. To emphasize its provisional character, which would at all times permit the admission of the Russian Zone, the document was called the Basic Law rather than a constitution. Four days later, the military governors recognized the Basic Law with the reservation that Berlin, although a state of West Germany, was not to be governed by the Bonn government nor to send voting delegates to its legislatures. The eleven states were then asked to ratify the Basic Law. Only the still particularistic Bavarian Landtag rejected it, and on May 23, the law was proclaimed in effect.

During the summer, the three Allies prepared to transfer power from Military Government to a new Allied High Commission, and the Germans held their first elections to the Bundestag, the newly created lower house of the West German legislature. The CDU/CSU coalition obtained 7,359,100 votes (31 percent) and 139 seats. With 6,935,000 votes, the SPD received 131 seats, while the FDP groups won 52. Eight other parties earned representation in the Bundestag: the Center with 10 seats, the KPD with 15, and various conservative parties with a combined total of 55. On September 12, Theodor Heuss of the FDP was elected first president of the Federal Republic of Germany, with its temporary capital established at Bonn. A few days later, Konrad Adenauer formed a coalition government of CDU, CSU, FDP, and the conservative DP, and was elected chancellor by an extraordinarily slim margin. Of the 402 deputies, only 202 cast their ballot for him.

The western Allies formally recognized the Federal Republic on September 21 and awarded it conditional sovereignty, subject to the limitations contained in the Occupation Statute. Two weeks later, the division of Germany became complete when the Russians turned their zone into the German Democratic Republic, under the presidency of Wilhelm Pieck and the premiership of the SED's Otto Grotewohl. Since that time Germany has been governed by two German administrations, each claiming to have the exclusive right to speak for the country as a whole.

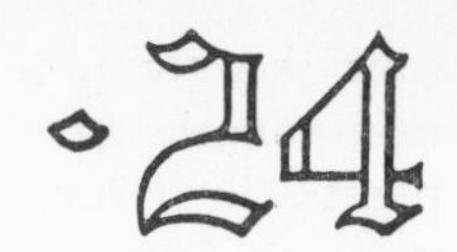

Germany's Troubled Resurgence: Division and the Resumption of Sovereignty, 1949–1955

Most foreign observers, especially those in the Communist orbit, look upon the division of Germany as twofold—with the German Federal Republic in the west and the German Democratic Republic in the east. The Germans themselves, however, speak of a threefold division: West Germany (the Federal Republic), Middle Germany (the German Democratic Republic), and East Germany (the lands east of the Oder-Neisse under Polish and Soviet administration). In accordance with the Potsdam Agreements, they cling to the hope that the Oder-Neisse boundary is temporary.

The dividing lines between these two—or three—parts of Germany gradually hardened after 1949, largely as a result of the growing tensions of the cold war. The Poles and the Russians treated their occupied lands east of the Oder-Neisse as permanent acquisitions; the Soviet Union and the Western powers, each in their own way, courted their respective protégés by awarding them more and more attributes of sovereignty—an anomalous reversal from the days of 1945. In this process, the western Allies generally took the first steps, and their actions were reluctantly emulated by the Russians, who at heart felt more hesitant about granting freedom of action to the East Germans.

With the coming into being of an East and a West Germany, the political, social, economic, and cultural development of the two states became so divergent that they must be discussed as separate entities, even though, according to international law, there are not two German states.

THE EVOLUTION OF THE GERMAN FEDERAL REPUBLIC

The Basic Law and the Occupation Statute

The Basic Law for the Federal Republic of Germany, with its 146 articles, is designed, according to the preamble, to permit Germany "to preserve its national and political unity and to serve world peace as an equal partner in a united Europe." Besides stressing European solidarity, the document underscores its "transitional" character, in view of the hope for the ultimate reunification of Germany. It emphasizes "the unity and freedom of Germany," and asserts that it speaks "on behalf of those Germans to whom participation was denied."

Opening with an extensive bill of rights, which stipulates that basic inalienable rights cannot be altered by constitutional amendments, the Basic Law defines the powers of the federal government versus those of the states, as well as the prerogatives of the various agencies of the central government. The legislature is bicameral, with most powers lodged in the lower house or *Bundestag,* elected every four years "in universal, free, equal, direct, and secret elections." The original number of 402 deputies was raised to 487 in 1953, in view of the considerable increase in population. West Berlin was permitted to send 8 (22 after 1953) nonvoting observers to the Bundestag, in order to underline Berlin's integration into West Germany without vitiating the separate occupation status of the city.

The upper house, the Bundesrat, representing the eleven states (reduced to nine in 1952 by amalgamation of three states into Baden-Württemberg, and increased to ten in 1957 with the admission of the Saar as a new state), enjoys the right to be kept informed "on the conduct of federal affairs," to veto certain legislation, and to ratify treaties, but in reality exerts relatively little influence. The federal president was given less authority than his counterpart had in the Weimar Republic. Elected by a federal convention (members of the Bundestag and "an equal number of members elected by the popular representative bodies of the *Länder*") rather than by popular suffrage, he may serve a maximum of two consecutive five-year terms. He may grant pardons and must sign treaties and accredit ambassadors; he appoints the federal chancellor in accordance with the choice of the Bundestag, but on the whole his prerogatives are largely ceremonial. By reducing the powers of the president, the Basic Law increased those of the federal chancellor, whose tenure of office was made more strictly dependent on the consent of the Bundestag. But in order to prevent recurrence of the governmental instability typical of the Weimar Republic and to force the Bundestag to follow a constructive course, Article 67 stipulates that the Bundestag's vote of no confidence is not valid until a successor has been chosen and a new cabinet approved. In this way, government vacancies are made impossible and the chancellorship is rendered more stable.

A large section of the Basic Law is devoted to circumscribing the jurisdiction of the federal government. The areas of foreign affairs, citizenship, postal and railroad service, criminal police and customs, inland waterways, and financial matters (like currency), are reserved to the federal government. In certain fields, such as civil and criminal law, refugees and expellees, public welfare, war damage, and compensation, there is concurrent jurisdiction between federal and state governments. But in everything else, ultimate sovereignty is reserved to the states. Over the years, the question of states' versus federal rights has caused considerable acrimony in German politics, and despite the CDU's vaunted devotion to federalism, the rights of the federal government have been gradually increased in various fields, including finance, communications, and education.

The Basic Law contains various innovations that reflect German feeling in the postwar period. The determination to prevent a revival of Nazism prompted Article 21, which stipulates that "parties, which according to their aims and behavior of their members seek to impair or abolish the free and democratic basic order or to jeopardize the existence of the Federal Republic of Germany, shall be unconstitutional." This article has been used to outlaw extremist groups. Similarly, Germany's new international or European orientation is strikingly underscored in Article 24 of the Basic Law, which specifies that "the Federation may, by legislation, transfer sovereign powers to international institutions," thus providing the government with authority to proceed boldly toward European integration.

The operation of the Basic Law was at first coupled with the limitations contained in the Occupation Statute. This document reserved for the Allied High Commission control over German disarmament and demilitarization, over the conduct of German foreign affairs, and over "the Ruhr, restitution, reparations, decartelization, . . . foreign interests in Germany and claims against Germany." The western Allies furthermore were allowed to station troops in Germany and to abrogate German legislation or countermand German action "if they consider that to do so is essential to security or to preserve democratic government in Germany."

The organization of federal ministries reflected some of Germany's postwar problems. Until the revision of the Occupation Statute in 1951, no Foreign Ministry was created. German foreign relations were handled by the Allies. In consonance with the new ideal of federalism and in an effort to avoid the pitfalls of Goebbels' Propaganda Ministry, no federal Ministry of Culture was established. Cultural and educational matters were left to the jurisdiction of the states. This decentralization led to great divergence among them, particularly in the educational system, and became an issue for considerable debate. Hence a cultural section was later set up in the federal Ministry of the Interior, and a permanent conference of the state ministers of culture was organized in order to coordinate educational matters throughout West Germany. On the other hand, several unusual federal ministries were created, in addition to the normal agencies found in most European countries. The Ministry for Expellee Affairs coordinated the equitable settlement of expelled persons in the various states; the Ministry of Housing dealt with reconstruction; the Ministry for All-German Affairs supervised relations between West Germany and East Germany, and kept alive the hope for eventual reunification; the Ministry for Economic Cooperation handled the Marshall Plan and later the numerous schemes for European economic integration.

The Political Life of the Young Republic

The early years after 1949 saw the development of a number of political trends that remained characteristic of West German politics. Unlike the situation that developed in the Weimar

Republic, extremist parties on the Right and the Left failed to gain momentum. None of them attracted many voters, some were declared unconstitutional, and those that survived remained at the fringe of the political spectrum. In contrast to the Weimar Republic, the proliferation of parties was steadily replaced by the growth of a few larger parties at the national level. This consolidation was furthered by a 1953 regulation stipulating that only parties obtaining at least 5 percent of all votes cast throughout West Germany, or three seats on the basis of direct suffrage in their constituencies, could gain representation in the Bundestag. In 1949, eleven parties earned seats in the Bundestag (counting the CDU/CSU as a single group). In the 1953 elections, only six parties won representation in Bonn. In 1957, the number shrank to four, and in 1961 to three. A further noteworthy difference from the Weimar days is that all parties operating at the national level are loyal to the democratic regime, so that political struggles are carried on within a framework freely accepted by all contenders.

Another trend was growing conservatism in the major parties, not only in the CDU and the FDP, but also in the SPD. Although the CDU's early platforms (see page 620) had stressed the need for socialization, its Düsseldorf program of 1949 rejected economic planning, nationalization, and controls over consumption. Instead, the party advocated a free market economy with reduced taxes on higher incomes and increased indirect levies. This shift in policy no doubt stemmed from various causes. The dismal example of economic planning in the Russian Zone served as a deterrent, while the sudden economic and industrial growth in the west, sparked by the currency reform of 1948 and by foreign aid, seemed to obviate the need for nationalization as a means for ensuring recovery. Pressure of Protestant industrial circles within the CDU and the strong influence of the United States government, all favoring a free economy, also contributed to the shift. There was also the growing influence within the party of its two conservative leaders: Konrad Adenauer, who was made CDU chairman in 1950, and Ludwig Erhard (1897–   ), who became vice-chancellor and federal minister of economics in Adenauer's first cabinet.

Konrad Adenauer, a lawyer and former member of the Center party and of the Prussian upper house, had served as lord mayor of Cologne from 1917 to 1933. During the Weimar period, he had gained many influential friends in Rhineland industrial and financial circles, and through his second wife, the daughter of a German-American professor (Ferdinand Zinsser), he numbered important Americans among his relatives and friends. One of his sisters-in-law had married Lewis W. Douglas, United States ambassador to London (1947–1950), another had become the wife of John Jay McCloy, United States high commissioner to Germany (1949–1952). In 1933, Adenauer had been dismissed by the Nazis and part of his property was confiscated. He spent the twelve years of National Socialist rule in political retirement, and although not engaged in any active anti-Nazi movement, he was three times incarcerated for brief periods. After the war, the British reinstated him as mayor of Cologne, but his decision to give priority to rebuilding the Cologne town hall rather than to reconstructing homes led to a dispute with British Military Government and his dismissal. Subsequently, he turned again to full-time politics and rapidly acquired paramount importance in the growing CDU.

Ludwig Erhard, who had been minister of economics in Bavaria and had lectured on economics at the University of Munich, brought to the CDU his stanch belief in free enterprise. He soon became the prophet of what he called Germany's "Social Market Economy," a system that stressed the free search for profits, combined with the employers' responsibility to the social security of the community. In a Social Market Economy, Erhard felt, there should be private initiative and free competition, but not unbridled *laissez faire*. While the federal government should interfere as little as possible in the nation's economic life, it should enforce the observance of social responsibility, particularly in areas of shortages, such as housing, and should intervene in times of crisis, such as unemployment or overconcentration of economic power. Similarly, the government should ensure the free interplay of economic forces by outlawing monopolistic cartels, except where needed for the rationalization of industry.

Erhard's economic theories found rapid acceptance in the CDU. At the party congress of 1950 held at Goslar, Erhard insisted that nationalization could never cement close bonds between workers and industry, whereas individual participation in industry through profit-sharing devices would best serve the economy. Hence the Ahlen program was abandoned and replaced by the Social Market Economy. In line with the new policy and under pressure from the United States (as well as from Britain after Churchill replaced Attlee in October 1951), the CDU then initiated the removal of price restrictions and a new tax program that favored industrial investment.

The bitter electoral campaign of 1953 was partly fought on the issue of economic recovery, for which the CDU claimed full credit. The SPD accused the government of being the tool of big industry; the CDU charged that the Socialists were getting financial support from East Germany. The voters evidently liked "the republic of prosperity." The CDU/CSU coalition increased its electoral support from 31 to 45.2 percent, while the SPD percentage remained more or less unchanged. To assure himself not merely a majority but the two-thirds margin required for the passage of constitutional amendments (in connection with rearmament) (see page 643). Adenauer formed a coalition comprising all parties (CDU, CSU, FDP, DP, Center, and the new Refugee party, for a total of 346 seats) except the SPD (151 seats).

The SPD, for its part, also grew markedly more conservative and, like most European Socialist parties, gradually abandoned its doctrinaire Marxism during the 1950s. To be sure, it rejected Erhard's Social Market Economy as harmful to wage earners, fought the tax reductions on the grounds that there were no guarantees that the freed capital would be used for socially beneficial investments, and opposed the increase of indirect taxes that burdened primarily the lower-income groups. But despite these disagreements with the CDU on economic and social theories as well as on foreign policy, the Socialist program became more moderate. The SPD helped channel the demands of the mammoth German Federation of Trade Unions (DGB), comprising some 40 percent of all trade-union members, toward seeking elaboration of the right of codetermination (see page 620) rather than nationalization. Its party chairman after 1952, Erich Ollenhauer (1901–), and Willy Brandt (1913–), the mayor of Berlin, its most influential leader after the late 1950s, were decidedly more concerned with immediate political, social, and economic gains than with the search for utopias. Moreover, the constant electoral success of the CDU (the party gained even more in the 1957 elections than it had in 1953) seemed to call for a revised program on the part of the SPD. In the new Socialist platform of 1959, total economic planning was no longer demanded. Instead, the Socialists called for "free competition as far as possible—economic planning as far as necessary," and advocated "the taming of the power of big business" without destroying private initiative.

Refugees and Expellees

Even after the initial postwar flood of refugees and expellees into West Germany had abated, the population of the western zones continued to grow at a rapid pace. Excesses of births over deaths amounted to a yearly average of almost 300,000. The influx of expellees from eastern Europe or from the territories beyond the Oder-Neisse, and of refugees from the Russian Zone, amounted to 900,000 in 1947 and 870,000 in 1948. Thereafter, expulsions from eastern Europe ceased, but the average number of refugees from the Russian Zone remained at over 300,000 a year. Between 1949, the year the two German states were created, and 1961, when the Berlin Wall was built, about 2.8 million Germans fled from East Germany and an additional 700,000 moved their domiciles from East to West Germany without requesting refugee status.

As a result of this migration, one of every five inhabitants of West Germany was either a refugee or an expellee. These uprooted persons were primarily concentrated in Schleswig-Holstein, Lower Saxony, and Bavaria. In 1947, they were awarded the same legal rights as other West Germans. Yet the tasks of the German states, at first exclusively responsible for housing and feeding them, were immense. Initially it proved impossible to integrate them into Germany's shattered economy. In August 1949, a first step was taken at the national level to solve the problem of relief. The Immediate Aid Act provided for special taxes on real estate and other private holdings to finance aid for refugees and expellees, as well as indemnification for those native Germans who had suffered war damage. Proceeds from this tax paid for subsistence, housing, education, replacement of lost savings for old age, and compensation for bomb damage.

With the creation of the Federal Republic and the establishment of the Ministry for Expellee Affairs, the federal government assumed the coordination of the numerous state laws for the rehabilitation of refugees and expellees, and helped settle the newcomers with housing, jobs, farms, and credit. In May 1950, it helped found a special Expellee Bank to speed up their economic integration. Finally, the Bundestag passed a comprehensive Equalization of Burdens Law in 1952, imposing a special levy of 50 percent (at the June 1948 value) on all real property in West Germany. Revenue from this tax, payable in quarterly installments over a period of thirty years, is accumulated in a federal Equalization of Burdens Fund, for the purpose of compensating expellees, refugees, and victims of air raids or of other war damage. Compensatory payments are made at a ratio of 5 to 10 percent for large losses, and up to 50 percent for small losses. Besides financing indemnities, the fund also pays for the retraining of expellees and refugees and for the establishment of new handicraft industries to employ the newcomers.

Despite such governmental solicitude, the plight of the refugees and expellees was at first bitter. As late as 1951 there were still some 2700 camps housing over 400,000 people. Even for those who had found housing and employment, integration into the social and political life was difficult. From the beginning, certain refugee groups had sought to form political parties of their own in order to further their demands for redress. But Military Government had refused to license such groups as political parties, ostensibly because their existence would render integration of the refugees and expellees more difficult. In reality it was also feared that such parties might be extremist in their views and fan irredentism for the lost eastern territories.

Nevertheless, the expellees founded numerous local associations, based on either the territory in which they were resettled (for example, *Land* Association of Expelled Germans in the Rhineland-Palatinate), or the region from which they had been expelled (such as the Union of Pomeranian Compatriots, Association of Carpathian Germans from Slovakia, and Union of Germans from Rumania). In August 1950, these associations held a joint rally in Stuttgart at which they signed "a solemn declaration to the German people and to the entire world" in the form of a "Charter of the German Expellees." They demanded a "reasonable repartition of the burdens of the last war" and "a sensible integration" of the expellees "into the life of the German people." But they also stressed their God-given right to live in their native land. Renouncing "all thought of revenge and retaliation," they proposed the establishment of a "free and united Europe" as one of the ways of regaining access to their lost homes.

In the same year, after licensing of new parties was no longer required, a special refugee party was formed in Schleswig-Holstein—the Block of Expellees and Victims of Injustice (BHE). Within six months, the BHE grew to be the second strongest party in Schleswig-Holstein, polling 23.4 percent of the vote in the *Landtag* (State legislature) elections. In January 1951, the BHE became a national party, with a platform for foreign affairs demanding restoration of the Saar and of the German territories in the east, as well as equal rights for Germany within the framework of a united Europe. In internal matters, the party opposed federalism, and stressed the need for an effective equalization of burdens and for compensation to expellees in the form of real-estate grants. Although the BHE counted among its members some extremists, its program on the whole was moderate and sufficiently vague to allow the party to enter a coalition government with the SPD in Hesse, while remaining a stanch opponent of the Socialists in Hanover. In 1952, the

BHE changed its party label to All-German Block (GB); in the federal elections of 1953 it polled 1.6 million votes and obtained 27 seats in the Bundestag. Such electoral success showed the potential political strength of the expellees.

Thereafter, the expellees continued to constitute a political and economic problem, but the GB failed to develop its potential. Although its party chairman (Waldemar Kraft) was given a post in Adenauer's cabinet after the 1953 elections, increasing prosperity, the gradual integration of the expellees into German life, and their tacit realization of the hopelessness of returning to their native lands sapped the strength of the GB. In 1957, it failed to poll sufficient votes in the federal elections to obtain representation in the Bundestag. Although it retained some importance in a few German states, even a political merger with the German party (DP) for the 1961 elections did not save it from political extinction at the national level.

Economic Rehabilitation

Foreign aid, the currency reform of 1948, the establishment of the Bonn government in 1949, growing financial and economic cooperation among the European nations, the managerial skill of German entrepreneurs, the hard work and cooperative attitude of German labor, and, above all, the new aura of hope and self-confidence pulled Germany out of the economic quagmire after 1950. West Germany's resurgence to third place among the industrial nations of the world by 1955, with a share of 7.1 percent of world trade, has often been labeled a "miracle."

The Federal Republic (with its 95,000 square miles as contrasted with the 181,000 square miles of the prewar Reich) had become a relatively small country with a vastly increased population. The influx of people had swelled the number of inhabitants by 25 percent and turned the Federal Republic into one of the world's most densely populated countries, with a density of over 500 people per square mile. Since the separated lands to the east had been areas producing a surplus of food, West Germany's food shortage was more acute than before the war. Hence Germany had to increase domestic food production and raise its industrial output so that a greater volume of exports would permit the importing of essential food and raw materials. On both counts, the West Germans proved eminently successful.

By 1955, agricultural output in the federal territory had been increased by 22 percent over prewar production. General industrial production was growing at three times the rate of some of Germany's neighbors. On the basis of 100 for 1948, the industrial index in 1955 stood at 297, as contrasted with 127 for France. With 49 percent of its national income derived from industry, Germany had become the most industrialized country in the world. In 1955 alone, it produced over 21 million tons of crude steel and built almost 1 million gross tons of merchant shipping, about half on consignment for other countries.

By 1955, West Germany was exporting 6.5 billion dollars worth of goods (motor vehicles, machinery, merchant vessels, precision instruments, electrical goods, chemicals, and the like), and had achieved a favorable balance of trade (about 300 million dollars). Within the European Payments Union, a financial cooperative organization embracing most European non-Communist countries, it had become the chief creditor. The *Deutsche mark* had become one of the world's most stable currencies, with Germany's gold and foreign exchange reserves standing at close to 3 billion dollars by the end of 1955.

Internally, the price and wage structure had been kept remarkably noninflationary. Unions cooperated with management, and strikes were rare. By the end of 1955, there was almost full employment, although some 10 percent of the expellees had not yet found adequate employment, largely because their skills were not in demand. A slight shortage of unskilled labor was even developing, and some Italian workers were being imported, the first of an ever-growing contingent of foreign laborers to find employment in the Federal Republic.

Despite this miraculous resurgence, which brought material comforts and self-satisfaction to the German middle class, vast problems remained to be solved. The housing shortage persisted. With 20 percent of housing in the Federal Republic destroyed by the war and an increase of 25 percent in the population, there was a shortage of about 5 million dwelling units. Although about 3.6 million units were built or rebuilt during the decade 1945–1955, the demand for adequate living space still far exceeded available housing. Moreover, it was doubtful whether the industrial boom could be sustained indefinitely, once the most urgent needs of reconstruction were met. The federal budget continued to be more or less balanced, although nearly half of all public expenditures was devoted to burdens arising from the war: relief for expellees and refugees, pensions, indemnification, and Allied occupation costs. The decision to force German rearmament and to oblige the Federal Republic to contribute more substantially to the defense of western Europe brought increased expenditures for which new sources of revenue had to be found.

CREATION OF THE GERMAN DEMOCRATIC REPUBLIC

Like the Federal Republic, the German Democratic Republic (DDR) was officially created in East Germany in the autumn of 1949. Immediately after the announcement of its establishment on October 7, West German Chancellor Adenauer declared it illegal on the grounds that it was not based on free elections; and on October 10, the Allied High Commission proclaimed that the DDR represented neither all of Germany nor East Germany. To this day, the western powers and the Bonn government have refused to recognize the *de jure* existence of the East German government. The West German press still calls East Germany "the Soviet Zone of Occupation" or "the so-called DDR." However, on a *de facto* basis, the governments of Bonn and of the DDR have continually been forced to deal with each other.

The Formation of the Government and Its Constitution

The Communist government of East Germany gradually evolved through a series of people's congresses by which the Russians hoped to bring about the formation of a Communist-dominated all-German central government.

After the Russian-supported SED failed to obtain 50 percent of the vote in the state elections of October 1946, the Communists decided to suspend all further free elections and to consolidate their position by resorting to a system of bloc politics and people's congresses. They created an Anti-Fascist Democratic Bloc, comprising not only the SED as well as the LDP and CDU —both of which were allowed to retain a sham existence—but also two new political parties and numerous mass organizations, all indirectly controlled by the SED. By granting mock representation to diverse groups within the state, the Russians wished to create the illusion of mass support for their regime and to impede the formation of an organized opposition. The mass organizations that, subject to Communist approval, sent delegates to the Anti-Fascist Democratic Bloc, included the compulsory Free Trade Union Federation (FDGB), the Free German Youth (FDJ), the Democratic Women's League of Germany (DFD), the Cultural League (KB), and the League of Nazi Victims (VVN). For the same reason, the Communists created two new political parties in 1948. The National Democratic party of Germany (NDPD) was to attract conservatives, nationalistic middle-class elements, former army officers, and ex-Nazis. Leadership of the NDPD was strictly controlled by the Communists, and, as part of the bloc, this new party became a useful device for binding the middle class to the regime and rendering it politically innocuous. Similarly, the Democratic Peasant party of Germany (DBD), also under strict Communist supervision, was set up to attract rural interests and wean them away from possible antigovernment activity.

The Anti-Fascist Democratic Bloc was then used to form the First People's Congress. In December 1947, the bloc parties and mass organizations delegated, without regular elections, representatives to a people's congress that in turn issued invitations to West German political parties. Although the western parties declined to send delegates, the congress alleged to speak for Germany as a whole, and demanded an immediate peace treaty together with an end to military occupation.

In March 1948, a Second People's Congress was convened through a similar device. This congress selected from its members a German People's Council of 400 delegates who were given advisory functions on governmental matters. The council then delegated a committee to draft a constitution for East Germany. The draft was published in October 1948 and submitted for popular discussion by means of press, radio, and political meetings. Again, it was the Communists' intention to demonstrate apparent popular approval for their work, and the German People's Council actually accepted some minor modifications in the draft. On March 19, 1949, the council finally approved the modified draft. National elections for a Third People's Congress were then held in May. The voters were presented with a single list of names of members of the bloc parties and the mass organizations, together called the "National Front." The list had been drawn up by the People's Council on the basis of the existing representative ratio of the various parties in the Second People's Congress. The ballot asked for approval of the official list and for a vote in favor of "German unity and a just peace," with voters given the choice of voting "yes" or "no" or invalidating their ballots. Of the total votes cast, 61.8 percent were affirmative but in East Berlin only 51.7 percent voted for this list.

On May 30, the Third People's Congress ratified the constitution, and elected a new People's Council of 330 delegates (70 additional delegates were to represent West Germany). But the Russians held up enactment of the constitution to await political developments in the west. After the western powers completed their establishment of the Federal Republic, the People's Council, on October 7, changed its name to "Provisional People's Chamber," by promulgating a special law without further reference to the electorate. At the same time, a provisional government of the DDR was appointed, a provisional upper house (*Länderkammer*) was formed, and the constitution was declared in force. All bodies were designated as "provisional" until confirmed by elections, eventually held in July 1950.

The constitution of the DDR stresses the sovereignty of the people and is extremely democratic in appearance. But, like the Russian constitution, it does not provide for a clear separation of power among the three branches of government nor for judicial review. In theory, the legislature is bicameral, whereas in fact East Germany is a unitary state. The upper house, representing the states, initially endowed with even less power than the Bundesrat of West Germany, was shorn of all significance in 1952, and although the lower house or people's chamber (*Volkskammer*) dominates the states as well as the executive, in reality the party elite controls all facets of government.

Centralization was applied everywhere, with even East Berlin incorporated into the new state, whose capital is Pankow, a working-class suburb of Berlin. Finances and police, social insurance, justice, and even cultural matters are all directed by central agencies. Actually, the constitution is less important for the functioning of everyday government than are the special government decrees, some of which overtly contradict the terms of the constitution. Significantly, the Russians did not impose an occupation statute, on the assumption that Communist control of the SED and the presence of Russian armed forces were sufficient to keep the new East German state in line with their policies.

The electoral system was also designed to keep the SED in power. Age requirements were low (eighteen for voting and twenty-one for eligibility for elected offices) in order to attract the pliable youth. National elections, held every four years, were retained as window dressing. The constitution stipulated "universal, equal, direct, and secret elections," but lacked the term "free," included in the Basic Law of the Federal Republic. For the 1950 elections to the lower house, the usual bloc list was compiled by the SED, but in view of the experience of 1949, the voters were no longer given the possibility of voting "no." The choice was between voting "yes" and casting an invalid ballot. Soon even secrecy of voting was abolished in many places. The new electoral code for the Trade Chambers stipulates: "Elections are secret. . . . Upon decision by the majority of those present, voting will be public." Under similar arrangements, most voting was soon made compulsory and public.

Economic Planning and Socialization

From their inception, the SED plans for the reconstruction of East Germany were based on the Soviet model, modified to meet German conditions. Proceeding from a Half Year Plan in 1948, followed by a Two-Year Plan for 1949–1950, the government inaugurated its first full-fledged Five-Year Plan in 1951. Directed primarily at doubling industrial production—particularly in fuel and energy, coal, iron, steel, chemicals, and machine tools—the plan called for increased "Socialist competition" and higher work norms. Although concerned largely with economic goals, the plan embraced all areas of public life, including transport, education, health and welfare, and even sports and culture. At the same time, socialization of industry and agriculture was intensified, particularly after 1952, so that by 1953 approximately 85 percent of the economy had been sequestered from private ownership. Rather than outright nationalization, however, a system of productive associations and semiprivate cooperatives was used in both agriculture and industry in order to permit a more gradual transition to socialism. Simultaneously the SED began its campaign to infiltrate and ultimately control all cultural and educational activities, its aim being to inculcate proletarian values in the coming generation. These efforts to dominate the youth soon led to a prolonged struggle with the German Protestant Church, which opposed the materialistic creed of the new regime.

Although the economic, social, and educational planning of the early years took East Germany far down the road toward socialism—and helped deepen the cleavage between East and West Germany—the SED and its Russian backers felt that progress was too slow. At a SED party conference in July 1952, it was decided to abandon the old "Anti-Fascist Democratic" order, which had been based on a compromise with the bourgeois. Instead, the party leaders called for the dictatorship of the proletariat and the accelerated implementation of true socialism. This decision created considerable unrest among large segments of the East German population, many of whom had already shown their unhappiness with economic restraints and lack of freedom by "voting with their feet," as the saying went—fleeing to West Germany.

On June 9, 1953, after barely eleven months, the "acceleration of socialism" was canceled. Faulty economic planning, inefficiency of the party bureaucracy, an impending economic crisis, the threatening restlessness of the population, as well as the general relaxation in the Socialist countries after the death of Stalin, forced Walter Ulbricht to adopt a "new course," which in some respects resembled Lenin's New Economic Policy of the 1920s. Without abandoning basic principles, the new course called for a temporary delay in the rapid sovietization of East Germany. It softened the demands of the Five-Year Plan; repudiated the call for the complete elimination of private enterprise; lowered the quotas of compulsory deliveries from farmers; promised an increase in food rations, consumer goods, and wages; announced a relaxation of travel restrictions to West Germany; and relented on some measures taken against religious institutions.

Even the announcement of the new course did not prevent the uprising of June 1953. On June 16, some workers in East Berlin went on strike to demonstrate against an increase of 10 percent in their daily work norms. Although the government canceled the demanded increase at noon, the strikers, joined by other Berliners, marched downtown, demanding free elections, the resignation of the SED government, and assurances of better living conditions. The Vopos (people's police) did not interfere with the march of the rioters.

On June 17, the riots spread to the suburbs. Some 12,000 workers from outlying districts entered Berlin to march on the ministries. They burned SED party offices and propaganda bureaus and, without organization or planning, attempted to gain control of certain sectors of the city. Although some Vopos joined the marchers, most of the police tried to put down the revolt. Early that afternoon the Russian commandant placed the city under martial law, and two Russian divisions with supporting tanks entered Berlin. After a few brief clashes, in which German workers fought Russian armor with bricks and sticks, the revolt was put down. The news of the risings caused similar revolts in various East German cities, but despite some temporary successes, all were quickly suppressed by Russian troops. The revolts of June 17 became a symbol of heroism and may have made Ulbricht's government temporarily somewhat cautious but they hardly altered the basic course of East Germany's development.

The new course was retained in most essentials until 1955, when the post-Stalin era of uncertainty ended with Nikita Khrushchev's ascension to power. Thereafter the economic development of East Germany, as well as its foreign policy, was more and more clearly subordinated to the over-all needs of the Soviet bloc, regardless of ideological refinements.

Despite the planning and the hard work of the population, economic recovery in East Germany was slow until 1955. Food shortages continued and rubble cluttered the streets. The new currency, issued in 1948, rapidly sank to a ratio of 3 to 1, and then 4 to 1 to West Germany's *Deutsche Mark,* since productivity remained insufficient to cover the enormous demands made by Russia and the satellites, and at the same time allow exports to non-Communist nations. Moreover, the population was shrinking and the labor force was being constantly depleted, as skilled workers and professional people fled to West Germany.

East Germany's Foreign Policy

The roles played by East and West Germany in international affairs during the period 1949 to 1955 were, of course, largely determined by the respective occupying powers. But whereas the western Allies accorded the West Germans a modicum of self-determination after 1951, Moscow retained tight control of East Germany's policies.

The Pankow regime continued to claim that it spoke for all Germans, and persisted in its demands for unification on terms that would assure the continued power of the SED. At the same time it initiated a program of rearmament. By 1950, the 220,000 Vopos were armed with automatic weapons and were receiving military training. An additional 50,000 "emergency units" were supplied with howitzers, antiaircraft guns, and tanks.

The Russians forced the East Germans to settle the border dispute with Poland so as to reconcile internal differences within the Communist camp. In June 1950, Walter Ulbricht, as deputy prime minister of East Germany, negotiated with Warsaw a bilateral accord, sanctioned by the Soviet Union, whereby the Oder-Neisse line was recognized as the permanent border between Germany and Poland. At the same time, Poland granted East Germany use of the harbor of Stettin, pending German reunification. Bonn immediately repudiated this agreement between Warsaw and Pankow, and London and Washington protested that the settlement of frontiers had to await a final peace treaty.

GERMANY IN THE INTERNATIONAL SCENE

Even after the Germans had been given control over most of their own internal affairs, the four occupying powers still faced the task of solving Germany's international problems: agreement on its permanent frontiers (the status of the Saar and of the lands beyond the Oder-Neisse); the question of reunification; the integration of Germany's economy with that of the rest of Europe; and the decision whether it should be permanently neutralized and disarmed, or permitted to join international power alignments. All these questions had to be solved before a peace treaty with a united Germany could be signed.

Allied Meetings and the German Peace Treaty

Immediately after the termination of the Berlin blockade in May 1949, the four powers held another foreign ministers' conference in Paris to discuss the German question. Again the meeting ended in a deadlock. After a considerable lull during 1950, when the eyes of the world were averted to the conflict in Korea, negotiations were resumed in the spring of 1951. But after 73 negotiating sessions in Paris, the deputy foreign ministers could report no progress. Thereafter, an almost constant stream of official and semiofficial communiqués crossed back and forth between Washington, London, Paris, and Moscow without bringing the four any closer to agreement.

During the early years of occupation, the main East-West disagreements over Germany had been economic and financial. In the 1950s, however, after each of the two Germanies had been integrated into the economic orbit of its respective occupying powers, the German question turned more and more into a political problem. The West now sought to rearm West Germany and to bind it ever closer into the NATO alliance, while Russia was determined to frustrate the Allied plans, if necessary by turning Germany into a neutralized nation.

In November 1952, Chancellor Adenauer once again called on Russia to permit German reunification by allowing "free all-German elections . . . under international supervision." Such elections were to be followed by the formation of a "Constituent National Assembly, which in turn would have to install an all-German government." Such a government could then conclude a negotiated peace with the four powers. The western Big Three supported this stand. The sequence in this proposed maneuver was all-important. Free elections had to precede the formation of an all-German government, for such elections were bound to produce a democratic, pro-western majority. The Russians, however, remained adamant in insisting on the reverse order: the four Allies were first to conclude peace with both German governments, a step the West rejected since it involved *de jure* recognition of Ulbricht's regime. Conclusion of peace was to be followed by the establishment of an all-German government by merging the governments of Bonn and Pankow, a proposal the West found unacceptable because it would have awarded the SED power out of proportion to its strength in a reunited Germany. As a third and last step, the Russians proposed the holding of elections.

Although under the Occupation Statute, negotiations of the German question with Russia were to be conducted by the western powers, the Bonn government frequently expressed its views on the issue. In June 1953, the Bundestag passed a resolution calling for elections, an all-German government, and a "freely negotiated peace treaty" in the sequence acceptable to the West, adding that the treaty should include the "settlement of all outstanding territorial questions" and should safeguard "freedom of action for an all-German parliament and an all-German government within the framework of the principles and the aims of the United Nations." By stressing "freedom of action," the West German legislature enunciated its opposition to the neutralization of Germany. In October of the same year, as the four powers once again prepared for a conference on Germany, Adenauer delivered a major foreign policy address to the Bundestag in which he defined the "central issues" for Germany as "restoration of its own independence," "reunification," and the "unification of free Europe and the integration of Germany into the European Community." He also hoped to forestall any possible inter-Allied bargain over the eastern border. "Following the numerous declarations by the *Bundestag* and the Federal Government," he announced, "the German people will never recognize the so-called Oder-Neisse frontier. But let me emphasize one thing here: the problem connected with the Oder-Neisse line shall never be settled by force but only by peaceful means."

Finally, in January 1954, a new Big Four conference was held in Berlin, the first full-fledged meeting of the foreign ministers in almost five years. The sessions alternated between the eastern and western sectors of the city, and lasted for almost four weeks. Russia was in the throes of the post-Stalin era, and the Korean War had been settled by an armistice; hence there was considerable hope that east-west differences over Germany could be bridged at the conference, despite the fact that Russia was still represented by the same V. M. Molotov who had proved intractable at previous meetings. Actually, the respective views announced in advance of the conference showed the divergence between the two positions: Russia sought to discuss global solutions to world problems, and for this purpose wanted Communist China to be represented; the West preferred to center the discussions on concluding an Austrian peace treaty and discussing means for reunifying Germany.

In the course of the Berlin conference, the west presented its joint program for Germany: general elections, followed by the formation of an all-German government, and the conclusion of a peace treaty. The only disagreement among the three western powers, which they tried unsuccessfully to hide from Russia, concerned Germany's international role after the conclusion of peace. Great Britain wished to leave a united Germany free to rearm and free to join NATO if the German people wished it; the United States believed that a united and rearmed Germany should be more or less compelled to join NATO; France preferred that a united Germany remain demilitarized. Russia for its part was primarily interested in preventing West German rearmament. Besides the usual Russian demand for establishment of a unified government in advance of elections, Molotov specified that such elections be held without international supervision, that a united Germany not be allowed to join the contemplated European Defense Community, and that the peace treaty for Germany be drafted not merely by the Big Four but by all former Allied powers. In addition, the Russians demanded an end to the stationing of atomic weapons on German soil—a reference to American atomic artillery. They also called for an "immediate ban on militaristic and fascist organizations and expulsion of Hitler officials from the West German Government"—a proposal that the East Germans might have used to deny authority to any anti-Communist official of Bonn.

In the end, the long conference resulted in another deadlock. It proved impossible to negotiate a treaty for Austria and no agreement was reached on the German question. Consequently, the western Allies proceeded with their plans for initiating the rearmament of Germany and for granting it full sovereignty.

The Courtship of the Federal Republic by the West

Unlike the Russians, who could dictate the political behavior of the East German regime through Communist party channels, the west found it more difficult to persuade the Federal Republic to adopt certain policies without infringing on the quasi-sovereign character of the Bonn government. Hence the years between 1949 and 1955 witnessed a long courtship of West Germany, full of gentle persuasion interspersed with more importunate pressure. The ultimate aim of the West was to assure the integration of a rearmed Germany into a western economic and military community, in return for the granting of full sovereignty to the Federal Republic.

An early step was taken in November 1949, when the Bonn government was allowed to participate in international organizations and to establish commercial and consular relations with other countries. The outbreak of the Korean War in June 1950 caused a redoubling of western efforts to erect an integrated European Defense Community with German participation, and to assure the pooling of western Europe's economic resources. As a first step, the Big Three issued a declaration in September, stating that they would consider an attack on the western zones or on West Berlin tantamount to an attack on themselves. This unilateral guarantee sought to prevent Germany from becoming another Korea, but it contained no stipulation that the Germans should themselves contribute to Europe's defense.

Chancellor Adenauer suggested as a preliminary measure that the Occupation Statute be replaced by negotiated agreements between Bonn and the three western powers. But at first the Allies were willing merely to revise the Occupation Statute, the first major revision being granted in March 1951. The Federal Republic was allowed to establish a Foreign Office (Adenauer himself became the first foreign minister) and a full-fledged diplomatic service. At the same time, restrictions on German industrial production were again reduced in conjunction with the signing of the Schuman Plan (see page 645), and shortly thereafter England, France, and the United States passed legislation to terminate the state of war with Germany—despite the absence of a formal peace treaty.

In September 1951, the three Allies notified Bonn that they were willing to replace the Occupation Statute with Contractual Agreements, provided the Germans would contribute armed forces to a European Defense Community (EDC), consisting of French, Italian, Dutch, Belgian, Luxemburgian, and German units. Rearming Germany, of course, presented countless problems. The French objected to it unless the proposed German forces be strictly subordinated to a non-German command, and the British viewed it with certain apprehensions.

Even many Germans were confused by the prospect. For six years, the Germans had been told that militarism was bad, and that Germany should remain permanently disarmed. The youth, in particular, had begun to accept the new antimilitary creed. As a result, there was a considerable feeling in Germany against rearming and in favor of neutralism. The neutralists, some of whom adopted the slogan "*Ohne mich*" ("Count me out"), were motivated by various reasons. Many merely reacted to the horrors of war and defeat, and resolved to keep Germany out of any future conflict. Some were nationalists who hoped to rid Germany of all outside interference and commitments by preaching a neutral course. Others were convinced that the Americans would inevitably withdraw to their own shores, and since they placed little confidence in Franco-British help, saw no reason for Germany alone to face the onslaught of Soviet Russia. Most of the neutralists, however, opposed rearmament simply because aligning the two Germanies with two opposing power blocs would tend to create a permanent division of Germany.

Although neutralist opinion was strong in the early 1950s, there were few organized groups to promote its tenets. The so-called Nauheim Circle favored neutrality as the only path to reunification, although some of its more nationalistic members demanded a neutral, independent, but remilitarized Germany, free to choose its own orientation in foreign affairs. Some leaders of the German Evangelical Church also advocated neutralism, presumably as the only way of reuniting the two separated branches of the German Protestant Church. Moreover, there were intellectual circles and democratic groups, such as those grouped around the magazine *Frankfurter Hefte,* which preached German neutrality as an essential preliminary step in the unification of Europe.

Despite this reluctance to rearm, shared to some extent by the SPD and the FDP, the western Allies negotiated with Bonn from November 1951 to May 1952 for the conclusion of Contractual Agreements. This "Convention on Relations between the Three Powers and the Federal Republic of Germany," signed on May 26, 1952, was to replace the Occupation Statute, grant virtual sovereignty to West Germany, and arrange for a defensive alliance between Germany and the western powers. The Allies were to retain control over the question of unification, and would be allowed to station troops on German soil. In return, Germany would "participate in the European Defense Community in order to contribute to the common defense of the free world." On the following day, the EDC treaty was signed in Paris, providing for integrated forces of the six European countries in close cooperation with NATO.

The mere signing of the Contractual Agreements and of the EDC Treaty brought no solution to the question of German rearmament. Lengthy parliamentary debates followed in the Allied capitals and at Bonn. America and England finally ratified the Contractual Agreements in late 1953. But France continued to hesitate, and in the summer of 1954, the French National Assembly finally rejected the EDC Treaty, which was an integral part of the Contractual Agreements. Within Germany, ratification also presented problems. The Bundestag approved the Contractual Agreements and the EDC Treaty in March 1953 by a vote of 224 to 165, and the Bundesrat ratified both in May. But President Heuss could not sign the treaties, since the SPD brought a lawsuit before the newly created Federal Constitutional Court, claiming that the treaties were unconstitutional, since the Basic Law made no provision for rearmament. Because amendments to the Basic Law require a two-thirds vote in both houses, and Adenauer's coalition did not command such a majority, an impasse had seemingly been reached. The campaign for the September 1953 elections centered in part on the issue of rearmament. The SPD insisted that arming West Germany and integrating it militarily into Western Europe would cause the permanent division of Germany. The CDU/CSU replied that only a strong Federal Republic, backed by the full weight of the western powers, could hope to gain the respect of Soviet Russia and successfully negotiate the reunification of Germany.

The September elections gave Adenauer the opportunity to form a new five-party coalition (see page 630) that assured him a two-thirds majority in both houses and thus sufficient votes to amend the Basic Law. Hence President Heuss signed the Contractual Agreements and the EDC Treaty in March 1954, even though the constitutional amendment permitting German rearmament was enacted only in 1956. Had France ratified EDC, West Germany would have assumed sovereignty in 1954.

After the failure of EDC, a new round of negotiations was started. The United States and other NATO powers urged France to find a solution for bringing the Federal Republic into the western defense network. In return for British guarantees to maintain troops on the Continent alongside those of France as a counterbalance to a rearmed Germany, France finally acquiesced. Details of new agreements were worked out at a London conference in October 1954 among representatives of the United States, Canada, Great Britain, France, Italy, West Germany, and the Benelux nations. These agreements were then included in the Paris Treaties, signed later in the same month by all NATO countries and by Chancellor Adenauer.

The Paris Treaties consisted of four main agreements. In the treaty of sovereignty for Germany, the United States, Britain, and France stated their intention of terminating the occupation of West Germany, *except* for West Berlin. They retained the right to station forces of "effective strength" on German soil for the "defense of the free world," and the responsibility for governing Berlin, defending Germany, and negotiating the question of reunification. In return for Adenauer's reassurance not to use force to obtain unification or to change existing boundaries, the Big Three pledged to recognize the Bonn government as the "only German government freely and legitimately constituted and entitled to speak . . . for the German people in international affairs," and they reiterated their declaration that an attack on West Berlin would be considered as an attack on themselves.

The second Paris agreement admitted West Germany and Italy to the Western European Union (WEU), an extension of the 1948 Brussels Pact that had created a fifty-year defense alliance among France, England, and the Benelux countries. The seven-nation WEU was given power to limit German armaments and armaments production, and to supervise the creation of a German army of half a million men, a tactical air force, and a small navy. Chancellor Adenauer gave assurances that Germany would not engage in the production of atomic, biological, or chemical weapons, and would refrain from building specified articles of war (mines, tanks, strategic bombers, guided missiles, and large warships or submarines), *unless* NATO specifically requested Germany to produce such items, and the WEU Council approved such a request. In the third treaty, West Germany was admitted to membership in NATO, with the provision that all of Germany's armed forces were to be integrated into WEU and NATO—a provision made to assuage the misgivings of France concerning German rearmament.

The last agreement reached in Paris attempted to solve the Saar question. In 1946, the French had begun to incorporate the rich Saar basin into the economic life of France, with the hope of ultimate political annexation. But the Saarlanders, who at first had seen advantages in a union with France, began to agitate for a return to Germany when the Federal Republic started its spiraling climb to prosperity. In 1951, the governments of Bonn and Paris agreed to postpone discussion of the Saar question until conclusion of a peace treaty; but in the following year, the Bundestag passed a resolution declaring that the Saar was German unless a plebiscite showed otherwise. The Paris Treaties of 1954 finally attempted a compromise by making the Saar independent, with economic ties with France but subject to international supervision by the WEU. This agreement, however, was subject to approval by the Saarlanders.

Thus the Paris Treaties paved the way for a return of sovereignty to a remilitarized West Germany. During the process of ratification, the treaties were heatedly debated in the various capitals. The German SPD, the Trade Union Federation, and many members of the FDP persisted in their opposition to rearmament until "all possibilities for negotiation on reunification have been exhausted." But in the end, the Bonn legislature as well as the other governments ratified the treaties. On May 5, 1955, ten years after the termination of World War II, the agreements were implemented, and West Germany attained its sovereignty.

In the same month, Russia and the west finally compromised on a state treaty for Austria containing a provision for its permanent neutrality.

Only the Saarlanders rejected the Paris agreements. After a heated election campaign, they voted in October 1955 overwhelmingly against international supervision, so that Bonn and Paris were forced to reopen negotiations. As one result of the increasingly friendly relations between the two countries, the Saar was incorporated into West Germany as a state in 1957, although it remained economically tied to France until 1959.

Consolidation of Western Europe

At the same time, West Germany was gradually being readmitted to the community of nations. In 1950, it became an associate member of the Council of Europe [1] and in 1951 obtained full membership. In the same year, West Germany joined various specialized agencies of the United Nations [2]—the World Health Organization, the International Labor Organization, and UNESCO—and became a signatory of GATT, the General Agreement on Tariffs and Trade. In 1952, it joined the World Bank and the International Monetary Fund.

But more decisive in the long run was the determination of the Adenauer government to effect a *rapprochement* with France and to cement the unity of western Europe, in particular of the so-called Inner Six (France, Italy, Germany, and Benelux—the nucleus of the later Common Market). The European Coal and Steel Community, proposed by France's Foreign Minister Robert Schuman in 1950 and inaugurated in 1952, although perhaps the most spectacular and successful, was only one of the new organizations demonstrating the new "European" spirit that animated West Germany. By pooling the coal and steel resources of the six participating countries and placing them under a supranational High Authority, the Schuman Plan aimed not merely at preventing a possible future war between France and Germany and at speeding up European economic recovery; rather, the plan was part of a general movement in western Europe that sought to overcome the narrow horizons of petty nationalism and fuse the participating states into an economic, social, military, and ultimately, perhaps, even political unit.

This new "internationalism" or "Europeanism" marked a significant departure from the traditional German political thought of the last hundred years. The CDU became firmly committed to it, and with certain reservations, even the SPD and FDP supported it. It became a popular creed with the young and the intellectuals, and gradually became an accepted tenet of foreign policy. Even those who looked upon "Europeanism" with distrust did not, like their predecessors in the Weimar period, regard "internationalists" as unpatriotic. This transformation alone provides hopeful evidence that, with the creation of the Federal Republic, Germany entered a new era.

[1] An organization, created in 1949 with headquarters in Strassburg, dedicated to the achievement of greater cultural, economic, social, and political unity of Europe.

[2] Pending unification, Germany could not join the United Nations itself, unless Russia and the West were to admit both Germanies, a move that would imply *de jure* recognition of East Germany.

Germany Today

THE CONTINUED DIVISION OF GERMANY

International Conferences and German Foreign Policy

In reply to the integration of a remilitarized Germany into the western defense system, the Russians accelerated the militarization of East Germany. They officially ended the war between East Germany and the Communist Bloc (Russia, China, Albania, Bulgaria, Czechoslovakia, Poland, and Rumania), and included the DDR in the Warsaw Pact, Russia's newly created eastern defense system.

Simultaneously, however, the first "thaw" in the cold war appeared after Khrushchev, together with Nikolai Bulganin, assumed power in the Kremlin. Settlement of the war in Indo-China and agreement on an Austrian treaty again raised hopes that the German problem might be solved. In consequence, the Big Four (Eisenhower, Eden, Faure, and the team of Bulganin and Khrushchev) met in Geneva in July of 1955 at the first full-fledged summit meeting since Potsdam. But the friendly atmosphere in Geneva could not conceal the serious differences between East and West. Before 1955, the German problem had already been complicated; now the two Germanies were aligned with opposing power blocs, the problem seemed well-nigh insoluble unless East and West would agree to a military disengagement in Germany.

After the failure of the summit meeting, the Bonn government itself became active in the international field, although the western Allies were still legally responsible for negotiating German reunification. Chancellor Adenauer journeyed to Washington and London, exchanged several visits with France's prime minister, and then went to Moscow in September 1955. The Moscow discussions on German reunification proved fruitless, since Khrushchev simply advised Adenauer to negotiate directly with the Pankow government. But Adenauer's plea for the release of all German prisoners of war still detained in Russia evoked Bulganin's promise to repatriate some 10,000 Germans—although Bonn insisted that this number was far below the total still held by the Russians. At the same time,

Bonn and Moscow agreed to establish diplomatic relations.

Adenauer's trip to Moscow raised his popularity at home. The Russians actually released some prisoners—to both East and West Germany. The establishment of diplomatic relations with Soviet Russia pleased those Germans who believed that only direct negotiations with the Communists might achieve reunification and that only Moscow could redraw the Oder-Neisse boundary short of war. It also appealed to those who favored a pro-eastern orientation because of the enticing possibilities for trade in eastern Europe. In some western circles, however, Adenauer's action raised apprehensions that Germany might make a bargain with the Kremlin reminiscent of the Rapallo Treaty of 1922 or the Nazi-Soviet Pact of 1939. To reassure the west, Adenauer reaffirmed to the press that he would abide by the Paris Treaties and seek reunification only with western support. And the new foreign minister, Heinrich von Brentano (1904–   ), asserted: "The German people will not permit themselves to be pulled out of this [western] community, nor will they separate themselves voluntarily from it."

Yet Adenauer's Moscow trip involved an anomaly. By awarding diplomatic recognition to Bonn while at the same time granting sovereignty to East Germany, Russia bolstered its assertion that *two* separate Germanies existed legally, and that Germany could be unified only by merging the two governments. Adenauer, however, claimed to be speaking for *all* Germans, including those in East Germany, and persisted in denying recognition to the Pankow regime on the grounds that the Ulbricht government was a mere puppet of the Russian occupation forces. His state secretary, Walter Hallstein (1901–   ), initiated what came to be known as the Hallstein Doctrine, whereby Bonn refused to maintain diplomatic relations with all nations that recognized East Germany. Over the next eight years, thirteen communist nations (including Cuba in 1963) formally recognized the DDR; and in accordance with the Hallstein Doctrine, Bonn severed, or refused to establish, diplomatic relations with these states (with the exception of Russia). No other governments gave *de jure* recognition to East Germany, although many neutrals, such as Egypt, Finland, and India, established close, informal relations and carried on extensive trade with the Pankow regime.

The Hallstein Doctrine, designed to stress the theoretical indivisibility of Germany, rendered Bonn's eastern policy somewhat inflexible. This rigidity was supported by France, especially after the advent of Charles de Gaulle in 1958, but was often criticized by the SPD and FDP, and tacitly deplored by London and Washington. Actually, the Hallstein Doctrine was not consistently enforced by Bonn: the very recognition of the Soviet Union violated its principles. Moreover, it was a legal and political stand that carefully avoided trade restrictions or other economic measures. In spite of the public adamancy of Chancellor Adenauer against all dealings with Pankow and the Soviet satellites, there was in fact considerable contact. Extensive trade was also maintained with Yugoslavia, even after diplomatic relations were severed when Tito recognized Ulbricht's regime. Trade with Russia increased constantly. By 1958, the Krupp industrial complex was selling

30 million dollars worth of machinery annually to the Russians, prompting Khrushchev himself to toast the "continued health and prosperity of the firm" of Krupp. Between 1956 and 1958, when de-Stalinization effected a temporary relaxation of Russian control over the satellites, there was also a tentative *rapprochement* between Bonn and Warsaw. Polish–West German trade was increased, and some cabinet members and politicians, although not Adenauer, weighed the possibility of a political bargain with Warsaw. They thought that Poland might be persuaded to allow German reunification on western terms in return for West German recognition of the permanence of the Oder-Neisse line. Such a settlement with Bonn might have strengthened Poland's hand vis-à-vis the Kremlin and helped remove it from Russian influence. It was also in accord with the new United States policy of aiding the satellites, in particular Poland, in order to loosen Moscow's grip on eastern Europe.

In the long run, nothing came of this plan, largely because it proved impossible seriously to impair communist solidarity in eastern Europe and because the Polish government feared the resurgence of a united, militarized Germany on its western border even more than it resented the presence of Russian armies on its own soil. This became clear when, in 1958, Poland's foreign minister, Adam Rapacki, proposed his plan for a "nuclear-free zone" in Poland, Czechoslovakia, and the two Germanies that would eventually permit the withdrawal of foreign armed forces and the unification of a neutral Germany. Rapacki's plan, supported by Moscow, Prague, and Pankow, was largely aimed at disengaging West Germany from NATO. Bonn, Paris, London, and Washington for their part, found Rapacki's proposals unacceptable.

But West German discussions with Warsaw and Moscow foundered not only over the question of disengagement from NATO but also over the Oder-Neisse line. Every German political party persists in championing Germany's right to recover the frontiers of 1937. The Federal Ministry for All-German Affairs continues to disseminate the view that the lands beyond the Oder-Neisse form a historical, cultural, and economic part of Germany. Journals such as the *Zeitschrift für Ostforschung* (*Journal for Research on the East*) and research institutions supported by public funds, such as the Johann Gottfried Herder Institute in Marburg, produce a plethora of literature depicting Polish mismanagement of the Oder-Neisse territories and tacitly urging their return to German administration.

To be sure, the younger generation has generally shown little interest in the eastern lands. The expellee party has largely lost its political power and many irredentist organizations have been dissolved—although a few pressure groups, such as the *Bund Vertriebener Deutscher* (Union of Expelled Germans) still exist. Among the "Europeanists" there is hope that Germany's former *Drang nach Osten* can be permanently sublimated in a community of western Europe. Moreover, prosperity has taken the edge off irredentism, the voices of moderation are strong, and foreign pressure, especially by France, is seeking to discourage German hopes of regaining the lost lands.

Yet irredentism is being kept alive, almost artificially. Even in the 1961 federal elections, few German politicians and newspapers felt it wise to take a public stand favoring abandonment of the lands beyond the Oder-Neisse, not even to gain a bargaining point for reunification. Despite private indifference, the public position that the Oder-Neisse question is not negotiable is being stanchly maintained, and reluctance to abandon the eastern territories remains one of the stumbling blocks to reunification and to a peace settlement.

Thus neither the first "thaw" in the cold war—labeled "spirit of Geneva" in the American press—nor Bonn's own diplomatic efforts produced the slightest advance toward a solution to the German problem. Understandably, neither East nor West devoted its full energies to getting Germany reunified. But it is also questionable how ardently the West Germans themselves desire reunification. Probably half the people of West Germany have relatives or friends in East Germany. Many cherish traditional ties that bind them to the East German lands, in which some had economic interests they hope to recover. They also recognize that a united Germany, with some 75 million inhabitants, would at once rank next to Russia as the dominant power in Europe and would become the unquestioned leader of the Common Market or any other large European union that may be created. Yet among the population at large, there is in fact considerable apathy toward the question of reunification. The political opposition in Germany also questions the sincerity of the Adenauer government and of the ruling circles, which publicly pay lip service to the demand for reunification but privately show less eagerness to press for a solution to the problem. In a reunited Germany, the CDU would lose its electoral advantage to the SPD; the strength of the Roman Catholic Church would wane with the inclusion of primarily Protestant East Germany; conservatives and industralists would face the difficulties of amalgamating the socialized economy of the East with their own system of free enterprise; and wealthy West Germany would have to share its affluence to help build up the economically less advanced east.

Meanwhile, despite the Hallstein Doctrine and despite tacit misgivings, the Federal Ministry for All-German Affairs and many other public and private agencies attempted to increase contacts between the two Germanies, so that during their period of separation, the two states would not grow apart irremediably. Travel restrictions were almost completely lifted. In 1957 alone, some three million East Germans visited the Federal Republic, and millions of West Germans paid visits to the DDR. Trade was expanded. Trade fairs, church meetings, youth congresses, scientific exchanges, sport competitions, cultural exchanges, and numerous other arrangements permitted contact between Germans from both sides of the "iron curtain." There was cooperation in transport and communication, in public health problems, and in such legal matters as restitution for damage suffered under National Socialism or the clearing up of wills, stocks, and personal records. At the same time, federal committees in West Germany studied economic and social changes in East Germany to prepare for adjustments required in the event of reunification.

In 1958, however, East German authorities began to hamper travel between the two states. Gradually contact was choked off, and the differences between East and West began to grow at an accelerated pace.

The Berlin Crises

After countless exchanges of diplomatic notes between East and West and a series of reciprocal visits by the British, German, and French heads of state in 1958, Khrushchev suddenly revived tensions by opening the first of a series of Berlin crises. In November 1958, he proposed that West Berlin be turned into a demilitarized, free city, perhaps under U.N. supervision and guarantee, and that the occupying powers immediately conclude peace with both Germanies. The Russian leader intimated that unless the western powers agreed to his proposal within six months, he would sign a separate peace treaty with the DDR and relinquish to the East Germans all Russian responsibilities for western military communications with Berlin by rail, highway, and air. This Russian demand turned 1959 into a critical year of feverish diplomatic activity. Despite serious disagreement among the western powers on how best to counter Russia's threat, Bonn and the Big Three shared the apprehension that implementation of Khrushchev's proposal might result in the loss of Berlin for the West and the permanent splitting of Germany. If control of access routes to Berlin were turned over to Ulbricht, the West would be forced to deal with the DDR in an official capacity and thereby would extend recognition to the regime. In consequence, the West would no longer be able to deny the validity of Russia's claim that two Germanies existed, and the western plan for reunification (see page 639) would have to be abandoned.

The year opened with threats and counterthreats, interspersed with Russian demands for a new summit meeting. After Chancellor Adenauer conferred with President Charles de Gaulle, and Prime Minister Harold Macmillan visited Bonn and Moscow, where Premier Khrushchev agreed to withdraw his six-month deadline, the powers arranged a foreign ministers' conference in Geneva. The ministers held thirty-one meetings during May and June. Although both sides ceded a few minor points, no solution was reached. The Russian threat to Berlin was not withdrawn but merely postponed, and to stress their determination Russian and East German authorities frequently harassed Allied traffic to Berlin.

Despite the patent incompatibility of the opposing views, a new thaw developed. Vice-President Richard Nixon went to Russia, and Premier Khrushchev visited the United States (September 1959) to discuss with President Eisenhower at Camp David ways of easing the cold war. While preparing for a new summit meeting, the four western Allies maneuvered to bridge their own differences. Eisenhower visited Bonn in August, and Adenauer journeyed to London in November and conferred with De Gaulle in Paris in early December.

The talks between Adenauer and De Gaulle opened an era of growing friendship between the two. Franco-German cooperation in the European Coal and Steel Community and in the Common Market (created in 1958), and perhaps a certain affinity between the two rigid and self-assured leaders, each of whom felt that he had personally restored his country to greatness, led to an ever-closer *rapprochement* between them. There were, of course, points of difference between France and Germany. Starting in 1959, De Gaulle pressed for a separate atomic force for western Europe and a more independent policy for France, whereas Adenauer was less convinced of the desirability of an "atomic third force" and remained more devoted to the closest possible relations with England and America. Moreover, De Gaulle was not averse to accepting the Oder-Neisse line as permanent, whereas Adenauer rejected such a position. But in regard to the general approach to negotiations with Russia, Bonn and Paris were in agreement and differed from the Anglo-American position. Washington and London appeared willing to make minor concessions to the Russians in order to secure a temporary settlement of the Berlin issue. Adenauer and De Gaulle, however, preferred to see the *status quo* in Berlin rather than to make concessions to the Russians, and they opposed discussing Berlin as a separate issue from the rest of the German problem.

The Paris Conference, officially committed to the discussion of Berlin, Germany, and world disarmament, finally opened on May 16, 1960. But even before its opening, "the spirit of Camp David" had evaporated. By late April, the Geneva disarmament talks had been suspended, and Khrushchev had reiterated his warning that he would sign a separate peace with the DDR and force the western powers out of Berlin unless they agreed to his proposals. The U-2 incident—the downing of an American reconnaissance plane deep inside Russia—was used by the Soviet Union as a pretext for terminating the summit conference barely three hours after it had started.

In 1961, Khrushchev again intimated that he expected to settle the Berlin issue by the end of the year, presumably in order to put pressure on the newly installed administration of John F. Kennedy and to take advantage of discord among the Allies and within West Germany. Adenauer visited Paris, London, and Washington in the spring, but the Franco-German stand remained more rigid than that of Great Britain and the United States. Within Germany, the election campaign showed that many groups were growing weary of Adenauer's lack of success on Berlin and reunification. The SPD and the FDP called for a new approach to "the German problem," without proffering specific alternatives. The CDU, on the other hand, reiterated its "absolute rejection of any step that might lead to a neutralization of Germany," and warned that the negotiations on Berlin might be harmed if the FDP and the SPD injected foreign policy into the election campaign.

In June, President Kennedy met Premier Khrushchev in Vienna. The meeting produced no changes, since the Russians persisted in demanding that Berlin be turned into a "free city," and stressed their readiness to sign a separate peace and unleash a third Berlin crisis. New harassments of Allied traffic to Berlin followed, and the borders between East and West Germany were closed almost completely. Despite Khrushchev's call for "peaceful coexistence," the East Germans soon began to restrict access also between East and West Berlin. As if sensing that the DDR would soon be turned into a huge barbed wire encampment and sealed off like other Russian satellites, over 30,000 East Germans and East Berliners used the last open escape route by fleeing to West Berlin in July, followed by 22,000 more in early August.

On August 13, 1961, Russia and the DDR suddenly announced the closure of the border between East and West Berlin, ostensibly to keep out West German saboteurs. A decree prohibited East Germans and East Berliners from entering West Berlin. East German army units and Vopos encircled the entire perimeter of West Berlin with barbed wire, which was replaced in the ensuing weeks by a wall of solid cement blocks, topped with broken glass and barbed wire.

Erection of the Berlin Wall was not merely a desperate measure to stop the flight of refugees, which was endangering East Germany's productive strength; it was also another attempt to weaken the resistance of West Berlin. The western powers did not try to prevent the construction of the wall. According to retired General Lucius Clay, the West is "responsible only for the independence, security, and well-being of West Berlin," whereas "East Berlin is a Soviet responsibility." But the West made plain its intention to remain in West Berlin and defend it. The wall, of course, caused much additional hardship to the people of Berlin, and imprisoned in East Germany all those who had hoped to flee to the West. But it failed to force the surrender of the city to East Germany.

Throughout 1962, the situation in Berlin remained unchanged. Occasional escapees tunneled or vaulted their way to freedom, and there were moments of tension when American and Russian tanks stood menacingly face to face at "Checkpoint Charlie," one of the few official crossing points between the west and the east of the city. Communist Vopos and West Berlin police sometimes exchanged gunfire during the escape of a refugee. But both sides were clearly determined not to let the Berlin issue erupt into open conflict. Among the western powers there continued to be different views on the best procedure to follow. Adenauer once again journeyed to Washington in November, and further cemented relations with France by an official visit of state to Paris, followed by a return visit by De Gaulle and ultimately by the signing of a treaty of friendship and cooperation between France and Germany in January 1963. But despite the division of the western powers into a Franco-German and an Anglo-American camp, the four states presented a firm, united front to the Kremlin in regard to Berlin.

But East–West negotiations at various diplomatic levels produced no progress. In repeated public statements, Khrushchev called for a German settlement and made vague allusions to possible unilateral action. In his New Year's message for 1963, he again advocated a "normalization" of the status of Berlin, suggesting as a minimum that Allied forces in Berlin be placed under United Nations control. But even when he visited East Berlin in January 1963 to attend the party congress of the East German Communists, he refrained from setting new deadlines or voicing further precise demands for a change in the status of Berlin. Khrushchev's hesitation resulted not merely from his preoccupation with internal economic problems and the Sino-Russian dispute; he was also reluctant to award Walter Ulbricht full freedom of action that the German Communist might misuse to the embarrassment of the Russians.

THE GERMAN DEMOCRATIC REPUBLIC

Under the strict tutelage of the Soviet Union, the East German Democratic Republic gradually emerged as a quasi-sovereign state in steps paralleling those taken by the west in regard to Bonn. In most cases, the Russians made their plans ahead of the western powers, but implemented them only in response to similar measures taken by the West. Moscow was more hesitant than the western powers to perpetuate the division of Germany, since the Communists had more to gain from converting Germany into a united but neutralized state, and thereby forcing Bonn's withdrawal from NATO.

Rearmament

As early as 1948, units of the people's police had been equipped with military weapons. A Vopo navy and air force had been created in 1950 and 1951, respectively, and the constitution had been amended in 1953 to permit rearmament. But the remilitarization of East Germany was publicly acknowledged only in 1955, when the DDR became an associate member of the Warsaw Pact. In the following year—officially in retaliation for the establishment of a West German army (*Bundeswehr*)—the East Germans established a Ministry of National Defense, under General Karl-Heinz Hoffman (1910–)—a reliable party member and friend of Ulbricht's—and set up the NVA, the National People's Army. To staff the NVA, some Vopo units were converted into regular armed forces and equipped largely with Russian and Czech weapons.

During the subsequent years, the East German forces grew relatively slowly. By 1961, they had reached 110,000 men, including army, navy, and air force, although a new target of 170,000 men was set. Alone among the Warsaw Pact nations, the DDR instituted no official draft, and instead filled its military ranks with "volunteers," most of whom enlisted because of pressure or enticements exerted through various party and organizational channels. Leadership in the NVA was entrusted to those deemed politically reliable rather than to those with military experience; hence former *Wehrmacht* officers were gradually pushed aside in favor of younger and better indoctrinated men. The ideal of a nonpolitical army, preached by Bonn, was alien to Pankow. Typical of those in the upper echelons of the officer corps is the head of the air force, Lieutenant General Heinz Kessler (1920–), who had deserted to the Red Army on June 22, 1941, received his Communist apprenticeship in Moscow as a student in the anti-Fascist school and as a member of the Russian-sponsored National Committee for a Free Germany, and is a member of the SED Central Committee.

The relatively modest size of the National People's Army stems partly from Russian precautions not to let the Germans create a single large military force that might escape their political control. For this reason, the Russians preferred to see the militarization of numerous other organizations, each of which can be controlled through separate channels. Thus the Border Security Police (some 50,000 men), the Factory Guard Police (some 8000), the Security Alert Police (some 30,000), the Security Guard Police (some 5000), the Railroad Security Police (some 7000), the District Alert Police (some 5000), and the

Workers' Militia (some 350,000)—all of whom receive military training and considerable armaments—add almost half a million men to the pool of available forces. In addition, about 400,000 young men and women of the Association for Sports and Technical Crafts receive paramilitary training in parachute jumping, piloting, and marksmanship.

Together with its official permission to rearm, Russia reluctantly granted the Ulbricht regime other symbols of sovereign status. In September 1955, the DDR assumed control over its own frontiers, forcing the West Germans to deal increasingly with East German authorities, whose *de jure* existence the West still refuses to recognize. In 1957, Russia promised that the 400,000-man Red Army stationed on East German soil would refrain from interfering in the internal affairs of the DDR. In 1959, the Russians even ceased demanding reimbursement for the cost of the occupation troops, giving the DDR more nearly the illusion of being a bona fide ally of the Soviet Union.

Economic Progress

Economic progress at first remained slow. The balance of trade was still unfavorable, essential foods were in short supply, and the First Five-Year Plan fell short of its goals. By 1957, industrial output—initially severely handicapped by indiscriminate Russian dismantling and by poor planning—began to grow significantly, although the Second Five-Pear Plan also fell behind schedule. Trade with the Russian bloc increased measurably, partly financed by extensive Russian credits. But despite increased industrial production, the economy as a whole suffered from the constant decline in population caused by the continued flights to West Germany. The DDR's population decreased from 20 million in 1948 to 17 million by 1960.

In the late 1950s, economic progress accelerated. In 1958, Ulbricht took a major step in his program of socialization, and at the same time attempted to assuage the discontent of the working population. Nationalization of small industry and the creation of state farms were now pushed vigorously, while food rationing was abolished and wages were increased. A concerted effort was made to raise the standard of living, although higher food prices partly wiped out the greater earning power of the workers. The drive for increased productivity was successful in industry at least. By 1959, the DDR had achieved a favorable balance of exports over imports and was increasing its trade not only with the Russian bloc and West Germany, but also with many nonaligned Near Eastern nations, such as Egypt and Iraq. Its recovery, in fact, placed East Germany in the industrial forefront of the Communist nations.

But the economic recovery was only one side of the coin, and was achieved under considerable strain. Ulbricht began to clamp down on travel to the West in order to slow down the exodus of refugees. He also resorted to a type of forced labor. After 1959, every child over eleven was forced to work one day a week on a farm or in a factory, and by 1960, all workers were assigned to jobs, regardless of personal preferences. Industrialization was stressed at the expense of consumer production, and agriculture was mismanaged and neglected. The forced collectivization in 1960 of all land remaining in private possession failed to increase the production of food. On the contrary, by 1961 new food shortages forced the reintroduction of rationing of fats and even of potatoes in some regions. At the same time, industrial production slowed down. Despite East Germany's industrial prowess, Ulbricht found himself in ever-deeper economic trouble. United States agencies in West Berlin distributed free food parcels to East Germans, who, much to the embarrassment of the Communist regime, flocked there to supplement their meager diet. The Bonn government offered free shipments of food, and began to use economic pressure as a lever for negotiating political concessions. In late 1960, Bonn bargained successfully for an easing of travel restrictions for West Germans visiting Berlin or East Germany, in return for the renewal of trade agreements (11 percent of East Germany's foreign trade was with West Germany). In 1963, when East Germany was severely handicapped by a lack of foreign credits, Bonn offered Ulbricht a loan of $100 million, provided West Berliners were permitted to pass through the Berlin Wall to visit East Berlin. Under pressure from Russia, the Pankow government eventually rejected this offer.

Ulbricht's Dictatorship

Neither the failure to relieve shortages nor changes in the Communist party line in Moscow prevented Walter Ulbricht from gradually consolidating his grip on the DDR and from converting East Germany into a dictatorship. Among all the Stalinist satellite leaders, Ulbricht proved the most durable and agile, capable of shifting with every change of wind from Moscow, yet retaining a measure of independent power. To achieve unquestioned rule over East Germany and, he hopes, ultimately over a united Germany, Ulbricht set out to suppress all opposition outside the SED, to eliminate rivals within his party, and to find a *modus vivendi* with Moscow.

Opposition at large that had not been channeled into innocuous pseudo parties centered around the Lutheran Church, led by Bishop Otto Dibelius (1880–), whose residence is in West Berlin but whose diocese includes East Berlin and parts of the DDR. The struggle between the Lutheran Church and the SED continued all through the 1950s and early 1960s, with inconclusive results. As in the days of Hitler, the issue provoked a split in the church. Certain Lutheran leaders, most of whom belong to the Pastors' League (*Pfarrerbund*), accept a narrow interpretation of St. Paul's admonition that "the powers that be are ordained of God," and hence favor close cooperation between the Lutheran Church and the Communist regime. On the other hand, Dibelius and a majority of pastors and church members, chastened by the experience of National Socialism, assert that a totalitarian government cannot be permitted to rule Christian consciences.

In order to gain greater political power and capture the confidence of the workers, Ulbricht tried various approaches. The "soft line" adopted in 1956, when thousands of political prisoners were pardoned and more contact with West Germany was permitted, was abandoned in 1958. "De-Stalinization" was followed by a purge of unreliable SED leaders. Meanwhile, use of the "National Front" (see page 635) for elections continued to ensure a malleable legislature. The elections of 1957 gave the candidates of the official list a vote of 99.5 percent, and the shadow president, Wilhelm Pieck, was easily re-elected to a third four-year term in the same year.

Yet in the face of new economic problems, Ulbricht required even more power and sought less cumbersome pretenses at playing democracy. His opportunity came with Pieck's death in 1960. Reminiscent of Hitler in 1934 at the death of Hindenburg, Ulbricht abolished the presidency and made himself chairman of a newly created Council of State. This council, whose twenty-three members were appointed for a term of four years by the SED—in reality by Ulbricht himself—was given power to promulgate legislation, sign international agreements, control foreign affairs, order elections, and even countermand existing legislation. At the same time, Ulbricht assumed the post of chairman of the new National Defense Council, with power over all land, sea, and air forces, while he retained his post as first party secretary of the SED. The fiction of a cabinet was retained, but Prime Minister Grotewohl, never very powerful, was in fact demoted to be a mere administrator. This new arrangement gave Ulbricht almost complete power over the state, under the guise of a collective party leadership. But when economic problems grew in 1962, responsibility for the failures was also placed more squarely at his feet. Arrests of discontents, stern reprisals, and dismissal of scapegoats only provoked further unrest.

Although the fate of the regime depends on the Soviet Union, the DDR at times took matters into its own hands. The Pankow regime repeatedly attempted bilateral negotiations with Bonn on questions of reunification, but Adenauer stanchly refused such overtures, although he increased commercial relations with Pankow. In answer, Ulbricht occasionally enacted his own reprisals, sometimes to the embarrassment of Russia. A favorite measure was interference with West German civilian traffic to West Berlin. The death strip of barbed wire and cleared fields, hermetically sealing off East Germany from the West, was another move revealing Ulbricht's desperation. And there is reason to believe that construction of the Berlin Wall initially was a measure conceived by Pankow and only reluctantly accepted by the Kremlin. At times, Ulbricht also seemed tempted to flirt with Communist China in an effort to bring pressure on Moscow for greater financial and political support. Despite his inherent distrust of Ulbricht, Khrushchev had no choice but to bolster the East German regime for fear of jeopardizing negotiations with the West. To raise the prestige of the Pankow government, he made frequent visits to East Berlin: 1955, 1957, 1959, 1960, 1963. At the SED Party Congress in January 1963, attended by Khrushchev, Vladislav Gomulka, and high-ranking delegates from all Communist countries, including Yugoslavia and China, the Russian leader again did his best to bolster Ulbricht's prestige, without, however, giving him greater freedom of action for solving the Berlin issue on his own terms.

THE FEDERAL REPUBLIC

West German Rearmament

The Paris Treaties called for a German army of 500,000 men, with a limited air force and navy. To create this army, the federal legislature amended the Basic Law to permit rearmament (March 6, 1956), and appointed as Commander in Chief General Hans Speidel (1897–), a former chief of staff to Rommel. At that time, 10,000 men were transferred from the 20,000 man Federal Frontier Protection Service to form the nucleus of the federal defense force, and a law was passed permitting the recruitment of 150,000 volunteers. At the same time, Adenauer turned over the Ministry of Defense, which had been created in 1955, to Franz Joseph Strauss (1915–), a ranking member of the CSU and former lieutenant in World War II, who had first served in the Bavarian government and after 1953 held various posts in Adenauer's cabinet. Only 70,000 volunteers had enrolled by the end of 1956; hence the Bundestag enacted compulsory military service, effective January 1957, despite the protest of the SPD, which still feared a revival of militarism.

During 1957, the West German defense force continued its slow expansion. The federal government built airplanes for NATO, and the first three German divisions of light armor were transferred to NATO command. German military morale was given a considerable boost when General Speidel was appointed commander in chief of all NATO land forces in Europe.

But German rearmament faced serious problems. The Bundestag had to frame new codes of military conduct and justice that would place greater responsibility on the judgment of officers and enlisted men without undermining the traditional army hierarchy of command. In addition to assuring internal democratization of the armed forces, Bonn had to establish firm civilian control over the military. Moreover, the military establishment required considerable financial expenditures. Many Germans were averse to seeing their funds diverted from buttressing economic growth to purchasing foreign weapons or financing an army. Also, the federal structure established by the Basic Law was not geared to large expenditures by the federal government, since it provided that the states retain the bulk of tax revenue (see page 660). These restrictions on Bonn's resources affected Germany's contributions toward NATO, as well as its ability to purchase British and American arms.

By 1958, the West German army had been expanded to seven divisions. As the Western European Union Council (see page 644) lifted its restrictions, the Germans increased the size of their naval vessels and air force. At the same time, Germany, Italy, and France decided to produce certain weapons jointly, such as tanks and fighter aircraft. With the French army deeply involved in the Algerian War and with De Gaulle withholding the bulk of his forces from NATO control, NATO planners began to rely increasingly on German contributions to western Europe's defense. As early as 1958, General Lauris Norstad, Supreme Allied Commander in Europe from 1956 to 1962, favored removing all remaining restrictions on German production and German use of conventional weapons. He also suggested that German artillery be equipped with nuclear warheads.

But the growth and equipment of the German army raised considerable debate. Minister Strauss urged that the federal defense force be awarded equal status with other western armies, even in its armaments. And there were some in Germany who thought that Germans should not be mere foot soldiers in an alliance in which only Americans controlled the nuclear arms. Hence Strauss also felt that nuclear weapons in German hands would be justified, an assertion that raised a storm of protest in and out of Germany.

As the army grew, Strauss also insisted on the need for German training bases as well as depots of strategic stockpiles further removed from the "iron curtain" than the federal territory. In early 1960, he negotiated for German bases in Spain, a move perhaps militarily sound, but diplomatically tactless, since most WEU countries looked askance on the dictatorial regime of Generalissimo Franco. The resulting Allied protests revealed the ingrained apprehensions about a possible revival of German militarism, and Strauss abandoned his negotiations. But gradual military integration with the western powers continued.

In 1961, German troops were provided training bases in England and France, and the federal defense force was equipped with an increased number of short-range missiles. However, its growth continued to be hampered by financial problems. And so long as NATO leaders were undecided whether to press for large, conventional land forces, or ask for small, highly mobile, heavily armed units, the Germans felt little incentive to expand their land armies. By the beginning of 1963, the combined total for all three branches of the federal armed forces amounted to only 398,000 men, in spite of the fact the Paris Treaties had stipulated 500,000, and United States military planners in NATO were calling for a new goal of 700,000.

Continued Prosperity

West Germany's economic boom continued after 1955. The economy grew at a rate of over 7 percent annually, until it slowed down in 1961. Production of crude steel rose to over 34 million tons a year (1961). Unemployment disappeared completely, and by 1962 over half a million foreign workers, mostly from Italy, Spain, and Greece, were employed in the Federal Republic. The European Common Market proved eminently successful in further stimulating the growth of German trade and industry, although not until 1962 was a tentative solution found to the problem of reducing agricultural tariffs among the six members. France and Holland, in particular, favored freer trade in order to export their agricultural surpluses, while Germany and Italy, with high costs of agricultural production, preferred to keep high tariffs on farm produce.

Germany's high rate of industrial production further increased its favorable balance of trade. By 1962, German exports were valued at 13.7 billion dollars, and imports at 12.4 billion. Consequently, Germany's gold and foreign reserve holdings stood at 6.3 billion dollars at the beginning of 1963. The value of the German mark became so high that in 1961 Bonn gave in to pressure from the western powers to aid the general balance of payments problems by revaluing its currency upward by 5 percent. Germany also increased its share of carrying the financial burdens of the western world, although not to the degree hoped for by the Allies. In 1953, at the London Debt Conference, the Bonn government had already agreed to pay 3.2 billion dollars over a period of thirty-five years for all prewar debts to the western powers. To help slow down the gold drain on the United States, Germany began in 1961 to repay its debts to the United States and Great Britain at an accelerated rate, and increased its foreign aid to underdeveloped countries to 1 billion dollars a year. Bonn also contributed to the Common Market Fund for aiding France's former overseas territories, joined the newly created Organization for Economic Cooperation and Development (OECD), and extended direct credits to nations in Africa and Asia.

Germany's industrial growth proceeded under the aegis of Ludwig Erhard's Social Market Economy. Economic controls were kept to a minimum, and social security programs vastly extended. But no measures were taken, as initially contemplated, to prevent the reconstitution of cartels. The decartelization of Krupp was constantly postponed, even though Chancellor Adenauer asserted in 1958 that "there is a great future danger that a handful of economic structures will control the German economy to such a degree that the government will be forced to take drastic steps against them. "By 1962, the Krupp industries had become Europe's largest steel producer, with a yearly turnover of 1 billion dollars and branches operating on every continent of the world.

As part of its program supporting private enterprise, the Bonn government attempted to decrease the government's role in business by "privatizing" (denationalizing) parts of the huge industrial empire (worth almost 2 billion dollars) it had inherited from the Nazis. Grouped together in three large holding companies, the government's interests in steel, coal, aluminum, zinc, lead, oil, shipbuilding, automobile construction, and other enterprises made it in some fields the largest single producer in Germany (for example, it controlled 72 percent of the total aluminum output, 42 percent of automobile production). But almost ten years passed before an acceptable method was devised for selling government enterprises without upsetting the economy and without allowing private corporations to increase to monopolistic proportions by buying up the government's shares. Erhard's program of privatization encountered strong opposition. Although the SPD had abandoned its demands for nationalization, the Socialists saw no reason for the government's divesting itself of basic industries it already owned. Moreover, the federal minister of finance opposed the scheme assiduously, partly because the federal government would lose badly needed revenue, since the increased taxes paid by private business would largely accrue to the states rather than to the central government.

In late 1958, a compromise on privatization was achieved. By selling shares in government-owned concerns only to people of limited income, the CDU could claim to promote "people's capitalism." In March 1959, an initial bloc of 300,000 shares of the Preussag coal and oil combine, each with a nominal value of 100 marks, was offered to the public. Only Germans with an annual income of less than the equivalent of 4000 dollars were permitted to purchase the stocks, with a maximum of 5 shares per person. Sold at 145 marks each, the shares soared to 237 within five months, although they subsequently declined to a more realistic level. After this successful experiment, which according to some critics, encouraged stock market speculation among the normally staid German middle class, the government turned to denationalizing the highly profitable Volkswagen Works. Two years of litigation were required to determine whether this enterprise, originally founded by Goering and the Nazi Labor Front, legally belonged to the state of Lower Saxony, whose legislature opposed privatization, or to the federal government. Also to be determined was whether compensation should be made to those Germans who had paid the Nazis for a Volkswagen on the strength of Goering's promises but had never received one. The courts eventually decided that the federal government was the legal owner of the enterprise, and that those who had paid for a Volkswagen before World War II should be permitted to purchase one at a considerable discount. In March 1961, shares were finally sold to small investors with limitations similar to those applied to the Preussag shares.

In the early 1960s, the German economy faced new problems. Even with 34 percent of the gross national product devoted to taxes—probably the highest percentage in the world—the federal budget was no longer balanced in 1962, and a deficit of 750 million dollars was forecast for 1963. In addition to disbursements for social services, assistance to agriculture and industry, there were extraordinary expenditures for restitution—including 822 million dollars to Israel for Jewish claims against Germany—for refugees and expellees, subsidies to West Berlin, occupation costs, and pensions to veterans. Above all, there was the question of financing the constantly rising defense budget, estimated at 4.6 billion dollars for 1963 (about 7 percent of the gross national product) out of a total federal budget of 15 billion dollars. In spite of the fact that West Germany is the richest country in western Europe, the federal government is constantly in financial straits because of the federalism embedded in the Basic Law. Its revenue is limited to customs duties, taxes on consumption (except beer), turnover taxes, and the special Equalization of Burdens Fund. The state governments, on the other hand, collect the profitable income and corporation taxes; the municipalities have their own local revenue. Since the receipts of the federal government do not suffice to pay for normal expenditures as well as for defense, annual agreements are negotiated between Bonn and the state governments concerning the share of state revenues to be turned over to the federal government. Since they involve the question of federal and states' rights, these negotiations engender constant political controversy.

The 1960s brought added economic problems. The trade-unions, which had scaled down their demands for years, now pressed for higher wages. A perceptible inflation set in, and economic growth slowed down. The gross national product, which stood at 67.7 billion dollars in 1960, was projected at about 100 billion dollars for 1970, indicating that the yearly rate of expansion had decreased to about 4 percent. At the same time, the growth of population was expected to slow down to an annual average of 0.8 percent, so that the Federal Republic was expected to reach about 57.6 million inhabitants by 1970.

Remnants of the Past

A 1959 cartoon in a Hamburg paper (*Die Welt*) depicted a set of volumes on German history on a shelf in a typical, comfortable German household. The collection showed a conspicuous gap for the years 1933 to 1945, the period of the Third Reich. The cartoon attacked the smug insouciance with which large segments of Germans view the Hitler years, an attitude greatly disturbing to many foreign observers and to some Germans as well. Prosperity and material comforts seem to have brought self-assurance, and a few billion marks of restitution have laid many troubled consciences to rest.

During the first decade after the war, the majority of the Germans buried the Hitler years in a deep silence. The history of 1933 to 1945 was not taught in the schools. Few Germans would have known how to teach it dispassionately, and few parents felt inclined to discuss it with their children. Those still believing in National Socialist dogma thought it unwise to admit the fact publicly. Those recognizing their folly, hesitated to confess to their children that they had participated in it.

In the late 1950s, brushing the Nazi era under the carpet gave way to a serious campaign of instructing the youth in the history of the Third Reich. With official support from the federal Ministry of the Interior and the state Ministries of Culture, high school and university courses offered undiluted analyses of Nazi excesses. German films, books, radio, television, and editorials presented frank portrayals of the Nazi terror. The Germans were being asked to live with their past.

Even this concerted campaign hardly modified the attitude of the bulk of the population. The blame for whatever had happened and whatever new horrors were discovered in the course of continued war crimes trials was always placed on others. Convinced neo-Nazis clung to the conviction that Hitler himself did not know of the atrocities committed by a "few" demented underlings. This persistent self-exoneration by most Germans often led many observers to decry the "unreconstructed mentality" of the Germans and to assert that German democracy today is skin-deep and fragile and may all too easily give way to a revival of Nazism.

Although it is unquestionably true that Nazi prejudices and concepts persist in certain segments of German thought, it should also be realized that an entire population can hardly be expected to wear sackcloth indefinitely.

WAR CRIMES TRIALS AND DENAZIFICATION After gaining sovereignty in 1955, the West Germans assumed complete control over all denazification measures and war crimes prosecutions, except where cases involved foreign nationals. Since jurisdiction over anti-Nazi legislation, trials, and amnesties resided in the state governments, there were widespread differences in the zeal with which former Nazis were found and brought to trial. In 1958, a Central Office for Nazi Crimes was set up in Ludwigsburg, largely in answer to complaints by foreigners as well as by Germans that some state governments were lax in ferreting out war crimes suspects who were hiding behind pseudonyms or in the obscurity of German villages. The new agency gathered evidence on Nazi criminals and coordinated the prosecution efforts of the various state governments. As a result, countless new clues were unearthed and many new suspects discovered. Supplied with documents by the Central Office, the local courts redoubled their efforts to try hundreds of concentration camp commandants, gas chamber operators, SS guards, and employers of slave labor. By 1962, the number of such trials had swollen to over 13,000, resulting in some 5000 convictions. The gruesome details revealed in these trials, which will continue until the statute of limitations becomes effective in May 1965, are accurately reported in German newspapers and avidly read for their sensational value, just as the trial of Adolf Eichmann in 1961–1962 in Israel received ample coverage in the German press.

Denazification as such is today a matter of the past. In all the states of West Germany, Nazis who were removed from their jobs because of membership in certain Nazi organizations—except those in category "A," major offenders—became re-employable after January 1, 1960, in accordance with the Third Law on the Termination of Denazification. Many had found employment long before in industry and commerce. Even some members of the state and federal governments were former Nazi party members—a fact frequently denounced by their political opponents in West Germany and by the Communist press in the East. The official attitude on the employment of former Nazis was succinctly stated by Gerhard Schroeder (1911–)—himself a nominal member of the NSDAP from 1933 to 1941—who served as federal minister of the interior before becoming foreign minister in 1961. Schroeder asserted that "there will be no second denazification" and that he saw no reason for not allowing "reformed" Nazis to serve the government, provided they had discarded their Nazi sentiments.

NEO-NAZIS Despite denazification, war crimes trials, and "re-education," there were individuals and organized groups who continued to embrace aspects of Nazi ideology. The small but active "Ludendorff movement," organized around a right-wing circle that included the general's widow, Mathilde Ludendorff, trumpeted its virulently anti-Semitic and anti-Christian "pure German" program until it was legally banned in May 1961. Small, rightist student organizations, such as the *Bund Nationaler Studenten* (League of National Students) and the *Nationale Jugend Deutschland* (National Youth of Germany), worshiped Nazi symbols and uniforms as well as Hitler's *Mein Kampf* while awaiting the dawning of a Fourth Reich.

The *Deutsche Reichspartei* (DRP), successor to the outlawed Social Reich party, became a major rallying point for ex-Nazis and young people who felt drawn to ultranationalism. Like the NSDAP, the DRP derides "American and French concepts of democracy and economy," republicanism, freedom of the press, and big business. It opposes NATO, the presence of "foreign soldiers on German soil," and European integration, is stanchly anti-Semitic, and champions "the great German future." In December 1959, the DRP became involved in anti-Semitic vandalism when two members of its Cologne branch were arrested for desecrating Cologne's new synagogue by painting swastikas and anti-Jewish slogans on its walls. For several weeks, a veritable rash of swastika-smearing and anti-Semitic incitements spread across Germany. Nazi symbols and slogans such as "Down with the Jews!" "Jews Get Out!" "Germany Awake!" and "Heil Hitler!" were daubed on Jewish homes, Catholic churches, and public buildings. A few of the apprehended vandals were members of student organizations typified by the *Bund Nationaler Studenten;* most were in their mid-twenties, and therefore had been about ten years old when Hitler died. Hence their anti-Semitism must have come from secondhand sources.

The anti-Semitic acts raised loud stirs of protest in Germany and in the forum of world opinion. Socialists and liberals held mass rallies; political and religious leaders, as well as journalists, denounced the incidents; Adenauer suggested that the hooligans receive a hiding on the spot, and his cabinet again considered promulgating special laws to deal with emergencies that might threaten the democratic order. Although these sporadic anti-Jewish outbreaks revealed a surprising residue of anti-Semitism in West Germany, which counts a Jewish population of only about thirty thousand, they shed little light on the remaining strength of Nazism: during the same months, similar swastika-daubings occured in Paris, London, New York, and other western cities.

Besides the DRP and the student organizations, there are other remnants of National Socialism and other neo-Nazi movements. The Association of the Victims of Denazification (VEB), with some 40,000 members, has been outlawed by the Ministry of the Interior on the national level, but is active in each state. Its aim is to obtain restitution and rehabilitation for those who suffered injustice from the denazification procedures, to expose atrocities committed during the period 1945 to 1947 by Allied and German guards in internment camps for Nazis, and to fight Communism with the skill and techniques acquired during their active participation in the National Socialist movement. Members of the VEB stress their political moderation, but their reverence for Hitler and his prophetic genius seems undiminished, and they assert that the horrors in the extermination camps were committed by a few criminals. A clique of unscrupulous Nazis, they believe, kept Hitler in the dark until almost the end of the war. Punishment, they insist, should have been reserved for those *few* who had actually committed atrocities, but not randomly inflicted on thousands of innocent party members "who had faithfully served an official political party which supported a state that was diplomatically recognized by all civilized nations of the world."

Some right-wing extremists, cognizant of the difficulty of reviving National Socialism, have seized upon the trend toward European integration as a vehicle for a new nationalistic supranationalism. The New European Movement (NEO), for example, established in Zurich in 1951 with strong German participation, would create a well-armed "Nation Europe" of some 300 million people, dominated by a racially oriented, dictatorially ruled Germany, and pitted in battle against "Bolshevist mongrels and capitalist Negroes"—its designation for east and west. Another group, the European Social Movement, also established in 1951, collaborated with neo-Fascists in various European capitals, particularly with the Italian Movimento Soziale Italiano (MIS). Otto Strasser, whose brother was assassinated in the June purge of 1934, founded the Social Movement in 1956, followed in 1957 by the Social Organic Order Movement (SORBE), both dedicated to recasting Europe on an authoritarian basis under the rule of a racial elite.

Finally, in 1962, dissatisfaction with existing political parties produced the resurrection of another remnant of the past. In Kassel, a small group of conservatives re-established the DNVP, the Nationalist party of Hugenberg that had helped topple the Weimar regime and had pushed Hitler into power in 1933. Although the party's founders stressed their allegiance to the democratic system of Bonn and set as their aim the reunification of Germany through Russian-American cooperation, the choice of the party label "DNVP" evoked concern among some observers.

Chancellor Democracy

Despite these remnants of the past and despite the gloomy predictions of some observers who almost by habit refuse to concede that Germans can be "reeducated," democracy has taken firm roots in West Germany in the eighteen years since the fall of Hitler. Extremism remains discredited and, unlike the Weimar period, even the thorniest problems—reunification and acceptance of the Oder-Neisse line—rarely stir unreasonable political passions. At the local level, individual political action has again acquired meaning, and civil rights on the whole are respected.

But at the level of national politics and party life, and especially in the functioning of the legislature and of the executive, West German parliamentary democracy has developed its own peculiar characteristics. Just as Bismarck fashioned institutions and a political atmosphere suitable to his personal modes of action, so Konrad Adenauer in the course of his fourteen years in office molded the Bonn government to fit his own somewhat authoritarian temper. In this the chancellor was aided by the rather flabby submissiveness of most Bonn parliamentarians and politicians, and by the traditional party structure that reserves most power to a few professional leaders.

ELECTIONS The 1957 federal elections revealed popular satisfaction with Adenauer's regime, particularly with Germany's economic progress. The CDU/CSU group made considerable gains, obtaining 50.3 percent of the votes and 54.3 percent of the Bundestag seats (270). Although assured of a majority for the CDU/CSU, Adenauer formed a coalition cabinet with the DP (17 seats), so as to obtain a better voting margin over the SPD, which gained an additional 1.5 million votes over 1953 and received 169 seats in the Bundestag. The only other party earning representation in Bonn, the FDP with its 41 seats, stayed out of the government, although it frequently supported Adenauer's legislative program. After the new Bundestag convened, Adenauer was elected for his third term as chancellor by a vote of 274 to 193.

During the next few years, the trend toward a two-party system remained evident in the state elections. The CDU and SPD continued to grow at the expense of the smaller parties. By 1959, CDU/CSU held a total of 570 seats in all eleven state legislatures as against 564 for the SPD, out of a grand total of 1345 seats. The Free Democrats (FDP) ran a poor third with 105 seats, with the remaining 106 shared by the other small parties. Despite the continued success of the CDU at the national level, the SPD added to its local strength. By 1959, it controlled five state governments (Hamburg, Lower Saxony, Bremen, Hesse, and West Berlin), and in subsequent Landtag elections in 1960 and 1962, it further increased its representation, particularly in North Rhine–Westphalia and Baden-Württemberg. In 1963, it scored a landslide victory of 62 percent in the West Berlin elections.

The CDU suffered its first major crisis in 1959. The electorate at large was grateful to their eighty-three-year-old chancellor, who was credited with gaining for West Germany the respect and prowess of a sovereign nation. But many felt that after ten years of rule, *der Alte* (the Old One) should gracefully retire to his rose garden on the banks of the Rhine and entrust the reins of government to a younger, more flexible candidate. Favored for such a post was Ludwig Erhard, popularly identified with Germany's prosperity. Moreover, Bonn parliamentarians and bureaucrats, and even members of the cabinet, chafed increasingly under the authoritarian and sometimes tactless manner in which the chancellor conducted the affairs of government. Adenauer handled foreign relations as though they were private matters, often refused to reveal negotiations to members of his own cabinet and party, frequently did not deign to answer criticism by the opposition, and did not permit cabinet members to make public statements without his approval.

Since Theodor Heuss's second term ended in July 1959 and he was not constitutionally re-eligible, some thought that Adenauer should be rewarded with the largely honorary post of president so that a new chancellor could be elected. In April, Adenauer agreed with the suggestion. He accepted his party's nomination as candidate for the presidency, and his election seemed assured. There remained the problem of finding a successor for the chancellorship from among the ranks of the CDU. The defects of "chancellor democracy" became at once apparent. Adenauer's one-man government had seemingly discouraged the development of suitable successors. Foreign Minister Brentano, sometimes considered the "heir apparent," was not favored by the leading circles in the CDU. Economics Minister Erhard seemed the more likely choice, although Adenauer distrusted his judgment in foreign affairs. But in June, while Erhard was on an official trip to Washington, Adenauer stunned Bonn by suddenly withdrawing his name as a presidential candidate. As official reason he indicated that the Berlin crisis, the Geneva Conference of Foreign Ministers, and other pressing foreign problems would make it unwise to change the leadership of the state. To his CDU colleagues he wrote: "I cannot, therefore, assume the responsibility of leaving my post during so critical a time."

It was symptomatic that the startled leaders of his own party grumblingly submitted to this decision. Although privately deploring their impotence, they continued to recognize the value of his leadership and his appeal with the voters at large. Consequently Adenauer remained chancellor. In July, the Electoral Assembly held its presidential election in Berlin—a symbolic gesture to underline the unity of West Berlin with West Germany. The CDU candidate was Heinrich Luebke (1894–), a former member of the Center party who had served Adenauer as minister of food and agriculture. In opposition, the Socialists supported Carlo Schmid (1896–), a long-time leader of the SPD and vice-president of the Bundestag; the FDP put up its own candidate (Max Becker). As expected, Luebke was elected second president of the Federal Republic—although he obtained only six more votes than the minimum required on the second ballot.

The chancellor's about-face evoked considerable criticism in the press and grumbling among the deputies. Eugen Gerstenmaier (1906–), the CDU president of the Bundestag, urged his colleagues to cease being "yes men" and to assert their parliamentary privileges. But most CDU deputies stifled their displeasure in view of the 1961 elections and Adenauer's proved attraction with the voters.

The 1961 elections were fought under the shadow of the new crisis provoked by the erection of the Berlin Wall. Although the German and Refugee parties merged in a vain attempt to regain national stature, the electoral campaign was waged essentially by three parties. Adenauer vaunted his past achievements and his seeming indispensability. Having discarded most Marxist slogans in order to appeal to the middle class, the Socialists counted on the dynamic and popular Willy Brandt to sweep the electorate. Most remarkable was the active campaign of Erich Mende's FDP, which urged the voters to put an end to the "sole dominance of the CDU/CSU with its concomitant dangers of overweening pride and misuse of power." The FDP vowed not to enter a coalition with the SPD, which it accused of desiring "the nationalization of man instead of the humanization of the state," and based its campaign on the theory that a two-party system was not proper "for German conditions in view of the ideological character of the two major parties." The FDP hoped to emulate the success of the Liberal party in England as a third force between Labor and Conservatives. It rejected the sectarian preferences of the CDU/CSU and the Socialist dogmas of the SPD, and called for a new approach to foreign problems; but it advanced few specific remedies in its own program. Above all, Erich Mende seemed bent on terminating Adenauer's rule.

The electoral results of September 1961 reflected the disenchantment of some of the voters. The CDU/CSU lost its majority, polling 45.3 percent and 242 seats (188 for CDU and 54 for CSU). The SPD rose to 36.3 percent and 190 seats, while the FDP, with 12.7 percent, obtained 67 seats. During seven weeks of negotiations for a new coalition, the FDP tried to implement its campaign promise of dislodging Adenauer immediately; but in the end, it had to accept the chancellor's statement that he would relinquish his post sometime before the 1965 elections, that he would seek new approaches to the question of reunification, and pursue a more forceful and independent course in foreign policy. After these backstage agreements, which provoked the resignation of Brentano, Adenauer formed his fourth coalition cabinet of 12 CDU, 3 CSU, and 5 FDP members. Thereafter he was elected to his fourth term as chancellor by the narrow margin of 258 to 239 (nays and abstentions). Twenty-six CDU members cast blank ballots to underline their disapproval of Adenauer's infatuation with power, and many delegates ostentatiously refused to applaud when his re-election was announced. Thus Adenauer remained and "chancellor democracy" survived.

THE END OF THE ADENAUER ERA A freak scandal in late October 1962 provoked a political crisis that revealed the latent discontent with Adenauer's obstinate resistance to retirement. After the publication of a controversial article describing defects in the armed forces as revealed in NATO maneuvers, Rudolph Augstein (1923–), the publisher, and four staff members of the news magazine *Der Spiegel* were arrested in the middle of the night on charges of treason. Simultaneously, the writer of the article was apprehended in Spain and summarily returned to Germany. Political leaders, newspapers, and civic organizations decried the method of arrest, and expressed fear that the government was infringing on freedom of the press. *Der Spiegel,* it was noted, specialized in vitriolic attacks on the government; its publisher was a firm supporter of the FDP and a well-known foe of Defense Minister Strauss. The Free Democrats, long bitter about the minor role reserved for them by Adenauer in the coalition cabinet, seized the occasion to vent their discontent. Erich Mende threatened to withdraw his party from the government coalition immediately, on the grounds that the FDP minister of justice (Wolfgang Stammberger) had not been consulted before the arrests were made.

The *Spiegel* affair thus engendered a prolonged government crisis. Adenauer's bland disregard for due process of law when, before any trial had convicted the accused, he publicly accused *Der Spiegel's* publisher of making "money out of committing treason," infuriated many parliamentary delegates. Cries of "Gestapo!" were increasingly hurled at government officials. Growing suspicion was raised by the role of Minister Strauss, who initially asserted that he had nothing to do with the affair, but later admitted that he had personally telephoned Madrid to order the arrest of *Der Spiegel's* correspondent.

Strauss blandly contended that attacks on him merely aided the Communist cause by discrediting the German government and the German armed forces. When the Free Democrats clamored for Strauss's dismissal from the cabinet, Adenauer at first refused to drop him because he was a leader of the Christian Socialists and the chancellor feared losing the support of the 54 CSU Bundestag delegates. Erich Mende, however, sought to acquire new power and make his the pivotal party in German politics by forcing the CDU to form a new coalition with the Free Democrats, but without the Christian Socialists. Such a combination would command 255 votes as opposed to a total of 244 for the Socialist party (190) and the Christian Socialists (54). Hence the five FDP ministers resigned on November 19, hinting that the party would be willing to re-enter a coalition with the Christian Democrats "free from problems of personalities"—referring to their hope for Strauss's and Adenauer's retirement.

While the country at large took up the slogan "Franz Joseph and Konrad out," the chancellor found a way of disposing of Strauss without firing him. He persuaded all cabinet members to resign, so that he could form an entirely new cabinet—without Strauss. Although Strauss's position was strengthened on November 25 when his

Christian Socialists were victorious in the Bavarian diet elections, he finally agreed to stay out of the new cabinet, while permitting his party to join the government coalition.

But the crisis was not yet over. There remained the question of Adenauer's own retirement. The FDP and even some CDU members pressed the chancellor to set a terminal date for his tenure in office. Moreover, the chancellor now became determined to use the crisis in order to limit the power and "partisan tactics" of the FDP. In a sudden and unexpected move to destroy the Free Democrats, he opened coalition talks with his traditional opponents, the Socialists. As a primary condition, he asked for their agreement to amend the electoral law so as further to disenfranchise the smaller parties—in other words, the Free Democrats. Surprisingly, the SPD showed a willingness to enter a coalition, provided Adenauer would promise to step down in the foreseeable future, but they were unwilling to consent to changes in the electoral law.

Hence Adenauer reopened negotiations with the FDP and regretfully gave in to that party's demand for setting a date for his retirement. On December 7, he announced that he would step down in the fall of 1963. Four days later, the seven-week crisis ended with the formation of a new coalition cabinet, including 11 Christian Democrats, 4 Christian Socialists, and 5 Free Democrats. Erhard and Schroeder retained their posts, and a newcomer to Bonn, Kai-Uwe von Hassel (1913–   ) of the CDU, received the Ministry of Defense vacated by Strauss. But Adenauer's authoritarianism had not been chastened: instead of being personally told by the chancellor, some former cabinet ministers heard through the press or through secretaries that they were not being reappointed.

The prolonged crisis had proved the resilience of "chancellor democracy" and the boundless tenacity of *der Alte*. But there was widespread criticism of the chancellor in the press and in the Bundestag, although some representatives still hesitated to be iconoclasts. Adenauer's regime, at any rate, had suffered a serious loss of prestige, and the new cabinet was at best a shaky stopgap. The FDP distrusted the chancellor who had tried his best to ruin it through electoral reform and Adenauer looked askance at the FDP for its efforts to unseat him. Above all, Adenauer persistently refused to name an heir, perhaps in fear of becoming a lame-duck ruler. Ludwig Erhard was still a likely successor and was also acceptable to the FDP. But despite his occasional temptation to rebel, he was a spiritless rival who meekly suffered Adenauer's continued efforts to embarrass him. And there were other contenders, around whom political cliques were forming, sowing dissension among the CDU: Brentano, Schroeder, Hassel, and others. Finally in the late spring of 1963, the party leaders of the CDU, notwithstanding Adenauer's misgivings, agreed to name Erhard as chancellor-designate, and in October Adenauer turned over the reins of government to Erhard.

Konrad Adenauer unquestionably had performed an immense service to Germany by re-creating economic and political stability, bridging the enmity with France, and making West Germany one of the major powers in the world. But like Bismarck, he had clung to power beyond his appointed time.

BIBLIOGRAPHY

More than most people, the Germans have been passionately devoted to the study of their history. The strong current of romanticism during much of the nineteenth century evoked in them a fondness for the past; the tradition of the scientific historical school of Leopold von Ranke and the delight of German scholars in painstaking research stimulated historical scholarship; their turbulent history over the past century furnished cogent reasons for studying the past—to bolster the drive for national unification, to render the new imperial institutions more venerable, to explain defeats and catastrophes.

But not only the Germans themselves have toiled over the history of their own people. Much has also been written about Germany by non-German scholars, particularly by the British. Germany's spectacular rise to nationhood in the late nineteenth century, its sometimes importune attitude in international affairs, and especially its development under National Socialism have awakened an ever-increasing interest among non-German historians and led them to focus their investigations on Germany's past.

In all countries that experience pronounced political shifts, historiography evinces the influence of political currents. France has its Jacobin, republican, Catholic, monarchist, Bonapartist, and socialist historians—to name but a few. So also German historical scholarship is rent between Catholics and Protestants, pro- and anti-Prussians, liberals and conservatives, federalists and centralists, and a myriad other tendencies. Moreover, the political and intellectual climate in which history is written is of vital importance. A book published in 1932 in Germany may be of almost any coloring, but one published in 1937 is bound to be at least moderately pro-Nazi. Similarly, non-German scholarship must be carefully weighed as to time-conditioned biases. Most books on Germany written between 1938 and 1945, for example, are likely to bear the imprint of anti-Teutonic passions. But such blanket indictments are naturally subject to exceptions, and it would be foolhardy indeed to attempt the construction of a chronological timetable of bias or of historical interpretation. The most one can do for the uninitiated reader is to provide him with a strong caveat before he undertakes his reading in the history of Germany.

Although this book is based primarily on German sources, the bibliography emphasizes works in English, since most studies in German are not available in the average library and since many readers lack the required knowledge of German to profit from such books. Because it is difficult in many cases to fit a given work into the compass of a particular chapter of this text, the bibliography has been arranged into larger units, following the general chronological outline of the book itself.

Bibliographic aids and collections of documents

For quick reference, consult the appropriate sections of W. H. Allison, G. M. Dutcher, S. B. Fay, and others, *A Guide to Historical Literature* (New York, 1931), or *The American Historical Association's Guide to Historical Literature,* edited by G. F. Howe, G. C. Boyce, T. R. S. Broughton, and others (New York, 1961). Louis J. Paetow's *Guide to the Study of Medieval History* (rev. ed., New York, 1931) with its succinctly categorized bibliographic and source references and useful historical outlines remains a pertinent tool, despite its dated materials. For German bibliographies, the most authoritative are still those by Friedrich Dahlmann and Georg Waitz, *Quellenkunde der Deutschen Geschichte* (Leipzig, 1932), and G. Gebhardt, *Handbuch der Deutschen Geschichte* (Stuttgart, 1930). The most recent is the four-volume *Handbuch der Deutschen Geschichte* (Marburg, 1952–1959) by O. Brandt, A. O. Meyer, and L. Just. Franz Schnabel's *Deutschlands Geschichtliche Quellen und Darstellungen in der Neuzeit* (Leipzig, 1931) gives sources as well as bibliographical aids. An indirect, but interesting tool for bibliographical studies is Edward Fueter's *Geschichte der Neueren Historiographie* (Munich, 1936), which discusses historical writing from Machiavelli to the Franco-Prussian War.

A brief collection of documents translated into English is available in L. Snyder's *Documents of German History* (New York, 1958). The number of volumes of collected source documents in German is considerable, and some have been listed in parts of this bibliography. Among those of wider range are *R. Oldenbourgs Geschichtliches Quellenwerk,* edited by E. Chudzinski, a ten-volume collection of letters, treaties, memoirs, and interviews from ancient times to the 1930s, most of them published in 1931; Teubner's *Quellensammlungen,* small booklets, of which hundreds have been published, each containing source material on a specific topic; *Geschichte in Quellen,* edited by W. Lautermann and M. Schlenke, of which the fifth volume on *Weltkriege und Revolutionen, 1914–1945* (Munich, 1961) is of particular interest. *Deutsche Reichsgeschichte in Dokumenten* (2 vols., Hanover, 1932–1934) edited by J. Hohlfeld, provides numerous official documents and statistics for the period 1849 to 1934. For foreign affairs under Bismarck and William II, see *Die Grosse Politik der Europäischen Kabinette, 1871–1914,* a forty-volume compendium of state papers from the German foreign office, edited by J. Lepsius, A. Mendelssohn-Bartholdy, and F. Thimme (Berlin, 1922–1927). Some interesting documents on German sociopolitical life can be found in *Die Zerstörung der Deutschen Politik, 1871–1933* (Frankfurt, 1959), H. Pross, editor. Useful though incomplete summaries of treaties are contained in K. Ploetz's *Konferenzen und Verträge* (2 vols., Bielefeld, 1953).

General works

Perhaps the best work dealing with German history from early times to the 1930s is the somewhat romanticized but well-documented *The Germans in History* (New York, 1945) by Prince H. zu Löwenstein. It is available in both English and German. For a political survey down to the Franco-Prussian War, there is still E. F. Henderson's *A Short History of Germany* (2 vols., New York, rev. ed., 1937), or G. M. Priest's *Germany since 1740* (Boston, 1915) for the years 1740–1914. K. F. Reinhardt's *Germany 2000 Years* (Milwaukee, 1950), which ends with the Weimar Republic, attempts an unsuccessful mixture of cultural and political developments and is overly encyclopedic, but can serve as a useful reference tool. The best brief discussion of social and intellectual trends of the nineteenth and early twentieth centuries is contained in K. S. Pinson's *Modern Germany* (New

York, 1954), which treats German history from 1815 to 1953. Veit Valentin's *The German People: Their History and Civilization from the Holy Roman Empire to the Third Reich* (New York, 1946) is overly burdened with emotional generalizations evoked by the author's revulsion toward Hitlerism. In the same category belongs A. J. P. Taylor's brief *The Course of German History* (New York, 1945), a diatribe against the Germans covering the period 1815 to 1939. The English translation, *The Epochs of German History* (London), 1930), of the conservative German historian Johannes Haller's survey of German history contains interesting insights into some problems of German history. Other recent general histories stressing mostly political developments are J. S. Davies, *From Charlemagne to Hitler* (London, 1948); R. Flenley, *Modern German History* (London, 1953) on the period 1640 to 1939; E. J. Passant, *A Short History of Germany, 1815–1945* (Cambridge, Engl., 1959), with considerable emphasis on economics; and M. Dill, Jr., *Germany, a Modern History* (Ann Arbor, Mich., 1961), with its useful surveys, particularly of the period 1871–1945.

Among works in German, the reader should be familiar with Wilhelm Oncken's monumental *Allgemeine Geschichte in Einzeldarstellungen* (46 volumes, Berlin, 1879–1893). Individual volumes of this series are written by different German scholars and are generally rich in factual information. The new *Deutsche Geschichte im Überblick* (Stuttgart, 1953), edited by P. Rassow, is a factual survey compiled by over a dozen collaborators. L. Stacke's *Deutsche Geschichte* (4 parts, Leipzig, 1888), which goes only up to 1871, and E. Orthbrandt's more recent, nationalistic *Deutsche Geschichte—Lebenslauf des Deutschen Volkes* (Laupheim, 1954), are both more valuable for their beautiful colored illustrations than for content. F. Stieve's *Geschichte des Deutschen Volkes* (Munich, 1944) might serve as a good example of Nazi-inspired interpretation; R. Wahl's poetic *Die Deutschen, eine Historie* (Munich, 1953) exhibits a not uncommon nationalistic, though anti-Prussian and pro-Austrian bias; while F. Schnabel's four-volume *Deutschland im 19ten Jahrhundert* (Berlin, 1931–1939), which actually goes only to 1848, typifies the liberal, anti-Prussian tendency combined with excellence of scholarship. Also noteworthy are K. Lamprecht's various works on German history, covering the entire period to 1910 on the basis of sociological and psychological interpretations, two disciplines then in their infancy (published between 1891 and 1913, a total of sixteen volumes).

Works specifically on Prussian history almost outnumber those on German history in general. *The Evolution of Prussia* (Oxford, 1946) by J. A. R. Marriott and C. G. Robertson, although a superficial treatment, is still the most useful political survey available in English. A classic of the Prussian historical school based on thorough research and devoted to the glorification of Prussia is J. Droysen's fourteen-volume *Geschichte der Preussischen Politik* (Leipzig, 1858–1886), which covers Prussian history to 1757. A good antidote to the Prussianism of Droysen is H. Prutz's four-volume *Preussische Geschichte* (Stuttgart, 1900–1902), a scholarly and well-balanced account of Prussia from its beginnings to 1888. *Die Hohenzollern und ihr Werk* (Berlin, 1916) by O. Hintze provides a nationalistic view of the Prussian monarchy in the eighteenth and nineteenth centuries. For economic, social, administrative, and judicial aspects of Prussia, consult the numerous works by G. Schmoller, published between 1894 and 1937. The Prussian army and military history received a thorough treatment in C. Jany's four-volume *Geschichte der Königlich Preussischen Armee* (Berlin, 1928–1933); more recently, the political implications were aired in W. Görlitz' *History of the German General Staff* (New York, 1953), and G. Craig's *The Politics of the Prussian Army, 1640–1945* (New York, 1956).

Because of the breadth of the topic,

there are few good books on German civilization as a whole. E. Richard's *History of German Civilization* (New York, 1911) presents but a cursory survey. The best is still Egon Friedell's *A Cultural History of The Modern Age* (3 vols., New York, 1930–1932), which reaches beyond the confines of Germany for the period from the Renaissance to 1914. Henri Lichtenberger's *Germany and Its Evolution in Modern Times* (New York, 1913) deals mostly with religion, art, and philosophy. Since the end of World War II, it has become popular to analyze "the German mentality," an undertaking of dubious scholarly value. Among the most successful of these analyses are E. Vermeil's *Germany's Three Reichs: Their History and Culture* (London, 1945), dealing with cultural and national characteristics in a moderate tone; Friedrich Meinecke's *The German Catastrophe: Reflections and Recollections* (Cambridge, Mass., 1950), a liberal humanist's thoughts on nineteenth- and twentieth-century Germany; Hans Kohn's collection of interpretive essays, *German History: Some New German Views* (Boston, 1954), and an intellectual history of Germany's last three centuries by the same author, *The Mind of Germany: The Education of a Nation* (New York, 1960). Noteworthy contributions to intellectual history are also K. S. Pinson's *Pietism as a Factor in the Rise of German Nationalism* (New York, 1934); L. Snyder's *German Nationalism: The Tragedy of a People* (Harrisburg, Penn., 1952), a collection of essays dealing with nationalism from Jahn to Hitler; and G. P. Gooch's *Studies in German History* (London, 1948).

Among more specialized general works, R. E. Dickinson's *Germany, a General and Regional Geography* (New York, 1953) is of great value. The influence and development of pamphlets and periodicals from the fifteenth century to World War I is well delineated in K. Schottenloher's *Flugblatt und Zeitung: ein Wegweiser durch das Gedruckte Tagesschrifttum* (Berlin, 1922). For constitutional developments to the twentieth century, see the standard manual by F. Hartung, *Deutsche Verfassungsgeschichte vom 15ten Jahrhundert bis zur Gegenwart* (Leipzig, 1922). E. Rupert's *State and Sovereignty in Modern Germany* (New Haven, Conn., 1928) deals only with the nineteenth century and Weimar; L. Dehio's *Germany and World Politics in the 20th Century* (New York, 1959) has a much broader scope. An interesting monograph is E. von Meier's *Französische Einflüsse auf die Staats– und Reichsentwicklung Preussens* (Munich, 1918). As a brief reference work on the histories of German political parties, primarily 1848 to Weimar, consult L. Bergsträsser's *Geschichte der politischen Parteien in Deutschland* (Munich, 1955). The early history of the Socialist party is dealt with in a propagandizing but scholarly fashion in F. Mehring's four-volume *Geschichte der Deutschen Sozialdemokratie* (Stuttgart, 1922).

Among books on Germany's relations with other powers in the earlier centuries, two in particular deserve listing: L. Reynaud, *Histoire générale de l'influence française en Allemagne* (Paris, 1915), and B. Schmitt, *England and Germany, 1740–1914* (Princeton, N. J., 1916).

There are, of course, countless histories of the various German states as well as regional treatments. Almost every state produced its own historians, who wrote on local developments or described German history from a particularistic viewpoint. For the study of the question of particularism and unification, research would have to take into account this added wealth of source material. An example is the three-volume study by M. Doeberl, *Bayern und Deutschland* (Munich, 1922–1926), an excellent analysis of the unification movement, 1848 to 1871, as seen from the point of view of Bavaria.

The vast field of German belletristic literature has been entirely omitted from this bibliography, although an adequate knowledge of German literature is indispensable to an understanding of the development of German political history. For reference, the reader might consult J. G. Robertson's *A History of German Literature* (rev. and enl. ed., London, 1961), a conventional survey of authors; E. Rose, *A History of German Literature* (New York, 1960); F. Martini, *Deutsche Literaturgeschichte von den Anfängen bis zur Gegenwart* (Stuttgart, 1960); or the new and as yet incomplete series of volumes, *Geschichte der Deutschen Literatur von den Anfängen bis zur Gegenwart* (Munich, 1949–) by H. A. W. de Boor and R. Newald, which promises to become one of the best comprehensive surveys. W. Scherer's standard, pedantic work, *Geschichte der Deutschen Literatur,* originally published in 1886, was reissued in revised form in 1948 (Vienna). Among recent or revised works in German, the following represent useful general surveys: *Annalen der Deutschen Literatur: Geschichte der Deutschen Literatur von den Anfängen bis zur Gegenwart* (Stuttgart, 1959–1962), edited by H. O. Burger and others; B. Boesch, editor, *Deutsche Literaturgeschichte in Grundzügen* (Bern, 1961); J. Klein, *Geschichte der Deutschen Lyrik, Von Luther bis zum Ausgang des Zweiten Weltkrieges* (Wiesbaden, 1957); H. Schneider, *Geschichte der Deutschen Dichtung nach ihren Epochen dargestellt* (2 vols., Bonn, 1949–1950); and T. C. van Stockum and J. van Dam, *Geschichte der Deutschen Literatur* (3d ed., Groningen, 1961).

The more recent periods are surveyed in F. Bertaux, *A Panorama of German Literature from 1871 to 1931* (New York, 1935); J. Bithell, *Modern German Literature, 1880–1950* (3d ed., London, 1959); A Soergel, *Dichtung und Dichter der Zeit: Vom Naturalismus bis zur Gegenwart* (2 vols., Düsseldorf, 1961–1962); and H. Friedman and O. Mann, *Deutsche Literatur im Zwanzigsten Jahrhundert—Gestalten und Strukturen* (2 vols., 4th ed., Heidelberg, 1961). See also E. Heller's *The Disinherited Mind: Essays in Modern German Literature and Thought* (Cambridge, Engl., 1952); Roy Pascal, *The German Novel* (Manchester, 1956); and H. M. Waidson, *The Modern German Novel: A Mid-twentieth Century Survey* (London, 1959).

The Middle Ages (Chapters 2–4)

G. Barraclough's *The Origins of Modern Germany* (Oxford, 1947), despite its misleading title, presents a good, although sketchy, orientation to medieval Germany, with emphasis on institutional developments. Greater detail is provided in W. Stubbs's two-volume *Germany in the Middle Ages* (London, 1908), although this work is not based on the best sources. J. W. Thompson's *Feudal Germany* (Chicago, 1928) is still useful to most students. Social and political matters are well covered in the two volumes by J. Bühler, *Deutsche Geschichte bis 1500* (Berlin, 1954), although the treatment of the fifteenth century is cursory.

The earlier medieval period has received much recent attention: M. Deanesly, *A History of Early Medieval Europe, 476–911* (London, 1956); H. Fichtenau, *The Carolingian Empire* (Oxford, 1957), a somewhat incomprehensive treatment; and a new revised edition of the excellent *Thought and Letters in Western Europe, A.D. 500–900* (New York, 1957) by M. L. Laistner.

There are numerous older works on the Empire at its zenith. E. F. Henderson's *History of Germany in the Middle Ages* (London, 1894), though giving background on the politics and culture of the earlier period, deals essentially with the years 911 to 1272. H. Fisher's *The Medieval Empire* (2 vols., London, 1898), though antiquated, is thorough for the period 918 to 1190. L. Bryce's *The Holy Roman Empire* (latest ed., London, 1919) has become a classic on the theoretical symbolism of the Empire. Karl Hampe's *Deutsche Kaisergeschichte in der Zeit der Salier und Staufer* (Leipzig, 1945) is a revised version of a well-documented earlier study.

The temper of medieval times is rendered most poetically by R. Huch in her *Deutsche Geschichte: Römisches Reich Deutscher Nation* (Berlin, 1934). For papal-imperial relations, see W. Ullmann, *The Growth of Papal Government in the Middle Ages* (London, 1955).

There exist, of course, numerous collections of medieval documents, particularly the vast 120-volume *Monumenta Germaniae* (Hanover, Berlin, 1826–1925). Of more interest to the ordinary reader are E. F. Henderson's *Select Documents of the Middle Ages* (London, 1898), and the two-volume *Quellenlesebuch zur Geschichte des Deutschen Mittelalters* (Leipzig, 1914).

From the list of biographies for this period, one can select only a few: Einhard, *Life of Charlemagne,* a biography by the emperor's contemporary, available in many editions and translations; H. W. C. Davis, *Charlemagne, the Hero of Two Nations* (New York, 1900); R. Winston, *Charlemagne: From the Hammer to the Cross* (Indianapolis, 1954); E. S. Duckett, *Alcuin, Friend of Charlemagne* (New York, 1951); and E. H. Kantorowitz, *Frederick the Second, 1194–1250* (New York, 1957).

1410 to 1648 (Chapters 5–8)

Much reinterpretation of the Reformation has recently been undertaken. For a lengthy bibliography, the reader is referred to H. J. Grimm's excellent survey, *The Reformation Era, 1500–1650* (New York, 1954).

A general picture of the religious and cultural life in the fifteenth century is contained in *Deutschland vor der Reformation—Eine Zeitenwende* (Berlin, 1934), by W. Andreas. A more penetrating analysis of humanism is presented in L. Spitz, *The Religious Renaissance of the German Humanists* (Cambridge, Mass., 1963). Histories of the Reformation itself exist in considerable numbers. Still important for factual details is the strongly pro-Protestant *History of the Reformation in Germany* (London, 3 vols., 1845–1847) by Leopold von Ranke, as well as Preserved Smith's *Life and Letters of Martin Luther* (Boston, 1911). Among important recent works are Gerhard Ritter's *Die Neugestaltung Europas im 16ten Jahrhundert* (Berlin, 1950); E. G. Schwiebert, *Luther and His Times* (St. Louis, 1951); R. H. Bainton, *The Reformation of the Sixteenth Century* (Boston, 1952); G. L. Mosse, *The Reformation* (New York, 1953); and H. Holborn, *A History of Germany: The Reformation* (New York, 1959), which covers the period 1495 to 1648.

The most solid work on the years 1618–1648 is still C. V. Wedgewood's *The Thirty Years' War* (London, 1938), while an excellent re-creation of the temper of the times is contained in R. Huch's *Der Dreissigjährige Krieg* (Berlin, 1958). *News and Rumor in Renaissance Europe* (New York, 1959), edited by G. T. Matthews, provides an interesting, brief collection of Fugger letters dealing with the period 1568 to 1604. Recommended from the many available biographies are K. Brandi's *Emperor Charles V* (London, 1949), and F. Watson's *Wallenstein, Soldier under Saturn* (Boston, 1938).

1640 to 1789 (Chapters 9 and 10)

Among the general works on the period, the best political treatment is still Leopold von Ranke's *History of Prussia* (3 vols., London, 1847–1848). A Waddington's *Histoire de Prusse* (2 vols., Paris, 1911–1922), which goes only to 1740, is a scholarly treatment, expectedly anti-Prussian in tone. Equally anti-Prussian and dealing heavily with institutional history is H. Tuttle's *History of Prussia* (4 vols., Boston, 1884–1896), which ends with the Seven Years' War. O. Hintze's *Historische und Politische Aufsätze* (4 vols., Berlin, 1908) contains some masterly discussions of Prussian social and institutional history of the seventeenth and eighteenth centuries.

Among shorter surveys, the most compact are S. B. Fay's *The Rise of Brandenburg-Prussia to 1786* (New York, 1937) and *Brandenburg-Preussen* (Hamburg, 1958) by W. von Etzdorf. A valuable textbook treatment of part of the period is found in C. T. Atkinson, *A History of Germany, 1715–1815* (London, 1908). The reader is also referred to G. Schilfert's *Deutschland von 1648–1789* (Berlin, 1959), a socialist-dialectical work, as a representative product of contemporary East German writing. Two recent works by Francis L. Carsten are of great value for this and the preceding period: *The Origins of Prussia* (Oxford, 1954) is a thoroughly documented study of Prussia's early development from the settlements of the twelfth century to the days of the Great Elector, with considerable emphasis on economics; *Princes and Parliaments from the fifteenth to the eighteenth century* (Oxford, 1959) deals with the estates and the administrative frameworks of Württemberg, Hesse, Saxony, Bavaria, and some Rhineland states.

Good treatments of German social and intellectual history during this period can be found in K. Biedermann's four-volume *Deutschland im 18ten Jahrhundert* (Leipzig, 1854–1880); E. Ermatinger's *Deutsche Kultur im Zeitalter der Aufklärung* (Potsdam, 1935); and W. H. Bruford's *Germany in the 18th Century: The Social Background of the Literary Revival* (Cambridge, Engl., 1935). A challenging book on intellectual trends is E. M. Butler's *The Tyranny of Greece over Germany* (Cambridge, Engl., 1935).

There are many good biographies for the period. On the Great Elector, consult M. Philippson, *Der Grosse Kurfürst, Friedrich Wilhelm von Brandenburg* (3 vols., Berlin, 1897–1903), A. Waddington's *Le Grand Electeur* (2 vols., Paris, 1905–1908), or the captivating *The Great Elector* (Chicago, 1947) by Ferdinand Schevill. Robert Ergang's *The Potsdam Führer* (New York, 1941) deals with King Frederick William I. The best cursory survey of Frederick II's reign is still W. F. Reddaway's *Frederick the Great and the Rise of Prussia* (New York, 1904). A more critical though still adulatory work is *König Friedrich der Grosse,* including *Friedrich der Grosse als Kronprinz* (4 vols., Stuttgart, 1912) by R. Koser, who was for many years director of the Prussian state archives. E. Lavisse's *Youth of Frederick the Great* (London, 1891), a translation from the French, contains an interesting though outdated psychological analysis of the king's early years. Among the standard biographies of Frederick are P. Gaxotte's *Frederick the Great* (New Haven, Conn., 1942) and G. P. Gooch's *Frederick the Great* (London, 1947), to which a translation of L. Reiner's *Friedrich der Grosse* (New York, 1960) has recently been added. S. K. Padover's *The Revolutionary Emperor: Joseph the Second* (New York, 1934) is a readable biography. A. von Arneth's ten-volume *Maria Theresia und Joseph II* (Vienna, 1863–1879) is a history of eighteenth-century Austria rather than a biographical treatise.

Among the more specialized works that should be mentioned are H. von Caemmerer, *Die Testamente der Kurfürsten von Brandenburg und der beiden ersten Könige von Preussen* (Munich, 1915), an analysis of the political views of the Prussian rulers before 1740; E. Dette's *Friedrich der Grosse und sein Heer* (Halle, 1914), a study of the Prussian army of the period; J. W. von Archenholtz' classic *Geschichte des Siebenjährigen Krieges in Deutschland* (Leipzig, 1793, 1904); H. W. Temperley's *Frederick the Great and Kaiser Joseph: an Episode of War and Diplomacy* (London, 1915), covering the period 1763 to 1779; and the recent book by H. Kaplan, *The First Partition of Poland* (New York, 1962).

1789 to 1850 (Chapters 11–13)

For the influence of the French Revolution and the Napoleonic occupation on Germany, see E. Saur's *Die Französische*

Revolution von 1789 in Zeitgenössischen Flugschriften und Dichtungen (Weimar, 1913); A. Stern, *Der Einfluss der Französischen Revolution auf das Deutsche Geistesleben* (Stuttgart, 1927), dealing mostly with repercussions in literature; G. P. Gooch, *Germany and the French Revolution* (London, 1920); and H. A. L. Fisher's *Studies in Napoleonic Statesmanship: Germany* (Oxford, 1923).

The transformation from cosmopolitanism to nationalism, particularly in Prussia, is discussed in L. Lévy-Bruhl's *L'Allemagne depuis Leipzig: Essai sur le développement de la conscience nationale en Allemagne, 1700–1848* (Paris, 1890); R. Aris' *History of Political Thought in Germany from 1789 to 1815* (London, 1936); E. N. Anderson's excellent *Nationalism and the Cultural Crisis in Prussia, 1806–1815* (New York, 1939); and to some extent in L. A. Willoughby's *Classical Age of German Literature, 1748–1805* (London, 1926).

One of the best works on Prussian reforms is still G. S. Ford's *Stein and the Era of Reforms in Prussia* (Princeton, N. J., 1922). As indicated in the subtitle, J. R. Seeley's *Life and Times of Stein: Germany and Prussia in the Napoleonic Age* (3 vols., London, 1878) deals not merely with Stein but with the entire period of reforms. Consult also B. Gebhardt, *Wilhelm von Humboldt als Staatsmann* (2 vols., Stuttgart, 1896–1899); A. G. Pundt, *Arndt and the Nationalist Awakening in Germany* (New York, 1935); and W. O. Shanahan, *Prussian Military Reforms, 1786–1813* (New York, 1945). An illuminating study of the problems of the smaller states is G. S. Ford's *Hanover and Prussia, 1795–1803: A Study in Neutrality* (New York, 1903).

Among works on Austria, there is an interesting biography by W. C. Langsam, *Francis the Good, the Education of an Emperor, 1768–1792* (New York, 1949). The implications of the termination of the Empire are discussed by H. von Srbik in *Das oesterreichische Kaisertum und das Ende des Heiligen Römischen Reiches, 1804–1806* (Berlin, 1927). Golo Mann's *Secretary of Europe: The Life of Friedrich Gentz, Enemy of Napoleon* (New Haven, Conn., 1946) gives insight into the diplomatic background of the period 1802 to 1815.

For the era after 1815, a general survey is contained in A. May's *The Age of Metternich* (New York, 1933). Heinrich von Treitschke's classic, pro-Prussian history covering the period 1815 to 1848 has been translated into English as *A History of Germany in the Nineteenth Century* (7 vols., New York, 1915–1919). A. W. Ward's *Germany, 1815–1890* (3 vols., Cambridge, Engl., 1916–1918) treats the earlier period largely as background to the unification movement. Invaluable for the cultural background of the period is J. G. Legge's *Rhyme and Revolution in Germany: A Study in German History, Life, Literature, and Character, 1813–1850* (London, 1918). A recent study of the period is T. S. Hamerow, *Restoration, Revolution, Reaction: Economics and Politics in Germany, 1815–1871* (Princeton, N. J., 1958).

The romantic and nationalistic flavor of this period is well illuminated in R. Kuehnemund's *Arminius or the Rise of a National Symbol in Literature* (Chapel Hill, N. C., 1953). A good example of the superpatriotism evident in many historical writings of the post-Napoleonic era is *A History of Germany* by F. Kohlrausch, originally published in 1816 and recently translated into English (New York, 1959).

For economic history, the most useful is J. H. Clapham, *The Economic Development of France and Germany, 1815–1914* (4th ed., Cambridge, Engl., 1955), which deals with agriculture, industry, communication, as well as finance during the entire nineteenth century. A good monograph is W. O. Henderson's *The Zollverein* (London, 1939).

The best biography on Metternich is by C. Algernon (New York, 1933). There are also important memoirs and collections of correspondence for the period, including, among others, those by Metternich, Frederick William IV, Radowitz, Camphausen, and Windisch-Grätz.

The most detailed study of the revolutionary years, including the upheavals in the lesser states, is V. Valentin's *Geschichte der Deutschen Revolution von 1848–1849* (2 vols., Berlin, 1930), of which the English version, entitled *1848, Chapters of German History* (London, 1940) is but a pale replica. The plight of the German liberals is stressed in L. B. Namier's *The Revolution of the Intellectuals* (London, 1944). P. Robertson's *Revolutions of 1848* (Princeton, N. J., 1952) attempts an analysis of the social make-up of the revolutionary groups. *Revolution and Counter-Revolution in Germany,* which Karl Marx and Friedrich Engels wrote in 1852 for *The New York Tribune,* is still one of the clearest analyses of the events of 1848, despite its exaggerated stress on the class struggle. Jacques Droz's *Les Révolutions allemandes de 1848* (Paris, 1957) is a recent addition to the growing volume of studies of the revolution.

The monographic work on the period is of great variety. V. Valentin's *Frankfurt/Main und die Revolution von 1848–1849* (Stuttgart, 1908) contains a detailed portrait of life in Germany's "temporary capital." K. Biedermann's *Erinnerungen aus der Paulskirche* (Leipzig, 1849) is a valuable description of the Frankfurt National Assembly by one of its members. E. Brandenburg's *Untersuchungen und Aktenstücke zur Geschichte der Reichsgründung* (2 vols., Leipzig, 1916) deals with the revolution and Prussia down to 1866. A useful work is L. D. Steefel, *The Schleswig-Holstein Question* (Cambridge, Mass., 1932). A little-known but interesting collection of documents is *1848: Der Vorkampf Deutscher Einheit und Freiheit. Urkunden, Berichte, Briefe* (Munich, 1914), edited by T. Klein.

1850 to 1871 (Chapters 13–14)

Most of the works dealing with the period of unification evince strong political coloring. H. von Sybel's seven-volume *The Founding of the German Empire by William I, Based Chiefly upon Prussian State Documents* (New York, 1890–1898) covers the period 1848–1870 and is a semiofficial history, conservative, and strongly pro-Bismarck. A shorter, strongly pro-Austrian work is H. Friedjung's *The Struggle for Supremacy in Germany: 1859–1866* (New York, 1935). J. W. Headlam's *Bismarck and the Foundation of the German Empire* (New York, 1899) is an adulatory, popularized rendition of Bismarck's achievements. Munroe Smith's *Bismarck and German Unity* (New York, 1923) attempts a more detached tone. H. von Srbik's *Deutsche Einheit: Idee und Wirklichkeit vom Heiligen Reich bis Königgrätz* (4 vols., Berlin, 1935–1939), dealing mainly with the Austro-German struggle from Olmütz to the Seven Weeks' War, is a nationalistic, Nazified work. Otto Pflanze's recent *Bismarck and the Development of Germany: 1815–1871* (Princeton, N. J., 1963) provides a contemporary critical appraisal of the chancellor.

On Bismarck himself, one must consult his own memoirs, which are of great value but must be analyzed critically. In addition, there exist fifteen volumes of his collected works (Berlin, 1924–1935), as well as the fourteen volumes of *Die Politischen Reden des Fürsten Bismarck* (Stuttgart, 1892–1905), edited by H. Kohl. The best—and quite critical—biography of the chancellor is by Erich Eyck (4 vols., Zurich, 1941–1944), which exists in an abridged English translation. For Bismarck's early life, consult E. Marcks's *Bismarck, eine Biographie, 1815–1851* (Stuttgart, 1951). C. G. Robertson's *Bismarck* (London, 1918) still remains a popular though brief biography.

Among the many studies of international relations of the period, the following deserve special consideration: W. E. Mosse, *The European Powers and the German Question, 1848–1871* (Cambridge, Engl., 1958), dealing with the unification of the 1860s; C. W. Clark, *Franz Joseph and Bismarck: The Diplomacy of Austria be-*

fore the War of 1866 (Cambridge, Mass., 1934); A. J. P. Taylor, *The Struggle for Mastery in Europe, 1848–1918* (Oxford, 1954); the anti-Prussian *The Origins of the War of 1870* (Cambridge, Mass., 1924), by R. H. Lord; and the anti-French *Napoleon III and the Rhine: The Origin of the War of 1870–1871* (New York, 1928), by Hermann Oncken.

For the growth of socialism during this period, consult W. H. Dawson's *German Socialism and Ferdinand Lassalle: A Biographical History of German Socialist Movements during This Century* (London, 1888). The revisionist Edouard Bernstein also wrote an interesting biography, *Ferdinand Lassalle as a Social Reformer* (London, 1893). The best recent biography is *Ferdinand Lassalle* (New Haven, Conn., 1947), by D. Footman. Another important biography for the period is W. O. Morris' *Moltke, a Biographical and Critical Study* (London, 1894).

1871 to 1890 (Chapter 15)

Many books dealing with the Bismarckian empire also cover the subsequent decades to World War I. Among the more important general histories of the Second Reich are R. H. Fife, Jr., *The German Empire between Two Wars: A Study of Political and Social Development of the Nation between 1871 and 1914* (New York, 1916), a fairly well-balanced analysis; G. Egelhaaf, *Geschichte der Neuesten Zeit, vom Frankfurter Frieden bis zur Gegenwart* (Stuttgart, 1918), heavily factual and quite conservative; A. Wahl, *Deutsche Geschichte von der Reichsgründung bis zum Ausbruch des Weltkrieges, 1871–1914* (4 vols., Stuttgart, 1926–1936), comprehensive and strongly pro-Bismarck; J. Ziekursch, *Politische Geschichte des neuen Deutschen Kaiserreiches* (3 vols., Frankfurt, 1925–1930), rather anti-Bismarck and republican; and F. Hartung, *Deutsche Geschichte, 1871–1919* (rev. ed., Stuttgart, 1952), nationalistic in tone.

For the foreign policy of the empire see E. Brandenburg's *From Bismarck to the World War: A History of German Foreign Policy, 1870–1914* (London, 1927); E. M. Carroll, *Germany and the Great Powers, 1866–1914: A Study in Public Opinion and Foreign Policy* (New York, 1938); and R. J. Sontag, *Germany and England, Background of Conflict, 1848–1918* (New York, 1938). For economic development, consult Gustav Stolper's *German Economy, 1870–1940: Issues and Trends* (New York, 1940), a brief survey; A. Gerschenkron, *Bread and Democracy in Germany* (Berkeley, Calif., 1943), a discussion of tariff problems between 1870 and 1914; and W. Sombart, *The German National Economy in the Nineteenth Century* (Berlin, 1903). G. Steinhausen's *Deutsche Geistes- und Kulturgeschichte von 1870 bis zur Gegenwart* (Halle, 1931) deals with social and economic trends as much as with intellectual development. G. P. Gooch, *Germany* (London, 1925) treats German culture under the empire to some extent.

For the Bismarckian empire proper, there are P. Matter's substantial *Bismarck et son temps* (3 vols., Paris, 1912–1914) and a new appraisal by W. Mommsen, *Bismarck: ein politisches Lebensbild* (Munich, 1959). W. H. Dawson's *The German Empire, 1867–1914, and the Unity Movement* (2 vols., New York, 1919) as well as his *Evolution of Modern Germany* (London, 1908) actually both deal primarily with Bismarck's period, the former concentrating on political questions, the latter dealing more with industrial and commercial developments. H. von Poschinger wrote a number of monumental monographs on specific aspects of Bismarck's career: *Fürst Bismarck und die Diplomaten, 1852–1890* (Hamburg, 1900), *Fürst Bismarck und die Parlamentarier* (3 vols., Breslau, 1894–1896), and *Fürst Bismarck und der Bundesrat, 1876–1890* (5 vols., Stuttgart, 1896–1901). Equally valuable is W. H. Dawson's *Prince Bismarck and State Socialism* (London, 1890), dealing with his social and economic legislation. For the colonial question, see P. Giordani, *The German Colonial Empire, Its Beginning and Ending* (London, 1916), and M. E. Townsend, *The Rise and Fall of Germany's Colonial Empire, 1884–1918* (New York, 1930).

Valuable for the period are also the memoirs of A. Bebel as well as the following biographies: P. Wiegler, *William I* (Boston, 1929); E. Newman, *Life of Richard Wagner* (4 vols., New York, 1933–1946); E. Hüsgen, *Ludwig Windthorst* (Cologne, 1907); and M. von Poschinger, *The Life of Emperor Frederick III* (New York, 1901).

1890 to 1914 (Chapters 16–18)

Much has been written on Emperor William II, most of it critical. A typical diatribe is M. Barrière's *Guillaume II et son Temps* (Paris, 1934), an emotional account of the period 1908 to 1914 based on contemporary newspapers. E. Ludwig attempts in his *William Hohenzollern, the Last of the Kaisers* (New York, 1927) an interesting though questionable psychological interpretation of the emperor's life. E. Eyck, *1890–1914: Das persönliche Regiment Wilhelms II* (Zurich, 1948) is frankly hostile to William's diplomatic and political activity, as is L. Reiners' *In Europa gehen die Lichter aus* (Munich, 1954), an anecdotal approach to the disintegration of William's empire. A more detached analysis was recently attempted by J. von Kürenberg in his *The Kaiser, A Life of William II* (London, 1954). There exist numerous compendiums of William's speeches, letters, and conversations, especially of his famous correspondence with Tsar Nicholas II of Russia. Moreover, he left two revealing books of his own: *My Early Life* (London, 1926), describing the years to 1888, and *Meine Vorfahren* (Berlin, 1929), a glorification of his own ancestors.

Numerous other memoirs shed interesting light on the period, particularly those of Holstein, Waldersee, Bülow, Hohenlohe-Schillingsfürst, and Tirpitz. J. Haller's *Philip Eulenburg: The Kaiser's Friend* (2 vols., New York, 1930), an attempted rehabilitation of the controversial diplomat, reveals much interesting information on William himself.

More specific aspects of the period are dealt with in the following works: J. A. Nichols, *Germany after Bismarck* (Cambridge, Mass., 1958), an analysis of the Caprivi era; O. Hammann, *The World Policy of Germany* (New York, 1927); E. L. Woodward, *Great Britain and the German Navy* (London, 1935); and A. S. Hurd and H. Castle, *German Sea Power, Its Rise, Progress, and Economic Basis* (London, 1913), all dealing with William's foreign policy and in particular with the naval problem. E. Kehr's *Schlachtflottenbau und Parteipolitik, 1894–1901* (Berlin, 1930) represents a brilliant analysis of the relationship of the naval program to domestic politics. Another study of pressure groups is contained in M. Wertheimer's *The Pan-German League, 1890–1918* (New York, 1924). For an experience in Social Darwinism, the reader is referred to F. von Bernhardi's *Germany and the Next War,* published in 1911 (Engl. transl., New York, 1914). For a good analysis of economic trends, see W. F. Bruck, *Economic and Social History of Germany from William II to Hitler* (London, 1938).

1914 to 1919 (Chapter 18)

For the military operations of the war itself, the reader can easily refer to special bibliographies. As did those of other nations, the General Staff of the German Army also issued its own monumental description of the war: *Der Grosse Krieg in Einzeldarstellungen* (39 vols., Oldenburg, 1918–1932).

Among the many tomes dealing with the origins of the war, it is sufficient to refer the reader to S. B. Fay, *Origins of the World War* (2 vols., New York, 1928); B. E.

Schmitt, *The Coming of the War* (2 vols., New York, 1930); and P. Renouvin, *Histoire des rélations internationales: de 1871 à 1914* (Paris, 1955).

A general discussion of the German home front during the war is contained in A. Mendelssohn-Bartholdy, *The War and German Society* (New Haven, Conn., 1937). F. Naumann's *Central Europe* (New York, 1917) provides a valuable sample of the conservative idea of a Greater Germany proposed during the early period of the war. For a discussion of the Socialist attitude toward the war, see E. R. Bevan, *German Social Democracy during the War* (London, 1918), an interesting description, although it lacks in perspective and accuracy; C. E. Schorske's more scholarly *German Social Democracy, 1905–1917* (Cambridge, Mass., 1955); and an informative collection of speeches and proclamations by Socialists, published by the Social Democratic party, *Die Deutsche Sozialdemokratie über Krieg und Frieden* (Berlin, 1916).

The best work on the revolution of 1918 is still A. Rosenberg's *The Birth of the German Republic, 1871–1918* (New York, 1931), which details the background of the revolution from a Socialist point of view. H. Rudin's *Armistice, 1918* (New Haven, Conn., 1944) provides further important background. *Die Novemberrevolution in Deutschland: Dokumente und Materialien* (Berlin, 1958) is a Communist compilation of interesting letters, newspaper articles, and proclamations for the period 1917–1919. In *Von Kiel bis Kapp: zur Geschichte der Deutschen Revolution* (Berlin, 1920), Gustav Noske defends his role in the revolutionary days. Among the most valuable, relatively unbiased works are those by R. H. Lutz: *The German Revolution, 1918–1919* (Stanford, Calif., 1922), and the collection of *Documents of the German Revolution: Fall of the German Empire, 1914–1918* (2 vols., Stanford, Calif., 1932).

In addition, much insight can be obtained from a critical reading of the memoirs of the period, especially those by Bethmann-Hollweg, Maximilian von Baden, Ludendorff, Hindenburg, Kiderlen-Wächter, and Scheidemann.

1919 to 1933 (Chapters 19–20)

The problem with most general histories of the Weimar Republic is that they were unable to place events in perspective or they were written with the sole aim of finding in Weimar the breeding ground for National Socialism. Among the many histories of the period, one can recommend only a few: S. W. Halperin, *Germany Tried Democracy, 1918–1933* (New York, 1946); H. Kraus, *The Crisis of German Democracy* (Princeton, N. J., 1933); and G. Scheele, *The Weimar Republic, Overture to the Third Reich* (London, 1945). A. Rosenberg, *A History of the Weimar Republic* (London, 1936) deals only with the early years. Both R. T. Clark's *The Fall of the German Republic* (London, 1935) and A. Brecht's *Prelude to Silence—The End of the German Republic* (Oxford, 1944) concentrate on the dying years of Weimar. A typical Nazi version is H. Schnee's *Deutsche Geschichte von Bismarck bis Hitler* (Paderborn, 1934) which, despite its misleading title, is centered on Hitler's movement in the days of the republic. E. Vermeil undertakes a general discussion of the men who shaped the ambience of Weimar in his *Doctrinaires de le révolution allemande, 1918–1939* (Paris, 1948).

A wealth of material on the foreign relations of Weimar is available in *Documents on German Foreign Policy, 1918–1945,* based mostly on documents captured during World War II and issued by the United States Department of State (1948–). For general questions of foreign affairs, see E. H. Carr, *The Twenty Years' Crisis, 1919–1939* (London, 1939); H. L. Bretton, *Stresemann and the Revision of Versailles* (Stanford, Calif., 1953); and H. W. Gatzke, *Stresemann and the Rearmament of Ger-*

many (Baltimore, 1954), which casts Stresemann more in the role of a Realpolitiker than that of peace-loving idealist. The particular problem of German-Russian relations has received much attention. R. Fischer's *Stalin and German Communism* (Cambridge, Mass., 1948) deals mostly with the 1920s; G. Hilger and A. G. Meyer, *The Incompatible Allies—A Memoir-History of German Soviet Relations, 1918–1941* (New York, 1953), and G. Freund, *Unholy Allies* (London, 1957) both deal with the Weimar and Nazi periods.

The nature of Weimar's democratic institutions is discussed by J. F. Coar in *The Old and the New Germany* (New York, 1924), an analysis of the Weimar Constitution; by F. M. Walkins in *The Failure of Constitutional Emergency Powers under the German Republic* (Cambridge, Mass., 1939); and to some extent by K. Epstein in *Matthias Erzberger and the Dilemma of German Democracy* (Princeton, N. J., 1959). K. Pritzkoleit in his somewhat satirical *Das kommandierte Wunder—Deutschlands Weg im 20ten Jahrhundert* (Munich, 1959) analyzes the socioeconomic forces inimical to Weimar institutions.

The early failure of the Socialists is discussed in A. J. Berlau's *The German Social Democratic Party, 1914–1921* (New York, 1949), and E. Waldman's *The Spartacist Uprising of 1919 and the Crisis of the German Socialist Movement* (Milwaukee, 1958). E. Anderson, *Hammer or Anvil: The Story of the German Working-Class Movement* (London, 1945) follows the plight of the Socialists into the Hitler period.

The conservative forerunners of National Socialism have recently received much attention from scholars. Most important are K. von Klemperer, *Germany's New Conservatism: Its History and Dilemma in the Twentieth Century* (Princeton, N. J., 1957); R. G. L. Waite, *Vanguard of Nazism: the Free Corps Movement in Postwar Germany, 1918–1923* (Cambridge, Mass., 1952); J. W. Wheeler-Bennett, *Nemesis of Power: The German Army in Politics, 1918–1945* (London, 1953); and H. J. Gordon, Jr., *The Reichswehr and the German Republic, 1919–1926* (Princeton, N. J. 1957).

The complex financial picture of Weimar is discussed by S. Flink in *The German Reichsbank and Economic Germany* (New York, 1930), dealing particularly with the period after 1923, while Hjalmar Schacht's *The Stabilization of the Mark* (London, 1927) deals with the period 1919–1923 and Schacht's own solution to the inflationary movement.

Two biographies of note are J. W. Wheeler-Bennett, *The Wooden Titan: Hindenburg in Twenty Years of German History, 1914–1934* (London, 1936), and C. H. von Kessler, *Walter Rathenau, sein Leben und sein Werk* (New York, 1930). Of fundamental importance are the official and private papers of Stresemann, most of them made available only recently. Martin Niemöller's autobiographical *From U-Boat to Pulpit* (New York, 1937) throws light on the period. The cultural trends are treated in M. Bonn, *Wandering Scholar* (New York, 1948).

1933 to 1945 (Chapters 20–22)

Rarely has a contemporary period been the object of so much analytical and pseudoanalytical writing as that of Hitler's Germany. The collections of published and unpublished documents made available since the end of World War II are overwhelming in size and numbers. Only a few sources can be indicated for those wishing to do further research: the forty-two volumes of *The Trial of the Major War Criminals before the International Military Tribunal* (1947–1949); innumerable series of documentary collections, in printed form or on microfilm, released by the United States Department of State; publications by the Wiener Library in London; collections at the Hoover Library at Stanford; materials at the Centre de documentation juive contemporaine in Paris.

For the background and early years of Nazi rule, see K. D. Bracher, *Die Auflösung der Weimarer Republik* (Stuttgart, 1957); C. B. Hoover, *Germany Enters the Third Reich* (New York, 1933); R. B. Rohan, *The Roots of National Socialism* (London, 1941); H. Lichtenberger, *The Third Reich* (New York, 1937); and the two collections of penetrating essays, one by M. Baumont, J. H. E. Fried, and others, *The Third Reich* (New York, 1955), the other by G. A. Almond, editor, *The Struggle for Democracy in Germany* (Chapel Hill, N. C., 1949). Among the best analyses of Nazi dictatorial practices are F. M. Marx, *Government in the Third Reich* (New York, 1937); F. L. Schumann, *The Nazi Dictatorship* (New York, 1939); the rather technical work by F. L. Neumann, *Behemoth, the Structure and Practice of National Socialism, 1933–1944* (Oxford, 1944); and *The Nazi State* (New York, 1943), by W. Ebenstein, who also wrote the penetrating *The German Record: A Political Portrait* (New York, 1945).

Two recent works attempt to cover the entire period of National Socialism: T. L. Jarman's *The Rise and Fall of Nazi Germany* (New York, 1956) and W. Shirer's censorious *The Rise and Fall of the Third Reich* (New York, 1960). A fairly typical German nationalistic and exculpatory book is E. Hemmerle's *Der Weg in die Katastrophe* (Munich, 1948).

On Hitler himself, see K. Heiden's *Der Führer: Hitler's Rise to Power* (Boston, 1944), which goes only to 1934, and Alan Bullock's excellent *Hitler, a Study in Tyranny* (New York, 1952). Much insight can be gained from a reading of Hitler's *Mein Kampf* as well as of various collections of his speeches and of reminiscences of those who surrounded him, such as Otto Dietrich's *Zwölf Jahre mit Hitler* (Munich, 1955), or H. R. Trevor-Roper's *Hitler's Secret Conversations, 1941–1944* (New York, 1953).

Among the legion of works on more limited topics, one might select the following: J. W. Wheeler-Bennett, *Munich, Prologue to Tragedy* (New York, 1948), one of the most lucid discussions of the 1938 crisis; A. Kolnai, *The War against the West* (London, 1938), a discussion of Nazi anti-intellectualism; and F. Littell, *The German Phoenix* (New York, 1960), containing a good treatment of religion under National Socialism. On the atmosphere of terror, see E. Kogon, *The Theory and Practice of Hell* (New York, 1951) as well as Otto Strasser's *Flight from Terror* (New York, 1943). The Bonn government itself (Bundeszentrale für Heimatdienst) has issued a number of documentary studies on Nazi persecutions, such as *Der neunte November 1938, "Reichskristallnacht"* (Bonn, 1953). G. Reitlinger's *The S.S., Alibi of a Nation* (London, 1956) deals with the problem of persecutions and of German responsibility.

Economics under National Socialism are treated in C. S. Guillebaud, *The Economic Recovery of Germany from 1933 to March 1938* (London, 1939), and B. H. Klein, *Germany's Economic Preparation for War* (Cambridge, Engl., 1959). To understand the intertwining of politics and economics in Nazi Germany, one must also examine German pamphlets, such as H. W. Bauer, *Kolonien oder nicht? Die Einstellung von Partei und Staat zum kolonialen Gedanken* (Leipzig, 1935), with a foreword by H. Schacht. An interesting work dealing with the division of Prussia is A. Brecht's *Federalism and Regionalism in Germany* (Oxford, 1945). Nazi excesses naturally also induced anti-German diatribes of fantastic proportions, such as L. Nizer's *What to Do with Germany* (New York, 1944).

The German underground movement has been subjected to much analysis. Among these, consult A. W. Dulles, *Germany's Underground* (New York, 1947); F. von Schlabrendorff, *They Almost Killed Hitler* (New York, 1947); H. B. Gisevius, *To the Bitter End* (Boston, 1947); H. Rothfels, *The German Opposition to Hitler* (Chicago, 1948); G. Ritter, *The German*

Resistance: Carl Goerdeler's Struggle against Tyranny (New York, 1958); and the *Diaries, 1938–1944* of Ulrich von Hassel (New York, 1947).

For the end of the Third Reich, H. R. Trevor-Roper's *The Last Days of Hitler* (New York, 1947) contains some debatable conclusions. There exist many German descriptions of the confusion in Germany during the last months of the war. Interesting are W. Lüdde-Neurath, *Regierung Doenitz, die letzten Tage des Dritten Reiches* (Göttingen, 1951), and J. Müller, *Sturz in den Abgrund, die letzten zehn Monate* (Offenbach, 1947).

The reader is also referred to the voluminous memoirs of the period, by Germans as well as non-Germans: Goebbels, Papen, Schacht, Doenitz, Thyssen, Goering, Rosenberg, Halder, Kesselring, Schwerin von Kroszigk, Raeder, as well as Schuschnigg, de Gaulle, Churchill, Eisenhower, Hull, Forrestal, Morgenthau, Byrnes, and Welles.

After 1945 (Chapters 23–25)

For the period of the occupation, there are many collections of documents, such as *Germany under Occupation* (Ann Arbor, Mich., 1949), edited by J. Pollock and others; *Germany, 1947–1949: The Story in Documents* (Washington, D.C., 1950), a United States Department of State publication; *Documents on Germany under Occupation, 1945–1954* (London, 1955), edited by B. Ruhm von Oppen; and many publications on all phases of the occupation published by the Office of Military Government and the later Office of the United States High Commissioner for Germany. Harold Zink's *American Military Government in Germany* (New York, 1947) and his *The United States in Germany, 1944–1955* (Princeton, N. J., 1957) provide excellent general surveys. Consult also E. H. Litchfield, *Governing Postwar Germany* (Ithaca, N. Y., 1952); L. H. Brown, *A Report on Germany* (New York, 1947); L. D. Clay, *Decision in Germany* (New York, 1950); J. Vernant, *The Refugee in the Postwar World* (New Haven, Conn., 1953); E. Schäfer, *Von Potsdam bis Bonn* (Lahr, 1950); and the controversial *Germany Is Our Problem* (New York, 1945) by Henry Morgenthau, Jr.

For general discussions of the German Federal Republic, consult E. Davidson, *The Death and Life of Germany* (New York, 1959) which contains useful bibliographical references. Prince H. zu Löwenstein's *Deutschlands Schicksaal, 1945–1957* (Bonn, 1957) also contains an excellent bibliography. A. Grosser, *The Colossus Again* (New York, 1955), E. McInnis, editor, *The Shaping of Postwar Germany* (New York, 1960), and W. Stahl, *The Politics of Postwar Germany* (New York, 1963), a collection of interesting essays, all deal with the problem of German democratic revival.

For studies of the establishment of the Bonn government, see the excellent *The Founding of the Federal Republic of Germany* (Chicago, 1958), by J. F. Golay. E. Plischke's brief *Contemporary Government of Germany* (Boston, 1961) analyzes governmental institutions in both Germanies and in Berlin; P. H. Merkl's *The Origin of the West German Republic* (New York, 1963) gives a thorough treatment of constitutional and political problems involved in the creation of the Basic Law and also contains a useful bibliography. E. L. Pinney's *Federalism, Bureaucracy, and Party Politics in Western Germany: The Role of Bundesrat* (Chapel Hill, N.C., 1963) analyzes the conservatism of the Bundesrat in the period 1949–1960. See also H. C. Wallich, *Mainsprings of the German Revival* (New Haven, Conn., 1955); the booklets *Facts about Germany,* published irregularly by the Press and Information Office of the Federal German Government; and W. Bosch, *Die Sozialstruktur in West and Mittel Deutschland* (Bonn, 1958).

Besides P. Weymar's semiofficial *Adenauer: His Authorized Biography* (New

York, 1957), two other works on the chancellor are worth consulting: E. Alexander, *Adenauer and the New Germany: The Chancellor of the Vanquished* (New York, 1957), and A. J. Heidenheimer, *Adenauer and the CDU* (The Hague, 1960). A biography of *Ernst Reuter* (Munich, 1957) was written by the mayor of Berlin, Willy Brandt, in collaboration with R. Löwenthal. Ludwig Erhard's socioeconomic views are presented in his *Wohlstand für Alle* (Düsseldorf, 1957).

Considerably less material is available on the German Democratic Republic. C. J. Friedrich's *The Soviet Zone of Germany* (New Haven, Conn., 1956) is an attempt at a general survey. For the earlier period, consult J. P. Nettl, *The Eastern Zone and Soviet Policy in Germany, 1945–1950* (London, 1951), and R. S. Lusser, editor, *Soviet Economic Policy in Postwar Germany* (New York, 1953). A. Baring's *Der 17te Juni 1953* (Bonn, 1957) is one of the best on the revolution in Berlin. The Bundesministerium für Gesamtdeutsche Fragen in Bonn as well as the Johann Gottfried Herder Institut in Marburg continue to publish voluminous material on East Germany and the lands beyond the Oder-Neisse line. Useful reference material can be found in *SBZ von A bis Z,* published occasionally by the Deutscher Bundesverlag in Bonn.

The questions of Berlin, unification, and German foreign policy have received ample treatment. J. L. Snell, *Wartime Origins of the East-West Dilemma over Germany* (New Orleans, 1959) furnishes useful background. The rearming of Germany is dealt with in *Germany Rejoins the Powers* (Stanford, Calif., 1959) by K. W. Deutsch and L. J. Edinger. Most valuable are Z. M. Szaz, *Germany's Eastern Frontiers: The Problem of the Oder-Neisse Line* (Chicago, 1960), and W. P. Davison, *West German Leadership and Foreign Policy* (Evanston, Ill., 1957). R. Fiedler's *Würfelspiel um Deutschland, 1944–1956, eine kritische Untersuchung der Zerstücklungs- und Wiedervereinigungspolitik* (Düsseldorf, 1957) is a well-documented study, highly critical of Allied policies. Two legal analyses of the problems of the sovereignty of the two Germanies are T. Eschenburg, *Die Deutsche Frage* (*Verfassungsprobleme der Wiedervereinigung*) (Munich, 1960), and G. Scheuer, *Die Rechtslage des Geteilten Deutschlands* (Frankfurt, 1960). A violent, Communistic diatribe on the division of Germany that might be read as an antidote to pro-Western books is K. Bittel, *Vom Potsdamer Abkommen zur Viermächte-Konferenz* (Berlin, 1953). Another problem of German boundaries is discussed in J. Freymond's *The Saar Conflict, 1945–1955* (New York, 1960). Three worthwhile books have appeared on the Berlin problem: E. Butler, *City Divided: Berlin, 1955* (New York, 1955); P. W. Davison, *The Berlin Blockade* (Princeton, N. J., 1958); and the recent *City on Leave: A History of Berlin, 1945–1962* (New York, 1963) by P. Windsor.

Index